This book belongs to:

_____

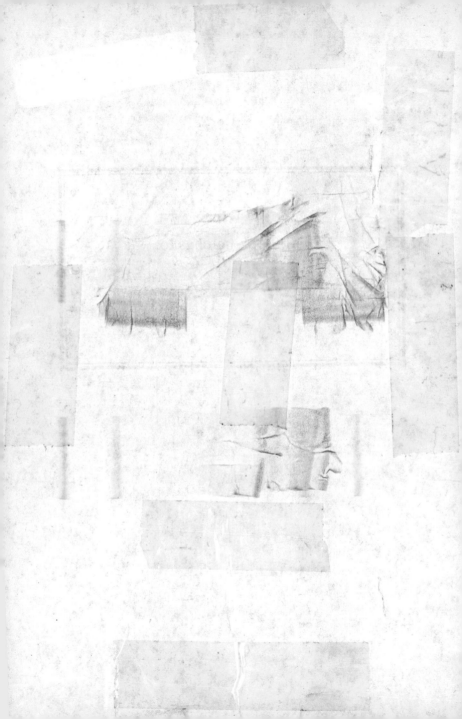

WEBSTER'S
Thesaurus
for Students

≡ FOURTH EDITION ≡

Created in Cooperation with the Editors of
MERRIAM-WEBSTER

FEDERAL
STREET
PRESS

A Division of Merriam-Webster, Incorporated
Springfield, Massachusetts

This edition published by
Federal Street Press
A Division of Merriam-Webster, Incorporated
P.O. Box 281
Springfield, MA 01102

Federal Street Press books are available for bulk purchase for sales promotion
and premium use. For details, write the manager of special sales,
Federal Street Press, P.O. Box 281, Springfield, MA 01102.

ISBN   978-1-59695-181-5

Printed in Canada

1st Printing   Marquis, Toronto, ON   1/2020   Jouve

Contents

Using the Thesaurus

As with any thesaurus, the heart of the book is the list of **synonyms** (*Syn*), words that have the same essential meaning as the one you have in mind. Yet sometimes you may be looking for a word that means the same and sometimes looking for a word that is only similar to your word. Thus, at many entries you will find a list of **related words** (*Rel*), or near synonyms, words that may be close to your notion when an exact match is not quite right. And many times you may be thinking of a word with opposite meaning, and that is where a list of **antonyms** (*Ant*) will be helpful.

All of the entries in this book are in alphabetical order. Each thesaurus main entry contains a full list of at least two synonyms and often a list of antonyms, so no matter what word you start with, you will find its synonyms listed.

> **adjacent** · having a border in common *Syn* abutting, adjoining, bordering, contiguous, flanking, fringing, joining, juxtaposed, skirting, touching, verging *Rel* close, closest, immediate, near, nearby, nearest, neighboring, next, next-door, nigh *Ant* nonadjacent
>
> **contiguous** *Syn* ADJACENT, abutting, adjoining, bordering, flanking, fringing, joining, juxtaposed, skirting, touching, verging *Ant* nonadjacent

The word *contiguous*, in the synonym list at the principal entry **adjacent**, has its own entry with the same synonyms and antonyms.

A unique feature of this book not found in many thesauruses is the appearance of the **meaning core**, marked by a small raised black dot. The meaning core is a definition-like statement of the central meaning shared by all of the words in the synonym list. The main entry for the principal synonym of the list will contain the meaning core and often a list of related words as well (as at **adjacent** above). At a main entry for a synonym that is not the principal synonym, that principal synonym will be listed first, in SMALL CAPITALS, (as at **contiguous** above) and this tells you where to look if you want to read the meaning core for that list or to see if there are any listed related words.

Entry words ordinarily conform to normal dictionary practice: nouns are normally styled as singulars; verbs as infinitives. Homographs (words spelled the same but having a different part of speech) are given separate entries with a functional label, indicating whether noun (*n*), verb (*vb*), adjective (*adj*), preposition (*prep*), or conjunction (*conj*).

> **contrary** *adj* **1** · given to opposing or resisting wishes, commands, conditions, or circumstances *Syn* balky, froward, perverse, restive, wayward *Rel* headstrong, intractable, recalcitrant, refractory, unruly *Ant* complaisant, good-natured . . .
>
> **contrary** *n* *Syn* OPPOSITE, antipode, antithesis, antonym, contradictory, converse, counter, reverse

Whenever two homographs come together and have the same part of speech but have different origins, they are marked with a superscript homograph number and a part of speech label.

> **desert**[1] *n* *Syn* DUE, merit
> **desert**[2] *n* *Syn* WASTE, badlands, wilderness

Headwords that are synonyms and alphabetically close to each other are sometimes listed together.

summon, summons · to demand or request the presence or service of *Syn* call, cite, convene, convoke, muster *Rel* bid, command, enjoin, order

Parentheses enclose a particle or particles usually associated with a word. They may accompany a main entry word or a word in a list.

approve (of) · to have a favorable opinion of *Syn* accept, care (for), countenance, favor, OK (*or* okay), subscribe (to) *Rel* acclaim, applaud, laud, praise, salute *Ant* disapprove (of), discountenance, disfavor, frown (on *or* upon)

Parentheses also enclose material indicating a typical or, occasionally, a sole object of reference.

recant *Syn* ABJURE, forswear, renounce, retract *Ant* pledge (*allegiance, a vow*), elect (*a way of life, a means to an end*)

Spelling variants are labeled as such at the main entry or in lists.

specter *or* **spectre** *Syn* GHOST, apparition, bogey, phantasm, phantom, poltergeist, shade, shadow, spirit, spook, vision, wraith
adequate 1 · of a level of quality that meets one's needs or standards *Syn* acceptable, all right, decent, fine, OK (*or* okay), passable, respectable, satisfactory . . .

Plural usage is indicated in the spelling of the main entry or when necessary at a specific sense.

movie 1 · a story told by . . . *Syn* film, motion picture . . . **2 movies** *pl* · the art or business of making a movie *Syn* cinema, film, motion pictures . . .

English and the Thesaurus

A Brief Look at the English Language

The English language is peculiarly rich in synonyms, which is not surprising considering its history. Over its history of more than a thousand years the language of England has woven together strands of the Celtic language, of earlier Roman words and later church Latin, and then of the Germanic tongues of the early invaders from the European continent.

Because English has so many words derived from Latin and from Greek by way of Latin, the casual observer might guess that English would be—like French, Spanish, and Italian—a Romance language derived from the Latin spoken by the ancient Romans. But although the Romans made a few visits to Britain in the first century A.D., long before the English were there (before there even was an England), English is not a Romance language. English is actually a member of the Germanic group, and thus a sister of such modern languages as Swedish, Dutch, and German.

We often speak of English as having its beginnings with the conquest and settlement of a large part of the island of Britain by Germanic tribes from the European continent in the fifth century, although the earliest written documents of the language belong to the seventh century. Of course these Germanic peoples did not suddenly begin to speak a new language the moment they arrived in England. They spoke the closely related Germanic languages of their continental homelands. And it was from these languages that the English language developed. In fact, the words *English* and *England* are derived from the name of one of these early Germanic peoples, the Angles.

From its beginnings English has been gradually changing and evolving, as language tends to do. To get a sense of how far evolution has taken us from the early tongue, we need only glance at a sample of Old English. Here is the beginning of the Lord's Prayer:

Fæder ūre, þu þe eart on heofonum: si þin nama gehālgod.
Tōbecume þin rīce. Geweorþe þin willa on eorþan swāswā on heofonum.

There is a certain continuity between the vocabularies of Old English and Modern English. Of the thousand most common Modern English words, four-fifths are of Old English origin. Think of such words as *asleep* and *awake* or *alive* and *dead*, words relating to the body, *blood, flesh, arm, leg, bone, tooth*—even words for the daily activities of farming, *acre, barn, plow, till*, or for after the harvest, *drink, eat, meal*.

Of the foreign languages affecting the Old English vocabulary, the most influential was Latin. Church terms especially, like *priest, vicar,* and *mass,* were borrowed from Latin, the language of the church. But words belonging to aspects of life other than the strictly religious, like *cap, inch, kiln, school,* and *noon,* also entered Old English from Latin. The Scandinavians, too, influenced the language of England during the Old English period. From the eighth century on, Vikings from Scandinavia raided and eventually settled in England, especially in the north and the east. In a few instances the influence of a Scandinavian word gave an English word a new meaning. Thus our *dream,* which meant "joy" in Old English, probably took on the now familiar sense "a series of thoughts, images, or emotions occurring during sleep" because its Scandinavian relative *draumr* had that meaning. A considerable number of common words, like *cross, fellow, ball,* and *raise,* also became naturalized as a result of the Viking incursions over the years. The initial consonants *sk-* often reveal the Scandinavian ancestry of words like *sky, skin,* and *skirt,* the last of which has persisted side by side with its native English relative *shirt.*

Additional foreign influence on English came about principally as a result of the Norman Conquest of 1066, which brought England under the rule of French speakers. The English language, though it did not die, was for a long time of only secondary importance in political, social, and cultural matters. French became the language of the upper classes in England. The lower classes continued to speak English, but many French words were borrowed into English. To this circumstance we owe, for example, a number of distinctions between the words used for animals in the pasture and the words for those animals prepared to be eaten. Living animals were under the care of English-speaking peasants; cooked, the animals were served to the French-speaking nobility. *Swine* in the sty became *pork* at the table, *cow* and *calf* became *beef* and *veal*. This Anglo-French also had an influence on the words used in the courts, such as *indict, jury,* and *verdict.*

English eventually reestablished itself as the major language of England, but the language did not lose its habit of borrowing. English still derives much of its learned vocabulary from Latin and Greek. We have also borrowed words from nearly all of the languages in Europe. From Modern French we have such words as *bikini, cliché,* and *discotheque; from* Dutch, *easel, gin,* and *yacht;* from German, *delicatessen, pretzel,* and *swindler;* from Swedish, *ombudsman* and *smorgasbord.* From Italian we have taken *carnival, fiasco,* and *pizza,* as well as many terms from music (including *piano*).

From the period of the Renaissance voyages of discovery through the days when the sun never set upon the British Empire and up to the present, a steady stream of new words has flowed into the language to match the new objects and experiences English speakers have encountered all over the globe. English has drawn words from India (*bandanna*), China (*gung ho*), and Japan (*tycoon*). Arabic has been a prolific source of words over the centuries, giving us *hazard, lute, magazine,* and a host of words beginning with the letter *a,* from *algebra* to *azimuth.*

How Meaning Has Developed

Whether borrowed or created, a word generally begins its life in English with one meaning. Yet no living language is static, and in time words develop new meanings and lose old ones. A word used in a specific sense may be extended, or generalized, to cover a host of similar senses. Our word *virtue* is derived from the Latin *virtus,* which originally meant "manliness." But we apply the term to any excellent quality possessed by man, woman, or beast; even inanimate objects have their *virtues.* In Latin, *decimare* meant "to select and kill a tenth part of" and described the Roman way of dealing with mutinous troops. Its English descendant, *decimate,* now simply means "to destroy a large part of."

The development of meaning can easily be followed in this example. Today when we think of the word *fast* we probably think of the sense involving great speed. But the word's oldest meaning is quite different: "firmly placed" or "immovable," as in "tent pegs set fast in the ground" and "a fast and impassable barrier." It is easy to see how this sense developed expanded uses, such as "a door that is stuck fast and won't open." We see something of this sense in the expression "fast asleep."

In time, users added senses, some of which are common today, from being "unable to leave something, as one's bed" to being "stable and unchangeable," which we find in such uses as "hard and fast rules" or "clothes that are colorfast." Then came the sense of being "steadfast" or "firmly or totally loyal," as in "they were fast friends."

The sense that is most common today, "quick, speedy," came later. It probably developed from an obsolete sense of the adverb meaning "near at hand," which may have led to another meaning "soon." From this obsolete sense of "soon" it is just a short step, in terms of language development, to the sense meaning "quick."

In addition to what could be thought of as a horizontal dimension of change—the extension or contraction of meaning—words also may rise and fall along a vertical scale of value. Perfectly unobjectionable words are sometimes used disparagingly or sarcastically. If we say, "You're a fine one to talk," we are using *fine* in a sense quite different from its usual meaning. If a word is used often enough in negative contexts, the negative coloring may eventually become an integral part of the meaning of the word. A *villain* was once a peasant. His social standing was not high, perhaps, but he was certainly not necessarily a scoundrel. *Scavenger* originally designated the collector of a particular kind of tax in late medieval England. *Puny* meant no more than "younger" when it first passed from French into English and its spelling was transformed. Only later did it acquire the derogatory meaning more familiar to us now.

The opposite process seems to take place somewhat less frequently, but change of meaning to a more positive sense does occasionally occur. In the fourteenth century *nice*, for example, meant "foolish." Its present meaning, of course, is quite different, and the attitude it conveys seems to have undergone a complete reversal from contempt to approval.

What Qualifies as a Synonym?

It is not surprising that with so much to work with, users of English have long been interested in synonyms as an element both in accuracy and in elegance in their expression. Synonyms relieve monotony and enhance expressiveness.

Earlier writers were clear on the meaning of *synonym*. They viewed synonyms as words meaning the same thing. Unfortunately, during the last century or so this simple, clear-cut meaning has become blurred. To many publishers of thesauruses the term has come to mean little more than words that are somewhat similar in meaning. But this loose definition is unsuitable for many people, since it deprives them of the guidance needed for finding the precise word in a particular context.

This thesaurus takes a different approach to describing the nature of a synonym. Groups of synonyms are organized around a segment of meaning that two or more words have in common. In order to create these groups, one has to analyze each word carefully, ignoring nonessential aspects such as connotations and implications and try to isolate the basic meaning, which we call an *elementary meaning*.

When we look at the synonymous relationship of words in terms of elementary meanings, the process of choosing synonyms is simpler and more exact. For example, it is easy to see that no term more restricted in definition than another word can be its synonym. For example, *station wagon* and *minivan* cannot be synonyms of *automobile*, nor can *biceps* be a synonym of *muscle*. Even though a very definite relationship exists between the members, *station wagon* and *minivan* are types of automobile and *biceps* is a type of muscle. So these words are narrower in their range of application. On the other hand, a word more broadly defined than another word in the dictionary may be considered a synonym of the other word so long as the two words share one or more elementary meanings. In order to pin down the area of shared meaning for you, each main entry in this work contains before its synonym list a *meaning core* which states the elementary meaning shared by all the words in that particular synonym group.

What is an Antonym?

Like the word *synonym, antonym* has been used by some writers with a great deal of vagueness and often applied loosely to words which show no real oppositeness when compared one to another. As in the case of synonyms, the relation needs to be seen as one between segments of meaning that can be isolated, rather than between words or dictionary senses of words. As is the case with synonyms, antonyms need to have one or more elementary meanings precisely opposite to or negating the same area of meaning of another word. This definition excludes from consideration as antonyms several classes of words that are sometimes treated as antonyms but that actually contain words which neither directly oppose nor directly negate the words with which they are said to be antonymous.

For example, some terms have such a relationship to each other that one can scarcely be used without suggesting the other (as *husband* and *wife, father* and *son, buyer* and *seller*), yet there is no real opposition or real negation between such pairs. These are merely *relative terms*—their relation is reciprocal or correlative rather than antonymous.

Complementary terms in a similar way are usually paired and have a reciprocal relationship to the point that one seems incomplete without the other (as in such pairs as *question* and *answer, seek* and *find*). This relation which involves no negation is better seen as sequential than antonymous.

And contrastive terms differ sharply from their "opposites" only in some parts of their meaning. They neither oppose nor negate fully, since they are significantly different in range of meaning and applicability, in emphasis, and in the suggestions they convey. An example is *destitute* (a strong word carrying suggestions of misery and distress) which is contrastive rather than antonymous with respect to *rich* (a rather neutral and matter-of-fact term), while *poor* (another neutral and matter-of-fact term) is the appropriate antonym of *rich*. Basically, contrastive words are only opposed incidentally; they do not meet head on.

What then is considered an antonym? True antonyms can be classified in three ways:

Opposites without intermediates: What is *perfect* can be in no way *imperfect;* you cannot at the same time *accept* and *reject* or *agree* and *disagree*.

Opposites with intermediates: Such words make up the extremes in a range of difference and are so completely opposed that the language allows no wider difference. Thus, a scale of excellence might include *superiority, adequacy, mediocrity*, and *inferiority*, but only *superiority* and *inferiority* are so totally opposed that each exactly negates what its opposite affirms.

Reverse opposites: These are words that are opposed in such a way that each means the undoing or nullification of what the other affirms. Such reverse opposites exactly oppose and fully negate the special features of their opposites. Thus, *disprove* so perfectly opposes and so clearly negates the implications of *prove* that it fits the concept of antonym, as does *unkind* with respect to *kind*.

In this book, antonyms, when they fit one of these criteria, are listed after the synonym to which they apply.

THESAURUS

A

A1 *Syn* EXCELLENT, bang-up, banner, capital, classic, crackerjack, dandy, divine, fabulous, fine, first-class, first-rate, grand, great, groovy, heavenly, jim-dandy, keen, marvelous (*or* marvellous), mean, neat, nifty, noble, par excellence, prime, sensational, splendid, stellar, sterling, superb, superior, superlative, supernal, swell, terrific, tip-top, top, top-notch, unsurpassed, wonderful *Ant* poor

aback *Syn* UNAWARES, suddenly, unaware, unexpectedly

abaft · toward or at the stern (of a vessel) *Syn* aft, astern *Rel* after, back, hind, hinder, posterior, rear *Ant* afore

abandon *n* · carefree freedom from constraint *Syn* abandonment, ease, lightheartedness, naturalness, spontaneity, unrestraint *Rel* ardor, enthusiasm, exuberance, fervor, spirit, warmth, zeal *Ant* constraint, restraint

abandon *vb* **1** · to quit absolutely *Syn* desert, forsake *Rel* cast, discard, junk, scrap *Ant* reclaim **2** *Syn* RELINQUISH, cede, leave, resign, surrender, waive, yield *Ant* keep

abandoned **1** · utterly depraved *Syn* dissolute, profligate, reprobate *Rel* debased, debauched, depraved, perverted *Ant* redeemed, regenerate **2** · left unoccupied or unused *Syn* derelict, deserted, disused, forgotten, forsaken, rejected, vacated *Rel* ignored, neglected, unattended, untended

abandonment *Syn* ABANDON, ease, lightheartedness, naturalness, spontaneity, unrestraint *Ant* constraint, restraint

abase · to lower in one's own estimation or in that of others *Syn* debase, degrade, demean, humble, humiliate *Rel* cower, cringe, fawn, toady, truckle *Ant* exalt, extol (*especially oneself*)

abash *Syn* EMBARRASS, discomfit, disconcert, faze, rattle *Ant* facilitate, relieve

abate **1** · to die down in force or intensity *Syn* ebb, subside, wane *Rel* decrease, diminish, dwindle *Ant* revive, rise **2** *Syn* DECREASE, diminish, dwindle, lessen, reduce *Ant* increase

abatement *Syn* DEDUCTION, discount, rebate

abbey *Syn* CLOISTER, convent, monastery, nunnery, priory

abbreviate *Syn* SHORTEN, abridge, curtail, retrench *Ant* elongate, extend, lengthen, prolong, protract

abdicate · to give up formally or definitely a position of trust, honor, or glory *Syn* renounce, resign *Rel* abandon, leave, relinquish, surrender *Ant* assume, usurp

abdomen *Syn* STOMACH, belly, gut, solar plexus, tummy

aberrant *Syn* DEVIANT, abnormal, anomalous, atypical, irregular, unnatural *Ant* natural, normal, regular, standard, typical

aberration **1** · mental disorder *Syn* alienation, derangement *Rel* dementia, insanity, lunacy *Ant* soundness (*of mind*) **2** *Syn* DEVIATION, deflection, divergence

abet *Syn* INCITE, foment, instigate *Ant* restrain

abettor **1** *Syn* ACCOMPLICE, accessory, cohort, confederate **2** *Syn* ALLY, backer, confederate, supporter, sympathizer

abeyance · a state of temporary inactivity *Syn* doldrums, dormancy, latency, quiescence, suspense, suspension *Rel* inaction, inertia, inertness, motionlessness *Ant* continuance, continuation

abeyant *Syn* LATENT, dormant, potential, quiescent *Ant* patent

abhor *Syn* HATE, abominate, detest, loathe *Ant* love

abhorrence · a feeling of extreme disgust or dislike *Syn* abomination, detestation, hate, hatred, loathing *Rel* distaste, repellency, repugnance *Ant* admiration, enjoyment

abhorrent **1** *Syn* HATEFUL, abominable, detestable, odious *Ant* lovable, sympathetic **2** *Syn* REPUGNANT, distasteful, invidious, obnoxious, repellent *Ant* congenial

abide **1** *Syn* BEAR (sense 2), brook, endure, stand, suffer, tolerate **2** *Syn* CONTINUE, endure, last, persist **3** *Syn* STAY, linger, remain, tarry, wait

ability · the physical or mental power to do something *Syn* capability, capacity, competence, competency, faculty *Rel* aptitude, aptness, endowment, facility, gift, knack, talent *Ant* disability, inability, incapability, incapacity, incompetence, incompetency, ineptitude, ineptness

abject *Syn* MEAN, ignoble, sordid

abjure · to abandon irrevocably and usually with solemnity or publicity *Syn* forswear, recant, renounce, retract *Rel* eschew, forbear, forgo *Ant* pledge (*allegiance, a vow*), elect (*a way of life, a means to an end*)

able *Syn* COMPETENT, capable, fit, good, qualified, suitable *Ant* incompetent, inept, poor, unfit, unqualified

abnegate *Syn* FORGO, eschew, forbear, sacrifice

abnegation *Syn* RENUNCIATION, self-abnegation, self-denial *Ant* indulgence, self-indulgence

abnormal *Syn* DEVIANT, aberrant, anomalous,

atypical, irregular, unnatural *Ant* natural, normal, regular, standard, typical

abode *Syn* HABITATION, domicile, dwelling, home, house, residence

abolish · to put an end to by formal action *Syn* abrogate, annul, cancel, dissolve, invalidate, negate, nullify, quash, repeal, rescind, void *Rel* countermand, override, overrule, overturn, veto

abominable *Syn* HATEFUL, abhorrent, detestable, odious *Ant* lovable, sympathetic

abominate *Syn* HATE, abhor, detest, loathe *Ant* love

abomination **1** · a person or thing from which one shrinks with intense dislike *Syn* anathema, bête noire, bugbear *Rel* annoyance, pest, plague *Ant* joy **2** *Syn* ABHORRENCE, detestation, hate, hatred, loathing *Ant* admiration, enjoyment

aboriginal *Syn* NATIVE, autochthonous, endemic, indigenous *Ant* alien, foreign

abortion *Syn* CANCELLATION, calling, calling off, dropping, recall, repeal, rescission, revocation *Ant* continuation

abortive *Syn* FUTILE, bootless, fruitless, vain *Ant* effective, effectual, efficacious, efficient, fruitful, productive, profitable, successful

abound *Syn* TEEM, overflow, swarm

abounding *Syn* RIFE, flush, fraught, replete, swarming, teeming, thick, thronging

about *prep* **1** · in reference to *Syn* concerning, regarding, respecting **2** *Syn* AROUND (sense 1), by, near, next to

about *adv* **1** *Syn* ALMOST, more or less, most, much, near, nearly, next to, nigh, practically, some, virtually, well-nigh **2** *Syn* AROUND (sense 2), over, round, through, throughout

above · to or in a higher place *Syn* aloft, over, overhead, skyward *Ant* below, beneath, under

aboveboard *Syn* STRAIGHTFORWARD, forthright *Ant* devious, indirect

abracadabra *Syn* GIBBERISH, hocus-pocus, mummery

abrade · to affect a surface by rubbing, scraping, or wearing away *Syn* chafe, excoriate, fret, gall *Rel* grate, grind, rasp, scrape, scratch

abridge *Syn* SHORTEN, abbreviate, curtail, retrench *Ant* elongate, extend, lengthen, prolong, protract

abridgment · a condensation of a larger work *Syn* abstract, brief, conspectus, epitome, synopsis *Rel* compendium, digest, précis, sketch, syllabus *Ant* expansion

abrogate *Syn* ABOLISH, annul, cancel, dissolve, invalidate, negate, nullify, quash, repeal, rescind, void

abrupt **1** *Syn* PRECIPITATE, hasty, headlong, impetuous, sudden *Ant* deliberate **2** *Syn* STEEP, precipitous, sheer

abscess · a localized swollen area of infection containing pus *Syn* boil, carbuncle, furuncle, pimple, pustule

abscond *Syn* ESCAPE (sense 1), decamp, flee, fly

absence *Syn* LACK, dearth, defect, privation, want

absent *Syn* ABSTRACTED, absentminded, distraught, preoccupied *Ant* alert

absentminded *Syn* ABSTRACTED, absent, distraught, preoccupied *Ant* alert

absolute **1** · exercising power or authority without external restraint *Syn* arbitrary, autocratic, despotic, tyrannical, tyrannous *Rel* authoritarian, totalitarian *Ant* limited, restrained **2** *Syn* PURE, sheer, simple *Ant* adulterated, applied (*of science*), contaminated, polluted **3** *Syn* ULTIMATE, categorical

absolution *Syn* PARDON, amnesty, forgiveness, remission, remittal *Ant* penalty, punishment, retribution

absolve *Syn* EXCULPATE, acquit, exonerate, vindicate *Ant* accuse, inculpate

absorb **1** · to take (something) in so as to become imbued with it or to make it a part of one's being *Syn* assimilate, imbibe *Rel* impregnate, saturate, soak *Ant* exude, give out **2** *Syn* MONOPOLIZE, consume, engross

absorbed *Syn* INTENT, engrossed, rapt *Ant* distracted

absorbing *Syn* INTERESTING, arresting, engaging, engrossing, enthralling, fascinating, gripping, immersing, intriguing, involving, riveting *Ant* boring, drab, dry, dull, heavy, monotonous, tedious, uninteresting

abstain *Syn* REFRAIN, forbear

abstemiousness *Syn* TEMPERANCE, abstinence, continence, sobriety *Ant* excessiveness, immoderacy, intemperance, intemperateness

abstinence *Syn* TEMPERANCE, abstemiousness, continence, sobriety *Ant* excessiveness, immoderacy, intemperance, intemperateness

abstract *adj* **1** · having conceptual rather than concrete existence *Syn* ideal, transcendent, transcendental *Rel* general, generic, universal *Ant* concrete **2** · dealing with or expressing a quality or idea *Syn* conceptual, theoretical *Rel* conjectural, hypothetical, speculative *Ant* concrete

abstract *n* *Syn* ABRIDGMENT, brief, conspectus, epitome, synopsis *Ant* expansion

abstract *vb* **1** *Syn* DETACH, disengage *Ant* affix, attach **2** *Syn* SUMMARIZE, digest, encapsulate, epitomize, outline, recap, recapitulate, sum up, wrap up

abstracted · inattentive to what presently claims or demands consideration *Syn* absent, absentminded, distraught, preoccupied *Rel* engrossed, intent *Ant* alert

abstruse *Syn* RECONDITE, esoteric, occult

absurd *Syn* FOOLISH, preposterous, silly *Ant* sensible

abundant *Syn* PLENTIFUL, ample, copious, plenteous *Ant* scant, scanty

abuse *n* · vehemently expressed condemnation

or disapproval *Syn* billingsgate, invective, obloquy, scurrility, vituperation *Rel* animadversion, aspersion, reflection, stricture *Ant* adulation

abuse *vb* **1** • to use or treat a person or thing improperly or wrongfully *Syn* ill-treat, maltreat, mistreat, misuse, outrage *Rel* damage, harm, hurt, impair, injure, mar, spoil *Ant* honor, respect **2** *Syn* ATTACK (sense 2), assail, belabor, blast, castigate, excoriate, jump (on), lambaste (*or* lambast), scathe, slam, vituperate

abusive • coarse, insulting, and contemptuous in character or utterance *Syn* contumelious, opprobrious, scurrilous, vituperative *Rel* affronting, insulting, offending, outraging *Ant* complementary, respectful

abutment *Syn* BUTTRESS, pier

abutting *Syn* ADJACENT, adjoining, bordering, contiguous, flanking, fringing, joining, juxtaposed, skirting, touching, verging *Ant* nonadjacent

abysm *Syn* GULF, abyss, chasm

abysmal *Syn* DEEP, profound

abyss *Syn* GULF, abysm, chasm

academic **1** • of or relating to schooling or learning especially at an advanced level *Syn* educational, scholarly, scholastic *Rel* bookish, pedantic, professorial *Ant* nonacademic, unacademic **2** *Syn* PEDANTIC, bookish, scholastic **3** *Syn* THEORETICAL, speculative

accede *Syn* ASSENT, acquiesce, agree, consent, subscribe *Ant* dissent

accelerate *Syn* HURRY (sense 1), hasten, quicken, rush, speed (up), whisk *Ant* decelerate, retard, slow (down)

accent *n* **1** *Syn* EMPHASIS, accentuation, stress **2** *Syn* INFLECTION, intonation

accent *vb* *Syn* EMPHASIZE, accentuate, feature, highlight, play (up), point (up), stress, underline, underscore *Ant* play (down)

accentuate *Syn* EMPHASIZE, accent, feature, highlight, play (up), point (up), stress, underline, underscore *Ant* play (down)

accentuation *Syn* EMPHASIS, accent, stress

accept **1** *Syn* APPROVE (OF), care (for), countenance, favor, OK (*or* okay), subscribe (to) *Ant* disapprove (of), discountenance, disfavor, frown (on *or* upon) **2** *Syn* RECEIVE, admit, take

acceptability *Syn* SUFFICIENCY, adequacy, satisfactoriness *Ant* inadequacy, insufficiency

acceptable *Syn* ADEQUATE, all right, decent, fine, OK (*or* okay), passable, respectable, satisfactory, tolerable *Ant* deficient, inadequate, lacking, unacceptable, unsatisfactory, wanting

acceptation *Syn* MEANING, import, sense, significance, signification

accession *Syn* ADDITION, accretion, increment

accessory *n* **1** *Syn* ACCOMPLICE, abettor,

cohort, confederate **2** *Syn* APPENDAGE, adjunct, appurtenance

accessory *adj* *Syn* AUXILIARY, adjuvant, ancillary, contributory, subservient, subsidiary

accident **1** • chance or a chance event bringing injury or loss *Syn* casualty, mishap *Rel* catastrophe, disaster **2** *Syn* CHANCE, fortune, hap, hazard, luck *Ant* law, principle

accidental • happening by chance *Syn* casual, chance, fluky, fortuitous, inadvertent, incidental, unintended, unintentional, unplanned, unpremeditated, unwitting *Rel* coincidental *Ant* deliberate, intended, intentional, planned, premeditated

acclaim **1** • to declare enthusiastic approval of *Syn* applaud, cheer, hail, laud, praise, salute, tout *Rel* ballyhoo *Ant* knock, pan, slam **2** *Syn* PRAISE, eulogize, extol, laud *Ant* blame

acclamation *Syn* APPLAUSE, cheering, cheers, ovation, plaudit(s), rave(s) *Ant* booing, hissing

acclimate *Syn* HARDEN (sense 2), acclimatize, season *Ant* soften

acclimatize *Syn* HARDEN (sense 2), acclimate, season *Ant* soften

accommodate **1** *Syn* ADAPT, adjust, conform, reconcile *Ant* unfit **2** *Syn* CONTAIN, hold **3** *Syn* OBLIGE, favor *Ant* disoblige

accompany • to go along with in order to provide assistance, protection, or companionship *Syn* attend, chaperone (*or* chaperon), convoy, escort, squire *Rel* associate, consort, pal (around), team (up)

accomplice • one associated with another in wrongdoing *Syn* abettor, accessory, cohort, confederate *Rel* collaborationist, collaborator, informant, informer

accomplish *Syn* PERFORM, achieve, discharge, effect, execute, fulfill

accomplished *Syn* CONSUMMATE, finished *Ant* crude

accomplishment **1** *Syn* ACQUIREMENT, acquisition, attainment **2** *Syn* FRUITION, achievement, actuality, attainment, consummation, fulfillment, realization *Ant* naught, nonfulfillment

accord *n* **1** *Syn* AGREEMENT, understanding **2** *Syn* HARMONY, concord, consonance *Ant* conflict

accord *vb* **1** *Syn* AGREE (sense 2), conform, correspond, harmonize, jibe, square, tally *Ant* differ (from) **2** *Syn* GRANT (sense 1), award, concede, vouchsafe

accordingly *Syn* THEREFORE, consequently, hence, so, then

accost *Syn* ADDRESS, greet, hail, salute

account *n* • a statement of actual events or conditions or of purported occurrences or conditions *Syn* chronicle, report, story, version

account *vb* **1** *Syn* CONSIDER (sense 2), deem, reckon, regard **2** *Syn* USE (sense 1), advantage, avail, profit, service

accountable *Syn* RESPONSIBLE, amenable, answerable, liable

account (for) *Syn* EXPLAIN (sense 2), explain away, rationalize

accoutre *or* **accouter** *Syn* FURNISH (sense 1), equip, fit (out), outfit, rig, supply *Ant* hold (back), keep (back), reserve, retain, withhold

accredit **1** *Syn* APPROVE, certify, endorse, sanction *Ant* disapprove **2** *Syn* ASCRIBE, assign, attribute, charge, credit, impute, refer **3** *Syn* AUTHORIZE, commission, license

accretion *Syn* ADDITION, accession, increment

accumulate **1** · to bring together so as to make a store or great quantity *Syn* amass, hoard *Rel* collect, gather *Ant* dissipate **2** *Syn* INCREASE (sense 2), appreciate, balloon, build (up), burgeon, enlarge, escalate, expand, mount, multiply, mushroom, proliferate, rise, snowball, swell, wax *Ant* contract, decrease, diminish, lessen, wane

accumulative *Syn* CUMULATIVE, additive, summative

accuracy *Syn* PRECISION, closeness, delicacy, exactitude, exactness, fineness, preciseness, rigorousness, veracity *Ant* coarseness, impreciseness, imprecision, inaccuracy, inexactness, roughness

accurate *Syn* CORRECT, exact, nice, precise, right *Ant* incorrect

accursed *Syn* EXECRABLE, cursed, damnable

accuse · to make a claim of wrongdoing against *Syn* charge, impeach, incriminate, indict *Rel* blame, castigate, censure, condemn, criticize, damn, denounce, fault, impugn, reproach, reprobate *Ant* absolve, acquit, clear, exculpate, exonerate, vindicate

accustom *Syn* HABITUATE, addict, inure

accustomed **1** · being in the habit or custom *Syn* given, habituated, used, wont *Rel* apt, inclined, liable, prone *Ant* unaccustomed, unused **2** *Syn* USUAL, customary, habitual, wonted

ace *Syn* EXPERT, adept, artist, authority, crackerjack, maestro, master, past master, scholar, shark, virtuoso, whiz, wizard *Ant* amateur

acerbity *Syn* ACRIMONY, asperity *Ant* suavity

ache *Syn* PAIN, pang, stitch, throe, twinge

achieve **1** *Syn* PERFORM, accomplish, discharge, effect, execute, fulfill **2** *Syn* REACH, attain, compass, gain

achievement **1** *Syn* FEAT, exploit **2** *Syn* FRUITION, accomplishment, actuality, attainment, consummation, fulfillment, realization *Ant* naught, nonfulfillment

acid *Syn* SOUR, acidulous, dry, tart

acidulous *Syn* SOUR, acid, dry, tart

acknowledge *Syn* ADMIT, agree, allow, concede, confess, grant, own (up) *Ant* deny

acknowledgment *Syn* CONFESSION, admission, avowal, concession

acme *Syn* SUMMIT, apex, apogee, climax, culmination, meridian, peak, pinnacle, zenith

acoustic *or* **acoustical** *Syn* AUDITORY, aural, auricular

acquaint *Syn* ENLIGHTEN (sense 1), advise, apprise, brief, clue, familiarize, fill in, inform, instruct, tell, wise (up)

acquaintance **1** · knowledge gained by personal experience *Syn* cognizance, familiarity *Rel* association, experience, exposure, intimacy, involvement *Ant* unfamiliarity **2** *Syn* FRIEND, confidant, intimate *Ant* foe

acquiesce *Syn* ASSENT, accede, agree, consent, subscribe *Ant* dissent

acquiescence *Syn* COMPLIANCE, resignation *Ant* forwardness

acquiescent **1** *Syn* COMPLIANT, resigned *Ant* forward **2** *Syn* PASSIVE, nonresistant, resigned, tolerant, tolerating, unresistant, unresisting, yielding *Ant* protesting, resistant, resisting, unyielding

acquire *Syn* EARN, attain, capture, carry, draw, gain, garner, get, land, make, obtain, procure, realize, secure, win *Ant* forfeit, lose

acquirement · a power or skill that is the fruit of exertion or effort *Syn* accomplishment, acquisition, attainment *Rel* achievement, feat

acquisition *Syn* ACQUIREMENT, accomplishment, attainment

acquisitive *Syn* COVETOUS, avaricious, grasping, greedy

acquisitiveness *Syn* GREED, avarice, avariciousness, avidity, covetousness, cupidity, greediness, rapaciousness, rapacity

acquit **1** *Syn* BEHAVE, comport, conduct, demean, deport, quit *Ant* misbehave **2** *Syn* EXCULPATE, absolve, exonerate, vindicate *Ant* accuse, inculpate

acrid *Syn* CAUSTIC, mordant, scathing *Ant* genial

acrimony · temper or language marked by irritation or some degree of anger or resentment *Syn* acerbity, asperity *Rel* bitterness *Ant* suavity

across · so as to intersect the length of something *Syn* athwart, crossways, crosswise

act *vb* **1** · to perform especially in an indicated way *Syn* behave, function, operate, react, work **2** · to assume the appearance or role of another person or character *Syn* impersonate, play **3** *Syn* SEEM, appear, look, make, sound

act *n* **1** *Syn* ACTION, deed **2** *Syn* FUNCTION, perform, serve, work

acting *Syn* TEMPORARY, ad interim, provisional *Ant* permanent

action **1** · something done or effected *Syn* act, deed *Rel* procedure, proceeding, process **2** *Syn* BATTLE, engagement **3** *Syn* SUIT, case, cause, lawsuit

activate **1** · to cause to function *Syn* actuate, crank (up), drive, move, propel, run, set off, spark, start, touch off, trigger, turn on *Rel* charge, electrify, energize, fire, fuel, generate, power, push *Ant* cut, deactivate, kill, shut off, turn off   **2** *Syn* VITALIZE, energize *Ant* atrophy

active · at work or in effective action *Syn* dynamic, live, operative *Rel* agile, brisk, nimble *Ant* inactive

actor · one who, for the entertainment or edification of an audience, takes part in an exhibition simulating happenings in real life *Syn* impersonator, mime, mimic, mummer, performer, player, thespian, trouper

actual · existing in fact and not merely as a possibility *Syn* concrete, existent, factual, real, true, very *Rel* attested, authenticated, confirmed, demonstrated, established, proven, substantiated, validated, verified *Ant* conjectural, hypothetical, ideal, nonexistent, possible, potential, theoretical

actuality **1** *Syn* EXISTENCE, being *Ant* nonexistence   **2** *Syn* FRUITION, accomplishment, achievement, attainment, consummation, fulfillment, realization *Ant* naught, nonfulfillment

actualize *Syn* REALIZE, embody, externalize, hypostatize, incarnate, materialize, objectify, reify

actuate *Syn* ACTIVATE, crank (up), drive, move, propel, run, set off, spark, start, touch off, trigger, turn on *Ant* cut, deactivate, kill, shut off, turn off

act up *Syn* CUT UP, clown (around), fool (around), horse (around), monkey (around), show off, skylark

acumen *Syn* DISCERNMENT, discrimination, insight, penetration, perception

acute **1** · of uncertain outcome *Syn* critical, crucial *Rel* climactic, culminating   **2** *Syn* SHARP, keen *Ant* blunt, dull   **3** *Syn* SHRILL, high-pitched, piping, screeching, shrieking, squeaking, squeaky, treble, whistling *Ant* bass, deep, low, throaty

ad *Syn* ANNOUNCEMENT, advertisement, bulletin, notice, notification, posting, release

adage *Syn* SAYING, aphorism, apothegm, epigram, maxim, motto, proverb, saw

adamant *Syn* OBSTINATE, adamantine, dogged, hard, hardened, hardheaded, hardhearted, headstrong, immovable, implacable, inflexible, mulish, obdurate, opinionated, ossified, pat, peevish, pertinacious, perverse, pigheaded, rigid, self-willed, stubborn, unbending, uncompromising, unrelenting, unyielding, willful (*or* wilful) *Ant* acquiescent, agreeable, amenable, compliant, complying, flexible, pliable, pliant, relenting, yielding

adamantine *Syn* OBSTINATE, adamant, dogged, hard, hardened, hardheaded, hardhearted, headstrong, immovable, implacable, inflexible, mulish, obdurate, opinionated, ossified, pat, peevish, pertinacious, perverse, pigheaded, rigid, self-willed, stubborn, unbending, uncompromising, unrelenting, unyielding, willful (*or* wilful) *Ant* acquiescent, agreeable, amenable, compliant, complying, flexible, pliable, pliant, relenting, yielding

adapt **1** · to bring into correspondence *Syn* accommodate, adjust, conform, reconcile *Rel* moderate, qualify, temper *Ant* unfit   **2** *Syn* EDIT, compile, redact, revise, rewrite

adaptable *Syn* PLASTIC, ductile, malleable, pliable, pliant

add **1** · to combine (numbers) into a single sum *Syn* foot (up), sum, total *Rel* calculate, cast, cipher, compute, figure, reckon, tally   **2** · to join (something) to a mass, quantity, or number so as to bring about an overall increase *Syn* adjoin, annex, append, tack (on) *Rel* affix, attach, fasten, fix, graft, hitch, tie *Ant* deduct, remove, subtract, take

added *Syn* ADDITIONAL, another, else, farther, further, more, other

addendum *Syn* APPENDIX, supplement

addict *n* **1** · a person who by habit and strong inclination indulges in something or the pursuit of something *Syn* devotee, habitué, votary   **2** *Syn* FAN, aficionado, buff, bug, devotee, enthusiast, fanatic, fancier, fiend, freak, lover, maniac, nut

addict *vb Syn* HABITUATE, accustom, inure

addition · a thing that serves to increase another in size, amount, or content *Syn* accession, accretion, increment

additional · resulting in an increase in amount or number *Syn* added, another, else, farther, further, more, other *Rel* accessory, collateral, extraneous, side, supplemental, supplementary

additive *Syn* CUMULATIVE, accumulative, summative

addle *Syn* CONFUSE, befuddle, fuddle, muddle *Ant* enlighten

address *vb* **1** · to speak to or less often to write or make a sign to a person in recognition or in order to obtain recognition *Syn* accost, greet, hail, salute *Rel* converse, speak, talk   **2** *Syn* DIRECT (sense 1), apply, devote *Ant* misdirect

address *n* **1** *Syn* SPEECH, harangue, homily, lecture, oration, sermon, talk   **2** *Syn* TACT, poise, savoir faire *Ant* awkwardness

add (to) *Syn* INCREASE (sense 1), aggrandize, amplify, augment, boost, compound, enlarge, escalate, expand, extend, multiply, raise, swell, up *Ant* abate, contract, decrease, diminish, lessen, lower, reduce, subtract (from)

adduce · to bring forward by way of explanation, proof, illustration, or demonstration *Syn* advance, allege, cite *Rel* exemplify, illustrate

adept *n Syn* EXPERT, ace, artist, authority, crackerjack, maestro, master, past master, scholar, shark, virtuoso, whiz, wizard *Ant* amateur

adept *adj Syn* PROFICIENT, expert, masterly, skilled, skillful *Ant* amateur, amateurish, inexperienced, inexpert, unexperienced, unpracticed, unprofessional, unseasoned, unskilled, unskillful

adequacy *Syn* SUFFICIENCY, acceptability, satisfactoriness *Ant* inadequacy, insufficiency

adequate **1** • of a level of quality that meets one's needs or standards *Syn* acceptable, all right, decent, fine, OK (*or* okay), passable, respectable, satisfactory, tolerable *Rel* agreeable, bearable, endurable, sufferable *Ant* deficient, inadequate, lacking, unacceptable, unsatisfactory, wanting **2** *Syn* SUFFICIENT, competent, enough

adhere *Syn* STICK, cleave, cling, cohere

adherence *Syn* ADHESION, bonding

adherent *Syn* FOLLOWER, convert, disciple, partisan, pupil, votary *Ant* leader

adhesion • a physical sticking to as if by glue *Syn* adherence, bonding *Rel* agglutination, clumping, cohesion

adieu *Syn* GOOD-BYE, au revoir, bon voyage, farewell, Godspeed *Ant* hello

ad interim *Syn* TEMPORARY, acting, provisional *Ant* permanent

adjacent • having a border in common *Syn* abutting, adjoining, bordering, contiguous, flanking, fringing, joining, juxtaposed, skirting, touching, verging *Rel* close, closest, immediate, near, nearby, nearest, neighboring, next, next-door, nigh *Ant* nonadjacent

adjoin *Syn* ADD (SENSE 2), annex, append, tack (on) *Ant* deduct, remove, subtract, take

adjoining *Syn* ADJACENT, abutting, bordering, contiguous, flanking, fringing, joining, juxtaposed, skirting, touching, verging *Ant* nonadjacent

adjourn • to bring to a formal close for a period of time *Syn* recess, suspend *Rel* break off, discontinue, intermit, interrupt

adjudge *Syn* JUDGE, adjudicate, arbitrate

adjudicate *Syn* JUDGE, adjudge, arbitrate

adjunct *Syn* APPENDAGE, accessory, appurtenance

adjure *Syn* BEG, beseech, entreat, implore, importune, supplicate

adjust **1** • to set right or to rights *Syn* fix, regulate *Rel* correct, rectify *Ant* derange **2** *Syn* ADAPT, accommodate, conform, reconcile *Ant* unfit

adjutant *Syn* ASSISTANT, aid, aide, apprentice, coadjutor, deputy, helper, sidekick

adjuvant *Syn* AUXILIARY, accessory, ancillary, contributory, subservient, subsidiary

administer *Syn* ENFORCE, apply, execute, implement

administration *Syn* RULE (sense 2), authority, governance, government, jurisdiction, regime, regimen

administrator *Syn* EXECUTIVE, director, manager, superintendent, supervisor

admirable • deserving of high regard or great approval *Syn* commendable, creditable, laudable, meritorious, praiseworthy *Rel* awesome, distinctive, distinguished, excellent, honorable, noteworthy, noticeable, outstanding, reputable, worthy *Ant* censurable, discreditable, reprehensible

admiration **1** *Syn* REGARD, esteem, respect *Ant* despite **2** *Syn* WONDER (sense 2), amazement, awe, wonderment

admire *Syn* REGARD, esteem, respect *Ant* despise

admissible *Syn* PERMISSIBLE, allowable, licensable *Ant* banned, barred, forbidden, impermissible, inadmissible, interdicted, prohibited, proscribed

admission *Syn* CONFESSION, acknowledgment, avowal, concession

admit **1** • to accept the truth or existence of (something) usually reluctantly *Syn* acknowledge, agree, allow, concede, confess, grant, own (up) *Rel* disburden, unburden, unload *Ant* deny **2** *Syn* ENTER (sense 2), introduce **3** *Syn* RECEIVE, accept, take

admixture **1** • an added ingredient that destroys the purity or genuineness of a substance *Syn* adulterant, alloy *Rel* accretion, addition **2** *Syn* BLEND, amalgam, amalgamation, combination, composite, compound, fusion, intermixture, mix, mixture

admonish *Syn* REPROVE, chide, rebuke, reprimand, reproach

admonishing *Syn* CAUTIONARY, admonitory, cautioning, warning

admonition *Syn* WARNING, alarm, alert, caution, forewarning, notice

admonitory *Syn* CAUTIONARY, admonishing, cautioning, warning

ado *Syn* STIR, bustle, flurry, fuss, pother *Ant* tranquillity

adolescence *Syn* YOUTH, puberty, pubescence *Ant* age

adolescent **1** *Syn* CALLOW, green, immature, inexperienced, juvenile, puerile, raw, unfledged, unripe, unripened *Ant* adult, experienced, grown-up, mature, ripe **2** *Syn* CHILDISH, babyish, immature, infantile, juvenile, kiddish, puerile *Ant* adult, grown-up, mature **3** *Syn* YOUNG, immature, juvenile, youngish, youthful *Ant* adult, full-grown, mature, matured

adopt • to make one's own what in some fashion one owes to another *Syn* embrace, espouse *Rel* appropriate, arrogate, usurp *Ant* discard, repudiate

adorable *Syn* LOVABLE, darling, dear, disarming, endearing, precious, sweet, winning *Ant* abhorrent, abominable, detestable, hateful, odious, unlovable

adoration *Syn* REVERENCE (sense 1), veneration, worship

adore **1** *Syn* IDOLIZE, adulate, canonize, deify, dote (on), worship **2** *Syn* REVERE, reverence, venerate, worship *Ant* flout

adorn · to add something unessential in order to enhance the appearance *Syn* beautify, bedeck, deck, decorate, embellish, garnish, ornament *Rel* enhance, heighten, intensify *Ant* disfigure

adroit *Syn* CLEVER, cunning, ingenious

adroitness *Syn* DEXTERITY (sense 1), cleverness, finesse, sleight *Ant* awkwardness, clumsiness, gawkiness

adulate *Syn* IDOLIZE, adore, canonize, deify, dote (on), worship

adulation 1 *Syn* COMPLIMENT, flattery *Ant* taunt 2 *Syn* WORSHIP, deification, idolatry, idolization, worshipping

adult *Syn* MATURE, grown-up, matured, mellow, ripe *Ant* childish, immature

adulterant *Syn* ADMIXTURE, alloy

adulterate · to alter fraudulently especially for profit *Syn* doctor, load, sophisticate, weight *Rel* corrupt, debase, vitiate *Ant* refine

adulterated *Syn* IMPURE, alloyed, contaminated, dilute, diluted, polluted, tainted, thinned, weakened *Ant* pure, unadulterated, unalloyed, uncontaminated, undiluted, unpolluted, untainted

adumbrate *Syn* SUGGEST (sense 2), shadow *Ant* manifest

adumbration *Syn* SHADE, penumbra, shadow, umbra, umbrage

advance *n* 1 · an instance of notable progress in the development of knowledge, technology, or skill *Syn* advancement, breakthrough, enhancement, improvement, refinement *Rel* amelioration, boost, heightening, increase, melioration, strengthening, upgrade, uplift, upswing, uptrend, upturn *Ant* setback 2 · forward movement in time or place *Syn* advancement, furtherance, going, headway, march, onrush, passage, process, procession, progress, progression *Rel* current, drift, flow, flux, stream, way *Ant* recession, regression, retrogression 3 *Syn* OVERTURE, approach, bid, tender

advance *vb* 1 · to move or put ahead *Syn* forward, further, promote *Rel* aid, assist, help *Ant* check, retard 2 *Syn* ADDUCE, allege, cite

advanced 1 *Syn* LIBERAL (sense 2), progressive, radical *Ant* authoritarian 2 *Syn* PREMATURE, forward, precocious, untimely *Ant* matured

advancement 1 · the act of raising a person in grade, rank, or dignity, or the honor that comes to one who is so raised *Syn* elevation, preferment, promotion *Ant* degradation, reduction (*in rank or status*) 2 *Syn* ADVANCE (sense 1), breakthrough, enhancement, improvement, refinement *Ant* setback 3 *Syn* ADVANCE (sense 2), furtherance, going, headway, march, onrush, passage, process, procession, progress, progression *Ant* recession, regression, retrogression

advantage 1 · a factor or set of factors in a competition or rivalry giving one person or side a position of superiority over the other *Syn* allowance, edge, handicap, odds *Rel* preeminence, superlativeness *Ant* disadvantage, handicap 2 *Syn* USE (sense 1), account, avail, profit, service

advantageous *Syn* BENEFICIAL, favorable, helpful, profitable, salutary *Ant* disadvantageous, unfavorable, unhelpful

adventure *n* · an undertaking, an exploit, or an experience involving hazards and requiring boldness *Syn* enterprise, quest *Rel* achievement, exploit, feat

adventure *vb* *Syn* ENDANGER, compromise, gamble (with), hazard, imperil, jeopardize, menace, risk, venture

adventurous · courting danger or exposing oneself to danger in a greater degree than is required for courage *Syn* daredevil, daring, foolhardy, rash, reckless, venturesome *Rel* audacious, bold, brave, doughty, intrepid *Ant* cautious, unadventurous

adversary *Syn* ENEMY, antagonist, foe, opponent *Ant* friend

adverse 1 · so opposed as to cause interference and often harmful or fatal interference *Syn* antagonistic, counter, counteractive *Rel* harmful, hurtful, injurious *Ant* propitious 2 *Syn* HARMFUL, bad, baleful, baneful, damaging, deleterious, detrimental, evil, hurtful, ill, injurious, mischievous, noxious, pernicious, prejudicial *Ant* harmless, innocent, innocuous, inoffensive, safe

adversity *Syn* MISFORTUNE, knock, misadventure, mischance, mishap *Ant* fortune, luck

advert *Syn* REFER, allude

advertise *Syn* ANNOUNCE, blaze, broadcast, declare, enunciate, placard, post, proclaim, promulgate, publicize, publish, sound

advertisement 1 *Syn* ANNOUNCEMENT, ad, bulletin, notice, notification, posting, release 2 *Syn* DECLARATION, announcement, broadcasting, proclamation, promulgation, publication

advice · an opinion suggesting a wise or proper course of action *Syn* counsel, guidance *Rel* recommendation, suggestion

advisable *Syn* EXPEDIENT, desirable, judicious, politic, prudent, tactical, wise *Ant* imprudent, inadvisable, inexpedient, injudicious, unwise

advise 1 *Syn* ENLIGHTEN (sense 1), acquaint, apprise, brief, clue, familiarize, fill in, inform, instruct, tell, wise (up) 2 *Syn* INFORM (sense 2), apprise, notify

advised *Syn* DELIBERATE, considered, designed, premeditated, studied *Ant* casual

advocate *n* 1 *Syn* EXPONENT, apostle, backer, booster, champion, friend, promoter, proponent, supporter *Ant* adversary, antagonist, opponent 2 *Syn* LAWYER, attorney, barrister, counsel, counselor, solicitor

advocate *vb Syn* SUPPORT (sense 2), back, champion, uphold

aerial *Syn* AIRY, ethereal *Ant* substantial

aesthete · a person conspicuous for his enjoyment and appreciation of the beautiful, the exquisite, or the choice *Syn* connoisseur, dilettante

affable 1 *Syn* AMIABLE, agreeable, genial, good-natured, good-tempered, gracious, nice, sweet, well-disposed *Ant* disagreeable, ill-natured, ill-tempered, ungracious, unpleasant 2 *Syn* GRACIOUS, cordial, genial, sociable *Ant* ungracious

affair 1 · something done or dealt with *Syn* business, concern, matter, thing 2 *Syn* AMOUR, intrigue, liaison

affect[1] *vb* · to produce or to have an effect upon a person or upon a thing capable of a reaction *Syn* impress, influence, strike, sway, touch *Rel* actuate, drive, impel, move

affect[2] *vb Syn* ASSUME, counterfeit, feign, pretend, sham, simulate

affectation *Syn* POSE, air, mannerism

affecting *Syn* MOVING, emotional, impressive, poignant, stirring, touching *Ant* unemotional, unimpressive

affection 1 *Syn* ATTACHMENT, love *Ant* aversion 2 *Syn* FEELING, emotion, passion, sentiment

affectionate *Syn* LOVING, devoted, doting, fond *Ant* unloving

affiliated *Syn* RELATED, allied, cognate, kindred

affinity *Syn* ATTRACTION, sympathy

affirm *Syn* ASSERT, aver, avouch, avow, declare, predicate, profess, protest, warrant *Ant* controvert, deny

affix *Syn* FASTEN, attach, fix *Ant* loose, loosen, unfasten

afflatus *Syn* INSPIRATION, frenzy, fury

afflict · to cause persistent suffering to *Syn* agonize, bedevil, curse, harrow, martyr, persecute, plague, rack, torment, torture *Rel* assail, attack, beset, set upon

affliction *Syn* TRIAL, cross, tribulation, visitation

affluent *Syn* RICH, opulent, wealthy *Ant* poor

afford *Syn* GIVE, bestow, confer, donate, present

affray *n Syn* CONTEST, combat, conflict, fight, fray

affray *vb Syn* FRIGHTEN, affright, alarm, fright, scare, startle, terrify, terrorize *Ant* reassure

affright *Syn* FRIGHTEN, affray, alarm, fright, scare, startle, terrify, terrorize *Ant* reassure

affront *n Syn* INSULT, barb, dart, dig, epithet, indignity, name, offense (*or* offence), outrage, put-down, sarcasm, slight, slur

affront *vb Syn* OFFEND, insult, outrage

aficionado *Syn* FAN, addict, buff, bug, devotee, enthusiast, fanatic, fancier, fiend, freak, lover, maniac, nut

afield *Syn* WRONG, amiss, astray, awry *Ant* aright, right, well

afraid *Syn* FEARFUL (sense 1), apprehensive *Ant* fearless, intrepid

aft *Syn* ABAFT, astern *Ant* afore

after *adv* · following in time or place *Syn* afterward (*or* afterwards), later, subsequently, thereafter *Rel* next *Ant* before, beforehand, earlier, previously

after *prep* · subsequent to in time or order *Syn* behind, following *Rel* next *Ant* ahead of, before, ere, previous to, prior to

aftereffect *Syn* EFFECT, aftermath, consequence, event, issue, outcome, result, sequel, upshot *Ant* cause

aftermath *Syn* EFFECT, aftereffect, consequence, event, issue, outcome, result, sequel, upshot *Ant* cause

afterward *or* **afterwards** *Syn* AFTER, later, subsequently, thereafter *Ant* before, beforehand, earlier, previously

against · in or into contact with *Syn* on, upon *Rel* alongside, next, next to

age *n* 1 · the period in one's life when one is old in years and declining in body or mind or both *Syn* dotage, senescence, senility *Ant* youth 2 · a long or seemingly long period of time *Syn* aeon (*or* eon), cycle, eternity *Rel* infinity 3 · an extent of time associated with a particular person or thing *Syn* day, epoch, era, period, time *Rel* cycle, generation, year

age *vb Syn* MATURE, develop, ripen

aged *Syn* ELDERLY, aging, ancient, geriatric, long-lived, old, older, senior *Ant* young, youthful

agency *Syn* AGENT (sense 2), instrument, instrumentality, machinery, means, medium, organ, vehicle

agenda *Syn* PROGRAM, schedule, timetable

agent 1 · a person who acts or does business for another *Syn* attorney, commissary, delegate, deputy, envoy, factor, procurator, proxy, representative *Rel* ambassador, emissary, foreign minister, legate, minister 2 · something used to achieve an end *Syn* agency, instrument, instrumentality, machinery, means, medium, organ, vehicle *Rel* determinant, expedient, factor, influence, ingredient, mechanism, tool

agglomerate *Syn* AGGREGATE, agglomeration, aggregation, conglomerate, conglomeration *Ant* constituent

agglomeration *Syn* AGGREGATE, agglomerate, aggregation, conglomerate, conglomeration *Ant* constituent

aggrandize 1 *Syn* EXALT, dignify, ennoble, enshrine, glorify, magnify *Ant* abase, degrade, demean, humble, humiliate 2 *Syn* INCREASE (sense 1), add (to), amplify, augment, boost, compound, enlarge, escalate, expand, extend, multiply, raise, swell, up *Ant* abate, contract, decrease, diminish, lessen, lower, reduce, subtract (from)

aggravate 1 *Syn* INTENSIFY, enhance, heighten *Ant* abate, allay, mitigate, temper 2 *Syn* IRRITATE, exasperate, nettle, peeve, provoke, rile

aggravating *Syn* ANNOYING, bothersome, disturbing, exasperating, frustrating, galling, irksome, irritating, maddening, nettling, peeving, pesty, rankling, riling, vexatious, vexing

aggregate 1 · a mass formed by parts or particles that are not merged into each other *Syn* agglomerate, agglomeration, aggregation, conglomerate, conglomeration *Rel* integrity, union, unity *Ant* constituent 2 *Syn* SUM, amount, number, quantity, total, whole

aggregation *Syn* AGGREGATE, agglomerate, agglomeration, conglomerate, conglomeration *Ant* constituent

aggression 1 *Syn* ATTACK (sense 2), assault, blitzkrieg, charge, descent, offense (*or* offence), offensive, onset, onslaught, raid, rush, strike 2 *Syn* BELLIGERENCE, aggressiveness, bellicosity, combativeness, contentiousness, disputatiousness, fight, militancy, pugnacity, scrappiness, truculence *Ant* pacifism

aggressive 1 · initiating hostile action in a struggle for supremacy *Syn* ATTACKING, offensive *Rel* encroaching, invading, trespassing *Ant* repelling, resisting 2 · conspicuously or obtrusively active or energetic *Syn* assertive, militant, pushing, pushy, self-assertive *Rel* energetic, strenuous, vigorous 3 *Syn* BELLIGERENT, argumentative, bellicose, combative, contentious, discordant, disputatious, gladiatorial, militant, pugnacious, quarrelsome, scrappy, truculent, warlike *Ant* nonbelligerent, pacific, peaceable, peaceful

aggressiveness *Syn* BELLIGERENCE, aggression, bellicosity, combativeness, contentiousness, disputatiousness, fight, militancy, pugnacity, scrappiness, truculence *Ant* pacifism

aggressor · one that starts armed conflict against another especially without reasonable cause *Syn* invader, raider *Rel* initiator, instigator

aggrieve *Syn* WRONG, oppress, persecute

agile · acting or moving with quickness and alacrity *Syn* brisk, nimble, spry *Rel* adroit, deft, dexterous *Ant* torpid

agility *Syn* DEXTERITY (sense 2), deftness, nimbleness, sleight, spryness *Ant* awkwardness, clumsiness, gawkiness

aging *Syn* ELDERLY, aged, ancient, geriatric, long-lived, old, older, senior *Ant* young, youthful

agitate 1 *Syn* DISCOMPOSE, disquiet, disturb, flurry, fluster, perturb, upset 2 *Syn* DISCUSS, argue, debate, dispute 3 *Syn* SHAKE (sense 2), convulse, rock

agitation *Syn* FRENZY, delirium, distraction, furor, furore, fury, hysteria, rage, rampage, uproar

agitator · a person who stirs up public feelings especially of discontent *Syn* demagogue, exciter, firebrand, fomenter, incendiary, inciter, instigator, rabble-rouser *Rel* advocate, alarmist, champion, demonstrator, exponent, extremist, insurgent, insurrectionist, marcher, objector, persuader, picketer, promoter, proponent, protester (*or* protestor), radical, rebel, reformer, revolter, revolutionary, revolutionist, subversive, supporter, troublemaker

agog *Syn* EAGER, anxious, athirst, avid, keen *Ant* listless

agonize 1 *Syn* AFFLICT, bedevil, curse, harrow, martyr, persecute, plague, rack, torment, torture 2 *Syn* WRITHE, squirm

agonizing *Syn* EXCRUCIATING, racking

agony *Syn* DISTRESS, dolor, misery, passion, suffering

agrarian *Syn* AGRICULTURAL, farming *Ant* nonagricultural

agree 1 · to come into or to be in harmony regarding a matter of opinion or a policy *Syn* coincide, concur *Rel* cooperate, unite *Ant* differ, disagree 2 · to exist or go together without conflict or incongruity *Syn* accord, conform, correspond, harmonize, jibe, square, tally *Ant* differ (from) 3 *Syn* ADMIT, acknowledge, allow, concede, confess, grant, own (up) *Ant* deny 4 *Syn* ASSENT, accede, acquiesce, consent, subscribe *Ant* dissent

agreeable 1 *Syn* AMIABLE, affable, genial, good-natured, good-tempered, gracious, nice, sweet, well-disposed *Ant* disagreeable, ill-natured, ill-tempered, ungracious, unpleasant 2 *Syn* PLEASANT, grateful, gratifying, pleasing, welcome *Ant* distasteful, harsh, unpleasant

agreement · a reconciliation of differences as to what should be done or not done *Syn* accord, understanding *Rel* cartel, concordat, contract, convention, entente, pact

agricultural · engaged in or concerned with agriculture *Syn* agrarian, farming *Rel* pastoral, rural *Ant* nonagricultural

agriculture · the science or the business of raising useful plants and animals *Syn* farming, husbandry

aground · resting on the shore or bottom of a body of water *Syn* beached, grounded, stranded *Rel* landed *Ant* afloat

ahead *Syn* ALONG, forth, forward, on, onward

ahead of *Syn* BEFORE, ere, of, previous to, prior to, to *Ant* after, following

aid *n* 1 *Syn* HELP, assistance 2 *Syn* ASSISTANT, adjutant, aide, apprentice, coadjutor, deputy, helper, sidekick

aid *vb* *Syn* HELP, assist *Ant* hinder

aide *Syn* ASSISTANT, adjutant, aid, apprentice, coadjutor, deputy, helper, sidekick

ail *Syn* TROUBLE, distress

ailment *Syn* DISEASE, complaint, condition, disorder, distemper, malady, syndrome

aim *vb* · to have as a controlling desire something beyond one's present power of attainment *Syn* aspire, pant *Rel* design, intend, propose, purpose

aim *n Syn* GOAL, ambition, aspiration, design, dream, end, intent, intention, mark, meaning, object, objective, plan, pretension, purpose, target, thing

aimlessly *Syn* HIT OR MISS, anyhow, anyway, anywise, desultorily, erratically, haphazard, haphazardly, helter-skelter, irregularly, randomly *Ant* methodically, systematically

air *n* **1** *Syn* AURA, atmosphere, climate, flavor, mood, note, temper **2** *Syn* MELODY, lay, song, strain, tune, warble **3** *Syn* POSE, affectation, mannerism

air *vb Syn* EXPRESS, broach, utter, vent, ventilate, voice *Ant* imply

airdrome *Syn* AIRPORT, airfield, airstrip, flying field, landing field, landing strip

airfield *Syn* AIRPORT, airdrome, airstrip, flying field, landing field, landing strip

airport · a place where airplanes take off and land *Syn* airdrome, airfield, airstrip, flying field, landing field, landing strip *Rel* air base, heliport

airstrip *Syn* AIRPORT, airdrome, airfield, flying field, landing field, landing strip

airy · as light and insubstantial as air *Syn* aerial, ethereal *Rel* rare, tenuous, thin *Ant* substantial

aisle *Syn* PASSAGE, arcade, cloister, corridor, gallery, hall, hallway, passageway

akin *Syn* ALIKE, analogous, comparable, correspondent, corresponding, like, matching, parallel, resembling, similar, such, suchlike *Ant* different, dissimilar, diverse, unlike

alacrity · cheerful readiness to do something *Syn* amenability, gameness, goodwill, willingness *Rel* celerity, quickness, rapidity, speed, speediness, swiftness

alarm *n* **1** *Syn* FEAR, consternation, dismay, dread, fright, horror, panic, terror, trepidation *Ant* fearlessness **2** *Syn* WARNING, admonition, alert, caution, forewarning, notice

alarm *vb Syn* FRIGHTEN, affray, affright, fright, scare, startle, terrify, terrorize *Ant* reassure

albeit *Syn* ALTHOUGH, howbeit, though, when, while

album *Syn* ANTHOLOGY, compilation, miscellany

alchemy *Syn* MAGIC, sorcery, thaumaturgy, witchcraft, witchery, wizardry

alcohol · a fermented or distilled beverage that can make a person drunk *Syn* booze, drink, grog, intoxicant, liquor, moonshine, spirits *Rel* ale, beer, brandy, gin, mead, mescal, rum, sake (*or* saki), table wine, tequila, vodka, whiskey (*or* whisky), wine

alcoholic *Syn* DRUNKARD, dipsomaniac, inebriate, soak, sot, tippler, toper, tosspot *Ant* teetotaler

alert *adj* **1** *Syn* INTELLIGENT, bright, brilliant, clever, knowing, quick-witted, smart *Ant* unintelligent **2** *Syn* WATCHFUL, vigilant, wide-awake

alert *n Syn* WARNING, admonition, alarm, caution, forewarning, notice

alert *vb Syn* WARN, caution, forewarn

alertness *Syn* VIGILANCE, attentiveness, lookout, surveillance, watch, watchfulness

alias *Syn* PSEUDONYM, incognito, nom de guerre, nom de plume, pen name

alibi **1** *Syn* APOLOGY, apologia, excuse, plea, pretext **2** *Syn* EXCUSE, defense, justification, plea, reason

alien *adj Syn* EXTRINSIC, extraneous, foreign *Ant* intrinsic

alien *n Syn* STRANGER, émigré, foreigner, immigrant, outlander, outsider

alienate **1** *Syn* ESTRANGE, disaffect, wean *Ant* reconcile **2** *Syn* TRANSFER, convey, deed

alienation **1** *Syn* ABERRATION, derangement *Ant* soundness (*of mind*) **2** *Syn* ESTRANGEMENT, disaffection, disgruntlement, souring *Ant* reconciliation

alight **1** · to come to rest after descending from the air *Syn* land, light, perch, roost, settle, touch down *Rel* belly-land, crash-land *Ant* take off **2** *Syn* DESCEND, dismount *Ant* ascend, climb

align *Syn* LINE, array, line up, range

alike · having qualities in common *Syn* akin, analogous, comparable, correspondent, corresponding, like, matching, parallel, resembling, similar, such, suchlike *Rel* commensurate, proportionate *Ant* different, dissimilar, diverse, unlike

alikeness *Syn* SIMILARITY, community, correspondence, likeness, parallelism, resemblance, similitude *Ant* dissimilarity, unlikeness

aliment *Syn* FOOD (sense 2), nourishment, nutriment, pabulum, pap, sustenance

alive **1** *Syn* AWARE, awake, cognizant, conscious, sensible *Ant* unaware **2** *Syn* CONSCIOUS, aware, cognizant, mindful, sensible, sentient *Ant* insensible, unaware, unconscious, unmindful **3** *Syn* LIVING, animate, animated, vital *Ant* lifeless

all *adj* **1** *Syn* WHOLE, entire, gross, total *Ant* partial **2** · including the entire membership of a group with no exceptions *Syn* each, every *Ant* no

all *adv Syn* APIECE, each, per capita

all-around **1** *Syn* VERSATILE, many-sided **2** *Syn* GENERAL (sense 2), bird's-eye, broad, nonspecific, overall *Ant* delineated, detailed, particularized, specific

allay *Syn* RELIEVE, alleviate, assuage, lighten, mitigate *Ant* alarm, embarrass, intensify

allege *Syn* ADDUCE, advance, cite

allegiance *Syn* FIDELITY, devotion, fealty, loyalty, piety *Ant* faithlessness, perfidy

allegory · a story intended to teach a basic truth or moral about life *Syn* fable, parable *Rel* morality play

allergic *Syn* ANTIPATHETIC, averse

alleviate *Syn* RELIEVE, allay, assuage, lighten, mitigate *Ant* alarm, embarrass, intensify

alliance · a chiefly political combination for a common object *Syn* coalition, confederacy, confederation, federation, fusion, league

allied *Syn* RELATED, affiliated, cognate, kindred

allocate *Syn* ALLOT, apportion, assign

allocation *Syn* APPROPRIATION, allotment, annuity, grant, subsidy

allot · to give as one's share, portion, role, or place *Syn* allocate, apportion, assign *Rel* deal, dispense, distribute, divide, dole

allotment *Syn* APPROPRIATION, allocation, annuity, grant, subsidy

all-out *Syn* EXHAUSTIVE, clean, complete, comprehensive, full-scale, out-and-out, thorough, thoroughgoing, total

allow 1 *Syn* ADMIT, acknowledge, agree, concede, confess, grant, own (up) *Ant* deny 2 *Syn* LET, leave, permit, suffer

allowable *Syn* PERMISSIBLE, admissible, licensable *Ant* banned, barred, forbidden, impermissible, inadmissible, interdicted, prohibited, proscribed

allowance 1 *Syn* ADVANTAGE, edge, handicap, odds *Ant* disadvantage, handicap 2 *Syn* PERMISSION, authorization, clearance, concurrence, consent, granting, leave, license (*or* licence), sanction, sufferance *Ant* interdiction, prohibition, proscription 3 *Syn* RATION, dole, pittance

alloy *Syn* ADMIXTURE, adulterant

alloyed *Syn* IMPURE, adulterated, contaminated, dilute, diluted, polluted, tainted, thinned, weakened *Ant* pure, unadulterated, unalloyed, uncontaminated, undiluted, unpolluted, untainted

all right *Syn* ADEQUATE, decent, fine, OK (*or* okay), passable, respectable, satisfactory, tolerable *Ant* deficient, inadequate, lacking, unacceptable, unsatisfactory, wanting

allude 1 *Syn* HINT, imply, indicate, infer, insinuate, intimate, suggest 2 *Syn* REFER, advert

allure 1 *Syn* ATTRACT, bewitch, captivate, charm, enchant, fascinate *Ant* repel 2 *Syn* LURE, beguile, decoy, entice, lead on, seduce, tempt

alluring *Syn* ATTRACTIVE, bewitching, captivating, charming, enchanting, fascinating *Ant* forbidding, repellent

ally *n* 1 · someone associated with another to give assistance or moral support *Syn* abettor, backer, confederate, supporter, sympathizer *Rel* well-wisher 2 *Syn* PARTNER, colleague, confederate, copartner *Ant* rival

ally *vb* · to form or enter into an association that furthers the interests of its members *Syn* associate, band, club, confederate, conjoin, cooperate, federate, league, unite *Rel* collaborate, gang (up), team (up) *Ant* break up, disband

almost · very close to but not completely *Syn* about, more or less, most, much, near, nearly, next to, nigh, practically, some, virtually, well-nigh *Rel* appreciably, by and large, chiefly, largely, mainly, mostly

alms *Syn* CONTRIBUTION, benefaction, beneficence, charity, donation, philanthropy

aloft *Syn* ABOVE, over, overhead, skyward *Ant* below, beneath, under

alone 1 · isolated from others *Syn* desolate, forlorn, lone, lonely, lonesome, lorn, solitary *Rel* lone, single, sole, unique *Ant* accompanied 2 *Syn* ONLY, lone, singular, sole, solitary, special, unique

along · toward or at a point lying in advance in space or time *Syn* ahead, forth, forward, on, onward *Rel* before

aloof *Syn* INDIFFERENT, detached, disinterested, incurious, unconcerned, uninterested *Ant* avid

aloud · with one's normal voice speaking the words *Syn* audibly, out, out loud *Rel* clearly, discernibly, distinctly, distinguishably, perceptibly, plainly *Ant* inaudibly, silently, soundlessly

alp *Syn* MOUNTAIN, mesa, mount, peak, volcano

alpha *Syn* BEGINNING, birth, commencement, dawn, genesis, inception, incipiency, launch, morning, onset, outset, start, threshold *Ant* close, conclusion, end, ending

alter 1 *Syn* CHANGE (sense 1), make over, modify, recast, redo, refashion, remake, remodel, revamp, revise, rework, vary *Ant* fix, freeze, set, stabilize 2 *Syn* STERILIZE (sense 1), castrate, emasculate, geld, mutilate, spay *Ant* fertilize

alteration *Syn* CHANGE (sense 1), modification, variation *Ant* monotony, uniformity

altercation *Syn* QUARREL, bickering, spat, squabble, tiff, wrangle

alternate *Syn* INTERMITTENT, periodic, recurrent *Ant* continual, incessant

alternation *Syn* CHANGE (sense 2), mutation, permutation, vicissitude

alternative *Syn* CHOICE, election, option, preference, selection

although · in spite of the fact that *Syn* albeit, howbeit, though, when, while *Rel* but, whereas

altitude *Syn* HEIGHT, elevation

altogether *Syn* CHIEFLY, basically, by and large, generally, largely, mainly, mostly, overall, predominantly, primarily, principally, substantially

altruistic *Syn* CHARITABLE, benevolent, eleemosynary, humane, humanitarian, philanthropic *Ant* uncharitable

amalgam *Syn* BLEND, admixture, amalgamation, combination, composite, compound, fusion, intermixture, mix, mixture

amalgamate *Syn* MIX, blend, coalesce, commingle, fuse, merge, mingle

amalgamation **1** *Syn* BLEND, admixture, amalgam, combination, composite, compound, fusion, intermixture, mix, mixture **2** *Syn* CONSOLIDATION, merger *Ant* dissolution

amass *Syn* ACCUMULATE, hoard *Ant* dissipate

amateur *n* · a person who follows a pursuit without attaining proficiency or a professional status *Syn* dabbler, dilettante, tyro *Rel* apprentice, novice, probationer *Ant* expert, professional

amateur *adj Syn* AMATEURISH, dilettante, inexperienced, inexpert, nonprofessional, unprofessional, unskilled, unskillful *Ant* ace, adept, consummate, crackerjack, expert, master, masterful, masterly, professional, virtuoso

amateurish · lacking or showing a lack of expert skill *Syn* amateur, dilettante, inexperienced, inexpert, nonprofessional, unprofessional, unskilled, unskillful *Rel* primitive, self-taught, uninitiated, unprepared, unqualified, unschooled, untaught, untrained, untutored *Ant* ace, adept, consummate, crackerjack, expert, master, masterful, masterly, professional, virtuoso

amative *Syn* EROTIC, amatory, amorous, aphrodisiac

amatory *Syn* EROTIC, amative, amorous, aphrodisiac

amaze *Syn* SURPRISE (sense 2), astonish, astound, flabbergast

amazement *Syn* WONDER (sense 2), admiration, awe, wonderment

ambassador · a person sent on a mission to represent another *Syn* delegate, emissary, envoy, legate, minister, representative *Rel* agent, attaché, consul, deputy, diplomat, foreign minister, nuncio, procurator, proxy

ambiguous *Syn* OBSCURE, cryptic, dark, enigmatic, equivocal, vague *Ant* distinct, obvious

ambition *Syn* GOAL, aim, aspiration, design, dream, end, intent, intention, mark, meaning, object, objective, plan, pretension, purpose, target, thing

ambitious · straining or exceeding the capacity of their authors or executants *Syn* pretentious, utopian *Rel* audacious, bold, brave *Ant* modest

amble *Syn* SAUNTER, stroll

ambrosial *Syn* FRAGRANT, aromatic, perfumed, redolent, savory, scented, sweet *Ant* fetid, foul, malodorous, noisome, putrid, ran-

cid, rank, reeking, reeky, smelly, stinking, stinky, strong

ambulant *Syn* ITINERANT, ambulatory, nomadic, peripatetic, vagrant

ambulatory *Syn* ITINERANT, ambulant, nomadic, peripatetic, vagrant

ambush *vb Syn* SURPRISE (sense 1), waylay

ameliorate *Syn* IMPROVE (sense 1), better, help *Ant* impair, worsen

amenability *Syn* ALACRITY, gameness, goodwill, willingness

amenable **1** *Syn* OBEDIENT, compliant, conformable, docile, law-abiding, submissive, tractable *Ant* contrary, disobedient, froward, insubordinate, intractable, rebellious, recalcitrant, refractory, unruly **2** *Syn* RESPONSIBLE, accountable, answerable, liable

amend *Syn* CORRECT, emend, rectify, redress, reform, remedy, revise

amends *Syn* REPARATION, indemnity, redress, restitution

amenity *Syn* COURTESY, attention, gallantry *Ant* discourtesy

amerce *Syn* PENALIZE, fine, mulct

American Indian · a member of any of the native peoples of the western hemisphere usually not including the Eskimos *Syn* Amerindian, Indian, Native American *Rel* mestizo

Amerindian *Syn* AMERICAN INDIAN, Indian, Native American

amiable · having an easygoing and pleasing manner especially in social situations *Syn* affable, agreeable, genial, good-natured, good-tempered, gracious, nice, sweet, well-disposed *Rel* amicable, cordial, friendly, neighborly *Ant* disagreeable, ill-natured, ill-tempered, ungracious, unpleasant

amicable · marked by or exhibiting goodwill or absence of antagonism *Syn* friendly, neighborly *Rel* pacific, peaceable, peaceful *Ant* antagonistic

amid *or* **amidst** *Syn* AMONG, mid, midst, through

amiss *Syn* WRONG, afield, astray, awry *Ant* aright, right, well

amity *Syn* FRIENDSHIP, comity, goodwill *Ant* animosity

amnesty *Syn* PARDON, absolution, forgiveness, remission, remittal *Ant* penalty, punishment, retribution

among · in or into the middle of *Syn* amid (*or* amidst), mid, midst, through *Rel* between, betwixt

amorous *Syn* EROTIC, amative, amatory, aphrodisiac

amorphous *Syn* FORMLESS, shapeless, unformed, unshaped, unstructured *Ant* formed, shaped, structured

amount **1** · a given or particular mass or aggregate of matter *Syn* measure, quantity, volume *Rel* body, portion **2** *Syn* SUM, aggregate, number, quantity, total, whole

amour · an instance of illicit sexual relationship *Syn* affair, intrigue, liaison

amour propre *Syn* CONCEIT, egoism, egotism, self-esteem, self-love *Ant* humility

ample 1 *Syn* PLENTIFUL, abundant, copious, plenteous *Ant* scant, scanty 2 *Syn* SPACIOUS, capacious, commodious

amplify 1 *Syn* EXPAND, dilate, distend, inflate, swell *Ant* abridge, circumscribe, contract 2 *Syn* INCREASE (sense 1), add (to), aggrandize, augment, boost, compound, enlarge, escalate, expand, extend, multiply, raise, swell, up *Ant* abate, contract, decrease, diminish, lessen, lower, reduce, subtract (from)

amplitude *Syn* EXPANSE, spread, stretch

amulet *Syn* FETISH, charm, talisman

amuse · to cause or enable one to pass one's time in pleasant or agreeable activity *Syn* divert, entertain, recreate *Rel* absorb, engross *Ant* bore

amusement · an agreeable activity or its effect *Syn* diversion, entertainment, recreation *Rel* absorption, engrossment *Ant* boredom

amusing *Syn* FUN, delightful, diverting, enjoyable, entertaining, pleasurable *Ant* boring, dull

anagogic *Syn* MYSTICAL, cabalistic, mystic

analgesic *Syn* ANODYNE, anesthetic *Ant* irritant, stimulant

analogous *Syn* ALIKE, akin, comparable, correspondent, corresponding, like, matching, parallel, resembling, similar, such, suchlike *Ant* different, dissimilar, diverse, unlike

analogue *Syn* PARALLEL, correlate, counterpart

analogy · a comparison between things essentially or generically different but strikingly alike in one or more pertinent aspects *Syn* metaphor, simile

analysis · separation of a whole into its fundamental elements or constituent parts *Syn* breakdown, dissection, resolution *Rel* division, separation *Ant* synthesis

analytical *Syn* LOGICAL, subtle *Ant* illogical

analyze · to identify and examine the basic elements or parts of (something) especially for discovering interrelationships *Syn* anatomize, assay, break down, dissect *Rel* assess, evaluate, examine, inspect, investigate, scrutinize

anarchic *Syn* LAWLESS, disorderly, lawbreaking, unruly *Ant* law-abiding, orderly

anarchy · a state in which there is widespread wrongdoing and disregard for rules and authority *Syn* chaos, lawlessness, misrule *Rel* commotion, tumult, uproar

anathema 1 *Syn* ABOMINATION, bête noire, bugbear *Ant* joy 2 *Syn* CURSE, imprecation, malediction *Ant* blessing

anathematize *Syn* EXECRATE, curse, damn, objurgate

anatomize *Syn* ANALYZE, assay, break down, dissect

anatomy *Syn* STRUCTURE, framework, skeleton

ancestor 1 · a person from whom one is descended *Syn* forebear, forefather, progenitor *Ant* descendant 2 · something belonging to an earlier time from which something else was later developed *Syn* antecedent, foregoer, forerunner, precursor, predecessor *Rel* archetype, model, original, prototype *Ant* descendant (*or* descendent)

ancestry · the line of ancestors from whom a person is descended *Syn* birth, blood, bloodline, breeding, descent, extraction, family tree, genealogy, line, lineage, origin, parentage, pedigree, stock, strain *Rel* heredity, succession *Ant* issue, posterity, progeny, seed

anchor *Syn* SECURE, moor, rivet

anchorite *Syn* RECLUSE, cenobite, eremite, hermit

ancient *adj Syn* ELDERLY, aged, aging, geriatric, long-lived, old, older, senior *Ant* young, youthful

ancient *n Syn* SENIOR CITIZEN, elder, goldenager, oldster, old-timer *Ant* youngster, youth

ancillary *Syn* AUXILIARY, accessory, adjuvant, contributory, subservient, subsidiary

anecdote *Syn* STORY, narrative, tale, yarn

anemic *Syn* PALE (sense 2), bloodless

anesthetic *n Syn* ANODYNE, analgesic *Ant* irritant, stimulant

anesthetic *adj Syn* INSENSIBLE, impassible, insensitive *Ant* sensible (*to or of something*)

angel 1 *Syn* LAMB, dove, innocent, sheep *Ant* wolf 2 *Syn* SPONSOR, backer, guarantor, patron, surety

anger *n* · an intense emotional state of displeasure with someone or something *Syn* angriness, furor, fury, indignation, irateness, ire, outrage, rage, spleen, wrath, wrathfulness *Rel* aggravation, annoyance, exasperation, irritation, vexation *Ant* delight, pleasure

anger *vb* · to make angry *Syn* antagonize, enrage, incense, inflame, infuriate, madden, outrage, rankle, rile, roil *Rel* affront, aggravate, annoy, cross, exasperate, get, irritate, nettle, offend, peeve, pique, provoke, put out, ruffle, vex *Ant* delight, gratify, please

angered *Syn* ANGRY, apoplectic, enraged, foaming, fuming, furious, incensed, indignant, inflamed, infuriated, irate, ireful, mad, outraged, rabid, riled, roiled, sore, steaming, wrathful, wroth *Ant* delighted, pleased

angle 1 *Syn* PHASE, aspect, facet, side 2 *Syn* POINT OF VIEW, slant, standpoint, viewpoint

angriness *Syn* ANGER, furor, fury, indignation, irateness, ire, outrage, rage, spleen, wrath, wrathfulness *Ant* delight, pleasure

angry · feeling or showing anger *Syn* angered, apoplectic, enraged, foaming, fuming, furious, incensed, indignant, inflamed, infuriated, irate, ireful, mad, outraged, rabid, riled, roiled, sore, steaming, wrathful, wroth *Rel* ranting, raving, stormy *Ant* delighted, pleased

anguish *Syn* SORROW, grief, heartache, heartbreak, regret, woe *Ant* joy

angular *Syn* LEAN, gaunt, lank, lanky, rawboned, scrawny, skinny, spare *Ant* fleshy

animadversion · a remark or statement that is an adverse criticism *Syn* aspersion, reflection, stricture *Rel* censure, criticism, reprehension *Ant* commendation

animadvert *Syn* REMARK, comment, commentate

animal *n* · one of the lower animals as distinguished from human beings *Syn* beast, brute, creature, critter *Rel* varmint, vermin

animal *adj* *Syn* CARNAL, fleshly, sensual *Ant* intellectual, spiritual

animate *vb* **1** · to give life, vigor, or spirit to *Syn* brace, energize, enliven, fire, invigorate, jazz (up), liven (up), pep (up), quicken, stimulate, vitalize, vivify *Rel* arouse, awake, awaken, raise, rouse, stir, wake (up) *Ant* damp, dampen, deaden, dull **2** *Syn* INFORM (sense 1), fire, inspire

animate *adj* *Syn* LIVING, alive, animated, vital *Ant* lifeless

animated **1** *Syn* LIVELY, gay, sprightly, vivacious *Ant* dull **2** *Syn* LIVING, alive, animate, vital *Ant* lifeless

animosity *Syn* ENMITY, animus, antagonism, antipathy, hostility, rancor *Ant* amity

animus *Syn* ENMITY, animosity, antagonism, antipathy, hostility, rancor *Ant* amity

annals *Syn* HISTORY, chronicle

annex *n* · an addition to a main (and often the original) building *Syn* ell, extension, wing *Rel* accretion, addition, increment

annex *vb* *Syn* ADD (sense 2), adjoin, append, tack (on) *Ant* deduct, remove, subtract, take

annihilation *Syn* DESTRUCTION, decimation, demolishment, demolition, desolation, devastation, extermination, extinction, havoc, loss, obliteration, ruin, ruination, wastage, wreckage *Ant* building, construction, erection, raising

announce · to make known openly or publicly *Syn* advertise, blaze, broadcast, declare, enunciate, placard, post, proclaim, promulgate, publicize, publish, sound *Rel* advise, apprise, inform, notify

announcement **1** · a published statement informing the public of a matter of general interest *Syn* ad, advertisement, bulletin, notice, notification, posting, release *Rel* advertising, ballyhoo, bill, billboard, boost, broadcast, broadside, buildup, campaign, circular, commercial, communication, dispatch, flier (*or* flyer), handbill, handout, message, newscast, placard, plug, poster, promotion, propaganda, publicity, report, sign, spot, telecast, word **2** *Syn* DECLARATION, advertisement,

broadcasting, proclamation, promulgation, publication

annoy **1** · to disturb and nervously upset a person *Syn* bother, irk, vex *Rel* aggravate, exasperate, irritate, nettle, rile *Ant* soothe **2** *Syn* WORRY, harass, harry, pester, plague, tantalize, tease

annoying · causing annoyance *Syn* aggravating, bothersome, disturbing, exasperating, frustrating, galling, irksome, irritating, maddening, nettling, peeving, pesty, rankling, riling, vexatious, vexing *Rel* burdensome, discomforting, displeasing, disquieting, distressing, importunate, inconveniencing

annuity *Syn* APPROPRIATION, allocation, allotment, grant, subsidy

annul *Syn* ABOLISH, abrogate, cancel, dissolve, invalidate, negate, nullify, quash, repeal, rescind, void

anodyne · something used to relieve or prevent pain *Syn* analgesic, anesthetic

anoint *Syn* OIL, cream, grease, lubricate

anomalous **1** *Syn* DEVIANT, aberrant, abnormal, atypical, irregular, unnatural *Ant* natural, normal, regular, standard, typical **2** *Syn* IRREGULAR, unnatural *Ant* regular

anomaly *Syn* PARADOX, antinomy

anon *Syn* SHORTLY, momentarily, presently, soon

another *Syn* ADDITIONAL, added, else, farther, further, more, other

answer *n* **1** · something spoken or written by way of return to a question or demand *Syn* rejoinder, reply, response, retort *Rel* defense, justification, rebuttal, refutation, vindication **2** · something attained by mental effort and especially by computation *Syn* result, solution *Rel* conclusion, determination, explanation, finding

answer *vb* **1** · to say, write, or do something in response *Syn* rejoin, reply, respond, retort *Rel* acknowledge, recognize **2** *Syn* SATISFY (sense 2), fulfill, meet **3** *Syn* SOLVE, break, crack, dope (out), figure out, puzzle (out), resolve, riddle, unravel, work, work out

answerable **1** *Syn* RESPONSIBLE, accountable, amenable, liable **2** *Syn* SOLVABLE, explainable, explicable, resolvable, soluble *Ant* inexplicable, insoluble, unexplainable, unsolvable

antagonism *Syn* ENMITY, animosity, animus, antipathy, hostility, rancor *Ant* amity

antagonist *Syn* ENEMY, adversary, foe, opponent *Ant* friend

antagonistic *Syn* ADVERSE, counter, counteractive *Ant* propitious

antagonize **1** *Syn* ANGER, enrage, incense, inflame, infuriate, madden, outrage, rankle, rile, roil *Ant* delight, gratify, please **2** *Syn* RESIST, combat, conflict, contest, fight, oppose, withstand *Ant* abide, submit

ante *Syn* BET, pot, stake, wager

antecedent *n* **1** *Syn* CAUSE, determinant, occasion, reason **2** *Syn* ANCESTOR (sense 2), foregoer, forerunner, precursor, predecessor *Ant* descendant (*or* descendent)

antecedent *adj Syn* PREVIOUS, anterior, foregoing, precedent, preceding, prior *Ant* after, ensuing, following, subsequent, succeeding

anterior *Syn* PREVIOUS, antecedent, foregoing, precedent, preceding, prior *Ant* after, ensuing, following, subsequent, succeeding

anthology · a collection of writings *Syn* album, compilation, miscellany *Rel* archives

anthropoid · resembling humans *Syn* anthropomorphic, anthropomorphous

anthropomorphic *Syn* ANTHROPOID, anthropomorphous

anthropomorphous *Syn* ANTHROPOID, anthropomorphic

antic *adj Syn* FANTASTIC, bizarre, grotesque

antic *n Syn* PRANK, caper, dido, monkeyshine

anticipate **1** *Syn* FORESEE, apprehend, divine, foreknow **2** *Syn* PREVENT (sense 1), forestall

anticipation *Syn* PROSPECT, foretaste, outlook

antidote *Syn* CORRECTIVE, check, control

antinomy *Syn* PARADOX, anomaly

antipathetic · having a natural dislike for something *Syn* allergic, averse *Rel* adverse, antagonistic, disgusted, disinclined, hostile, intolerant, loath (*or* loth), nauseated, negative, opposed, opposing, reluctant, repelled, repulsed, resistant, resisting, revolted, shocked, squeamish, turned off, uncongenial, unfriendly, unsympathetic, unwilling

antipathy *Syn* ENMITY, animosity, animus, antagonism, hostility, rancor *Ant* amity

antipodal *Syn* OPPOSITE, antipodean, antithetical, antonymous, contradictory, contrary

antipode *Syn* OPPOSITE, antithesis, antonym, contradictory, contrary, converse, counter, reverse

antipodean *Syn* OPPOSITE, antipodal, antithetical, antonymous, contradictory, contrary

antiquated *Syn* OBSOLETE, archaic, dated, moth-eaten, outdated, outmoded, out-of-date, outworn, passé *Ant* new

antisocial *Syn* UNSOCIAL, asocial, nonsocial *Ant* social

antithesis *Syn* OPPOSITE, antipode, antonym, contradictory, contrary, converse, counter, reverse

antithetical *Syn* OPPOSITE, antipodal, antipodean, antonymous, contradictory, contrary

antonym *Syn* OPPOSITE, antipode, antithesis, contradictory, contrary, converse, counter, reverse

antonymous *Syn* OPPOSITE, antipodal, antipodean, antithetical, contradictory, contrary

anxiety *Syn* CARE, concern, solicitude, worry

anxious **1** *Syn* EAGER, agog, athirst, avid, keen *Ant* listless **2** *Syn* WORRIED, careful, concerned, solicitous

anyhow *Syn* HIT OR MISS, aimlessly, anyway, anywise, desultorily, erratically, haphazard, haphazardly, helter-skelter, irregularly, randomly *Ant* methodically, systematically

anyway *Syn* HIT OR MISS, aimlessly, anyhow, anywise, desultorily, erratically, haphazard, haphazardly, helter-skelter, irregularly, randomly *Ant* methodically, systematically

anywise **1** *Syn* AT ALL, ever **2** *Syn* HIT OR MISS, aimlessly, anyhow, anyway, desultorily, erratically, haphazard, haphazardly, helter-skelter, irregularly, randomly *Ant* methodically, systematically

apart · into parts or to pieces *Syn* asunder, piecemeal *Ant* together

apartment *Syn* ROOM (sense 1), chamber

apathetic *Syn* IMPASSIVE, phlegmatic, stoic, stolid *Ant* responsive

apathy **1** *Syn* IMPASSIVITY, phlegm, stoicism, stolidity **2** *Syn* INDIFFERENCE, casualness, disinterestedness, disregard, insouciance, nonchalance, unconcern *Ant* concern, interest, regard

ape *Syn* COPY, imitate, mimic, mock *Ant* originate

aperçu *Syn* COMPENDIUM, digest, pandect, précis, sketch, survey, syllabus

aperture · an opening allowing passage through or in and out *Syn* interstice, orifice *Rel* bore, perforation, prick, puncture

apex *Syn* SUMMIT, acme, apogee, climax, culmination, meridian, peak, pinnacle, zenith

aphorism *Syn* SAYING, adage, apothegm, epigram, maxim, motto, proverb, saw

aphrodisiac *Syn* EROTIC, amative, amatory, amorous

apiece **1** · for each one *Syn* all, each, per capita *Rel* apart, independently, individually, respectively, separately, singly **2** *Syn* EACH, individually, respectively, severally

aplomb **1** *Syn* CONFIDENCE, assurance, self-assurance, self-confidence, self-possession *Ant* diffidence **2** *Syn* EQUANIMITY, calmness, composure, coolheadedness, coolness, imperturbability, placidity, self-possession, serenity, tranquillity (*or* tranquility) *Ant* agitation, discomposure, perturbation

apocalypse *Syn* DISASTER, calamity, cataclysm, catastrophe

apocryphal *Syn* FICTITIOUS, fabulous, legendary, mythical *Ant* historical

apogee *Syn* SUMMIT, acme, apex, climax, culmination, meridian, peak, pinnacle, zenith

apologia *Syn* APOLOGY, alibi, excuse, plea, pretext

apology · the reason or reasons offered in explanation or defense of something (as an act, a policy, or a view) *Syn* alibi, apologia, excuse, plea, pretext *Rel* defense, justification, vindication

apoplectic *Syn* ANGRY, angered, enraged, foaming, fuming, furious, incensed, indignant, inflamed, infuriated, irate, ireful, mad, outraged, rabid, riled, roiled, sore, steaming, wrathful, wroth *Ant* delighted, pleased

apostasy *Syn* DEFECTION, desertion

apostate *Syn* RENEGADE, backslider, recreant, turncoat *Ant* adherent, loyalist

apostle *Syn* EXPONENT, advocate, backer, booster, champion, friend, promoter, proponent, supporter *Ant* adversary, antagonist, opponent

apothecary *Syn* DRUGGIST, chemist, pharmacist

apothegm *Syn* SAYING, adage, aphorism, epigram, maxim, motto, proverb, saw

apotheosis *Syn* PARAGON, nonesuch, nonpareil

appall *Syn* DISMAY, daunt, horrify *Ant* cheer

appalling *Syn* FEARFUL (sense 2), awful, dreadful, frightful, horrible, horrific, shocking, terrible, terrific

appanage *Syn* RIGHT, birthright, perquisite, prerogative, privilege

apparatus 1 *Syn* EQUIPMENT, gear, machinery, matériel, outfit, paraphernalia, tackle 2 *Syn* MACHINE, engine, machinery, mechanism, motor

apparel *vb Syn* CLOTHE, array, attire, dress, robe *Ant* unclothe

apparel *n Syn* CLOTHES, attire, clothing, dress, raiment

apparent 1 · not actually being what appearance indicates *Syn* illusory, ostensible, seeming *Rel* false, wrong *Ant* real 2 *Syn* EVIDENT, clear, distinct, manifest, obvious, palpable, patent, plain 3 *Syn* VISIBLE, observable, seeable, visual *Ant* invisible, unseeable

apparently · to all outward appearances *Syn* evidently, ostensibly, presumably, seemingly, supposedly *Rel* externally, outwardly, visibly

apparition *Syn* GHOST, bogey, phantasm, phantom, poltergeist, shade, shadow, specter (*or* spectre), spirit, spook, vision, wraith

appeal *n Syn* PRAYER, petition, plea, suit

appeal *vb Syn* PRAY, petition, plead, sue

appear 1 · to come out into view *Syn* emerge, loom *Rel* arrive, come *Ant* disappear, vanish 2 *Syn* SEEM, act, look, make, sound

appearance · the outward show presented by a person or thing *Syn* aspect, look, semblance

appease *Syn* PACIFY, conciliate, disarm, mollify, placate, propitiate *Ant* anger, enrage, incense, infuriate, madden, outrage

appellation *Syn* NAME, denomination, designation, style, title

append *Syn* ADD (sense 2), adjoin, annex, tack (on) *Ant* deduct, remove, subtract, take

appendage · something regarded as additional and at the same time as subsidiary to another object *Syn* accessory, adjunct, appurtenance

appendix · additional matter subjoined to a book *Syn* addendum, supplement

apperception *Syn* RECOGNITION, assimilation, identification

appertain *Syn* BEAR (sense 3), apply, belong, pertain, relate

appetite 1 *Syn* DESIRE, lust, passion, urge *Ant* distaste 2 *Syn* LIKING, fancy, favor, fondness, like, love, partiality, preference, relish, shine, taste, use *Ant* aversion, disfavor, dislike, distaste, hatred, loathing

appetizing *Syn* PALATABLE, flavorsome, relishing, sapid, savory, tasty, toothsome *Ant* distasteful, unpalatable

applaud 1 · to demonstrate one's feeling, and especially one's approbation or joy, audibly and enthusiastically *Syn* cheer, root *Rel* acclaim, extol, praise *Ant* boo, hiss 2 *Syn* ACCLAIM, cheer, hail, laud, praise, salute, tout *Ant* knock, pan, slam 3 *Syn* COMMEND, compliment, recommend *Ant* admonish, censure

applause · enthusiastic and usually public expression of approval *Syn* acclamation, cheering, cheers, ovation, plaudit(s), rave(s) *Rel* clapping *Ant* booing, hissing

appliance 1 *Syn* GADGET, contraption, contrivance, gimmick, gizmo (*or* gismo), jigger 2 *Syn* IMPLEMENT, instrument, tool, utensil

applicable *Syn* PERTINENT, apposite, apropos, germane, material, pointed, relative, relevant *Ant* extraneous, immaterial, inapplicable, irrelevant, pointless

applicant *Syn* CANDIDATE, aspirant, campaigner, contender, hopeful, prospect, seeker

application *Syn* ATTENTION (sense 1), concentration, study *Ant* inattention

appliqué *Syn* OVERLAY, superimpose, superpose

apply 1 *Syn* BEAR (sense 3), appertain, belong, pertain, relate 2 *Syn* DIRECT (sense 1), address, devote *Ant* misdirect 3 *Syn* ENFORCE, administer, execute, implement 4 *Syn* EXERT, exercise, ply, put out, wield 5 *Syn* RESORT, go, refer, turn 6 *Syn* USE, avail, employ, utilize

appoint 1 · to decide upon (the time or date for an event) usually from a position of authority *Syn* designate, fix, name, set *Rel* adopt, assign, choose, determine, establish, opt (for), pick, pin down, prefer, select, settle, single (out), specify 2 · to pick (someone) by one's authority for a specific position or duty *Syn* assign, attach, commission, constitute, designate, detail, name *Rel* authorize, delegate, depute, deputize *Ant* discharge, dismiss, expel, fire

appointment *Syn* ENGAGEMENT, assignation, date, rendezvous, tryst

apportion 1 · to divide something carefully and distribute it among a number *Syn* parcel, portion, prorate, ration *Rel* accord, award, grant 2 *Syn* ALLOT, allocate, assign

apposite *Syn* PERTINENT, applicable, apropos, germane, material, pointed, relative, relevant *Ant* extraneous, immaterial, inapplicable, irrelevant, pointless

appraise *Syn* ESTIMATE (sense 1), assay, assess, evaluate, rate, value

appreciable *Syn* PERCEPTIBLE, detectable, discernible, distinguishable, palpable, sensible *Ant* impalpable, imperceptible, inappreciable, indistinguishable, insensible

appreciate **1** · to hold in high estimation *Syn* cherish, prize, treasure, value *Rel* admire, esteem, regard, respect *Ant* despise **2** *Syn* INCREASE (sense 2), accumulate, balloon, build (up), burgeon, enlarge, escalate, expand, mount, multiply, mushroom, proliferate, rise, snowball, swell, wax *Ant* contract, decrease, diminish, lessen, wane **3** *Syn* UNDERSTAND, comprehend

appreciation **1** *Syn* COMPREHENSION, apprehension, grasp, grip, perception, understanding **2** *Syn* THANKS, appreciativeness, gratefulness, gratitude, thankfulness *Ant* ingratitude, thanklessness, ungratefulness

appreciativeness *Syn* THANKS, appreciation, gratefulness, gratitude, thankfulness *Ant* ingratitude, thanklessness, ungratefulness

apprehend **1** *Syn* ARREST (sense 2), attach, detain **2** *Syn* FORESEE, anticipate, divine, foreknow

apprehension **1** *Syn* COMPREHENSION, appreciation, grasp, grip, perception, understanding **2** · fear (or an instance of it) that something is going wrong or will go wrong *Syn* foreboding, misgiving, presentiment *Rel* alarm, dread, fear, panic *Ant* confidence **3** *Syn* ARREST, attachment, detention

apprehensive *Syn* FEARFUL (sense 1), afraid *Ant* fearless, intrepid

apprentice *Syn* ASSISTANT, adjutant, aid, aide, coadjutor, deputy, helper, sidekick

apprise **1** *Syn* ENLIGHTEN (sense 1), acquaint, advise, brief, clue, familiarize, fill in, inform, instruct, tell, wise (up) **2** *Syn* INFORM (sense 2), advise, notify

approach *vb* **1** · to come or draw close (to) *Syn* approximate, near *Rel* accost, address **2** *Syn* MATCH, equal, rival, touch

approach *n Syn* OVERTURE, advance, bid, tender

approaching *Syn* FORTHCOMING, coming, imminent, impending, nearing, oncoming, pending, upcoming *Ant* late, recent

approbation *Syn* APPROVAL, blessing, favor, imprimatur, OK (*or* okay) *Ant* disapprobation, disapproval, disfavor

appropriate *vb Syn* ARROGATE, confiscate, preempt, usurp *Ant* renounce, yield

appropriate *adj Syn* FIT, apt, felicitous, fitting, happy, meet, proper, suitable *Ant* unfit

appropriately *Syn* PROPERLY, congruously, correctly, fittingly, happily, meetly, rightly, suitably *Ant* improperly, inappropriately, incongruously, incorrectly, unsuitably, wrongly

appropriateness · the quality or state of being especially suitable or fitting *Syn* aptness, felicitousness, fitness, fittingness, rightness, seemliness, suitability, suitableness *Rel* agreeableness, compatibility, congruity, harmoniousness *Ant* inappropriateness, inaptness, infelicity, unfitness

appropriation · a sum of money allotted for a specific use by official or formal action *Syn* allocation, allotment, annuity, grant, subsidy *Rel* advance, allowance, benefit, endowment, fund, stipend, trust

approval · an acceptance of something as satisfactory *Syn* approbation, blessing, favor, imprimatur, OK (*or* okay) *Rel* backing, endorsement, sanction, support *Ant* disapprobation, disapproval, disfavor

approve · to have or to express a favorable opinion of *Syn* accredit, certify, endorse, sanction *Rel* applaud, commend, compliment *Ant* disapprove

approve (of) · to have a favorable opinion of *Syn* accept, care (for), countenance, favor, OK (*or* okay), subscribe (to) *Rel* acclaim, applaud, laud, praise, salute *Ant* disapprove (of), discountenance, disfavor, frown (on *or* upon)

approximate *Syn* APPROACH, near

appurtenance *Syn* APPENDAGE, accessory, adjunct

apropos *Syn* PERTINENT, applicable, apposite, germane, material, pointed, relative, relevant *Ant* extraneous, immaterial, inapplicable, irrelevant, pointless

apt **1** *Syn* FIT, appropriate, felicitous, fitting, happy, meet, proper, suitable *Ant* unfit **2** *Syn* PRONE (sense 1), given, inclined, tending *Ant* erect **3** *Syn* QUICK, prompt, ready *Ant* sluggish

aptitude *Syn* GIFT (sense 2), bent, faculty, genius, knack, talent, turn

aptness *Syn* APPROPRIATENESS, felicitousness, fitness, fittingness, rightness, seemliness, suitability, suitableness *Ant* inappropriateness, inaptness, infelicity, unfitness

aqueduct *Syn* CHANNEL, canal, conduit, duct

arbiter **1** *Syn* JUDGE, arbitrator, referee, umpire **2** *Syn* MEDIATOR, arbitrator, conciliator, go-between, intercessor, intermediary, interposer, middleman, peacemaker

arbitrary *Syn* ABSOLUTE, autocratic, despotic, tyrannical, tyrannous *Ant* limited, restrained

arbitrate *Syn* JUDGE, adjudge, adjudicate

arbitrator **1** *Syn* JUDGE, arbiter, referee, umpire **2** *Syn* MEDIATOR, arbiter, conciliator, go-between, intercessor, intermediary, interposer, middleman, peacemaker

arc *Syn* CURVE, arch, bow

arcade *Syn* PASSAGE, aisle, cloister, corridor, gallery, hall, hallway, passageway

arcane *Syn* MYSTERIOUS, inscrutable

arch **1** *Syn* CURVE, arc, bow **2** *Syn* SAUCY, pert

archaic *Syn* OBSOLETE, antiquated, dated, moth-eaten, outdated, outmoded, out-of-date, outworn, passé

architect *Syn* ARTIST, artificer, artisan

archive *Syn* DOCUMENT, monument, record

arctic *Syn* COLD, chilly, cool, freezing, frigid, frosty, gelid, glacial, icy *Ant* hot

ardent *Syn* FERVENT, blazing, burning, charged, emotional, fervid, feverish, fiery, flaming, glowing, hot-blooded, impassioned, passionate, red-hot, vehement, warm, warm-blooded *Ant* cold, cool, dispassionate, impassive, unemotional

ardor *Syn* PASSION, enthusiasm, fervor, zeal

arduous *Syn* HARD, difficult *Ant* easy

area **1** · a distinguishable extent of surface and especially of the earth's surface *Syn* belt, region, tract, zone *Rel* district, locality **2** *Syn* REGION, demesne, field, zone **3** *Syn* SIZE, dimensions, extent, magnitude, volume

argot *Syn* TERMINOLOGY, cant, dialect, jargon, language, lingo, patois, patter, slang, vocabulary

argue **1** *Syn* DISCUSS, agitate, debate, dispute **2** *Syn* INDICATE, attest, bespeak, betoken, prove **3** *Syn* PERSUADE, convince, get, induce, move, prevail (on *or* upon), satisfy, talk (into), win (over)

argument **1** · a vigorous and often heated discussion of a moot question *Syn* controversy, dispute *Rel* argumentation, debate, disputation **2** *Syn* REASON (sense 1), ground, proof **3** *Syn* SUBJECT, leitmotiv, matter, motif, motive, subject matter, text, theme, topic

argumentation · the act or art of argument or an exercise of one's powers of argument *Syn* debate, dialectic, disputation, forensic *Rel* argument, controversy, dispute

argumentative *Syn* BELLIGERENT, aggressive, bellicose, combative, contentious, discordant, disputatious, gladiatorial, militant, pugnacious, quarrelsome, scrappy, truculent, warlike *Ant* nonbelligerent, pacific, peaceable, peaceful

arise **1** *Syn* ASCEND, climb, lift, mount, rise, soar, up, uprise, upsweep, upturn *Ant* decline, descend, dip, drop, fall (off) **2** *Syn* BEGIN (sense 1), commence, dawn, form, materialize, originate, set in, spring, start *Ant* cease, end, stop **3** *Syn* SPRING, derive, emanate, flow, issue, originate, proceed, rise, stem

aristocracy **1** · a body of persons who constitute a socially superior caste *Syn* county, elite, gentry, nobility, society *Ant* people, proletariat **2** *Syn* OLIGARCHY, plutocracy

aristocrat · a person of high birth or social station *Syn* GENTLEPERSON, noble, patrician *Ant* commoner, peasant, peon

arithmetic *Syn* CALCULATION, ciphering, computation, figures, figuring, reckoning

armistice *Syn* TRUCE, cease-fire, peace

armory · a place where military arms are stored *Syn* arsenal, depot, dump, magazine *Rel* fort, fortress, stronghold

army *Syn* MULTITUDE, host, legion

aroma *Syn* SMELL, odor, scent

aromatic **1** *Syn* FRAGRANT, ambrosial, perfumed, redolent, savory, scented, sweet *Ant* fetid, foul, malodorous, noisome, putrid, rancid, rank, reeking, reeky, smelly, stinking, stinky, strong **2** *Syn* ODOROUS, balmy, fragrant, redolent *Ant* malodorous, odorless

around **1** · close to *Syn* about, by, near, next to *Rel* alongside, beside **2** · in random positions within the boundaries of *Syn* about, over, round, through, throughout *Rel* on

arouse *Syn* STIR, awaken, rally, rouse, waken

arrange **1** *Syn* NEGOTIATE, concert **2** *Syn* ORDER, marshal, methodize, organize, systematize

arrant *Syn* OUTRIGHT, out-and-out, unmitigated

array *vb* **1** *Syn* CLOTHE, apparel, attire, dress, robe *Ant* unclothe **2** *Syn* LINE, align, line up, range

array *n* **1** *Syn* FINERY, best, bravery, caparison, feather, frippery, full dress, gaiety, regalia **2** *Syn* DISPLAY, parade, pomp

arrear *Syn* DEBT, debit, indebtedness, liability, obligation

arrest *n* · seizing and holding under restraint or in custody by authority of the law *Syn* apprehension, attachment, detention *Rel* seizing, seizure, taking

arrest *vb* **1** · to stop in midcourse *Syn* check, interrupt *Rel* interfere, interpose, intervene *Ant* activate, quicken **2** · to seize and hold under restraint or in custody by authority of the law *Syn* apprehend, attach, detain *Rel* seize, take

arresting **1** *Syn* INTERESTING, absorbing, engaging, engrossing, enthralling, fascinating, gripping, immersing, intriguing, involving, riveting *Ant* boring, drab, dry, dull, heavy, monotonous, tedious, uninteresting **2** *Syn* NOTICEABLE, conspicuous, outstanding, prominent, remarkable, salient, signal, striking

arrogance · an exaggerated sense of one's importance that shows itself in the making of excessive or unjustified claims *Syn* haughtiness, imperiousness, loftiness, lordliness, masterfulness, peremptoriness, pompousness, presumptuousness, pretense (*or* pretence), pretension, pretentiousness, self-importance, superciliousness, superiority *Rel* authoritativeness, bossiness, dominance, high-handedness *Ant* humility, modesty

arrogant **1** · having a feeling of superiority that shows itself in an overbearing attitude *Syn* cavalier, haughty, highfalutin, high-handed, high-hat, imperious, important, lofty, lordly, masterful, overweening, peremptory, pompous, presumptuous, pretentious, supercilious, superior, uppish, uppity *Rel* authoritarian, bossy, dominant, dominating, domineering, magisterial, pontificating *Ant* humble, modest **2** *Syn* PROUD (sense 1), disdainful, haughty, insolent, lordly, overbearing, supercilious *Ant* ashamed, humble

arrogate · to seize or take over in a highhanded manner *Syn* appropriate, confiscate, preempt, usurp *Rel* grab, seize, take *Ant* renounce, yield

arsenal *Syn* ARMORY, depot, dump, magazine

arsonist · a person who deliberately and unlawfully sets fire to a building or other property *Syn* firebug, incendiary *Rel* igniter (*or* ignitor)

art **1** · the faculty of performing or executing expertly what is planned or devised *Syn* artifice, craft, cunning, skill **2** *Syn* TRADE, craft, handicraft, profession

artery *Syn* WAY, course, pass, passage, route

artful *Syn* SLY, crafty, cunning, foxy, guileful, insidious, tricky, wily

article **1** *Syn* ESSAY, composition, paper, theme **2** *Syn* PARAGRAPH, clause, count, plank, verse **3** *Syn* THING, object

articled *Syn* BOUND, bond, indentured

articulate *adj* · able to express oneself clearly and well *Syn* eloquent, fluent, well-spoken *Rel* facile, glib, smooth-tongued, voluble *Ant* inarticulate

articulate *vb* **1** · to form speech sounds *Syn* enunciate, pronounce **2** *Syn* PHRASE, clothe, couch, express, formulate, put, say, state, word

articulation *Syn* JOINT, suture

artifact *Syn* WORK (sense 3), opus, product, production

artifice **1** *Syn* ART, craft, cunning, skill **2** *Syn* TRICKERY, chicanery, hanky-panky, jugglery, legerdemain, subterfuge, wile **3** *Syn* TRICK, feint, gambit, maneuver, ploy, ruse, stratagem, wile

artificer **1** *Syn* ARTISAN, craftsman, handicrafter, tradesman **2** *Syn* ARTIST, architect, artisan

artificial **1** · not brought into being by nature but by human art or effort or by some process of manufacture *Syn* ersatz, factitious, synthetic *Rel* fabricated, fashioned, manufactured *Ant* natural **2** *Syn* IMITATION, bogus, factitious, fake, false, man-made, mimic, mock, sham, simulated, substitute, synthetic *Ant* genuine, natural, real **3** *Syn* INSINCERE, backhanded, double-dealing, feigned, hypocritical, left-handed, mealy, mealymouthed, two-faced, unctuous *Ant* genuine, heartfelt, honest, sincere, unfeigned

artisan **1** · a person whose occupation requires skill with the hands *Syn* artificer, craftsman, handicrafter, tradesman *Rel* artist, maker **2** *Syn* ARTIST, architect, artificer **3** *Syn* WORKER, craftsman, hand, handicraftsman, laborer, mechanic, operative, roustabout, workingman, workman *Ant* idler

artist **1** · one who makes something beautiful or useful or both *Syn* architect, artificer, artisan *Rel* craftsman, worker, workman **2** *Syn* EXPERT, ace, adept, authority, crackerjack, maestro, master, past master, scholar, shark, virtuoso, whiz, wizard *Ant* amateur

artless *Syn* NATURAL, ingenuous, naive, simple, unaffected, unsophisticated

artlessly *Syn* NATURALLY (sense 3), guilelessly, ingenuously, innocently, naively, sincerely, unaffectedly, unfeignedly, unpretentiously *Ant* affectedly, artificially, hypocritically, insincerely, pretentiously, unnaturally

as *Syn* BECAUSE, for, inasmuch as, since

ascend · to move or extend upward *Syn* arise, climb, lift, mount, rise, soar, up, uprise, upsweep, upturn *Rel* boost, elevate, raise, uplift, upraise *Ant* decline, descend, dip, drop, fall (off)

ascendancy *Syn* SUPREMACY, dominance, dominion, predominance, preeminence, sovereignty

ascertain *Syn* DISCOVER, determine, learn, unearth

ascetic *Syn* SEVERE, austere, stern *Ant* tender, tolerant

ascribe · to lay something (creditable, discreditable, or neutral) to the account of a person or thing *Syn* accredit, assign, attribute, charge, credit, impute, refer *Rel* affix, attach, fasten

aseptic *Syn* SANITARY, germfree, hygienic, sterile *Ant* insanitary, unhygienic, unsanitary

ash · the remains of combustible material after it has been destroyed by fire *Syn* cinders, clinkers, embers

ashamed **1** · acutely or manifestly conscious of embarrassment and humiliation *Syn* chagrined, mortified *Rel* abashed, discomfited, embarrassed *Ant* proud **2** *Syn* GUILTY, contrite, hangdog, penitent, remorseful, repentant, shamed, shamefaced *Ant* impenitent, remorseless, shameless, unashamed, unrepentant

ashen *Syn* PALE (sense 1), ashy, livid, pallid, wan *Ant* florid, flush, rubicund, ruddy, sanguine

ashy *Syn* PALE (sense 1), ashen, livid, pallid, wan *Ant* florid, flush, rubicund, ruddy, sanguine

asinine *Syn* SIMPLE, fatuous, foolish, silly *Ant* wise

ask **1** · to address a person in an attempt to elicit information *Syn* catechize, examine, inquire, interrogate, query, question, quiz **2** · to seek to obtain by making one's wants or desires known *Syn* request, solicit *Rel* appeal, petition, plead, pray, sue

askance · with distrust *Syn* distrustfully, doubtfully, doubtingly, dubiously, mistrustfully, skeptically, suspiciously *Rel* hesitantly, hesitatingly, incredulously, questioningly, quizzically, unbelievingly *Ant* trustfully, trustingly

askew *Syn* AWRY, aslant, cockeyed, crooked, listing, lopsided, oblique, skewed, slanted, slanting, slantwise, tilted, tipping, uneven *Ant* even, level, straight

aslant *Syn* AWRY, askew, cockeyed, crooked, listing, lopsided, oblique, skewed, slanted, slanting, slantwise, tilted, tipping, uneven *Ant* even, level, straight

asleep *Syn* NUMB, benumbed, dead, insensitive, numbed, unfeeling *Ant* feeling, sensitive

asocial *Syn* UNSOCIAL, antisocial, nonsocial *Ant* social

aspect 1 *Syn* APPEARANCE, look, semblance **2** *Syn* PHASE, angle, facet, side

asperity *Syn* ACRIMONY, acerbity *Ant* suavity

asperse *Syn* SLANDER, blacken, defame, libel, malign, smear, traduce, vilify

aspersion *Syn* ANIMADVERSION, reflection, stricture *Ant* commendation

asphyxiate *Syn* SUFFOCATE, choke, smother, stifle, strangle, throttle

aspirant *Syn* CANDIDATE, applicant, campaigner, contender, hopeful, prospect, seeker

aspiration *Syn* GOAL, aim, ambition, design, dream, end, intent, intention, mark, meaning, object, objective, plan, pretension, purpose, target, thing

aspire *Syn* AIM, pant

assail 1 *Syn* ATTACK (sense 1), assault, bombard, storm **2** *Syn* ATTACK (sense 2), abuse, belabor, blast, castigate, excoriate, jump (on), lambaste (*or* lambast), scathe, slam, vituperate

assassin · one who can be hired to murder *Syn* bravo, cutthroat, gunman *Rel* killer, murderer, slayer

assassinate *Syn* KILL, dispatch, execute, murder, slay

assault *vb Syn* ATTACK (sense 1), assail, bombard, storm

assault *n* **1** *Syn* ATTACK (sense 1), onset, onslaught **2** *Syn* ATTACK (sense 2), aggression, blitzkrieg, charge, descent, offense (*or* offence), offensive, onset, onslaught, raid, rush, strike

assay 1 *Syn* ANALYZE, anatomize, break down, dissect **2** *Syn* ATTEMPT, endeavor, essay, seek, strive, try **3** *Syn* ESTIMATE (sense 1), appraise, assess, evaluate, rate, value

assemblage *Syn* GATHERING, assembly, collection, congregation

assemble 1 *Syn* BUILD, construct, erect, fabricate, make, make up, piece, put up, raise, rear, set up *Ant* disassemble, dismantle, take down **2** *Syn* GATHER, collect, congregate

assembly *Syn* GATHERING, assemblage, collection, congregation

assent · concurrence with what someone else has stated or proposed *Syn* accede, acquiesce, agree, consent, subscribe *Rel* accept, receive *Ant* dissent

assert 1 · to state positively usually either in anticipation of denial or objection or in the face of it *Syn* affirm, aver, avouch, avow, declare, predicate, profess, protest, warrant *Rel* adduce, advance, allege, cite *Ant* controvert, deny **2** *Syn* MAINTAIN, defend, justify, vindicate

assertive *Syn* AGGRESSIVE (sense 1), militant, pushing, pushy, self-assertive

assess 1 *Syn* ESTIMATE (sense 1), appraise, assay, evaluate, rate, value **2** *Syn* IMPOSE, charge, exact, fine, lay, levy, put *Ant* remit

assessment *Syn* TAX, duty, imposition, impost, levy

assets *Syn* POSSESSIONS, belongings, effects, means, resources

assiduous *Syn* BUSY, diligent, industrious, sedulous *Ant* idle, unoccupied

assign 1 *Syn* ALLOT, allocate, apportion **2** *Syn* ASCRIBE, accredit, attribute, charge, credit, impute, refer **3** *Syn* PRESCRIBE, define **4** *Syn* APPOINT (sense 2), attach, commission, constitute, designate, detail, name *Ant* discharge, dismiss, expel, fire

assignation *Syn* ENGAGEMENT, appointment, date, rendezvous, tryst

assignment 1 *Syn* CHORE, duty, job, stint, task **2** *Syn* MISSION, charge, job, operation, post

assimilate 1 *Syn* ABSORB, imbibe *Ant* exude, give out **2** *Syn* EMBODY (sense 1), incorporate, integrate

assimilation *Syn* RECOGNITION, apperception, identification

assist *Syn* HELP, aid *Ant* hinder

assistance *Syn* HELP, aid

assistant · a person who helps a more skilled person *Syn* adjutant, aid, aide, apprentice, coadjutor, deputy, helper, sidekick *Rel* employee, hand, help, helpmate, helpmeet, hireling, laborer, mate, worker

associate *n* · a person frequently found in the company of another *Syn* companion, comrade, crony *Rel* ally, colleague, confederate, partner

associate *vb* **1** *Syn* ALLY, band, club, confederate, conjoin, cooperate, federate, league, unite *Ant* break up, disband **2** *Syn* JOIN, combine, conjoin, connect, link, relate, unite *Ant* disjoin, part **3** *Syn* SOCIALIZE, fraternize, hobnob, mingle, mix

association · a body of persons who unite in the pursuit of a common aim or object *Syn* club, order, society

assort · to arrange in systematic order or according to some definite method of arrangement or distribution *Syn* classify, pigeonhole, sort *Rel* arrange, methodize, order, systematize

assorted *Syn* MISCELLANEOUS, heterogeneous, motley, promiscuous

assuage *Syn* RELIEVE, allay, alleviate, lighten, mitigate *Ant* alarm, embarrass, intensify

assume 1 · to put on a false or deceptive appearance *Syn* affect, counterfeit, feign, pretend, sham, simulate *Rel* camouflage, cloak, disguise, dissemble, mask 2 *Syn* PRESUPPOSE, posit, postulate, premise, presume

assumption · something that is taken for granted or advanced as fact *Syn* posit, postulate, premise, presumption, presupposition *Rel* hypothesis, theory

assurance 1 *Syn* CERTAINTY, certitude, conviction *Ant* uncertainty 2 *Syn* CONFIDENCE, aplomb, self-assurance, self-confidence, self-possession *Ant* diffidence

assure *Syn* ENSURE, cinch, guarantee, guaranty, insure, secure

assured *Syn* CONFIDENT, presumptuous, sanguine, sure *Ant* apprehensive, diffident

astern *Syn* ABAFT, aft *Ant* afore

astonish *Syn* SURPRISE (sense 2), amaze, astound, flabbergast

astound *Syn* SURPRISE (sense 2), amaze, astonish, flabbergast

astral *Syn* STARRY, sidereal, stellar

astray *Syn* WRONG, afield, amiss, awry *Ant* aright, right, well

astute *Syn* SHREWD, perspicacious, sagacious

asunder *Syn* APART, piecemeal *Ant* together

asylum *Syn* SHELTER, cover, refuge, retreat, sanctuary

at all · in any way or respect *Syn* anywise, ever *Rel* somehow, someway

athirst *Syn* EAGER, agog, anxious, avid, keen *Ant* listless

athletic *Syn* MUSCULAR, brawny, burly, husky, sinewy

athletics · physical activities engaged in for exercise or play *Syn* games, sports

athwart *Syn* ACROSS, crossways, crosswise

atmosphere *Syn* AURA, air, climate, flavor, mood, note, temper

atom *Syn* PARTICLE, bit, iota, jot, mite, smidgen, tittle, whit

atomic *Syn* TINY, bitty, infinitesimal, microminiature, microscopic, miniature, minute, teeny, teeny-weeny, wee *Ant* astronomical, colossal, cosmic, elephantine, enormous, giant, gigantic, herculean, heroic, huge, immense, mammoth, massive, monster, monstrous, monumental, mountainous, prodigious, titanic, tremendous

atrabilious *Syn* MELANCHOLIC, hypochondriac, melancholy

atrocious *Syn* OUTRAGEOUS, heinous, monstrous

attach 1 *Syn* ARREST (sense 2), apprehend, detain 2 *Syn* FASTEN, affix, fix *Ant* loose, loosen, unfasten 3 *Syn* APPOINT (sense 2), assign, commission, constitute, designate, detail, name *Ant* discharge, dismiss, expel, fire

attachment 1 · the feeling which animates a person who is genuinely fond of someone or something *Syn* affection, love *Rel* devotedness, fondness *Ant* aversion 2 *Syn* ARREST, apprehension, detention

attack *n* 1 · an attempt made on another or on others to injure, destroy, or defame *Syn* assault, onset, onslaught *Rel* action, battle 2 · the act or action of setting upon with force or violence *Syn* aggression, assault, blitzkrieg, charge, descent, offense (*or* offence), offensive, onset, onslaught, raid, rush, strike *Rel* ambuscade, ambush 3 · a sudden experiencing of a physical or mental disorder *Syn* bout, case, fit, seizure, siege, spell *Rel* recurrence, relapse

attack *vb* 1 · to make an onslaught upon *Syn* assail, assault, bombard, storm *Rel* battle, contend, fight, war 2 · to criticize harshly and usually publicly *Syn* abuse, assail, belabor, blast, castigate, excoriate, jump (on), lambaste (*or* lambast), scathe, slam, vituperate *Rel* berate, harangue, harass, harry, revile, scold

attain 1 *Syn* EARN, acquire, capture, carry, draw, gain, garner, get, land, make, obtain, procure, realize, secure, win *Ant* forfeit, lose 2 *Syn* REACH, achieve, compass, gain

attainment 1 *Syn* ACQUIREMENT, accomplishment, acquisition 2 *Syn* FRUITION, accomplishment, achievement, actuality, consummation, fulfillment, realization *Ant* naught, nonfulfillment

attempt *n* · an effort to do or accomplish something *Syn* crack, endeavor, essay, fling, go, pass, shot, stab, trial, try, whack *Rel* bid, striving, struggle, throes, undertaking

attempt *vb* · to make an effort to do *Syn* assay, endeavor, essay, seek, strive, try *Rel* fight, strain, struggle, toil, trouble, work

attend 1 *Syn* ACCOMPANY, chaperone (*or* chaperon), convoy, escort, squire 2 *Syn* LISTEN, hark, hear, hearken, heed, mind *Ant* ignore, tune out 3 *Syn* TEND, mind, watch

attendant *Syn* ESCORT, companion, guard, guide

attention 1 · the direct focusing of the mind especially on something to be learned, worked out, or dealt with *Syn* application, concentration, study *Rel* assiduity, diligence, industriousness, sedulousness *Ant* inattention 2 · a state of being aware *Syn* awareness, cognizance, ear, eye, heed, notice, observance, observation *Rel* advisement, care, concern, consideration, regard, watch 3 *Syn* COURTESY, amenity, gallantry *Ant* discourtesy

attentiveness *Syn* VIGILANCE, alertness, lookout, surveillance, watch, watchfulness

attenuate *Syn* THIN, dilute, extenuate, rarefy *Ant* thicken

attest 1 *Syn* CERTIFY, vouch, witness 2 *Syn* INDICATE, argue, bespeak, betoken, prove 3 *Syn* TESTIFY, depose, swear, witness

attire *vb Syn* CLOTHE, apparel, array, dress, robe *Ant* unclothe

attire *n Syn* CLOTHES, apparel, clothing, dress, raiment

attitude 1 *Syn* POSITION, stand 2 *Syn* POSTURE, pose

attorney 1 *Syn* AGENT (sense 1), commissary, delegate, deputy, envoy, factor, procurator, proxy, representative 2 *Syn* LAWYER, advocate, barrister, counsel, counselor, solicitor

attract · to draw another by exerting an irresistible or compelling influence *Syn* allure, bewitch, captivate, charm, enchant, fascinate *Rel* court, invite, solicit *Ant* repel

attraction · the relationship between persons or things that are involuntarily or naturally drawn together *Syn* affinity, sympathy

attractive 1 · drawing another by exerting a compelling influence *Syn* alluring, bewitching, captivating, charming, enchanting, fascinating *Rel* beautiful, bonny, comely, fair, lovely, pretty *Ant* forbidding, repellent 2 *Syn* BEAUTIFUL, beauteous, comely, cute, fair, gorgeous, handsome, knockout, lovely, pretty, ravishing, sightly, stunning, taking *Ant* homely, ill-favored, plain, ugly, unattractive, unbeautiful, unhandsome, unlovely, unpretty, unsightly

attribute *vb Syn* ASCRIBE, accredit, assign, charge, credit, impute, refer

attribute *n* 1 *Syn* CHARACTERISTIC, character, feature, mark, peculiarity, point, property, quality, trait 2 *Syn* SYMBOL, emblem, type

attrition *Syn* PENITENCE, compunction, contrition, remorse, repentance

attune *Syn* HARMONIZE, tune

atypical *Syn* DEVIANT, aberrant, abnormal, anomalous, irregular, unnatural *Ant* natural, normal, regular, standard, typical

audacious *Syn* BRAVE, bold, courageous, dauntless, doughty, fearless, intrepid, unafraid, undaunted, valiant, valorous *Ant* craven

audacity *Syn* EFFRONTERY, brashness, brass, brassiness, brazenness, cheek, cheekiness, chutzpah, gall, nerve, nerviness, pertness, presumption, presumptuousness, sauce, sauciness, temerity

audibly *Syn* ALOUD, out, out loud *Ant* inaudibly, silently, soundlessly

audit *n Syn* INSPECTION, check, checkup, examination, review, scan, scrutiny, survey

audit *vb Syn* SCRUTINIZE, examine, inspect, scan

auditory · of, relating to, or experienced through the sense of hearing *Syn* acoustic (*or* acoustical), aural, auricular *Rel* audible, clear, discernible, distinct, distinguishable, heard, perceptible

augment *Syn* INCREASE (sense 1), add (to), aggrandize, amplify, boost, compound, enlarge, escalate, expand, extend, multiply, raise, swell, up *Ant* abate, contract, decrease, diminish, lessen, lower, reduce, subtract (from)

augur *vb Syn* FORETELL, forebode, forecast, portend, predict, presage, prognosticate, prophesy

augur *n Syn* PROPHET, diviner, forecaster, foreseer, foreteller, fortune-teller, futurist, prognosticator, prophesier, seer, soothsayer

auguring *Syn* PREDICTION, cast, forecast, forecasting, foretelling, predicting, presaging, prognosis, prognosticating, prognostication, prophecy, soothsaying

augury *Syn* OMEN, auspice, boding, foreboding, foreshadowing, portent, prefiguring, presage

august 1 *Syn* DIGNIFIED, imposing, solemn, staid, stately *Ant* flighty, frivolous, giddy, goofy, silly, undignified 2 *Syn* GRAND, grandiose, imposing, magnificent, majestic, noble, stately

augustness *Syn* MAGNIFICENCE, brilliance, gloriousness, glory, grandeur, grandness, majesty, nobility, nobleness, resplendence, splendor, stateliness, stupendousness, sublimeness, superbness

auld lang syne *Syn* PAST, history, yesterday, yesteryear, yore

aura · a special quality or impression associated with something *Syn* air, atmosphere, climate, flavor, mood, note, temper *Rel* feel, feeling, sensation, sense, spirit

aural *Syn* AUDITORY, acoustic (*or* acoustical), auricular

aureate *Syn* RHETORICAL, bombastic, euphuistic, flowery, grandiloquent, magniloquent

au revoir *Syn* GOOD-BYE, adieu, bon voyage, farewell, Godspeed *Ant* hello

auricular *Syn* AUDITORY, acoustic (*or* acoustical), aural

auspice *Syn* OMEN, augury, boding, foreboding, foreshadowing, portent, prefiguring, presage

auspicious *Syn* FAVORABLE, benign, propitious *Ant* antagonistic, unfavorable

austere *Syn* SEVERE, ascetic, stern *Ant* tender, tolerant

autarchic *Syn* FREE, autarkic, autonomous, independent, sovereign *Ant* bond

autarchy *Syn* FREEDOM (sense 1), autarky, autonomy, independence, sovereignty *Ant* bondage

autarkic *Syn* FREE, autarchic, autonomous, independent, sovereign *Ant* bond

autarky *Syn* FREEDOM (sense 1), autarchy, autonomy, independence, sovereignty *Ant* bondage

authentic · being exactly as appears or is claimed *Syn* bona fide, genuine, veritable *Rel* authoritarian, dictatorial *Ant* spurious

authenticate *Syn* CONFIRM, corroborate, substantiate, validate, verify *Ant* contradict, deny

author *Syn* MAKER, creator

authoritarian **1** *Syn* BOSSY, autocratic, despotic, dictatorial, domineering, imperious, masterful, overbearing, peremptory, tyrannical, tyrannous **2** *Syn* DICTATORIAL, doctrinaire, dogmatic, magisterial

authority **1** *Syn* EXPERT, ace, adept, artist, crackerjack, maestro, master, past master, scholar, shark, virtuoso, whiz, wizard *Ant* amateur **2** *Syn* INFLUENCE, credit, prestige, weight **3** *Syn* RULE (sense 2), administration, governance, government, jurisdiction, regime, regimen

authorization *Syn* PERMISSION, allowance, clearance, concurrence, consent, granting, leave, license (*or* licence), sanction, sufferance *Ant* interdiction, prohibition, proscription

authorize · to invest with power or the right to act *Syn* accredit, commission, license *Rel* empower, enable

autobiography *Syn* BIOGRAPHY, confessions, life, memoir

autochthonous *Syn* NATIVE, aboriginal, endemic, indigenous *Ant* alien, foreign

autocrat *Syn* MONARCH, ruler, sovereign

autocratic **1** *Syn* ABSOLUTE, arbitrary, despotic, tyrannical, tyrannous *Ant* limited, restrained **2** *Syn* BOSSY, authoritarian, despotic, dictatorial, domineering, imperious, masterful, overbearing, peremptory, tyrannical, tyrannous

automatic *Syn* SPONTANEOUS, impulsive, instinctive, mechanical

autonomous *Syn* FREE, autarchic, autarkic, independent, sovereign *Ant* bond

autonomy *Syn* FREEDOM (sense 1), autarchy, autarky, independence, sovereignty *Ant* bondage

autopsy · examination of a dead body especially to find out the cause of death *Syn* postmortem, postmortem examination *Rel* dissection

auxiliary · supplying aid or support *Syn* accessory, adjuvant, ancillary, contributory, subservient, subsidiary *Rel* secondary, subordinate, tributary

avail *n* **1** *Syn* BENEFIT, profit *Ant* harm **2** *Syn* USE (sense 1), account, advantage, profit, service

avail *vb* *Syn* USE, apply, employ, utilize

avarice *Syn* GREED, acquisitiveness, avariciousness, avidity, covetousness, cupidity, greediness, rapaciousness, rapacity

avaricious *Syn* COVETOUS, acquisitive, grasping, greedy

avariciousness *Syn* GREED, acquisitiveness, avarice, avidity, covetousness, cupidity, greediness, rapaciousness, rapacity

avenge · to punish in kind the wrongdoer

responsible *Syn* retaliate, revenge *Rel* castigate, chasten, chastise, discipline, penalize, punish, scourge

aver *Syn* ASSERT, affirm, avouch, avow, declare, predicate, profess, protest, warrant *Ant* controvert, deny

average **1** · what is typical of a group, class, or series *Syn* norm, normal, par, standard *Rel* golden mean, mean, median, middle **2** *Syn* MEDIUM, fair, indifferent, mediocre, middling, moderate, second-rate

averse **1** *Syn* ANTIPATHETIC, allergic **2** *Syn* DISINCLINED, hesitant, indisposed, loath, reluctant

aversion **1** *Syn* DISGUST, distaste, loathing, nausea, repugnance, repulsion, revulsion **2** *Syn* DISLIKE, disfavor, distaste *Ant* liking

avert **1** *Syn* PREVENT (sense 2), forestall, help, obviate, preclude **2** *Syn* TURN (sense 2), deflect, divert, sheer

avid *Syn* EAGER, agog, anxious, athirst, keen *Ant* listless

avidity *Syn* GREED, acquisitiveness, avarice, avariciousness, covetousness, cupidity, greediness, rapaciousness, rapacity

avoid *Syn* ESCAPE (sense 2), elude, eschew, evade, shun

avouch *Syn* ASSERT, affirm, aver, avow, declare, predicate, profess, protest, warrant *Ant* controvert, deny

avow *Syn* ASSERT, affirm, aver, avouch, declare, predicate, profess, protest, warrant *Ant* controvert, deny

avowal *Syn* CONFESSION, acknowledgment, admission, concession

await *Syn* EXPECT, hope, look *Ant* despair of

awake **1** *Syn* AWARE, alive, cognizant, conscious, sensible *Ant* unaware **2** *Syn* WAKEFUL, sleepless, wide-awake *Ant* asleep, dormant, dozing, napping, resting, sleeping, slumbering

awaken *Syn* STIR, arouse, rally, rouse, waken

award *n* · something given in recognition of achievement *Syn* decoration, distinction, honor, plume, premium, prize *Rel* badge, crown, cup, laurel, medal, order, ribbon, trophy

award *vb* *Syn* GRANT (sense 1), accord, concede, vouchsafe

aware **1** · having knowledge of something *Syn* alive, awake, cognizant, conscious, sensible *Rel* certain, positive, sure *Ant* unaware **2** *Syn* CONSCIOUS, alive, cognizant, mindful, sensible, sentient *Ant* insensible, unaware, unconscious, unmindful

awareness *Syn* ATTENTION (sense 2), cognizance, ear, eye, heed, notice, observance, observation

awe **1** *Syn* REVERENCE (sense 2), fear **2** *Syn* WONDER (sense 2), admiration, amazement, wonderment

awful *adj* *Syn* FEARFUL (sense 2), appalling, dreadful, frightful, horrible, horrific, shocking, terrible, terrific

awful *adv Syn* VERY, awfully, beastly, deadly, especially, exceedingly, extra, extremely, far, frightfully, full, greatly, heavily, highly, hugely, jolly, mightily, mighty, mortally, most, much, particularly, rattling, real, right, so, something, super, terribly, too, whacking *Ant* little, negligibly, nominally, slightly

awfully *Syn* VERY, awful, beastly, deadly, especially, exceedingly, extra, extremely, far, frightfully, full, greatly, heavily, highly, hugely, jolly, mightily, mighty, mortally, most, much, particularly, rattling, real, right, so, something, super, terribly, too, whacking *Ant* little, negligibly, nominally, slightly

awkward **1** · not marked by ease (as of performance, movement, or social conduct) *Syn* clumsy, gauche, inept, maladroit *Rel* rigid, stiff, wooden *Ant* deft, graceful, handy **2** *Syn* CUMBERSOME, clumsy, cranky, cumbrous, ungainly, unhandy, unwieldy *Ant* handy

awning *Syn* CANOPY, ceiling, roof, tent

awry *adj* · inclined or twisted to one side *Syn* askew, aslant, cockeyed, crooked, listing, lopsided, oblique, skewed, slanted, slanting, slantwise, tilted, tipping, uneven *Rel* asymmetrical (*or* asymmetric), contorted, disordered, distorted, irregular, unbalanced, unsymmetrical *Ant* even, level, straight

awry *adv Syn* WRONG, afield, amiss, astray *Ant* aright, right, well

axiom *Syn* PRINCIPLE, fundamental, law, theorem

B

babble *Syn* CHAT, blab, cackle, chatter, converse, gab, gabble, gas, jabber, jaw, palaver, patter, prate, prattle, rap, rattle, run on, talk, twitter, visit

babe *Syn* BABY, child, infant, newborn

babel **1** *Syn* DIN, clamor, hubbub, hullabaloo, pandemonium, racket, uproar *Ant* quiet **2** *Syn* MADHOUSE, bedlam, circus, hell

babushka *Syn* BANDANNA, handkerchief, kerchief, mantilla

baby *n* · a recently born person *Syn* babe, child, infant, newborn *Rel* cherub

baby *vb* · to treat with great or excessive care *Syn* coddle, dandle, mollycoddle, nurse, pamper, spoil *Rel* cater (to), humor, indulge *Ant* discipline

babyish *Syn* CHILDISH, adolescent, immature, infantile, juvenile, kiddish, puerile *Ant* adult, grown-up, mature

back *adj* · being at or in the part of something opposite the front part *Syn* hind, hindmost, posterior, rear, rearward *Ant* anterior, fore, forward, front

back *vb* **1** *Syn* RECEDE, retract, retreat, retrograde *Ant* advance, proceed **2** *Syn* SUPPORT (sense 2), advocate, champion, uphold

back *n Syn* SPINE, backbone, chine, vertebrae

backbiting *Syn* DETRACTION, calumny, scandal, slander

backbone **1** *Syn* SPINE, back, chine, vertebrae **2** *Syn* FORTITUDE, grit, guts, pluck, sand *Ant* pusillanimity

back down *Syn* RENEGE, back off, cop out

backdrop *Syn* BACKGROUND, environment, milieu, mise-en-scène, setting

backer **1** *Syn* ALLY, abettor, confederate, supporter, sympathizer **2** *Syn* EXPONENT, advocate, apostle, booster, champion, friend, promoter, proponent, supporter *Ant* adversary, antagonist, opponent **3** *Syn* SPONSOR, angel, guarantor, patron, surety

background · the place, time, and circumstances in which something occurs *Syn* backdrop, environment, milieu, mise-en-scène, setting

backhanded *Syn* INSINCERE, artificial, double-dealing, feigned, hypocritical, left-handed, mealy, mealymouthed, two-faced, unctuous *Ant* genuine, heartfelt, honest, sincere, unfeigned

back off *Syn* RENEGE, back down, cop out

backside *Syn* BUTTOCKS, bottom, breech, butt, fanny, hams, haunches, posterior, rear, rump, seat

backslide *Syn* LAPSE, relapse

backslider *Syn* RENEGADE, apostate, recreant, turncoat *Ant* adherent, loyalist

back talk · disrespectful or argumentative talk given in response to a command or request *Syn* cheek, impertinence, impudence, insolence, sass, sauce *Rel* comeback, rejoinder, retort, riposte, wisecrack

backup *Syn* SUBSTITUTE, pinch hitter, relief, replacement, reserve, stand-in, sub

backward · not moving or going ahead *Syn* regressive, retrograde, retrogressive *Rel* dilatory, laggard, slow *Ant* advanced

backwater *Syn* FRONTIER, backwoods, bush, hinterland, up-country

backwoods *Syn* FRONTIER, backwater, bush, hinterland, up-country

bad *adj* **1** · deviating from the dictates of moral law *Syn* evil, ill, naughty, wicked *Rel* iniquitous, vicious, villainous *Ant* good

2 · not measuring up to a standard of what is satisfactory *Syn* poor, wrong *Ant* good **3** *Syn* FAULTY, defective, flawed, imperfect *Ant* faultless, flawless, impeccable, perfect **4** *Syn* HARMFUL, adverse, baleful, baneful, damaging, deleterious, detrimental, evil, hurtful, ill, injurious, mischievous, noxious, pernicious, prejudicial *Ant* harmless, innocent, innocuous, inoffensive, safe **5** *Syn* SAD (sense 1), blue, brokenhearted, crestfallen, dejected, depressed, despondent, disconsolate, doleful, down, downcast, downhearted, droopy, forlorn, gloomy, glum, heartbroken, heartsick, heartsore, inconsolable, joyless, low, low-spirited, melancholy, miserable, mournful, saddened, sorrowful, sorry, unhappy, woebegone, woeful, wretched *Ant* blissful, buoyant, buoyed, cheerful, cheery, chipper, delighted, glad, gladdened, gladsome, gleeful, happy, joyful, joyous, jubilant, sunny, upbeat **6** *Syn* UNPLEASANT, disagreeable, displeasing, distasteful, nasty, rotten, sour, uncongenial, unlovely, unpleasing, unsatisfying, unwelcome *Ant* agreeable, congenial, good, grateful, gratifying, nice, palatable, pleasant, pleasing, pleasurable, satisfying, welcome

bad *n* *Syn* EVIL, evildoing, ill, immorality, iniquity, sin, villainy, wrong *Ant* good, morality, right, virtue

badge *Syn* SIGN (sense 1), mark, note, symptom, token

badger *Syn* BAIT, chivy, heckle, hector, hound, ride

badlands *Syn* WASTE, desert, wilderness

badly · in an unsatisfactory way *Syn* inadequately, poorly, unacceptably, unsatisfactorily *Rel* rottenly *Ant* acceptably, adequately, all right, fine, good, palatably, passably, so-so, tolerably

baffle *Syn* FRUSTRATE, balk, circumvent, foil, outwit, thwart *Ant* fulfill

bag *n* **1** · a container made of a flexible material and open or opening at the top *Syn* pouch, sack **2** *Syn* PURSE, handbag, pocketbook

bag *vb* *Syn* CATCH, capture, ensnare, entrap, snare, trap *Ant* miss

bail *vb* *Syn* DIP (sense 2), dish, ladle, scoop, spoon

bail *n* *Syn* GUARANTEE, bond, guaranty, security, surety

bailiwick *Syn* FIELD, domain, province, sphere, territory

bait · to persist in tormenting or harassing another *Syn* badger, chivy, heckle, hector, hound, ride *Rel* annoy, harass, harry, worry

bake *Syn* DRY, dehydrate, desiccate, parch *Ant* moisten, wet

balance *n* **1** · the stability or efficiency resulting from the equalization or exact adjustment of opposing forces *Syn* equilibrium, equipoise, poise, tension **2** *Syn* REMAINDER,

leavings, remains, remnant, residue, residuum, rest **3** *Syn* SYMMETRY, harmony, proportion

balance *vb* **1** *Syn* COMPENSATE, counterbalance, counterpoise, countervail, offset **2** *Syn* EQUALIZE, equate, even, level **3** *Syn* STABILIZE, ballast, poise, steady, trim

balanced *Syn* SANE, clearheaded, lucid, normal, right, stable *Ant* crazed, crazy, demented, deranged, insane, lunatic, mad, maniacal, mental, unbalanced, unsound

bald *Syn* BARE, barren, naked, nude *Ant* covered

balderdash *Syn* NONSENSE, bull, bunk, drivel, gobbledygook, poppycock, rot, trash, twaddle

bale *Syn* BUNDLE, bunch, pack, package, packet, parcel

baleful **1** *Syn* DEADLY, deathly, fatal, fell, killer, lethal, mortal, murderous, pestilent, vital *Ant* healthful, healthy, nonfatal, nonlethal, wholesome **2** *Syn* HARMFUL, adverse, bad, baneful, damaging, deleterious, detrimental, evil, hurtful, ill, injurious, mischievous, noxious, pernicious, prejudicial *Ant* harmless, innocent, innocuous, inoffensive, safe **3** *Syn* OMINOUS, dire, foreboding, inauspicious, menacing, portentous, sinister, threatening **4** *Syn* SINISTER, malefic, maleficent, malign

balk **1** *Syn* DEMUR, boggle, jib, scruple, shy, stick, stickle, strain *Ant* accede **2** *Syn* FRUSTRATE, baffle, circumvent, foil, outwit, thwart *Ant* fulfill

balky **1** *Syn* CONTRARY, froward, perverse, restive, wayward *Ant* complaisant, good-natured **2** *Syn* DISOBEDIENT, contrary, defiant, froward, insubordinate, intractable, rebellious, recalcitrant, refractory, restive, ungovernable, unruly, untoward, wayward, willful (*or* wilful) *Ant* amenable, compliant, docile, obedient, tractable

ball *Syn* DANCE, cotillion, formal, hop, prom

ballast *Syn* STABILIZE, balance, poise, steady, trim

balloon *Syn* INCREASE (sense 2), accumulate, appreciate, build (up), burgeon, enlarge, escalate, expand, mount, multiply, mushroom, proliferate, rise, snowball, swell, wax *Ant* contract, decrease, diminish, lessen, wane

ballot *Syn* SUFFRAGE, franchise, vote

ballyhoo *Syn* PUBLICITY, promotion, propaganda

balmy **1** *Syn* CLEMENT, equable, gentle, mild, moderate, temperate *Ant* harsh, inclement, intemperate, severe **2** *Syn* ODOROUS, aromatic, fragrant, redolent *Ant* malodorous, odorless **3** *Syn* SOFT, bland, gentle, lenient, mild, smooth *Ant* hard, stern

balustrade *Syn* RAILING, banister, guardrail, rail

bamboozle *Syn* DUPE, befool, gull, hoax, hoodwink, trick

ban *n Syn* PROHIBITION (sense 2), embargo, interdict, interdiction, proscription, veto *Ant* prescription

ban *vb Syn* FORBID, bar, enjoin, interdict, outlaw, prohibit, proscribe *Ant* allow, let, permit, suffer

banal 1 *Syn* INSIPID, flat, inane, jejune, vapid, wishy-washy *Ant* sapid, zestful 2 *Syn* STALE, commonplace, hackney, hackneyed, moth-eaten, musty, stereotyped, threadbare, tired, trite *Ant* fresh, new, original

band *vb Syn* ALLY, associate, club, confederate, conjoin, cooperate, federate, league, unite *Ant* break up, disband

band *n* 1 *Syn* BOND, tie 2 *Syn* COMPANY, party, troop, troupe 3 *Syn* STRIP, fillet, ribbon, stripe

bandanna *or* **bandana** · a scarf worn on the head *Syn* babushka, handkerchief, kerchief, mantilla *Rel* shawl

bandwagon *Syn* CAMPAIGN, cause, crusade, drive, movement

bandy *Syn* EXCHANGE, interchange

bane *Syn* POISON, toxin, venom, virus

baneful *Syn* HARMFUL, adverse, bad, baleful, damaging, deleterious, detrimental, evil, hurtful, ill, injurious, mischievous, noxious, pernicious, prejudicial *Ant* harmless, innocent, innocuous, inoffensive, safe

bang *Syn* THRILL, exhilaration, kick, titillation

bangle *Syn* PENDANT, charm, lavalier

bang-up *Syn* EXCELLENT, A1, banner, capital, classic, crackerjack, dandy, divine, fabulous, fine, first-class, first-rate, grand, great, groovy, heavenly, jim-dandy, keen, marvelous (*or* marvellous), mean, neat, nifty, noble, par excellence, prime, sensational, splendid, stellar, sterling, superb, superior, superlative, supernal, swell, terrific, tip-top, top, top-notch, unsurpassed, wonderful *Ant* poor

banish · to remove by authority or force from a country, state, or sovereignty *Syn* deport, exile, expatriate, extradite, ostracize, transport *Rel* eject, expel, oust

banister *Syn* RAILING, balustrade, guardrail, rail

bank *n* 1 *Syn* HEAP, cock, mass, pile, shock, stack 2 *Syn* SHOAL, bar, reef 3 *Syn* SHORE, beach, coast, foreshore, littoral, strand

bank *vb* 1 *Syn* HEAP, cock, mass, pile, shock, stack 2 *Syn* RELY (ON), count, depend, reckon, trust

banner *adj Syn* EXCELLENT, A1, bang-up, capital, classic, crackerjack, dandy, divine, fabulous, fine, first-class, first-rate, grand, great, groovy, heavenly, jim-dandy, keen, marvelous (*or* marvellous), mean, neat, nifty, noble, par excellence, prime, sensational, splendid, stellar, sterling, superb, superior, superlative, supernal, swell, terrific, tip-top, top, top-notch, unsurpassed, wonderful *Ant* poor

banner *n Syn* FLAG, color, ensign, jack, pendant, pennant, pennon, standard, streamer

banning *Syn* PROHIBITION (sense 1), barring, enjoining, forbidding, interdicting, interdiction, outlawing, prohibiting, proscribing, proscription *Ant* prescription

banquet *Syn* DINNER, feast

banter *n* · good-natured teasing or exchanging of clever remarks *Syn* chaff, give-and-take, jesting, joshing, persiflage, raillery, repartee *Rel* barb, crack, dig, gag, jest, joke, quip, sally, wisecrack, witticism

banter *vb* 1 · to make fun of good-naturedly *Syn* chaff, jolly, josh, kid, rag, rib *Rel* deride, rally, ridicule, twit 2 *Syn* JOKE, fool, fun, jest, jive, josh, kid, quip, wisecrack

bar *n* 1 *Syn* ENCUMBRANCE, block, chain, clog, crimp, deterrent, drag, embarrassment, fetter, handicap, hindrance, hurdle, impediment, inhibition, interference, let, manacle, obstacle, obstruction, shackles, stop, stumbling block, trammel *Ant* aid, assistance, benefit, help 2 *Syn* BARROOM, café, groggery, grogshop, pub, saloon, tavern 3 *Syn* SHOAL, bank, reef

bar *vb* 1 *Syn* FORBID, ban, enjoin, interdict, outlaw, prohibit, proscribe *Ant* allow, let, permit, suffer 2 *Syn* HINDER, block, dam, impede, obstruct *Ant* further

barb *Syn* INSULT, affront, dart, dig, epithet, indignity, name, offense (*or* offence), outrage, put-down, sarcasm, slight, slur

barbarian · of, relating to, or characteristic of people that are not fully civilized *Syn* barbaric, barbarous, savage *Ant* civilized

barbaric *Syn* BARBARIAN, barbarous, savage *Ant* civilized

barbarism · a word or expression which offends against standards of correctness *Syn* corruption, impropriety, solecism, vernacularism, vulgarism

barbarity *Syn* CRUELTY, brutality, cruelness, heartlessness, inhumanity, sadism, savageness, savagery, viciousness, wantonness *Ant* benignity, compassion, good-heartedness, humanity, kindheartedness, kindness, sympathy

barbarous 1 *Syn* BARBARIAN, barbaric, savage *Ant* civilized 2 *Syn* FIERCE, cruel, fell, ferocious, inhuman, savage, truculent *Ant* mild, tame

bard *Syn* POET, minstrel, poetaster, rhymer, rhymester, troubadour, versifier

bare *adj* 1 · lacking naturally or conventionally appropriate covering or clothing *Syn* bald, barren, naked, nude *Rel* denuded, divested, stripped *Ant* covered 2 *Syn* MERE, very

bare *vb Syn* STRIP, denude, dismantle, divest *Ant* furnish, invest

barefaced *Syn* SHAMELESS, brash, brazen, impudent

bareness *Syn* VACANCY (sense 2), emptiness, vacuity *Ant* fullness

bargain *vb* · to talk over or dispute the terms of a purchase *Syn* chaffer, deal, dicker, haggle, horse-trade, negotiate, palter *Rel* argue, bicker, clash, quibble, squabble, wrangle

bargain *n Syn* CONTRACT, cartel, compact, concordat, convention, entente, pact, treaty

bark *vb* · to make the sound of or a sound suggestive of a dog *Syn* bay, growl, howl, snarl, yap, yelp *Rel* bawl, bellow, roar, vociferate

bark *n Syn* SKIN, hide, peel, pelt, rind

baroque *Syn* ORNATE, flamboyant, florid, rococo *Ant* austere, chaste

barrage · a rapid or overwhelming outpouring of many things at once *Syn* bombardment, cannonade, fusillade, hail, salvo, shower, storm, volley *Rel* broadside, burst, deluge, flood, flood tide, flush, gush, inundation, outburst, outflow, outpouring, overflow, spate, surge, torrent

barrel *n Syn* CASK, firkin, hogshead, keg, pipe, puncheon

barrel *vb Syn* HURRY (sense 2), bolt, bowl, breeze, career, course, dash, fly, hasten, hotfoot (it), hump, hurtle, hustle, pelt, race, rip, rocket, run, rush, rustle, scoot, scurry, scuttle, shoot, speed, step (along), tear, trot, whirl, whisk, zip, zoom *Ant* crawl, creep, poke

barren **1** *Syn* BARE, bald, naked, nude *Ant* covered **2** *Syn* STERILE, impotent, infertile, unfruitful *Ant* exuberant, fertile

barricade *Syn* BARRIER, fence, hedge, wall

barrier · a physical object that blocks the way *Syn* barricade, fence, hedge, wall *Rel* bar, encumbrance, handicap, hindrance, hurdle, impediment, obstacle, obstruction, roadblock, stop

barring *Syn* PROHIBITION (sense 1), banning, enjoining, forbidding, interdicting, interdiction, outlawing, prohibiting, proscribing, proscription *Ant* prescription

barrister *Syn* LAWYER, advocate, attorney, counsel, counselor, solicitor

barroom · a place of business where alcoholic beverages are sold to be consumed on the premises *Syn* bar, café, groggery, grogshop, pub, saloon, tavern *Rel* cabaret, dive, joint, nightclub, roadhouse, speakeasy

basal *Syn* FUNDAMENTAL, basic, radical, underlying

base *adj* · deserving of contempt because of the absence of higher values *Syn* low, vile *Rel* abject, ignoble, mean, sordid *Ant* noble

base *n* **1** · something on which another thing is reared or built or by which it is supported or fixed in place *Syn* basis, foundation, ground, groundwork *Ant* top **2** *Syn* CENTER (sense 2), capital, core, cynosure, eye, focus, heart, hub, mecca, nucleus, seat

base *vb* · to supply or to serve as a basis *Syn* found, ground, rest, stay *Rel* support, sustain

baseless · not justified or justifiable in any way *Syn* groundless, unfounded, unwarranted *Rel* false, wrong

bashful *Syn* SHY, coy, diffident, modest *Ant* obtrusive

basic **1** *Syn* ELEMENTARY, elemental, essential, fundamental, rudimentary, underlying *Ant* advanced **2** *Syn* FUNDAMENTAL, basal, radical, underlying

basically *Syn* CHIEFLY, altogether, by and large, generally, largely, mainly, mostly, overall, predominantly, primarily, principally, substantially

basis *Syn* BASE, foundation, ground, groundwork *Ant* top

baste *Syn* BEAT, belabor, buffet, pound, pummel, thrash

bastion *Syn* BULWARK, breastwork, parapet, rampart

bathe *Syn* WET, douse, drench, soak, souse, wash, water *Ant* dry

batter *Syn* MAIM, cripple, mangle, mutilate

battle *n* · a hostile meeting between opposing military forces *Syn* action, engagement *Rel* brush, encounter, skirmish

battle *vb Syn* CONTEND, fight, war

bauble *Syn* KNICKKNACK, curio, curiosity, gaud, gewgaw, novelty, ornamental, trinket

bawl *vb* **1** *Syn* ROAR, bellow, bluster, clamor, howl, ululate, vociferate **2** *Syn* SCOLD, berate, chew out, jaw, rail, rate, revile, tonguelash, upbraid, vituperate, wig

bawl *n Syn* ROAR, bellow, bluster, ululation, vociferation

bay *vb Syn* BARK, growl, howl, snarl, yap, yelp

bay *n Syn* COMPARTMENT, cabin, cell, chamber, cubicle

bazaar *Syn* STORE, emporium, shop

be · to have actuality or reality *Syn* exist, live, subsist

beach *Syn* SHORE, bank, coast, foreshore, littoral, strand

beached *Syn* AGROUND, grounded, stranded *Ant* afloat

beak *Syn* BILL, neb, nib

beaming *Syn* BRIGHT, brilliant, effulgent, incandescent, lambent, lucent, luminous, lustrous, radiant, refulgent *Ant* dim, dull

bear *vb* **1** · to bring forth as products *Syn* produce, turn out, yield *Rel* breed, generate, propagate, reproduce **2** · to sustain something trying or painful *Syn* abide, brook, endure, stand, suffer, tolerate *Rel* accept, receive **3** · to have a connection especially logically *Syn* appertain, apply, belong, pertain, relate *Rel* affect, concern **4** *Syn* CARRY, convey, transmit, transport **5** *Syn* PRESS, bear down, crowd, jam, squeeze

bear *n Syn* GROUCH, complainer, crab, crank, croaker, curmudgeon, fusser, griper, grouser, growler, grumbler, grump, murmurer, mutterer, whiner

bearable · capable of being endured *Syn* endurable, sufferable, supportable, sustainable, tolerable *Rel* acceptable, allowable, livable, reasonable *Ant* insufferable, insupportable, intolerable, unbearable, unendurable, unsupportable

beard *Syn* FACE, brave, challenge, dare, defy *Ant* avoid

bear down *Syn* PRESS, bear, crowd, jam, squeeze

bearing · the way in which or the quality by which a person outwardly manifests personality *Syn* demeanor, deportment, mien, port, presence *Rel* attitude, pose, posture

beast *Syn* ANIMAL, brute, creature, critter

beastly *adj Syn* BRUTAL, bestial, brute, brutish, feral

beastly *adv Syn* VERY, awful, awfully, deadly, especially, exceedingly, extra, extremely, far, frightfully, full, greatly, heavily, highly, hugely, jolly, mightily, mighty, mortally, most, much, particularly, rattling, real, right, so, something, super, terribly, too, whacking *Ant* little, negligibly, nominally, slightly

beat *vb* **1** · to strike repeatedly *Syn* baste, belabor, buffet, pound, pummel, thrash *Rel* box, clout, cuff, hit, punch, slap, slug, smite, strike, swat **2** *Syn* CONQUER, defeat, lick, overcome, overthrow, reduce, rout, subdue, subjugate, surmount, vanquish **3** *Syn* PULSATE, palpitate, pulse, throb

beat *n* **1** *Syn* PULSATION, palpitation, pulse, throb **2** *Syn* RHYTHM, cadence, measure, meter

beatitude *Syn* HAPPINESS, blessedness, bliss, felicity *Ant* unhappiness

beau **1** *Syn* BOYFRIEND, fellow, man, swain **2** *Syn* FOP, buck, coxcomb, dandy, dude, exquisite

beau ideal *Syn* MODEL, example, exemplar, ideal, mirror, pattern, standard

beauteous *Syn* BEAUTIFUL, attractive, comely, cute, fair, gorgeous, handsome, knockout, lovely, pretty, ravishing, sightly, stunning, taking *Ant* homely, ill-favored, plain, ugly, unattractive, unbeautiful, unhandsome, unlovely, unpretty, unsightly

beautiful · very pleasing to look at *Syn* attractive, beauteous, comely, cute, fair, gorgeous, handsome, knockout, lovely, pretty, ravishing, sightly, stunning, taking *Rel* alluring, appealing, charming, dainty, delicate, delightful, elegant, exquisite, eye-catching, flawless, glamorous, glorious, perfect, personable, prepossessing, presentable, radiant, resplendent, splendid, statuesque, sublime, superb *Ant* homely, ill-favored, plain, ugly, unattractive, unbeautiful, unhandsome, unlovely, unpretty, unsightly

beautify *Syn* ADORN, bedeck, deck, decorate, embellish, garnish, ornament *Ant* disfigure

beauty *Syn* JIM-DANDY, corker, crackerjack, dandy, knockout, nifty, pip

because · for the reason that *Syn* as, for, inasmuch as, since

because of · as the result of *Syn* due to, owing to, through, with

beckon *Syn* MOTION, flag, gesture, signal, wave

becloud *Syn* OBSCURE, bedim, befog, cloud, darken, dim, eclipse, fog, obfuscate *Ant* illuminate, illumine

beclouded *Syn* OVERCAST, clouded, cloudy, dull, hazed, hazy, heavy, lowering, overclouded *Ant* clear, cloudless

become · to eventually have as a state or quality *Syn* come, get, go, grow, run, turn, wax *Rel* alter, change, metamorphose, modify, mutate, transfigure, transform, transmute

bedeck *Syn* ADORN, beautify, deck, decorate, embellish, garnish, ornament *Ant* disfigure

bedevil *Syn* AFFLICT, agonize, curse, harrow, martyr, persecute, plague, rack, torment, torture

bedim *Syn* OBSCURE, becloud, befog, cloud, darken, dim, eclipse, fog, obfuscate *Ant* illuminate, illumine

bedlam *Syn* MADHOUSE, babel, circus, hell

beef *Syn* COMPLAIN, bellyache, carp, crab, croak, fuss, gripe, grouse, growl, grumble, kick, moan, murmur, mutter, repine, squawk, wail, whine, yammer *Ant* rejoice

beetle *Syn* BULGE, jut, overhang, project, protrude, stick out

befall *Syn* HAPPEN, betide, chance, occur, transpire

befog *Syn* OBSCURE, becloud, bedim, cloud, darken, dim, eclipse, fog, obfuscate *Ant* illuminate, illumine

befool *Syn* DUPE, bamboozle, gull, hoax, hoodwink, trick

before · earlier than *Syn* ahead of, ere, of, previous to, prior to, to *Rel* till, until, up to *Ant* after, following

beforehand *Syn* EARLY, betimes, soon *Ant* late

befoul **1** *Syn* CONTAMINATE, defile, foul, poison, pollute, taint *Ant* decontaminate, purify **2** *Syn* DIRTY, begrime, besmirch, blacken, foul, grime, mire, muddy, smirch, smudge, soil, stain, sully *Ant* clean, cleanse

befuddle *Syn* CONFUSE, addle, fuddle, muddle *Ant* enlighten

beg · to ask or request urgently *Syn* adjure, beseech, entreat, implore, importune, supplicate *Rel* ask, request, solicit

beget *Syn* GENERATE, breed, engender, get, procreate, propagate, reproduce, sire

beggar · a person who lives by public begging *Syn* mendicant, panhandler *Rel* bum, drifter, hobo, tramp, vagabond, vagrant

beggarly *Syn* CONTEMPTIBLE, cheap, despicable, pitiable, scurvy, shabby, sorry *Ant* admirable, estimable, formidable

begin **1** · to come into existence *Syn* arise,

commence, dawn, form, materialize, originate, set in, spring, start *Rel* be, breathe, exist, live, subsist *Ant* cease, end, stop **2** · to take the first step in (a process or course of action) *Syn* commence, embark (on *or* upon), enter (into *or* upon), get off, kick off, launch, open, start, strike (into) *Rel* create, generate, inaugurate, initiate, innovate, invent, originate *Ant* conclude, end, finish, terminate

beginner · a person who is just starting out in a field of activity *Syn* colt, fledgling, freshman, greenhorn, neophyte, newbie, newcomer, novice, recruit, rookie, tenderfoot, tyro *Rel* amateur, apprentice, cub, dilettante, learner, probationer, student, trainee *Ant* old hand, old-timer, vet, veteran

beginning · the point at which something begins *Syn* alpha, birth, commencement, dawn, genesis, inception, incipiency, launch, morning, onset, outset, start, threshold *Rel* creation, inauguration, initiation, institution, origination *Ant* close, conclusion, end, ending

begrime *Syn* DIRTY, befoul, besmirch, blacken, foul, grime, mire, muddy, smirch, smudge, soil, stain, sully *Ant* clean, cleanse

begrudge *Syn* COVET, envy, grudge

beguile 1 *Syn* DECEIVE, betray, delude, double-cross, mislead *Ant* enlighten, undeceive **2** *Syn* LURE, allure, decoy, entice, lead on, seduce, tempt

behave 1 · to act or to cause oneself to do something in a certain way *Syn* acquit, comport, conduct, demean, deport, quit *Rel* bear, carry *Ant* misbehave **2** *Syn* ACT (sense 1), function, operate, react, work

behavior · one's actions in general or on a particular occasion *Syn* conduct, deportment *Rel* bearing, demeanor, mien

behemoth *Syn* GIANT, blockbuster, colossus, jumbo, leviathan, mammoth, monster, titan, whale, whopper *Ant* dwarf, midget, mini, miniature, peewee, pygmy, runt, shrimp

behest *Syn* COMMAND, bidding, dictate, injunction, mandate, order

behind *Syn* AFTER, following *Ant* ahead of, before, ere, previous to, prior to

behindhand *Syn* TARDY, late, overdue *Ant* prompt

behold *Syn* SEE (sense 1), contemplate, descry, discern, espy, note, notice, observe, perceive, remark, survey, view

beholder *Syn* SPECTATOR, bystander, eyewitness, kibitzer, looker-on, observer, onlooker, witness

being 1 *Syn* ENTITY, creature, individual, person **2** *Syn* EXISTENCE, actuality *Ant* nonexistence

belabor 1 *Syn* ATTACK (sense 2), abuse, assail, blast, castigate, excoriate, jump (on), lambaste (*or* lambast), scathe, slam, vituperate **2** *Syn* BEAT, baste, buffet, pound, pummel, thrash

belch 1 · to eject (gas) from the stomach by way of the mouth or matter from a containing cavity by way of an opening *Syn* burp, disgorge, regurgitate, spew, throw up, vomit *Rel* eject, expel **2** *Syn* ERUPT (sense 2), disgorge, eject, expel, jet, spew, spout, spurt

beleaguer *Syn* BESIEGE, blockade, invest

belie *Syn* MISREPRESENT, falsify, garble

belief 1 · the act of one who assents intellectually to something proposed or offered for acceptance as true or the state of mind of one who so assents *Syn* credence, credit, faith *Rel* assurance, certainty, certitude, conviction *Ant* disbelief, unbelief **2** *Syn* OPINION, conviction, persuasion, sentiment, view

believable *Syn* PLAUSIBLE, colorable, credible, specious

believe 1 · to have as an opinion *Syn* consider, deem, feel, figure, guess, hold, imagine, suppose, think *Rel* esteem, regard, view **2** · to regard as right or true *Syn* accept, credit, swallow, trust *Rel* account, accredit, understand *Ant* disbelieve, discredit, reject

belittle *Syn* DECRY, deprecate, derogate, detract, disparage, minimize *Ant* extol

bellicose *Syn* BELLIGERENT, aggressive, argumentative, combative, contentious, discordant, disputatious, gladiatorial, militant, pugnacious, quarrelsome, scrappy, truculent, warlike *Ant* nonbelligerent, pacific, peaceable, peaceful

bellicosity *Syn* BELLIGERENCE, aggression, aggressiveness, combativeness, contentiousness, disputatiousness, fight, militancy, pugnacity, scrappiness, truculence *Ant* pacifism

belligerence · an inclination to fight or quarrel *Syn* aggression, aggressiveness, bellicosity, combativeness, contentiousness, disputatiousness, fight, militancy, pugnacity, scrappiness, truculence *Rel* antagonism, fierceness, hostility, unfriendliness *Ant* pacifism

belligerent · feeling or displaying eagerness to fight *Syn* aggressive, argumentative, bellicose, combative, contentious, discordant, disputatious, gladiatorial, militant, pugnacious, quarrelsome, scrappy, truculent, warlike *Rel* antagonistic, fierce, hostile, hot-tempered *Ant* nonbelligerent, pacific, peaceable, peaceful

bellow *vb Syn* ROAR, bawl, bluster, clamor, howl, ululate, vociferate

bellow *n Syn* ROAR, bawl, bluster, ululation, vociferation

belly *Syn* STOMACH, abdomen, gut, solar plexus, tummy

bellyache *Syn* COMPLAIN, beef, carp, crab, croak, fuss, gripe, grouse, growl, grumble, kick, moan, murmur, mutter, repine, squawk, wail, whine, yammer *Ant* rejoice

belong *Syn* BEAR (sense 3), appertain, apply, pertain, relate

belongings *Syn* POSSESSIONS, assets, effects, means, resources

beloved *Syn* SWEETHEART, darling, dear, flame, honey, love, sweet

below · in a lower position relative to some other object or place *Syn* beneath, under, underneath *Ant* above

belt *Syn* AREA, region, tract, zone

bemoan *Syn* REGRET, deplore, lament, repent, rue

bemuse *Syn* DAZE, benumb, paralyze, petrify, stun, stupefy

bend *Syn* CURVE, twist

beneath *Syn* BELOW, under, underneath *Ant* above

benefaction *Syn* CONTRIBUTION, alms, beneficence, charity, donation, philanthropy

benefactor · one that helps another with gifts or money *Syn* donator, donor, patron *Rel* almsgiver, philanthropist

beneficence *Syn* CONTRIBUTION, alms, benefaction, charity, donation, philanthropy

beneficial · conferring benefits or promoting or contributing to personal or social well-being *Syn* advantageous, favorable, helpful, profitable, salutary *Rel* gratifying, rewarding, satisfying *Ant* disadvantageous, unfavorable, unhelpful

benefit · to do good or to be of advantage to someone *Syn* avail, profit *Rel* ameliorate, better, improve *Ant* harm

benevolent *Syn* CHARITABLE, altruistic, eleemosynary, humane, humanitarian, philanthropic *Ant* uncharitable

benighted *Syn* IGNORANT, dark, illiterate, nonliterate, simple, uneducated, uninstructed, unlearned, unlettered, unread, unschooled, untaught, untutored *Ant* educated, knowledgeable, literate, schooled

benign **1** *Syn* FAVORABLE, auspicious, propitious *Ant* antagonistic, unfavorable **2** *Syn* KIND, benignant, kindly *Ant* unkind

benignant *Syn* KIND, benign, kindly *Ant* unkind

bent *Syn* GIFT (sense 2), aptitude, faculty, genius, knack, talent, turn

benumb *Syn* DAZE, bemuse, paralyze, petrify, stun, stupefy

benumbed *Syn* NUMB, asleep, dead, insensitive, numbed, unfeeling *Ant* feeling, sensitive

bequeath *Syn* WILL, devise, leave, legate

berate *Syn* SCOLD, bawl, chew out, jaw, rail, rate, revile, tongue-lash, upbraid, vituperate, wig

berth **1** *Syn* ROOM (sense 2), clearance, elbow room, leeway, margin, play **2** *Syn* WHARF, dock, jetty, levee, pier, quay, slip

beseech *Syn* BEG, adjure, entreat, implore, importune, supplicate

beset *Syn* INFEST, overrun *Ant* disinfest

besiege · to surround (as a fortified place) with armed forces for the purpose of capturing or preventing commerce and communication *Syn* beleaguer, blockade, invest *Rel* barricade, block, cut off, dam, encircle

besmirch *Syn* DIRTY, befoul, begrime, blacken, foul, grime, mire, muddy, smirch, smudge, soil, stain, sully *Ant* clean, cleanse

besotted *Syn* FOND, infatuated, insensate

bespangled *Syn* SPOTTED, flecked, marbled, mottled, spangled, spattered, speckled, sprinkled, stippled

bespeak *Syn* INDICATE, argue, attest, betoken, prove

best **1** *Syn* ELITE, choice, cream, elect, fat, flower, pick, prime, upper crust **2** *Syn* FINERY, array, bravery, caparison, feather, frippery, full dress, gaiety, regalia

bestial *Syn* BRUTAL, beastly, brute, brutish, feral

bestow *Syn* GIVE, afford, confer, donate, present

bestrew *Syn* SCATTER (sense 2), dot, pepper, sow, spray, sprinkle, strew

bet *n* · something (as money) staked on a winner-take-all basis on the outcome of an uncertainty *Syn* ante, pot, stake, wager

bet *vb* · to risk (something) on the outcome of an uncertain event *Syn* gamble, go, lay, stake, wager *Rel* bid, offer

bête noire *Syn* ABOMINATION, anathema, bugbear *Ant* joy

bethink *Syn* REMEMBER, mind, recall, recollect, remind, reminisce *Ant* forget

betide *Syn* HAPPEN, befall, chance, occur, transpire

betimes *Syn* EARLY, beforehand, soon *Ant* late

betoken *Syn* INDICATE, argue, attest, bespeak, prove

betray **1** *Syn* DECEIVE, beguile, delude, double-cross, mislead *Ant* enlighten, undeceive **2** *Syn* REVEAL, disclose, discover, divulge, tell *Ant* conceal

betrayal · the act or fact of violating the trust or confidence of another *Syn* disloyalty, double cross, faithlessness, falseness, falsity, infidelity, perfidy, sellout, treachery, treason, unfaithfulness *Rel* abandonment, desertion

betrayer *Syn* TRAITOR, double-crosser, quisling, recreant, turncoat

betrothed · the person to whom one is engaged to be married *Syn* fiancé, fiancée, intended *Rel* admirer, beau, beloved, boyfriend, darling, dear, favorite, fellow, flame, girlfriend, honey, love, lover, steady, swain, sweet, sweetheart, valentine

better *adj* · more worthy or more pleasing than another or others *Syn* preferable, superior *Rel* choice, dainty, delicate

better *n* *Syn* SUPERIOR, elder, senior *Ant* inferior, subordinate, underling

better *vb* *Syn* IMPROVE (sense 1), ameliorate, help *Ant* impair, worsen

bettor *or* **better** · one that bets (as on the outcome of a contest or sports event) *Syn* gambler, wagerer *Rel* dicer

bewilder *Syn* PUZZLE, confound, distract, dumbfound, mystify, nonplus, perplex

bewitch *Syn* ATTRACT, allure, captivate, charm, enchant, fascinate *Ant* repel

bewitching *Syn* ATTRACTIVE, alluring, captivating, charming, enchanting, fascinating *Ant* forbidding, repellent

beyond *prep* 1 · on or to the farther side of *Syn* over, past *Rel* outside 2 · out of the reach or sphere of *Syn* outside, outside of, without *Rel* except *Ant* within

beyond *adv Syn* FARTHER, further

bias *n* 1 · an attitude that always favors one way of feeling or acting especially without considering any other possibilities *Syn* favor, one-sidedness, partiality, partisanship, prejudice *Rel* favoritism, nepotism *Ant* impartiality, neutrality, objectivity, open-mindedness 2 *Syn* PREDILECTION, partiality, prejudice, prepossession *Ant* aversion

bias *vb Syn* INCLINE, dispose, predispose *Ant* disincline, indispose

bickering *Syn* QUARREL, altercation, spat, squabble, tiff, wrangle

bid *vb* 1 *Syn* COMMAND, charge, direct, enjoin, instruct, order *Ant* comply, obey 2 *Syn* INVITE, court, solicit, woo

bid *n Syn* OVERTURE, advance, approach, tender

bidding *Syn* COMMAND, behest, dictate, injunction, mandate, order

big *Syn* LARGE, bulky, considerable, goodly, good-sized, grand, great, handsome, hefty, hulking, largish, outsize, oversize (*or* oversized), sizable (*or* sizeable), substantial, tidy, voluminous *Ant* little, puny, small, undersized

bigoted *Syn* INTOLERANT, narrow, narrow-minded, prejudiced, small-minded *Ant* broadminded, liberal, open-minded, tolerant, unprejudiced

bill · the jaws of a bird together with their horny covering *Syn* beak, neb, nib

billingsgate *Syn* ABUSE, invective, obloquy, scurrility, vituperation *Ant* adulation

binary *Syn* DOUBLE, bipartite, dual, duplex, twin *Ant* single

biography · an account of the events and circumstances of a person's life *Syn* autobiography, confessions, life, memoir

biologic *Syn* DRUG, medicinal, pharmaceutical, simple

biotope *Syn* HABITAT, range, station

bipartite *Syn* DOUBLE, binary, dual, duplex, twin *Ant* single

bird's-eye *Syn* GENERAL (sense 2), all-around, broad, nonspecific, overall *Ant* delineated, detailed, particularized, specific

birth 1 *Syn* ANCESTRY, blood, bloodline, breeding, descent, extraction, family tree, genealogy, line, lineage, origin, parentage, pedigree, stock, strain *Ant* issue, posterity, progeny, seed 2 *Syn*

BEGINNING, alpha, commencement, dawn, genesis, inception, incipiency, launch, morning, onset, outset, start, threshold *Ant* close, conclusion, end, ending

birthright 1 *Syn* HERITAGE, inheritance, patrimony 2 *Syn* RIGHT, appanage, perquisite, prerogative, privilege

bit *Syn* PARTICLE, atom, iota, jot, mite, smidgen, tittle, whit

bite *vb* · to attack with or as if with the teeth *Syn* champ, gnash, gnaw *Rel* consume, devour, eat

bite *n Syn* CHILL, bitterness, bleakness, chilliness, nip, rawness, sharpness

biting *Syn* INCISIVE, clear-cut, crisp, cutting, trenchant

bitterness *Syn* CHILL, bite, bleakness, chilliness, nip, rawness, sharpness

bitty *Syn* TINY, atomic, infinitesimal, microminiature, microscopic, miniature, minute, teeny, teeny-weeny, wee *Ant* astronomical, colossal, cosmic, elephantine, enormous, giant, gigantic, herculean, heroic, huge, immense, mammoth, massive, monster, monstrous, monumental, mountainous, prodigious, titanic, tremendous

bizarre *Syn* FANTASTIC, antic, grotesque

blab 1 *Syn* CHAT, babble, cackle, chatter, converse, gab, gabble, gas, jabber, jaw, palaver, patter, prate, prattle, rap, rattle, run on, talk, twitter, visit 2 *Syn* GOSSIP, tattle

blackball *Syn* EXCLUDE, debar, disbar, eliminate, rule out, shut out, suspend *Ant* admit, include

blacken 1 *Syn* DIRTY, befoul, begrime, besmirch, foul, grime, mire, muddy, smirch, smudge, soil, stain, sully *Ant* clean, cleanse 2 *Syn* SLANDER, asperse, defame, libel, malign, smear, traduce, vilify

blackguard *Syn* VILLAIN, knave, miscreant, rapscallion, rascal, rogue, scamp, scoundrel

blackout *Syn* FAINT, coma, insensibility, knockout, swoon

black out *Syn* FAINT, pass out, swoon *Ant* come around, come round, come to, revive

blame *n* · responsibility for misdeed or delinquency *Syn* culpability, fault, guilt *Rel* accountability, answerability, responsibility

blame *vb Syn* CRITICIZE, censure, condemn, denounce, reprehend, reprobate

blameworthy · deserving reproach and punishment for a wrong, sinful, or criminal act, practice, or condition *Syn* culpable, guilty *Ant* blameless

blanch *Syn* WHITEN, bleach, blench, decolorize, dull, fade, pale, wash out *Ant* blacken, darken, deepen

bland *Syn* SOFT, balmy, gentle, lenient, mild, smooth *Ant* hard, stern

blandish *Syn* COAX, blarney, cajole, softsoap, wheedle

blank *adj Syn* EMPTY, vacant, vacuous, void *Ant* full

blank *n Syn* VACANCY (sense 1), blankness, emptiness, vacuity, void *Ant* fullness

blanket *Syn* GENERAL (sense 1), common, generic, global, overall, universal *Ant* individual, particular

blankness *Syn* VACANCY (sense 1), blank, emptiness, vacuity, void *Ant* fullness

blarney *Syn* COAX, blandish, cajole, soft-soap, wheedle

blasphemous *Syn* IMPIOUS, profane, sacrilegious *Ant* pious, reverent

blasphemy 1 · impious or irreverent speech *Syn* cursing, profanity, swearing *Rel* affront, indignity, insult *Ant* adoration 2 *Syn* PROFANATION, desecration, sacrilege

blast *n* · severe, sudden, or surprising ruin or injury *Syn* blight, nip *Rel* destruction

blast *vb* 1 · to ruin or to injure severely, suddenly, or surprisingly *Syn* blight, nip *Rel* destroy 2 *Syn* ATTACK (sense 2), abuse, assail, belabor, castigate, excoriate, jump (on), lambaste (*or* lambast), scathe, slam, vituperate

blatant 1 *Syn* EGREGIOUS, conspicuous, flagrant, glaring, gross, obvious, patent, pronounced, rank, striking 2 *Syn* VOCIFEROUS, boisterous, clamorous, obstreperous, strident

blaze *n* · brightly burning light or fire *Syn* flame, flare, glare, glow *Rel* fire, firing, igniting, ignition, kindling

blaze *vb* 1 · to burn or appear to burn brightly *Syn* flame, flare, glare, glow *Rel* illuminate, illumine, light 2 *Syn* ANNOUNCE, advertise, broadcast, declare, enunciate, placard, post, proclaim, promulgate, publicize, publish, sound

blazing *Syn* FERVENT, ardent, burning, charged, emotional, fervid, feverish, fiery, flaming, glowing, hot-blooded, impassioned, passionate, red-hot, vehement, warm, warm-blooded *Ant* cold, cool, dispassionate, impassive, unemotional

bleach *Syn* WHITEN, blanch, blench, decolorize, dull, fade, pale, wash out *Ant* blacken, darken, deepen

bleak *Syn* DISMAL, cheerless, desolate, dispiriting, dreary

bleakness *Syn* CHILL, bite, bitterness, chilliness, nip, rawness, sharpness

bleed 1 *Syn* EXUDE, ooze, percolate, seep, strain, sweat, weep 2 *Syn* FLEECE, cheat, chisel, cozen, defraud, hustle, mulct, rook, shortchange, skin, squeeze, stick, sting, swindle, victimize

blemish · something that spoils the appearance or completeness of a thing *Syn* defect, deformity, disfigurement, fault, flaw, imperfection, mark, pockmark, scar *Rel* abnormality, distortion, irregularity, malformation

blench 1 *Syn* RECOIL, flinch, quail, shrink, wince *Ant* confront, defy 2 *Syn* WHITEN, blanch, bleach, decolorize, dull, fade, pale, wash out *Ant* blacken, darken, deepen

blend *n* · a distinct entity formed by the combining of two or more different things *Syn* admixture, amalgam, amalgamation, combination, composite, compound, fusion, intermixture, mix, mixture *Rel* coalescence, concoction, incorporation, intermingling, mingling

blend *vb Syn* MIX, amalgamate, coalesce, commingle, fuse, merge, mingle

blessed *Syn* HOLY (sense 2), consecrated, hallowed, sacred, sacrosant, sanctified *Ant* unconsecrated, unhallowed

blessedness 1 *Syn* HOLINESS, devoutness, godliness, piety, piousness, sainthood, saintliness, saintship, sanctity *Ant* godlessness, impiety, ungodliness, unholiness 2 *Syn* HAPPINESS, beatitude, bliss, felicity *Ant* unhappiness

blessing 1 *Syn* APPROVAL, approbation, favor, imprimatur, OK (*or* okay) *Ant* disapprobation, disapproval, disfavor 2 *Syn* CONSECRATION, hallowing, sanctification

blight *n Syn* BLAST, nip

blight *vb Syn* BLAST, nip

blind · lacking the power of sight *Syn* eyeless, sightless, stone blind *Rel* unobservant, unobserving *Ant* sighted

bliss *Syn* HAPPINESS, beatitude, blessedness, felicity *Ant* unhappiness

blithe *Syn* CHEERFUL (sense 1), blithesome, bright, buoyant, cheery, chipper, gay, gladsome, lightsome, sunny, upbeat *Ant* dour, gloomy, glum, morose, saturnine, sulky, sullen

blithesome 1 *Syn* CHEERFUL (sense 1), blithe, bright, buoyant, cheery, chipper, gay, gladsome, lightsome, sunny, upbeat *Ant* dour, gloomy, glum, morose, saturnine, sulky, sullen 2 *Syn* MERRY, festive, gay, gleeful, jocose, jocund, jolly, jovial, laughing, mirthful, sunny

blitzkrieg *Syn* ATTACK (sense 2), aggression, assault, charge, descent, offense (*or* offence), offensive, onset, onslaught, raid, rush, strike

bloc 1 *Syn* COMBINATION, combine, faction, party, ring 2 *Syn* FACTION, body, coalition, party, sect, set, side, wing

block *n Syn* ENCUMBRANCE, bar, chain, clog, crimp, deterrent, drag, embarrassment, fetter, handicap, hindrance, hurdle, impediment, inhibition, interference, let, manacle, obstacle, obstruction, shackles, stop, stumbling block, trammel *Ant* aid, assistance, benefit, help

block *vb Syn* HINDER, bar, dam, impede, obstruct *Ant* further

blockade *Syn* BESIEGE, beleaguer, invest

blockbuster *Syn* GIANT, behemoth, colossus, jumbo, leviathan, mammoth, monster, titan, whale, whopper *Ant* dwarf, midget, mini, miniature, peewee, pygmy, runt, shrimp

blond *or* **blonde** · of a pale yellow or yellowish brown color *Syn* fair, flaxen, golden, sandy, straw, tawny *Rel* gold, light, white *Ant* dark

blood *Syn* ANCESTRY, birth, bloodline, breeding, descent, extraction, family tree, genealogy, line, lineage, origin, parentage, pedigree, stock, strain *Ant* issue, posterity, progeny, seed

bloodless *Syn* PALE (sense 2), anemic

bloodline *Syn* ANCESTRY, birth, blood, breeding, descent, extraction, family tree, genealogy, line, lineage, origin, parentage, pedigree, stock, strain *Ant* issue, posterity, progeny, seed

bloodthirsty · eager for or marked by the shedding of blood, extreme violence, or killing *Syn* bloody, homicidal, murdering, murderous, sanguinary, sanguine *Rel* barbaric, barbarous, cruel, heartless, inhumane, sadistic, savage, vicious, wanton

bloody **1** · affected by or involving the shedding of blood *Syn* gory, sanguinary, sanguine, sanguineous **2** *Syn* BLOODTHIRSTY, homicidal, murdering, murderous, sanguinary, sanguine

bloom *n Syn* BLOSSOM, blow, flower

bloom *vb* **1** *Syn* BLOSSOM, blow, flower **2** *Syn* BLUSH, color, crimson, flush, glow, redden

blossom *n* · the period or state of florescence of a seed plant *Syn* bloom, blow, flower

blossom *vb* · to become florescent *Syn* bloom, blow, flower

blot *Syn* STIGMA, brand, stain

blotch *Syn* SPOT, dapple, dot, fleck, freckle, marble, mottle, pepper, speck, speckle, splotch, sprinkle, stipple

blot out *Syn* ERASE, cancel, delete, efface, expunge, obliterate

blow *vb Syn* BLOSSOM, bloom, flower

blow *n Syn* BLOSSOM, bloom, flower

blowsy *Syn* SLATTERNLY, dowdy, frowzy

blubber *Syn* CRY, keen, wail, weep, whimper

blue *Syn* SAD (sense 1), bad, brokenhearted, crestfallen, dejected, depressed, despondent, disconsolate, doleful, down, downcast, downhearted, droopy, forlorn, gloomy, glum, heartbroken, heartsick, heartsore, inconsolable, joyless, low, low-spirited, melancholy, miserable, mournful, saddened, sorrowful, sorry, unhappy, woebegone, woeful, wretched *Ant* blissful, buoyant, buoyed, cheerful, cheery, chipper, delighted, glad, gladdened, gladsome, gleeful, happy, joyful, joyous, jubilant, sunny, upbeat

bluejacket *Syn* MARINER, gob, sailor, seaman, tar

blueprint *n Syn* SKETCH, delineate, diagram, draft, outline, plot, trace

blueprint *vb Syn* SKETCH, delineation, diagram, draft, outline, plot, tracing

blues *Syn* SADNESS, dejection, depression, desolation, despondency, disconsolateness, dispiritedness, doldrums, downheartedness, dreariness, dumps, forlornness, gloom, gloominess, heartsickness, joylessness, melancholy, mopes, oppression, unhappiness *Ant* bliss, blissfulness, ecstasy, elatedness, elation, euphoria, exhilaration, exuberance, exultation, felicity, gladness, gladsomeness, happiness, heaven, intoxication, joy, joyfulness, joyousness, jubilation, rapture, rapturousness

bluff · abrupt and unceremonious in speech or manner *Syn* blunt, brusque, crusty, curt, gruff *Rel* hearty, sincere *Ant* smooth, suave

blunder *n Syn* ERROR, bull, faux pas, howler, lapse, mistake, slip

blunder *vb Syn* STUMBLE, bumble, flounder, galumph, lollop, lumber, lurch, trip

blunt **1** *Syn* BLUFF, brusque, crusty, curt, gruff *Ant* smooth, suave **2** *Syn* DULL (sense 1), obtuse *Ant* lively

blurb *Syn* CRITICISM, critique, puff, review

blush · to develop a rosy facial color (as from excitement or embarrassment) *Syn* bloom, color, crimson, flush, glow, redden *Rel* rouge

bluster *vb* **1** *Syn* RANT, fulminate, rave, spout **2** *Syn* ROAR, bawl, bellow, clamor, howl, ululate, vociferate

bluster *n Syn* ROAR, bawl, bellow, ululation, vociferation

board *Syn* HARBOR, entertain, house, lodge, shelter

boarder *Syn* TENANT, lodger, renter, roomer *Ant* landlord

boast · to give vent in speech to one's pride in oneself or something intimately connected with oneself *Syn* brag, crow, gasconade, vaunt *Rel* flaunt, parade, show *Ant* depreciate (*oneself, one's accomplishments*)

boat · a floating structure designed to carry persons or goods over water *Syn* craft, ship, vessel

bob *Syn* CLIP, crop, curtail, cut, cut back, dock, lop (off), nip, pare, prune, shave, shear, snip, trim

bobble *Syn* BOTCH, bungle, butcher, flub, foozle, foul up, fumble, louse up, mangle, mess (up), muff, murder

bodily · of or relating to the human body *Syn* corporal, corporeal, physical, somatic *Rel* animal, carnal, fleshly, sensual

boding *Syn* OMEN, augury, auspice, foreboding, foreshadowing, portent, prefiguring, presage

body **1** · the dead physical substance of a human being or animal *Syn* cadaver, carcass, corpse **2** *Syn* FACTION, bloc, coalition, party, sect, set, side, wing

bog *Syn* SWAMP, fen, marsh, marshland, mire, morass, muskeg, slough, swampland

bogey *Syn* GHOST, apparition, phantasm, phantom, poltergeist, shade, shadow, specter (*or* spectre), spirit, spook, vision, wraith

boggle *Syn* DEMUR, balk, jib, scruple, shy, stick, stickle, strain *Ant* accede

bogus **1** *Syn* COUNTERFEIT, fake, phony, pinchbeck, pseudo, sham, spurious *Ant* bona fide, genuine **2** *Syn* IMITATION, artificial, factitious, fake, false, man-made, mimic, mock, sham, simulated, substitute, synthetic *Ant* genuine, natural, real

boil *vb* · to prepare (as food) in a liquid heated to the point where it emits considerable steam *Syn* parboil, seethe, simmer, stew

boil *n* *Syn* ABSCESS, carbuncle, furuncle, pimple, pustule

boisterous **1** · being rough or noisy in a high-spirited way *Syn* knockabout, rambunctious, raucous, rowdy *Rel* rampageous, riotous, stormy, tempestuous, turbulent, violent *Ant* orderly **2** *Syn* VOCIFEROUS, blatant, clamorous, obstreperous, strident

bold *Syn* BRAVE, audacious, courageous, dauntless, doughty, fearless, intrepid, unafraid, undaunted, valiant, valorous *Ant* craven

bolster *Syn* SUPPORT (sense 1), brace, buttress, prop, sustain

bolt *Syn* HURRY (sense 2), barrel, bowl, breeze, career, course, dash, fly, hasten, hotfoot (it), hump, hurtle, hustle, pelt, race, rip, rocket, run, rush, rustle, scoot, scurry, scuttle, shoot, speed, step (along), tear, trot, whirl, whisk, zip, zoom *Ant* crawl, creep, poke

bombard *Syn* ATTACK (sense 1), assail, assault, storm

bombardment *Syn* BARRAGE, cannonade, fusillade, hail, salvo, shower, storm, volley

bombast · speech or writing characterized by high-flown pomposity or pretentiousness of language disproportionate to the thought or subject matter *Syn* fustian, rant, rhapsody, rodomontade *Rel* grandiloquence, magniloquence, rhetoric

bombastic *Syn* RHETORICAL, aureate, euphuistic, flowery, grandiloquent, magniloquent

bona fide *Syn* AUTHENTIC, genuine, veritable *Ant* spurious

bond *n* **1** · something which serves to bind or bring two or more things firmly together *Syn* band, tie **2** *Syn* GUARANTEE, bail, guaranty, security, surety

bond *adj* *Syn* BOUND, articled, indentured

bonding *Syn* ADHESION, adherence

bondman *Syn* SLAVE (sense 1), bondsman, chattel, thrall *Ant* freeman

bondsman *Syn* SLAVE (sense 1), bondman, chattel, thrall *Ant* freeman

bonus · something given in addition to what is ordinarily expected or owed *Syn* dividend, extra, gratuity, gravy, lagniappe, perquisite, tip *Rel* fillip

bon vivant *Syn* EPICURE, gastronome, glutton, gourmand, gourmet

bon voyage *Syn* GOOD-BYE, adieu, au revoir, farewell, Godspeed *Ant* hello

booby *Syn* FOOL (sense 2), goose, half-wit, jackass, lunatic, nincompoop, ninny, nitwit, nut, simpleton, turkey, yo-yo

bookish **1** · suggestive of the vocabulary used in books *Syn* erudite, learned, literary *Rel* academic, pedantic, scholastic *Ant* colloquial, nonliterary **2** *Syn* PEDANTIC, academic, scholastic

boon *adj* *Syn* CONVIVIAL, companionable, extroverted, gregarious, outgoing, sociable, social *Ant* antisocial, introverted, reclusive, unsociable

boon *n* *Syn* GIFT (sense 1), favor, gratuity, largess, present

boorish *Syn* CLOWNISH, churlish, cloddish, loutish, uncouth *Ant* civil, courteous, courtly, cultivated, genteel, gentlemanly, ladylike, polished, polite, refined, well-bred

boost **1** *Syn* INCREASE (sense 1), add (to), aggrandize, amplify, augment, compound, enlarge, escalate, expand, extend, multiply, raise, swell, up *Ant* abate, contract, decrease, diminish, lessen, lower, reduce, subtract (from) **2** *Syn* LIFT, elevate, heave, hoist, raise, rear *Ant* lower

booster *Syn* EXPONENT, advocate, apostle, backer, champion, friend, promoter, proponent, supporter *Ant* adversary, antagonist, opponent

bootleg *Syn* SMUGGLED, contraband

bootless *Syn* FUTILE, abortive, fruitless, vain *Ant* effective, effectual, efficacious, efficient, fruitful, productive, profitable, successful

bootlicker *Syn* PARASITE, favorite, hanger-on, leech, lickspittle, sponge, sponger, sycophant, toady

booty *Syn* SPOIL, loot, plunder, prize, swag

booze *Syn* ALCOHOL, drink, grog, intoxicant, liquor, moonshine, spirits

border *n* · the line or relatively narrow space which marks the limit or outermost bound of something *Syn* brim, brink, edge, margin, rim, verge *Rel* bound, confine, end, limit

border *vb* · to serve as a border for *Syn* bound, fringe, margin, rim, skirt *Rel* edge, hem, trim

bordering *Syn* ADJACENT, abutting, adjoining, contiguous, flanking, fringing, joining, juxtaposed, skirting, touching, verging *Ant* nonadjacent

bore *Syn* PERFORATE, drill, prick, punch, puncture

boredom *Syn* TEDIUM, doldrums, ennui

boring · causing weariness, restlessness, or lack of interest *Syn* drab, dreary, dry, dull, flat, heavy, humdrum, jading, leaden, monotonous, pedestrian, ponderous, stodgy, stuffy, stupid, tame, tedious, tiresome, tiring, unanimated, uninteresting, wearisome, weary, wearying *Rel* undramatic, unentertaining, uneventful, unexciting, uninspiring, unnewsworthy, unrewarding, unsatisfying, unsensational, unspectacular *Ant* absorbing, engaging, engrossing, gripping, interesting, intriguing, involving

boss · the person (as an employer or supervisor) who tells people and especially workers what to do *Syn* captain, chief, foreman, head, headman, helmsman, kingpin, leader, master, taskmaster *Rel* administrator, commander, director, executive, general, manager, overseer, principal, standard-bearer, straw boss, superintendent, superior, supervisor

bossy · fond of ordering people around *Syn* authoritarian, autocratic, despotic, dictatorial, domineering, imperious, masterful, overbearing, peremptory, tyrannical, tyrannous *Rel* arrogant, disdainful, haughty, lofty, lordly, proud, supercilious, superior

botch · to make or do (something) in a clumsy or unskillful way *Syn* bobble, bungle, butcher, flub, foozle, foul up, fumble, louse up, mangle, mess (up), muff, murder *Rel* blunder, goof (up), gum (up)

bother *vb Syn* ANNOY, irk, vex *Ant* soothe

bother *n Syn* COMMOTION, bustle, clatter, disturbance, furor, furore, fuss, hubbub, hullabaloo, hurly-burly, pandemonium, pother, row, ruckus, ruction, rumpus, shindy, squall, stew, stir, storm, to-do, tumult, turmoil, uproar, welter, whirl

bothersome *Syn* ANNOYING, aggravating, disturbing, exasperating, frustrating, galling, irksome, irritating, maddening, nettling, peeving, pesty, rankling, riling, vexatious, vexing

bottom *Syn* BUTTOCKS, backside, breech, butt, fanny, hams, haunches, posterior, rear, rump, seat

bough *Syn* SHOOT, branch, limb

bounce *Syn* DISMISS, cashier, discharge, drop, fire, sack

bound *adj* · obliged to serve a master or in a clearly defined capacity for a certain number of years by the terms of a contract or mutual agreement *Syn* articled, bond, indentured

bound *n* 1 *Syn* BORDER, fringe, margin, rim, skirt 2 *Syn* JUMP, leap, spring, vault

bound *vb* 1 *Syn* JUMP, leap, spring, vault 2 *Syn* LIMIT, confine, end, term 3 *Syn* SKIP, curvet, hop, lollop, lope, ricochet

boundless *Syn* INFINITE, endless, illimitable, immeasurable, indefinite, limitless, measureless, unbounded, unfathomable, unlimited *Ant* bounded, circumscribed, confined, definite, finite, limited, restricted

bounteous *Syn* LIBERAL (sense 1), bountiful, generous, handsome, munificent, openhanded *Ant* close

bountiful *Syn* LIBERAL (sense 1), bounteous, generous, handsome, munificent, openhanded *Ant* close

bouquet *Syn* FRAGRANCE, incense, perfume, redolence *Ant* stench, stink

bout 1 *Syn* ATTACK (sense 3), case, fit, seizure, siege, spell 2 *Syn* SPELL, go, shift, stint, tour, trick, turn

bow *n Syn* CURVE, arc, arch

bow *vb* 1 *Syn* FLEX, buckle, crook *Ant* extend 2 *Syn* YIELD, capitulate, cave, defer, relent, submit, succumb

bowl *Syn* HURRY (sense 2), barrel, bolt, breeze, career, course, dash, fly, hasten, hotfoot (it), hump, hurtle, hustle, pelt, race, rip, rocket, run, rush, rustle, scoot, scurry, scuttle, shoot, speed, step (along), tear, trot, whirl, whisk, zip, zoom *Ant* crawl, creep, poke

box *n Syn* CHEST, caddy, case, casket, locker, trunk

box *vb Syn* STRIKE, clout, cuff, hit, punch, slap, slog, slug, smite, swat

boy · a male person who has not yet reached adulthood *Syn* lad, laddie, nipper, shaver, sonny, stripling, tad *Rel* adolescent, juvenile, kid, minor, moppet, teenager, youngster, youth

boyfriend · a male romantic companion *Syn* beau, fellow, man, swain *Rel* admirer, crush, steady

brace *vb* 1 *Syn* ANIMATE, energize, enliven, fire, invigorate, jazz (up), liven (up), pep (up), quicken, stimulate, vitalize, vivify *Ant* damp, dampen, deaden, dull 2 *Syn* SUPPORT (sense 1), bolster, buttress, prop, sustain

brace *n* 1 *Syn* COUPLE, pair, yoke 2 *Syn* PAIR, couple, duo, twain, twosome

bracing *Syn* TONIC, invigorating, refreshing, restorative, reviving, stimulating, stimulative, vitalizing

brag *Syn* BOAST, crow, gasconade, vaunt *Ant* depreciate (*oneself, one's accomplishments*)

braid *n* · a length of something formed of three or more strands woven together *Syn* lace, lacing, plait *Rel* pigtail, rickrack (*or* ricrac), stripe

braid *vb* 1 · to form into a braid *Syn* plait, pleat *Rel* interlace, interweave, weave 2 *Syn* WEAVE, crochet, knit, plait, tat

brain *Syn* MIND, intellect, intelligence, psyche, soul, wit

brake *vb Syn* SLOW, decelerate, retard *Ant* accelerate, hasten, hurry, quicken, rush, speed (up), step up

brake *n Syn* THICKET, brushwood, chaparral, coppice, copse, covert

branch *Syn* SHOOT, bough, limb

brand *vb Syn* MARK, label, stamp, tag, ticket

brand *n* 1 *Syn* MARK, label, stamp, tag, ticket 2 *Syn* STIGMA, blot, stain

brandish *Syn* SWING (sense 1), flourish, shake, thrash, wave

brash *Syn* SHAMELESS, barefaced, brazen, impudent

brashness *Syn* EFFRONTERY, audacity, brass, brassiness, brazenness, cheek, cheekiness, chutzpah, gall, nerve, nerviness, pertness, presumption, presumptuousness, sauce, sauciness, temerity

brass *Syn* EFFRONTERY, audacity, brashness, brassiness, brazenness, cheek, cheekiness, chutzpah, gall, nerve, nerviness, pertness, presumption, presumptuousness, sauce, sauciness, temerity

brassiness *Syn* EFFRONTERY, audacity, brashness, brass, brazenness, cheek, cheekiness, chutzpah, gall, nerve, nerviness, pertness, presumption, presumptuousness, sauce, sauciness, temerity

brave *adj* • having or showing no fear when faced with something dangerous, difficult, or unknown *Syn* audacious, bold, courageous, dauntless, doughty, fearless, intrepid, unafraid, undaunted, valiant, valorous *Rel* adventurous, daredevil, daring, venturesome *Ant* craven

brave *vb Syn* FACE, beard, challenge, dare, defy *Ant* avoid

bravery **1** *Syn* COURAGE, courageousness, daring, dauntlessness, doughtiness, fearlessness, gallantry, greatheartedness, guts, hardihood, heart, heroism, intrepidity, intrepidness, nerve, stoutness, valor *Ant* cowardice, cowardliness, cravenness, dastardliness, spinelessness, yellowness **2** *Syn* FINERY, array, best, caparison, feather, frippery, full dress, gaiety, regalia

bravo *Syn* ASSASSIN, cutthroat, gunman

brawl • a noisy fight or quarrel *Syn* broil, fracas, melee, row, rumpus, scrap *Rel* affray, conflict, contest, fight, fray

brawny *Syn* MUSCULAR, athletic, burly, husky, sinewy

brazen *Syn* SHAMELESS, barefaced, brash, impudent

brazenness *Syn* EFFRONTERY, audacity, brashness, brass, brassiness, cheek, cheekiness, chutzpah, gall, nerve, nerviness, pertness, presumption, presumptuousness, sauce, sauciness, temerity

breach **1** • the act or the offense of failing to keep the law or to do what the law, duty, or obligation requires *Syn* contravention, infraction, infringement, transgression, trespass, violation *Ant* observance **2** • a pulling apart in relations or in connections *Syn* break, rent, rift, rupture, schism, split *Rel* division, separation, severance

bread *Syn* LIVING, bread and butter, keep, livelihood, maintenance, subsistence, support, sustenance

bread and butter *Syn* LIVING, bread, keep, livelihood, maintenance, subsistence, support, sustenance

break *n* **1** • a lapse in continuity *Syn* gap, hiatus, interim, interruption, interval, lacuna *Rel* division, separation, severance **2** *Syn* OPPORTUNITY, chance, occasion, time **3** *Syn* PAUSE, breath, breather, interruption, lull, recess **4** *Syn* BREACH, rent, rift, rupture, schism, split

break *vb* **1** • to come apart or cause to come apart *Syn* burst, bust, crack, shatter, shiver, snap *Rel* crumble, decay, disintegrate *Ant* cleave (*together*), keep (*of laws*) **2** *Syn* SOLVE, answer, crack, dope (out), figure out, puzzle (out), resolve, riddle, unravel, work, work out

breakdown *Syn* ANALYSIS, dissection, resolution *Ant* synthesis

break down *Syn* ANALYZE, anatomize, assay, dissect

break out *Syn* ERUPT (sense 1), burst (forth), explode, flame, flare (up)

breakthrough *Syn* ADVANCE (sense 1), advancement, enhancement, improvement, refinement *Ant* setback

breastwork *Syn* BULWARK, bastion, parapet, rampart

breath *Syn* PAUSE, break, breather, interruption, lull, recess

breather *Syn* PAUSE, break, breath, interruption, lull, recess

breech *Syn* BUTTOCKS, backside, bottom, butt, fanny, hams, haunches, posterior, rear, rump, seat

breed *vb Syn* GENERATE, beget, engender, get, procreate, propagate, reproduce, sire

breed *n Syn* VARIETY (sense 2), clone, cultivar, race, stock, strain, subspecies

breeding **1** *Syn* ANCESTRY, birth, blood, bloodline, descent, extraction, family tree, genealogy, line, lineage, origin, parentage, pedigree, stock, strain *Ant* issue, posterity, progeny, seed **2** *Syn* CULTURE, cultivation, refinement

breeze *n Syn* CINCH, child's play, duck soup, picnic, pushover, snap *Ant* chore, headache, labor

breeze *vb Syn* HURRY (sense 2), barrel, bolt, bowl, career, course, dash, fly, hasten, hotfoot (it), hump, hurtle, hustle, pelt, race, rip, rocket, run, rush, rustle, scoot, scurry, scuttle, shoot, speed, step (along), tear, trot, whirl, whisk, zip, zoom *Ant* crawl, creep, poke

bribable *Syn* VENAL, corruptible, purchasable *Ant* incorruptible, uncorruptible

bridle **1** *Syn* RESTRAIN, check, curb, inhibit *Syn* RESTRAIN, bridle, check, curb, inhibit *Ant* abandon (*oneself*), activate, impel, incite **2** *Syn* STRUT, bristle, swagger

brief *n Syn* ABRIDGMENT, abstract, conspectus, epitome, synopsis *Ant* expansion

brief *vb Syn* ENLIGHTEN (sense 1), acquaint, advise, apprise, clue, familiarize, fill in, inform, instruct, tell, wise (up)

briefly *Syn* SUCCINCTLY, compactly, concisely, crisply, laconically, pithily, summarily, tersely *Ant* diffusely, long-windedly, verbosely, wordily

brig *Syn* JAIL, guardroom, hoosegow, jug, lockup, pen, penitentiary, prison, stockade

bright **1** • actually or seemingly shining or

glowing with light *Syn* beaming, brilliant, effulgent, incandescent, lambent, lucent, luminous, lustrous, radiant, refulgent *Rel* enlightened, illuminated, illumined, lighted, lightened *Ant* dim, dull **2** *Syn* CHEERFUL (sense 1), blithe, blithesome, buoyant, cheery, chipper, gay, gladsome, lightsome, sunny, upbeat *Ant* dour, gloomy, glum, morose, saturnine, sulky, sullen **3** *Syn* CHEERFUL (sense 2), cheering, cheery, gay, glad *Ant* bleak, cheerless, dark, depressing, dismal, dreary, gloomy, gray **4** *Syn* INTELLIGENT, alert, brilliant, clever, knowing, quick-witted, smart *Ant* unintelligent

brilliance *Syn* MAGNIFICENCE, augustness, gloriousness, glory, grandeur, grandness, majesty, nobility, nobleness, resplendence, splendor, stateliness, stupendousness, sublimeness, superbness

brilliant **1** *Syn* BRIGHT, beaming, effulgent, incandescent, lambent, lucent, luminous, lustrous, radiant, refulgent *Ant* dim, dull **2** *Syn* INTELLIGENT, alert, bright, clever, knowing, quick-witted, smart *Ant* unintelligent

brim *Syn* BORDER, brink, edge, margin, rim, verge

bring · to convey from one place to another *Syn* fetch, take *Rel* bear, carry, convey *Ant* remove, withdraw

bring about *Syn* EFFECT, cause, create, effectuate, engender, generate, induce, make, produce, prompt, result (in), spawn, work, yield

brink *Syn* BORDER, brim, edge, margin, rim, verge

brisk *Syn* AGILE, nimble, spry *Ant* torpid

bristle *Syn* STRUT, bridle, swagger

bristly *Syn* HAIRY (sense 1), fleecy, furry, hirsute, rough, shaggy, unshorn, woolly *Ant* bald, furless, hairless, shorn, smooth

brittle *Syn* FRAGILE, crisp, frangible, friable, short *Ant* tough

broach *Syn* EXPRESS, air, utter, vent, ventilate, voice *Ant* imply

broad **1** · having horizontal extent *Syn* deep, wide *Rel* extended, extensive *Ant* narrow **2** *Syn* EXTENSIVE, expansive, extended, far-flung, far-reaching, wide, widespread *Ant* narrow **3** *Syn* GENERAL (sense 2), all-around, bird's-eye, nonspecific, overall *Ant* delineated, detailed, particularized, specific

broadcast **1** *Syn* ANNOUNCE, advertise, blaze, declare, enunciate, placard, post, proclaim, promulgate, publicize, publish, sound **2** *Syn* STREW, scatter, sow, straw

broadcasting *Syn* DECLARATION, advertisement, announcement, proclamation, promulgation, publication

broadside *Syn* SIDEWAYS, edgewise, sidewise

Brobdingnagian *Syn* HUGE, colossal, cyclopean, elephantine, enormous, gargantuan, giant, gigantean, gigantic, Herculean, immense, mammoth, titanic, vast *Ant* bitty, diminutive, microscopic (*or* microscopical), midget, miniature, minute, pocket, pygmy, teeny, teeny-weeny, tiny, wee

broil *Syn* BRAWL, fracas, melee, row, rumpus, scrap

brokenhearted *Syn* SAD (sense 1), bad, blue, crestfallen, dejected, depressed, despondent, disconsolate, doleful, down, downcast, downhearted, droopy, forlorn, gloomy, glum, heartbroken, heartsick, heartsore, inconsolable, joyless, low, low-spirited, melancholy, miserable, mournful, saddened, sorrowful, sorry, unhappy, woebegone, woeful, wretched *Ant* blissful, buoyant, buoyed, cheerful, cheery, chipper, delighted, glad, gladdened, gladsome, gleeful, happy, joyful, joyous, jubilant, sunny, upbeat

bromide *Syn* COMMONPLACE, cliché, platitude, truism

brook *Syn* BEAR (sense 2), abide, endure, stand, suffer, tolerate

browbeat *Syn* INTIMIDATE, bulldoze, bully, cow

brownie *Syn* FAIRY, elf, fay, pixie (*also* pixy), sprite

bruise *vb Syn* CRUSH (sense 1), macerate, mash, smash, squash

bruise *n Syn* WOUND, contusion, lesion, trauma, traumatism

bruit (about) *Syn* RUMOR, circulate, noise (about), whisper

brush *vb* · to touch lightly in passing *Syn* glance, graze, shave, skim *Rel* contact, touch

brush *n Syn* ENCOUNTER, skirmish

brushwood *Syn* THICKET, brake, chaparral, coppice, copse, covert

brusque *Syn* BLUFF, blunt, crusty, curt, gruff *Ant* smooth, suave

brutal · characteristic of an animal in nature, action, or instinct *Syn* beastly, bestial, brute, brutish, feral *Rel* animal, carnal, fleshly, sensual

brutality *Syn* CRUELTY, barbarity, cruelness, heartlessness, inhumanity, sadism, savageness, savagery, viciousness, wantonness *Ant* benignity, compassion, good-heartedness, humanity, kindheartedness, kindness, sympathy

brute *n Syn* ANIMAL, beast, creature, critter

brute *adj Syn* BRUTAL, beastly, bestial, brutish, feral

brutish *Syn* BRUTAL, beastly, bestial, brute, feral

buccaneer *Syn* PIRATE, corsair, freebooter, privateer

buck *Syn* FOP, beau, coxcomb, dandy, dude, exquisite

buckaroo *Syn* COWBOY, cowhand, cowman, cowpoke, cowpuncher

buckle *Syn* FLEX, bow, crook *Ant* extend

bucolic *Syn* RURAL, pastoral, rustic *Ant* urban

buff *n Syn* FAN, addict, aficionado, bug, devotee, enthusiast, fanatic, fancier, fiend, freak, lover, maniac, nut

buff *vb Syn* POLISH, burnish, dress, gloss, grind, rub, shine, smooth

buffed *Syn* GLOSSY, burnished, glistening, lustrous, polished, rubbed, satin, satiny, sleek *Ant* dim, dull, flat, lusterless, matte

buffer *Syn* CUSHION, gentle, soften

buffet *vb Syn* BEAT, baste, belabor, pound, pummel, thrash

buffet *n Syn* CABINET, closet, cupboard, hutch, locker, sideboard

bug *Syn* FAN, addict, aficionado, buff, devotee, enthusiast, fanatic, fancier, fiend, freak, lover, maniac, nut

bugbear *Syn* ABOMINATION, anathema, bête noire *Ant* joy

build *vb ·* to form by putting together parts or materials *Syn* assemble, construct, erect, fabricate, make, make up, piece, put up, raise, rear, set up *Rel* fashion, forge, frame, manufacture, mold, produce, shape *Ant* disassemble, dismantle, take down

build *n Syn* PHYSIQUE, constitution, habit

building · something built as a dwelling, shelter, or place for human activity *Syn* edifice, structure *Rel* construction, erection

build (up) *Syn* INCREASE (sense 2), accumulate, appreciate, balloon, burgeon, enlarge, escalate, expand, mount, multiply, mushroom, proliferate, rise, snowball, swell, wax *Ant* contract, decrease, diminish, lessen, wane

bulge *vb ·* to extend outward beyond the usual and normal line *Syn* beetle, jut, overhang, project, protrude, stick out *Rel* dilate, distend, expand, swell

bulge *n Syn* PROJECTION, protrusion, protuberance

bulk · a body of usually material substance that constitutes a thing or unit *Syn* mass, volume *Rel* figure, form, shape

bulky **1** *Syn* LARGE, big, considerable, goodly, good-sized, grand, great, handsome, hefty, hulking, largish, outsize, oversize (*or* oversized), sizable (*or* sizeable), substantial, tidy, voluminous *Ant* little, puny, small, undersized **2** *Syn* MASSIVE, massy, monumental, substantial

bull **1** *Syn* ERROR, blunder, faux pas, howler, lapse, mistake, slip **2** *Syn* NONSENSE, balderdash, bunk, drivel, gobbledygook, poppycock, rot, trash, twaddle

bulldoze *Syn* INTIMIDATE, browbeat, bully, cow

bulletin *Syn* ANNOUNCEMENT, ad, advertisement, notice, notification, posting, release

bully *Syn* INTIMIDATE, browbeat, bulldoze, cow

bulwark · an aboveground defensive structure that forms part of a fortification *Syn* bastion, breastwork, parapet, rampart *Rel* citadel, fort, fortress, stronghold

bum *Syn* VAGABOND, hobo, tramp, truant, vagrant

bumble *Syn* STUMBLE, blunder, flounder, galumph, lollop, lumber, lurch, trip

bummer *Syn* DISAPPOINTMENT (sense 2), letdown

bump · to come or cause to come into violent contact or close or direct opposition *Syn* clash, collide, conflict *Rel* hit, smite, strike

bumpkin *Syn* HICK, clodhopper, countryman, provincial, rustic, yokel *Ant* cosmopolitan, sophisticate

bunch **1** *Syn* BUNDLE, bale, pack, package, packet, parcel **2** *Syn* GROUP, cluster, lot, parcel

bundle · things done up for storage, sale, or carriage *Syn* bale, bunch, pack, package, packet, parcel *Rel* assemblage, collection, gathering

bungle *Syn* BOTCH, bobble, butcher, flub, foozle, foul up, fumble, louse up, mangle, mess (up), muff, murder

bunk *Syn* NONSENSE, balderdash, bull, drivel, gobbledygook, poppycock, rot, trash, twaddle

buoyant **1** *Syn* CHEERFUL (sense 1), blithe, blithesome, bright, cheery, chipper, gay, gladsome, lightsome, sunny, upbeat *Ant* dour, gloomy, glum, morose, saturnine, sulky, sullen

buoyant **2** *Syn* ELASTIC (sense 2), effervescent, expansive, resilient, volatile *Ant* depressed

burden *vb ·* to lay a heavy load upon or to lie like a heavy load upon a person or thing *Syn* charge, cumber, encumber, lade, load, saddle, tax, weigh, weight *Rel* depress, oppress, weigh

burden *n* **1** *Syn* LOAD, cargo, freight, lading **2** *Syn* OBLIGATION, charge, commitment, duty, need, responsibility **3** *Syn* SUBSTANCE, core, gist, pith, purport

burdensome *Syn* ONEROUS, exacting, oppressive

bureaucrat · a worker in a government agency *Syn* functionary, public servant *Rel* clerk, officeholder, official

burg *Syn* CITY, megalopolis, metropolis, municipality, town

burgeon *Syn* INCREASE (sense 2), accumulate, appreciate, balloon, build (up), enlarge, escalate, expand, mount, multiply, mushroom, proliferate, rise, snowball, swell, wax *Ant* contract, decrease, diminish, lessen, wane

burglar *Syn* THIEF, larcener, larcenist, robber

burglarize *Syn* ROB, loot, plunder, rifle

burglary *Syn* THEFT, larceny, robbery

burlesque *n Syn* CARICATURE, parody, travesty

burlesque *vb Syn* CARICATURE, parody, travesty

burly *Syn* MUSCULAR, athletic, brawny, husky, sinewy

burn · to injure by exposure to fire or intense heat *Syn* char, scorch, sear, singe *Rel* fire, ignite, kindle, light

burning *Syn* FERVENT, ardent, blazing,

charged, emotional, fervid, feverish, fiery, flaming, glowing, hot-blooded, impassioned, passionate, red-hot, vehement, warm, warm-blooded *Ant* cold, cool, dispassionate, impassive, unemotional

burnish *Syn* POLISH, buff, dress, gloss, grind, rub, shine, smooth

burnished *Syn* GLOSSY, buffed, glistening, lustrous, polished, rubbed, satin, satiny, sleek *Ant* dim, dull, flat, lusterless, matte

burnout *Syn* FATIGUE, collapse, exhaustion, lassitude, prostration, tiredness, weariness *Ant* refreshment, rejuvenation, revitalization

burp *Syn* BELCH, disgorge, regurgitate, spew, throw up, vomit

burst *vb Syn* BREAK, bust, crack, shatter, shiver, snap *Ant* cleave (*together*), keep (*of laws*)

burst *n Syn* OUTBREAK, flare, flare-up, flash, flicker, flurry, flutter, outburst, spurt

burst (forth) *Syn* ERUPT (sense 1), break out, explode, flame, flare (up)

bury *Syn* HIDE, cache, conceal, ensconce, screen, secrete

bush *Syn* FRONTIER, backwater, backwoods, hinterland, up-country

business 1 · one of the forms or branches of human endeavor which have for their objective the supplying of commodities *Syn* commerce, industry, trade, traffic **2** *Syn* WORK (sense 2), calling, employment, occupation, pursuit **3** *Syn* AFFAIR, concern, matter, thing

bust *Syn* BREAK, burst, crack, shatter, shiver, snap *Ant* cleave (*together*), keep (*of laws*)

bustle 1 *Syn* COMMOTION, bother, clatter, disturbance, furor, furore, fuss, hubbub, hullabaloo, hurly-burly, pandemonium, pother, row, ruckus, ruction, rumpus, shindy, squall, stew, stir, storm, to-do, tumult, turmoil, uproar, welter, whirl **2** *Syn* STIR, ado, flurry, fuss, pother *Ant* tranquillity

busy · actively engaged or occupied in work or in accomplishing a purpose or intention *Syn* assiduous, diligent, industrious, sedulous *Rel* absorbed, engrossed, intent *Ant* idle, unoccupied

busybody · a person who meddles in the affairs of others *Syn* interferer, interloper, intruder, kibitzer, meddler *Rel* peeper, peeping Tom, snoop, snooper, spy

butcher 1 *Syn* BOTCH, bobble, bungle, flub, foozle, foul up, fumble, louse up, mangle, mess (up), muff, murder **2** *Syn* MASSACRE, mow (down), slaughter

butchery *Syn* MASSACRE, carnage, pogrom, slaughter

butt 1 *Syn* BUTTOCKS, backside, bottom, breech, fanny, hams, haunches, posterior, rear, rump, seat **2** *Syn* LAUGHINGSTOCK, mark, mock, mockery, target

butt in *Syn* INTERFERE, intrude, meddle, mess, nose, obtrude, poke, pry, snoop

buttocks · the part of the body upon which someone sits *Syn* backside, bottom, breech, butt, fanny, hams, haunches, posterior, rear, rump, seat

buttress *n ·* auxiliary structures designed to serve as a prop, shore, or support for a wall (as of a building) *Syn* abutment, pier

buttress *vb Syn* SUPPORT (sense 1), bolster, brace, prop, sustain

buy · to get possession of (something) by giving money in exchange for *Syn* pick up, purchase, take *Rel* acquire, get, obtain, procure, secure

by 1 · using as a means of approach or action *Syn* through, with **2** *Syn* AROUND (sense 1), about, near, next to

by and large *Syn* CHIEFLY, altogether, basically, generally, largely, mainly, mostly, overall, predominantly, primarily, principally, substantially

bygone *Syn* EXTINCT, dead, defunct, departed, expired, gone, vanished *Ant* alive, existent, existing, extant, living

bylaw *Syn* RULE (sense 1), ground rule, regulation

by-product *Syn* DERIVATIVE, offshoot, outgrowth, spin-off *Ant* origin, root, source

bystander *Syn* SPECTATOR, beholder, eyewitness, kibitzer, looker-on, observer, onlooker, witness

byword *Syn* CATCHWORD, shibboleth, slogan

C

cabal *Syn* PLOT, conspiracy, intrigue, machination

cabalistic *Syn* MYSTICAL, anagogic, mystic

cabin 1 *Syn* COMPARTMENT, bay, cell, chamber, cubicle **2** *Syn* SHACK, camp, hovel, hut, hutch, shanty

cabinet · a storage case typically having doors and shelves *Syn* buffet, closet, cupboard, hutch, locker, sideboard *Rel* bookcase, secretary

cable *Syn* CORD, lace, lacing, line, rope, string, wire

cache *vb* **1** *Syn* HIDE, bury, conceal, ensconce, screen, secrete **2** *Syn* HOARD, lay away, lay up, put by, salt away, squirrel (away), stash, stockpile, store, stow

cache *n* *Syn* STORE, deposit, hoard, reserve

cackle *Syn* CHAT, babble, blab, chatter, converse, gab, gabble, gas, jabber, jaw, palaver, patter, prate, prattle, rap, rattle, run on, talk, twitter, visit

cadaver *Syn* BODY, carcass, corpse

cadaverous *Syn* HAGGARD, careworn, pinched, wasted, worn

caddy *Syn* CHEST, box, case, casket, locker, trunk

cadence *Syn* RHYTHM, beat, measure, meter

café **1** *Syn* BARROOM, bar, groggery, grogshop, pub, saloon, tavern **2** *Syn* RESTAURANT, diner, grill

cage *Syn* ENCLOSE, coop, corral, envelop, fence, pen, wall

cajole *Syn* COAX, blandish, blarney, soft-soap, wheedle

cake *Syn* HARDEN (sense 1), indurate, petrify, solidify *Ant* soften

calamitous *Syn* UNLUCKY, disastrous, hapless, ill-fated, ill-starred, luckless, unfortunate *Ant* fortunate, happy, lucky

calamity *Syn* DISASTER, apocalypse, cataclysm, catastrophe

calculate **1** · to determine something (as cost, speed, or quantity) by mathematical processes *Syn* compute, estimate, reckon *Rel* consider, study, weigh **2** *Syn* ESTIMATE (sense 2), call, conjecture, figure, gauge, guess, judge, make, place, put, reckon, suppose

calculating *Syn* CAUTIOUS, chary, circumspect, wary *Ant* adventurous, temerarious

calculation **1** · the act or process of performing mathematical operations to find a value *Syn* arithmetic, ciphering, computation, figures, figuring, reckoning *Rel* mathematics **2** *Syn* CAUTION, chariness, circumspection, wariness *Ant* adventurousness, temerity

caliber *Syn* QUALITY (sense 2), stature

call *vb* **1** *Syn* ESTIMATE (sense 2), calculate, conjecture, figure, gauge, guess, judge, make, place, put, reckon, suppose **2** *Syn* SUMMON, cite, convene, convoke, muster

call *n* *Syn* VISIT, visitation

caller *Syn* VISITOR, guest, visitant

calling **1** *Syn* CANCELLATION, abortion, calling off, dropping, recall, repeal, rescission, revocation *Ant* continuation **2** *Syn* OCCUPATION, employment, line, profession, trade, vocation, work **3** *Syn* WORK (sense 2), business, employment, occupation, pursuit

calling off *Syn* CANCELLATION, abortion, calling, dropping, recall, repeal, rescission, revocation *Ant* continuation

callous *Syn* HARDENED, indurated *Ant* softened

callow **1** · lacking in adult experience or maturity *Syn* adolescent, green, immature, inexperienced, juvenile, puerile, raw, unfledged, unripe, unripened *Rel* babyish, childish, infantile *Ant* adult, experienced, grown-up, mature, ripe **2** *Syn* RUDE (sense 1), crude, green, raw, rough, uncouth *Ant* civil, urbane

calm *adj* · quiet and free from all that disturbs or excites *Syn* halcyon, peaceful, placid, serene, tranquil *Rel* noiseless, quiet, still, stilly *Ant* agitated, stormy

calm *n* · a state of freedom from storm or disturbance *Syn* calmness, hush, peace, peacefulness, placidity, quiet, quietness, quietude, repose, restfulness, sereneness, serenity, still, stillness, tranquillity (*or* tranquility) *Rel* lull, pause, respite *Ant* bustle, commotion, hubbub, hurly-burly, pandemonium, tumult, turmoil, uproar

calm *vb* · to relieve or to bring to an end whatever distresses, agitates, or disturbs *Syn* compose, lull, quiet, quieten, settle, soothe, still, tranquilize *Rel* allay, alleviate, assuage, mitigate, relieve *Ant* agitate, arouse

calmness **1** *Syn* CALM, hush, peace, peacefulness, placidity, quiet, quietness, quietude, repose, restfulness, sereneness, serenity, still, stillness, tranquillity (*or* tranquility) *Ant* bustle, commotion, hubbub, hurly-burly, pandemonium, tumult, turmoil, uproar **2** *Syn* EQUANIMITY, aplomb, composure, coolheadedness, coolness, imperturbability, placidity, self-possession, serenity, tranquillity (*or* tranquility) *Ant* agitation, discomposure, perturbation

calumny *Syn* DETRACTION, backbiting, scandal, slander

camaraderie *Syn* COMPANIONSHIP, company, comradeship, fellowship, society

camouflage *Syn* DISGUISE, cloak, dissemble, mask

camp *Syn* SHACK, cabin, hovel, hut, hutch, shanty

campaign · a series of activities undertaken to achieve a goal *Syn* bandwagon, cause, crusade, drive, movement *Rel* attack, march, offensive

campaigner *Syn* CANDIDATE, applicant, aspirant, contender, hopeful, prospect, seeker

camper · a motor vehicle that is specially equipped for living while traveling *Syn* caravan, mobile home, motor home, trailer *Rel* van

canal *Syn* CHANNEL, aqueduct, conduit, duct

cancel **1** *Syn* ABOLISH, abrogate, annul, dissolve, invalidate, negate, nullify, quash, repeal, rescind, void **2** *Syn* ERASE, blot out, delete, efface, expunge, obliterate

cancellation · the act of putting an end to something planned or previously agreed to *Syn* abortion, calling, calling off, dropping, recall, repeal, rescission, revocation *Rel* annulment, invalidation, neutralization, nullification *Ant* continuation

candid *Syn* FRANK, open, plain *Ant* reticent

candidate · one who seeks an office, honor, position, or award *Syn* applicant, aspirant, campaigner, contender, hopeful, prospect, seeker *Rel* competitor, contestant, entrant

candor · the free expression of one's true feelings and opinions *Syn* directness, forthrightness, frankness, openheartedness, openness, plainness, straightforwardness *Rel* earnestness, sincerity, sobriety *Ant* dissembling, pretense (*or* pretence)

cannonade *Syn* BARRAGE, bombardment, fusillade, hail, salvo, shower, storm, volley

canon *Syn* LAW, ordinance, precept, regulation, rule, statute

canonize *Syn* IDOLIZE, adore, adulate, deify, dote (on), worship

canopy · a raised covering over something for decoration or protection *Syn* awning, ceiling, roof, tent *Rel* screen, shade, shelter, shield, sunshade

cant 1 *Syn* HYPOCRISY, dissembling, dissimulation, insincerity, piousness, sanctimoniousness *Ant* genuineness, sincerity 2 *Syn* TERMINOLOGY, argot, dialect, jargon, language, lingo, patois, patter, slang, vocabulary

canvass · to go around and approach (people) with a request for opinions or information *Syn* poll, solicit, survey *Rel* interrogate, interview, question

canyon · a narrow opening between hillsides or mountains that can be used for passage *Syn* defile, flume, gap, gorge, gulch, gulf, notch, pass, ravine *Rel* abyss, chasm, cirque, cleft, crevasse, crevice, fissure

capability *Syn* ABILITY, capacity, competence, competency, faculty *Ant* disability, inability, incapability, incapacity, incompetence, incompetency, ineptitude, ineptness

capable *Syn* COMPETENT, able, fit, good, qualified, suitable *Ant* incompetent, inept, poor, unfit, unqualified

capacious *Syn* SPACIOUS, ample, commodious

capacity 1 *Syn* ABILITY, capability, competence, competency, faculty *Ant* disability, inability, incapability, incapacity, incompetence, incompetency, ineptitude, ineptness 2 *Syn* ROLE, function, job, part, place, position, purpose, task, work

caparison *Syn* FINERY, array, best, bravery, feather, frippery, full dress, gaiety, regalia

caper *Syn* PRANK, antic, dido, monkeyshine

capital *n Syn* CENTER (sense 2), base, core, cynosure, eye, focus, heart, hub, mecca, nucleus, seat

capital *adj* 1 *Syn* CHIEF, foremost, leading, main, principal *Ant* subordinate 2 *Syn* EXCELLENT, A1, bang-up, banner, classic, crackerjack, dandy, divine, fabulous, fine, first-class, first-rate, grand, great, groovy, heavenly, jim-dandy, keen, marvelous (*or* marvellous), mean, neat, nifty, noble, par excellence, prime, sensational, splendid, stellar, sterling, superb, superior, superlative, supernal, swell, terrific, tip-top, top, top-notch, unsurpassed, wonderful *Ant* poor

capitulate *Syn* YIELD, bow, cave, defer, relent, submit, succumb

capitulation *Syn* SURRENDER, submission

caprice *Syn* WHIM, fancy, freak, notion, vagary, whimsy

capricious 1 *Syn* INCONSTANT, fickle, mercurial, unstable *Ant* constant 2 *Syn* WHIMSICAL, freakish, impulsive

capsize *Syn* OVERTURN, overthrow, subvert, upset

capsule *Syn* PILL, lozenge, tablet

captain *Syn* BOSS, chief, foreman, head, headman, helmsman, kingpin, leader, master, taskmaster

caption *Syn* INSCRIPTION, legend

captious *Syn* CRITICAL, carping, caviling, censorious, faultfinding, hypercritical *Ant* uncritical

captivate *Syn* ATTRACT, allure, bewitch, charm, enchant, fascinate *Ant* repel

captivating *Syn* ATTRACTIVE, alluring, bewitching, charming, enchanting, fascinating *Ant* forbidding, repellent

capture 1 *Syn* CATCH, bag, ensnare, entrap, snare, trap *Ant* miss 2 *Syn* EARN, acquire, attain, carry, draw, gain, garner, get, land, make, obtain, procure, realize, secure, win *Ant* forfeit, lose

caravan *Syn* CAMPER, mobile home, motor home, trailer

carbon copy *Syn* COPY, duplicate, duplication, facsimile, imitation, reduplication, replica, replication, reproduction *Ant* original

carbuncle *Syn* ABSCESS, boil, furuncle, pimple, pustule

carcass *Syn* BODY, cadaver, corpse

cardinal *Syn* ESSENTIAL, fundamental, vital

care 1 · a troubled or engrossed state of mind or the thing that causes this *Syn* anxiety, concern, solicitude, worry *Rel* effort, exertion, pains, trouble 2 *Syn* CUSTODY, guardianship, keeping, safekeeping, trust, ward

career *Syn* HURRY (sense 2), barrel, bolt, bowl, breeze, course, dash, fly, hasten, hotfoot (it), hump, hurtle, hustle, pelt, race, rip, rocket, run, rush, rustle, scoot, scurry, scuttle, shoot, speed, step (along), tear, trot, whirl, whisk, zip, zoom *Ant* crawl, creep, poke

care (for) *Syn* APPROVE (OF), accept, countenance, favor, OK (*or* okay), subscribe (to) *Ant* disapprove (of), discountenance, disfavor, frown (on *or* upon)

carefree · having or showing a lack of concern or seriousness *Syn* careless, cavalier, devil-may-care, easygoing, gay, happy-go-lucky, insouciant, lighthearted, unconcerned *Rel* breezy, nonchalant *Ant* careworn

careful 1 · marked by close attention to details or care in execution or performance *Syn* meticulous, punctilious, punctual, scrupulous *Rel* cautious, circumspect, wary *Ant* careless **2** *Syn* WORRIED, anxious, concerned, solicitous

careless 1 · showing lack of concern or attention *Syn* heedless, inadvertent, thoughtless *Rel* lax, neglectful, negligent, remiss, slack *Ant* careful **2** *Syn* CAREFREE, cavalier, devil-may-care, easygoing, gay, happy-go-lucky, insouciant, lighthearted, unconcerned *Ant* careworn **3** *Syn* NEGLIGENT, derelict, lax, neglectful, neglecting, remiss, slack *Ant* attentive, careful, conscientious

caress · to show affection or love by touching or handling *Syn* cosset, cuddle, dandle, fondle, pet *Rel* coquet, dally, flirt, toy, trifle

careworn *Syn* HAGGARD, cadaverous, pinched, wasted, worn

cargo *Syn* LOAD, burden, freight, lading

caricature *n* **1** · a grotesque or bizarre imitation of something *Syn* burlesque, parody, travesty *Rel* humor, sarcasm, satire, wit **2** *Syn* EXAGGERATION, coloring, elaboration, embellishment, embroidering, hyperbole, magnification, overstatement, padding, stretching *Ant* understatement

caricature *vb* · to make a grotesque or bizarre imitation of something *Syn* burlesque, parody, travesty *Rel* ape, copy, imitate, mimic, mock

carnage *Syn* MASSACRE, butchery, pogrom, slaughter

carnal · characterized by physical rather than intellectual or spiritual orientation *Syn* animal, fleshly, sensual *Rel* bodily, corporal, corporeal, physical, somatic *Ant* intellectual, spiritual

carnival *Syn* FESTIVAL, celebration, festivity, fete (*or* fête), fiesta, gala, jubilee

carol *Syn* SING, chant, descant, hymn, intone, trill, troll, warble

carp 1 *Syn* COMPLAIN, beef, bellyache, crab, croak, fuss, gripe, grouse, growl, grumble, kick, moan, murmur, mutter, repine, squawk, wail, whine, yammer *Ant* rejoice **2** *Syn* QUIBBLE, cavil, fuss, nitpick

carper *Syn* CRITIC, castigator, caviler (*or* caviller), censurer, faultfinder, nitpicker, railer, scold

carping *Syn* CRITICAL, captious, caviling, censorious, faultfinding, hypercritical *Ant* uncritical

carry 1 · to be the agent or the means whereby something or someone is moved from one place to another *Syn* bear, convey, transmit, transport *Rel* bring, fetch, take **2** *Syn* EARN, acquire, attain, capture, draw, gain, garner, get, land, make, obtain, procure, realize, secure, win *Ant* forfeit, lose

carry away *Syn* ENTRANCE, enrapture, enthrall (*or* enthral), overjoy, ravish, transport

carry on *Syn* PERSEVERE, persist

cartel 1 · a number of businesses or enterprises united for commercial advantage *Syn* combination, combine, syndicate, trust *Rel* chain, conglomerate, multinational **2** *Syn* CONTRACT, bargain, compact, concordat, convention, entente, pact, treaty **3** *Syn* MONOPOLY, corner, pool, syndicate, trust

carve 1 · to cut an outline or a shape out of or into some substance *Syn* chisel, engrave, etch, incise, sculpt, sculpture *Rel* fashion, form, make, shape **2** *Syn* CUT, chop, hew, slash, slit

cascade *Syn* WATERFALL, cataract, fall(s)

case 1 *Syn* ATTACK (sense 3), bout, fit, seizure, siege, spell **2** *Syn* CHEST, box, caddy, casket, locker, trunk **3** *Syn* EXAMPLE, exemplar, illustration, instance, representative, sample, specimen **4** *Syn* SUIT, action, cause, lawsuit

casement *Syn* WINDOW, oriel

cash *Syn* MONEY, coin, coinage, currency, legal tender, specie

cashier *Syn* DISMISS, bounce, discharge, drop, fire, sack

cask · an enclosed wooden vessel for holding beverages *Syn* barrel, firkin, hogshead, keg, pipe, puncheon *Rel* tub, vat

casket *Syn* CHEST, box, caddy, case, locker, trunk

cast *vb* **1** *Syn* DISCARD, junk, molt, scrap, shed, slough **2** *Syn* THROW, fling, hurl, pitch, sling, toss

cast *n* *Syn* PREDICTION, auguring, forecast, forecasting, foretelling, predicting, presaging, prognosis, prognosticating, prognostication, prophecy, soothsaying

castaway *Syn* OUTCAST, derelict, pariah, reprobate, untouchable

castigate 1 *Syn* ATTACK (sense 2), abuse, assail, belabor, blast, excoriate, jump (on), lambaste (*or* lambast), scathe, slam, vituperate **2** *Syn* PUNISH, chasten, chastise, correct, discipline *Ant* excuse, pardon

castigating *Syn* PUNITIVE, chastening, chastising, correcting, correctional, corrective, disciplinary, disciplining, penal, penalizing

castigator *Syn* CRITIC, carper, caviler (*or* caviller), censurer, faultfinder, nitpicker, railer, scold

castle *Syn* MANSION, château, countryseat, estate, hacienda, hall, manor, manor house, palace, villa

castrate *Syn* STERILIZE (sense 1), alter, emasculate, geld, mutilate, spay *Ant* fertilize

casual 1 *Syn* ACCIDENTAL, chance, fluky, fortuitous, inadvertent, incidental, unintended, unintentional, unplanned, unpremeditated, unwitting *Ant* deliberate, intended, intentional, planned, premeditated **2** *Syn* FITFUL, choppy, discontinuous, erratic, intermittent, irregular, occasional, spasmodic, sporadic, spotty,

unsteady *Ant* constant, continuous, regular, steady **3** *Syn* RANDOM, chance, chancy, desultory, haphazard, happy-go-lucky, hit-or-miss *Ant* methodical, nonrandom, orderly, systematic

casualness *Syn* INDIFFERENCE, apathy, disinterestedness, disregard, insouciance, nonchalance, unconcern *Ant* concern, interest, regard

casualty *Syn* ACCIDENT, mishap

cataclysm **1** *Syn* CONVULSION, paroxysm, storm, tempest, tumult, upheaval, uproar **2** *Syn* DISASTER, apocalypse, calamity, catastrophe

cataclysmal *or* **cataclysmic** *Syn* CONVULSIVE, stormy, tempestuous, tumultuous

catalog *n Syn* LIST, inventory, register, roll, roster, schedule, table

catalog *vb Syn* RECORD, enroll, list, register

cataract **1** *Syn* FLOOD, deluge, inundation, spate, torrent **2** *Syn* WATERFALL, cascade, fall(s)

catastrophe *Syn* DISASTER, apocalypse, calamity, cataclysm

catch · to come to possess or control by or as if by seizing *Syn* bag, capture, ensnare, entrap, snare, trap *Rel* clutch, grab, grasp, seize, snatch, take *Ant* miss

catching *Syn* INFECTIOUS (sense 1), communicable, contagious

catchword · a phrase that catches the eye or the ear and is repeated so often that it becomes a formula *Syn* byword, shibboleth, slogan *Rel* caption, inscription, legend

catechize *Syn* ASK (sense 1), examine, inquire, interrogate, query, question, quiz

categorical **1** *Syn* EXPLICIT, definite, express, specific *Ant* ambiguous **2** *Syn* ULTIMATE, absolute

cater · to furnish with what satisfies the appetite or desires *Syn* pander, purvey *Rel* accouter, appoint, equip, furnish

catholic *Syn* UNIVERSAL (sense 1), cosmic, cosmopolitan, ecumenical *Ant* particular

catnap *Syn* SLEEP, doze, drowse, nap, slumber, snooze

cause *n* **1** · that (as a person, fact, or condition) which is responsible for an effect *Syn* antecedent, determinant, occasion, reason *Rel* goad, impulse, incentive, inducement, motive, spring, spur **2** *Syn* CAMPAIGN, bandwagon, crusade, drive, movement **3** *Syn* SUIT, action, case, lawsuit

cause *vb Syn* EFFECT, bring about, create, effectuate, engender, generate, induce, make, produce, prompt, result (in), spawn, work, yield

caustic · stingingly incisive *Syn* acrid, mordant, scathing *Rel* biting, cutting, incisive, trenchant *Ant* genial

caution *n* **1** · careful prudence especially in reducing or avoiding risk or danger *Syn* calculation, chariness, circumspection, wariness *Rel* alertness, vigilance, watchfulness *Ant* adventurousness, temerity **2** *Syn* WARNING, admonition, alarm, alert, forewarning, notice

caution *vb Syn* WARN, alert, forewarn

cautionary · serving as or offering a warning *Syn* admonishing, admonitory, cautioning, warning *Rel* didactic, moralistic, moralizing

cautioning *Syn* CAUTIONARY, admonishing, admonitory, warning

cautious · prudently watchful and discreet in the face of danger or risk *Syn* calculating, chary, circumspect, wary *Rel* alert, vigilant, watchful *Ant* adventurous, temerarious

cavalcade *Syn* PROCESSION, cortege, motorcade, parade

cavalier **1** *Syn* ARROGANT, haughty, highfalutin, high-handed, high-hat, imperious, important, lofty, lordly, masterful, overweening, peremptory, pompous, presumptuous, pretentious, supercilious, superior, uppish, uppity *Ant* humble, modest **2** *Syn* CAREFREE, careless, devil-may-care, easygoing, gay, happy-go-lucky, insouciant, lighthearted, unconcerned *Ant* careworn

cave *Syn* YIELD, bow, capitulate, defer, relent, submit, succumb

cavil *Syn* QUIBBLE, carp, fuss, nitpick

caviler *or* **caviller** *Syn* CRITIC, carper, castigator, censurer, faultfinder, nitpicker, railer, scold

caviling *Syn* CRITICAL, captious, carping, censorious, faultfinding, hypercritical *Ant* uncritical

cavity *Syn* HOLE, hollow, pocket, vacuum, void

cease *Syn* STOP, desist, discontinue, quit

cease-fire *Syn* TRUCE, armistice, peace

cede *Syn* RELINQUISH, abandon, leave, resign, surrender, waive, yield *Ant* keep

ceiling *Syn* CANOPY, awning, roof, tent

celebrate *Syn* KEEP (sense 1), commemorate, observe, solemnize *Ant* break

celebrated *Syn* FAMOUS, famed, noted, notorious, prominent, renowned, star, well-known *Ant* anonymous, obscure, unknown

celebration *Syn* FESTIVAL, carnival, festivity, fete (*or* fête), fiesta, gala, jubilee

celebrity *Syn* FAME, éclat, glory, honor, notoriety, renown, reputation, repute *Ant* infamy, obscurity

celestial · of, relating to, or suggesting heaven *Syn* Elysian, empyreal, empyrean, heavenly, supernal *Rel* ethereal, supernatural, transcendent, transcendental, unearthly, unworldly *Ant* hellish, infernal

cell *Syn* COMPARTMENT, bay, cabin, chamber, cubicle

cenobite *Syn* RECLUSE, anchorite, eremite, hermit

censorious *Syn* CRITICAL, captious, carping, caviling, faultfinding, hypercritical *Ant* uncritical

censure *n* · an often public or formal expression of disapproval *Syn* condemnation, denunciation, rebuke, reprimand, reproach, reproof, stricture *Rel* admonishment, admonition, castigation, chastisement, punishment *Ant* citation, commendation, endorsement

censure *vb Syn* CRITICIZE, blame, condemn, denounce, reprehend, reprobate

censurer *Syn* CRITIC, carper, castigator, caviler (*or* caviller), faultfinder, nitpicker, railer, scold

center *n* **1** · an area or point that is an equal distance from all points along an edge or outer surface *Syn* core, middle, midpoint, midst *Rel* inside, interior *Ant* perimeter, periphery **2** · a thing or place that is of greatest importance to an activity or interest *Syn* base, capital, core, cynosure, eye, focus, heart, hub, mecca, nucleus, seat *Rel* focus, headquarters

center *vb* · to draw to or fix upon a center *Syn* centralize, concentrate, focus *Rel* depend, hang, hinge, turn

central · dominant or most important *Syn* focal, pivotal *Rel* dominant, paramount, predominant, preponderant

centralize *Syn* CENTER, concentrate, focus

cerebral *Syn* MENTAL, intellectual, intelligent, psychic

ceremonial *adj* · characterized or marked by attention to the forms, procedures, and details prescribed as right, proper, or requisite *Syn* ceremonious, conventional, formal, solemn *Rel* liturgical, ritualistic

ceremonial *n Syn* FORM (sense 2), ceremony, formality, liturgy, rite, ritual

ceremonious *Syn* CEREMONIAL, conventional, formal, solemn

ceremony *Syn* FORM (sense 2), ceremonial, formality, liturgy, rite, ritual

certain **1** · bound to follow in obedience to the laws of nature or of thought *Syn* inevitable, necessary *Ant* probable, supposed **2** *Syn* INEVITABLE, inescapable, necessary, sure, unavoidable *Ant* avoidable, escapable, uncertain, unsure **3** *Syn* SURE, cocksure, positive *Ant* unsure

certainty · a state of mind in which one is free from doubt *Syn* assurance, certitude, conviction *Rel* belief, credence, faith *Ant* uncertainty

certify **1** · to testify to the truth or genuineness of something *Syn* attest, vouch, witness *Rel* assert, aver, avouch, avow, profess **2** *Syn* APPROVE, accredit, endorse, sanction *Ant* disapprove

certitude *Syn* CERTAINTY, assurance, conviction *Ant* uncertainty

chafe *Syn* ABRADE, excoriate, fret, gall

chaff *n Syn* BANTER, give-and-take, jesting, joshing, persiflage, raillery, repartee

chaff *vb* **1** *Syn* BANTER, jolly, josh, kid, rag, rib **2** *Syn* TEASE, jive, josh, kid, rally, razz, rib, ride, roast

chaffer *Syn* BARGAIN, deal, dicker, haggle, horse-trade, negotiate, palter

chagrined *Syn* ASHAMED, mortified *Ant* proud

chain **1** *Syn* ENCUMBRANCE, bar, block, clog, crimp, deterrent, drag, embarrassment, fetter, handicap, hindrance, hurdle, impediment, inhibition, interference, let, manacle, obstacle, obstruction, shackles, stop, stumbling block, trammel *Ant* aid, assistance, benefit, help **2** *Syn* SUCCESSION, progression, sequence, series, string, train

challenge *vb* **1** · to invite (someone) to take part in a contest or to perform a feat *Syn* dare, defy, stump *Rel* beard, brave, brazen, breast, confront, face, outbrave **2** *Syn* FACE, beard, brave, dare, defy *Ant* avoid

challenge *n Syn* OBJECTION, complaint, demur, expostulation, fuss, protest, question, remonstrance

challenger *Syn* COMPETITOR, competition, contender, contestant, rival

chamber **1** *Syn* COMPARTMENT, bay, cabin, cell, cubicle **2** *Syn* ROOM (sense 1), apartment

champ *Syn* BITE, gnash, gnaw

champion *n* **1** *Syn* EXPONENT, advocate, apostle, backer, booster, friend, promoter, proponent, supporter *Ant* adversary, antagonist, opponent **2** *Syn* VICTOR, conqueror, vanquisher, winner

champion *vb Syn* SUPPORT (sense 2), advocate, back, uphold

chance *n* **1** · something that happens without an apparent or determinable cause or as a result of unpredictable forces *Syn* accident, fortune, hap, hazard, luck *Rel* contingency, emergency, exigency, juncture, pass *Ant* law, principle **2** *Syn* OPPORTUNITY, break, occasion, time **3** *Syn* PROBABILITY, odds, percentage

chance *adj* **1** *Syn* ACCIDENTAL, casual, fluky, fortuitous, inadvertent, incidental, unintended, unintentional, unplanned, unpremeditated, unwitting *Ant* deliberate, intended, intentional, planned, premeditated **2** *Syn* RANDOM, casual, chancy, desultory, haphazard, happy-go-lucky, hit-or-miss *Ant* methodical, nonrandom, orderly, systematic

chance *vb Syn* HAPPEN, befall, betide, occur, transpire

chance (upon) *Syn* HAPPEN (on *or* upon), encounter, find, hit (upon), meet, stumble (on *or* onto)

chancy *Syn* RANDOM, casual, chance, desultory, haphazard, happy-go-lucky, hit-or-miss *Ant* methodical, nonrandom, orderly, systematic

change *n* **1** · a making different *Syn* alteration, modification, variation *Rel* diversity, variety *Ant* monotony, uniformity **2** · a result of a making different *Syn* alternation, mutation, permutation, vicissitude *Rel* conversion, metamorphosis, transformation, transmogrification, transmutation

change *vb* **1** · to make different in some way *Syn* alter, make over, modify, recast, redo, refashion, remake, remodel, revamp, revise, rework, vary *Rel* deform, metamorphose, mutate *Ant* fix, freeze, set, stabilize **2** · to pass from one form, state, or level to another *Syn* fluctuate, mutate, shift, vary *Rel* metamorphose, transmute *Ant* stabilize **3** · to give up (something) and take something else in return *Syn* commute, exchange, shift, substitute, swap, switch, trade *Rel* interchange

changeable · having or showing a marked capacity for changes or a marked tendency to alter under slight provocation *Syn* changeful, mutable, protean, variable *Rel* capricious, fickle, inconstant, mercurial, unstable *Ant* stable, unchangeable

changeful *Syn* CHANGEABLE, mutable, protean, variable *Ant* stable, unchangeable

channel *n* **1** · something through which a fluid (as water) is led or flows *Syn* aqueduct, canal, conduit, duct *Rel* pass, passage, way **2** *Syn* STRAIT, narrows, passage, sound

channel *vb* · to cause to move to a central point or along a restricted pathway *Syn* channelize, conduct, direct, funnel, pipe, siphon *Rel* carry, convey, transmit

channelize *Syn* CHANNEL, conduct, direct, funnel, pipe, siphon

chant *Syn* SING, carol, descant, hymn, intone, trill, troll, warble

chaos **1** *Syn* ANARCHY, lawlessness, misrule **2** *Syn* CONFUSION, clutter, disarray, disorder, jumble, muddle, snarl

chaotic *Syn* MESSY, cluttered, confused, disarranged, disarrayed, disheveled (*or* dishevelled), disordered, disorderly, higgledy-piggledy, hugger-mugger, jumbled, littered, messed, muddled, mussed, mussy, pell-mell, rumpled, sloppy, topsy-turvy, tousled, tumbled, unkempt, untidy, upside-down *Ant* neat, ordered, orderly, organized, shipshape, snug, tidied, tidy, trim

chaparral *Syn* THICKET, brake, brushwood, coppice, copse, covert

chaperone *or* **chaperon** *Syn* ACCOMPANY, attend, convoy, escort, squire

char *Syn* BURN, scorch, sear, singe

character **1** · an arbitrary or conventional device that is used in writing and in printing, but is neither a word nor a phrase nor a picture *Syn* mark, sign, symbol **2** *Syn* CHARACTERISTIC, attribute, feature, mark, peculiarity, point, property, quality, trait **3** *Syn*

CREDENTIAL, recommendation, reference, testimonial **4** *Syn* DISPOSITION, complexion, individuality, personality, temper, temperament **5** *Syn* ECCENTRIC, codger, crackbrain, crackpot, crank, kook, nut, oddball, screwball, weirdo **6** *Syn* TYPE, description, ilk, kidney, kind, nature, sort, stripe

characteristic *adj* · being or revealing a quality specific or identifying to an individual or group *Syn* distinctive, individual, peculiar *Rel* especial, particular, special, specific

characteristic *n* · something that sets apart an individual from others of the same kind *Syn* attribute, character, feature, mark, peculiarity, point, property, quality, trait *Rel* badge, indication, sign

characterize · to be a peculiar or significant quality or feature of something *Syn* distinguish, mark, qualify *Rel* demarcate, differentiate, distinguish

charge *vb* **1** *Syn* ACCUSE, impeach, incriminate, indict *Ant* absolve, acquit, clear, exculpate, exonerate, vindicate **2** *Syn* ASCRIBE, accredit, assign, attribute, credit, impute, refer **3** *Syn* BURDEN, cumber, encumber, lade, load, saddle, tax, weigh, weight **4** *Syn* COMMAND, bid, direct, enjoin, instruct, order *Ant* comply, obey **5** *Syn* IMPOSE, assess, exact, fine, lay, levy, put *Ant* remit

charge *n* **1** *Syn* ATTACK (sense 2), aggression, assault, blitzkrieg, descent, offense (*or* offence), offensive, onset, onslaught, raid, rush, strike **2** *Syn* MISSION, assignment, job, operation, post **3** *Syn* OBLIGATION, burden, commitment, duty, need, responsibility **4** *Syn* PRICE, cost, expense **5** · a formal claim of criminal wrongdoing against a person *Syn* complaint, count, indictment, rap *Rel* accusation, allegation

charged *Syn* FERVENT, ardent, blazing, burning, emotional, fervid, feverish, fiery, flaming, glowing, hot-blooded, impassioned, passionate, red-hot, vehement, warm, warm-blooded *Ant* cold, cool, dispassionate, impassive, unemotional

chariness *Syn* CAUTION, calculation, circumspection, wariness *Ant* adventurousness, temerity

charitable · having or showing interest in or being concerned with the welfare of others *Syn* altruistic, benevolent, eleemosynary, humane, humanitarian, philanthropic *Rel* bounteous, bountiful, generous, liberal, munificent, openhanded *Ant* uncharitable

charity **1** *Syn* CONTRIBUTION, alms, benefaction, beneficence, donation, philanthropy **2** *Syn* MERCY, clemency, grace, lenity

charlatan *Syn* IMPOSTOR, faker, mountebank, quack

charley horse *Syn* CRAMP, crick, spasm

charm *vb* *Syn* ATTRACT, allure, bewitch, captivate, enchant, fascinate *Ant* repel

charm *n* **1** *Syn* FETISH, amulet, talisman **2** *Syn* PENDANT, bangle, lavalier

charmer *Syn* MAGICIAN (sense 1), conjurer (*or* conjuror), enchanter, necromancer, sorcerer, voodoo, witch, wizard

charming *Syn* ATTRACTIVE, alluring, bewitching, captivating, enchanting, fascinating *Ant* forbidding, repellent

chart *n* · a stylized or symbolic depiction of something incapable of direct verbal or pictorial representation *Syn* graph, map *Rel* design, plan, plot, project, scheme

chart *vb* · to make a representation of something with a chart *Syn* graph, map

charter *Syn* HIRE, lease, let, rent

chary *Syn* CAUTIOUS, calculating, circumspect, wary *Ant* adventurous, temerarious

chase *Syn* PURSUIT, chasing, dogging, following, hounding, pursuing, shadowing, tagging, tailing, tracing, tracking, trailing

chasing *Syn* PURSUIT, chase, dogging, following, hounding, pursuing, shadowing, tagging, tailing, tracing, tracking, trailing

chasm *Syn* GULF, abysm, abyss

chaste · free from all taint of what is lewd or salacious *Syn* decent, modest, pure *Rel* ethical, moral, righteous, virtuous *Ant* bizarre (*of style, effect*), immoral, lewd, wanton

chasten *Syn* PUNISH, castigate, chastise, correct, discipline *Ant* excuse, pardon

chasteness *Syn* CHASTITY, modesty, purity *Ant* immodesty, impurity, unchastity

chastening *Syn* PUNITIVE, castigating, chastising, correcting, correctional, corrective, disciplinary, disciplining, penal, penalizing

chastise *Syn* PUNISH, castigate, chasten, correct, discipline *Ant* excuse, pardon

chastising *Syn* PUNITIVE, castigating, chastening, correcting, correctional, corrective, disciplinary, disciplining, penal, penalizing

chastity · the quality or state of being morally pure *Syn* chasteness, modesty, purity *Rel* goodness, righteousness, virtuousness *Ant* immodesty, impurity, unchastity

chat *n* · friendly, informal conversation or an instance of this *Syn* chatter, chitchat, gabfest, gossip, palaver, rap, small talk, table talk, talk, tête-à-tête *Rel* colloquy, conference, discourse, parley, powwow, symposium

chat *vb* · to engage in casual or rambling conversation *Syn* babble, blab, cackle, chatter, converse, gab, gabble, gas, jabber, jaw, palaver, patter, prate, prattle, rap, rattle, run on, talk, twitter, visit *Rel* gossip, tattle

château *Syn* MANSION, castle, countryseat, estate, hacienda, hall, manor, manor house, palace, villa

chattel *Syn* SLAVE (sense 1), bondman, bondsman, thrall *Ant* freeman

chatter *vb* *Syn* CHAT, babble, blab, cackle, converse, gab, gabble, gas, jabber, jaw, pala-

ver, patter, prate, prattle, rap, rattle, run on, talk, twitter, visit

chatter *n* *Syn* CHAT, chitchat, gabfest, gossip, palaver, rap, small talk, table talk, talk, tête-à-tête

cheap *Syn* CONTEMPTIBLE, beggarly, despicable, pitiable, scurvy, shabby, sorry *Ant* admirable, estimable, formidable

cheat *Syn* FLEECE, bleed, chisel, cozen, defraud, hustle, mulct, rook, shortchange, skin, squeeze, stick, sting, swindle, victimize

check *vb* **1** *Syn* ARREST (sense 1), interrupt *Ant* activate, quicken **2** *Syn* RESTRAIN, bridle, curb, inhibit *Ant* abandon (*oneself*), activate, impel, incite

check *n* **1** *Syn* CORRECTIVE, antidote, control **2** *Syn* INSPECTION, audit, checkup, examination, review, scan, scrutiny, survey **3** *Syn* RESTRICTION, condition, constraint, curb, fetter, limitation, restraint

checked *Syn* VARIEGATED, checkered, dappled, motley, parti-colored, piebald, pied, skewbald

checkered *Syn* VARIEGATED, checked, dappled, motley, parti-colored, piebald, pied, skewbald

checkup *Syn* INSPECTION, audit, check, examination, review, scan, scrutiny, survey

cheek **1** *Syn* BACK TALK, impertinence, impudence, insolence, sass, sauce **2** *Syn* EFFRONTERY, audacity, brashness, brass, brassiness, brazenness, cheekiness, chutzpah, gall, nerve, nerviness, pertness, presumption, presumptuousness, sauce, sauciness, temerity

cheekiness *Syn* EFFRONTERY, audacity, brashness, brass, brassiness, brazenness, cheek, chutzpah, gall, nerve, nerviness, pertness, presumption, presumptuousness, sauce, sauciness, temerity

cheep *vb* *Syn* CHIRP, chirrup, chitter, peep, tweet, twitter

cheep *n* *Syn* CHIRP, chirrup, chitter, peep, tweet, twitter

cheer **1** *Syn* ACCLAIM, applaud, hail, laud, praise, salute, tout *Ant* knock, pan, slam **2** *Syn* APPLAUD, root *Ant* boo, hiss **3** *Syn* ENCOURAGE, embolden, hearten, inspirit, nerve, steel *Ant* discourage

cheerful **1** · having or showing a good mood or disposition *Syn* blithe, blithesome, bright, buoyant, cheery, chipper, gay, gladsome, lightsome, sunny, upbeat *Rel* hopeful, optimistic, sanguine *Ant* dour, gloomy, glum, morose, saturnine, sulky, sullen **2** · serving to lift one's spirits *Syn* bright, cheering, cheery, gay, glad *Rel* gladdening, heartening, heartwarming *Ant* bleak, cheerless, dark, depressing, dismal, dreary, gloomy, gray **3** *Syn* GLAD, happy, joyful, joyous, lighthearted *Ant* sad

cheering *n* *Syn* APPLAUSE, acclamation,

cheers, ovation, plaudit(s), rave(s) *Ant* booing, hissing

cheering *adj* **1** *Syn* CHEERFUL (sense 2), bright, cheery, gay, glad *Ant* bleak, cheerless, dark, depressing, dismal, dreary, gloomy, gray **2** *Syn* HEARTWARMING, comforting, encouraging, fulfilling, gladdening, gratifying, heartening, rewarding, satisfying *Ant* depressing, discouraging, disheartening, dispiriting

cheerless *Syn* DISMAL, bleak, desolate, dispiriting, dreary

cheers *Syn* APPLAUSE, acclamation, cheering, ovation, plaudit(s), rave(s) *Ant* booing, hissing

cheery **1** *Syn* CHEERFUL (sense 1), blithe, blithesome, bright, buoyant, chipper, gay, gladsome, lightsome, sunny, upbeat *Ant* dour, gloomy, glum, morose, saturnine, sulky, sullen **2** *Syn* CHEERFUL (sense 2), bright, cheering, gay, glad *Ant* bleak, cheerless, dark, depressing, dismal, dreary, gloomy, gray

cheeseparing *Syn* STINGY, close, closefisted, miserly, niggardly, parsimonious, pennypinching, penurious, tight, tightfisted *Ant* generous

chemist *Syn* DRUGGIST, apothecary, pharmacist

cherish **1** *Syn* APPRECIATE, prize, treasure, value *Ant* despise **2** *Syn* NURSE, cultivate, foster, nurture

chest · a covered rectangular container for storing or transporting things *Syn* box, caddy, case, casket, locker, trunk *Rel* crate

chesterfield *Syn* COUCH, davenport, divan, lounge, settee, sofa

chew out *Syn* SCOLD, bawl, berate, jaw, rail, rate, revile, tongue-lash, upbraid, vituperate, wig

chic *Syn* STYLISH, dashing, fashionable, modish, smart

chicane *Syn* DECEPTION, chicanery, doubledealing, fraud, trickery

chicanery **1** *Syn* DECEPTION, chicane, double-dealing, fraud, trickery **2** *Syn* TRICKERY, artifice, hanky-panky, jugglery, legerdemain, subterfuge, wile

chicken *adj* *Syn* COWARDLY, chickenhearted, craven, dastardly, lily-livered, pusillanimous, recreant, spineless, unheroic, yellow *Ant* brave, courageous, daring, dauntless, doughty, fearless, gallant, greathearted, gutsy, hardy, heroic, intrepid, lionhearted, stalwart, stout, stouthearted, valiant, valorous

chicken *n* *Syn* COWARD, craven, dastard, poltroon, recreant *Ant* hero, stalwart, valiant

chickenhearted *Syn* COWARDLY, chicken, craven, dastardly, lily-livered, pusillanimous, recreant, spineless, unheroic, yellow *Ant* brave, courageous, daring, dauntless, doughty, fearless, gallant, greathearted, gutsy, hardy, heroic, intrepid, lionhearted, stalwart, stout, stouthearted, valiant, valorous

chide *Syn* REPROVE, admonish, rebuke, reprimand, reproach

chief *adj* · first in importance or in standing *Syn* capital, foremost, leading, main, principal *Rel* dominant, paramount, predominant, preponderant, preponderating, sovereign *Ant* subordinate

chief *n* **1** · the person in whom resides authority or ruling power *Syn* chieftain, head, headman, leader, master *Rel* governor, ruler **2** *Syn* BOSS, captain, foreman, head, headman, helmsman, kingpin, leader, master, taskmaster **3** *Syn* HEAD, commanding, first, foremost, high, lead, leading, managing, preeminent, premier, presiding, primary, prime, principal, supreme

chiefly **1** · for the most part *Syn* altogether, basically, by and large, generally, largely, mainly, mostly, overall, predominantly, primarily, principally, substantially *Rel* nearly, practically, virtually **2** *Syn* LARGELY, generally, greatly, mainly, mostly, principally

chieftain *Syn* CHIEF, head, headman, leader, master

child *Syn* BABY, babe, infant, newborn

childish · having or showing the annoying qualities (as silliness) associated with children *Syn* adolescent, babyish, immature, infantile, juvenile, kiddish, puerile *Rel* boyish, girlish *Ant* adult, grown-up, mature

child's play **1** *Syn* CINCH, breeze, duck soup, picnic, pushover, snap *Ant* chore, headache, labor **2** *Syn* TRIFLE, frippery, nothing, triviality

chill · an uncomfortable degree of coolness *Syn* bite, bitterness, bleakness, chilliness, nip, rawness, sharpness *Rel* briskness, crispness

chilliness *Syn* CHILL, bite, bitterness, bleakness, nip, rawness, sharpness

chilly *Syn* COLD, arctic, cool, freezing, frigid, frosty, gelid, glacial, icy *Ant* hot

chimerical *Syn* IMAGINARY, fanciful, fantastic, quixotic, visionary *Ant* actual, real

chine *Syn* SPINE, back, backbone, vertebrae

chink *Syn* CRACK, cleft, cranny, crevasse, crevice, fissure

chipper *Syn* CHEERFUL (sense 1), blithe, blithesome, bright, buoyant, cheery, gay, gladsome, lightsome, sunny, upbeat *Ant* dour, gloomy, glum, morose, saturnine, sulky, sullen

chirp *n* · the little sounds characteristic of small animals or sounds that suggest such small animal sounds *Syn* cheep, chirrup, chitter, peep, tweet, twitter

chirp *vb* · to make a short, sharp, and usually repetitive sound *Syn* cheep, chirrup, chitter, peep, tweet, twitter

chirrup *n* *Syn* CHIRP, cheep, chitter, peep, tweet, twitter

chirrup *vb* *Syn* CHIRP, cheep, chitter, peep, tweet, twitter

chisel 1 *Syn* CARVE, engrave, etch, incise, sculpt, sculpture 2 *Syn* FLEECE, bleed, cheat, cozen, defraud, hustle, mulct, rook, short-change, skin, squeeze, stick, sting, swindle, victimize

chitchat *Syn* CHAT, chatter, gabfest, gossip, palaver, rap, small talk, table talk, talk, tête-à-tête

chitter *n Syn* CHIRP, cheep, chirrup, peep, tweet, twitter

chitter *vb Syn* CHIRP, cheep, chirrup, peep, tweet, twitter

chivalrous *Syn* CIVIL, courteous, courtly, gallant, polite *Ant* rude, uncivil

chivy *Syn* BAIT, badger, heckle, hector, hound, ride

choice *adj* · having qualities that appeal to a fine or highly refined taste *Syn* dainty, delicate, elegant, exquisite, rare, recherché *Rel* incomparable, peerless, preeminent, superlative, supreme, surpassing *Ant* indifferent, medium

choice *n* 1 · the act or opportunity of choosing or the thing chosen *Syn* alternative, election, option, preference, selection 2 *Syn* ELITE, best, cream, elect, fat, flower, pick, prime, upper crust

choke *Syn* SUFFOCATE, asphyxiate, smother, stifle, strangle, throttle

choleric *Syn* IRASCIBLE, cranky, cross, splenetic, testy, touchy

choose · to fix upon one of a number of things as the one to be taken, accepted, or adopted *Syn* cull, elect, opt, pick, prefer, select, single *Rel* adopt, embrace, espouse *Ant* eschew, reject

choosy *or* **choosey** *Syn* SELECTIVE, particular, picky *Ant* nonselective

chop 1 · to cut into small pieces *Syn* dice, hash, mince *Rel* chip, grind, mash, puree, slice 2 *Syn* CUT, carve, hew, slash, slit

choppy *Syn* FITFUL, casual, discontinuous, erratic, intermittent, irregular, occasional, spasmodic, sporadic, spotty, unsteady *Ant* constant, continuous, regular, steady

chore · a piece of work that needs to be done regularly *Syn* assignment, duty, job, stint, task *Rel* endeavor, enterprise, project, undertaking

chow *Syn* MEAL, feed, mess, repast, table

chronic *Syn* INVETERATE, confirmed, deep-rooted, deep-seated

chronicle 1 *Syn* ACCOUNT, report, story, version 2 *Syn* HISTORY, annals

chthonian *Syn* INFERNAL, chthonic, Hadean, hellish, stygian, Tartarean *Ant* supernal

chthonic *Syn* INFERNAL, chthonian, Hadean, hellish, stygian, Tartarean *Ant* supernal

chubby *Syn* FLESHY, corpulent, fat, obese, plump, portly, rotund, stout *Ant* scrawny, skinny

chummy *Syn* FAMILIAR, close, confidential, intimate, thick *Ant* aloof

chump *Syn* DUPE, gull, pigeon, sap, sucker, tool

chunky *Syn* STOCKY, dumpy, squat, stubby, thick, thickset

church *Syn* RELIGION, communion, creed, denomination, faith, persuasion, sect

churlish *Syn* CLOWNISH, boorish, cloddish, loutish, uncouth *Ant* civil, courteous, courtly, cultivated, genteel, gentlemanly, ladylike, polished, polite, refined, well-bred

chutzpah *Syn* EFFRONTERY, audacity, brashness, brass, brassiness, brazenness, cheek, cheekiness, gall, nerve, nerviness, pertness, presumption, presumptuousness, sauce, sauciness, temerity

cinch *n* · something that is easy to do *Syn* breeze, child's play, duck soup, picnic, pushover, snap *Rel* nothing *Ant* chore, headache, labor

cinch *vb Syn* ENSURE, assure, guarantee, guaranty, insure, secure

cinders *Syn* ASH, clinkers, embers

cinema *Syn* MOVIE (sense 2), film, motion pictures, pictures, screen

ciphering *Syn* CALCULATION, arithmetic, computation, figures, figuring, reckoning

circle 1 *Syn* SURROUND, compass, encircle, encompass, environ, gird, girdle, hem, ring 2 *Syn* TURN (sense 1), eddy, gyrate, pirouette, revolve, rotate, spin, swirl, twirl, wheel, whirl

circuit *Syn* CIRCUMFERENCE, compass, perimeter, periphery

circuitous *Syn* INDIRECT, roundabout *Ant* direct, forthright, straightforward

circulate 1 *Syn* RUMOR, bruit (about), noise (about), whisper 2 *Syn* SPREAD, diffuse, disseminate, propagate, radiate

circumference · a continuous line enclosing an area or space *Syn* circuit, compass, perimeter, periphery *Rel* contour, outline

circumlocution *Syn* VERBIAGE, periphrasis, pleonasm, redundancy, tautology

circumscribe *Syn* LIMIT, confine, restrict *Ant* widen

circumspect *Syn* CAUTIOUS, calculating, chary, wary *Ant* adventurous, temerarious

circumspection *Syn* CAUTION, calculation, chariness, wariness *Ant* adventurousness, temerity

circumstance *Syn* OCCURRENCE, episode, event, incident

circumstantial · dealing with a matter fully and usually point by point *Syn* detailed, itemized, minute, particular, particularized *Rel* accurate, correct, exact, nice, precise *Ant* abridged, summary

circumvent *Syn* FRUSTRATE, baffle, balk, foil, outwit, thwart *Ant* fulfill

circus *Syn* MADHOUSE, babel, bedlam, hell

citadel *Syn* FORT, fastness, fortress, stronghold

citation *Syn* ENCOMIUM, eulogy, panegyric, tribute

cite **1** *Syn* ADDUCE, advance, allege **2** *Syn* QUOTE, repeat **3** *Syn* SUMMON, call, convene, convoke, muster

citizen · a person who is regarded as a member of a sovereign state, entitled to its protection, and subject to its laws *Syn* national, subject *Ant* alien

city · a thickly settled and highly populated area *Syn* burg, megalopolis, metropolis, municipality, town *Rel* borough

civil · observant of the forms required by good breeding *Syn* chivalrous, courteous, courtly, gallant, polite *Rel* amiable, complaisant, obliging *Ant* rude, uncivil

civility *Syn* POLITENESS, courteousness, courtesy, gentility, graciousness, mannerliness *Ant* discourteousness, discourtesy, impoliteness, incivility, rudeness, ungraciousness

civilized *Syn* CULTIVATED, cultured, genteel, polished, refined *Ant* philistine, uncivilized, uncultured, unpolished, unrefined

claim *n* · an actual or alleged right to demand something as one's possession, quality, power, or prerogative *Syn* pretense, pretension, title *Rel* affirmation, assertion, declaration, protestation

claim *vb Syn* DEMAND, exact, require

clamor *n Syn* DIN, babel, hubbub, hullabaloo, pandemonium, racket, uproar *Ant* quiet

clamor *vb Syn* ROAR, bawl, bellow, bluster, howl, ululate, vociferate

clamorous *Syn* VOCIFEROUS, blatant, boisterous, obstreperous, strident

clam up *Syn* SHUT UP, hush, quiet (down) *Ant* speak, talk

clandestine *Syn* SECRET, covert, furtive, stealthy, surreptitious, underhand, underhanded

clarify *Syn* EXPLAIN (sense 1), clear (up), construe, demonstrate, elucidate, explicate, expound, illuminate, illustrate, interpret, spell out *Ant* obscure

clash *vb Syn* BUMP, collide, conflict

clash *n Syn* IMPACT, collision, concussion, impingement, jar, jolt, percussion, shock

class *n Syn* ELEGANCE, elegancy, grace, gracefulness, handsomeness, majesty, refinement, stateliness

class *vb* · to order a number of things according to a scale or to place a thing in its due order *Syn* gradate, grade, graduate, rank, rate *Rel* divide, part, separate

classic *Syn* EXCELLENT, A1, bang-up, banner, capital, crackerjack, dandy, divine, fabulous, fine, first-class, first-rate, grand, great, groovy, heavenly, jim-dandy, keen, marvelous (*or* marvellous), mean, neat, nifty, noble, par excellence, prime, sensational, splendid, stellar, sterling, superb, superior, superlative, supernal, swell, terrific, tip-top, top, topnotch, unsurpassed, wonderful *Ant* poor

classify *Syn* ASSORT, pigeonhole, sort

clatter *Syn* COMMOTION, bother, bustle, disturbance, furor, furore, fuss, hubbub, hullabaloo, hurly-burly, pandemonium, pother, row, ruckus, ruction, rumpus, shindy, squall, stew, stir, storm, to-do, tumult, turmoil, uproar, welter, whirl

clause *Syn* PARAGRAPH, article, count, plank, verse

clean *adj Syn* EXHAUSTIVE, all-out, complete, comprehensive, full-scale, out-and-out, thorough, thoroughgoing, total

clean (out) *Syn* DEPLETE, consume, drain, exhaust, expend, spend, use up *Ant* renew, replace

clear *adj* **1** · having the property of being literally or figuratively seen through *Syn* diaphanous, limpid, lucid, pellucid, translucent, transparent *Rel* bright, luminous *Ant* confused, turbid **2** · quickly and easily understood *Syn* lucid, perspicuous *Rel* definite, explicit, express *Ant* abstruse, unintelligible **3** *Syn* EVIDENT, apparent, distinct, manifest, obvious, palpable, patent, plain

clear *vb* **1** *Syn* RID, disabuse, purge, unburden **2** *Syn* EMPTY, evacuate, vacate, void *Ant* fill, load

clearance **1** *Syn* PERMISSION, allowance, authorization, concurrence, consent, granting, leave, license (*or* licence), sanction, sufferance *Ant* interdiction, prohibition, proscription **2** *Syn* ROOM (sense 2), berth, elbow room, leeway, margin, play

clear-cut *Syn* INCISIVE, biting, crisp, cutting, trenchant

clearheaded *Syn* SANE, balanced, lucid, normal, right, stable *Ant* crazed, crazy, demented, deranged, insane, lunatic, mad, maniacal, mental, unbalanced, unsound

clear (up) *Syn* EXPLAIN (sense 1), clarify, construe, demonstrate, elucidate, explicate, expound, illuminate, illustrate, interpret, spell out *Ant* obscure

cleave¹ *vb Syn* STICK, adhere, cling, cohere

cleave² *vb Syn* TEAR, rend, rip, rive, split

cleft *Syn* CRACK, chink, cranny, crevasse, crevice, fissure

clemency **1** *Syn* FORBEARANCE, indulgence, leniency, mercifulness, tolerance *Ant* anger, vindictiveness **2** *Syn* MERCY, charity, grace, lenity

clement **1** · marked by temperatures that are neither too high nor too low *Syn* balmy, equable, gentle, mild, moderate, temperate *Rel* clear, cloudless, fair, rainless, sunny, sunshiny *Ant* harsh, inclement, intemperate, severe **2** *Syn* FORBEARING, indulgent, lenient, merciful, tolerant *Ant* unrelenting

clemently *Syn* FORBEARINGLY, indulgently, leniently, mercifully, tolerantly

clever **1** · having or showing a high degree of practical intelligence or skill in contrivance *Syn* adroit, cunning, ingenious *Rel* deft, dexterous, handy **2** *Syn* INTELLIGENT, alert, bright, brilliant, knowing, quick-witted, smart *Ant* unintelligent

cleverness *Syn* DEXTERITY (sense 1), adroitness, finesse, sleight *Ant* awkwardness, clumsiness, gawkiness

cliché *Syn* COMMONPLACE, bromide, platitude, truism

climate *Syn* AURA, air, atmosphere, flavor, mood, note, temper

climax 1 *Syn* SUMMIT, acme, apex, apogee, culmination, meridian, peak, pinnacle, zenith **2** *Syn* TURNING POINT, landmark, milestone

climb *Syn* ASCEND, arise, lift, mount, rise, soar, up, uprise, upsweep, upturn *Ant* decline, descend, dip, drop, fall (off)

cling *Syn* STICK, adhere, cleave, cohere

clinkers *Syn* ASH, cinders, embers

clip · to make (as hair) shorter with or as if with the use of shears *Syn* bob, crop, curtail, cut, cut back, dock, lop (off), nip, pare, prune, shave, shear, snip, trim *Rel* manicure, mow

cloak *Syn* DISGUISE, camouflage, dissemble, mask

clod *Syn* OAF, gawk, hulk, lout, lubber, lug

cloddish *Syn* CLOWNISH, boorish, churlish, loutish, uncouth *Ant* civil, courteous, courtly, cultivated, genteel, gentlemanly, ladylike, polished, polite, refined, well-bred

clodhopper *Syn* HICK, bumpkin, countryman, provincial, rustic, yokel *Ant* cosmopolitan, sophisticate

clog *n* *Syn* ENCUMBRANCE, bar, block, chain, crimp, deterrent, drag, embarrassment, fetter, handicap, hindrance, hurdle, impediment, inhibition, interference, let, manacle, obstacle, obstruction, shackles, stop, stumbling block, trammel *Ant* aid, assistance, benefit, help

clog *vb* *Syn* HAMPER, fetter, hog-tie, manacle, shackle, trammel *Ant* assist (*persons*), expedite (*work, projects*)

cloister 1 · a place of retirement from the world for members of a religious community *Syn* abbey, convent, monastery, nunnery, priory **2** *Syn* PASSAGE, aisle, arcade, corridor, gallery, hall, hallway, passageway

cloistered *Syn* SECLUDED, covert, isolated, quiet, remote, retired, secret, sheltered

clone *Syn* VARIETY (sense 2), breed, cultivar, race, stock, strain, subspecies

close *adj* **1** · not far (as in place, time, or relationship) from the point, position, or relation that is indicated or understood *Syn* near, nearby, nigh *Rel* abutting, adjacent, adjoining, contiguous *Ant* remote, remotely **2** · having constituent parts that are massed tightly together *Syn* compact, dense, thick *Rel* compressed, condensed, constricted *Ant* open **3** *Syn* FAMILIAR, chummy, confidential, intimate, thick *Ant* aloof **4** *Syn* SILENT (sense

1), close-lipped, closemouthed, reserved, reticent, secretive, taciturn, tight-lipped, uncommunicative *Ant* talkative **5** *Syn* SECRETIVE, closemouthed, dark, reticent, uncommunicative *Ant* communicative, open **6** *Syn* STINGY, cheeseparing, closefisted, miserly, niggardly, parsimonious, penny-pinching, penurious, tight, tightfisted *Ant* generous

close *n* *Syn* FINALE, closing, conclusion, consummation, end, ending, finis, finish, windup *Ant* beginning, dawn, opening, start

closefisted *Syn* STINGY, cheeseparing, close, miserly, niggardly, parsimonious, penny-pinching, penurious, tight, tightfisted *Ant* generous

close-lipped *Syn* SILENT (sense 1), close, closemouthed, reserved, reticent, secretive, taciturn, tight-lipped, uncommunicative *Ant* talkative

closemouthed 1 *Syn* SECRETIVE, close, dark, reticent, uncommunicative *Ant* communicative, open **2** *Syn* SILENT (sense 1), close, close-lipped, reserved, reticent, secretive, taciturn, tight-lipped, uncommunicative *Ant* talkative

closeness 1 *Syn* PRECISION, accuracy, delicacy, exactitude, exactness, fineness, preciseness, rigorousness, veracity *Ant* coarseness, impreciseness, imprecision, inaccuracy, inexactness, roughness **2** *Syn* PROXIMITY, contiguity, immediacy, nearness *Ant* distance, remoteness

closet *Syn* CABINET, buffet, cupboard, hutch, locker, sideboard

closing *Syn* FINALE, close, conclusion, consummation, end, ending, finis, finish, windup *Ant* beginning, dawn, opening, start

clot *Syn* COAGULATE, congeal, curdle, jell, jelly, set

clothe 1 · to cover with or as if with garments *Syn* apparel, array, attire, dress, robe *Ant* unclothe **2** *Syn* PHRASE, articulate, couch, express, formulate, put, say, state, word

clothes · a person's garments considered collectively *Syn* apparel, attire, clothing, dress, raiment

clothing *Syn* CLOTHES, apparel, attire, dress, raiment

cloud *Syn* OBSCURE, becloud, bedim, befog, darken, dim, eclipse, fog, obfuscate *Ant* illuminate, illumine

cloudburst *Syn* RAIN (sense 1), deluge, downpour, rainfall, rainstorm, storm, wet

clouded *Syn* OVERCAST, beclouded, cloudy, dull, hazed, hazy, heavy, lowering, overclouded *Ant* clear, cloudless

cloudy *Syn* OVERCAST, beclouded, clouded, dull, hazed, hazy, heavy, lowering, overclouded *Ant* clear, cloudless

clout *Syn* STRIKE, box, cuff, hit, punch, slap, slog, slug, smite, swat

clown (around) *Syn* CUT UP, act up, fool

(around), horse (around), monkey (around), show off, skylark

clowning *Syn* HORSEPLAY, foolery, high jinks, horsing (around), monkeying, monkeyshines, roughhouse, roughhousing, shenanigans, skylarking, tomfoolery

clownish · having or showing crudely insensitive or impolite manners *Syn* boorish, churlish, cloddish, loutish, uncouth *Rel* coarse, ill-bred, uncultivated, unpolished, unrefined *Ant* civil, courteous, courtly, cultivated, genteel, gentlemanly, ladylike, polished, polite, refined, well-bred

cloy *Syn* SATIATE, glut, gorge, pall, sate, surfeit

club *vb Syn* ALLY, associate, band, confederate, conjoin, cooperate, federate, league, unite *Ant* break up, disband

club *n Syn* ASSOCIATION, order, society

clue *Syn* ENLIGHTEN (sense 1), acquaint, advise, apprise, brief, familiarize, fill in, inform, instruct, tell, wise (up)

clumsy 1 *Syn* AWKWARD, gauche, inept, maladroit *Ant* deft, graceful, handy 2 *Syn* CUMBERSOME, awkward, cranky, cumbrous, ungainly, unhandy, unwieldy *Ant* handy

cluster *Syn* GROUP, bunch, lot, parcel

clutch 1 *Syn* HOLD, grasp, grip 2 *Syn* TAKE, grab, grasp, seize, snatch

clutter *Syn* CONFUSION, chaos, disarray, disorder, jumble, muddle, snarl

cluttered *Syn* MESSY, chaotic, confused, disarranged, disarrayed, disheveled (*or* dishevelled), disordered, disorderly, higgledypiggledy, hugger-mugger, jumbled, littered, messed, muddled, mussed, mussy, pellmell, rumpled, sloppy, topsy-turvy, tousled, tumbled, unkempt, untidy, upside-down *Ant* neat, ordered, orderly, organized, shipshape, snug, tidied, tidy, trim

coadjutor *Syn* ASSISTANT, adjutant, aid, aide, apprentice, deputy, helper, sidekick

coagulate · to alter by chemical reaction from a liquid to a more or less firm jelly *Syn* clot, congeal, curdle, jell, jelly, set *Rel* harden, solidify

coalesce *Syn* MIX, amalgamate, blend, commingle, fuse, merge, mingle

coalition 1 *Syn* ALLIANCE, confederacy, confederation, federation, fusion, league 2 *Syn* FACTION, bloc, body, party, sect, set, side, wing

coarse · offensive to good taste or morals *Syn* gross, obscene, ribald, vulgar *Rel* callow, crude, green, raw, rough, rude, uncouth *Ant* fine, refined

coast *n Syn* SHORE, bank, beach, foreshore, littoral, strand

coast *vb Syn* SLIDE, glide, glissade, skid, slip, slither, toboggan

coax · to get (someone) to do something by gentle urging, special attention, or flattery *Syn*

blandish, blarney, cajole, soft-soap, wheedle *Rel* adulate, flatter, overpraise

cock *n Syn* HEAP, bank, mass, pile, shock, stack

cock *vb Syn* HEAP, bank, mass, pile, shock, stack

cockeyed *Syn* AWRY, askew, aslant, crooked, listing, lopsided, oblique, skewed, slanted, slanting, slantwise, tilted, tipping, uneven *Ant* even, level, straight

cocksure *Syn* SURE, certain, positive *Ant* unsure

coddle *Syn* BABY, dandle, mollycoddle, nurse, pamper, spoil *Ant* abuse, ill-treat, ill-use, maltreat, mishandle, mistreat, misuse

codger *Syn* ECCENTRIC, character, crackbrain, crackpot, crank, kook, nut, oddball, screwball, weirdo

coerce *Syn* FORCE, compel, constrain, oblige

coercion *Syn* FORCE, compulsion, constraint, duress, restraint, violence

coetaneous *Syn* CONTEMPORARY, coeval, coincident, concomitant, concurrent, contemporaneous, simultaneous, synchronous

coeval *Syn* CONTEMPORARY, coetaneous, coincident, concomitant, concurrent, contemporaneous, simultaneous, synchronous

cogent · having the power to persuade *Syn* compelling, conclusive, convincing, decisive, effective, forceful, persuasive, satisfying, strong, telling *Rel* sound, valid, well-founded *Ant* inconclusive, indecisive, ineffective, unconvincing

cogitate *Syn* THINK (sense 2), deliberate, reason, reflect, speculate

cognate *Syn* RELATED, affiliated, allied, kindred

cognizance 1 *Syn* ACQUAINTANCE, familiarity *Ant* unfamiliarity 2 *Syn* ATTENTION (sense 2), awareness, ear, eye, heed, notice, observance, observation

cognizant 1 *Syn* AWARE, alive, awake, conscious, sensible *Ant* unaware 2 *Syn* CONSCIOUS, alive, aware, mindful, sensible, sentient *Ant* insensible, unaware, unconscious, unmindful

cohere *Syn* STICK, adhere, cleave, cling

cohort *Syn* ACCOMPLICE, abettor, accessory, confederate

coil *Syn* WIND, curl, entwine, twine, twist, wreathe

coiling *Syn* SPIRAL, corkscrew, helical, screwlike, winding

coin *Syn* MONEY, cash, coinage, currency, legal tender, specie

coinage *Syn* MONEY, cash, coin, currency, legal tender, specie

coincide *Syn* AGREE (sense 1), concur *Ant* differ, disagree

coincident *Syn* CONTEMPORARY, coetaneous, coeval, concomitant, concurrent, contemporaneous, simultaneous, synchronous

cold · having a temperature below that which

is normal or comfortable *Syn* arctic, chilly, cool, freezing, frigid, frosty, gelid, glacial, icy *Ant* hot

collapse *Syn* FATIGUE, burnout, exhaustion, lassitude, prostration, tiredness, weariness *Ant* refreshment, rejuvenation, revitalization

collate *Syn* COMPARE, contrast

collateral *Syn* SUBORDINATE, dependent, secondary, subject, tributary *Ant* chief, dominant, leading

collation *Syn* COMPARISON, contrast, parallel

colleague *Syn* PARTNER, ally, confederate, copartner *Ant* rival

collect *Syn* GATHER, assemble, congregate

collected *Syn* COOL, composed, imperturbable, nonchalant, unflappable, unruffled *Ant* agitated, ardent

collection *Syn* GATHERING, assemblage, assembly, congregation

collide *Syn* BUMP, clash, conflict

collision *Syn* IMPACT, clash, concussion, impingement, jar, jolt, percussion, shock

color *n* **1** · a property or attribute of a visible thing recognizable only when rays of light fall upon it and serving to distinguish them otherwise visually identical (as shape or size) *Syn* hue, shade, tinge, tint, tone **2** *Syn* PIGMENT, coloring, dye, dyestuff, stain, tincture **3** *Syn* FLAG, banner, ensign, jack, pendant, pennant, pennon, standard, streamer

color *vb* *Syn* BLUSH, bloom, crimson, flush, glow, redden

colorable *Syn* PLAUSIBLE, believable, credible, specious

colorful · marked by a variety of usually vivid colors *Syn* motley, multicolored, polychromatic, polychrome, varicolored, variegated *Rel* brave, bright, brilliant, gay *Ant* colorless, monochromatic, solid

coloring **1** *Syn* EXAGGERATION, caricature, elaboration, embellishment, embroidering, hyperbole, magnification, overstatement, padding, stretching *Ant* understatement **2** *Syn* PIGMENT, color, dye, dyestuff, stain, tincture

colorless · lacking an addition of color *Syn* uncolored, undyed, unpainted, unstained, white *Rel* clear, limpid, liquid, lucent, pellucid, transparent *Ant* colored, dyed, painted, stained, tinged, tinted

colossal *Syn* HUGE, Brobdingnagian, cyclopean, elephantine, enormous, gargantuan, giant, gigantean, gigantic, Herculean, immense, mammoth, titanic, vast *Ant* bitty, diminutive, microscopic (*or* microscopical), midget, miniature, minute, pocket, pygmy, teeny, teeny-weeny, tiny, wee

colossus *Syn* GIANT, behemoth, blockbuster, jumbo, leviathan, mammoth, monster, titan, whale, whopper *Ant* dwarf, midget, mini, miniature, peewee, pygmy, runt, shrimp

colt *Syn* BEGINNER, fledgling, freshman, greenhorn, neophyte, newbie, newcomer, novice, recruit, rookie, tenderfoot, tyro *Ant* old hand, old-timer, vet, veteran

column *Syn* PILLAR, pilaster

coma *Syn* FAINT, blackout, insensibility, knockout, swoon

comatose *Syn* LETHARGIC, sluggish, torpid *Ant* energetic, vigorous

comb *Syn* SEEK, ferret out, hunt, ransack, rummage, scour, search

combat *n* *Syn* CONTEST, affray, conflict, fight, fray

combat *vb* *Syn* RESIST, antagonize, conflict, contest, fight, oppose, withstand *Ant* abide, submit

combative *Syn* BELLIGERENT, aggressive, argumentative, bellicose, contentious, discordant, disputatious, gladiatorial, militant, pugnacious, quarrelsome, scrappy, truculent, warlike *Ant* nonbelligerent, pacific, peaceable, peaceful

combativeness *Syn* BELLIGERENCE, aggression, aggressiveness, bellicosity, contentiousness, disputatiousness, fight, militancy, pugnacity, scrappiness, truculence *Ant* pacifism

combination **1** · a union, either of individuals or of organized interests, for mutual support in obtaining common political or private ends *Syn* bloc, combine, faction, party, ring *Rel* cartel, corner, monopoly, pool, syndicate, trust **2** *Syn* BLEND, admixture, amalgam, amalgamation, composite, compound, fusion, intermixture, mix, mixture **3** *Syn* CARTEL, combine, syndicate, trust

combine *n* **1** *Syn* CARTEL, combination, syndicate, trust **2** *Syn* COMBINATION, bloc, faction, party, ring

combine *vb* **1** *Syn* JOIN, associate, conjoin, connect, link, relate, unite *Ant* disjoin, part **2** *Syn* UNITE, concur, conjoin, cooperate *Ant* part

combustible · showing a tendency to catch or be set on fire *Syn* flammable, incendiary, inflammable, inflammatory *Rel* burnable

come *Syn* BECOME, get, go, grow, run, turn, wax

come around *Syn* COME TO, come round, revive

comedown · a loss of status *Syn* decline, descent, down, downfall, fall *Rel* breakdown, collapse, crash, meltdown, ruin, undoing *Ant* aggrandizement, ascent, exaltation, rise, up

comedy · humorous entertainment *Syn* farce, humor, slapstick *Rel* burlesque, parody, satire

comely *Syn* BEAUTIFUL, attractive, beauteous, cute, fair, gorgeous, handsome, knockout, lovely, pretty, ravishing, sightly, stunning, taking *Ant* homely, ill-favored, plain, ugly, unattractive, unbeautiful, unhandsome, unlovely, unpretty, unsightly

come round *Syn* COME TO, come around, revive

comestibles *Syn* FOOD (sense 1), feed, fodder, forage, provender, provisions, viands, victuals

come to · to gain consciousness again *Syn* come around, come round, revive *Rel* pull through, rally, recover

comfort *vb* · to give or offer a person help or assistance in relieving his suffering or sorrow *Syn* console, solace *Rel* delight, gladden, please, rejoice *Ant* afflict, bother

comfort *n Syn* REST, ease, leisure, relaxation, repose

comfortable · enjoying or providing condition or circumstances which make for one's contentment and security *Syn* cozy, easy, restful, snug *Rel* comforting, consoling, solacing *Ant* miserable, uncomfortable

comforting *Syn* HEARTWARMING, cheering, encouraging, fulfilling, gladdening, gratifying, heartening, rewarding, satisfying *Ant* depressing, discouraging, disheartening, dispiriting

comic *Syn* LAUGHABLE, comical, droll, farcical, funny, ludicrous, ridiculous, risible

comical *Syn* LAUGHABLE, comic, droll, farcical, funny, ludicrous, ridiculous, risible

coming *Syn* FORTHCOMING, approaching, imminent, impending, nearing, oncoming, pending, upcoming *Ant* late, recent

comity *Syn* FRIENDSHIP, amity, goodwill *Ant* animosity

command *n* · a direction that must or should be obeyed *Syn* behest, bidding, dictate, injunction, mandate, order *Rel* charge, charging, direction, instruction

command *vb* · to issue orders to someone to give, get, or do something *Syn* bid, charge, direct, enjoin, instruct, order *Rel* conduct, control, direct, manage *Ant* comply, obey

commanding *Syn* HEAD, chief, first, foremost, high, lead, leading, managing, preeminent, premier, presiding, primary, prime, principal, supreme

commemorate *Syn* KEEP (sense 1), celebrate, observe, solemnize *Ant* break

commemorative *Syn* MEMORIAL, keepsake, memento, monument, remembrance, reminder, souvenir, token

commence **1** *Syn* BEGIN (sense 1), arise, dawn, form, materialize, originate, set in, spring, start *Ant* cease, end, stop **2** *Syn* BEGIN (sense 2), embark (on *or* upon), enter (into *or* upon), get off, kick off, launch, open, start, strike (into) *Ant* conclude, end, finish, terminate

commencement *Syn* BEGINNING, alpha, birth, dawn, genesis, inception, incipiency, launch, morning, onset, outset, start, threshold *Ant* close, conclusion, end, ending

commend · to voice or otherwise manifest to others one's warm approval *Syn* applaud, compliment, recommend *Rel* acclaim, eulogize, extol, laud, praise *Ant* admonish, censure

commendable *Syn* ADMIRABLE, creditable, laudable, meritorious, praiseworthy *Ant* censurable, discreditable, reprehensible

commensurable *Syn* PROPORTIONAL, commensurate, proportionate

commensurate *Syn* PROPORTIONAL, commensurable, proportionate

comment *vb Syn* REMARK, animadvert, commentate

comment *n Syn* REMARK, commentary, note, obiter dictum, observation

commentary *Syn* REMARK, comment, note, obiter dictum, observation

commentate *Syn* REMARK, animadvert, comment

commerce **1** · the buying and selling of goods especially on a large scale and between different places *Syn* business, marketplace, trade, traffic *Rel* free trade **2** *Syn* BUSINESS, industry, trade, traffic

commercial · fit or likely to be sold especially on a large scale *Syn* marketable, salable (*or* saleable) *Rel* mass-produced, wholesale *Ant* noncommercial, nonsalable, uncommercial, unmarketable, unsalable

commingle *Syn* MIX, amalgamate, blend, coalesce, fuse, merge, mingle

commiseration *Syn* SYMPATHY, compassion, condolence, empathy, pity, ruth

commissary *Syn* AGENT (sense 1), attorney, delegate, deputy, envoy, factor, procurator, proxy, representative

commission **1** *Syn* AUTHORIZE, accredit, license **2** *Syn* APPOINT (sense 2), assign, attach, constitute, designate, detail, name *Ant* discharge, dismiss, expel, fire

commit · to assign to a person or place for some definite end or purpose (as custody or safekeeping) *Syn* confide, consign, entrust, relegate *Rel* move, remove, shift, transfer

commitment *Syn* OBLIGATION, burden, charge, duty, need, responsibility

commodious *Syn* SPACIOUS, ample, capacious

common **1** · generally met with and not in any way special, strange, or unusual *Syn* familiar, ordinary, popular, vulgar *Rel* current, prevailing, prevalent, rife *Ant* exceptional, uncommon **2** *Syn* GENERAL (sense 1), blanket, generic, global, overall, universal *Ant* individual, particular **3** *Syn* RECIPROCAL (sense 1), mutual

commonly *Syn* NATURALLY (sense 1), generally, normally, ordinarily, typically, usually *Ant* abnormally, atypically, extraordinarily, uncommonly, unusually

commonplace *n* · an idea or expression lacking in originality or freshness *Syn* bromide, cliché, platitude, truism *Rel* expression, idiom, locution, phrase

commonplace *adj Syn* STALE, banal, hackney, hackneyed, moth-eaten, musty, stereotyped, threadbare, tired, trite *Ant* fresh, new, original

common sense **1** • the ability to make intelligent decisions especially in everyday matters *Syn* discreetness, discretion, horse sense, levelheadedness, prudence, sense, sensibleness, wisdom, wit *Rel* street smarts *Ant* imprudence, indiscretion **2** *Syn* SENSE, good sense, gumption, horse sense, judgment, wisdom

commonwealth *Syn* NATION, country, land, sovereignty, state

commotion • a state of noisy, confused activity *Syn* bother, bustle, clatter, disturbance, furor, furore, fuss, hubbub, hullabaloo, hurly-burly, pandemonium, pother, row, ruckus, ruction, rumpus, shindy, squall, stew, stir, storm, to-do, tumult, turmoil, uproar, welter, whirl *Rel* cacophony, clamor, din, howl, hue and cry, noise, outcry, racket, roar

communicable *Syn* INFECTIOUS (sense 1), catching, contagious

communicate • to cause (something) to pass from one to another *Syn* convey, impart, spread, transfer, transfuse, transmit *Rel* deliver, hand over, surrender, turn over

communion **1** *Syn* RAPPORT, fellowship, rapprochement **2** *Syn* RELIGION, church, creed, denomination, faith, persuasion, sect

community *Syn* SIMILARITY, alikeness, correspondence, likeness, parallelism, resemblance, similitude *Ant* dissimilarity, unlikeness

commute *Syn* CHANGE (sense 3), exchange, shift, substitute, swap, switch, trade

compact *vb* • to bring or gather together the parts, particles, elements, or units of a thing so as to form a close mass or an integral whole *Syn* concentrate, consolidate, unify *Rel* compress, condense, contract

compact *adj Syn* CLOSE (sense 2), dense, thick *Ant* open

compact *n Syn* CONTRACT, bargain, cartel, concordat, convention, entente, pact, treaty

compactly *Syn* SUCCINCTLY, briefly, concisely, crisply, laconically, pithily, summarily, tersely *Ant* diffusely, long-windedly, verbosely, wordily

companion **1** *Syn* ASSOCIATE, comrade, crony **2** *Syn* ESCORT, attendant, guard, guide

companionable *Syn* CONVIVIAL, boon, extroverted, gregarious, outgoing, sociable, social *Ant* antisocial, introverted, reclusive, unsociable

companionship • the feeling of closeness and friendship that exists between companions *Syn* camaraderie, company, comradeship, fellowship, society *Rel* amity, benevolence, cordiality, friendliness, friendship, goodwill, kindliness

company **1** • a group of persons who are associated in a joint endeavor or who are assembled for a common end *Syn* band, party, troop, troupe *Rel* circle, clique, coterie, set **2** *Syn* COMPANIONSHIP, camaraderie, comradeship, fellowship, society

comparable *Syn* ALIKE, akin, analogous, correspondent, corresponding, like, matching, parallel, resembling, similar, such, suchlike *Ant* different, dissimilar, diverse, unlike

compare • to set two or more things side by side in order to show likenesses and differences *Syn* collate, contrast *Rel* approach, equal, match, rival, touch

comparison • a setting of things side by side so as to discover or exhibit their likenesses and differences *Syn* collation, contrast, parallel *Rel* affinity, analogy, likeness, resemblance, similarity, similitude

compartment • one of the parts into which an enclosed space is divided *Syn* bay, cabin, cell, chamber, cubicle *Rel* cubbyhole, pigeonhole

compass *n* **1** *Syn* CIRCUMFERENCE, circuit, perimeter, periphery **2** *Syn* RANGE, gamut, horizon, ken, orbit, purview, radius, reach, scope, sweep

compass *vb* **1** *Syn* REACH, achieve, attain, gain **2** *Syn* SURROUND, circle, encircle, encompass, environ, gird, girdle, hem, ring

compassion *Syn* SYMPATHY, commiseration, condolence, empathy, pity, ruth

compassionate *Syn* TENDER, responsive, sympathetic, warm, warmhearted *Ant* callous, severe

compatible **1** *Syn* CONSISTENT, conformable (to), congruous, consonant, correspondent (with *or* to), harmonious, nonconflicting *Ant* conflicting, incompatible, incongruous, inconsistent, inharmonious, unharmonious **2** *Syn* CONSONANT, congenial, congruous, consistent, sympathetic *Ant* dissonant (*in music*), inconstant

compel *Syn* FORCE, coerce, constrain, oblige

compelling *Syn* COGENT, conclusive, convincing, decisive, effective, forceful, persuasive, satisfying, strong, telling *Ant* inconclusive, indecisive, ineffective, unconvincing

compendious **1** *Syn* CONCISE, laconic, pithy, succinct, summary, terse *Ant* redundant **2** *Syn* ENCYCLOPEDIC, complete, comprehensive, full, global, inclusive, in-depth, omnibus, panoramic, universal

compendium • a condensed treatment of a subject *Syn* aperçu, digest, pandect, précis, sketch, survey, syllabus *Rel* abridgement, abstract, brief, conspectus, epitome

compensate **1** • to make up for or to undo the effects of *Syn* balance, counterbalance, counterpoise, countervail, offset *Rel* counteract, negative, neutralize **2** *Syn* PAY, indemnify, recompense, reimburse, remunerate, repay, satisfy

compete 1 · to strive to gain the mastery or upper hand *Syn* contend, contest *Rel* battle, fight 2 *Syn* RIVAL, emulate, vie

competence *Syn* ABILITY, capability, capacity, competency, faculty *Ant* disability, inability, incapability, incapacity, incompetence, incompetency, ineptitude, ineptness

competency *Syn* ABILITY, capability, capacity, competence, faculty *Ant* disability, inability, incapability, incapacity, incompetence, incompetency, ineptitude, ineptness

competent 1 · having the required skills for an acceptable level of performance *Syn* able, capable, fit, good, qualified, suitable *Rel* accomplished, ace, adept, experienced, expert, master, masterful, masterly, practiced (*or* practised), prepared, proficient, schooled, seasoned, skilled, skillful, trained, veteran *Ant* incompetent, inept, poor, unfit, unqualified 2 *Syn* SUFFICIENT, adequate, enough

competition *Syn* COMPETITOR, challenger, contender, contestant, rival

competitor · one who strives for the same thing as another *Syn* challenger, competition, contender, contestant, rival *Rel* finalist, semifinalist

compilation *Syn* ANTHOLOGY, album, miscellany

compile *Syn* EDIT, adapt, redact, revise, rewrite

complacence · an often unjustified feeling of being pleased with oneself or with one's situation or achievements *Syn* complacency, conceit, conceitedness, ego, egotism, pompousness, pride, pridefulness, self-admiration, self-conceit, self-esteem, self-importance, self-satisfaction, smugness, vaingloriousness, vainglory, vainness, vanity *Rel* assurance, confidence, self-assurance, self-confidence *Ant* humbleness, humility, modesty

complacency *Syn* COMPLACENCE, conceit, conceitedness, ego, egotism, pompousness, pride, pridefulness, self-admiration, self-conceit, self-esteem, self-importance, self-satisfaction, smugness, vaingloriousness, vainglory, vainness, vanity *Ant* humbleness, humility, modesty

complacent 1 · feeling or showing an often excessive or unjustified satisfaction in one's possessions, attainments, accomplishments, or virtues *Syn* priggish, self-complacent, self-satisfied, smug *Rel* assured, confident, self-assured, self-confident, self-possessed 2 *Syn* CONCEITED, egoistic, egotistic (*or* egotistical), important, overweening, pompous, prideful, proud, self-conceited, self-important, self-satisfied, smug, stuck-up, vain, vainglorious *Ant* humble, modest

complain · to express dissatisfaction, pain, or resentment usually tiresomely *Syn* beef, bellyache, carp, crab, croak, fuss, gripe, grouse, growl, grumble, kick, moan, murmur, mut-

ter, repine, squawk, wail, whine, yammer *Rel* object (to), protest, quarrel (with) *Ant* rejoice

complainer *Syn* GROUCH, bear, crab, crank, croaker, curmudgeon, fusser, griper, grouser, growler, grumbler, grump, murmurer, mutterer, whiner

complaint 1 *Syn* DISEASE, ailment, condition, disorder, distemper, malady, syndrome *Syn* OBJECTION, complaint, demur, expostulation, fuss, protest, question, remonstrance 2 *Syn* OBJECTION, challenge, demur, expostulation, fuss, protest, question, remonstrance 3 *Syn* CHARGE, count, indictment, rap

complemental *Syn* RECIPROCAL (sense 2), complementary, convertible, correlative, corresponding

complementary *Syn* RECIPROCAL (sense 2), complemental, convertible, correlative, corresponding

complete *vb Syn* CONCLUDE (sense 1), conclude, end, finish, terminate

complete *adj* 1 *Syn* ENCYCLOPEDIC, compendious, comprehensive, full, global, inclusive, in-depth, omnibus, panoramic, universal 2 *Syn* EXHAUSTIVE, all-out, clean, comprehensive, full-scale, out-and-out, thorough, thoroughgoing, total 3 *Syn* FULL, plenary, replete *Ant* empty

complex *adj* · having parts or elements that are more or less confusingly interrelated *Syn* complicated, intricate, involved, knotty *Rel* amalgamated, blended, fused, merged, mingled, mixed *Ant* simple

complex *n Syn* SYSTEM, network, organism, scheme *Ant* chaos

complexion *Syn* DISPOSITION, character, individuality, personality, temper, temperament

compliance · passive or weak agreement to what is asked or demanded *Syn* acquiescence, resignation *Rel* amenableness, docility, obedience, tractableness *Ant* forwardness

compliant 1 · manifesting acceptance (as of another's will or something disagreeable) *Syn* acquiescent, resigned *Rel* amenable, docile, obedient, tractable *Ant* forward 2 *Syn* OBEDIENT, amenable, conformable, docile, law-abiding, submissive, tractable *Ant* contrary, disobedient, froward, insubordinate, intractable, rebellious, recalcitrant, refractory, unruly

complicated *Syn* COMPLEX, intricate, involved, knotty *Ant* simple

compliment *n* · praise addressed directly to a person *Syn* adulation, flattery *Rel* encomium, eulogy, panegyric, tribute *Ant* taunt

compliment *vb Syn* COMMEND, applaud, recommend *Ant* admonish, censure

compliments · best wishes *Syn* congratulations, felicitations, greetings, regards, respects *Rel* approval, blessing, endorsement

comply *Syn* OBEY, mind *Ant* command, order

component *Syn* ELEMENT, constituent, factor, ingredient *Ant* composite, compound (*in science*)

comport *Syn* BEHAVE, acquit, conduct, demean, deport, quit *Ant* misbehave

compose *Syn* CALM, lull, quiet, quieten, settle, soothe, still, tranquilize *Ant* agitate, arouse

composed *Syn* COOL, collected, imperturbable, nonchalant, unflappable, unruffled *Ant* agitated, ardent

composite *Syn* BLEND, admixture, amalgam, amalgamation, combination, compound, fusion, intermixture, mix, mixture

composition *Syn* ESSAY, article, paper, theme

composure *Syn* EQUANIMITY, aplomb, calmness, coolheadedness, coolness, imperturbability, placidity, self-possession, serenity, tranquillity (*or* tranquility) *Ant* agitation, discomposure, perturbation

compound 1 *Syn* BLEND, admixture, amalgam, amalgamation, combination, composite, fusion, intermixture, mix, mixture 2 *Syn* INCREASE (sense 1), add (to), aggrandize, amplify, augment, boost, enlarge, escalate, expand, extend, multiply, raise, swell, up *Ant* abate, contract, decrease, diminish, lessen, lower, reduce, subtract (from)

comprehend 1 *Syn* INCLUDE, embrace, imply, involve, subsume *Ant* exclude 2 *Syn* UNDERSTAND, appreciate

comprehension · the knowledge gained from the process of coming to know or understand something *Syn* appreciation, apprehension, grasp, grip, perception, understanding *Rel* absorption, assimilation, uptake

comprehensive 1 *Syn* ENCYCLOPEDIC, compendious, complete, full, global, inclusive, in-depth, omnibus, panoramic, universal 2 *Syn* EXHAUSTIVE, all-out, clean, complete, full-scale, out-and-out, thorough, thoroughgoing, total

compress *Syn* CONTRACT, condense, constrict, deflate, shrink *Ant* expand

compromise *Syn* ENDANGER, adventure, gamble (with), hazard, imperil, jeopardize, menace, risk, venture

compulsion *Syn* FORCE, coercion, constraint, duress, restraint, violence

compulsive · caused by or suggestive of an irresistible urge *Syn* impulsive, obsessive *Rel* irrepressible, uncontrollable

compulsory *Syn* MANDATORY, forced, imperative, incumbent, involuntary, necessary, nonelective, obligatory, peremptory, required *Ant* elective, optional, voluntary

compunction 1 *Syn* PENITENCE, attrition, contrition, remorse, repentance 2 *Syn* QUALM, misgiving, scruple

computation *Syn* CALCULATION, arithmetic, ciphering, figures, figuring, reckoning

compute *Syn* CALCULATE, estimate, reckon

comrade *Syn* ASSOCIATE, companion, crony

comradeship *Syn* COMPANIONSHIP, camaraderie, company, fellowship, society

conation *Syn* WILL, volition

concave *Syn* HOLLOW, dented, depressed, indented, recessed, sunken *Ant* bulging, convex, protruding, protuberant

conceal *Syn* HIDE, bury, cache, ensconce, screen, secrete

concede 1 *Syn* ADMIT, acknowledge, agree, allow, confess, grant, own (up) *Ant* deny 2 *Syn* GRANT (sense 1), accord, award, vouchsafe

conceit 1 · an attitude of regarding oneself with favor *Syn* amour propre, egotism, self-esteem, self-love *Rel* pride, vainglory, vanity *Ant* humility 2 *Syn* COMPLACENCE, complacency, conceitedness, ego, egotism, pompousness, pride, pridefulness, self-admiration, self-conceit, self-esteem, self-importance, self-satisfaction, smugness, vaingloriousness, vainglory, vainness, vanity *Ant* humbleness, humility, modesty

conceited · having too high an opinion of oneself *Syn* complacent, egoistic, egotistic (*or* egotistical), important, overweening, pompous, prideful, proud, self-conceited, self-important, self-satisfied, smug, stuck-up, vain, vainglorious *Rel* boastful, braggart, bragging *Ant* humble, modest

conceitedness *Syn* COMPLACENCE, complacency, conceit, ego, egotism, pompousness, pride, pridefulness, self-admiration, self-conceit, self-esteem, self-importance, self-satisfaction, smugness, vaingloriousness, vainglory, vainness, vanity *Ant* humbleness, humility, modesty

conceivably *Syn* PERHAPS, maybe, mayhap, perchance, possibly

conceive *Syn* THINK (sense 1), envisage, envision, fancy, imagine, realize

concentrate 1 *Syn* CENTER, centralize, focus 2 *Syn* COMPACT, consolidate, unify

concentration *Syn* ATTENTION (sense 1), application, study *Ant* inattention

concept *Syn* IDEA, conception, impression, notion, thought

conception *Syn* IDEA, concept, impression, notion, thought

conceptual *Syn* ABSTRACT (sense 2), theoretical *Ant* concrete

concern 1 *Syn* AFFAIR, business, matter, thing 2 *Syn* CARE, anxiety, solicitude, worry

concerned *Syn* WORRIED, anxious, careful, solicitous

concerning *Syn* ABOUT, regarding, respecting

concert *Syn* NEGOTIATE, arrange

concession *Syn* CONFESSION, acknowledgment, admission, avowal

conciliate *Syn* PACIFY, appease, disarm, mollify, placate, propitiate *Ant* anger, enrage, incense, infuriate, madden, outrage

conciliator *Syn* MEDIATOR, arbiter, arbitrator,

go-between, intercessor, intermediary, inter-poser, middleman, peacemaker

concise · presented with or given to brev-ity of expression *Syn* compendious, laconic, pithy, succinct, summary, terse *Rel* com-pressed, condensed *Ant* redundant

concisely *Syn* SUCCINCTLY, briefly, com-pactly, crisply, laconically, pithily, summar-ily, tersely *Ant* diffusely, long-windedly, verbosely, wordily

conclude 1 · to bring to a natural or ap-propriate close *Syn* complete, end, finish, terminate 2 *Syn* INFER, deduce, gather, judge

concluding *Syn* LAST, eventual, final, latest, terminal, ultimate *Ant* first

conclusion 1 *Syn* FINALE, close, closing, con-summation, end, ending, finis, finish, windup *Ant* beginning, dawn, opening, start 2 *Syn* IN-FERENCE (sense 1), deduction, judgment

conclusive 1 · having or manifesting quali-ties that bring something to a finish or end *Syn* decisive, definitive, determinative *Rel* cogent, compelling, convincing, telling, valid *Ant* inconclusive 2 *Syn* COGENT, compel-ling, convincing, decisive, effective, force-ful, persuasive, satisfying, strong, telling *Ant* inconclusive, indecisive, ineffective, uncon-vincing

concoct 1 *Syn* CONTRIVE, devise, frame, in-vent 2 *Syn* INVENT, contrive, cook (up), de-vise, fabricate, make up, manufacture, think (up)

concomitant *Syn* CONTEMPORARY, coetane-ous, coeval, coincident, concurrent, contem-poraneous, simultaneous, synchronous

concord *Syn* HARMONY, accord, consonance *Ant* conflict

concordat *Syn* CONTRACT, bargain, cartel, compact, convention, entente, pact, treaty

concourse *Syn* JUNCTION, confluence

concrete *Syn* ACTUAL, existent, factual, real, true, very *Ant* conjectural, hypothetical, ideal, nonexistent, possible, potential, theoretical

concur 1 *Syn* AGREE (sense 1), coincide *Ant* differ, disagree 2 *Syn* UNITE, combine, con-join, cooperate *Ant* part

concurrence *Syn* PERMISSION, allowance, authorization, clearance, consent, granting, leave, license (*or* licence), sanction, suffer-ance *Ant* interdiction, prohibition, proscrip-tion

concurrent *Syn* CONTEMPORARY, coetaneous, coeval, coincident, concomitant, contempo-raneous, simultaneous, synchronous

concussion *Syn* IMPACT, clash, collision, im-pingement, jar, jolt, percussion, shock

condemn 1 *Syn* CRITICIZE, blame, censure, denounce, reprehend, reprobate 2 *Syn* SEN-TENCE, damn, doom, proscribe

condemnation *Syn* CENSURE, denunciation, rebuke, reprimand, reproach, reproof, stric-ture *Ant* citation, commendation, endorse-ment

condense *Syn* CONTRACT, compress, con-strict, deflate, shrink *Ant* expand

condescend *Syn* STOOP, deign

condign *Syn* DUE, rightful

condition *n* 1 · something that limits or qualifies an agreement or offer *Syn* provi-sion, proviso, reservation, stipulation, strings, terms *Rel* prerequisite, requirement, requi-site 2 *Syn* DISEASE, ailment, complaint, dis-order, distemper, malady, syndrome 3 *Syn* RESTRICTION, check, constraint, curb, fetter, limitation, restraint 4 *Syn* STATE, mode, pos-ture, situation, status

condition *vb* *Syn* PREPARE, fit, qualify, ready

conditional *Syn* DEPENDENT, contingent, rel-ative *Ant* absolute, infinite, original

condolence *Syn* SYMPATHY, commiseration, compassion, empathy, pity, ruth

condone *Syn* EXCUSE, forgive, pardon, remit *Ant* punish

conduct *vb* 1 · to use one's skill, authority, or other powers in order to lead, guide, com-mand, or dominate persons or things *Syn* con-trol, direct, manage *Rel* oversee, supervise 2 *Syn* BEHAVE, acquit, comport, demean, de-port, quit *Ant* misbehave 3 *Syn* CHANNEL, channelize, direct, funnel, pipe, siphon

conduct *n* *Syn* BEHAVIOR, deportment

conduit *Syn* CHANNEL, aqueduct, canal, duct

confederacy *Syn* ALLIANCE, coalition, con-federation, federation, fusion, league

confederate *n* 1 *Syn* ACCOMPLICE, abet-tor, accessory, cohort 2 *Syn* ALLY, abettor, backer, supporter, sympathizer 3 *Syn* PART-NER, ally, colleague, copartner *Ant* rival

confederate *vb* *Syn* ALLY, associate, band, club, conjoin, cooperate, federate, league, unite *Ant* break up, disband

confederation *Syn* ALLIANCE, coalition, con-federacy, federation, fusion, league

confer 1 · to give the ownership or benefit of (something) formally or publicly *Syn* ac-cord, award, grant *Rel* bestow, contribute, donate, give, present 2 *Syn* GIVE, afford, be-stow, donate, present

confess *Syn* ADMIT, acknowledge, agree, al-low, concede, grant, own (up) *Ant* deny

confession · an open declaration of some-thing (as a fault or the commission of an of-fense) about oneself *Syn* acknowledgment, admission, avowal, concession *Rel* allowance

confessions *Syn* BIOGRAPHY, autobiography, life, memoir

confidant *Syn* FRIEND, acquaintance, intimate *Ant* foe

confide *Syn* COMMIT, consign, entrust, rel-egate

confidence 1 · a feeling or showing of ad-equacy or reliance on oneself and one's pow-ers *Syn* aplomb, assurance, self-assurance, self-confidence, self-possession *Rel* courage, mettle, resolution, spirit, tenacity *Ant* diffidence **2** *Syn* TRUST, dependence, faith, reliance *Ant* mistrust

confident · not inhibited by doubts, fears, or a sense of inferiority *Syn* assured, presumptuous, sanguine, sure *Rel* bold, brave, courageous, dauntless, fearless, intrepid, unafraid, undaunted, valiant *Ant* apprehensive, diffident

confidential *Syn* FAMILIAR, chummy, close, intimate, thick *Ant* aloof

configuration *Syn* FORM (sense 1), conformation, figure, shape

confine *n Syn* LIMIT, bound, end, term

confine *vb Syn* LIMIT, circumscribe, restrict *Ant* widen

confirm · to attest to the truth, genuineness, accuracy, or validity of something *Syn* authenticate, corroborate, substantiate, validate, verify *Rel* back, support, uphold *Ant* contradict, deny

confirmed *Syn* INVETERATE, chronic, deep-rooted, deep-seated

confiscate *Syn* ARROGATE, appropriate, preempt, usurp *Ant* renounce, yield

conflagration *Syn* FIRE, holocaust

conflict *vb* **1** *Syn* BUMP, clash, collide **2** *Syn* RESIST, antagonize, combat, contest, fight, oppose, withstand *Ant* abide, submit

conflict *n* **1** *Syn* CONTEST, affray, combat, fight, fray **2** *Syn* DISCORD, contention, difference, dissension, schism, strife, variance

confluence *Syn* JUNCTION, concourse

conform **1** *Syn* ADAPT, accommodate, adjust, reconcile *Ant* unfit **2** *Syn* AGREE (sense 2), accord, correspond, harmonize, jibe, square, tally *Ant* differ (from)

conformable **1** *Syn* OBEDIENT, amenable, compliant, docile, law-abiding, submissive, tractable *Ant* contrary, disobedient, froward, insubordinate, intractable, rebellious, recalcitrant, refractory, unruly **2** *Syn* CONSISTENT, compatible, congruous, consonant, correspondent (with *or* to), harmonious, nonconflicting *Ant* conflicting, incompatible, incongruous, inconsistent, inharmonious, unharmonious

conformation *Syn* FORM (sense 1), configuration, figure, shape

confound **1** *Syn* MISTAKE, confuse *Ant* recognize **2** *Syn* PUZZLE, bewilder, distract, dumbfound, mystify, nonplus, perplex

confront *Syn* MEET, encounter, face *Ant* avoid

confuse **1** · to make unclear in mind or purpose *Syn* addle, befuddle, fuddle, muddle *Rel* bewilder, confound, mystify, perplex, puzzle *Ant* enlighten **2** *Syn* DISORDER, derange, disarrange, disarray, discompose, dishevel, dislocate, disorganize, disrupt, disturb, hash, jumble, mess (up), mix (up), muddle, muss, rumple, scramble, shuffle, tousle, tumble,

upset *Ant* arrange, array, draw up, marshal, order, organize, range, regulate, straighten (up), tidy **3** *Syn* MISTAKE, confound *Ant* recognize

confused *Syn* MESSY, chaotic, cluttered, disarranged, disarrayed, disheveled (*or* dishevelled), disordered, disorderly, higgledy-piggledy, hugger-mugger, jumbled, littered, messed, muddled, mussed, mussy, pell-mell, rumpled, sloppy, topsy-turvy, tousled, tumbled, unkempt, untidy, upside-down *Ant* neat, ordered, orderly, organized, shipshape, snug, tidied, tidy, trim

confusion · a condition in which things are not in their normal or proper places or relationships *Syn* chaos, clutter, disarray, disorder, jumble, muddle, snarl *Rel* derangement, disarrangement, disorganization, disturbance

confute *Syn* DISPROVE, controvert, rebut, refute *Ant* demonstrate, prove

congeal *Syn* COAGULATE, clot, curdle, jell, jelly, set

congenial *Syn* CONSONANT, compatible, congruous, consistent, sympathetic *Ant* dissonant (*in music*), inconstant

congenital *Syn* INNATE, hereditary, inborn, inbred, inherited *Ant* acquired

conglomerate *Syn* AGGREGATE, agglomerate, agglomeration, aggregation, conglomeration *Ant* constituent

conglomeration *Syn* AGGREGATE, agglomerate, agglomeration, aggregation, conglomerate *Ant* constituent

congratulations *Syn* COMPLIMENTS, felicitations, greetings, regards, respects

congregate *Syn* GATHER, assemble, collect

congregation *Syn* GATHERING, assemblage, assembly, collection

congruous **1** *Syn* CONSISTENT, compatible, conformable (to), consonant, correspondent (with *or* to), harmonious, nonconflicting *Ant* conflicting, incompatible, incongruous, inconsistent, inharmonious, unharmonious **2** *Syn* CONSONANT, compatible, congenial, consistent, sympathetic *Ant* dissonant (*in music*), inconstant

congruously *Syn* PROPERLY, appropriately, correctly, fittingly, happily, meetly, rightly, suitably *Ant* improperly, inappropriately, incongruously, incorrectly, unsuitably, wrongly

conjectural *Syn* SUPPOSED, hypothetical, purported, putative, reputed, suppositious, supposititious *Ant* certain

conjecture *n* · an opinion or judgment based on little or no evidence *Syn* guess, supposition, surmise *Rel* hypothesis, theory, thesis

conjecture *vb Syn* ESTIMATE (sense 2), calculate, call, figure, gauge, guess, judge, make, place, put, reckon, suppose

conjoin **1** *Syn* ALLY, associate, band, club, confederate, cooperate, federate, league, unite *Ant* break up, disband **2** *Syn* JOIN, associate, combine, connect, link, relate, unite *Ant* disjoin, part **3** *Syn* UNITE, combine, concur, cooperate *Ant* part

conjugal *Syn* MARITAL, connubial, married, matrimonial, nuptial, wedded

conjurer *or* **conjuror 1** *Syn* MAGICIAN (sense 1), charmer, enchanter, necromancer, sorcerer, voodoo, witch, wizard **2** *Syn* MAGICIAN (sense 2), prestidigitator, trickster

connect *Syn* JOIN, associate, combine, conjoin, link, relate, unite *Ant* disjoin, part

connoisseur *Syn* AESTHETE, dilettante

connubial *Syn* MARITAL, conjugal, married, matrimonial, nuptial, wedded

conquer · to get the better of or to bring into subjection by force or strategy *Syn* beat, defeat, lick, overcome, overthrow, reduce, rout, subdue, subjugate, surmount, vanquish *Rel* baffle, balk, circumvent, foil, frustrate, outwit, thwart

conqueror *Syn* VICTOR, champion, vanquisher, winner

conquest *Syn* VICTORY, triumph *Ant* defeat

conscientious *Syn* UPRIGHT, honest, honorable, just, scrupulous

conscious 1 · having specified facts or feelings actively impressed on the mind *Syn* alive, aware, cognizant, mindful, sensible, sentient *Rel* attentive, heedful, observant, regardful, vigilant, watchful *Ant* insensible, unaware, unconscious, unmindful **2** *Syn* AWARE, alive, awake, cognizant, sensible *Ant* unaware

consciously *Syn* INTENTIONALLY, deliberately, designedly, knowingly, purposefully, purposely, willfully, wittingly *Ant* inadvertently, unconsciously, unintentionally, unknowingly, unwittingly

consecrate *Syn* DEVOTE, dedicate, hallow

consecrated *Syn* HOLY (sense 2), blessed, hallowed, sacred, sacrosanct, sanctified *Ant* unconsecrated, unhallowed

consecration · the act of making something holy through religious ritual *Syn* blessing, hallowing, sanctification *Rel* dedication

consecutive · following one after the other in order *Syn* sequent, sequential, serial, successive *Rel* ensuing, following, succeeding *Ant* inconsecutive

consent 1 *Syn* ASSENT, accede, acquiesce, agree, subscribe *Ant* dissent **2** *Syn* PERMISSION, allowance, authorization, clearance, concurrence, granting, leave, license (*or* licence), sanction, sufferance *Ant* interdiction, prohibition, proscription

consequence 1 *Syn* EFFECT, aftereffect, aftermath, event, issue, outcome, result, sequel, upshot *Ant* cause **2** *Syn* IMPORTANCE, import, moment, significance, weight *Ant* unimportance

consequently *Syn* THEREFORE, accordingly, hence, so, then

conservative · tending to favor established ideas, conditions, or institutions *Syn* orthodox, traditional *Rel* hidebound, old-fashioned, reactionary *Ant* liberal, nontraditional, progressive

conserve *Syn* SAVE, preserve *Ant* consume, spend

consider 1 · to give serious thought to *Syn* contemplate, excogitate, study, weigh *Rel* meditate, muse, ponder, ruminate **2** · to come to view, judge, or classify *Syn* account, deem, reckon, regard *Rel* conceive, fancy, imagine, think **3** *Syn* BELIEVE (sense 1), deem, feel, figure, guess, hold, imagine, suppose, think *Ant* disbelieve, discredit, reject

considerable *Syn* LARGE, big, bulky, goodly, good-sized, grand, great, handsome, hefty, hulking, largish, outsize, oversize (*or* oversized), sizable (*or* sizeable), substantial, tidy, voluminous *Ant* little, puny, small, undersized

considered *Syn* DELIBERATE, advised, designed, premeditated, studied *Ant* casual

consign *Syn* COMMIT, confide, entrust, relegate

consistent 1 · not having or showing any apparent conflict *Syn* compatible, conformable (to), congruous, consonant, correspondent (with *or* to), harmonious, nonconflicting *Rel* appropriate, fitting, meet, suitable *Ant* conflicting, incompatible, incongruous, inconsistent, inharmonious, unharmonious **2** *Syn* CONSONANT, compatible, congenial, congruous, sympathetic *Ant* dissonant (*in music*), inconstant

console *Syn* COMFORT, solace *Ant* afflict, bother

consolidate *Syn* COMPACT, concentrate, unify

consolidation · a union of two or more business corporations *Syn* amalgamation, merger *Ant* dissolution

consonance *Syn* HARMONY, accord, concord *Ant* conflict

consonant 1 · conforming (as to a pattern, standard, or relationship) without discord or difficulty *Syn* compatible, congenial, congruous, consistent, sympathetic *Rel* accordant, according, agreeable, agreeing, conformable, conforming, harmonious, harmonizing *Ant* dissonant (*in music*), inconstant **2** *Syn* CONSISTENT, compatible, conformable (to), congruous, correspondent (with *or* to), harmonious, nonconflicting *Ant* conflicting, incompatible, incongruous, inconsistent, inharmonious, unharmonious

consort *Syn* SPOUSE, mate, partner

conspectus *Syn* ABRIDGMENT, abstract, brief, epitome, synopsis *Ant* expansion

conspicuous 1 *Syn* EGREGIOUS, blatant, flagrant, glaring, gross, obvious, patent, pronounced, rank, striking **2** *Syn* NOTICEABLE, arresting, outstanding, prominent, remarkable, salient, signal, striking

conspiracy *Syn* PLOT, cabal, intrigue, machination

conspire *Syn* PLOT, contrive, intrigue, machinate, scheme

constant 1 *Syn* CONTINUAL, continuous, incessant, perennial, perpetual, unremitting *Ant* intermittent 2 *Syn* FAITHFUL, devoted, devout, fast, good, loyal, pious, staunch (*or* stanch), steadfast, steady, true, true-blue *Ant* disloyal, faithless, false, fickle, inconstant, perfidious, recreant, traitorous, treacherous, unfaithful, untrue 3 *Syn* STEADY, equable, even, uniform *Ant* jumpy, nervous, unsteady

consternation *Syn* FEAR, alarm, dismay, dread, fright, horror, panic, terror, trepidation *Ant* fearlessness

constituent *Syn* ELEMENT, component, factor, ingredient *Ant* composite, compound (*in science*)

constitute *Syn* APPOINT (sense 2), assign, attach, commission, designate, detail, name *Ant* discharge, dismiss, expel, fire

constitution *Syn* PHYSIQUE, build, habit

constitutional *adj Syn* INHERENT, essential, ingrained, intrinsic *Ant* adventitious

constitutional *n Syn* WALK, perambulation, ramble, range, saunter, stroll, turn

constitutionally *Syn* NATURALLY (sense 2), inherently, innately, intrinsically *Ant* affectedly, artificially, hypocritically, insincerely, pretentiously, unnaturally

constrain *Syn* FORCE, coerce, compel, oblige

constraint 1 *Syn* FORCE, coercion, compulsion, duress, restraint, violence 2 *Syn* RESTRICTION, check, condition, curb, fetter, limitation, restraint

constrict *Syn* CONTRACT, compress, condense, deflate, shrink *Ant* expand

construct *Syn* BUILD, assemble, erect, fabricate, make, make up, piece, put up, raise, rear, set up *Ant* disassemble, dismantle, take down

construe *Syn* EXPLAIN (sense 1), clarify, clear (up), demonstrate, elucidate, explicate, expound, illuminate, illustrate, interpret, spell out *Ant* obscure

consume 1 *Syn* DEPLETE, clean (out), drain, exhaust, expend, spend, use up *Ant* renew, replace 2 *Syn* EAT, devour, ingest, swallow 3 *Syn* MONOPOLIZE, absorb, engross 4 *Syn* WASTE, dissipate, fritter, squander *Ant* conserve, save

consummate · brought to completion or perfection *Syn* accomplished, finished *Rel* entire, intact, perfect, whole *Ant* crude

consummation 1 *Syn* FINALE, close, closing, conclusion, end, ending, finis, finish, windup *Ant* beginning, dawn, opening, start 2 *Syn* FRUITION, accomplishment, achievement, actuality, attainment, fulfillment, realization *Ant* naught, nonfulfillment

contagious *Syn* INFECTIOUS (sense 1), catching, communicable

contain · to have or be capable of having within *Syn* accommodate, hold *Rel* admit, receive, take

container · something into which a liquid or smaller objects can be put for storage or transportation *Syn* holder, receptacle, vessel *Rel* cartridge

contaminate · to make unfit for use by the addition of something harmful or undesirable *Syn* befoul, defile, foul, poison, pollute, taint *Rel* infect *Ant* decontaminate, purify

contaminated *Syn* IMPURE, adulterated, alloyed, dilute, diluted, polluted, tainted, thinned, weakened *Ant* pure, unadulterated, unalloyed, uncontaminated, undiluted, unpolluted, untainted

contemn *Syn* DESPISE, disdain, scorn, scout *Ant* appreciate

contemplate 1 *Syn* CONSIDER (sense 1), excogitate, study, weigh 2 *Syn* SEE (sense 1), behold, descry, discern, espy, note, notice, observe, perceive, remark, survey, view

contemplative 1 · given to or marked by long, quiet thinking *Syn* meditative, melancholy, pensive, reflective, ruminant, thoughtful *Rel* introspective, retrospective *Ant* unreflective 2 *Syn* THOUGHTFUL (sense 1), meditative, pensive, reflective, speculative *Ant* thoughtless

contemporaneous *Syn* CONTEMPORARY, coetaneous, coeval, coincident, concomitant, concurrent, simultaneous, synchronous

contemporary 1 · existing, living, or occurring at the same time *Syn* coetaneous, coeval, coincident, concomitant, concurrent, contemporaneous, simultaneous, synchronous *Rel* existing, living, subsisting 2 *Syn* MODERN, current, hot, mod, modernistic, new, newfangled, new-fashioned, present-day, red-hot, space-age, ultramodern, up-to-date *Ant* antiquated, archaic, dated, fusty, musty, noncontemporary, oldfangled, old-fashioned, old-time, out-of-date, passé

contempt · open dislike for someone or something considered unworthy of one's concern or respect *Syn* despite, despitefulness, disdain, scorn *Rel* abhorrence, abomination, execration, hate, hatred, loathing *Ant* admiration, esteem, regard, respect

contemptible · arousing or deserving scorn or disdain *Syn* beggarly, cheap, despicable, pitiable, scurvy, shabby, sorry *Rel* abhorrent, abominable, detestable, hateful, odious *Ant* admirable, estimable, formidable

contend 1 · to strive in opposition to someone or something *Syn* battle, fight, war *Rel* altercate, quarrel, squabble, wrangle 2 *Syn* COMPETE, contest

contender 1 *Syn* CANDIDATE, applicant, aspirant, campaigner, hopeful, prospect, seeker 2 *Syn* COMPETITOR, challenger, competition, contestant, rival

content · feeling that one's needs or desires have been met *Syn* contented, gratified, happy, pleased, satisfied *Rel* delighted, glad, joyful, joyous, jubilant *Ant* discontent, discontented, displeased, dissatisfied, malcontent, unhappy

contented *Syn* CONTENT, gratified, happy, pleased, satisfied *Ant* discontent, discontented, displeased, dissatisfied, malcontent, unhappy

contention *Syn* DISCORD, conflict, difference, dissension, schism, strife, variance

contentious *Syn* BELLIGERENT, aggressive, argumentative, bellicose, combative, discordant, disputatious, gladiatorial, militant, pugnacious, quarrelsome, scrappy, truculent, warlike *Ant* nonbelligerent, pacific, peaceable, peaceful

contentiousness *Syn* BELLIGERENCE, aggression, aggressiveness, bellicosity, combativeness, disputatiousness, fight, militancy, pugnacity, scrappiness, truculence *Ant* pacifism

contest *n* · a battle between opposing forces for supremacy, for power, or for possessions *Syn* affray, combat, conflict, fight, fray *Rel* brush, encounter, skirmish

contest *vb* **1** *Syn* COMPETE, contend **2** *Syn* RESIST, antagonize, combat, conflict, fight, oppose, withstand *Ant* abide, submit

contestant *Syn* COMPETITOR, challenger, competition, contender, rival

contiguity *Syn* PROXIMITY, closeness, immediacy, nearness *Ant* distance, remoteness

contiguous *Syn* ADJACENT, abutting, adjoining, bordering, flanking, fringing, joining, juxtaposed, skirting, touching, verging *Ant* nonadjacent

continence *Syn* TEMPERANCE, abstemiousness, abstinence, sobriety *Ant* excessiveness, immoderacy, intemperance, intemperateness

continent *Syn* SOBER, temperate, unimpassioned *Ant* drunk, excited

contingency *Syn* JUNCTURE, crisis, emergency, exigency, pass, pinch, strait

contingent *Syn* DEPENDENT, conditional, relative *Ant* absolute, infinite, original

continual · characterized by continued occurrence or recurrence over a relatively long period of time *Syn* constant, continuous, incessant, perennial, perpetual, unremitting *Rel* endless, everlasting, interminable, unceasing *Ant* intermittent

continuance *Syn* CONTINUATION, duration, endurance, persistence, subsistence *Ant* ending, termination

continuation · uninterrupted or lasting existence *Syn* continuance, duration, endurance, persistence, subsistence *Rel* elongation, extension, lengthening, prolongation *Ant* ending, termination

continue **1** · to remain indefinitely in existence or in a given condition or course *Syn* abide, endure, last, persist *Rel* remain, stay **2** *Syn* RESUME, renew, reopen, restart

continuous *Syn* CONTINUAL, constant, incessant, perennial, perpetual, unremitting *Ant* intermittent

contort *Syn* DEFORM, distort, warp

contour *Syn* OUTLINE, profile, silhouette, skyline

contraband *Syn* SMUGGLED, bootleg

contract *n* **1** · an agreement reached after negotiation and ending in an exchange of promises between the parties concerned *Syn* bargain, cartel, compact, concordat, convention, entente, pact, treaty **2** *Syn* PROMISE, covenant, engage, pledge, plight

contract *vb* · to decrease in bulk, volume, or content *Syn* compress, condense, constrict, deflate, shrink *Rel* decrease, diminish, dwindle, reduce *Ant* expand

contradict *Syn* DENY, contravene, gainsay, impugn, negative, traverse *Ant* concede, confirm

contradiction *Syn* DENIAL (sense 2), disallowance, disavowal, disclaimer, negation, rejection, repudiation *Ant* acknowledgment, admission, avowal, confirmation

contradictory *adj* *Syn* OPPOSITE, antipodal, antipodean, antithetical, antonymous, contrary

contradictory *n* *Syn* OPPOSITE, antipode, antithesis, antonym, contrary, converse, counter, reverse

contraption **1** *Syn* DEVICE, contrivance, gadget **2** *Syn* GADGET, appliance, contrivance, gimmick, gizmo (*or* gismo), jigger

contrariness *Syn* DISOBEDIENCE, defiance, frowardness, insubordination, intractability, rebelliousness, recalcitrance, refractoriness, unruliness, willfulness *Ant* amenability, compliance, docility, obedience

contrary *adj* **1** · given to opposing or resisting wishes, commands, conditions, or circumstances *Syn* balky, froward, perverse, restive, wayward *Rel* headstrong, intractable, recalcitrant, refractory, unruly *Ant* complaisant, good-natured **2** *Syn* DISOBEDIENT, balky, defiant, froward, insubordinate, intractable, rebellious, recalcitrant, refractory, restive, ungovernable, unruly, untoward, wayward, willful (*or* wilful) *Ant* amenable, compliant, docile, obedient, tractable **3** *Syn* OPPOSITE, antipodal, antipodean, antithetical, antonymous, contradictory

contrary *n* *Syn* OPPOSITE, antipode, antithesis, antonym, contradictory, converse, counter, reverse

contrast *vb* *Syn* COMPARE, collate

contrast *n* *Syn* COMPARISON, collation, parallel

contravene *Syn* DENY, contradict, gainsay, impugn, negative, traverse *Ant* concede, confirm

contravention *Syn* BREACH (sense 1), infraction, infringement, transgression, trespass, violation

contribution · a gift of money or its equivalent to a charity, humanitarian cause, or public institution *Syn* alms, benefaction, beneficence, charity, donation, philanthropy *Rel* offering, tithe

contributory *Syn* AUXILIARY, accessory, adjuvant, ancillary, subservient, subsidiary

contrite *Syn* GUILTY, ashamed, hangdog, penitent, remorseful, repentant, shamed, shamefaced *Ant* impenitent, remorseless, shameless, unashamed, unrepentant

contrition *Syn* PENITENCE, attrition, compunction, remorse, repentance

contrivance **1** *Syn* DEVICE, contraption, gadget **2** *Syn* GADGET, appliance, contraption, gimmick, gizmo (*or* gismo), jigger

contrive **1** *Syn* ENGINEER, finagle, finesse, frame, machinate, maneuver, manipulate, mastermind, negotiate, wangle **2** *Syn* INVENT, concoct, cook (up), devise, fabricate, make up, manufacture, think (up) **3** *Syn* PLOT, conspire, intrigue, machinate, scheme

control *vb Syn* CONDUCT, direct, manage

control *n Syn* CORRECTIVE, antidote, check

controversy *Syn* ARGUMENT, dispute

controvert *Syn* DISPROVE, confute, rebut, refute *Ant* demonstrate, prove

contumacious *Syn* INSUBORDINATE, factious, mutinous, rebellious, seditious

contumelious *Syn* ABUSIVE, opprobrious, scurrilous, vituperative *Ant* complementary, respectful

contusion *Syn* WOUND, bruise, lesion, trauma, traumatism

conundrum *Syn* MYSTERY, enigma, problem, puzzle, riddle

convalesce **1** · to become healthy and strong again after illness or weakness *Syn* gain, heal, mend, rally, recover, recuperate, snap back *Rel* come around, come round, come to, improve, pick up, revive **2** *Syn* IMPROVE (sense 2), gain, recover, recuperate

convenance *Syn* FORM (sense 3), convention, usage

convene *Syn* SUMMON, call, cite, convoke, muster

convent *Syn* CLOISTER, abbey, monastery, nunnery, priory

convention **1** *Syn* CONTRACT, bargain, cartel, compact, concordat, entente, pact, treaty **2** *Syn* FORM (sense 3), convenance, usage

conventional *Syn* CEREMONIAL, ceremonious, formal, solemn

converse *vb* **1** *Syn* CHAT, babble, blab, cackle, chatter, gab, gabble, gas, jabber, jaw, palaver, patter, prate, prattle, rap, rattle, run on, talk, twitter, visit **2** *Syn* SPEAK, talk

converse *n Syn* OPPOSITE, antipode, antithesis, antonym, contradictory, contrary, counter, reverse

conversion *Syn* TRANSFORMATION, metamorphosis, transfiguration, transmogrification, transmutation

convert *n Syn* FOLLOWER, adherent, disciple, partisan, pupil, votary *Ant* leader

convert *vb* **1** · to change in form, appearance, or use *Syn* make over, metamorphose, transfigure, transform *Rel* adjust, alter, modify **2** *Syn* TRANSFORM, metamorphose, transfigure, transmogrify, transmute

convertible *Syn* RECIPROCAL (sense 2), complemental, complementary, correlative, corresponding

convey **1** *Syn* CARRY, bear, transmit, transport **2** *Syn* COMMUNICATE, impart, spread, transfer, transfuse, transmit **3** *Syn* TRANSFER, alienate, deed

convict *Syn* CRIMINAL, culprit, delinquent, felon, malefactor

conviction **1** *Syn* CERTAINTY, assurance, certitude *Ant* uncertainty **2** *Syn* OPINION, belief, persuasion, sentiment, view

convince *Syn* PERSUADE, argue, get, induce, move, prevail (on *or* upon), satisfy, talk (into), win (over)

convincing *Syn* COGENT, compelling, conclusive, decisive, effective, forceful, persuasive, satisfying, strong, telling *Ant* inconclusive, indecisive, ineffective, unconvincing

convivial · likely to seek or enjoy the company of others *Syn* boon, companionable, extroverted, gregarious, outgoing, sociable, social *Rel* cordial, friendly, hospitable *Ant* antisocial, introverted, reclusive, unsociable

convoke *Syn* SUMMON, call, cite, convene, muster

convoy *Syn* ACCOMPANY, attend, chaperone (*or* chaperon), escort, squire

convulse *Syn* SHAKE (sense 2), agitate, rock

convulsion **1** · a violent disturbance (as of the political or social order) *Syn* cataclysm, paroxysm, storm, tempest, tumult, upheaval, uproar *Rel* overthrow, overturn, revolution, subversion, upset **2** *Syn* FIT, paroxysm, spasm

convulsive · marked by sudden or violent disturbance *Syn* cataclysmal (*or* cataclysmic), stormy, tempestuous, tumultuous *Rel* fitful, spasmodic, sporadic

cook (up) *Syn* INVENT, concoct, contrive, devise, fabricate, make up, manufacture, think (up)

cool **1** · showing or seeming to show freedom from agitation or excitement *Syn* collected, composed, imperturbable, nonchalant, unflappable, unruffled *Rel* calm, placid, serene, tranquil *Ant* agitated, ardent **2** *Syn* COLD, arctic, chilly, freezing, frigid, frosty, gelid, glacial, icy *Ant* hot

coolheadedness *Syn* EQUANIMITY, aplomb, calmness, composure, coolness, imperturbability, placidity, self-possession, serenity, tranquillity (*or* tranquility) *Ant* agitation, discomposure, perturbation

coolness *Syn* EQUANIMITY, aplomb, calmness, composure, coolheadedness, imperturbability, placidity, self-possession, serenity, tranquillity (*or* tranquility) *Ant* agitation, discomposure, perturbation

coop *Syn* ENCLOSE, cage, corral, envelop, fence, pen, wall

cooperate **1** *Syn* ALLY, associate, band, club, confederate, conjoin, federate, league, unite *Ant* break up, disband **2** *Syn* UNITE, combine, concur, conjoin *Ant* part

coordinate *Syn* EQUAL, counterpart, equivalent, fellow, like, match, parallel, peer, rival

cop *Syn* STEAL, filch, lift, pilfer, pinch, purloin, snitch, swipe

copartner *Syn* PARTNER, ally, colleague, confederate *Ant* rival

copious *Syn* PLENTIFUL, abundant, ample, plenteous *Ant* scant, scanty

cop out *Syn* RENEGE, back down, back off

coppice *Syn* THICKET, brake, brushwood, chaparral, copse, covert

copse *Syn* THICKET, brake, brushwood, chaparral, coppice, covert

copy *n* · something that is made to look exactly like something else *Syn* carbon copy, duplicate, duplication, facsimile, imitation, reduplication, replica, replication, reproduction *Rel* counterfeit, dummy, fake, forgery, image, impression, imprint, likeness, mock-up, phony, print, re-creation, reconstruction, semblance, shadow, sham, simulation *Ant* original

copy *vb* · to make something like an already existing thing in form, appearance, or obvious or salient characteristics *Syn* ape, imitate, mimic, mock *Ant* originate

cord · a length of braided, flexible material that is used for tying or connecting things *Syn* cable, lace, lacing, line, rope, string, wire *Rel* guy, lanyard, stay

cordial *Syn* GRACIOUS, affable, genial, sociable *Ant* ungracious

core **1** *Syn* CENTER (sense 1), middle, midpoint, midst *Ant* perimeter, periphery **2** *Syn* CENTER (sense 2), base, capital, cynosure, eye, focus, heart, hub, mecca, nucleus, seat **3** *Syn* CRUX, gist, heart, nub, pith, pivot **4** *Syn* SUBSTANCE, burden, gist, pith, purport

corker *Syn* JIM-DANDY, beauty, crackerjack, dandy, knockout, nifty, pip

corkscrew *Syn* SPIRAL, coiling, helical, screwlike, winding

corner *Syn* MONOPOLY, cartel, pool, syndicate, trust

corny · appealing to the emotions in an obvious and tiresome way *Syn* maudlin, mawkish, mushy, saccharine, sappy, schmaltzy, sentimental, sloppy, sugarcoated, sugary *Rel*

dreamy, moonstruck, nostalgic *Ant* unsentimental

corporal *Syn* BODILY, corporeal, physical, somatic

corporeal **1** *Syn* BODILY, corporal, physical, somatic **2** *Syn* MATERIAL, objective, phenomenal, physical, sensible *Ant* immaterial

corpse *Syn* BODY, cadaver, carcass

corpulent *Syn* FLESHY, chubby, fat, obese, plump, portly, rotund, stout *Ant* scrawny, skinny

corral *Syn* ENCLOSE, cage, coop, envelop, fence, pen, wall

correct *adj* · conforming to standard, fact, or truth *Syn* accurate, exact, nice, precise, right *Rel* faultless, flawless, impeccable *Ant* incorrect

correct *vb* **1** · to set or make right something which is wrong *Syn* amend, emend, rectify, redress, reform, remedy, revise *Rel* ameliorate, better, improve **2** *Syn* PUNISH, castigate, chasten, chastise, discipline *Ant* excuse, pardon

correctable *Syn* REMEDIABLE, fixable, rectifiable, repairable, reparable *Ant* incorrigible, irremediable, irreparable

correcting *Syn* PUNITIVE, castigating, chastening, chastising, correctional, corrective, disciplinary, disciplining, penal, penalizing

correctional *Syn* PUNITIVE, castigating, chastening, chastising, correcting, corrective, disciplinary, disciplining, penal, penalizing

corrective *n* · something which serves to keep another thing in its desired place or condition *Syn* antidote, check, control

corrective *adj* **1** *Syn* CURATIVE, remedial, restorative, sanative **2** *Syn* PUNITIVE, castigating, chastening, chastising, correcting, correctional, disciplinary, disciplining, penal, penalizing

correctly *Syn* PROPERLY, appropriately, congruously, fittingly, happily, meetly, rightly, suitably *Ant* improperly, inappropriately, incongruously, incorrectly, unsuitably, wrongly

correlate *Syn* PARALLEL, analogue, counterpart

correlative *Syn* RECIPROCAL (sense 2), complemental, complementary, convertible, corresponding

correspond *Syn* AGREE (sense 2), accord, conform, harmonize, jibe, square, tally *Ant* differ (from)

correspondence *Syn* SIMILARITY, alikeness, community, likeness, parallelism, resemblance, similitude *Ant* dissimilarity, unlikeness

correspondent *adj* **1** *Syn* ALIKE, akin, analogous, comparable, corresponding, like, matching, parallel, resembling, similar, such, suchlike *Ant* different, dissimilar, diverse, unlike **2** *Syn* CONSISTENT, compatible, conformable (to), congruous, consonant, harmonious, nonconflicting *Ant* conflicting, incompatible, incongruous, inconsistent, inharmonious, unharmonious

correspondent *n Syn* REPORTER, journalist

corresponding **1** *Syn* ALIKE, akin, analogous, comparable, correspondent, like, matching, parallel, resembling, similar, such, suchlike *Ant* different, dissimilar, diverse, unlike **2** *Syn* RECIPROCAL (sense 2), complemental, complementary, convertible, correlative

corridor *Syn* PASSAGE, aisle, arcade, cloister, gallery, hall, hallway, passageway

corroborate *Syn* CONFIRM, authenticate, substantiate, validate, verify *Ant* contradict, deny

corrupt *adj* **1** · having or showing lowered moral character or standards *Syn* debased, debauched, decadent, degenerate, degraded, demoralized, depraved, dissipated, dissolute, perverse, perverted, reprobate, warped *Rel* crooked, cutthroat, dishonest, unethical, unprincipled, unscrupulous *Ant* uncorrupted **2** *Syn* VICIOUS, degenerate, flagitious, infamous, iniquitous, nefarious, villainous *Ant* virtuous

corrupt *vb Syn* DEBASE, debauch, deprave, pervert, vitiate *Ant* amend (*morals, character*), elevate (*taste, way of life*)

corrupted *Syn* DEBASED, debauched, depraved, perverted, vitiated

corruptible *Syn* VENAL, bribable, purchasable *Ant* incorruptible, uncorruptible

corruption *Syn* BARBARISM, impropriety, solecism, vernacularism, vulgarism

corsair *Syn* PIRATE, buccaneer, freebooter, privateer

cortege *Syn* PROCESSION, cavalcade, motorcade, parade

coruscate *Syn* FLASH, glance, gleam, glint, glisten, glitter, scintillate, sparkle, twinkle

cosmic *Syn* UNIVERSAL (sense 1), catholic, cosmopolitan, ecumenical *Ant* particular

cosmopolitan *n* · a person with the outlook, experience, and manners thought to be typical of big city dwellers *Syn* metropolitan, sophisticate *Rel* urbanite *Ant* bumpkin, hick, provincial, rustic, yokel

cosmopolitan *adj* **1** *Syn* UNIVERSAL (sense 1), catholic, cosmic, ecumenical *Ant* particular **2** *Syn* WORLDLY-WISE, smart, sophisticated, worldly *Ant* ingenuous, innocent, naive, unsophisticated, unworldly, wide-eyed

cosset *Syn* CARESS, cuddle, dandle, fondle, pet

cost *Syn* PRICE, charge, expense

costly · having a high value or valuation, especially in terms of money *Syn* dear, expensive, invaluable, precious, priceless, valuable *Rel* excessive, exorbitant, extravagant *Ant* cheap

cotillion *Syn* DANCE, ball, formal, hop, prom

couch *n* · a long upholstered piece of furniture designed for several sitters *Syn* chesterfield, davenport, divan, lounge, settee, sofa *Rel* love seat

couch *vb Syn* PHRASE, articulate, clothe, express, formulate, put, say, state, word

counsel **1** *Syn* ADVICE, guidance **2** *Syn* LAWYER, advocate, attorney, barrister, counselor, solicitor

counselor *Syn* LAWYER, advocate, attorney, barrister, counsel, solicitor

count *vb* **1** · to ascertain the total of units in a collection by noting one after another *Syn* enumerate, number, tell *Rel* calculate, compute, estimate, reckon **2** *Syn* MATTER, import, mean, signify, weigh **3** *Syn* RELY (ON), bank, depend, reckon, trust

count *n* **1** *Syn* CHARGE, complaint, indictment, rap **2** *Syn* PARAGRAPH, article, clause, plank, verse

countenance *vb* **1** *Syn* APPROVE (OF), accept, care (for), favor, OK (*or* okay), subscribe (to) *Ant* disapprove (of), discountenance, disfavor, frown (on *or* upon) **2** *Syn* FAVOR, encourage *Ant* disapprove

countenance *n Syn* FACE, mug, physiognomy, puss, visage

counter *adj Syn* ADVERSE, antagonistic, counteractive *Ant* propitious

counter *n Syn* OPPOSITE, antipode, antithesis, antonym, contradictory, contrary, converse, reverse

counteract *Syn* NEUTRALIZE, negative

counteractive *Syn* ADVERSE, antagonistic, counter *Ant* propitious

counterbalance *Syn* COMPENSATE, balance, counterpoise, countervail, offset

counterfeit *adj* · being an imitation intended to mislead or deceive *Syn* bogus, fake, phony, pinchbeck, pseudo, sham, spurious *Rel* feigned, pretended, simulated *Ant* bona fide, genuine

counterfeit *vb Syn* ASSUME, affect, feign, pretend, sham, simulate

counterpart **1** *Syn* EQUAL, coordinate, equivalent, fellow, like, match, parallel, peer, rival **2** *Syn* PARALLEL, analogue, correlate

counterpoise *Syn* COMPENSATE, balance, counterbalance, countervail, offset

countervail *Syn* COMPENSATE, balance, counterbalance, counterpoise, offset

countless · too many to be counted *Syn* innumerable, numberless, uncountable, uncounted, unnumbered, untold *Rel* endless, infinite, unlimited, vast *Ant* countable

country *Syn* NATION, commonwealth, land, sovereignty, state

countryman *Syn* HICK, bumpkin, clodhopper, provincial, rustic, yokel *Ant* cosmopolitan, sophisticate

countryseat *Syn* MANSION, castle, château, estate, hacienda, hall, manor, manor house, palace, villa

county *Syn* ARISTOCRACY, elite, gentry, nobility, society *Ant* people, proletariat

coup *Syn* REBELLION, insurrection, mutiny, putsch, revolt, revolution, uprising

couple **1** · two things of the same kind *Syn* brace, pair, yoke **2** *Syn* PAIR, brace, duo, twain, twosome

courage · strength of mind to carry on in spite of danger *Syn* bravery, courageousness, daring, dauntlessness, doughtiness, fearlessness, gallantry, greatheartedness, guts, hardihood, heart, heroism, intrepidity, intrepidness, nerve, stoutness, valor *Rel* backbone, fiber, fortitude, grit, gumption, mettle, pluck, spunk *Ant* cowardice, cowardliness, cravenness, dastardliness, spinelessness, yellowness

courageous *Syn* BRAVE, audacious, bold, dauntless, doughty, fearless, intrepid, unafraid, undaunted, valiant, valorous *Ant* craven

courageousness *Syn* COURAGE, bravery, daring, dauntlessness, doughtiness, fearlessness, gallantry, greatheartedness, guts, hardihood, heart, heroism, intrepidity, intrepidness, nerve, stoutness, valor *Ant* cowardice, cowardliness, cravenness, dastardliness, spinelessness, yellowness

course *vb Syn* HURRY (sense 2), barrel, bolt, bowl, breeze, career, dash, fly, hasten, hotfoot (it), hump, hurtle, hustle, pelt, race, rip, rocket, run, rush, rustle, scoot, scurry, scuttle, shoot, speed, step (along), tear, trot, whirl, whisk, zip, zoom *Ant* crawl, creep, poke

course *n Syn* WAY, artery, pass, passage, route

court *Syn* INVITE, bid, solicit, woo

courteous *Syn* CIVIL, chivalrous, courtly, gallant, polite *Ant* rude, uncivil

courteousness *Syn* POLITENESS, civility, courtesy, gentility, graciousness, mannerliness *Ant* discourteousness, discourtesy, impoliteness, incivility, rudeness, ungraciousness

courtesy **1** · a manner or an act which promotes agreeable or pleasant social relations *Syn* amenity, attention, gallantry *Rel* affability, cordiality, geniality, graciousness *Ant* discourtesy **2** *Syn* POLITENESS, civility, courteousness, gentility, graciousness, mannerliness *Ant* discourteousness, discourtesy, impoliteness, incivility, rudeness, ungraciousness

courtly *Syn* CIVIL, chivalrous, courteous, gallant, polite *Ant* rude, uncivil

covenant *Syn* PROMISE, contract, engage, pledge, plight

cover *vb* **1** · to put or place or to be put or placed over or around *Syn* envelop, overspread, shroud, veil, wrap *Rel* conceal, hide, screen *Ant* bare **2** *Syn* TRAVERSE, crisscross, cross, cut (across), follow, go, pass (over), proceed (along), travel

cover *n Syn* SHELTER, asylum, refuge, retreat, sanctuary

covert *adj* **1** *Syn* SECLUDED, cloistered, isolated, quiet, remote, retired, secret, sheltered **2** *Syn* SECRET, clandestine, furtive, stealthy, surreptitious, underhand, underhanded

covert *n Syn* THICKET, brake, brushwood, chaparral, coppice, copse

covet **1** · to desire selfishly to have something for one's own *Syn* begrudge, envy, grudge **2** *Syn* DESIRE, crave, want, wish

covetous **1** · having or manifesting a strong desire for especially material possessions *Syn* acquisitive, avaricious, grasping, greedy *Rel* envious, jealous **2** *Syn* ENVIOUS, invidious, jaundiced, jealous, resentful

covetousness *Syn* GREED, acquisitiveness, avarice, avariciousness, avidity, cupidity, greediness, rapaciousness, rapacity

cow *Syn* INTIMIDATE, browbeat, bulldoze, bully

coward · a person who shows a shameful lack of courage in the face of danger *Syn* chicken, craven, dastard, poltroon, recreant *Rel* defeatist, quitter *Ant* hero, stalwart, valiant

cowardly · having or showing a shameful lack of courage *Syn* chicken, chickenhearted, craven, dastardly, lily-livered, pusillanimous, recreant, spineless, unheroic, yellow *Rel* diffident, fainthearted, fearful, timid, timorous *Ant* brave, courageous, daring, dauntless, doughty, fearless, gallant, greathearted, gutsy, hardy, heroic, intrepid, lionhearted, stalwart, stout, stouthearted, valiant, valorous

cowboy · a man who tends cattle or horses at a ranch or on the range *Syn* buckaroo, cowhand, cowman, cowpoke, cowpuncher *Rel* cowgirl

cower *Syn* FAWN, cringe, toady, truckle *Ant* domineer

cowhand *Syn* COWBOY, buckaroo, cowman, cowpoke, cowpuncher

cowman *Syn* COWBOY, buckaroo, cowhand, cowpoke, cowpuncher

cowpoke *Syn* COWBOY, buckaroo, cowhand, cowman, cowpuncher

cowpuncher *Syn* COWBOY, buckaroo, cowhand, cowman, cowpoke

coxcomb *Syn* FOP, beau, buck, dandy, dude, exquisite

coy *Syn* SHY, bashful, diffident, modest *Ant* obtrusive

cozen *Syn* FLEECE, bleed, cheat, chisel, defraud, hustle, mulct, rook, shortchange, skin, squeeze, stick, sting, swindle, victimize

cozy *Syn* COMFORTABLE, easy, restful, snug *Ant* miserable, uncomfortable

crab *vb Syn* COMPLAIN, beef, bellyache, carp, croak, fuss, gripe, grouse, growl, grumble, kick, moan, murmur, mutter, repine, squawk, wail, whine, yammer *Ant* rejoice

crab *n Syn* GROUCH, bear, complainer, crank, croaker, curmudgeon, fusser, griper, grouser, growler, grumbler, grump, murmurer, mutterer, whiner

crabbed *Syn* SULLEN, dour, gloomy, glum, morose, saturnine, sulky, surly

crack *n* **1 ·** an opening, break, or discontinuity made by or as if by splitting or rupture *Syn* chink, cleft, cranny, crevasse, crevice, fissure *Rel* breach, rent, rift, split **2** *Syn* JOKE, gag, jape, jest, quip, wisecrack, witticism **3** *Syn* ATTEMPT, endeavor, essay, fling, go, pass, shot, stab, trial, try, whack

crack *vb* **1** *Syn* BREAK, burst, bust, shatter, shiver, snap *Ant* cleave (*together*), keep (*of laws*) **2** *Syn* SOLVE, answer, break, dope (out), figure out, puzzle (out), resolve, riddle, unravel, work, work out

crackbrain *Syn* ECCENTRIC, character, codger, crackpot, crank, kook, nut, oddball, screwball, weirdo

crackerjack *adj Syn* EXCELLENT, A1, bang-up, banner, capital, classic, dandy, divine, fabulous, fine, first-class, first-rate, grand, great, groovy, heavenly, jim-dandy, keen, marvelous (*or* marvellous), mean, neat, nifty, noble, par excellence, prime, sensational, splendid, stellar, sterling, superb, superior, superlative, supernal, swell, terrific, tip-top, top, top-notch, unsurpassed, wonderful *Ant* poor

crackerjack *n* **1** *Syn* EXPERT, ace, adept, artist, authority, maestro, master, past master, scholar, shark, virtuoso, whiz, wizard *Ant* amateur **2** *Syn* JIM-DANDY, beauty, corker, dandy, knockout, nifty, pip

crackpot *Syn* ECCENTRIC, character, codger, crackbrain, crank, kook, nut, oddball, screwball, weirdo

craft **1** *Syn* ART, artifice, cunning, skill **2** *Syn* TRADE, art, handicraft, profession **3** *Syn* BOAT, ship, vessel

craftsman **1** *Syn* ARTISAN, artificer, handicrafter, tradesman **2** *Syn* WORKER, artisan, hand, handicraftsman, laborer, mechanic, operative, roustabout, workingman, workman *Ant* idler

crafty *Syn* SLY, artful, cunning, foxy, guileful, insidious, tricky, wily

cram *Syn* PACK, crowd, ram, stuff, tamp

cramp · a painful sudden tightening of a muscle *Syn* charley horse, crick, spasm *Rel* contraction, jerk, stitch, twinge, twitch

crank **1** *Syn* ECCENTRIC, character, codger, crackbrain, crackpot, kook, nut, oddball, screwball, weirdo **2** *Syn* GROUCH, bear, complainer, crab, croaker, curmudgeon, fusser, griper, grouser, growler, grumbler, grump, murmurer, mutterer, whiner

crank (up) *Syn* ACTIVATE, actuate, drive, move, propel, run, set off, spark, start, touch off, trigger, turn on *Ant* cut, deactivate, kill, shut off, turn off

cranky **1** *Syn* CUMBERSOME, awkward, clumsy, cumbrous, ungainly, unhandy, unwieldy *Ant* handy **2** *Syn* IRASCIBLE, choleric, cross, splenetic, testy, touchy

cranny *Syn* CRACK, chink, cleft, crevasse, crevice, fissure

crass *Syn* STUPID, dense, dull, dumb, slow *Ant* intelligent

crave *Syn* DESIRE, covet, want, wish

craven *adj Syn* COWARDLY, chicken, chickenhearted, dastardly, lily-livered, pusillanimous, recreant, spineless, unheroic, yellow *Ant* brave, courageous, daring, dauntless, doughty, fearless, gallant, greathearted, gutsy, hardy, heroic, intrepid, lionhearted, stalwart, stout, stouthearted, valiant, valorous

craven *n Syn* COWARD, chicken, dastard, poltroon, recreant, *Ant* hero, stalwart, valiant

craze *Syn* FASHION, cry, dernier cri, fad, mode, rage, style, vogue

crazed *Syn* INSANE, crazy, demented, deranged, lunatic, mad, maniac, non compos mentis *Ant* sane

crazy *Syn* INSANE, crazed, demented, deranged, lunatic, mad, maniac, non compos mentis *Ant* sane

cream *n Syn* ELITE, best, choice, elect, fat, flower, pick, prime, upper crust

cream *vb Syn* OIL, anoint, grease, lubricate

create **1** *Syn* EFFECT, bring about, cause, effectuate, engender, generate, induce, make, produce, prompt, result (in), spawn, work, yield **2** *Syn* FOUND, establish, institute, organize

creator *Syn* MAKER, author

creature **1** *Syn* ANIMAL, beast, brute, critter **2** *Syn* ENTITY, being, individual, person

credence *Syn* BELIEF, credit, faith *Ant* disbelief, unbelief

credential · something presented by one person to another in proof that he is what or who he claims to be *Syn* character, recommendation, reference, testimonial *Rel* accreditation, certification, endorsement, sanction

credible *Syn* PLAUSIBLE, believable, colorable, specious

credit *vb Syn* ASCRIBE, accredit, assign, attribute, charge, impute, refer

credit *n* **1** *Syn* BELIEF, credence, faith *Ant* disbelief, unbelief **2** *Syn* INFLUENCE, authority, prestige, weight

creditable *Syn* ADMIRABLE, commendable, laudable, meritorious, praiseworthy *Ant* censurable, discreditable, reprehensible

credulity · readiness to believe the claims of others without sufficient evidence *Syn* credulousness, gullibility, naivete *Rel* artlessness, simplicity, unsophistication *Ant* incredulity, skepticism

credulousness *Syn* CREDULITY, gullibility, naivete *Ant* incredulity, skepticism

creed *Syn* RELIGION, church, communion, denomination, faith, persuasion, sect

creepy *Syn* EERIE, haunting, spooky, uncanny, unearthly, weird

crestfallen *Syn* SAD (sense 1), bad, blue, brokenhearted, dejected, depressed, despondent, disconsolate, doleful, down, downcast, downhearted, droopy, forlorn, gloomy, glum, heartbroken, heartsick, heartsore, inconsolable, joyless, low, low-spirited, melancholy, miserable, mournful, saddened, sorrowful, sorry, unhappy, woebegone, woeful, wretched *Ant* blissful, buoyant, buoyed, cheerful, cheery, chipper, delighted, glad, gladdened, gladsome, gleeful, happy, joyful, joyous, jubilant, sunny, upbeat

crevasse *Syn* CRACK, chink, cleft, cranny, crevice, fissure

crevice *Syn* CRACK, chink, cleft, cranny, crevasse, fissure

crick *Syn* CRAMP, charley horse, spasm

crime *Syn* OFFENSE (sense 2), scandal, sin, vice

criminal · one who has committed a usually serious offense especially against the law *Syn* convict, culprit, delinquent, felon, malefactor *Rel* offender, sinner

crimp *Syn* ENCUMBRANCE, bar, block, chain, clog, deterrent, drag, embarrassment, fetter, handicap, hindrance, hurdle, impediment, inhibition, interference, let, manacle, obstacle, obstruction, shackles, stop, stumbling block, trammel *Ant* aid, assistance, benefit, help

crimson *Syn* BLUSH, bloom, color, flush, glow, redden

cringe *Syn* FAWN, cower, toady, truckle *Ant* domineer

cripple *Syn* MAIM, batter, mangle, mutilate

crisis *Syn* JUNCTURE, contingency, emergency, exigency, pass, pinch, strait

crisp **1** *Syn* FRAGILE, brittle, frangible, friable, short *Ant* tough **2** *Syn* INCISIVE, biting, clear-cut, cutting, trenchant

crisply *Syn* SUCCINCTLY, briefly, compactly, concisely, laconically, pithily, summarily, tersely *Ant* diffusely, long-windedly, verbosely, wordily

crisscross *Syn* TRAVERSE, cover, cross, cut (across), follow, go, pass (over), proceed (along), travel

criterion *Syn* STANDARD, gauge, touchstone, yardstick

critic · a person given to harsh judgments and to finding faults *Syn* carper, castigator, caviler (*or* caviller), censurer, faultfinder, nitpicker, railer, scold *Rel* belittler, derider, detractor

critical **1** · exhibiting the spirit of one who detects and points out faults or defects *Syn* captious, carping, caviling, censorious, faultfinding, hypercritical *Rel* judicious *Ant* uncritical **2** *Syn* ACUTE, crucial **3** *Syn* CRUCIAL, key, pivotal, vital

criticism · a discourse presenting one's con-

clusions after examining a work of art and especially of literature *Syn* blurb, critique, puff, review

criticize · to find fault with someone or something openly, often publicly, and with varying degrees of severity *Syn* blame, censure, condemn, denounce, reprehend, reprobate *Rel* examine, inspect, scan, scrutinize

critique *Syn* CRITICISM, blurb, puff, review

critter *Syn* ANIMAL, beast, brute, creature

croak *Syn* COMPLAIN, beef, bellyache, carp, crab, fuss, gripe, grouse, growl, grumble, kick, moan, murmur, mutter, repine, squawk, wail, whine, yammer *Ant* rejoice

croaker *Syn* GROUCH, bear, complainer, crab, crank, curmudgeon, fusser, griper, grouser, growler, grumbler, grump, murmurer, mutterer, whiner

crochet *Syn* WEAVE, braid, knit, plait, tat

crony *Syn* ASSOCIATE, companion, comrade

crook *Syn* FLEX, bow, buckle *Ant* extend

crooked **1** · not straight or straightforward *Syn* devious, oblique *Rel* askew, awry *Ant* straight **2** *Syn* AWRY, askew, aslant, cockeyed, listing, lopsided, oblique, skewed, slanted, slanting, slantwise, tilted, tipping, uneven *Ant* even, level, straight

crop *Syn* CLIP, bob, curtail, cut, cut back, dock, lop (off), nip, pare, prune, shave, shear, snip, trim

cross *adj* *Syn* IRASCIBLE, choleric, cranky, splenetic, testy, touchy

cross *vb* *Syn* TRAVERSE, cover, crisscross, cut (across), follow, go, pass (over), proceed (along), travel

cross *n* *Syn* TRIAL, affliction, tribulation, visitation

crossways *Syn* ACROSS, athwart, crosswise

crosswise *Syn* ACROSS, athwart, crossways

crow *Syn* BOAST, brag, gasconade, vaunt *Ant* depreciate (*oneself, one's accomplishments*)

crowd *n* · a more or less closely assembled multitude usually of persons *Syn* crush, horde, mob, press, rout, throng *Rel* army, host, legion, multitude

crowd *vb* **1** *Syn* PACK, cram, ram, stuff, tamp **2** *Syn* PRESS, bear, bear down, jam, squeeze

crucial **1** · of the greatest possible importance *Syn* critical, key, pivotal, vital *Rel* decisive, life-and-death **2** *Syn* ACUTE, critical

crude *Syn* RUDE (sense 1), callow, green, raw, rough, uncouth *Ant* civil, urbane

cruel *Syn* FIERCE, barbarous, fell, ferocious, inhuman, savage, truculent *Ant* mild, tame

cruelness *Syn* CRUELTY, barbarity, brutality, heartlessness, inhumanity, sadism, savageness, savagery, viciousness, wantonness *Ant* benignity, compassion, good-heartedness, humanity, kindheartedness, kindness, sympathy

cruelty · the willful infliction of pain and suffering on others *Syn* barbarity, brutality, cruelness, heartlessness, inhumanity, sadism, savageness, savagery, viciousness, wantonness *Rel* mercilessness, ruthlessness *Ant* benignity, compassion, good-heartedness, humanity, kindheartedness, kindness, sympathy

cruise *Syn* JOURNEY, excursion, expedition, jaunt, pilgrimage, tour, trip, voyage

crumble 1 *Syn* DECAY, decompose, disintegrate, putrefy, rot, spoil 2 *Syn* DETERIORATE, decay, decline, degenerate, descend, ebb, rot, sink, worsen *Ant* ameliorate, improve, meliorate

crusade *Syn* CAMPAIGN, bandwagon, cause, drive, movement

crusader *Syn* ZEALOT, fanatic, militant, partisan

crush *vb* 1 · to reduce or be reduced to a pulpy or broken mass *Syn* bruise, macerate, mash, smash, squash *Rel* crowd, jam, press, squeeze 2 · to bring to an end by destroying or defeating *Syn* extinguish, quash, quell, quench, suppress *Rel* demolish, destroy

crush *n Syn* CROWD, horde, mob, press, rout, throng

crusty *Syn* BLUFF, blunt, brusque, curt, gruff *Ant* smooth, suave

crux · the central part or aspect of something under consideration *Syn* core, gist, heart, nub, pith, pivot *Rel* course, direction, drift, tenor

cry *vb* · to show grief, pain, or distress by tears and usually inarticulate utterances *Syn* blubber, keen, wail, weep, whimper *Rel* bemoan, bewail, deplore, lament

cry *n* 1 *Syn* FASHION, craze, dernier cri, fad, mode, rage, style, vogue 2 *Syn* SLOGAN, shibboleth, watchword

crying *Syn* PRESSING, exigent, imperative, importunate, insistent, instant, urgent

cryptic *Syn* OBSCURE, ambiguous, dark, enigmatic, equivocal, vague *Ant* distinct, obvious

cubicle *Syn* COMPARTMENT, bay, cabin, cell, chamber

cuddle *Syn* CARESS, cosset, dandle, fondle, pet

cuff *Syn* STRIKE, box, clout, hit, punch, slap, slog, slug, smite, swat

cull *Syn* CHOOSE, elect, opt, pick, prefer, select, single *Ant* eschew, reject

culmination *Syn* SUMMIT, acme, apex, apogee, climax, meridian, peak, pinnacle, zenith

culpability *Syn* BLAME, fault, guilt

culpable *Syn* BLAMEWORTHY, guilty *Ant* blameless

culprit *Syn* CRIMINAL, convict, delinquent, felon, malefactor

cultivar *Syn* VARIETY (sense 2), breed, clone, race, stock, strain, subspecies

cultivate *Syn* NURSE, cherish, foster, nurture

cultivated · having or showing a taste for the fine arts and gracious living *Syn* civilized, cultured, genteel, polished, refined *Rel* cerebral, highbrow, intellectual *Ant* philistine,

uncivilized, uncultured, unpolished, unrefined

cultivation *Syn* CULTURE, breeding, refinement

culture · enlightenment and excellence of taste acquired by intellectual and aesthetic training *Syn* breeding, cultivation, refinement

cultured *Syn* CULTIVATED, civilized, genteel, polished, refined *Ant* philistine, uncivilized, uncultured, unpolished, unrefined

cumber *Syn* BURDEN, charge, encumber, lade, load, saddle, tax, weigh, weight

cumbersome 1 · difficult to use or operate especially because of size, weight, or design *Syn* awkward, clumsy, cranky, cumbrous, ungainly, unhandy, unwieldy *Rel* uncontrollable, unmanageable *Ant* handy 2 *Syn* HEAVY, cumbrous, hefty, ponderous, weighty *Ant* light

cumbrous 1 *Syn* CUMBERSOME, awkward, clumsy, cranky, ungainly, unhandy, unwieldy *Ant* handy 2 *Syn* HEAVY, cumbersome, hefty, ponderous, weighty *Ant* light

cumulative · increasing or produced by the addition of like or assimilable things *Syn* accumulative, additive, summative *Rel* accumulated, amassed

cunning *n* 1 *Syn* ART, artifice, craft, skill 2 *Syn* DECEIT, dissimulation, duplicity, guile

cunning *adj* 1 *Syn* CLEVER, adroit, ingenious 2 *Syn* SLY, artful, crafty, foxy, guileful, insidious, tricky, wily

cupboard *Syn* CABINET, buffet, closet, hutch, locker, sideboard

cupidity *Syn* GREED, acquisitiveness, avarice, avariciousness, avidity, covetousness, greediness, rapaciousness, rapacity

curative · returning or tending to return to a state of normalcy or health *Syn* corrective, remedial, restorative, sanative *Rel* curing, healing, remedying

curb *vb Syn* RESTRAIN, bridle, check, inhibit *Ant* abandon (*oneself*), activate, impel, incite

curb *n Syn* RESTRICTION, check, condition, constraint, fetter, limitation, restraint

curdle *Syn* COAGULATE, clot, congeal, jell, jelly, set

cure *vb* · to rectify an unhealthy or undesirable condition especially by some specific treatment *Syn* heal, remedy

cure *n Syn* REMEDY, medicament, medication, medicine, physic, specific

curio *Syn* KNICKKNACK, bauble, curiosity, gaud, gewgaw, novelty, ornamental, trinket

curiosity *Syn* KNICKKNACK, bauble, curio, gaud, gewgaw, novelty, ornamental, trinket

curious 1 · interested in what is not one's personal or proper concern *Syn* inquisitive, nosy, prying, snoopy *Rel* interfering, intermeddling, meddling, tampering *Ant* incurious, uninterested 2 *Syn* STRANGE, eccentric, erratic, odd, outlandish, peculiar, quaint, queer, singular, unique *Ant* familiar

curl *Syn* WIND, coil, entwine, twine, twist, wreathe

curmudgeon *Syn* GROUCH, bear, complainer, crab, crank, croaker, fusser, griper, grouser, growler, grumbler, grump, murmurer, mutterer, whiner

currency *Syn* MONEY, cash, coin, coinage, legal tender, specie

current *n Syn* FLOW, flood, flux, stream, tide

current *adj* **1** *Syn* MODERN, contemporary, hot, mod, modernistic, new, newfangled, new-fashioned, present-day, red-hot, space-age, ultramodern, up-to-date *Ant* antiquated, archaic, dated, fusty, musty, noncontemporary, old-fangled, old-fashioned, old-time, out-of-date, passé **2** *Syn* PRESENT, extant, ongoing, present-day *Ant* ago, future, past **3** *Syn* PREVAILING, prevalent, rife

curse *n* · a denunciation that conveys a wish or threat of evil *Syn* anathema, imprecation, malediction *Rel* execration, objurgation *Ant* blessing

curse *vb* **1** *Syn* AFFLICT, agonize, bedevil, harrow, martyr, persecute, plague, rack, torment, torture **2** *Syn* EXECRATE, anathematize, damn, objurgate

cursed *Syn* EXECRABLE, accursed, damnable

cursing *Syn* BLASPHEMY, profanity, swearing *Ant* adoration

cursory *Syn* SUPERFICIAL, shallow, uncritical *Ant* deep, profound

curt *Syn* BLUFF, blunt, brusque, crusty, gruff *Ant* smooth, suave

curtail **1** *Syn* CLIP, bob, crop, cut, cut back, dock, lop (off), nip, pare, prune, shave, shear, snip, trim **2** *Syn* SHORTEN, abbreviate, abridge, retrench *Ant* elongate, extend, lengthen, prolong, protract

curve *n* · a line or something which follows a line that is neither straight nor angular but rounded *Syn* arc, arch, bow *Rel* circuit, circumference, compass

curve *vb* · to swerve or cause to swerve from a straight line or course *Syn* bend, twist *Rel* deflect, divert, turn

curvet *Syn* SKIP, bound, hop, lollop, lope, ricochet

cushion · to lessen the shock of *Syn* buffer, gentle, soften *Rel* baffle, dampen, deaden, dull

custodian *Syn* PROTECTOR, defender, guard, protection

custody · responsibility for the safety and well-being of someone or something *Syn* care, guardianship, keeping, safekeeping, trust, ward *Rel* control, governorship, management, superintendence, supervision

custom *Syn* HABIT, fashion, pattern, practice, trick, way, wont

customary *Syn* USUAL, accustomed, habitual, wonted

cut **1** · to penetrate and divide something with a sharp-bladed tool or instrument *Syn* carve, chop, hew, slash, slit *Rel* cleave, rive, split, tear **2** *Syn* CLIP, bob, crop, curtail, cut back, crop, lop (off), nip, pare, prune, shave, shear, snip, trim

cut (across) *Syn* TRAVERSE, cover, crisscross, cross, follow, go, pass (over), proceed (along), travel

cut back *Syn* CLIP, bob, crop, curtail, cut, dock, lop (off), nip, pare, prune, shave, shear, snip, trim

cute *Syn* BEAUTIFUL, attractive, beauteous, comely, fair, gorgeous, handsome, knockout, lovely, pretty, ravishing, sightly, stunning, taking *Ant* homely, ill-favored, plain, ugly, unattractive, unbeautiful, unhandsome, unlovely, unpretty, unsightly

cutthroat *n Syn* ASSASSIN, bravo, gunman

cutthroat *adj Syn* UNPRINCIPLED, immoral, Machiavellian, unconscionable, unethical, unmoral, unscrupulous *Ant* ethical, moral, principled, scrupulous

cutting *Syn* INCISIVE, biting, clear-cut, crisp, trenchant

cut up · to engage in attention-getting playful or boisterous behavior *Syn* act up, clown (around), fool (around), horse (around), monkey (around), show off, skylark *Rel* carry on, misbehave

cyclone *Syn* TORNADO, twister

cyclopean *Syn* HUGE, Brobdingnagian, colossal, elephantine, enormous, gargantuan, giant, gigantean, gigantic, Herculean, immense, mammoth, titanic, vast *Ant* bitty, diminutive, microscopic (*or* microscopical), midget, miniature, minute, pocket, pygmy, teeny, teeny-weeny, tiny, wee

cynical · deeply and often contemptuously distrustful *Syn* misanthropic, pessimistic *Rel* flouting, girding, scoffing, sneering

cynosure *Syn* CENTER (sense 2), base, capital, core, eye, focus, heart, hub, mecca, nucleus, seat

D

dabbler *Syn* AMATEUR, dilettante, tyro *Ant* expert, professional

daily *adj* · occurring, done, produced, or appearing every day *Syn* day-to-day, diurnal *Rel* alternate, cyclical, intermittent, periodic, recurrent, recurring, regular

dainty **1** *Syn* CHOICE, delicate, elegant, exquisite, rare, recherché *Ant* indifferent, medium **2** *Syn* NICE, fastidious, finical, finicking, finicky, fussy, particular, pernickety, persnickety, squeamish

dais *Syn* PLATFORM, podium, rostrum, stage, stand

dally *Syn* FLIRT, frivol, trifle

dam *n* · a bank of earth constructed to control water *Syn* dike, embankment, levee *Rel* breakwater, jetty, seawall

dam *vb* *Syn* HINDER, bar, block, impede, obstruct *Ant* further

damage *vb* *Syn* INJURE, harm, hurt, impair, mar, spoil *Ant* aid

damage *n* *Syn* INJURY, harm, hurt, mischief

damages *Syn* FINE, forfeit, forfeiture, mulct, penalty

damaging *Syn* HARMFUL, adverse, bad, baleful, baneful, deleterious, detrimental, evil, hurtful, ill, injurious, mischievous, noxious, pernicious, prejudicial *Ant* harmless, innocent, innocuous, inoffensive, safe

dame *Syn* GENTLEWOMAN, lady, noblewoman

damn **1** *Syn* EXECRATE, anathematize, curse, objurgate **2** *Syn* SENTENCE, condemn, doom, proscribe

damnable *Syn* EXECRABLE, accursed, cursed

damp *Syn* WET, dank, humid, moist *Ant* dry

dance · a social gathering for dancing *Syn* ball, cotillion, formal, hop, prom *Rel* blowout, celebration, event, festival, festivity, fete (*or* fête), gala, masquerade, mixer, party, reception, shindig, soiree (*or* soirée)

dandle **1** *Syn* BABY, coddle, mollycoddle, nurse, pamper, spoil *Ant* abuse, ill-treat, illuse, maltreat, mishandle, mistreat, misuse **2** *Syn* CARESS, cosset, cuddle, fondle, pet

dandy *adj* *Syn* EXCELLENT, A1, bang-up, banner, capital, classic, crackerjack, divine, fabulous, fine, first-class, first-rate, grand, great, groovy, heavenly, jim-dandy, keen, marvelous (*or* marvellous), mean, neat, nifty, noble, par excellence, prime, sensational, splendid, stellar, sterling, superb, superior, superlative, supernal, swell, terrific, tip-top, top, top-notch, unsurpassed, wonderful *Ant* poor

dandy *n* **1** *Syn* FOP, beau, buck, coxcomb, dude, exquisite **2** *Syn* JIM-DANDY, beauty, corker, crackerjack, knockout, nifty, pip

danger **1** · something that may cause injury or harm *Syn* hazard, menace, peril, pitfall, risk, threat, trouble *Rel* snare, trap **2** · the state of not being protected from injury, harm, or evil *Syn* distress, endangerment, imperilment, jeopardy, peril, risk, trouble *Rel* exposure, liability, vulnerability *Ant* safeness, safety, security

dangerous · attended by or involving the possibility of loss, evil, injury, or harm *Syn* hazardous, perilous, precarious, risky *Rel* insecure, unsafe *Ant* safe, secure

dangle *Syn* HANG, sling, suspend

dank *Syn* WET, damp, humid, moist *Ant* dry

dapple *Syn* SPOT, blotch, dot, fleck, freckle, marble, mottle, pepper, speck, speckle, splotch, sprinkle, stipple

dappled *Syn* VARIEGATED, checked, checkered, motley, parti-colored, piebald, pied, skewbald

dare **1** *Syn* CHALLENGE, defy, stump **2** *Syn* FACE, beard, brave, challenge, defy *Ant* avoid

daredevil *Syn* ADVENTUROUS, daring, foolhardy, rash, reckless, venturesome *Ant* cautious, unadventurous

daring *adj* *Syn* ADVENTUROUS, daredevil, foolhardy, rash, reckless, venturesome *Ant* cautious, unadventurous

daring *n* *Syn* COURAGE, bravery, courageousness, dauntlessness, doughtiness, fearlessness, gallantry, greatheartedness, guts, hardihood, heart, heroism, intrepidity, intrepidness, nerve, stoutness, valor *Ant* cowardice, cowardliness, cravenness, dastardliness, spinelessness, yellowness

dark **1** · deficient in light *Syn* dim, dusky, gloomy, murky, obscure *Ant* light **2** *Syn* IGNORANT, benighted, illiterate, nonliterate, simple, uneducated, uninstructed, unlearned, unlettered, unread, unschooled, untaught, untutored *Ant* educated, knowledgeable, literate, schooled **3** *Syn* OBSCURE, ambiguous, cryptic, enigmatic, equivocal, vague *Ant* distinct, obvious **4** *Syn* SECRETIVE, close, closemouthed, reticent, uncommunicative *Ant* communicative, open

darken *Syn* OBSCURE, becloud, bedim, befog, cloud, dim, eclipse, fog, obfuscate *Ant* illuminate, illumine

darling *n* **1** *Syn* FAVORITE, minion, pet, preference **2** *Syn* SWEETHEART, beloved, dear, flame, honey, love, sweet

darling *adj* *Syn* LOVABLE, adorable, dear, disarming, endearing, precious, sweet, winning *Ant* abhorrent, abominable, detestable, hateful, odious, unlovable

dart *vb* *Syn* FLY, float, sail, scud, shoot, skim

dart *n Syn* INSULT, affront, barb, dig, epithet, indignity, name, offense (*or* offence), outrage, put-down, sarcasm, slight, slur

dash *vb Syn* HURRY (sense 2), barrel, bolt, bowl, breeze, career, course, fly, hasten, hotfoot (it), hump, hurtle, hustle, pelt, race, rip, rocket, run, rush, rustle, scoot, scurry, scuttle, shoot, speed, step (along), tear, trot, whirl, whisk, zip, zoom *Ant* crawl, creep, poke

dash *n* **1** *Syn* TOUCH, shade, smack, soupçon, spice, strain, streak, suggestion, suspicion, tincture, tinge, vein **2** *Syn* VIGOR, drive, élan, esprit, punch, spirit, verve, vim

dashing *Syn* STYLISH, chic, fashionable, modish, smart

dashingly *Syn* SMARTLY, nattily, sharply, sprucely *Ant* sloppily, slovenly

dastard *Syn* COWARD, chicken, craven, poltroon, recreant *Ant* hero, stalwart, valiant

dastardly *Syn* COWARDLY, chicken, chickenhearted, craven, lily-livered, pusillanimous, recreant, spineless, unheroic, yellow *Ant* brave, courageous, daring, dauntless, doughty, fearless, gallant, greathearted, gutsy, hardy, heroic, intrepid, lionhearted, stalwart, stout, stouthearted, valiant, valorous

date *Syn* ENGAGEMENT, appointment, assignation, rendezvous, tryst

dated *Syn* OBSOLETE, antiquated, archaic, moth-eaten, outdated, out-of-date, outmoded, outworn, passé

datum *Syn* FACT, detail, nicety, particular, particularity, point

daunt **1** *Syn* DISCOURAGE (sense 1), demoralize, dishearten, dismay, dispirit, unnerve *Ant* embolden, encourage, hearten, nerve, steel **2** *Syn* DISMAY, appall, horrify *Ant* cheer

dauntless *Syn* BRAVE, audacious, bold, courageous, doughty, fearless, intrepid, unafraid, undaunted, valiant, valorous *Ant* craven

dauntlessness *Syn* COURAGE, bravery, courageousness, daring, doughtiness, fearlessness, gallantry, greatheartedness, guts, hardihood, heart, heroism, intrepidity, intrepidness, nerve, stoutness, valor *Ant* cowardice, cowardliness, cravenness, dastardliness, spinelessness, yellowness

davenport *Syn* COUCH, chesterfield, divan, lounge, settee, sofa

dawdle *Syn* DELAY (sense 2), lag, loiter, procrastinate *Ant* hasten, hurry

dawn *n Syn* BEGINNING, alpha, birth, commencement, genesis, inception, incipiency, launch, morning, onset, outset, start, threshold *Ant* close, conclusion, end, ending

dawn *vb Syn* BEGIN (sense 1), arise, commence, form, materialize, originate, set in, spring, start *Ant* cease, end, stop

day *Syn* AGE (sense 3), epoch, era, period, time

daydream *Syn* FANCY, dream, fantasy, nightmare, phantasm, phantasy, vision *Ant* reality

daydreaming *Syn* REVERIE, study, trance, woolgathering

day-to-day *Syn* DAILY, diurnal

daze *vb* · to dull or deaden the powers of the mind through some disturbing experience or influence *Syn* bemuse, benumb, paralyze, petrify, stun, stupefy *Rel* bewilder, confound, mystify, puzzle

daze *n Syn* HAZE (sense 2), fog, muddle, spin

dazzled *Syn* GIDDY, dizzy, swimming, vertiginous

dead **1** · devoid of life *Syn* deceased, defunct, departed, inanimate, late, lifeless *Rel* alive **2** *Syn* EXTINCT, bygone, defunct, departed, expired, gone, vanished *Ant* alive, existent, existing, extant, living **3** *Syn* NUMB, asleep, benumbed, insensitive, numbed, unfeeling *Ant* feeling, sensitive

deadlock *Syn* DRAW, stalemate, standoff, tie

deadly *adj* · likely to cause or capable of causing death *Syn* baleful, deathly, fatal, fell, killer, lethal, mortal, murderous, pestilent, vital *Rel* baneful, destructive, harmful, noxious, pernicious *Ant* healthful, healthy, nonfatal, nonlethal, wholesome

deadly *adv Syn* VERY, awful, awfully, beastly, especially, exceedingly, extra, extremely, far, frightfully, full, greatly, heavily, highly, hugely, jolly, mightily, mighty, mortally, most, much, particularly, rattling, real, right, so, something, super, terribly, too, whacking *Ant* little, negligibly, nominally, slightly

deal *n Syn* SALE, trade, transaction

deal *vb* **1** *Syn* BARGAIN, chaffer, dicker, haggle, horse-trade, negotiate, palter **2** *Syn* DISTRIBUTE, dispense, divide, dole *Ant* amass, collect **3** *Syn* TREAT, handle **4** *Syn* MARKET, merchandise, put up, retail, sell, vend *Ant* buy, purchase

dealer *Syn* MERCHANT, merchandiser, trader, tradesman, trafficker

dear *adj* **1** *Syn* COSTLY, expensive, invaluable, precious, priceless, valuable *Ant* cheap **2** *Syn* LOVABLE, adorable, darling, disarming, endearing, precious, sweet, winning *Ant* abhorrent, abominable, detestable, hateful, odious, unlovable

dear *n Syn* SWEETHEART, beloved, darling, flame, honey, love, sweet

dearth **1** *Syn* DEFICIENCY, deficit, failure, famine, inadequacy, insufficiency, lack, paucity, poverty, scantiness, scarceness, scarcity, shortage, want *Ant* abundance, adequacy, amplitude, plenitude, plenty, sufficiency **2** *Syn* LACK, absence, defect, privation, want

death · the end or the ending of life *Syn* decease, demise, passing *Ant* life

deathless *Syn* IMMORTAL, undying, unfading *Ant* mortal

deathly *Syn* DEADLY, baleful, fatal, fell, killer, lethal, mortal, murderous, pestilent, vital

Ant healthful, healthy, nonfatal, nonlethal, wholesome

debar *Syn* EXCLUDE, blackball, disbar, eliminate, rule out, shut out, suspend *Ant* admit, include

debase 1 · to cause a person or thing to become impaired and lowered in quality or character *Syn* corrupt, debauch, deprave, pervert, vitiate *Rel* contaminate, defile, pollute, taint *Ant* amend (*morals, character*), elevate (*taste, way of life*) 2 *Syn* ABASE, degrade, demean, humble, humiliate *Ant* exalt, extol (*especially oneself*)

debased 1 · being lowered in quality or character *Syn* corrupted, debauched, depraved, perverted, vitiated *Rel* decadent, degenerate, degenerated, deteriorated 2 *Syn* CORRUPT, debauched, decadent, degenerate, degraded, demoralized, depraved, dissipated, dissolute, perverse, perverted, reprobate, warped *Ant* uncorrupted

debate *n* *Syn* ARGUMENTATION, dialectic, disputation, forensic

debate *vb* *Syn* DISCUSS, agitate, argue, dispute

debauch *Syn* DEBASE, corrupt, deprave, pervert, vitiate *Ant* amend (*morals, character*), elevate (*taste, way of life*)

debauched 1 *Syn* CORRUPT, debased, decadent, degenerate, degraded, demoralized, depraved, dissipated, dissolute, perverse, perverted, reprobate, warped *Ant* uncorrupted 2 *Syn* DEBASED, corrupted, depraved, perverted, vitiated

debilitate *Syn* WEAKEN, enervate, enfeeble, sap, soften *Ant* strengthen

debit *Syn* DEBT, arrear, indebtedness, liability, obligation

debonair *Syn* SUAVE, smooth, sophisticated, urbane *Ant* boorish, churlish, clownish, loutish, uncouth

debris *Syn* REFUSE, garbage, offal, rubbish, trash, waste

debt · something, and especially a sum of money, that is owed *Syn* arrear, debit, indebtedness, liability, obligation

decadence *Syn* DETERIORATION, declension, decline, degeneration, devolution *Ant* amelioration, improvement

decadent *Syn* CORRUPT, debased, debauched, degenerate, degraded, demoralized, depraved, dissipated, dissolute, perverse, perverted, reprobate, warped *Ant* uncorrupted

decamp *Syn* ESCAPE (sense 1), abscond, flee, fly

decay 1 · to undergo or to cause to undergo destructive changes *Syn* crumble, decompose, disintegrate, putrefy, rot, spoil *Rel* debilitate, enfeeble, sap, undermine, weaken 2 *Syn* DETERIORATE, crumble, decline, degenerate, descend, ebb, rot, sink, worsen *Ant* ameliorate, improve, meliorate

decease *Syn* DEATH, demise, passing *Ant* life

deceased *Syn* DEAD, defunct, departed, inanimate, late, lifeless

deceit · the act or practice of imposing upon the credulity of others by dishonesty, fraud, or trickery *Syn* cunning, dissimulation, duplicity, guile *Rel* chicane, chicanery, deception, double-dealing, fraud, trickery

deceive · to lead astray or into evil or to frustrate by underhandedness or craft *Syn* beguile, betray, delude, double-cross, mislead *Rel* cheat, cozen, defraud, overreach *Ant* enlighten, undeceive

decelerate *Syn* SLOW, brake, retard *Ant* accelerate, hasten, hurry, quicken, rush, speed (up), step up

decency *Syn* DECORUM, dignity, etiquette, propriety *Ant* indecorum, license

decent 1 *Syn* ADEQUATE, acceptable, all right, fine, OK (*or* okay), passable, respectable, satisfactory, tolerable *Ant* deficient, inadequate, lacking, unacceptable, unsatisfactory, wanting 2 *Syn* CHASTE, modest, pure *Ant* bizarre (*of style, effect*); immoral, lewd, wanton 3 *Syn* DECOROUS, nice, proper, seemly *Ant* blatant, indecorous

deception · the act or practice of deliberately deceiving *Syn* chicane, chicanery, double-dealing, fraud, trickery *Rel* cunning, deceit, dissimulation, duplicity, guile

deceptive *Syn* MISLEADING, delusive, delusory

decide · to come or to cause to come to a conclusion *Syn* determine, resolve, rule, settle *Rel* conclude, gather, judge

decided · free from any doubt, wavering, or ambiguity *Syn* decisive, determined, resolved *Rel* definite, definitive

decimation *Syn* DESTRUCTION, annihilation, demolishment, demolition, desolation, devastation, extermination, extinction, havoc, loss, obliteration, ruin, ruination, wastage, wreckage *Ant* building, construction, erection, raising

decisive 1 *Syn* COGENT, compelling, conclusive, convincing, effective, forceful, persuasive, satisfying, strong, telling *Ant* inconclusive, indecisive, ineffective, unconvincing 2 *Syn* CONCLUSIVE, definitive, determinative *Ant* inconclusive 3 *Syn* DECIDED, determined, resolved

deck *Syn* ADORN, beautify, bedeck, decorate, embellish, garnish, ornament *Ant* disfigure

declaration · the act of making known openly or publicly *Syn* advertisement, announcement, broadcasting, proclamation, promulgation, publication

declare 1 *Syn* ANNOUNCE, advertise, blaze, broadcast, enunciate, placard, post, proclaim, promulgate, publicize, publish, sound 2 *Syn* ASSERT, affirm, aver, avouch, avow, predicate, profess, protest, warrant *Ant* controvert, deny

declass *Syn* DEGRADE, demote, disrate, reduce *Ant* elevate

declension *Syn* DETERIORATION, decadence, decline, degeneration, devolution *Ant* amelioration, improvement

decline *vb* **1** · to turn away by not accepting, receiving, or considering *Syn* refuse, reject, repudiate, spurn *Rel* balk, boggle, demur, jib, scruple, shy, stick, stickle *Ant* accept **2** *Syn* DETERIORATE, crumble, decay, degenerate, descend, ebb, rot, sink, worsen *Ant* ameliorate, improve, meliorate

decline *n* **1** *Syn* COMEDOWN, descent, down, downfall, fall *Ant* aggrandizement, ascent, exaltation, rise, up **2** *Syn* DETERIORATION, decadence, declension, degeneration, devolution *Ant* amelioration, improvement

decolorize *Syn* WHITEN, blanch, bleach, blench, dull, fade, pale, wash out *Ant* blacken, darken, deepen

decompose *Syn* DECAY, crumble, disintegrate, putrefy, rot, spoil

decorate *Syn* ADORN, beautify, bedeck, deck, embellish, garnish, ornament *Ant* disfigure

decoration *Syn* AWARD, distinction, honor, plume, premium, prize

decorous · conforming to an accepted standard of what is right or fitting or is regarded as good form *Syn* decent, nice, proper, seemly *Rel* ceremonial, ceremonious, conventional, formal *Ant* blatant, indecorous

decorticate *Syn* SKIN, flay, pare, peel

decorum · the quality or character of rightness, fitness, or honorableness in behavior or conduct *Syn* decency, dignity, etiquette, propriety *Rel* ceremoniousness, conventionality, formality *Ant* indecorum, license

decoy *Syn* LURE, allure, beguile, entice, lead on, seduce, tempt

decrease · to make or grow less especially gradually *Syn* abate, diminish, dwindle, lessen, reduce *Rel* abbreviate, abridge, curtail, retrench, shorten *Ant* increase

decree *Syn* DICTATE, impose, ordain, prescribe

decrepit *Syn* WEAK, feeble, fragile, frail, infirm *Ant* strong

decry · to indicate one's low opinion of something *Syn* belittle, deprecate, derogate, detract, disparage, minimize *Rel* disapprove *Ant* extol

dedicate *Syn* DEVOTE, consecrate, hallow

deduce *Syn* INFER, conclude, gather, judge

deducible *Syn* DEDUCTIVE, derivable, inferable, reasoned

deduction **1** · an amount subtracted from a gross sum *Syn* abatement, discount, rebate **2** *Syn* INFERENCE (sense 1), conclusion, judgment

deductive · being or provable by reasoning in which the conclusion follows necessarily from given information *Syn* deducible, derivable, inferable, reasoned *Rel* conjectural,

hypothetical, purported, supposed, suppositional

deed *n* *Syn* ACTION, act

deed *vb* *Syn* TRANSFER, alienate, convey

deem **1** *Syn* BELIEVE (sense 1), consider, feel, figure, guess, hold, imagine, suppose, think *Ant* disbelieve, discredit, reject **2** *Syn* CONSIDER (sense 2), account, reckon, regard

deep *adj* **1** · having great extension downward or inward *Syn* abysmal, profound **2** *Syn* BROAD, wide *Ant* narrow

deep *n* *Syn* THICK, depth, height, middle, midst

deep-rooted *Syn* INVETERATE, chronic, confirmed, deep-seated

deep-seated *Syn* INVETERATE, chronic, confirmed, deep-rooted

defamatory *Syn* LIBELOUS, scandalous, slanderous

defame *Syn* SLANDER, asperse, blacken, libel, malign, smear, traduce, vilify

default *Syn* FAILURE, dereliction, miscarriage, neglect

defeat *Syn* CONQUER, beat, lick, overcome, overthrow, reduce, rout, subdue, subjugate, surmount, vanquish

defect **1** *Syn* BLEMISH, deformity, disfigurement, fault, flaw, imperfection, mark, pockmark, scar **2** *Syn* LACK, absence, dearth, privation, want

defection · conscious abandonment of allegiance or duty *Syn* apostasy, desertion *Rel* alienation, disaffection, estrangement

defective *Syn* FAULTY, bad, flawed, imperfect *Ant* faultless, flawless, impeccable, perfect

defend **1** · to keep secure from danger or against attack *Syn* guard, protect, safeguard, shield *Rel* avert, prevent, ward *Ant* attack, combat **2** *Syn* MAINTAIN, assert, justify, vindicate

defendable *Syn* TENABLE, defensible, justifiable, maintainable, supportable, sustainable *Ant* indefensible, insupportable, unjustifiable, untenable

defender *Syn* PROTECTOR, custodian, guard, protection

defense *Syn* EXCUSE, alibi, justification, plea, reason

defensible *Syn* TENABLE, defendable, justifiable, maintainable, supportable, sustainable *Ant* indefensible, insupportable, unjustifiable, untenable

defer **1** *Syn* POSTPONE, delay, hold off (on), hold up, put off, shelve **2** *Syn* YIELD, bow, capitulate, cave, relent, submit, succumb

deference *Syn* HONOR, homage, obeisance, reverence

deferential *Syn* RESPECTFUL, dutiful, regardful *Ant* disrespectful

defiance **1** *Syn* DISOBEDIENCE, contrariness, frowardness, insubordination, intractability, rebelliousness, recalcitrance, refractoriness, unruliness, willfulness *Ant* amenability, compliance, docility, obedience **2** *Syn* RE-SISTANCE, opposition *Ant* acquiescence

defiant *Syn* DISOBEDIENT, balky, contrary, froward, insubordinate, intractable, rebellious, recalcitrant, refractory, restive, ungovernable, unruly, untoward, wayward, willful (*or* wilful) *Ant* amenable, compliant, docile, obedient, tractable

deficiency 1 · a falling short of an essential or desirable amount or number *Syn* dearth, deficit, failure, famine, inadequacy, insufficiency, lack, paucity, poverty, scantiness, scarceness, scarcity, shortage, want *Rel* absence, omission *Ant* abundance, adequacy, amplitude, plenitude, plenty, sufficiency **2** *Syn* IMPERFECTION, fault, shortcoming *Ant* perfection

deficit *Syn* DEFICIENCY, dearth, failure, famine, inadequacy, insufficiency, lack, paucity, poverty, scantiness, scarceness, scarcity, shortage, want *Ant* abundance, adequacy, amplitude, plenitude, plenty, sufficiency

defile *n* *Syn* CANYON, flume, gap, gorge, gulch, gulf, notch, pass, ravine

defile *vb* **1** *Syn* CONTAMINATE, befoul, foul, poison, pollute, taint *Ant* decontaminate, purify **2** *Syn* DESECRATE, profane, violate

define *Syn* PRESCRIBE, assign

definite *Syn* EXPLICIT, categorical, express, specific *Ant* ambiguous

definitive *Syn* CONCLUSIVE, decisive, determinative *Ant* inconclusive

deflate *Syn* CONTRACT, compress, condense, constrict, shrink *Ant* expand

deflect *Syn* TURN (sense 2), avert, divert, sheer

deflection *Syn* DEVIATION, aberration, divergence

deform · to mar or spoil by or as if by twisting *Syn* contort, distort, warp *Rel* batter, cripple, maim, mangle, mutilate

deformity *Syn* BLEMISH, defect, disfigurement, fault, flaw, imperfection, mark, pockmark, scar

defraud *Syn* FLEECE, bleed, cheat, chisel, cozen, hustle, mulct, rook, shortchange, skin, squeeze, stick, sting, swindle, victimize

deftness *Syn* DEXTERITY (sense 2), agility, nimbleness, sleight, spryness *Ant* awkwardness, clumsiness, gawkiness

defunct 1 *Syn* DEAD, deceased, departed, inanimate, late, lifeless **2** *Syn* EXTINCT, bygone, dead, departed, expired, gone, vanished *Ant* alive, existent, existing, extant, living

defy 1 *Syn* CHALLENGE, dare, stump **2** *Syn* FACE, beard, brave, challenge, dare *Ant* avoid

degenerate *adj* **1** *Syn* CORRUPT, debased, debauched, decadent, degraded, demoralized, depraved, dissipated, dissolute, perverse, perverted, reprobate, warped *Ant* uncorrupted **2** *Syn* VICIOUS, corrupt, flagi-

tious, infamous, iniquitous, nefarious, villainous *Ant* virtuous

degenerate *vb* *Syn* DETERIORATE, crumble, decay, decline, descend, ebb, rot, sink, worsen *Ant* ameliorate, improve, meliorate

degeneration *Syn* DETERIORATION, decadence, declension, decline, devolution *Ant* amelioration, improvement

degrade 1 · to lower in station, rank, or grade *Syn* declass, demote, disrate, reduce *Rel* abase, debase, humble, humiliate *Ant* elevate **2** *Syn* ABASE, debase, demean, humble, humiliate *Ant* exalt, extol (*especially oneself*)

degraded *Syn* CORRUPT, debased, debauched, decadent, degenerate, demoralized, depraved, dissipated, dissolute, perverse, perverted, reprobate, warped *Ant* uncorrupted

dehydrate *Syn* DRY, bake, desiccate, parch *Ant* moisten, wet

deification *Syn* WORSHIP, adulation, idolatry, idolization, worshipping

deify *Syn* IDOLIZE, adore, adulate, canonize, dote (on), worship

deign *Syn* STOOP, condescend

dejected *Syn* SAD (sense 1), bad, blue, brokenhearted, crestfallen, depressed, despondent, disconsolate, doleful, down, downcast, downhearted, droopy, forlorn, gloomy, glum, heartbroken, heartsick, heartsore, inconsolable, joyless, low, low-spirited, melancholy, miserable, mournful, saddened, sorrowful, sorry, unhappy, woebegone, woeful, wretched *Ant* blissful, buoyant, buoyed, cheerful, cheery, chipper, delighted, glad, gladdened, gladsome, gleeful, happy, joyful, joyous, jubilant, sunny, upbeat

dejection *Syn* SADNESS, blues, depression, desolation, despondency, disconsolateness, dispiritedness, doldrums, downheartedness, dreariness, dumps, forlornness, gloom, gloominess, heartsickness, joylessness, melancholy, mopes, oppression, unhappiness *Ant* bliss, blissfulness, ecstasy, elatedness, elation, euphoria, exhilaration, exuberance, exultation, felicity, gladness, gladsomeness, happiness, heaven, intoxication, joy, joyfulness, joyousness, jubilation, rapture, rapturousness

delay *n* · an instance or period of being prevented from going about one's business *Syn* detainment, holdup, wait *Rel* deferment, postponement

delay *vb* **1** · to cause to be late or behind in movement or progress *Syn* detain, retard, slacken, slow *Rel* block, hinder, impede, obstruct *Ant* expedite, hasten **2** · to move or act slowly so that progress is hindered or work remains undone or unfinished *Syn* dawdle, lag, loiter, procrastinate *Rel* linger, stay, tarry, wait *Ant* hasten, hurry **3** *Syn* POSTPONE, defer, hold off (on), hold up, put off, shelve

delectable *Syn* DELIGHTFUL, delicious, luscious *Ant* boring, distressing, horrid

delectation *Syn* PLEASURE, delight, enjoyment, fruition, joy *Ant* anger, displeasure, vexation

delegate 1 · a person who stands in place of another or others *Syn* deputy, representative 2 *Syn* AGENT (sense 1), attorney, commissary, deputy, envoy, factor, procurator, proxy, representative 3 *Syn* AMBASSADOR, emissary, envoy, legate, minister, representative

delete *Syn* ERASE, blot out, cancel, efface, expunge, obliterate

deleterious *Syn* HARMFUL, adverse, bad, baleful, baneful, damaging, detrimental, evil, hurtful, ill, injurious, mischievous, noxious, pernicious, prejudicial *Ant* harmless, innocent, innocuous, inoffensive, safe

deliberate *adj* 1 · arrived at after due thought *Syn* advised, considered, designed, premeditated, studied *Rel* planned, projected, schemed *Ant* casual 2 *Syn* VOLUNTARY, intentional, willful, willing *Ant* instinctive, involuntary 3 *Syn* SLOW, dilatory, laggard, leisurely *Ant* fast

deliberate *vb* *Syn* THINK (sense 2), cogitate, reason, reflect, speculate

deliberately *Syn* INTENTIONALLY, consciously, designedly, knowingly, purposefully, purposely, willfully, wittingly *Ant* inadvertently, unconsciously, unintentionally, unknowingly, unwittingly

delicacy *Syn* PRECISION, accuracy, closeness, exactitude, exactness, fineness, preciseness, rigorousness, veracity *Ant* coarseness, impreciseness, imprecision, inaccuracy, inexactness, roughness

delicate *Syn* CHOICE, dainty, elegant, exquisite, rare, recherché *Ant* indifferent, medium

delicious *Syn* DELIGHTFUL, delectable, luscious *Ant* boring, distressing, horrid

delight *vb* *Syn* PLEASE, gladden, gratify, regale, rejoice, tickle *Ant* anger, displease, vex

delight *n* *Syn* PLEASURE, delectation, enjoyment, fruition, joy *Ant* anger, displeasure, vexation

delightful 1 · highly pleasing to the senses or to aesthetic taste *Syn* delectable, delicious, luscious *Rel* alluring, attractive, charming, enchanting, fascinating *Ant* boring, distressing, horrid 2 *Syn* FUN, amusing, diverting, enjoyable, entertaining, pleasurable *Ant* boring, dull

delineate 1 *Syn* REPRESENT, depict, limn, picture, portray 2 *Syn* SKETCH, blueprint, diagram, draft, outline, plot, trace

delineation *Syn* SKETCH, blueprint, diagram, draft, outline, plot, tracing

delinquent *Syn* CRIMINAL, convict, culprit, felon, malefactor

deliquesce *Syn* LIQUEFY, fuse, melt, thaw

delirious *Syn* FURIOUS, frantic, frenetic, frenzied, rabid, wild

delirium 1 *Syn* FRENZY, agitation, distraction, furor, furore, fury, hysteria, rage, rampage, uproar 2 *Syn* MANIA, frenzy, hysteria

deliver 1 *Syn* RESCUE, ransom, reclaim, redeem, save 2 *Syn* FURNISH (sense 2), feed, give, hand, hand over, provide, supply *Ant* hold (back), keep (back), reserve, retain, withhold

deliverer *Syn* SAVIOR, redeemer, rescuer, saver

delude *Syn* DECEIVE, beguile, betray, double-cross, mislead *Ant* enlighten, undeceive

deluge *n* 1 *Syn* FLOOD, cataract, inundation, spate, torrent 2 *Syn* RAIN (sense 1), cloudburst, downpour, rainfall, rainstorm, storm, wet

deluge *vb* *Syn* FLOOD, drown, engulf, inundate, overflow, overwhelm, submerge, submerse, swamp *Ant* drain

delusion · something which is believed to be or is accepted as being true or real but which is actually false or unreal *Syn* hallucination, illusion, mirage *Rel* chicane, chicanery, deception, trickery

delusive *Syn* MISLEADING, deceptive, delusory

delusory *Syn* MISLEADING, deceptive, delusive

deluxe *Syn* LUXURIOUS, lavish, luxuriant, opulent, palatial, plush, sumptuous *Ant* ascetic, austere, humble, Spartan

delve *Syn* DIG, excavate, grub, spade

delve (into) *Syn* EXPLORE, dig (into), inquire (into), investigate, look (into), probe, research

demagogue *Syn* AGITATOR, exciter, firebrand, fomenter, incendiary, inciter, instigator, rabble-rouser

demand · to ask or call for something as due or as necessary or as strongly desired *Syn* claim, exact, require *Rel* ask, request, solicit

demarcate *Syn* DISTINGUISH, differentiate, discriminate *Ant* confound

demean 1 *Syn* ABASE, debase, degrade, humble, humiliate *Ant* exalt, extol (*especially oneself*) 2 *Syn* BEHAVE, acquit, comport, conduct, deport, quit *Ant* misbehave

demeanor *Syn* BEARING, deportment, mien, port, presence

demented *Syn* INSANE, crazed, crazy, deranged, lunatic, mad, maniac, non compos mentis *Ant* sane

demesne *Syn* REGION, area, field, zone

demise *Syn* DEATH, decease, passing *Ant* life

democratic · of, relating to, or favoring political democracy *Syn* popular, republican, self-governing, self-ruling *Rel* representative *Ant* undemocratic

demolish *Syn* DESTROY, raze

demolishment *Syn* DESTRUCTION, annihilation, decimation, demolition, desolation, devastation, extermination, extinction, havoc, loss, obliteration, ruin, ruination, wastage, wreckage *Ant* building, construction, erection, raising

demolition *Syn* DESTRUCTION, annihilation, decimation, demolishment, desolation, devastation, extermination, extinction, havoc, loss, obliteration, ruin, ruination, wastage, wreckage *Ant* building, construction, erection, raising

demon *or* **daemon** · an evil spirit *Syn* devil, fiend, ghoul, imp, incubus *Rel* apparition, bogey, brownie, dwarf, elf, faerie, fairy, familiar, fay, ghost, gnome, goblin, gremlin, hobgoblin, leprechaun, monster, ogre, phantasm, phantom, pixie, poltergeist, puck, shade, shadow, specter (*or* spectre), spirit, spook, sprite, troll, vision, wraith

demoniac *Syn* FIENDISH, demonic, devilish, diabolic, diabolical

demonic *Syn* FIENDISH, demoniac, devilish, diabolic, diabolical

demonstrate 1 *Syn* EXPLAIN (sense 1), clarify, clear (up), construe, elucidate, explicate, expound, illuminate, illustrate, interpret, spell out *Ant* obscure 2 *Syn* PROVE, test, try *Ant* disprove 3 *Syn* SHOW (sense 1), evidence, evince, manifest *Ant* disguise

demonstration *Syn* PROOF, test, trial

demonstrative · showing feeling freely *Syn* effusive, emotional, uninhibited, unreserved, unrestrained *Rel* dramatic, histrionic, melodramatic, theatrical *Ant* inhibited, reserved, restrained, undemonstrative, unemotional

demoralize *Syn* DISCOURAGE (sense 1), daunt, dishearten, dismay, dispirit, unnerve *Ant* embolden, encourage, hearten, nerve, steel

demoralized *Syn* CORRUPT, debased, debauched, decadent, degenerate, degraded, depraved, dissipated, dissolute, perverse, perverted, reprobate, warped *Ant* uncorrupted

demote *Syn* DEGRADE, declass, disrate, reduce *Ant* elevate

demur *vb* · to hesitate or show reluctance because of difficulties in the way *Syn* balk, boggle, jib, scruple, shy, stick, stickle, strain *Rel* falter, hesitate, vacillate, waver *Ant* accede

demur *n* *Syn* OBJECTION, challenge, complaint, expostulation, fuss, protest, question, remonstrance

denial 1 · an unwillingness to grant something asked for *Syn* disallowance, nay, no, refusal, rejection *Rel* decline, rebuff, repudiation *Ant* allowance, grant 2 · a refusal to confirm the truth of a statement *Syn* contradiction, disallowance, disavowal, disclaimer, negation, rejection, repudiation *Rel* disproof, rebuttal, refutation *Ant* acknowledgment, admission, avowal, confirmation

denizen *Syn* INHABITANT, dweller, habitant, occupant, resident, resider *Ant* transient

denomination 1 *Syn* NAME, appellation, designation, style, title 2 *Syn* RELIGION, church, communion, creed, faith, persuasion, sect

denote *Syn* MEAN, import, signify

denounce *Syn* CRITICIZE, blame, censure, condemn, reprehend, reprobate

dense 1 *Syn* CLOSE (sense 2), compact, thick *Ant* open 2 *Syn* STUPID, crass, dull, dumb, slow *Ant* intelligent

dented *Syn* HOLLOW, concave, depressed, indented, recessed, sunken *Ant* bulging, convex, protruding, protuberant

denude *Syn* STRIP, bare, dismantle, divest *Ant* furnish, invest

denunciation *Syn* CENSURE, condemnation, rebuke, reprimand, reproach, reproof, stricture *Ant* citation, commendation, endorsement

deny · to refuse to accept as true or valid *Syn* contradict, contravene, gainsay, impugn, negative, traverse *Rel* decline, refuse, reject, repudiate *Ant* concede, confirm

depart 1 *Syn* GO, leave, quit, retire, withdraw *Ant* come 2 *Syn* SWERVE, deviate, digress, diverge, veer

departed 1 *Syn* DEAD, deceased, defunct, inanimate, late, lifeless 2 *Syn* EXTINCT, bygone, dead, defunct, expired, vanished *Ant* alive, existent, existing, extant, living

depend 1 · to rest or to be contingent upon something uncertain, variable, or indeterminable *Syn* hang, hinge, turn 2 · to place reliance or trust *Syn* count, lean, reckon, rely *Rel* commit, confide, entrust, trust 3 *Syn* RELY (ON), bank, count, reckon, trust

dependable · worthy of one's trust *Syn* good, reliable, responsible, safe, solid, steady, sure, tried, tried-and-true, true, trustworthy, trusty *Rel* attested, authenticated, blameless, confirmed, constant, devoted, effective, faithful, fast, firm, honest, infallible, irreproachable, loyal, proven, sincere, single-minded, sound, staunch (*or* stanch), steadfast, strong, telling, unerring, unimpeachable, unquestionable, valid, validated, verified *Ant* irresponsible, undependable, unreliable, untrustworthy

dependence *Syn* TRUST, confidence, faith, reliance *Ant* mistrust

dependent 1 · determined or conditioned by another *Syn* conditional, contingent, relative *Rel* exposed, liable, open, subject, susceptible *Ant* absolute, infinite, original 2 *Syn* SUBORDINATE, collateral, secondary, subject, tributary *Ant* chief, dominant, leading

depict *Syn* REPRESENT, delineate, limn, picture, portray

deplete · to make complete use of *Syn* clean (out), consume, drain, exhaust, expend, spend, use up *Rel* decrease, diminish, lessen, reduce *Ant* renew, replace

deplorable *Syn* REGRETTABLE, distressful, distressing, grievous, heartbreaking, heartrending, lamentable, unfortunate, woeful

deplore *Syn* REGRET, bemoan, lament, repent, rue

deport 1 *Syn* BANISH, exile, expatriate, extradite, ostracize, transport 2 *Syn* BEHAVE, acquit, comport, conduct, demean, quit *Ant* misbehave

deportment 1 *Syn* BEARING, demeanor, mien, port, presence 2 *Syn* BEHAVIOR, conduct

depose *Syn* TESTIFY, attest, swear, witness

deposit 1 · matter which settles to the bottom of a liquid *Syn* dregs, grounds, lees, precipitate, sediment 2 *Syn* STORE, cache, hoard, reserve

depository *Syn* STOREHOUSE, depot, magazine, repository, storage, stowage, warehouse

depot 1 *Syn* ARMORY, arsenal, dump, magazine 2 *Syn* STOREHOUSE, depository, magazine, repository, storage, stowage, warehouse

deprave *Syn* DEBASE, corrupt, debauch, pervert, vitiate *Ant* amend (*morals, character*), elevate (*taste, way of life*)

depraved 1 *Syn* CORRUPT, debased, debauched, decadent, degenerate, degraded, demoralized, dissipated, dissolute, perverse, perverted, reprobate, warped *Ant* uncorrupted 2 *Syn* DEBASED, corrupted, debauched, perverted, vitiated

deprecate 1 *Syn* DECRY, belittle, derogate, detract, disparage, minimize *Ant* extol 2 *Syn* DISAPPROVE (OF), discountenance, disfavor, dislike, frown (on), reprove *Ant* approve, favor, like

depreciative *Syn* DEROGATORY, depreciatory, disparaging, pejorative, slighting

depreciatory *Syn* DEROGATORY, depreciative, disparaging, pejorative, slighting

depress · to lower in spirit or mood *Syn* oppress, weigh *Rel* ail, distress, trouble *Ant* cheer, elate

depressed 1 *Syn* HOLLOW, concave, dented, indented, recessed, sunken *Ant* bulging, convex, protruding, protuberant 2 *Syn* SAD (sense 1), bad, blue, brokenhearted, crestfallen, dejected, despondent, disconsolate, doleful, down, downcast, downhearted, droopy, forlorn, gloomy, glum, heartbroken, heartsick, heartsore, inconsolable, joyless, low, low-spirited, melancholy, miserable, mournful, saddened, sorrowful, sorry, unhappy, woebegone, woeful, wretched *Ant* blissful, buoyant, buoyed, cheerful, cheery, chipper, delighted, glad, gladdened, gladsome, gleeful, happy, joyful, joyous, jubilant, sunny, upbeat

depressing *Syn* SAD (sense 2), dismal, drear, dreary, heartbreaking, heartrending, melancholy, pathetic, saddening, sorry, tearful, teary *Ant* cheering, cheery, glad, happy

depression *Syn* SADNESS, blues, dejection, desolation, despondency, disconsolateness, dispiritedness, doldrums, downhearted-ness, dreariness, dumps, forlornness, gloom, gloominess, heartsickness, joylessness, melancholy, mopes, oppression, unhappiness *Ant* bliss, blissfulness, ecstasy, elatedness, elation, euphoria, exhilaration, exuberance, exultation, felicity, gladness, gladsomeness, happiness, heaven, intoxication, joy, joyfulness, joyousness, jubilation, rapture, rapturousness

deprived · kept from having the necessities of life or a healthful environment *Syn* disadvantaged, underprivileged *Rel* impoverished, needy, poor *Ant* privileged

depth *Syn* THICK, deep, height, middle, midst

deputy 1 *Syn* AGENT (sense 1), attorney, commissary, delegate, envoy, factor, procurator, proxy, representative 2 *Syn* DELEGATE, representative 3 *Syn* ASSISTANT, adjutant, aid, aide, apprentice, coadjutor, helper, sidekick

deracinate *Syn* EXTERMINATE, eradicate, extirpate, uproot, wipe

derange *Syn* DISORDER, confuse, disarrange, disarray, discompose, dishevel, dislocate, disorganize, disrupt, disturb, hash, jumble, mess (up), mix (up), muddle, muss, rumple, scramble, shuffle, tousle, tumble, upset *Ant* arrange, array, draw up, marshal, order, organize, range, regulate, straighten (up), tidy

deranged *Syn* INSANE, crazed, crazy, demented, lunatic, mad, maniac, non compos mentis *Ant* sane

derangement *Syn* ABERRATION, alienation *Ant* soundness (*of mind*)

derelict *adj* 1 *Syn* ABANDONED (sense 2), deserted, disused, forgotten, forsaken, rejected, vacated 2 *Syn* NEGLIGENT, careless, lax, neglectful, neglecting, remiss, slack *Ant* attentive, careful, conscientious

derelict *n* *Syn* OUTCAST, castaway, pariah, reprobate, untouchable

dereliction *Syn* FAILURE, default, miscarriage, neglect

deride *Syn* RIDICULE, mock, rally, taunt, twit

derivable *Syn* DEDUCTIVE, deducible, inferable, reasoned

derivative · something that naturally develops or is developed from something else *Syn* by-product, offshoot, outgrowth, spin-off *Rel* aftereffect, aftermath, consequence, copy, descendant (*or* descendent), duplicate, facsimile, replica, reproduction, result, side effect *Ant* origin, root, source

derive *Syn* SPRING, arise, emanate, flow, issue, originate, proceed, rise, stem

dernier cri *Syn* FASHION, craze, cry, fad, mode, rage, style, vogue

derogate *Syn* DECRY, belittle, deprecate, detract, disparage, minimize *Ant* extol

derogatory · designed or tending to belittle *Syn* depreciative, depreciatory, disparaging, pejorative, slighting *Rel* belittling, decrying, minimizing

descant 1 *Syn* DISCOURSE, dilate, expatiate 2 *Syn* SING, carol, chant, hymn, intone, trill, troll, warble

descend 1 · to get or come down from a height *Syn* alight, dismount *Ant* ascend, climb 2 *Syn* DETERIORATE, crumble, decay, decline, degenerate, ebb, rot, sink, worsen *Ant* ameliorate, improve, meliorate

descendants *Syn* OFFSPRING, issue, posterity, progeny, young

descent 1 *Syn* ANCESTRY, birth, blood, bloodline, breeding, extraction, family tree, genealogy, line, lineage, origin, parentage, pedigree, stock, strain *Ant* issue, posterity, progeny, seed 2 *Syn* ATTACK (sense 2), aggression, assault, blitzkrieg, charge, offense (*or* offence), offensive, onset, onslaught, raid, rush, strike 3 *Syn* COMEDOWN, decline, down, downfall, fall *Ant* aggrandizement, ascent, exaltation, rise, up

describe *Syn* RELATE, narrate, recite, recount, rehearse, report, state

description *Syn* TYPE, character, ilk, kidney, kind, nature, sort, stripe

descry *Syn* SEE (sense 1), behold, contemplate, discern, espy, note, notice, observe, perceive, remark, survey, view

desecrate · to treat (a sacred place or object) shamefully or with great disrespect *Syn* defile, profane, violate *Rel* blaspheme, curse, swear

desecration *Syn* PROFANATION, blasphemy, sacrilege

desert *vb Syn* ABANDON, forsake *Ant* reclaim

desert[1] *n Syn* DUE, merit

desert[2] *n Syn* WASTE, badlands, wilderness

deserted *Syn* ABANDONED (sense 2), derelict, disused, forgotten, forsaken, rejected, vacated

desertion *Syn* DEFECTION, apostasy

deserve · to be or become worthy of *Syn* earn, merit, rate *Rel* gain, get, win

deserving *Syn* WORTHY, good, meritorious *Ant* no-good, undeserving, valueless, worthless

desiccate *Syn* DRY, bake, dehydrate, parch *Ant* moisten, wet

design *n* 1 *Syn* FIGURE, device, motif, pattern 2 *Syn* GOAL, aim, ambition, aspiration, dream, end, intent, intention, mark, meaning, object, objective, plan, pretension, purpose, target, thing 3 *Syn* PLAN, plot, project, scheme

design *vb* 1 *Syn* INTEND, mean, propose, purpose 2 *Syn* PLAN, plot, project, scheme

designate 1 *Syn* APPOINT (sense 1), fix, name, set 2 *Syn* APPOINT (sense 2), assign, attach, commission, constitute, detail, name *Ant* discharge, dismiss, expel, fire

designation *Syn* NAME, appellation, denomination, style, title

designed *Syn* DELIBERATE, advised, considered, premeditated, studied *Ant* casual

designedly *Syn* INTENTIONALLY, consciously, deliberately, knowingly, purposefully, purposely, willfully, wittingly *Ant* inadvertently, unconsciously, unintentionally, unknowingly, unwittingly

desirable *Syn* EXPEDIENT, advisable, judicious, politic, prudent, tactical, wise *Ant* imprudent, inadvisable, inexpedient, injudicious, unwise

desire *n* · a longing for something that promises enjoyment or satisfaction *Syn* appetite, lust, passion, urge *Rel* hankering, hunger, hungering, longing, pining, thirst, thirsting, yearning *Ant* distaste

desire *vb* · to have a longing for something *Syn* covet, crave, want, wish *Rel* hanker, hunger, long, pine, thirst, yearn

desist *Syn* STOP, cease, discontinue, quit

desolate 1 *Syn* ALONE, forlorn, lone, lonely, lonesome, lorn, solitary *Ant* accompanied 2 *Syn* DISMAL, bleak, cheerless, dispiriting, dreary

desolation 1 *Syn* DESTRUCTION, annihilation, decimation, demolishment, demolition, devastation, extermination, extinction, havoc, loss, obliteration, ruin, ruination, wastage, wreckage *Ant* building, construction, erection, raising 2 *Syn* SADNESS, blues, dejection, depression, despondency, disconsolateness, dispiritedness, doldrums, downheartedness, dreariness, dumps, forlornness, gloom, gloominess, heartsickness, joylessness, melancholy, mopes, oppression, unhappiness *Ant* bliss, blissfulness, ecstasy, elatedness, elation, euphoria, exhilaration, exuberance, exultation, felicity, gladness, gladsomeness, happiness, heaven, intoxication, joy, joyfulness, joyousness, jubilation, rapture, rapturousness

despair *Syn* DESPONDENCY, desperation, forlornness, hopelessness *Ant* lightheartedness

despairing *Syn* DESPONDENT, desperate, forlorn, hopeless *Ant* lighthearted

desperate *Syn* DESPONDENT, despairing, forlorn, hopeless *Ant* lighthearted

desperation *Syn* DESPONDENCY, despair, forlornness, hopelessness *Ant* lightheartedness

despicable *Syn* CONTEMPTIBLE, beggarly, cheap, pitiable, scurvy, shabby, sorry *Ant* admirable, estimable, formidable

despise 1 · to regard as beneath one's notice and as unworthy of attention or interest *Syn* contemn, disdain, scorn, scout *Rel* abhor, abominate, detest, hate, loathe *Ant* appreciate 2 *Syn* SCORN (sense 1), disregard, flout *Ant* honor, respect

despite *n* 1 · the feeling or attitude of despising *Syn* contempt, disdain, scorn 2 *Syn* CONTEMPT, despitefulness, disdain, scorn *Ant* admiration, esteem, regard, respect 3 *Syn* MALICE, grudge, ill will, malevolence, malignancy, malignity, spite, spleen *Ant* charity

despite *prep Syn* NOTWITHSTANDING, in spite of

despitefulness *Syn* CONTEMPT, despite, disdain, scorn *Ant* admiration, esteem, regard, respect

despoil *Syn* RAVAGE, devastate, pillage, sack, spoliate, waste

despondency 1 · the state or feeling of having lost hope *Syn* despair, desperation, forlornness, hopelessness *Rel* blues, dejection, depression, dumps, melancholia, melancholy, sadness *Ant* lightheartedness 2 *Syn* SADNESS, blues, dejection, depression, desolation, disconsolateness, dispiritedness, doldrums, downheartedness, dreariness, dumps, forlornness, gloom, gloominess, heartsickness, joylessness, melancholy, mopes, oppression, unhappiness *Ant* bliss, blissfulness, ecstasy, elatedness, elation, euphoria, exhilaration, exuberance, exultation, felicity, gladness, gladsomeness, happiness, heaven, intoxication, joy, joyfulness, joyousness, jubilation, rapture, rapturousness

despondent 1 · having lost all or nearly all hope *Syn* despairing, desperate, forlorn, hopeless *Rel* grieving, mourning, sorrowing *Ant* lighthearted 2 *Syn* SAD (sense 1), bad, blue, brokenhearted, crestfallen, dejected, depressed, disconsolate, doleful, down, downcast, downhearted, droopy, forlorn, gloomy, glum, heartbroken, heartsick, heartsore, inconsolable, joyless, low, low-spirited, melancholy, miserable, mournful, saddened, sorrowful, sorry, unhappy, woebegone, woeful, wretched *Ant* blissful, buoyant, buoyed, cheerful, cheery, chipper, delighted, glad, gladdened, gladsome, gleeful, happy, joyful, joyous, jubilant, sunny, upbeat

despotic 1 *Syn* ABSOLUTE, arbitrary, autocratic, tyrannical, tyrannous *Ant* limited, restrained 2 *Syn* BOSSY, authoritarian, autocratic, dictatorial, domineering, imperious, masterful, overbearing, peremptory, tyrannical, tyrannous

destiny *Syn* FATE, doom, lot, portion

destitute 1 *Syn* DEVOID, void 2 *Syn* POOR, impecunious, indigent, necessitous, needy, penniless, poverty-stricken *Ant* rich

destitution *Syn* POVERTY, indigence, penury, privation, want *Ant* riches

destroy · to bring to ruin *Syn* demolish, raze *Rel* dilapidate, ruin, wreck

destruction · the state or fact of being rendered nonexistent, physically unsound, or useless *Syn* annihilation, decimation, demolishment, demolition, desolation, devastation, extermination, extinction, havoc, loss, obliteration, ruin, ruination, wastage, wreckage *Rel* depredation, despoilment, despoliation *Ant* building, construction, erection, raising

desultorily *Syn* HIT OR MISS, aimlessly, anyhow, anyway, anywise, erratically, haphaz-

ard, haphazardly, helter-skelter, irregularly, randomly *Ant* methodically, systematically

desultory *Syn* RANDOM, casual, chance, chancy, haphazard, happy-go-lucky, hit-or-miss *Ant* methodical, nonrandom, orderly, systematic

detach · to remove one thing from another with which it is in union or association *Syn* abstract, disengage *Rel* divorce, part, separate, sever, sunder *Ant* affix, attach

detached *Syn* INDIFFERENT, aloof, disinterested, incurious, unconcerned, uninterested *Ant* avid

detachment · lack of favoritism toward one side or another *Syn* disinterestedness, impartiality, neutrality, objectivity *Rel* equitableness, fairness *Ant* bias, favor, favoritism, one-sidedness, partiality, partisanship, prejudice

detail *n* 1 *Syn* FACT, datum, nicety, particular, particularity, point 2 *Syn* ITEM, particular 3 *Syn* PART, division, fraction, fragment, member, parcel, piece, portion, section, sector, segment *Ant* whole

detail *vb Syn* APPOINT (sense 2), assign, attach, commission, constitute, designate, detail, name *Ant* discharge, dismiss, expel, fire

detailed *Syn* CIRCUMSTANTIAL, itemized, minute, particular, particularized *Ant* abridged, summary

detain 1 *Syn* ARREST (sense 2), apprehend, attach 2 *Syn* DELAY (sense 1), retard, slacken, slow *Ant* expedite, hasten 3 *Syn* KEEP (sense 2), hold back, keep back, keep out, reserve, retain, withhold *Ant* relinquish

detainment *Syn* DELAY, holdup, wait

detectable *Syn* PERCEPTIBLE, appreciable, discernible, distinguishable, palpable, sensible *Ant* impalpable, imperceptible, inappreciable, indistinguishable, insensible

detention *Syn* ARREST, apprehension, attachment

deter *Syn* DISCOURAGE (sense 2), dissuade, inhibit *Ant* encourage, persuade

deteriorate · to become worse or of less value *Syn* crumble, decay, decline, degenerate, descend, ebb, rot, sink, worsen *Rel* recede, wane *Ant* ameliorate, improve, meliorate

deterioration · a falling from a higher to a lower level in quality, character, or vitality *Syn* decadence, declension, decline, degeneration, devolution *Rel* impairment, spoiling *Ant* amelioration, improvement

determinant *Syn* CAUSE, antecedent, occasion, reason

determinative *Syn* CONCLUSIVE, decisive, definitive *Ant* inconclusive

determine 1 *Syn* DECIDE, resolve, rule, settle 2 *Syn* DISCOVER, ascertain, learn, unearth

determined *Syn* DECIDED, decisive, resolved

deterrent *Syn* ENCUMBRANCE, bar, block, chain, clog, crimp, drag, embarrassment, fetter, handicap, hindrance, hurdle, impediment, inhibition, interference, let, manacle, obstacle, obstruction, shackles, stop, stumbling block, trammel *Ant* aid, assistance, benefit, help

detest *Syn* HATE, abhor, abominate, loathe *Ant* love

detestable *Syn* HATEFUL, abhorrent, abominable, odious *Ant* lovable, sympathetic

detestation *Syn* ABHORRENCE, abomination, hate, hatred, loathing *Ant* admiration, enjoyment

detract *Syn* DECRY, belittle, deprecate, derogate, disparage, minimize *Ant* extol

detraction · the expression of damaging or malicious opinions *Syn* backbiting, calumny, scandal, slander *Rel* damage, harm, hurt, injury

detrimental *Syn* HARMFUL, adverse, bad, baleful, baneful, damaging, deleterious, evil, hurtful, ill, injurious, mischievous, noxious, pernicious, prejudicial *Ant* harmless, innocent, innocuous, inoffensive, safe

devastate *Syn* RAVAGE, despoil, pillage, sack, spoliate, waste

devastation *Syn* DESTRUCTION, annihilation, decimation, demolishment, demolition, desolation, extermination, extinction, havoc, loss, obliteration, ruin, ruination, wastage, wreckage *Ant* building, construction, erection, raising

develop 1 *Syn* MATURE, age, ripen 2 *Syn* UNFOLD, elaborate, evolve, perfect

deviant · departing from some accepted standard of what is normal *Syn* aberrant, abnormal, anomalous, atypical, irregular, unnatural *Rel* extraordinary, preternatural *Ant* natural, normal, regular, standard, typical

deviate *Syn* SWERVE, depart, digress, diverge, veer

deviation · departure from a straight course or procedure or from a norm or standard *Syn* aberration, deflection, divergence

device 1 · something usually of a mechanical character that performs a function or effects a desired end *Syn* contraption, contrivance, gadget *Rel* appliance, implement, instrument, tool, utensil 2 *Syn* FIGURE, design, motif, pattern

devil *Syn* DEMON, fiend, ghoul, imp, incubus

devilish *Syn* FIENDISH, demoniac, demonic, diabolic, diabolical

devil-may-care *Syn* CAREFREE, careless, cavalier, easygoing, gay, happy-go-lucky, insouciant, lighthearted, unconcerned *Ant* careworn

devious *Syn* CROOKED, oblique *Ant* straight

devise 1 *Syn* INVENT, concoct, contrive, cook (up), fabricate, make up, manufacture, think (up) 2 *Syn* WILL, bequeath, leave, legate

devoid · showing a want or lack *Syn* destitute, void *Rel* bare, barren

devolution *Syn* DETERIORATION, decadence, declension, decline, degeneration *Ant* amelioration, improvement

devote 1 · to set apart for a particular and often a better or higher use or end *Syn* consecrate, dedicate, hallow *Rel* commit, confide, consign, entrust 2 *Syn* DIRECT (sense 1), address, apply *Ant* misdirect

devoted 1 *Syn* FAITHFUL, constant, devout, fast, good, loyal, pious, staunch (*or* stanch), steadfast, steady, true, true-blue *Ant* disloyal, faithless, false, fickle, inconstant, perfidious, recreant, traitorous, treacherous, unfaithful, untrue 2 *Syn* LOVING, affectionate, doting, fond *Ant* unloving

devotee 1 *Syn* ADDICT, habitué, votary 2 *Syn* FAN, addict, aficionado, buff, bug, enthusiast, fanatic, fancier, fiend, freak, lover, maniac, nut

devotion *Syn* FIDELITY, allegiance, fealty, loyalty, piety *Ant* faithlessness, perfidy

devour *Syn* EAT, consume, ingest, swallow

devout 1 *Syn* HOLY (sense 1), godly, pious, religious, sainted, saintly *Ant* faithless, godless, impious, irreligious, ungodly, unholy 2 *Syn* FAITHFUL, constant, devoted, fast, good, loyal, pious, staunch (*or* stanch), steadfast, steady, true, true-blue *Ant* disloyal, faithless, false, fickle, inconstant, perfidious, recreant, traitorous, treacherous, unfaithful, untrue

devoutness *Syn* HOLINESS, blessedness, godliness, piety, piousness, sainthood, saintliness, saintship, sanctity *Ant* godlessness, impiety, ungodliness, unholiness

dexterity 1 · mental skill or quickness *Syn* adroitness, cleverness, finesse, sleight *Rel* ability, prowess, talent 2 · ease and grace in physical activity *Syn* agility, deftness, nimbleness, sleight, spryness *Rel* coordination *Ant* awkwardness, clumsiness, gawkiness 3 *Syn* READINESS, ease, facility

diabolic *Syn* FIENDISH, demoniac, demonic, devilish, diabolical

diabolical *Syn* FIENDISH, demoniac, demonic, devilish, diabolic

diagram *vb Syn* SKETCH, blueprint, delineate, draft, outline, plot, trace

diagram *n Syn* SKETCH, blueprint, delineation, draft, outline, plot, tracing

dialect 1 *Syn* LANGUAGE (sense 1), idiom, speech, tongue 2 *Syn* TERMINOLOGY, argot, cant, jargon, language, lingo, patois, patter, slang, vocabulary

dialectic *Syn* ARGUMENTATION, debate, disputation, forensic

diaphanous *Syn* CLEAR (sense 1), limpid, lucid, pellucid, translucent, transparent *Ant* confused, turbid

diatribe *Syn* TIRADE, jeremiad, philippic *Ant* eulogy

dice *Syn* CHOP, hash, mince

dicker *Syn* BARGAIN, chaffer, deal, haggle, horse-trade, negotiate, palter

dictate *vb* · to lay down expressly something to be followed, observed, obeyed, or accepted *Syn* decree, impose, ordain, prescribe *Rel* control, direct, manage

dictate *n Syn* COMMAND, behest, bidding, injunction, mandate, order

dictatorial 1 · imposing one's will or opinions on others *Syn* authoritarian, doctrinaire, dogmatic, magisterial *Rel* domineering, imperative, imperious, masterful, peremptory 2 *Syn* BOSSY, authoritarian, autocratic, despotic, domineering, imperious, masterful, overbearing, peremptory, tyrannical, tyrannous

diction *Syn* LANGUAGE (sense 2), phraseology, phrasing, style, vocabulary

dido *Syn* PRANK, antic, caper, monkeyshine

differ · to be unlike or out of harmony *Syn* disagree, dissent, vary *Rel* depart, deviate, diverge *Ant* agree

difference 1 *Syn* DISCORD, conflict, contention, dissension, schism, strife, variance 2 *Syn* DISSIMILARITY, distinction, divergence, divergency, unlikeness *Ant* similarity

different · unlike in kind or character *Syn* disparate, divergent, diverse, various *Rel* distinct, separate, several *Ant* alike, identical, same

differentiate *Syn* DISTINGUISH, demarcate, discriminate *Ant* confound

difficult *Syn* HARD, arduous *Ant* easy

difficulty · something which demands effort and endurance if it is to be overcome or one's end achieved *Syn* hardship, rigor, vicissitude *Rel* impediment, obstacle, obstruction, snag

diffident *Syn* SHY, bashful, coy, modest *Ant* obtrusive

diffuse *vb Syn* SPREAD, circulate, disseminate, propagate, radiate

diffuse *adj Syn* WORDY, prolix, redundant, verbose *Ant* compact, concise, crisp, pithy, succinct, terse

dig *vb* · to loosen and turn over or remove (as soil) with or as if with a spade *Syn* delve, excavate, grub, spade *Rel* enter, penetrate, pierce, probe

dig *n Syn* INSULT, affront, barb, dart, epithet, indignity, name, offense (*or* offence), outrage, put-down, sarcasm, slight, slur

digest *n Syn* COMPENDIUM, aperçu, pandect, précis, sketch, survey, syllabus

digest *vb Syn* SUMMARIZE, abstract, encapsulate, epitomize, outline, recap, recapitulate, sum up, wrap up

dig (into) *Syn* EXPLORE, delve (into), inquire (into), investigate, look (into), probe, research

digit *Syn* NUMBER, figure, integer, numeral

dignified · having or showing a serious and reserved manner *Syn* august, imposing, solemn, staid, stately *Rel* decorous, formal, proper, seemly *Ant* flighty, frivolous, giddy, goofy, silly, undignified

dignify 1 · to enhance the status of or raise in human estimation *Syn* ennoble, glorify, honor *Rel* elevate, lift, raise 2 *Syn* EXALT, aggrandize, ennoble, enshrine, glorify, magnify *Ant* abase, degrade, demean, humble, humiliate

dignity *Syn* DECORUM, decency, etiquette, propriety *Ant* indecorum, license

digress *Syn* SWERVE, depart, deviate, diverge, veer

digression · a departure from a subject or theme *Syn* divagation, episode, excursus

dike *Syn* DAM, embankment, levee

dilapidate *Syn* RUIN, wreck

dilapidated *Syn* SHABBY, dingy, faded, seedy, threadbare

dilate 1 *Syn* DISCOURSE, descant, expatiate 2 *Syn* EXPAND, amplify, distend, inflate, swell *Ant* abridge, circumscribe, contract

dilatory *Syn* SLOW, deliberate, laggard, leisurely *Ant* fast

dilemma *Syn* PREDICAMENT, fix, jam, pickle, plight, quandary, scrape

dilettante *n* 1 *Syn* AESTHETE, connoisseur 2 *Syn* AMATEUR, dabbler, tyro *Ant* expert, professional

dilettante *adj Syn* AMATEURISH, amateur, inexperienced, inexpert, nonprofessional, unprofessional, unskilled, unskillful *Ant* ace, adept, consummate, crackerjack, expert, master, masterful, masterly, professional, virtuoso

diligent *Syn* BUSY, assiduous, industrious, sedulous *Ant* idle, unoccupied

dilute 1 *Syn* IMPURE, adulterated, alloyed, contaminated, diluted, polluted, tainted, thinned, weakened *Ant* pure, unadulterated, unalloyed, uncontaminated, undiluted, unpolluted, untainted 2 *Syn* THIN, attenuate, extenuate, rarefy *Ant* thicken

diluted *Syn* IMPURE, adulterated, alloyed, contaminated, dilute, polluted, tainted, thinned, weakened *Ant* pure, unadulterated, unalloyed, uncontaminated, undiluted, unpolluted, untainted

dim *adj Syn* DARK, dusky, gloomy, murky, obscure *Ant* light

dim *vb Syn* OBSCURE, becloud, bedim, befog, cloud, darken, eclipse, fog, obfuscate *Ant* illuminate, illumine

dimensions *Syn* SIZE, area, extent, magnitude, volume

diminish *Syn* DECREASE, abate, dwindle, lessen, reduce *Ant* increase

din · a disturbing or confusing welter of sounds *Syn* babel, clamor, hubbub, hullabaloo, pandemonium, racket, uproar *Rel* blatancy, boisterousness, clamorousness, stridency *Ant* quiet

diner *Syn* RESTAURANT, café, grill

dingy *Syn* SHABBY, dilapidated, faded, seedy, threadbare

dinner · a usually elaborate meal served to guests or to a group often to mark an occasion or honor an individual *Syn* banquet, feast

dip 1 · to plunge a person or thing into or as if into liquid *Syn* duck, dunk, immerse, souse, submerge 2 · to remove a liquid or a loose or soft substance from a container by means of an implement shaped to hold liquid *Syn* bail, dish, ladle, scoop, spoon

dipsomaniac *Syn* DRUNKARD, alcoholic, inebriate, soak, sot, tippler, toper, tosspot *Ant* teetotaler

dire *Syn* OMINOUS, baleful, foreboding, inauspicious, menacing, portentous, sinister, threatening

direct 1 · to turn or bend one's attention or efforts toward a certain object or objective *Syn* address, apply, devote *Rel* bend 2 · to turn something toward its appointed or intended mark or goal *Syn* aim, lay, level, point, train *Rel* engineer, guide, lead, pilot, steer *Ant* misdirect 3 *Syn* CHANNEL, channelize, conduct, funnel, pipe, siphon 4 *Syn* COMMAND, bid, charge, enjoin, instruct, order *Ant* comply, obey 5 *Syn* CONDUCT, control, manage

directly *Syn* PRESENTLY, shortly, soon

directness *Syn* CANDOR, forthrightness, frankness, openheartedness, openness, plainness, straightforwardness *Ant* dissembling, pretense (*or* pretence)

director *Syn* EXECUTIVE, administrator, manager, superintendent, supervisor

dirty *adj* · conspicuously unclean or impure *Syn* filthy, foul, nasty, squalid *Ant* clean

dirty *vb* · to make dirty *Syn* befoul, begrime, besmirch, blacken, foul, grime, mire, muddy, smirch, smudge, soil, stain, sully *Rel* contaminate, defile, pollute, taint *Ant* clean, cleanse

disabuse *Syn* RID, clear, purge, unburden

disadvantage · a feature of someone or something that creates difficulty for achieving success *Syn* drawback, handicap, liability, minus, penalty, strike *Rel* stranglehold *Ant* advantage, asset, edge, plus

disadvantaged *Syn* DEPRIVED, underprivileged *Ant* privileged

disaffect *Syn* ESTRANGE, alienate, wean *Ant* reconcile

disaffection *Syn* ESTRANGEMENT, alienation, disgruntlement, souring *Ant* reconciliation

disagree *Syn* DIFFER, dissent, vary *Ant* agree

disagreeable *Syn* UNPLEASANT, bad, displeasing, distasteful, nasty, rotten, sour, uncongenial, unlovely, unpleasing, unsatisfying, unwelcome *Ant* agreeable, congenial, good, grateful, gratifying, nice, palatable, pleasant, pleasing, pleasurable, satisfying, welcome

disallow *Syn* DISCLAIM, disavow, disown, repudiate *Ant* claim

disallowance 1 *Syn* DENIAL (sense 1), nay, no, refusal, rejection *Ant* allowance, grant 2 *Syn* DENIAL (sense 2), contradiction, disavowal, disclaimer, negation, rejection, repudiation *Ant* acknowledgment, admission, avowal, confirmation

disappear *Syn* VANISH, evanesce, evaporate, fade *Ant* appear, loom

disappointment 1 · the emotion felt when one's expectations are not met *Syn* dismay, dissatisfaction, frustration, letdown *Rel* disenchantment, disillusionment *Ant* contentment, gratification, satisfaction 2 · something that disappoints *Syn* bummer, letdown *Rel* anticlimax, failure, fiasco, fizzle

disapprove (of) · to hold an unfavorable opinion of *Syn* deprecate, discountenance, disfavor, dislike, frown (on), reprove *Rel* blame, censure, condemn, criticize, denounce, reprehend, reprobate *Ant* approve, favor, like

disarm *Syn* PACIFY, appease, conciliate, mollify, placate, propitiate *Ant* anger, enrage, incense, infuriate, madden, outrage

disarming *Syn* LOVABLE, adorable, darling, dear, endearing, precious, sweet, winning *Ant* abhorrent, abominable, detestable, hateful, odious, unlovable

disarrange *Syn* DISORDER, confuse, derange, disarray, discompose, dishevel, dislocate, disorganize, disrupt, disturb, hash, jumble, mess (up), mix (up), muddle, muss, rumple, scramble, shuffle, tousle, tumble, upset *Ant* arrange, array, draw up, marshal, order, organize, range, regulate, straighten (up), tidy

disarranged *Syn* MESSY, chaotic, cluttered, confused, disarrayed, disheveled (*or* dishevelled), disordered, disorderly, higgledy-piggledy, hugger-mugger, jumbled, littered, messed, muddled, mussed, mussy, pell-mell, rumpled, sloppy, topsy-turvy, tousled, tumbled, unkempt, untidy, upside-down *Ant* neat, ordered, orderly, organized, shipshape, snug, tidied, tidy, trim

disarray *n* *Syn* CONFUSION, chaos, clutter, disorder, jumble, muddle, snarl

disarray *vb* *Syn* DISORDER, confuse, derange, disarrange, discompose, dishevel, dislocate, disorganize, disrupt, disturb, hash, jumble, mess (up), mix (up), muddle, muss, rumple, scramble, shuffle, tousle, tumble, upset *Ant* arrange, array, draw up, marshal, order, organize, range, regulate, straighten (up), tidy

disarrayed *Syn* MESSY, chaotic, cluttered, confused, disarranged, disheveled (*or* dishevelled), disordered, disorderly, higgledy-piggledy, hugger-mugger, jumbled, littered, messed, muddled, mussed, mussy, pell-mell, rumpled, sloppy, topsy-turvy, tousled, tumbled, unkempt, untidy, upside-down *Ant* neat, ordered, orderly, organized, shipshape, snug, tidied, tidy, trim

disaster · an event bringing great damage, loss, or destruction *Syn* apocalypse, calamity, cataclysm, catastrophe *Rel* accident, casualty, mishap

disastrous *Syn* UNLUCKY, calamitous, hapless, ill-fated, ill-starred, luckless, unfortunate *Ant* fortunate, happy, lucky

disavow *Syn* DISCLAIM, disallow, disown, repudiate *Ant* claim

disavowal *Syn* DENIAL (sense 2), contradiction, disallowance, disclaimer, negation, rejection, repudiation *Ant* acknowledgment, admission, avowal, confirmation

disbar *Syn* EXCLUDE, blackball, debar, eliminate, rule out, shut out, suspend *Ant* admit, include

disbelief *Syn* UNBELIEF, incredulity *Ant* belief

disbeliever *Syn* SKEPTIC, doubter, questioner, unbeliever

disburse *Syn* SPEND, expend *Ant* save

discard · to get rid of *Syn* cast, junk, molt, scrap, shed, slough *Rel* abandon, desert, forsake

discern *Syn* SEE (sense 1), behold, contemplate, descry, espy, note, notice, observe, perceive, remark, survey, view

discernible *Syn* PERCEPTIBLE, appreciable, detectable, distinguishable, palpable, sensible *Ant* impalpable, imperceptible, inappreciable, indistinguishable, insensible

discernment · a power to see what is not evident to the average mind *Syn* acumen, discrimination, insight, penetration, perception *Rel* intuition, reason, understanding

discharge **1** *Syn* DISMISS, bounce, cashier, drop, fire, sack **2** *Syn* FREE, emancipate, liberate, manumit, release **3** *Syn* PERFORM, accomplish, achieve, effect, execute, fulfill

disciple *Syn* FOLLOWER, adherent, convert, partisan, pupil, votary *Ant* leader

disciplinary *Syn* PUNITIVE, castigating, chastening, chastising, correcting, correctional, corrective, disciplining, penal, penalizing

discipline *n* *Syn* MORALE, esprit de corps

discipline *vb* **1** *Syn* PUNISH, castigate, chasten, chastise, correct *Ant* excuse, pardon **2** *Syn* TEACH, educate, instruct, school, train

disciplining *Syn* PUNITIVE, castigating, chastening, chastising, correcting, correctional, corrective, disciplinary, penal, penalizing

disclaim · to refuse to admit, accept, or approve *Syn* disallow, disavow, disown, repudiate *Rel* contradict, deny, gainsay, traverse *Ant* claim

disclaimer *Syn* DENIAL (sense 2), contradiction, disallowance, disavowal, negation, rejection, repudiation *Ant* acknowledgment, admission, avowal, confirmation

disclose *Syn* REVEAL, betray, discover, divulge, tell *Ant* conceal

disclosure *Syn* REVELATION (sense 2), divulgence, exposure

discomfit *Syn* EMBARRASS, abash, disconcert, faze, rattle *Ant* facilitate, relieve

discomforting *Syn* TROUBLESOME, discomposing, disquieting, distressing, disturbing, perturbing, troubling, troublous, unsettling,

upsetting, worrisome *Ant* reassuring, untroublesome

discommode *Syn* INCONVENIENCE, disoblige, disturb, incommode, trouble *Ant* accommodate, oblige

discompose **1** · to excite one so as to destroy one's capacity for clear or collected thought or prompt action *Syn* agitate, disquiet, disturb, flurry, fluster, perturb, upset *Rel* discomfit, disconcert, embarrass, faze, rattle **2** *Syn* DISORDER, confuse, derange, disarrange, disarray, dishevel, dislocate, disorganize, disrupt, disturb, hash, jumble, mess (up), mix (up), muddle, muss, rumple, scramble, shuffle, tousle, tumble, upset *Ant* arrange, array, draw up, marshal, order, organize, range, regulate, straighten (up), tidy

discomposing *Syn* TROUBLESOME, discomforting, disquieting, distressing, disturbing, perturbing, troubling, troublous, unsettling, upsetting, worrisome *Ant* reassuring, untroublesome

disconcert *Syn* EMBARRASS, abash, discomfit, faze, rattle *Ant* facilitate, relieve

disconsolate *Syn* SAD (sense 1), bad, blue, brokenhearted, crestfallen, dejected, depressed, despondent, doleful, down, downcast, downhearted, droopy, forlorn, gloomy, glum, heartbroken, heartsick, heartsore, inconsolable, joyless, low, low-spirited, melancholy, miserable, mournful, saddened, sorrowful, sorry, unhappy, woebegone, woeful, wretched *Ant* blissful, buoyant, buoyed, cheerful, cheery, chipper, delighted, glad, gladdened, gladsome, gleeful, happy, joyful, joyous, jubilant, sunny, upbeat

disconsolateness *Syn* SADNESS, blues, dejection, depression, desolation, despondency, dispiritedness, doldrums, downheartedness, dreariness, dumps, forlornness, gloom, gloominess, heartsickness, joylessness, melancholy, mopes, oppression, unhappiness *Ant* bliss, blissfulness, ecstasy, elatedness, elation, euphoria, exhilaration, exuberance, exultation, felicity, gladness, gladsomeness, happiness, heaven, intoxication, joy, joyfulness, joyousness, jubilation, rapture, rapturousness

discontinue *Syn* STOP, cease, desist, quit

discontinuous *Syn* FITFUL, casual, choppy, erratic, intermittent, irregular, occasional, spasmodic, sporadic, spotty, unsteady *Ant* constant, continuous, regular, steady

discord · a state or condition marked by disagreement and lack of harmony *Syn* conflict, contention, difference, dissension, schism, strife, variance *Rel* discrepancy, incompatibility, incongruity, inconsistency, inconsonance, uncongeniality

discordant **1** *Syn* BELLIGERENT, aggressive, argumentative, bellicose, combative, contentious, disputatious, gladiatorial, militant, pugnacious, quarrelsome, scrappy, truculent, warlike *Ant* nonbelligerent, pacific, peaceable, peaceful **2** *Syn* INCONSONANT, discrepant, incompatible, incongruous, inconsistent, uncongenial, unsympathetic *Ant* consonant

discount *Syn* DEDUCTION, abatement, rebate

discountenance *Syn* DISAPPROVE (OF), deprecate, disfavor, dislike, frown (on), reprove *Ant* approve, favor, like

discourage 1 · to lessen the courage or confidence of *Syn* daunt, demoralize, dishearten, dismay, dispirit, unnerve *Rel* browbeat, bully, cow, intimidate *Ant* embolden, encourage, hearten, nerve, steel **2** · to steer (a person) from an activity or course of action *Syn* deter, dissuade, inhibit *Rel* divert *Ant* encourage, persuade

discourse *n* · a systematic, serious, and often learned exposition of a subject or topic *Syn* disquisition, dissertation, monograph, thesis, treatise *Rel* article, essay, paper

discourse *vb* · to talk or sometimes write especially formally and at length upon a subject *Syn* descant, dilate, expatiate *Rel* argue, discuss, dispute

discourteous *Syn* IMPOLITE, ill-bred, ill-mannered, impertinent, inconsiderate, rude, thoughtless, uncalled-for, uncivil, ungracious, unmannerly *Ant* civil, considerate, courteous, genteel, gracious, mannerly, polite, thoughtful, well-bred

discover 1 · to find out something not previously known *Syn* ascertain, determine, learn, unearth *Rel* discern, espy, observe, perceive **2** *Syn* REVEAL, betray, disclose, divulge, tell *Ant* conceal

discreet *Syn* PRUDENT, foresighted, forethoughtful, provident

discreetness *Syn* COMMON SENSE, discretion, horse sense, levelheadedness, prudence, sense, sensibleness, wisdom, wit *Ant* imprudence, indiscretion

discrepant *Syn* INCONSONANT, discordant, incompatible, incongruous, inconsistent, uncongenial, unsympathetic *Ant* consonant

discrete *Syn* DISTINCT, separate, several

discretion 1 *Syn* COMMON SENSE, discreetness, horse sense, levelheadedness, prudence, sense, sensibleness, wisdom, wit *Ant* imprudence, indiscretion **2** *Syn* PRUDENCE, foresight, forethought, providence

discretionary *Syn* OPTIONAL, elective, voluntary *Ant* compulsory, mandatory, nonelective, obligatory, required

discriminate *Syn* DISTINGUISH, demarcate, differentiate *Ant* confound

discrimination *Syn* DISCERNMENT, acumen, insight, penetration, perception

discuss · to exchange views about something in order to arrive at the truth or to convince others *Syn* agitate, argue, debate, dispute *Rel*

elucidate, explain, explicate, expound, interpret

disdain *n* *Syn* CONTEMPT, despite, despitefulness, scorn *Ant* admiration, esteem, regard, respect

disdain *vb* *Syn* DESPISE, contemn, scorn, scout *Ant* appreciate

disdainful *Syn* PROUD (sense 1), arrogant, haughty, insolent, lordly, overbearing, supercilious *Ant* ashamed, humble

disease · an impairment of the normal state of the living body that interferes with normal bodily functions *Syn* ailment, complaint, condition, disorder, distemper, malady, syndrome

diseased *Syn* UNWHOLESOME, morbid, pathological, sickly *Ant* wholesome

disembarrass *Syn* EXTRICATE, disencumber, disentangle, untangle

disencumber *Syn* EXTRICATE, disembarrass, disentangle, untangle

disengage *Syn* DETACH, abstract *Ant* affix, attach

disentangle *Syn* EXTRICATE, disembarrass, disencumber, untangle

disfavor *vb* *Syn* DISAPPROVE (OF), deprecate, discountenance, dislike, frown (on), reprove *Ant* approve, favor, like

disfavor *n* *Syn* DISLIKE, aversion, distaste *Ant* liking

disfigurement *Syn* BLEMISH, defect, deformity, fault, flaw, imperfection, mark, pockmark, scar

disgorge 1 *Syn* BELCH, burp, regurgitate, spew, throw up, vomit **2** *Syn* ERUPT (sense 2), belch, eject, expel, jet, spew, spout, spurt

disgrace · the state of suffering loss of esteem and of enduring reproach *Syn* dishonor, disrepute, ignominy, infamy, obloquy, odium, opprobrium, shame *Rel* abasement, debasement, degradation, humbling, humiliation *Ant* esteem, respect

disgruntlement *Syn* ESTRANGEMENT, alienation, disaffection, souring *Ant* reconciliation

disguise · to alter so as to hide the true appearance or character of *Syn* camouflage, cloak, dissemble, mask *Rel* conceal, hide

disgust *n* · a dislike so strong as to cause stomach upset or queasiness *Syn* aversion, distaste, loathing, nausea, repugnance, repulsion, revulsion *Rel* abhorrence, abomination, execration, hate, hatred

disgust *vb* · to cause to feel disgust *Syn* nauseate, repel, repulse, revolt, sicken, turn off *Rel* displease, distress

dish *Syn* DIP (sense 2), bail, ladle, scoop, spoon

dishearten *Syn* DISCOURAGE (sense 1), daunt, demoralize, dismay, dispirit, unnerve *Ant* embolden, encourage, hearten, nerve, steel

dishevel *Syn* DISORDER, confuse, derange, disarrange, disarray, discompose, dislocate, disorganize, disrupt, disturb, hash, jumble, mess (up), mix (up), muddle, muss, rumple, scramble, shuffle, tousle, tumble, upset *Ant* arrange, array, draw up, marshal, order, organize, range, regulate, straighten (up), tidy

disheveled 1 *Syn* SLIPSHOD, sloppy, slovenly, unkempt 2 *Syn* MESSY, chaotic, cluttered, confused, disarranged, disarrayed, disordered, disorderly, higgledy-piggledy, hugger-mugger, jumbled, littered, messed, muddled, mussed, mussy, pell-mell, rumpled, sloppy, topsy-turvy, tousled, tumbled, unkempt, untidy, upside-down *Ant* neat, ordered, orderly, organized, shipshape, snug, tidied, tidy, trim

dishonor *Syn* DISGRACE, disrepute, ignominy, infamy, obloquy, odium, opprobrium, shame *Ant* esteem, respect

disinclination *Syn* RELUCTANCE, hesitance, hesitancy, unwillingness *Ant* inclination, willingness

disinclined · lacking the will or the desire to do something *Syn* averse, hesitant, indisposed, loath, reluctant *Rel* antipathetic, unsympathetic

disinfect *Syn* STERILIZE (sense 2), fumigate, sanitize

disintegrate *Syn* DECAY, crumble, decompose, putrefy, rot, spoil

disinterested *Syn* INDIFFERENT, aloof, detached, incurious, unconcerned, uninterested *Ant* avid

disinterestedness 1 *Syn* DETACHMENT, impartiality, neutrality, objectivity *Ant* bias, favor, favoritism, one-sidedness, partiality, partisanship, prejudice 2 *Syn* INDIFFERENCE, apathy, casualness, disregard, insouciance, nonchalance, unconcern *Ant* concern, interest, regard

dislike *n* · a feeling of aversion or disapproval *Syn* aversion, disfavor, distaste *Rel* detestation, hate, hatred *Ant* liking

dislike *vb Syn* DISAPPROVE (OF), deprecate, discountenance, disfavor, frown (on), reprove *Ant* approve, favor, like

dislocate *Syn* DISORDER, confuse, derange, disarrange, disarray, discompose, dishevel, disorganize, disrupt, disturb, hash, jumble, mess (up), mix (up), muddle, muss, rumple, scramble, shuffle, tousle, tumble, upset *Ant* arrange, array, draw up, marshal, order, organize, range, regulate, straighten (up), tidy

disloyal *Syn* FAITHLESS, false, perfidious, traitorous, treacherous *Ant* faithful

disloyalty *Syn* BETRAYAL, double cross, faithlessness, falseness, falsity, infidelity, perfidy, sellout, treachery, treason, unfaithfulness

dismal 1 · devoid of all that makes for cheer or comfort *Syn* bleak, cheerless, desolate, dispiriting, dreary *Rel* dark, gloomy, murky 2 *Syn* SAD (sense 2), depressing, drear, dreary, heartbreaking, heartrending, melancholy, pathetic, saddening, sorry, tearful, teary *Ant* cheering, cheery, glad, happy

dismantle *Syn* STRIP, bare, denude, divest *Ant* furnish, invest

dismay *vb* 1 · to unnerve and check by arousing fear, apprehension, or aversion *Syn* appall, daunt, horrify *Rel* bewilder, confound, dumbfound, mystify, nonplus, perplex, puzzle *Ant* cheer 2 *Syn* DISCOURAGE (sense 1), daunt, demoralize, dishearten, dispirit, unnerve *Ant* embolden, encourage, hearten, nerve, steel

dismay *n* 1 *Syn* DISAPPOINTMENT (sense 1), dissatisfaction, frustration, letdown *Ant* contentment, gratification, satisfaction 2 *Syn* FEAR, alarm, consternation, dread, fright, horror, panic, terror, trepidation *Ant* fearlessness

dismiss · to let go from one's employ or service *Syn* bounce, cashier, discharge, drop, fire, sack

dismount *Syn* DESCEND, alight *Ant* ascend, climb

disobedience · refusal to obey *Syn* contrariness, defiance, frowardness, insubordination, intractability, rebelliousness, recalcitrance, refractoriness, unruliness, willfulness *Rel* disrespect, impudence, insolence, rudeness *Ant* amenability, compliance, docility, obedience

disobedient · given to resisting authority or another's control *Syn* balky, contrary, defiant, froward, insubordinate, intractable, rebellious, recalcitrant, refractory, restive, ungovernable, unruly, untoward, wayward, willful (*or* wilful) *Rel* insurgent, mutinous *Ant* amenable, compliant, docile, obedient, tractable

disoblige *Syn* INCONVENIENCE, discommode, disturb, incommode, trouble *Ant* accommodate, oblige

disorder *vb* · to undo the proper order or arrangement of *Syn* confuse, derange, disarrange, disarray, discompose, dishevel, dislocate, disorganize, disrupt, disturb, hash, jumble, mess (up), mix (up), muddle, muss, rumple, scramble, shuffle, tousle, tumble, upset *Rel* embroil, entangle, snarl, tangle *Ant* arrange, array, draw up, marshal, order, organize, range, regulate, straighten (up), tidy

disorder *n* 1 *Syn* CONFUSION, chaos, clutter, disarray, jumble, muddle, snarl 2 *Syn* DISEASE, ailment, complaint, condition, distemper, malady, syndrome

disordered *Syn* MESSY, chaotic, cluttered, confused, disarranged, disarrayed, disheveled (*or* dishevelled), disorderly, higgledy-piggledy, hugger-mugger, jumbled, littered, messed, muddled, mussed, mussy, pell-mell, rumpled, sloppy, topsy-turvy, tousled, tumbled, unkempt, untidy, upside-down *Ant* neat, ordered, orderly, organized, shipshape, snug, tidied, tidy, trim

disorderly 1 *Syn* LAWLESS, anarchic, law-breaking, unruly *Ant* law-abiding, orderly 2 *Syn* MESSY, chaotic, cluttered, confused, disarranged, disarrayed, disheveled (*or* dishevelled), disordered, higgledy-piggledy, hugger-mugger, jumbled, littered, messed, muddled, mussed, mussy, pell-mell, rumpled, sloppy, topsy-turvy, tousled, tumbled, unkempt, untidy, upside-down *Ant* neat, ordered, orderly, organized, shipshape, snug, tidied, tidy, trim

disorganize *Syn* DISORDER, confuse, derange, disarrange, disarray, discompose, dishevel, dislocate, disrupt, disturb, hash, jumble, mess (up), mix (up), muddle, muss, rumple, scramble, shuffle, tousle, tumble, upset *Ant* arrange, array, draw up, marshal, order, organize, range, regulate, straighten (up), tidy

disown *Syn* DISCLAIM, disallow, disavow, repudiate *Ant* claim

disparage *Syn* DECRY, belittle, deprecate, derogate, detract, minimize *Ant* extol

disparaging *Syn* DEROGATORY, depreciative, depreciatory, pejorative, slighting

disparate *Syn* DIFFERENT, divergent, diverse, various *Ant* alike, identical, same

dispassionate *Syn* FAIR, equitable, impartial, just, objective, unbiased, uncolored *Ant* unfair

dispatch n 1 *Syn* HASTE, expedition, hurry, speed *Ant* deliberation 2 *Syn* LETTER, epistle, memorandum, message, missive, note, report

dispatch vb 1 *Syn* KILL, assassinate, execute, murder, slay 2 *Syn* SEND, forward, remit, route, ship, transmit *Ant* accept, receive

dispel *Syn* SCATTER (sense 1), disperse, dissipate

dispensable *Syn* UNNECESSARY, gratuitous, needless, nonessential, uncalled-for, unessential, unwarranted *Ant* essential, indispensable, necessary, needed, needful, required

dispense *Syn* DISTRIBUTE, deal, divide, dole *Ant* amass, collect

disperse *Syn* SCATTER (sense 1), dispel, dissipate

dispirit *Syn* DISCOURAGE (sense 1), daunt, demoralize, dishearten, dismay, unnerve *Ant* embolden, encourage, hearten, nerve, steel

dispiritedness *Syn* SADNESS, blues, dejection, depression, desolation, despondency, disconsolateness, doldrums, downheartedness, dreariness, dumps, forlornness, gloom, gloominess, heartsickness, joylessness, melancholy, mopes, oppression, unhappiness *Ant* bliss, blissfulness, ecstasy, elatedness, elation, euphoria, exhilaration, exuberance, exultation, felicity, gladness, gladsomeness, happiness, heaven, intoxication, joy, joyfulness, joyousness, jubilation, rapture, rapturousness

dispiriting *Syn* DISMAL, bleak, cheerless, desolate, dreary

displace *Syn* REPLACE, supersede, supplant

display n · a striking or spectacular show or exhibition for the sake of effect *Syn* array, parade, pomp *Rel* ostentation, ostentatiousness, pretension, pretentiousness, show, showiness

display vb *Syn* SHOW (sense 2), exhibit, expose, flaunt, parade *Ant* disguise

displeasing *Syn* UNPLEASANT, bad, disagreeable, distasteful, nasty, rotten, sour, uncongenial, unlovely, unpleasing, unsatisfying, unwelcome *Ant* agreeable, congenial, good, grateful, gratifying, nice, palatable, pleasant, pleasing, pleasurable, satisfying, welcome

disport n *Syn* PLAY, frolic, gambol, rollick, romp, sport *Ant* work

disport vb *Syn* PLAY, frolic, gambol, rollick, romp, sport

dispose *Syn* INCLINE, bias, predispose *Ant* disincline, indispose

disposition · the prevailing and dominant quality or qualities which distinguish or identify a person or group *Syn* character, complexion, individuality, personality, temper, temperament

disprove · to show by presenting evidence that something is not true *Syn* confute, controvert, rebut, refute *Rel* contravene, impugn, negative, traverse *Ant* demonstrate, prove

disputation *Syn* ARGUMENTATION, debate, dialectic, forensic

disputatious *Syn* BELLIGERENT, aggressive, argumentative, bellicose, combative, contentious, discordant, gladiatorial, militant, pugnacious, quarrelsome, scrappy, truculent, warlike *Ant* nonbelligerent, pacific, peaceable, peaceful

disputatiousness *Syn* BELLIGERENCE, aggression, aggressiveness, bellicosity, combativeness, contentiousness, fight, militancy, pugnacity, scrappiness, truculence *Ant* pacifism

dispute n *Syn* ARGUMENT, controversy

dispute vb *Syn* DISCUSS, agitate, argue, debate

disquiet vb *Syn* DISCOMPOSE, agitate, disturb, flurry, fluster, perturb, upset

disquiet n *Syn* UNREST, ferment, restiveness, restlessness, turmoil, uneasiness *Ant* calm, ease, peace, quiet

disquieting *Syn* TROUBLESOME, discomforting, discomposing, distressing, disturbing, perturbing, troubling, troublous, unsettling, upsetting, worrisome *Ant* reassuring, untroublesome

disquisition *Syn* DISCOURSE, dissertation, monograph, thesis, treatise

disrate *Syn* DEGRADE, declass, demote, reduce *Ant* elevate

disregard n *Syn* INDIFFERENCE, apathy, casualness, disinterestedness, insouciance, nonchalance, unconcern *Ant* concern, interest, regard

disregard vb 1 *Syn* NEGLECT, forget, ignore, omit, overlook, slight *Ant* cherish 2 *Syn*

SCORN (sense 1), despise, flout *Ant* honor, respect

disrepute *Syn* DISGRACE, dishonor, ignominy, infamy, obloquy, odium, opprobrium, shame *Ant* esteem, respect

disrupt *Syn* DISORDER, confuse, derange, disarrange, disarray, discompose, dishevel, dislocate, disorganize, disturb, hash, jumble, mess (up), mix (up), muddle, muss, rumple, scramble, shuffle, tousle, tumble, upset *Ant* arrange, array, draw up, marshal, order, organize, range, regulate, straighten (up), tidy

dissatisfaction *Syn* DISAPPOINTMENT (sense 1), dismay, frustration, letdown *Ant* contentment, gratification, satisfaction

dissect *Syn* ANALYZE, anatomize, assay, break down

dissection *Syn* ANALYSIS, breakdown, resolution *Ant* synthesis

dissemble *Syn* DISGUISE, camouflage, cloak, mask

dissembling *Syn* HYPOCRISY, cant, dissimulation, insincerity, piousness, sanctimoniousness *Ant* genuineness, sincerity

disseminate *Syn* SPREAD, circulate, diffuse, propagate, radiate

dissension *Syn* DISCORD, conflict, contention, difference, schism, strife, variance

dissent *vb Syn* DIFFER, disagree, vary *Ant* agree

dissent *n Syn* HERESY, dissidence, heterodoxy, nonconformity *Ant* conformity, orthodoxy

dissenter *Syn* HERETIC, dissident, nonconformist *Ant* conformer, conformist

dissertation *Syn* DISCOURSE, disquisition, monograph, thesis, treatise

disservice · unfair or inadequate treatment of someone or something or an instance of this *Syn* injury, injustice, raw deal, wrong *Rel* insult, offense, outrage *Ant* justice

dissidence *Syn* HERESY, dissent, heterodoxy, nonconformity *Ant* conformity, orthodoxy

dissimilarity · lack of agreement or correspondence or an instance of this *Syn* difference, distinction, divergence, divergency, unlikeness *Rel* disparity, diversity *Ant* similarity

dissimulation 1 *Syn* DECEIT, cunning, duplicity, guile 2 *Syn* HYPOCRISY, cant, dissembling, insincerity, piousness, sanctimoniousness *Ant* genuineness, sincerity

dissipate 1 *Syn* SCATTER (sense 1), dispel, disperse 2 *Syn* WASTE, consume, fritter, squander *Ant* conserve, save

dissipated *Syn* CORRUPT, debased, debauched, decadent, degenerate, degraded, demoralized, depraved, dissolute, perverse, perverted, reprobate, warped *Ant* uncorrupted

dissolute 1 *Syn* ABANDONED (sense 1), profligate, reprobate *Ant* redeemed, regenerate 2 *Syn* CORRUPT, debased, debauched, decadent, degenerate, degraded, demoralized, depraved, dissipated, perverse, perverted, reprobate, warped *Ant* uncorrupted

dissolve *Syn* ABOLISH, abrogate, annul, cancel, invalidate, negate, nullify, quash, repeal, rescind, void

dissuade *Syn* DISCOURAGE (sense 2), deter, inhibit *Ant* encourage, persuade

distant · not close in space, time, or relationship *Syn* far, faraway, far-off, remote, removed

distaste 1 *Syn* DISGUST, aversion, loathing, nausea, repugnance, repulsion, revulsion 2 *Syn* DISLIKE, aversion, disfavor *Ant* liking

distasteful 1 *Syn* REPUGNANT, abhorrent, invidious, obnoxious, repellent *Ant* congenial 2 *Syn* UNPLEASANT, bad, disagreeable, displeasing, nasty, rotten, sour, uncongenial, unlovely, unpleasing, unsatisfying, unwelcome *Ant* agreeable, congenial, good, grateful, gratifying, nice, palatable, pleasant, pleasing, pleasurable, satisfying, welcome

distemper *Syn* DISEASE, ailment, complaint, condition, disorder, malady, syndrome

distend *Syn* EXPAND, amplify, dilate, inflate, swell *Ant* abridge, circumscribe, contract

distinct 1 · capable of being distinguished as differing *Syn* discrete, separate, several *Rel* distinctive, individual, peculiar 2 *Syn* EVIDENT, apparent, clear, manifest, obvious, palpable, patent, plain

distinction 1 *Syn* AWARD, decoration, honor, plume, premium, prize 2 *Syn* DISSIMILARITY, difference, divergence, divergency, unlikeness *Ant* similarity 3 *Syn* EXCELLENCE, excellency, merit, value, virtue *Ant* deficiency

distinctive *Syn* CHARACTERISTIC, individual, peculiar

distinguish 1 · to recognize the differences between *Syn* demarcate, differentiate, discriminate *Rel* divide, part, separate *Ant* confound 2 *Syn* CHARACTERIZE, mark, qualify

distinguishable *Syn* PERCEPTIBLE, appreciable, detectable, discernible, palpable, sensible *Ant* impalpable, imperceptible, inappreciable, indistinguishable, insensible

distinguished *Syn* EMINENT, illustrious, noble, notable, noteworthy, outstanding, preeminent, prestigious, signal, star, superior

distort *Syn* DEFORM, contort, warp

distract *Syn* PUZZLE, bewilder, confound, dumbfound, mystify, nonplus, perplex

distraction *Syn* FRENZY, agitation, delirium, furor, furore, fury, hysteria, rage, rampage, uproar

distraught *Syn* ABSTRACTED, absent, absentminded, preoccupied *Ant* alert

distress *n* 1 · the state of being in great trouble or in mental or physical anguish *Syn* agony, dolor, misery, passion, suffering *Rel* affliction, trial, tribulation 2 *Syn* DANGER (sense 2), endangerment, imperilment, jeopardy, peril, risk, trouble *Ant* safeness, safety, security

distress

distress *vb Syn* TROUBLE, ail

distressful *Syn* REGRETTABLE, deplorable, distressing, grievous, heartbreaking, heart-rending, lamentable, unfortunate, woeful

distressing **1** *Syn* REGRETTABLE, deplorable, distressful, grievous, heartbreaking, heartrending, lamentable, unfortunate, woeful **2** *Syn* TROUBLESOME, discomforting, discomposing, disquieting, disturbing, perturbing, troubling, troublous, unsettling, upsetting, worrisome *Ant* reassuring, untroublesome

distribute · to give out, usually in shares, to each member of a group *Syn* deal, dispense, divide, dole *Rel* allocate, allot, apportion, assign *Ant* amass, collect

district *Syn* LOCALITY, neighborhood, vicinity

distrust *vb* · to have no trust or confidence in *Syn* doubt, mistrust, question, suspect *Rel* disbelieve, discount, discredit, negate *Ant* trust

distrust *n Syn* DOUBT, distrustfulness, incertitude, misgiving, mistrust, mistrustfulness, skepticism, suspicion, uncertainty *Ant* assurance, belief, certainty, certitude, confidence, conviction, sureness, surety, trust

distrustfully *Syn* ASKANCE, doubtfully, doubtingly, dubiously, mistrustfully, skeptically, suspiciously *Ant* trustfully, trustingly

distrustfulness *Syn* DOUBT, distrust, incertitude, misgiving, mistrust, mistrustfulness, skepticism, suspicion, uncertainty *Ant* assurance, belief, certainty, certitude, confidence, conviction, sureness, surety, trust

disturb **1** *Syn* DISCOMPOSE, agitate, disquiet, flurry, fluster, perturb, upset **2** *Syn* DISORDER, confuse, derange, disarrange, disarray, discompose, dishevel, dislocate, disorganize, disrupt, hash, jumble, mess (up), mix (up), muddle, muss, rumple, scramble, shuffle, tousle, tumble, upset *Ant* arrange, array, draw up, marshal, order, organize, range, regulate, straighten (up), tidy **3** *Syn* INCONVENIENCE, discommode, disoblige, incommode, trouble *Ant* accommodate, oblige

disturbance *Syn* COMMOTION, bother, bustle, clatter, furor, furore, fuss, hubbub, hullabaloo, hurly-burly, pandemonium, pother, row, ruckus, ruction, rumpus, shindy, squall, stew, stir, storm, to-do, tumult, turmoil, uproar, welter, whirl

disturbing **1** *Syn* ANNOYING, aggravating, bothersome, exasperating, frustrating, galling, irksome, irritating, maddening, nettling, peeving, pesty, rankling, riling, vexatious, vexing **2** *Syn* TROUBLESOME, discomforting, discomposing, disquieting, distressing, perturbing, troubling, troublous, unsettling, upsetting, worrisome *Ant* reassuring, untroublesome

disused *Syn* ABANDONED (sense 2), derelict, deserted, forgotten, forsaken, rejected, vacated

dither *Syn* SHAKE (sense 1), quake, quaver, quiver, shimmy, shiver, shudder, teeter, totter, tremble, wobble

diurnal *Syn* DAILY, day-to-day

divagation *Syn* DIGRESSION, episode, excursus

divan *Syn* COUCH, chesterfield, davenport, lounge, settee, sofa

dive *Syn* PLUNGE, pitch

diverge *Syn* SWERVE, depart, deviate, digress, veer

divergence **1** *Syn* DEVIATION, aberration, deflection **2** *Syn* DISSIMILARITY, difference, distinction, divergency, unlikeness *Ant* similarity

divergency *Syn* DISSIMILARITY, difference, distinction, divergence, unlikeness *Ant* similarity

divergent *Syn* DIFFERENT, disparate, diverse, various *Ant* alike, identical, same

divers *Syn* MANY, multifarious, numerous, several, sundry, various *Ant* few

diverse *Syn* DIFFERENT, disparate, divergent, various *Ant* alike, identical, same

diversion *Syn* AMUSEMENT, entertainment, recreation *Ant* boredom

divert **1** *Syn* AMUSE, entertain, recreate *Ant* bore **2** *Syn* TURN (sense 2), avert, deflect, sheer

diverting *Syn* FUN, amusing, delightful, enjoyable, entertaining, pleasurable *Ant* boring, dull

divest *Syn* STRIP, bare, denude, dismantle *Ant* furnish, invest

divide **1** *Syn* DISTRIBUTE, deal, dispense, dole *Ant* amass, collect **2** *Syn* SEPARATE, divorce, part, sever, sunder *Ant* combine

dividend *Syn* BONUS, extra, gratuity, gravy, lagniappe, perquisite, tip

divine *adj Syn* EXCELLENT, A1, bang-up, banner, capital, classic, crackerjack, dandy, fabulous, fine, first-class, first-rate, grand, great, groovy, heavenly, jim-dandy, keen, marvelous (*or* marvellous), mean, neat, nifty, noble, par excellence, prime, sensational, splendid, stellar, sterling, superb, superior, superlative, supernal, swell, terrific, tip-top, top, top-notch, unsurpassed, wonderful *Ant* poor

divine *vb Syn* FORESEE, anticipate, apprehend, foreknow

diviner *Syn* PROPHET, augur, forecaster, foreseer, foreteller, fortune-teller, futurist, prognosticator, prophesier, seer, soothsayer

division *Syn* PART, detail, fraction, fragment, member, parcel, piece, portion, section, sector, segment *Ant* whole

divorce *Syn* SEPARATE, divide, part, sever, sunder *Ant* combine

divulge *Syn* REVEAL, betray, disclose, discover, tell *Ant* conceal

divulgence *Syn* REVELATION (sense 2), disclosure, exposure

dizzy *Syn* GIDDY, dazzled, swimming, vertiginous

docile *Syn* OBEDIENT, amenable, compliant, conformable, law-abiding, submissive, tractable *Ant* contrary, disobedient, froward, insubordinate, intractable, rebellious, recalcitrant, refractory, unruly

dock *vb Syn* CLIP, bob, crop, curtail, cut, cut back, lop (off), nip, pare, prune, shave, shear, snip, trim

dock *n Syn* WHARF, berth, jetty, levee, pier, quay, slip

doctor *Syn* ADULTERATE, load, sophisticate, weight *Ant* refine

doctrinaire *Syn* DICTATORIAL, authoritarian, dogmatic, magisterial

doctrine · a principle accepted as valid and authoritative *Syn* dogma, tenet *Rel* instruction, teaching

document 1 · something preserved and serving as evidence (as of an event, a situation, or the culture of the period) *Syn* archive, monument, record *Rel* evidence, testimony 2 *Syn* PAPER, instrument

dodge · to avoid or evade by some maneuver or shift *Syn* duck, fence, malinger, parry, shirk, sidestep *Rel* avoid, elude, escape, evade *Ant* face

dogged 1 *Syn* OBSTINATE, adamant, adamantine, hard, hardened, hardheaded, hardhearted, headstrong, immovable, implacable, inflexible, mulish, obdurate, opinionated, ossified, pat, peevish, pertinacious, perverse, pigheaded, rigid, self-willed, stubborn, unbending, uncompromising, unrelenting, unyielding, willful (*or* wilful) *Ant* acquiescent, agreeable, amenable, compliant, complying, flexible, pliable, pliant, relenting, yielding 2 *Syn* PERSISTENT, insistent, patient, persevering, pertinacious, tenacious

dogging *Syn* PURSUIT, chase, chasing, following, hounding, pursuing, shadowing, tagging, tailing, tracing, tracking, trailing

dogma *Syn* DOCTRINE, tenet

dogmatic *Syn* DICTATORIAL, authoritarian, doctrinaire, magisterial

doldrums 1 *Syn* ABEYANCE, dormancy, latency, quiescence, suspense, suspension *Ant* continuance, continuation 2 *Syn* SADNESS, blues, dejection, depression, desolation, despondency, disconsolateness, dispiritedness, downheartedness, dreariness, dumps, forlornness, gloom, gloominess, heartsickness, joylessness, melancholy, mopes, oppression, unhappiness *Ant* bliss, blissfulness, ecstasy, elatedness, elation, euphoria, exhilaration, exuberance, exultation, felicity, gladness, gladsomeness, happiness, heaven, intoxication, joy, joyfulness, joyousness, jubilation, rapture, rapturousness 3 *Syn* TEDIUM, boredom, ennui

dole *vb Syn* DISTRIBUTE, deal, dispense, divide *Ant* amass, collect

dole *n Syn* RATION, allowance, pittance

doleful 1 *Syn* MELANCHOLY, dolorous, lugubrious, plaintive, rueful 2 *Syn* SAD (sense 1), bad, blue, brokenhearted, crestfallen, dejected, depressed, despondent, disconsolate, down, downcast, downhearted, droopy, forlorn, gloomy, glum, heartbroken, heartsick, heartsore, inconsolable, joyless, low, lowspirited, melancholy, miserable, mournful, saddened, sorrowful, sorry, unhappy, woebegone, woeful, wretched *Ant* blissful, buoyant, buoyed, cheerful, cheery, chipper, delighted, glad, gladdened, gladsome, gleeful, happy, joyful, joyous, jubilant, sunny, upbeat

dolor *Syn* DISTRESS, agony, misery, passion, suffering

dolorous *Syn* MELANCHOLY, doleful, lugubrious, plaintive, rueful

domain *Syn* FIELD, bailiwick, province, sphere, territory

domestic *Syn* SERVANT, flunky, lackey, menial, retainer, steward *Ant* master

domicile *Syn* HABITATION, abode, dwelling, home, house, residence

dominance *Syn* SUPREMACY, ascendancy, dominion, predominance, preeminence, sovereignty

dominant · superior to all others in power, influence, position, or rank *Syn* paramount, predominant, preponderant, preponderating, sovereign *Rel* prevailing, prevalent *Ant* subordinate

domineering 1 *Syn* BOSSY, authoritarian, autocratic, despotic, dictatorial, imperious, masterful, overbearing, peremptory, tyrannical, tyrannous 2 *Syn* MASTERFUL, imperative, imperious, peremptory

dominion *Syn* SUPREMACY, ascendancy, dominance, predominance, preeminence, sovereignty

donate *Syn* GIVE, afford, bestow, confer, present

donation *Syn* CONTRIBUTION, alms, benefaction, beneficence, charity, philanthropy

donator *Syn* BENEFACTOR, donor, patron

donor *Syn* BENEFACTOR, donator, patron

doom *n Syn* FATE, destiny, lot, portion

doom *vb Syn* SENTENCE, condemn, damn, proscribe

door · an entrance to a place *Syn* doorway, gate, gateway, portal, postern *Rel* access, entrance, entrée, entry, ingress

doorway *Syn* DOOR, gate, gateway, portal, postern

dope (out) *Syn* SOLVE, answer, break, crack, figure out, puzzle (out), resolve, riddle, unravel, work, work out

dormancy *Syn* ABEYANCE, doldrums, latency, quiescence, suspense, suspension *Ant* continuance, continuation

dormant *Syn* LATENT, abeyant, potential, quiescent *Ant* patent

dot 1 *Syn* SCATTER (sense 2), bestrew, pepper, sow, spray, sprinkle, strew 2 *Syn* SPOT, blotch, dapple, fleck, freckle, marble, mottle, pepper, speck, speckle, splotch, sprinkle, stipple

dotage *Syn* AGE (sense 1), senescence, senility

dote *Syn* LIKE, enjoy, fancy, love, relish *Ant* dislike

dote (on) *Syn* IDOLIZE, adore, adulate, canonize, deify, worship

doting *Syn* LOVING, affectionate, devoted, fond *Ant* unloving

double · consisting of two members or parts that are usually joined *Syn* binary, bipartite, dual, duplex, twin *Rel* mated, paired *Ant* single

double cross *Syn* BETRAYAL, disloyalty, faithlessness, falseness, falsity, infidelity, perfidy, sellout, treachery, treason, unfaithfulness

double-cross *Syn* DECEIVE, beguile, betray, delude, mislead *Ant* enlighten, undeceive

double-crosser *Syn* TRAITOR, betrayer, quisling, recreant, turncoat

double-dealing *n Syn* DECEPTION, chicane, chicanery, fraud, trickery

double-dealing *adj Syn* INSINCERE, artificial, backhanded, feigned, hypocritical, left-handed, mealy, mealymouthed, two-faced, unctuous *Ant* genuine, heartfelt, honest, sincere, unfeigned

doubt *n* · a feeling or attitude that one does not know the truth, truthfulness, or trustworthiness of someone or something *Syn* distrust, distrustfulness, incertitude, misgiving, mistrust, mistrustfulness, skepticism, suspicion, uncertainty *Rel* disbelief, incredulity, unbelief *Ant* assurance, belief, certainty, certitude, confidence, conviction, sureness, surety, trust

doubt *vb Syn* DISTRUST, mistrust, question, suspect *Ant* trust

doubter *Syn* SKEPTIC, disbeliever, questioner, unbeliever

doubtful 1 · not affording assurance of the worth, soundness, success, or certainty of something or someone *Syn* dubious, problematic, questionable *Rel* distrustful, distrusting, mistrustful, mistrusting *Ant* cocksure, positive 2 *Syn* IMPROBABLE, dubious, far-fetched, flimsy, questionable, unapt, unlikely *Ant* likely, probable

doubtfully *Syn* ASKANCE, distrustfully, doubtingly, dubiously, mistrustfully, skeptically, suspiciously *Ant* trustfully, trustingly

doubtingly *Syn* ASKANCE, distrustfully, doubtfully, dubiously, mistrustfully, skeptically, suspiciously *Ant* trustfully, trustingly

doubtless *Syn* PROBABLY, likely, presumably *Ant* improbably

doughtiness *Syn* COURAGE, bravery, courageousness, daring, dauntlessness, fearlessness, gallantry, greatheartedness, guts, hardihood, heart, heroism, intrepidity, intrep-

idness, nerve, stoutness, valor *Ant* cowardice, cowardliness, cravenness, dastardliness, spinelessness, yellowness

doughty *Syn* BRAVE, audacious, bold, courageous, dauntless, fearless, intrepid, unafraid, undaunted, valiant, valorous *Ant* craven

dour *Syn* SULLEN, crabbed, gloomy, glum, morose, saturnine, sulky, surly

douse *Syn* WET, bathe, drench, soak, souse, wash, water *Ant* dry

dove *Syn* LAMB, angel, innocent, sheep *Ant* wolf

dowdily *Syn* SLOPPILY, slovenly, unstylishly *Ant* nattily, sharply, smartly, sprucely

dowdy *Syn* SLATTERNLY, blowsy, frowzy

dower · to furnish or provide with a gift *Syn* endow, endue *Rel* accouter, appoint, equip, furnish, outfit

down *n* 1 *Syn* COMEDOWN, decline, descent, downfall, fall *Ant* aggrandizement, ascent, exaltation, rise, up 2 *Syn* PLAIN, grassland, prairie, savanna, steppe, tundra, veld (*or* veldt)

down *adj Syn* SAD (sense 1), bad, blue, brokenhearted, crestfallen, dejected, depressed, despondent, disconsolate, doleful, downcast, downhearted, droopy, forlorn, gloomy, glum, heartbroken, heartsick, heartsore, inconsolable, joyless, low, low-spirited, melancholy, miserable, mournful, saddened, sorrowful, sorry, unhappy, woebegone, woeful, wretched *Ant* blissful, buoyant, buoyed, cheerful, cheery, chipper, delighted, glad, gladdened, gladsome, gleeful, happy, joyful, joyous, jubilant, sunny, upbeat

downcast *Syn* SAD (sense 1), bad, blue, brokenhearted, crestfallen, dejected, depressed, despondent, disconsolate, doleful, down, downhearted, droopy, forlorn, gloomy, glum, heartbroken, heartsick, heartsore, inconsolable, joyless, low, low-spirited, melancholy, miserable, mournful, saddened, sorrowful, sorry, unhappy, woebegone, woeful, wretched *Ant* blissful, buoyant, buoyed, cheerful, cheery, chipper, delighted, glad, gladdened, gladsome, gleeful, happy, joyful, joyous, jubilant, sunny, upbeat

downfall *Syn* COMEDOWN, decline, descent, down, fall *Ant* aggrandizement, ascent, exaltation, rise, up

downhearted *Syn* SAD (sense 1), bad, blue, brokenhearted, crestfallen, dejected, depressed, despondent, disconsolate, doleful, down, downcast, droopy, forlorn, gloomy, glum, heartbroken, heartsick, heartsore, inconsolable, joyless, low, low-spirited, melancholy, miserable, mournful, saddened, sorrowful, sorry, unhappy, woebegone, woeful, wretched *Ant* blissful, buoyant, buoyed, cheerful, cheery, chipper, delighted, glad, gladdened, gladsome, gleeful, happy, joyful, joyous, jubilant, sunny, upbeat

downheartedness *Syn* SADNESS, blues, dejection, depression, desolation, despondency, disconsolateness, dispiritedness, doldrums, dreariness, dumps, forlornness, gloom, gloominess, heartsickness, joylessness, melancholy, mopes, oppression, unhappiness *Ant* bliss, blissfulness, ecstasy, elatedness, elation, euphoria, exhilaration, exuberance, exultation, felicity, gladness, gladsomeness, happiness, heaven, intoxication, joy, joyfulness, joyousness, jubilation, rapture, rapturousness

downpour *Syn* RAIN (sense 1), cloudburst, deluge, rainfall, rainstorm, storm, wet

doze *Syn* SLEEP, catnap, drowse, nap, slumber, snooze

drab *Syn* BORING, dreary, dry, dull, flat, heavy, humdrum, jading, leaden, monotonous, pedestrian, ponderous, stodgy, stuffy, stupid, tame, tedious, tiresome, tiring, unanimated, uninteresting, wearisome, weary, wearying *Ant* absorbing, engaging, engrossing, gripping, interesting, intriguing, involving

draft *vb Syn* SKETCH, blueprint, delineate, diagram, outline, plot, trace

draft *n Syn* SKETCH, blueprint, delineation, diagram, outline, plot, tracing

drag *n Syn* ENCUMBRANCE, bar, block, chain, clog, crimp, deterrent, embarrassment, fetter, handicap, hindrance, hurdle, impediment, inhibition, interference, let, manacle, obstacle, obstruction, shackles, stop, stumbling block, trammel *Ant* aid, assistance, benefit, help

drag *vb Syn* PULL, draw, hale, haul, tow, tug

drain *Syn* DEPLETE, clean (out), consume, exhaust, expend, spend, use up *Ant* renew, replace

dramatic · of, relating to, or suggestive of plays, or the performance of a play *Syn* dramaturgic, histrionic, melodramatic, theatrical

dramaturgic *Syn* DRAMATIC, histrionic, melodramatic, theatrical

draw *n* · an indecisive ending to a contest or competition *Syn* deadlock, stalemate, standoff, tie

draw *vb* **1** *Syn* EARN, acquire, attain, capture, carry, gain, garner, get, land, make, obtain, procure, realize, secure, win *Ant* forfeit, lose **2** *Syn* PULL, drag, hale, haul, tow, tug

drawback *Syn* DISADVANTAGE, handicap, liability, minus, penalty, strike *Ant* advantage, asset, edge, plus

dread *Syn* FEAR, alarm, consternation, dismay, fright, horror, panic, terror, trepidation *Ant* fearlessness

dreadful *Syn* FEARFUL (sense 2), appalling, awful, frightful, horrible, horrific, shocking, terrible, terrific

dream **1** *Syn* FANCY, daydream, fantasy, nightmare, phantasm, phantasy, vision *Ant* reality **2** *Syn* GOAL, aim, ambition, aspiration, design, end, intent, intention, mark, meaning, object, objective, plan, pretension, purpose, target, thing

dreamer *Syn* IDEALIST, romantic, romanticist, utopian, visionary *Ant* pragmatist, realist

drear *Syn* SAD (sense 2), depressing, dismal, dreary, heartbreaking, heartrending, melancholy, pathetic, saddening, sorry, tearful, teary *Ant* cheering, cheery, glad, happy

dreariness *Syn* SADNESS, blues, dejection, depression, desolation, despondency, disconsolateness, dispiritedness, doldrums, downheartedness, dumps, forlornness, gloom, gloominess, heartsickness, joylessness, melancholy, mopes, oppression, unhappiness *Ant* bliss, blissfulness, ecstasy, elatedness, elation, euphoria, exhilaration, exuberance, exultation, felicity, gladness, gladsomeness, happiness, heaven, intoxication, joy, joyfulness, joyousness, jubilation, rapture, rapturousness

dreary **1** *Syn* BORING, drab, dry, dull, flat, heavy, humdrum, jading, leaden, monotonous, pedestrian, ponderous, stodgy, stuffy, stupid, tame, tedious, tiresome, tiring, unanimated, uninteresting, wearisome, weary, wearying *Ant* absorbing, engaging, engrossing, gripping, interesting, intriguing, involving **2** *Syn* DISMAL, bleak, cheerless, desolate, dispiriting **3** *Syn* SAD (sense 2), depressing, dismal, drear, heartbreaking, heartrending, melancholy, pathetic, saddening, sorry, tearful, teary *Ant* cheering, cheery, glad, happy

dregs *Syn* DEPOSIT, grounds, lees, precipitate, sediment

drench **1** *Syn* SOAK, impregnate, saturate, sop, steep, waterlog **2** *Syn* WET, bathe, douse, soak, souse, wash, water *Ant* dry

dress *adj* · relating to or suitable for wearing to an event requiring elegant dress and manners *Syn* dressy, formal *Rel* costume *Ant* casual, informal, sporty

dress *vb* **1** *Syn* CLOTHE, apparel, array, attire, robe *Ant* unclothe **2** *Syn* POLISH, buff, burnish, gloss, grind, rub, shine, smooth

dress *n Syn* CLOTHES, apparel, attire, clothing, raiment

dressy *Syn* DRESS, formal *Ant* casual, informal, sporty

drift *Syn* TENDENCY, tenor, trend

drifter *Syn* NOMAD, gadabout, rambler, roamer, rover, stroller, vagabond, wanderer, wayfarer

drill **1** *Syn* PERFORATE, bore, prick, punch, puncture **2** *Syn* PRACTICE, exercise

drink *Syn* ALCOHOL, booze, grog, intoxicant, liquor, moonshine, spirits

drive *vb Syn* ACTIVATE, actuate, crank (up), move, propel, run, set off, spark, start, touch off, trigger, turn on *Ant* cut, deactivate, kill, shut off, turn off

drive *n* **1** *Syn* CAMPAIGN, bandwagon, cause, crusade, movement **2** *Syn* VIGOR, dash, élan, esprit, punch, spirit, verve, vim

drivel

drivel *Syn* NONSENSE, balderdash, bull, bunk, gobbledygook, poppycock, rot, trash, twaddle

droll *Syn* LAUGHABLE, comic, comical, farcical, funny, ludicrous, risible

drone *Syn* LAZYBONES, idler, loafer, slouch, slug, sluggard *Ant* doer, go-getter, hummer, hustler, rustler, self-starter

droop · to become literally or figuratively limp through loss of vigor or freshness *Syn* flag, sag, wilt *Rel* drop, fall, sink, slump, subside

droopy *Syn* SAD (sense 1), bad, blue, brokenhearted, crestfallen, dejected, depressed, despondent, disconsolate, doleful, down, downcast, downhearted, forlorn, gloomy, glum, heartbroken, heartsick, heartsore, inconsolable, joyless, low, low-spirited, melancholy, miserable, mournful, saddened, sorrowful, sorry, unhappy, woebegone, woeful, wretched *Ant* blissful, buoyant, buoyed, cheerful, cheery, chipper, delighted, glad, gladdened, gladsome, gleeful, happy, joyful, joyous, jubilant, sunny, upbeat

drop 1 *Syn* DISMISS, bounce, cashier, discharge, fire, sack 2 *Syn* FALL, sink, slump, subside *Ant* rise

dropping *Syn* CANCELLATION, abortion, calling, calling off, recall, repeal, rescission, revocation *Ant* continuation

drown *Syn* FLOOD, deluge, engulf, inundate, overflow, overwhelm, submerge, submerse, swamp *Ant* drain

drowse *Syn* SLEEP, catnap, doze, nap, slumber, snooze

drowsiness *Syn* SLEEPINESS, somnolence *Ant* insomnia, sleeplessness, wakefulness

drowsy *Syn* SLEEPY, slumberous, somnolent

drudge *n Syn* SLAVE (sense 2), drudger, grubber, laborer, peon, plugger, slogger, toiler, worker *Ant* freeman

drudge *vb Syn* LABOR, endeavor, grub, hump, hustle, moil, peg (away), plod, plow, plug, slave, slog, strain, strive, struggle, sweat, toil, travail, work *Ant* dabble, fiddle (around), fool (around), mess (around), putter (around)

drudger *Syn* SLAVE (sense 2), drudge, grubber, laborer, peon, plugger, slogger, toiler, worker *Ant* freeman

drudgery *Syn* WORK (sense 1), grind, labor, toil, travail *Ant* fun, play

drug · a substance used by itself or in a mixture for the treatment or in the diagnosis of disease *Syn* biologic, medicinal, pharmaceutical, simple *Rel* cure, medicament, medication, medicine, physic, remedy, specific

druggist · one who deals in medicinal drugs *Syn* apothecary, chemist, pharmacist

drunk · having the faculties impaired by alcohol *Syn* drunken, inebriated, intoxicated, tight, tipsy *Rel* befuddled, confused, fuddled *Ant* sober

drunkard · one who is habitually drunk *Syn* alcoholic, dipsomaniac, inebriate, soak, sot, tippler, toper, tosspot *Ant* teetotaler

drunken *Syn* DRUNK, inebriated, intoxicated, tight, tipsy *Ant* sober

dry *vb* · to treat or to affect so as to deprive of moisture *Syn* bake, dehydrate, desiccate, parch *Rel* deplete, drain, exhaust *Ant* moisten, wet

dry *adj* 1 *Syn* BORING, drab, dreary, dull, flat, heavy, humdrum, jading, leaden, monotonous, pedestrian, ponderous, stodgy, stuffy, stupid, tame, tedious, tiresome, tiring, unanimated, uninteresting, wearisome, weary, wearying *Ant* absorbing, engaging, engrossing, gripping, interesting, intriguing, involving 2 *Syn* SOUR, acid, acidulous, tart

dry run *Syn* REHEARSAL, practice, trial

dual *Syn* DOUBLE, binary, bipartite, duplex, twin *Ant* single

dubious 1 *Syn* DOUBTFUL, problematic, questionable *Ant* cocksure, positive 2 *Syn* IMPROBABLE, doubtful, far-fetched, flimsy, questionable, unapt, unlikely *Ant* likely, probable

dubiously *Syn* ASKANCE, distrustfully, doubtfully, doubtingly, mistrustfully, skeptically, suspiciously *Ant* trustfully, trustingly

duck 1 *Syn* DIP (sense 1), dunk, immerse, souse, submerge 2 *Syn* DODGE, fence, malinger, parry, shirk, sidestep *Ant* face

duck soup *Syn* CINCH, breeze, child's play, picnic, pushover, snap *Ant* chore, headache, labor

duct *Syn* CHANNEL, aqueduct, canal, conduit

ductile *Syn* PLASTIC, adaptable, malleable, pliable, pliant

dude 1 *Syn* FOP, beau, buck, coxcomb, dandy, exquisite 2 *Syn* MAN (sense 1), fellow, gent, gentleman, guy, male

dudgeon *Syn* OFFENSE (sense 1), huff, pique, resentment, umbrage

due *adj* · being in accordance with what is just and appropriate *Syn* condign, rightful *Rel* appropriate, fit, fitting, meet, proper, suitable

due *n* · what is justly owed to a person (sometimes a thing), especially as a recompense or compensation *Syn* desert, merit *Rel* compensation, payment, recompense, recompensing, repayment, satisfaction

due to *Syn* BECAUSE OF, owing to, through, with

dulcet *Syn* SWEET, engaging, winning, winsome *Ant* bitter, sour

dull *adj* 1 · lacking sharpness of edge or point *Syn* blunt, obtuse *Ant* feeling, poignant (*sensation, reaction*), sharp 2 *Syn* BORING, drab, dreary, dry, flat, heavy, humdrum, jading, leaden, monotonous, pedestrian, ponderous, stodgy, stuffy, stupid, tame, tedious, tiresome, tiring, unanimated, uninteresting, wearisome, weary, wearying *Ant* absorbing, engaging, engrossing, gripping, interesting, intriguing, involving **3** *Syn* OVERCAST, beclouded, clouded, cloudy, hazed, hazy, heavy, lowering, overclouded *Ant* clear, cloudless **4** *Syn* STUPID, crass, dense, dumb, slow *Ant* intelligent

dull *vb Syn* WHITEN, blanch, bleach, blench, decolorize, fade, pale, wash out *Ant* blacken, darken, deepen

dumb 1 *Syn* SILENT (sense 3), mum, mute, speechless, uncommunicative, wordless **2** *Syn* STUPID, crass, dense, dull, slow *Ant* intelligent

dumbfound *Syn* PUZZLE, bewilder, confound, distract, mystify, nonplus, perplex

dump *Syn* ARMORY, arsenal, depot, magazine

dumps *Syn* SADNESS, blues, dejection, depression, desolation, despondency, disconsolateness, dispiritedness, doldrums, downheartedness, dreariness, forlornness, gloom, gloominess, heartsickness, joylessness, melancholy, mopes, oppression, unhappiness *Ant* bliss, blissfulness, ecstasy, elatedness, elation, euphoria, exhilaration, exuberance, exultation, felicity, gladness, gladsomeness, happiness, heaven, intoxication, joy, joyfulness, joyousness, jubilation, rapture, rapturousness

dumpy *Syn* STOCKY, chunky, squat, stubby, thick, thickset

dunk *Syn* DIP (sense 1), duck, immerse, souse, submerge

duo *Syn* PAIR, brace, couple, twain, twosome

dupe *n* · one who is easily deceived or cheated *Syn* chump, gull, pigeon, sap, sucker, tool *Rel* victim

dupe *vb* · mean to delude by underhanded means or methods *Syn* bamboozle, befool, gull, hoax, hoodwink, trick *Rel* beguile, betray, deceive, delude, double-cross, mislead

duplex *Syn* DOUBLE, binary, bipartite, dual, twin *Ant* single

duplicate *Syn* COPY, carbon copy, duplication, facsimile, imitation, reduplication, replica, replication, reproduction *Ant* original

duplication *Syn* COPY, carbon copy, duplicate, facsimile, imitation, reduplication, replica, replication, reproduction *Ant* original

duplicity *Syn* DECEIT, cunning, dissimulation, guile

durable *Syn* LASTING, perdurable, permanent, perpetual, stable *Ant* fleeting

duration *Syn* CONTINUATION, continuance, endurance, persistence, subsistence *Ant* ending, termination

duress *Syn* FORCE, coercion, compulsion, constraint, restraint, violence

dusky *Syn* DARK, dim, gloomy, murky, obscure *Ant* light

dutiful *Syn* RESPECTFUL, deferential, regardful *Ant* disrespectful

duty 1 *Syn* CHORE, assignment, job, stint, task **2** *Syn* FUNCTION, office, province **3** *Syn* OBLIGATION, burden, charge, commitment, need, responsibility **4** *Syn* TAX, assessment, imposition, impost, levy

dwarf · a living thing much smaller than others of its kind *Syn* midget, pygmy, runt

dwell *Syn* RESIDE, live, lodge, put up, sojourn, stay, stop

dweller *Syn* INHABITANT, denizen, habitant, occupant, resident, resider *Ant* transient

dwelling *Syn* HABITATION, abode, domicile, home, house, residence

dwindle *Syn* DECREASE, abate, diminish, lessen, reduce *Ant* increase

dye *Syn* PIGMENT, color, coloring, dyestuff, stain, tincture

dyestuff *Syn* PIGMENT, color, coloring, dye, stain, tincture

dynamic *Syn* ACTIVE, live, operative *Ant* inactive

E

each *adv* **1** · by, for, or to every one of the many *Syn* apiece, individually, respectively, severally **2** *Syn* APIECE, all, per capita

each *adj Syn* ALL, every *Ant* no

eager · moved by a strong and urgent desire or interest *Syn* agog, anxious, athirst, avid, keen *Rel* coveting, craving, desiring *Ant* listless

ear *Syn* ATTENTION (sense 2), awareness, cognizance, eye, heed, notice, observance, observation

early · at or nearly at the beginning of a spec-

ified or implied period of time *Syn* beforehand, betimes, soon *Ant* late

earn 1 · to receive as return for effort *Syn* acquire, attain, capture, carry, draw, gain, garner, get, land, make, obtain, procure, realize, secure, win *Rel* clear, net *Ant* forfeit, lose **2** *Syn* DESERVE, merit, rate

earnest *n Syn* PLEDGE, hostage, pawn, token

earnest *adj Syn* SERIOUS, grave, sedate, sober, solemn, somber, staid *Ant* flippant, light

earnestness · a mental state free of jesting or

trifling *Syn* gravity, intentness, seriousness, soberness, sobriety, solemnity *Rel* deliberation, determination, firmness, purposefulness, resolve *Ant* frivolity, levity, lightheartedness

earsplitting *Syn* LOUD, hoarse, raucous, stentorian, stertorous, strident *Ant* low, low-pitched

earth · the entire area or extent of space in which human beings think of themselves as living and acting *Syn* globe, planet, world *Rel* cosmos, macrocosm, universe

earthly · of, belonging to, or characteristic of the earth or life on earth *Syn* earthy, mundane, sublunary, terrestrial, worldly *Rel* profane, secular, temporal

earthy *Syn* EARTHLY, mundane, sublunary, terrestrial, worldly

ease *n* **1** *Syn* ABANDON, abandonment, lightheartedness, naturalness, spontaneity, unrestraint *Ant* constraint, restraint **2** *Syn* READINESS, dexterity, facility **3** *Syn* REST, comfort, leisure, relaxation, repose

ease *vb Syn* SLACKEN, loosen, relax, slack *Ant* strain, stretch, tense, tighten

easily · without difficulty *Syn* effortlessly, facilely, fluently, freely, handily, lightly, painlessly, readily, smoothly *Rel* ably, adeptly, adroitly, competently, dexterously, efficiently, expertly, proficiently, skillfully *Ant* arduously, laboriously

easy **1** · causing or involving little or no difficulty *Syn* effortless, facile, light, simple, smooth *Ant* hard **2** *Syn* COMFORTABLE, cozy, restful, snug *Ant* miserable, uncomfortable

easygoing *Syn* CAREFREE, careless, cavalier, devil-may-care, gay, happy-go-lucky, insouciant, lighthearted, unconcerned *Ant* careworn

eat · to take food into the stomach through the mouth *Syn* consume, devour, ingest, swallow *Rel* bite, champ, gnaw

ebb **1** *Syn* ABATE, subside, wane *Ant* revive, rise **2** *Syn* DETERIORATE, crumble, decay, decline, degenerate, descend, rot, sink, worsen *Ant* ameliorate, improve, meliorate

eccentric *n* · a person of odd or whimsical habits *Syn* character, codger, crackbrain, crackpot, crank, kook, nut, oddball, screwball, weirdo *Rel* bohemian, maverick, nonconformist

eccentric *adj Syn* STRANGE, curious, erratic, odd, outlandish, peculiar, quaint, queer, singular, unique *Ant* familiar

echelon *Syn* LINE, file, rank, row, tier

echo *Syn* REPEAT (sense 2), parrot, quote

éclat *Syn* FAME, celebrity, glory, honor, notoriety, renown, reputation, repute *Ant* infamy, obscurity

eclipse *Syn* OBSCURE, becloud, bedim, befog, cloud, darken, dim, fog, obfuscate *Ant* illuminate, illumine

economical *Syn* FRUGAL, economizing, provident, scrimping, sparing, thrifty *Ant* prodigal, wasteful

economize · to avoid unnecessary waste or expense *Syn* save, scrimp, skimp *Rel* conserve, husband, manage *Ant* waste

economizing *Syn* FRUGAL, economical, provident, scrimping, sparing, thrifty *Ant* prodigal, wasteful

economy · careful management of material resources *Syn* frugality, husbandry, providence, scrimping, skimping, thrift *Rel* conservation, saving *Ant* wastefulness

ecstasy · a state of overwhelming usually pleasurable emotion *Syn* elation, euphoria, exhilaration, heaven, intoxication, paradise, rapture, rhapsody, transport *Rel* exaltation *Ant* depression

ecstatic · experiencing or marked by overwhelming usually pleasurable emotion *Syn* elated, enraptured, entranced, euphoric, exhilarated, intoxicated, rapturous, rhapsodic *Rel* exultant, jubilant, triumphant *Ant* depressed

ecumenical *Syn* UNIVERSAL (sense 1), catholic, cosmic, cosmopolitan *Ant* particular

eddy *n* · a swirling mass especially of water *Syn* maelstrom, vortex, whirlpool

eddy *vb Syn* TURN (sense 1), circle, gyrate, pirouette, revolve, rotate, spin, swirl, twirl, wheel, whirl

edge *n* **1** *Syn* ADVANTAGE, allowance, handicap, odds *Ant* disadvantage, handicap **2** *Syn* BORDER, brim, brink, margin, rim, verge

edge *vb Syn* SHARPEN, grind, hone, strop, whet *Ant* blunt, dull

edgewise *Syn* SIDEWAYS, broadside, sidewise

edifice *Syn* BUILDING, structure

edify *Syn* ENLIGHTEN (sense 1), educate, nurture

edit · to prepare material for publication *Syn* adapt, compile, redact, revise, rewrite *Rel* fabricate, fashion, form, make

edition · the total number of copies of the same work printed during a stretch of time *Syn* impression, printing, reissue, reprinting

educate **1** *Syn* ENLIGHTEN (sense 1), edify, nurture **2** *Syn* TEACH, discipline, instruct, school, train

educated · having or displaying advanced knowledge or education *Syn* erudite, knowledgeable, learned, literate, scholarly, well-read *Rel* civilized, cultivated, cultured *Ant* ignorant, illiterate, uneducated

education **1** · the act or process of imparting knowledge or skills to another *Syn* instruction, schooling, teaching, training, tutelage, tutoring *Rel* coaching, conditioning, cultivation, preparation, readying **2** · the understanding and information gained from being educated *Syn* erudition, knowledge, learnedness, learning, scholarship, science *Rel* culture, edification, enlightenment

educational *Syn* ACADEMIC, scholarly, scholastic *Ant* nonacademic, unacademic

educator *Syn* TEACHER, instructor, pedagogue, preceptor, schoolteacher

educe · to bring or draw out what is hidden, latent, or reserved *Syn* elicit, evoke, extort, extract *Rel* drag, draw, pull

eerie · fearfully and mysteriously strange or fantastic *Syn* creepy, haunting, spooky, uncanny, unearthly, weird *Rel* ghostly, spectral

efface *Syn* ERASE, blot out, cancel, delete, expunge, obliterate

effect *n* · a condition, situation, or occurrence ascribable to a cause *Syn* aftereffect, aftermath, consequence, event, issue, outcome, result, sequel, upshot *Ant* cause

effect *vb* **1** · to be the cause of (a situation, action, or state of mind) *Syn* bring about, cause, create, effectuate, engender, generate, induce, make, produce, prompt, result (in), spawn, work, yield *Rel* decide, determine **2** *Syn* PERFORM, accomplish, achieve, discharge, execute, fulfill

effective **1** · producing or capable of producing a result *Syn* effectual, efficacious, efficient *Rel* forceful, forcible, potent, powerful *Ant* futile, ineffective **2** *Syn* COGENT, compelling, conclusive, convincing, decisive, forceful, persuasive, satisfying, strong, telling *Ant* inconclusive, indecisive, ineffective, unconvincing

effects *Syn* POSSESSIONS, assets, belongings, means, resources

effectual *Syn* EFFECTIVE, efficacious, efficient *Ant* futile, ineffective

effectuate *Syn* EFFECT, bring about, cause, create, engender, generate, induce, make, produce, prompt, result (in), spawn, work, yield

effeminate · of or relating to a man characterized by qualities traditionally associated with women *Syn* effete, epicene

effervescent *Syn* ELASTIC (sense 2), buoyant, expansive, resilient, volatile *Ant* depressed

effete *Syn* EFFEMINATE, epicene

efficacious *Syn* EFFECTIVE, effectual, efficient *Ant* futile, ineffective

efficient *Syn* EFFECTIVE, effectual, efficacious *Ant* futile, ineffective

effigy *Syn* IMAGE, icon, mask, photograph, portrait, statue

effort · the active use or expenditure of physical or mental power to produce a desired result *Syn* exertion, pains, trouble *Rel* labor, toil, travail, work *Ant* ease

effortless *Syn* EASY, facile, light, simple, smooth *Ant* hard

effortlessly *Syn* EASILY, facilely, fluently, freely, handily, lightly, painlessly, readily, smoothly *Ant* arduously, laboriously

effrontery · shameless boldness *Syn* audacity, brashness, brass, brassiness, brazenness, cheek, cheekiness, chutzpah, gall, nerve,

nerviness, pertness, presumption, presumptuousness, sauce, sauciness, temerity *Rel* arrogance, assurance, cockiness, confidence, overconfidence, sanguinity, self-assurance, self-confidence

effulgent *Syn* BRIGHT, beaming, brilliant, incandescent, lambent, lucent, luminous, lustrous, radiant, refulgent *Ant* dim, dull

effusive *Syn* DEMONSTRATIVE, emotional, uninhibited, unreserved, unrestrained *Ant* inhibited, reserved, restrained, undemonstrative, unemotional

egg (on) *Syn* URGE, encourage, exhort, goad, press, prod, prompt

ego *Syn* COMPLACENCE, complacency, conceit, conceitedness, egotism, pompousness, pride, pridefulness, self-admiration, self-conceit, self-esteem, self-importance, self-satisfaction, smugness, vaingloriousness, vainglory, vainness, vanity *Ant* humbleness, humility, modesty

egocentric · overly concerned with one's own desires, needs, or interests *Syn* egoistic, egotistic (*or* egotistical), self-centered, selfish, self-seeking *Rel* complacent, conceited, self-conceited, self-directed, self-important, self-indulgent, self-satisfied, smug, vain *Ant* selfless

egoism *Syn* CONCEIT, amour propre, egotism, self-esteem, self-love *Ant* humility

egoistic **1** *Syn* CONCEITED, complacent, egotistic (*or* egotistical), important, overweening, pompous, prideful, proud, self-conceited, self-important, self-satisfied, smug, stuck-up, vain, vainglorious *Ant* humble, modest **2** *Syn* EGOCENTRIC, egotistic (*or* egotistical), self-centered, selfish, self-seeking *Ant* selfless

egotism **1** *Syn* COMPLACENCE, complacency, conceit, conceitedness, ego, pompousness, pride, pridefulness, self-admiration, self-conceit, self-esteem, self-importance, self-satisfaction, smugness, vaingloriousness, vainglory, vainness, vanity *Ant* humbleness, humility, modesty **2** *Syn* CONCEIT, amour propre, egoism, self-esteem, self-love *Ant* humility

egotistic *or* **egotistical** **1** *Syn* CONCEITED, complacent, egoistic, important, overweening, pompous, prideful, proud, self-conceited, self-important, self-satisfied, smug, stuck-up, vain, vainglorious *Ant* humble, modest **2** *Syn* EGOCENTRIC, egoistic, self-centered, selfish, self-seeking *Ant* selfless

egregious · very noticeable especially for being incorrect or bad *Syn* blatant, conspicuous, flagrant, glaring, gross, obvious, patent, pronounced, rank, striking *Rel* clear, distinct, evident, notable, outstanding, plain, salient

eject *Syn* ERUPT (sense 2), belch, disgorge, expel, jet, spew, spout, spurt

elaborate *Syn* UNFOLD, develop, evolve, perfect

elaboration *Syn* EXAGGERATION, caricature,

coloring, embellishment, embroidering, hyperbole, magnification, overstatement, padding, stretching *Ant* understatement

élan *Syn* VIGOR, dash, drive, esprit, punch, spirit, verve, vim

elapse *Syn* PASS, expire, pass away

elastic 1 · able to endure strain without being permanently affected or injured *Syn* flexible, resilient, springy, supple *Rel* ductile, pliable, pliant *Ant* rigid 2 · able to recover quickly from depression and maintain high spirits *Syn* buoyant, effervescent, expansive, resilient, volatile *Rel* high-spirited, mettlesome, spirited *Ant* depressed

elate · to fill with great joy *Syn* elevate, enrapture, exhilarate, overjoy, transport *Rel* excite, inspire, stimulate, uplift *Ant* depress

elated *Syn* ECSTATIC, enraptured, entranced, euphoric, exhilarated, intoxicated, rapturous, rhapsodic *Ant* depressed

elation *Syn* ECSTASY, euphoria, exhilaration, heaven, intoxication, paradise, rapture, rhapsody, transport *Ant* depression

elbow room *Syn* ROOM (sense 2), berth, clearance, leeway, margin, play

elder 1 *Syn* SENIOR CITIZEN, ancient, golden-ager, oldster, old-timer *Ant* youngster, youth 2 *Syn* SUPERIOR, better, senior *Ant* inferior, subordinate, underling

elderly · being of advanced years and especially past middle age *Syn* aged, aging, ancient, geriatric, long-lived, old, older, senior *Rel* adult, grown-up, mature, middle-aged *Ant* young, youthful

elect *vb Syn* CHOOSE, cull, opt, pick, prefer, select, single *Ant* eschew, reject

elect *n Syn* ELITE, best, choice, cream, fat, flower, pick, prime, upper crust

elect *adj Syn* SELECT, exclusive, picked *Ant* indiscriminate

election *Syn* CHOICE, alternative, option, preference, selection

elective *Syn* OPTIONAL, discretionary, voluntary *Ant* compulsory, mandatory, nonelective, obligatory, required

electrify *Syn* THRILL, enthuse

eleemosynary *Syn* CHARITABLE, altruistic, benevolent, humane, humanitarian, philanthropic *Ant* uncharitable

elegance · dignified or restrained beauty of form, appearance, or style *Syn* class, elegancy, grace, gracefulness, handsomeness, majesty, refinement, stateliness *Rel* grandeur, lavishness, luxuriousness, magnificence, ornateness, richness, splendor

elegancy *Syn* ELEGANCE, class, grace, gracefulness, handsomeness, majesty, refinement, stateliness

elegant *Syn* CHOICE, dainty, delicate, exquisite, rare, recherché *Ant* indifferent, medium

element · one of the parts of a compound or complex whole *Syn* component, constituent,

factor, ingredient *Rel* fundamental, principle *Ant* composite, compound (*in science*)

elemental *Syn* ELEMENTARY, basic, essential, fundamental, rudimentary, underlying *Ant* advanced

elementary · of or relating to the simplest facts or theories of a subject *Syn* basic, elemental, essential, fundamental, rudimentary, underlying *Rel* primal, primary, prime *Ant* advanced

elephantine *Syn* HUGE, Brobdingnagian, colossal, cyclopean, enormous, gargantuan, giant, gigantean, gigantic, Herculean, immense, mammoth, titanic, vast *Ant* bitty, diminutive, microscopic (*or* microscopical), midget, miniature, minute, pocket, pygmy, teeny, teenyweeny, tiny, wee

elevate 1 *Syn* ELATE, enrapture, exhilarate, overjoy, transport *Ant* depress 2 *Syn* LIFT, boost, heave, hoist, raise, rear *Ant* lower

elevation 1 *Syn* ADVANCEMENT, preferment, promotion *Ant* degradation, reduction (*in rank or status*) 2 *Syn* HEIGHT, altitude

elf *Syn* FAIRY, brownie, fay, pixie (*also* pixy), sprite

elicit *Syn* EDUCE, evoke, extort, extract

eliminate *Syn* EXCLUDE, blackball, debar, disbar, rule out, shut out, suspend *Ant* admit, include

elite 1 · individuals carefully selected as being the best of a class *Syn* best, choice, cream, elect, fat, flower, pick, prime, upper crust *Rel* aristocracy, (the) establishment, gentry, nobility, society, (the) top, upper class 2 *Syn* ARISTOCRACY, county, gentry, nobility, society *Ant* people, proletariat

ell *Syn* ANNEX, extension, wing

elongate *Syn* EXTEND, lengthen, prolong, protract *Ant* abridge, shorten

elongated *Syn* LONG (sense 1), extended, king-size (*or* king-sized), lengthy *Ant* brief, short

eloquent 1 *Syn* ARTICULATE, fluent, well-spoken *Ant* inarticulate 2 *Syn* EXPRESSIVE, meaning, meaningful, pregnant, revealing, significant, suggestive

else *Syn* ADDITIONAL, added, another, farther, further, more, other

elucidate *Syn* EXPLAIN (sense 1), clarify, clear (up), construe, demonstrate, explicate, expound, illuminate, illustrate, interpret, spell out *Ant* obscure

elude *Syn* ESCAPE (sense 2), avoid, eschew, evade, shun

Elysian *Syn* CELESTIAL, empyreal, empyrean, heavenly, supernal *Ant* hellish, infernal

emanate *Syn* SPRING, arise, derive, flow, issue, originate, proceed, rise, stem

emancipate *Syn* FREE, discharge, liberate, manumit, release

emasculate *Syn* STERILIZE (sense 1), alter, castrate, geld, mutilate, spay *Ant* fertilize

embankment *Syn* DAM, dike, levee

embargo *Syn* PROHIBITION (sense 2), ban, interdict, interdiction, proscription, veto *Ant* prescription

embark (on *or* **upon)** *Syn* BEGIN (sense 2), commence, enter (into *or* upon), get off, kick off, launch, open, start, strike (into) *Ant* conclude, end, finish, terminate

embarrass · to distress by confusing or confounding *Syn* abash, discomfit, disconcert, faze, rattle *Rel* discompose, disturb, flurry, fluster, perturb *Ant* facilitate, relieve

embarrassment *Syn* ENCUMBRANCE, bar, block, chain, clog, crimp, deterrent, drag, fetter, handicap, hindrance, hurdle, impediment, inhibition, interference, let, manacle, obstacle, obstruction, shackles, stop, stumbling block, trammel *Ant* aid, assistance, benefit, help

embellish *Syn* ADORN, beautify, bedeck, deck, decorate, garnish, ornament *Ant* disfigure

embellishment *Syn* EXAGGERATION, caricature, coloring, elaboration, embroidering, hyperbole, magnification, overstatement, padding, stretching *Ant* understatement

embers *Syn* ASH, cinders, clinkers

emblem *Syn* SYMBOL, attribute, type

embodiment · a visible representation of something abstract (as a quality) *Syn* epitome, incarnation, manifestation, personification *Rel* exemplification, incorporation, substantiation

embody **1** · to make a part of a body or system *Syn* assimilate, incorporate, integrate *Rel* amalgamate, blend, combine, commingle, fuse, intermingle, merge, mingle **2** · to represent in visible form *Syn* epitomize, incarnate, manifest, materialize, personalize, personify, substantiate *Rel* actualize, realize **3** *Syn* REALIZE, actualize, externalize, hypostatize, incarnate, materialize, objectify, reify

embolden *Syn* ENCOURAGE, cheer, hearten, inspirit, nerve, steel *Ant* discourage

embrace **1** *Syn* ADOPT, espouse *Ant* discard, repudiate **2** *Syn* INCLUDE, comprehend, imply, involve, subsume *Ant* exclude

embroidering *Syn* EXAGGERATION, caricature, coloring, elaboration, embellishment, hyperbole, magnification, overstatement, padding, stretching *Ant* understatement

emend *Syn* CORRECT, amend, rectify, redress, reform, remedy, revise

emerge *Syn* APPEAR, loom *Ant* disappear, vanish

emergency *Syn* JUNCTURE, contingency, crisis, exigency, pass, pinch, strait

emigrant · a person who leaves one country in order to settle in another *Syn* immigrant, migrant *Rel* alien, emigré, exile, expatriate, foreigner, fugitive, refugee

emigrate *Syn* MIGRATE, immigrate

émigré *Syn* STRANGER, alien, foreigner, immigrant, outlander, outsider

eminent · standing above others in rank, importance, or achievement *Syn* distinguished, illustrious, noble, notable, noteworthy, outstanding, preeminent, prestigious, signal, star, superior *Rel* celebrated, famed, famous, glorious, honored, renowned, reputable

emissary *Syn* AMBASSADOR, delegate, envoy, legate, minister, representative

emolument *Syn* WAGE, fee, hire, pay, salary, stipend

emotion *Syn* FEELING, affection, passion, sentiment

emotional **1** *Syn* DEMONSTRATIVE, effusive, uninhibited, unreserved, unrestrained *Ant* inhibited, reserved, restrained, undemonstrative, unemotional **2** *Syn* FERVENT, ardent, blazing, burning, charged, fervid, feverish, fiery, flaming, glowing, hot-blooded, impassioned, passionate, red-hot, vehement, warm, warm-blooded *Ant* cold, cool, dispassionate, impassive, unemotional **3** *Syn* MOVING, affecting, impressive, poignant, stirring, touching *Ant* unemotional, unimpressive

empathy *Syn* SYMPATHY, commiseration, compassion, condolence, pity, ruth

emphasis · exerted force or special stress that gives impressiveness or importance to something *Syn* accent, accentuation, stress

emphasize · to indicate the importance of by giving prominent display *Syn* accent, accentuate, feature, highlight, play (up), point (up), stress, underline, underscore *Rel* focus, identify, pinpoint, spotlight *Ant* play (down)

employ *Syn* USE, apply, avail, utilize

employment **1** *Syn* OCCUPATION, calling, line, profession, trade, vocation, work **2** *Syn* WORK (sense 2), business, calling, occupation, pursuit

emporium *Syn* STORE, bazaar, shop

emptiness **1** *Syn* VACANCY (sense 1), blank, blankness, vacuity, void *Ant* fullness **2** *Syn* VACANCY (sense 2), bareness, vacuity *Ant* fullness

empty *adj* **1** · lacking the contents that could or should be present *Syn* blank, vacant, vacuous, void *Rel* destitute, devoid, void *Ant* full **2** *Syn* MEANINGLESS, inane, pointless, senseless *Ant* meaningful **3** *Syn* VAIN, hollow, idle, nugatory, otiose

empty *vb* · to remove the contents of *Syn* clear, evacuate, vacate, void *Rel* deplete, drain, eliminate, exhaust *Ant* fill, load

empyreal *Syn* CELESTIAL, Elysian, empyrean, heavenly, supernal *Ant* hellish, infernal

empyrean *Syn* CELESTIAL, Elysian, empyreal, heavenly, supernal *Ant* hellish, infernal

emulate *Syn* RIVAL, compete, vie

enact · to put into effect through legislative or authoritative action *Syn* lay down, legislate, make, pass *Rel* bring about, effect *Ant* repeal, rescind, revoke

encapsulate *Syn* SUMMARIZE, abstract, digest,

epitomize, outline, recap, recapitulate, sum up, wrap up

enchant *Syn* ATTRACT, allure, bewitch, captivate, charm, fascinate *Ant* repel

enchanter *Syn* MAGICIAN (sense 1), charmer, conjurer (*or* conjuror), necromancer, sorcerer, voodoo, witch, wizard

enchanting *Syn* ATTRACTIVE, alluring, bewitching, captivating, charming, fascinating *Ant* forbidding, repellent

enchantress *Syn* SIREN, seductress, temptress

encircle *Syn* SURROUND, circle, compass, encompass, environ, gird, girdle, hem, ring

enclose · to shut in or confine by or as if by barriers *Syn* cage, coop, corral, envelop, fence, pen, wall *Rel* circumscribe, confine, limit, restrict

encomium · a more or less formal and public expression of praise *Syn* citation, eulogy, panegyric, tribute *Rel* extollation, extolling, laudation, lauding, praise, praising

encompass *Syn* SURROUND, circle, compass, encircle, environ, gird, girdle, hem, ring

encounter *n* · a sudden, hostile, and usually brief confrontation or dispute between factions or persons *Syn* brush, skirmish *Rel* battle, engagement

encounter *vb* 1 *Syn* HAPPEN (on *or* upon), chance (upon), find, hit (upon), meet, stumble (on *or* onto) 2 *Syn* MEET, confront, face *Ant* avoid

encourage 1 · to fill with courage or strength of purpose especially in preparation for a hard task *Syn* cheer, embolden, hearten, inspirit, nerve, steel *Rel* excite, galvanize, pique, provoke, quicken, stimulate *Ant* discourage 2 *Syn* FAVOR, countenance *Ant* disapprove 3 *Syn* URGE, egg (on), exhort, goad, press, prod, prompt

encouraging *Syn* HEARTWARMING, cheering, comforting, fulfilling, gladdening, gratifying, heartening, rewarding, satisfying *Ant* depressing, discouraging, disheartening, dispiriting

encroach *Syn* TRESPASS, entrench, infringe, invade

encumber *Syn* BURDEN, charge, cumber, lade, load, saddle, tax, weigh, weight

encumbrance · something that makes movement or progress more difficult *Syn* bar, block, chain, clog, crimp, deterrent, drag, embarrassment, fetter, handicap, hindrance, hurdle, impediment, inhibition, interference, let, manacle, obstacle, obstruction, shackles, stop, stumbling block, trammel *Rel* catch, hitch, rub, snag *Ant* aid, assistance, benefit, help

encyclopedic · covering everything or all important points *Syn* compendious, complete, comprehensive, full, global, inclusive, in-depth, omnibus, panoramic, universal *Rel* broad, catholic, extensive, far-reaching, general, overall, sweeping, vast, wide

end *n* 1 · the point at which something

ceases *Syn* ending, termination, terminus *Rel* close, closing, completion, concluding, conclusion, finish, finishing *Ant* beginning 2 *Syn* FINALE, close, closing, conclusion, consummation, ending, finis, finish, windup *Ant* beginning, dawn, opening, start 3 *Syn* GOAL, aim, ambition, aspiration, design, dream, intent, intention, mark, meaning, object, objective, plan, pretension, purpose, target, thing

end *vb* 1 *Syn* CONCLUDE (sense 1), complete, finish, terminate 2 *Syn* LIMIT, bound, confine, term

endanger · to place in danger *Syn* adventure, compromise, gamble (with), hazard, imperil, jeopardize, menace, risk, venture *Rel* intimidate, threaten

endangerment *Syn* DANGER (sense 2), distress, imperilment, jeopardy, peril, risk, trouble *Ant* safeness, safety, security

endearing *Syn* LOVABLE, adorable, darling, dear, disarming, precious, sweet, winning *Ant* abhorrent, abominable, detestable, hateful, odious, unlovable

endeavor *vb* 1 *Syn* ATTEMPT, assay, essay, seek, strive, try 2 *Syn* LABOR, drudge, grub, hump, hustle, moil, peg (away), plod, plow, plug, slave, slog, strain, strive, struggle, sweat, toil, travail, work *Ant* dabble, fiddle (around), fool (around), mess (around), putter (around)

endeavor *n* *Syn* ATTEMPT, crack, essay, fling, go, pass, shot, stab, trial, try, whack

endemic *Syn* NATIVE, aboriginal, autochthonous, indigenous *Ant* alien, foreign

ending 1 *Syn* END, termination, terminus *Ant* beginning 2 *Syn* FINALE, close, closing, conclusion, consummation, end, finis, finish, windup *Ant* beginning, dawn, opening, start

endless 1 *Syn* EVERLASTING, interminable, unceasing *Ant* transitory 2 *Syn* INFINITE, boundless, illimitable, immeasurable, indefinite, limitless, measureless, unbounded, unfathomable, unlimited *Ant* bounded, circumscribed, confined, definite, finite, limited, restricted

endorse *Syn* APPROVE, accredit, certify, sanction *Ant* disapprove

endow *Syn* DOWER, endue

endue *Syn* DOWER, endow

endurable *Syn* BEARABLE, sufferable, supportable, sustainable, tolerable *Ant* insufferable, insupportable, intolerable, unbearable, unendurable, unsupportable

endurance *Syn* CONTINUATION, continuance, duration, persistence, subsistence *Ant* ending, termination

endure 1 *Syn* BEAR (sense 2), abide, brook, stand, suffer, tolerate 2 *Syn* CONTINUE, abide, last, persist

enemy · one that is hostile toward another *Syn* adversary, antagonist, foe, opponent *Rel* archenemy *Ant* friend

energetic *Syn* VIGOROUS, lusty, nervous, strenuous *Ant* languorous, lethargic

energize **1** *Syn* ANIMATE, brace, enliven, fire, invigorate, jazz (up), liven (up), pep (up), quicken, stimulate, vitalize, vivify *Ant* damp, dampen, deaden, dull **2** *Syn* STRENGTHEN, fortify, invigorate, reinforce *Ant* weaken **3** *Syn* VITALIZE, activate *Ant* atrophy

energy *Syn* POWER (sense 1), force, might, puissance, strength *Ant* impotence

enervate *Syn* WEAKEN, debilitate, enfeeble, sap, soften *Ant* strengthen

enervated *Syn* LISTLESS, lackadaisical, languid, languishing, languorous, limp, spiritless *Ant* ambitious, animated, energetic, enterprising, motivated

enfeeble *Syn* WEAKEN, debilitate, enervate, sap, soften *Ant* strengthen

enforce · to carry out effectively *Syn* administer, apply, execute, implement *Rel* effect, effectuate

engage *Syn* PROMISE, contract, covenant, pledge, plight

engagement **1** · a promise to be in an agreed place at a specified time, usually for a particular purpose *Syn* appointment, assignation, date, rendezvous, tryst **2** *Syn* BATTLE, action

engaging **1** *Syn* INTERESTING, absorbing, arresting, engrossing, enthralling, fascinating, gripping, immersing, intriguing, involving, riveting *Ant* boring, drab, dry, dull, heavy, monotonous, tedious, uninteresting **2** *Syn* SWEET, dulcet, winning, winsome *Ant* bitter, sour

engender **1** *Syn* EFFECT, bring about, cause, create, effectuate, generate, induce, make, produce, prompt, result (in), spawn, work, yield **2** *Syn* GENERATE, beget, breed, get, procreate, propagate, reproduce, sire

engine *Syn* MACHINE, apparatus, machinery, mechanism, motor

engineer **1** · to plan out usually with subtle skill or care *Syn* contrive, finagle, finesse, frame, machinate, maneuver, manipulate, mastermind, negotiate, wangle *Rel* intrigue, plot, scheme **2** *Syn* GUIDE, lead, pilot, steer *Ant* misguide

engrave *Syn* CARVE, chisel, etch, incise, sculpt, sculpture

engross *Syn* MONOPOLIZE, absorb, consume

engrossed *Syn* INTENT, absorbed, rapt *Ant* distracted

engrossing *Syn* INTERESTING, absorbing, arresting, engaging, enthralling, fascinating, gripping, immersing, intriguing, involving, riveting *Ant* boring, drab, dry, dull, heavy, monotonous, tedious, uninteresting

engulf *Syn* FLOOD, deluge, drown, inundate, overflow, overwhelm, submerge, submerse, swamp *Ant* drain

enhance *Syn* INTENSIFY, aggravate, heighten *Ant* abate, allay, mitigate, temper

enhancement *Syn* ADVANCE (sense 1), advancement, breakthrough, improvement, refinement *Ant* setback

enigma *Syn* MYSTERY, conundrum, problem, puzzle, riddle

enigmatic *Syn* OBSCURE, ambiguous, cryptic, dark, equivocal, vague *Ant* distinct, obvious

enjoin **1** *Syn* COMMAND, bid, charge, direct, instruct, order *Ant* comply, obey **2** *Syn* FORBID, ban, bar, interdict, outlaw, prohibit, proscribe *Ant* allow, let, permit, suffer

enjoining *Syn* PROHIBITION (sense 1), banning, barring, forbidding, interdicting, interdiction, outlawing, prohibiting, proscribing, proscription *Ant* prescription

enjoy **1** *Syn* HAVE, hold, own, possess **2** *Syn* LIKE, dote, fancy, love, relish *Ant* dislike

enjoyable *Syn* FUN, amusing, delightful, diverting, entertaining, pleasurable *Ant* boring, dull

enjoyment *Syn* PLEASURE, delectation, delight, fruition, joy *Ant* anger, displeasure, vexation

enlarge **1** *Syn* INCREASE (sense 1), add (to), aggrandize, amplify, augment, boost, compound, escalate, expand, extend, multiply, raise, swell, up *Ant* abate, contract, decrease, diminish, lessen, lower, reduce, subtract (from) **2** *Syn* INCREASE (sense 2), accumulate, appreciate, balloon, build (up), burgeon, escalate, expand, mount, multiply, mushroom, proliferate, rise, snowball, swell, wax *Ant* contract, decrease, diminish, lessen, wane

enlighten **1** · to give information to *Syn* acquaint, advise, apprise, brief, clue, familiarize, fill in, inform, instruct, tell, wise (up) *Rel* clarify, clear (up), construe, elucidate, explain, explicate, expound, illuminate, illustrate, interpret, spell out **2** · to provide (someone) with moral or spiritual understanding *Syn* edify, educate, nurture *Rel* elevate, ennoble, lift, uplift **3** *Syn* ILLUMINATE, illustrate, light, lighten *Ant* darken, obscure

enliven *Syn* ANIMATE, brace, energize, fire, invigorate, jazz (up), liven (up), pep (up), quicken, stimulate, vitalize, vivify *Ant* damp, dampen, deaden, dull

enmesh *Syn* ENTANGLE, ensnare, entrap, mesh, snare, tangle, trap *Ant* disentangle

enmity · deep-seated dislike or ill will or a manifestation of such a feeling *Syn* animosity, animus, antagonism, antipathy, hostility, rancor *Rel* abhorrence, detestation, hate, hatred, loathing *Ant* amity

ennoble **1** *Syn* DIGNIFY, glorify, honor **2** *Syn* EXALT, aggrandize, dignify, enshrine, glorify, magnify *Ant* abase, degrade, demean, humble, humiliate

ennui *Syn* TEDIUM, boredom, doldrums

enormous *Syn* HUGE, Brobdingnagian, colossal, cyclopean, elephantine, gargantuan, giant, gigantean, gigantic, Herculean, immense, mammoth, titanic, vast *Ant* bitty, diminutive, microscopic (*or* microscopical), midget, miniature, minute, pocket, pygmy, teeny, teeny-weeny, tiny, wee

enough *Syn* SUFFICIENT, adequate, competent

enrage *Syn* ANGER, antagonize, incense, inflame, infuriate, madden, outrage, rankle, rile, roil *Ant* delight, gratify, please

enraged *Syn* ANGRY, angered, apoplectic, foaming, fuming, furious, incensed, indignant, inflamed, infuriated, irate, ireful, mad, outraged, rabid, riled, roiled, sore, steaming, wrathful, wroth *Ant* delighted, pleased

enrapture 1 *Syn* ELATE, elevate, exhilarate, overjoy, transport *Ant* depress 2 *Syn* ENTRANCE, carry away, enthrall (*or* enthral), overjoy, ravish, transport

enraptured *Syn* ECSTATIC, elated, entranced, euphoric, exhilarated, intoxicated, rapturous, rhapsodic *Ant* depressed

enroll *Syn* RECORD, catalog, list, register

ensconce *Syn* HIDE, bury, cache, conceal, screen, secrete

enshrine *Syn* EXALT, aggrandize, dignify, ennoble, glorify, magnify *Ant* abase, degrade, demean, humble, humiliate

ensign *Syn* FLAG, banner, color, jack, pendant, pennant, pennon, standard, streamer

ensnare 1 *Syn* CATCH, bag, capture, entrap, snare, trap *Ant* miss 2 *Syn* ENTANGLE, enmesh, entrap, mesh, snare, tangle, trap *Ant* disentangle

ensue *Syn* FOLLOW (sense 1), succeed, supervene *Ant* forsake (*a teacher or teachings*), precede

ensure · to make sure, certain, or safe *Syn* assure, cinch, guarantee, guaranty, insure, secure *Rel* attest, certify, vouch, warrant, witness

entangle · to catch or hold as if in a net *Syn* enmesh, ensnare, entrap, mesh, snare, tangle, trap *Rel* bag, capture, collar *Ant* disentangle

entente *Syn* CONTRACT, bargain, cartel, compact, concordat, convention, pact, treaty

enter 1 · to make way into something so as to reach or pass through the interior *Syn* penetrate, pierce, probe *Rel* encroach, entrench, invade, trespass *Ant* issue from 2 · to cause or permit to go in or get in *Syn* admit, introduce *Rel* insert, insinuate, intercalate, interpolate, introduce

enter (into *or* **upon)** *Syn* BEGIN (sense 2), commence, embark (on *or* upon), get off, kick off, launch, open, start, strike (into) *Ant* conclude, end, finish, terminate

enterprise *Syn* ADVENTURE, quest

entertain 1 *Syn* AMUSE, divert, recreate *Ant* bore 2 *Syn* HARBOR, board, house, lodge, shelter

entertaining *Syn* FUN, amusing, delightful, diverting, enjoyable, pleasurable *Ant* boring, dull

entertainment *Syn* AMUSEMENT, diversion, recreation *Ant* boredom

enthrall *or* **enthral** *Syn* ENTRANCE, carry away, enrapture, overjoy, ravish, transport

enthralling *Syn* INTERESTING, absorbing, arresting, engaging, engrossing, fascinating, gripping, immersing, intriguing, involving, riveting *Ant* boring, drab, dry, dull, heavy, monotonous, tedious, uninteresting

enthuse 1 *Syn* GUSH (sense 2), fuss, rave, rhapsodize, slobber 2 *Syn* THRILL, electrify

enthusiasm *Syn* PASSION, ardor, fervor, zeal

enthusiast 1 · a person who manifests excessive ardor, fervor, or devotion in an attachment to some cause, idea, party, or church *Syn* fanatic, zealot *Rel* addict, devotee, votary 2 *Syn* FAN, addict, aficionado, buff, bug, devotee, fanatic, fancier, fiend, freak, lover, maniac, nut

entice *Syn* LURE, allure, beguile, decoy, lead on, seduce, tempt

entire 1 *Syn* PERFECT, intact, whole *Ant* imperfect 2 *Syn* WHOLE, all, gross, total *Ant* partial

entity · one that has real and independent existence *Syn* being, creature, individual, person

entrance · to fill with overwhelming emotion (as wonder or delight) *Syn* carry away, enrapture, enthrall (*or* enthral), overjoy, ravish, transport *Rel* delight, gladden, gratify, please, satisfy

entranced *Syn* ECSTATIC, elated, enraptured, euphoric, exhilarated, intoxicated, rapturous, rhapsodic *Ant* depressed

entrap 1 *Syn* CATCH, bag, capture, ensnare, snare, trap *Ant* miss 2 *Syn* ENTANGLE, enmesh, ensnare, mesh, snare, tangle, trap *Ant* disentangle

entreat *Syn* BEG, adjure, beseech, implore, importune, supplicate

entrench *Syn* TRESPASS, encroach, infringe, invade

entrust *Syn* COMMIT, confide, consign, relegate

entwine *Syn* WIND, coil, curl, twine, twist, wreathe

enumerate *Syn* COUNT, number, tell

enunciate 1 *Syn* ANNOUNCE, advertise, blaze, broadcast, declare, placard, post, proclaim, promulgate, publicize, publish, sound 2 *Syn* ARTICULATE, pronounce

envelop 1 *Syn* COVER, overspread, shroud, veil, wrap *Ant* bare 2 *Syn* ENCLOSE, cage, coop, corral, fence, pen, wall

envious · having or showing mean resentment of another's possessions or advantages *Syn* covetous, invidious, jaundiced, jealous, resentful *Rel* begrudging, grudging

environ *Syn* SURROUND, circle, compass, encircle, encompass, gird, girdle, hem, ring

environment *Syn* BACKGROUND, backdrop, milieu, mise-en-scène, setting

envisage *Syn* THINK (sense 1), conceive, envision, fancy, imagine, realize

envision *Syn* THINK (sense 1), conceive, envisage, fancy, imagine, realize

envoy **1** *Syn* AGENT (sense 1), attorney, commissary, delegate, deputy, factor, procurator, proxy, representative **2** *Syn* AMBASSADOR, delegate, emissary, legate, minister, representative

envy *Syn* COVET, begrudge, grudge

ephemeral *Syn* MOMENTARY, evanescent, flash, fleeting, fugitive, impermanent, passing, short-lived, temporary, transient, transitory *Ant* enduring, eternal, everlasting, lasting, long-lived, permanent, perpetual

epicene *Syn* EFFEMINATE, effete

epicure · one who takes great pleasure in eating and drinking *Syn* bon vivant, gastronome, glutton, gourmand, gourmet *Rel* aesthete, connoisseur, dilettante

epicurean *Syn* SENSUOUS, luxurious, sybaritic, voluptuous

epigram *Syn* SAYING, adage, aphorism, apothegm, maxim, motto, proverb, saw

episode **1** *Syn* DIGRESSION, divagation, excursus **2** *Syn* OCCURRENCE, circumstance, event, incident

epistle *Syn* LETTER, dispatch, memorandum, message, missive, note, report

epithet *Syn* INSULT, affront, barb, dart, dig, indignity, name, offense (*or* offence), outrage, put-down, sarcasm, slight, slur

epitome **1** *Syn* ABRIDGMENT, abstract, brief, conspectus, synopsis *Ant* expansion **2** *Syn* EMBODIMENT, incarnation, manifestation, personification

epitomize **1** *Syn* EMBODY (sense 2), incarnate, manifest, materialize, personalize, personify, substantiate **2** *Syn* SUMMARIZE, abstract, digest, encapsulate, outline, recap, recapitulate, sum up, wrap up

epoch *Syn* AGE (sense 3), day, era, period, time

equable **1** *Syn* CLEMENT, balmy, gentle, mild, moderate, temperate *Ant* harsh, inclement, intemperate, severe **2** *Syn* STEADY, constant, even, uniform *Ant* jumpy, nervous, unsteady

equal *n* · one that is equal to another in status, achievement, or value *Syn* coordinate, counterpart, equivalent, fellow, like, match, parallel, peer, rival *Rel* analogue (*or* analog), associate, colleague, companion, competitor, double, mate, partner, twin

equal *vb Syn* MATCH, approach, rival, touch

equal *adj Syn* SAME, equivalent, identic, identical, selfsame, tantamount, very *Ant* different

equalize · to make equal in amount, degree, or status *Syn* balance, equate, even, level *Rel* accommodate, adjust, compensate, fit

equanimity · evenness of emotions or temper

Syn aplomb, calmness, composure, coolheadedness, coolness, imperturbability, placidity, self-possession, serenity, tranquillity (*or* tranquility) *Rel* assurance, confidence, poise, self-assurance, self-confidence *Ant* agitation, discomposure, perturbation

equate *Syn* EQUALIZE, balance, even, level

equilibrium *Syn* BALANCE, equipoise, poise, tension

equip *Syn* FURNISH (sense 1), accoutre (*or* accouter), fit (out), outfit, rig, supply *Ant* hold (back), keep (back), reserve, retain, withhold

equipment · items needed for the performance of a task or useful in effecting a given end *Syn* apparatus, gear, machinery, matériel, outfit, paraphernalia, tackle

equipoise *Syn* BALANCE, equilibrium, poise, tension

equitable *Syn* FAIR, dispassionate, impartial, just, objective, unbiased, uncolored *Ant* unfair

equivalent *n Syn* EQUAL, coordinate, counterpart, fellow, like, match, parallel, peer, rival

equivalent *adj Syn* SAME, equal, identic, identical, selfsame, tantamount, very *Ant* different

equivocal *Syn* OBSCURE, ambiguous, cryptic, dark, enigmatic, vague *Ant* distinct, obvious

equivocate *Syn* LIE, fib, palter, prevaricate

era *Syn* AGE (sense 3), day, epoch, period, time

eradicate *Syn* EXTERMINATE, deracinate, extirpate, uproot, wipe

erase · to strike, rub, or scrape out something so that it no longer has effect or existence *Syn* blot out, cancel, delete, efface, expunge, obliterate *Rel* annul, negate, nullify

ere *Syn* BEFORE, ahead of, of, previous to, prior to, to *Ant* after, following

erect *adj* · rising straight up *Syn* perpendicular, plumb, raised, standing, upright, upstanding, vertical *Rel* elevated, lifted, upended, upraised *Ant* flat, recumbent

erect *vb Syn* BUILD, assemble, construct, fabricate, make, make up, piece, put up, raise, rear, set up *Ant* disassemble, dismantle, take down

eremite *Syn* RECLUSE, anchorite, cenobite, hermit

erotic · of, devoted to, affected by, or tending to arouse sexual love or desire *Syn* amative, amatory, amorous, aphrodisiac *Rel* ardent, fervent, fervid, impassioned, passionate, perfervid

erratic **1** *Syn* FITFUL, casual, choppy, discontinuous, intermittent, irregular, occasional, spasmodic, sporadic, spotty, unsteady *Ant* constant, continuous, regular, steady **2** *Syn* STRANGE, curious, eccentric, odd, outlandish, peculiar, quaint, queer, singular, unique *Ant* familiar

erratically *Syn* HIT OR MISS, aimlessly, anyhow,

anyway, anywise, desultorily, haphazard, haphazardly, helter-skelter, irregularly, randomly *Ant* methodically, systematically

erroneousness *Syn* FALLACY (sense 2), fallaciousness, falseness, falsity, untruth *Ant* truth

error 1 · something (as an act, statement, or belief) that departs from what is or is generally held to be acceptable *Syn* blunder, bull, faux pas, howler, lapse, mistake, slip 2 *Syn* FALLACY (sense 1), falsehood, falsity, illusion, misconception, myth, old wives' tale, untruth *Ant* truth, verity

errorless *Syn* IMPECCABLE, faultless, flawless

ersatz *Syn* ARTIFICIAL, factitious, synthetic *Ant* natural

erstwhile *Syn* FORMER, late, old, onetime, past, sometime, whilom

erudite 1 *Syn* BOOKISH, learned, literary *Ant* colloquial, nonliterary 2 *Syn* EDUCATED, knowledgeable, learned, literate, scholarly, well-read *Ant* ignorant, illiterate, uneducated 3 *Syn* LEARNED, scholarly

erudition 1 *Syn* EDUCATION (sense 2), knowledge, learnedness, learning, scholarship, science 2 *Syn* KNOWLEDGE, information, learning, lore, scholarship, science *Ant* ignorance

erupt 1 · to develop suddenly and violently *Syn* break out, burst (forth), explode, flame, flare (up) *Rel* burgeon, mushroom, snowball 2 · to throw out or off (something from within) often violently *Syn* belch, disgorge, eject, expel, jet, spew, spout, spurt *Rel* gush, pour, stream, surge

escalate 1 *Syn* INCREASE (sense 1), add (to), aggrandize, amplify, augment, boost, compound, enlarge, expand, extend, multiply, raise, swell, up *Ant* abate, contract, decrease, diminish, lessen, lower, reduce, subtract (from) 2 *Syn* INCREASE (sense 2), accumulate, appreciate, balloon, build (up), burgeon, enlarge, expand, mount, multiply, mushroom, proliferate, rise, snowball, swell, wax *Ant* contract, decrease, diminish, lessen, wane

escape 1 · to run away especially from something that limits one's freedom or threatens one's well-being *Syn* abscond, decamp, flee, fly 2 · to get away or keep away from what one does not wish to incur, endure, or encounter *Syn* avoid, elude, eschew, evade, shun

eschew 1 *Syn* ESCAPE (sense 2), avoid, elude, evade, shun 2 *Syn* FORGO, abnegate, forbear, sacrifice

escort *n* · one that accompanies another for protection, guidance, or as a courtesy *Syn* attendant, companion, guard, guide *Rel* chaperone (*or* chaperon), conductor, leader, pilot, shadow, sidekick, squire

escort *vb* *Syn* ACCOMPANY, attend, chaperone (*or* chaperon), convoy, squire

esoteric *Syn* RECONDITE, abstruse, occult

especial *Syn* SPECIAL, individual, particular, specific

especially *Syn* VERY, awful, awfully, beastly, deadly, exceedingly, extra, extremely, far, frightfully, full, greatly, heavily, highly, hugely, jolly, mightily, mighty, mortally, most, much, particularly, rattling, real, right, so, something, super, terribly, too, whacking *Ant* little, negligibly, nominally, slightly

espousal *Syn* MARRIAGE, matrimony, nuptial, wedding, wedlock

espouse *Syn* ADOPT, embrace *Ant* discard, repudiate

esprit *Syn* VIGOR, dash, drive, élan, punch, spirit, verve, vim

esprit de corps *Syn* MORALE, discipline

espy *Syn* SEE (sense 1), behold, contemplate, descry, discern, note, notice, observe, perceive, remark, survey, view

essay *n* 1 · a relatively brief discourse written for others' reading or consideration *Syn* article, composition, paper, theme 2 *Syn* ATTEMPT, crack, endeavor, fling, go, pass, shot, stab, trial, try, whack

essay *vb* *Syn* ATTEMPT, assay, endeavor, seek, strive, try

essential 1 · so important as to be indispensable *Syn* cardinal, fundamental, vital *Rel* basal, basic, underlying 2 *Syn* ELEMENTARY, basic, elemental, fundamental, rudimentary, underlying *Ant* advanced 3 *Syn* INHERENT, constitutional, ingrained, intrinsic *Ant* adventitious 4 *Syn* NEEDFUL, indispensable, necessary, requisite

establish 1 *Syn* FOUND, create, institute, organize 2 *Syn* SET, fix, settle

estate *Syn* MANSION, castle, château, countryseat, hacienda, hall, manor, manor house, palace, villa

esteem *n* *Syn* REGARD, admiration, respect *Ant* despite

esteem *vb* *Syn* REGARD, admire, respect *Ant* despise

estimate 1 · to judge a thing with respect to its worth *Syn* appraise, assay, assess, evaluate, rate, value *Rel* adjudge, adjudicate, judge 2 · to decide the size, amount, number, or distance of (something) without actual measurement *Syn* calculate, call, conjecture, figure, gauge, guess, judge, make, place, put, reckon, suppose 3 *Syn* CALCULATE, compute, reckon

estrange · to cause one to break a bond or tie of affection or loyalty *Syn* alienate, disaffect, wean *Rel* divide, divorce, part, separate, sever, sunder *Ant* reconcile

estrangement · the loss of friendship or affection *Syn* alienation, disaffection, disgruntlement, souring *Rel* antagonism, embitterment, envenoming *Ant* reconciliation

etch *Syn* CARVE, chisel, engrave, incise, sculpt, sculpture

ethereal *Syn* AIRY, aerial *Ant* substantial

ethical *Syn* MORAL, noble, righteous, virtuous

ethics · the code of good conduct for an individual or group *Syn* morality, morals, principles, standards *Rel* customs, etiquette, manners, mores

etiquette *Syn* DECORUM, decency, dignity, propriety *Ant* indecorum, license

eulogize *Syn* PRAISE, acclaim, extol, laud *Ant* blame

eulogy *Syn* ENCOMIUM, citation, panegyric, tribute

euphoria *Syn* ECSTASY, elation, exhilaration, heaven, intoxication, paradise, rapture, rhapsody, transport *Ant* depression

euphoric *Syn* ECSTATIC, elated, enraptured, entranced, exhilarated, intoxicated, rapturous, rhapsodic *Ant* depressed

euphuistic *Syn* RHETORICAL, aureate, bombastic, flowery, grandiloquent, magniloquent

evacuate *Syn* EMPTY, clear, vacate, void *Ant* fill, load

evade *Syn* ESCAPE (sense 2), avoid, elude, eschew, shun

evaluate *Syn* ESTIMATE (sense 1), appraise, assay, assess, rate, value

evanesce *Syn* VANISH, disappear, evaporate, fade *Ant* appear, loom

evanescent *Syn* MOMENTARY, ephemeral, flash, fleeting, fugitive, impermanent, passing, short-lived, temporary, transient, transitory *Ant* enduring, eternal, everlasting, lasting, long-lived, permanent, perpetual

evaporate *Syn* VANISH, disappear, evanesce, fade *Ant* appear, loom

even *vb Syn* EQUALIZE, balance, equate, level

even *adj* **1** *Syn* LEVEL, flat, flush, plain, plane, smooth **2** *Syn* STEADY, constant, equable, uniform *Ant* jumpy, nervous, unsteady

event **1** *Syn* EFFECT, aftereffect, aftermath, consequence, issue, outcome, result, sequel, upshot *Ant* cause **2** *Syn* OCCURRENCE, circumstance, episode, incident

eventual *Syn* LAST, concluding, final, latest, terminal, ultimate *Ant* first

ever *Syn* AT ALL, anywise

everlasting · continuing on and on without end *Syn* endless, interminable, unceasing *Rel* boundless, eternal, infinite *Ant* transitory

every *Syn* ALL, each *Ant* no

evidence *Syn* SHOW (sense 1), demonstrate, evince, manifest *Ant* disguise

evident · readily perceived or apprehended *Syn* apparent, clear, distinct, manifest, obvious, palpable, patent, plain *Rel* appreciable, perceptible, ponderable, sensible, tangible

evidently *Syn* APPARENTLY, ostensibly, presumably, seemingly, supposedly

evil *n* · that which is morally unacceptable *Syn* bad, evildoing, ill, immorality, iniquity, sin, villainy, wrong *Rel* atrociousness, bad-ness, evilness, heinousness, nefariousness, sinfulness, vileness, wickedness *Ant* good, morality, right, virtue

evil *adj* **1** *Syn* BAD (sense 1), ill, naughty, wicked *Ant* good **2** *Syn* HARMFUL, adverse, bad, baleful, baneful, damaging, deleterious, detrimental, hurtful, ill, injurious, mischievous, noxious, pernicious, prejudicial *Ant* harmless, innocent, innocuous, inoffensive, safe

evildoing *Syn* EVIL, bad, ill, immorality, iniquity, sin, villainy, wrong *Ant* good, morality, right, virtue

evince *Syn* SHOW (sense 1), demonstrate, evidence, manifest *Ant* disguise

evoke *Syn* EDUCE, elicit, extort, extract

evolve *Syn* UNFOLD, develop, elaborate, perfect

exact *adj Syn* CORRECT, accurate, nice, precise, right *Ant* incorrect

exact *vb* **1** *Syn* DEMAND, claim, require **2** *Syn* IMPOSE, assess, charge, fine, lay, levy, put *Ant* remit

exacting *Syn* ONEROUS, burdensome, oppressive

exactitude *Syn* PRECISION, accuracy, closeness, delicacy, exactness, fineness, preciseness, rigorousness, veracity *Ant* coarseness, impreciseness, imprecision, inaccuracy, inexactness, roughness

exactly *Syn* STRICTLY, precisely, rigidly, rigorously *Ant* imprecisely, inexactly, loosely

exactness *Syn* PRECISION, accuracy, closeness, delicacy, exactitude, fineness, preciseness, rigorousness, veracity *Ant* coarseness, impreciseness, imprecision, inaccuracy, inexactness, roughness

exaggerate *Syn* OVERSTATE, overdo, overdraw, put on *Ant* understate

exaggeration · the representation of something in terms that go beyond the facts *Syn* caricature, coloring, elaboration, embellishment, embroidering, hyperbole, magnification, overstatement, padding, stretching *Rel* amplification, enhancement *Ant* understatement

exalt · to enhance the status of *Syn* aggrandize, dignify, ennoble, enshrine, glorify, magnify *Rel* boost, elevate, lift, promote, raise, upgrade, uplift *Ant* abase, degrade, demean, humble, humiliate

examination *Syn* INSPECTION, audit, check, checkup, review, scan, scrutiny, survey

examine **1** *Syn* ASK (sense 1), catechize, inquire, interrogate, query, question, quiz **2** *Syn* SCRUTINIZE, audit, inspect, scan

example **1** · one of a group or collection that shows what the whole is like *Syn* case, exemplar, illustration, instance, representative, sample, specimen *Rel* cross section **2** *Syn* MODEL, beau ideal, exemplar, ideal, mirror, pattern, standard

exasperate *Syn* IRRITATE, aggravate, nettle, peeve, provoke, rile

exasperating *Syn* ANNOYING, aggravating, bothersome, disturbing, frustrating, galling, irksome, irritating, maddening, nettling, peeving, pesty, rankling, riling, vexatious, vexing

excavate *Syn* DIG, delve, grub, spade

exceed · to go or to be beyond a stated or implied limit, measure, or degree *Syn* excel, outdo, outstrip, surpass, transcend

exceedingly *Syn* VERY, awful, awfully, beastly, deadly, especially, extra, extremely, far, frightfully, full, greatly, heavily, highly, hugely, jolly, mightily, mighty, mortally, most, much, particularly, rattling, real, right, so, something, super, terribly, too, whacking *Ant* little, negligibly, nominally, slightly

excel *Syn* EXCEED, outdo, outstrip, surpass, transcend

excellence · a quality that gives something special worth *Syn* distinction, excellency, merit, value, virtue *Rel* advantage, edge, superiority *Ant* deficiency

excellency *Syn* EXCELLENCE, distinction, merit, value, virtue *Ant* deficiency

excellent · of the very best kind *Syn* A1, bang-up, banner, capital, classic, crackerjack, dandy, divine, fabulous, fine, first-class, first-rate, grand, great, groovy, heavenly, jim-dandy, keen, marvelous (*or* marvellous), mean, neat, nifty, noble, par excellence, prime, sensational, splendid, stellar, sterling, superb, superior, superlative, supernal, swell, terrific, tip-top, top, top-notch, unsurpassed, wonderful *Rel* OK, acceptable, adequate, all right, decent, good, passable, satisfactory, tolerable *Ant* poor

exceptionable *Syn* OBJECTIONABLE, unacceptable, undesirable, unwanted, unwelcome

exceptional · being out of the ordinary *Syn* extraordinary, phenomenal, unusual, unwonted *Rel* conspicuous, noticeable, outstanding, prominent, remarkable, salient, signal *Ant* average, common

excess · the state or an instance of going beyond what is usual, proper, or needed *Syn* fat, overabundance, overage, overflow, overkill, overmuch, oversupply, superabundance, superfluity, surfeit, surplus *Rel* abundance, bounty, plentitude, plenty, profusion, sufficiency *Ant* deficiency, deficit, insufficiency

excessive · going beyond a normal or acceptable limit *Syn* exorbitant, extravagant, extreme, immoderate, inordinate *Rel* extra, spare, superfluous, supernumerary, surplus *Ant* deficient

exchange 1 · to give and receive reciprocally *Syn* bandy, interchange 2 *Syn* CHANGE (sense 3), commute, shift, substitute, swap, switch, trade

excitable · easily excited by nature *Syn* flighty, fluttery, high-strung, jittery, jumpy, nervous, skittish, spooky *Rel* hot-blooded, mercurial, temperamental, unstable, volatile, volcanic *Ant* unflappable

excitant *Syn* STIMULUS, impetus, incitement, stimulant

excite *Syn* PROVOKE, galvanize, pique, quicken, stimulate

exciter *Syn* AGITATOR, demagogue, firebrand, fomenter, incendiary, inciter, instigator, rabble-rouser

exciting *Syn* PROVOCATIVE, inciting, instigating, piquing, provoking, stimulating

exclude · to prevent the participation, consideration, or inclusion of *Syn* blackball, debar, disbar, eliminate, rule out, shut out, suspend *Rel* bar, block, hinder *Ant* admit, include

exclusive *Syn* SELECT, elect, picked *Ant* indiscriminate

excogitate *Syn* CONSIDER (sense 1), contemplate, study, weigh

excoriate 1 *Syn* ABRADE, chafe, fret, gall 2 *Syn* ATTACK (sense 2), abuse, assail, belabor, blast, castigate, jump (on), lambaste (*or* lambast), scathe, slam, vituperate

excruciating · intensely or unbearably painful *Syn* agonizing, racking *Rel* tormenting, torturing

exculpate · to free from alleged fault or guilt *Syn* absolve, acquit, exonerate, vindicate *Rel* explain, justify, rationalize *Ant* accuse, inculpate

excursion *Syn* JOURNEY, cruise, expedition, jaunt, pilgrimage, tour, trip, voyage

excursus *Syn* DIGRESSION, divagation, episode

excusable *Syn* VENIAL, forgivable, pardonable, remittable *Ant* inexcusable, mortal, unforgivable, unpardonable

excuse *n* 1 · an explanation that frees one from fault or blame *Syn* alibi, defense, justification, plea, reason *Rel* acknowledgment, apology, atonement, confession, cop-out, guise, out, pretense (*or* pretence), pretext, rationale, rationalization 2 *Syn* APOLOGY, alibi, apologia, plea, pretext

excuse *vb* · to exact neither punishment nor redress for or from *Syn* condone, forgive, pardon, remit *Rel* account, explain, justify, rationalize *Ant* punish

execrable · so odious as to be utterly detestable *Syn* accursed, cursed, damnable *Rel* atrocious, heinous, monstrous, outrageous

execrate · to denounce violently *Syn* anathematize, curse, damn, objurgate *Rel* censure, condemn, denounce, reprehend, reprobate

execute 1 *Syn* ENFORCE, administer, apply, implement 2 *Syn* KILL, assassinate, dispatch, murder, slay 3 *Syn* PERFORM, accomplish, achieve, discharge, effect, fulfill

executive · a person who manages or directs

Syn administrator, director, manager, superintendent, supervisor *Rel* officer, official

exemplar 1 *Syn* EXAMPLE, case, illustration, instance, representative, sample, specimen **2** *Syn* MODEL, beau ideal, example, ideal, mirror, pattern, standard

exercise *n* • repeated activity or exertion *Syn* drill, practice *Rel* act, action, deed

exercise *vb Syn* EXERT, apply, ply, put out, wield

exert • to bring to bear especially forcefully or effectively *Syn* apply, exercise, ply, put out, wield *Rel* employ, use, utilize

exertion *Syn* EFFORT, pains, trouble *Ant* ease

exhaust 1 *Syn* DEPLETE, clean (out), consume, drain, expend, spend, use up *Ant* renew, replace **2** *Syn* TIRE, fatigue, jade, tucker, weary

exhaustion *Syn* FATIGUE, burnout, collapse, lassitude, prostration, tiredness, weariness *Ant* refreshment, rejuvenation, revitalization

exhaustive • trying all possibilities *Syn* all-out, clean, complete, comprehensive, full-scale, out-and-out, thorough, thoroughgoing, total *Rel* broad, extensive, far-reaching, indepth, wide

exhibit *n Syn* EXHIBITION, exposition, fair, show

exhibit *vb Syn* SHOW (sense 2), display, expose, flaunt, parade *Ant* disguise

exhibition • a public display of objects of interest *Syn* exhibit, exposition, fair, show

exhilarate *Syn* ELATE, elevate, enrapture, overjoy, transport *Ant* depress

exhilarated *Syn* ECSTATIC, elated, enraptured, entranced, euphoric, intoxicated, rapturous, rhapsodic *Ant* depressed

exhilaration 1 *Syn* ECSTASY, elation, euphoria, heaven, intoxication, paradise, rapture, rhapsody, transport *Ant* depression **2** *Syn* THRILL, bang, kick, titillation

exhort *Syn* URGE, egg (on), encourage, goad, press, prod, prompt

exigency 1 *Syn* JUNCTURE, contingency, crisis, emergency, pass, pinch, strait **2** *Syn* NEED, necessity

exigent *Syn* PRESSING, crying, imperative, importunate, insistent, instant, urgent

exiguous *Syn* MEAGER, scant, scanty, scrimpy, skimpy, spare, sparse *Ant* ample, copious

exile *Syn* BANISH, deport, expatriate, extradite, ostracize, transport

exist *Syn* BE, live, subsist

existence • the state or fact of having independent reality *Syn* actuality, being *Rel* condition, situation, state, status *Ant* nonexistence

existent *Syn* ACTUAL, concrete, factual, real, true, very *Ant* conjectural, hypothetical, ideal, nonexistent, possible, potential, theoretical

exonerate *Syn* EXCULPATE, absolve, acquit, vindicate *Ant* accuse, inculpate

exorbitant *Syn* EXCESSIVE, extravagant, extreme, immoderate, inordinate *Ant* deficient

exordium *Syn* INTRODUCTION, foreword, preamble, preface, prelude, prologue

exotic • excitingly or mysteriously unusual *Syn* fantastic, glamorous, marvelous (*or* marvellous), outlandish, romantic, strange *Rel* colorful, picturesque, quaint

expand 1 • to increase or become increased in size, bulk, or volume *Syn* amplify, dilate, distend, inflate, swell *Rel* augment, enlarge, increase *Ant* abridge, circumscribe, contract **2** *Syn* INCREASE (sense 1), add (to), aggrandize, amplify, augment, boost, compound, enlarge, escalate, extend, multiply, raise, swell, up *Ant* abate, contract, decrease, diminish, lessen, lower, reduce, subtract (from) **3** *Syn* INCREASE (sense 2), accumulate, appreciate, balloon, build (up), burgeon, enlarge, escalate, mount, multiply, mushroom, proliferate, rise, snowball, swell, wax *Ant* contract, decrease, diminish, lessen, wane

expanse • a significantly large area or range *Syn* amplitude, spread, stretch *Rel* compass, orbit, range, reach, scope, sweep

expansive 1 *Syn* ELASTIC (sense 2), buoyant, effervescent, resilient, volatile *Ant* depressed **2** *Syn* EXTENSIVE, broad, extended, far-flung, far-reaching, wide, widespread *Ant* narrow

expatiate *Syn* DISCOURSE, descant, dilate

expatriate *Syn* BANISH, deport, exile, extradite, ostracize, transport

expect • to anticipate in the mind *Syn* await, hope, look *Rel* anticipate, apprehend, divine, foreknow, foresee *Ant* despair of

expedient *adj* • suitable for bringing about a desired result under the circumstances *Syn* advisable, desirable, judicious, politic, prudent, tactical, wise *Rel* advantageous, beneficial, profitable *Ant* imprudent, inadvisable, inexpedient, injudicious, unwise

expedient *n Syn* RESOURCE, makeshift, resort, shift, stopgap, substitute, surrogate

expedition 1 *Syn* HASTE, dispatch, hurry, speed *Ant* deliberation **2** *Syn* JOURNEY, cruise, excursion, jaunt, pilgrimage, tour, trip, voyage

expeditious *Syn* FAST, fleet, hasty, quick, rapid, speedy, swift *Ant* slow

expel *Syn* ERUPT (sense 2), belch, disgorge, eject, jet, spew, spout, spurt

expend 1 *Syn* DEPLETE, clean (out), consume, drain, exhaust, spend, use up *Ant* renew, replace **2** *Syn* SPEND, disburse *Ant* save

expense *Syn* PRICE, charge, cost

expensive *Syn* COSTLY, dear, invaluable, precious, priceless, valuable *Ant* cheap

expensively *Syn* HIGH, extravagantly, grandly, lavishly, luxuriously, opulently, richly, sumptuously *Ant* austerely, humbly, modestly, plainly, simply

experience · to pass through the process of actually coming to know or to feel *Syn* suffer, sustain, undergo *Rel* behold, perceive, see, survey, view

expert *n* · a person with a high level of knowledge or skill in a field *Syn* ace, adept, artist, authority, crackerjack, maestro, master, past master, scholar, shark, virtuoso, whiz, wizard *Rel* pro, professional *Ant* amateur

expert *adj Syn* PROFICIENT, adept, masterly, skilled, skillful *Ant* amateur, amateurish, inexperienced, inexpert, unexperienced, unpracticed, unprofessional, unseasoned, unskilled, unskillful

expire *Syn* PASS, elapse, pass away

expired *Syn* EXTINCT, bygone, dead, defunct, departed, gone, vanished *Ant* alive, existent, existing, extant, living

explain **1** · to make the meaning of something understood or more comprehensible *Syn* clarify, clear (up), construe, demonstrate, elucidate, explicate, expound, illuminate, illustrate, interpret, spell out *Rel* decipher, decode *Ant* obscure **2** · to give the reason for or cause of *Syn* account (for), explain away, rationalize *Rel* condone, excuse, forgive, justify

explainable *Syn* SOLVABLE, answerable, explicable, resolvable, soluble *Ant* inexplicable, insoluble, unexplainable, unsolvable

explain away *Syn* EXPLAIN (sense 2), account (for), rationalize

explicable *Syn* SOLVABLE, answerable, explainable, resolvable, soluble *Ant* inexplicable, insoluble, unexplainable, unsolvable

explicate *Syn* EXPLAIN (sense 1), clarify, clear (up), construe, demonstrate, elucidate, expound, illuminate, illustrate, interpret, spell out *Ant* obscure

explicit · characterized by full precise expression and meaning that is perfectly clear *Syn* categorical, definite, express, specific *Rel* accurate, exact, precise *Ant* ambiguous

explode *Syn* ERUPT (sense 1), break out, burst (forth), flame, flare (up)

exploit *Syn* FEAT, achievement

explore · to search through or into *Syn* delve (into), dig (into), inquire (into), investigate, look (into), probe, research *Rel* examine, inspect, sift, study, view

exponent · a person who actively supports or favors a cause *Syn* advocate, apostle, backer, booster, champion, friend, promoter, proponent, supporter *Rel* loyalist, partisan, stalwart *Ant* adversary, antagonist, opponent

expose *Syn* SHOW (sense 2), display, exhibit, flaunt, parade *Ant* disguise

exposé *Syn* EXPOSITION, exposure

exposed *Syn* LIABLE, open, prone, sensitive, subject, susceptible *Ant* exempt, immune

exposition **1** · a setting forth or laying open of a thing or things hitherto not known or fully understood *Syn* exposé, exposure **2** *Syn* EXHIBITION, exhibit, fair, show

expostulate *Syn* OBJECT, kick, protest, remonstrate *Ant* acquiesce

expostulation *Syn* OBJECTION, challenge, complaint, demur, fuss, protest, question, remonstrance

exposure **1** *Syn* EXPOSITION, exposé **2** *Syn* REVELATION (sense 2), disclosure, divulgence

expound *Syn* EXPLAIN (sense 1), clarify, clear (up), construe, demonstrate, elucidate, explicate, illuminate, illustrate, interpret, spell out *Ant* obscure

express *vb* **1** · to let out what one feels or thinks *Syn* air, broach, utter, vent, ventilate, voice *Rel* speak, talk *Ant* imply **2** *Syn* PHRASE, articulate, clothe, couch, formulate, put, say, state, word

express *adj Syn* EXPLICIT, categorical, definite, specific *Ant* ambiguous

expression *Syn* PHRASE, idiom, locution

expressive · clearly conveying a special meaning (as one's mood) *Syn* eloquent, meaning, meaningful, pregnant, revealing, significant, suggestive *Rel* evocative, flavorful, graphic, pictorial, redolent, reminiscent, rich, sententious, vivid, weighty

expunge *Syn* ERASE, blot out, cancel, delete, efface, obliterate

exquisite *adj* **1** *Syn* CHOICE, dainty, delicate, elegant, rare, recherché *Ant* indifferent, medium **2** *Syn* INTENSE, fierce, vehement, violent *Ant* subdued

exquisite *n Syn* FOP, beau, buck, coxcomb, dandy, dude

extant *Syn* PRESENT, current, ongoing, present-day *Ant* ago, future, past

extemporaneous · composed, devised, or done at the moment rather than beforehand *Syn* extemporary, extempore, impromptu, improvised, offhand, unpremeditated *Rel* impulsive, spontaneous

extemporary *Syn* EXTEMPORANEOUS, extempore, impromptu, improvised, offhand, unpremeditated

extempore *Syn* EXTEMPORANEOUS, extemporary, impromptu, improvised, offhand, unpremeditated

extend **1** · to make or become longer *Syn* elongate, lengthen, prolong, protract *Rel* augment, enlarge, increase *Ant* abridge, shorten **2** *Syn* INCREASE (sense 1), add (to), aggrandize, amplify, augment, boost, compound, enlarge, escalate, expand, multiply, raise, swell, up *Ant* abate, contract, decrease, diminish, lessen, lower, reduce, subtract (from)

extended **1** *Syn* EXTENSIVE, broad, expansive, far-flung, far-reaching, wide, widespread *Ant* narrow **2** *Syn* LONG (sense 1), elongated, king-size (*or* king-sized), lengthy *Ant* brief, short **3** *Syn* LONG (sense 2), far, great, lengthy, long-lived, long-range, long-term, marathon *Ant* brief, short, short-lived, short-range, short-term

extension *Syn* ANNEX, ell, wing

extensive · having considerable extent *Syn* broad, expansive, extended, far-flung, far-reaching, wide, widespread *Rel* comprehensive, general, global, inclusive *Ant* narrow

extent *Syn* SIZE, area, dimensions, magnitude, volume

extenuate 1 *Syn* PALLIATE, gloss, gloze, whiten, whitewash 2 *Syn* THIN, attenuate, dilute, rarefy *Ant* thicken

exterior *Syn* OUTER, external, outside, outward *Ant* inner

exterminate · to destroy utterly *Syn* deracinate, eradicate, extirpate, uproot, wipe *Rel* abate, abolish, annihilate, extinguish

extermination *Syn* DESTRUCTION, annihilation, decimation, demolishment, demolition, desolation, devastation, extinction, havoc, loss, obliteration, ruin, ruination, wastage, wreckage *Ant* building, construction, erection, raising

external *Syn* OUTER, exterior, outside, outward *Ant* inner

externalize *Syn* REALIZE, actualize, embody, hypostatize, incarnate, materialize, objectify, reify

extinct · no longer existing *Syn* bygone, dead, defunct, departed, expired, gone, vanished *Rel* nonexistent *Ant* alive, existent, existing, extant, living

extinction *Syn* DESTRUCTION, annihilation, decimation, demolishment, demolition, desolation, devastation, extermination, havoc, loss, obliteration, ruin, ruination, wastage, wreckage *Ant* building, construction, erection, raising

extinguish *Syn* CRUSH (sense 2), quash, quell, quench, suppress

extirpate *Syn* EXTERMINATE, deracinate, eradicate, uproot, wipe

extol *Syn* PRAISE, acclaim, eulogize, laud *Ant* blame

extort *Syn* EDUCE, elicit, evoke, extract

extra *n Syn* BONUS, dividend, gratuity, gravy, lagniappe, perquisite, tip

extra *adj Syn* SUPERFLUOUS, spare, supernumerary, surplus

extra *adv Syn* VERY, awful, awfully, beastly, deadly, especially, exceedingly, extremely, far, frightfully, full, greatly, heavily, highly, hugely, jolly, mightily, mighty, mortally, most, much, particularly, rattling, real, right, so, something, super, terribly, too, whacking *Ant* little, negligibly, nominally, slightly

extract *Syn* EDUCE, elicit, evoke, extort

extraction *Syn* ANCESTRY, birth, blood, bloodline, breeding, descent, family tree, genealogy, line, lineage, origin, parentage, pedigree, stock, strain *Ant* issue, posterity, progeny, seed

extradite *Syn* BANISH, deport, exile, expatriate, ostracize, transport

extraneous 1 *Syn* EXTRINSIC, alien, foreign *Ant* intrinsic 2 *Syn* IRRELEVANT, immaterial, inapplicable *Ant* applicable, apposite, apropos, germane, material, pertinent, relevant

extraordinary *Syn* EXCEPTIONAL, phenomenal, unusual, unwonted *Ant* average, common

extravagant 1 *Syn* EXCESSIVE, exorbitant, extreme, immoderate, inordinate *Ant* deficient 2 *Syn* PRODIGAL, profligate, spendthrift, squandering, thriftless, unthrifty, wasteful *Ant* conserving, economical, economizing, frugal, scrimping, skimping, thrifty

extravagantly *Syn* HIGH, expensively, grandly, lavishly, luxuriously, opulently, richly, sumptuously *Ant* austerely, humbly, modestly, plainly, simply

extreme *Syn* EXCESSIVE, exorbitant, extravagant, immoderate, inordinate *Ant* deficient

extremely *Syn* VERY, awful, awfully, beastly, deadly, especially, exceedingly, extra, far, frightfully, full, greatly, heavily, highly, hugely, jolly, mightily, mighty, mortally, most, much, particularly, rattling, real, right, so, something, super, terribly, too, whacking *Ant* little, negligibly, nominally, slightly

extremist *Syn* RADICAL, revolutionary, revolutionist *Ant* moderate

extricate · to free or release from what binds or holds back *Syn* disembarrass, disencumber, disentangle, untangle *Rel* abstract, detach, disengage

extrinsic · external to a thing, its essential nature, or its original character *Syn* alien, extraneous, foreign *Rel* exterior, external, outer, outside, outward *Ant* intrinsic

extroverted *Syn* CONVIVIAL, boon, companionable, gregarious, outgoing, sociable, social *Ant* antisocial, introverted, reclusive, unsociable

exuberant *Syn* PROFUSE, lavish, lush, luxuriant, prodigal *Ant* scant, scanty, spare

exude · to flow forth slowly through small openings *Syn* bleed, ooze, percolate, seep, strain, sweat, weep *Rel* dribble, drip, trickle

exultant · having or expressing feelings of joy or triumph *Syn* exulting, glorying, jubilant, rejoicing, triumphant *Rel* ecstatic, elated, euphoric

exulting *Syn* EXULTANT, glorying, jubilant, rejoicing, triumphant

eye 1 *Syn* ATTENTION (sense 2), awareness, cognizance, ear, heed, notice, observance, observation 2 *Syn* CENTER (sense 2), base, capital, core, cynosure, focus, heart, hub, mecca, nucleus, seat

eyeless *Syn* BLIND, sightless, stone blind *Ant* sighted

eyewitness *Syn* SPECTATOR, beholder, bystander, kibitzer, looker-on, observer, onlooker, witness

F

fable 1 *Syn* ALLEGORY, parable 2 *Syn* FICTION, fabrication, figment

fabricate 1 *Syn* BUILD, assemble, construct, erect, make, make up, piece, put up, raise, rear, set up *Ant* disassemble, dismantle, take down 2 *Syn* INVENT, concoct, contrive, cook (up), devise, make up, manufacture, think (up) 3 *Syn* MAKE, fashion, forge, form, manufacture, shape

fabrication *Syn* FICTION, fable, figment

fabulous 1 *Syn* EXCELLENT, A1, bang-up, banner, capital, classic, crackerjack, dandy, divine, fine, first-class, first-rate, grand, great, groovy, heavenly, jim-dandy, keen, marvelous (*or* marvellous), mean, neat, nifty, noble, par excellence, prime, sensational, splendid, stellar, sterling, superb, superior, superlative, supernal, swell, terrific, tip-top, top, top-notch, unsurpassed, wonderful *Ant* poor 2 *Syn* FICTITIOUS, apocryphal, legendary, mythical *Ant* historical

face *n* 1 · the front part of a human or sometimes animal head including the mouth, nose, eyes, forehead, and cheeks *Syn* countenance, mug, physiognomy, puss, visage 2 *Syn* GRIMACE, frown, lower, mouth, pout, scowl

face *vb* 1 · to confront with courage or boldness *Syn* beard, brave, challenge, dare, defy *Rel* confront, encounter, meet *Ant* avoid 2 *Syn* MEET, confront, encounter *Ant* avoid

facet *Syn* PHASE, angle, aspect, side

facetious 1 *Syn* FLIPPANT, flip, pert, smart, smart-alecky (*or* smart-aleck) *Ant* earnest, sincere 2 *Syn* WITTY, humorous, jocose, jocular

facetiousness *Syn* FRIVOLITY, flightiness, flippancy, frivolousness, levity, light-headedness, lightness

facile *Syn* EASY, effortless, light, simple, smooth *Ant* hard

facilely *Syn* EASILY, effortlessly, fluently, freely, handily, lightly, painlessly, readily, smoothly *Ant* arduously, laboriously

facility *Syn* READINESS, dexterity, ease

facsimile *Syn* COPY, carbon copy, duplicate, duplication, imitation, reduplication, replica, replication, reproduction *Ant* original

fact · a single piece of information *Syn* datum, detail, nicety, particular, particularity, point *Rel* article, item

faction 1 · a group of people acting together within a larger group *Syn* bloc, body, coalition, party, sect, set, side, wing *Rel* crew, gang, pack, team 2 *Syn* COMBINATION, bloc, combine, party, ring

factious *Syn* INSUBORDINATE, contumacious, mutinous, rebellious, seditious

factitious 1 *Syn* ARTIFICIAL, ersatz, synthetic *Ant* natural 2 *Syn* IMITATION, artificial, bogus, fake, false, man-made, mimic, mock, sham, simulated, substitute, synthetic *Ant* genuine, natural, real

factor 1 *Syn* AGENT (sense 1), attorney, commissary, delegate, deputy, envoy, procurator, proxy, representative 2 *Syn* ELEMENT, component, constituent, ingredient *Ant* composite, compound (*in science*)

factual *Syn* ACTUAL, concrete, existent, real, true, very *Ant* conjectural, hypothetical, ideal, nonexistent, possible, potential, theoretical

faculty 1 *Syn* ABILITY, capability, capacity, competence, competency *Ant* disability, inability, incapability, incapacity, incompetence, incompetency, ineptitude, ineptness 2 *Syn* GIFT (sense 2), aptitude, bent, genius, knack, talent, turn 3 *Syn* POWER (sense 2), function

fad *Syn* FASHION, craze, cry, dernier cri, mode, rage, style, vogue

fade 1 *Syn* VANISH, disappear, evanesce, evaporate *Ant* appear, loom 2 *Syn* WHITEN, blanch, bleach, blench, decolorize, dull, pale, wash out *Ant* blacken, darken, deepen

faded *Syn* SHABBY, dilapidated, dingy, seedy, threadbare

failing *Syn* FAULT, foible, frailty, vice *Ant* merit

failure 1 · an omission on the part of someone or something of what is expected or required *Syn* default, dereliction, miscarriage, neglect *Rel* failing, fault 2 *Syn* DEFICIENCY, dearth, deficit, famine, inadequacy, insufficiency, lack, paucity, poverty, scantiness, scarceness, scarcity, shortage, want *Ant* abundance, adequacy, amplitude, plenitude, plenty, sufficiency

faineant *Syn* LAZY, indolent, slothful *Ant* industrious

faint *n* · a temporary or permanent state of unconsciousness *Syn* blackout, coma, insensibility, knockout, swoon *Rel* daze, stupor, trance

faint *vb* · to lose consciousness *Syn* black out, pass out, swoon *Rel* break down, collapse *Ant* come around, come round, come to, revive

faintheartedness *Syn* TIMIDITY, timidness, timorousness *Ant* audaciousness, audacity, boldness, guts, nerve

fair *adj* 1 · characterized by honesty, justice, and freedom from improper influence *Syn* dispassionate, equitable, impartial, just, objective, unbiased, uncolored *Rel* detached, disinterested, indifferent *Ant* unfair **2** *Syn* BEAUTIFUL, attractive, beauteous, comely, cute, gorgeous, handsome, knockout, lovely, pretty, ravishing, sightly, stunning, taking *Ant* homely, ill-favored, plain, ugly, unattractive, unbeautiful, unhandsome, unlovely, unpretty, unsightly **3** *Syn* BLOND, flaxen, golden, sandy, straw, tawny *Ant* dark **4** *Syn* MEDIUM, average, indifferent, mediocre, middling, moderate, second-rate

fair *n Syn* EXHIBITION, exhibit, exposition, show

fairy · an imaginary being usually having a small human form and magical powers *Syn* BROWNIE, elf, fay, pixie (*also* pixy), sprite *Rel* dwarf, gnome, goblin, gremlin, hobgoblin, imp, leprechaun, troll

faith **1** *Syn* BELIEF, credence, credit *Ant* disbelief, unbelief **2** *Syn* RELIGION, church, communion, creed, denomination, persuasion, sect **3** *Syn* TRUST, confidence, dependence, reliance *Ant* mistrust

faithful · firm in one's allegiance to someone or something *Syn* constant, devoted, devout, fast, good, loyal, pious, staunch (*or* stanch), steadfast, steady, true, true-blue *Rel* dependable, dutiful, reliable, tried, trustworthy *Ant* disloyal, faithless, false, fickle, inconstant, perfidious, recreant, traitorous, treacherous, unfaithful, untrue

faithless · not true to allegiance or duty *Syn* disloyal, false, perfidious, traitorous, treacherous *Rel* capricious, fickle, inconstant, unstable *Ant* faithful

faithlessness *Syn* BETRAYAL, disloyalty, double cross, falseness, falsity, infidelity, perfidy, sellout, treachery, treason, unfaithfulness

fake **1** *Syn* COUNTERFEIT, bogus, phony, pinchbeck, pseudo, sham, spurious *Ant* bona fide, genuine **2** *Syn* IMITATION, artificial, bogus, factitious, false, man-made, mimic, mock, sham, simulated, substitute, synthetic *Ant* genuine, natural, real

faker *Syn* IMPOSTOR, charlatan, mountebank, quack

fall *vb* · to go or to let go downward freely *Syn* drop, sink, slump, subside *Rel* alight, descend, dismount *Ant* rise

fall *n Syn* COMEDOWN, decline, descent, down, downfall *Ant* aggrandizement, ascent, exaltation, rise, up

fallacious *Syn* ILLOGICAL, invalid, irrational, nonrational, unreasonable, unreasoning, unsound, weak *Ant* logical, rational, reasonable, sound, valid

fallaciousness *Syn* FALLACY (sense 2), erroneousness, falseness, falsity, untruth *Ant* truth

fallacy **1** · a false idea or belief *Syn* error, falsehood, falsity, illusion, misconception, myth, old wives' tale, untruth *Rel* superstition *Ant* truth, verity **2** · the quality or state of being false *Syn* erroneousness, fallaciousness, falseness, falsity, untruth *Rel* speciousness, spuriousness *Ant* truth

fall(s) *Syn* WATERFALL, cascade, cataract

false **1** *Syn* FAITHLESS, disloyal, perfidious, traitorous, treacherous *Ant* faithful **2** *Syn* IMITATION, artificial, bogus, factitious, fake, man-made, mimic, mock, sham, simulated, substitute, synthetic *Ant* genuine, natural, real

falsehood **1** *Syn* FALLACY (sense 1), error, falsity, illusion, misconception, myth, old wives' tale, untruth *Ant* truth, verity **2** *Syn* LIE, fib, misrepresentation, story, untruth *Ant* truth

falseness **1** *Syn* BETRAYAL, disloyalty, double cross, faithlessness, falsity, infidelity, perfidy, sellout, treachery, treason, unfaithfulness **2** *Syn* FALLACY (sense 2), erroneousness, fallaciousness, falsity, untruth *Ant* truth

falsify *Syn* MISREPRESENT, belie, garble

falsity **1** *Syn* BETRAYAL, disloyalty, double cross, faithlessness, falseness, infidelity, perfidy, sellout, treachery, treason, unfaithfulness **2** *Syn* FALLACY (sense 1), error, falsehood, illusion, misconception, myth, old wives' tale, untruth *Ant* truth, verity **3** *Syn* FALLACY (sense 2), erroneousness, fallaciousness, falseness, untruth *Ant* truth

falter *Syn* HESITATE, vacillate, waver *Ant* dive (in), plunge (in)

faltering *Syn* HESITATION, hesitance, hesitancy, indecision, irresolution, shilly-shallying, vacillation, wavering, wobbling

fame · the state of being widely known for one's deeds *Syn* celebrity, éclat, glory, honor, notoriety, renown, reputation, repute *Rel* acclaim, acclamation, applause *Ant* infamy, obscurity

famed *Syn* FAMOUS, celebrated, noted, notorious, prominent, renowned, star, well-known *Ant* anonymous, obscure, unknown

familiar **1** · near to one another because of frequent association or shared interests *Syn* chummy, close, confidential, intimate, thick *Rel* amicable, friendly, neighborly *Ant* aloof **2** *Syn* COMMON, ordinary, popular, vulgar *Ant* exceptional, uncommon

familiarity **1** *Syn* ACQUAINTANCE, cognizance *Ant* unfamiliarity **2** *Syn* IMPROPRIETY (sense 1), gaffe, indiscretion, solecism *Ant* amenity, civility, courtesy, formality, gesture

familiarize *Syn* ENLIGHTEN (sense 1), acquaint, advise, apprise, brief, clue, fill in, inform, instruct, tell, wise (up)

family tree *Syn* ANCESTRY, birth, blood, bloodline, breeding, descent, extraction, genealogy, line, lineage, origin, parentage, pedigree, stock, strain *Ant* issue, posterity, progeny, seed

famine *Syn* DEFICIENCY, dearth, deficit, failure, inadequacy, insufficiency, lack, paucity, poverty, scantiness, scarceness, scarcity, shortage, want *Ant* abundance, adequacy, amplitude, plenitude, plenty, sufficiency

famous · widely known *Syn* celebrated, famed, noted, notorious, prominent, renowned, star, well-known *Rel* fabled, fabulous, legendary *Ant* anonymous, obscure, unknown

fan · a person with a strong and habitual liking for something *Syn* addict, aficionado, buff, bug, devotee, enthusiast, fanatic, fancier, fiend, freak, lover, maniac, nut *Rel* groupie

fanatic 1 *Syn* ENTHUSIAST, zealot 2 *Syn* FAN, addict, aficionado, buff, bug, devotee, enthusiast, fancier, fiend, freak, lover, maniac, nut 3 *Syn* ZEALOT, crusader, militant, partisan

fancier *Syn* FAN, addict, aficionado, buff, bug, devotee, enthusiast, fanatic, fiend, freak, lover, maniac, nut

fanciful *Syn* IMAGINARY, chimerical, fantastic, quixotic, visionary *Ant* actual, real

fancy *n* 1 · a vivid idea or image present in the mind but having no concrete or objective reality *Syn* daydream, dream, fantasy, nightmare, phantasm, phantasy, vision *Rel* fable, fabrication, fiction, figment *Ant* reality 2 *Syn* IMAGINATION, fantasy 3 *Syn* LIKING, appetite, favor, fondness, like, love, partiality, preference, relish, shine, taste, use *Ant* aversion, disfavor, dislike, distaste, hatred, loathing 4 *Syn* WHIM, caprice, freak, notion, vagary, whimsy

fancy *vb* 1 *Syn* LIKE, dote, enjoy, love, relish *Ant* dislike 2 *Syn* THINK (sense 1), conceive, envisage, envision, imagine, realize

fanny *Syn* BUTTOCKS, backside, bottom, breech, butt, hams, haunches, posterior, rear, rump, seat

fantastic 1 · conceived or made without reference to reality *Syn* antic, bizarre, grotesque *Rel* conceived, fancied, imagined 2 *Syn* EXOTIC, glamorous, marvelous (*or* marvellous), outlandish, romantic, strange 3 *Syn* IMAGINARY, chimerical, fanciful, quixotic, visionary *Ant* actual, real

fantasy 1 *Syn* FANCY, daydream, dream, nightmare, phantasm, phantasy, vision *Ant* reality 2 *Syn* IMAGINATION, fancy

far *adj* 1 *Syn* DISTANT, faraway, far-off, remote, removed 2 *Syn* LONG (sense 2), extended, great, lengthy, long-lived, long-range, long-term, marathon *Ant* brief, short, short-lived, short-range, short-term

far *adv* *Syn* VERY, awful, awfully, beastly, deadly, especially, exceedingly, extra, extremely, frightfully, full, greatly, heavily, highly, hugely, jolly, mightily, mighty, mortally, most, much, particularly, rattling, real, right, so, something, super, terribly, too, whacking *Ant* little, negligibly, nominally, slightly

faraway *Syn* DISTANT, far, far-off, remote, removed

farce *Syn* COMEDY, humor, slapstick

farcical *Syn* LAUGHABLE, comic, comical, droll, funny, ludicrous, ridiculous, risible

farewell *Syn* GOOD-BYE, adieu, au revoir, bon voyage, Godspeed *Ant* hello

far-fetched *Syn* IMPROBABLE, doubtful, dubious, flimsy, questionable, unapt, unlikely *Ant* likely, probable

far-flung *Syn* EXTENSIVE, broad, expansive, extended, far-reaching, wide, widespread *Ant* narrow

farming *adj Syn* AGRICULTURAL, agrarian *Ant* nonagricultural

farming *n Syn* AGRICULTURE, husbandry

far-off *Syn* DISTANT, far, faraway, remote, removed

far-reaching *Syn* EXTENSIVE, broad, expansive, extended, far-flung, wide, widespread *Ant* narrow

farther *adv* · at or to a greater distance or more avanced point *Syn* beyond, further

farther *adj Syn* ADDITIONAL, added, another, else, further, more, other

fascinate *Syn* ATTRACT, allure, bewitch, captivate, charm, enchant *Ant* repel

fascinating 1 *Syn* ATTRACTIVE, alluring, bewitching, captivating, charming, enchanting *Ant* forbidding, repellent 2 *Syn* INTERESTING, absorbing, arresting, engaging, engrossing, enthralling, gripping, immersing, intriguing, involving, riveting *Ant* boring, drab, dry, dull, heavy, monotonous, tedious, uninteresting

fashion *n* 1 · the prevailing or accepted custom *Syn* craze, cry, dernier cri, fad, mode, rage, style, vogue *Rel* drift, tendency, trend 2 *Syn* HABIT, custom, pattern, practice, trick, way, wont 3 *Syn* METHOD, manner, mode, system, way

fashion *vb Syn* MAKE, fabricate, forge, form, manufacture, shape

fashionable *Syn* STYLISH, chic, dashing, modish, smart

fashionableness *Syn* POPULARITY, favor, hotness, modishness, vogue *Ant* disfavor, unpopularity

fast 1 · moving, proceeding, or acting with great celerity *Syn* expeditious, fleet, hasty, quick, rapid, speedy, swift *Ant* slow 2 *Syn* FAITHFUL, constant, devoted, devout, good, loyal, pious, staunch (*or* stanch), steadfast, steady, true, true-blue *Ant* disloyal, faithless, false, fickle, inconstant, perfidious, recreant, traitorous, treacherous, unfaithful, untrue

fasten · to cause one thing to hold to another *Syn* affix, attach, fix *Rel* anchor, moor, rivet, secure *Ant* loose, loosen, unfasten

fastidious *Syn* NICE, dainty, finical, finicking, finicky, fussy, particular, pernickety, persnickety, squeamish

fastness *Syn* FORT, citadel, fortress, stronghold

fat *n* **1** *Syn* ELITE, best, choice, cream, elect, flower, pick, prime, upper crust **2** *Syn* EXCESS, overabundance, overage, overflow, overkill, overmuch, oversupply, superabundance, superfluity, surfeit, surplus *Ant* deficiency, deficit, insufficiency

fat *adj* **1** *Syn* FERTILE, fecund, fruitful, luxuriant, productive, prolific, rich *Ant* barren, infertile, sterile, unfruitful, unproductive **2** *Syn* FLESHY, chubby, corpulent, obese, plump, portly, rotund, stout *Ant* scrawny, skinny

fatal *Syn* DEADLY, baleful, deathly, fell, killer, lethal, mortal, murderous, pestilent, vital *Ant* healthful, healthy, nonfatal, nonlethal, wholesome

fate · whatever is destined or inevitably decreed for one *Syn* destiny, doom, lot, portion *Rel* consequence, effect, issue, outcome, result, upshot

fathom · to measure depth typically with a weighted line *Syn* plumb, sound

fatigue *n* · a complete depletion of energy or strength *Syn* burnout, collapse, exhaustion, lassitude, prostration, tiredness, weariness *Rel* debilitation, enervation, faintness, feebleness, weakness *Ant* refreshment, rejuvenation, revitalization

fatigue *vb* *Syn* TIRE, exhaust, jade, tucker, weary

fatuous *Syn* SIMPLE, asinine, foolish, silly *Ant* wise

fault **1** · an imperfection in character or an ingrained moral weakness *Syn* failing, foible, frailty, vice *Rel* infirmity, weakness *Ant* merit **2** *Syn* BLAME, culpability, guilt **3** *Syn* BLEMISH, defect, deformity, disfigurement, flaw, imperfection, mark, pockmark, scar **4** *Syn* IMPERFECTION, deficiency, shortcoming *Ant* perfection

faultfinder *Syn* CRITIC, carper, castigator, caviler (*or* caviller), censurer, nitpicker, railer, scold

faultfinding *Syn* CRITICAL, captious, carping, caviling, censorious, hypercritical *Ant* uncritical

faultless *Syn* IMPECCABLE, errorless, flawless

faulty · having a fault *Syn* bad, defective, flawed, imperfect *Rel* fallible *Ant* faultless, flawless, impeccable, perfect

faux pas *Syn* ERROR, blunder, bull, howler, lapse, mistake, slip

favor *vb* **1** · to give the support of one's approval to *Syn* countenance, encourage *Rel* approve, endorse *Ant* disapprove **2** *Syn* APPROVE (OF), accept, care (for), countenance, OK (*or* okay), subscribe (to) *Ant* disapprove

(of), discountenance, disfavor, frown (on *or* upon) **3** *Syn* OBLIGE, accommodate *Ant* disoblige

favor *n* **1** *Syn* APPROVAL, approbation, blessing, imprimatur, OK (*or* okay) *Ant* disapprobation, disapproval, disfavor **2** *Syn* BIAS, one-sidedness, partiality, partisanship, prejudice *Ant* impartiality, neutrality, objectivity, open-mindedness **3** *Syn* GIFT (sense 1), boon, gratuity, largess, present **4** *Syn* LIKING, appetite, fancy, fondness, like, love, partiality, preference, relish, shine, taste, use *Ant* aversion, disfavor, dislike, distaste, hatred, loathing **5** *Syn* POPULARITY, fashionableness, hotness, modishness, vogue *Ant* disfavor, unpopularity

favorable **1** · being of good omen or presaging a happy or successful outcome *Syn* auspicious, benign, propitious *Rel* advantageous, beneficial, profitable *Ant* antagonistic, unfavorable **2** *Syn* BENEFICIAL, advantageous, helpful, profitable, salutary *Ant* disadvantageous, unfavorable, unhelpful

favorite **1** · a person or thing that is preferred over others *Syn* darling, minion, pet, preference *Rel* beloved, dear **2** *Syn* PARASITE, bootlicker, hanger-on, leech, lickspittle, sponge, sponger, sycophant, toady

fawn · to behave abjectly before a superior *Syn* cower, cringe, toady, truckle *Rel* blandish, cajole, coax, wheedle *Ant* domineer

fawner *Syn* SYCOPHANT, flunky, toady

fay *Syn* FAIRY, brownie, elf, pixie (*also* pixy), sprite

faze *Syn* EMBARRASS, abash, discomfit, disconcert, rattle *Ant* facilitate, relieve

fealty *Syn* FIDELITY, allegiance, devotion, loyalty, piety *Ant* faithlessness, perfidy

fear **1** · agitation or dismay which overcomes one in the anticipation or in the presence of danger *Syn* alarm, consternation, dismay, dread, fright, horror, panic, terror, trepidation *Rel* apprehension, foreboding, misgiving, presentiment *Ant* fearlessness **2** *Syn* REVERENCE (sense 2), awe

fearful **1** · inspired or moved by fear *Syn* afraid, apprehensive *Rel* timid, timorous *Ant* fearless, intrepid **2** · causing fear *Syn* appalling, awful, dreadful, frightful, horrible, horrific, shocking, terrible, terrific *Rel* alarming, frightening, terrifying

fearless *Syn* BRAVE, audacious, bold, courageous, dauntless, doughty, intrepid, unafraid, undaunted, valiant, valorous *Ant* craven

fearlessness *Syn* COURAGE, bravery, courageousness, daring, dauntlessness, doughtiness, gallantry, greatheartedness, guts, hardihood, heart, heroism, intrepidity, intrepidness, nerve, stoutness, valor *Ant* cowardice, cowardliness, cravenness, dastardliness, spinelessness, yellowness

feasible *Syn* POSSIBLE, practicable

feast *Syn* DINNER, banquet

feat · a remarkable deed or performance *Syn* achievement, exploit *Rel* act, action, deed

feather *Syn* FINERY, array, best, bravery, caparison, frippery, full dress, gaiety, regalia

feature *n Syn* CHARACTERISTIC, attribute, character, mark, peculiarity, point, property, quality, trait

feature *vb Syn* EMPHASIZE, accent, accentuate, highlight, play (up), point (up), stress, underline, underscore *Ant* play (down)

fecund *Syn* FERTILE, fat, fruitful, luxuriant, productive, prolific, rich *Ant* barren, infertile, sterile, unfruitful, unproductive

fecundity *Syn* FERTILITY, fruitfulness, prolificacy *Ant* infertility, sterility

federate *Syn* ALLY, associate, band, club, confederate, conjoin, cooperate, league, unite *Ant* break up, disband

federation *Syn* ALLIANCE, coalition, confederacy, confederation, fusion, league

fee *Syn* WAGE, emolument, hire, pay, salary, stipend

feeble *Syn* WEAK, decrepit, fragile, frail, infirm *Ant* strong

feed *vb* **1** · to provide the food that one needs or desires *Syn* graze, nourish, pasture *Rel* cherish, foster, nurse, nurture *Ant* starve **2** *Syn* FURNISH (sense 2), deliver, give, hand, hand over, provide, supply *Ant* hold (back), keep (back), reserve, retain, withhold

feed *n* **1** *Syn* FOOD (sense 1), comestibles, fodder, forage, provender, provisions, viands, victuals **2** *Syn* MEAL, chow, mess, repast, table

feel **1** *Syn* BELIEVE (sense 1), consider, deem, figure, guess, hold, imagine, suppose, think *Ant* disbelieve, discredit, reject **2** *Syn* TOUCH, handle, palpate, paw

feeling **1** · subjective response or reaction *Syn* affection, emotion, passion, sentiment *Rel* affecting, affection, impressing, impression, touching **2** *Syn* SENSATION (sense 2), sense, sensibility

feign *Syn* ASSUME, affect, counterfeit, pretend, sham, simulate

feigned *Syn* INSINCERE, artificial, backhanded, double-dealing, hypocritical, lefthanded, mealy, mealymouthed, two-faced, unctuous *Ant* genuine, heartfelt, honest, sincere, unfeigned

feint *Syn* TRICK, artifice, gambit, maneuver, ploy, ruse, stratagem, wile

felicitations *Syn* COMPLIMENTS, congratulations, greetings, regards, respects

felicitous *Syn* FIT, appropriate, apt, fitting, happy, meet, proper, suitable *Ant* unfit

felicitousness *Syn* APPROPRIATENESS, aptness, fitness, fittingness, rightness, seemliness, suitability, suitableness *Ant* inappropriateness, inaptness, infelicity, unfitness

felicity *Syn* HAPPINESS, beatitude, blessedness, bliss *Ant* unhappiness

fell **1** *Syn* DEADLY, baleful, deathly, fatal, killer, lethal, mortal, murderous, pestilent, vital *Ant* healthful, healthy, nonfatal, nonlethal, wholesome **2** *Syn* FIERCE, barbarous, cruel, ferocious, inhuman, savage, truculent *Ant* mild, tame

fellow **1** *Syn* BOYFRIEND, beau, man, swain **2** *Syn* EQUAL, coordinate, counterpart, equivalent, like, match, parallel, peer, rival **3** *Syn* MAN, dude, gent, gentleman, guy, male

fellowship **1** *Syn* COMPANIONSHIP, camaraderie, company, comradeship, society **2** *Syn* RAPPORT, communion, rapprochement

felon *Syn* CRIMINAL, convict, culprit, delinquent, malefactor

female *adj* · of, relating to, or marked by qualities traditionally associated with women *Syn* feminine, ladylike, womanish, womanlike, womanly *Ant* male

female *n Syn* WOMAN (sense 1), lady

feminine *Syn* FEMALE, ladylike, womanish, womanlike, womanly *Ant* male

fen *Syn* SWAMP, bog, marsh, marshland, mire, morass, muskeg, slough, swampland

fence *n Syn* BARRIER, barricade, hedge, wall

fence *vb* **1** *Syn* DODGE, duck, malinger, parry, shirk, sidestep *Ant* face **2** *Syn* ENCLOSE, cage, coop, corral, envelop, pen, wall

feral *Syn* BRUTAL, beastly, bestial, brute, brutish

ferment *Syn* UNREST, disquiet, restiveness, restlessness, turmoil, uneasiness *Ant* calm, ease, peace, quiet

ferocious *Syn* FIERCE, barbarous, cruel, fell, inhuman, savage, truculent *Ant* mild, tame

ferret out *Syn* SEEK, comb, hunt, ransack, rummage, scour, search

fertile · producing abundantly *Syn* fat, fecund, fruitful, luxuriant, productive, prolific, rich *Rel* bearing, producing, yielding *Ant* barren, infertile, sterile, unfruitful, unproductive

fertility · the quality or state of being fertile *Syn* fecundity, fruitfulness, prolificacy *Ant* infertility, sterility

fervent · having or expressing great depth of feeling *Syn* ardent, blazing, burning, charged, emotional, fervid, feverish, fiery, flaming, glowing, hot-blooded, impassioned, passionate, red-hot, vehement, warm, warm-blooded *Rel* gushing, maudlin, mawkish, mushy, sentimental *Ant* cold, cool, dispassionate, impassive, unemotional

fervid *Syn* FERVENT, ardent, blazing, burning, charged, emotional, feverish, fiery, flaming, glowing, hot-blooded, impassioned, passionate, red-hot, vehement, warm, warm-blooded *Ant* cold, cool, dispassionate, impassive, unemotional

fervor *Syn* PASSION, ardor, enthusiasm, zeal

festival · a time or program of special events

and entertainment in honor of something *Syn* carnival, celebration, festivity, fete (*or* fête), fiesta, gala, jubilee *Rel* jamboree, jollification, merrymaking, revel, revelry

festive *Syn* MERRY, blithesome, gay, gleeful, jocose, jocund, jolly, jovial, laughing, mirthful, sunny

festivity *Syn* FESTIVAL, carnival, celebration, fete (*or* fête), fiesta, gala, jubilee

fetch *Syn* BRING, take *Ant* remove, withdraw

fete *or* **fête** *Syn* FESTIVAL, carnival, celebration, festivity, fiesta, gala, jubilee

fetid *Syn* MALODOROUS, fusty, musty, noisome, putrid, rancid, rank, stinking *Ant* odorous

fetish · an object believed to be endowed with the virtue of averting evil or of bringing good fortune *Syn* amulet, charm, talisman

fetter *n* 1 *Syn* ENCUMBRANCE, bar, block, chain, clog, crimp, deterrent, drag, embarrassment, handicap, hindrance, hurdle, impediment, inhibition, interference, let, manacle, obstacle, obstruction, shackles, stop, stumbling block, trammel *Ant* aid, assistance, benefit, help 2 *Syn* RESTRICTION, check, condition, constraint, curb, limitation, restraint

fetter *vb Syn* HAMPER, clog, hog-tie, manacle, shackle, trammel *Ant* assist (*persons*), expedite (*work, projects*)

feverish *Syn* FERVENT, ardent, blazing, burning, charged, emotional, fervid, fiery, flaming, glowing, hot-blooded, impassioned, passionate, red-hot, vehement, warm, warm-blooded *Ant* cold, cool, dispassionate, impassive, unemotional

fiancé *Syn* BETROTHED, fiancée, intended

fiancée *Syn* BETROTHED, fiancé, intended

fib *vb Syn* LIE, equivocate, palter, prevaricate

fib *n Syn* LIE, falsehood, misrepresentation, story, untruth *Ant* truth

fickle *Syn* INCONSTANT, capricious, mercurial, unstable *Ant* constant

fiction · a story, account, explanation, or conception which is an invention of the human mind *Syn* fable, fabrication, figment *Rel* anecdote, narrative, story, tale, yarn

fictitious · having the character of something invented or imagined as opposed to something true or genuine *Syn* apocryphal, fabulous, legendary, mythical *Rel* created, invented *Ant* historical

fidelity · faithfulness to something to which one is bound by a pledge or duty *Syn* allegiance, devotion, fealty, loyalty, piety *Rel* constancy, faithfulness, staunchness, steadfastness *Ant* faithlessness, perfidy

fidgety *Syn* IMPATIENT, jittery, jumpy, nervous, restive, restless, uneasy, unquiet *Ant* patient

field 1 · a limited area of knowledge or endeavor to which pursuits, activities, and interests are confined *Syn* bailiwick, domain, province, sphere, territory *Rel* bounds, confines, limits 2 *Syn* REGION, area, demesne, zone

fiend 1 *Syn* DEMON, devil, ghoul, imp, incubus 2 *Syn* FAN, addict, aficionado, buff, bug, devotee, enthusiast, fanatic, fancier, freak, lover, maniac, nut

fiendish · having or manifesting qualities associated with devils, demons, and fiends *Syn* demoniac, demonic, devilish, diabolic, diabolical *Rel* hellish, infernal

fierce 1 · displaying fury or malignity in looks or actions *Syn* barbarous, cruel, fell, ferocious, inhuman, savage, truculent *Rel* menacing, threatening *Ant* mild, tame 2 *Syn* INTENSE, exquisite, vehement, violent *Ant* subdued

fiery 1 *Syn* FERVENT, ardent, blazing, burning, charged, emotional, fervid, feverish, flaming, glowing, hot-blooded, impassioned, passionate, red-hot, vehement, warm, warm-blooded *Ant* cold, cool, dispassionate, impassive, unemotional 2 *Syn* SPIRITED, gingery, high-spirited, mettlesome, peppery, spunky *Ant* spiritless

fiesta *Syn* FESTIVAL, carnival, celebration, festivity, fete (*or* fête), gala, jubilee

fight *n* 1 *Syn* BELLIGERENCE, aggression, aggressiveness, bellicosity, combativeness, contentiousness, disputatiousness, militancy, pugnacity, scrappiness, truculence *Ant* pacifism 2 *Syn* CONTEST, affray, combat, conflict, fray

fight *vb* 1 *Syn* CONTEND, battle, war 2 *Syn* RESIST, antagonize, combat, conflict, contest, oppose, withstand *Ant* abide, submit

figment *Syn* FICTION, fable, fabrication

figure *n* 1 · a unit in a decorative composition (as in fabric) *Syn* design, device, motif, pattern 2 *Syn* FORM (sense 1), configuration, conformation, shape 3 *Syn* NUMBER, digit, integer, numeral

figure *vb* 1 *Syn* BELIEVE (sense 1), consider, deem, feel, guess, hold, imagine, suppose, think *Ant* disbelieve, discredit, reject 2 *Syn* ESTIMATE (sense 2), calculate, call, conjecture, gauge, guess, judge, make, place, put, reckon, suppose

figure out *Syn* SOLVE, answer, break, crack, dope (out), puzzle (out), resolve, riddle, unravel, work, work out

figures *Syn* CALCULATION, arithmetic, ciphering, computation, figuring, reckoning

figuring *Syn* CALCULATION, arithmetic, ciphering, computation, figures, reckoning

filch *Syn* STEAL, cop, lift, pilfer, pinch, purloin, snitch, swipe

file *Syn* LINE, echelon, rank, row, tier

fillet *Syn* STRIP, band, ribbon, stripe

fill in *Syn* ENLIGHTEN (sense 1), acquaint, advise, apprise, brief, clue, familiarize, inform, instruct, tell, wise (up)

film 1 *Syn* MOVIE (sense 1), motion picture, moving picture, picture **2** *Syn* MOVIE (sense 2), cinema, motion pictures, pictures, screen

filthy *Syn* DIRTY, foul, nasty, squalid *Ant* clean

finagle *Syn* ENGINEER, contrive, finesse, frame, machinate, maneuver, manipulate, mastermind, negotiate, wangle

final *Syn* LAST, concluding, eventual, latest, terminal, ultimate *Ant* first

finale · the last part of a process or action *Syn* close, closing, conclusion, consummation, end, ending, finis, finish, windup *Rel* apex, climax, crescendo, culmination, peak, summit, zenith *Ant* beginning, dawn, opening, start

financial · of or relating to the possession, making, borrowing, lending, or expenditure of money *Syn* fiscal, monetary, pecuniary

find *Syn* HAPPEN (on *or* upon), chance (upon), encounter, hit (upon), meet, stumble (on *or* onto)

fine *n* · a sum of money to be paid as a punishment *Syn* damages, forfeit, forfeiture, mulct, penalty *Rel* reparations

fine *adj* **1** *Syn* ADEQUATE, acceptable, all right, decent, OK (*or* okay), passable, respectable, satisfactory, tolerable *Ant* deficient, inadequate, lacking, unacceptable, unsatisfactory, wanting **2** *Syn* EXCELLENT, A1, bang-up, banner, capital, classic, crackerjack, dandy, divine, fabulous, first-class, first-rate, grand, great, groovy, heavenly, jim-dandy, keen, marvelous (*or* marvellous), mean, neat, nifty, noble, par excellence, prime, sensational, splendid, stellar, sterling, superb, superior, superlative, supernal, swell, terrific, tip-top, top, top-notch, unsurpassed, wonderful *Ant* poor

fine *vb* **1** *Syn* IMPOSE, assess, charge, exact, lay, levy, put *Ant* remit **2** *Syn* PENALIZE, amerce, mulct

fineness *Syn* PRECISION, accuracy, closeness, delicacy, exactitude, exactness, preciseness, rigorousness, veracity *Ant* coarseness, impreciseness, imprecision, inaccuracy, inexactness, roughness

finery · dressy clothing *Syn* array, best, bravery, caparison, feather, frippery, full dress, gaiety, regalia *Rel* apparel, attire, costume, duds, raiment

finesse *n* *Syn* DEXTERITY (sense 1), adroitness, cleverness, sleight *Ant* awkwardness, clumsiness, gawkiness

finesse *vb* *Syn* ENGINEER, contrive, finagle, frame, machinate, maneuver, manipulate, mastermind, negotiate, wangle

finical *Syn* NICE, dainty, fastidious, finicking, finicky, fussy, particular, pernickety, persnickety, squeamish

finicking *Syn* NICE, dainty, fastidious, finical, finicky, fussy, particular, pernickety, persnickety, squeamish

finicky *Syn* NICE, dainty, fastidious, finical, finicking, fussy, particular, pernickety, persnickety, squeamish

finis *Syn* FINALE, close, closing, conclusion, consummation, end, ending, finish, windup *Ant* beginning, dawn, opening, start

finish *vb* *Syn* CONCLUDE (sense 1), complete, end, terminate

finish *n* *Syn* FINALE, close, closing, conclusion, consummation, end, ending, finis, windup *Ant* beginning, dawn, opening, start

finished *Syn* CONSUMMATE, accomplished *Ant* crude

fire *n* · a destructive burning *Syn* conflagration, holocaust *Rel* blaze, flame, flare, glare

fire *vb* **1** *Syn* ANIMATE, brace, energize, enliven, invigorate, jazz (up), liven (up), pep (up), quicken, stimulate, vitalize, vivify *Ant* damp, dampen, deaden, dull **2** *Syn* DISMISS, bounce, cashier, discharge, drop, sack **3** *Syn* INFORM (sense 1), animate, inspire **4** *Syn* LIGHT, ignite, kindle

firebrand *Syn* AGITATOR, demagogue, exciter, fomenter, incendiary, inciter, instigator, rabble-rouser

firebug *Syn* ARSONIST, incendiary

firkin *Syn* CASK, barrel, hogshead, keg, pipe, puncheon

firm · having a texture or consistency that resists deformation by external force *Syn* hard, solid *Rel* close, compact, dense, thick *Ant* flabby, loose

first *Syn* HEAD, chief, commanding, foremost, high, lead, leading, managing, preeminent, premier, presiding, primary, prime, principal, supreme

first-class *Syn* EXCELLENT, A1, bang-up, banner, capital, classic, crackerjack, dandy, divine, fabulous, fine, first-rate, grand, great, groovy, heavenly, jim-dandy, keen, marvelous (*or* marvellous), mean, neat, nifty, noble, par excellence, prime, sensational, splendid, stellar, sterling, superb, superior, superlative, supernal, swell, terrific, tip-top, top, top-notch, unsurpassed, wonderful *Ant* poor

first-rate *Syn* EXCELLENT, A1, bang-up, banner, capital, classic, crackerjack, dandy, divine, fabulous, fine, first-class, grand, great, groovy, heavenly, jim-dandy, keen, marvelous (*or* marvellous), mean, neat, nifty, noble, par excellence, prime, sensational, splendid, stellar, sterling, superb, superior, superlative, supernal, swell, terrific, tip-top, top, top-notch, unsurpassed, wonderful *Ant* poor

fiscal *Syn* FINANCIAL, monetary, pecuniary

fissure *Syn* CRACK, chink, cleft, cranny, crevasse, crevice

fit *adj* **1** · right with respect to some end, need, use, or circumstances *Syn* appropriate, apt, felicitous, fitting, happy, meet, proper, suitable *Rel* adaptable, adapted, adjustable, adjusted, conformable, conformed *Ant* unfit **2** *Syn* COMPETENT, able, capable, good, qualified, suitable *Ant* incompetent, inept, poor, unfit, unqualified

fit *n* **1** · an episode of bodily or mental disorder or excess *Syn* convulsion, paroxysm, spasm **2** *Syn* ATTACK (sense 3), bout, case, seizure, siege, spell

fit *vb* PREPARE, condition, qualify, ready

fitful · lacking in steadiness or regularity of occurrence *Syn* casual, choppy, discontinuous, erratic, intermittent, irregular, occasional, spasmodic, sporadic, spotty, unsteady *Rel* convulsive, sudden, violent *Ant* constant, continuous, regular, steady

fitness **1** *Syn* APPROPRIATENESS, aptness, felicitousness, fittingness, rightness, seemliness, suitability, suitableness *Ant* inappropriateness, inaptness, infelicity, unfitness **2** *Syn* HEALTH, healthiness, heartiness, robustness, soundness, wellness, wholeness, wholesomeness *Ant* illness, sickness, unhealthiness, unsoundness

fit (out) *Syn* FURNISH (sense 1), accoutre (*or* accouter), equip, outfit, rig, supply *Ant* hold (back), keep (back), reserve, retain, withhold

fitting *Syn* FIT, appropriate, apt, felicitous, happy, meet, proper, suitable *Ant* unfit

fittingly *Syn* PROPERLY, appropriately, congruously, correctly, happily, meetly, rightly, suitably *Ant* improperly, inappropriately, incongruously, incorrectly, unsuitably, wrongly

fittingness *Syn* APPROPRIATENESS, aptness, felicitousness, fitness, rightness, seemliness, suitability, suitableness *Ant* inappropriateness, inaptness, infelicity, unfitness

fix *vb* **1** *Syn* ADJUST, regulate *Ant* derange **2** *Syn* APPOINT (sense 1), designate, name, set *Ant* discharge, dismiss, expel, fire **3** *Syn* FASTEN, affix, attach *Ant* loose, loosen, unfasten **4** *Syn* SET, establish, settle

fix *n* *Syn* PREDICAMENT, dilemma, jam, pickle, plight, quandary, scrape

fixable *Syn* REMEDIABLE, correctable, rectifiable, repairable, reparable *Ant* incorrigible, irremediable, irreparable

flabbergast *Syn* SURPRISE (sense 2), amaze, astonish, astound

flabby *Syn* LIMP, flaccid, flimsy, floppy, sleazy

flaccid *Syn* LIMP, flabby, flimsy, floppy, sleazy

flag *n* · a piece of fabric that is used as a symbol (as of a nation) or as a signaling device *Syn* banner, color, ensign, jack, pendant, pennant, pennon, standard, streamer

flag *vb* **1** *Syn* DROOP, sag, wilt **2** *Syn* MOTION, beckon, gesture, signal, wave

flagitious *Syn* VICIOUS, corrupt, degenerate,

infamous, iniquitous, nefarious, villainous *Ant* virtuous

flagrant **1** · bad or objectionable *Syn* glaring, gross, rank *Rel* atrocious, heinous, monstrous, outrageous **2** *Syn* EGREGIOUS, blatant, conspicuous, glaring, gross, obvious, patent, pronounced, rank, striking

flair *Syn* LEANING, penchant, proclivity, propensity *Ant* distaste

flamboyance *Syn* OSTENTATION, flashiness, garishness, gaudiness, glitz, ostentatiousness, pretentiousness, showiness, swank *Ant* austerity, plainness, severity

flamboyant **1** *Syn* GAUDY, flashy, garish, glitzy, loud, ostentatious, splashy, swank (*or* swanky), tawdry *Ant* conservative, quiet, understated **2** *Syn* ORNATE, baroque, florid, rococo *Ant* austere, chaste

flame *n* **1** *Syn* BLAZE, flare, glare, glow **2** *Syn* SWEETHEART, beloved, darling, dear, honey, love, sweet

flame *vb* **1** *Syn* BLAZE, flare, glare, glow **2** *Syn* ERUPT (sense 1), break out, burst (forth), explode, flare (up)

flaming *Syn* FERVENT, ardent, blazing, burning, charged, emotional, fervid, feverish, fiery, glowing, hot-blooded, impassioned, passionate, red-hot, vehement, warm, warm-blooded *Ant* cold, cool, dispassionate, impassive, unemotional

flammable *Syn* COMBUSTIBLE, incendiary, inflammable, inflammatory

flanking *Syn* ADJACENT, abutting, adjoining, bordering, contiguous, fringing, joining, juxtaposed, skirting, touching, verging *Ant* nonadjacent

flapjack *Syn* PANCAKE, griddle cake, hotcake, slapjack

flare *vb* *Syn* BLAZE, flame, glare, glow

flare *n* **1** *Syn* BLAZE, flame, glare, glow **2** *Syn* OUTBREAK, burst, flare-up, flash, flicker, flurry, flutter, outburst, spurt

flare (up) *Syn* ERUPT (sense 1), break out, burst (forth), explode, flame

flare-up *Syn* OUTBREAK, burst, flare, flash, flicker, flurry, flutter, outburst, spurt

flash *vb* · to shoot forth light (as in rays or sparks) *Syn* coruscate, glance, gleam, glint, glisten, glitter, scintillate, sparkle, twinkle *Rel* dart, fly, shoot

flash *n* **1** *Syn* INSTANT, jiffy, minute, moment, second, shake, split second, trice, twinkle, twinkling, wink **2** *Syn* OUTBREAK, burst, flare, flare-up, flicker, flurry, flutter, outburst, spurt

flash *adj* *Syn* MOMENTARY, ephemeral, evanescent, fleeting, fugitive, impermanent, passing, short-lived, temporary, transient, transitory *Ant* enduring, eternal, everlasting, lasting, long-lived, permanent, perpetual

flashiness *Syn* OSTENTATION, flamboyance, garishness, gaudiness, glitz, ostentatiousness, pretentiousness, showiness, swank *Ant* austerity, plainness, severity

flashy *Syn* GAUDY, flamboyant, garish, glitzy, loud, ostentatious, splashy, swank (*or* swanky), tawdry *Ant* conservative, quiet, understated

flat **1** *Syn* BORING, drab, dreary, dry, dull, heavy, humdrum, jading, leaden, monotonous, pedestrian, ponderous, stodgy, stuffy, stupid, tame, tedious, tiresome, tiring, unanimated, uninteresting, wearisome, weary, wearying *Ant* absorbing, engaging, engrossing, gripping, interesting, intriguing, involving **2** *Syn* INSIPID, banal, inane, jejune, vapid, wishy-washy *Ant* sapid, zestful **3** *Syn* LEVEL, even, flush, plain, plane, smooth

flattery *Syn* COMPLIMENT, adulation *Ant* taunt

flatulent *Syn* INFLATED, tumid, turgid *Ant* pithy

flaunt *Syn* SHOW (sense 2), display, exhibit, expose, parade *Ant* disguise

flavor **1** *Syn* AURA, air, atmosphere, climate, mood, note, temper **2** *Syn* TASTE (sense 1), relish, savor, smack, tang *Ant* antipathy

flavorsome *Syn* PALATABLE, appetizing, relishing, sapid, savory, tasty, toothsome *Ant* distasteful, unpalatable

flaw *Syn* BLEMISH, defect, deformity, disfigurement, fault, imperfection, mark, pockmark, scar

flawed *Syn* FAULTY, bad, defective, imperfect *Ant* faultless, flawless, impeccable, perfect

flawless *Syn* IMPECCABLE, errorless, faultless

flaxen *Syn* BLOND, fair, golden, sandy, straw, tawny *Ant* dark

flay *Syn* SKIN, decorticate, pare, peel

fleck *Syn* SPOT, blotch, dapple, dot, freckle, marble, mottle, pepper, speck, speckle, splotch, sprinkle, stipple

flecked *Syn* SPOTTED, bespangled, marbled, mottled, spangled, spattered, speckled, sprinkled, stippled

fledgling *Syn* BEGINNER, colt, freshman, greenhorn, neophyte, newbie, newcomer, novice, recruit, rookie, tenderfoot, tyro *Ant* old hand, old-timer, vet, veteran

flee *Syn* ESCAPE (sense 1), abscond, decamp, fly

fleece · to rob by the use of trickery or threats *Syn* bleed, cheat, chisel, cozen, defraud, hustle, mulct, rook, shortchange, skin, squeeze, stick, sting, swindle, victimize *Rel* extort, wrench, wrest, wring

fleecy *Syn* HAIRY (sense 1), bristly, furry, hirsute, rough, shaggy, unshorn, woolly *Ant* bald, furless, hairless, shorn, smooth

fleer *Syn* SCOFF, flout, gibe, gird, jeer, sneer

fleet *Syn* FAST, expeditious, hasty, quick, rapid, speedy, swift *Ant* slow

fleeting *Syn* MOMENTARY, ephemeral, evanescent, flash, fugitive, impermanent, passing, short-lived, temporary, transient, transitory

Ant enduring, eternal, everlasting, lasting, long-lived, permanent, perpetual

fleshly *Syn* CARNAL, animal, sensual *Ant* intellectual, spiritual

fleshy · thick and heavy in body because of superfluous fat *Syn* chubby, corpulent, fat, obese, plump, portly, rotund, stout *Rel* brawny, burly, husky, muscular *Ant* scrawny, skinny

flex · to bend *Syn* bow, buckle, crook *Rel* bend, curve, twist *Ant* extend

flexible **1** *Syn* ELASTIC (sense 1), resilient, springy, supple *Ant* rigid **2** *Syn* WILLOWY, limber, lissome, lithe, pliable, pliant, supple *Ant* inflexible, rigid, stiff

flexuous *Syn* WINDING, serpentine, sinuous, tortuous *Ant* straight

flicker *vb Syn* FLIT, flitter, flutter, hover

flicker *n Syn* OUTBREAK, burst, flare, flare-up, flash, flurry, flutter, outburst, spurt

flightiness **1** *Syn* FRIVOLITY, facetiousness, flippancy, frivolousness, levity, light-headedness, lightness **2** *Syn* LIGHTNESS, flippancy, frivolity, levity, light-mindedness, volatility *Ant* seriousness

flighty *Syn* EXCITABLE, fluttery, high-strung, jittery, jumpy, nervous, skittish, spooky *Ant* unflappable

flimsy **1** *Syn* IMPROBABLE, doubtful, dubious, far-fetched, questionable, unapt, unlikely *Ant* likely, probable **2** *Syn* LIMP, flabby, flaccid, floppy, sleazy

flinch *Syn* RECOIL, blench, quail, shrink, wince *Ant* confront, defy

fling *n Syn* ATTEMPT, crack, endeavor, essay, go, pass, shot, stab, trial, try, whack

fling *vb Syn* THROW, cast, hurl, pitch, sling, toss

flip *Syn* FLIPPANT, facetious, pert, smart, smart-alecky (*or* smart-aleck) *Ant* earnest, sincere

flippancy **1** *Syn* FRIVOLITY, facetiousness, flightiness, frivolousness, levity, light-headedness, lightness **2** *Syn* LIGHTNESS, flightiness, frivolity, levity, light-mindedness, volatility *Ant* seriousness

flippant · making light of something usually regarded as serious or sacred *Syn* facetious, flip, pert, smart, smart-alecky (*or* smart-aleck) *Rel* flighty, frivolous *Ant* earnest, sincere

flirt · to show a liking for someone just for fun *Syn* dally, frivol, trifle *Rel* josh, kid, put on, razz, rib, tease

flit · to move or fly briskly, irregularly, and usually intermittently *Syn* flicker, flitter, flutter, hover *Rel* dart, float, fly, scud, skim

flitter *Syn* FLIT, flicker, flutter, hover

float *Syn* FLY, dart, sail, scud, shoot, skim

flood *n* **1** · a great or overwhelming flow of or as if of water *Syn* cataract, deluge, inundation, spate, torrent *Rel* current, flow, stream, tide **2** *Syn* FLOW, current, flux, stream, tide

flood *vb* • to cover or become filled with a flood *Syn* deluge, drown, engulf, inundate, overflow, overwhelm, submerge, submerse, swamp *Rel* overcome, overrun *Ant* drain

floppy *Syn* LIMP, flabby, flaccid, flimsy, sleazy

florid *Syn* ORNATE, baroque, flamboyant, rococo *Ant* austere, chaste

flounder *Syn* STUMBLE, blunder, bumble, galumph, lollop, lumber, lurch, trip

flourish **1** *Syn* SUCCEED, prosper, thrive *Ant* attempt, fail **2** *Syn* SWING (sense 1), brandish, shake, thrash, wave

flout **1** *Syn* SCOFF, fleer, gibe, gird, jeer, sneer **2** *Syn* SCORN (sense 1), despise, disregard *Ant* honor, respect

flow *n* • something suggestive of running water *Syn* current, flood, flux, stream, tide *Rel* progression, sequence, series, succession

flow *vb* *Syn* SPRING, arise, derive, emanate, issue, originate, proceed, rise, stem

flower *n* **1** *Syn* BLOSSOM, bloom, blow **2** *Syn* ELITE, best, choice, cream, elect, fat, pick, prime, upper crust

flower *vb* *Syn* BLOSSOM, bloom, blow

flowery *Syn* RHETORICAL, aureate, bombastic, euphuistic, grandiloquent, magniloquent

flub *Syn* BOTCH, bobble, bungle, butcher, foozle, foul up, fumble, louse up, mangle, mess (up), muff, murder

fluctuate **1** *Syn* CHANGE (sense 2), mutate, shift, vary *Ant* stabilize **2** *Syn* SWING (sense 2), oscillate, pendulate, sway, undulate, vibrate, waver

fluent *Syn* ARTICULATE, eloquent, well-spoken *Ant* inarticulate

fluently *Syn* EASILY, effortlessly, facilely, freely, handily, lightly, painlessly, readily, smoothly *Ant* arduously, laboriously

fluky *Syn* ACCIDENTAL, casual, chance, fortuitous, inadvertent, incidental, unintended, unintentional, unplanned, unpremeditated, unwitting *Ant* deliberate, intended, intentional, planned, premeditated

flume *Syn* CANYON, defile, gap, gorge, gulch, gulf, notch, pass, ravine

flunky **1** *Syn* SERVANT, domestic, lackey, menial, retainer, steward *Ant* master **2** *Syn* SYCOPHANT, fawner, toady

flurry *vb* *Syn* DISCOMPOSE, agitate, disquiet, disturb, fluster, perturb, upset

flurry *n* **1** *Syn* OUTBREAK, burst, flare, flare-up, flash, flicker, flutter, outburst, spurt **2** *Syn* STIR, ado, bustle, fuss, pother *Ant* tranquillity

flush *vb* *Syn* BLUSH, bloom, color, crimson, glow, redden

flush *adj* **1** *Syn* LEVEL, even, flat, plain, plane, smooth **2** *Syn* RIFE, abounding,

fraught, replete, swarming, teeming, thick, thronging

fluster *Syn* DISCOMPOSE, agitate, disquiet, disturb, flurry, perturb, upset

flutter *vb* *Syn* FLIT, flicker, flitter, hover

flutter *n* *Syn* OUTBREAK, burst, flare, flare-up, flash, flicker, flurry, outburst, spurt

fluttery *Syn* EXCITABLE, flighty, high-strung, jittery, jumpy, nervous, skittish, spooky *Ant* unflappable

flux *Syn* FLOW, current, flood, stream, tide

fly **1** • to pass lightly or quickly over or above a surface *Syn* dart, float, sail, scud, shoot, skim *Rel* flicker, flit, flitter, flutter, hover **2** *Syn* ESCAPE (sense 1), abscond, decamp, flee **3** *Syn* HURRY (sense 2), barrel, bolt, bowl, breeze, career, course, dash, hasten, hotfoot (it), hump, hurtle, hustle, pelt, race, rip, rocket, run, rush, rustle, scoot, scurry, scuttle, shoot, speed, step (along), tear, trot, whirl, whisk, zip, zoom *Ant* crawl, creep, poke

flying field *Syn* AIRPORT, airdrome, airfield, airstrip, landing field, landing strip

foam • a mass of bubbles gathering in or on the surface of a liquid or something as insubstantial as such a mass *Syn* froth, lather, scum, spume, suds, yeast

foaming *Syn* ANGRY, angered, apoplectic, enraged, fuming, furious, incensed, indignant, inflamed, infuriated, irate, ireful, mad, outraged, rabid, riled, roiled, sore, steaming, wrathful, wroth *Ant* delighted, pleased

focal *Syn* CENTRAL, pivotal

focus *vb* *Syn* CENTER, centralize, concentrate

focus *n* *Syn* CENTER (sense 2), base, capital, core, cynosure, eye, heart, hub, mecca, nucleus, seat

fodder *Syn* FOOD (sense 1), comestibles, feed, forage, provender, provisions, viands, victuals

foe *Syn* ENEMY, adversary, antagonist, opponent *Ant* friend

fog *n* **1** *Syn* HAZE (sense 1), mist, murk, reek, smog, soup **2** *Syn* HAZE (sense 2), daze, muddle, spin

fog *vb* *Syn* OBSCURE, becloud, bedim, befog, cloud, darken, dim, eclipse, obfuscate *Ant* illuminate, illumine

foible *Syn* FAULT, failing, frailty, vice *Ant* merit

foil *Syn* FRUSTRATE, baffle, balk, circumvent, outwit, thwart *Ant* fulfill

folklore • the body of customs, beliefs, stories, and sayings associated with a people, thing, or place *Syn* legend, lore, myth, mythology, tradition *Rel* information, knowledge, wisdom

follow **1** • to come after in time *Syn* ensue, succeed, supervene **2** • to go after or on the trail of *Syn* chase, pursue, tag, tail, trail *Rel* accompany, attend, convoy *Ant* forsake (*a teacher or* *teachings*), precede **3** *Syn* TRAVERSE, cover, crisscross, cross, cut (across), go, pass (over), proceed (along), travel

follower · one who follows the teachings of another *Syn* adherent, convert, disciple, partisan, pupil, votary *Rel* devotee, flunky, hanger-on, henchman, lackey, satellite, stooge, sycophant, toady, yes-man *Ant* leader

following *prep Syn* AFTER, behind *Ant* ahead of, before, ere, previous to, prior to

following *n Syn* PURSUIT, chase, chasing, dogging, hounding, pursuing, shadowing, tagging, tailing, tracing, tracking, trailing

foment *Syn* INCITE, abet, instigate *Ant* restrain

fomenter *Syn* AGITATOR, demagogue, exciter, firebrand, incendiary, inciter, instigator, rabble-rouser

fond 1 · made blindly or stupidly foolish *Syn* besotted, infatuated, insensate *Rel* asinine, fatuous, foolish, silly, simple **2** *Syn* LOVING, affectionate, devoted, doting *Ant* unloving

fondle *Syn* CARESS, cosset, cuddle, dandle, pet

fondness *Syn* LIKING, appetite, fancy, favor, like, love, partiality, preference, relish, shine, taste, use *Ant* aversion, disfavor, dislike, distaste, hatred, loathing

food 1 · things that are edible for human beings or animals *Syn* comestibles, feed, fodder, forage, provender, provisions, viands, victuals **2** · material which feeds and supports the mind or the spirit *Syn* aliment, nourishment, nutriment, pabulum, pap, sustenance

fool *n* **1** · a person formerly kept in a royal or noble household to amuse with jests and pranks *Syn* jester, motley *Rel* buffoon, clown, comedian, comedienne, comic, cutup, harlequin, zany **2** · a person who lacks good sense or judgment *Syn* booby, goose, half-wit, jackass, lunatic, nincompoop, ninny, nitwit, nut, simpleton, turkey, yo-yo *Rel* daredevil

fool *vb Syn* JOKE, banter, fun, jest, jive, josh, kid, quip, wisecrack

fool (around) *Syn* CUT UP, act up, clown (around), horse (around), monkey (around), show off, skylark

foolery *Syn* HORSEPLAY, clowning, high jinks, horsing (around), monkeying, monkeyshines, roughhouse, roughhousing, shenanigans, skylarking, tomfoolery

foolhardy *Syn* ADVENTUROUS, daredevil, daring, rash, reckless, venturesome *Ant* cautious, unadventurous

foolish 1 · felt to be ridiculous because not exhibiting good sense *Syn* absurd, preposterous, silly *Rel* laughable, ludicrous, ridiculous *Ant* sensible **2** *Syn* SIMPLE, asinine, fatuous, silly *Ant* wise

foot (it) *Syn* WALK, hoof (it), leg (it), pad, step, traipse, tread

foot (up) *Syn* ADD (sense 1), sum, total *Ant* deduct, remove, subtract, take

foozle *Syn* BOTCH, bobble, bungle, butcher, flub, foul up, fumble, louse up, mangle, mess (up), muff, murder

fop · a man who is conspicuously fashionable or elegant in dress or manners *Syn* beau, buck, coxcomb, dandy, dude, exquisite

for *Syn* BECAUSE, as, inasmuch as, since

forage *Syn* FOOD (sense 1), comestibles, feed, fodder, provender, provisions, viands, victuals

forbear 1 *Syn* FORGO, abnegate, eschew, sacrifice **2** *Syn* REFRAIN, abstain

forbearance 1 · a disinclination to be severe or rigorous *Syn* clemency, indulgence, leniency, mercifulness, tolerance *Rel* longanimity, long-suffering, patience *Ant* anger, vindictiveness **2** *Syn* PATIENCE, longanimity, long-suffering, resignation *Ant* impatience

forbearing · disinclined by nature, disposition, or circumstances to be severe or rigorous *Syn* clement, indulgent, lenient, merciful, tolerant *Rel* gentle, mild, soft *Ant* unrelenting

forbearingly · in a forbearing manner *Syn* clemently, indulgently, leniently, mercifully, tolerantly

forbid · to order not to do or use or to be done or used *Syn* ban, bar, enjoin, interdict, outlaw, prohibit, proscribe *Rel* deter, discourage, dissuade *Ant* allow, let, permit, suffer

forbidding *Syn* PROHIBITION (sense 1), banning, barring, enjoining, interdicting, interdiction, outlawing, prohibiting, proscribing, proscription *Ant* prescription

force *n* **1** · the exercise of power in order to impose one's will on a person or to have one's will with a thing *Syn* coercion, compulsion, constraint, duress, restraint, violence *Rel* fierceness, intensity, vehemence **2** *Syn* POWER (sense 1), energy, might, puissance, strength *Ant* impotence

force *vb* · to cause a person or thing to yield to pressure *Syn* coerce, compel, constrain, oblige *Rel* drive, impel, move

forced 1 · produced or kept up through effort *Syn* labored, strained *Rel* coerced, compelled, constrained **2** *Syn* MANDATORY, compulsory, imperative, incumbent, involuntary, necessary, nonelective, obligatory, peremptory, required *Ant* elective, optional, voluntary

forceful 1 *Syn* COGENT, compelling, conclusive, convincing, decisive, effective, persuasive, satisfying, strong, telling *Ant* inconclusive, indecisive, ineffective, unconvincing **2** *Syn* POWERFUL, forcible, potent, puissant *Ant* inefficacious, powerless

forcible *Syn* POWERFUL, forceful, potent, puissant *Ant* inefficacious, powerless

forebear *Syn* ANCESTOR (sense 1), forefather, progenitor *Ant* descendant (*or* descendent)

forebode *Syn* FORETELL, augur, forecast, portend, predict, presage, prognosticate, prophesy

foreboding *n* **1** *Syn* OMEN, augury, auspice, boding, foreshadowing, portent, prefiguring, presage **2** *Syn* PREMONITION, presage, presentiment

foreboding *adj* *Syn* OMINOUS, baleful, dire, inauspicious, menacing, portentous, sinister, threatening

forecast *vb* *Syn* FORETELL, augur, forebode, portend, predict, presage, prognosticate, prophesy

forecast *n* *Syn* PREDICTION, auguring, cast, forecasting, foretelling, predicting, presaging, prognosis, prognosticating, prognostication, prophecy, soothsaying

forecaster *Syn* PROPHET, augur, diviner, foreseer, foreteller, fortune-teller, futurist, prognosticator, prophesier, seer, soothsayer

forecasting *Syn* PREDICTION, auguring, cast, forecast, foretelling, predicting, presaging, prognosis, prognosticating, prognostication, prophecy, soothsaying

forefather *Syn* ANCESTOR (sense 1), forebear, progenitor *Ant* descendant (*or* descendent)

foregoer *Syn* ANCESTOR (sense 2), antecedent, forerunner, precursor, predecessor *Ant* descendant (*or* descendent)

foregoing *Syn* PREVIOUS, antecedent, anterior, precedent, preceding, prior *Ant* after, ensuing, following, subsequent, succeeding

foreign *Syn* EXTRINSIC, alien, extraneous *Ant* intrinsic

foreigner *Syn* STRANGER, alien, émigré, immigrant, outlander, outsider

foreknow *Syn* FORESEE, anticipate, apprehend, divine

foreknowledge *Syn* FORESIGHT (sense 1), prescience *Ant* improvidence, shortsightedness

foreman *Syn* BOSS, captain, chief, head, headman, helmsman, kingpin, leader, master, taskmaster

foremost **1** *Syn* CHIEF, capital, leading, main, principal *Ant* subordinate **2** *Syn* HEAD, chief, commanding, first, high, lead, leading, managing, preeminent, premier, presiding, primary, prime, principal, supreme

forensic *Syn* ARGUMENTATION, debate, dialectic, disputation

forerunner **1** · one that goes before or in some way announces the coming of another *Syn* harbinger, herald, precursor *Rel* anticipator **2** *Syn* ANCESTOR (sense 2), antecedent, foregoer, precursor, predecessor *Ant* descendant (*or* descendent)

foresee · to know or expect in advance that something will happen or come into existence or be made manifest *Syn* anticipate,

apprehend, divine, foreknow *Rel* forecast, foretell, predict, prognosticate, prophesy

foreseer *Syn* PROPHET, augur, diviner, forecaster, foreteller, fortune-teller, futurist, prognosticator, prophesier, seer, soothsayer

foreshadowing *Syn* OMEN, augury, auspice, boding, foreboding, portent, prefiguring, presage

foreshore *Syn* SHORE, bank, beach, coast, littoral, strand

foresight **1** · the special ability to see or know about events before they actually occur *Syn* foreknowledge, prescience *Rel* premonition, presentiment **2** · concern or preparation for the future *Syn* farsightedness, foresightedness, forethought, prescience, providence *Rel* precaution, premeditation *Ant* improvidence, shortsightedness **3** *Syn* PRUDENCE, discretion, forethought, providence

foresighted *Syn* PRUDENT, discreet, forethoughtful, provident

forestall **1** *Syn* PREVENT (sense 1), anticipate **2** *Syn* PREVENT (sense 2), avert, help, obviate, preclude

foretaste *Syn* PROSPECT, anticipation, outlook

foretell · to tell something before it happens through special knowledge or occult power *Syn* augur, forebode, forecast, portend, predict, presage, prognosticate, prophesy *Rel* anticipate, apprehend, divine, foreknow, foresee

foreteller *Syn* PROPHET, augur, diviner, forecaster, foreseer, fortune-teller, futurist, prognosticator, prophesier, seer, soothsayer

foretelling *Syn* PREDICTION, auguring, cast, forecast, forecasting, predicting, presaging, prognosis, prognosticating, prognostication, prophecy, soothsaying

forethought *Syn* PRUDENCE, discretion, foresight, providence

forethoughtful *Syn* PRUDENT, discreet, foresighted, provident

forewarn *Syn* WARN, alert, caution

forewarning *Syn* WARNING, admonition, alarm, alert, caution, notice

foreword *Syn* INTRODUCTION, exordium, preamble, preface, prelude, prologue

forfeit *Syn* FINE, damages, forfeiture, mulct, penalty

forfeiture *Syn* FINE, damages, forfeit, mulct, penalty

forge *Syn* MAKE, fabricate, fashion, form, manufacture, shape

forget *Syn* NEGLECT, disregard, ignore, omit, overlook, slight *Ant* cherish

forgetful · losing or letting go from one's mind something once known or learned *Syn* oblivious, unmindful *Rel* lax, neglectful, negligent, remiss, slack

forgivable *Syn* VENIAL, excusable, pardonable,

remittable Ant inexcusable, mortal, unforgivable, unpardonable

forgive Syn EXCUSE, condone, pardon, remit Ant punish

forgiveness Syn PARDON, absolution, amnesty, remission, remittal Ant penalty, punishment, retribution

forgo · to deny oneself something for the sake of an end Syn abnegate, eschew, forbear, sacrifice Rel abandon, relinquish, surrender, waive

forgotten Syn ABANDONED (sense 2), derelict, deserted, disused, forsaken, rejected, vacated

forlorn 1 Syn ALONE, desolate, lone, lonely, lonesome, lorn, solitary Ant accompanied 2 Syn DESPONDENT, despairing, desperate, hopeless Ant lighthearted 3 Syn SAD (sense 1), bad, blue, brokenhearted, crestfallen, dejected, depressed, despondent, disconsolate, doleful, down, downcast, downhearted, droopy, gloomy, glum, heartbroken, heartsick, heartsore, inconsolable, joyless, low, lowspirited, melancholy, miserable, mournful, saddened, sorrowful, sorry, unhappy, woebegone, woeful, wretched Ant blissful, buoyant, buoyed, cheerful, cheery, chipper, delighted, glad, gladdened, gladsome, gleeful, happy, joyful, joyous, jubilant, sunny, upbeat

forlornness 1 Syn DESPONDENCY, despair, desperation, hopelessness Ant lightheartedness 2 Syn SADNESS, blues, dejection, depression, desolation, despondency, disconsolateness, dispiritedness, doldrums, downheartedness, dreariness, dumps, gloom, gloominess, heartsickness, joylessness, melancholy, mopes, oppression, unhappiness Ant bliss, blissfulness, ecstasy, elatedness, elation, euphoria, exhilaration, exuberance, exultation, felicity, gladness, gladsomeness, happiness, heaven, intoxication, joy, joyfulness, joyousness, jubilation, rapture, rapturousness

form n 1 · outward appearance of something as distinguished from the substance of which it is made Syn configuration, conformation, figure, shape Rel contour, outline, profile, silhouette 2 · conduct regulated by an external control (as custom or a formal protocol of procedure) Syn ceremonial, ceremony, formality, liturgy, rite, ritual Rel procedure, proceeding, process 3 · a fixed or accepted way of doing or sometimes of expressing something Syn convenance, convention, usage

form vb 1 Syn BEGIN (sense 1), arise, commence, dawn, materialize, originate, set in, spring, start Ant cease, end, stop 2 Syn MAKE, fabricate, fashion, forge, manufacture, shape

formal adj 1 Syn CEREMONIAL, ceremonious, conventional, solemn 2 Syn DRESS, dressy Ant casual, informal, sporty

formal n Syn DANCE, ball, cotillion, hop, prom

formality Syn FORM (sense 2), ceremonial, ceremony, liturgy, rite, ritual

formalize Syn STANDARDIZE, homogenize, normalize, regularize

former · having been such at some previous time Syn erstwhile, late, old, onetime, past, sometime, whilom Rel bygone, dead, extinct

formless · having no definite or recognizable form Syn amorphous, shapeless, unformed, unshaped, unstructured Rel characterless, featureless, nondescript Ant formed, shaped, structured

formulate Syn PHRASE, articulate, clothe, couch, express, put, say, state, word

forsake Syn ABANDON, desert Ant reclaim

forsaken Syn ABANDONED (sense 2), derelict, deserted, disused, forgotten, rejected, vacated

forswear Syn ABJURE, recant, renounce, retract Ant pledge (allegiance, a vow), elect (a way of life, a means to an end)

fort · a structure or place offering resistance to a hostile force Syn citadel, fastness, fortress, stronghold

forth 1 Syn ALONG, ahead, forward, on, onward 2 Syn ONWARD, forward

forthcoming · being soon to appear or take place Syn approaching, coming, imminent, impending, nearing, oncoming, pending, upcoming Rel future Ant late, recent

forthright Syn STRAIGHTFORWARD, aboveboard Ant devious, indirect

forthrightness Syn CANDOR, directness, frankness, openheartedness, openness, plainness, straightforwardness Ant dissembling, pretense (or pretence)

fortify Syn STRENGTHEN, energize, invigorate, reinforce Ant weaken

fortitude · a quality of character combining courage and staying power Syn backbone, grit, guts, pluck, sand Rel courage, mettle, resolution, spirit, tenacity Ant pusillanimity

fortress Syn FORT, citadel, fastness, stronghold

fortuitous Syn ACCIDENTAL, casual, chance, fluky, inadvertent, incidental, unintended, unintentional, unplanned, unpremeditated, unwitting Ant deliberate, intended, intentional, planned, premeditated

fortunate Syn LUCKY, happy, providential Ant unlucky

fortune Syn CHANCE, accident, hap, hazard, luck Ant law, principle

fortune-teller Syn PROPHET, augur, diviner, forecaster, foreseer, foreteller, futurist, prognosticator, prophesier, seer, soothsayer

forward vb 1 Syn ADVANCE (sense 1), further, promote Ant check, retard 2 Syn SEND, dispatch, remit, route, ship, transmit Ant accept, receive

forward *adv* **1** *Syn* ALONG, ahead, forth, on, onward (*or* onwards) **2** *Syn* ONWARD, forth

forward *adj* *Syn* PREMATURE, advanced, precocious, untimely *Ant* matured

foster *Syn* NURSE, cherish, cultivate, nurture

foul *vb* **1** *Syn* CONTAMINATE, befoul, defile, poison, pollute, taint *Ant* decontaminate, purify **2** *Syn* DIRTY, befoul, begrime, besmirch, blacken, grime, mire, muddy, smirch, smudge, soil, stain, sully *Ant* clean, cleanse

foul *adj* *Syn* DIRTY, filthy, nasty, squalid *Ant* clean

foul up *Syn* BOTCH, bobble, bungle, butcher, flub, foozle, fumble, louse up, mangle, mess (up), muff, murder

found **1** · to set going or to bring into existence *Syn* create, establish, institute, organize *Rel* begin, commence, inaugurate, initiate, start **2** *Syn* BASE, ground, rest, stay

foundation *Syn* BASE, basis, ground, groundwork *Ant* top

foxy *Syn* SLY, artful, crafty, cunning, guileful, insidious, tricky, wily

fracas *Syn* BRAWL, broil, melee, row, rumpus, scrap

fraction *Syn* PART, detail, division, fragment, member, parcel, piece, portion, section, sector, segment *Ant* whole

fractious *Syn* IRRITABLE, fretful, huffy, peevish, pettish, petulant, querulous, snappish, waspish *Ant* easygoing

fragile **1** · easily broken *Syn* brittle, crisp, frangible, friable, short *Ant* tough **2** *Syn* WEAK, decrepit, feeble, frail, infirm *Ant* strong

fragment *Syn* PART, detail, division, fraction, member, parcel, piece, portion, section, sector, segment *Ant* whole

fragrance · a sweet or pleasant odor *Syn* bouquet, incense, perfume, redolence *Rel* aroma, odor, scent, smell *Ant* stench, stink

fragrant **1** · having a pleasant smell *Syn* ambrosial, aromatic, perfumed, redolent, savory, scented, sweet *Rel* flowery, fruity, pungent, spicy *Ant* fetid, foul, malodorous, noisome, putrid, rancid, rank, reeking, reeky, smelly, stinking, stinky, strong **2** *Syn* ODOROUS, aromatic, balmy, redolent *Ant* malodorous, odorless

frail *Syn* WEAK, decrepit, feeble, fragile, infirm *Ant* strong

frailty *Syn* FAULT, failing, foible, vice *Ant* merit

frame *Syn* ENGINEER, contrive, finagle, finesse, machinate, maneuver, manipulate, mastermind, negotiate, wangle

framework *Syn* STRUCTURE, anatomy, skeleton

franchise *Syn* SUFFRAGE, ballot, vote

frangible *Syn* FRAGILE, brittle, crisp, friable, short *Ant* tough

frank · marked by free, forthright, and sincere expression *Syn* candid, open, plain *Rel*

ingenuous, naive, natural, simple, unsophisticated *Ant* reticent

frankness *Syn* CANDOR, directness, forthrightness, openheartedness, openness, plainness, straightforwardness *Ant* dissembling, pretense (*or* pretence)

frantic *Syn* FURIOUS, delirious, frenetic, frenzied, rabid, wild

fraternize *Syn* SOCIALIZE, associate, hobnob, mingle, mix

fraud *Syn* DECEPTION, chicane, chicanery, double-dealing, trickery

fraught *Syn* RIFE, abounding, flush, replete, swarming, teeming, thick, thronging

fray *Syn* CONTEST, affray, combat, conflict, fight

freak **1** *Syn* FAN, addict, aficionado, buff, bug, devotee, enthusiast, fanatic, fancier, fiend, lover, maniac, nut **2** *Syn* WHIM, caprice, fancy, notion, vagary, whimsy

freakish *Syn* WHIMSICAL, capricious, impulsive

freckle *Syn* SPOT, blotch, dapple, dot, fleck, marble, mottle, pepper, speck, speckle, splotch, sprinkle, stipple

free *adj* · not subject to the rule or control of another *Syn* autarchic, autarkic, autonomous, independent, sovereign *Rel* delivered, emancipated, enfranchised, freed, liberated, released *Ant* bond

free *vb* · to relieve from constraint or restraint *Syn* discharge, emancipate, liberate, manumit, release *Rel* deliver, enfranchise

freebooter *Syn* PIRATE, buccaneer, corsair, privateer

freedom **1** · the state or condition of not being subject to external rule or control *Syn* autarchy, autarky, autonomy, independence, sovereignty *Rel* delivery, emancipation, enfranchisement, liberation, manumission, release *Ant* bondage **2** · the power or condition of acting without compulsion *Syn* liberty, license *Rel* exemption, immunity *Ant* necessity

freely *Syn* EASILY, effortlessly, facilely, fluently, handily, lightly, painlessly, readily, smoothly *Ant* arduously, laboriously

freezing *Syn* COLD, arctic, chilly, cool, frigid, frosty, gelid, glacial, icy *Ant* hot

freight *Syn* LOAD, burden, cargo, lading

frenetic *Syn* FURIOUS, delirious, frantic, frenzied, rabid, wild

frenzied *Syn* FURIOUS, delirious, frantic, frenetic, rabid, wild

frenzy **1** · a state of wildly excited activity or emotion *Syn* agitation, delirium, distraction, furor, furore, fury, hysteria, rage, rampage, uproar *Rel* chaos, confusion, disorder, turmoil **2** *Syn* INSPIRATION, afflatus, fury **3** *Syn* MANIA, delirium, hysteria

frequently *Syn* OFTEN, oft, oftentimes

fresh *Syn* NEW, modern, modernistic, newfangled, new-fashioned, novel, original *Ant* old

freshman *Syn* BEGINNER, colt, fledgling, greenhorn, neophyte, newbie, newcomer, novice, recruit, rookie, tenderfoot, tyro *Ant* old hand, old-timer, vet, veteran

fret *Syn* ABRADE, chafe, excoriate, gall

fretful *Syn* IRRITABLE, fractious, huffy, peevish, pettish, petulant, querulous, snappish, waspish *Ant* easygoing

friable *Syn* FRAGILE, brittle, crisp, frangible, short *Ant* tough

friar *Syn* RELIGIOUS, monk, nun

friend 1 · a person, and especially one not related by blood, with whom one is on good and usually familiar terms *Syn* acquaintance, confidant, intimate *Rel* associate, companion, comrade, crony *Ant* foe **2** *Syn* EXPONENT, advocate, apostle, backer, booster, champion, promoter, proponent, supporter *Ant* adversary, antagonist, opponent

friendly *Syn* AMICABLE, neighborly *Ant* antagonistic

friendship · the relation existing between persons, communities, states, or peoples that are in accord and in sympathy with each other *Syn* amity, comity, goodwill *Rel* affinity, attraction, sympathy *Ant* animosity

fright *n Syn* FEAR, alarm, consternation, dismay, dread, horror, panic, terror, trepidation *Ant* fearlessness

fright *vb Syn* FRIGHTEN, affray, affright, alarm, scare, startle, terrify, terrorize *Ant* reassure

frighten · to strike or to fill with fear or dread *Syn* affray, affright, alarm, fright, scare, startle, terrify, terrorize *Rel* appall, daunt, dismay, horrify *Ant* reassure

frightful *Syn* FEARFUL (sense 2), appalling, awful, dreadful, horrible, horrific, shocking, terrible, terrific

frightfully *Syn* VERY, awful, awfully, beastly, deadly, especially, exceedingly, extra, extremely, far, full, greatly, heavily, highly, hugely, jolly, mightily, mighty, mortally, most, much, particularly, rattling, real, right, so, something, super, terribly, too, whacking *Ant* little, negligibly, nominally, slightly

frigid *Syn* COLD, arctic, chilly, cool, freezing, frosty, gelid, glacial, icy *Ant* hot

fringe *Syn* BORDER, bound, margin, rim, skirt

fringing *Syn* ADJACENT, abutting, adjoining, bordering, contiguous, flanking, joining, juxtaposed, skirting, touching, verging *Ant* nonadjacent

frippery 1 *Syn* FINERY, array, best, bravery, caparison, feather, full dress, gaiety, regalia **2** *Syn* TRIFLE, child's play, nothing, triviality

fritter *Syn* WASTE, consume, dissipate, squander *Ant* conserve, save

frivol *Syn* FLIRT, dally, trifle

frivolity 1 · a lack of seriousness often at an improper time *Syn* facetiousness, flightiness, flippancy, frivolousness, levity, light-headedness, lightness *Rel* cheerfulness, gaiety, glee, high-spiritedness, lightheartedness, merriment, mirth **2** *Syn* LIGHTNESS, flightiness, flippancy, levity, light-mindedness, volatility *Ant* seriousness

frivolous *Syn* UNIMPORTANT, inconsequential, inconsiderable, insignificant, little, minor, minute, negligible, slight, small, small-fry, trifling, trivial *Ant* big, consequential, eventful, important, major, material, meaningful, momentous, significant, substantial, weighty

frivolousness *Syn* FRIVOLITY, facetiousness, flightiness, flippancy, levity, light-headedness, lightness

frolic *n Syn* PLAY, disport, gambol, rollick, romp, sport *Ant* work

frolic *vb Syn* PLAY, disport, gambol, rollick, romp, sport

frolicsome *Syn* PLAYFUL, impish, mischievous, roguish, sportive, waggish

frontier · a rural region that forms the edge of the settled or developed part of a country *Syn* backwater, backwoods, bush, hinterland, upcountry *Rel* country, countryside, sticks

frosty *Syn* COLD, arctic, chilly, cool, freezing, frigid, gelid, glacial, icy *Ant* hot

froth *Syn* FOAM, lather, scum, spume, suds, yeast

froward 1 *Syn* CONTRARY, balky, perverse, restive, wayward *Ant* complaisant, good-natured **2** *Syn* DISOBEDIENT, balky, contrary, defiant, insubordinate, intractable, rebellious, recalcitrant, refractory, restive, ungovernable, unruly, untoward, wayward, willful (*or* wilful) *Ant* amenable, compliant, docile, obedient, tractable **3** *Syn* UNCONTROLLABLE, headstrong, intractable, recalcitrant, refractory, ungovernable, unmanageable, unruly, untoward, wayward, willful (*or* wilful) *Ant* controllable, governable, tractable

frowardness *Syn* DISOBEDIENCE, contrariness, defiance, insubordination, intractability, rebelliousness, recalcitrance, refractoriness, unruliness, willfulness *Ant* amenability, compliance, docility, obedience

frown *vb* · to look with anger or disapproval *Syn* glare, gloom, glower, lower, scowl *Rel* gape, gaze, ogle, stare *Ant* beam, smile

frown *n Syn* GRIMACE, face, lower, mouth, pout, scowl

frown (on) *Syn* DISAPPROVE (OF), deprecate, discountenance, disfavor, dislike, reprove *Ant* approve, favor, like

frowzy *Syn* SLATTERNLY, blowsy, dowdy

frugal · careful in the management of money or resources *Syn* economical, economizing, provident, scrimping, sparing, thrifty *Rel* conserving, preserving, saving *Ant* prodigal, wasteful

frugality *Syn* ECONOMY, husbandry, providence, scrimping, skimping, thrift *Ant* wastefulness

fruitful *Syn* FERTILE, fat, fecund, luxuriant, productive, prolific, rich *Ant* barren, infertile, sterile, unfruitful, unproductive

fruitfulness *Syn* FERTILITY, fecundity, prolificacy *Ant* infertility, sterility

fruition 1 · the state of being actual or complete *Syn* accomplishment, achievement, actuality, attainment, consummation, fulfillment, realization *Ant* naught, nonfulfillment 2 *Syn* PLEASURE, delectation, delight, enjoyment, joy *Ant* anger, displeasure, vexation

fruitless *Syn* FUTILE, abortive, bootless, vain *Ant* effective, effectual, efficacious, efficient, fruitful, productive, profitable, successful

frustrate · to come between a person and his or her aim or desire or to defeat another's plan *Syn* baffle, balk, circumvent, foil, outwit, thwart *Rel* counteract, negative, neutralize *Ant* fulfill

frustrating *Syn* ANNOYING, aggravating, bothersome, disturbing, exasperating, galling, irksome, irritating, maddening, nettling, peeving, pesty, rankling, riling, vexatious, vexing

frustration *Syn* DISAPPOINTMENT (sense 1), dismay, dissatisfaction, letdown *Ant* contentment, gratification, satisfaction

fuddle *Syn* CONFUSE, addle, befuddle, muddle *Ant* enlighten

fugitive *Syn* MOMENTARY, ephemeral, evanescent, flash, fleeting, impermanent, passing, short-lived, temporary, transient, transitory *Ant* enduring, eternal, everlasting, lasting, long-lived, permanent, perpetual

fulfill 1 *Syn* PERFORM, accomplish, achieve, discharge, effect, execute 2 *Syn* SATISFY (sense 2), answer, meet

fulfilling *Syn* HEARTWARMING, cheering, comforting, encouraging, gladdening, gratifying, heartening, rewarding, satisfying *Ant* depressing, discouraging, disheartening, dispiriting

fulfillment *Syn* FRUITION, accomplishment, achievement, actuality, attainment, consummation, realization *Ant* naught, nonfulfillment

full *adj* 1 · containing all that is wanted or needed or possible *Syn* complete, plenary, replete *Rel* comprehending, comprehensive, including, inclusive *Ant* empty 2 *Syn* ENCYCLOPEDIC, compendious, complete, comprehensive, global, inclusive, in-depth, omnibus, panoramic, universal

full *adv* *Syn* VERY, awful, awfully, beastly, deadly, especially, exceedingly, extra, extremely, far, frightfully, greatly, heavily, highly, hugely, jolly, mightily, mighty, mortally, most, much, particularly, rattling, real, right, so, something, super, terribly, too,

whacking *Ant* little, negligibly, nominally, slightly

full dress *Syn* FINERY, array, best, bravery, caparison, feather, frippery, gaiety, regalia

full-scale *Syn* EXHAUSTIVE, all-out, clean, complete, comprehensive, out-and-out, thorough, thoroughgoing, total

fulminate *Syn* RANT, bluster, rave, spout

fumble *Syn* BOTCH, bobble, bungle, butcher, flub, foozle, foul up, louse up, mangle, mess (up), muff, murder

fumigate *Syn* STERILIZE (sense 2), disinfect, sanitize

fuming *Syn* ANGRY, angered, apoplectic, enraged, foaming, furious, incensed, indignant, inflamed, infuriated, irate, ireful, mad, outraged, rabid, riled, roiled, sore, steaming, wrathful, wroth *Ant* delighted, pleased

fun *adj* · providing amusement or enjoyment *Syn* amusing, delightful, diverting, enjoyable, entertaining, pleasurable *Rel* agreeable, beguiling, pleasant *Ant* boring, dull

fun *n* · action or speech that is intended to amuse or arouse laughter *Syn* game, jest, play, sport *Rel* amusement, diversion, entertainment, recreation

fun *vb* *Syn* JOKE, banter, fool, jest, jive, josh, kid, quip, wisecrack

function *n* 1 · acts or operations expected of a person or thing *Syn* duty, office, province *Rel* end, goal, intention, object, objective, purpose 2 *Syn* POWER (sense 2), faculty 3 *Syn* ROLE, capacity, job, part, place, position, purpose, task, work

function *vb* 1 · to have a certain purpose *Syn* act, perform, serve, work *Rel* operate, run 2 *Syn* ACT (sense 1), behave, operate, react, work

functionary *Syn* BUREAUCRAT, public servant

fundamental *adj* 1 · forming or affecting the groundwork, roots, or lowest part of something *Syn* basal, basic, radical, underlying *Rel* primal, primary, prime, primordial 2 *Syn* ELEMENTARY, basic, elemental, essential, rudimentary, underlying *Ant* advanced 3 *Syn* ESSENTIAL, cardinal, vital

fundamental *n* *Syn* PRINCIPLE, axiom, law, theorem

funnel *Syn* CHANNEL, channelize, conduct, direct, pipe, siphon

funny *Syn* LAUGHABLE, comic, comical, droll, farcical, ludicrous, ridiculous, risible

furious 1 · marked by uncontrollable excitement especially under the stress of a powerful emotion *Syn* delirious, frantic, frenetic, frenzied, rabid, wild *Rel* excited, provoked, stimulated 2 *Syn* ANGRY, angered, apoplectic, enraged, foaming, fuming, incensed, indignant, inflamed, infuriated, irate, ireful, mad, outraged, rabid, riled, roiled, sore, steaming, wrathful, wroth *Ant* delighted, pleased

furnish 1 · to provide (someone) with what is needed for a task or activity *Syn* accoutre (*or* accouter), equip, fit (out), outfit, rig, supply *Rel* stock, store 2 · to put (something) into the possession of someone for use or consumption *Syn* deliver, feed, give, hand, hand over, provide, supply *Rel* administer, dispense, distribute, dole (out), mete (out), parcel (out) *Ant* hold (back), keep (back), reserve, retain, withhold

furor 1 *Syn* ANGER, angriness, fury, indignation, irateness, ire, outrage, rage, spleen, wrath, wrathfulness *Ant* delight, pleasure 2 *Syn* COMMOTION, bother, bustle, clatter, disturbance, furore, fuss, hubbub, hullabaloo, hurly-burly, pandemonium, pother, row, ruckus, ruction, rumpus, shindy, squall, stew, stir, storm, to-do, tumult, turmoil, uproar, welter, whirl 3 *Syn* FRENZY, agitation, delirium, distraction, furore, fury, hysteria, rage, rampage, uproar

furore 1 *Syn* COMMOTION, bother, bustle, clatter, disturbance, furor, fuss, hubbub, hullabaloo, hurly-burly, pandemonium, pother, row, ruckus, ruction, rumpus, shindy, squall, stew, stir, storm, to-do, tumult, turmoil, uproar, welter, whirl 2 *Syn* FRENZY, agitation, delirium, distraction, furor, fury, hysteria, rage, rampage, uproar

furry 1 *Syn* HAIRY (sense 1), bristly, fleecy, hirsute, rough, shaggy, unshorn, woolly *Ant* bald, furless, hairless, shorn, smooth 2 *Syn* HAIRY (sense 2), fuzzy, rough, shaggy, woolly

further *adj Syn* ADDITIONAL, added, another, else, farther, more, other

further *vb Syn* ADVANCE (sense 1), forward, promote *Ant* check, retard

further *adv Syn* FARTHER, beyond

furtherance *Syn* ADVANCE (sense 2), advancement, going, headway, march, onrush, passage, process, procession, progress, progression *Ant* recession, regression, retrogression

furtive *Syn* SECRET, clandestine, covert, stealthy, surreptitious, underhand, underhanded

furuncle *Syn* ABSCESS, boil, carbuncle, pimple, pustule

fury 1 *Syn* ANGER, angriness, furor, indignation, irateness, ire, outrage, rage, spleen, wrath, wrathfulness *Ant* delight, pleasure 2 *Syn* FRENZY, agitation, delirium, distraction, furor, furore, hysteria, rage, rampage, uproar 3 *Syn* INSPIRATION, afflatus, frenzy

fuse 1 *Syn* LIQUEFY, deliquesce, melt, thaw 2 *Syn* MIX, amalgamate, blend, coalesce, commingle, merge, mingle

fusillade *Syn* BARRAGE, bombardment, cannonade, hail, salvo, shower, storm, volley

fusion 1 *Syn* ALLIANCE, coalition, confederacy, confederation, federation, league 2 *Syn* BLEND, admixture, amalgam, amalgamation, combination, composite, compound, intermixture, mix, mixture

fuss *n* 1 *Syn* COMMOTION, bother, bustle, clatter, disturbance, furor, furore, hubbub, hullabaloo, hurly-burly, pandemonium, pother, row, ruckus, ruction, rumpus, shindy, squall, stew, stir, storm, to-do, tumult, turmoil, uproar, welter, whirl 2 *Syn* STIR, ado, bustle, flurry, pother *Ant* tranquillity 3 *Syn* OBJECTION, challenge, complaint, demur, expostulation, protest, question, remonstrance

fuss *vb* 1 *Syn* COMPLAIN, beef, bellyache, carp, crab, croak, gripe, grouse, growl, grumble, kick, moan, murmur, mutter, repine, squawk, wail, whine, yammer *Ant* rejoice 2 *Syn* GUSH (sense 2), enthuse, rave, rhapsodize, slobber 3 *Syn* QUIBBLE, carp, cavil, nitpick

fusser *Syn* GROUCH, bear, complainer, crab, crank, croaker, curmudgeon, griper, grouser, growler, grumbler, grump, murmurer, mutterer, whiner

fussy *Syn* NICE, dainty, fastidious, finical, finicking, finicky, particular, pernickety, persnickety, squeamish

fustian *Syn* BOMBAST, rant, rhapsody, rodomontade

fusty *Syn* MALODOROUS, fetid, musty, noisome, putrid, rancid, rank, stinking *Ant* odorous

futile · barren of result *Syn* abortive, bootless, fruitless, vain *Rel* idle, nugatory, otiose, vain *Ant* effective, effectual, efficacious, efficient, fruitful, productive, profitable, successful

futurist *Syn* PROPHET, augur, diviner, forecaster, foreseer, foreteller, fortune-teller, prognosticator, prophesier, seer, soothsayer

fuzzy *Syn* HAIRY (sense 2), furry, rough, shaggy, woolly

G

gab *Syn* CHAT, babble, blab, cackle, chatter, converse, gabble, gas, jabber, jaw, palaver, patter, prate, prattle, rap, rattle, run on, talk, twitter, visit

gabble *Syn* CHAT, babble, blab, cackle, chatter, converse, gab, gas, jabber, jaw, palaver, patter, prate, prattle, rap, rattle, run on, talk, twitter, visit

gabfest *Syn* CHAT, chatter, chitchat, gossip, palaver, rap, small talk, table talk, talk, tête-à-tête

gad *Syn* WANDER, gallivant, meander, prowl, ramble, range, roam, rove, stray, traipse

gadabout *Syn* NOMAD, drifter, rambler, roamer, rover, stroller, vagabond, wanderer, wayfarer

gadget 1 · an interesting and often novel device with a practical use *Syn* appliance, contraption, contrivance, gimmick, gizmo (*or* gismo), jigger *Rel* implement, instrument, tool, utensil 2 *Syn* DEVICE, contraption, contrivance

gaffe *Syn* IMPROPRIETY (sense 1), familiarity, indiscretion, solecism *Ant* amenity, civility, courtesy, formality, gesture

gag *Syn* JOKE, crack, jape, jest, quip, wisecrack, witticism

gaiety *Syn* FINERY, array, best, bravery, caparison, feather, frippery, full dress, regalia

gain 1 *Syn* CONVALESCE, heal, mend, rally, recover, recuperate, snap back 2 *Syn* EARN, acquire, attain, capture, carry, draw, garner, get, land, make, obtain, procure, realize, secure, win *Ant* forfeit, lose 3 *Syn* GET, obtain, procure, secure, win 4 *Syn* IMPROVE (sense 2), convalesce, recover, recuperate 5 *Syn* REACH, achieve, attain, compass

gainful *Syn* PAYING, lucrative, profitable, remunerative

gainsay *Syn* DENY, contradict, contravene, impugn, negative, traverse *Ant* concede, confirm

gal *Syn* GIRLFRIEND, lady, woman

gala *Syn* FESTIVAL, carnival, celebration, festivity, fete (*or* fête), fiesta, jubilee

gall *vb Syn* ABRADE, chafe, excoriate, fret

gall *n Syn* EFFRONTERY, audacity, brashness, brass, brassiness, brazenness, cheek, cheekiness, chutzpah, nerve, nerviness, pertness, presumption, presumptuousness, sauce, sauciness, temerity

gallant *Syn* CIVIL, chivalrous, courteous, courtly, polite *Ant* rude, uncivil

gallantry 1 *Syn* COURAGE, bravery, courageousness, daring, dauntlessness, doughtiness, fearlessness, greatheartedness, guts, hardihood, heart, heroism, intrepidity, intrepidness, nerve, stoutness, valor *Ant* cowardice, cowardliness, cravenness, dastardliness, spinelessness, yellowness 2 *Syn* COURTESY, amenity, attention *Ant* discourtesy 3 *Syn* HEROISM, prowess, valor

gallery *Syn* PASSAGE, aisle, arcade, cloister, corridor, hall, hallway, passageway

galling *Syn* ANNOYING, aggravating, bothersome, disturbing, exasperating, frustrating, irksome, irritating, maddening, nettling, peeving, pesty, rankling, riling, vexatious, vexing

gallivant *Syn* WANDER, gad, meander, prowl, ramble, range, roam, rove, stray, traipse

galumph *Syn* STUMBLE, blunder, bumble, flounder, lollop, lumber, lurch, trip

galvanize *Syn* PROVOKE, excite, pique, quicken, stimulate

gambit *Syn* TRICK, artifice, feint, maneuver, ploy, ruse, stratagem, wile

gamble *Syn* BET, go, lay, stake, wager

gambler *Syn* BETTOR, wagerer

gamble (with) *Syn* ENDANGER, adventure, compromise, hazard, imperil, jeopardize, menace, risk, venture

gambol *n Syn* PLAY, disport, frolic, rollick, romp, sport *Ant* work

gambol *vb Syn* PLAY, disport, frolic, rollick, romp, sport

game *Syn* FUN, jest, play, sport

gameness *Syn* ALACRITY, amenability, goodwill, willingness

games *Syn* ATHLETICS, sports

gamut *Syn* RANGE, compass, horizon, ken, orbit, purview, radius, reach, scope, sweep

gangling *Syn* LANKY, gangly, rangy, spindling, spindly

gangly *Syn* LANKY, gangling, rangy, spindling, spindly

gap 1 *Syn* BREAK, hiatus, interim, interruption, interval, lacuna 2 *Syn* CANYON, defile, flume, gorge, gulch, gulf, notch, pass, ravine

gape 1 · to look long and hard in wonder or surprise *Syn* gawk, gaze, goggle, peer, rubberneck, stare *Rel* glare, gloat, glower 2 *Syn* GAZE, glare, gloat, peer, stare

garbage *Syn* REFUSE, debris, offal, rubbish, trash, waste

garble *Syn* MISREPRESENT, belie, falsify

gargantuan *Syn* HUGE, Brobdingnagian, colossal, cyclopean, elephantine, enormous, giant, gigantean, gigantic, herculean, immense, mammoth, titanic, vast *Ant* bitty, diminutive, microscopic (*or* microscopical), midget, miniature, minute, pocket, pygmy, teeny, teeny-weeny, tiny, wee

garish *Syn* GAUDY, flamboyant, flashy, glitzy, loud, ostentatious, splashy, swank (*or* swanky), tawdry *Ant* conservative, quiet, understated

garishness *Syn* OSTENTATION, flamboyance, flashiness, gaudiness, glitz, ostentatiousness, pretentiousness, showiness, swank *Ant* austerity, plainness, severity

garner 1 *Syn* EARN, acquire, attain, capture, carry, draw, gain, get, land, make, obtain, procure, realize, secure, win *Ant* forfeit, lose **2** *Syn* REAP, gather, glean, harvest

garnish *Syn* ADORN, beautify, bedeck, deck, decorate, embellish, ornament *Ant* disfigure

garrulity *Syn* TALKATIVENESS, garrulousness, glibness, loquaciousness, loquacity, volubility *Ant* silence

garrulous *Syn* TALKATIVE, glib, loquacious, voluble *Ant* closemouthed, laconic, reserved, reticent, taciturn, tight-lipped

garrulousness *Syn* TALKATIVENESS, garrulity, glibness, loquaciousness, loquacity, volubility *Ant* silence

gas *Syn* CHAT, babble, blab, cackle, chatter, converse, gab, gabble, jabber, jaw, palaver, patter, prate, prattle, rap, rattle, run on, talk, twitter, visit

gasconade *Syn* BOAST, brag, crow, vaunt *Ant* depreciate (*oneself, one's accomplishments*)

gastronome *Syn* EPICURE, bon vivant, glutton, gourmand, gourmet

gate *Syn* DOOR, doorway, gateway, portal, postern

gateway *Syn* DOOR, doorway, gate, portal, postern

gather 1 · to come or bring together *Syn* assemble, collect, congregate *Rel* accumulate, amass, hoard **2** *Syn* INFER, conclude, deduce, judge **3** *Syn* REAP, garner, glean, harvest

gathering · a number of individuals come or brought together *Syn* assemblage, assembly, collection, congregation *Rel* crowd, crush, horde, mob, press, rout, throng

gauche *Syn* AWKWARD, clumsy, inept, maladroit *Ant* deft, graceful, handy

gaud *Syn* KNICKKNACK, bauble, curio, curiosity, gewgaw, novelty, ornamental, trinket

gaudiness *Syn* OSTENTATION, flamboyance, flashiness, garishness, glitz, ostentatiousness, pretentiousness, showiness, swank *Ant* austerity, plainness, severity

gaudy · excessively showy *Syn* flamboyant, flashy, garish, glitzy, loud, ostentatious, splashy, swank (*or* swanky), tawdry *Rel* meretricious, pretentious *Ant* conservative, quiet, understated

gauge *n Syn* STANDARD, criterion, touchstone, yardstick

gauge *vb Syn* ESTIMATE (sense 2), calculate, call, conjecture, figure, guess, judge, make, place, put, reckon, suppose

gaunt *Syn* LEAN, angular, lank, lanky, rawboned, scrawny, skinny, spare *Ant* fleshy

gawk *vb Syn* GAPE, gaze, goggle, peer, rubberneck, stare

gawk *n Syn* OAF, clod, hulk, lout, lubber, lug

gay 1 *Syn* CAREFREE, careless, cavalier, devil-may-care, easygoing, happy-go-lucky, insouciant, lighthearted, unconcerned *Ant* careworn **2** *Syn* CHEERFUL (sense 1), blithe, blithesome, bright, buoyant, cheery, chipper, gladsome, lightsome, sunny, upbeat *Ant* dour, gloomy, glum, morose, saturnine, sulky, sullen **3** *Syn* CHEERFUL (sense 2), bright, cheering, cheery, glad *Ant* bleak, cheerless, dark, depressing, dismal, dreary, gloomy, gray **4** *Syn* LIVELY, animated, sprightly, vivacious *Ant* dull **5** *Syn* MERRY, blithesome, festive, gleeful, jocose, jocund, jolly, jovial, laughing, mirthful, sunny

gaze 1 · to look at long and attentively *Syn* gape, glare, gloat, peer, stare *Rel* look, see, watch **2** *Syn* GAPE, gawk, goggle, peer, rubberneck, stare

gear *Syn* EQUIPMENT, apparatus, machinery, matériel, outfit, paraphernalia, tackle

geld *Syn* STERILIZE (sense 1), alter, castrate, emasculate, mutilate, spay *Ant* fertilize

gelid *Syn* COLD, arctic, chilly, cool, freezing, frigid, frosty, glacial, icy *Ant* hot

genealogy *Syn* ANCESTRY, birth, blood, bloodline, breeding, descent, extraction, family tree, line, lineage, origin, parentage, pedigree, stock, strain *Ant* issue, posterity, progeny, seed

general 1 · belonging or relating to the whole *Syn* blanket, common, generic, global, overall, universal *Rel* broad, collective, comprehensive, extensive, pervasive, sweeping, ubiquitous, wholesale, wide, widespread *Ant* individual, particular **2** · relating to the main elements and not to specific details *Syn* all-around, bird's-eye, broad, nonspecific, overall *Rel* comprehensive, inclusive *Ant* delineated, detailed, particularized, specific

generally 1 *Syn* CHIEFLY, altogether, basically, by and large, largely, mainly, mostly, overall, predominantly, primarily, principally, substantially **2** *Syn* LARGELY, chiefly, greatly, mainly, mostly, principally **3** *Syn* NATURALLY (sense 1), commonly, normally, ordinarily, typically, usually *Ant* abnormally, atypically, extraordinarily, uncommonly, unusually

generate 1 · to give life or origin to or to bring into existence by or as if by natural processes *Syn* beget, breed, engender, get, procreate, propagate, reproduce, sire *Rel* bear, produce, yield **2** *Syn* EFFECT, bring about, cause, create, effectuate, engender, induce, make, produce, prompt, result (in), spawn, work, yield

generic *Syn* GENERAL (sense 1), blanket,

common, global, overall, universal *Ant* individual, particular

generous *Syn* LIBERAL (sense 1), bounteous, bountiful, handsome, munificent, openhanded *Ant* close

genesis *Syn* BEGINNING, alpha, birth, commencement, dawn, inception, incipiency, launch, morning, onset, outset, start, threshold *Ant* close, conclusion, end, ending

genial **1** *Syn* AMIABLE, affable, agreeable, good-natured, good-tempered, gracious, nice, sweet, well-disposed *Ant* disagreeable, ill-natured, ill-tempered, ungracious, unpleasant **2** *Syn* GRACIOUS, affable, cordial, sociable *Ant* ungracious

genius *Syn* GIFT (sense 2), aptitude, bent, faculty, knack, talent, turn

gent *Syn* MAN (sense 1), dude, fellow, gentleman, guy, male

genteel *Syn* CULTIVATED, civilized, cultured, polished, refined *Ant* philistine, uncivilized, uncultured, unpolished, unrefined

gentility *Syn* POLITENESS, civility, courteousness, courtesy, graciousness, mannerliness *Ant* discourteousness, discourtesy, impoliteness, incivility, rudeness, ungraciousness

gentle *adj* **1** *Syn* CLEMENT, balmy, equable, mild, moderate, temperate *Ant* harsh, inclement, intemperate, severe **2** *Syn* SOFT, balmy, bland, lenient, mild, smooth *Ant* hard, stern

gentle *vb* *Syn* CUSHION, buffer, soften

gentleman **1** · a man of high birth or social position *Syn* lord, nobleman **2** *Syn* MAN, dude, fellow, gent, guy, male

gentleperson *Syn* ARISTOCRAT, noble, patrician

gentlewoman · a woman of high birth or social position *Syn* dame, lady, noblewoman

gentry *Syn* ARISTOCRACY, county, elite, nobility, society *Ant* people, proletariat

genuine *Syn* AUTHENTIC, bona fide, veritable *Ant* spurious

geriatric *Syn* ELDERLY, aged, aging, ancient, long-lived, old, older, senior *Ant* young, youthful

germane *Syn* PERTINENT, applicable, apposite, apropos, material, pointed, relative, relevant *Ant* extraneous, immaterial, inapplicable, irrelevant, pointless

germfree *Syn* SANITARY, aseptic, hygienic, sterile *Ant* insanitary, unhygienic, unsanitary

gesture *Syn* MOTION, beckon, flag, signal, wave

get **1** · to come into possession of *Syn* gain, obtain, procure, secure, win *Rel* bring, fetch **2** *Syn* BECOME, come, go, grow, run, turn, wax **3** *Syn* EARN, acquire, attain, capture, carry, draw, gain, garner, land, make, obtain, procure, realize, secure, win *Ant* forfeit, lose **4** *Syn* GENERATE, beget, breed, engender, procreate, propagate, reproduce, sire **5** *Syn* PERSUADE, argue, convince, induce, move,

prevail (on *or* upon), satisfy, talk (into), win (over)

get off *Syn* BEGIN (sense 2), commence, embark (on *or* upon), enter (into *or* upon), kick off, launch, open, start, strike (into) *Ant* conclude, end, finish, terminate

gewgaw *Syn* KNICKKNACK, bauble, curio, curiosity, gaud, novelty, ornamental, trinket

ghastly · horrifying and repellent in appearance or aspect *Syn* grim, grisly, gruesome, lurid, macabre *Rel* deadly, deathly

ghost · the soul of a dead person thought of especially as appearing to living people *Syn* apparition, bogey, phantasm, phantom, poltergeist, shade, shadow, specter (*or* spectre), spirit, spook, vision, wraith *Rel* banshee, demon (*or* daemon), familiar (*or* familiar spirit), genie, imp, incubus, puck, vampire, zombie

ghoul *Syn* DEMON, devil, fiend, imp, incubus

giant *n* · something that is unusually large and powerful *Syn* behemoth, blockbuster, colossus, jumbo, leviathan, mammoth, monster, titan, whale, whopper *Rel* amazon *Ant* dwarf, midget, mini, miniature, peewee, pygmy, runt, shrimp

giant *adj* *Syn* HUGE, Brobdingnagian, colossal, cyclopean, elephantine, enormous, gargantuan, gigantean, gigantic, Herculean, immense, mammoth, titanic, vast *Ant* bitty, diminutive, microscopic (*or* microscopical), midget, miniature, minute, pocket, pygmy, teeny, teeny-weeny, tiny, wee

gibberish · speech or actions that are esoteric in nature and suggest the magical, strange, or unknown *Syn* abracadabra, hocus-pocus, mummery

gibe *Syn* SCOFF, fleer, flout, gird, jeer, sneer

giddy · affected by a sensation of being whirled about or around *Syn* dazzled, dizzy, swimming, vertiginous *Rel* reeling, whirling

gift **1** · something, often of value but not necessarily material, given freely to another for his benefit or pleasure *Syn* boon, favor, gratuity, largess, present *Rel* alms, benefaction, contribution, donation **2** · a special ability or a capacity for a definite kind of activity or achievement *Syn* aptitude, bent, faculty, genius, knack, talent, turn *Rel* dowry, endowment

gigantean *Syn* HUGE, Brobdingnagian, colossal, cyclopean, elephantine, enormous, gargantuan, giant, gigantic, Herculean, immense, mammoth, titanic, vast *Ant* bitty, diminutive, microscopic (*or* microscopical), midget, miniature, minute, pocket, pygmy, teeny, teeny-weeny, tiny, wee

gigantic *Syn* HUGE, Brobdingnagian, colossal, cyclopean, elephantine, enormous, gargantuan, giant, gigantean, Herculean, immense, mammoth, titanic, vast *Ant* bitty, diminutive, microscopic (*or* microscopical), midget, miniature, minute, pocket, pygmy, teeny, teeny-weeny, tiny, wee

gimmick *Syn* GADGET, appliance, contraption, contrivance, gizmo (*or* gismo), jigger

gingery *Syn* SPIRITED, fiery, high-spirited, mettlesome, peppery, spunky *Ant* spiritless

gird 1 *Syn* SCOFF, fleer, flout, gibe, jeer, sneer 2 *Syn* SURROUND, circle, compass, encircle, encompass, environ, girdle, hem, ring

girdle *Syn* SURROUND, circle, compass, encircle, encompass, environ, gird, hem, ring

girl • a female person who has not yet reached adulthood *Syn* lass, lassie, miss, missy *Rel* adolescent, juvenile, kid, minor, moppet, teenager, youngster

girlfriend • a female romantic companion *Syn* gal, lady, woman *Rel* beloved, darling, sweetheart

gist 1 *Syn* CRUX, core, heart, nub, pith, pivot 2 *Syn* SUBSTANCE, burden, core, pith, purport

give 1 • to convey something or make something over or available to another *Syn* afford, bestow, confer, donate, present *Rel* accord, award, concede, grant, vouchsafe 2 *Syn* FURNISH (sense 2), deliver, feed, hand, hand over, provide, supply *Ant* hold (back), keep (back), reserve, retain, withhold

give-and-take *Syn* BANTER, chaff, jesting, joshing, persiflage, raillery, repartee

given 1 *Syn* ACCUSTOMED, habituated, used, wont *Ant* unaccustomed, unused 2 *Syn* PRONE (sense 1), apt, inclined, tending *Ant* erect

gizmo *or* **gismo** *Syn* GADGET, appliance, contraption, contrivance, gimmick, jigger

glacial *Syn* COLD, arctic, chilly, cool, freezing, frigid, frosty, gelid, icy *Ant* hot

glad 1 • characterized by or expressing the mood of one who is pleased or delighted *Syn* cheerful, happy, joyful, joyous, lighthearted *Rel* delighted, gratified, pleased, rejoiced, tickled *Ant* sad 2 *Syn* CHEERFUL (sense 2), bright, cheering, cheery, gay *Ant* bleak, cheerless, dark, depressing, dismal, dreary, gloomy, gray

gladden *Syn* PLEASE, delight, gratify, regale, rejoice, tickle *Ant* anger, displease, vex

gladdening *Syn* HEARTWARMING, cheering, comforting, encouraging, fulfilling, gratifying, heartening, rewarding, satisfying *Ant* depressing, discouraging, disheartening, dispiriting

gladiatorial *Syn* BELLIGERENT, aggressive, argumentative, bellicose, combative, contentious, discordant, disputatious, militant, pugnacious, quarrelsome, scrappy, truculent, warlike *Ant* nonbelligerent, pacific, peaceable, peaceful

gladsome *Syn* CHEERFUL (sense 1), blithe, blithesome, bright, buoyant, cheery, chipper, gay, lightsome, sunny, upbeat *Ant* dour, gloomy, glum, morose, saturnine, sulky, sullen

glamorize *Syn* IDEALIZE, glorify, romanticize

glamorous *Syn* EXOTIC, fantastic, marvelous (*or* marvellous), outlandish, romantic, strange

glance 1 *Syn* BRUSH, graze, shave, skim 2 *Syn* FLASH, coruscate, gleam, glint, glisten, glitter, scintillate, sparkle, twinkle 3 *Syn* LOOK, glimpse, peek, peep, sight, view

glare *n Syn* BLAZE, flame, flare, glow

glare *vb* 1 *Syn* BLAZE, flame, flare, glow 2 *Syn* FROWN, gloom, glower, lower, scowl *Ant* beam, smile 3 *Syn* GAZE, gape, gloat, peer, stare

glaring 1 *Syn* EGREGIOUS, blatant, conspicuous, flagrant, gross, obvious, patent, pronounced, rank, striking 2 *Syn* FLAGRANT, gross, rank

glaze *Syn* LUSTER, gloss, sheen

gleam *Syn* FLASH, coruscate, glance, glint, glisten, glitter, scintillate, sparkle, twinkle

glean *Syn* REAP, garner, gather, harvest

glee *Syn* MIRTH, hilarity, jollity

gleeful *Syn* MERRY, blithesome, festive, gay, jocose, jocund, jolly, jovial, laughing, mirthful, sunny

glib *Syn* TALKATIVE, garrulous, loquacious, voluble *Ant* closemouthed, laconic, reserved, reticent, taciturn, tight-lipped

glibness *Syn* TALKATIVENESS, garrulity, garrulousness, loquaciousness, loquacity, volubility *Ant* silence

glide *Syn* SLIDE, coast, glissade, skid, slip, slither, toboggan

glimpse *Syn* LOOK, glance, peek, peep, sight, view

glint *Syn* FLASH, coruscate, glance, gleam, glisten, glitter, scintillate, sparkle, twinkle

glissade *Syn* SLIDE, coast, glide, skid, slip, slither, toboggan

glisten *Syn* FLASH, coruscate, glance, gleam, glint, glitter, scintillate, sparkle, twinkle

glistening *Syn* GLOSSY, buffed, burnished, lustrous, polished, rubbed, satin, satiny, sleek *Ant* dim, dull, flat, lusterless, matte

glitter *Syn* FLASH, coruscate, glance, gleam, glint, glisten, scintillate, sparkle, twinkle

glitz *Syn* OSTENTATION, flamboyance, flashiness, garishness, gaudiness, ostentatiousness, pretentiousness, showiness, swank *Ant* austerity, plainness, severity

glitzy *Syn* GAUDY, flamboyant, flashy, garish, loud, ostentatious, splashy, swank (*or* swanky), tawdry *Ant* conservative, quiet, understated

gloat *Syn* GAZE, gape, glare, peer, stare

global 1 *Syn* ENCYCLOPEDIC, compendious, complete, comprehensive, full, inclusive, indepth, omnibus, panoramic, universal 2 *Syn* GENERAL (sense 1), blanket, common, generic, overall, universal *Ant* individual, particular

globe *Syn* EARTH, planet, world

gloom *vb Syn* FROWN, glare, glower, lower, scowl *Ant* beam, smile

gloom *n Syn* SADNESS, blues, dejection, depression, desolation, despondency, disconsolateness,dispiritedness,doldrums,downheartedness, dreariness, dumps, forlornness, gloominess, heartsickness, joylessness, melancholy, mopes, oppression, unhappiness *Ant* bliss, blissfulness, ecstasy, elatedness, elation, euphoria, exhilaration, exuberance, exultation, felicity, gladness, gladsomeness, happiness, heaven, intoxication, joy, joyfulness, joyousness, jubilation, rapture, rapturousness

gloominess *Syn* SADNESS, blues, dejection, depression, desolation, despondency, disconsolateness, dispiritedness, doldrums, downheartedness, dreariness, dumps, forlornness, gloom, heartsickness, joylessness, melancholy, mopes, oppression, unhappiness *Ant* bliss, blissfulness, ecstasy, elatedness, elation, euphoria, exhilaration, exuberance, exultation, felicity, gladness, gladsomeness, happiness, heaven, intoxication, joy, joyfulness, joyousness, jubilation, rapture, rapturousness

gloomy 1 *Syn* DARK, dim, dusky, murky, obscure *Ant* light 2 *Syn* SAD (sense 1), bad, blue, brokenhearted, crestfallen, dejected, depressed, despondent, disconsolate, doleful, down, downcast, downhearted, droopy, forlorn, glum, heartbroken, heartsick, heartsore, inconsolable, joyless, low, low-spirited, melancholy, miserable, mournful, saddened, sorrowful, sorry, unhappy, woebegone, woeful, wretched *Ant* blissful, buoyant, buoyed, cheerful, cheery, chipper, delighted, glad, gladdened, gladsome, gleeful, happy, joyful, joyous, jubilant, sunny, upbeat 3 *Syn* SULLEN, crabbed, dour, glum, morose, saturnine, sulky, surly

glorify 1 *Syn* DIGNIFY, ennoble, honor 2 *Syn* EXALT, aggrandize, dignify, ennoble, enshrine, magnify *Ant* abase, degrade, demean, humble, humiliate 3 *Syn* IDEALIZE, glamorize, romanticize

glorious *Syn* SPLENDID, gorgeous, resplendent, sublime, superb

gloriousness *Syn* MAGNIFICENCE, augustness, brilliance, glory, grandeur, grandness, majesty, nobility, nobleness, resplendence, splendor, stateliness, stupendousness, sublimeness, superbness

glory 1 *Syn* FAME, celebrity, éclat, honor, notoriety, renown, reputation, repute *Ant* infamy, obscurity 2 *Syn* MAGNIFICENCE, augustness, brilliance, gloriousness, grandeur, grandness, majesty, nobility, nobleness, resplendence, splendor, stateliness, stupendousness, sublimeness, superbness

glorying *Syn* EXULTANT, exulting, jubilant, rejoicing, triumphant

gloss *n Syn* LUSTER, glaze, sheen

gloss *vb* 1 *Syn* PALLIATE, extenuate, gloze, whiten, whitewash 2 *Syn* POLISH, buff, burnish, dress, grind, rub, shine, smooth

glossy 1 · having a shiny surface or finish *Syn* buffed, burnished, glistening, lustrous, polished, rubbed, satin, satiny, sleek *Rel* silken, silky, slick, slippery *Ant* dim, dull, flat, lusterless, matte 2 *Syn* SLEEK, satiny, silken, silky, slick, velvety

glow *n Syn* BLAZE, flame, flare, glare

glow *vb* 1 *Syn* BLAZE, flame, flare, glare 2 *Syn* BLUSH, bloom, color, crimson, flush, redden

glower *Syn* FROWN, glare, gloom, lower, scowl *Ant* beam, smile

glowing *Syn* FERVENT, ardent, blazing, burning, charged, emotional, fervid, feverish, fiery, flaming, hot-blooded, impassioned, passionate, red-hot, vehement, warm, warm-blooded *Ant* cold, cool, dispassionate, impassive, unemotional

gloze *Syn* PALLIATE, extenuate, gloss, whiten, whitewash

glum 1 *Syn* SAD (sense 1), bad, blue, brokenhearted, crestfallen, dejected, depressed, despondent, disconsolate, doleful, down, downcast, downhearted, droopy, forlorn, gloomy, heartbroken, heartsick, heartsore, inconsolable, joyless, low, low-spirited, melancholy, miserable, mournful, saddened, sorrowful, sorry, unhappy, woebegone, woeful, wretched *Ant* blissful, buoyant, buoyed, cheerful, cheery, chipper, delighted, glad, gladdened, gladsome, gleeful, happy, joyful, joyous, jubilant, sunny, upbeat 2 *Syn* SULLEN, crabbed, dour, gloomy, morose, saturnine, sulky, surly

glut *Syn* SATIATE, cloy, gorge, pall, sate, surfeit

glutton 1 · one who eats greedily or too much *Syn* gorger, gormandizer, gourmand, hog, overeater, stuffer, swiller *Rel* feaster, trencherman 2 *Syn* EPICURE, bon vivant, gastronome, glutton, gourmet

gluttonous *Syn* VORACIOUS, rapacious, ravening, ravenous

gnash *Syn* BITE, champ, gnaw

gnaw *Syn* BITE, champ, gnash

go *vb* 1 · to move out of or away from where one is *Syn* depart, leave, quit, retire, withdraw *Rel* abscond, decamp, escape, flee, fly *Ant* come 2 *Syn* BET, gamble, lay, stake, wager 3 *Syn* BECOME, come, get, grow, run, turn, wax 4 *Syn* RESORT, apply, refer, turn 5 *Syn* TRAVERSE, cover, crisscross, cross, cut (across), follow, pass (over), proceed (along), travel

go *n* 1 *Syn* ATTEMPT, crack, endeavor, essay, fling, pass, shot, stab, trial, try, whack 2 *Syn* SPELL, bout, shift, stint, tour, trick, turn

goad *n Syn* MOTIVE, impulse, incentive, inducement, spring, spur

goad *vb Syn* URGE, egg (on), encourage, exhort, press, prod, prompt

goal · something that one hopes or intends to accomplish *Syn* aim, ambition, aspiration, design, dream, end, intent, intention, mark, meaning, object, objective, plan, pretension, purpose, target, thing *Rel* plot, project, scheme

gob *Syn* MARINER, bluejacket, sailor, seaman, tar

gobbledygook *Syn* NONSENSE, balderdash, bull, bunk, drivel, poppycock, rot, trash, twaddle

go-between *Syn* MEDIATOR, arbiter, arbitrator, conciliator, intercessor, intermediary, interposer, middleman, peacemaker

godless *Syn* IRRELIGIOUS, nonreligious, ungodly, unreligious *Ant* religious

godliness *Syn* HOLINESS, blessedness, devoutness, piety, piousness, sainthood, saintliness, saintship, sanctity *Ant* godlessness, impiety, ungodliness, unholiness

godly *Syn* HOLY (sense 1), devout, pious, religious, sainted, saintly *Ant* faithless, godless, impious, irreligious, ungodly, unholy

Godspeed *Syn* GOOD-BYE, adieu, au revoir, bon voyage, farewell *Ant* hello

goggle *Syn* GAPE, gawk, gaze, peer, rubberneck, stare

going *Syn* ADVANCE (sense 2), advancement, furtherance, headway, march, onrush, passage, process, procession, progress, progression *Ant* recession, regression, retrogression

golden *Syn* BLOND, fair, flaxen, sandy, straw, tawny *Ant* dark

golden-ager *Syn* SENIOR CITIZEN, ancient, elder, oldster, old-timer *Ant* youngster, youth

gone *Syn* EXTINCT, bygone, dead, defunct, departed, expired, vanished *Ant* alive, existent, existing, extant, living

good 1 *Syn* COMPETENT, able, capable, fit, qualified, suitable *Ant* incompetent, inept, poor, unfit, unqualified **2** *Syn* DEPENDABLE, reliable, responsible, safe, solid, steady, sure, tried, tried-and-true, true, trustworthy, trusty *Ant* irresponsible, undependable, unreliable, untrustworthy **3** *Syn* FAITHFUL, constant, devoted, devout, fast, loyal, pious, staunch (*or* stanch), steadfast, steady, true, true-blue *Ant* disloyal, faithless, false, fickle, inconstant, perfidious, recreant, traitorous, treacherous, unfaithful, untrue **4** *Syn* WORTHY, deserving, meritorious *Ant* no-good, undeserving, valueless, worthless

good-bye *or* **good-by** · an expression of good wishes at parting *Syn* adieu, au revoir, bon voyage, farewell, Godspeed *Rel* leavetaking, send-off *Ant* hello

goodly *Syn* LARGE, big, bulky, considerable, good-sized, grand, great, handsome, hefty, hulking, largish, outsize, oversize (*or* oversized), sizable (*or* sizeable), substantial, tidy, voluminous *Ant* little, puny, small, undersized

good-natured *Syn* AMIABLE, affable, agreeable, genial, good-tempered, gracious, nice, sweet, well-disposed *Ant* disagreeable, ill-natured, ill-tempered, ungracious, unpleasant

goodness · moral excellence *Syn* morality, rectitude, virtue *Rel* nobility, righteousness, virtuousness *Ant* badness, evil

good sense *Syn* SENSE, common sense, gumption, horse sense, judgment, wisdom

good-sized *Syn* LARGE, big, bulky, considerable, goodly, grand, great, handsome, hefty, hulking, largish, outsize, oversize (*or* oversized), sizable (*or* sizeable), substantial, tidy, voluminous *Ant* little, puny, small, undersized

good-tempered *Syn* AMIABLE, affable, agreeable, genial, good-natured, gracious, nice, sweet, well-disposed *Ant* disagreeable, ill-natured, ill-tempered, ungracious, unpleasant

goodwill 1 *Syn* ALACRITY, amenability, gameness, willingness **2** *Syn* FRIENDSHIP, amity, comity *Ant* animosity

goose *Syn* FOOL (sense 2), booby, half-wit, jackass, lunatic, nincompoop, ninny, nitwit, nut, simpleton, turkey, yo-yo

gorge *n Syn* CANYON, defile, flume, gap, gulch, gulf, notch, pass, ravine

gorge *vb Syn* SATIATE, cloy, glut, pall, sate, surfeit

gorgeous 1 *Syn* BEAUTIFUL, attractive, beauteous, comely, cute, fair, handsome, knockout, lovely, pretty, ravishing, sightly, stunning, taking *Ant* homely, ill-favored, plain, ugly, unattractive, unbeautiful, unhandsome, unlovely, unpretty, unsightly **2** *Syn* SPLENDID, glorious, resplendent, sublime, superb

gorger *Syn* GLUTTON, gormandizer, gourmand, hog, overeater, stuffer, swiller

gormandizer *Syn* GLUTTON, gorger, gourmand, hog, overeater, stuffer, swiller

gory *Syn* BLOODY, sanguinary, sanguine, sanguineous

gossip *vb* · to disclose something, often of questionable veracity, that is better kept to oneself *Syn* blab, tattle

gossip *n* **1** *Syn* CHAT, chatter, chitchat, gabfest, palaver, rap, small talk, table talk, talk, tête-à-tête **2** *Syn* REPORT, hearsay, rumor

gourmand 1 *Syn* EPICURE, bon vivant, gastronome, glutton, gourmet **2** *Syn* GLUTTON, gorger, gormandizer, hog, overeater, stuffer, swiller

gourmet *Syn* EPICURE, bon vivant, gastronome, glutton, gourmand

governance *Syn* RULE (sense 2), administration, authority, government, jurisdiction, regime, regimen

government *Syn* RULE (sense 2), administration, authority, governance, jurisdiction, regime, regimen

grab *Syn* TAKE, clutch, grasp, seize, snatch

grace 1 *Syn* ELEGANCE, class, elegancy, gracefulness, handsomeness, majesty, refinement, stateliness 2 *Syn* MERCY, charity, clemency, lenity

gracefulness *Syn* ELEGANCE, class, elegancy, grace, handsomeness, majesty, refinement, stateliness

graceless *Syn* INAPPROPRIATE, improper, inapt, incongruous, incorrect, indecorous, inept, infelicitous, unapt, unbecoming, unfit, unhappy, unseemly, unsuitable, wrong *Ant* appropriate, becoming, befitting, correct, decorous, felicitous, fit, fitting, genteel, happy, meet, proper, right, seemly, suitable

gracious 1 · marked by kindly courtesy *Syn* affable, cordial, genial, sociable *Ant* amiable, complaisant, obliging *Ant* ungracious 2 *Syn* AMIABLE, affable, agreeable, genial, good-natured, good-tempered, nice, sweet, well-disposed *Ant* disagreeable, ill-natured, ill-tempered, ungracious, unpleasant

graciousness *Syn* POLITENESS, civility, courteousness, courtesy, gentility, mannerliness *Ant* discourteousness, discourtesy, impoliteness, incivility, rudeness, ungraciousness

gradate *Syn* CLASS, grade, graduate, rank, rate

gradation · difference or variation between two things that are nearly alike *Syn* nuance, shade *Rel* difference, dissimilarity, distinction, divergence

gradational *Syn* GRADUAL, incremental, phased, piecemeal, step-by-step *Ant* sudden

grade *Syn* CLASS, gradate, graduate, rank, rate

gradual · proceeding or changing by steps or degrees *Syn* gradational, incremental, phased, piecemeal, step-by-step *Rel* progressive, stepped, tapered *Ant* sudden

graduate *Syn* CLASS, gradate, grade, rank, rate

grand 1 · large, handsome, dignified, and impressive *Syn* august, grandiose, imposing, magnificent, majestic, noble, stately *Rel* luxurious, opulent, sumptuous 2 *Syn* EXCELLENT, A1, bang-up, banner, capital, classic, crackerjack, dandy, divine, fabulous, fine, first-class, first-rate, great, groovy, heavenly, jim-dandy, keen, marvelous (*or* marvellous), mean, neat, nifty, noble, par excellence, prime, sensational, splendid, stellar, sterling, superb, superior, superlative, supernal, swell, terrific, tip-top, top, top-notch, unsurpassed, wonderful *Ant* poor 3 *Syn* LARGE, big, bulky, considerable, goodly, good-sized, great, handsome, hefty, hulking, largish, outsize, oversize (*or* oversized), sizable (*or* sizeable), substantial, tidy, voluminous *Ant* little, puny, small, undersized

grandeur *Syn* MAGNIFICENCE, augustness, brilliance, gloriousness, glory, grandness, majesty, nobility, nobleness, resplendence, splendor, stateliness, stupendousness, sublimeness, superbness

grandiloquent *Syn* RHETORICAL, aureate, bombastic, euphuistic, flowery, magniloquent

grandiose *Syn* GRAND, august, imposing, magnificent, majestic, noble, stately

grandly *Syn* HIGH, expensively, extravagantly, lavishly, luxuriously, opulently, richly, sumptuously *Ant* austerely, humbly, modestly, plainly, simply

grandness *Syn* MAGNIFICENCE, augustness, brilliance, gloriousness, glory, grandeur, majesty, nobility, nobleness, resplendence, splendor, stateliness, stupendousness, sublimeness, superbness

grant *vb* 1 · to give as a favor or as a right *Syn* accord, award, concede, vouchsafe *Rel* bestow, confer, donate, give, present 2 *Syn* ADMIT, acknowledge, agree, allow, concede, confess, own (up) *Ant* deny

grant *n* *Syn* APPROPRIATION, allocation, allotment, annuity, subsidy

granting *Syn* PERMISSION, allowance, authorization, clearance, concurrence, consent, leave, license (*or* licence), sanction, sufferance *Ant* interdiction, prohibition, proscription

graph *n* *Syn* CHART, map

graph *vb* *Syn* CHART, map

graphic · giving a clear visual impression especially in words *Syn* pictorial, picturesque, vivid *Rel* clear, lucid, perspicuous

grapple *Syn* WRESTLE, scuffle, tussle

grasp *n* 1 *Syn* COMPREHENSION, appreciation, apprehension, grip, perception, understanding 2 *Syn* HOLD, clutch, grip

grasp *vb* *Syn* TAKE, clutch, grab, seize, snatch

grasping *Syn* COVETOUS, acquisitive, avaricious, greedy

grassland *Syn* PLAIN, down, prairie, savanna, steppe, tundra, veld (*or* veldt)

grate *Syn* SCRAPE, grind, rasp, scratch

grateful *Syn* PLEASANT, agreeable, gratifying, pleasing, welcome *Ant* distasteful, harsh, unpleasant

gratefulness *Syn* THANKS, appreciation, appreciativeness, gratitude, thankfulness *Ant* ingratitude, thanklessness, ungratefulness

gratified *Syn* CONTENT, contented, happy, pleased, satisfied *Ant* discontent, discontented, displeased, dissatisfied, malcontent, unhappy

gratify *Syn* PLEASE, delight, gladden, regale, rejoice, tickle *Ant* anger, displease, vex

gratifying 1 *Syn* HEARTWARMING, cheering, comforting, encouraging, fulfilling, gladdening, heartening, rewarding, satisfying *Ant* depressing, discouraging, disheartening, dispiriting 2 *Syn* PLEASANT, agreeable, gratifying, pleasing, welcome *Ant* distasteful, harsh, unpleasant

gratitude *Syn* THANKS, appreciation, appreciativeness, gratefulness, thankfulness *Ant* ingratitude, thanklessness, ungratefulness

gratuitous 1 *Syn* SUPEREROGATORY, uncalled-for, wanton 2 *Syn* UNNECESSARY, dispensable, needless, nonessential, uncalled-for, unessential, unwarranted *Ant* essential, indispensable, necessary, needed, needful, required

gratuity 1 *Syn* BONUS, dividend, extra, gravy, lagniappe, perquisite, tip 2 *Syn* GIFT (sense 1), boon, favor, largess, present

grave *Syn* SERIOUS, earnest, sedate, sober, solemn, somber, staid *Ant* flippant, light

gravity *Syn* EARNESTNESS, intentness, seriousness, soberness, sobriety, solemnity *Ant* frivolity, levity, lightheartedness

gravy *Syn* BONUS, dividend, extra, gratuity, lagniappe, perquisite, tip

graze 1 *Syn* BRUSH, glance, shave, skim 2 *Syn* FEED, nourish, pasture *Ant* starve

grease *Syn* OIL, anoint, cream, lubricate

great 1 *Syn* EXCELLENT, A1, bang-up, banner, capital, classic, crackerjack, dandy, divine, fabulous, fine, first-class, first-rate, grand, groovy, heavenly, jim-dandy, keen, marvelous (*or* marvellous), mean, neat, nifty, noble, par excellence, prime, sensational, splendid, stellar, sterling, superb, superior, superlative, supernal, swell, terrific, tip-top, top, top-notch, unsurpassed, wonderful *Ant* poor 2 *Syn* LARGE, big, bulky, considerable, goodly, good-sized, grand, handsome, hefty, hulking, largish, outsize, oversize (*or* oversized), sizable (*or* sizeable), substantial, tidy, voluminous *Ant* little, puny, small, undersized 3 *Syn* LONG (sense 2), extended, far, lengthy, long-lived, long-range, long-term, marathon *Ant* brief, short, short-lived, short-range, short-term

greatheartedness *Syn* COURAGE, bravery, courageousness, daring, dauntlessness, doughtiness, fearlessness, gallantry, guts, hardihood, heart, heroism, intrepidity, intrepidness, nerve, stoutness, valor *Ant* cowardice, cowardliness, cravenness, dastardliness, spinelessness, yellowness

greatly 1 *Syn* LARGELY, chiefly, generally, mainly, mostly, principally 2 *Syn* VERY, awful, awfully, beastly, deadly, especially, exceedingly, extra, extremely, far, frightfully, full, heavily, highly, hugely, jolly, mightily, mighty, mortally, most, much, particularly, rattling, real, right, so, something, super, terribly, too, whacking *Ant* little, negligibly, nominally, slightly

greed · an intense selfish desire for wealth or possessions *Syn* acquisitiveness, avarice, avariciousness, avidity, covetousness, cupidity, greediness, rapaciousness, rapacity *Rel* materialism, possessiveness

greediness *Syn* GREED, acquisitiveness, avarice, avariciousness, avidity, covetousness, cupidity, rapaciousness, rapacity

greedy *Syn* COVETOUS, acquisitive, avaricious, grasping

green 1 *Syn* CALLOW, adolescent, immature, inexperienced, juvenile, puerile, raw, unfledged, unripe, unripened *Ant* adult, experienced, grown-up, mature, ripe 2 *Syn* RUDE (sense 1), callow, crude, raw, rough, uncouth *Ant* civil, urbane

greenhorn *Syn* BEGINNER, colt, fledgling, freshman, neophyte, newbie, newcomer, novice, recruit, rookie, tenderfoot, tyro *Ant* old hand, old-timer, vet, veteran

greet *Syn* ADDRESS, accost, hail, salute

greetings *Syn* COMPLIMENTS, congratulations, felicitations, regards, respects

gregarious *Syn* CONVIVIAL, boon, companionable, extroverted, outgoing, sociable, social *Ant* antisocial, introverted, reclusive, unsociable

griddle cake *Syn* PANCAKE, flapjack, hotcake, slapjack

grief *Syn* SORROW, anguish, heartache, heartbreak, regret, woe *Ant* joy

grieve · to feel or express sorrow or grief *Syn* mourn, sorrow *Rel* bear, endure, suffer *Ant* rejoice

grievous *Syn* REGRETTABLE, deplorable, distressful, distressing, heartbreaking, heartrending, lamentable, unfortunate, woeful

grill *Syn* RESTAURANT, café, diner

grim 1 · being extremely obdurate or firm in action or purpose *Syn* implacable, merciless, relentless, unrelenting *Rel* adamant, inexorable, inflexible, obdurate *Ant* lenient 2 *Syn* GHASTLY, grisly, gruesome, lurid, macabre

grimace · a twisting of the facial features in disgust or disapproval *Syn* face, frown, lower, mouth, pout, scowl *Rel* flinch, squinch, wince

grime *Syn* DIRTY, befoul, begrime, besmirch, blacken, foul, mire, muddy, smirch, smudge, soil, stain, sully *Ant* clean, cleanse

grin *n Syn* SMILE, simper, smirk *Ant* frown

grin *vb Syn* SMILE, simper, smirk *Ant* frown

grind *vb* 1 *Syn* POLISH, buff, burnish, dress, gloss, rub, shine, smooth 2 *Syn* SCRAPE, grate, rasp, scratch 3 *Syn* SHARPEN, edge, hone, strop, whet *Ant* blunt, dull

grind *n Syn* WORK (sense 1), drudgery, labor, toil, travail *Ant* play

grip 1 *Syn* COMPREHENSION, appreciation, apprehension, grasp, grip, understanding 2 *Syn* HOLD, clutch, grasp

gripe *Syn* COMPLAIN, beef, bellyache, carp, crab, croak, fuss, grouse, growl, grumble, kick, moan, murmur, mutter, repine, squawk, wail, whine, yammer *Ant* rejoice

griper *Syn* GROUCH, bear, complainer, crab, crank, croaker, curmudgeon, fusser, grouser, growler, grumbler, grump, murmurer, mutterer, whiner

gripping *Syn* INTERESTING, absorbing, arresting, engaging, engrossing, enthralling, fascinating, immersing, intriguing, involving, riveting *Ant* boring, drab, dry, dull, heavy, monotonous, tedious, uninteresting

grisly *Syn* GHASTLY, grim, gruesome, lurid, macabre

grit *Syn* FORTITUDE, backbone, guts, pluck, sand *Ant* pusillanimity

groan *n* **1** *Syn* LAMENT, howl, keen, lamentation, moan, plaint, wail *Ant* exultation, rejoicing **2** *Syn* SIGH, moan, sob

groan *vb Syn* SIGH, moan, sob

grog *Syn* ALCOHOL, booze, drink, intoxicant, liquor, moonshine, spirits

groggery *Syn* BARROOM, bar, café, grogshop, pub, saloon, tavern

grogshop *Syn* BARROOM, bar, café, groggery, pub, saloon, tavern

groovy *Syn* EXCELLENT, A1, bang-up, banner, capital, classic, crackerjack, dandy, divine, fabulous, fine, first-class, first-rate, grand, great, heavenly, jim-dandy, keen, marvelous (*or* marvellous), mean, neat, nifty, noble, par excellence, prime, sensational, splendid, stellar, sterling, superb, superior, superlative, supernal, swell, terrific, tip-top, top, top-notch, unsurpassed, wonderful *Ant* poor

gross 1 *Syn* COARSE, obscene, ribald, vulgar *Ant* fine, refined **2** *Syn* EGREGIOUS, blatant, conspicuous, flagrant, glaring, obvious, patent, pronounced, rank, striking **3** *Syn* FLAGRANT, glaring, rank **4** *Syn* WHOLE, all, entire, total *Ant* partial

grotesque *Syn* FANTASTIC, antic, bizarre

grouch · an irritable and complaining person *Syn* bear, complainer, crab, crank, croaker, curmudgeon, fusser, griper, grouser, growler, grumbler, grump, murmurer, mutterer, whiner *Rel* fulminator, malcontent, sorehead

ground *n* **1** *Syn* BASE, basis, foundation, groundwork *Ant* top **2** *Syn* REASON (sense 1), argument, proof

ground *vb Syn* BASE, found, rest, stay

grounded *Syn* AGROUND, beached, stranded *Ant* afloat

groundless 1 · having no basis in reason or fact *Syn* invalid, nonvalid, unfounded, ungrounded, unreasonable, unsubstantiated, unsupported, unwarranted *Rel* illogical, irrational, nonlogical, unconscionable, unsound *Ant* good, hard, just, justified, reasonable, reasoned, substantiated, valid, well-founded **2** *Syn* BASELESS, unfounded, unwarranted

ground rule *Syn* RULE (sense 1), bylaw, regulation

grounds *Syn* DEPOSIT, dregs, lees, precipitate, sediment

groundwork *Syn* BASE, basis, foundation, ground *Ant* top

group · a collection or assemblage of persons or things *Syn* bunch, cluster, lot, parcel *Rel* band, company, party, troop, troupe

grouse *Syn* COMPLAIN, beef, bellyache, carp, crab, croak, fuss, gripe, growl, grumble,

kick, moan, murmur, mutter, repine, squawk, wail, whine, yammer *Ant* rejoice

grouser *Syn* GROUCH, bear, complainer, crab, crank, croaker, curmudgeon, fusser, griper, growler, grumbler, grump, murmurer, mutterer, whiner

grovel *Syn* WALLOW, welter

grow *Syn* BECOME, come, get, go, run, turn, wax

growl 1 *Syn* BARK, bay, howl, snarl, yap, yelp **2** *Syn* COMPLAIN, beef, bellyache, carp, crab, croak, fuss, gripe, grouse, grumble, kick, moan, murmur, mutter, repine, squawk, wail, whine, yammer *Ant* rejoice

growler *Syn* GROUCH, bear, complainer, crab, crank, croaker, curmudgeon, fusser, griper, grouser, grumbler, grump, murmurer, mutterer, whiner

grown-up *Syn* MATURE, adult, matured, mellow, ripe *Ant* childish, immature

grub 1 *Syn* DIG, delve, excavate, spade **2** *Syn* LABOR, drudge, endeavor, hump, hustle, moil, peg (away), plod, plow, plug, slave, slog, strain, strive, struggle, sweat, toil, travail, work *Ant* dabble, fiddle (around), fool (around), mess (around), putter (around)

grubber *Syn* SLAVE (sense 2), drudge, drudger, laborer, peon, plugger, slogger, toiler, worker *Ant* freeman

grudge *vb Syn* COVET, begrudge, envy

grudge *n Syn* MALICE, despite, ill will, malevolence, malignancy, malignity, spite, spleen *Ant* charity

gruesome *Syn* GHASTLY, grim, grisly, lurid, macabre

gruff *Syn* BLUFF, blunt, brusque, crusty, curt *Ant* smooth, suave

grumble *Syn* COMPLAIN, beef, bellyache, carp, crab, croak, fuss, gripe, grouse, growl, kick, moan, murmur, mutter, repine, squawk, wail, whine, yammer *Ant* rejoice

grumbler *Syn* GROUCH, bear, complainer, crab, crank, croaker, curmudgeon, fusser, griper, grouser, growler, grump, murmurer, mutterer, whiner

grump *Syn* GROUCH, bear, complainer, crab, crank, croaker, curmudgeon, fusser, griper, grouser, growler, grumbler, murmurer, mutterer, whiner

guarantee *n* · an assurance for the fulfillment of a condition or a person who provides such assurance *Syn* bail, bond, guaranty, security, surety *Rel* earnest, pledge, token

guarantee *vb Syn* ENSURE, assure, cinch, guaranty, insure, secure

guarantor *Syn* SPONSOR, angel, backer, patron, surety

guaranty *vb Syn* ENSURE, assure, cinch, guarantee, insure, secure

guaranty *n Syn* GUARANTEE, bail, bond, security, surety

guard *vb Syn* DEFEND, protect, safeguard, shield *Ant* attack, combat

guard

guard *n* **1** *Syn* ESCORT, attendant, companion, guide **2** *Syn* PROTECTOR, custodian, defender, protection

guardianship *Syn* CUSTODY, care, keeping, safekeeping, trust, ward

guardrail *Syn* RAILING, balustrade, banister, rail

guardroom *Syn* JAIL, brig, hoosegow, jug, lockup, pen, penitentiary, prison, stockade

guess *vb* **1** *Syn* BELIEVE (sense 1), consider, deem, feel, figure, hold, imagine, suppose, think *Ant* disbelieve, discredit, reject **2** *Syn* ESTIMATE (sense 2), calculate, call, conjecture, figure, gauge, judge, make, place, put, reckon, suppose

guess *n* *Syn* CONJECTURE, supposition, surmise

guest *Syn* VISITOR, caller, visitant

guidance *Syn* ADVICE, counsel

guide *vb* • to put or lead on a course or into the way to be followed *Syn* engineer, lead, pilot, steer *Rel* accompany, chaperon, conduct, convoy, escort *Ant* misguide

guide *n* *Syn* ESCORT, attendant, companion, guard

guile *Syn* DECEIT, cunning, dissimulation, duplicity

guileful *Syn* SLY, artful, crafty, cunning, foxy, insidious, tricky, wily

guilelessly *Syn* NATURALLY (sense 3), artlessly, ingenuously, innocently, naively, sincerely, unaffectedly, unfeignedly, unpretentiously *Ant* affectedly, artificially, hypocritically, insincerely, pretentiously, unnaturally

guilt *Syn* BLAME, culpability, fault

guilty **1** • suffering from or expressive of a feeling of responsibility for wrongdoing *Syn* ashamed, contrite, hangdog, penitent, remorseful, repentant, shamed, shamefaced *Rel* apologetic, sorry *Ant* impenitent, remorseless, shameless, unashamed, unrepentant **2** *Syn* BLAMEWORTHY, culpable *Ant* blameless

gulch *Syn* CANYON, defile, flume, gap, gorge, gulf, notch, pass, ravine

gulf **1** • a hollow place of vast width and depth *Syn* abysm, abyss, chasm **2** *Syn* CANYON, defile, flume, gap, gorge, gulch, notch, pass, ravine

gull *vb* *Syn* DUPE, bamboozle, befool, hoax, hoodwink, trick

gull *n* *Syn* DUPE, chump, pigeon, sap, sucker, tool

gullibility *Syn* CREDULITY, credulousness, naivete *Ant* incredulity, skepticism

gumption **1** *Syn* COMMON SENSE, discreetness, discretion, horse sense, levelheadedness, prudence, sense, sensibleness, wisdom, wit *Ant* imprudence, indiscretion **2** *Syn* SENSE, common sense, good sense, horse sense, judgment, wisdom

gunman *Syn* ASSASSIN, bravo, cutthroat

gush **1** • to flow out in great quantities or with force *Syn* jet, pour, rush, spew, spout, spurt, squirt *Rel* cascade, issue, roll, run, stream *Ant* dribble, drip, drop, trickle **2** • to make an exaggerated display of affection or enthusiasm *Syn* enthuse, fuss, rave, rhapsodize, slobber *Rel* dote (on), fawn **3** *Syn* POUR, sluice, stream

gut *Syn* STOMACH, abdomen, belly, solar plexus, tummy

guts **1** *Syn* COURAGE, bravery, courageousness, daring, dauntlessness, doughtiness, fearlessness, gallantry, greatheartedness, hardihood, heart, heroism, intrepidity, intrepidness, nerve, stoutness, valor *Ant* cowardice, cowardliness, cravenness, dastardliness, spinelessness, yellowness **2** *Syn* FORTITUDE, backbone, grit, pluck, sand *Ant* pusillanimity

guy *Syn* MAN (sense 1), dude, fellow, gent, gentleman, male

gyrate *Syn* TURN (sense 1), circle, eddy, pirouette, revolve, rotate, spin, swirl, twirl, wheel, whirl

H

habit **1** • a usual manner of behaving or doing *Syn* custom, fashion, pattern, practice, trick, way, wont *Rel* addiction **2** *Syn* PHYSIQUE, build, constitution

habitant *Syn* INHABITANT, denizen, dweller, occupant, resident, resider *Ant* transient

habitat • the place in which a particular kind of organism lives or grows *Syn* biotope, range, station

habitation • the place where one lives *Syn* abode, domicile, dwelling, home, house, residence

habitual *Syn* USUAL, accustomed, customary, wonted

habituate • to make used to something *Syn* accustom, addict, inure *Rel* discipline, school, teach, train

habituated *Syn* ACCUSTOMED, given, used, wont *Ant* unaccustomed, unused

habitué *Syn* ADDICT, devotee, votary

hacienda *Syn* MANSION, castle, château, countryseat, estate, hall, manor, manor house, palace, villa

hack *Syn* MERCENARY, hireling

hackney *Syn* STALE, banal, commonplace, hackneyed, moth-eaten, musty, stereotyped, threadbare, tired, trite *Ant* fresh, new, original

hackneyed *Syn* STALE, banal, commonplace, hackney, moth-eaten, musty, stereotyped, threadbare, tired, trite *Ant* fresh, new, original

Hadean *Syn* INFERNAL, chthonian, chthonic, hellish, stygian, Tartarean *Ant* supernal

haggard · thin and drawn by or as if by worry, fatigue, hunger, or illness *Syn* cadaverous, careworn, pinched, wasted, worn *Rel* gaunt, lean, scrawny, skinny

haggle *Syn* BARGAIN, chaffer, deal, dicker, horse-trade, negotiate, palter

hail *vb* **1** *Syn* ACCLAIM, applaud, cheer, laud, praise, salute, tout *Ant* knock, pan, slam **2** *Syn* ADDRESS, accost, greet, salute

hail *n* **1** *Syn* BARRAGE, bombardment, cannonade, fusillade, salvo, shower, storm, volley **2** *Syn* RAIN (sense 2), shower, storm

hairy 1 · covered with or as if with hair *Syn* bristly, fleecy, furry, hirsute, rough, shaggy, unshorn, woolly *Rel* bearded, mustachioed, whiskered *Ant* bald, furless, hairless, shorn, smooth **2** · made of or resembling hair *Syn* furry, fuzzy, rough, shaggy, woolly *Rel* downy, fluffy, nappy

halcyon *Syn* CALM, peaceful, placid, serene, tranquil *Ant* agitated, stormy

hale *adj Syn* HEALTHY, robust, sound, well, wholesome *Ant* unhealthy

hale *vb Syn* PULL, drag, draw, haul, tow, tug

halfway *Syn* MIDDLE, intermediary, intermediate, medial, median, medium, mid, middlemost, midmost, midway *Ant* extreme, farthermost, farthest, furthermost, furthest, outermost, outmost, remotest, utmost

half-wit *Syn* FOOL (sense 2), booby, goose, jackass, lunatic, nincompoop, ninny, nitwit, nut, simpleton, turkey, yo-yo

hall 1 *Syn* MANSION, castle, château, countryseat, estate, hacienda, manor, manor house, palace, villa **2** *Syn* PASSAGE, aisle, arcade, cloister, corridor, gallery, hallway, passageway

hallow *Syn* DEVOTE, consecrate, dedicate

hallowed *Syn* HOLY (sense 2), blessed, consecrated, sacred, sacrosanct, sanctified *Ant* unconsecrated, unhallowed

hallowing *Syn* CONSECRATION, blessing, sanctification

hallucination *Syn* DELUSION, illusion, mirage

hallway *Syn* PASSAGE, aisle, arcade, cloister, corridor, gallery, hall, passageway

hamper · to hinder or impede in moving, progressing, or acting freely *Syn* clog, fetter, hog-tie, manacle, shackle, trammel *Rel* bar, block, hinder, impede, obstruct *Ant* assist (*persons*), expedite (*work, projects*)

hams *Syn* BUTTOCKS, backside, bottom, breech, butt, fanny, haunches, posterior, rear, rump, seat

hand *n Syn* WORKER, artisan, craftsman, handicraftsman, laborer, mechanic, operative, roustabout, workingman, workman *Ant* idler

hand *vb Syn* FURNISH (sense 2), deliver, feed, give, hand over, provide, supply *Ant* hold (back), keep (back), reserve, retain, withhold

handbag *Syn* PURSE, bag, pocketbook

handicap 1 *Syn* ADVANTAGE, allowance, edge, odds *Ant* disadvantage, handicap **2** *Syn* DISADVANTAGE, drawback, liability, minus, penalty, strike *Ant* advantage, asset, edge, plus **3** *Syn* ENCUMBRANCE, bar, block, chain, clog, crimp, deterrent, drag, embarrassment, fetter, hindrance, hurdle, impediment, inhibition, interference, let, manacle, obstacle, obstruction, shackles, stop, stumbling block, trammel *Ant* aid, assistance, benefit, help

handicraft *Syn* TRADE, art, craft, profession

handicrafter *Syn* ARTISAN, artificer, craftsman, tradesman

handicraftsman *Syn* WORKER, artisan, craftsman, hand, laborer, mechanic, operative, roustabout, workingman, workman *Ant* idler

handily *Syn* EASILY, effortlessly, facilely, fluently, freely, lightly, painlessly, readily, smoothly *Ant* arduously, laboriously

handkerchief *Syn* BANDANNA, babushka, kerchief, mantilla

handle 1 · to deal with or manage usually with dexterity or efficiency *Syn* manipulate, ply, swing, wield *Rel* brandish, flourish, shake, swing, wave **2** *Syn* TOUCH, feel, palpate, paw **3** *Syn* TREAT, deal

hand over *Syn* FURNISH (sense 2), deliver, feed, give, hand, provide, supply *Ant* hold (back), keep (back), reserve, retain, withhold

handsome 1 *Syn* BEAUTIFUL, attractive, beauteous, comely, cute, fair, gorgeous, knockout, lovely, pretty, ravishing, sightly, stunning, taking *Ant* homely, ill-favored, plain, ugly, unattractive, unbeautiful, unhandsome, unlovely, unpretty, unsightly **2** *Syn* LARGE, big, bulky, considerable, goodly, good-sized, grand, great, hefty, hulking, largish, outsize, oversize (*or* oversized), sizable (*or* sizeable), substantial, tidy, voluminous *Ant* little, puny, small, undersized **3** *Syn* LIBERAL (sense 1), bounteous, bountiful, generous, munificent, openhanded *Ant* close

handsomeness *Syn* ELEGANCE, class, elegancy, grace, gracefulness, majesty, refinement, stateliness

hang 1 · to place or be placed so as to be supported at one point or side usually at the top *Syn* dangle, sling, suspend *Rel* adhere, cling, stick **2** *Syn* DEPEND (sense 1), hinge, turn

hangdog *Syn* GUILTY, ashamed, contrite,

penitent, remorseful, repentant, shamed, shamefaced *Ant* impenitent, remorseless, shameless, unashamed, unrepentant

hanger-on *Syn* PARASITE, bootlicker, favorite, leech, lickspittle, sponge, sponger, sycophant, toady

hangout · a place for spending time or for socializing *Syn* haunt, rendezvous, resort *Rel* camp, canteen, club, clubhouse, den, harbor, haven, nest, refuge, retreat

hanker *Syn* LONG, hunger, pine, thirst, yearn

hanky-panky *Syn* TRICKERY, artifice, chicanery, jugglery, legerdemain, subterfuge, wile

hap *Syn* CHANCE, accident, fortune, hazard, luck *Ant* law, principle

haphazard *adv Syn* HIT OR MISS, aimlessly, anyhow, anyway, anywise, desultorily, erratically, haphazardly, helter-skelter, irregularly, randomly *Ant* methodically, systematically

haphazard *adj Syn* RANDOM, casual, chance, chancy, desultory, happy-go-lucky, hit-or-miss *Ant* methodical, nonrandom, orderly, systematic

haphazardly *Syn* HIT OR MISS, aimlessly, anyhow, anyway, anywise, desultorily, erratically, haphazard, helter-skelter, irregularly, randomly *Ant* methodically, systematically

hapless *Syn* UNLUCKY, calamitous, disastrous, ill-fated, ill-starred, luckless, unfortunate *Ant* fortunate, happy, lucky

happen · to come to pass or to come about *Syn* befall, betide, chance, occur, transpire

happen (on or upon) · to come upon unexpectedly or by chance *Syn* chance (upon), encounter, find, hit (upon), meet, stumble (on *or* onto) *Rel* confront, face

happily *Syn* PROPERLY, appropriately, congruously, correctly, fittingly, meetly, rightly, suitably *Ant* improperly, inappropriately, incongruously, incorrectly, unsuitably, wrongly

happiness · a state of well-being or pleasurable satisfaction *Syn* beatitude, blessedness, bliss, felicity *Rel* content, contentedness, satisfaction, satisfiedness *Ant* unhappiness

happy **1** *Syn* CONTENT, contented, gratified, pleased, satisfied *Ant* discontent, discontented, displeased, dissatisfied, malcontent, unhappy **2** *Syn* FIT, appropriate, apt, felicitous, fitting, meet, proper, suitable *Ant* unfit **3** *Syn* GLAD, cheerful, joyful, joyous, lighthearted *Ant* sad **4** *Syn* LUCKY, fortunate, providential *Ant* unlucky

happy-go-lucky **1** *Syn* CAREFREE, careless, cavalier, devil-may-care, easygoing, gay, insouciant, lighthearted, unconcerned *Ant* careworn **2** *Syn* RANDOM, casual, chance, chancy, desultory, haphazard, hit-or-miss *Ant* methodical, nonrandom, orderly, systematic

harangue *Syn* SPEECH, address, homily, lecture, oration, sermon, talk

harass *Syn* WORRY, annoy, harry, pester, plague, tantalize, tease

harbinger *Syn* FORERUNNER, herald, precursor

harbor *n* · a place where seacraft may ride secure *Syn* haven, port

harbor *vb* · to provide with shelter or refuge *Syn* board, entertain, house, lodge, shelter *Rel* cherish, foster, nurse, nurture

hard **1** · demanding great toil or effort *Syn* arduous, difficult *Rel* burdensome, exacting, onerous, oppressive *Ant* easy **2** *Syn* FIRM, solid *Ant* flabby, loose **3** *Syn* OBSTINATE, adamant, adamantine, dogged, hardened, hardheaded, hardhearted, headstrong, immovable, implacable, inflexible, mulish, obdurate, opinionated, ossified, pat, peevish, pertinacious, perverse, pigheaded, rigid, self-willed, stubborn, unbending, uncompromising, unrelenting, unyielding, willful (*or* wilful) *Ant* acquiescent, agreeable, amenable, compliant, complying, flexible, pliable, pliant, relenting, yielding

harden **1** · to make or to become physically hard or solid *Syn* cake, indurate, petrify, solidify *Rel* compact, concentrate, consolidate *Ant* soften **2** · to make proof against hardship, strain, or exposure *Syn* acclimate, acclimatize, season *Rel* accustom, habituate, inure *Ant* soften

hardened **1** · grown or become hard *Syn* callous, indurated *Rel* compacted, concentrated, consolidated *Ant* softened **2** *Syn* OBSTINATE, adamant, adamantine, dogged, hard, hardheaded, hardhearted, headstrong, immovable, implacable, inflexible, mulish, obdurate, opinionated, ossified, pat, peevish, pertinacious, perverse, pigheaded, rigid, self-willed, stubborn, unbending, uncompromising, unrelenting, unyielding, willful (*or* wilful) *Ant* acquiescent, agreeable, amenable, compliant, complying, flexible, pliable, pliant, relenting, yielding

hardheaded *Syn* OBSTINATE, adamant, adamantine, dogged, hard, hardened, hardhearted, headstrong, immovable, implacable, inflexible, mulish, obdurate, opinionated, ossified, pat, peevish, pertinacious, perverse, pigheaded, rigid, self-willed, stubborn, unbending, uncompromising, unrelenting, unyielding, willful (*or* wilful) *Ant* acquiescent, agreeable, amenable, compliant, complying, flexible, pliable, pliant, relenting, yielding

hardhearted *Syn* OBSTINATE, adamant, adamantine, dogged, hard, hardened, hardheaded, headstrong, immovable, implacable, inflexible, mulish, obdurate, opinionated, ossified, pat, peevish, pertinacious, perverse, pigheaded, rigid, self-willed, stubborn, unbending, uncompromising, unrelenting, unyielding, willful (*or* wilful) *Ant* acquiescent, agreeable, amenable, compliant, complying, flexible, pliable, pliant, relenting, yielding

hardihood *Syn* COURAGE, bravery, courageousness, daring, dauntlessness, doughtiness, fearlessness, gallantry, greatheartedness, guts, heart, heroism, intrepidity, intrepidness, nerve, stoutness, valor *Ant* cowardice, cowardliness, cravenness, dastardliness, spinelessness, yellowness

hardness *Syn* SEVERITY, harshness, inflexibility, rigidity, rigidness, rigorousness, sternness, strictness *Ant* flexibility, gentleness, laxness, mildness

hardship *Syn* DIFFICULTY, rigor, vicissitude

hark *Syn* LISTEN, attend, hear, hearken, heed, mind *Ant* ignore, tune out

harm *vb* *Syn* INJURE, damage, hurt, impair, mar, spoil *Ant* aid

harm *n* *Syn* INJURY, damage, hurt, mischief

harmful · causing or capable of causing harm *Syn* adverse, bad, baleful, baneful, damaging, deleterious, detrimental, evil, hurtful, ill, injurious, mischievous, noxious, pernicious, prejudicial *Rel* hostile, inimical, unfriendly *Ant* harmless, innocent, innocuous, inoffensive, safe

harmless · not having hurtful or injurious qualities *Syn* innocent, innocuous, inoffensive, unoffending *Ant* harmful

harmonious *Syn* CONSISTENT, compatible, conformable (to), congruous, consonant, correspondent (with *or* to), nonconflicting *Ant* conflicting, incompatible, incongruous, inconsistent, inharmonious, unharmonious

harmonize **1** · to bring into consonance or accord *Syn* attune, tune *Rel* adapt, adjust, reconcile **2** *Syn* AGREE (sense 2), accord, conform, correspond, jibe, square, tally *Ant* differ (from)

harmony **1** · the effect produced when different things come together without clashing or disagreement *Syn* accord, concord, consonance *Rel* articulation, concatenation, integration *Ant* conflict **2** *Syn* SYMMETRY, balance, proportion

harrow *Syn* AFFLICT, agonize, bedevil, curse, martyr, persecute, plague, rack, torment, torture

harry *Syn* WORRY, annoy, harass, pester, plague, tantalize, tease

harsh *Syn* ROUGH, rugged, scabrous, uneven *Ant* smooth

harshness *Syn* SEVERITY, hardness, inflexibility, rigidity, rigidness, rigorousness, sternness, strictness *Ant* flexibility, gentleness, laxness, mildness

harvest *Syn* REAP, garner, gather, glean

hash **1** *Syn* CHOP, dice, mince **2** *Syn* DISORDER, confuse, derange, disarrange, disarray, discompose, dishevel, dislocate, disorganize, disrupt, disturb, jumble, mess (up), mix (up), muddle, muss, rumple, scramble, shuffle, tousle, tumble, upset *Ant* arrange, array, draw up, marshal, order, organize, range, regulate, straighten (up), tidy

haste · rapidity of motion or action *Syn* dispatch, expedition, hurry, speed *Rel* alacrity, celerity, legerity *Ant* deliberation

hasten **1** *Syn* HURRY (sense 1), accelerate, quicken, rush, speed (up), whisk *Ant* decelerate, retard, slow (down) **2** *Syn* HURRY (sense 2), barrel, bolt, bowl, breeze, career, course, dash, fly, hotfoot (it), hump, hurtle, hustle, pelt, race, rip, rocket, run, rush, rustle, scoot, scurry, scuttle, shoot, speed, step (along), tear, trot, whirl, whisk, zip, zoom *Ant* crawl, creep, poke

hasty **1** *Syn* FAST, expeditious, fleet, quick, rapid, speedy, swift *Ant* slow **2** *Syn* PRECIPITATE, abrupt, headlong, impetuous, sudden *Ant* deliberate

hate *vb* · to feel extreme enmity or dislike *Syn* abhor, abominate, detest, loathe *Rel* contemn, despise, disdain, scorn *Ant* love

hate *n* *Syn* ABHORRENCE, abomination, detestation, hatred, loathing *Ant* admiration, enjoyment

hateful · deserving of or arousing hate *Syn* abhorrent, abominable, detestable, odious *Rel* antipathetic, averse, unsympathetic *Ant* lovable, sympathetic

hatred *Syn* ABHORRENCE, abomination, detestation, hate, loathing *Ant* admiration, enjoyment

haughtiness *Syn* ARROGANCE, imperiousness, loftiness, lordliness, masterfulness, peremptoriness, pompousness, presumptuousness, pretense (*or* pretence), pretension, pretentiousness, self-importance, superciliousness, superiority *Ant* humility, modesty

haughty **1** *Syn* ARROGANT, cavalier, highfalutin, high-handed, high-hat, imperious, important, lofty, lordly, masterful, overweening, peremptory, pompous, presumptuous, pretentious, supercilious, superior, uppish, uppity *Ant* humble, modest **2** *Syn* PROUD (sense 1), arrogant, disdainful, insolent, lordly, overbearing, supercilious *Ant* ashamed, humble

haul *Syn* PULL, drag, draw, hale, tow, tug

haunches *Syn* BUTTOCKS, backside, bottom, breech, butt, fanny, hams, posterior, rear, rump, seat

haunt *Syn* HANGOUT, rendezvous, resort

haunting *Syn* EERIE, creepy, spooky, uncanny, unearthly, weird

have · to keep, control, or experience as one's own *Syn* enjoy, hold, own, possess

haven *Syn* HARBOR, port

have (to) *Syn* NEED (sense 1), must, ought (to), shall, should *Ant* have, hold

havoc *Syn* DESTRUCTION, annihilation, decimation, demolishment, demolition, desolation, devastation, extermination, extinction, loss, obliteration, ruin, ruination, wastage, wreckage *Ant* building, construction, erection, raising

hazard *n* **1** *Syn* CHANCE, accident, fortune, hap, luck *Ant* law, principle **2** *Syn* DANGER (sense 1), menace, peril, pitfall, risk, threat, trouble *Ant* safeness, safety, security

hazard *vb* *Syn* ENDANGER, adventure, compromise, gamble (with), imperil, jeopardize, menace, risk, venture

hazardous *Syn* DANGEROUS, perilous, precarious, risky *Ant* safe, secure

haze **1** · an atmospheric condition in which suspended particles in the air rob it of its transparency *Syn* fog, mist, murk, reek, smog, soup *Rel* cloud, fume, miasma, smoke, steam **2** · a state of mental confusion *Syn* daze, fog, muddle, spin *Rel* reverie, stupor, trance

hazed *Syn* OVERCAST, beclouded, clouded, cloudy, dull, hazy, heavy, lowering, overclouded *Ant* clear, cloudless

hazy *Syn* OVERCAST, beclouded, clouded, cloudy, dull, hazed, heavy, lowering, overclouded *Ant* clear, cloudless

head *adj* · highest in rank or authority *Syn* chief, commanding, first, foremost, high, lead, leading, managing, preeminent, premier, presiding, primary, prime, principal, supreme *Rel* high-level, senior

head *n* **1** *Syn* BOSS, captain, chief, foreman, headman, helmsman, kingpin, leader, master, taskmaster **2** *Syn* CHIEF, chieftain, headman, leader, master

headlong *Syn* PRECIPITATE, abrupt, hasty, impetuous, sudden *Ant* deliberate

headman **1** *Syn* BOSS, captain, chief, foreman, head, helmsman, kingpin, leader, master, taskmaster **2** *Syn* CHIEF, chieftain, head, leader, master

headstrong **1** *Syn* OBSTINATE, adamant, adamantine, dogged, hard, hardened, hardheaded, hardhearted, immovable, implacable, inflexible, mulish, obdurate, opinionated, ossified, pat, peevish, pertinacious, perverse, pigheaded, rigid, self-willed, stubborn, unbending, uncompromising, unrelenting, unyielding, willful (*or* wilful) *Ant* acquiescent, agreeable, amenable, compliant, complying, flexible, pliable, pliant, relenting, yielding **2** *Syn* UNCONTROLLABLE, froward, intractable, recalcitrant, refractory, ungovernable, unmanageable, unruly, untoward, wayward, willful (*or* wilful) *Ant* controllable, governable, tractable **3** *Syn* UNRULY, intractable, recalcitrant, refractory, ungovernable, willful *Ant* docile, tractable

headway **1** *Syn* ADVANCE (sense 2), advancement, furtherance, going, march, onrush, passage, process, procession, progress, progression *Ant* recession, regression, retrogression **2** *Syn* SPEED, impetus, momentum, pace, velocity

heal **1** *Syn* CONVALESCE, gain, mend, rally, recover, recuperate, snap back **2** *Syn* CURE, remedy

health · the condition of being sound in body *Syn* fitness, healthiness, heartiness, robustness, soundness, wellness, wholeness, wholesomeness *Rel* fettle, shape *Ant* illness, sickness, unhealthiness, unsoundness

healthful · conducive or beneficial to the health or soundness of body or mind *Syn* healthy, hygienic, salubrious, salutary, sanitary, wholesome *Rel* advantageous, beneficial, profitable

healthiness *Syn* HEALTH, fitness, heartiness, robustness, soundness, wellness, wholeness, wholesomeness *Ant* illness, sickness, unhealthiness, unsoundness

healthy **1** · having or manifesting health of mind or body or indicative of such health *Syn* hale, robust, sound, well, wholesome *Rel* energetic, lusty, vigorous *Ant* unhealthy **2** *Syn* HEALTHFUL, hygienic, salubrious, salutary, sanitary, wholesome

heap *n* · a quantity of things brought together into a more or less compact group *Syn* bank, cock, mass, pile, shock, stack *Rel* aggregate, aggregation, conglomerate, conglomeration

heap *vb* · to bring a number of things together into a more or less compact group or collection *Syn* bank, cock, mass, pile, shock, stack *Rel* accumulate, amass, hoard

hear *Syn* LISTEN, attend, hark, hearken, heed, mind *Ant* ignore, tune out

hearken *Syn* LISTEN, attend, hark, hear, heed, mind *Ant* ignore, tune out

hearsay *Syn* REPORT, gossip, rumor

heart **1** *Syn* CENTER (sense 2), base, capital, core, cynosure, eye, focus, hub, mecca, nucleus, seat **2** *Syn* COURAGE, bravery, courageousness, daring, dauntlessness, doughtiness, fearlessness, gallantry, greatheartedness, guts, hardihood, heroism, intrepidity, intrepidness, nerve, stoutness, valor *Ant* cowardice, cowardliness, cravenness, dastardliness, spinelessness, yellowness **3** *Syn* CRUX, core, gist, nub, pith, pivot

heartache *Syn* SORROW, anguish, grief, heartbreak, regret, woe *Ant* joy

heartbreak *Syn* SORROW, anguish, grief, heartache, regret, woe *Ant* joy

heartbreaking **1** *Syn* REGRETTABLE, deplorable, distressful, distressing, grievous, heartrending, lamentable, unfortunate, woeful **2** *Syn* SAD (sense 2), depressing, dismal, drear, dreary, heartrending, melancholy, pathetic, saddening, sorry, tearful, teary *Ant* cheering, cheery, glad, happy

heartbroken *Syn* SAD (sense 1), bad, blue, brokenhearted, crestfallen, dejected, depressed, despondent, disconsolate, doleful, down, downcast, downhearted, droopy, forlorn, gloomy, glum, heartsick, heartsore, inconsolable, joyless, low, low-spirited, melancholy, miserable, mournful, saddened, sorrowful, sorry, unhappy, woebegone, woeful, wretched *Ant* blissful, buoyant, buoyed, cheerful, cheery, chipper, delighted, glad, gladdened, gladsome, gleeful, happy, joyful, joyous, jubilant, sunny, upbeat

hearten *Syn* ENCOURAGE, cheer, embolden, inspirit, nerve, steel *Ant* discourage

heartening *Syn* HEARTWARMING, cheering, comforting, encouraging, fulfilling, gladdening, gratifying, rewarding, satisfying *Ant* depressing, discouraging, disheartening, dispiriting

heartfelt *Syn* SINCERE, hearty, unfeigned, wholehearted, whole-souled *Ant* insincere

heartiness *Syn* HEALTH, fitness, healthiness, robustness, soundness, wellness, wholeness, wholesomeness *Ant* illness, sickness, unhealthiness, unsoundness

heartlessness *Syn* CRUELTY, barbarity, brutality, cruelness, inhumanity, sadism, savageness, savagery, viciousness, wantonness *Ant* benignity, compassion, good-heartedness, humanity, kindheartedness, kindness, sympathy

heartrending **1** *Syn* REGRETTABLE, deplorable, distressful, distressing, grievous, heartbreaking, lamentable, unfortunate, woeful **2** *Syn* SAD (sense 2), depressing, dismal, drear, dreary, heartbreaking, melancholy, pathetic, saddening, sorry, tearful, teary *Ant* cheering, cheery, glad, happy

heartsick *Syn* SAD (sense 1), bad, blue, brokenhearted, crestfallen, dejected, depressed, despondent, disconsolate, doleful, down, downcast, downhearted, droopy, forlorn, gloomy, glum, heartbroken, heartsore, inconsolable, joyless, low, low-spirited, melancholy, miserable, mournful, saddened, sorrowful, sorry, unhappy, woebegone, woeful, wretched *Ant* blissful, buoyant, buoyed, cheerful, cheery, chipper, delighted, glad, gladdened, gladsome, gleeful, happy, joyful, joyous, jubilant, sunny, upbeat

heartsickness *Syn* SADNESS, blues, dejection, depression, desolation, despondency, disconsolateness, dispiritedness, doldrums, downheartedness, dreariness, dumps, forlornness, gloom, gloominess, joylessness, melancholy, mopes, oppression, unhappiness *Ant* bliss, blissfulness, ecstasy, elatedness, elation, euphoria, exhilaration, exuberance, exultation, felicity, gladness, gladsomeness, happiness, heaven, intoxication, joy, joyfulness, joyousness, jubilation, rapture, rapturousness

heartsore *Syn* SAD (sense 1), bad, blue, brokenhearted, crestfallen, dejected, depressed, despondent, disconsolate, doleful, down, downcast, downhearted, droopy, forlorn,

gloomy, glum, heartbroken, heartsick, inconsolable, joyless, low, low-spirited, melancholy, miserable, mournful, saddened, sorrowful, sorry, unhappy, woebegone, woeful, wretched *Ant* blissful, buoyant, buoyed, cheerful, cheery, chipper, delighted, glad, gladdened, gladsome, gleeful, happy, joyful, joyous, jubilant, sunny, upbeat

heartwarming · making one feel good inside *Syn* cheering, comforting, encouraging, fulfilling, gladdening, gratifying, heartening, rewarding, satisfying *Rel* affecting, inspiring, moving, poignant, stirring, touching *Ant* depressing, discouraging, disheartening, dispiriting

hearty *Syn* SINCERE, heartfelt, unfeigned, wholehearted, whole-souled *Ant* insincere

heave *Syn* LIFT, boost, elevate, hoist, raise, rear *Ant* lower

heaven *Syn* ECSTASY, elation, euphoria, exhilaration, intoxication, paradise, rapture, rhapsody, transport *Ant* depression

heavenly **1** *Syn* CELESTIAL, Elysian, empyreal, empyrean, supernal *Ant* hellish, infernal **2** *Syn* EXCELLENT, A1, bang-up, banner, capital, classic, crackerjack, dandy, divine, fabulous, fine, first-class, first-rate, grand, great, groovy, jim-dandy, keen, marvelous (*or* marvellous), mean, neat, nifty, noble, par excellence, prime, sensational, splendid, stellar, sterling, superb, superior, superlative, supernal, swell, terrific, tip-top, top, top-notch, unsurpassed, wonderful *Ant* poor

heavily *Syn* VERY, awful, awfully, beastly, deadly, especially, exceedingly, extra, extremely, far, frightfully, full, greatly, highly, hugely, jolly, mightily, mighty, mortally, most, much, particularly, rattling, real, right, so, something, super, terribly, too, whacking *Ant* little, negligibly, nominally, slightly

heavy **1** · having great weight *Syn* cumbersome, cumbrous, hefty, ponderous, weighty *Rel* firm, hard, solid *Ant* light **2** *Syn* BORING, drab, dreary, dry, dull, flat, humdrum, jading, leaden, monotonous, pedestrian, ponderous, stodgy, stuffy, stupid, tame, tedious, tiresome, tiring, unanimated, uninteresting, wearisome, weary, wearying *Ant* absorbing, engaging, engrossing, gripping, interesting, intriguing, involving **3** *Syn* OVERCAST, beclouded, clouded, cloudy, dull, hazed, hazy, lowering, overclouded *Ant* clear, cloudless

heckle *Syn* BAIT, badger, chivy, hector, hound, ride

hector *Syn* BAIT, badger, chivy, heckle, hound, ride

hedge *Syn* BARRIER, barricade, fence, wall

heed *n Syn* ATTENTION (sense 2), awareness, cognizance, ear, eye, notice, observance, observation

heed *vb Syn* LISTEN, attend, hark, hear, hearken, mind *Ant* ignore, tune out

heedless *Syn* CARELESS, inadvertent, thoughtless *Ant* careful

hefty 1 *Syn* HEAVY, cumbersome, cumbrous, ponderous, weighty *Ant* light **2** *Syn* LARGE, big, bulky, considerable, goodly, good-sized, grand, great, handsome, hulking, largish, outsize, oversize (*or* oversized), sizable (*or* sizeable), substantial, tidy, voluminous *Ant* little, puny, small, undersized

height 1 · the distance a thing rises above the level on which it stands *Syn* altitude, elevation **2** *Syn* THICK, deep, depth, middle, midst

heighten *Syn* INTENSIFY, aggravate, enhance *Ant* abate, allay, mitigate, temper

heinous *Syn* OUTRAGEOUS, atrocious, monstrous

helical *Syn* SPIRAL, coiling, corkscrew, screwlike, winding

hell *Syn* MADHOUSE, babel, bedlam, circus

hellish *Syn* INFERNAL, chthonian, chthonic, Hadean, stygian, Tartarean *Ant* supernal

helmsman *Syn* BOSS, captain, chief, foreman, head, headman, kingpin, leader, master, taskmaster

help *n* · an act or instance of giving what will benefit or assist *Syn* aid, assistance *Rel* cooperation, union, uniting

help *vb* **1** · to give assistance or support *Syn* aid, assist *Rel* back, champion, support, uphold *Ant* hinder **2** *Syn* IMPROVE (sense 1), ameliorate, better *Ant* impair, worsen **3** *Syn* PREVENT (sense 2), avert, forestall, obviate, preclude

helper *Syn* ASSISTANT, adjutant, aid, aide, apprentice, coadjutor, deputy, sidekick

helpful *Syn* BENEFICIAL, advantageous, favorable, profitable, salutary *Ant* disadvantageous, unfavorable, unhelpful

helpless *Syn* POWERLESS, impotent, weak *Ant* mighty, potent, powerful, puissant, strong

helter-skelter *Syn* HIT OR MISS, aimlessly, anyhow, anyway, anywise, desultorily, erratically, haphazard, haphazardly, irregularly, randomly *Ant* methodically, systematically

hem *Syn* SURROUND, circle, compass, encircle, encompass, environ, gird, girdle, ring

hence *Syn* THEREFORE, accordingly, consequently, so, then

herald *Syn* FORERUNNER (sense 1), harbinger, precursor

Herculean *Syn* HUGE, Brobdingnagian, colossal, cyclopean, elephantine, enormous, gargantuan, giant, gigantean, gigantic, immense, mammoth, titanic, vast *Ant* bitty, diminutive, microscopic (*or* microscopical), midget, miniature, minute, pocket, pygmy, teeny, teeny-weeny, tiny, wee

hereditary *Syn* INNATE, congenital, inborn, inbred, inherited *Ant* acquired

heresy · departure from a generally accepted theory, opinion, or practice *Syn* dissent, dissidence, heterodoxy, nonconformity *Rel* error, fallacy, falsehood, misbelief, misconception, myth *Ant* conformity, orthodoxy

heretic · one who believes, teaches, or advocates something opposed to accepted beliefs *Syn* dissenter, dissident, nonconformist *Rel* apostate, defector, renegade, schismatic, separationist, separatist *Ant* conformer, conformist

heritage · something which one receives or is entitled to receive by succession *Syn* birthright, inheritance, patrimony

hermit *Syn* RECLUSE, anchorite, cenobite, eremite

heroism 1 · conspicuous courage or bravery *Syn* gallantry, prowess, valor *Rel* bravery, dauntlessness, doughtiness, intrepidity **2** *Syn* COURAGE, bravery, courageousness, daring, dauntlessness, doughtiness, fearlessness, gallantry, greatheartedness, guts, hardihood, heart, intrepidity, intrepidness, nerve, stoutness, valor *Ant* cowardice, cowardliness, cravenness, dastardliness, spinelessness, yellowness

hesitance 1 *Syn* HESITATION, faltering, hesitancy, indecision, irresolution, shilly-shallying, vacillation, wavering, wobbling **2** *Syn* RELUCTANCE, disinclination, hesitancy, unwillingness *Ant* inclination, willingness

hesitancy 1 *Syn* HESITATION, faltering, hesitance, indecision, irresolution, shilly-shallying, vacillation, wavering, wobbling **2** *Syn* RELUCTANCE, disinclination, hesitance, unwillingness *Ant* inclination, willingness

hesitant *Syn* DISINCLINED, averse, indisposed, loath, reluctant

hesitate · to show irresolution or uncertainty *Syn* falter, vacillate, waver *Rel* balk, boggle, demur, scruple, shy, stick, stickle *Ant* dive (in), plunge (in)

hesitation · the act or an instance of pausing because of uncertainty about the right course of action *Syn* faltering, hesitance, hesitancy, indecision, irresolution, shilly-shallying, vacillation, wavering, wobbling *Rel* delay, hawing, procrastination, waiting

heterodoxy *Syn* HERESY, dissent, dissidence, nonconformity *Ant* conformity, orthodoxy

heterogeneous *Syn* MISCELLANEOUS, assorted, motley, promiscuous

hew *Syn* CUT, carve, chop, slash, slit

hiatus *Syn* BREAK, gap, interim, interruption, interval, lacuna

hick · an awkward or simple person especially from a small town or the country *Syn* bumpkin, clodhopper, countryman, provincial, rustic, yokel *Rel* boor, clod, gawk, lout, oaf *Ant* cosmopolitan, sophisticate

hide *vb* · to withdraw or to withhold from sight or observation *Syn* bury, cache, conceal, ensconce, screen, secrete *Rel* camouflage, cloak, disguise, dissemble, mask

hide *n Syn* SKIN, bark, peel, pelt, rind

hideous *Syn* UGLY, ill-favored, unsightly *Ant* beautiful

higgledy-piggledy *Syn* MESSY, chaotic, cluttered, confused, disarranged, disarrayed, disheveled (*or* dishevelled), disordered, disorderly, hugger-mugger, jumbled, littered, messed, muddled, mussed, mussy, pell-mell, rumpled, sloppy, topsy-turvy, tousled, tumbled, unkempt, untidy, upside-down *Ant* neat, ordered, orderly, organized, shipshape, snug, tidied, tidy, trim

high **1** · having a relatively great upward extension *Syn* lofty, tall *Rel* elevated, lifted, raised, reared *Ant* low **2** · in a luxurious manner *Syn* expensively, extravagantly, grandly, lavishly, luxuriously, opulently, richly, sumptuously *Rel* imposingly, impressively, magnificently, splendidly *Ant* austerely, humbly, modestly, plainly, simply **3** *Syn* HEAD, chief, commanding, first, foremost, lead, leading, managing, preeminent, premier, presiding, primary, prime, principal, supreme

highfalutin *Syn* ARROGANT, cavalier, haughty, high-handed, high-hat, imperious, important, lofty, lordly, masterful, overweening, peremptory, pompous, presumptuous, pretentious, supercilious, superior, uppish, uppity *Ant* humble, modest

high-handed *Syn* ARROGANT, cavalier, haughty, highfalutin, high-hat, imperious, important, lofty, lordly, masterful, overweening, peremptory, pompous, presumptuous, pretentious, supercilious, superior, uppish, uppity *Ant* humble, modest

high-hat *Syn* ARROGANT, cavalier, haughty, highfalutin, high-handed, imperious, important, lofty, lordly, masterful, overweening, peremptory, pompous, presumptuous, pretentious, supercilious, superior, uppish, uppity *Ant* humble, modest

high jinks *Syn* HORSEPLAY, clowning, foolery, horsing (around), monkeying, monkeyshines, roughhouse, roughhousing, shenanigans, skylarking, tomfoolery

highlight *Syn* EMPHASIZE, accent, accentuate, feature, play (up), point (up), stress, underline, underscore *Ant* play (down)

highly *Syn* VERY, awful, awfully, beastly, deadly, especially, exceedingly, extra, extremely, far, frightfully, full, greatly, heavily, hugely, jolly, mightily, mighty, mortally, most, much, particularly, rattling, real, right, so, something, super, terribly, too, whacking *Ant* little, negligibly, nominally, slightly

high-pitched *Syn* SHRILL, acute, piping, screeching, shrieking, squeaking, squeaky, treble, whistling *Ant* bass, deep, low, throaty

high-spirited *Syn* SPIRITED, fiery, gingery, mettlesome, peppery, spunky *Ant* spiritless

high-strung *Syn* EXCITABLE, flighty, fluttery,

jittery, jumpy, nervous, skittish, spooky *Ant* unflappable

hilarity *Syn* MIRTH, glee, jollity

hind *Syn* BACK, hindmost, posterior, rear, rearward *Ant* anterior, fore, forward, front

hinder · to put obstacles in the way *Syn* bar, block, dam, impede, obstruct *Rel* arrest, check, interrupt *Ant* further

hindmost *Syn* BACK, hind, posterior, rear, rearward *Ant* anterior, fore, forward, front

hindrance *Syn* ENCUMBRANCE, bar, block, chain, clog, crimp, deterrent, drag, embarrassment, fetter, handicap, hurdle, impediment, inhibition, interference, let, manacle, obstacle, obstruction, shackles, stop, stumbling block, trammel *Ant* aid, assistance, benefit, help

hinge *Syn* DEPEND (sense 1), hang, turn

hint · to convey an idea indirectly *Syn* allude, imply, indicate, infer, insinuate, intimate, suggest *Rel* advert, mention, point, refer, signal, signify

hinterland *Syn* FRONTIER, backwater, backwoods, bush, up-country

hire *vb* · to take or engage something or grant the use of something for a stipulated price or rate *Syn* charter, lease, let, rent *Rel* get, obtain, procure, secure

hire *n Syn* WAGE, emolument, fee, pay, salary, stipend

hireling *Syn* MERCENARY, hack

hirsute *Syn* HAIRY (sense 1), bristly, fleecy, furry, rough, shaggy, unshorn, woolly *Ant* bald, furless, hairless, shorn, smooth

history **1** · a chronological record of events *Syn* annals, chronicle **2** *Syn* PAST, auld lang syne, yesterday, yesteryear, yore

histrionic *Syn* DRAMATIC, dramaturgic, melodramatic, theatrical

hit *Syn* STRIKE, box, clout, cuff, punch, slap, slog, slug, smite, swat

hit or miss · without definite aim, direction, rule, or method *Syn* aimlessly, anyhow, anyway, anywise, desultorily, erratically, haphazard, haphazardly, helter-skelter, irregularly, randomly *Rel* capriciously, carelessly, casually, indiscriminately, informally, offhand, offhandedly, promiscuously, whimsically *Ant* methodically, systematically

hit-or-miss *Syn* RANDOM, casual, chance, chancy, desultory, haphazard, happy-go-lucky *Ant* methodical, nonrandom, orderly, systematic

hit (upon) *Syn* HAPPEN (on *or* upon), chance (upon), encounter, find, meet, stumble (on *or* onto)

hoard *vb* **1** · to put (something of future use or value) in a safe or secret place *Syn* cache, lay away, lay up, put by, salt away, squirrel (away), stash, stockpile, store, stow *Rel* accumulate, acquire, amass, assemble, collect, concentrate, garner, gather, round up, scrape (together) **2** *Syn* ACCUMULATE, amass *Ant* dissipate

hoard *n Syn* STORE, cache, deposit, reserve

hoarse *Syn* LOUD, earsplitting, raucous, stentorian, stertorous, strident *Ant* low, low-pitched

hoax *Syn* DUPE, bamboozle, befool, gull, hoodwink, trick

hobnob *Syn* SOCIALIZE, associate, fraternize, mingle, mix

hobo *Syn* VAGABOND, bum, tramp, truant, vagrant

hocus-pocus *Syn* GIBBERISH, abracadabra, mummery

hog *Syn* GLUTTON, gorger, gormandizer, gourmand, overeater, stuffer, swiller

hogshead *Syn* CASK, barrel, firkin, keg, pipe, puncheon

hog-tie *Syn* HAMPER, clog, fetter, manacle, shackle, trammel *Ant* assist (*persons*), expedite (*work, projects*)

hoist *Syn* LIFT, boost, elevate, heave, raise, rear *Ant* lower

hold *n* · the act or manner of grasping or holding *Syn* clutch, grasp, grip *Rel* ownership, possession

hold *vb* **1** *Syn* BELIEVE (sense 1), consider, deem, feel, figure, guess, imagine, suppose, think *Ant* disbelieve, discredit, reject **2** *Syn* CONTAIN, accommodate **3** *Syn* HAVE, enjoy, own, possess

hold back *Syn* KEEP (sense 2), detain, keep back, keep out, reserve, retain, withhold *Ant* relinquish

holder 1 *Syn* CONTAINER, receptacle, vessel **2** *Syn* PROPRIETOR, owner, possessor

hold off (on) *Syn* POSTPONE, defer, delay, hold up, put off, shelve

holdup *Syn* DELAY, detainment, wait

hold up *Syn* POSTPONE, defer, delay, hold off (on), put off, shelve

hole · a space within the substance of a body or mass *Syn* cavity, hollow, pocket, vacuum, void *Rel* aperture, interstice, orifice

holiness · the quality or state of being spiritually pure or virtuous *Syn* blessedness, devoutness, godliness, piety, piousness, sainthood, saintliness, saintship, sanctity *Rel* asceticism, devotion, morality, prayerfulness, religiousness, spirituality *Ant* godlessness, impiety, ungodliness, unholiness

holler *n Syn* SHOUT, scream, screech, shriek, squeal, whoop, yell

holler *vb Syn* SHOUT, scream, screech, shriek, squeal, whoop, yell

hollow *adj* **1** · curved inward *Syn* concave, dented, depressed, indented, recessed, sunken *Rel* alveolar, cavernous, cuplike, cupped *Ant* bulging, convex, protruding, protuberant **2** *Syn* VAIN, empty, idle, nugatory, otiose

hollow *n Syn* HOLE, cavity, pocket, vacuum, void

holocaust *Syn* FIRE, conflagration

holy 1 · showing devotion to God and to a life of virtue *Syn* devout, godly, pious, religious, sainted, saintly *Rel* ascetic, prayerful, reverent, reverential, spiritual, worshipful *Ant* faithless, godless, impious, irreligious, ungodly, unholy **2** · set apart or worthy of veneration by association with God *Syn* blessed, consecrated, hallowed, sacred, sacrosanct, sanctified *Rel* adored, enshrined, glorified, revered, venerated, worshipped *Ant* unconsecrated, unhallowed

homage *Syn* HONOR, deference, obeisance, reverence

home *Syn* HABITATION, abode, domicile, dwelling, house, residence

homely *Syn* PLAIN, simple, unpretentious *Ant* lovely

homicidal *Syn* BLOODTHIRSTY, bloody, murdering, murderous, sanguinary, sanguine

homily *Syn* SPEECH, address, harangue, lecture, oration, sermon, talk

homogenize *Syn* STANDARDIZE, formalize, normalize, regularize

hone *Syn* SHARPEN, edge, grind, strop, whet *Ant* blunt, dull

honest 1 *Syn* TRUTHFUL, veracious *Ant* dishonest, fibbing, lying, mendacious, prevaricating, untruthful **2** *Syn* UPRIGHT, conscientious, honorable, just, scrupulous

honesty · uprightness as evidenced in character and actions *Syn* honor, integrity, probity *Rel* truth, veracity, verity *Ant* dishonesty

honey *Syn* SWEETHEART, beloved, darling, dear, flame, love, sweet

honor *n* **1** · respect or esteem shown one as his or her due or claimed by one as a right *Syn* deference, homage, obeisance, reverence *Rel* acknowledgment, recognition **2** *Syn* AWARD, decoration, distinction, plume, premium, prize **3** *Syn* FAME, celebrity, éclat, glory, notoriety, renown, reputation, repute *Ant* infamy, obscurity **4** *Syn* HONESTY, integrity, probity *Ant* dishonesty

honor *vb Syn* DIGNIFY, ennoble, glorify

honorable *Syn* UPRIGHT, conscientious, honest, just, scrupulous

hoodwink *Syn* DUPE, bamboozle, befool, gull, hoax, trick

hoof (it) *Syn* WALK, foot (it), leg (it), pad, step, traipse, tread

hoosegow *Syn* JAIL, brig, guardroom, jug, lockup, pen, penitentiary, prison, stockade

hop *n Syn* DANCE, ball, cotillion, formal, prom

hop *vb Syn* SKIP, bound, curvet, lollop, lope, ricochet

hope *Syn* EXPECT, await, look *Ant* despair of

hopeful *adj* · having or showing confidence that the end or outcome will be favorable *Syn* optimistic, roseate, rose-colored *Rel* awaiting, expecting, hoping *Ant* despairing, hopeless

hopeful *n Syn* CANDIDATE, applicant, aspirant, campaigner, contender, prospect, seeker

hopeless 1 *Syn* DESPONDENT, despairing, desperate, forlorn *Ant* lighthearted **2** *Syn* IMPOSSIBLE, unachievable, unattainable, unsolvable *Ant* achievable, attainable, doable, feasible, possible, realizable, workable

hopelessness *Syn* DESPONDENCY, despair, desperation, forlornness *Ant* lightheartedness

horde *Syn* CROWD, crush, mob, press, rout, throng

horizon *Syn* RANGE, compass, gamut, ken, orbit, purview, radius, reach, scope, sweep

horrendous *Syn* HORRIBLE, horrid, horrific *Ant* fascinating

horrible 1 · inspiring horror or abhorrence *Syn* horrendous, horrid, horrific *Rel* abhorrent, abominable, detestable, hateful *Ant* fascinating **2** *Syn* FEARFUL (sense 2), appalling, awful, dreadful, frightful, horrific, shocking, terrible, terrific

horrid *Syn* HORRIBLE, horrendous, horrific *Ant* fascinating

horrific 1 *Syn* FEARFUL (sense 2), appalling, awful, dreadful, frightful, horrible, shocking, terrible, terrific **2** *Syn* HORRIBLE, horrendous, horrid *Ant* fascinating

horrify *Syn* DISMAY, appall, daunt *Ant* cheer

horror *Syn* FEAR, alarm, consternation, dismay, dread, fright, panic, terror, trepidation *Ant* fearlessness

horse (around) *Syn* CUT UP, act up, clown (around), fool (around), monkey (around), show off, skylark

horseplay · wildly playful or mischievous behavior *Syn* clowning, foolery, high jinks, horsing (around), monkeying, monkeyshines, roughhouse, roughhousing, shenanigans, skylarking, tomfoolery *Rel* buffoonery, clownishness, foolishness, funning, jesting, joking, nonsense, waggery

horse sense 1 *Syn* COMMON SENSE, discreetness, discretion, gumption, levelheadedness, prudence, sense, sensibleness, wisdom, wit *Ant* imprudence, indiscretion **2** *Syn* SENSE, common sense, good sense, gumption, judgment, wisdom

horse-trade *Syn* BARGAIN, chaffer, deal, dicker, haggle, negotiate, palter

horsing (around) *Syn* HORSEPLAY, clowning, foolery, high jinks, monkeying, monkeyshines, roughhouse, roughhousing, shenanigans, skylarking, tomfoolery

host *Syn* MULTITUDE, army, legion

hostage *Syn* PLEDGE, earnest, pawn, token

hostility *Syn* ENMITY, animosity, animus, antagonism, antipathy, rancor *Ant* amity

hot *Syn* MODERN, contemporary, current, mod, modernistic, new, newfangled, new-fashioned, present-day, red-hot, space-age, ultramodern, up-to-date *Ant* antiquated, archaic, dated, fusty, musty, noncontemporary, oldfangled, old-fashioned, old-time, out-of-date, passé

hot-blooded *Syn* FERVENT, ardent, blazing, burning, charged, emotional, fervid, feverish, fiery, flaming, glowing, impassioned, passionate, red-hot, vehement, warm, warm-blooded *Ant* cold, cool, dispassionate, impassive, unemotional

hotcake *Syn* PANCAKE, flapjack, griddle cake, slapjack

hotfoot (it) *Syn* HURRY (sense 2), barrel, bolt, bowl, breeze, career, course, dash, fly, hasten, hump, hurtle, hustle, pelt, race, rip, rocket, run, rush, rustle, scoot, scurry, scuttle, shoot, speed, step (along), tear, trot, whirl, whisk, zip, zoom *Ant* crawl, creep, poke

hotness *Syn* POPULARITY, fashionableness, favor, modishness, vogue *Ant* disfavor, unpopularity

hound *Syn* BAIT, badger, chivy, heckle, hector, ride

hounding *Syn* PURSUIT, chase, chasing, dogging, following, pursuing, shadowing, tagging, tailing, tracing, tracking, trailing

house *n Syn* HABITATION, abode, domicile, dwelling, home, residence

house *vb Syn* HARBOR, board, entertain, lodge, shelter

hovel *Syn* SHACK, cabin, camp, hut, hutch, shanty

hover *Syn* FLIT, flicker, flitter, flutter

howbeit *Syn* ALTHOUGH, albeit, though, when, while

howl *vb* **1** *Syn* BARK, bay, growl, snarl, yap, yelp **2** *Syn* ROAR, bawl, bellow, bluster, clamor, ululate, vociferate **3** *Syn* SCREAM, screech, shriek, shrill, squall, squeal, yell, yelp

howl *n Syn* LAMENT, groan, keen, lamentation, moan, plaint, wail *Ant* exultation, rejoicing

howler *Syn* ERROR, blunder, bull, faux pas, lapse, mistake, slip

hub *Syn* CENTER (sense 2), base, capital, core, cynosure, eye, focus, heart, mecca, nucleus, seat

hubbub 1 *Syn* COMMOTION, bother, bustle, clatter, disturbance, furor, furore, fuss, hullabaloo, hurly-burly, pandemonium, pother, row, ruckus, ruction, rumpus, shindy, squall, stew, stir, storm, to-do, tumult, turmoil, uproar, welter, whirl **2** *Syn* DIN, babel, clamor, hullabaloo, pandemonium, racket, uproar *Ant* quiet

hue *Syn* COLOR, shade, tinge, tint, tone

huff *Syn* OFFENSE (sense 1), dudgeon, pique, resentment, umbrage

huffy *Syn* IRRITABLE, fractious, fretful, peevish, pettish, petulant, querulous, snappish, waspish *Ant* easygoing

huge · exceedingly or excessively large *Syn* Brobdingnagian, colossal, cyclopean, elephantine, enormous, gargantuan, giant, gigantean, gigantic, Herculean, immense, mammoth, titanic, vast *Rel* monstrous, monumental, prodigious, stupendous, tremendous *Ant* bitty, diminutive, microscopic (*or* microscopical), midget, miniature, minute, pocket, pygmy, teeny, teeny-weeny, tiny, wee

hugely *Syn* VERY, awful, awfully, beastly, deadly, especially, exceedingly, extra, extremely, far, frightfully, full, greatly, heavily, highly, jolly, mightily, mighty, mortally, most, much, particularly, rattling, real, right, so, something, super, terribly, too, whacking *Ant* little, negligibly, nominally, slightly

hugger-mugger *Syn* MESSY, chaotic, cluttered, confused, disarranged, disarrayed, disheveled (*or* dishevelled), disordered, disorderly, higgledy-piggledy, jumbled, littered, messed, muddled, mussed, mussy, pell-mell, rumpled, sloppy, topsy-turvy, tousled, tumbled, unkempt, untidy, upside-down *Ant* neat, ordered, orderly, organized, shipshape, snug, tidied, tidy, trim

hulk *Syn* OAF, clod, gawk, lout, lubber, lug

hulking *Syn* LARGE, big, bulky, considerable, goodly, good-sized, grand, great, handsome, hefty, largish, outsize, oversize (*or* oversized), sizable (*or* sizeable), substantial, tidy, voluminous *Ant* little, puny, small, undersized

hullabaloo **1** *Syn* COMMOTION, bother, bustle, clatter, disturbance, furor, furore, fuss, hubbub, hurly-burly, pandemonium, pother, row, ruckus, ruction, rumpus, shindy, squall, stew, stir, storm, to-do, tumult, turmoil, uproar, welter, whirl **2** *Syn* DIN, babel, clamor, hubbub, pandemonium, racket, uproar *Ant* quiet

humane *Syn* CHARITABLE, altruistic, benevolent, eleemosynary, humanitarian, philanthropic *Ant* uncharitable

humanitarian *Syn* CHARITABLE, altruistic, benevolent, eleemosynary, humane, philanthropic *Ant* uncharitable

humble *adj* · lacking all signs of pride, aggressiveness, or self-assertiveness *Syn* lowly, meek, modest *Rel* subdued, submissive, tame

humble *vb* *Syn* abase, debase, degrade, demean, humiliate *Ant* exalt, extol (*especially oneself*)

humdrum *Syn* BORING, drab, dreary, dry, dull, flat, heavy, jading, leaden, monotonous, pedestrian, ponderous, stodgy, stuffy, stupid, tame, tedious, tiresome, tiring, unanimated, uninteresting, wearisome, weary, wearying *Ant* absorbing, engaging, engrossing, gripping, interesting, intriguing, involving

humid *Syn* WET, damp, dank, moist *Ant* dry

humiliate *Syn* ABASE, debase, degrade, demean, humble *Ant* exalt, extol (*especially oneself*)

humor **1** *Syn* COMEDY, farce, slapstick **2** *Syn* MOOD, temper, vein **3** *Syn* WIT, irony, repartee, sarcasm, satire

humorous *Syn* WITTY, facetious, jocose, jocular

hump **1** *Syn* HURRY (sense 2), barrel, bolt, bowl, breeze, career, course, dash, fly, hasten, hotfoot (it), hurtle, hustle, pelt, race, rip, rocket, run, rush, rustle, scoot, scurry, scuttle, shoot, speed, step (along), tear, trot, whirl, whisk, zip, zoom *Ant* crawl, creep, poke **2** *Syn* LABOR, drudge, endeavor, grub, hustle, moil, peg (away), plod, plow, plug, slave, slog, strain, strive, struggle, sweat, toil, travail, work *Ant* dabble, fiddle (around), fool (around), mess (around), putter (around)

hunger *Syn* LONG, hanker, pine, thirst, yearn

hunt *Syn* SEEK, comb, ferret out, ransack, rummage, scour, search

hurdle *Syn* ENCUMBRANCE, bar, block, chain, clog, crimp, deterrent, drag, embarrassment, fetter, handicap, hindrance, impediment, inhibition, interference, let, manacle, obstacle, obstruction, shackles, stop, stumbling block, trammel *Ant* aid, assistance, benefit, help

hurl *Syn* THROW, cast, fling, pitch, sling, toss

hurly-burly *Syn* COMMOTION, bother, bustle, clatter, disturbance, furor, furore, fuss, hubbub, hullabaloo, pandemonium, pother, row, ruckus, ruction, rumpus, shindy, squall, stew, stir, storm, to-do, tumult, turmoil, uproar, welter, whirl

hurricane · a violent rotating storm originating in the tropics and often moving into temperate latitudes *Syn* tropical storm, typhoon *Rel* whirlwind, whirly

hurry *vb* **1** · to cause to move or proceed fast or faster *Syn* accelerate, hasten, quicken, rush, speed (up), whisk *Rel* drive, goad, prod, propel, push, race, spur, stir, urge *Ant* decelerate, retard, slow (down) **2** · to proceed or move quickly *Syn* barrel, bolt, bowl, breeze, career, course, dash, fly, hasten, hotfoot (it), hump, hurtle, hustle, pelt, race, rip, rocket, run, rush, rustle, scoot, scurry, scuttle, shoot, speed, step (along), tear, trot, whirl, whisk, zip, zoom *Rel* dart, flit, scamper, scud, scuffle *Ant* crawl, creep, poke

hurry *n* *Syn* HASTE, dispatch, expedition, speed *Ant* deliberation

hurt *vb* *Syn* INJURE, damage, harm, impair, mar, spoil *Ant* aid

hurt *n* *Syn* INJURY, damage, harm, mischief

hurtful *Syn* HARMFUL, adverse, bad, baleful, baneful, damaging, deleterious, detrimental, evil, ill, injurious, mischievous, noxious, pernicious, prejudicial *Ant* harmless, innocent, innocuous, inoffensive, safe

hurtle *Syn* HURRY (sense 2), barrel, bolt, bowl, breeze, career, course, dash, fly, hasten, hotfoot (it), hump, hustle, pelt, race, rip, rocket, run, rush, rustle, scoot, scurry, scuttle, shoot, speed, step (along), tear, trot, whirl, whisk, zip, zoom *Ant* crawl, creep, poke

husbandry **1** *Syn* AGRICULTURE, farming **2** *Syn* ECONOMY, frugality, providence, scrimping, skimping, thrift *Ant* wastefulness

hush *n* **1** *Syn* CALM, calmness, peace, peacefulness, placidity, quiet, quietness, quietude, repose, restfulness, sereneness, serenity, still, stillness, tranquillity (*or* tranquility) *Ant* bustle, commotion, hubbub, hurly-burly, pandemonium, tumult, turmoil, uproar **2** *Syn* SILENCE, quiet, quietness, quietude, still, stillness *Ant* noise, sound

hush *vb Syn* SHUT UP, clam up, quiet (down) *Ant* speak, talk

hushed *Syn* SILENT (sense 2), muted, noiseless, quiet, quieted, soundless, still *Ant* noisy, unquiet

husky *Syn* MUSCULAR, athletic, brawny, burly, sinewy

hustle **1** *Syn* FLEECE, bleed, cheat, chisel, cozen, defraud, mulct, rook, shortchange, skin, squeeze, stick, sting, swindle, victimize **2** *Syn* HURRY (sense 2), barrel, bolt, bowl, breeze, career, course, dash, fly, hasten, hotfoot (it), hump, hurtle, pelt, race, rip, rocket, run, rush, rustle, scoot, scurry, scuttle, shoot, speed, step (along), tear, trot, whirl, whisk, zip, zoom *Ant* crawl, creep, poke **3** *Syn* LABOR, drudge, endeavor, fag, grub, hump, moil, peg (away), plod, plow, plug, slave, slog, strain, strive, struggle, sweat, toil, travail, work *Ant* dabble, fiddle (around), fool (around), mess (around), putter (around)

hut *Syn* SHACK, cabin, camp, hovel, hutch, shanty

hutch **1** *Syn* CABINET, buffet, closet, cupboard, locker, sideboard **2** *Syn* SHACK, cabin, camp, hovel, hut, shanty

hygienic **1** *Syn* HEALTHFUL, healthy, salubrious, salutary, sanitary, wholesome **2** *Syn* SANITARY, aseptic, germfree, sterile *Ant* insanitary, unhygienic, unsanitary

hymn *Syn* SING, carol, chant, descant, intone, trill, troll, warble

hyperbole *Syn* EXAGGERATION, caricature, coloring, elaboration, embellishment, embroidering, magnification, overstatement, padding, stretching *Ant* understatement

hypercritical *Syn* CRITICAL, captious, carping, caviling, censorious, faultfinding *Ant* uncritical

hypochondriac *Syn* MELANCHOLIC, atrabilious, melancholy

hypocrisy · the pretending of having virtues, principles, or beliefs that one in fact does not have *Syn* cant, dissembling, dissimulation, insincerity, piousness, sanctimoniousness *Rel* deception, deceptiveness, dishonesty, falsity, pretense, pretension, pretentiousness, self-righteousness, self-satisfaction *Ant* genuineness, sincerity

hypocritical *Syn* INSINCERE, double-dealing, feigned, left-handed, mealy, mealymouthed, two-faced, unctuous *Ant* genuine, heartfelt, honest, sincere, unfeigned

hypostatize *Syn* REALIZE, actualize, embody, externalize, incarnate, materialize, objectify, reify

hypothesis *Syn* THEORY, proposition, supposition

hypothetical *Syn* SUPPOSED, conjectural, purported, putative, reputed, suppositious, supposititious *Ant* certain

hysteria **1** *Syn* FRENZY, agitation, delirium, distraction, furor, furore, fury, rage, rampage, uproar **2** *Syn* MANIA, delirium, frenzy

I

icon *Syn* IMAGE, effigy, mask, photograph, portrait, statue

iconoclast *Syn* REBEL, insurgent

icy *Syn* COLD, arctic, chilly, cool, freezing, frigid, frosty, gelid, glacial *Ant* hot

idea · what exists in the mind as a representation as of something comprehended or as a formulation as of a plan *Syn* concept, conception, impression, notion, thought *Rel* belief, conviction, opinion, sentiment, view

ideal *adj Syn* ABSTRACT (sense 1), transcendent, transcendental *Ant* concrete

ideal *n Syn* MODEL, beau, example, exemplar, ideal, mirror, pattern, standard

idealist · one whose conduct is guided more by the image of perfection than by the real world *Syn* dreamer, romantic, romanticist, utopian, visionary *Rel* sentimentalist *Ant* pragmatist, realist

idealize · to represent or think of as better

than reality *Syn* glamorize, glorify, romanticize *Rel* daydream, imagine, romance, theorize, vision

identic *Syn* SAME, equal, equivalent, identical, selfsame, tantamount, very *Ant* different

identical *Syn* SAME, equal, equivalent, identic, selfsame, tantamount, very *Ant* different

identification *Syn* RECOGNITION, apperception, assimilation

idiom 1 *Syn* LANGUAGE (sense 1), dialect, speech, tongue 2 *Syn* PHRASE, expression, locution

idle *vb* · to spend time not in work but in idleness *Syn* laze, loaf, loll, lounge *Rel* relax, repose, rest

idle *adj* 1 *Syn* INACTIVE, inert, passive, supine *Ant* active, live 2 *Syn* VAIN, empty, hollow, nugatory, otiose

idler *Syn* LAZYBONES, drone, loafer, slouch, slug, sluggard *Ant* doer, go-getter, hummer, hustler, rustler, self-starter

idolatry *Syn* WORSHIP, adulation, deification, idolization, worshipping

idolization *Syn* WORSHIP, adulation, deification, idolatry, worshipping

idolize · to love or admire too much *Syn* adore, adulate, canonize, deify, dote (on), worship *Rel* appreciate, cherish, esteem, prize, treasure, value

ignite *Syn* LIGHT, fire, kindle

ignoble *Syn* MEAN, abject, sordid

ignominy *Syn* DISGRACE, dishonor, disrepute, ignominy, infamy, obloquy, odium, opprobrium, shame *Ant* esteem, respect

ignorant · lacking in education or the knowledge gained from books *Syn* benighted, dark, illiterate, nonliterate, simple, uneducated, uninstructed, unlearned, unlettered, unread, unschooled, untaught, untutored *Rel* lowbrow, uncultivated, uncultured *Ant* educated, knowledgeable, literate, schooled

ignore *Syn* NEGLECT, disregard, forget, omit, overlook, slight *Ant* cherish

ilk *Syn* TYPE, character, description, kidney, kind, nature, sort, stripe

ill 1 *Syn* BAD (sense 1), evil, naughty, wicked *Ant* good 2 *Syn* EVIL, bad, evildoing, immorality, iniquity, sin, villainy, wrong *Ant* good, morality, right, virtue 3 *Syn* HARMFUL, adverse, bad, baleful, baneful, damaging, deleterious, detrimental, evil, hurtful, injurious, mischievous, noxious, pernicious, prejudicial *Ant* harmless, innocent, innocuous, inoffensive, safe

ill-advised *Syn* INDISCREET, imprudent, inadvisable, injudicious, tactless, unadvisable, unwise *Ant* advisable, discreet, judicious, prudent, tactful, wise

ill-bred *Syn* IMPOLITE, discourteous, illmannered, impertinent, inconsiderate, rude, thoughtless, uncalled-for, uncivil, ungracious, unmannerly *Ant* civil, considerate, courteous, genteel, gracious, mannerly, polite, thoughtful, well-bred

illegal *Syn* UNLAWFUL, illegitimate, illicit *Ant* lawful

illegitimate *Syn* UNLAWFUL, illegal, illicit *Ant* lawful

ill-fated *Syn* UNLUCKY, calamitous, disastrous, hapless, ill-starred, luckless, unfortunate *Ant* fortunate, happy, lucky

ill-favored *Syn* UGLY, hideous, unsightly *Ant* beautiful

illicit *Syn* UNLAWFUL, illegal, illegitimate *Ant* lawful

illimitable *Syn* INFINITE, boundless, endless, immeasurable, indefinite, limitless, measureless, unbounded, unfathomable, unlimited *Ant* bounded, circumscribed, confined, definite, finite, limited, restricted

illiterate *Syn* IGNORANT, benighted, dark, nonliterate, simple, uneducated, uninstructed, unlearned, unlettered, unread, unschooled, untaught, untutored *Ant* educated, knowledgeable, literate, schooled

ill-mannered *Syn* IMPOLITE, discourteous, ill-bred, impertinent, inconsiderate, rude, thoughtless, uncalled-for, uncivil, ungracious, unmannerly *Ant* civil, considerate, courteous, genteel, gracious, mannerly, polite, thoughtful, well-bred

illogical · not using or following good reasoning *Syn* fallacious, invalid, irrational, nonrational, unreasonable, unreasoning, unsound, weak *Rel* misleading, specious *Ant* logical, rational, reasonable, sound, valid

ill-starred *Syn* UNLUCKY, calamitous, disastrous, hapless, ill-fated, luckless, unfortunate *Ant* fortunate, happy, lucky

ill-treat *Syn* ABUSE, maltreat, mistreat, misuse, outrage *Ant* honor, respect

illuminate, illumine 1 · to fill with or to throw light upon *Syn* enlighten, illustrate, light, lighten *Rel* fire, kindle *Ant* darken, obscure 2 *Syn* EXPLAIN (sense 1), clarify, clear (up), construe, demonstrate, elucidate, explicate, expound, illustrate, interpret, spell out *Ant* obscure

illusion 1 *Syn* DELUSION, hallucination, mirage 2 *Syn* FALLACY (sense 1), error, falsehood, falsity, misconception, myth, old wives' tale, untruth *Ant* truth, verity

illusory *Syn* APPARENT, ostensible, seeming *Ant* real

illustrate 1 *Syn* EXPLAIN (sense 1), clarify, clear (up), construe, demonstrate, elucidate, explicate, expound, illuminate, interpret, spell out *Ant* obscure 2 *Syn* ILLUMINATE, enlighten, light, lighten *Ant* darken, obscure

illustration *Syn* EXAMPLE, case, exemplar, instance, representative, sample, specimen

illustrious *Syn* EMINENT, distinguished, noble, notable, noteworthy, outstanding, preeminent, prestigious, signal, star, superior

ill will *Syn* MALICE, despite, grudge, malevolence, malignancy, malignity, spite, spleen *Ant* charity

image 1 · a lifelike representation especially of a living being *Syn* effigy, icon, mask, photograph, portrait, statue *Rel* copy, duplicate, facsimile, replica, reproduction **2** *Syn* SENSATION (sense 1), percept, sense-datum, sensum

imaginary · unreal or unbelievable or conceiving such unreal or unbelievable things *Syn* chimerical, fanciful, fantastic, quixotic, visionary *Rel* apocryphal, fabulous, fictitious, legendary, mythical *Ant* actual, real

imagination · the power or function of the mind by which mental images of things are formed or the exercise of that power *Syn* fancy, fantasy *Rel* creation, invention

imagine 1 *Syn* BELIEVE (sense 1), consider, deem, feel, figure, guess, hold, suppose, think *Ant* disbelieve, discredit, reject **2** *Syn* THINK (sense 1), conceive, envisage, envision, fancy, realize

imbibe *Syn* ABSORB, assimilate *Ant* exude, give out

imbue *Syn* INFUSE, ingrain, inoculate, leaven, suffuse

imitate *Syn* COPY, ape, mimic, mock *Ant* originate

imitation · being such in appearance only and made with or manufactured from usually cheaper materials *Syn* artificial, bogus, factitious, fake, false, man-made, mimic, mock, sham, simulated, substitute, synthetic *Rel* adulterated, affected, concocted, counterfeit, cultured, deceptive, doctored, dummy, fabricated, feigned, forged, fraudulent, fudged, juggled, manipulated, manufactured, misleading, phony, pseudo, spurious, tampered (with), unauthentic *Ant* genuine, natural, real

imitation *n Syn* COPY, carbon copy, duplicate, duplication, facsimile, reduplication, replica, replication *Ant* original

immaterial 1 · not composed of matter *Syn* incorporeal, spiritual *Ant* material **2** *Syn* IRRELEVANT, extraneous, inapplicable *Ant* applicable, apposite, apropos, germane, material, pertinent, relevant

immature 1 · not fully developed *Syn* unmatured, unmellow, unripe *Rel* callow, crude, green, rude *Ant* mature **2** *Syn* CALLOW, adolescent, green, inexperienced, juvenile, puerile, raw, unfledged, unripe, unripened *Ant* adult, experienced, grown-up, mature, ripe **3** *Syn* CHILDISH, adolescent, babyish, infantile, juvenile, kiddish, puerile *Ant* adult, grown-up, mature **4** *Syn* YOUNG, adolescent, juvenile, youngish, youthful *Ant* adult, full-grown, mature, matured

immeasurable *Syn* INFINITE, boundless, endless, illimitable, indefinite, limitless, measureless, unbounded, unfathomable, un-

limited *Ant* bounded, circumscribed, confined, definite, finite, limited, restricted

immediacy *Syn* PROXIMITY, closeness, contiguity, nearness *Ant* distance, remoteness

immense *Syn* HUGE, Brobdingnagian, colossal, cyclopean, elephantine, enormous, gargantuan, giant, gigantean, gigantic, Herculean, mammoth, titanic, vast *Ant* bitty, diminutive, microscopic (*or* microscopical), midget, miniature, minute, pocket, pygmy, teeny, teeny-weeny, tiny, wee

immerse *Syn* DIP (sense 1), duck, dunk, souse, submerge

immersing *Syn* INTERESTING, absorbing, arresting, engaging, engrossing, enthralling, fascinating, gripping, intriguing, involving, riveting *Ant* boring, drab, dry, dull, heavy, monotonous, tedious, uninteresting

immigrant 1 *Syn* EMIGRANT, migrant **2** *Syn* STRANGER, alien, émigré, foreigner, outlander, outsider

immigrate *Syn* MIGRATE, emigrate

imminent *Syn* FORTHCOMING, approaching, coming, impending, nearing, oncoming, pending, upcoming *Ant* late, recent

immobile *Syn* IMMOVABLE, immotive *Ant* movable

immoderate *Syn* EXCESSIVE, exorbitant, extravagant, extreme, inordinate *Ant* deficient

immoral *Syn* UNPRINCIPLED, cutthroat, Machiavellian, unconscionable, unethical, unmoral, unscrupulous *Ant* ethical, moral, principled, scrupulous

immorality *Syn* EVIL, bad, evildoing, ill, iniquity, sin, villainy, wrong *Ant* good, morality, right, virtue

immortal · not subject to death or decay *Syn* deathless, undying, unfading *Rel* endless, everlasting *Ant* mortal

immotive *Syn* IMMOVABLE, immobile *Ant* movable

immovable 1 · incapable of moving or being moved *Syn* immobile, immotive *Ant* movable **2** *Syn* OBSTINATE, adamant, adamantine, dogged, hard, hardened, hardheaded, hardhearted, headstrong, implacable, inflexible, mulish, obdurate, opinionated, ossified, pat, peevish, pertinacious, perverse, pigheaded, rigid, self-willed, stubborn, unbending, uncompromising, unrelenting, unyielding, willful (*or* wilful) *Ant* acquiescent, agreeable, amenable, compliant, complying, flexible, pliable, pliant, relenting, yielding

immure *Syn* IMPRISON, incarcerate, intern, jail

imp *Syn* DEMON, devil, fiend, ghoul, incubus

impact · a forcible or enforced contact between two or more things *Syn* clash, collision, concussion, impingement, jar, jolt, percussion, shock *Rel* hit, hitting, slap, slapping, smiting, striking, stroke

impair *Syn* INJURE, damage, harm, hurt, mar, spoil *Ant* aid

impalpable

impalpable *Syn* IMPERCEPTIBLE, inappreciable, indistinguishable, insensible *Ant* appreciable, discernible, palpable, perceptible, sensible

impart *Syn* COMMUNICATE, convey, spread, transfer, transfuse, transmit

impartial *Syn* FAIR, dispassionate, equitable, just, objective, unbiased, uncolored *Ant* unfair

impartiality *Syn* DETACHMENT, disinterestedness, neutrality, objectivity *Ant* bias, favor, favoritism, one-sidedness, partiality, partisanship, prejudice

impassable · not allowing passage *Syn* impenetrable, impermeable, impervious *Ant* passable

impassible *Syn* INSENSIBLE, anesthetic, insensitive *Ant* sensible (*to or of something*)

impassioned *Syn* FERVENT, ardent, blazing, burning, charged, emotional, fervid, feverish, fiery, flaming, glowing, hot-blooded, passionate, red-hot, vehement, warm, warm-blooded *Ant* cold, cool, dispassionate, impassive, unemotional

impassive · unresponsive to what might normally excite interest or emotion *Syn* apathetic, phlegmatic, stoic, stolid *Rel* collected, composed, cool, imperturbable *Ant* responsive

impassivity, impassiveness · unresponsiveness to something that might normally excite interest or emotion *Syn* apathy, phlegm, stoicism, stolidity

impatient · manifesting signs of unrest or an inability to keep still or quiet *Syn* fidgety, jittery, jumpy, nervous, restive, restless, uneasy, unquiet *Rel* fretful, irritable, querulous, snappish, waspish *Ant* patient

impeach *Syn* ACCUSE, charge, incriminate, indict *Ant* absolve, acquit, clear, exculpate, exonerate, vindicate

impeccable · absolutely correct and beyond criticism *Syn* errorless, faultless, flawless *Rel* inerrant, infallible, unerring

impecunious *Syn* POOR, destitute, indigent, necessitous, needy, penniless, poverty-stricken *Ant* rich

impede *Syn* HINDER, bar, block, dam, obstruct *Ant* further

impediment *Syn* ENCUMBRANCE, bar, block, chain, clog, crimp, deterrent, drag, embarrassment, fetter, handicap, hindrance, hurdle, inhibition, interference, let, manacle, obstacle, obstruction, shackles, stop, stumbling block, trammel *Ant* aid, assistance, benefit, help

impending *Syn* FORTHCOMING, approaching, coming, imminent, nearing, oncoming, pending, upcoming *Ant* late, recent

impenetrable **1** *Syn* IMPASSABLE, impermeable, impervious *Ant* passable **2** *Syn* INCOMPREHENSIBLE, unfathomable, unintelligible *Ant* fathomable, intelligible, understandable

impenetrate *Syn* PERMEATE, impregnate, interpenetrate, penetrate, pervade, saturate

impenitent *Syn* REMORSELESS, unrepentant *Ant* contrite, guilty, penitent, regretful, remorseful, repentant, sorry

imperative **1** *Syn* MANDATORY, compulsory, forced, incumbent, involuntary, necessary, nonelective, obligatory, peremptory, required *Ant* elective, optional, voluntary **2** *Syn* MASTERFUL, domineering, imperious, peremptory **3** *Syn* PRESSING, crying, exigent, importunate, insistent, instant, urgent

imperceptible · not perceptible by a sense or by the mind *Syn* impalpable, inappreciable, indistinguishable, insensible *Rel* inaudible, intangible, invisible *Ant* appreciable, discernible, palpable, perceptible, sensible

imperfect *Syn* FAULTY, bad, defective, flawed *Ant* faultless, flawless, impeccable, perfect

imperfection **1** · an instance of failure to reach a standard of excellence or perfection *Syn* deficiency, fault, shortcoming *Rel* dereliction, failure, neglect *Ant* perfection **2** *Syn* BLEMISH, defect, deformity, disfigurement, fault, flaw, mark, pockmark, scar

imperial *Syn* KINGLY, princely, queenly, regal, royal

imperil *Syn* ENDANGER, adventure, compromise, gamble (with), hazard, jeopardize, menace, risk, venture

imperilment *Syn* DANGER (sense 2), distress, endangerment, jeopardy, peril, risk, trouble *Ant* safeness, safety, security

imperious **1** *Syn* ARROGANT, cavalier, haughty, highfalutin, high-handed, high-hat, important, lofty, lordly, masterful, overweening, peremptory, pompous, presumptuous, pretentious, supercilious, superior, uppish, uppity *Ant* humble, modest **2** *Syn* BOSSY, authoritarian, autocratic, despotic, dictatorial, domineering, masterful, overbearing, peremptory, tyrannical, tyrannous **3** *Syn* MASTERFUL, domineering, imperative, peremptory

imperiousness *Syn* ARROGANCE, haughtiness, loftiness, lordliness, masterfulness, peremptoriness, pompousness, presumptuousness, pretense (*or* pretence), pretension, pretentiousness, self-importance, superciliousness, superiority *Ant* humility, modesty

impermanent *Syn* MOMENTARY, ephemeral, evanescent, flash, fleeting, fugitive, passing, short-lived, temporary, transient, transitory *Ant* enduring, eternal, everlasting, lasting, long-lived, permanent, perpetual

impermeable *Syn* IMPASSABLE, impenetrable, impervious *Ant* passable

impersonate *Syn* ACT (sense 2), play

impersonator *Syn* ACTOR, mime, mimic, mummer, performer, player, thespian, trouper

impertinence *Syn* BACK TALK, cheek, impudence, insolence, sass, sauce

impertinent *Syn* IMPOLITE, discourteous, ill-bred, ill-mannered, inconsiderate, rude, thoughtless, uncalled-for, uncivil, ungracious, unmannerly *Ant* civil, considerate, courteous, genteel, gracious, mannerly, polite, thoughtful, well-bred

imperturbability *Syn* EQUANIMITY, aplomb, calmness, composure, coolheadedness, coolness, placidity, self-possession, serenity, tranquillity (*or* tranquility) *Ant* agitation, discomposure, perturbation

imperturbable 1 *Syn* COOL, collected, composed, nonchalant, unflappable, unruffled *Ant* agitated, ardent 2 *Syn* UNFLAPPABLE, nerveless, unshakable *Ant* perturbable, shakable

impervious *Syn* IMPASSABLE, impenetrable, impermeable *Ant* passable

impetuous *Syn* PRECIPITATE, abrupt, hasty, headlong, sudden *Ant* deliberate

impetus 1 *Syn* SPEED, headway, momentum, pace, velocity 2 *Syn* STIMULUS, excitant, incitement, stimulant

impingement *Syn* IMPACT, clash, collision, concussion, jar, jolt, percussion, shock

impious · lacking in reverence for what is sacred or divine *Syn* blasphemous, profane, sacrilegious *Rel* flagitious, iniquitous, nefarious *Ant* pious, reverent

impish *Syn* PLAYFUL, frolicsome, mischievous, roguish, sportive, waggish

implacable 1 *Syn* GRIM, merciless, relentless, unrelenting *Ant* lenient 2 *Syn* OBSTINATE, adamant, adamantine, dogged, hard, hardened, hardheaded, hardhearted, headstrong, immovable, inflexible, mulish, obdurate, opinionated, ossified, pat, peevish, pertinacious, perverse, pigheaded, rigid, self-willed, stubborn, unbending, uncompromising, unrelenting, unyielding, willful (*or* wilful) *Ant* acquiescent, agreeable, amenable, compliant, complying, flexible, pliable, pliant, relenting, yielding

implant · to introduce into the mind *Syn* inculcate, instill *Rel* imbue, infuse, ingrain, inoculate, leaven

implement *n* · a relatively simple device for performing work *Syn* appliance, instrument, tool, utensil *Rel* apparatus, machine, mechanism

implement *vb* *Syn* ENFORCE, administer, apply, execute

implicit · understood although not put into words *Syn* implied, tacit, unexpressed, unspoken, unvoiced, wordless *Rel* inferred *Ant* explicit, express, expressed, spoken, stated

implied *Syn* IMPLICIT, tacit, unexpressed, unspoken, unvoiced, wordless *Ant* explicit, express, expressed, spoken, stated

implore *Syn* BEG, adjure, beseech, entreat, importune, supplicate

imply 1 *Syn* HINT, allude, indicate, infer, insinuate, intimate, suggest 2 *Syn* INCLUDE,

comprehend, embrace, involve, subsume *Ant* exclude

impolite · showing a lack of manners or consideration for others *Syn* discourteous, ill-bred, ill-mannered, impertinent, inconsiderate, rude, thoughtless, uncivil, ungracious, unmannerly *Rel* audacious, bold, bold-faced, brash, brassy, disrespectful, impudent, insolent, saucy, shameless *Ant* civil, considerate, courteous, genteel, gracious, mannerly, polite, thoughtful, well-bred

import *n* 1 *Syn* IMPORTANCE, consequence, moment, significance, weight *Ant* unimportance 2 *Syn* MEANING, acceptation, sense, significance, signification

import *vb* 1 *Syn* MATTER, count, mean, signify, weigh 2 *Syn* MEAN, denote, signify

importance · the quality or state of being of notable worth or influence *Syn* consequence, import, moment, significance, weight *Rel* conspicuousness, prominence, saliency *Ant* unimportance

important 1 *Syn* ARROGANT, cavalier, haughty, highfalutin, high-handed, high-hat, imperious, lofty, lordly, masterful, overweening, peremptory, pompous, presumptuous, pretentious, supercilious, superior, uppish, uppity *Ant* humble, modest 2 *Syn* CONCEITED, complacent, egoistic, egotistic (*or* egotistical), overweening, pompous, prideful, proud, self-conceited, self-important, self-satisfied, smug, stuck-up, vain, vainglorious *Ant* humble, modest

importunate *Syn* PRESSING, crying, exigent, imperative, insistent, instant, urgent

importune *Syn* BEG, adjure, beseech, entreat, implore, supplicate

impose 1 · to establish or apply as a charge or penalty *Syn* assess, charge, exact, fine, lay, levy, put *Rel* dock, mulct, penalize, tax *Ant* remit 2 *Syn* DICTATE, decree, ordain, prescribe

imposing 1 *Syn* DIGNIFIED, august, solemn, staid, stately *Ant* flighty, frivolous, giddy, goofy, silly, undignified 2 *Syn* GRAND, august, grandiose, magnificent, majestic, noble, stately

imposition *Syn* TAX, assessment, duty, impost, levy

impossible · incapable of being solved or accomplished *Syn* hopeless, unachievable, unattainable, unsolvable *Rel* impracticable, impractical *Ant* achievable, attainable, doable, feasible, possible, realizable, workable

impost *Syn* TAX, assessment, duty, imposition, levy

impostor · a person who fraudulently pretends to be someone or something else *Syn* charlatan, faker, mountebank, quack *Rel* cheat, fake, fraud, humbug, imposture

impotence *Syn* INABILITY, inadequacy, incapability, incapacity, incompetence, ineptitude, powerlessness *Ant* ability, adequacy, capability, capacity, competence, potency

impotent 1 *Syn* POWERLESS, helpless, weak *Ant* mighty, potent, powerful, puissant, strong **2** *Syn* STERILE, barren, infertile, unfruitful *Ant* exuberant, fertile

impracticable *Syn* IMPRACTICAL, inoperable, nonpractical, unusable, unworkable, useless *Ant* applicable, feasible, functional, operable, operational, practicable, practical, usable, useful, workable

impractical · not capable of being put to use or account *Syn* impracticable, inoperable, nonpractical, unusable, unworkable, useless *Rel* unsuitable *Ant* applicable, feasible, functional, operable, operational, practicable, practical, usable, useful, workable

imprecation *Syn* CURSE, anathema, malediction *Ant* blessing

impregnable *Syn* INVINCIBLE, indomitable, inexpugnable, invulnerable, unassailable, unconquerable

impregnate 1 *Syn* PERMEATE, impenetrate, interpenetrate, penetrate, pervade, saturate **2** *Syn* SOAK, drench, saturate, sop, steep, waterlog

impress *vb Syn* AFFECT, influence, strike, sway, touch

impress *n Syn* IMPRESSION, imprint, print, stamp

impressible *Syn* SENTIENT, impressionable, responsive, sensitive, susceptible

impression 1 · the perceptible trace or traces left by pressure *Syn* impress, imprint, print, stamp *Rel* trace, track, vestige **2** *Syn* EDITION, printing, reissue, reprinting **3** *Syn* IDEA, concept, conception, notion, thought

impressionable *Syn* SENTIENT, impressible, responsive, sensitive, susceptible

impressive *Syn* MOVING, affecting, emotional, poignant, stirring, touching *Ant* unemotional, unimpressive

imprimatur *Syn* APPROVAL, approbation, blessing, favor, OK (*or* okay) *Ant* disapprobation, disapproval, disfavor

imprint *Syn* IMPRESSION, impress, print, stamp

imprison · to confine closely so that escape is impossible or unlikely *Syn* immure, incarcerate, intern, jail *Rel* circumscribe, confine, limit, restrict

improbable · not likely to be true or to occur *Syn* doubtful, dubious, far-fetched, flimsy, questionable, unapt, unlikely *Rel* implausible, impossible, inconceivable, incredible, last, unbelievable, unthinkable *Ant* likely, probable

impromptu *Syn* EXTEMPORANEOUS, extemporary, extempore, improvised, offhand, unpremeditated

improper 1 *Syn* INAPPROPRIATE, graceless, inapt, incongruous, incorrect, indecorous, inept, infelicitous, unapt, unbecoming, un-

fit, unhappy, unseemly, unsuitable, wrong *Ant* appropriate, becoming, befitting, correct, decorous, felicitous, fit, fitting, genteel, happy, meet, proper, right, seemly, suitable **2** *Syn* UNFIT, inappropriate, inapt, infelicitous, unfitting, unhappy, unsuitable *Ant* fit

impropriety 1 · a socially improper or unsuitable act or remark *Syn* familiarity, gaffe, indiscretion, solecism *Rel* blunder, error, flub, fumble, goof, lapse, miscue, misstep, mistake, slip, slipup, stumble *Ant* amenity, civility, courtesy, formality, gesture **2** · the quality or state of not being socially proper *Syn* inappropriateness, incorrectness, indecency, unfitness *Rel* coarseness, crudeness *Ant* appropriateness, correctness, decency, decorousness, fitness, propriety, rightness, seemliness, suitability **3** *Syn* BARBARISM, corruption, solecism, vernacularism, vulgarism

improve 1 · to make more acceptable or bring nearer to some standard *Syn* ameliorate, better, help *Rel* benefit, profit *Ant* impair, worsen **2** · to grow or become better (as in health or well-being) *Syn* convalesce, gain, recover, recuperate

improvement *Syn* ADVANCE (sense 1), advancement, breakthrough, enhancement, refinement *Ant* setback

improvised *Syn* EXTEMPORANEOUS, extemporary, extempore, impromptu, offhand, unpremeditated

imprudent *Syn* INDISCREET, ill-advised, inadvisable, injudicious, tactless, unadvisable, unwise *Ant* advisable, discreet, judicious, prudent, tactful, wise

impudence *Syn* BACK TALK, cheek, impertinence, insolence, sass, sauce

impudent *Syn* SHAMELESS, barefaced, brash, brazen

impugn *Syn* DENY, contradict, contravene, gainsay, negative, traverse *Ant* concede, confirm

impulse *Syn* MOTIVE, goad, incentive, inducement, spring, spur

impulsive 1 *Syn* COMPULSIVE, obsessive **2** *Syn* SPONTANEOUS, automatic, instinctive, mechanical **3** *Syn* WHIMSICAL, capricious, freakish

impure · containing foreign or lower-grade substances *Syn* adulterated, alloyed, contaminated, dilute, diluted, polluted, tainted, thinned, weakened *Rel* befouled, besmirched, corrupted, debased, defiled, dirtied, fouled, soiled, spoiled, sullied *Ant* pure, unadulterated, unalloyed, uncontaminated, undiluted, unpolluted, untainted

impute *Syn* ASCRIBE, accredit, assign, attribute, charge, credit, refer

inability · the lack of sufficient ability, power, or means *Syn* impotence, inadequacy, incapability, incapacity, incompetence, ineptitude, powerlessness *Rel* inaptitude *Ant* ability, adequacy, capability, capacity, competence, potency

inactive · not engaged in work or activity *Syn* idle, inert, passive, supine *Rel* abeyant, dormant, latent, potential, quiescent *Ant* active, live

inadequacy 1 *Syn* DEFICIENCY, dearth, deficit, failure, famine, insufficiency, lack, paucity, poverty, scantiness, scarceness, scarcity, shortage, want *Ant* abundance, adequacy, amplitude, plenitude, plenty, sufficiency 2 *Syn* INABILITY, impotence, incapability, incapacity, incompetence, ineptitude, powerlessness *Ant* ability, adequacy, capability, capacity, competence, potency

inadequately *Syn* BADLY, poorly, unacceptably, unsatisfactorily *Ant* acceptably, adequately, all right, fine, good, palatably, passably, so-so, tolerably

inadvertent 1 *Syn* ACCIDENTAL, casual, chance, fluky, fortuitous, incidental, unintended, unintentional, unplanned, unpremeditated, unwitting *Ant* deliberate, intended, intentional, planned, premeditated 2 *Syn* CARELESS, heedless, thoughtless *Ant* careful

inadvisable *Syn* INDISCREET, ill-advised, imprudent, injudicious, tactless, unadvisable, unwise *Ant* advisable, discreet, judicious, prudent, tactful, wise

inane 1 *Syn* INSIPID, banal, flat, jejune, vapid, wishy-washy *Ant* sapid, zestful 2 *Syn* MEANINGLESS, empty, pointless, senseless *Ant* meaningful

inanimate *Syn* DEAD, deceased, defunct, departed, late, lifeless

inapplicable *Syn* IRRELEVANT, extraneous, immaterial *Ant* applicable, apposite, apropos, germane, material, pertinent, relevant

inappreciable *Syn* IMPERCEPTIBLE, impalpable, indistinguishable, insensible *Ant* appreciable, discernible, palpable, perceptible, sensible

inappropriate 1 · not appropriate for a particular occasion or situation *Syn* graceless, improper, inapt, incongruous, incorrect, indecorous, inept, infelicitous, unapt, unbecoming, unfit, unhappy, unseemly, unsuitable, wrong *Rel* inopportune, unfortunate, unseasonable, untimely *Ant* appropriate, becoming, befitting, correct, decorous, felicitous, fit, fitting, genteel, happy, meet, proper, right, seemly, suitable 2 *Syn* UNFIT, improper, inapt, infelicitous, unfitting, unhappy, unsuitable *Ant* fit

inappropriateness *Syn* IMPROPRIETY (sense 2), incorrectness, indecency, unfitness *Ant* appropriateness, correctness, decency, decorousness, fitness, propriety, rightness, seemliness, suitability

inapt 1 *Syn* INAPPROPRIATE, graceless, improper, incongruous, incorrect, indecorous,

inept, infelicitous, unapt, unbecoming, unfit, unhappy, unseemly, unsuitable, wrong *Ant* appropriate, becoming, befitting, correct, decorous, felicitous, fit, fitting, genteel, happy, meet, proper, right, seemly, suitable 2 *Syn* UNFIT, improper, inappropriate, infelicitous, unfitting, unhappy, unsuitable *Ant* fit

inarticulate *Syn* MUTE, speechless, voiceless

inasmuch as *Syn* BECAUSE, as, for, since

inaugurate *Syn* INITIATE, induct, install, invest

inauspicious *Syn* OMINOUS, baleful, dire, foreboding, menacing, portentous, sinister, threatening

inborn *Syn* INNATE, congenital, hereditary, inbred, inherited *Ant* acquired

inbred *Syn* INNATE, congenital, hereditary, inborn, inherited *Ant* acquired

incandescent *Syn* BRIGHT, beaming, brilliant, effulgent, lambent, lucent, luminous, lustrous, radiant, refulgent *Ant* dim, dull

incapability *Syn* INABILITY, impotence, inadequacy, incapacity, incompetence, ineptitude, powerlessness *Ant* ability, adequacy, capability, capacity, competence, potency

incapable *Syn* INCOMPETENT, inept, inexpert, unfit, unqualified, unskilled, unskillful *Ant* able, capable, competent, expert, fit, qualified, skilled, skillful

incapacity *Syn* INABILITY, impotence, inadequacy, incapability, incompetence, ineptitude, powerlessness *Ant* ability, adequacy, capability, capacity, competence, potency

incarcerate *Syn* IMPRISON, immure, intern, jail

incarnate 1 *Syn* EMBODY (sense 2), epitomize, manifest, materialize, personalize, personify, substantiate 2 *Syn* REALIZE, actualize, embody, externalize, hypostatize, materialize, objectify, reify

incarnation *Syn* EMBODIMENT, epitome, manifestation, personification

incendiary *n* 1 *Syn* AGITATOR, demagogue, exciter, firebrand, fomenter, inciter, instigator, rabble-rouser 2 *Syn* ARSONIST, firebug

incendiary *adj Syn* COMBUSTIBLE, flammable, inflammable, inflammatory

incense 1 *Syn* ANGER, antagonize, enrage, inflame, infuriate, madden, outrage, rankle, rile, roil *Ant* delight, gratify, please 2 *Syn* FRAGRANCE, bouquet, perfume, redolence *Ant* stench, stink

incensed *Syn* ANGRY, angered, apoplectic, enraged, foaming, fuming, furious, indignant, inflamed, infuriated, irate, ireful, mad, outraged, rabid, riled, roiled, sore, steaming, wrathful, wroth *Ant* delighted, pleased

incentive *Syn* MOTIVE, goad, impulse, inducement, spring, spur

inception 1 *Syn* BEGINNING, alpha, birth, commencement, dawn, genesis, incipiency, launch, morning, onset, outset, start, threshold *Ant* close, conclusion, end, ending **2** *Syn* ORIGIN, prime mover, provenance, provenience, root, source

incertitude *Syn* DOUBT, distrust, distrustfulness, misgiving, mistrust, mistrustfulness, skepticism, suspicion, uncertainty *Ant* assurance, belief, certainty, certitude, confidence, conviction, sureness, surety, trust

incessant *Syn* CONTINUAL, constant, continuous, perennial, perpetual, unremitting *Ant* intermittent

incident *Syn* OCCURRENCE, circumstance, episode, event

incidental *Syn* ACCIDENTAL, casual, chance, fluky, fortuitous, inadvertent, unintended, unintentional, unplanned, unpremeditated, unwitting *Ant* deliberate, intended, intentional, planned, premeditated

incipiency *Syn* BEGINNING, alpha, birth, commencement, dawn, genesis, inception, launch, morning, onset, outset, start, threshold *Ant* close, conclusion, end, ending

incise *Syn* CARVE, chisel, engrave, etch, sculpt, sculpture

incisive · having, manifesting, or suggesting a keen alertness of mind *Syn* biting, clearcut, crisp, cutting, trenchant *Rel* concise, laconic, succinct, terse

incite · to spur to action *Syn* abet, foment, instigate *Rel* excite, galvanize, pique, provoke, stimulate *Ant* restrain

incitement *Syn* STIMULUS, excitant, impetus, stimulant

inciter *Syn* AGITATOR, demagogue, exciter, firebrand, fomenter, incendiary, instigator, rabble-rouser

inciting *Syn* PROVOCATIVE, exciting, instigating, piquing, provoking, stimulating

incline 1 · to influence one to have or to take an attitude toward something *Syn* bias, dispose, predispose *Rel* affect, influence, sway *Ant* disincline, indispose **2** *Syn* SLANT, lean, slope

inclined *Syn* PRONE (sense 1), apt, given, tending *Ant* erect

include · to contain within as part of the whole *Syn* comprehend, embrace, imply, involve, subsume *Rel* accommodate, contain, hold *Ant* exclude

inclusive *Syn* ENCYCLOPEDIC, compendious, complete, comprehensive, full, global, indepth, omnibus, panoramic, universal

incognito *Syn* PSEUDONYM, alias, nom de guerre, nom de plume, pen name

incommode *Syn* INCONVENIENCE, discommode, disoblige, disturb, trouble *Ant* accommodate, oblige

incomparable *Syn* SUPREME, peerless, preeminent, superlative, surpassing, transcendent

incompatible *Syn* INCONSONANT, discordant, discrepant, incongruous, inconsistent, uncongenial, unsympathetic *Ant* consonant

incompetence *Syn* INABILITY, impotence, inadequacy, incapability, incapacity, ineptitude, powerlessness *Ant* ability, adequacy, capability, capacity, competence, potency

incompetent · lacking qualities (as knowledge, skill, or ability) required to do a job *Syn* incapable, inept, inexpert, unfit, unqualified, unskilled, unskillful *Rel* ineffective, ineffectual, inefficient *Ant* able, capable, competent, expert, fit, qualified, skilled, skillful

incompletely *Syn* PARTLY, part, partially *Ant* completely, entirely, totally, wholly

incomprehensible · impossible to understand *Syn* impenetrable, unfathomable, unintelligible *Rel* abstruse, baffling, bewildering, confounding, confusing, cryptic, enigmatic, esoteric, inscrutable, mysterious, mystifying, obscure, perplexing, puzzling, recondite, unanswerable, unknowable *Ant* fathomable, intelligible, understandable

incongruous 1 *Syn* INAPPROPRIATE, graceless, improper, inapt, incorrect, indecorous, inept, infelicitous, unapt, unbecoming, unfit, unhappy, unseemly, unsuitable, wrong *Ant* appropriate, becoming, befitting, correct, decorous, felicitous, fit, fitting, genteel, happy, meet, proper, right, seemly, suitable **2** *Syn* INCONSONANT, discordant, discrepant, incompatible, inconsistent, uncongenial, unsympathetic *Ant* consonant

inconsequential *Syn* UNIMPORTANT, frivolous, inconsiderable, insignificant, little, minor, minute, negligible, slight, small, small-fry, trifling, trivial *Ant* big, consequential, eventful, important, major, material, meaningful, momentous, significant, substantial, weighty

inconsiderable *Syn* UNIMPORTANT, frivolous, inconsequential, insignificant, little, minor, minute, negligible, slight, small, small-fry, trifling, trivial *Ant* big, consequential, eventful, important, major, material, meaningful, momentous, significant, substantial, weighty

inconsiderate *Syn* IMPOLITE, discourteous, ill-bred, ill-mannered, impertinent, rude, thoughtless, uncalled-for, uncivil, ungracious, unmannerly *Ant* civil, considerate, courteous, genteel, gracious, mannerly, polite, thoughtful, well-bred

inconsistent *Syn* INCONSONANT, discordant, discrepant, incompatible, incongruous, uncongenial, unsympathetic *Ant* consonant

inconsolable *Syn* SAD (sense 1), bad, blue, brokenhearted, crestfallen, dejected, depressed, despondent, disconsolate, doleful, down, downcast, downhearted, droopy, forlorn, gloomy, glum, heartbroken, heartsick, heartsore, joyless, low, low-spirited, melancholy, miserable, mournful, saddened, sorrowful, sorry, unhappy, woebegone, woeful, wretched *Ant* blissful, buoyant, buoyed, cheerful, cheery, chipper, delighted, glad, gladdened, gladsome, gleeful, happy, joyful, joyous, jubilant, sunny, upbeat

inconsonant · not in agreement with or not agreeable to *Syn* discordant, discrepant, incompatible, incongruous, inconsistent, uncongenial, unsympathetic *Ant* consonant

inconspicuous *Syn* UNOBTRUSIVE, unnoticeable *Ant* conspicuous, noticeable

inconstant · lacking firmness or steadiness (as in purpose or devotion) *Syn* capricious, fickle, mercurial, unstable *Rel* changeable, changeful, mutable, protean, variable *Ant* constant

incontestable *Syn* IRREFUTABLE, incontrovertible, indisputable, indubitable, unanswerable, undeniable, unquestionable *Ant* answerable, debatable, disputable, questionable

incontrovertible *Syn* IRREFUTABLE, incontestable, indisputable, indubitable, unanswerable, undeniable, unquestionable *Ant* answerable, debatable, disputable, questionable

inconvenience · to cause discomfort to or trouble for *Syn* discommode, disoblige, disturb, incommode, trouble *Rel* burden, encumber, saddle, weigh *Ant* accommodate, oblige

incorporate *Syn* EMBODY (sense 1), assimilate, integrate

incorporeal *Syn* IMMATERIAL, spiritual *Ant* material

incorrect *Syn* INAPPROPRIATE, graceless, improper, inapt, incongruous, indecorous, inept, infelicitous, unapt, unbecoming, unfit, unhappy, unseemly, unsuitable, wrong *Ant* appropriate, becoming, befitting, correct, decorous, felicitous, fit, fitting, genteel, happy, meet, proper, right, seemly, suitable

incorrectness *Syn* IMPROPRIETY (sense 2), inappropriateness, indecency, unfitness *Ant* appropriateness, correctness, decency, decorousness, fitness, propriety, rightness, seemliness, suitability

increase **1** · to make greater in size, amount, or number *Syn* add (to), aggrandize, amplify, augment, boost, compound, enlarge, escalate, expand, extend, multiply, raise, swell, up *Rel* skyrocket *Ant* abate, contract, decrease, diminish, lessen, lower, reduce, subtract (from) **2** · to become greater in extent, volume, amount, or number *Syn* accumulate, appreciate, balloon, build (up), burgeon, enlarge, escalate, expand, mount, multiply, mushroom, proliferate, rise, snowball, swell, wax *Rel* rocket, skyrocket *Ant* contract, decrease, diminish, lessen, wane

incredulity *Syn* UNBELIEF, disbelief *Ant* belief

increment *Syn* ADDITION, accession, accretion

incremental *Syn* GRADUAL, gradational, phased, piecemeal, step-by-step *Ant* sudden

incriminate *Syn* ACCUSE, charge, impeach, indict *Ant* absolve, acquit, clear, exculpate, exonerate, vindicate

incubus *Syn* DEMON, devil, fiend, ghoul, imp

inculcate *Syn* IMPLANT, instill

incumbent *Syn* MANDATORY, compulsory, forced, imperative, involuntary, necessary, nonelective, obligatory, peremptory, required *Ant* elective, optional, voluntary

incurious *Syn* INDIFFERENT, aloof, detached, disinterested, unconcerned, uninterested *Ant* avid

incursion *Syn* INVASION, inroad, raid

indebtedness *Syn* DEBT, arrear, debit, liability, obligation

indecency *Syn* IMPROPRIETY (sense 2), inappropriateness, incorrectness, unfitness *Ant* appropriateness, correctness, decency, decorousness, fitness, propriety, rightness, seemliness, suitability

indecision *Syn* HESITATION, faltering, hesitance, hesitancy, irresolution, shilly-shallying, vacillation, wavering, wobbling

indecorous *Syn* INAPPROPRIATE, graceless, improper, inapt, incongruous, incorrect, inept, infelicitous, unapt, unbecoming, unfit, unhappy, unseemly, unsuitable, wrong *Ant* appropriate, becoming, befitting, correct, decorous, felicitous, fit, fitting, genteel, happy, meet, proper, right, seemly, suitable

indefatigable · capable of prolonged and arduous effort *Syn* tireless, unflagging, untiring, unwearied, unwearying, weariless *Rel* assiduous, busy, diligent, industrious, sedulous

indefensible *Syn* INEXCUSABLE, unforgivable, unjustifiable, unpardonable, unwarrantable *Ant* defensible, excusable, forgivable, justifiable, pardonable

indefinable *Syn* UNUTTERABLE, indescribable, ineffable, inexpressible, unspeakable

indefinite *Syn* INFINITE, boundless, endless, illimitable, immeasurable, limitless, measureless, unbounded, unfathomable, unlimited *Ant* bounded, circumscribed, confined, definite, finite, limited, restricted

indemnify *Syn* PAY, compensate, recompense, reimburse, remunerate, repay, satisfy

indemnity *Syn* REPARATION, amends, redress, restitution

indented *Syn* HOLLOW, concave, dented, depressed, recessed, sunken *Ant* bulging, convex, protruding, protuberant

indentured *Syn* BOUND, articled, bond

independence *Syn* FREEDOM (sense 1), autarchy, autarky, autonomy, sovereignty *Ant* bondage

independent **1** *Syn* FREE, autarchic, autar-

kic, autonomous, sovereign *Ant* bond **2** *Syn*
SELF-SUFFICIENT, self-reliant, self-supporting
Ant dependent, reliant

in-depth *Syn* ENCYCLOPEDIC, compendious,
complete, comprehensive, full, global, inclusive, omnibus, panoramic, universal

indescribable *Syn* UNUTTERABLE, indefinable, ineffable, inexpressible, unspeakable

Indian *Syn* AMERICAN INDIAN, Amerindian,
Native American

indicate **1** · to give evidence of or to serve
as ground for a valid or reasonable inference
Syn argue, attest, bespeak, betoken, prove
Rel hint, intimate, suggest **2** *Syn* HINT, allude, imply, infer, insinuate, intimate, suggest

indict *Syn* ACCUSE, charge, impeach, incriminate *Ant* absolve, acquit, clear, exculpate, exonerate, vindicate

indictment *Syn* CHARGE, complaint, count,
rap

indifference · lack of interest or concern *Syn*
apathy, casualness, disinterestedness, disregard, insouciance, nonchalance, unconcern
Rel halfheartedness, lukewarmness *Ant* concern, interest, regard

indifferent **1** · not showing or feeling interest *Syn* aloof, detached, disinterested,
incurious, unconcerned, uninterested *Rel* dispassionate, fair, impartial, unbiased *Ant* avid
2 *Syn* MEDIUM, average, fair, mediocre, middling, moderate, second-rate

indigence *Syn* POVERTY, destitution, penury,
privation, want *Ant* riches

indigenous *Syn* NATIVE, aboriginal, autochthonous, endemic *Ant* alien, foreign

indigent *Syn* POOR, destitute, impecunious,
necessitous, needy, penniless, poverty-
stricken *Ant* rich

indignant *Syn* ANGRY, angered, apoplectic,
enraged, foaming, fuming, furious, incensed,
inflamed, infuriated, irate, ireful, mad, outraged, rabid, riled, roiled, sore, steaming,
wrathful, wroth *Ant* delighted, pleased

indignation *Syn* ANGER, angriness, furor,
fury, irateness, ire, outrage, rage, spleen,
wrath, wrathfulness *Ant* delight, pleasure

indignity *Syn* INSULT, affront, barb, dart, dig,
epithet, name, offense (*or* offence), outrage,
put-down, sarcasm, slight, slur

indirect · deviating from a direct line or
straightforward course *Syn* circuitous, roundabout *Rel* crooked, devious, oblique *Ant* direct, forthright, straightforward

indiscreet · showing poor judgment especially in personal relationships or social
situations *Syn* ill-advised, imprudent, inadvisable, injudicious, tactless, unadvisable,
unwise *Rel* dumb, idiotic, moronic, stupid
Ant advisable, discreet, judicious, prudent,
tactful, wise

indiscretion *Syn* IMPROPRIETY (sense 1), fa-

miliarity, gaffe, solecism *Ant* amenity, civility, courtesy, formality, gesture

indiscriminate · including all or nearly all
within the range of choice, operation, or effectiveness *Syn* sweeping, wholesale *Rel*
assorted, heterogeneous, miscellaneous, motley, promiscuous *Ant* discriminating, selective

indispensable *Syn* NEEDFUL, essential, necessary, requisite

indisposed *Syn* DISINCLINED, averse, hesitant, loath, reluctant

indisputable *Syn* IRREFUTABLE, incontestable, incontrovertible, indubitable, unanswerable, undeniable, unquestionable *Ant*
answerable, debatable, disputable, questionable

indistinguishable *Syn* IMPERCEPTIBLE, impalpable, inappreciable, insensible *Ant* appreciable, discernible, palpable, perceptible,
sensible

individual *adj* **1** *Syn* CHARACTERISTIC, distinctive, peculiar **2** *Syn* SPECIAL, especial,
particular, specific

individual *n Syn* ENTITY, being, creature, person

individuality *Syn* DISPOSITION, character,
complexion, personality, temper, temperament

individually *Syn* EACH, apiece, respectively,
severally

indolent *Syn* LAZY, faineant, slothful *Ant* industrious

indomitable *Syn* INVINCIBLE, impregnable,
inexpugnable, invulnerable, unassailable, unconquerable

indubitable *Syn* IRREFUTABLE, incontestable,
incontrovertible, indisputable, unanswerable,
undeniable, unquestionable *Ant* answerable,
debatable, disputable, questionable

induce **1** *Syn* EFFECT, bring about, cause,
create, effectuate, engender, generate, make,
produce, prompt, result (in), spawn, work,
yield **2** *Syn* PERSUADE, argue, convince,
get, move, prevail (on *or* upon), satisfy, talk
(into), win (over)

inducement *Syn* MOTIVE, goad, impulse, incentive, spring, spur

induct *Syn* INITIATE, inaugurate, install, invest

indulgence *Syn* FORBEARANCE, clemency,
leniency, mercifulness, tolerance *Ant* anger,
vindictiveness

indulgent *Syn* FORBEARING, clement, lenient,
merciful, tolerant *Ant* unrelenting

indulgently *Syn* FORBEARINGLY, clemently,
leniently, mercifully, tolerantly

indurate *Syn* HARDEN (sense 1), cake, petrify,
solidify *Ant* soften

indurated *Syn* HARDENED, callous *Ant* softened

industrious *Syn* BUSY, assiduous, diligent,
sedulous *Ant* idle, unoccupied

industry *Syn* BUSINESS, commerce, trade, traffic

inebriate *Syn* DRUNKARD, alcoholic, dipsomaniac, soak, sot, tippler, toper, tosspot *Ant* teetotaler

inebriated *Syn* DRUNK, drunken, intoxicated, tight, tipsy *Ant* sober

ineffable *Syn* UNUTTERABLE, indefinable, indescribable, inexpressible, unspeakable

ineffective · not producing or incapable of producing an intended result *Syn* ineffectual, inefficacious, inefficient *Rel* abortive, bootless, fruitless, futile, vain *Ant* effective

ineffectual *Syn* INEFFECTIVE, inefficacious, inefficient *Ant* effective

inefficacious *Syn* INEFFECTIVE, ineffectual, inefficient *Ant* effective

inefficient *Syn* INEFFECTIVE, ineffectual, inefficacious *Ant* effective

inept **1** *Syn* AWKWARD, clumsy, gauche, maladroit *Ant* deft, graceful, handy **2** *Syn* INAPPROPRIATE, graceless, improper, inapt, incongruous, incorrect, indecorous, infelicitous, unapt, unbecoming, unfit, unhappy, unseemly, unsuitable, wrong *Ant* appropriate, becoming, befitting, correct, decorous, felicitous, fit, fitting, genteel, happy, meet, proper, right, seemly, suitable **3** *Syn* INCOMPETENT, incapable, inexpert, unfit, unqualified, unskilled, unskillful *Ant* able, capable, competent, expert, fit, qualified, skilled, skillful

ineptitude *Syn* INABILITY, impotence, inadequacy, incapability, incapacity, incompetence, powerlessness *Ant* ability, adequacy, capability, capacity, competence, potency

inerrable *Syn* INFALLIBLE, inerrant, unerring *Ant* fallible

inerrant *Syn* INFALLIBLE, inerrable, unerring *Ant* fallible

inert *Syn* INACTIVE, idle, passive, supine *Ant* active, live

inescapable *Syn* INEVITABLE, certain, necessary, sure, unavoidable *Ant* avoidable, escapable, uncertain, unsure

inevitable **1** · impossible to avoid or evade *Syn* certain, inescapable, necessary, sure, unavoidable *Rel* decided, definite, settled *Ant* avoidable, escapable, uncertain, unsure **2** *Syn* CERTAIN, necessary *Ant* probable, supposed

inexcusable · too bad to be excused or justified *Syn* indefensible, unforgivable, unjustifiable, unpardonable, unwarrantable *Rel* insufferable, insupportable, intolerable, unbearable, unendurable *Ant* defensible, excusable, forgivable, justifiable, pardonable

inexperienced **1** *Syn* AMATEURISH, amateur, dilettante, inexpert, nonprofessional, unprofessional, unskilled, unskillful *Ant* ace, adept, consummate, crackerjack, expert, master, masterful, masterly, professional, virtuoso **2** *Syn* CALLOW, adolescent, green, immature,

juvenile, puerile, raw, unfledged, unripe, unripened *Ant* adult, experienced, grown-up, mature, ripe

inexpert **1** *Syn* AMATEURISH, amateur, dilettante, inexperienced, nonprofessional, unprofessional, unskilled, unskillful *Ant* ace, adept, consummate, crackerjack, expert, master, masterful, masterly, professional, virtuoso **2** *Syn* INCOMPETENT, incapable, inept, unfit, unqualified, unskilled, unskillful *Ant* able, capable, competent, expert, fit, qualified, skilled, skillful

inexpressible *Syn* UNUTTERABLE, indefinable, indescribable, ineffable, unspeakable

inexpugnable *Syn* INVINCIBLE, impregnable, indomitable, invulnerable, unassailable, unconquerable

infallible · incapable of making mistakes or errors *Syn* inerrable, inerrant, unerring *Rel* certain, inevitable, necessary *Ant* fallible

infamous *Syn* VICIOUS, corrupt, degenerate, flagitious, iniquitous, nefarious, villainous *Ant* virtuous

infamy *Syn* DISGRACE, dishonor, disrepute, ignominy, obloquy, odium, opprobrium, shame *Ant* esteem, respect

infant *Syn* BABY, babe, child, newborn

infantile *Syn* CHILDISH, adolescent, babyish, immature, juvenile, kiddish, puerile *Ant* adult, grown-up, mature

infatuated *Syn* FOND, besotted, insensate

infectious · transmissible by infection *Syn* catching, communicable, contagious *Rel* mephitic, pestilent, pestilential, poisonous, toxic, virulent

infelicitous **1** *Syn* INAPPROPRIATE, graceless, improper, inapt, incongruous, incorrect, indecorous, inept, unapt, unbecoming, unfit, unhappy, unseemly, unsuitable, wrong *Ant* appropriate, becoming, befitting, correct, decorous, felicitous, fit, fitting, genteel, happy, meet, proper, right, seemly, suitable **2** *Syn* UNFIT, improper, inappropriate, inapt, unfitting, unhappy, unsuitable *Ant* fit

infer **1** · to arrive at by reasoning from evidence or from premises *Syn* conclude, deduce, gather, judge *Rel* reason, speculate, think **2** *Syn* HINT, allude, imply, indicate, insinuate, intimate, suggest

inferable *Syn* DEDUCTIVE, deducible, derivable, reasoned

inference · the deriving of a conclusion by reasoning *Syn* conclusion, deduction, judgment

inferior *n* *Syn* UNDERLING, junior, subordinate *Ant* senior, superior

inferior *adj* *Syn* LESSER, junior, less, lower, minor, smaller, subordinate, under *Ant* greater, higher, major, more, primary, prime, senior, superior

infernal · of or relating to a nether world of the dead *Syn* chthonian, chthonic, Hadean, hellish, stygian, Tartarean *Rel* demoniac, devilish, diabolical, fiendish *Ant* supernal

infertile *Syn* STERILE, barren, impotent, unfruitful *Ant* exuberant, fertile

infest · to spread or swarm over in a troublesome manner *Syn* beset, overrun *Rel* abound, swarm, teem *Ant* disinfest

infidelity *Syn* BETRAYAL, disloyalty, double cross, faithlessness, falseness, falsity, perfidy, sellout, treachery, treason, unfaithfulness

infinite · being or seeming to be without limits *Syn* boundless, endless, illimitable, immeasurable, indefinite, limitless, measureless, unbounded, unfathomable, unlimited *Rel* abysmal, bottomless *Ant* bounded, circumscribed, confined, definite, finite, limited, restricted

infinitesimal *Syn* TINY, atomic, bitty, microminiature, microscopic, miniature, minute, teeny, teeny-weeny, wee *Ant* astronomical, colossal, cosmic, elephantine, enormous, giant, gigantic, herculean, heroic, huge, immense, mammoth, massive, monster, monstrous, monumental, mountainous, prodigious, titanic, tremendous

infirm *Syn* WEAK, decrepit, feeble, fragile, frail *Ant* strong

inflame *Syn* ANGER, antagonize, enrage, incense, infuriate, madden, outrage, rankle, rile, roil *Ant* delight, gratify, please

inflamed *Syn* ANGRY, angered, apoplectic, enraged, foaming, fuming, furious, incensed, indignant, infuriated, irate, ireful, mad, outraged, rabid, riled, roiled, sore, steaming, wrathful, wroth *Ant* delighted, pleased

inflammable *Syn* COMBUSTIBLE, flammable, incendiary, inflammatory

inflammatory *Syn* COMBUSTIBLE, flammable, incendiary, inflammable

inflate *Syn* EXPAND, amplify, dilate, distend, swell *Ant* abridge, circumscribe, contract

inflated · swollen with or as if with something insubstantial *Syn* flatulent, tumid, turgid *Rel* aureate, bombastic, flowery, grandiloquent, magniloquent, rhetorical *Ant* pithy

inflection · a particular manner of employing the sounds of the voice in speech *Syn* accent, intonation *Rel* articulation, enunciation, pronunciation

inflexibility *Syn* SEVERITY, hardness, harshness, rigidity, rigidness, rigorousness, sternness, strictness *Ant* flexibility, gentleness, laxness, mildness

inflexible **1** *Syn* OBSTINATE, adamant, adamantine, dogged, hard, hardened, hardheaded, hardhearted, headstrong, immovable, implacable, mulish, obdurate, opinionated, ossified, pat, peevish, pertinacious, perverse, pigheaded, rigid, self-willed, stubborn, unbending, uncompromising, unrelenting, unyielding, willful (*or* wilful) *Ant* acquiescent, agreeable, amenable, compliant, complying, flexible, pliable, pliant, relenting, yielding **2** *Syn* STIFF, rigid, stark, tense, wooden *Ant* relaxed, supple

influence *n* · power exerted over the minds or behavior of others *Syn* authority, credit, prestige, weight *Rel* actuation, drive, driving, impelling, impulsion

influence *vb Syn* AFFECT, impress, strike, sway, touch

inform **1** · to stimulate (as mental powers) to higher or more intense activity *Syn* animate, fire, inspire *Rel* imbue, infuse, inoculate, leaven **2** · to make one aware of something *Syn* acquaint, advise, apprise, notify *Rel* communicate, impart **3** *Syn* ENLIGHTEN (sense 1), advise, apprise, brief, clue, familiarize, fill in, instruct, tell, wise (up)

information **1** *Syn* KNOWLEDGE, erudition, learning, lore, scholarship, science *Ant* ignorance **2** *Syn* NEWS, intelligence, item, story, tidings, word

infraction *Syn* BREACH (sense 1), contravention, infringement, transgression, trespass, violation

infrequent · not common or abundant *Syn* occasional, rare, scarce, sporadic, uncommon *Rel* exceptional *Ant* frequent

infrequently *Syn* SELDOM, little, rarely *Ant* frequently, often

infringe *Syn* TRESPASS, encroach, entrench, invade

infringement *Syn* BREACH (sense 1), contravention, infraction, transgression, trespass, violation

infuriate *Syn* ANGER, antagonize, enrage, incense, inflame, madden, outrage, rankle, rile, roil *Ant* delight, gratify, please

infuriated *Syn* ANGRY, angered, apoplectic, enraged, foaming, fuming, furious, incensed, indignant, inflamed, irate, ireful, mad, outraged, rabid, riled, roiled, sore, steaming, wrathful, wroth *Ant* delighted, pleased

infuse · to introduce one thing into another so as to affect it throughout *Syn* imbue, ingrain, inoculate, leaven, suffuse *Rel* impenetrate, impregnate, permeate, pervade, saturate

ingeminate *Syn* REPEAT (sense 1), iterate, re-iterate

ingenious *Syn* CLEVER, adroit, cunning

ingenuous *Syn* NATURAL, artless, naive, simple, unaffected, unsophisticated

ingenuously *Syn* NATURALLY (sense 3), artlessly, guilelessly, innocently, naively, sincerely, unaffectedly, unfeignedly, unpretentiously *Ant* affectedly, artificially, hypocritically, insincerely, pretentiously, unnaturally

ingest *Syn* EAT, consume, devour, swallow

ingrain *Syn* INFUSE, imbue, inoculate, leaven, suffuse

ingrained *Syn* INHERENT, constitutional, essential, intrinsic *Ant* adventitious

ingredient *Syn* ELEMENT, component, constituent, factor *Ant* composite, compound (*in science*)

inhabitant · one who lives permanently in a place *Syn* denizen, dweller, habitant, occupant, resident, resider *Rel* aborigine, native *Ant* transient

inherent · being a part, element, or quality of a thing's inmost being *Syn* constitutional, essential, ingrained, intrinsic *Rel* congenital, inborn, inbred, innate *Ant* adventitious

inherently *Syn* NATURALLY (sense 2), constitutionally, innately, intrinsically *Ant* affectedly, artificially, hypocritically, insincerely, pretentiously, unnaturally

inheritance *Syn* HERITAGE, birthright, patrimony

inherited *Syn* INNATE, congenital, hereditary, inborn, inbred *Ant* acquired

inhibit **1** *Syn* DISCOURAGE (sense 2), deter, dissuade *Ant* encourage, persuade **2** *Syn* RESTRAIN, bridle, check, curb *Ant* abandon (*oneself*), activate, impel, incite

inhibition *Syn* ENCUMBRANCE, bar, block, chain, clog, crimp, deterrent, drag, embarrassment, fetter, handicap, hindrance, hurdle, impediment, interference, let, manacle, obstacle, obstruction, shackles, stop, stumbling block, trammel *Ant* aid, assistance, benefit, help

inhuman *Syn* FIERCE, barbarous, cruel, fell, ferocious, savage, truculent *Ant* mild, tame

inhumanity *Syn* CRUELTY, barbarity, brutality, cruelness, heartlessness, sadism, savageness, savagery, viciousness, wantonness *Ant* benignity, compassion, good-heartedness, humanity, kindheartedness, kindness, sympathy

iniquitous *Syn* VICIOUS, corrupt, degenerate, flagitious, infamous, nefarious, villainous *Ant* virtuous

iniquity *Syn* EVIL, bad, evildoing, ill, immorality, sin, villainy, wrong *Ant* good, morality, right, virtue

initial · marking a beginning or constituting a start *Syn* original, primordial *Rel* beginning, commencing, starting *Ant* final

initiate · to put through the formalities for becoming a member or an official *Syn* inaugurate, induct, install, invest *Rel* admit, enter, introduce

initiative *Syn* MANDATE, plebiscite, referendum

injudicious *Syn* INDISCREET, ill-advised, imprudent, inadvisable, tactless, unadvisable, unwise *Ant* advisable, discreet, judicious, prudent, tactful, wise

injunction *Syn* COMMAND, behest, bidding, dictate, mandate, order

injure · to deplete the soundness, strength, effectiveness, or perfection of something *Syn* damage, harm, hurt, impair, mar, spoil *Rel* deface, disfigure *Ant* aid

injurious *Syn* HARMFUL, adverse, bad, baleful, baneful, damaging, deleterious, detrimental, evil, hurtful, ill, mischievous, noxious, pernicious, prejudicial *Ant* harmless, innocent, innocuous, inoffensive, safe

injury **1** · the act or the result of inflicting something that causes loss or pain *Syn* damage, harm, hurt, mischief *Rel* agony, distress, misery, suffering **2** *Syn* DISSERVICE, injustice, raw deal, wrong *Ant* justice

injustice *Syn* DISSERVICE, injury, raw deal, wrong *Ant* justice

innate · not acquired after birth *Syn* congenital, hereditary, inborn, inbred, inherited *Rel* constitutional, essential, ingrained, inherent, intrinsic *Ant* acquired

innately *Syn* NATURALLY (sense 2), constitutionally, inherently, intrinsically *Ant* affectedly, artificially, hypocritically, insincerely, pretentiously, unnaturally

inner · situated further in *Syn* inside, interior, internal, intestine, inward *Rel* central, focal, middle, nuclear *Ant* outer

innocent *adj Syn* HARMLESS, innocuous, inoffensive, unoffending *Ant* harmful

innocent *n Syn* LAMB, angel, dove, sheep *Ant* wolf

innocently *Syn* NATURALLY (sense 3), artlessly, guilelessly, ingenuously, naively, sincerely, unaffectedly, unfeignedly, unpretentiously *Ant* affectedly, artificially, hypocritically, insincerely, pretentiously, unnaturally

innocuous *Syn* HARMLESS, innocent, inoffensive, unoffending *Ant* harmful

innumerable *Syn* COUNTLESS, numberless, uncountable, uncounted, unnumbered, untold *Ant* countable

inoculate *Syn* INFUSE, imbue, ingrain, leaven, suffuse

inoffensive *Syn* HARMLESS, innocent, innocuous, unoffending *Ant* harmful

inoperable *Syn* IMPRACTICAL, impracticable, nonpractical, unusable, unworkable, useless *Ant* applicable, feasible, functional, operable, operational, practicable, practical, usable, useful, workable

inordinate *Syn* EXCESSIVE, exorbitant, extravagant, extreme, immoderate *Ant* deficient

inquest *Syn* INQUIRY, inquisition, investigation, probe, research

inquire *Syn* ASK (sense 1), catechize, examine, interrogate, query, question, quiz

inquire (into) *Syn* EXPLORE, delve (into), dig (into), investigate, look (into), probe, research

inquiry · a search for truth, knowledge, or information *Syn* inquest, inquisition, investigation, probe, research *Rel* catechizing, interrogation, questioning

inquisition *Syn* INQUIRY, inquest, investigation, probe, research

inquisitive *Syn* CURIOUS, nosy, prying, snoopy *Ant* incurious, uninterested

inroad *Syn* INVASION, incursion, raid

insane · afflicted by or manifesting unsoundness of mind or an inability to control one's rational processes *Syn* crazed, crazy, demented, deranged, lunatic, mad, maniac, non compos mentis *Rel* irrational, unreasonable *Ant* sane

insanity · a deranged state of mind or serious mental disorder *Syn* lunacy, mania, psychosis *Rel* aberration, alienation, derangement *Ant* sanity

inscription · something written, printed, or engraved (as on a coin or a medal or under or over a picture) to indicate or describe the purpose or the nature of the thing *Syn* caption, legend

inscrutable *Syn* MYSTERIOUS, arcane

insensate *Syn* FOND, besotted, infatuated

insensibility *Syn* FAINT, blackout, coma, knockout, swoon

insensible 1 · unresponsive to stimuli or to external influences *Syn* anesthetic, impassible, insensitive *Rel* blunt, dull, obtuse *Ant* sensible (*to or of something*) 2 *Syn* IMPERCEPTIBLE, impalpable, inappreciable, indistinguishable *Ant* appreciable, discernible, palpable, perceptible, sensible

insensitive 1 *Syn* INSENSIBLE, anesthetic, impassible *Ant* sensible (*to or of something*) 2 *Syn* NUMB, asleep, benumbed, dead, numbed, unfeeling *Ant* feeling, sensitive

insert *Syn* INTRODUCE, insinuate, intercalate, interject, interpolate, interpose *Ant* abstract, withdraw

inside *Syn* INNER, interior, internal, intestine, inward *Ant* outer

insidious *Syn* SLY, artful, crafty, cunning, foxy, guileful, tricky, wily

insight *Syn* DISCERNMENT, acumen, discrimination, penetration, perception

insignificant *Syn* UNIMPORTANT, frivolous, inconsequential, inconsiderable, little, minor, minute, negligible, slight, small, small-fry, trifling, trivial *Ant* big, consequential, eventful, important, major, material, meaningful, momentous, significant, substantial, weighty

insincere · not being or expressing what one appears to be or express *Syn* artificial, backhanded, double-dealing, feigned, hypocritical, left-handed, mealy, mealymouthed, two-faced, unctuous *Rel* empty, hollow, meaningless *Ant* genuine, heartfelt, honest, sincere, unfeigned

insincerity *Syn* HYPOCRISY, cant, dissembling, dissimulation, piousness, sanctimoniousness *Ant* genuineness, sincerity

insinuate 1 *Syn* HINT, allude, imply, indicate, infer, intimate, suggest 2 *Syn* INTRODUCE, insert, intercalate, interject, interpolate, interpose *Ant* abstract, withdraw

insipid · devoid of qualities that make for spirit and character *Syn* banal, flat, inane, jejune, vapid, wishy-washy *Rel* rare, slight, tenuous, thin *Ant* sapid, zestful

insistent 1 *Syn* PERSISTENT, dogged, patient, persevering, pertinacious, tenacious 2 *Syn* PRESSING, crying, exigent, imperative, importunate, instant, urgent

insolence *Syn* BACK TALK, cheek, impertinence, impudence, sass, sauce

insolent *Syn* PROUD (sense 1), arrogant, disdainful, haughty, lordly, overbearing, supercilious *Ant* ashamed, humble

insouciance *Syn* INDIFFERENCE, apathy, casualness, disinterestedness, disregard, nonchalance, unconcern *Ant* concern, interest, regard

insouciant *Syn* CAREFREE, careless, cavalier, devil-may-care, easygoing, gay, happy-go-lucky, lighthearted, unconcerned *Ant* careworn

inspect *Syn* SCRUTINIZE, audit, examine, scan

inspection · a close look at or over someone or something in order to judge condition *Syn* audit, check, checkup, examination, review, scan, scrutiny, survey *Rel* analysis, dissection

inspiration · a divine or seemingly divine imparting of knowledge or power *Syn* afflatus, frenzy, fury *Rel* enlightenment, illumination

inspire *Syn* INFORM (sense 1), animate, fire

inspirit *Syn* ENCOURAGE, cheer, embolden, hearten, nerve, steel *Ant* discourage

in spite of *Syn* NOTWITHSTANDING, despite

install *Syn* INITIATE, inaugurate, induct, invest

instance *n Syn* EXAMPLE, case, exemplar, illustration, representative, sample, specimen

instance *vb Syn* MENTION, name, specify

instant *n* · a very small space of time *Syn* flash, jiffy, minute, moment, second, shake, split second, trice, twinkle, twinkling, wink *Rel* microsecond, nanosecond

instant *adj Syn* PRESSING, crying, exigent, imperative, importunate, insistent, urgent

instigate *Syn* INCITE, abet, foment *Ant* restrain

instigating *Syn* PROVOCATIVE, exciting, inciting, piquing, provoking, stimulating

instigator *Syn* AGITATOR, demagogue, exciter, firebrand, fomenter, incendiary, inciter, rabble-rouser

instill *Syn* IMPLANT, inculcate

instinctive *Syn* SPONTANEOUS, automatic, impulsive, mechanical

institute *Syn* FOUND, create, establish, organize

instruct 1 *Syn* COMMAND, bid, charge, direct, enjoin, order *Ant* comply, obey **2** *Syn* ENLIGHTEN (sense 1), acquaint, advise, apprise, brief, clue, familiarize, fill in, inform, tell, wise (up) **3** *Syn* TEACH, discipline, educate, school, train

instruction *Syn* EDUCATION (sense 1), schooling, teaching, training, tutelage, tutoring

instructor *Syn* TEACHER, educator, pedagogue, preceptor, schoolteacher

instrument **1** *Syn* AGENT (sense 2), agency, instrumentality, machinery, means, medium, organ, vehicle **2** *Syn* IMPLEMENT, appliance, tool, utensil

instrument *Syn* PAPER, document

instrumentality *Syn* AGENT (sense 2), agency, instrument, machinery, means, medium, organ, vehicle

insubordinate **1** · unwilling to submit to authority *Syn* contumacious, factious, mutinous, rebellious, seditious *Rel* intractable, recalcitrant, refractory, ungovernable, unruly **2** *Syn* DISOBEDIENT, balky, contrary, defiant, froward, intractable, rebellious, recalcitrant, refractory, restive, ungovernable, unruly, untoward, wayward, willful (*or* wilful) *Ant* amenable, compliant, docile, obedient, tractable

insubordination *Syn* DISOBEDIENCE, contrariness, defiance, frowardness, intractability, rebelliousness, recalcitrance, refractoriness, unruliness, willfulness *Ant* amenability, compliance, docility, obedience

insufferable *Syn* UNBEARABLE, insupportable, intolerable, unendurable, unsupportable *Ant* endurable, sufferable, supportable, tolerable

insufficiency *Syn* DEFICIENCY, dearth, deficit, failure, famine, inadequacy, lack, paucity, poverty, scantiness, scarceness, scarcity, shortage, want *Ant* abundance, adequacy, amplitude, plenitude, plenty, sufficiency

insular · having the narrow and limited outlook characteristic of geographic isolation *Syn* local, parochial, provincial, small-town *Rel* insulated, isolated, secluded

insulate *Syn* ISOLATE, seclude, segregate, sequester

insulation *Syn* ISOLATION, secludedness, seclusion, segregation, separateness, sequestration, solitariness, solitude

insult *n* · an act or expression showing scorn and usually intended to hurt another's feelings *Syn* affront, barb, dart, dig, epithet, indignity, name, offense (*or* offence), outrage, put-down, sarcasm, slight, slur *Rel* abuse, attack, criticism, disapproval, disgrace, dishonor, gibe (*or* jibe), invective, jeer, opprobrium, shame, slam, sneer, taunt, torment, torture, vituperation

insult *vb Syn* OFFEND, affront, outrage

insupportable *Syn* UNBEARABLE, insufferable, intolerable, unendurable, unsupportable *Ant* endurable, sufferable, supportable, tolerable

insure *Syn* ENSURE, assure, cinch, guarantee, guaranty, secure

insurgent *Syn* REBEL, iconoclast

insurrection *Syn* REBELLION, coup, mutiny, putsch, revolt, revolution, uprising

intact *Syn* PERFECT, entire, whole *Ant* imperfect

integer *Syn* NUMBER, digit, figure, numeral

integrate *Syn* EMBODY (sense 1), assimilate, incorporate

integrity **1** *Syn* HONESTY, honor, probity *Ant* dishonesty **2** *Syn* UNITY, solidarity, union

intellect *Syn* MIND, brain, intelligence, psyche, soul, wit

intellectual *Syn* MENTAL, cerebral, intelligent, psychic

intelligence **1** *Syn* MIND, brain, intellect, psyche, soul, wit **2** *Syn* NEWS, information, item, story, tidings, word

intelligent **1** · mentally quick or keen *Syn* alert, bright, brilliant, clever, knowing, quick-witted, smart *Rel* acute, keen, sharp *Ant* unintelligent **2** *Syn* MENTAL, cerebral, intellectual, psychic

intend · to have in mind as a purpose or goal *Syn* design, mean, propose, purpose *Rel* aim, aspire

intended *Syn* BETROTHED, fiancé, fiancée

intense · extreme in degree, power, or effect *Syn* exquisite, fierce, vehement, violent *Rel* aggravated, enhanced, heightened, intensified *Ant* subdued

intensify · to increase markedly in degree or measure *Syn* aggravate, enhance, heighten *Rel* accent, accentuate, emphasize, stress *Ant* abate, allay, mitigate, temper

intent *adj* · having one's mind or attention deeply fixed *Syn* absorbed, engrossed, rapt *Rel* attending, attentive, minding, watching *Ant* distracted

intent *n Syn* GOAL, aim, ambition, aspiration, design, dream, end, intention, mark, meaning, object, objective, plan, pretension, purpose, target, thing

intention · what one intends to accomplish or attain *Syn* aim, design, end, goal, intent, object, objective, purpose *Rel* plan, project, scheme

intentional *Syn* VOLUNTARY, deliberate, willful, willing *Ant* instinctive, involuntary

intentionally · with full awareness of what one is doing *Syn* consciously, deliberately, designedly, knowingly, purposefully, purposely, willfully, wittingly *Rel* calculatingly, studiedly *Ant* inadvertently, unconsciously, unintentionally, unknowingly, unwittingly

intentness *Syn* EARNESTNESS, gravity, seriousness, soberness, sobriety, solemnity *Ant* frivolity, levity, lightheartedness

intercalate Syn INTRODUCE, insert, insinuate, interject, interpolate, interpose Ant abstract, withdraw

intercede Syn INTERVENE, interpose, mediate

intercessor Syn MEDIATOR, arbiter, arbitrator, conciliator, go-between, intermediary, interposer, middleman, peacemaker

interchange Syn EXCHANGE, bandy

interdict vb Syn FORBID, ban, bar, enjoin, outlaw, prohibit, proscribe Ant allow, let, permit, suffer

interdict n Syn PROHIBITION (sense 2), ban, embargo, interdiction, proscription, veto Ant prescription

interdicting Syn PROHIBITION (sense 1), banning, barring, enjoining, forbidding, interdiction, outlawing, prohibiting, proscribing, proscription Ant prescription

interdiction 1 Syn PROHIBITION (sense 1), banning, barring, enjoining, forbidding, interdicting, outlawing, prohibiting, proscribing, proscription Ant prescription 2 Syn PROHIBITION (sense 2), ban, embargo, interdict, proscription, veto Ant prescription

interesting · holding the attention or provoking interest Syn absorbing, arresting, engaging, engrossing, enthralling, fascinating, gripping, immersing, intriguing, involving, riveting Rel breathtaking, electric, electrifying, exciting, exhilarating, galvanizing, inspiring, rousing, stimulating, stirring, thrilling Ant boring, drab, dry, dull, heavy, monotonous, tedious, uninteresting

interfere · to interest oneself in what is not one's concern Syn butt in, intrude, meddle, mess, nose, obtrude, poke, pry, snoop Rel intercede, interpose, intervene

interference Syn ENCUMBRANCE, bar, block, chain, clog, crimp, deterrent, drag, embarrassment, fetter, handicap, hindrance, hurdle, impediment, inhibition, let, manacle, obstacle, obstruction, shackles, stop, stumbling block, trammel Ant aid, assistance, benefit, help

interferer Syn BUSYBODY, interloper, intruder, kibitzer, meddler

interfering Syn INTRUSIVE, intruding, meddlesome, meddling, nosy (or nosey), obtrusive, officious, presumptuous, prying, snoopy Ant unobtrusive

interim Syn BREAK, gap, hiatus, interruption, interval, lacuna

interior Syn INNER, inside, internal, intestine, inward Ant outer

interject Syn INTRODUCE, insert, insinuate, intercalate, interpolate, interpose Ant abstract, withdraw

interloper Syn BUSYBODY, interferer, intruder, kibitzer, meddler

intermediary Syn MEDIATOR, arbiter, arbitrator, conciliator, go-between, intercessor, interposer, middleman, peacemaker

intermediary Syn MIDDLE, halfway, intermediate, medial, median, medium, mid, middlemost, midmost, midway Ant extreme, farthermost, farthest, furthermost, furthest, outermost, outmost, remotest, utmost

intermediate Syn MIDDLE, halfway, intermediary, medial, median, medium, mid, middlemost, midmost, midway Ant extreme, farthermost, farthest, furthermost, furthest, outermost, outmost, remotest, utmost

interminable Syn EVERLASTING, endless, unceasing Ant transitory

intermittent 1 · occurring or appearing in interrupted sequence Syn alternate, periodic, recurrent Rel arrested, checked, interrupted Ant continual, incessant 2 Syn FITFUL, casual, choppy, discontinuous, erratic, irregular, occasional, spasmodic, sporadic, spotty, unsteady Ant constant, continuous, regular, steady

intermixture Syn BLEND, admixture, amalgam, amalgamation, combination, composite, compound, fusion, mix, mixture

intern Syn IMPRISON, immure, incarcerate, jail

internal Syn INNER, inside, interior, intestine, inward Ant outer

interpenetrate Syn PERMEATE, impenetrate, impregnate, penetrate, pervade, saturate

interpolate Syn INTRODUCE, insert, insinuate, intercalate, interject, interpose Ant abstract, withdraw

interpose 1 Syn INTERVENE, intercede, mediate 2 Syn INTRODUCE, insert, insinuate, intercalate, interject, interpolate Ant abstract, withdraw

interposer Syn MEDIATOR, arbiter, arbitrator, conciliator, go-between, intercessor, intermediary, middleman, peacemaker

interpret Syn EXPLAIN (sense 1), clarify, clear (up), construe, demonstrate, elucidate, explicate, expound, illuminate, illustrate, spell out Ant obscure

interrogate Syn ASK (sense 1), catechize, examine, inquire, query, question, quiz

interrupt Syn ARREST (sense 1), check Ant activate, quicken

interruption 1 Syn BREAK, gap, hiatus, interim, interval, lacuna 2 Syn PAUSE, break, breath, breather, lull, recess

interstice Syn APERTURE, orifice

interval Syn BREAK, gap, hiatus, interim, interruption, lacuna

intervene · to act as a go-between for opposing sides Syn intercede, interpose, mediate Rel butt in, interfere, intrude, meddle, obtrude, pry, snoop

intestine Syn INNER, inside, interior, internal, inward Ant outer

intimate adj Syn FAMILIAR, chummy, close, confidential, thick Ant aloof

intimate n Syn FRIEND, acquaintance, confidant Ant foe

intimate *vb Syn* HINT, allude, imply, indicate, infer, insinuate, suggest

intimidate · to frighten into submission *Syn* browbeat, bulldoze, bully, cow *Rel* frighten, terrify, terrorize

intolerable *Syn* UNBEARABLE, insufferable, insupportable, unendurable, unsupportable *Ant* endurable, sufferable, supportable, tolerable

intolerant · unwilling to grant other people social rights or to accept other viewpoints *Syn* bigoted, narrow, narrow-minded, prejudiced, small-minded *Rel* conservative, hidebound, old-fashioned, reactionary *Ant* broad-minded, liberal, open-minded, tolerant, unprejudiced

intonation *Syn* INFLECTION, accent

intone *Syn* SING, carol, chant, descant, hymn, trill, troll, warble

intoxicant *Syn* ALCOHOL, booze, drink, grog, liquor, moonshine, spirits

intoxicated 1 *Syn* DRUNK, drunken, inebriated, tight, tipsy *Ant* sober 2 *Syn* ECSTATIC, elated, enraptured, entranced, euphoric, exhilarated, rapturous, rhapsodic *Ant* depressed

intoxication *Syn* ECSTASY, elation, euphoria, exhilaration, heaven, paradise, rapture, rhapsody, transport *Ant* depression

intractability *Syn* DISOBEDIENCE, contrariness, defiance, frowardness, insubordination, rebelliousness, recalcitrance, refractoriness, unruliness, willfulness *Ant* amenability, compliance, docility, obedience

intractable 1 *Syn* DISOBEDIENT, balky, contrary, defiant, froward, insubordinate, rebellious, recalcitrant, refractory, restive, ungovernable, unruly, untoward, wayward, willful (*or* wilful) *Ant* amenable, compliant, docile, obedient, tractable 2 *Syn* UNCONTROLLABLE, froward, headstrong, recalcitrant, refractory, ungovernable, unmanageable, unruly, untoward, wayward, willful (*or* wilful) *Ant* controllable, governable, tractable 3 *Syn* UNRULY, headstrong, recalcitrant, refractory, ungovernable, willful *Ant* docile, tractable

intrepid *Syn* BRAVE, audacious, bold, courageous, dauntless, doughty, fearless, unafraid, undaunted, valiant, valorous *Ant* craven

intrepidity *Syn* COURAGE, bravery, courageousness, daring, dauntlessness, doughtiness, fearlessness, gallantry, greatheartedness, guts, hardihood, heart, heroism, intrepidness, nerve, stoutness, valor *Ant* cowardice, cowardliness, cravenness, dastardliness, spinelessness, yellowness

intrepidness *Syn* COURAGE, bravery, courageousness, daring, dauntlessness, doughtiness, fearlessness, gallantry, greatheartedness, guts, hardihood, heart, heroism, intrepidity, nerve, stoutness, valor *Ant* cowardice, cowardliness, cravenness, dastardliness, spinelessness, yellowness

intricate *Syn* COMPLEX, complicated, involved, knotty *Ant* simple

intrigue *n* 1 *Syn* AMOUR, affair, liaison 2 *Syn* PLOT, cabal, conspiracy, machination

intrigue *vb Syn* PLOT, conspire, contrive, machinate, scheme

intriguing *Syn* INTERESTING, absorbing, arresting, engaging, engrossing, enthralling, fascinating, gripping, immersing, involving, riveting *Ant* boring, drab, dry, dull, heavy, monotonous, tedious, uninteresting

intrinsic *Syn* INHERENT, constitutional, essential, ingrained *Ant* adventitious

intrinsically *Syn* NATURALLY (sense 2), constitutionally, inherently, innately *Ant* affectedly, artificially, hypocritically, insincerely, pretentiously, unnaturally

introduce 1 · to put among or between others *Syn* insert, insinuate, intercalate, interject, interpolate, interpose *Ant* abstract, withdraw 2 *Syn* ENTER (sense 2), admit

introduction · something that serves as a preliminary or antecedent *Syn* exordium, foreword, preamble, preface, prelude, prologue

introductory *Syn* PRELIMINARY, prefatory, preparatory

intrude *Syn* INTERFERE, butt in, meddle, mess, nose, obtrude, poke, pry, snoop

intruder *Syn* BUSYBODY, interferer, interloper, kibitzer, meddler

intruding *Syn* INTRUSIVE, interfering, meddlesome, meddling, nosy (*or* nosey), obtrusive, officious, presumptuous, prying, snoopy *Ant* unobtrusive

intrusive · thrusting oneself where one is not welcome or invited *Syn* interfering, intruding, meddlesome, meddling, nosy (*or* nosey), obtrusive, officious, presumptuous, prying, snoopy *Rel* bold, brazen, impertinent, impudent, insolent, rude *Ant* unobtrusive

intuition *Syn* REASON (sense 2), understanding

inundate *Syn* FLOOD, deluge, drown, engulf, overflow, overwhelm, submerge, submerse, swamp *Ant* drain

inundation *Syn* FLOOD, cataract, deluge, spate, torrent

inure *Syn* HABITUATE, accustom, addict

invade *Syn* TRESPASS, encroach, entrench, infringe

invader *Syn* AGGRESSOR, raider

invalid 1 *Syn* GROUNDLESS, nonvalid, unfounded, ungrounded, unreasonable, unsubstantiated, unsupported, unwarranted *Ant* good, hard, just, justified, reasonable, reasoned, substantiated, valid, well-founded 2 *Syn* ILLOGICAL, fallacious, irrational, nonrational, unreasonable, unreasoning, unsound, weak *Ant* logical, rational, reasonable, sound, valid

invalidate *Syn* ABOLISH, abrogate, annul, cancel, dissolve, negate, nullify, quash, repeal, rescind, void

invaluable *Syn* COSTLY, dear, expensive, precious, priceless, valuable *Ant* cheap

invariant *Syn* UNIFORM, steady, unchanging, undeviating, unvarying, unwavering *Ant* changing, deviating, varying

invasion · a hostile entrance into the territory of another *Syn* incursion, inroad, raid *Rel* aggression, attack, offense, offensive

invective *Syn* ABUSE, billingsgate, obloquy, scurrility, vituperation *Ant* adulation

invent · to create or think of by clever use of the imagination *Syn* concoct, contrive, cook (up), devise, fabricate, make up, manufacture, think (up) *Rel* coin, contrive, create, design, hatch, produce

inventory *Syn* LIST, catalog, register, roll, roster, schedule, table

invert *Syn* REVERSE, transpose

invest **1** *Syn* BESIEGE, beleaguer, blockade **2** *Syn* INITIATE, inaugurate, induct, install

investigate *Syn* EXPLORE, delve (into), dig (into), inquire (into), look (into), probe, research

investigation *Syn* INQUIRY, inquest, inquisition, probe, research

inveterate · so firmly established that change is almost impossible *Syn* chronic, confirmed, deep-rooted, deep-seated *Rel* accustomed, addicted, habituated

invidious **1** *Syn* ENVIOUS, covetous, jaundiced, jealous, resentful **2** *Syn* REPUGNANT, abhorrent, distasteful, obnoxious, repellent *Ant* congenial

invigorate **1** *Syn* ANIMATE, brace, energize, enliven, fire, jazz (up), liven (up), pep (up), quicken, stimulate, vitalize, vivify *Ant* damp, dampen, deaden, dull **2** *Syn* STRENGTHEN, energize, fortify, reinforce *Ant* weaken

invigorating *Syn* TONIC, bracing, refreshing, restorative, reviving, stimulating, stimulative, vitalizing

invincible · incapable of being conquered *Syn* impregnable, indomitable, inexpugnable, invulnerable, unassailable, unconquerable *Rel* dauntless, intrepid, undaunted

inviolable *Syn* SACRED, inviolate, sacrosanct

inviolate *Syn* SACRED, inviolable, sacrosanct

invite · to request the presence or participation of *Syn* bid, court, solicit, woo *Rel* ask, request

involuntary *Syn* MANDATORY, compulsory, forced, imperative, incumbent, necessary, nonelective, obligatory, peremptory, required *Ant* elective, optional, voluntary

involve *Syn* INCLUDE, comprehend, embrace, imply, subsume *Ant* exclude

involved *Syn* COMPLEX, complicated, intricate, knotty *Ant* simple

involving *Syn* INTERESTING, absorbing, arresting, engaging, engrossing, enthralling, fascinating, gripping, immersing, intriguing, riveting *Ant* boring, drab, dry, dull, heavy, monotonous, tedious, uninteresting

invulnerable *Syn* INVINCIBLE, impregnable, indomitable, inexpugnable, unassailable, unconquerable

inward *Syn* INNER, inside, interior, internal, intestine *Ant* outer

iota *Syn* PARTICLE, atom, bit, jot, mite, smidgen, tittle, whit

irascible · easily aroused to anger *Syn* choleric, cranky, cross, splenetic, testy, touchy *Rel* fractious, huffy, irritable, peevish, petulant, querulous, snappish, waspish

irate *Syn* ANGRY, angered, apoplectic, enraged, foaming, fuming, furious, incensed, indignant, inflamed, infuriated, ireful, mad, outraged, rabid, riled, roiled, sore, steaming, wrathful, wroth *Ant* delighted, pleased

irateness *Syn* ANGER, angriness, furor, fury, indignation, ire, outrage, rage, spleen, wrath, wrathfulness *Ant* delight, pleasure

ire *Syn* ANGER, angriness, furor, fury, indignation, irateness, outrage, rage, spleen, wrath, wrathfulness *Ant* delight, pleasure

ireful *Syn* ANGRY, angered, apoplectic, enraged, foaming, fuming, furious, incensed, indignant, inflamed, infuriated, irate, mad, outraged, rabid, riled, roiled, sore, steaming, wrathful, wroth *Ant* delighted, pleased

irenic *Syn* PACIFIC, pacifist, pacifistic, peaceable, peaceful *Ant* bellicose

iridescent *Syn* PRISMATIC, opalescent, opaline

irk *Syn* ANNOY, bother, vex *Ant* soothe

irksome *Syn* ANNOYING, aggravating, bothersome, disturbing, exasperating, frustrating, galling, irritating, maddening, nettling, peeving, pesty, rankling, riling, vexatious, vexing

ironic *Syn* SARCASTIC, sardonic, satiric

irony *Syn* WIT, humor, repartee, sarcasm, satire

irrational *Syn* ILLOGICAL, fallacious, invalid, nonrational, unreasonable, unreasoning, unsound, weak *Ant* logical, rational, reasonable, sound, valid

irrefutable · not capable of being challenged or proved wrong *Syn* incontestable, incontrovertible, indisputable, indubitable, unanswerable, undeniable, unquestionable *Rel* certain, definite, positive, sure *Ant* answerable, debatable, disputable, questionable

irregular **1** · not conforming to rule, law, or custom *Syn* anomalous, unnatural *Rel* aberrant, abnormal, atypical *Ant* regular **2** *Syn* DEVIANT, aberrant, abnormal, anomalous, atypical, unnatural *Ant* natural, normal, regular, standard, typical **3** *Syn* FITFUL, casual, choppy, discontinuous, erratic, intermittent, occasional, spasmodic, sporadic, spotty, unsteady *Ant* constant, continuous, regular, steady

irregularly *Syn* HIT OR MISS, aimlessly, anyhow, anyway, anywise, desultorily, erratically, haphazard, haphazardly, helter-skelter, randomly *Ant* methodically, systematically

irrelevant · not having anything to do with the matter at hand *Syn* extraneous, immaterial, inapplicable *Rel* inconsequential, insignificant, unimportant *Ant* applicable, apposite, apropos, germane, material, pertinent, relevant

irreligious · lacking religious emotions, doctrines, or practices *Syn* godless, nonreligious, ungodly, unreligious *Rel* blasphemous, impious, profane, sacrilegious *Ant* religious

irresolution *Syn* HESITATION, faltering, hesitance, hesitancy, indecision, shilly-shallying, vacillation, wavering, wobbling

irritable · easily exasperated *Syn* fractious, fretful, huffy, peevish, pettish, petulant, querulous, snappish, waspish *Rel* choleric, cranky, cross, irascible, splenetic, testy, touchy *Ant* easygoing

irritate · to excite a feeling of anger or annoyance *Syn* aggravate, exasperate, nettle, peeve, provoke, rile *Rel* annoy, bother, irk, vex

irritating *Syn* ANNOYING, aggravating, bothersome, disturbing, exasperating, frustrating, galling, irksome, maddening, nettling, peeving, pesty, rankling, riling, vexatious, vexing

isolate · to set apart from others *Syn* insulate, seclude, segregate, sequester *Rel* abstract, detach, disengage

isolated *Syn* SECLUDED, cloistered, covert, quiet, remote, retired, secret, sheltered

isolation · the state of being alone or kept apart from others *Syn* insulation, secludedness, seclusion, segregation, separateness, sequestration, solitariness, solitude *Rel* loneliness, lonesomeness

issue *n* **1** *Syn* EFFECT, aftereffect, aftermath, consequence, event, outcome, result, sequel, upshot *Ant* cause **2** *Syn* OFFSPRING, descendants, posterity, progeny, young

issue *vb Syn* SPRING, arise, derive, emanate, flow, originate, proceed, rise, stem

item **1** · one of the distinct parts of a whole *Syn* detail, particular *Rel* article, object, thing **2** *Syn* NEWS, information, intelligence, story, tidings, word

itemized *Syn* CIRCUMSTANTIAL, detailed, minute, particular, particularized *Ant* abridged, summary

iterate *Syn* REPEAT (sense 1), ingeminate, reiterate

itinerant · traveling from place to place *Syn* ambulant, ambulatory, nomadic, peripatetic, vagrant *Rel* rambling, ranging, roaming, roving, straying, wandering

J

jabber *Syn* CHAT, babble, blab, cackle, chatter, converse, gab, gabble, gas, jaw, palaver, patter, prate, prattle, rap, rattle, run on, talk, twitter, visit

jack *Syn* FLAG, banner, color, ensign, pendant, pennant, pennon, standard, streamer

jackass *Syn* FOOL (sense 2), booby, goose, half-wit, lunatic, nincompoop, ninny, nitwit, nut, simpleton, turkey, yo-yo

jade *Syn* TIRE, exhaust, fatigue, tucker, weary

jading *Syn* BORING, drab, dreary, dry, dull, flat, heavy, humdrum, leaden, monotonous, pedestrian, ponderous, stodgy, stuffy, stupid, tame, tedious, tiresome, tiring, unanimated, uninteresting, wearisome, weary, wearying *Ant* absorbing, engaging, engrossing, gripping, interesting, intriguing, involving

jail *n* · a place of confinement for persons held in lawful custody *Syn* brig, guardroom, hoosegow, jug, lockup, pen, penitentiary, prison, stockade *Rel* bull pen

jail *vb Syn* IMPRISON, immure, incarcerate, intern

jam *n Syn* PREDICAMENT, dilemma, fix, pickle, plight, quandary, scrape

jam *vb Syn* PRESS, bear, bear down, crowd, squeeze

jape *Syn* JOKE, crack, gag, jest, quip, wisecrack, witticism

jar *Syn* IMPACT, clash, collision, concussion, impingement, jolt, percussion, shock

jargon *Syn* TERMINOLOGY, argot, cant, dialect, language, lingo, patois, patter, slang, vocabulary

jaundiced *Syn* ENVIOUS, covetous, invidious, jealous, resentful

jaunt *Syn* JOURNEY, cruise, excursion, expedition, pilgrimage, tour, trip, voyage

jaw **1** *Syn* CHAT, babble, blab, cackle, chatter, converse, gab, gabble, gas, jabber, palaver, patter, prate, prattle, rap, rattle, run on, talk, twitter, visit **2** *Syn* SCOLD, bawl, berate, chew out, rail, rate, revile, tongue-lash, upbraid, vituperate, wig

jazz (up) *Syn* ANIMATE, brace, energize, enliven, fire, invigorate, liven (up), pep (up), quicken, stimulate, vitalize, vivify *Ant* damp, dampen, deaden, dull

jealous *Syn* ENVIOUS, covetous, invidious, jaundiced, resentful

jeer *Syn* SCOFF, fleer, flout, gibe, gird, sneer

jejune *Syn* INSIPID, banal, flat, inane, vapid, wishy-washy *Ant* sapid, zestful

jell *Syn* COAGULATE, clot, congeal, curdle, jelly, set

jelly *Syn* COAGULATE, clot, congeal, curdle, jell, set

jeopardize *Syn* ENDANGER, adventure, compromise, gamble (with), hazard, imperil, menace, risk, venture

jeopardy *Syn* DANGER (sense 2), distress, endangerment, imperilment, peril, risk, trouble *Ant* safeness, safety, security

jeremiad *Syn* TIRADE, diatribe, philippic *Ant* eulogy

jerk · to make a sudden sharp quick movement *Syn* snap, twitch, yank *Rel* drag, pull

jest *n* 1 *Syn* FUN, game, play, sport 2 *Syn* JOKE, crack, gag, jape, quip, wisecrack, witticism

jest *vb* *Syn* JOKE, banter, fool, fun, jive, josh, kid, quip, wisecrack

jester *Syn* FOOL (sense 1), motley

jesting *Syn* BANTER, chaff, give-and-take, joshing, persiflage, raillery, repartee

jet 1 *Syn* ERUPT (sense 2), belch, disgorge, eject, expel, spew, spout, spurt 2 *Syn* GUSH (sense 1), pour, rush, spew, spout, spurt, squirt *Ant* dribble, drip, drop, trickle

jetty *Syn* WHARF, berth, dock, levee, pier, quay, slip

jib *Syn* DEMUR, balk, boggle, scruple, shy, stick, stickle, strain *Ant* accede

jibe *Syn* AGREE (sense 2), accord, conform, correspond, harmonize, square, tally *Ant* differ (from)

jiffy *Syn* INSTANT, flash, minute, moment, second, shake, split second, trice, twinkle, twinkling, wink

jigger *Syn* GADGET, appliance, contraption, contrivance, gimmick, gizmo (*or* gismo)

jim-dandy *adj* *Syn* EXCELLENT, A1, bang-up, banner, capital, classic, crackerjack, dandy, divine, fabulous, fine, first-class, first-rate, grand, great, groovy, heavenly, keen, marvelous (*or* marvellous), mean, neat, nifty, noble, par excellence, prime, sensational, splendid, stellar, sterling, superb, superior, superlative, supernal, swell, terrific, tip-top, top, top-notch, unsurpassed, wonderful *Ant* poor

jim-dandy *n* · something very good of its kind *Syn* beauty, corker, crackerjack, dandy, knockout, nifty, pip *Rel* marvel, wonder

jittery 1 *Syn* EXCITABLE, flighty, fluttery, high-strung, jumpy, nervous, skittish, spooky *Ant* unflappable 2 *Syn* IMPATIENT, fidgety, jumpy, nervous, restive, restless, uneasy, unquiet *Ant* patient

jive 1 *Syn* JOKE, banter, fool, fun, jest, josh, kid, quip, wisecrack 2 *Syn* TEASE, chaff, josh, kid, rally, razz, rib, ride, roast

job 1 *Syn* CHORE, assignment, duty, stint, task 2 *Syn* MISSION, assignment, charge, operation, post 3 *Syn* ROLE, capacity, function, part, place, position, purpose, task, work

jocose 1 *Syn* MERRY, blithesome, festive, gay, gleeful, jocund, jolly, jovial, laughing, mirthful, sunny 2 *Syn* WITTY, facetious, humorous, jocular

jocular *Syn* WITTY, facetious, humorous, jocose

jocund *Syn* MERRY, blithesome, festive, gay, gleeful, jocose, jolly, jovial, laughing, mirthful, sunny

jog *n* *Syn* POKE, nudge, prod

jog *vb* *Syn* POKE, nudge, prod

join · to bring or come together into some manner of union *Syn* associate, combine, conjoin, connect, link, relate, unite *Rel* concur, cooperate *Ant* disjoin, part

joining *Syn* ADJACENT, abutting, adjoining, bordering, contiguous, flanking, fringing, juxtaposed, skirting, touching, verging *Ant* nonadjacent

joint · a place where two or more things are united *Syn* articulation, suture

joke *n* · something said or done to provoke laughter *Syn* crack, gag, jape, jest, quip, wisecrack, witticism *Rel* antic, caper, dido, monkeyshine, prank

joke *vb* · to make jokes *Syn* banter, fool, fun, jest, jive, josh, kid, quip, wisecrack *Rel* chaff, mock, rally, razz, rib, ridicule, tease

jollity *Syn* MIRTH, glee, hilarity

jolly *vb* *Syn* BANTER, chaff, josh, kid, rag, rib

jolly *adj* *Syn* MERRY, blithesome, festive, gay, gleeful, jocose, jocund, jovial, laughing, mirthful, sunny

jolly *adv* *Syn* VERY, awful, awfully, beastly, deadly, especially, exceedingly, extra, extremely, far, frightfully, full, greatly, heavily, highly, hugely, mightily, mighty, mortally, most, much, particularly, rattling, real, right, so, something, super, terribly, too, whacking *Ant* little, negligibly, nominally, slightly

jolt *Syn* IMPACT, clash, collision, concussion, impingement, jar, percussion, shock

josh 1 *Syn* BANTER, chaff, jolly, kid, rag, rib 2 *Syn* JOKE, banter, fool, fun, jest, jive, kid, quip, wisecrack 3 *Syn* TEASE, chaff, jive, kid, rally, razz, rib, ride, roast

joshing *Syn* BANTER, chaff, give-and-take, jesting, persiflage, raillery, repartee

jot *Syn* PARTICLE, atom, bit, iota, mite, smidgen, tittle, whit

journal · a publication that appears at regular intervals *Syn* magazine, newspaper, organ, periodical, review

journalist *Syn* REPORTER, correspondent

journey · travel or a passage from one place to another *Syn* cruise, excursion, expedition, jaunt, pilgrimage, tour, trip, voyage

jovial *Syn* MERRY, blithesome, festive, gay,

gleeful, jocose, jocund, jolly, laughing, mirthful, sunny

joy *Syn* PLEASURE, delectation, delight, enjoyment, fruition *Ant* anger, displeasure, vexation

joyful *Syn* GLAD, cheerful, happy, joyous, lighthearted *Ant* sad

joyless *Syn* SAD (sense 1), bad, blue, brokenhearted, crestfallen, dejected, depressed, despondent, disconsolate, doleful, down, downcast, downhearted, droopy, forlorn, gloomy, glum, heartbroken, heartsick, heartsore, inconsolable, low, low-spirited, melancholy, miserable, mournful, saddened, sorrowful, sorry, unhappy, woebegone, woeful, wretched *Ant* blissful, buoyant, buoyed, cheerful, cheery, chipper, delighted, glad, gladdened, gladsome, gleeful, happy, joyful, joyous, jubilant, sunny, upbeat

joylessness *Syn* SADNESS, blues, dejection, depression, desolation, despondency, disconsolateness, dispiritedness, doldrums, downheartedness, dreariness, dumps, forlornness, gloom, gloominess, heartsickness, melancholy, mopes, oppression, unhappiness *Ant* bliss, blissfulness, ecstasy, elatedness, elation, euphoria, exhilaration, exuberance, exultation, felicity, gladness, gladsomeness, happiness, heaven, intoxication, joy, joyfulness, joyousness, jubilation, rapture, rapturousness

joyous *Syn* GLAD, cheerful, happy, joyful, lighthearted *Ant* sad

jubilant *Syn* EXULTANT, exulting, glorying, rejoicing, triumphant

jubilee *Syn* FESTIVAL, carnival, celebration, festivity, fete (*or* fête), fiesta, gala

judge *n* · a person who impartially decides unsettled questions or controversial issues *Syn* arbiter, arbitrator, referee, umpire

judge *vb* **1** · to decide something in dispute or controversy upon its merits and upon evidence *Syn* adjudge, adjudicate, arbitrate *Rel* decide, determine, rule, settle **2** *Syn* ESTIMATE (sense 2), calculate, call, conjecture, figure, gauge, guess, make, place, put, reckon, suppose **3** *Syn* INFER, conclude, deduce, gather

judgment 1 *Syn* INFERENCE (sense 1), conclusion, deduction **2** *Syn* SENSE, common sense, good sense, gumption, horse sense, wisdom

judicious 1 *Syn* EXPEDIENT, advisable, desirable, politic, prudent, tactical, wise *Ant* imprudent, inadvisable, inexpedient, injudicious, unwise **2** *Syn* WISE, prudent, sage, sane, sapient, sensible *Ant* simple

jug *Syn* JAIL, brig, guardroom, hoosegow, lockup, pen, penitentiary, prison, stockade

jugglery *Syn* TRICKERY, artifice, chicanery, hanky-panky, legerdemain, subterfuge, wile

jumble *n* *Syn* CONFUSION, chaos, clutter, disarray, disorder, muddle, snarl

jumble *vb* *Syn* DISORDER, confuse, derange, disarrange, disarray, discompose, dishevel, dislocate, disorganize, disrupt, disturb, hash, mess (up), mix (up), muddle, muss, rumple, scramble, shuffle, tousle, tumble, upset *Ant* arrange, array, draw up, marshal, order, organize, range, regulate, straighten (up), tidy

jumbled *Syn* MESSY, chaotic, cluttered, confused, disarranged, disarrayed, disheveled (*or* dishevelled), disordered, disorderly, higgledy-piggledy, hugger-mugger, littered, messed, muddled, mussed, mussy, pell-mell, rumpled, sloppy, topsy-turvy, tousled, tumbled, unkempt, untidy, upside-down *Ant* neat, ordered, orderly, organized, shipshape, snug, tidied, tidy, trim

jumbo *Syn* GIANT, behemoth, blockbuster, colossus, leviathan, mammoth, monster, titan, whale, whopper *Ant* dwarf, midget, mini, miniature, peewee, pygmy, runt, shrimp

jump *n* · a sudden move through space *Syn* bound, leap, spring, vault

jump *vb* · to move suddenly through space by or as if by muscular action *Syn* bound, leap, spring, vault

jump (on) *Syn* ATTACK (sense 2), abuse, assail, belabor, blast, castigate, excoriate, lambaste (*or* lambast), scathe, slam, vituperate

jumpy 1 *Syn* EXCITABLE, flighty, fluttery, high-strung, jittery, nervous, skittish, spooky *Ant* unflappable **2** *Syn* IMPATIENT, fidgety, jittery, nervous, restive, restless, uneasy, unquiet *Ant* patient

junction · the act, state, or place of meeting or uniting *Syn* concourse, confluence

juncture · a critical or crucial time or state of affairs *Syn* contingency, crisis, emergency, exigency, pass, pinch, strait *Rel* condition, posture, situation, state, status

junior *adj* *Syn* LESSER, inferior, less, lower, minor, smaller, subordinate, under *Ant* greater, higher, major, more, primary, prime, senior, superior

junior *n* *Syn* UNDERLING, inferior, subordinate *Ant* senior, superior

junk *Syn* DISCARD, cast, molt, scrap, shed, slough

jurisdiction *Syn* RULE (sense 2), administration, authority, governance, government, regime, regimen

just 1 *Syn* FAIR, dispassionate, equitable, impartial, objective, unbiased, uncolored *Ant* unfair **2** *Syn* UPRIGHT, conscientious, honest, honorable, scrupulous

justifiable *Syn* TENABLE, defendable, defensible, maintainable, supportable, sustainable *Ant* indefensible, insupportable, unjustifiable, untenable

justification *Syn* EXCUSE, alibi, defense, plea, reason

justify *Syn* MAINTAIN, assert, defend, vindicate

jut Syn BULGE, beetle, overhang, project, protrude, stick out

juvenile 1 Syn CALLOW, adolescent, green, immature, inexperienced, puerile, raw, unfledged, unripe, unripened Ant adult, experienced, grown-up, mature, ripe 2 Syn CHILDISH, adolescent, babyish, immature, infantile, kiddish, puerile Ant adult, grown-up, mature 3 Syn YOUNG, adolescent, immature, youngish, youthful Ant adult, full-grown, mature, matured

juxtaposed Syn ADJACENT, abutting, adjoining, bordering, contiguous, flanking, fringing, joining, skirting, touching, verging Ant nonadjacent

K

keen vb Syn CRY, blubber, wail, weep, whimper

keen adj 1 Syn EAGER, agog, anxious, athirst, avid Ant listless 2 Syn EXCELLENT, A1, bang-up, banner, capital, classic, crackerjack, dandy, divine, fabulous, fine, first-class, first-rate, grand, great, groovy, heavenly, jim-dandy, marvelous (or marvellous), mean, neat, nifty, noble, par excellence, prime, sensational, splendid, stellar, sterling, superb, superior, superlative, supernal, swell, terrific, tip-top, top, top-notch, unsurpassed, wonderful Ant poor 3 Syn SHARP, acute Ant blunt, dull

keen n Syn LAMENT, groan, howl, lamentation, moan, plaint, wail Ant exultation, rejoicing

keep vb 1 · to notice or honor a day, occasion, or deed Syn celebrate, commemorate, observe, solemnize Rel regard, respect Ant break 2 · to hold in one's possession or under one's control Syn detain, hold back, keep back, keep out, reserve, retain, withhold Rel conserve, preserve, save Ant relinquish

keep n Syn LIVING, bread, bread and butter, livelihood, maintenance, subsistence, support, sustenance

keep back Syn KEEP (sense 2), detain, hold back, keep out, reserve, retain, withhold Ant relinquish

keeping Syn CUSTODY, care, guardianship, safekeeping, trust, ward

keep out Syn KEEP (sense 2), detain, hold back, keep back, reserve, retain, withhold Ant relinquish

keepsake Syn MEMORIAL, commemorative, memento, monument, remembrance, reminder, souvenir, token

keg Syn CASK, barrel, firkin, hogshead, pipe, puncheon

ken Syn RANGE, compass, gamut, horizon, orbit, purview, radius, reach, scope, sweep

kerchief Syn BANDANNA, babushka, handkerchief, mantilla

key Syn CRUCIAL, critical, pivotal, vital

kibitzer 1 Syn BUSYBODY, interferer, interloper, intruder, meddler 2 Syn SPECTATOR, beholder, bystander, eyewitness, looker-on, observer, onlooker, witness

kick vb 1 Syn COMPLAIN, beef, bellyache, carp, crab, croak, fuss, gripe, grouse, growl, grumble, moan, murmur, mutter, repine, squawk, wail, whine, yammer Ant rejoice 2 Syn OBJECT, expostulate, protest, remonstrate Ant acquiesce

kick n Syn THRILL, bang, exhilaration, titillation

kick off Syn BEGIN (sense 2), commence, embark (on or upon), enter (into or upon), get off, launch, open, start, strike (into) Ant conclude, end, finish, terminate

kid 1 Syn BANTER, chaff, jolly, josh, rag, rib 2 Syn JOKE, banter, fool, fun, jest, jive, josh, quip, wisecrack 3 Syn TEASE, chaff, jive, josh, rally, razz, rib, ride, roast

kiddish Syn CHILDISH, adolescent, babyish, immature, infantile, juvenile, puerile Ant adult, grown-up, mature

kidney Syn TYPE, character, description, ilk, kind, nature, sort, stripe

kill · to deprive of life Syn assassinate, dispatch, execute, murder, slay

killer Syn DEADLY, baleful, deathly, fatal, fell, lethal, mortal, murderous, pestilent, vital Ant healthful, healthy, nonfatal, nonlethal, wholesome

kin Syn RELATIVE, kinsman, relation

kind adj · showing or having a gentle considerate nature Syn benign, benignant, kindly Rel altruistic, benevolent, charitable, eleemosynary, humane, humanitarian, philanthropic Ant unkind

kind n Syn TYPE, character, description, ilk, kidney, nature, sort, stripe

kindle Syn LIGHT, fire, ignite

kindly Syn KIND, benign, benignant Ant unkind

kindred Syn RELATED, affiliated, allied, cognate

kingly · of, relating to, or befitting one who occupies a throne Syn imperial, princely, queenly, regal, royal

kingpin *Syn* BOSS, captain, chief, foreman, head, headman, helmsman, leader, master, taskmaster

king-size *or* **king-sized** *Syn* LONG (sense 1), elongated, extended, lengthy *Ant* brief, short

kinsman *Syn* RELATIVE, kin, relation

knack *Syn* GIFT (sense 2), aptitude, bent, faculty, genius, talent, turn

knave *Syn* VILLAIN, blackguard, miscreant, rapscallion, rascal, rogue, scamp, scoundrel

knickknack · a small object displayed for its attractiveness or interest *Syn* bauble, curio, curiosity, gaud, gewgaw, novelty, ornamental, trinket *Rel* bric-a-brac, trumpery

knit *Syn* WEAVE, braid, crochet, plait, tat

knock *n* **1** *Syn* MISFORTUNE, adversity, misadventure, mischance, mishap *Ant* fortune, luck **2** *Syn* TAP, rap, thud, thump

knock *vb* *Syn* TAP, rap, thud, thump

knockabout *Syn* BOISTEROUS, rambunctious, raucous, rowdy *Ant* orderly

knockout *adj* *Syn* BEAUTIFUL, attractive, beauteous, comely, cute, fair, gorgeous, handsome, lovely, pretty, ravishing, sightly, stunning, taking *Ant* homely, ill-favored, plain, ugly, unattractive, unbeautiful, unhandsome, unlovely, unpretty, unsightly

knockout *n* **1** *Syn* FAINT, blackout, coma, insensibility, swoon **2** *Syn* JIM-DANDY, beauty, corker, crackerjack, dandy, nifty, pip

knotty *Syn* COMPLEX, complicated, intricate, involved *Ant* simple

knowing *Syn* INTELLIGENT, alert, bright, brilliant, clever, quick-witted, smart *Ant* unintelligent

knowingly *Syn* INTENTIONALLY, consciously, deliberately, designedly, purposefully, purposely, willfully, wittingly *Ant* inadvertently, unconsciously, unintentionally, unknowingly, unwittingly

knowledge **1** · what is or can be known by an individual or by mankind *Syn* erudition, information, learning, lore, scholarship, science *Ant* ignorance **2** *Syn* EDUCATION (sense 2), erudition, learnedness, learning, scholarship, science

knowledgeable *Syn* EDUCATED, erudite, learned, literate, scholarly, well-read *Ant* ignorant, illiterate, uneducated

kook *Syn* ECCENTRIC, character, codger, crackbrain, crackpot, crank, nut, oddball, screwball, weirdo

L

label *n* *Syn* MARK, brand, stamp, tag, ticket

label *vb* *Syn* MARK, brand, stamp, tag, ticket

labor *vb* · to devote serious and sustained effort *Syn* drudge, endeavor, grub, hump, hustle, moil, peg (away), plod, plow, plug, slave, slog, strain, strive, struggle, sweat, toil, travail, work *Rel* apply (oneself), attempt, buckle (down), hammer (away), pitch in *Ant* dabble, fiddle (around), fool (around), mess (around), putter (around)

labor *n* *Syn* WORK (sense 1), drudgery, grind, toil, travail *Ant* play

labored *Syn* FORCED, strained

laborer **1** *Syn* SLAVE (sense 2), drudge, drudger, grubber, peon, plugger, slogger, toiler, worker *Ant* freeman **2** *Syn* WORKER, artisan, craftsman, hand, handicraftsman, mechanic, operative, roustabout, workingman, workman *Ant* idler

lace **1** *Syn* BRAID, lacing, plait **2** *Syn* CORD, cable, lacing, line, rope, string, wire

lacing **1** *Syn* BRAID, lace, plait **2** *Syn* CORD, cable, lace, line, rope, string, wire

lack *n* **1** · the fact or state of being wanting or deficient *Syn* absence, dearth, defect, privation, want *Rel* exigency, necessity, need **2** *Syn* DEFICIENCY, dearth, deficit, failure, famine, inadequacy, insufficiency, paucity, poverty, scantiness, scarceness, scarcity, shortage, want *Ant* abundance, adequacy, amplitude, plenitude, plenty, sufficiency

lack *vb* · to be without something and especially something essential or greatly needed *Syn* need, require, want

lackadaisical *Syn* LISTLESS, enervated, languid, languishing, languorous, limp, spiritless *Ant* ambitious, animated, energetic, enterprising, motivated

lackey *Syn* SERVANT, domestic, flunky, menial, retainer, steward *Ant* master

laconic *Syn* CONCISE, compendious, pithy, succinct, summary, terse *Ant* redundant

laconically *Syn* SUCCINCTLY, briefly, compactly, concisely, crisply, pithily, summarily, tersely *Ant* diffusely, long-windedly, verbosely, wordily

lacuna *Syn* BREAK, gap, hiatus, interim, interruption, interval

lad *Syn* BOY, laddie, nipper, shaver, sonny, stripling, tad, youth

laddie *Syn* BOY, lad, nipper, shaver, sonny, stripling, tad, youth

lade *Syn* BURDEN, charge, cumber, encumber, load, saddle, tax, weigh, weight

lading *Syn* LOAD, burden, cargo, freight

ladle *Syn* DIP (sense 2), bail, dish, scoop, spoon

lady 1 *Syn* WOMAN, female 2 *Syn* GIRL-FRIEND, gal, woman 3 *Syn* GENTLEWOMAN, dame, noblewoman

ladylike *Syn* FEMALE, feminine, womanish, womanlike, womanly *Ant* male

lag *Syn* DELAY (sense 2), dawdle, loiter, procrastinate *Ant* hasten, hurry

laggard *Syn* SLOW, deliberate, dilatory, leisurely *Ant* fast

laggardly *Syn* SLOW, leisurely, slowly, sluggishly, tardily *Ant* apace, briskly, fast, fleetly, full tilt, hastily, quick, quickly, rapidly, snappily, speedily, swift, swiftly

lagniappe *Syn* BONUS, dividend, extra, gratuity, gravy, perquisite, tip

lamb · an innocent or gentle person *Syn* angel, dove, innocent, sheep *Rel* cherub, saint *Ant* wolf

lambaste *or* **lambast** *Syn* ATTACK (sense 2), abuse, assail, belabor, blast, castigate, excoriate, jump (on), scathe, slam, vituperate

lambent *Syn* BRIGHT, beaming, brilliant, effulgent, incandescent, lucent, luminous, lustrous, radiant, refulgent *Ant* dim, dull

lament *n* · a crying out in grief *Syn* groan, howl, keen, lamentation, moan, plaint, wail *Rel* grieving, mourning, weeping *Ant* exultation, rejoicing

lament *vb* *Syn* REGRET, bemoan, deplore, repent, rue

lamentable *Syn* REGRETTABLE, deplorable, distressful, distressing, grievous, heartbreaking, heartrending, unfortunate, woeful

lamentation *Syn* LAMENT, groan, howl, keen, moan, plaint, wail *Ant* exultation, rejoicing

land *vb* 1 *Syn* ALIGHT, light, perch, roost, settle, touch down *Ant* take off 2 *Syn* EARN, acquire, attain, capture, carry, draw, gain, garner, get, make, obtain, procure, realize, secure, win *Ant* forfeit, lose

land *n* *Syn* NATION, commonwealth, country, sovereignty, state

landing field *Syn* AIRPORT, airdrome, airfield, airstrip, flying field, landing strip

landing strip *Syn* AIRPORT, airdrome, airfield, airstrip, flying field, landing field

landmark *Syn* TURNING POINT, climax, milestone

language 1 · a body or system of words and phrases used by a large community or by a people, a nation, or a group of nations *Syn* dialect, idiom, speech, tongue *Rel* argot, cant, jargon, lingo, patois, slang, vernacular 2 · oral or written expression or a quality of such expression that is dependent on the variety, arrangement, or expressiveness of words *Syn* diction, phraseology, phrasing, style, vocabulary 3 *Syn* TERMINOLOGY, argot, cant, dialect, jargon, lingo, patois, patter, slang, vocabulary

languid *Syn* LISTLESS, enervated, lackadaisical, languishing, languorous, limp, spiritless

Ant ambitious, animated, energetic, enterprising, motivated

languishing *Syn* LISTLESS, enervated, lackadaisical, languid, languorous, limp, spiritless *Ant* ambitious, animated, energetic, enterprising, motivated

languor *Syn* LETHARGY, lassitude, stupor, torpidity, torpor *Ant* vigor

languorous *Syn* LISTLESS, enervated, lackadaisical, languid, languishing, limp, spiritless *Ant* ambitious, animated, energetic, enterprising, motivated

lank *Syn* LEAN, angular, gaunt, lanky, rawboned, scrawny, skinny, spare *Ant* fleshy

lanky 1 · being tall, thin and usually loose-jointed *Syn* gangling, gangly, rangy, spindling, spindly *Rel* angular, bony, gaunt, lank, rawboned, scrawny, skinny 2 *Syn* LEAN, angular, gaunt, lank, rawboned, scrawny, skinny, spare *Ant* fleshy

lap *Syn* OVERLAP, overlay, overlie, overspread

lapse *vb* · to fall from a better or higher state into a lower or poorer one *Syn* backslide, relapse *Rel* return, revert

lapse *n* *Syn* ERROR, blunder, bull, faux pas, howler, mistake, slip

larcener *Syn* THIEF, burglar, larcenist, robber

larcenist *Syn* THIEF, burglar, larcener, robber

larceny *Syn* THEFT, burglary, robbery

large · of a size greater than average of its kind *Syn* big, bulky, considerable, goodly, good-sized, grand, great, handsome, hefty, hulking, largish, outsize, oversize (*or* oversized), sizable (*or* sizeable), substantial, tidy, voluminous *Rel* abundant, ample, appreciable, astronomical, bumper, capacious, cavernous, colossal, commodious, copious, enormous, excessive, exorbitant, extravagant, extreme, fat, gigantic, gross, heroic, huge, immense, immoderate, inordinate, jumbo, king-size (*or* king-sized), major, mammoth, massive, monolithic, monstrous, monumental, plentiful, prodigious, roomy, spacious, staggering, stupendous, super, thick, tremendous, vast, vasty, whacking, whopping *Ant* little, puny, small, undersized

largely 1 · in a reasonably inclusive manner *Syn* chiefly, generally, greatly, mainly, mostly, principally 2 *Syn* CHIEFLY, altogether, basically, by and large, generally, mainly, mostly, overall, predominantly, primarily, principally, substantially

largess *Syn* GIFT (sense 1), boon, favor, gratuity, present

largish *Syn* LARGE, big, bulky, considerable, goodly, good-sized, grand, great, handsome, hefty, hulking, outsize, oversize (*or* oversized), sizable (*or* sizeable), substantial, tidy, voluminous *Ant* little, puny, small, undersized

lascivious *Syn* LICENTIOUS, lecherous, lewd, libertine, libidinous, lustful, wanton *Ant* continent

lead

lass *Syn* GIRL, lassie, miss, missy

lassie *Syn* GIRL, lass, miss, missy

lassitude **1** *Syn* FATIGUE, burnout, collapse, exhaustion, prostration, tiredness, weariness *Ant* refreshment, rejuvenation, revitalization **2** *Syn* LETHARGY, languor, stupor, torpidity, torpor *Ant* vigor

last *adj* · following all others as in time, order, or importance *Syn* concluding, eventual, final, latest, terminal, ultimate *Ant* first

last *vb Syn* CONTINUE, abide, endure, persist

lasting · enduring so long as to seem fixed or established *Syn* durable, perdurable, permanent, perpetual, stable *Rel* abiding, continuing, enduring, persistent, persisting *Ant* fleeting

late **1** *Syn* DEAD, deceased, defunct, departed, inanimate, lifeless **2** *Syn* FORMER, erstwhile, old, onetime, past, sometime, whilom **3** *Syn* TARDY, behindhand, overdue *Ant* prompt

latency *Syn* ABEYANCE, doldrums, dormancy, quiescence, suspense, suspension *Ant* continuance, continuation

latent · not now showing signs of activity or existence *Syn* abeyant, dormant, potential, quiescent *Rel* concealed, hidden *Ant* patent

later *Syn* AFTER, afterward (*or* afterwards), subsequently, thereafter *Ant* before, beforehand, earlier, previously

latest *Syn* LAST, concluding, eventual, final, terminal, ultimate *Ant* first

lather *Syn* FOAM, froth, scum, spume, suds, yeast

laud **1** *Syn* ACCLAIM, applaud, cheer, hail, praise, salute, tout *Ant* knock, pan, slam **2** *Syn* PRAISE, acclaim, eulogize, extol *Ant* blame

laudable *Syn* ADMIRABLE, commendable, creditable, meritorious, praiseworthy *Ant* censurable, discreditable, reprehensible

laughable · provoking laughter or mirth *Syn* comic, comical, droll, farcical, funny, ludicrous, ridiculous, risible *Rel* amusing, diverting, entertaining

laughing *Syn* MERRY, blithesome, festive, gay, gleeful, jocose, jocund, jolly, jovial, mirthful, sunny

laughingstock · a person or thing that is made fun of *Syn* butt, mark, mock, mockery, target *Rel* chump, dupe, fall guy, fool, gull, monkey, pigeon, sap, sucker, victim

launch *n Syn* BEGINNING, alpha, birth, commencement, dawn, genesis, inception, incipiency, morning, onset, outset, start, threshold *Ant* close, conclusion, end, ending

launch *vb Syn* BEGIN (sense 2), commence, embark (on *or* upon), enter (into *or* upon), get off, kick off, open, start, strike (into) *Ant* conclude, end, finish, terminate

lavalier *Syn* PENDANT, bangle, charm

lavish **1** *Syn* LUXURIOUS, deluxe, luxuriant, opulent, palatial, plush, sumptuous *Ant* ascetic, austere, humble, Spartan **2** *Syn* PROFUSE, exuberant, lush, luxuriant, prodigal *Ant* scant, scanty, spare

lavishly *Syn* HIGH, expensively, extravagantly, grandly, luxuriously, opulently, richly, sumptuously *Ant* austerely, humbly, modestly, plainly, simply

law **1** · a principle governing action or procedure *Syn* canon, ordinance, precept, regulation, rule, statute *Rel* command, dictate, mandate **2** *Syn* PRINCIPLE, axiom, fundamental, theorem

law-abiding *Syn* OBEDIENT, amenable, compliant, conformable, docile, submissive, tractable *Ant* contrary, disobedient, froward, insubordinate, intractable, rebellious, recalcitrant, refractory, unruly

lawbreaking *Syn* LAWLESS, anarchic, disorderly, unruly *Ant* law-abiding, orderly

lawful · being in accordance with law *Syn* legal, legitimate, licit *Rel* condign, due, rightful *Ant* unlawful

lawless · not restrained by or under the control of legal authority *Syn* anarchic, disorderly, lawbreaking, unruly *Rel* defiant, insubordinate, mutinous, rebellious, refractory, riotous *Ant* law-abiding, orderly

lawlessness *Syn* ANARCHY, chaos, misrule

lawsuit *Syn* SUIT, action, case, cause

lawyer · a person authorized to practice law in the courts or to serve clients in the capacity of legal agent or adviser *Syn* advocate, attorney, barrister, counsel, counselor, solicitor

lax **1** *Syn* LOOSE, relaxed, slack *Ant* strict, tight **2** *Syn* NEGLIGENT, careless, derelict, neglectful, neglecting, remiss, slack *Ant* attentive, careful, conscientious

lay *vb* **1** *Syn* BET, gamble, go, stake, wager **2** *Syn* IMPOSE, assess, charge, exact, fine, levy, put *Ant* remit

lay *n Syn* MELODY, air, song, strain, tune, warble

lay *adj Syn* PROFANE, secular, temporal *Ant* sacred

lay away *Syn* HOARD, cache, lay up, put by, salt away, squirrel (away), stash, stockpile, store, stow

lay down *Syn* ENACT, legislate, make, pass *Ant* repeal, rescind, revoke

lay up *Syn* HOARD, cache, lay away, put by, salt away, squirrel (away), stash, stockpile, store, stow

laze *Syn* IDLE, loaf, loll, lounge

lazy · not easily aroused to activity *Syn* faineant, indolent, slothful *Rel* idle, inactive, inert, passive, supine *Ant* industrious

lazybones · a lazy person *Syn* drone, idler, loafer, slouch, slug, sluggard *Rel* bum, ne'er-do-well *Ant* doer, go-getter, hummer, hustler, rustler, self-starter

lead *vb Syn* GUIDE, engineer, pilot, steer *Ant* misguide

lead *adj Syn* HEAD, chief, commanding, first, foremost, high, leading, managing, preeminent, premier, presiding, primary, prime, principal, supreme

leaden *Syn* BORING, drab, dreary, dry, dull, flat, heavy, humdrum, jading, monotonous, pedestrian, ponderous, stodgy, stuffy, stupid, tame, tedious, tiresome, tiring, unanimated, uninteresting, wearisome, weary, wearying *Ant* absorbing, engaging, engrossing, gripping, interesting, intriguing, involving

leader 1 *Syn* BOSS, captain, chief, foreman, head, headman, helmsman, kingpin, master, taskmaster **2** *Syn* CHIEF, chieftain, head, headman, master

leading 1 *Syn* CHIEF, capital, foremost, main, principal *Ant* subordinate **2** *Syn* HEAD, chief, commanding, first, foremost, high, lead, managing, preeminent, premier, presiding, primary, prime, principal, supreme

lead on *Syn* LURE, allure, beguile, decoy, entice, seduce, tempt

league *n Syn* ALLIANCE, coalition, confederacy, confederation, federation, fusion

league *vb Syn* ALLY, associate, band, club, confederate, conjoin, cooperate, federate, unite *Ant* break up, disband

lean *adj* · thin because of an absence of excess flesh *Syn* angular, gaunt, lank, lanky, rawboned, scrawny, skinny, spare *Rel* slender, slight, slim, thin *Ant* fleshy

lean *vb Syn* SLANT, incline, slope

leaning · a strong instinct or liking for something *Syn* flair, penchant, proclivity, propensity *Rel* bias, partiality, predilection, prejudice, prepossession *Ant* distaste

leap *vb Syn* JUMP, bound, spring, vault

leap *n Syn* JUMP, bound, spring, vault

learn *Syn* DISCOVER, ascertain, determine, unearth

learned 1 · possessing or manifesting unusually wide and deep knowledge *Syn* erudite, scholarly *Rel* cultivated, cultured **2** *Syn* BOOKISH, erudite, literary *Ant* colloquial, nonliterary **3** *Syn* EDUCATED, erudite, knowledgeable, literate, scholarly, well-read *Ant* ignorant, illiterate, uneducated

learnedness *Syn* EDUCATION (sense 2), erudition, knowledge, learning, scholarship, science

learning 1 *Syn* EDUCATION (sense 2), erudition, knowledge, learnedness, scholarship, science **2** *Syn* KNOWLEDGE, erudition, information, lore, scholarship, science *Ant* ignorance

lease *Syn* HIRE, charter, let, rent

least *Syn* MINIMAL, littlest, lowest, minimum, slightest *Ant* full, greatest, largest, maximum, top, topmost, utmost

leave *vb* **1** *Syn* GO, depart, quit, retire, withdraw *Ant* come **2** *Syn* LET, allow, permit, suffer **3** *Syn* RELINQUISH, abandon, cede,

resign, surrender, waive, yield *Ant* keep **4** *Syn* WILL, bequeath, devise, legate

leave *n Syn* PERMISSION, allowance, authorization, clearance, concurrence, consent, granting, license (*or* licence), sanction, sufferance *Ant* interdiction, prohibition, proscription

leaven *Syn* INFUSE, imbue, ingrain, inoculate, suffuse

leavings *Syn* REMAINDER, balance, remains, remnant, residue, residuum, rest

lecherous *Syn* LICENTIOUS, lascivious, lewd, libertine, libidinous, lustful, wanton *Ant* continent

lecture *Syn* SPEECH, address, harangue, homily, oration, sermon, talk

leech *Syn* PARASITE, bootlicker, favorite, hanger-on, lickspittle, sponge, sponger, sycophant, toady

lees *Syn* DEPOSIT, dregs, grounds, precipitate, sediment

leeway *Syn* ROOM (sense 2), berth, clearance, elbow room, margin, play

left-handed *Syn* INSINCERE, artificial, backhanded, double-dealing, feigned, hypocritical, mealy, mealymouthed, two-faced, unctuous *Ant* genuine, heartfelt, honest, sincere, unfeigned

legal *Syn* LAWFUL, legitimate, licit *Ant* unlawful

legal tender *Syn* MONEY, cash, coin, coinage, currency, specie

legate *n Syn* AMBASSADOR, delegate, emissary, envoy, minister, representative

legate *vb Syn* WILL, bequeath, devise, leave

legend 1 *Syn* FOLKLORE, lore, myth, mythology, tradition **2** *Syn* INSCRIPTION, caption **3** *Syn* MYTH, saga

legendary *Syn* FICTITIOUS, apocryphal, fabulous, mythical *Ant* historical

legerdemain *Syn* TRICKERY, artifice, chicanery, hanky-panky, jugglery, subterfuge, wile

legion *Syn* MULTITUDE, army, host

legislate *Syn* ENACT, lay down, make, pass *Ant* repeal, rescind, revoke

leg (it) *Syn* WALK, foot (it), hoof (it), pad, step, traipse, tread

legitimate *Syn* LAWFUL, legal, licit *Ant* unlawful

leisure *Syn* REST, comfort, ease, relaxation, repose

leisurely *adj Syn* SLOW, deliberate, dilatory, laggard *Ant* fast

leisurely *adv Syn* SLOW, laggardly, slowly, sluggishly, tardily *Ant* apace, briskly, fast, fleetly, full tilt, hastily, quick, quickly, rapidly, snappily, speedily, swift, swiftly

leitmotiv *Syn* SUBJECT, argument, matter, motif, motive, subject matter, text, theme, topic

lengthen *Syn* EXTEND, elongate, prolong, protract *Ant* abridge, shorten

lengthy 1 *Syn* LONG (sense 1), elongated, extended, king-size (*or* king-sized) *Ant* brief, short 2 *Syn* LONG (sense 2), extended, far, great, long-lived, long-range, long-term, marathon *Ant* brief, short, short-lived, short-range, short-term

leniency *Syn* FORBEARANCE, clemency, indulgence, mercifulness, tolerance *Ant* anger, vindictiveness

lenient 1 *Syn* FORBEARING, clement, indulgent, merciful, tolerant *Ant* unrelenting 2 *Syn* SOFT, balmy, bland, gentle, mild, smooth *Ant* hard, stern

leniently *Syn* FORBEARINGLY, clemently, indulgently, mercifully, tolerantly

lenity *Syn* MERCY, charity, clemency, grace

lesion *Syn* WOUND, bruise, contusion, trauma, traumatism

less *Syn* LESSER, inferior, junior, lower, minor, smaller, subordinate, under *Ant* greater, higher, major, more, primary, prime, senior, superior

lessen *Syn* DECREASE, abate, diminish, dwindle, reduce *Ant* increase

lesser · having not so great importance or rank as another *Syn* inferior, junior, less, lower, minor, smaller, subordinate, under *Rel* little, mean, small *Ant* greater, higher, major, more, primary, prime, senior, superior

let *vb* 1 · to neither forbid nor prevent *Syn* allow, leave, permit, suffer *Rel* accredit, approve, certify, endorse, sanction 2 *Syn* HIRE, charter, lease, rent

let *n* *Syn* ENCUMBRANCE, bar, block, chain, clog, crimp, deterrent, drag, embarrassment, fetter, handicap, hindrance, hurdle, impediment, inhibition, interference, manacle, obstacle, obstruction, shackles, stop, stumbling block, trammel *Ant* aid, assistance, benefit, help

letdown 1 *Syn* DISAPPOINTMENT (sense 1), dismay, dissatisfaction, frustration *Ant* contentment, gratification, satisfaction 2 *Syn* DISAPPOINTMENT (sense 2), bummer

lethal *Syn* DEADLY, baleful, deathly, fatal, fell, killer, mortal, murderous, pestilent, vital *Ant* healthful, healthy, nonfatal, nonlethal, wholesome

lethargic · deficient in alertness or activity *Syn* comatose, sluggish, torpid *Rel* idle, inactive, inert, passive, supine *Ant* energetic, vigorous

lethargy · physical or mental inertness *Syn* languor, lassitude, stupor, torpidity, torpor *Rel* comatoseness, sluggishness *Ant* vigor

letter · a direct or personal written or printed message addressed to a person or organization *Syn* dispatch, epistle, memorandum, message, missive, note, report

levee 1 *Syn* DAM, dike, embankment 2 *Syn* WHARF, berth, dock, jetty, pier, quay, slip

level *adj* · having a surface without bends, curves, or irregularities *Syn* even, flat, flush, plain, plane, smooth *Rel* akin, alike, identical, like, parallel, similar, uniform

level *vb* *Syn* EQUALIZE, balance, equate, even

levelheadedness *Syn* COMMON SENSE, discreetness, discretion, horse sense, prudence, sense, sensibleness, wisdom, wit *Ant* imprudence, indiscretion

leviathan *Syn* GIANT, behemoth, blockbuster, colossus, jumbo, mammoth, monster, titan, whale, whopper *Ant* dwarf, midget, mini, miniature, peewee, pygmy, runt, shrimp

levity 1 *Syn* FRIVOLITY, facetiousness, flightiness, flippancy, frivolousness, lightheadedness, lightness 2 *Syn* LIGHTNESS, flightiness, flippancy, frivolity, light-mindedness, volatility *Ant* seriousness

levy *vb* *Syn* IMPOSE, assess, charge, exact, fine, lay, put *Ant* remit

levy *n* *Syn* TAX, assessment, duty, imposition, impost

lewd *Syn* LICENTIOUS, lascivious, lecherous, libertine, libidinous, lustful, wanton *Ant* continent

liability 1 *Syn* DEBT, arrear, debit, indebtedness, obligation 2 *Syn* DISADVANTAGE, drawback, handicap, minus, penalty, strike *Ant* advantage, asset, edge, plus

liable 1 · being by nature or through circumstances likely to experience something adverse *Syn* exposed, open, prone, sensitive, subject, susceptible *Ant* exempt, immune 2 *Syn* RESPONSIBLE, accountable, amenable, answerable

liaison *Syn* AMOUR, affair, intrigue

libel *Syn* SLANDER, asperse, blacken, defame, malign, smear, traduce, vilify

libelous *or* **libellous** · causing or intended to cause unjust injury to a person's good name *Syn* defamatory, scandalous, slanderous *Rel* erroneous, false, inaccurate, incorrect, inexact, invalid, off, unsound, untrue, wrong

liberal 1 · giving or given freely and unstintingly *Syn* bounteous, bountiful, generous, handsome, munificent, openhanded *Rel* exuberant, lavish, prodigal, profuse *Ant* close 2 · not bound by what is orthodox, established, or traditional *Syn* advanced, progressive, radical *Rel* forbearing, indulgent, lenient, tolerant *Ant* authoritarian

liberate *Syn* FREE, discharge, emancipate, manumit, release

libertine *Syn* LICENTIOUS, lascivious, lecherous, lewd, libidinous, lustful, wanton *Ant* continent

liberty *Syn* FREEDOM (sense 2), license *Ant* necessity

libidinous *Syn* LICENTIOUS, lascivious, lecherous, lewd, libertine, lustful, wanton *Ant* continent

licensable *Syn* PERMISSIBLE, admissible, allowable *Ant* banned, barred, forbidden, impermissible, inadmissible, interdicted, prohibited, proscribed

license *vb Syn* AUTHORIZE, accredit, commission

license *n* **1** *Syn* FREEDOM (sense 2), liberty *Ant* necessity **2** *Syn* PERMISSION, allowance, authorization, clearance, concurrence, consent, granting, leave, sanction, sufferance *Ant* interdiction, prohibition, proscription

licentious · lacking moral restraint especially in a disregarding of sexual restraints *Syn* lascivious, lecherous, lewd, libertine, libidinous, lustful, wanton *Rel* abandoned, dissolute, profligate, reprobate *Ant* continent

licit *Syn* LAWFUL, legal, legitimate *Ant* unlawful

lick *Syn* CONQUER, beat, defeat, overcome, overthrow, reduce, rout, subdue, subjugate, surmount, vanquish

lickspittle *Syn* PARASITE, bootlicker, favorite, hanger-on, leech, sponge, sponger, sycophant, toady

lie *n* · a statement or declaration that is not true *Syn* falsehood, fib, misrepresentation, story, untruth *Rel* equivocation, fib, fibbing, prevarication *Ant* truth

lie *vb* · to tell an untruth *Syn* equivocate, fib, palter, prevaricate *Rel* beguile, deceive, delude, mislead

life *Syn* BIOGRAPHY, autobiography, confessions, memoir

lifeless *Syn* DEAD, deceased, defunct, departed, inanimate, late

lift **1** · to move from a lower to a higher place or position *Syn* boost, elevate, heave, hoist, raise, rear *Rel* arise, ascend, levitate, mount, rise, rocket, soar, surge, tower *Ant* lower **2** *Syn* ASCEND, arise, climb, mount, rise, soar, up, uprise, upsweep, upturn *Ant* decline, descend, dip, drop, fall (off) **3** *Syn* STEAL, cop, filch, pilfer, pinch, purloin, snitch, swipe

light *vb* **1** · to cause something to start burning *Syn* fire, ignite, kindle **2** *Syn* ALIGHT, land, perch, roost, settle, touch down *Ant* take off **3** *Syn* ILLUMINATE, enlighten, illustrate, lighten *Ant* darken, obscure

light *adj Syn* EASY, effortless, facile, simple, smooth *Ant* hard

lighten **1** *Syn* ILLUMINATE, enlighten, illustrate, light *Ant* darken, obscure **2** *Syn* RELIEVE, allay, alleviate, assuage, mitigate *Ant* alarm, embarrass, intensify

light-headedness *Syn* FRIVOLITY, facetiousness, flightiness, flippancy, frivolousness, levity, lightness

lighthearted **1** *Syn* CAREFREE, careless, cavalier, devil-may-care, easygoing, gay, happy-go-lucky, insouciant, unconcerned *Ant* careworn **2** *Syn* GLAD, cheerful, happy, joyful, joyous *Ant* sad

lightheartedness *Syn* ABANDON, abandonment, ease, naturalness, spontaneity, unrestraint *Ant* constraint, restraint

lightly *Syn* EASILY, effortlessly, facilely, fluently, freely, handily, painlessly, readily, smoothly *Ant* arduously, laboriously

light-mindedness *Syn* LIGHTNESS, flightiness, flippancy, frivolity, levity, volatility *Ant* seriousness

lightness **1** · gaiety or indifference where seriousness and attention are called for *Syn* flightiness, flippancy, frivolity, levity, light-mindedness, volatility *Rel* buoyancy, effervescence, elasticity, expansiveness, resiliency *Ant* seriousness **2** *Syn* FRIVOLITY, facetiousness, flightiness, flippancy, frivolousness, levity, light-headedness

lightsome *Syn* CHEERFUL (sense 1), blithe, blithesome, bright, buoyant, cheery, chipper, gay, gladsome, sunny, upbeat *Ant* dour, gloomy, glum, morose, saturnine, sulky, sullen

like *vb* · to feel attraction toward or take pleasure in *Syn* dote, enjoy, fancy, love, relish *Rel* choose, elect, prefer, select *Ant* dislike

like *adj* **1** *Syn* ALIKE, akin, analogous, comparable, correspondent, corresponding, matching, parallel, resembling, similar, such, suchlike *Ant* different, dissimilar, diverse, unlike **2** *Syn* EQUAL, coordinate, counterpart, equivalent, fellow, match, parallel, peer, rival

like *n Syn* LIKING, appetite, fancy, favor, fondness, love, partiality, preference, relish, shine, taste, use *Ant* aversion, disfavor, dislike, distaste, hatred, loathing

likely *adj Syn* PROBABLE, possible *Ant* certain, improbable

likely *adv Syn* PROBABLY, doubtless, presumably *Ant* improbably

likeness *n Syn* SIMILARITY, alikeness, community, correspondence, parallelism, resemblance, similitude *Ant* dissimilarity, unlikeness

liking · positive regard for something *Syn* appetite, fancy, favor, fondness, like, love, partiality, preference, relish, shine, taste, use *Rel* craving, desire, longing, thirst, yen *Ant* aversion, disfavor, dislike, distaste, hatred, loathing

lily-livered *Syn* COWARDLY, chicken, chickenhearted, craven, dastardly, pusillanimous, recreant, spineless, unheroic, yellow *Ant* brave, courageous, daring, dauntless, doughty, fearless, gallant, greathearted, gutsy, hardy, heroic, intrepid, lionhearted, stalwart, stout, stouthearted, valiant, valorous

limb *Syn* SHOOT, bough, branch

limber **1** *Syn* SUPPLE, lissome, lithe, lithesome **2** *Syn* WILLOWY, flexible, lissome, lithe, pliable, pliant, supple *Ant* inflexible, rigid, stiff

limit *n* · a material or immaterial point beyond which something does not or cannot extend

Syn bound, confine, end, term *Rel* circumscription, confinement, limitation, restriction

limit *vb* · to set bounds for *Syn* circumscribe, confine, restrict *Rel* assign, define, prescribe *Ant* widen

limitation *Syn* RESTRICTION, check, condition, constraint, curb, fetter, restraint

limitless *Syn* INFINITE, boundless, endless, illimitable, immeasurable, indefinite, measureless, unbounded, unfathomable, unlimited *Ant* bounded, circumscribed, confined, definite, finite, limited, restricted

limn *Syn* REPRESENT, delineate, depict, picture, portray

limp **1** · deficient in firmness of texture, substance, or structure *Syn* flabby, flaccid, flimsy, floppy, sleazy *Rel* lax, loose, relaxed, slack **2** *Syn* LISTLESS, enervated, lackadaisical, languid, languishing, languorous, spiritless *Ant* ambitious, animated, energetic, enterprising, motivated

limpid *Syn* CLEAR (sense 1), diaphanous, lucid, pellucid, translucent, transparent *Ant* confused, turbid

line *n* **1** · a series of things arranged in continuous or uniform order *Syn* echelon, file, rank, row, tier *Rel* chain, progression, sequence, series, succession **2** *Syn* ANCESTRY, birth, blood, bloodline, breeding, descent, extraction, family tree, genealogy, lineage, origin, parentage, pedigree, stock, strain *Ant* issue, posterity, progeny, seed **3** *Syn* CORD, cable, lace, lacing, rope, string, wire **4** *Syn* OCCUPATION, calling, employment, profession, trade, vocation, work

line *vb* · to arrange in a line or in lines *Syn* align, array, line up, range *Rel* arrange, marshal, order

lineage *Syn* ANCESTRY, birth, blood, bloodline, breeding, descent, extraction, family tree, genealogy, line, origin, parentage, pedigree, stock, strain *Ant* issue, posterity, progeny, seed

line up *Syn* LINE, align, array, range

linger *Syn* STAY, abide, remain, tarry, wait

lingo *Syn* TERMINOLOGY, argot, cant, dialect, jargon, language, patois, patter, slang, vocabulary

link *Syn* JOIN, associate, combine, conjoin, connect, relate, unite *Ant* disjoin, part

liquefy · to convert or to become converted to a liquid state *Syn* deliquesce, fuse, melt, thaw

liquor *Syn* ALCOHOL, booze, drink, grog, intoxicant, moonshine, spirits

lissome **1** *Syn* SUPPLE, limber, lithe, lithesome **2** *Syn* WILLOWY, flexible, limber, lithe, pliable, pliant, supple *Ant* inflexible, rigid, stiff

list *n* · a series of items (as names) written down or printed as a memorandum or record *Syn* catalog, inventory, register, roll, roster, schedule, table

list *vb Syn* RECORD, catalog, enroll, register

listen · to pay attention especially through the act of hearing *Syn* attend, hark, hear, hearken, heed, mind *Ant* ignore, tune out

listing *Syn* AWRY, askew, aslant, cockeyed, crooked, lopsided, oblique, skewed, slanted, slanting, slantwise, tilted, tipping, uneven *Ant* even, level, straight

listless · lacking bodily energy or motivation *Syn* enervated, lackadaisical, languid, languishing, languorous, limp, spiritless *Rel* indolent, lazy, slothful *Ant* ambitious, animated, energetic, enterprising, motivated

literary *Syn* BOOKISH, erudite, learned *Ant* colloquial, nonliterary

literate *Syn* EDUCATED, erudite, knowledgeable, learned, scholarly, well-read *Ant* ignorant, illiterate, uneducated

lithe **1** *Syn* SUPPLE, limber, lissome, lithesome **2** *Syn* WILLOWY, flexible, limber, lissome, pliable, pliant, supple *Ant* inflexible, rigid, stiff

lithesome *Syn* SUPPLE, limber, lissome, lithe

littered *Syn* MESSY, chaotic, cluttered, confused, disarranged, disarrayed, disheveled (*or* dishevelled), disordered, disorderly, higgledy-piggledy, hugger-mugger, jumbled, messed, muddled, mussed, mussy, pell-mell, rumpled, sloppy, topsy-turvy, tousled, tumbled, unkempt, untidy, upside-down *Ant* neat, ordered, orderly, organized, shipshape, snug, tidied, tidy, trim

little *adv Syn* SELDOM, infrequently, rarely *Ant* frequently, often

little *adj Syn* UNIMPORTANT, frivolous, inconsequential, inconsiderable, insignificant, minor, minute, negligible, slight, small, small-fry, trifling, trivial *Ant* big, consequential, eventful, important, major, material, meaningful, momentous, significant, substantial, weighty

littlest *Syn* MINIMAL, least, lowest, minimum, slightest *Ant* full, greatest, largest, maximum, top, topmost, utmost

littoral *Syn* SHORE, bank, beach, coast, foreshore, strand

liturgy *Syn* FORM (sense 2), ceremonial, ceremony, formality, rite, ritual

live *adj Syn* ACTIVE, dynamic, operative *Ant* inactive

live *vb* **1** *Syn* BE, exist, subsist **2** *Syn* RESIDE, dwell, lodge, put up, sojourn, stay, stop

livelihood *Syn* LIVING, bread, bread and butter, keep, maintenance, subsistence, support, sustenance

lively · keenly alive and spirited *Syn* animated, gay, sprightly, vivacious *Rel* agile, brisk, nimble, spry *Ant* dull

liven (up) *Syn* ANIMATE, brace, energize, enliven, fire, invigorate, jazz (up), pep (up), quicken, stimulate, vitalize, vivify *Ant* damp, dampen, deaden, dull

livid *Syn* PALE (sense 1), ashen, ashy, pallid, wan *Ant* florid, flush, rubicund, ruddy, sanguine

living *adj* · having or showing life *Syn* alive, animate, animated, vital *Rel* being, existing, subsisting *Ant* lifeless

living *n* · supplies or resources needed to live *Syn* bread, bread and butter, keep, livelihood, maintenance, subsistence, support, sustenance

load *n* · something which is carried, conveyed, or transported from one place to another *Syn* burden, cargo, freight, lading

load *vb* **1** *Syn* ADULTERATE, doctor, sophisticate, weight *Ant* refine **2** *Syn* BURDEN, charge, cumber, encumber, lade, saddle, tax, weigh, weight

loaf *Syn* IDLE, laze, loll, lounge

loafer *Syn* LAZYBONES, drone, idler, slouch, slug, sluggard *Ant* doer, go-getter, hummer, hustler, rustler, self-starter

loath *Syn* DISINCLINED, averse, hesitant, indisposed, reluctant

loathe *Syn* HATE, abhor, abominate, detest *Ant* love

loathing **1** *Syn* ABHORRENCE, abomination, detestation, hate, hatred *Ant* admiration, enjoyment **2** *Syn* DISGUST, aversion, distaste, nausea, repugnance, repulsion, revulsion

loathsome *Syn* OFFENSIVE, repugnant, repulsive, revolting

local *Syn* INSULAR, parochial, provincial, small-town

locality · a more or less definitely circumscribed place or region *Syn* district, neighborhood, vicinity *Rel* area, belt, region, tract, zone

location *Syn* PLACE, position, site, situation, spot, station

locker **1** *Syn* CABINET, buffet, closet, cupboard, hutch, sideboard **2** *Syn* CHEST, box, caddy, case, casket, trunk

lockup *Syn* JAIL, brig, guardroom, hoosegow, jug, pen, penitentiary, prison, stockade

locomotion *Syn* MOTION, move, movement, stir

locution *Syn* PHRASE, expression, idiom

lodge **1** *Syn* HARBOR, board, entertain, house, shelter **2** *Syn* RESIDE, dwell, live, put up, sojourn, stay, stop

lodger *Syn* TENANT, boarder, renter, roomer *Ant* landlord

loftiness *Syn* ARROGANCE, haughtiness, imperiousness, lordliness, masterfulness, peremptoriness, pompousness, presumptuousness, pretense (*or* pretence), pretension, pretentiousness, self-importance, superciliousness, superiority *Ant* humility, modesty

lofty **1** *Syn* ARROGANT, cavalier, haughty, highfalutin, high-handed, high-hat, imperious, important, lordly, masterful, overweening, peremptory, pompous, presumptuous, pretentious, supercilious, superior, uppish,

uppity *Ant* humble, modest **2** *Syn* HIGH, tall *Ant* low

logical · having or showing skill in thinking or reasoning *Syn* analytical, subtle *Rel* cogent, compelling, convincing, sound, telling, valid *Ant* illogical

logistic *Syn* STRATEGIC, tactical

logistics *Syn* STRATEGY, tactics

loiter *Syn* DELAY (sense 2), dawdle, lag, procrastinate *Ant* hasten, hurry

loll *Syn* IDLE, laze, loaf, lounge

lollop **1** *Syn* SKIP, bound, curvet, hop, lope, ricochet **2** *Syn* STUMBLE, blunder, bumble, flounder, galumph, lumber, lurch, trip

lone **1** *Syn* ALONE, desolate, forlorn, lonely, lonesome, lorn, solitary *Ant* accompanied **2** *Syn* ONLY, alone, singular, sole, solitary, special, unique **3** *Syn* SINGLE, particular, separate, sole, solitary, unique *Ant* accompanied, conjugal, supported

lonely *Syn* ALONE, desolate, forlorn, lone, lonesome, lorn, solitary *Ant* accompanied

lonesome *Syn* ALONE, desolate, forlorn, lone, lonely, lorn, solitary *Ant* accompanied

long *adj* **1** · of great extent from end to end *Syn* elongated, extended, king-size (*or* king-sized), lengthy *Rel* extensive, far-reaching, longish, outstretched *Ant* brief, short **2** · lasting for a considerable time *Syn* extended, far, great, lengthy, long-lived, long-range, long-term, marathon *Rel* endless, everlasting, interminable, persistent *Ant* brief, short, short-lived, short-range, short-term

long *vb* · to have a strong desire for something *Syn* hanker, hunger, pine, thirst, yearn *Rel* covet, crave, desire, want, wish

longanimity *Syn* PATIENCE, forbearance, long-suffering, resignation *Ant* impatience

long-lived **1** *Syn* ELDERLY, aged, aging, ancient, geriatric, old, older, senior *Ant* young, youthful **2** *Syn* LONG (sense 2), extended, far, great, lengthy, long-range, long-term, marathon *Ant* brief, short, short-lived, short-range, short-term

long-range *Syn* LONG (sense 2), extended, far, great, lengthy, long-lived, long-term, marathon *Ant* brief, short, short-lived, short-range, short-term

long-suffering *Syn* PATIENCE, forbearance, longanimity, resignation *Ant* impatience

long-term *Syn* LONG (sense 2), extended, far, great, lengthy, long-lived, long-range, marathon *Ant* brief, short, short-lived, short-range, short-term

look *n* **1** · the directing of one's eyes in order to see *Syn* glance, glimpse, peek, peep, sight, view *Rel* gaze, gazing, stare, staring **2** *Syn* APPEARANCE, aspect, semblance

look *vb* **1** *Syn* EXPECT, await, hope *Ant* despair of **2** *Syn* SEEM, act, appear, make, sound **3** *Syn* SEE (sense 2), watch

looker-on *Syn* SPECTATOR, beholder, bystander, eyewitness, kibitzer, observer, onlooker, witness

look (into) *Syn* EXPLORE, delve (into), dig (into), inquire (into), investigate, probe, research

lookout *Syn* VIGILANCE, alertness, attentiveness, surveillance, watch, watchfulness

loom *Syn* APPEAR, emerge *Ant* disappear, vanish

loose · not tightly bound, held, restrained, or stretched *Syn* lax, relaxed, slack *Rel* flabby, flaccid, flimsy, limp *Ant* strict, tight

loosen *Syn* SLACKEN, ease, relax, slack *Ant* strain, stretch, tense, tighten

loot 1 *Syn* ROB, burglarize, plunder, rifle 2 *Syn* SPOIL, booty, plunder, prize, swag

lope *Syn* SKIP, bound, curvet, hop, lollop, ricochet

lop (off) *Syn* CLIP, bob, crop, curtail, cut, cut back, dock, nip, pare, prune, shave, shear, snip, trim

lopsided *Syn* AWRY, askew, aslant, cockeyed, crooked, listing, oblique, skewed, slanted, slanting, slantwise, tilted, tipping, uneven *Ant* even, level, straight

loquacious *Syn* TALKATIVE, garrulous, glib, voluble *Ant* closemouthed, laconic, reserved, reticent, taciturn, tight-lipped

loquaciousness *Syn* TALKATIVENESS, garrulity, garrulousness, glibness, loquacity, volubility *Ant* silence

loquacity *Syn* TALKATIVENESS, garrulity, garrulousness, glibness, loquaciousness, volubility *Ant* silence

lord *Syn* GENTLEMAN, nobleman

lordliness *Syn* ARROGANCE, haughtiness, imperiousness, loftiness, masterfulness, peremptoriness, pompousness, presumptuousness, pretense (*or* pretence), pretension, pretentiousness, self-importance, superciliousness, superiority *Ant* humility, modesty

lordly 1 *Syn* ARROGANT, cavalier, haughty, highfalutin, high-handed, high-hat, imperious, important, lofty, masterful, overweening, peremptory, pompous, presumptuous, pretentious, supercilious, superior, uppish, uppity *Ant* humble, modest 2 *Syn* PROUD (sense 1), arrogant, disdainful, haughty, insolent, overbearing, supercilious *Ant* ashamed, humble

lore 1 *Syn* FOLKLORE, legend, myth, mythology, tradition 2 *Syn* KNOWLEDGE, erudition, information, learning, scholarship, science *Ant* ignorance

lorn *Syn* ALONE, desolate, forlorn, lone, lonely, lonesome, solitary *Ant* accompanied

loss *Syn* DESTRUCTION, annihilation, decimation, demolishment, demolition, desolation, devastation, extermination, extinction, havoc, obliteration, ruin, ruination, wastage, wreckage *Ant* building, construction, erection, raising

lot 1 *Syn* FATE, destiny, doom, portion 2 *Syn* GROUP, bunch, cluster, parcel

loud 1 · marked by intensity or volume of sound *Syn* earsplitting, hoarse, raucous, stentorian, stertorous, strident *Ant* low, low-pitched 2 *Syn* GAUDY, flamboyant, flashy, garish, glitzy, ostentatious, splashy, swank (*or* swanky), tawdry *Ant* conservative, quiet, understated

lounge *n* *Syn* COUCH, chesterfield, davenport, divan, settee, sofa

lounge *vb* *Syn* IDLE, laze, loaf, loll

louse up *Syn* BOTCH, bobble, bungle, butcher, flub, foozle, foul up, fumble, mangle, mess (up), muff, murder

lout *Syn* OAF, clod, gawk, hulk, lubber, lug

loutish *Syn* CLOWNISH, boorish, churlish, cloddish, uncouth *Ant* civil, courteous, courtly, cultivated, genteel, gentlemanly, ladylike, polished, polite, refined, well-bred

lovable · having qualities that tend to make one loved *Syn* adorable, darling, dear, disarming, endearing, precious, sweet, winning *Rel* embraceable, kissable *Ant* abhorrent, abominable, detestable, hateful, odious, unlovable

love *vb* *Syn* LIKE, dote, enjoy, fancy, relish *Ant* dislike

love *n* 1 *Syn* ATTACHMENT, affection *Ant* aversion 2 *Syn* LIKING, appetite, fancy, favor, fondness, like, partiality, preference, relish, shine, taste, use *Ant* aversion, disfavor, dislike, distaste, hatred, loathing 3 *Syn* SWEETHEART, beloved, darling, dear, flame, honey, sweet

lovely *Syn* BEAUTIFUL, attractive, beauteous, comely, cute, fair, gorgeous, handsome, knockout, pretty, ravishing, sightly, stunning, taking *Ant* homely, ill-favored, plain, ugly, unattractive, unbeautiful, unhandsome, unlovely, unpretty, unsightly

lover *Syn* FAN, addict, aficionado, buff, bug, devotee, enthusiast, fanatic, fancier, fiend, freak, maniac, nut

loving · feeling or expressing love *Syn* affectionate, devoted, doting, fond *Rel* amatory, amorous, erotic *Ant* unloving

low 1 *Syn* BASE, vile *Ant* noble 2 *Syn* SAD (sense 1), bad, blue, brokenhearted, crestfallen, dejected, depressed, despondent, disconsolate, doleful, down, downcast, downhearted, droopy, forlorn, gloomy, glum, heartbroken, heartsick, heartsore, inconsolable, joyless, low-spirited, melancholy, miserable, mournful, saddened, sorrowful, sorry, unhappy, woebegone, woeful, wretched *Ant* blissful, buoyant, buoyed, cheerful, cheery, chipper, delighted, glad, gladdened, gladsome, gleeful, happy, joyful, joyous, jubilant, sunny, upbeat

lower *adj* *Syn* LESSER, inferior, junior, less, minor, smaller, subordinate, under *Ant* greater, higher, major, more, primary, prime, senior, superior

lower *vb* *Syn* FROWN, glare, gloom, glower, scowl *Ant* beam, smile

lower *n Syn* GRIMACE, face, frown, mouth, pout, scowl

lowering *Syn* OVERCAST, beclouded, clouded, cloudy, dull, hazed, hazy, heavy, overclouded *Ant* clear, cloudless

lowest *Syn* MINIMAL, least, littlest, minimum, slightest *Ant* full, greatest, largest, maximum, top, topmost, utmost

lowly *Syn* HUMBLE, meek, modest

low-spirited *Syn* SAD (sense 1), bad, blue, brokenhearted, crestfallen, dejected, depressed, despondent, disconsolate, doleful, down, downcast, downhearted, droopy, forlorn, gloomy, glum, heartbroken, heartsick, heartsore, inconsolable, joyless, low, melancholy, miserable, mournful, saddened, sorrowful, sorry, unhappy, woebegone, woeful, wretched *Ant* blissful, buoyant, buoyed, cheerful, cheery, chipper, delighted, glad, gladdened, gladsome, gleeful, happy, joyful, joyous, jubilant, sunny, upbeat

loyal *Syn* FAITHFUL, constant, devoted, devout, fast, good, pious, staunch (*or* stanch), steadfast, steady, true, true-blue *Ant* disloyal, faithless, false, fickle, inconstant, perfidious, recreant, traitorous, treacherous, unfaithful, untrue

loyalty *Syn* FIDELITY, allegiance, devotion, fealty, piety *Ant* faithlessness, perfidy

lozenge *Syn* PILL, capsule, tablet

lubber *Syn* OAF, clod, gawk, hulk, lout, lug

lubricate *Syn* OIL, anoint, cream, grease

lucent *Syn* BRIGHT, beaming, brilliant, effulgent, incandescent, lambent, luminous, lustrous, radiant, refulgent *Ant* dim, dull

lucid **1** *Syn* CLEAR (sense 1), diaphanous, limpid, pellucid, translucent, transparent *Ant* confused, turbid **2** *Syn* CLEAR (sense 2), perspicuous *Ant* abstruse, unintelligible **3** *Syn* SANE, balanced, clearheaded, normal, right, stable *Ant* crazed, crazy, demented, deranged, insane, lunatic, mad, maniacal, mental, unbalanced, unsound

luck *Syn* CHANCE, accident, fortune, hap, hazard *Ant* law, principle

luckless *Syn* UNLUCKY, calamitous, disastrous, hapless, ill-fated, ill-starred, unfortunate *Ant* fortunate, happy, lucky

lucky • meeting with unforeseen success *Syn* fortunate, happy, providential *Rel* auspicious, benign, favorable, propitious *Ant* unlucky

lucrative *Syn* PAYING, gainful, profitable, remunerative

ludicrous *Syn* LAUGHABLE, comic, comical, droll, farcical, funny, ridiculous, risible

lug *Syn* OAF, clod, gawk, hulk, lout, lubber

lugubrious *Syn* MELANCHOLY, doleful, dolorous, plaintive, rueful

lull *vb Syn* CALM, compose, quiet, quieten, settle, soothe, still, tranquilize *Ant* agitate, arouse

lull *n Syn* PAUSE, break, breath, breather, interruption, recess

lumber *Syn* STUMBLE, blunder, bumble, flounder, galumph, lollop, lurch, trip

luminous *Syn* BRIGHT, beaming, brilliant, effulgent, incandescent, lambent, lucent, lustrous, radiant, refulgent *Ant* dim, dull

lunacy *Syn* INSANITY, mania, psychosis *Ant* sanity

lunatic *n Syn* FOOL (sense 2), booby, goose, half-wit, jackass, nincompoop, ninny, nitwit, nut, simpleton, turkey, yo-yo

lunatic *adj Syn* INSANE, crazed, crazy, demented, deranged, mad, maniac, non compos mentis *Ant* sane

lurch *Syn* STUMBLE, blunder, bumble, flounder, galumph, lollop, lumber, trip

lure • to lead away from a usual or proper course by offering some pleasure or advantage *Syn* allure, beguile, decoy, entice, lead on, seduce, tempt *Rel* inveigle, persuade, rope (in), snow

lurid *Syn* GHASTLY, grim, grisly, gruesome, macabre

lurk • to behave so as to escape attention *Syn* skulk, slink, sneak *Rel* conceal, hide, secrete

luscious *Syn* DELIGHTFUL, delectable, delicious *Ant* boring, distressing, horrid

lush *Syn* PROFUSE, exuberant, lavish, luxuriant, prodigal *Ant* scant, scanty, spare

lust *Syn* DESIRE, appetite, passion, urge *Ant* distaste

luster • the quality or condition of shining by reflected light *Syn* glaze, gloss, sheen *Rel* iridescence, opalescence

lustful *Syn* LICENTIOUS, lascivious, lecherous, lewd, libertine, libidinous, wanton *Ant* continent

lustrous **1** *Syn* BRIGHT, beaming, brilliant, effulgent, incandescent, lambent, lucent, luminous, radiant, refulgent *Ant* dim, dull **2** *Syn* GLOSSY, buffed, burnished, glistening, polished, rubbed, satin, satiny, sleek *Ant* dim, dull, flat, lusterless, matte

lusty *Syn* VIGOROUS, energetic, nervous, strenuous *Ant* languorous, lethargic

luxuriant **1** *Syn* FERTILE, fat, fecund, fruitful, productive, prolific, rich *Ant* barren, infertile, sterile, unfruitful, unproductive **2** *Syn* LUXURIOUS, deluxe, lavish, opulent, palatial, plush, sumptuous *Ant* ascetic, austere, humble, Spartan **3** *Syn* PROFUSE, exuberant, lavish, lush, prodigal *Ant* scant, scanty, spare

luxurious **1** • showing obvious signs of wealth and comfort *Syn* deluxe, lavish, luxuriant, opulent, palatial, plush, sumptuous *Rel* costly, expensive *Ant* ascetic, austere, humble, Spartan **2** *Syn* SENSUOUS, epicurean, sybaritic, voluptuous

luxuriously *Syn* HIGH, expensively, extravagantly, grandly, lavishly, opulently, richly, sumptuously *Ant* austerely, humbly, modestly, plainly, simply

lyric *Syn* POEM, song, verse

M

macabre *Syn* GHASTLY, grim, grisly, gruesome, lurid

macerate *Syn* CRUSH (sense 1), bruise, mash, smash, squash

Machiavellian *Syn* UNPRINCIPLED, cutthroat, immoral, unconscionable, unethical, unmoral, unscrupulous *Ant* ethical, moral, principled, scrupulous

machinate **1** *Syn* ENGINEER, contrive, finagle, finesse, frame, maneuver, manipulate, mastermind, negotiate, wangle **2** *Syn* PLOT, conspire, contrive, intrigue, scheme

machination *Syn* PLOT, cabal, conspiracy, intrigue

machine · a device or system by which energy can be converted into useful work *Syn* apparatus, engine, machinery, mechanism, motor *Rel* contraption, contrivance, device, gadget

machinery **1** *Syn* AGENT (sense 2), agency, instrument, instrumentality, means, medium, organ, vehicle **2** *Syn* EQUIPMENT, apparatus, gear, matériel, outfit, paraphernalia, tackle **3** *Syn* MACHINE, apparatus, engine, mechanism, motor

mad **1** *Syn* ANGRY, angered, apoplectic, enraged, foaming, fuming, furious, incensed, indignant, inflamed, infuriated, irate, ireful, outraged, rabid, riled, roiled, sore, steaming, wrathful, wroth *Ant* delighted, pleased **2** *Syn* INSANE, crazed, crazy, demented, deranged, lunatic, maniac, non compos mentis *Ant* sane

madden *Syn* ANGER, antagonize, enrage, incense, inflame, infuriate, outrage, rankle, rile, roil *Ant* delight, gratify, please

maddening *Syn* ANNOYING, aggravating, bothersome, disturbing, exasperating, frustrating, galling, irksome, irritating, nettling, peeving, pesty, rankling, riling, vexatious, vexing

madhouse · a place of uproar or confusion *Syn* babel, bedlam, circus, hell *Rel* commotion, havoc, pandemonium, racket, ruckus, tumult, turmoil

maelstrom *Syn* EDDY, vortex, whirlpool

maestro *Syn* EXPERT, ace, adept, artist, authority, crackerjack, master, past master, scholar, shark, virtuoso, whiz, wizard *Ant* amateur

magazine **1** *Syn* ARMORY, arsenal, depot, dump **2** *Syn* STOREHOUSE, depository, depot, repository, storage, stowage, warehouse **3** *Syn* JOURNAL, newspaper, organ, periodical, review

magic · the use of means (as charms or spells) believed to have supernatural power over natural forces *Syn* alchemy, sorcery, thaumaturgy, witchcraft, witchery, wizardry

magician **1** · a person skilled in using supernatural forces *Syn* charmer, conjurer (*or* conjuror), enchanter, necromancer, sorcerer, voodoo, witch, wizard *Rel* enchantress, hag, hex, sorceress, warlock **2** · one who practices tricks and illusions for entertainment *Syn* conjurer (*or* conjuror), prestidigitator, trickster *Rel* charmer, enchanter, enchantress

magisterial *Syn* DICTATORIAL, authoritarian, doctrinaire, dogmatic

magnification *Syn* EXAGGERATION, caricature, coloring, elaboration, embellishment, embroidering, hyperbole, overstatement, padding, stretching *Ant* understatement

magnificence · impressiveness of beauty on a large scale *Syn* augustness, brilliance, gloriousness, glory, grandeur, grandness, majesty, nobility, nobleness, resplendence, splendor, stateliness, stupendousness, sublimeness, superbness *Rel* awesomeness, marvelousness, wondrousness

magnificent *Syn* GRAND, august, grandiose, imposing, majestic, noble, stately

magnify *Syn* EXALT, aggrandize, dignify, ennoble, enshrine, glorify *Ant* abase, degrade, demean, humble, humiliate

magniloquent *Syn* RHETORICAL, aureate, bombastic, euphuistic, flowery, grandiloquent

magnitude *Syn* SIZE, area, dimensions, extent, volume

maim · to injure so severely as to cause lasting damage *Syn* batter, cripple, mangle, mutilate *Rel* damage, injure, mar, spoil

main *Syn* CHIEF, capital, foremost, leading, principal *Ant* subordinate

mainly **1** *Syn* CHIEFLY, altogether, basically, by and large, generally, largely, mostly, overall, predominantly, primarily, principally, substantially **2** *Syn* LARGELY, chiefly, generally, greatly, mostly, principally

maintain · to uphold as true, right, just, or reasonable *Syn* assert, defend, justify, vindicate *Rel* affirm, aver, avouch, avow, declare, profess, protest

maintainable *Syn* TENABLE, defendable, defensible, justifiable, supportable, sustainable *Ant* indefensible, insupportable, unjustifiable, untenable

maintenance *Syn* LIVING, bread, bread and butter, keep, livelihood, subsistence, support, sustenance

majestic *Syn* GRAND, august, grandiose, imposing, magnificent, noble, stately

majesty **1** *Syn* ELEGANCE, class, elegancy, grace, gracefulness, handsomeness, refinement, stateliness **2** *Syn* MAGNIFICENCE, augustness, brilliance, gloriousness, glory, grandeur, grandness, nobility, nobleness, resplendence, splendor, stateliness, stupendousness, sublimeness, superbness

make 1 · to bring something into being by forming, shaping, combining, or altering materials *Syn* fabricate, fashion, forge, form, manufacture, shape *Rel* bear, produce, turn out, yield **2** *Syn* BUILD, assemble, construct, erect, fabricate, make up, piece, put up, raise, rear, set up *Ant* disassemble, dismantle, take down **3** *Syn* EARN, acquire, attain, capture, carry, draw, gain, garner, get, land, obtain, procure, realize, secure, win *Ant* forfeit, lose **4** *Syn* EFFECT, bring about, cause, create, effectuate, engender, generate, induce, produce, prompt, result (in), spawn, work, yield **5** *Syn* ENACT, lay down, legislate, pass *Ant* repeal, rescind, revoke **6** *Syn* ESTIMATE (sense 2), calculate, call, conjecture, figure, gauge, guess, judge, place, put, reckon, suppose **7** *Syn* SEEM, act, appear, look, sound

make-believe *Syn* PRETENSE, pretension

make over 1 *Syn* CHANGE (sense 1), alter, modify, recast, redo, refashion, remake, remodel, revamp, revise, rework, vary *Ant* fix, freeze, set, stabilize **2** *Syn* CONVERT, metamorphose, transfigure, transform

maker · one who brings something into being or existence *Syn* author, creator

makeshift *Syn* RESOURCE, expedient, resort, shift, stopgap, substitute, surrogate

make up 1 *Syn* BUILD, assemble, construct, erect, fabricate, make, piece, put up, raise, rear, set up *Ant* disassemble, dismantle, take down **2** *Syn* INVENT, concoct, contrive, cook (up), devise, fabricate, manufacture, think (up)

maladroit *Syn* AWKWARD, clumsy, gauche, inept *Ant* deft, graceful, handy

malady *Syn* DISEASE, ailment, complaint, condition, disorder, distemper, syndrome

male *adj ·* of, relating to, or marked by qualities traditionally associated with men *Syn* manful, manlike, manly, mannish, masculine, virile *Ant* female

male *n Syn* MAN, dude, fellow, gent, gentleman, guy

malediction *Syn* CURSE, anathema, imprecation *Ant* blessing

malefactor *Syn* CRIMINAL, convict, culprit, delinquent, felon

malefic *Syn* SINISTER, baleful, maleficent, malign

maleficent *Syn* SINISTER, baleful, malefic, malign

malevolence *Syn* MALICE, despite, grudge, ill will, malignancy, malignity, spite, spleen *Ant* charity

malevolent *Syn* MALICIOUS, malign, malignant, spiteful

malfeasance *Syn* MISCONDUCT, misbehavior, misdoing, wrongdoing

malice · the desire to see another experience pain, injury, or distress *Syn* despite, grudge, ill will, malevolence, malignancy, malignity, spite, spleen *Rel* maliciousness, spitefulness *Ant* charity

malicious · having, showing, or indicative of intense often vicious ill will *Syn* malevolent, malign, malignant, spiteful *Rel* poisonous, venomous

malign *adj* **1** *Syn* MALICIOUS, malevolent, malignant, spiteful **2** *Syn* SINISTER, baleful, malefic, maleficent

malign *vb Syn* SLANDER, asperse, blacken, defame, libel, smear, traduce, vilify

malignancy *Syn* MALICE, despite, grudge, ill will, malevolence, malignity, spite, spleen *Ant* charity

malignant *Syn* MALICIOUS, malevolent, malign, spiteful

malignity *Syn* MALICE, despite, grudge, ill will, malevolence, malignancy, spite, spleen *Ant* charity

malinger *Syn* DODGE, duck, fence, parry, shirk, sidestep *Ant* face

malleable *Syn* PLASTIC, adaptable, ductile, pliable, pliant

malodorous · having an unpleasant smell *Syn* fetid, fusty, musty, noisome, putrid, rancid, rank, stinking *Ant* odorous

maltreat *Syn* ABUSE, ill-treat, mistreat, misuse, outrage *Ant* honor, respect

mammoth 1 *Syn* GIANT, behemoth, blockbuster, colossus, jumbo, leviathan, monster, titan, whale, whopper *Ant* dwarf, midget, mini, miniature, peewee, pygmy, runt, shrimp **2** *Syn* HUGE, Brobdingnagian, colossal, cyclopean, elephantine, enormous, gargantuan, giant, gigantean, gigantic, Herculean, immense, titanic, vast *Ant* bitty, diminutive, microscopic (*or* microscopical), midget, miniature, minute, pocket, pygmy, teeny, teeny-weeny, tiny, wee

man 1 · an adult male human being *Syn* dude, fellow, gent, gentleman, guy, male **2** *Syn* BOYFRIEND, beau, fellow, swain

manacle *n Syn* ENCUMBRANCE, bar, block, chain, clog, crimp, deterrent, drag, embarrassment, fetter, handicap, hindrance, hurdle, impediment, inhibition, interference, let, obstacle, obstruction, shackles, stop, stumbling block, trammel *Ant* aid, assistance, benefit, help

manacle *vb Syn* HAMPER, clog, fetter, hog-tie, shackle, trammel *Ant* assist (*persons*), expedite (*work, projects*)

manage *Syn* CONDUCT, control, direct

manager *Syn* EXECUTIVE, administrator, director, superintendent, supervisor

managing *Syn* HEAD, chief, commanding, first, foremost, high, lead, leading, preeminent, premier, presiding, primary, prime, principal, supreme

mandate 1 · an authorization to take a political action given to a representative *Syn* initiative, plebiscite, referendum **2** *Syn* COMMAND, behest, bidding, dictate, injunction, order

mandatory · forcing one's compliance or participation by or as if by law *Syn* compulsory, forced, imperative, incumbent, involuntary, necessary, nonelective, obligatory, peremptory, required *Rel* all-important, essential, indispensable, needed, requisite *Ant* elective, optional, voluntary

maneuver *vb Syn* ENGINEER, contrive, finagle, finesse, frame, machinate, manipulate, mastermind, negotiate, wangle

maneuver *n Syn* TRICK, artifice, feint, gambit, ploy, ruse, stratagem, wile

manful *Syn* MALE, manlike, manly, mannish, masculine, virile *Ant* female

mangle 1 *Syn* BOTCH, bobble, bungle, butcher, flub, foozle, foul up, fumble, louse up, mess (up), muff, murder **2** *Syn* MAIM, batter, cripple, mutilate

manhood *Syn* VIRILITY, manliness, masculinity *Ant* femininity

mania 1 · a state of mind in which there is loss of control over emotional, nervous, or mental processes *Syn* delirium, frenzy, hysteria *Rel* dejection, depression, melancholia, melancholy, sadness **2** *Syn* INSANITY, lunacy, psychosis *Ant* sanity

maniac *n Syn* FAN, addict, aficionado, buff, bug, devotee, enthusiast, fanatic, fancier, fiend, freak, lover, nut

maniac *adj Syn* INSANE, crazed, crazy, demented, deranged, lunatic, mad, non compos mentis *Ant* sane

manifest *vb* **1** *Syn* EMBODY (sense 2), epitomize, incarnate, materialize, personalize, personify, substantiate **2** *Syn* SHOW (sense 1), demonstrate, evidence, evince *Ant* disguise

manifest *adj Syn* EVIDENT, apparent, clear, distinct, obvious, palpable, patent, plain

manifestation *Syn* EMBODIMENT, epitome, incarnation, personification

manipulate 1 *Syn* ENGINEER, contrive, finagle, finesse, frame, machinate, maneuver, mastermind, negotiate, wangle **2** *Syn* HANDLE, ply, swing, wield

manlike *Syn* MALE, manful, manly, mannish, masculine, virile *Ant* female

manliness *Syn* VIRILITY, manhood, masculinity *Ant* femininity

manly *Syn* MALE, manful, manlike, mannish, masculine, virile *Ant* female

man-made *Syn* IMITATION, artificial, bogus, factitious, fake, false, mimic, mock, sham, simulated, substitute, synthetic *Ant* genuine, natural, real

manner *Syn* METHOD, fashion, mode, system, way

mannerism *Syn* POSE, affectation, air

mannerliness *Syn* POLITENESS, civility, courteousness, courtesy, gentility, graciousness *Ant* discourteousness, discourtesy, impoliteness, incivility, rudeness, ungraciousness

mannish *Syn* MALE, manful, manlike, manly, masculine, virile *Ant* female

manor *Syn* MANSION, castle, château, countryseat, estate, hacienda, hall, manor house, palace, villa

manor house *Syn* MANSION, castle, château, countryseat, estate, hacienda, hall, manor, palace, villa

mansion · a large impressive residence *Syn* castle, château, countryseat, estate, hacienda, hall, manor, manor house, palace, villa *Rel* showplace

mantilla *Syn* BANDANNA, babushka, handkerchief, kerchief

manufacture 1 *Syn* INVENT, concoct, contrive, cook (up), devise, fabricate, make up, think (up) **2** *Syn* MAKE, fabricate, fashion, forge, form, shape

manumit *Syn* FREE, discharge, emancipate, liberate, release

many · amounting to or being one at a large indefinite number *Syn* divers, multifarious, numerous, several, sundry, various *Ant* few

many-sided *Syn* VERSATILE, all-around

map *n Syn* CHART, graph

map *vb Syn* CHART, graph

mar *Syn* INJURE, damage, harm, hurt, impair, spoil *Ant* aid

marathon *Syn* LONG (sense 2), extended, far, great, lengthy, long-lived, long-range, long-term *Ant* brief, short, short-lived, short-range, short-term

marble *Syn* SPOT, blotch, dapple, dot, fleck, freckle, mottle, pepper, speck, speckle, splotch, sprinkle, stipple

marbled *Syn* SPOTTED, bespangled, flecked, spangled, spattered, speckled, sprinkled, stippled

march *Syn* ADVANCE (sense 2), advancement, furtherance, going, headway, onrush, passage, process, procession, progress, progression *Ant* recession, regression, retrogression

margin *vb Syn* BORDER, bound, fringe, rim, skirt

margin *n* **1** *Syn* BORDER, brim, brink, edge, rim, verge **2** *Syn* ROOM (sense 2), berth, clearance, elbow room, leeway, play

marine 1 · of or relating to the sea *Syn* maritime, oceanic, pelagic *Rel* abyssal, deep-sea, deepwater, saltwater **2 ·** of or relating to the navigation of the sea *Syn* maritime, nautical, naval

mariner · a person engaged in sailing or handling a ship *Syn* bluejacket, gob, sailor, seaman, tar

marital · of or relating to marriage *Syn* conjugal, connubial, married, matrimonial, nuptial, wedded *Rel* espoused, matched, mated

maritime   **1** *Syn* MARINE (sense 1), oceanic, pelagic   **2** *Syn* MARINE (sense 2), nautical, naval

mark *n*   **1** · a symbol or device used for identification or indication of ownership *Syn* brand, label, stamp, tag, ticket   **2** *Syn* BLEMISH, defect, deformity, disfigurement, fault, flaw, imperfection, pockmark, scar   **3** *Syn* CHARACTERISTIC, attribute, character, feature, peculiarity, point, property, quality, trait   **4** *Syn* CHARACTER, sign, symbol   **5** *Syn* GOAL, aim, ambition, aspiration, design, dream, end, intent, intention, meaning, object, objective, plan, pretension, purpose, target, thing   **6** *Syn* LAUGHINGSTOCK, butt, mock, mockery, target   **7** *Syn* SIGN (sense 1), badge, note, symptom, token

mark *vb*   **1** · to affix, attach, or impress something which serves for identification *Syn* brand, label, stamp, tag, ticket *Rel* impress, imprint, print   **2** *Syn* CHARACTERIZE, distinguish, qualify

market · to offer for sale to the public *Syn* deal (in), merchandise, put up, retail, sell, vend *Rel* wholesale *Ant* buy, purchase

marketable *Syn* COMMERCIAL, salable (*or* saleable) *Ant* noncommercial, nonsalable, uncommercial, unmarketable, unsalable

marriage · acts by which two people are joined as spouses or the state of being joined as spouses *Syn* espousal, matrimony, nuptial, wedding, wedlock

married *Syn* MARITAL, conjugal, connubial, matrimonial, nuptial, wedded

marsh *Syn* SWAMP, bog, fen, marshland, mire, morass, muskeg, slough, swampland

marshal *Syn* ORDER, arrange, methodize, organize, systematize

marshland *Syn* SWAMP, bog, fen, marsh, mire, morass, muskeg, slough, swampland

martial · of, relating to, or suited for war or a warrior *Syn* military, warlike *Rel* bellicose, belligerent, combative, pugnacious

martyr *Syn* AFFLICT, agonize, bedevil, curse, harrow, persecute, plague, rack, torment, torture

marvel *Syn* WONDER (sense 1), miracle, phenomenon, prodigy

marvelous *or* **marvellous**   **1** *Syn* EXCELLENT, A1, bang-up, banner, capital, classic, crackerjack, dandy, divine, fabulous, fine, first-class, first-rate, grand, great, groovy, heavenly, jim-dandy, keen, mean, neat, nifty, noble, par excellence, prime, sensational, splendid, stellar, sterling, superb, superior, superlative, supernal, swell, terrific, tip-top, top, top-notch, unsurpassed, wonderful *Ant* poor   **2** *Syn* EXOTIC, fantastic, glamorous, outlandish, romantic, strange

masculine *Syn* MALE, manful, manlike, manly, mannish, virile *Ant* female

masculinity *Syn* VIRILITY, manhood, manliness *Ant* femininity

mash *Syn* CRUSH (sense 1), bruise, macerate, smash, squash

mask *vb* *Syn* DISGUISE, camouflage, cloak, dissemble

mask *n* *Syn* IMAGE, effigy, icon, photograph, portrait, statue

mass *n*   **1** *Syn* BULK, volume   **2** *Syn* HEAP, bank, cock, pile, shock, stack

mass *vb* *Syn* HEAP, bank, cock, pile, shock, stack

massacre *n* · the act or an instance of killing a number of usually helpless or unresisting human beings under circumstances of atrocity or cruelty *Syn* butchery, carnage, pogrom, slaughter *Rel* assassination, killing, murder, murdering, slaying

massacre *vb* · to kill on a large scale *Syn* butcher, mow (down), slaughter *Rel* assassinate, execute, murder, slay

massive · impressively large or heavy *Syn* bulky, massy, monumental, substantial *Rel* heavy, ponderous, weighty

massy *Syn* MASSIVE, bulky, monumental, substantial

master   **1** *Syn* BOSS, captain, chief, foreman, head, headman, helmsman, kingpin, leader, taskmaster   **2** *Syn* CHIEF, chieftain, head, headman, leader   **3** *Syn* EXPERT, ace, adept, artist, authority, crackerjack, maestro, past master, scholar, shark, virtuoso, whiz, wizard *Ant* amateur

masterful   **1** · tending to impose one's will on others *Syn* DICTATORIAL, domineering, imperative, imperious, peremptory *Rel* authoritarian, doctrinaire, dogmatic, magisterial, oracular   **2** *Syn* ARROGANT, cavalier, haughty, highfalutin, high-handed, high-hat, imperious, important, lofty, lordly, overweening, peremptory, pompous, presumptuous, pretentious, supercilious, superior, uppish, uppity *Ant* humble, modest   **3** *Syn* BOSSY, authoritarian, autocratic, despotic, dictatorial, domineering, imperious, overbearing, peremptory, tyrannical, tyrannous

masterfulness *Syn* ARROGANCE, haughtiness, imperiousness, loftiness, lordliness, peremptoriness, pompousness, presumptuousness, pretense (*or* pretence), pretension, pretentiousness, self-importance, superciliousness, superiority *Ant* humility, modesty

masterly *Syn* PROFICIENT, adept, expert, skilled, skillful *Ant* amateur, amateurish, inexperienced, inexpert, unexperienced, unpracticed, unprofessional, unseasoned, unskilled, unskillful

mastermind *Syn* ENGINEER, contrive, finagle, finesse, frame, machinate, maneuver, manipulate, negotiate, wangle

match *vb* · to come up to or nearly up to the level or standard of *Syn* approach, equal, rival, touch *Rel* accord, agree, conform, correspond, harmonize, square

match *n Syn* EQUAL, coordinate, counterpart, equivalent, fellow, like, parallel, peer, rival

matching *Syn* ALIKE, akin, analogous, comparable, correspondent, corresponding, like, parallel, resembling, similar, such, suchlike *Ant* different, dissimilar, diverse, unlike

mate *Syn* SPOUSE, consort, partner

material *adj* **1** · of or belonging to actuality *Syn* corporeal, objective, phenomenal, physical, sensible *Rel* animal, carnal, fleshly, sensual *Ant* immaterial **2** *Syn* PERTINENT, applicable, apposite, apropos, germane, pointed, relative, relevant *Ant* extraneous, immaterial, inapplicable, irrelevant, pointless

material *n Syn* MATTER, stuff, substance

materialize **1** *Syn* BEGIN (sense 1), arise, commence, dawn, form, originate, set in, spring, start *Ant* cease, end, stop **2** *Syn* EMBODY (sense 2), epitomize, incarnate, manifest, personalize, personify, substantiate **3** *Syn* REALIZE, actualize, embody, externalize, hypostatize, incarnate, objectify, reify

matériel *Syn* EQUIPMENT, apparatus, gear, machinery, outfit, paraphernalia, tackle

matrimonial *Syn* MARITAL, conjugal, connubial, married, nuptial, wedded

matrimony *Syn* MARRIAGE, espousal, nuptial, wedding, wedlock

matter *n* **1** · what goes into the makeup or forms the being of a thing whether physical or not *Syn* material, stuff, substance **2** *Syn* AFFAIR, business, concern, thing **3** *Syn* SUBJECT, argument, leitmotiv, motif, motive, subject matter, text, theme, topic

matter *vb* · to be of importance *Syn* count, import, mean, signify, weigh *Rel* affect, influence, sway

matter-of-fact *Syn* PROSAIC, prosy

mature *adj* · having attained the normal peak of natural growth and development *Syn* adult, grown-up, matured, mellow, ripe *Ant* childish, immature

mature *vb* · to become fully developed or ripe *Syn* age, develop, ripen *Rel* acclimate, acclimatize, harden, season

matured *Syn* MATURE, adult, grown-up, mellow, ripe *Ant* childish, immature

maudlin **1** *Syn* CORNY, mawkish, mushy, saccharine, sappy, schmaltzy, sentimental, sloppy, sugarcoated, sugary *Ant* unsentimental **2** *Syn* SENTIMENTAL, mawkish, mushy, romantic, slushy, soppy

mawkish **1** *Syn* CORNY, maudlin, mushy, saccharine, sappy, schmaltzy, sentimental, sloppy, sugarcoated, sugary *Ant* unsentimental **2** *Syn* SENTIMENTAL, maudlin, mushy, romantic, slushy, soppy

maxim *Syn* SAYING, adage, aphorism, apothegm, epigram, motto, proverb, saw

maybe *Syn* PERHAPS, conceivably, mayhap, perchance, possibly

mayhap *Syn* PERHAPS, conceivably, maybe, perchance, possibly

meager · falling short of what is normal, necessary, or desirable *Syn* exiguous, scant, scanty, scrimpy, skimpy, spare, sparse *Rel* rare, slender, slight, slim, tenuous, thin *Ant* ample, copious

meal · food eaten or prepared for eating at one time *Syn* chow, feed, mess, repast, table *Rel* board

mealy *Syn* INSINCERE, artificial, backhanded, double-dealing, feigned, hypocritical, left-handed, mealymouthed, two-faced, unctuous *Ant* genuine, heartfelt, honest, sincere, unfeigned

mealymouthed *Syn* INSINCERE, artificial, backhanded, double-dealing, feigned, hypocritical, left-handed, mealy, two-faced, unctuous *Ant* genuine, heartfelt, honest, sincere, unfeigned

mean *adj* **1** · being below the normal standards of human decency and dignity *Syn* abject, ignoble, sordid *Rel* base, low, vile **2** *Syn* EXCELLENT, A1, bang-up, banner, capital, classic, crackerjack, dandy, divine, fabulous, fine, first-class, first-rate, grand, great, groovy, heavenly, jim-dandy, keen, marvelous (*or* marvellous), neat, nifty, noble, par excellence, prime, sensational, splendid, stellar, sterling, superb, superior, superlative, supernal, swell, terrific, tip-top, top, top-notch, unsurpassed, wonderful *Ant* poor

mean *vb* **1** · to convey (as an idea) to the mind *Syn* denote, import, signify *Rel* bear, carry, convey, transmit **2** *Syn* INTEND, design, propose, purpose **3** *Syn* MATTER, count, import, signify, weigh

meander *Syn* WANDER, gad, gallivant, prowl, ramble, range, roam, rove, stray, traipse

meaning *n* **1** · the idea that something conveys to the mind *Syn* acceptation, import, sense, significance, signification *Rel* hint, hinting, implication, intimation, suggestion **2** *Syn* GOAL, aim, ambition, aspiration, design, dream, end, intent, intention, mark, object, objective, plan, pretension, purpose, target, thing

meaning *adj Syn* EXPRESSIVE, eloquent, meaningful, pregnant, revealing, significant, suggestive

meaningful *Syn* EXPRESSIVE, eloquent, meaning, pregnant, revealing, significant, suggestive

meaningless · having no meaning *Syn* empty, inane, pointless, senseless *Rel* insignificant, trivial, unimportant *Ant* meaningful

means 1 *Syn* AGENT (sense 2), agency, instrument, instrumentality, machinery, medium, organ, vehicle 2 *Syn* POSSESSIONS, assets, belongings, effects, resources

measly *Syn* PETTY, paltry, picayune, picayunish, puny, trifling, trivial *Ant* gross, important, momentous

measure 1 *Syn* AMOUNT, quantity, volume 2 *Syn* RHYTHM, beat, cadence, meter

measureless *Syn* INFINITE, boundless, endless, illimitable, immeasurable, indefinite, limitless, unbounded, unfathomable, unlimited *Ant* bounded, circumscribed, confined, definite, finite, limited, restricted

mecca *Syn* CENTER (sense 2), base, capital, core, cynosure, eye, focus, heart, hub, nucleus, seat

mechanic *Syn* WORKER, artisan, craftsman, hand, handicraftsman, laborer, operative, roustabout, workingman, workman *Ant* idler

mechanical *Syn* SPONTANEOUS, automatic, impulsive, instinctive

mechanism *Syn* MACHINE, apparatus, engine, machinery, motor

meddle *Syn* INTERFERE, butt in, intrude, mess, nose, obtrude, poke, pry, snoop

meddler *Syn* BUSYBODY, interferer, interloper, intruder, kibitzer

meddlesome *Syn* INTRUSIVE, interfering, intruding, meddling, nosy (*or* nosey), obtrusive, officious, presumptuous, prying, snoopy *Ant* unobtrusive

meddling *Syn* INTRUSIVE, interfering, intruding, meddlesome, nosy (*or* nosey), obtrusive, officious, presumptuous, prying, snoopy *Ant* unobtrusive

medial *Syn* MIDDLE, halfway, intermediary, intermediate, median, medium, mid, middlemost, midmost, midway *Ant* extreme, farthermost, farthest, furthermost, furthest, outermost, outmost, remotest, utmost

median *Syn* MIDDLE, halfway, intermediary, intermediate, medial, medium, mid, middlemost, midmost, midway *Ant* extreme, farthermost, farthest, furthermost, furthest, outermost, outmost, remotest, utmost

mediate *Syn* INTERVENE, intercede, interpose

mediator · one who works with opposing sides in order to bring about an agreement *Syn* arbiter, arbitrator, conciliator, go-between, intercessor, intermediary, interposer, middleman, peacemaker *Rel* moderator

medicament *Syn* REMEDY, cure, medication, medicine, physic, specific

medication *Syn* REMEDY, cure, medicament, medicine, physic, specific

medicinal *Syn* DRUG, biologic, pharmaceutical, simple

medicine *Syn* REMEDY, cure, medicament, medication, physic, specific

mediocre *Syn* MEDIUM, average, fair, indifferent, middling, moderate, second-rate

meditate *Syn* PONDER, muse, ruminate

meditative 1 *Syn* CONTEMPLATIVE, melancholy, pensive, reflective, ruminant, thoughtful *Ant* unreflective 2 *Syn* THOUGHTFUL (sense 1), contemplative, pensive, reflective, speculative *Ant* thoughtless

medium *adj* 1 · about midway between the extremes of a scale, measurement, or evaluation *Syn* average, fair, indifferent, mediocre, middling, moderate, second-rate *Rel* average, mean, median, par 2 *Syn* MIDDLE, halfway, intermediary, intermediate, medial, median, mid, middlemost, midmost, midway *Ant* extreme, farthermost, farthest, furthermost, furthest, outermost, outmost, remotest, utmost

medium *n Syn* AGENT (sense 2), agency, instrument, instrumentality, machinery, means, organ, vehicle

meek *Syn* HUMBLE, lowly, modest

meet *vb* 1 · to come together face-to-face or as if face-to-face *Syn* confront, encounter, face *Rel* accost, address, greet, salute *Ant* avoid 2 *Syn* HAPPEN (on *or* upon), chance (upon), encounter, find, hit (upon), stumble (on *or* onto)

meet *adj* 1 *Syn* FIT, appropriate, apt, felicitous, fitting, happy, proper, suitable *Ant* unfit 2 *Syn* SATISFY (sense 2), answer, fulfill

meetly *Syn* PROPERLY, appropriately, congruously, correctly, fittingly, happily, rightly, suitably *Ant* improperly, inappropriately, incongruously, incorrectly, unsuitably, wrongly

megalopolis *Syn* CITY, burg, metropolis, municipality, town

melancholic · gloomy or depressed especially as a manifestation of one's temperament or state of health *Syn* atrabilious, hypochondriac, melancholy *Rel* despairing, desperate, despondent, forlorn, hopeless

melancholy *adj* 1 · expressing or suggesting sorrow or mourning *Syn* doleful, dolorous, lugubrious, plaintive, rueful *Rel* moving, pathetic, poignant, touching 2 *Syn* CONTEMPLATIVE, meditative, pensive, reflective, ruminant, thoughtful *Ant* unreflective 3 *Syn* MELANCHOLIC, atrabilious, hypochondriac 4 *Syn* SAD (sense 1), bad, blue, brokenhearted, crestfallen, dejected, depressed, despondent, disconsolate, doleful, down, downcast, downhearted, droopy, forlorn, gloomy, glum, heartbroken, heartsick, heartsore, inconsolable, joyless, low, low-spirited, miserable, mournful, saddened, sorrowful, sorry, unhappy, woebegone, woeful, wretched *Ant* blissful, buoyant, buoyed, cheerful, cheery, chipper, delighted, glad, gladdened, gladsome, gleeful, happy, joyful, joyous, jubilant, sunny, upbeat 5 *Syn* SAD (sense 2), depressing, dismal, drear, dreary, heartbreaking, heartrending, pathetic, saddening, sorry, tearful, teary *Ant* cheering, cheery, glad, happy

melancholy *n Syn* SADNESS, blues, dejection, depression, desolation, despondency, disconsolateness, dispiritedness, doldrums, downheartedness, dreariness, dumps, forlornness, gloom, gloominess, heartsickness, joylessness, mopes, oppression, unhappiness *Ant* bliss, blissfulness, ecstasy, elatedness, elation, euphoria, exhilaration, exuberance, exultation, felicity, gladness, gladsomeness, happiness, heaven, intoxication, joy, joyfulness, joyousness, jubilation, rapture, rapturousness

melee *Syn* BRAWL, broil, fracas, row, rumpus, scrap

mellow *Syn* MATURE, adult, grown-up, matured, ripe *Ant* childish, immature

melodramatic *Syn* DRAMATIC, dramaturgic, histrionic, theatrical

melody · a rhythmic series of musical tones arranged to give a pleasing effect *Syn* air, lay, song, strain, tune, warble *Rel* descant

melt *Syn* LIQUEFY, deliquesce, fuse, thaw

member *Syn* PART, detail, division, fraction, fragment, parcel, piece, portion, section, sector, segment *Ant* whole

memento *Syn* MEMORIAL, commemorative, keepsake, monument, remembrance, reminder, souvenir, token

memoir *Syn* BIOGRAPHY, autobiography, confessions, life

memorable *Syn* NOTEWORTHY, notable

memorandum *Syn* LETTER, dispatch, epistle, message, missive, note, report

memorial · something that serves to keep alive the memory of a person or event *Syn* commemorative, keepsake, memento, monument, remembrance, reminder, souvenir, token *Rel* memorabilia

memory · the capacity for or the act of remembering or the thing remembered *Syn* mind, recollection, remembrance, reminiscence, souvenir *Rel* brain, intellect, intelligence, soul, wit *Ant* oblivion

menace *n Syn* DANGER (sense 1), hazard, peril, pitfall, risk, threat, trouble *Ant* safeness, safety, security

menace *vb Syn* ENDANGER, adventure, compromise, gamble (with), hazard, imperil, jeopardize, risk, venture

menacing *Syn* OMINOUS, baleful, dire, foreboding, inauspicious, portentous, sinister, threatening

mend 1 · to put into good order something that is injured, damaged, or defective *Syn* patch, rebuild, repair *Rel* ameliorate, better, help, improve 2 *Syn* CONVALESCE, gain, heal, rally, recover, recuperate, snap back

mendicant *Syn* BEGGAR, panhandler

menial *n Syn* SERVANT, domestic, flunky, lackey, retainer, steward *Ant* master

menial *adj Syn* SUBSERVIENT, obsequious, servile, slavish *Ant* domineering, overbearing

mental · of or relating to the mind *Syn* cerebral, intellectual, intelligent, psychic

mention · to refer to someone or something in a clear unmistakable manner *Syn* instance, name, specify *Rel* advert, allude, refer

mephitic *Syn* POISONOUS, miasmal, miasmatic, miasmic, pestilent, pestilential, toxic, venomous, virulent *Ant* nonpoisonous, nontoxic, nonvenomous

mercenary · one who serves merely for pay or sordid advantage *Syn* hack, hireling *Rel* abject, ignoble, mean, sordid

merchandise *Syn* MARKET, deal (in), put up, retail, sell, vend *Ant* buy, purchase

merchandiser *Syn* MERCHANT, dealer, trader, tradesman, trafficker

merchant · a buyer and seller of goods for profit *Syn* dealer, merchandiser, trader, tradesman, trafficker *Rel* businessman

merciful *Syn* FORBEARING, clement, indulgent, lenient, tolerant *Ant* unrelenting

mercifully *Syn* FORBEARINGLY, clemently, indulgently, leniently, tolerantly

mercifulness *Syn* FORBEARANCE, clemency, indulgence, leniency, tolerance *Ant* anger, vindictiveness

merciless *Syn* GRIM, implacable, relentless, unrelenting *Ant* lenient

mercurial *Syn* INCONSTANT, capricious, fickle, unstable *Ant* constant

mercy · a disposition to show compassion or kindness *Syn* charity, clemency, grace, lenity *Rel* commiseration, compassion, pity, ruth, sympathy

mere · being as stated with nothing more added or extra *Syn* bare, very

merge *Syn* MIX, amalgamate, blend, coalesce, commingle, fuse, mingle

merger *Syn* CONSOLIDATION, amalgamation *Ant* dissolution

meridian *Syn* SUMMIT, acme, apex, apogee, climax, culmination, peak, pinnacle, zenith

merit *vb Syn* DESERVE, earn, rate

merit *n* 1 *Syn* DUE, desert 2 *Syn* EXCELLENCE, distinction, excellency, value, virtue *Ant* deficiency

meritorious 1 *Syn* ADMIRABLE, commendable, creditable, laudable, praiseworthy *Ant* censurable, discreditable, reprehensible 2 *Syn* WORTHY, deserving, good *Ant* no-good, undeserving, valueless, worthless

merry · indicative of or marked by high spirits or good humor *Syn* blithesome, festive, gay, gleeful, jocose, jocund, jolly, jovial, laughing, mirthful, sunny *Rel* amused, beaming, chuckling, giggling, smiling

mesa *Syn* MOUNTAIN, alp, mount, peak, volcano

mesh *Syn* ENTANGLE, enmesh, ensnare, entrap, snare, tangle, trap *Ant* disentangle

mess *vb Syn* INTERFERE, butt in, intrude, meddle, nose, obtrude, poke, pry, snoop

mess *n Syn* MEAL, chow, feed, repast, table

message *Syn* LETTER, dispatch, epistle, memorandum, missive, note, report

messed *Syn* MESSY, chaotic, cluttered, confused, disarranged, disarrayed, disheveled (*or* dishevelled), disordered, disorderly, higgledy-piggledy, hugger-mugger, jumbled, littered, muddled, mussed, mussy, pellmell, rumpled, sloppy, topsy-turvy, tousled, tumbled, unkempt, untidy, upside-down *Ant* neat, ordered, orderly, organized, shipshape, snug, tidied, tidy, trim

mess (up) 1 *Syn* BOTCH, bobble, bungle, butcher, flub, foozle, foul up, fumble, louse up, mangle, muff, murder **2** *Syn* DISORDER, confuse, derange, disarrange, disarray, discompose, dishevel, dislocate, disorganize, disrupt, disturb, hash, jumble, mix (up), muddle, muss, rumple, scramble, shuffle, tousle, tumble, upset *Ant* arrange, array, draw up, marshal, order, organize, range, regulate, straighten (up), tidy

messy · lacking in order, neatness, and often cleanliness *Syn* chaotic, cluttered, confused, disarranged, disarrayed, disheveled (*or* dishevelled), disordered, disorderly, higgledy-piggledy, hugger-mugger, jumbled, littered, messed, muddled, mussed, mussy, pellmell, rumpled, sloppy, topsy-turvy, tousled, tumbled, unkempt, untidy, upside-down *Rel* besmirched, blackened, dingy, dirty, filthy, foul, grimy, grubby, grungy, mucky, nasty, soiled, spotted, squalid, stained, sullied, unclean, uncleanly *Ant* neat, ordered, orderly, organized, shipshape, snug, tidied, tidy, trim

metamorphose 1 *Syn* CONVERT, make over, transfigure, transform **2** *Syn* TRANSFORM, convert, transfigure, transmogrify, transmute

metamorphosis *Syn* TRANSFORMATION, conversion, transfiguration, transmogrification, transmutation

metaphor *Syn* ANALOGY, simile

metaphrase *Syn* TRANSLATION, paraphrase, version

meter *Syn* RHYTHM, beat, cadence, measure

method · the means taken or procedure followed in achieving an end *Syn* fashion, manner, mode, system, way *Rel* procedure, proceeding, process

methodical *Syn* ORDERLY, regular, systematic *Ant* chaotic, disorderly

methodize *Syn* ORDER, arrange, marshal, organize, systematize

meticulous *Syn* CAREFUL, punctilious, punctual, scrupulous *Ant* careless

metropolis *Syn* CITY, burg, megalopolis, municipality, town

metropolitan *Syn* COSMOPOLITAN, sophisticate *Ant* bumpkin, hick, provincial, rustic, yokel

mettlesome *Syn* SPIRITED, fiery, gingery, high-spirited, peppery, spunky *Ant* spiritless

miasmal *Syn* POISONOUS, mephitic, miasmatic, miasmic, pestilent, pestilential, toxic, venomous, virulent *Ant* nonpoisonous, nontoxic, nonvenomous

miasmatic *Syn* POISONOUS, mephitic, miasmal, miasmic, pestilent, pestilential, toxic, venomous, virulent *Ant* nonpoisonous, nontoxic, nonvenomous

miasmic *Syn* POISONOUS, mephitic, miasmal, miasmatic, pestilent, pestilential, toxic, venomous, virulent *Ant* nonpoisonous, nontoxic, nonvenomous

microminiature *Syn* TINY, atomic, bitty, infinitesimal, microscopic, miniature, minute, teeny, teeny-weeny, wee *Ant* astronomical, colossal, cosmic, elephantine, enormous, giant, gigantic, herculean, heroic, huge, immense, mammoth, massive, monster, monstrous, monumental, mountainous, prodigious, titanic, tremendous

microscopic *Syn* TINY, atomic, bitty, infinitesimal, microminiature, miniature, minute, teeny, teeny-weeny, wee *Ant* astronomical, colossal, cosmic, elephantine, enormous, giant, gigantic, herculean, heroic, huge, immense, mammoth, massive, monster, monstrous, monumental, mountainous, prodigious, titanic, tremendous

mid *prep Syn* AMONG, amid (*or* amidst), midst, through

mid *adj Syn* MIDDLE, halfway, intermediary, intermediate, medial, median, medium, middlemost, midmost, midway *Ant* extreme, farthermost, farthest, furthermost, furthest, outermost, outmost, remotest, utmost

middle *adj* · occupying a position equally distant from the ends or extremes *Syn* halfway, intermediary, intermediate, medial, median, medium, mid, middlemost, midmost, midway *Rel* equidistant *Ant* extreme, farthermost, farthest, furthermost, furthest, outermost, outmost, remotest, utmost

middle *n* **1** *Syn* CENTER (sense 1), core, midpoint, midst *Ant* perimeter, periphery **2** *Syn* THICK, deep, depth, height, midst

middleman *Syn* MEDIATOR, arbiter, arbitrator, conciliator, go-between, intercessor, intermediary, interposer, peacemaker

middlemost *Syn* MIDDLE, halfway, intermediary, intermediate, medial, median, medium, mid, midmost, midway *Ant* extreme, farthermost, farthest, furthermost, furthest, outermost, outmost, remotest, utmost

middling *Syn* MEDIUM, average, fair, indifferent, mediocre, moderate, second-rate

midget *Syn* DWARF, pygmy, runt

midmost *Syn* MIDDLE, halfway, intermediary, intermediate, medial, median, medium, mid, middlemost, midway *Ant* extreme, farthermost, farthest, furthermost, furthest, outermost, outmost, remotest, utmost

midpoint *Syn* CENTER (sense 1), core, middle, midst *Ant* perimeter, periphery

midst *prep Syn* AMONG, amid (*or* amidst), mid, through

midst *n* **1** *Syn* CENTER (sense 1), core, middle, midpoint *Ant* perimeter, periphery **2** *Syn* THICK, deep, depth, height, middle

midway *Syn* MIDDLE, halfway, intermediary, intermediate, medial, median, medium, mid, middlemost, midmost *Ant* extreme, farthermost, farthest, furthermost, furthest, outermost, outmost, remotest, utmost

mien *Syn* BEARING, demeanor, deportment, port, presence

might *Syn* POWER (sense 1), energy, force, puissance, strength *Ant* impotence

mightily *Syn* VERY, awful, awfully, beastly, deadly, especially, exceedingly, extra, extremely, far, frightfully, full, greatly, heavily, highly, hugely, jolly, mighty, mortally, most, much, particularly, rattling, real, right, so, something, super, terribly, too, whacking *Ant* little, negligibly, nominally, slightly

mighty *Syn* VERY, awful, awfully, beastly, deadly, especially, exceedingly, extra, extremely, far, frightfully, full, greatly, heavily, highly, hugely, jolly, mightily, mortally, most, much, particularly, rattling, real, right, so, something, super, terribly, too, whacking *Ant* little, negligibly, nominally, slightly

migrant *Syn* EMIGRANT, immigrant

migrate · to move from one country, place, or locality to another *Syn* emigrate, immigrate

mild **1** *Syn* CLEMENT, balmy, equable, gentle, moderate, temperate *Ant* harsh, inclement, intemperate, severe **2** *Syn* SOFT, balmy, bland, gentle, lenient, smooth *Ant* hard, stern

milestone *Syn* TURNING POINT, climax, landmark

milieu *Syn* BACKGROUND, backdrop, environment, mise-en-scène, setting

militancy *Syn* BELLIGERENCE, aggression, aggressiveness, bellicosity, combativeness, contentiousness, disputatiousness, fight, pugnacity, scrappiness, truculence *Ant* pacifism

militant *n Syn* ZEALOT, crusader, fanatic, partisan

militant *adj* **1** *Syn* BELLIGERENT, aggressive, argumentative, bellicose, combative, contentious, discordant, disputatious, gladiatorial, pugnacious, quarrelsome, scrappy, truculent, warlike *Ant* nonbelligerent, pacific, peaceable, peaceful **2** *Syn* AGGRESSIVE (sense 1), assertive, pushing, pushy, self-assertive

military *Syn* MARTIAL, warlike

mime *Syn* ACTOR, impersonator, mimic, mummer, performer, player, thespian, trouper

mimic *n Syn* ACTOR, impersonator, mime,

mummer, performer, player, thespian, trouper

mimic *vb Syn* COPY, ape, imitate, mock *Ant* originate

mimic *adj Syn* IMITATION, artificial, bogus, factitious, fake, false, man-made, mock, sham, simulated, substitute, synthetic *Ant* genuine, natural, real

mince *Syn* CHOP, dice, hash

mind *n* **1** · the element or complex of elements in an individual that feels, perceives, thinks, wills, and especially reasons *Syn* brain, intellect, intelligence, psyche, soul, wit *Rel* faculty, function, power **2** *Syn* MEMORY, recollection, remembrance, reminiscence, souvenir *Ant* oblivion

mind *vb* **1** *Syn* LISTEN, attend, hark, hear, hearken, heed *Ant* ignore, tune out **2** *Syn* OBEY, comply *Ant* command, order **3** *Syn* REMEMBER, bethink, recall, recollect, remind, reminisce *Ant* forget **4** *Syn* TEND, attend, watch

mindful *Syn* CONSCIOUS, alive, aware, cognizant, sensible, sentient *Ant* insensible, unaware, unconscious, unmindful

mingle **1** *Syn* MIX, amalgamate, blend, coalesce, commingle, fuse, merge **2** *Syn* SOCIALIZE, associate, fraternize, hobnob, mix

miniature *Syn* TINY, atomic, bitty, infinitesimal, microminiature, microscopic, minute, teeny, teeny-weeny, wee *Ant* astronomical, colossal, cosmic, elephantine, enormous, giant, gigantic, herculean, heroic, huge, immense, mammoth, massive, monster, monstrous, monumental, mountainous, prodigious, titanic, tremendous

minimal · being the least in amount, number, or size possible *Syn* least, littlest, lowest, minimum, slightest *Rel* fewer, lesser, low, slight, small, smaller *Ant* full, greatest, largest, maximum, top, topmost, utmost

minimize *Syn* DECRY, belittle, deprecate, derogate, detract, disparage *Ant* extol

minimum *Syn* MINIMAL, least, littlest, lowest, slightest *Ant* full, greatest, largest, maximum, top, topmost, utmost

minion *Syn* FAVORITE, pet, preference

minister *Syn* AMBASSADOR, delegate, emissary, envoy, legate, representative

minor **1** *Syn* LESSER, inferior, junior, less, lower, smaller, subordinate, under *Ant* greater, higher, major, more, primary, prime, senior, superior **2** *Syn* UNIMPORTANT, frivolous, inconsequential, inconsiderable, insignificant, little, minute, negligible, slight, small, small-fry, trifling, trivial *Ant* big, consequential, eventful, important, major, material, meaningful, momentous, significant, substantial, weighty

minstrel *Syn* POET, bard, poetaster, rhymer, rhymester, troubadour, versifier

minus *Syn* DISADVANTAGE, drawback, handicap, liability, penalty, strike *Ant* advantage, asset, edge, plus

minute *adj* **1** *Syn* CIRCUMSTANTIAL, detailed, itemized, particular, particularized *Ant* abridged, summary **2** *Syn* TINY, atomic, bitty, infinitesimal, microminiature, microscopic, miniature, teeny, teeny-weeny, wee *Ant* astronomical, colossal, cosmic, elephantine, enormous, giant, gigantic, herculean, heroic, huge, immense, mammoth, massive, monster, monstrous, monumental, mountainous, prodigious, titanic, tremendous **3** *Syn* UNIMPORTANT, frivolous, inconsequential, inconsiderable, insignificant, little, minor, negligible, slight, small, small-fry, trifling, trivial *Ant* big, consequential, eventful, important, major, material, meaningful, momentous, significant, substantial, weighty

minute *n* *Syn* INSTANT, flash, jiffy, moment, second, shake, split second, trice, twinkle, twinkling, wink

miracle *Syn* WONDER (sense 1), marvel, phenomenon, prodigy

miraculous *Syn* SUPERNATURAL, preternatural, superhuman, supranatural

mirage *Syn* DELUSION, hallucination, illusion

mire *vb* *Syn* DIRTY, befoul, begrime, besmirch, blacken, foul, grime, muddy, smirch, smudge, soil, stain, sully *Ant* clean, cleanse

mire *n* *Syn* SWAMP, bog, fen, marsh, marshland, morass, muskeg, slough, swampland

mirror *Syn* MODEL, beau ideal, example, exemplar, ideal, pattern, standard

mirth · a mood or temper characterized by joy and high spirits and usually manifested in laughter and merrymaking *Syn* glee, hilarity, jollity *Rel* cheer, cheerfulness, gladness, happiness, joyfulness, lightheartedness

mirthful *Syn* MERRY, blithesome, festive, gay, gleeful, jocose, jocund, jolly, jovial, laughing, sunny

misadventure *Syn* MISFORTUNE, adversity, knock, mischance, mishap *Ant* fortune, luck

misanthropic *Syn* CYNICAL, pessimistic

misapprehend *Syn* MISUNDERSTAND, misconstrue, misinterpret, misread, miss, mistake *Ant* apprehend, catch, comprehend, conceive, fathom, grasp, know, make out, penetrate, perceive, savvy, see, seize, take in, understand

misbehavior *Syn* MISCONDUCT, malfeasance, misdoing, wrongdoing

miscalculate · to make an incorrect judgment regarding *Syn* misconceive, misjudge, mistake *Rel* misconstrue, misinterpret, misunderstand

miscarriage *Syn* FAILURE, default, dereliction, neglect

miscellaneous · consisting of diverse things or members *Syn* assorted, heterogeneous, motley, promiscuous *Rel* different, disparate, divergent, diverse, various

miscellany *Syn* ANTHOLOGY, album, compilation

mischance *Syn* MISFORTUNE, adversity, knock, misadventure, mishap *Ant* fortune, luck

mischief *Syn* INJURY, damage, harm, hurt

mischievous **1** *Syn* HARMFUL, adverse, bad, baleful, baneful, damaging, deleterious, detrimental, evil, hurtful, ill, injurious, noxious, pernicious, prejudicial *Ant* harmless, innocent, innocuous, inoffensive, safe **2** *Syn* PLAYFUL, frolicsome, impish, roguish, sportive, waggish

misconceive *Syn* MISCALCULATE, misjudge, mistake

misconception *Syn* FALLACY (sense 1), error, falsehood, falsity, illusion, myth, old wives' tale, untruth *Ant* truth, verity

misconduct · improper or illegal behavior *Syn* malfeasance, misbehavior, misdoing, wrongdoing *Rel* malefaction, misdeed, sin, wrong

misconstrue *Syn* MISUNDERSTAND, misapprehend, misinterpret, misread, miss, mistake *Ant* apprehend, catch, comprehend, conceive, fathom, grasp, know, make out, penetrate, perceive, savvy, see, seize, take in, understand

miscreant *Syn* VILLAIN, blackguard, knave, rapscallion, rascal, rogue, scamp, scoundrel

misdoing *Syn* MISCONDUCT, malfeasance, misbehavior, wrongdoing

mise-en-scène *Syn* BACKGROUND, backdrop, environment, milieu, setting

miserable *Syn* SAD (sense 1), bad, blue, brokenhearted, crestfallen, dejected, depressed, despondent, disconsolate, doleful, down, downcast, downhearted, droopy, forlorn, gloomy, glum, heartbroken, heartsick, heartsore, inconsolable, joyless, low, low-spirited, melancholy, mournful, saddened, sorrowful, sorry, unhappy, woebegone, woeful, wretched *Ant* blissful, buoyant, buoyed, cheerful, cheery, chipper, delighted, glad, gladdened, gladsome, gleeful, happy, joyful, joyous, jubilant, sunny, upbeat

miserly *Syn* STINGY, cheeseparing, close, closefisted, niggardly, parsimonious, pennypinching, penurious, tight, tightfisted *Ant* generous

misery *Syn* DISTRESS, agony, dolor, passion, suffering

misfortune · bad luck or an example of this *Syn* adversity, knock, misadventure, mischance, mishap *Rel* calamity, cataclysm, catastrophe, disaster *Ant* fortune, luck

misgiving **1** *Syn* DOUBT, distrust, distrustfulness, incertitude, mistrust, mistrustfulness, skepticism, suspicion, uncertainty *Ant* assurance, belief, certainty, certitude, confidence, conviction, sureness, surety, trust **2** *Syn* QUALM, compunction, scruple

mishap 1 *Syn* ACCIDENT, casualty 2 *Syn* MISFORTUNE, adversity, knock, misadventure, mischance *Ant* fortune, luck

misinterpret *Syn* MISUNDERSTAND, misapprehend, misconstrue, misread, miss, mistake *Ant* apprehend, catch, comprehend, conceive, fathom, grasp, know, make out, penetrate, perceive, savvy, see, seize, take in, understand

misjudge *Syn* MISCALCULATE, misconceive, mistake

mislead *Syn* DECEIVE, beguile, betray, delude, double-cross *Ant* enlighten, undeceive

misleading · having an appearance or character that leads one astray or into error *Syn* deceptive, delusive, delusory *Rel* casuistical, fallacious, sophistical

misread *Syn* MISUNDERSTAND, misapprehend, misconstrue, misinterpret, miss, mistake *Ant* apprehend, catch, comprehend, conceive, fathom, grasp, know, make out, penetrate, perceive, savvy, see, seize, take in, understand

misrepresent · to give a false or misleading representation of usually with an intent to deceive *Syn* belie, falsify, garble *Rel* camouflage, cloak, disguise, dissemble, mask

misrepresentation *Syn* LIE, falsehood, fib, story, untruth *Ant* truth

misrule *Syn* ANARCHY, chaos, lawlessness

miss *vb Syn* MISUNDERSTAND, misapprehend, misconstrue, misinterpret, misread, mistake *Ant* apprehend, catch, comprehend, conceive, fathom, grasp, know, make out, penetrate, perceive, savvy, see, seize, take in, understand

miss *n Syn* GIRL, lass, lassie, missy

mission · a specific task with which a person or group is charged *Syn* assignment, charge, job, operation, post *Rel* burden, chore, duty, need, obligation, requirement, responsibility

missive *Syn* LETTER, dispatch, epistle, memorandum, message, note, report

missy *Syn* GIRL, lass, lassy, miss

mist *Syn* HAZE (sense 1), fog, murk, reek, smog, soup

mistake *vb* 1 · to take one thing to be another *Syn* confound, confuse *Rel* addle, muddle *Ant* recognize 2 *Syn* MISCALCULATE, misconceive, misjudge 3 *Syn* MISUNDERSTAND, misapprehend, misconstrue, misinterpret, misread, miss *Ant* apprehend, catch, comprehend, conceive, fathom, grasp, know, make out, penetrate, perceive, savvy, see, seize, take in, understand

mistake *n Syn* ERROR, blunder, bull, faux pas, howler, lapse, slip

mistreat *Syn* ABUSE, ill-treat, maltreat, misuse, outrage *Ant* honor, respect

mistrust *vb Syn* DISTRUST, doubt, question, suspect *Ant* trust

mistrust *n Syn* DOUBT, distrust, distrustfulness, incertitude, misgiving, mistrustfulness, skepticism, suspicion, uncertainty *Ant* assurance, belief, certainty, certitude, confidence, conviction, sureness, surety, trust

mistrustfully *Syn* ASKANCE, distrustfully, doubtfully, doubtingly, dubiously, skeptically, suspiciously *Ant* trustfully, trustingly

mistrustfulness *Syn* DOUBT, distrust, distrustfulness, incertitude, misgiving, mistrust, skepticism, suspicion, uncertainty *Ant* assurance, belief, certainty, certitude, confidence, conviction, sureness, surety, trust

misunderstand · to fail to understand the true or actual meaning of *Syn* misapprehend, misconstrue, misinterpret, misread, miss, mistake *Rel* misconceive *Ant* apprehend, catch, comprehend, conceive, fathom, grasp, know, make out, penetrate, perceive, savvy, see, seize, take in, understand

misuse *Syn* ABUSE, ill-treat, maltreat, mistreat, outrage *Ant* honor, respect

mite *Syn* PARTICLE, atom, bit, iota, jot, smidgen, tittle, whit

mitigate *Syn* RELIEVE, allay, alleviate, assuage, lighten *Ant* alarm, embarrass, intensify

mix *vb* 1 · to combine or be combined into a more or less uniform whole *Syn* amalgamate, blend, coalesce, commingle, fuse, merge, mingle *Rel* combine, conjoin, join, unite 2 *Syn* SOCIALIZE, associate, fraternize, hobnob, mingle

mix *n Syn* BLEND, admixture, amalgam, amalgamation, combination, composite, compound, fusion, intermixture, mixture

mixture *Syn* BLEND, admixture, amalgam, amalgamation, combination, composite, compound, fusion, intermixture, mix

mix (up) *Syn* DISORDER, confuse, derange, disarrange, disarray, discompose, dishevel, dislocate, disorganize, disrupt, disturb, hash, jumble, mess (up), muddle, muss, rumple, scramble, shuffle, tousle, tumble, upset *Ant* arrange, array, draw up, marshal, order, organize, range, regulate, straighten (up), tidy

moan *vb* 1 *Syn* COMPLAIN, beef, bellyache, carp, crab, croak, fuss, gripe, grouse, growl, grumble, kick, murmur, mutter, repine, squawk, wail, whine, yammer *Ant* rejoice 2 *Syn* SIGH, groan, sob

moan *n* 1 *Syn* LAMENT, groan, howl, keen, lamentation, plaint, wail *Ant* exultation, rejoicing 2 *Syn* SIGH, groan, sob

mob *Syn* CROWD, crush, horde, press, rout, throng

mobile *Syn* MOVABLE, motive *Ant* immovable, stationary

mobile home *Syn* CAMPER, caravan, motor home, trailer

mock *vb* 1 *Syn* COPY, ape, imitate, mimic *Ant* originate 2 *Syn* RIDICULE, deride, rally, taunt, twit

mock *adj Syn* IMITATION, artificial, bogus, factitious, fake, false, man-made, mimic, sham, simulated, substitute, synthetic *Ant* genuine, natural, real

mock *n Syn* LAUGHINGSTOCK, butt, mark, mockery, target

mockery *Syn* LAUGHINGSTOCK, butt, mark, mock, target

mod *Syn* MODERN, contemporary, current, hot, modernistic, new, newfangled, new-fashioned, present-day, red-hot, space-age, ultramodern, up-to-date *Ant* antiquated, archaic, dated, fusty, musty, noncontemporary, oldfangled, old-fashioned, old-time, out-of-date, passé

mode 1 *Syn* FASHION, craze, cry, dernier cri, fad, rage, style, vogue 2 *Syn* METHOD, fashion, manner, system, way 3 *Syn* STATE, condition, posture, situation, status

model · someone or something set before one for guidance or imitation *Syn* beau ideal, example, exemplar, ideal, mirror, pattern, standard *Rel* criterion, gauge, standard, touchstone

moderate *vb* · to modify something so as to avoid an extreme or to keep within bounds *Syn* qualify, temper *Rel* abate, decrease, diminish, lessen, reduce

moderate *adj* 1 *Syn* CLEMENT, balmy, equable, gentle, mild, temperate *Ant* harsh, inclement, intemperate, severe 2 *Syn* MEDIUM, average, fair, indifferent, mediocre, middling, second-rate

modern 1 · being or involving the latest methods, concepts, information, or styles *Syn* contemporary, current, hot, mod, modernistic, new, newfangled, new-fashioned, present-day, red-hot, space-age, ultramodern, up-to-date *Rel* fashionable, in, modish, stylish *Ant* antiquated, archaic, dated, fusty, musty, noncontemporary, oldfangled, old-fashioned, old-time, out-of-date, passé 2 *Syn* NEW, fresh, modernistic, newfangled, new-fashioned, novel, original *Ant* old

modernistic 1 *Syn* MODERN, contemporary, current, hot, mod, new, newfangled, new-fashioned, present-day, red-hot, space-age, ultramodern, up-to-date *Ant* antiquated, archaic, dated, fusty, musty, noncontemporary, oldfangled, old-fashioned, old-time, out-of-date, passé 2 *Syn* NEW, fresh, modern, newfangled, new-fashioned, novel, original *Ant* old

modest 1 *Syn* CHASTE, decent, pure *Ant* bizarre (*of style, effect*), immoral, lewd, wanton 2 *Syn* HUMBLE, lowly, meek 3 *Syn* SHY, bashful, coy, diffident *Ant* obtrusive

modesty *Syn* CHASTITY, chasteness, purity *Ant* immodesty, impurity, unchastity

modification *Syn* CHANGE (sense 1), alteration, variation *Ant* monotony, uniformity

modify *Syn* CHANGE (sense 1), alter, make over, recast, redo, refashion, remake, remodel, revamp, revise, rework, vary *Ant* fix, freeze, set, stabilize

modish *Syn* STYLISH, chic, dashing, fashionable, smart

modishness *Syn* POPULARITY, fashionableness, favor, hotness, vogue *Ant* disfavor, unpopularity

moil *Syn* LABOR, drudge, endeavor, grub, hump, hustle, peg (away), plod, plow, plug, slave, slog, strain, strive, struggle, sweat, toil, travail, work *Ant* dabble, fiddle (around), fool (around), mess (around), putter (around)

moist *Syn* WET, damp, dank, humid *Ant* dry

mollify *Syn* PACIFY, appease, conciliate, disarm, placate, propitiate *Ant* anger, enrage, incense, infuriate, madden, outrage

mollycoddle *Syn* BABY, coddle, dandle, nurse, pamper, spoil *Ant* abuse, ill-treat, ill-use, maltreat, mishandle, mistreat, misuse

molt *Syn* DISCARD, cast, junk, scrap, shed, slough

moment 1 *Syn* IMPORTANCE, consequence, import, significance, weight *Ant* unimportance 2 *Syn* INSTANT, flash, jiffy, minute, second, shake, split second, trice, twinkle, twinkling, wink

momentarily *Syn* SHORTLY, anon, presently, soon

momentary · lasting only for a short time *Syn* ephemeral, evanescent, flash, fleeting, fugitive, impermanent, passing, short-lived, temporary, transient, transitory *Rel* brief, short *Ant* enduring, eternal, everlasting, lasting, long-lived, permanent, perpetual

momentum *Syn* SPEED, headway, impetus, pace, velocity

monarch · one who rules over a people with a sole, supreme, and usually hereditary authority *Syn* autocrat, ruler, sovereign *Rel* authoritarian, czar, despot, dictator, emperor, empress, kaiser, king, lord, mogul, overlord, potentate, prince, queen, royalty, satrap, sultan, tyrant

monastery *Syn* CLOISTER, abbey, convent, nunnery, priory

monetary *Syn* FINANCIAL, fiscal, pecuniary

money · something (as pieces of stamped metal or paper certificates) customarily and legally used as a medium of exchange *Syn* cash, coin, coinage, currency, legal tender, specie

monk *Syn* RELIGIOUS, friar, nun

monkey (around) *Syn* CUT UP, act up, clown (around), fool (around), horse (around), show off, skylark

monkeying *Syn* HORSEPLAY, clowning, foolery, high jinks, horsing (around), monkeyshines, roughhouse, roughhousing, shenanigans, skylarking, tomfoolery

monkeyshine *Syn* PRANK, antic, caper, dido

monkeyshines *Syn* HORSEPLAY, clowning,

foolery, high jinks, horsing (around), monkeying, roughhouse, roughhousing, shenanigans, skylarking, tomfoolery

monograph Syn DISCOURSE, disquisition, dissertation, thesis, treatise

monopolize · to take up completely Syn absorb, consume, engross Rel have, hold, own, possess

monopoly · exclusive possession or control Syn cartel, corner, pool, syndicate, trust

monotonous Syn BORING, drab, dreary, dry, dull, flat, heavy, humdrum, jading, leaden, pedestrian, ponderous, stodgy, stuffy, stupid, tame, tedious, tiresome, tiring, unanimated, uninteresting, wearisome, weary, wearying Ant absorbing, engaging, engrossing, gripping, interesting, intriguing

monster Syn GIANT, behemoth, blockbuster, colossus, jumbo, leviathan, mammoth, titan, whale, whopper Ant dwarf, midget, mini, miniature, peewee, pygmy, runt, shrimp

monstrous 1 · extremely impressive Syn monumental, prodigious, stupendous, tremendous Rel colossal, enormous, gigantic, huge, immense, mammoth, vast 2 Syn OUTRAGEOUS, atrocious, heinous

monument 1 Syn DOCUMENT, archive, record 2 Syn MEMORIAL, commemorative, keepsake, memento, remembrance, reminder, souvenir, token

monumental 1 Syn MASSIVE, bulky, massy, substantial 2 Syn MONSTROUS, prodigious, stupendous, tremendous

mood 1 · a state of mind in which an emotion or set of emotions gains ascendancy Syn humor, temper, vein Rel character, disposition, individuality, personality, temperament 2 Syn AURA, air, atmosphere, climate, flavor, note, temper

moonshine Syn ALCOHOL, booze, drink, grog, intoxicant, liquor, spirits

moor Syn SECURE, anchor, rivet

mope Syn SULK, pout

mopes Syn SADNESS, blues, dejection, depression, desolation, despondency, disconsolateness, dispiritedness, doldrums, downheartedness, dreariness, dumps, forlornness, gloom, gloominess, heartsickness, joylessness, melancholy, oppression, unhappiness Ant bliss, blissfulness, ecstasy, elatedness, elation, euphoria, exhilaration, exuberance, exultation, felicity, gladness, gladsomeness, happiness, heaven, intoxication, joy, joyfulness, joyousness, jubilation, rapture, rapturousness

moral · conforming to a standard of what is right and good Syn ethical, noble, righteous, virtuous Rel good, right

morale · a sense of common purpose or dedication with respect to a group Syn discipline, esprit de corps Rel drive, spirit, vigor

morality 1 Syn ETHICS, morals, principles,

standards 2 Syn GOODNESS, rectitude, virtue Ant badness, evil

morally Syn VIRTUALLY, practically

morals Syn ETHICS, morality, principles, standards

morass Syn SWAMP, bog, fen, marsh, marshland, mire, muskeg, slough, swampland

morbid Syn UNWHOLESOME, diseased, pathological, sickly Ant wholesome

mordant Syn CAUSTIC, acrid, scathing Ant genial

more Syn ADDITIONAL, added, another, else, farther, further, other

more or less Syn ALMOST, about, most, much, near, nearly, next to, nigh, practically, some, virtually, well-nigh

morning Syn BEGINNING, alpha, birth, commencement, dawn, genesis, inception, incipiency, launch, onset, outset, start, threshold Ant close, conclusion, end, ending

morose Syn SULLEN, crabbed, dour, gloomy, glum, saturnine, sulky, surly

mortal Syn DEADLY, baleful, deathly, fatal, fell, killer, lethal, murderous, pestilent, vital Ant healthful, healthy, nonfatal, nonlethal, wholesome

mortally Syn VERY, awful, awfully, beastly, deadly, especially, exceedingly, extra, extremely, far, frightfully, full, greatly, heavily, highly, hugely, jolly, mightily, mighty, most, much, particularly, rattling, real, right, so, something, super, terribly, too, whacking Ant little, negligibly, nominally, slightly

mortified Syn ASHAMED, chagrined Ant proud

most 1 Syn ALMOST, about, more or less, much, near, nearly, next to, nigh, practically, some, virtually, well-nigh 2 Syn VERY, awful, awfully, beastly, deadly, especially, exceedingly, extra, extremely, far, frightfully, full, greatly, heavily, highly, hugely, jolly, mightily, mighty, mortally, much, particularly, rattling, real, right, so, something, super, terribly, too, whacking Ant little, negligibly, nominally, slightly

mostly 1 Syn CHIEFLY, altogether, basically, by and large, generally, largely, mainly, overall, predominantly, primarily, principally, substantially 2 Syn LARGELY, chiefly, generally, greatly, mainly, principally

moth-eaten Syn OBSOLETE, antiquated, archaic, dated, outdated, out-of-date, outmoded, outworn, passé

moth-eaten Syn STALE, banal, commonplace, hackney, hackneyed, musty, stereotyped, threadbare, tired, trite Ant fresh, new, original

motif 1 Syn FIGURE, design, device, pattern 2 Syn SUBJECT, argument, leitmotiv, matter, motive, subject matter, text, theme, topic

motion n · the act or an instance of moving Syn locomotion, move, movement, stir Rel headway, impetus, momentum, pace, speed, velocity

motion *vb* · to direct or notify by a movement or gesture *Syn* beckon, flag, gesture, signal, wave *Rel* gesticulate, pantomime, sign

motion picture *Syn* MOVIE (sense 1), film, moving picture, picture

motion pictures *Syn* MOVIE (sense 2), cinema, film, pictures, screen

motive *n* **1** · a stimulus to action *Syn* goad, impulse, incentive, inducement, spring, spur *Rel* antecedent, cause, determinant, reason **2** *Syn* SUBJECT, argument, leitmotiv, matter, motif, subject matter, text, theme, topic

motive *adj Syn* MOVABLE, mobile *Ant* immovable, stationary

motley *adj* **1** *Syn* COLORFUL, multicolored, polychromatic, polychrome, varicolored, variegated *Ant* colorless, monochromatic, solid **2** *Syn* MISCELLANEOUS, assorted, heterogeneous, promiscuous **3** *Syn* VARIEGATED, checked, checkered, dappled, parti-colored, piebald, pied, skewbald

motley *n Syn* FOOL (sense 1), jester

motor *Syn* MACHINE, apparatus, engine, machinery, mechanism

motorcade *Syn* PROCESSION, cavalcade, cortege, parade

motor home *Syn* CAMPER, caravan, mobile home, trailer

mottle *Syn* SPOT, blotch, dapple, dot, fleck, freckle, marble, pepper, speck, speckle, splotch, sprinkle, stipple

mottled *Syn* SPOTTED, bespangled, flecked, marbled, spangled, spattered, speckled, sprinkled, stippled

motto *Syn* SAYING, adage, aphorism, apothegm, epigram, maxim, proverb, saw

mount *vb* **1** *Syn* ASCEND, arise, climb, lift, rise, soar, up, uprise, upsweep, upturn *Ant* decline, descend, dip, drop, fall (off) **2** *Syn* INCREASE (sense 2), accumulate, appreciate, balloon, build (up), burgeon, enlarge, escalate, expand, multiply, mushroom, proliferate, rise, snowball, swell, wax *Ant* contract, decrease, diminish, lessen, wane

mount *n Syn* MOUNTAIN, alp, mesa, peak, volcano

mountain · a relatively steep and high elevation of land *Syn* alp, mesa, mount, peak, volcano *Rel* altitude, elevation, height

mountebank *Syn* IMPOSTOR, charlatan, faker, quack

mourn *Syn* GRIEVE, sorrow *Ant* rejoice

mournful *Syn* SAD (sense 1), bad, blue, brokenhearted, crestfallen, dejected, depressed, despondent, disconsolate, doleful, down, downcast, downhearted, droopy, forlorn, gloomy, glum, heartbroken, heartsick, heartsore, inconsolable, joyless, low, low-spirited, melancholy, miserable, saddened, sorrowful, sorry, unhappy, woebegone, woeful, wretched *Ant* blissful, buoyant, buoyed, cheerful, cheery, chipper, delighted, glad, gladdened, gladsome, gleeful, happy, joyful, joyous, jubilant, sunny, upbeat

mouth *Syn* GRIMACE, face, frown, lower, pout, scowl

movable · capable of moving or of being moved *Syn* mobile, motive *Rel* changeable, changeful, mutable, variable *Ant* immovable, stationary

move *vb* **1** · to change or to cause to change from one place to another *Syn* remove, shift, transfer *Rel* displace, replace, supersede, supplant **2** *Syn* ACTIVATE, actuate, crank (up), drive, propel, run, set off, spark, start, touch off, trigger, turn on *Ant* cut, deactivate, kill, shut off, turn off **3** *Syn* PERSUADE, argue, convince, get, induce, prevail (on *or* upon), satisfy, talk (into), win (over)

move *n Syn* MOTION, locomotion, movement, stir

movement **1** *Syn* CAMPAIGN, bandwagon, cause, crusade, drive **2** *Syn* MOTION, locomotion, move, stir

movie **1** · a story told by means of a series of continuously projected pictures and a sound track *Syn* film, motion picture, moving picture, picture *Rel* animated cartoon, cartoon, docudrama, documentary, feature **2 movies** *pl* · the art or business of making a movie *Syn* cinema, film, motion pictures, pictures, screen *Rel* show business

moving · having the power to affect the feelings or sympathies *Syn* affecting, emotional, impressive, poignant, stirring, touching *Rel* eloquent, expressive, meaningful, significant *Ant* unemotional, unimpressive

moving picture *Syn* MOVIE (sense 1), film, motion picture, picture

mow (down) *Syn* MASSACRE, butcher, slaughter

much **1** *Syn* ALMOST, about, more or less, most, near, nearly, next to, nigh, practically, some, virtually, well-nigh **2** *Syn* VERY, awful, awfully, beastly, deadly, especially, exceedingly, extra, extremely, far, frightfully, full, greatly, heavily, highly, hugely, jolly, mightily, mighty, mortally, most, particularly, rattling, real, right, so, something, super, terribly, too, whacking *Ant* little, negligibly, nominally, slightly

muddle *vb* **1** *Syn* CONFUSE, addle, befuddle, fuddle *Ant* enlighten **2** *Syn* DISORDER, confuse, derange, disarrange, disarray, discompose, dishevel, dislocate, disorganize, disrupt, disturb, hash, jumble, mess (up), mix (up), muss, rumple, scramble, shuffle, tousle, tumble, upset *Ant* arrange, array, draw up, marshal, order, organize, range, regulate, straighten (up), tidy

muddle *n* **1** *Syn* CONFUSION, chaos, clutter, disarray, disorder, jumble, snarl **2** *Syn* HAZE (sense 2), daze, fog, spin

muddled *Syn* MESSY, chaotic, cluttered, confused, disarranged, disarrayed, disheveled (*or* dishevelled), disordered, disorderly, higgledy-piggledy, hugger-mugger, jumbled, littered, messed, mussed, mussy, pell-mell, rumpled, sloppy, topsy-turvy, tousled, tumbled, unkempt, untidy, upside-down *Ant* neat, ordered, orderly, organized, shipshape, snug, tidied, tidy, trim

muddy 1 *Syn* DIRTY, befoul, begrime, besmirch, blacken, foul, grime, mire, smirch, smudge, soil, stain, sully *Ant* clean, cleanse **2** *Syn* TURBID, roily *Ant* clear, limpid

muff *Syn* BOTCH, bobble, bungle, butcher, flub, foozle, foul up, fumble, louse up, mangle, mess (up), murder

mug *Syn* FACE, countenance, physiognomy, puss, visage

mulct *n Syn* FINE, damages, forfeit, forfeiture, penalty

mulct *vb* **1** *Syn* FLEECE, bleed, cheat, chisel, cozen, defraud, hustle, rook, shortchange, skin, squeeze, stick, sting, swindle, victimize **2** *Syn* PENALIZE, amerce, fine

mulish *Syn* OBSTINATE, adamant, adamantine, dogged, hard, hardened, hardheaded, hardhearted, headstrong, immovable, implacable, inflexible, obdurate, opinionated, ossified, pat, peevish, pertinacious, perverse, pigheaded, rigid, self-willed, stubborn, unbending, uncompromising, unrelenting, unyielding, willful (*or* wilful) *Ant* acquiescent, agreeable, amenable, compliant, complying, flexible, pliable, pliant, relenting, yielding

multicolored *Syn* COLORFUL, motley, polychromatic, polychrome, varicolored, variegated *Ant* colorless, monochromatic, solid

multifarious *Syn* MANY, divers, numerous, several, sundry, various *Ant* few

multiply 1 *Syn* INCREASE (sense 1), add (to), aggrandize, amplify, augment, boost, compound, enlarge, escalate, expand, extend, raise, swell, up *Ant* abate, contract, decrease, diminish, lessen, lower, reduce, subtract (from) **2** *Syn* INCREASE (sense 2), accumulate, appreciate, balloon, build (up), burgeon, enlarge, escalate, expand, mount, mushroom, proliferate, rise, snowball, swell, wax *Ant* contract, decrease, diminish, lessen, wane

multitude · a very large number of individuals or things *Syn* army, host, legion *Rel* crowd, crush, horde, mob, press, throng

mum *Syn* SILENT (sense 3), dumb, mute, speechless, uncommunicative, wordless *Ant* communicative, speaking, talking

mummer *Syn* ACTOR, impersonator, mime, mimic, performer, player, thespian, trouper

mummery *Syn* GIBBERISH, abracadabra, hocus-pocus

mundane *Syn* EARTHLY, earthy, sublunary, terrestrial, worldly

municipality *Syn* CITY, burg, megalopolis, metropolis, town

munificent *Syn* LIBERAL (sense 1), bounteous, bountiful, generous, handsome, openhanded *Ant* close

murder 1 *Syn* KILL, assassinate, dispatch, execute, slay **2** *Syn* BOTCH, bobble, bungle, butcher, flub, foozle, foul up, fumble, louse up, mangle, mess (up), muff

murdering *Syn* BLOODTHIRSTY, bloody, homicidal, murderous, sanguinary, sanguine

murderous 1 *Syn* BLOODTHIRSTY, bloody, homicidal, murdering, sanguinary, sanguine **2** *Syn* DEADLY, baleful, deathly, fatal, fell, killer, lethal, mortal, pestilent, vital *Ant* healthful, healthy, nonfatal, nonlethal, wholesome

murk *Syn* HAZE (sense 1), fog, mist, reek, smog, soup

murky *Syn* DARK, dim, dusky, gloomy, obscure *Ant* light

murmur *Syn* COMPLAIN, beef, bellyache, carp, crab, croak, fuss, gripe, grouse, growl, grumble, kick, moan, mutter, repine, squawk, wail, whine, yammer *Ant* rejoice

murmurer *Syn* GROUCH, bear, complainer, crab, crank, croaker, curmudgeon, fusser, griper, grouser, growler, grumbler, grump, mutterer, whiner

muscular · strong and powerful in build or action *Syn* athletic, brawny, burly, husky, sinewy *Rel* hale, healthy, robust, sound

muse *Syn* PONDER, meditate, ruminate

mushroom *Syn* INCREASE (sense 2), accumulate, appreciate, balloon, build (up), burgeon, enlarge, escalate, expand, mount, multiply, proliferate, rise, snowball, swell, wax *Ant* contract, decrease, diminish, lessen, wane

mushy 1 *Syn* CORNY, maudlin, mawkish, saccharine, sappy, schmaltzy, sentimental, sloppy, sugarcoated, sugary *Ant* unsentimental **2** *Syn* SENTIMENTAL, maudlin, mawkish, romantic, slushy, soppy

muskeg *Syn* SWAMP, bog, fen, marsh, marshland, mire, morass, slough, swampland

muss *Syn* DISORDER, confuse, derange, disarrange, disarray, discompose, dishevel, dislocate, disorganize, disrupt, disturb, hash, jumble, mess (up), mix (up), muddle, rumple, scramble, shuffle, tousle, tumble, upset *Ant* arrange, array, ray, up, marshal, order, organize, range, regulate, straighten (up), tidy

mussed *Syn* MESSY, chaotic, cluttered, confused, disarranged, disarrayed, disheveled (*or* dishevelled), disordered, disorderly, higgledy-piggledy, hugger-mugger, jumbled, littered, messed, muddled, mussy, pell-mell, rumpled, sloppy, topsy-turvy, tousled, tumbled, unkempt, untidy, upside-down *Ant* neat, ordered, orderly, organized, shipshape, snug, tidied, tidy, trim

mussy *Syn* MESSY, chaotic, cluttered, confused, disarranged, disarrayed, disheveled (*or* dishevelled), disordered, disorderly, higgledy-piggledy, hugger-mugger, jumbled, littered, messed, muddled, mussed, pellmell, rumpled, sloppy, topsy-turvy, tousled, tumbled, unkempt, untidy, upside-down *Ant* neat, ordered, orderly, organized, shipshape, snug, tidied, tidy, trim

must *Syn* NEED (sense 1), have (to), ought (to), shall, should *Ant* have, hold

muster *Syn* SUMMON, call, cite, convene, convoke

musty **1** *Syn* MALODOROUS, fetid, fusty, noisome, putrid, rancid, rank, stinking *Ant* odorous **2** *Syn* STALE, banal, commonplace, hackney, hackneyed, moth-eaten, stereotyped, threadbare, tired, trite *Ant* fresh, new, original

mutable *Syn* CHANGEABLE, changeful, protean, variable *Ant* stable, unchangeable

mutate *Syn* CHANGE (sense 2), fluctuate, shift, vary *Ant* stabilize

mutation *Syn* CHANGE (sense 2), alternation, permutation, vicissitude

mute **1** · unable to speak *Syn* inarticulate, speechless, voiceless *Rel* mum, nonspeaking, quiet, silent, wordless **2** *Syn* SILENT (sense 3), dumb, mum, speechless, uncommunicative, wordless

muted *Syn* SILENT (sense 2), hushed, noiseless, quiet, quieted, soundless, still *Ant* noisy, unquiet

mutilate **1** *Syn* MAIM, batter, cripple, mangle **2** *Syn* STERILIZE (sense 1), alter, castrate, emasculate, geld, spay *Ant* fertilize

mutinous *Syn* INSUBORDINATE, contumacious, factious, rebellious, seditious

mutiny *Syn* REBELLION, coup, insurrection, putsch, revolt, revolution, uprising

mutter *Syn* COMPLAIN, beef, bellyache, carp, crab, croak, fuss, gripe, grouse, growl, grumble, kick, moan, murmur, repine, squawk, wail, whine, yammer

mutterer *Syn* GROUCH, bear, complainer, crab, crank, croaker, curmudgeon, fusser, griper, grouser, growler, grumbler, grump, murmurer, whiner

mutual *Syn* RECIPROCAL (sense 1), common

mysterious · being beyond one's power to discover, understand, or explain *Syn* arcane, inscrutable *Rel* abstruse, esoteric, occult, recondite

mystery · something which baffles or perplexes *Syn* conundrum, enigma, problem, puzzle, riddle

mystic *Syn* MYSTICAL, anagogic, cabalistic

mystical · having a spiritual meaning or reality that is neither apparent to the senses nor obvious to the intelligence *Syn* anagogic, cabalistic, mystic *Rel* abysmal, deep, profound

mystify *Syn* PUZZLE, bewilder, confound, distract, dumbfound, nonplus, perplex

myth **1** · a traditional story of ostensibly historical content whose origin has been lost *Syn* legend, saga *Rel* fable, fabrication, fiction, figment **2** *Syn* FALLACY (sense 1), error, falsehood, falsity, illusion, misconception, old wives' tale, untruth *Ant* truth, verity **3** *Syn* FOLKLORE, legend, lore, mythology, tradition

mythical *Syn* FICTITIOUS, apocryphal, fabulous, legendary *Ant* historical

mythology *Syn* FOLKLORE, legend, lore, myth, tradition

N

naive *Syn* NATURAL, artless, ingenuous, simple, unaffected, unsophisticated

naively *Syn* NATURALLY (sense 3), artlessly, guilelessly, ingenuously, innocently, sincerely, unaffectedly, unfeignedly, unpretentiously *Ant* affectedly, artificially, hypocritically, insincerely, pretentiously, unnaturally

naivete *Syn* CREDULITY, credulousness, gullibility *Ant* incredulity, skepticism

naked *Syn* BARE, bald, barren, nude *Ant* covered

name *n* **1** · the word or combination of words by which something is called and by means of which it can be distinguished or identified *Syn* appellation, denomination, designation, style, title **2** *Syn* INSULT, affront, barb, dart, dig, epithet, indignity, offense (*or* offence), outrage, put-down, sarcasm, slight, slur

name *vb* **1** *Syn* APPOINT (sense 1), designate, fix, set *Ant* discharge, dismiss, expel, fire **2** *Syn* MENTION, instance, specify **3** *Syn* APPOINT (sense 2), assign, attach, commission, constitute, designate, detail *Ant* discharge, dismiss, expel, fire

nap *Syn* SLEEP, catnap, doze, drowse, slumber, snooze

narrate *Syn* RELATE, describe, recite, recount, rehearse, report, state

narrative *Syn* STORY, anecdote, tale, yarn

narrow *Syn* INTOLERANT, bigoted, narrow-minded, prejudiced, small-minded *Ant* broad-minded, liberal, open-minded, tolerant, unprejudiced

narrow-minded *Syn* INTOLERANT, bigoted, narrow, prejudiced, small-minded *Ant* broad-minded, liberal, open-minded, tolerant, unprejudiced

narrows *Syn* STRAIT, channel, passage, sound

nasty 1 *Syn* DIRTY, filthy, foul, squalid *Ant* clean **2** *Syn* UNPLEASANT, bad, disagreeable, displeasing, distasteful, rotten, sour, uncongenial, unlovely, unpleasing, unsatisfying, unwelcome *Ant* agreeable, congenial, good, grateful, gratifying, nice, palatable, pleasant, pleasing, pleasurable, satisfying, welcome

nation · a body of people composed of one or more nationalities usually with its own territory and government *Syn* commonwealth, country, land, sovereignty, state *Rel* city-state

national *Syn* CITIZEN, subject *Ant* alien

native · belonging to a particular place by birth or origin *Syn* aboriginal, autochthonous, endemic, indigenous *Ant* alien, foreign

Native American *Syn* AMERICAN INDIAN, Amerindian, Indian

nattily *Syn* SMARTLY, dashingly, sharply, sprucely *Ant* sloppily, slovenly

natural 1 · free from pretension or calculation *Syn* artless, ingenuous, naive, simple, unaffected, unsophisticated *Rel* impulsive, instinctive, spontaneous **2** *Syn* REGULAR, normal, typical *Ant* irregular

naturally 1 · according to the usual course of things *Syn* commonly, generally, normally, ordinarily, typically, usually *Rel* customarily, habitually, regularly, routinely *Ant* abnormally, atypically, extraordinarily, uncommonly, unusually **2** · by natural character or ability *Syn* constitutionally, inherently, innately, intrinsically *Rel* elementally, essentially, fundamentally **3** · without any attempt to impress by deception or exaggeration *Syn* artlessly, guilelessly, ingenuously, innocently, naively, sincerely, unaffectedly, unfeignedly, unpretentiously *Rel* genuinely, honestly, simply, truly *Ant* affectedly, artificially, hypocritically, insincerely, pretentiously, unnaturally

naturalness *Syn* ABANDON, abandonment, ease, lightheartedness, spontaneity, unrestraint *Ant* constraint, restraint

nature *Syn* TYPE, character, description, ilk, kidney, kind, sort, stripe

naughty *Syn* BAD (sense 1), evil, ill, wicked *Ant* good

nausea *Syn* DISGUST, aversion, distaste, loathing, repugnance, repulsion, revulsion

nauseate *Syn* DISGUST, repel, repulse, revolt, sicken, turn off

nautical *Syn* MARINE (sense 2), maritime, naval

naval *Syn* MARINE (sense 2), maritime, nautical

nay *Syn* DENIAL (sense 1), disallowance, no, refusal, rejection *Ant* allowance, grant

near *adv Syn* ALMOST, about, more or less, most, much, nearly, next to, nigh, practically, some, virtually, well-nigh

near *adj Syn* CLOSE (sense 1), nearby, nigh *Ant* remote

near *n Syn* APPROACH, approximate

near *prep Syn* AROUND (sense 1), about, by, next to

nearby *Syn* CLOSE (sense 1), near, nigh *Ant* remote, remotely

nearing *Syn* FORTHCOMING, approaching, coming, imminent, impending, oncoming, pending, upcoming *Ant* late, recent

nearly *Syn* ALMOST, about, more or less, most, much, near, next to, nigh, practically, some, virtually, well-nigh

nearness *Syn* PROXIMITY, closeness, contiguity, immediacy *Ant* distance, remoteness

neat 1 · manifesting care and orderliness *Syn* shipshape, snug, spick-and-span, tidy, trig, trim *Rel* clean, cleanly *Ant* filthy **2** *Syn* EXCELLENT, A1, bang-up, banner, capital, classic, crackerjack, dandy, divine, fabulous, fine, first-class, first-rate, grand, great, groovy, heavenly, jim-dandy, keen, marvelous (*or* marvellous), mean, nifty, noble, par excellence, prime, sensational, splendid, stellar, sterling, superb, superior, superlative, supernal, swell, terrific, tip-top, top, top-notch, unsurpassed, wonderful *Ant* poor

neb *Syn* BILL, beak, nib

necessary 1 *Syn* CERTAIN, inevitable *Ant* probable, supposed **2** *Syn* INEVITABLE, certain, inescapable, sure, unavoidable *Ant* avoidable, escapable, uncertain, unsure **3** *Syn* MANDATORY, compulsory, forced, imperative, incumbent, involuntary, nonelective, obligatory, peremptory, required *Ant* elective, optional, voluntary **4** *Syn* NEEDFUL, essential, indispensable, requisite

necessitous *Syn* POOR, destitute, impecunious, indigent, needy, penniless, poverty-stricken *Ant* rich

necessity *Syn* NEED, exigency

necromancer *Syn* MAGICIAN (sense 1), charmer, conjurer (*or* conjuror), enchanter, sorcerer, voodoo, witch, wizard

need *n* **1** · a pressing lack of something essential *Syn* exigency, necessity *Rel* pressure, strain, stress **2** *Syn* OBLIGATION, burden, charge, commitment, duty, responsibility

need *vb* **1** · to be under necessity or obligation to *Syn* have (to), must, ought (to), shall, should *Rel* will **2** · to have as a requirement *Syn* demand, necessitate, require, take, want, warrant *Rel* entail, involve *Ant* have, hold **3** *Syn* LACK, require, want

needful · required for supply or relief *Syn*

essential, indispensable, necessary, requisite *Rel* lacked, needed, required, wanted

needless *Syn* UNNECESSARY, dispensable, gratuitous, nonessential, uncalled-for, unessential, unwarranted *Ant* essential, indispensable, necessary, needed, needful, required

needy *Syn* POOR, destitute, impecunious, indigent, necessitous, penniless, poverty-stricken *Ant* rich

nefarious *Syn* VICIOUS, corrupt, degenerate, flagitious, infamous, iniquitous, villainous *Ant* virtuous

negate *Syn* ABOLISH, abrogate, annul, cancel, dissolve, invalidate, nullify, quash, repeal, rescind, void

negation *Syn* DENIAL (sense 2), contradiction, disallowance, disavowal, disclaimer, rejection, repudiation *Ant* acknowledgment, admission, avowal, confirmation

negative 1 *Syn* DENY, contradict, contravene, gainsay, impugn, traverse *Ant* concede, confirm **2** *Syn* NEUTRALIZE, counteract

neglect *vb* • to pass over without giving due attention *Syn* disregard, forget, ignore, omit, overlook, slight *Ant* cherish

neglect *n* *Syn* FAILURE, default, dereliction, miscarriage

neglectful *Syn* NEGLIGENT, careless, derelict, lax, neglecting, remiss, slack *Ant* attentive, careful, conscientious

neglecting *Syn* NEGLIGENT, careless, derelict, lax, neglectful, remiss, slack *Ant* attentive, careful, conscientious

negligent • failing to give proper care and attention *Syn* careless, derelict, lax, neglectful, neglecting, remiss, slack *Rel* heedless, incautious, irresponsible, reckless, wild *Ant* attentive, careful, conscientious

negligible *Syn* UNIMPORTANT, frivolous, inconsequential, inconsiderable, insignificant, little, minor, minute, slight, small, small-fry, trifling, trivial *Ant* big, consequential, eventful, important, major, material, meaningful, momentous, significant, substantial, weighty

negotiate 1 • to bring about by mutual agreement *Syn* arrange, concert **2** *Syn* BARGAIN, chaffer, deal, dicker, haggle, horse-trade, palter **3** *Syn* ENGINEER, contrive, finagle, finesse, frame, machinate, maneuver, manipulate, mastermind, wangle

neighborhood *Syn* LOCALITY, district, vicinity

neighborly *Syn* AMICABLE, friendly *Ant* antagonistic

neophyte *Syn* BEGINNER, colt, fledgling, freshman, greenhorn, newbie, newcomer, novice, recruit, rookie, tenderfoot, tyro *Ant* old hand, old-timer, vet, veteran

nerve *n* **1** *Syn* COURAGE, bravery, courageousness, daring, dauntlessness, doughtiness, fearlessness, gallantry, greatheartedness, guts, hardihood, heart, heroism, intrepidity,

intrepidness, stoutness, valor *Ant* cowardice, cowardliness, cravenness, dastardliness, spinelessness, yellowness **2** *Syn* EFFRONTERY, audacity, brashness, brass, brassiness, brazenness, cheek, cheekiness, chutzpah, gall, nerviness, pertness, presumption, presumptuousness, sauce, sauciness, temerity

nerve *vb* *Syn* ENCOURAGE, cheer, embolden, hearten, inspirit, steel *Ant* discourage

nerveless *Syn* UNFLAPPABLE, imperturbable, unshakable *Ant* perturbable, shakable

nerviness *Syn* EFFRONTERY, audacity, brashness, brass, brassiness, brazenness, cheek, cheekiness, chutzpah, gall, nerve, pertness, presumption, presumptuousness, sauce, sauciness, temerity

nervous 1 *Syn* EXCITABLE, flighty, fluttery, high-strung, jittery, jumpy, skittish, spooky *Ant* unflappable **2** *Syn* IMPATIENT, fidgety, jittery, jumpy, restive, restless, uneasy, unquiet *Ant* patient **3** *Syn* VIGOROUS, energetic, lusty, strenuous *Ant* languorous, lethargic

nettle *Syn* IRRITATE, aggravate, exasperate, peeve, provoke, rile

nettling *Syn* ANNOYING, aggravating, bothersome, disturbing, exasperating, frustrating, galling, irksome, irritating, maddening, peeving, pesty, rankling, riling, vexatious, vexing

network *Syn* SYSTEM, complex, organism, scheme *Ant* chaos

neutrality *Syn* DETACHMENT, disinterestedness, impartiality, objectivity *Ant* bias, favor, favoritism, one-sidedness, partiality, partisanship, prejudice

neutralize • to make inoperative or ineffective usually by means of an opposite force, influence, or effect *Syn* counteract, negative *Rel* compensate, counterbalance, counterpoise, countervail

new 1 • having recently come into existence or use *Syn* fresh, modern, modernistic, newfangled, new-fashioned, novel, original *Ant* old **2** *Syn* MODERN, contemporary, current, hot, mod, modernistic, newfangled, newfashioned, present-day, red-hot, space-age, ultramodern, up-to-date *Ant* antiquated, archaic, dated, fusty, musty, noncontemporary, oldfangled, old-fashioned, old-time, out-of-date, passé

newbie *Syn* BEGINNER, colt, fledgling, freshman, greenhorn, neophyte, newcomer, novice, recruit, rookie, tenderfoot, tyro *Ant* old hand, old-timer, vet, veteran

newborn *Syn* BABY, babe, child, infant

newcomer *Syn* BEGINNER, colt, fledgling, freshman, greenhorn, neophyte, newbie, novice, recruit, rookie, tenderfoot, tyro *Ant* old hand, old-timer, vet, veteran

newfangled 1 *Syn* MODERN, contemporary, current, hot, mod, modernistic, new, newfashioned, present-day, red-hot, space-age, ultramodern, up-to-date *Ant* antiquated, archaic, dated, fusty, musty, noncontemporary, oldfangled, old-fashioned, old-time, out-of-date, passé **2** *Syn* NEW, fresh, modern, modernistic, new-fashioned, novel, original *Ant* old

new-fashioned *Syn* NEW, fresh, modern, modernistic, newfangled, novel, original *Ant* old

news · a report of recent events or facts not previously known *Syn* information, intelligence, item, story, tidings, word *Rel* announcement, communication, message

newspaper *Syn* JOURNAL, magazine, organ, periodical, review

next to *adv Syn* ALMOST, about, more or less, most, much, near, nearly, nigh, practically, some, virtually, well-nigh

next to *prep Syn* AROUND (sense 1), about, by, near

nib *Syn* BILL, beak, neb

nice 1 · having or displaying exacting standards *Syn* dainty, fastidious, finical, finicking, finicky, fussy, particular, pernickety, persnickety, squeamish *Rel* judicious, sage, sapient, wise **2** *Syn* AMIABLE, affable, agreeable, genial, good-natured, good-tempered, gracious, sweet, well-disposed *Ant* disagreeable, ill-natured, ill-tempered, ungracious, unpleasant **3** *Syn* CORRECT, accurate, exact, precise, right *Ant* incorrect **4** *Syn* DECOROUS, decent, proper, seemly *Ant* blatant, indecorous

nicety *Syn* FACT, datum, detail, particular, particularity, point

nifty *adj Syn* EXCELLENT, A1, bang-up, banner, capital, classic, crackerjack, dandy, divine, fabulous, fine, first-class, first-rate, grand, great, groovy, heavenly, jim-dandy, keen, marvelous (*or* marvellous), mean, neat, noble, par excellence, prime, sensational, splendid, stellar, sterling, superb, superior, superlative, supernal, swell, terrific, tip-top, top, top-notch, unsurpassed, wonderful *Ant* poor

nifty *n Syn* JIM-DANDY, beauty, corker, crackerjack, dandy, knockout, pip

niggardly *Syn* STINGY, cheeseparing, close, closefisted, miserly, parsimonious, pennypinching, penurious, tight, tightfisted *Ant* generous

nigh *adv Syn* ALMOST, about, more or less, most, much, near, nearly, next to, practically, some, virtually, well-nigh

nigh *adj Syn* CLOSE (sense 1), near, nearby *Ant* remote

night *Syn* NIGHTLY, nocturnal *Ant* daily

nightly · of, relating to, or associated with the night *Syn* night, nocturnal *Ant* daily

nightmare *Syn* FANCY, daydream, dream, fantasy, phantasm, phantasy, vision *Ant* reality

nimble *Syn* AGILE, brisk, spry *Ant* torpid

nimbleness *Syn* DEXTERITY (sense 2), agility, deftness, sleight, spryness *Ant* awkwardness, clumsiness, gawkiness

nincompoop *Syn* FOOL (sense 2), booby, goose, half-wit, jackass, lunatic, ninny, nitwit, nut, simpleton, turkey, yo-yo

ninny *Syn* FOOL (sense 2), booby, goose, half-wit, jackass, lunatic, nincompoop, nitwit, nut, simpleton, turkey, yo-yo

nip *vb* **1** *Syn* BLAST, blight **2** *Syn* CLIP, bob, crop, curtail, cut, cut back, dock, lop (off), pare, prune, shave, shear, snip, trim

nip *n* **1** *Syn* BLAST, blight **2** *Syn* CHILL, bite, bitterness, bleakness, chilliness, rawness, sharpness

nipper *Syn* BOY, lad, laddie, shaver, sonny, stripling, tad, youth

nitpick *Syn* QUIBBLE, carp, cavil, fuss

nitpicker *Syn* CRITIC, carper, castigator, caviler (*or* caviller), censurer, faultfinder, railer, scold

nitwit *Syn* FOOL (sense 2), booby, goose, half-wit, jackass, lunatic, nincompoop, ninny, simpleton, turkey, yo-yo

no *Syn* DENIAL (sense 1), disallowance, nay, refusal, rejection *Ant* allowance, grant

nobility 1 *Syn* ARISTOCRACY, county, elite, gentry, society *Ant* people, proletariat **2** *Syn* MAGNIFICENCE, augustness, brilliance, gloriousness, glory, grandeur, grandness, majesty, nobleness, resplendence, splendor, stateliness, stupendousness, sublimeness, superbness

noble *adj* **1** *Syn* EMINENT, distinguished, illustrious, notable, noteworthy, outstanding, preeminent, prestigious, signal, star, superior **2** *Syn* EXCELLENT, A1, bang-up, banner, capital, classic, crackerjack, dandy, divine, fabulous, fine, first-class, first-rate, grand, great, groovy, heavenly, jim-dandy, keen, marvelous (*or* marvellous), mean, neat, nifty, par excellence, prime, sensational, splendid, stellar, sterling, superb, superior, superlative, supernal, swell, terrific, tip-top, top, top-notch, unsurpassed, wonderful *Ant* poor **3** *Syn* GRAND, august, grandiose, imposing, magnificent, majestic, stately **4** *Syn* MORAL, ethical, righteous, virtuous

noble *n Syn* ARISTOCRAT, gentleperson, patrician

nobleman *n Syn* GENTLEMAN, lord

nobleness *Syn* MAGNIFICENCE, augustness, brilliance, gloriousness, glory, grandeur, grandness, majesty, nobility, resplendence, splendor, stateliness, stupendousness, sublimeness, superbness

noblewoman *Syn* GENTLEWOMAN, dame, lady

nocturnal *Syn* NIGHTLY, night *Ant* daily

noise (about) *Syn* RUMOR, bruit (about), circulate, whisper

noiseless 1 *Syn* SILENT (sense 2), hushed,

muted, quiet, quieted, soundless, still *Ant* noisy, unquiet **2** *Syn* STILL, quiet, silent, stilly *Ant* noisy, stirring

noisome *Syn* MALODOROUS, fetid, fusty, musty, putrid, rancid, rank, stinking

nomad · a person who roams about without a fixed route or destination *Syn* drifter, gadabout, rambler, roamer, rover, stroller, vagabond, wanderer, wayfarer *Rel* laggard, straggler

nomadic *Syn* ITINERANT, ambulant, ambulatory, peripatetic, vagrant

nom de guerre *Syn* PSEUDONYM, alias, incognito, nom de plume, pen name

nom de plume *Syn* PSEUDONYM, alias, incognito, nom de guerre, pen name

nonchalance *Syn* INDIFFERENCE, apathy, casualness, disinterestedness, disregard, insouciance, unconcern *Ant* concern, interest, regard

nonchalant *Syn* COOL, collected, composed, imperturbable, unflappable, unruffled *Ant* agitated, ardent

non compos mentis *Syn* INSANE, crazed, crazy, demented, deranged, lunatic, mad, maniac *Ant* sane

nonconflicting *Syn* CONSISTENT, compatible, conformable (to), congruous, consonant, correspondent (with *or* to), harmonious *Ant* conflicting, incompatible, incongruous, inconsistent, inharmonious, unharmonious

nonconformist *Syn* HERETIC, dissenter, dissident *Ant* conformer, conformist

nonconformity *Syn* HERESY, dissent, dissidence, heterodoxy *Ant* conformity, orthodoxy

nonelective *Syn* MANDATORY, compulsory, forced, imperative, incumbent, involuntary, necessary, obligatory, peremptory, required *Ant* elective, optional, voluntary

nonessential *Syn* UNNECESSARY, dispensable, gratuitous, needless, uncalled-for, unessential, unwarranted *Ant* essential, indispensable, necessary, needed, needful, required

nonesuch *Syn* PARAGON, apotheosis, nonpareil

nonliterate *Syn* IGNORANT, benighted, dark, illiterate, simple, uneducated, uninstructed, unlearned, unlettered, unread, unschooled, untaught, untutored *Ant* educated, knowledgeable, literate, schooled

nonpareil *Syn* PARAGON, apotheosis, nonesuch

nonplus *Syn* PUZZLE, bewilder, confound, distract, dumbfound, mystify, perplex

nonpractical *Syn* IMPRACTICAL, impracticable, inoperable, unusable, unworkable, useless *Ant* applicable, feasible, functional, operable, operational, practicable, practical, usable, useful, workable

nonprofessional *Syn* AMATEURISH, amateur, dilettante, inexperienced, inexpert, unprofessional, unskilled, unskillful *Ant* ace, adept, consummate, crackerjack, expert, master, masterful, masterly, professional, virtuoso

nonrational *Syn* ILLOGICAL, fallacious, invalid, irrational, unreasonable, unreasoning, unsound, weak *Ant* logical, rational, reasonable, sound, valid

nonreligious *Syn* IRRELIGIOUS, godless, ungodly, unreligious *Ant* religious

nonresistant *Syn* PASSIVE, acquiescent, resigned, tolerant, tolerating, unresistant, unresisting, yielding *Ant* protesting, resistant, resisting, unyielding

nonsense · something said or proposed that seems senseless or absurd *Syn* balderdash, bull, bunk, drivel, gobbledygook, poppycock, rot, trash, twaddle *Rel* absurdity, foolishness, preposterousness, silliness

nonsocial *Syn* UNSOCIAL, antisocial, asocial *Ant* social

nonspecific *Syn* GENERAL (sense 2), all-around, bird's-eye, broad, overall *Ant* delineated, detailed, particularized, specific

nonvalid *Syn* GROUNDLESS, invalid, unfounded, ungrounded, unreasonable, unsubstantiated, unsupported, unwarranted *Ant* good, hard, just, justified, reasonable, reasoned, substantiated, valid, well-founded

norm *Syn* AVERAGE, normal, par, standard

normal **1** *Syn* AVERAGE, norm, par, standard **2** *Syn* REGULAR, natural, typical *Ant* irregular **3** *Syn* SANE, balanced, clearheaded, lucid, right, stable *Ant* crazed, crazy, demented, deranged, insane, lunatic, mad, maniacal, mental, unbalanced, unsound

normalize *Syn* STANDARDIZE, formalize, homogenize, regularize

normally *Syn* NATURALLY (sense 1), commonly, generally, ordinarily, typically, usually *Ant* abnormally, atypically, extraordinarily, uncommonly, unusually

nose *Syn* INTERFERE, butt in, intrude, meddle, mess, obtrude, poke, pry, snoop

nosy **1** *Syn* CURIOUS, inquisitive, prying, snoopy *Ant* incurious, uninterested **2** *Syn* INTRUSIVE, interfering, intruding, meddlesome, meddling, obtrusive, officious, presumptuous, prying, snoopy *Ant* unobtrusive

notable **1** *Syn* EMINENT, distinguished, illustrious, noble, noteworthy, outstanding, preeminent, prestigious, signal, star, superior **2** *Syn* NOTEWORTHY, memorable

notch *Syn* CANYON, defile, flume, gap, gorge, gulch, gulf, pass, ravine

note *n* **1** *Syn* AURA, air, atmosphere, climate, flavor, mood, temper **2** *Syn* LETTER, dispatch, epistle, memorandum, message, missive, report **3** *Syn* REMARK, comment, commentary, obiter dictum, observation **4** *Syn* SIGN (sense 1), badge, mark, symptom, token

note *vb Syn* SEE (sense 1), behold, contemplate, descry, discern, espy, notice, observe, perceive, remark, survey, view

noted *Syn* FAMOUS, celebrated, famed, notorious, prominent, renowned, star, well-known *Ant* anonymous, obscure, unknown

noteworthy 1 · having some quality that attracts one's attention *Syn* memorable, notable *Rel* conspicuous, noticeable, prominent, remarkable **2** *Syn* EMINENT, distinguished, illustrious, noble, notable, outstanding, preeminent, prestigious, signal, star, superior

nothing *Syn* TRIFLE, child's play, frippery, triviality

notice *n* **1** *Syn* ANNOUNCEMENT, ad, advertisement, bulletin, notification, posting, release **2** *Syn* ATTENTION (sense 2), awareness, cognizance, ear, eye, heed, observance, observation **3** *Syn* WARNING, admonition, alarm, alert, caution, forewarning

notice *vb* **1** *Syn* SEE (sense 1), behold, contemplate, descry, discern, espy, note, observe, perceive, remark, survey, view

noticeable · attracting notice or attention *Syn* arresting, conspicuous, outstanding, prominent, remarkable, salient, signal, striking *Rel* evident, manifest, obvious, palpable, patent

notification *Syn* ANNOUNCEMENT, ad, advertisement, bulletin, notice, posting, release

notify *Syn* INFORM (sense 2), advise, apprise

notion 1 *Syn* IDEA, concept, conception, impression, thought **2** *Syn* WHIM, caprice, fancy, freak, vagary, whimsy

notoriety *Syn* FAME, celebrity, éclat, glory, honor, renown, reputation, repute *Ant* infamy, obscurity

notorious *Syn* FAMOUS, celebrated, famed, noted, prominent, renowned, star, well-known *Ant* anonymous, obscure, unknown

notwithstanding · without being prevented or obstructed by *Syn* despite, in spite of

nourish *Syn* FEED, graze, pasture *Ant* starve

nourishing *Syn* NUTRITIOUS, nutrient, nutritional, nutritive *Ant* nonnutritious

nourishment *Syn* FOOD (sense 2), aliment, nutriment, pabulum, pap, sustenance

novel *Syn* NEW, fresh, modern, modernistic, newfangled, new-fashioned, original *Ant* old

novelty *Syn* KNICKKNACK, bauble, curio, curiosity, gaud, gewgaw, ornamental, trinket

novice *Syn* BEGINNER, colt, fledgling, freshman, greenhorn, neophyte, newbie, newcomer, recruit, rookie, tenderfoot, tyro *Ant* old hand, old-timer, vet, veteran

noxious *Syn* HARMFUL, adverse, bad, baleful, baneful, damaging, deleterious, detrimental, evil, hurtful, ill, injurious, mischievous, pernicious, prejudicial *Ant* harmless, innocent, innocuous, inoffensive, safe

nuance *Syn* GRADATION, shade

nub *Syn* CRUX, core, gist, heart, pith, pivot

nucleus *Syn* CENTER (sense 2), base, capital, core, cynosure, eye, focus, heart, hub, mecca, seat

nude *Syn* BARE, bald, barren, naked *Ant* covered

nudge *n Syn* POKE, jog, prod

nudge *vb Syn* POKE, jog, prod

nugatory *Syn* VAIN, empty, hollow, idle, otiose

nullify *Syn* ABOLISH, abrogate, annul, cancel, dissolve, invalidate, negate, quash, repeal, rescind, void

numb · lacking in sensation or feeling *Syn* asleep, benumbed, dead, insensitive, numbed, unfeeling *Rel* chilled, nipped *Ant* feeling, sensitive

numbed *Syn* NUMB, asleep, benumbed, dead, insensitive, unfeeling *Ant* feeling, sensitive

number *n* **1 ·** a character by which an arithmetical value is designated *Syn* digit, figure, integer, numeral **2** *Syn* SUM, aggregate, amount, quantity, total, whole

number *vb Syn* COUNT, enumerate, tell

numberless *Syn* COUNTLESS, innumerable, uncountable, uncounted, unnumbered, untold *Ant* countable

numeral *Syn* NUMBER, digit, figure, integer

numerous *Syn* MANY, divers, multifarious, several, sundry, various *Ant* few

nun *Syn* RELIGIOUS, friar, monk

nunnery *Syn* CLOISTER, abbey, convent, monastery, priory

nuptial *adj Syn* MARITAL, conjugal, connubial, married, matrimonial, wedded

nuptial *n Syn* MARRIAGE, espousal, matrimony, wedding, wedlock

nurse 1 · to promote the growth, development, or progress of *Syn* cherish, cultivate, foster, nurture *Rel* feed, nourish **2** *Syn* BABY, coddle, dandle, mollycoddle, pamper, spoil *Ant* abuse, ill-treat, ill-use, maltreat, mishandle, mistreat, misuse

nurture 1 *Syn* ENLIGHTEN (sense 1), edify, educate **2** *Syn* NURSE, cherish, cultivate, foster

nut 1 *Syn* ECCENTRIC, character, codger, crackbrain, crackpot, crank, kook, oddball, screwball, weirdo **2** *Syn* FAN, addict, aficionado, buff, bug, devotee, enthusiast, fanatic, fancier, fiend, freak, lover, maniac **3** *Syn* FOOL (sense 2), booby, goose, half-wit, jackass, lunatic, nincompoop, ninny, nitwit, simpleton, turkey, yo-yo

nutrient *Syn* NUTRITIOUS, nourishing, nutritional, nutritive *Ant* nonnutritious

nutriment *Syn* FOOD (sense 2), aliment, nourishment, pabulum, pap, sustenance

nutritional *Syn* NUTRITIOUS, nourishing, nutrient, nutritive *Ant* nonnutritious

nutritious · providing the substances necessary for health and bodily growth *Syn* nourishing, nutrient, nutritional, nutritive *Rel* dietary, dietetic *Ant* nonnutritious

nutritive *Syn* NUTRITIOUS, nourishing, nutrient, nutritional *Ant* nonnutritious

O

oaf · a big clumsy often slow-witted person *Syn* clod, gawk, hulk, lout, lubber, lug *Rel* chump, loser, schlemiel, turkey

oath *Syn* PROMISE, pledge, troth, vow, word

obdurate *Syn* OBSTINATE, adamant, adamantine, dogged, hard, hardened, hardheaded, hardhearted, headstrong, immovable, implacable, inflexible, mulish, opinionated, ossified, pat, peevish, pertinacious, perverse, pigheaded, rigid, self-willed, stubborn, unbending, uncompromising, unrelenting, unyielding, willful (*or* wilful) *Ant* acquiescent, agreeable, amenable, compliant, complying, flexible, pliable, pliant, relenting, yielding

obedient · readily giving in to the command or authority of another *Syn* amenable, compliant, conformable, docile, law-abiding, submissive, tractable *Rel* acquiescent, agreeable, amiable, obliging *Ant* contrary, disobedient, froward, insubordinate, intractable, rebellious, recalcitrant, refractory, unruly

obeisance *Syn* HONOR, deference, homage, reverence

obese *Syn* FLESHY, chubby, corpulent, fat, plump, portly, rotund, stout *Ant* scrawny, skinny

obey · to follow the wish, direction, or command of another *Syn* comply, mind *Rel* bow, defer, submit, succumb, yield *Ant* command, order

obfuscate *Syn* OBSCURE, becloud, bedim, befog, cloud, darken, dim, eclipse, fog *Ant* illuminate, illumine

obiter dictum *Syn* REMARK, comment, commentary, note, observation

object *vb* · to oppose by arguing against *Syn* expostulate, kick, protest, remonstrate *Rel* balk, boggle, demur, jib, scruple, shy, stick, stickle *Ant* acquiesce

object *n* **1** *Syn* GOAL, aim, ambition, aspiration, design, dream, end, intent, intention, mark, meaning, objective, plan, pretension, purpose, target, thing **2** *Syn* THING, article

objectify *Syn* REALIZE, actualize, embody, externalize, hypostatize, incarnate, materialize, reify

objection *n* · a feeling or declaration of disapproval or dissent *Syn* challenge, complaint, demur, expostulation, fuss, protest, question, remonstrance *Rel* compunction, doubt, misgiving, qualm, scruple

objectionable · arousing or likely to arouse objection *Syn* exceptionable, unacceptable, undesirable, unwanted, unwelcome

objective *adj* **1** *Syn* FAIR, dispassionate, equitable, impartial, just, unbiased, uncolored

Ant unfair **2** *Syn* MATERIAL, corporeal, phenomenal, physical, sensible *Ant* immaterial

objective *n* *Syn* GOAL, aim, ambition, aspiration, design, dream, end, intent, intention, mark, meaning, object, plan, pretension, purpose, target, thing

objectivity *Syn* DETACHMENT, disinterestedness, impartiality, neutrality *Ant* bias, favor, favoritism, one-sidedness, partiality, partisanship, prejudice

objurgate *Syn* EXECRATE, anathematize, curse, damn

obligation **1** · something one must do because of prior agreement *Syn* burden, charge, commitment, duty, need, responsibility *Rel* pledge, promise **2** *Syn* DEBT, arrear, debit, indebtedness, liability

obligatory *Syn* MANDATORY, compulsory, forced, imperative, incumbent, involuntary, necessary, nonelective, peremptory, required *Ant* elective, optional, voluntary

oblige **1** · to do a service or courtesy *Syn* accommodate, favor *Rel* gratify, please *Ant* disoblige **2** *Syn* FORCE, coerce, compel, constrain

oblique **1** *Syn* AWRY, askew, aslant, cockeyed, crooked, listing, lopsided, skewed, slanted, slanting, slantwise, tilted, tipping, uneven *Ant* even, level, straight **2** *Syn* CROOKED, devious *Ant* straight

obliterate *Syn* ERASE, blot out, cancel, delete, efface, expunge

obliteration *Syn* DESTRUCTION, annihilation, decimation, demolishment, demolition, desolation, devastation, extermination, extinction, havoc, loss, ruin, ruination, wastage, wreckage *Ant* building, construction, erection, raising

oblivious *Syn* FORGETFUL, unmindful

obloquy **1** *Syn* ABUSE, billingsgate, invective, scurrility, vituperation *Ant* adulation **2** *Syn* DISGRACE, dishonor, disrepute, ignominy, infamy, odium, opprobrium, shame *Ant* esteem, respect

obnoxious *Syn* REPUGNANT, abhorrent, distasteful, invidious, repellent *Ant* congenial

obscene *Syn* COARSE, gross, ribald, vulgar *Ant* fine, refined

obscure *adj* **1** · not clearly understandable *Syn* ambiguous, cryptic, dark, enigmatic, equivocal, vague *Rel* abstruse, esoteric, occult, recondite *Ant* distinct, obvious **2** *Syn* DARK, dim, dusky, gloomy, murky *Ant* light

obscure *vb* · to make dark, dim, or indistinct *Syn* becloud, bedim, befog, cloud, darken, dim, eclipse, fog, obfuscate *Rel* conceal, hide, screen *Ant* illuminate, illumine

obsequious *Syn* SUBSERVIENT, menial, servile, slavish *Ant* domineering, overbearing

observable *Syn* VISIBLE, apparent, seeable, visual *Ant* invisible, unseeable

observance *Syn* ATTENTION (sense 2), awareness, cognizance, ear, eye, heed, notice, observation

observation 1 *Syn* ATTENTION (sense 2), awareness, cognizance, ear, eye, heed, notice, observance **2** *Syn* REMARK, comment, commentary, note, obiter dictum

observe 1 *Syn* KEEP (sense 1), celebrate, commemorate, solemnize *Ant* break **2** *Syn* SEE (sense 1), behold, contemplate, descry, discern, espy, note, notice, perceive, remark, survey, view

observer *Syn* SPECTATOR, beholder, bystander, eyewitness, kibitzer, looker-on, onlooker, witness

obsessive *Syn* COMPULSIVE, impulsive

obsolete · having passed its time of use or usefulness *Syn* antiquated, archaic, dated, moth-eaten, outdated, out-of-date, outmoded, outworn, passé *Rel* aging, obsolescent

obstacle *Syn* ENCUMBRANCE, bar, block, chain, clog, crimp, deterrent, drag, embarrassment, fetter, handicap, hindrance, hurdle, impediment, inhibition, interference, let, manacle, obstruction, shackles, stop, stumbling block, trammel *Ant* aid, assistance, benefit, help

obstinate · sticking to an opinion, purpose, or course of action in spite of reason, arguments, or persuasion *Syn* adamant, adamantine, dogged, hard, hardened, hardheaded, hardhearted, headstrong, immovable, implacable, inflexible, mulish, obdurate, opinionated, ossified, pat, peevish, pertinacious, perverse, pigheaded, rigid, self-willed, stubborn, unbending, uncompromising, unrelenting, unyielding, willful (*or* wilful) *Rel* hidebound, narrow-minded *Ant* acquiescent, agreeable, amenable, compliant, complying, flexible, pliable, pliant, relenting, yielding

obstreperous *Syn* VOCIFEROUS, blatant, boisterous, clamorous, strident

obstruct *Syn* HINDER, bar, block, dam, impede *Ant* further

obstruction *Syn* ENCUMBRANCE, bar, block, chain, clog, crimp, deterrent, drag, embarrassment, fetter, handicap, hindrance, hurdle, impediment, inhibition, interference, let, manacle, obstacle, shackles, stop, stumbling block, trammel *Ant* aid, assistance, benefit, help

obtain 1 *Syn* EARN, acquire, attain, capture, carry, draw, gain, garner, get, land, make, procure, realize, secure, win *Ant* forfeit, lose **2** *Syn* GET, gain, procure, secure, win

obtrude *Syn* INTERFERE, butt in, intrude, meddle, mess, nose, poke, pry, snoop

obtrusive *Syn* INTRUSIVE, interfering, intruding, meddlesome, meddling, nosy (*or* nosey), officious, presumptuous, prying, snoopy *Ant* unobtrusive

obtuse *Syn* DULL (sense 1), blunt *Ant* lively

obviate *Syn* PREVENT (sense 2), avert, forestall, help, preclude

obvious 1 *Syn* EGREGIOUS, blatant, conspicuous, flagrant, glaring, gross, patent, pronounced, rank, striking **2** *Syn* EVIDENT, apparent, clear, distinct, manifest, palpable, patent, plain

occasion 1 *Syn* CAUSE, antecedent, determinant, reason **2** *Syn* OPPORTUNITY, break, chance, time

occasional 1 *Syn* FITFUL, casual, choppy, discontinuous, erratic, intermittent, irregular, spasmodic, sporadic, spotty, unsteady *Ant* constant, continuous, regular, steady **2** *Syn* INFREQUENT, rare, scarce, sporadic, uncommon *Ant* frequent

occult *Syn* RECONDITE, abstruse, esoteric

occupant *Syn* INHABITANT, denizen, dweller, habitant, resident, resider *Ant* transient

occupation 1 · the activity by which one regularly makes a living *Syn* calling, employment, line, profession, trade, vocation, work *Rel* racket **2** *Syn* WORK (sense 2), business, calling, employment, pursuit

occur *Syn* HAPPEN, befall, betide, chance, transpire

occurrence · something that happens or takes place *Syn* circumstance, episode, event, incident *Rel* appearance, emergence

oceanic *Syn* MARINE (sense 1), maritime, pelagic

odd *Syn* STRANGE, curious, eccentric, erratic, outlandish, peculiar, quaint, queer, singular, unique *Ant* familiar

oddball *Syn* ECCENTRIC, character, codger, crackbrain, crackpot, crank, kook, nut, screwball, weirdo

odds 1 *Syn* ADVANTAGE, allowance, edge, handicap *Ant* disadvantage, handicap **2** *Syn* PROBABILITY, chance, percentage

odious *Syn* HATEFUL, abhorrent, abominable, detestable *Ant* lovable, sympathetic

odium *Syn* DISGRACE, dishonor, disrepute, ignominy, infamy, obloquy, opprobrium, shame *Ant* esteem, respect

odor *Syn* SMELL, aroma, scent

odorous · emitting and diffusing scent *Syn* aromatic, balmy, fragrant, redolent *Ant* malodorous, odorless

of *Syn* BEFORE, ahead, ere, of, previous to, prior to, to *Ant* after, following

offal *Syn* REFUSE, debris, garbage, rubbish, trash, waste

offend · to cause hurt feelings or deep resentment *Syn* affront, insult, outrage *Rel* annoy, bother, irk, vex

offense 1 · an emotional response to a slight or indignity *Syn* dudgeon, huff, pique, resentiment, umbrage *Rel* affront, indignity, insult **2** · a transgression of law *Syn* crime, scandal, sin, vice *Rel* grievance, injury, injustice, wrong **3** *Syn* ATTACK (sense 2), aggression, assault, blitzkrieg, charge, descent, offensive, onset, onslaught, raid, rush, strike **4** *Syn* INSULT, affront, barb, dart, dig, epithet, indignity, name, outrage, put-down, sarcasm, slight, slur

offensive *adj* · utterly distasteful or unpleasant to the senses or sensibilities *Syn* loathsome, repugnant, repulsive, revolting *Rel* abhorrent, distasteful, invidious, obnoxious, repellent

offensive *n* *Syn* ATTACK (sense 2), aggression, assault, blitzkrieg, charge, descent, offense (*or* offence), onset, onslaught, raid, rush, strike

offer *vb* · to put something before another for acceptance or consideration *Syn* prefer, present, proffer, tender *Rel* bestow, confer, give

offer *n* *Syn* PROPOSAL, proffer, proposition, suggestion

offhand *Syn* EXTEMPORANEOUS, extemporary, extempore, impromptu, improvised, unpremeditated

office *Syn* FUNCTION, duty, province

officious *Syn* INTRUSIVE, interfering, intruding, meddlesome, meddling, nosy (*or* nosey), snoopy *Ant* unobtrusive

offset *Syn* COMPENSATE, balance, counterbalance, counterpoise, countervail

offshoot *Syn* DERIVATIVE, by-product, outgrowth, spin-off *Ant* origin, root, source

offspring · those who follow in direct parental line *Syn* descendants, issue, posterity, progeny, young

oft *Syn* OFTEN, frequently, oftentimes

often · many times *Syn* frequently, oft, oftentimes

oftentimes *Syn* OFTEN, frequently, oft

oil · to smear, rub over, or lubricate with oil or an oily substance *Syn* anoint, cream, grease, lubricate

OK *or* **okay** *adj* *Syn* ADEQUATE, acceptable, all right, decent, fine, passable, respectable, satisfactory, tolerable *Ant* deficient, inadequate, lacking, unacceptable, unsatisfactory, wanting

OK *or* **okay** *n* *Syn* APPROVAL, approbation, blessing, favor, imprimatur *Ant* disapproval, disfavor

OK *or* **okay** *vb* *Syn* APPROVE (OF), accept, care (for), countenance, favor, subscribe (to) *Ant* disapprove (of), discountenance, disfavor, frown (on *or* upon)

old **1** *Syn* ELDERLY, aged, aging, ancient, geriatric, long-lived, older, senior *Ant* young, youthful **2** *Syn* FORMER, erstwhile, late, onetime, past, sometime, whilom

older *Syn* ELDERLY, aged, aging, ancient, geriatric, long-lived, old, senior *Ant* young, youthful

oldster *Syn* SENIOR CITIZEN, ancient, elder, golden-ager, old-timer *Ant* youngster, youth

old-timer *Syn* SENIOR CITIZEN, ancient, elder, golden-ager, oldster *Ant* youngster, youth

old wives' tale *Syn* FALLACY (sense 1), error, falsehood, falsity, illusion, misconception, myth, untruth *Ant* truth, verity

oligarchy · government by, or a state governed by, the few *Syn* aristocracy, plutocracy

omen · something believed to be a sign or warning of a future event *Syn* augury, auspice, boding, foreboding, foreshadowing, portent, prefiguring, presage *Rel* forerunner, harbinger, herald, precursor

ominous · being or showing a sign of evil or calamity to come *Syn* baleful, dire, foreboding, inauspicious, menacing, portentous, sinister, threatening *Rel* dark, gloomy

omit *Syn* NEGLECT, disregard, forget, ignore, overlook, slight *Ant* cherish

omnibus *Syn* ENCYCLOPEDIC, compendious, complete, comprehensive, full, global, inclusive, in-depth, panoramic, universal

on *prep* *Syn* AGAINST, upon

on *adv* *Syn* ALONG, ahead, forth, forward, onward

oncoming *Syn* FORTHCOMING, approaching, coming, imminent, impending, nearing, pending, upcoming *Ant* late, recent

onerous · imposing great hardship or strain *Syn* burdensome, exacting, oppressive *Rel* cumbersome, cumbrous, heavy, hefty, ponderous, weighty

one-sidedness *Syn* BIAS, favor, partiality, partisanship, prejudice *Ant* impartiality, neutrality, objectivity, open-mindedness

onetime *Syn* FORMER, erstwhile, late, old, past, sometime, whilom

ongoing *Syn* PRESENT, current, extant, present-day *Ant* ago, future, past

onlooker *Syn* SPECTATOR, beholder, bystander, eyewitness, kibitzer, looker-on, observer, witness

only · being the one or ones of a class with no other members *Syn* alone, lone, singular, sole, solitary, special, unique *Rel* solo, unaccompanied, unattended

onrush *Syn* ADVANCE (sense 2), advancement, furtherance, going, headway, march, passage, process, procession, progress, progression *Ant* recession, regression, retrogression

onset **1** *Syn* ATTACK (sense 1), assault, onslaught **2** *Syn* ATTACK (sense 2), aggression, assault, blitzkrieg, charge, descent, offense (*or* offence), offensive, onslaught, raid, rush, strike **3** *Syn* BEGINNING, alpha, birth, commencement, dawn, genesis, inception, incipiency, launch, morning, outset, start, threshold *Ant* close, conclusion, end, ending

onslaught 1 *Syn* ATTACK (sense 1), assault, onset 2 *Syn* ATTACK (sense 2), aggression, assault, blitzkrieg, charge, descent, offense (*or* offence), offensive, onset, raid, rush, strike

onward 1 · toward or at a point lying ahead in space or time *Syn* forth, forward 2 *Syn* ALONG, ahead, forth, forward, on

ooze *Syn* EXUDE, bleed, percolate, seep, strain, sweat, weep

opalescent *Syn* PRISMATIC, iridescent, opaline

opaline *Syn* PRISMATIC, iridescent, opalescent

open *vb Syn* BEGIN (sense 2), commence, embark (on *or* upon), enter (into *or* upon), get off, kick off, launch, start, strike (into) *Ant* conclude, end, finish, terminate

open *adj* 1 *Syn* FRANK, candid, plain *Ant* reticent *Syn* LIABLE, exposed, prone, sensitive, subject, susceptible *Ant* exempt, immune

open-air *Syn* OUTDOOR, out-of-door (*or* out-of-doors) *Ant* indoor

openhanded *Syn* LIBERAL (sense 1), bounteous, bountiful, generous, handsome, munificent *Ant* close

openheartedness *Syn* CANDOR, directness, forthrightness, frankness, openness, plainness, straightforwardness *Ant* dissembling, pretense (*or* pretence)

openness *Syn* CANDOR, directness, forthrightness, frankness, openheartedness, plainness, straightforwardness *Ant* dissembling, pretense (*or* pretence)

operate *Syn* ACT (sense 1), behave, function, react, work

operation *Syn* MISSION, assignment, charge, job, post

operative *adj Syn* ACTIVE, dynamic, live *Ant* inactive

operative *n Syn* WORKER, artisan, craftsman, hand, handicraftsman, laborer, mechanic, roustabout, workingman, workman *Ant* idler

opinion · a judgment one holds as true *Syn* belief, conviction, persuasion, sentiment, view *Rel* concept, conception, idea, impression, notion, thought

opinionated *Syn* OBSTINATE, adamant, adamantine, dogged, hard, hardened, hardheaded, hardhearted, headstrong, immovable, implacable, inflexible, mulish, obdurate, ossified, pat, peevish, pertinacious, perverse, pigheaded, rigid, self-willed, stubborn, unbending, uncompromising, unrelenting, unyielding, willful (*or* wilful) *Ant* acquiescent, agreeable, amenable, compliant, complying, flexible, pliable, pliant, relenting, yielding

opponent *Syn* ENEMY, adversary, antagonist, foe *Ant* friend

opportune *Syn* SEASONABLE, pat, timely, well-timed *Ant* unseasonable

opportunity · a state of affairs or a combination of circumstances favorable to some end *Syn* break, chance, occasion, time *Rel* contingency, emergency, juncture, pass

oppose *Syn* RESIST, antagonize, combat, conflict, contest, fight, withstand *Ant* abide, submit

opposite *adj* · so far apart as to be or to seem irreconcilable *Syn* antipodal, antipodean, antithetical, antonymous, contradictory, contrary *Rel* converse, reverse

opposite *n* · something that is exactly opposed or contrary *Syn* antipode, antithesis, antonym, contradictory, contrary, converse, counter, reverse

opposition *Syn* RESISTANCE, defiance *Ant* acquiescence

oppress 1 *Syn* DEPRESS, weigh *Ant* cheer, elate 2 *Syn* WRONG, aggrieve, persecute

oppression *Syn* SADNESS, blues, dejection, depression, desolation, despondency, disconsolateness, dispiritedness, doldrums, downheartedness, dreariness, dumps, forlornness, gloom, gloominess, heartsickness, joylessness, melancholy, mopes, unhappiness *Ant* bliss, blissfulness, ecstasy, elatedness, elation, euphoria, exhilaration, exuberance, exultation, felicity, gladness, gladsomeness, happiness, heaven, intoxication, joy, joyfulness, joyousness, jubilation, rapture, rapturousness

oppressive *Syn* ONEROUS, burdensome, exacting

opprobrious *Syn* ABUSIVE, contumelious, scurrilous, vituperative *Ant* complementary, respectful

opprobrium *Syn* DISGRACE, dishonor, disrepute, ignominy, infamy, obloquy, odium, shame *Ant* esteem, respect

opt *Syn* CHOOSE, cull, elect, pick, prefer, select, single *Ant* eschew, reject

optimistic *Syn* HOPEFUL, roseate, rose-colored *Ant* despairing, hopeless

option *Syn* CHOICE, alternative, election, preference, selection

optional · subject to one's freedom of choice *Syn* discretionary, elective, voluntary *Rel* alternative, chosen *Ant* compulsory, mandatory, nonelective, obligatory, required

opulent 1 *Syn* LUXURIOUS, deluxe, lavish, luxuriant, palatial, plush, sumptuous *Ant* ascetic, austere, humble, Spartan 2 *Syn* RICH, affluent, wealthy *Ant* poor

opulently *Syn* HIGH, expensively, extravagantly, grandly, lavishly, luxuriously, richly, sumptuously *Ant* austerely, humbly, modestly, plainly, simply

opus *Syn* WORK (sense 3), artifact, product, production

oral 1 *Syn* VERBAL, spoken, unwritten *Ant* written 2 *Syn* VOCAL (sense 1), uttered, voiced *Ant* nonvocal

oration *Syn* SPEECH, address, harangue, homily, lecture, sermon, talk

orbit *Syn* RANGE, compass, gamut, horizon, ken, purview, radius, reach, scope, sweep

ordain *Syn* DICTATE, decree, impose, prescribe

order *vb* **1** · to put persons or things into their proper places in relation to each other *Syn* arrange, marshal, methodize, organize, systematize *Rel* adjust, regulate **2** *Syn* COMMAND, bid, charge, direct, enjoin, instruct *Ant* comply, obey

order *n* **1** *Syn* ASSOCIATION, club, society **2** *Syn* COMMAND, behest, bidding, dictate, injunction, mandate

orderly · following a set arrangement, design, or pattern *Syn* methodical, regular, systematic *Rel* neat, spick-and-span, tidy, trim *Ant* chaotic, disorderly

ordinance *Syn* LAW, canon, precept, regulation, rule, statute

ordinarily *Syn* NATURALLY (sense 1), commonly, generally, normally, typically, usually *Ant* abnormally, atypically, extraordinarily, uncommonly, unusually

ordinary *Syn* COMMON, familiar, popular, vulgar *Ant* exceptional, uncommon

organ **1** *Syn* AGENT (sense 2), agency, instrument, instrumentality, machinery, means, medium, vehicle **2** *Syn* JOURNAL, magazine, newspaper, periodical, review

organism *Syn* SYSTEM, complex, network, scheme *Ant* chaos

organize **1** *Syn* FOUND, create, establish, institute **2** *Syn* ORDER, arrange, marshal, methodize, systematize

oriel *Syn* WINDOW, casement

orifice *Syn* APERTURE, interstice

origin **1** · the point at which something begins its course or its existence *Syn* inception, prime mover, provenance, provenience, root, source *Rel* beginning, commencement, initiation, starting **2** *Syn* ANCESTRY, birth, blood, bloodline, breeding, descent, extraction, family tree, genealogy, line, lineage, parentage, pedigree, stock, strain *Ant* issue, posterity, progeny, seed

original **1** *Syn* INITIAL, primordial *Ant* final **2** *Syn* NEW, fresh, modern, modernistic, newfangled, new-fashioned, novel *Ant* old

originate **1** *Syn* BEGIN (sense 1), arise, commence, dawn, form, materialize, set in, spring, start *Ant* cease, end, stop **2** *Syn* SPRING, arise, derive, emanate, flow, issue, proceed, rise, stem

ornament *Syn* ADORN, beautify, bedeck, deck, decorate, embellish, garnish *Ant* disfigure

ornamental *Syn* KNICKKNACK, bauble, curio, curiosity, gaud, gewgaw, novelty, trinket

ornate · elaborately and often pretentiously decorated or designed *Syn* baroque, flamboyant, florid, rococo *Rel* adorned, decorated, embellished, ornamented *Ant* austere, chaste

orotund *Syn* RESONANT, resounding, ringing, sonorous, vibrant

orthodox *Syn* CONSERVATIVE, traditional *Ant* liberal, nontraditional, progressive

oscillate *Syn* SWING (sense 2), fluctuate, pendulate, sway, undulate, vibrate, waver

ossified *Syn* OBSTINATE, adamant, adamantine, dogged, hard, hardened, hardheaded, hardhearted, headstrong, immovable, implacable, inflexible, mulish, obdurate, opinionated, pat, peevish, pertinacious, perverse, pigheaded, rigid, self-willed, stubborn, unbending, uncompromising, unrelenting, unyielding, willful (*or* wilful) *Ant* acquiescent, agreeable, amenable, compliant, complying, flexible, pliable, pliant, relenting, yielding

ostensible *Syn* APPARENT, illusory, seeming *Ant* real

ostensibly *Syn* APPARENTLY, evidently, presumably, seemingly, supposedly

ostentation · excessive or unnecessary display *Syn* flamboyance, flashiness, garishness, gaudiness, glitz, ostentatiousness, pretentiousness, showiness, swank *Rel* extravaganza, pageant, parade, show *Ant* austerity, plainness, severity

ostentatious **1** *Syn* GAUDY, flamboyant, flashy, garish, glitzy, loud, splashy, swank (*or* swanky), tawdry *Ant* conservative, quiet, understated **2** *Syn* SHOWY, pretentious

ostentatiousness *Syn* OSTENTATION, flamboyance, flashiness, garishness, gaudiness, glitz, pretentiousness, showiness, swank *Ant* austerity, plainness, severity

ostracize *Syn* BANISH, deport, exile, expatriate, extradite, transport

other *Syn* ADDITIONAL, added, another, else, farther, further, more

otiose *Syn* VAIN, empty, hollow, idle, nugatory

ought (to) *Syn* NEED (sense 1), have (to), must, shall, should *Ant* have, hold

out **1** *Syn* ALOUD, audibly, out loud *Ant* inaudibly, silently, soundlessly **2** *Syn* OUTDOORS, outside *Ant* indoors

out-and-out **1** *Syn* EXHAUSTIVE, all-out, clean, complete, comprehensive, full-scale, thorough, thoroughgoing, total **2** *Syn* OUTRIGHT, arrant, unmitigated

outbreak · a sudden and usually temporary growth of activity *Syn* burst, flare, flare-up, flash, flicker, flurry, flutter, outburst, spurt *Rel* binge, jag, spree

outburst *Syn* OUTBREAK, burst, flare, flare-up, flash, flicker, flurry, flutter, spurt

outcast · one that is cast out or refused acceptance by society *Syn* castaway, derelict, pariah, reprobate, untouchable *Rel* hobo, tramp, vagabond, vagrant

outcome *Syn* EFFECT, aftereffect, aftermath, consequence, event, issue, result, sequel, upshot *Ant* cause

outdated *Syn* OBSOLETE, antiquated, archaic, dated, moth-eaten, out-of-date, outmoded, outworn, passé

outdo *Syn* EXCEED, excel, outstrip, surpass, transcend

outdoor · of, relating to, or held in the open air *Syn* open-air, out-of-door (*or* out-of-doors) *Rel* airy *Ant* indoor

outdoors · in or into the open air *Syn* out, outside *Rel* without *Ant* indoors

outer · being or located outside something *Syn* exterior, external, outside, outward *Rel* alien, extraneous, extrinsic, foreign *Ant* inner

outfit *n Syn* EQUIPMENT, apparatus, gear, machinery, matériel, paraphernalia, tackle

outfit *vb Syn* FURNISH (sense 1), accoutre (*or* accouter), equip, fit (out), rig, supply *Ant* hold (back), keep (back), reserve, retain, withhold

outgoing *Syn* CONVIVIAL, boon, companionable, extroverted, gregarious, sociable, social *Ant* antisocial, introverted, reclusive, unsociable

outgrowth *Syn* DERIVATIVE, by-product, offshoot, spin-off *Ant* origin, root, source

outlander *Syn* STRANGER, alien, émigré, foreigner, immigrant, outsider

outlandish **1** *Syn* EXOTIC, fantastic, glamorous, marvelous (*or* marvellous), romantic, strange **2** *Syn* STRANGE, curious, eccentric, erratic, odd, peculiar, quaint, queer, singular, unique *Ant* familiar

outlast *Syn* OUTLIVE, survive

outlaw *Syn* FORBID, ban, bar, enjoin, interdict, prohibit, proscribe *Ant* allow, let, permit, suffer

outlawing *Syn* PROHIBITION (sense 1), banning, barring, enjoining, forbidding, interdicting, interdiction, prohibiting, proscribing, proscription *Ant* prescription

outline *n* **1** · the line that bounds and gives form to something *Syn* contour, profile, silhouette, skyline *Rel* configuration, conformation, figure, form, shape **2** *Syn* SKETCH, blueprint, delineation, diagram, draft, plot, tracing

outline *vb* **1** *Syn* SKETCH, blueprint, delineate, diagram, draft, plot, trace **2** *Syn* SUMMARIZE, abstract, digest, encapsulate, epitomize, recap, recapitulate, sum up, wrap up

outlive · to remain in existence longer than *Syn* outlast, survive *Rel* abide, continue, endure, persist

outlook *Syn* PROSPECT, anticipation, foretaste

out loud *Syn* ALOUD, audibly, out *Ant* inaudibly, silently, soundlessly

outmoded *Syn* OBSOLETE, antiquated, archaic, dated, moth-eaten, outdated, out-of-date, outworn, passé

out-of-date *Syn* OBSOLETE, antiquated, archaic, dated, moth-eaten, outdated, outmoded, outworn, passé

out-of-door *or* **out-of-doors** *Syn* OUTDOOR, open-air *Ant* indoor

outrage *vb* **1** *Syn* ABUSE, ill-treat, maltreat, mistreat, misuse *Ant* honor, respect **2** *Syn* ANGER, antagonize, enrage, incense, inflame, infuriate, madden, rankle, rile, roil *Ant* delight, gratify, please **3** *Syn* OFFEND, affront, insult

outrage *n* **1** *Syn* ANGER, angriness, furor, fury, indignation, irateness, ire, rage, spleen, wrath, wrathfulness *Ant* delight, pleasure **2** *Syn* INSULT, affront, barb, dart, dig, epithet, indignity, name, offense (*or* offence), put-down, sarcasm, slight, slur

outraged *Syn* ANGRY, angered, apoplectic, enraged, foaming, fuming, furious, incensed, indignant, inflamed, infuriated, irate, ireful, mad, rabid, riled, roiled, sore, steaming, wrathful, wroth *Ant* delighted, pleased

outrageous · enormously or flagrantly bad or horrible *Syn* atrocious, heinous, monstrous *Rel* flagrant, glaring, gross, rank

outrank *Syn* OUTWEIGH, overbalance, overshadow, overweigh

outright · being exactly what is stated *Syn* arrant, out-and-out, unmitigated

outset *Syn* BEGINNING, alpha, birth, commencement, dawn, genesis, inception, incipiency, launch, morning, onset, start, threshold *Ant* close, conclusion, end, ending

outside *adv Syn* OUTDOORS, out *Ant* indoors

outside *adj Syn* OUTER, exterior, external, outward *Ant* inner

outside *prep Syn* BEYOND (sense 2), outside of, without *Ant* within

outside of *Syn* BEYOND (sense 2), outside, without *Ant* within

outsider *Syn* STRANGER, alien, émigré, foreigner, immigrant, outlander

outsize *Syn* LARGE, big, bulky, considerable, goodly, good-sized, grand, great, handsome, hefty, hulking, largish, oversize (*or* oversized), sizable (*or* sizeable), substantial, tidy, voluminous *Ant* little, puny, small, undersized

outstanding **1** *Syn* EMINENT, distinguished, illustrious, noble, notable, noteworthy, preeminent, prestigious, signal, star, superior **2** *Syn* NOTICEABLE, arresting, conspicuous, prominent, remarkable, salient, signal, striking

outstrip *Syn* EXCEED, excel, outdo, surpass, transcend

outward *Syn* OUTER, exterior, external, outside *Ant* inner

outweigh · to be greater in importance than *Syn* outrank, overbalance, overshadow, overweigh *Rel* count, import, matter, mean, signify, weigh

outwit *Syn* FRUSTRATE, baffle, balk, circumvent, foil, thwart *Ant* fulfill

outworn *Syn* OBSOLETE, antiquated, archaic,

dated, moth-eaten, outdated, out-of-date, outmoded, passé

ovation *Syn* APPLAUSE, acclamation, cheering, cheers, plaudit(s), rave(s) *Ant* booing, hissing

over *adv Syn* ABOVE, aloft, overhead, skyward *Ant* below, beneath, under

over *prep* **1** *Syn* AROUND (sense 2), about, round, through, throughout **2** *Syn* BEYOND (sense 1), past *Ant* within

overabundance *Syn* EXCESS, fat, overage, overflow, overkill, overmuch, oversupply, superabundance, superfluity, surfeit, surplus *Ant* deficiency, deficit, insufficiency

overage *Syn* EXCESS, fat, overabundance, overflow, overkill, overmuch, oversupply, superabundance, superfluity, surfeit, surplus *Ant* deficiency, deficit, insufficiency

overall *adv Syn* CHIEFLY, altogether, basically, by and large, generally, largely, mainly, mostly, predominantly, primarily, principally, substantially

overall *adj* **1** *Syn* GENERAL (sense 1), blanket, common, generic, global, universal *Ant* individual, particular **2** *Syn* GENERAL (sense 2), all-around, bird's-eye, broad, nonspecific *Ant* delineated, detailed, particularized, specific

overbalance *Syn* OUTWEIGH, outrank, overshadow, overweigh

overbearing **1** *Syn* BOSSY, authoritarian, autocratic, despotic, dictatorial, domineering, imperious, masterful, peremptory, tyrannical, tyrannous **2** *Syn* PROUD (sense 1), arrogant, disdainful, haughty, insolent, lordly, supercilious *Ant* ashamed, humble

overcast · covered over by clouds *Syn* beclouded, clouded, cloudy, dull, hazed, hazy, heavy, lowering, overclouded *Rel* bedimmed, befogged, blackened, darkened, darksome, dim, dimmed, dulled, dusky, misty, murky, obscure, obscured, overshadowed *Ant* clear, cloudless

overclouded *Syn* OVERCAST, beclouded, clouded, cloudy, dull, hazed, hazy, heavy, lowering *Ant* clear, cloudless

overcome *Syn* CONQUER, beat, defeat, lick, overthrow, reduce, rout, subdue, subjugate, surmount, vanquish

overdo *Syn* OVERSTATE, exaggerate, overdraw, put on *Ant* understate

overdraw *Syn* OVERSTATE, exaggerate, overdo, put on *Ant* understate

overdue *Syn* TARDY, behindhand, late *Ant* prompt

overeater *Syn* GLUTTON, gorger, gormandizer, gourmand, hog, stuffer, swiller

overflow *n* **1** *Syn* EXCESS, fat, overabundance, overage, overkill, overmuch, oversupply, superabundance, superfluity, surfeit, surplus *Ant* deficiency, deficit, insufficiency **2** *Syn* FLOOD, deluge, drown, engulf, inundate, overwhelm, submerge, submerse, swamp *Ant* drain

overflow *vb Syn* TEEM, abound, swarm

overhang *Syn* BULGE, beetle, jut, project, protrude, stick out

overhead *Syn* ABOVE, aloft, over, skyward *Ant* below, beneath, under

overjoy **1** *Syn* ELATE, elevate, enrapture, exhilarate, transport *Ant* depress **2** *Syn* ENTRANCE, carry away, enrapture, enthrall (*or* enthral), ravish, transport

overkill *Syn* EXCESS, fat, overabundance, overage, overflow, overmuch, oversupply, superabundance, superfluity, surfeit, surplus *Ant* deficiency, deficit, insufficiency

overlap · to lie over parts of one another *Syn* lap, overlay, overlie, overspread *Rel* shingle

overlay **1** · to lay or spread over or across *Syn* appliqué, superimpose, superpose **2** *Syn* OVERLAP, lap, overlie, overspread

overlie *Syn* OVERLAP, lap, overlay, overspread

overlook *Syn* NEGLECT, disregard, forget, ignore, omit, slight *Ant* cherish

overmuch *Syn* EXCESS, fat, overabundance, overage, overflow, overkill, oversupply, superabundance, superfluity, surfeit, surplus *Ant* deficiency, deficit, insufficiency

overrun *Syn* INFEST, beset *Ant* disinfest

overshadow *Syn* OUTWEIGH, outrank, overbalance, overweigh

oversight · the function or duty of watching or guarding for the sake of proper control or direction *Syn* supervision, surveillance *Rel* control, controlling, direction, management

oversize *or* **oversized** *Syn* LARGE, big, bulky, considerable, goodly, good-sized, grand, great, handsome, hefty, hulking, largish, outsize, sizable (*or* sizeable), substantial, tidy, voluminous *Ant* little, puny, small, undersized

overspread **1** *Syn* COVER, envelop, shroud, veil, wrap *Ant* bare **2** *Syn* OVERLAP, lap, overlay, overlie

overstate · to describe or express in too strong terms *Syn* exaggerate, overdo, overdraw, put on *Rel* color, elaborate, embellish, embroider, magnify, pad, stretch *Ant* understate

overstatement *Syn* EXAGGERATION, caricature, coloring, elaboration, embellishment, embroidering, hyperbole, magnification, padding, stretching *Ant* understatement

oversupply *Syn* EXCESS, fat, overabundance, overage, overflow, overkill, overmuch, superabundance, superfluity, surfeit, surplus *Ant* deficiency, deficit, insufficiency

overthrow **1** *Syn* CONQUER, beat, defeat, lick, overcome, reduce, rout, subdue, subjugate, surmount, vanquish **2** *Syn* OVERTURN, capsize, subvert, upset

overture · an action taken to win the favor or approval of another person or party *Syn* ad-

vance, approach, bid, tender *Rel* proposal,
proposition

overturn · to turn from an upright or proper
position *Syn* capsize, overthrow, subvert, upset *Rel* invert, reverse, transpose

overweening 1 *Syn* ARROGANT, cavalier,
haughty, highfalutin, high-handed, high-hat,
imperious, important, lofty, lordly, masterful, peremptory, pompous, presumptuous,
pretentious, supercilious, superior, uppish,
uppity *Ant* humble, modest **2** *Syn* CON-
CEITED, complacent, egoistic, egotistic (*or*
egotistical), important, pompous, prideful,

proud, self-conceited, self-important, self-
satisfied, smug, stuck-up, vain, vainglorious
Ant humble, modest

overweigh *Syn* OUTWEIGH, outrank, overbalance, overshadow

overwhelm *Syn* FLOOD, deluge, drown, engulf, inundate, overflow, submerge, submerse, swamp *Ant* drain

owing to *Syn* BECAUSE OF, due to, through, with

own *Syn* HAVE, enjoy, hold, possess

owner *Syn* PROPRIETOR, holder, possessor

own (up) *Syn* ADMIT, acknowledge, agree, allow, concede, confess, grant *Ant* deny

P

pabulum *Syn* FOOD (sense 2), aliment, nourishment, nutriment, pap, sustenance

pace *Syn* SPEED, headway, impetus, momentum, velocity

pacific · affording or promoting peace *Syn*
irenic, pacifist, pacifistic, peaceable, peaceful
Rel calm, placid, serene, tranquil *Ant* bellicose

pacifist *Syn* PACIFIC, irenic, pacifistic, peaceable, peaceful *Ant* bellicose

pacifistic *Syn* PACIFIC, irenic, pacifist, peaceable, peaceful *Ant* bellicose

pacify · to lessen the anger or agitation of *Syn*
appease, conciliate, disarm, mollify, placate,
propitiate *Rel* calm, comfort, console, content, quiet, soothe *Ant* anger, enrage, incense,
infuriate, madden, outrage

pack *vb* · to fill a limited space with more
than is practicable or fitting *Syn* cram, crowd,
ram, stuff, tamp *Rel* compact, consolidate

pack *n* *Syn* BUNDLE, bale, bunch, package,
packet, parcel

package *Syn* BUNDLE, bale, bunch, pack,
packet, parcel

packet *Syn* BUNDLE, bale, bunch, pack, package, parcel

pact *Syn* CONTRACT, bargain, cartel, compact,
concordat, convention, entente, treaty

pad *Syn* WALK, foot (it), hoof (it), leg (it),
step, traipse, tread

padding *Syn* EXAGGERATION, caricature,
coloring, elaboration, embellishment, embroidering, hyperbole, magnification, overstatement, stretching *Ant* understatement

pain · a bodily sensation that causes acute discomfort or suffering *Syn* ache, pang, stitch,
throe, twinge *Rel* agony, distress, passion,
suffering

painlessly *Syn* EASILY, effortlessly, facilely,
fluently, freely, handily, lightly, readily,
smoothly *Ant* arduously, laboriously

pains *Syn* EFFORT, exertion, trouble *Ant* ease

pair 1 · two things of the same or similar
kind that match or are considered together
Syn brace, couple, duo, twain, twosome *Rel*
span, yoke **2** *Syn* COUPLE, brace, yoke

palace *Syn* MANSION, castle, château, countryseat, estate, hacienda, hall, manor, manor
house, villa

palatable · agreeable or pleasant to the taste
Syn appetizing, flavorsome, relishing, sapid,
savory, tasty, toothsome *Rel* delectable, delicious, delightful, luscious *Ant* distasteful, unpalatable

palatial *Syn* LUXURIOUS, deluxe, lavish, luxuriant, opulent, plush, sumptuous *Ant* ascetic,
austere, humble, Spartan

palaver *vb* *Syn* CHAT, babble, blab, cackle,
chatter, converse, gab, gabble, gas, jabber,
jaw, patter, prate, prattle, rap, rattle, run on,
talk, twitter, visit

palaver *n* *Syn* CHAT, chatter, chitchat, gabfest,
gossip, rap, small talk, table talk, talk, tête-à-
tête

pale *adj* **1** · deficient in color or in intensity
of color *Syn* ashen, ashy, livid, pallid, wan
Rel ghastly, macabre *Ant* florid, flush, rubicund, ruddy, sanguine **2** · being weak and
thin in substance or in vital qualities *Syn*
anemic, bloodless *Rel* inane, insipid, jejune,
wishy-washy

pale *vb* *Syn* WHITEN, blanch, bleach, blench,
decolorize, dull, fade, wash out *Ant* blacken,
darken, deepen

pall *Syn* SATIATE, cloy, glut, gorge, sate, surfeit

palliate · to give a speciously fine appearance
to what is base, evil, or erroneous *Syn* extenuate, gloss, gloze, whiten, whitewash *Rel*
alleviate, lighten, mitigate, relieve

pallid *Syn* PALE (sense 1), ashen, ashy, livid,

wan *Ant* florid, flush, rubicund, ruddy, sanguine

palpable 1 *Syn* EVIDENT, apparent, clear, distinct, manifest, obvious, patent, plain **2** *Syn* PERCEPTIBLE, appreciable, detectable, discernible, distinguishable, sensible *Ant* impalpable, imperceptible, inappreciable, indistinguishable, insensible **3** *Syn* TANGIBLE, touchable *Ant* impalpable, intangible

palpate *Syn* TOUCH, feel, handle, paw

palpitate *Syn* PULSATE, beat, pulse, throb

palpitation *Syn* PULSATION, beat, pulse, throb

palter 1 *Syn* BARGAIN, chaffer, deal, dicker, haggle, horse-trade, negotiate **2** *Syn* LIE, equivocate, fib, prevaricate

paltry *Syn* PETTY, measly, picayune, picayunish, puny, trifling, trivial *Ant* gross, important, momentous

pamper *Syn* BABY, coddle, dandle, mollycoddle, nurse, spoil *Ant* abuse, ill-treat, ill-use, maltreat, mishandle, mistreat, misuse

pancake · a flat cake made from thin batter and cooked on both sides (as on a griddle) *Syn* flapjack, griddle cake, hotcake, slapjack *Rel* crepe (*or* crêpe), waffle

pandect *Syn* COMPENDIUM, aperçu, précis, sketch, survey, syllabus

pandemonium 1 *Syn* COMMOTION, bother, bustle, clatter, disturbance, furor, furore, fuss, hubbub, hullabaloo, hurly-burly, pother, row, ruckus, ruction, rumpus, shindy, squall, stew, stir, storm, to-do, tumult, turmoil, uproar, welter, whirl **2** *Syn* DIN, babel, clamor, hubbub, hullabaloo, racket, uproar *Ant* quiet

pander *Syn* CATER, purvey

panegyric *Syn* ENCOMIUM, citation, eulogy, tribute

pang *Syn* PAIN, ache, stitch, throe, twinge

panhandler *Syn* BEGGAR, mendicant

panic *Syn* FEAR, alarm, consternation, dismay, dread, fright, horror, terror, trepidation *Ant* fearlessness

panoramic *Syn* ENCYCLOPEDIC, compendious, complete, comprehensive, full, global, inclusive, in-depth, omnibus, universal

pant *Syn* AIM, aspire

pap *Syn* FOOD (sense 2), aliment, nourishment, nutriment, pabulum, sustenance

paper · a written or printed statement that is of value as a source of information or proof of a right, contention, or claim *Syn* document, instrument **2** *Syn* ESSAY, article, composition, theme

par *Syn* AVERAGE, norm, normal, standard

parable *Syn* ALLEGORY, fable

parade *n* **1** *Syn* DISPLAY, array, pomp **2** *Syn* PROCESSION, cavalcade, cortege, motorcade

parade *vb* *Syn* SHOW (sense 2), display, exhibit, expose, flaunt *Ant* disguise

paradise *Syn* ECSTASY, elation, euphoria, exhilaration, heaven, intoxication, rapture, rhapsody, transport *Ant* depression

paradox · an expression or revelation of an inner or inherent contradiction *Syn* anomaly, antinomy

paragon · a model of excellence or perfection *Syn* apotheosis, nonesuch, nonpareil

paragraph · one of the several and individually distinct statements of a discourse or instrument, each of which deals with a particular point or item *Syn* article, clause, count, plank, verse

parallel *n* **1** · one that corresponds to or closely resembles another *Syn* analogue, correlate, counterpart **2** *Syn* COMPARISON, collation, contrast **3** *Syn* EQUAL, coordinate, counterpart, equivalent, fellow, like, match, peer, rival

parallel *adj* *Syn* ALIKE, akin, analogous, comparable, correspondent, corresponding, like, matching, resembling, similar, such, suchlike *Ant* different, dissimilar, diverse, unlike

parallelism *Syn* SIMILARITY, alikeness, community, correspondence, likeness, resemblance, similitude *Ant* dissimilarity, unlikeness

paralyze *Syn* DAZE, bemuse, benumb, petrify, stun, stupefy

paramount *Syn* DOMINANT, predominant, preponderant, preponderating, sovereign *Ant* subordinate

parapet *Syn* BULWARK, bastion, breastwork, rampart

paraphernalia *Syn* EQUIPMENT, apparatus, gear, machinery, matériel, outfit, tackle

paraphrase *vb* · to express something (as a text or statement) in different words *Syn* rephrase, restate, reword, translate *Rel* summarize *Ant* quote

paraphrase *n* *Syn* TRANSLATION, metaphrase, version

parasite · a usually obsequious flatterer or self-seeker *Syn* bootlicker, favorite, hanger-on, leech, lickspittle, sponge, sponger, sycophant, toady *Rel* cringer, fawner, truckler

parboil *Syn* BOIL, seethe, simmer, stew

parcel *vb* *Syn* APPORTION, portion, prorate, ration

parcel *n* **1** *Syn* BUNDLE, bale, bunch, pack, package, packet **2** *Syn* GROUP, bunch, cluster, lot **3** *Syn* PART, detail, division, fraction, fragment, member, piece, portion, section, sector, segment *Ant* whole

parch *Syn* DRY, bake, dehydrate, desiccate *Ant* moisten, wet

pardon *n* · release from the guilt or penalty of an offense *Syn* absolution, amnesty, forgiveness, remission, remittal *Ant* penalty, punishment, retribution

pardon *vb* *Syn* EXCUSE, condone, forgive, remit *Ant* punish

pardonable *Syn* VENIAL, excusable, forgivable, remittable *Ant* inexcusable, mortal, unforgivable, unpardonable

pare 1 *Syn* CLIP, bob, crop, curtail, cut, cut back, dock, lop (off), nip, prune, shave, shear, snip, trim 2 *Syn* SKIN, decorticate, flay, peel

parentage *Syn* ANCESTRY, birth, blood, bloodline, breeding, descent, extraction, family tree, genealogy, line, lineage, origin, pedigree, stock, strain *Ant* issue, posterity, progeny, seed

par excellence *Syn* EXCELLENT, A1, bangup, banner, capital, classic, crackerjack, dandy, divine, fabulous, fine, first-class, first-rate, grand, great, groovy, heavenly, jim-dandy, keen, marvelous (*or* marvellous), mean, neat, nifty, noble, prime, sensational, splendid, stellar, sterling, superb, superior, superlative, supernal, swell, terrific, tip-top, top, top-notch, unsurpassed, wonderful *Ant* poor

pariah *Syn* OUTCAST, castaway, derelict, reprobate, untouchable

parochial *Syn* INSULAR, local, provincial, small-town

parody *n Syn* CARICATURE, burlesque, travesty

parody *vb Syn* CARICATURE, burlesque, travesty

paroxysm 1 *Syn* CONVULSION, cataclysm, storm, tempest, tumult, upheaval, uproar 2 *Syn* FIT, convulsion, spasm

parrot *Syn* REPEAT (sense 2), echo, quote

parry *Syn* DODGE, duck, fence, malinger, shirk, sidestep *Ant* face

parsimonious *Syn* STINGY, cheeseparing, close, closefisted, miserly, niggardly, pennypinching, penurious, tight, tightfisted *Ant* generous

part *n* · something less than the whole *Syn* detail, division, fraction, fragment, member, parcel, piece, portion, section, sector, segment *Ant* whole 2 *Syn* ROLE, capacity, function, job, place, position, purpose, task, work

part *adv Syn* PARTLY, incompletely, partially *Ant* completely, entirely, totally, wholly

part *vb Syn* SEPARATE, divide, divorce, sever, sunder *Ant* combine

partake *Syn* SHARE, participate

partaker *Syn* PARTICIPANT, participator, party, sharer *Ant* nonparticipant

partiality 1 *Syn* BIAS, favor, one-sidedness, partisanship, prejudice *Ant* impartiality, neutrality, objectivity, open-mindedness 2 *Syn* LIKING, appetite, fancy, favor, fondness, like, love, preference, relish, shine, taste, use *Ant* aversion, disfavor, dislike, distaste, hatred, loathing 3 *Syn* PREDILECTION, bias, prejudice, prepossession *Ant* aversion

partially *Syn* PARTLY, incompletely, part *Ant* completely, entirely, totally, wholly

participant · one who takes part in something *Syn* partaker, participator, party, sharer *Rel* actor *Ant* nonparticipant

participate *Syn* SHARE, partake

participator *Syn* PARTICIPANT, partaker, party, sharer *Ant* nonparticipant

particle · a tiny or insignificant amount, part, or piece *Syn* atom, bit, iota, jot, mite, smidgen, tittle, whit

parti-colored *Syn* VARIEGATED, checked, checkered, dappled, motley, piebald, pied, skewbald

particular *adj* 1 *Syn* CIRCUMSTANTIAL, detailed, itemized, minute, particularized *Ant* abridged, summary 2 *Syn* NICE, dainty, fastidious, finical, finicking, finicky, fussy, pernickety, persnickety, squeamish 3 *Syn* SELECTIVE, choosy (*or* choosey), picky *Ant* nonselective 4 *Syn* SINGLE, lone, separate, sole, solitary, unique *Ant* accompanied, conjugal, supported 5 *Syn* SPECIAL, especial, individual, specific

particular *n* 1 *Syn* FACT, datum, detail, nicety, particularity, point 2 *Syn* ITEM, detail

particularity *Syn* FACT, datum, detail, nicety, particular, point

particularized *Syn* CIRCUMSTANTIAL, detailed, itemized, minute, particular *Ant* abridged, summary

particularly *Syn* VERY, awful, awfully, beastly, deadly, especially, exceedingly, extra, extremely, far, frightfully, full, greatly, heavily, highly, hugely, jolly, mightily, mighty, mortally, most, much, rattling, real, right, so, something, super, terribly, too, whacking *Ant* little, negligibly, nominally, slightly

partisan 1 *Syn* FOLLOWER, adherent, convert, disciple, pupil, votary *Ant* leader 2 *Syn* ZEALOT, crusader, fanatic, militant

partisanship *Syn* BIAS, favor, one-sidedness, partiality, prejudice *Ant* impartiality, neutrality, objectivity, open-mindedness

partly · in some measure or degree *Syn* incompletely, part, partially *Rel* in part *Ant* completely, entirely, totally, wholly

partner 1 · one associated in action with another *Syn* ally, colleague, confederate, copartner *Ant* rival 2 *Syn* SPOUSE, consort, mate

party 1 *Syn* COMBINATION, bloc, combine, faction, ring 2 *Syn* COMPANY, band, troop, troupe 3 *Syn* FACTION, bloc, body, coalition, sect, set, side, wing 4 *Syn* PARTICIPANT, partaker, participator, sharer *Ant* nonparticipant

pass *vb* 1 · move or come to a termination or end *Syn* elapse, expire, pass away *Rel* depart, go, leave, quit, withdraw 2 *Syn* ENACT, lay down, legislate, make *Ant* repeal, rescind, revoke

pass *n* 1 *Syn* ATTEMPT, crack, endeavor, essay, fling, go, shot, stab, trial, try, whack 2 *Syn* CANYON, defile, flume, gap, gorge, gulch, gulf, notch, ravine 3 *Syn* JUNCTURE, contingency, crisis, emergency, exigency, pinch, strait **4** *Syn* WAY, artery, course, passage, route

passable *Syn* ADEQUATE, acceptable, all right, decent, fine, OK (*or* okay), respectable, satisfactory, tolerable *Ant* deficient, inadequate, lacking, unacceptable, unsatisfactory, wanting

passage **1** · a typically long narrow way connecting parts of a building *Syn* aisle, arcade, cloister, corridor, gallery, hall, hallway, passageway **2** *Syn* ADVANCE (sense 2), advancement, furtherance, going, headway, march, onrush, process, procession, progress, progression *Ant* recession, regression, retrogression **3** *Syn* STRAIT, channel, narrows, sound **4** *Syn* WAY, artery, course, pass, route

passageway *Syn* PASSAGE, aisle, arcade, cloister, corridor, gallery, hall, hallway

pass away *Syn* PASS, elapse, expire

passé *Syn* OBSOLETE, antiquated, archaic, dated, moth-eaten, outdated, out-of-date, outmoded, outworn

passing *n Syn* DEATH, decease, demise *Ant* life

passing *adj Syn* MOMENTARY, ephemeral, evanescent, flash, fleeting, fugitive, impermanent, short-lived, temporary, transient, transitory *Ant* enduring, eternal, everlasting, lasting, long-lived, permanent, perpetual

passion **1** · intense emotion compelling action *Syn* ardor, enthusiasm, fervor, zeal *Rel* ecstasy, rapture, transport **2** *Syn* DESIRE, appetite, lust, urge *Ant* distaste **3** *Syn* DISTRESS, agony, dolor, misery, suffering **4** *Syn* FEELING, affection, emotion, sentiment

passionate *Syn* FERVENT, ardent, blazing, burning, charged, emotional, fervid, feverish, fiery, flaming, glowing, hot-blooded, impassioned, red-hot, vehement, warm, warm-blooded *Ant* cold, cool, dispassionate, impassive, unemotional

passive **1** · receiving or enduring without offering resistance *Syn* acquiescent, nonresistant, resigned, tolerant, tolerating, unresistant, unresisting, yielding *Rel* forbearing, long-suffering, patient, uncomplaining *Ant* protesting, resistant, resisting, unyielding **2** *Syn* INACTIVE, idle, inert, supine *Ant* active, live

pass out *Syn* FAINT, black out, swoon *Ant* come around, come round, come to, revive

pass (over) *Syn* TRAVERSE, cover, crisscross, cross, cut (across), follow, go, proceed (along), travel

past *n* · the events or experience of former times *Syn* auld lang syne, history, yesterday, yesteryear, yore *Rel* bygone

past *prep Syn* BEYOND (sense 1), over *Ant* within

past *adj Syn* FORMER, erstwhile, late, old, onetime, sometime, whilom

past master *Syn* EXPERT, ace, adept, artist, authority, crackerjack, maestro, master, scholar, shark, virtuoso, whiz, wizard *Ant* amateur

pastoral *Syn* RURAL, bucolic, rustic *Ant* urban

pasture *Syn* FEED, graze, nourish *Ant* starve

pat **1** *Syn* OBSTINATE, adamant, adamantine, dogged, hard, hardened, hardheaded, hardhearted, headstrong, immovable, implacable, inflexible, mulish, obdurate, opinionated, ossified, peevish, pertinacious, perverse, pigheaded, rigid, self-willed, stubborn, unbending, uncompromising, unrelenting, unyielding, willful (*or* wilful) *Ant* acquiescent, agreeable, amenable, compliant, complying, flexible, pliable, pliant, relenting, yielding **2** *Syn* SEASONABLE, opportune, timely, well-timed *Ant* unseasonable

patch *Syn* MEND, rebuild, repair

patent **1** *Syn* EGREGIOUS, blatant, conspicuous, flagrant, glaring, gross, obvious, pronounced, rank, striking **2** *Syn* EVIDENT, apparent, clear, distinct, manifest, obvious, palpable, plain

pathetic *Syn* SAD (sense 2), depressing, dismal, drear, dreary, heartbreaking, heartrending, melancholy, saddening, sorry, tearful, teary *Ant* cheering, cheery, glad, happy

pathological *Syn* UNWHOLESOME, diseased, morbid, sickly *Ant* wholesome

patience · the power or capacity to endure without complaint something difficult or disagreeable *Syn* forbearance, longanimity, long-suffering, resignation *Rel* perseverance, persistence *Ant* impatience

patient *Syn* PERSISTENT, dogged, insistent, persevering, pertinacious, tenacious

patois *Syn* TERMINOLOGY, argot, cant, dialect, jargon, language, lingo, patter, slang, vocabulary

patrician *Syn* ARISTOCRAT, gentleperson, noble

patrimony *Syn* HERITAGE, birthright, inheritance

patron **1** *Syn* BENEFACTOR, donator, donor **2** *Syn* SPONSOR, angel, backer, guarantor, surety

patter *vb Syn* CHAT, babble, blab, cackle, chatter, converse, gab, gabble, gas, jabber, jaw, palaver, prate, prattle, rap, rattle, run on, talk, twitter, visit

patter *n Syn* TERMINOLOGY, argot, cant, dialect, jargon, language, lingo, patois, slang, vocabulary

pattern **1** *Syn* HABIT, custom, fashion, practice, trick, way, wont **2** *Syn* MODEL, beau ideal, example, exemplar, ideal, mirror, standard **3** *Syn* FIGURE, design, device, motif

paucity *Syn* DEFICIENCY, dearth, deficit, failure, famine, inadequacy, insufficiency, lack, poverty, scantiness, scarceness, scarcity, shortage, want *Ant* abundance, adequacy, amplitude, plenitude, plenty, sufficiency

pause · a momentary halt in an activity *Syn* break, breath, breather, interruption, lull, recess *Rel* time-out

paw *Syn* TOUCH, feel, handle, palpate

pawn *Syn* PLEDGE, earnest, hostage, token

pay *vb* · to give money or its equivalent in return for something *Syn* compensate, indemnify, recompense, reimburse, remunerate, repay, satisfy

pay *n Syn* WAGE, emolument, fee, hire, salary, stipend

paying · yielding a profit *Syn* gainful, lucrative, profitable, remunerative

peace **1** *Syn* CALM, calmness, hush, peacefulness, placidity, quiet, quietness, quietude, repose, restfulness, sereneness, serenity, still, stillness, tranquillity (*or* tranquility) *Ant* bustle, commotion, hubbub, hurly-burly, pandemonium, tumult, turmoil, uproar **2** *Syn* TRUCE, armistice, cease-fire

peaceable *Syn* PACIFIC, irenic, pacifist, pacifistic, peaceful *Ant* bellicose

peaceful **1** *Syn* CALM, halcyon, placid, serene, tranquil *Ant* agitated, stormy **2** *Syn* PACIFIC, irenic, pacifist, pacifistic, peaceable *Ant* bellicose

peacefulness *Syn* CALM, calmness, hush, peace, placidity, quiet, quietness, quietude, repose, restfulness, sereneness, serenity, still, stillness, tranquillity (*or* tranquility) *Ant* bustle, commotion, hubbub, hurly-burly, pandemonium, tumult, turmoil, uproar

peacemaker *Syn* MEDIATOR, arbiter, arbitrator, conciliator, go-between, intercessor, intermediary, interposer, middleman

peak **1** *Syn* MOUNTAIN, alp, mesa, mount, volcano **2** *Syn* SUMMIT, acme, apex, apogee, climax, culmination, meridian, pinnacle, zenith

peculiar **1** *Syn* CHARACTERISTIC, distinctive, individual **2** *Syn* STRANGE, curious, eccentric, erratic, odd, outlandish, quaint, queer, singular, unique *Ant* familiar

peculiarity *Syn* CHARACTERISTIC, attribute, character, feature, mark, point, property, quality, trait

pecuniary *Syn* FINANCIAL, fiscal, monetary

pedagogue *Syn* TEACHER, educator, instructor, preceptor, schoolteacher

pedantic · too narrowly concerned with scholarly matters *Syn* academic, bookish, scholastic *Rel* erudite, learned

pedestrian *Syn* BORING, drab, dreary, dry, dull, flat, heavy, humdrum, jading, leaden, monotonous, ponderous, stodgy, stuffy, stupid, tame, tedious, tiresome, tiring, unanimated, uninteresting, wearisome, weary, wearying *Ant* absorbing, engaging, engrossing, gripping, interesting, intriguing, involving

pedigree *Syn* ANCESTRY, birth, blood, bloodline, breeding, descent, extraction, family tree, genealogy, line, lineage, origin, parentage, stock, strain *Ant* issue, posterity, progeny, seed

peek *Syn* LOOK, glance, glimpse, peep, sight, view

peel *n Syn* SKIN, bark, hide, pelt, rind

peel *vb Syn* SKIN, decorticate, flay, pare

peep *vb Syn* CHIRP, cheep, chirrup, chitter, tweet, twitter

peep *n* **1** *Syn* CHIRP, cheep, chirrup, chitter, tweet, twitter **2** *Syn* LOOK, glance, glimpse, peek, sight, view

peer *n Syn* EQUAL, coordinate, counterpart, equivalent, fellow, like, match, parallel, rival

peer *vb* **1** *Syn* GAPE, gawk, gaze, goggle, rubberneck, stare **2** *Syn* GAZE, gape, glare, gloat, stare

peerless *Syn* SUPREME, incomparable, preeminent, superlative, surpassing, transcendent

peeve *Syn* IRRITATE, aggravate, exasperate, nettle, provoke, rile

peeving *Syn* ANNOYING, aggravating, bothersome, disturbing, exasperating, frustrating, galling, irksome, irritating, maddening, nettling, pesty, rankling, riling, vexatious, vexing

peevish **1** *Syn* IRRITABLE, fractious, fretful, huffy, pettish, petulant, querulous, snappish, waspish *Ant* easygoing **2** *Syn* OBSTINATE, adamant, adamantine, dogged, hard, hardened, hardheaded, hardhearted, headstrong, immovable, implacable, inflexible, mulish, obdurate, opinionated, ossified, pat, pertinacious, perverse, pigheaded, rigid, self-willed, stubborn, unbending, uncompromising, unrelenting, unyielding, willful (*or* wilful) *Ant* acquiescent, agreeable, amenable, compliant, complying, flexible, pliable, pliant, relenting, yielding

peg (away) *Syn* LABOR, drudge, endeavor, grub, hump, hustle, moil, plod, plow, plug, slave, slog, strain, strive, struggle, sweat, toil, travail, work *Ant* dabble, fiddle (around), fool (around), mess (around), putter (around)

pejorative *Syn* DEROGATORY, depreciative, depreciatory, disparaging, slighting

pelagic *Syn* MARINE (sense 1), maritime, oceanic

pell-mell *Syn* MESSY, chaotic, cluttered, confused, disarranged, disarrayed, disheveled (*or* dishevelled), disordered, disorderly, higgledy-piggledy, hugger-mugger, jumbled, littered, messed, muddled, mussed, mussy, rumpled, sloppy, topsy-turvy, tousled, tumbled, unkempt, untidy, upside-down *Ant* neat, ordered, orderly, organized, shipshape, snug, tidied, tidy, trim

pellucid *Syn* CLEAR (sense 1), diaphanous, limpid, lucid, translucent, transparent *Ant* confused, turbid

pelt *vb Syn* HURRY (sense 2), barrel, bolt, bowl, breeze, career, course, dash, fly, hasten, hotfoot (it), hump, hurtle, hustle, race, rip, rocket, run, rush, rustle, scoot, scurry, scuttle, shoot, speed, step (along), tear, trot, whirl, whisk, zip, zoom *Ant* crawl, creep, poke

pelt *n Syn* SKIN, bark, hide, peel, rind

pen *vb Syn* ENCLOSE, cage, coop, corral, envelop, fence, wall

pen *n Syn* JAIL, brig, guardroom, hoosegow, jug, lockup, penitentiary, prison, stockade

penal *Syn* PUNITIVE, castigating, chastening, chastising, correcting, correctional, corrective, disciplinary, disciplining, penalizing

penalize · to inflict a penalty on *Syn* amerce, fine, mulct *Rel* chasten, correct, discipline, punish

penalizing *Syn* PUNITIVE, castigating, chastening, chastising, correcting, correctional, corrective, disciplinary, disciplining, penal

penalty **1** *Syn* DISADVANTAGE, drawback, handicap, liability, minus, strike *Ant* advantage, asset, edge, plus **2** *Syn* FINE, damages, forfeit, forfeiture, mulct

penchant *Syn* LEANING, flair, proclivity, propensity *Ant* distaste

pendant **1** · an ornament worn on a chain around the neck or wrist *Syn* bangle, charm, lavalier *Rel* locket, teardrop **2** *Syn* FLAG, banner, color, ensign, jack, pennant, pennon, standard, streamer

pendent *Syn* SUSPENDED, pendulous

pending *Syn* FORTHCOMING, approaching, coming, imminent, impending, nearing, oncoming, upcoming *Ant* late, recent

pendulate *Syn* SWING (sense 2), fluctuate, oscillate, sway, undulate, vibrate, waver

pendulous *Syn* SUSPENDED, pendent

penetrate **1** *Syn* ENTER (sense 1), pierce, probe *Ant* issue from **2** *Syn* PERMEATE, impenetrate, impregnate, interpenetrate, pervade, saturate

penetration *Syn* DISCERNMENT, acumen, discrimination, insight, perception

penitence · regret for sin or wrongdoing *Syn* attrition, compunction, contrition, remorse, repentance *Rel* anguish, regret, sorrow

penitent *Syn* GUILTY, ashamed, contrite, hangdog, remorseful, repentant, shamed, shamefaced *Ant* impenitent, remorseless, shameless, unashamed, unrepentant

penitentiary *Syn* JAIL, brig, guardroom, hoosegow, jug, lockup, pen, prison, stockade

pen name *Syn* PSEUDONYM, alias, incognito, nom de guerre, nom de plume

pennant *Syn* FLAG, banner, color, ensign, jack, pendant, pennon, standard, streamer

penniless *Syn* POOR, destitute, impecunious, indigent, necessitous, needy, poverty-stricken *Ant* rich

pennon *Syn* FLAG, banner, color, ensign, jack, pendant, pennant, standard, streamer

penny-pinching *Syn* STINGY, cheeseparing, close, closefisted, miserly, niggardly, parsimonious, penurious, tight, tightfisted *Ant* generous

pensive **1** *Syn* CONTEMPLATIVE, meditative, melancholy, reflective, ruminant, thoughtful *Ant* unreflective **2** *Syn* THOUGHTFUL (sense 1), contemplative, meditative, reflective, speculative *Ant* thoughtless

penumbra *Syn* SHADE, adumbration, shadow, umbra, umbrage

penurious *Syn* STINGY, cheeseparing, close, closefisted, miserly, niggardly, parsimonious, penny-pinching, tight, tightfisted *Ant* generous

penury *Syn* POVERTY, destitution, indigence, privation, want *Ant* riches

peon *Syn* SLAVE (sense 2), drudge, drudger, grubber, laborer, plugger, slogger, toiler, worker *Ant* freeman

pepper **1** *Syn* SCATTER (sense 2), bestrew, dot, sow, spray, sprinkle, strew **2** *Syn* SPOT, blotch, dapple, dot, fleck, freckle, marble, mottle, speck, speckle, splotch, sprinkle, stipple

peppery *Syn* SPIRITED, fiery, gingery, highspirited, mettlesome, spunky *Ant* spiritless

pep (up) *Syn* ANIMATE, brace, energize, enliven, fire, invigorate, jazz (up), liven (up), quicken, stimulate, vitalize, vivify *Ant* damp, dampen, deaden, dull

perambulation *Syn* WALK, constitutional, ramble, range, saunter, stroll, turn

per capita *Syn* APIECE, all, each

perceive *Syn* SEE (sense 1), behold, contemplate, descry, discern, espy, note, notice, observe, remark, survey, view

percentage *Syn* PROBABILITY, chance, odds

percept *Syn* SENSATION (sense 1), image, sense-datum, sensum

perceptible · able to be perceived by a sense or by the mind *Syn* appreciable, detectable, discernible, distinguishable, palpable, sensible *Rel* audible, observable, tangible, visible *Ant* impalpable, imperceptible, inappreciable, indistinguishable, insensible

perception **1** *Syn* COMPREHENSION, appreciation, apprehension, grasp, grip, understanding **2** *Syn* DISCERNMENT, acumen, discrimination, insight, penetration

perch *Syn* ALIGHT, land, light, roost, settle, touch down *Ant* take off

perchance *Syn* PERHAPS, conceivably, maybe, mayhap, possibly

percolate *Syn* EXUDE, bleed, ooze, seep, strain, sweat, weep

percussion *Syn* IMPACT, clash, collision, concussion, impingement, jar, jolt, shock

perdurable *Syn* LASTING, durable, permanent, perpetual, stable *Ant* fleeting

peremptoriness *Syn* ARROGANCE, haughtiness, imperiousness, loftiness, lordliness, masterfulness, pompousness, presumptuousness, pretense (*or* pretence), pretension, pretentiousness, self-importance, superciliousness, superiority *Ant* humility, modesty

peremptory 1 *Syn* ARROGANT, cavalier, haughty, highfalutin, high-handed, high-hat, imperious, important, lofty, lordly, masterful, overweening, pompous, presumptuous, pretentious, supercilious, superior, uppish, uppity *Ant* humble, modest 2 *Syn* BOSSY, authoritarian, autocratic, despotic, dictatorial, domineering, imperious, masterful, overbearing, tyrannical, tyrannous 3 *Syn* MANDATORY, compulsory, forced, imperative, incumbent, involuntary, necessary, nonelective, obligatory, required *Ant* elective, optional, voluntary 4 *Syn* MASTERFUL, domineering, imperative, imperious

perennial *Syn* CONTINUAL, constant, continuous, incessant, perpetual, unremitting *Ant* intermittent

perfect *n* · not lacking or faulty in any particular *Syn* entire, intact, whole *Rel* absolute, pure, sheer, simple *Ant* imperfect

perfect *vb* *Syn* UNFOLD, develop, elaborate, evolve

perfidious *Syn* FAITHLESS, disloyal, false, traitorous, treacherous *Ant* faithful

perfidy *Syn* BETRAYAL, disloyalty, double cross, faithlessness, falseness, falsity, infidelity, sellout, treachery, treason, unfaithfulness

perforate · to pierce through so as to leave a hole *Syn* bore, drill, prick, punch, puncture *Rel* enter, penetrate, pierce, probe

perform 1 · to carry out or into effect *Syn* accomplish, achieve, discharge, effect, execute, fulfill *Rel* attain, compass, gain, reach 2 *Syn* FUNCTION, act, serve, work

performer *Syn* ACTOR, impersonator, mime, mimic, mummer, player, thespian, trouper

perfume *Syn* FRAGRANCE, bouquet, incense, redolence *Ant* stench, stink

perfumed *Syn* FRAGRANT, ambrosial, aromatic, redolent, savory, scented, sweet *Ant* fetid, foul, malodorous, noisome, putrid, rancid, rank, reeking, reeky, smelly, stinking, stinky, strong

perhaps · it is possible *Syn* conceivably, maybe, mayhap, perchance, possibly *Rel* likely, probably

peril 1 *Syn* DANGER (sense 1), hazard, menace, pitfall, risk, threat, trouble *Ant* safeness, safety, security 2 *Syn* DANGER (sense 2), distress, endangerment, imperilment, jeopardy, risk, trouble *Ant* safeness, safety, security

perilous *Syn* DANGEROUS, hazardous, precarious, risky *Ant* safe, secure

perimeter *Syn* CIRCUMFERENCE, circuit, compass, periphery

period *Syn* AGE (sense 3), day, epoch, era, time

periodic *Syn* INTERMITTENT, alternate, recurrent *Ant* continual, incessant

periodical *Syn* JOURNAL, magazine, newspaper, organ, review

peripatetic *Syn* ITINERANT, ambulant, ambulatory, nomadic, vagrant

periphery *Syn* CIRCUMFERENCE, circuit, compass, perimeter

periphrasis *Syn* VERBIAGE, circumlocution, pleonasm, redundancy, tautology

permanent *Syn* LASTING, durable, perdurable, perpetual, stable *Ant* fleeting

permeate · to pass or cause to pass through every part of a thing *Syn* impenetrate, impregnate, interpenetrate, penetrate, pervade, saturate *Rel* imbue, infuse, ingrain

permissible · that may be permitted *Syn* admissible, allowable, licensable *Rel* acceptable, bearable, endurable, tolerable *Ant* banned, barred, forbidden, impermissible, inadmissible, interdicted, prohibited, proscribed

permission · the approval by someone in authority for the doing of something *Syn* allowance, authorization, clearance, concurrence, consent, granting, leave, license (*or* licence), sanction, sufferance *Rel* imprimatur, seal, signature, stamp *Ant* interdiction, prohibition, proscription

permit *Syn* LET, allow, leave, suffer

permutation *Syn* CHANGE (sense 2), alternation, mutation, vicissitude

pernicious *Syn* HARMFUL, adverse, bad, baleful, baneful, damaging, deleterious, detrimental, evil, hurtful, ill, injurious, mischievous, noxious, prejudicial *Ant* harmless, innocent, innocuous, inoffensive, safe

pernickety *Syn* NICE, dainty, fastidious, finical, finicking, finicky, fussy, particular, persnickety, squeamish

perpendicular 1 *Syn* ERECT, plumb, raised, standing, upright, upstanding, vertical *Ant* flat, recumbent 2 *Syn* VERTICAL, plumb *Ant* horizontal

perpetual 1 *Syn* CONTINUAL, constant, continuous, incessant, perennial, unremitting *Ant* intermittent 2 *Syn* LASTING, durable, perdurable, permanent, stable *Ant* fleeting

perplex *Syn* PUZZLE, bewilder, confound, distract, dumbfound, mystify, nonplus

perquisite 1 *Syn* BONUS, dividend, extra, gratuity, gravy, lagniappe, tip 2 *Syn* RIGHT, appanage, birthright, prerogative, privilege

persecute 1 *Syn* AFFLICT, agonize, bedevil, curse, harrow, martyr, plague, rack, torment, torture 2 *Syn* WRONG, aggrieve, oppress

persevere · to continue despite difficulties, opposition, or discouragement *Syn* carry on, persist *Rel* hang on

persevering *Syn* PERSISTENT, dogged, insistent, patient, pertinacious, tenacious

persiflage *Syn* BANTER, chaff, give-and-take, jesting, joshing, raillery, repartee

persist 1 *Syn* CONTINUE, abide, endure, last
2 *Syn* PERSEVERE, carry on

persistence *Syn* CONTINUATION, continuance,
duration, endurance, subsistence *Ant* ending,
termination

persistent · continuing despite difficulties,
opposition, or discouragement *Syn* dogged,
insistent, patient, persevering, pertinacious,
tenacious *Rel* assured, certain, dedicated, determined, firm, intent, positive, resolute, resolved, single-minded, sure

persnickety *Syn* NICE, dainty, fastidious, finical, finicking, finicky, fussy, particular, pernickety, squeamish

person *Syn* ENTITY, being, creature, individual

personality *Syn* DISPOSITION, character, complexion, individuality, temper, temperament

personalize *Syn* EMBODY (sense 2), epitomize, incarnate, manifest, materialize, personify, substantiate

personification *Syn* EMBODIMENT, epitome,
incarnation, manifestation

personify *Syn* EMBODY (sense 2), epitomize,
incarnate, manifest, materialize, personalize,
substantiate

perspicacious *Syn* SHREWD, astute, sagacious

perspicuous *Syn* CLEAR (sense 2), lucid *Ant*
abstruse, unintelligible

persuade · to cause (someone) to agree with a
belief or course of action by using arguments
or earnest request *Syn* argue, convince, get,
induce, move, prevail (on *or* upon), satisfy,
talk (into), win (over) *Rel* cajole, coax, exhort, urge

persuasion 1 *Syn* OPINION, belief, conviction, sentiment, view 2 *Syn* RELIGION,
church, communion, creed, denomination,
faith, sect

persuasive *Syn* COGENT, compelling, conclusive, convincing, decisive, effective,
forceful, satisfying, strong, telling *Ant* inconclusive, indecisive, ineffective, unconvincing

pert 1 *Syn* FLIPPANT, facetious, flip, smart,
smart-alecky (*or* smart-aleck) *Ant* earnest,
sincere 2 *Syn* SAUCY, arch

pertain *Syn* BEAR (sense 3), appertain, apply,
belong, relate

pertinacious 1 *Syn* OBSTINATE, adamant, adamantine, dogged, hard, hardened,
hardheaded, hardhearted, headstrong, immovable, implacable, inflexible, mulish, obdurate, opinionated, ossified, pat, peevish,
perverse, pigheaded, rigid, self-willed, stubborn, unbending, uncompromising, unrelenting, unyielding, willful (*or* wilful) *Ant*
acquiescent, agreeable, amenable, compliant,
complying, flexible, pliable, pliant, relenting,
yielding 2 *Syn* PERSISTENT, dogged, insistent, patient, persevering, tenacious

pertinent · having to do with the matter at
hand *Syn* applicable, apposite, apropos, germane, material, pointed, relative, relevant
Rel appropriate, apt, fit, fitting, suitable *Ant*
extraneous, immaterial, inapplicable, irrelevant, pointless

pertness *Syn* EFFRONTERY, audacity, brashness, brass, brassiness, brazenness, cheek,
cheekiness, chutzpah, gall, nerve, nerviness,
presumption, presumptuousness, sauce, sauciness, temerity

perturb *Syn* DISCOMPOSE, agitate, disquiet,
disturb, flurry, fluster, upset

perturbing *Syn* TROUBLESOME, discomforting, discomposing, disquieting, distressing,
disturbing, troubling, troublous, unsettling,
upsetting, worrisome *Ant* reassuring, untroublesome

pervade *Syn* PERMEATE, impenetrate, impregnate, interpenetrate, penetrate, saturate

perverse 1 *Syn* CORRUPT, debased, debauched, decadent, degenerate, degraded,
demoralized, depraved, dissipated, dissolute,
perverted, reprobate, warped *Ant* uncorrupted 2 *Syn* OBSTINATE, adamant, adamantine, dogged, hard, hardened, hardheaded,
hardhearted, headstrong, immovable, implacable, inflexible, mulish, obdurate, opinionated, ossified, pat, peevish, pertinacious,
pigheaded, rigid, self-willed, stubborn, unbending, uncompromising, unrelenting, unyielding, willful (*or* wilful) *Ant* acquiescent,
agreeable, amenable, compliant, complying,
flexible, pliable, pliant, relenting, yielding
3 *Syn* CONTRARY, balky, froward, perverse,
restive, wayward *Ant* complaisant, good-natured

pervert *Syn* DEBASE, corrupt, debauch, deprave, vitiate *Ant* amend (*morals, character*),
elevate (*taste, way of life*)

perverted 1 *Syn* CORRUPT, debased, debauched, decadent, degenerate, degraded,
demoralized, depraved, dissipated, dissolute,
perverse, reprobate, warped *Ant* uncorrupted
2 *Syn* DEBASED, corrupted, debauched, depraved, vitiated

pessimistic *Syn* CYNICAL, misanthropic

pester *Syn* WORRY, annoy, harass, harry,
plague, tantalize, tease

pestilent 1 *Syn* DEADLY, baleful, deathly, fatal, fell, killer, lethal, mortal, murderous, vital *Ant* healthful, healthy, nonfatal, nonlethal,
wholesome 2 *Syn* POISONOUS, mephitic,
miasmal, miasmatic, miasmic, pestilential,
toxic, venomous, virulent *Ant* nonpoisonous,
nontoxic, nonvenomous

pestilential *Syn* POISONOUS, mephitic, miasmal, miasmatic, miasmic, pestilent, toxic,
venomous, virulent *Ant* nonpoisonous, nontoxic, nonvenomous

pesty *Syn* ANNOYING, aggravating, bothersome, disturbing, exasperating, frustrating,
galling, irksome, irritating, maddening, net-

tling, peeving, rankling, riling, vexatious, vexing

pet *vb Syn* CARESS, cosset, cuddle, dandle, fondle

pet *n Syn* FAVORITE, darling, minion, preference

petition *n Syn* PRAYER, appeal, plea, suit

petition *vb Syn* PRAY, appeal, plead, sue

petitioner *Syn* SUPPLICANT, pleader, solicitor, suitor, suppliant

petrify 1 *Syn* DAZE, bemuse, benumb, paralyze, stun, stupefy 2 *Syn* HARDEN (sense 1), cake, indurate, solidify *Ant* soften

pettish *Syn* IRRITABLE, fractious, fretful, huffy, peevish, petulant, querulous, snappish, waspish *Ant* easygoing

petty · being often contemptibly insignificant or unimportant *Syn* measly, paltry, picayune, picayunish, puny, trifling, trivial *Rel* diminutive, little, minute, small *Ant* gross, important, momentous

petulant *Syn* IRRITABLE, fractious, fretful, huffy, peevish, pettish, querulous, snappish, waspish *Ant* easygoing

phantasm 1 *Syn* FANCY, daydream, dream, fantasy, nightmare, phantasy, vision *Ant* reality 2 *Syn* GHOST, apparition, bogey, phantom, poltergeist, shade, shadow, specter (*or* spectre), spirit, spook, vision, wraith

phantasy *Syn* FANCY, daydream, dream, fantasy, nightmare, phantasm, vision *Ant* reality

phantom *Syn* GHOST, apparition, bogey, phantasm, poltergeist, shade, shadow, specter (*or* spectre), spirit, spook, vision, wraith

pharmaceutical *Syn* DRUG, biologic, medicinal, simple

pharmacist *Syn* DRUGGIST, apothecary, chemist

phase · one of the possible ways of viewing or being presented to view *Syn* angle, aspect, facet, side *Rel* condition, posture, situation, state

phased *Syn* GRADUAL, gradational, incremental, piecemeal, step-by-step *Ant* sudden

phenomenal 1 *Syn* EXCEPTIONAL, extraordinary, unusual, unwonted *Ant* average, common 2 *Syn* MATERIAL, corporeal, objective, physical, sensible *Ant* immaterial

phenomenon *Syn* WONDER (sense 1), marvel, miracle, prodigy

philanthropic *Syn* CHARITABLE, altruistic, benevolent, eleemosynary, humane, humanitarian *Ant* uncharitable

philanthropy *Syn* CONTRIBUTION, alms, benefaction, beneficence, charity, donation

philippic *Syn* TIRADE, diatribe, jeremiad *Ant* eulogy

phlegm *Syn* IMPASSIVITY, apathy, stoicism, stolidity

phlegmatic *Syn* IMPASSIVE, apathetic, stoic, stolid *Ant* responsive

phony *Syn* COUNTERFEIT, bogus, fake, pinch-

beck, pseudo, sham, spurious *Ant* bona fide, genuine

photograph *Syn* IMAGE, effigy, icon, mask, portrait, statue

phrase *n* · a group of words which, taken together, express a notion and may be used as a part of a sentence *Syn* expression, idiom, locution

phrase *vb* · to convey in appropriate or telling terms *Syn* articulate, clothe, couch, express, formulate, put, say, state, word *Rel* craft, frame

phraseology *Syn* LANGUAGE (sense 2), diction, phrasing, style, vocabulary

phrasing *Syn* LANGUAGE (sense 2), diction, phraseology, style, vocabulary

physic *Syn* REMEDY, cure, medicament, medication, medicine, specific

physical 1 *Syn* BODILY, corporal, corporeal, somatic 2 *Syn* MATERIAL, corporeal, objective, phenomenal, sensible

physiognomy *Syn* FACE, countenance, mug, puss, visage

physique · bodily makeup or type *Syn* build, constitution, habit *Rel* body

picayune *Syn* PETTY, measly, paltry, picayunish, puny, trifling, trivial *Ant* gross, important, momentous

picayunish *Syn* PETTY, measly, paltry, picayune, puny, trifling, trivial *Ant* gross, important, momentous

pick *vb Syn* CHOOSE, cull, elect, opt, prefer, select, single *Ant* eschew, reject

pick *n Syn* ELITE, best, choice, cream, elect, fat, flower, prime, upper crust

picked *Syn* SELECT, elect, exclusive *Ant* indiscriminate

pickle *Syn* PREDICAMENT, dilemma, fix, jam, plight, quandary, scrape

pick up *Syn* BUY, purchase, take

picky *Syn* SELECTIVE, choosy (*or* choosey), particular *Ant* nonselective

picnic *Syn* CINCH, breeze, child's play, duck soup, pushover, snap *Ant* chore, headache, labor

pictorial *Syn* GRAPHIC, picturesque, vivid

picture *n Syn* MOVIE (sense 1), film, motion, moving picture, picture

picture *vb Syn* REPRESENT, delineate, depict, limn, portray

pictures *Syn* MOVIE (sense 2), cinema, film, motion, pictures, screen

picturesque *Syn* GRAPHIC, pictorial, vivid

piebald *Syn* VARIEGATED, checked, checkered, dappled, motley, parti-colored, pied, skewbald

piece *vb Syn* BUILD, assemble, construct, erect, fabricate, make, make up, put up, raise, rear, set up *Ant* disassemble, dismantle, take down

piece *n Syn* PART, detail, division, fraction, fragment, member, parcel, portion, section, sector, segment *Ant* whole

piecemeal 1 *Syn* APART, asunder *Ant* together 2 *Syn* GRADUAL, gradational, incremental, phased, step-by-step *Ant* sudden

pied *Syn* VARIEGATED, checked, checkered, dappled, motley, parti-colored, piebald, skewbald

pier 1 *Syn* BUTTRESS, abutment 2 *Syn* WHARF, berth, dock, jetty, levee, quay, slip

pierce *Syn* ENTER (sense 1), penetrate, probe *Ant* issue from

piety 1 *Syn* FIDELITY, allegiance, devotion, fealty, loyalty *Ant* faithlessness, perfidy 2 *Syn* HOLINESS, blessedness, devoutness, godliness, piousness, sainthood, saintliness, saintship, sanctity *Ant* godlessness, impiety, ungodliness, unholiness

pigeon *Syn* DUPE, chump, gull, sap, sucker, tool

pigeonhole *Syn* ASSORT, classify, sort

pigheaded *Syn* OBSTINATE, adamant, adamantine, dogged, hard, hardened, hardheaded, hardhearted, headstrong, immovable, implacable, inflexible, mulish, obdurate, opinionated, ossified, pat, peevish, pertinacious, perverse, rigid, self-willed, stubborn, unbending, uncompromising, unrelenting, unyielding, willful (*or* wilful) *Ant* acquiescent, agreeable, amenable, compliant, complying, flexible, pliable, pliant, relenting, yielding

pigment · a substance used to color other materials *Syn* color, coloring, dye, dyestuff, stain, tincture *Rel* cast, hue, shade, tinge, tint, tone

pilaster *Syn* PILLAR, column

pile *vb Syn* HEAP, bank, cock, mass, shock, stack

pile *n Syn* HEAP, bank, cock, mass, shock, stack

pilfer *Syn* STEAL, cop, filch, lift, pinch, purloin, snitch, swipe

pilgrimage *Syn* JOURNEY, cruise, excursion, expedition, jaunt, tour, trip, voyage

pill · a small mass containing medicine to be taken orally *Syn* capsule, lozenge, tablet *Rel* drug, medication, pharmaceutical, specific

pillage *Syn* RAVAGE, despoil, devastate, sack, spoliate, waste

pillar · a firm upright support for a superstructure *Syn* column, pilaster

pilot *Syn* GUIDE, engineer, lead, steer *Ant* misguide

pimple *Syn* ABSCESS, boil, carbuncle, furuncle, pustule

pinch *n Syn* JUNCTURE, contingency, crisis, emergency, exigency, pass, strait

pinch *vb Syn* STEAL, cop, filch, lift, pilfer, purloin, snitch, swipe

pinchbeck *Syn* COUNTERFEIT, bogus, fake, phony, pseudo, sham, spurious *Ant* bona fide, genuine

pinched *Syn* HAGGARD, cadaverous, careworn, wasted, worn

pinch hitter *Syn* SUBSTITUTE, backup, relief, replacement, reserve, stand-in, sub

pine *Syn* LONG, hanker, hunger, thirst, yearn

pinnacle *Syn* SUMMIT, acme, apex, apogee, climax, culmination, meridian, peak, zenith

pious 1 *Syn* HOLY (sense 1), devout, godly, religious, sainted, saintly *Ant* faithless, godless, impious, irreligious, ungodly, unholy 2 *Syn* FAITHFUL, constant, devoted, fast, good, loyal, staunch (*or* stanch), steadfast, steady, true, true-blue *Ant* disloyal, faithless, false, fickle, inconstant, perfidious, recreant, traitorous, treacherous, unfaithful, untrue

piousness *Syn* HOLINESS, blessedness, devoutness, godliness, piety, sainthood, saintliness, saintship, sanctity *Ant* godlessness, impiety, ungodliness, unholiness

piousness *Syn* HYPOCRISY, cant, dissembling, dissimulation, insincerity, sanctimoniousness *Ant* genuineness, sincerity

pip *Syn* JIM-DANDY, beauty, corker, crackerjack, dandy, knockout, nifty

pipe *n Syn* CASK, barrel, firkin, hogshead, keg, puncheon

pipe *vb Syn* CHANNEL, channelize, conduct, direct, funnel, siphon

piping *Syn* SHRILL, acute, high-pitched, screeching, shrieking, squeaking, squeaky, treble, whistling *Ant* bass, deep, low, throaty

piquant *Syn* PUNGENT, poignant, racy, snappy, spicy *Ant* bland

pique *n Syn* OFFENSE (sense 1), dudgeon, huff, resentment, umbrage

pique *vb* 1 *Syn* PRIDE, plume, preen 2 *Syn* PROVOKE, excite, galvanize, quicken, stimulate

piquing *Syn* PROVOCATIVE, exciting, inciting, instigating, provoking, stimulating

pirate · a robber on the high seas *Syn* buccaneer, corsair, freebooter, privateer

pirouette *Syn* TURN (sense 1), circle, eddy, gyrate, revolve, rotate, spin, swirl, twirl, wheel, whirl

pitch 1 *Syn* PLUNGE, dive 2 *Syn* THROW, cast, fling, hurl, sling, toss

piteous *Syn* PITIFUL, pitiable *Ant* cruel

pitfall *Syn* DANGER (sense 1), hazard, menace, peril, risk, threat, trouble *Ant* safeness, safety, security

pith 1 *Syn* CRUX, core, gist, heart, nub, pivot 2 *Syn* SUBSTANCE, burden, core, gist, purport

pithily *Syn* SUCCINCTLY, briefly, compactly, concisely, crisply, laconically, summarily, tersely *Ant* diffusely, long-windedly, verbosely, wordily

pithy *Syn* CONCISE, compendious, laconic, succinct, summary, terse *Ant* redundant

pitiable 1 *Syn* CONTEMPTIBLE, beggarly, cheap, despicable, scurvy, shabby, sorry *Ant* admirable, estimable, formidable 2 *Syn* PITIFUL, piteous *Ant* cruel

pitiful · arousing or deserving pity *Syn* piteous, pitiable *Rel* affecting, moving, pathetic, touching *Ant* cruel

pittance *Syn* RATION, allowance, dole

pity *Syn* SYMPATHY, commiseration, compassion, condolence, empathy, ruth

pivot *Syn* CRUX, core, gist, heart, nub, pith

pivotal 1 *Syn* CENTRAL, focal 2 *Syn* CRUCIAL, critical, key, vital

pixie *also* **pixy** *Syn* FAIRY, brownie, elf, fay, sprite

placard *Syn* ANNOUNCE, advertise, blaze, broadcast, declare, enunciate, post, proclaim, promulgate, publicize, publish, sound

placate *Syn* PACIFY, appease, conciliate, disarm, mollify, propitiate *Ant* anger, enrage, incense, infuriate, madden, outrage

place *n* 1 · the portion of space occupied by or chosen for something *Syn* location, position, site, situation, spot, station *Rel* district, locality, vicinity 2 *Syn* ROLE, capacity, function, job, part, position, purpose, task, work

place *vb* *Syn* ESTIMATE (sense 2), calculate, call, conjecture, figure, gauge, guess, judge, make, put, reckon, suppose

placid *Syn* CALM, halcyon, peaceful, serene, tranquil *Ant* agitated, stormy

placidity 1 *Syn* CALM, calmness, hush, peace, peacefulness, quiet, quietness, quietude, repose, restfulness, sereneness, serenity, still, stillness, tranquillity (*or* tranquility) *Ant* bustle, commotion, hubbub, hurly-burly, pandemonium, tumult, turmoil, uproar 2 *Syn* EQUANIMITY, aplomb, calmness, composure, coolheadedness, coolness, imperturbability, self-possession, serenity, tranquillity (*or* tranquility) *Ant* agitation, discomposure, perturbation

plague 1 *Syn* AFFLICT, agonize, bedevil, curse, harrow, martyr, persecute, rack, torment, torture 2 *Syn* WORRY, annoy, harass, harry, pester, tantalize, tease

plain *adj* 1 · free from all ostentation or superficial embellishment *Syn* homely, simple, unpretentious *Rel* hideous, ill-favored, ugly, unsightly *Ant* lovely 2 *Syn* EVIDENT, apparent, clear, distinct, manifest, obvious, palpable, patent 3 *Syn* FRANK, candid, open *Ant* reticent 4 *Syn* LEVEL, even, flat, flush, plane, smooth

plain *n* · a broad area of level or rolling treeless country *Syn* down, grassland, prairie, savanna, steppe, tundra, veld (*or* veldt) *Rel* pampas

plainness *Syn* CANDOR, directness, forthrightness, frankness, openheartedness, openness, straightforwardness *Ant* dissembling, pretense (*or* pretence)

plaint *Syn* LAMENT, groan, howl, keen, lamentation, moan, wail *Ant* exultation, rejoicing

plaintive *Syn* MELANCHOLY, doleful, dolorous, lugubrious, rueful

plait *n* *Syn* BRAID, lace, lacing

plait *vb* 1 *Syn* BRAID, pleat 2 *Syn* WEAVE, braid, crochet, knit, tat

plan *n* 1 · a method devised for making or doing something or achieving an end *Syn* design, plot, project, scheme *Rel* intent, intention, purpose 2 *Syn* GOAL, aim, ambition, aspiration, design, dream, end, intent, intention, mark, meaning, object, objective, pretension, purpose, target, thing

plan *vb* · to formulate a plan for arranging, realizing, or achieving something *Syn* design, plot, project, scheme *Rel* intend, propose, purpose

plane *Syn* LEVEL, even, flat, flush, plain, smooth

planet *Syn* EARTH, globe, world

plank *Syn* PARAGRAPH, article, clause, count, verse

plastic · susceptible of being modified in form or nature *Syn* adaptable, ductile, malleable, pliable, pliant *Rel* elastic, flexible, resilient, supple

platform · a level usually raised surface *Syn* dais, podium, rostrum, stage, stand *Rel* altar, pulpit

platitude *Syn* COMMONPLACE, bromide, cliché, truism

plaudit(s) *Syn* APPLAUSE, acclamation, cheering, cheers, ovation, rave(s) *Ant* booing, hissing

plausible · appearing worthy of belief *Syn* believable, colorable, credible, specious *Rel* bland, diplomatic, politic, smooth, suave

play *n* 1 · activity engaged in for amusement *Syn* disport, frolic, gambol, rollick, romp, sport *Rel* delectation, delight, enjoyment, pleasure *Ant* work 2 *Syn* FUN, game, jest, sport 3 *Syn* ROOM (sense 2), berth, clearance, elbow room, leeway, margin

play *vb* 1 · to engage in an activity for amusement or recreation *Syn* disport, frolic, gambol, rollick, romp, sport *Rel* amuse, divert, entertain, recreate 2 *Syn* ACT (sense 2), impersonate

player *Syn* ACTOR, impersonator, mime, mimic, mummer, performer, thespian, trouper

playful · given to or characterized by play, jests, or tricks *Syn* frolicsome, impish, mischievous, roguish, sportive, waggish *Rel* gay, lively, sprightly

play (up) *Syn* EMPHASIZE, accent, accentuate, feature, highlight, point (up), stress, underline, underscore *Ant* play (down)

plea 1 *Syn* APOLOGY, alibi, apologia, excuse, pretext 2 *Syn* EXCUSE, alibi, defense, justification, reason 3 *Syn* PRAYER, appeal, petition, suit

plead *Syn* PRAY, appeal, petition, sue

pleader *Syn* SUPPLICANT, petitioner, solicitor, suitor, suppliant

pleasant · highly acceptable to the mind or the senses *Syn* agreeable, grateful, gratifying, pleasing, welcome *Rel* alluring, attractive, charming *Ant* distasteful, harsh, unpleasant

please · to give or be a source of pleasure to *Syn* delight, gladden, gratify, regale, rejoice, tickle *Rel* content, satisfy *Ant* anger, displease, vex

pleased *Syn* CONTENT, contented, gratified, happy, satisfied *Ant* discontent, discontented, displeased, dissatisfied, malcontent, unhappy

pleasing *Syn* PLEASANT, agreeable, grateful, gratifying, welcome *Ant* distasteful, harsh, unpleasant

pleasurable *Syn* FUN, amusing, delightful, diverting, enjoyable, entertaining *Ant* boring, dull

pleasure · the agreeable emotion accompanying the expectation, acquisition, or possession of something good or greatly desired *Syn* delectation, delight, enjoyment, fruition, joy *Rel* bliss, felicity, happiness *Ant* anger, displeasure, vexation

pleat *Syn* BRAID, plait

plebiscite *Syn* MANDATE, initiative, referendum

pledge 1 · something given or held as a sign of another's good faith or intentions *Syn* earnest, hostage, pawn, token *Rel* bail, bond, guarantee, guaranty, security, surety 2 *Syn* PROMISE, contract, covenant, engage, plight 3 *Syn* PROMISE, oath, troth, vow, word

plenary *Syn* FULL, complete, replete *Ant* empty

plenteous *Syn* PLENTIFUL, abundant, ample, copious *Ant* scant, scanty

plentiful · being more than enough without being excessive *Syn* abundant, ample, copious, plenteous *Rel* fruitful, prolific *Ant* scant, scanty

pleonasm *Syn* VERBIAGE, circumlocution, periphrasis, redundancy, tautology

pliable 1 *Syn* PLASTIC, adaptable, ductile, malleable, pliant 2 *Syn* WILLOWY, flexible, limber, lissome, lithe, pliant, supple *Ant* inflexible, rigid, stiff

pliant 1 *Syn* PLASTIC, adaptable, ductile, malleable, pliable 2 *Syn* WILLOWY, flexible, limber, lissome, lithe, pliable, supple *Ant* inflexible, rigid, stiff

plight 1 *Syn* PREDICAMENT, dilemma, fix, jam, pickle, quandary, scrape 2 *Syn* PROMISE, contract, covenant, engage, pledge

plod *Syn* LABOR, drudge, endeavor, grub, hump, hustle, moil, peg (away), plow, plug, slave, slog, strain, strive, struggle, sweat, toil, travail, work *Ant* dabble, fiddle (around), fool (around), mess (around), putter (around)

plot *n* 1 · a plan secretly devised to accomplish an evil or treacherous end *Syn* cabal, conspiracy, intrigue, machination *Rel* contraption, contrivance, device 2 *Syn* PLAN,

design, project, scheme 3 *Syn* SKETCH, blueprint, delineation, diagram, draft, outline, tracing

plot *vb* 1 · to engage in a secret plan to accomplish evil or unlawful ends *Syn* conspire, contrive, intrigue, machinate, scheme *Rel* brew, concoct, cook (up), hatch 2 *Syn* PLAN, design, project, scheme 3 *Syn* SKETCH, blueprint, delineate, diagram, draft, outline, trace

plow *Syn* LABOR, drudge, endeavor, grub, hump, hustle, moil, peg (away), plod, plug, slave, slog, strain, strive, struggle, sweat, toil, travail, work *Ant* dabble, fiddle (around), fool (around), mess (around), putter (around)

ploy *Syn* TRICK, artifice, feint, gambit, maneuver, ruse, stratagem, wile

pluck *Syn* FORTITUDE, backbone, grit, guts, sand *Ant* pusillanimity

plug *Syn* LABOR, drudge, endeavor, grub, hump, hustle, moil, peg (away), plod, plow, slave, slog, strain, strive, struggle, sweat, toil, travail, work *Ant* dabble, fiddle (around), fool (around), mess (around), putter (around)

plugger *Syn* SLAVE (sense 2), drudge, drudger, grubber, laborer, peon, slogger, toiler, worker *Ant* freeman

plumb *n* 1 *Syn* ERECT, perpendicular, raised, standing, upright, upstanding, vertical *Ant* flat, recumbent 2 *Syn* VERTICAL, perpendicular *Ant* horizontal

plumb *vb Syn* FATHOM, sound

plume *n Syn* AWARD, decoration, distinction, honor, premium, prize

plume *vb Syn* PRIDE, pique, preen

plump *Syn* FLESHY, chubby, corpulent, fat, obese, portly, rotund, stout *Ant* scrawny, skinny

plunder *vb Syn* ROB, burglarize, loot, rifle

plunder *n Syn* SPOIL, booty, loot, prize, swag

plunge · to thrust or cast oneself or something into or as if into deep water *Syn* dive, pitch *Rel* dip, immerse, submerge

plush *Syn* LUXURIOUS, deluxe, lavish, luxuriant, opulent, palatial, sumptuous *Ant* ascetic, austere, humble, Spartan

plutocracy *Syn* OLIGARCHY, aristocracy

ply 1 *Syn* EXERT, apply, exercise, put out, wield 2 *Syn* HANDLE, manipulate, swing, wield

pocket *Syn* HOLE, cavity, hollow, vacuum, void

pocketbook *Syn* PURSE, bag, handbag

pockmark *Syn* BLEMISH, defect, deformity, disfigurement, fault, flaw, imperfection, mark, scar

podium *Syn* PLATFORM, dais, rostrum, stage, stand

poem · a composition using rhythm and often rhyme to create a lyrical effect *Syn* lyric, song, verse *Rel* English sonnet, ballad, blank verse, elegy, epic, epigram, free verse, haiku, jingle, lament, lay, limerick, minstrelsy, ode, poesy, poetry, psalm, rhyme, sonnet

poet · a writer of verse *Syn* bard, minstrel, poetaster, rhymer, rhymester, troubadour, versifier *Rel* author, creator, maker

poetaster *Syn* POET, bard, minstrel, rhymer, rhymester, troubadour, versifier

pogrom *Syn* MASSACRE, butchery, carnage, slaughter

poignant 1 *Syn* MOVING, affecting, emotional, impressive, stirring, touching *Ant* unemotional, unimpressive 2 *Syn* PUNGENT, piquant, racy, snappy, spicy *Ant* bland

point 1 *Syn* CHARACTERISTIC, attribute, character, feature, mark, peculiarity, property, quality, trait 2 *Syn* FACT, datum, detail, nicety, particular, particularity

pointed *Syn* PERTINENT, applicable, apposite, apropos, germane, material, relative, relevant *Ant* extraneous, immaterial, inapplicable, irrelevant, pointless

pointless *Syn* MEANINGLESS, empty, inane, senseless *Ant* meaningful

point of view · a position from which something is considered or evaluated *Syn* angle, slant, standpoint, viewpoint *Rel* attitude, position, stand

point (up) *Syn* EMPHASIZE, accent, accentuate, feature, highlight, play (up), stress, underline, underscore *Ant* play (down)

poise *n* 1 *Syn* BALANCE, equilibrium, equipoise, tension 2 *Syn* TACT, address, savoir faire *Ant* awkwardness

poise *vb* *Syn* STABILIZE, balance, ballast, steady, trim

poison *n* · something that harms, interferes with, or destroys the activity, progress, or welfare of something else *Syn* bane, toxin, venom, virus

poison *vb* *Syn* CONTAMINATE, befoul, defile, foul, pollute, taint *Ant* decontaminate, purify

poisonous · having the properties or effects of poison *Syn* mephitic, miasmal, miasmatic, miasmic, pestilent, pestilential, toxic, venomous, virulent *Rel* deadly, fatal, lethal, mortal *Ant* nonpoisonous, nontoxic, nonvenomous

poke *n* · a quick thrust with or as if with the hand *Syn* jog, nudge, prod

poke *vb* 1 · to thrust something into so as to stir up, urge on, or attract attention *Syn* jog, nudge, prod *Rel* push, shove, thrust 2 *Syn* INTERFERE, butt in, intrude, meddle, mess, nose, obtrude, pry, snoop

polish · to make smooth or glossy usually by repeatedly applying surface pressure *Syn* buff, burnish, dress, gloss, grind, rub, shine, smooth *Rel* sleek, slick

polished 1 *Syn* CULTIVATED, civilized, cultured, genteel, refined *Ant* philistine, uncivilized, uncultured, unpolished, unrefined 2 *Syn* GLOSSY, buffed, burnished, glistening, lustrous, rubbed, satin, satiny, sleek *Ant* dim, dull, flat, lusterless, matte

polite *Syn* CIVIL, chivalrous, courteous, courtly, gallant *Ant* rude, uncivil

politeness · speech or behavior that is a sign of good breeding *Syn* civility, courteousness, courtesy, gentility, graciousness, mannerliness *Rel* attentiveness, consideration, thoughtfulness *Ant* discourteousness, discourtesy, impoliteness, incivility, rudeness, ungraciousness

politic *Syn* EXPEDIENT, advisable, desirable, judicious, prudent, tactical, wise *Ant* imprudent, inadvisable, inexpedient, injudicious, unwise

politician · a person engaged in the art or science of government *Syn* politico, statesman

politico *Syn* POLITICIAN, statesman

poll *Syn* CANVASS, solicit, survey

pollute *Syn* CONTAMINATE, befoul, defile, foul, poison, taint *Ant* decontaminate, purify

polluted *Syn* IMPURE, adulterated, alloyed, contaminated, dilute, diluted, tainted, thinned, weakened *Ant* pure, unadulterated, unalloyed, uncontaminated, undiluted, unpolluted, untainted

poltergeist *Syn* GHOST, apparition, bogey, phantasm, phantom, shade, shadow, specter (*or* spectre), spirit, spook, vision, wraith

poltroon *Syn* COWARD, chicken, craven, dastard, recreant *Ant* hero, stalwart, valiant

polychromatic *Syn* COLORFUL, motley, multicolored, polychrome, varicolored, variegated *Ant* colorless, monochromatic, solid

polychrome *Syn* COLORFUL, motley, multicolored, polychromatic, varicolored, variegated *Ant* colorless, monochromatic, solid

pomp *Syn* DISPLAY, array, parade

pompous 1 *Syn* ARROGANT, cavalier, haughty, highfalutin, high-handed, high-hat, imperious, important, lofty, lordly, masterful, overweening, peremptory, presumptuous, pretentious, supercilious, superior, uppish, uppity *Ant* humble, modest 2 *Syn* CONCEITED, complacent, egoistic, egotistic (*or* egotistical), important, overweening, prideful, proud, self-conceited, self-important, self-satisfied, smug, stuck-up, vain, vainglorious *Ant* humble, modest

pompousness 1 *Syn* ARROGANCE, haughtiness, imperiousness, loftiness, lordliness, masterfulness, peremptoriness, presumptuousness, pretense (*or* pretence), pretension, pretentiousness, self-importance, superciliousness, superiority *Ant* humility, modesty 2 *Syn* COMPLACENCE, complacency, conceit, conceitedness, ego, egotism, pride, pridefulness, self-admiration, self-conceit, self-esteem, self-importance, self-satisfaction, smugness, vaingloriousness, vainglory, vainness, vanity *Ant* humbleness, humility, modesty

ponder · to consider or examine attentively or deliberately *Syn* meditate, muse, ruminate *Rel* consider, contemplate, weigh

ponderous **1** *Syn* BORING, drab, dreary, dry, dull, flat, heavy, humdrum, jading, leaden, monotonous, pedestrian, stodgy, stuffy, stupid, tame, tedious, tiresome, tiring, unanimated, uninteresting, wearisome, weary, wearying *Ant* absorbing, engaging, engrossing, gripping, interesting, intriguing, involving **2** *Syn* HEAVY, cumbersome, cumbrous, hefty, weighty *Ant* light

pool *Syn* MONOPOLY, cartel, corner, syndicate, trust

poor **1** · lacking money or material possessions *Syn* destitute, impecunious, indigent, necessitous, needy, penniless, poverty-stricken *Ant* rich **2** *Syn* BAD (sense 2), wrong *Ant* good

poorly *Syn* BADLY, inadequately, unacceptably, unsatisfactorily *Ant* acceptably, adequately, all right, fine, good, palatably, passably, so-so, tolerably

poppycock *Syn* NONSENSE, balderdash, bull, bunk, drivel, gobbledygook, rot, trash, twaddle

popular **1** *Syn* COMMON, familiar, ordinary, vulgar *Ant* exceptional, uncommon **2** *Syn* DEMOCRATIC, republican, self-governing, self-ruling *Ant* undemocratic

popularity · the state of enjoying widespread approval *Syn* fashionableness, favor, hotness, modishness, vogue *Rel* craze, fad, mode, rage, style, trend *Ant* disfavor, unpopularity

port[1] *n* *Syn* BEARING, demeanor, deportment, mien, presence

port[2] *n* *Syn* HARBOR, haven

portal *Syn* DOOR, doorway, gate, gateway, postern

portend *Syn* FORETELL, augur, forebode, forecast, predict, presage, prognosticate, prophesy

portent *Syn* OMEN, augury, auspice, boding, foreboding, foreshadowing, prefiguring, presage

portentous *Syn* OMINOUS, baleful, dire, foreboding, inauspicious, menacing, sinister, threatening

portion *vb* *Syn* APPORTION, parcel, prorate, ration

portion *n* **1** *Syn* FATE, destiny, doom, lot **2** *Syn* PART, detail, division, fraction, fragment, member, parcel, piece, section, sector, segment *Ant* whole

portly *Syn* FLESHY, chubby, corpulent, fat, obese, plump, rotund, stout *Ant* scrawny, skinny

portrait *Syn* IMAGE, effigy, icon, mask, photograph, statue

portray *Syn* REPRESENT, delineate, depict, limn, picture

pose *n* **1** · an adopted way of speaking or behaving *Syn* affectation, air, mannerism **2** *Syn* POSTURE, attitude

pose *vb* *Syn* PROPOSE, propound

posit *n* *Syn* ASSUMPTION, postulate, premise, presumption, presupposition

posit *vb* *Syn* PRESUPPOSE, assume, postulate, premise, presume

position **1** · a firmly held point of view or way of regarding something *Syn* attitude, stand *Rel* angle, point of view, slant, standpoint, viewpoint **2** *Syn* PLACE, location, site, situation, spot, station **3** *Syn* ROLE, capacity, function, job, part, place, purpose, task, work

positive *Syn* SURE, certain, cocksure *Ant* unsure

possess *Syn* HAVE, enjoy, hold, own

possessions · all the items that taken together constitute a person's or group's property or wealth *Syn* assets, belongings, effects, means, resources

possessor *Syn* PROPRIETOR, holder, owner

possible **1** · capable of being realized *Syn* feasible, practicable *Rel* practical **2** *Syn* PROBABLE, likely *Ant* certain, improbable

possibly *Syn* PERHAPS, conceivably, maybe, mayhap, perchance

post *vb* *Syn* ANNOUNCE, advertise, blaze, broadcast, declare, enunciate, placard, proclaim, promulgate, publicize, publish, sound

post *n* *Syn* MISSION, assignment, charge, job, operation

posterior **1** *Syn* BACK, hind, hindmost, rear, rearward *Ant* anterior, fore, forward, front **2** *Syn* BUTTOCKS, backside, bottom, breech, butt, fanny, hams, haunches, rear, rump, seat

posterity *Syn* OFFSPRING, descendants, issue, progeny, young

postern *Syn* DOOR, doorway, gate, gateway, portal

posting *Syn* ANNOUNCEMENT, ad, advertisement, bulletin, notice, notification, release

postmortem *Syn* AUTOPSY, postmortem examination

postmortem examination *Syn* AUTOPSY, postmortem

postpone · to assign to a later time *Syn* defer, delay, hold off (on), hold up, put off, shelve *Rel* suspend

postulate *n* *Syn* ASSUMPTION, posit, premise, presumption, presupposition

postulate *vb* *Syn* PRESUPPOSE, assume, posit, premise, presume

posture **1** · the position or bearing of the body *Syn* attitude, pose *Rel* bearing, deportment, mien **2** *Syn* STATE, condition, mode, situation, status

pot *Syn* BET, ante, stake, wager

potent *Syn* POWERFUL, forceful, forcible, puissant *Ant* inefficacious, powerless

potential *Syn* LATENT, abeyant, dormant, quiescent *Ant* patent

pother **1** *Syn* COMMOTION, bother, bustle,

clatter, disturbance, furor, furore, fuss, hub-bub, hullabaloo, hurly-burly, pandemonium, row, ruckus, ruction, rumpus, shindy, squall, stew, stir, storm, to-do, tumult, turmoil, up-roar, welter, whirl **2** *Syn* STIR, ado, bustle, flurry, fuss *Ant* tranquillity

pouch *Syn* BAG, sack

pound *Syn* BEAT, baste, belabor, buffet, pum-mel, thrash

pour 1 · to send forth or come forth abun-dantly *Syn* gush, sluice, stream *Rel* appear, emerge **2** *Syn* GUSH (sense 1), jet, rush, spew, spout, spurt, squirt *Ant* dribble, drip, drop, trickle

pout *n Syn* GRIMACE, face, frown, lower, mouth, scowl

pout *vb Syn* SULK, mope

poverty 1 · the state of one with insufficient resources *Syn* destitution, indigence, penury, privation, want *Rel* exigency, necessity, need *Ant* riches **2** *Syn* DEFICIENCY, dearth, deficit, failure, famine, inadequacy, insuffi-ciency, lack, paucity, scantiness, scarceness, scarcity, shortage, want *Ant* abundance, ad-equacy, amplitude, plenitude, plenty, suffi-ciency

poverty-stricken *Syn* POOR, destitute, impe-cunious, indigent, necessitous, needy, penni-less *Ant* rich

power 1 · the ability to exert effort *Syn* en-ergy, force, might, puissance, strength *Rel* ability, capability, capacity *Ant* impotence **2** · the ability of a living being to perform in a given way or a capacity for a particular kind of performance *Syn* faculty, function

powerful · having or manifesting power to effect great or striking results *Syn* forceful, forcible, potent, puissant *Rel* able, capable, competent *Ant* inefficacious, powerless

powerless · unable to act or achieve one's purpose *Syn* helpless, impotent, weak *Rel* incapable, incompetent, ineffective, ineffec-tual, inept, unfit, useless *Ant* mighty, potent, powerful, puissant, strong

powerlessness *Syn* INABILITY, impotence, inadequacy, incapability, incapacity, incom-petence, ineptitude *Ant* ability, adequacy, ca-pability, capacity, competence, potency

practicable *Syn* POSSIBLE, feasible

practically 1 *Syn* ALMOST, about, more or less, most, much, near, nearly, next to, nigh, some, virtually, well-nigh **2** *Syn* VIRTU-ALLY, morally

practice *vb* · to perform or cause one to per-form an act or series of acts repeatedly in or-der to master or strengthen a skill or ability *Syn* drill, exercise *Rel* execute, fulfill, perform

practice *n* **1** *Syn* EXERCISE, drill **2** *Syn* HABIT, custom, fashion, pattern, trick, way, wont **3** *Syn* REHEARSAL, dry run, trial

prairie *Syn* PLAIN, down, grassland, savanna, steppe, tundra, veld (*or* veldt)

praise 1 · to express approval of or esteem for *Syn* acclaim, eulogize, extol, laud *Rel* ap-plaud, commend, compliment *Ant* blame **2** *Syn* ACCLAIM, applaud, cheer, hail, laud, sa-lute, tout *Ant* knock, pan, slam

praiseworthy *Syn* ADMIRABLE, commend-able, creditable, laudable, meritorious *Ant* censurable, discreditable, reprehensible

prank · a playful or mischievous act intended as a joke *Syn* caper, antic, monkeyshine, dido *Rel* frolic, gambol, play, rollick, sport

prate *Syn* CHAT, babble, blab, cackle, chatter, converse, gab, gabble, gas, jabber, jaw, pa-laver, patter, prattle, rap, rattle, run on, talk, twitter, visit

prattle *Syn* CHAT, babble, blab, cackle, chatter, converse, gab, gabble, gas, jabber, jaw, pala-ver, patter, prate, rap, rattle, run on, talk, twit-ter, visit

pray · to request or make a request for in a humble, beseeching manner *Syn* appeal, peti-tion, plead, sue *Rel* beg, beseech, entreat, im-plore, supplicate

prayer · an earnest and usually a formal re-quest for something *Syn* appeal, petition, plea, suit *Rel* begging, beseeching, entreaty, imploring, supplication

preamble *Syn* INTRODUCTION, exordium, foreword, preface, prelude, prologue

precarious *Syn* DANGEROUS, hazardous, per-ilous, risky *Ant* safe, secure

precedent *Syn* PREVIOUS, antecedent, ante-rior, foregoing, preceding, prior *Ant* after, ensuing, following, subsequent, succeeding

preceding *Syn* PREVIOUS, antecedent, ante-rior, foregoing, precedent, prior *Ant* after, en-suing, following, subsequent, succeeding

precept *Syn* LAW, canon, ordinance, regula-tion, rule, statute

preceptor *Syn* TEACHER, educator, instructor, pedagogue, schoolteacher

precious 1 *Syn* COSTLY, dear, expensive, invaluable, priceless, valuable *Ant* cheap **2** *Syn* LOVABLE, adorable, darling, dear, disarm-ing, endearing, sweet, winning *Ant* abhorrent, abominable, detestable, hateful, odious, un-lovable

precipitate *adj* · showing undue haste or un-expectedness *Syn* abrupt, hasty, headlong, impetuous, sudden *Rel* headstrong, refrac-tory, willful *Ant* deliberate

precipitate *n Syn* DEPOSIT, dregs, grounds, lees, sediment

precipitous *Syn* STEEP, abrupt, sheer

précis *Syn* COMPENDIUM, aperçu, digest, pan-dect, sketch, survey, syllabus

precise *Syn* CORRECT, accurate, exact, nice, right *Ant* incorrect

precisely *Syn* STRICTLY, exactly, rigidly, rig-orously *Ant* imprecisely, inexactly, loosely

preciseness *Syn* PRECISION, accuracy, close-ness, delicacy, exactitude, exactness, fineness, rigorousness, veracity *Ant* coarseness, impreciseness, imprecision, inaccuracy, inexactness, roughness

precision · the quality or state of being very accurate *Syn* accuracy, closeness, delicacy, exactitude, exactness, fineness, preciseness, rigorousness, veracity *Rel* correctness, rightness, strictness, truth *Ant* coarseness, impreciseness, imprecision, inaccuracy, inexactness, roughness

preclude *Syn* PREVENT (sense 2), avert, forestall, help, obviate

precocious *Syn* PREMATURE, advanced, forward, untimely *Ant* matured

precursor 1 *Syn* FORERUNNER, harbinger, herald 2 *Syn* ANCESTOR (sense 2), antecedent, foregoer, forerunner, predecessor *Ant* descendant (*or* descendent)

predecessor *Syn* ANCESTOR (sense 2), antecedent, foregoer, forerunner, precursor *Ant* descendant (*or* descendent)

predicament · a difficult, perplexing, or trying situation *Syn* dilemma, fix, jam, pickle, plight, quandary, scrape *Rel* condition, posture, situation, state

predicate *Syn* ASSERT, affirm, aver, avouch, avow, declare, profess, protest, warrant *Ant* controvert, deny

predict *Syn* FORETELL, augur, forebode, forecast, portend, presage, prognosticate, prophesy

predicting *Syn* PREDICTION, auguring, cast, forecast, forecasting, foretelling, presaging, prognosis, prognosticating, prognostication, prophecy, soothsaying

prediction · a declaration that something will happen in the future *Syn* auguring, cast, forecast, forecasting, foretelling, predicting, presaging, prognosis, prognosticating, prognostication, prophecy, soothsaying *Rel* augury, omen, portent, sign

predilection · an attitude of mind that predisposes one to favor something *Syn* bias, partiality, prejudice, prepossession *Rel* flair, leaning, proclivity, propensity *Ant* aversion

predispose *Syn* INCLINE, bias, dispose *Ant* disincline, indispose

predominance *Syn* SUPREMACY, ascendancy, dominance, dominion, preeminence, sovereignty

predominant *Syn* DOMINANT, paramount, preponderant, preponderating, sovereign *Ant* subordinate

predominantly *Syn* CHIEFLY, altogether, basically, by and large, generally, largely, mainly, mostly, overall, primarily, principally, substantially

preeminence *Syn* SUPREMACY, ascendancy, dominance, dominion, predominance, sovereignty

preeminent 1 *Syn* EMINENT, distinguished, illustrious, noble, notable, noteworthy, outstanding, prestigious, signal, star, superior 2 *Syn* HEAD, chief, commanding, first, foremost, high, lead, leading, managing, premier, presiding, primary, prime, principal, supreme 3 *Syn* SUPREME, incomparable, peerless, superlative, surpassing, transcendent

preempt *Syn* ARROGATE, appropriate, confiscate, usurp *Ant* renounce, yield

preen *Syn* PRIDE, pique, plume

preface *Syn* INTRODUCTION, exordium, foreword, preamble, prelude, prologue

prefatory *Syn* PRELIMINARY, introductory, preparatory

prefer 1 *Syn* CHOOSE, cull, elect, opt, pick, select, single *Ant* eschew, reject 2 *Syn* OFFER, present, proffer, tender

preferable *Syn* BETTER, superior

preference 1 *Syn* CHOICE, alternative, election, option, selection 2 *Syn* FAVORITE, darling, minion, pet 3 *Syn* LIKING, appetite, fancy, favor, fondness, like, love, partiality, relish, shine, taste, use *Ant* aversion, disfavor, dislike, distaste, hatred, loathing

preferment *Syn* ADVANCEMENT, elevation, promotion *Ant* degradation, reduction (*in rank or status*)

prefiguring *Syn* OMEN, augury, auspice, boding, foreboding, foreshadowing, portent, presage

pregnant *Syn* EXPRESSIVE, eloquent, meaning, meaningful, revealing, significant, suggestive

prejudice 1 *Syn* BIAS, favor, one-sidedness, partiality, partisanship *Ant* impartiality, neutrality, objectivity, open-mindedness 2 *Syn* PREDILECTION, bias, partiality, prepossession *Ant* aversion

prejudiced *Syn* INTOLERANT, bigoted, narrow, narrow-minded, small-minded *Ant* broadminded, liberal, open-minded, tolerant, unprejudiced

prejudicial *Syn* HARMFUL, adverse, bad, baleful, baneful, damaging, deleterious, detrimental, evil, hurtful, ill, injurious, mischievous, noxious, pernicious *Ant* harmless, innocent, innocuous, inoffensive, safe

preliminary · serving to make ready the way for something that follows *Syn* introductory, prefatory, preparatory *Rel* primal, primary

prelude *Syn* INTRODUCTION, exordium, foreword, preamble, preface, prologue

premature · unduly early in coming, happening, or developing *Syn* advanced, forward, precocious, untimely *Rel* immature, unmatured, unmellow, unripe *Ant* matured

premeditated *Syn* DELIBERATE, advised, considered, designed, studied *Ant* casual

premier *Syn* HEAD, chief, commanding, first, foremost, high, lead, leading, managing, preeminent, presiding, primary, prime, principal, supreme

premise *n Syn* ASSUMPTION, posit, postulate, presumption, presupposition

premise *vb Syn* PRESUPPOSE, assume, posit, postulate, presume

premium *Syn* AWARD, decoration, distinction, honor, plume, prize

premonition · a feeling that something bad will happen *Syn* foreboding, presage, presentiment *Rel* anticipation, foreknowledge

preoccupied *Syn* ABSTRACTED, absent, absentminded, distraught *Ant* alert

preparatory *Syn* PRELIMINARY, introductory, prefatory

prepare · to make ready beforehand usually for some purpose, use, or activity *Syn* condition, fit, qualify, ready *Rel* furnish, provide, supply

preponderant *Syn* DOMINANT, paramount, predominant, preponderating, sovereign *Ant* subordinate

preponderating *Syn* DOMINANT, paramount, predominant, preponderant, sovereign *Ant* subordinate

prepossession *Syn* PREDILECTION, bias, partiality, prejudice *Ant* aversion

preposterous *Syn* FOOLISH, absurd, silly *Ant* sensible

prerequisite *Syn* REQUIREMENT, requisite

prerogative *Syn* RIGHT, appanage, birthright, perquisite, privilege

presage *vb Syn* FORETELL, augur, forebode, forecast, portend, predict, prognosticate, prophesy

presage *n* 1 *Syn* OMEN, augury, auspice, boding, foreboding, foreshadowing, portent, prefiguring 2 *Syn* PREMONITION, foreboding, presentiment

presaging *Syn* PREDICTION, auguring, cast, forecast, forecasting, foretelling, predicting, prognosis, prognosticating, prognostication, prophecy, soothsaying

prescience *Syn* FORESIGHT (sense 1), foreknowledge *Ant* improvidence, shortsightedness

prescribe 1 · to fix arbitrarily or authoritatively for the sake of order or of a clear understanding *Syn* assign, define *Rel* establish, fix, set, settle 2 *Syn* DICTATE, decree, impose, ordain

prescription *Syn* RECEIPT, recipe

presence *Syn* BEARING, demeanor, deportment, mien, port

present *adj* · existing or in progress right now *Syn* current, extant, ongoing, present-day *Rel* contemporary, mod, modern, new, newfangled, new-fashioned, now, recent, red-hot, space-age, ultramodern, up-to-date *Ant* ago, future, past

present *n Syn* GIFT (sense 1), boon, favor, gratuity, largess

present *vb* 1 *Syn* GIVE, afford, bestow, confer, donate 2 *Syn* OFFER, prefer, proffer, tender

present-day 1 *Syn* MODERN, contemporary, current, hot, mod, modernistic, newfangled, new, new-fashioned, red-hot, space-age, ultramodern, up-to-date *Ant* antiquated, archaic, dated, fusty, musty, noncontemporary, oldfangled, old-fashioned, old-time, out-of-date, passé 2 *Syn* PRESENT, current, extant, ongoing *Ant* ago, future, past

presentiment *Syn* PREMONITION, foreboding, presage

presently 1 · without undue time lapse *Syn* directly, shortly, soon 2 *Syn* SHORTLY, anon, momentarily, soon

preserve *Syn* SAVE, conserve *Ant* consume, spend

presiding *Syn* HEAD, chief, commanding, first, foremost, high, lead, leading, managing, preeminent, premier, primary, prime, principal, supreme

press *vb* 1 · to act upon through steady pushing or thrusting force exerted in contact *Syn* bear, bear down, crowd, jam, squeeze *Rel* propel, push, shove, thrust 2 *Syn* URGE, egg (on), encourage, exhort, goad, prod, prompt

press *n Syn* CROWD, crush, horde, mob, rout, throng

pressing · demanding or claiming especially immediate attention *Syn* crying, exigent, imperative, importunate, insistent, instant, urgent *Rel* direct, immediate

pressure *Syn* STRESS, strain, tension

prestidigitator *Syn* MAGICIAN (sense 2), conjurer (*or* conjuror), trickster

prestige *Syn* INFLUENCE, authority, credit, weight

prestigious *Syn* EMINENT, distinguished, illustrious, noble, notable, noteworthy, outstanding, preeminent, signal, star, superior

presumably 1 *Syn* APPARENTLY, evidently, ostensibly, seemingly, supposedly 2 *Syn* PROBABLY, doubtless, likely *Ant* improbably

presume *Syn* PRESUPPOSE, assume, posit, postulate, premise

presumption 1 *Syn* ASSUMPTION, posit, postulate, premise, presupposition 2 *Syn* EFFRONTERY, audacity, brashness, brass, brassiness, brazenness, cheek, cheekiness, chutzpah, gall, nerve, nerviness, pertness, presumptuousness, sauce, sauciness, temerity

presumptuous 1 *Syn* ARROGANT, cavalier, haughty, highfalutin, high-handed, high-hat, imperious, important, lofty, lordly, masterful, overweening, peremptory, pompous, pretentious, supercilious, superior, uppish, uppity *Ant* humble, modest 2 *Syn* CONFIDENT, assured, sanguine, sure *Ant* apprehensive, diffident 3 *Syn* INTRUSIVE, interfering, intruding, meddlesome, meddling, nosy (*or* nosey), obtrusive, officious, prying, snoopy *Ant* unobtrusive

presumptuousness 1 *Syn* ARROGANCE, haughtiness, imperiousness, loftiness, lordliness, masterfulness, peremptoriness, pompousness, pretense (*or* pretence), pretension, pretentiousness, self-importance, superciliousness, superiority *Ant* humility, modesty **2** *Syn* EFFRONTERY, audacity, brashness, brass, brassiness, brazenness, cheek, cheekiness, chutzpah, gall, nerve, nerviness, pertness, presumption, sauce, sauciness, temerity

presuppose • to take something for granted or as true or existent especially as a basis for action or reasoning *Syn* assume, posit, postulate, premise, presume *Rel* conjecture, guess, surmise

presupposition *Syn* ASSUMPTION, posit, postulate, premise, presumption

pretend *Syn* ASSUME, affect, counterfeit, feign, sham, simulate

pretense 1 • the offering of something false as real or true *Syn* make-believe, pretension *Rel* deceit, deception, fake, fraud, humbug, imposture, sham **2** *Syn* CLAIM, pretension, title **3** *Syn* ARROGANCE, haughtiness, imperiousness, loftiness, lordliness, masterfulness, peremptoriness, pompousness, presumptuousness, pretension, pretentiousness, self-importance, superciliousness, superiority *Ant* humility, modesty

pretension 1 *Syn* ARROGANCE, haughtiness, imperiousness, loftiness, lordliness, masterfulness, peremptoriness, pompousness, presumptuousness, pretense (*or* pretence), pretentiousness, self-importance, superciliousness, superiority *Ant* humility, modesty **2** *Syn* CLAIM, pretense, title **3** *Syn* GOAL, aim, ambition, aspiration, design, dream, end, intent, intention, mark, meaning, object, objective, plan, purpose, target, thing **4** *Syn* PRETENSE, make-believe

pretentious 1 *Syn* AMBITIOUS (sense 2), utopian *Ant* modest **2** *Syn* ARROGANT, cavalier, haughty, highfalutin, high-handed, high-hat, imperious, important, lofty, lordly, masterful, overweening, peremptory, pompous, presumptuous, supercilious, superior, uppish, uppity *Ant* humble, modest **3** *Syn* SHOWY, ostentatious

pretentiousness 1 *Syn* ARROGANCE, haughtiness, imperiousness, loftiness, lordliness, masterfulness, peremptoriness, pompousness, presumptuousness, pretense (*or* pretence), pretension, self-importance, superciliousness, superiority *Ant* humility, modesty **2** *Syn* OSTENTATION, flamboyance, flashiness, garishness, gaudiness, glitz, ostentatiousness, showiness, swank *Ant* austerity, plainness, severity

preternatural *Syn* SUPERNATURAL, miraculous, superhuman, supranatural

pretext *Syn* APOLOGY, alibi, apologia, excuse, plea

pretty *Syn* BEAUTIFUL, attractive, beauteous, comely, cute, fair, gorgeous, handsome, knockout, lovely, ravishing, sightly, stunning, taking *Ant* homely, ill-favored, plain, ugly, unattractive, unbeautiful, unhandsome, unlovely, unpretty, unsightly

prevailing • general (as in circulation, acceptance, or use) in a given place or at a given time *Syn* current, prevalent, rife *Rel* dominant, predominant, preponderant

prevail (on *or* **upon)** *Syn* PERSUADE, argue, convince, get, induce, move, satisfy, talk (into), win (over)

prevalent *Syn* PREVAILING, current, rife

prevaricate *Syn* LIE, equivocate, fib, palter

prevent 1 • to deal with beforehand *Syn* anticipate, forestall *Rel* baffle, balk, foil, frustrate, thwart **2** • to stop from advancing or occurring *Syn* avert, forestall, help, obviate, preclude *Rel* anticipate, provide

previous • going before another in time or order *Syn* antecedent, anterior, foregoing, precedent, preceding, prior *Rel* advance, early, premature *Ant* after, ensuing, following, subsequent, succeeding

previous to *Syn* BEFORE, ahead of, ere, of, prior to, to *Ant* after, following

prey *Syn* VICTIM, quarry

price • the quantity of one thing that is exchanged or demanded in barter or sale for another *Syn* charge, cost, expense

priceless *Syn* COSTLY, dear, expensive, invaluable, precious, valuable *Ant* cheap

prick *Syn* PERFORATE, bore, drill, punch, puncture

pride *n* **1** • an attitude of inordinate self-esteem or superiority *Syn* vainglory, vanity *Rel* arrogance, disdain, disdainfulness, haughtiness, insolence, superciliousness *Ant* humility, shame **2** *Syn* COMPLACENCE, complacency, conceit, conceitedness, ego, egotism, pompousness, pridefulness, self-admiration, self-conceit, self-esteem, self-importance, self-satisfaction, smugness, vaingloriousness, vainglory, vainness, vanity *Ant* humbleness, humility, modesty

pride *vb* • to congratulate oneself because of something one is, has, or has done or achieved *Syn* pique, plume, preen *Rel* boast, brag, crow, gasconade, vaunt

prideful *Syn* CONCEITED, complacent, egoistic, egotistic (*or* egotistical), important, overweening, pompous, proud, self-conceited, self-important, self-satisfied, smug, stuck-up, vain, vainglorious *Ant* humble, modest

pridefulness *Syn* COMPLACENCE, complacency, conceit, conceitedness, ego, egotism, pompousness, pride, self-admiration, self-conceit, self-esteem, self-importance, self-satisfaction, smugness, vaingloriousness, vainglory, vainness, vanity *Ant* humbleness, humility, modesty

process

priggish 1 *Syn* COMPLACENT, self-compla-cent, self-satisfied, smug **2** *Syn* PRIM, prissy, prudish, puritanical, straitlaced, stuffy

prim · excessively concerned with what one re-gards as proper or right *Syn* priggish, prissy, prudish, puritanical, straitlaced, stuffy *Rel* cor-rect, nice, precise

primal *Syn* PRIMARY, prime, primeval, primi-tive, primordial, pristine

primarily *Syn* CHIEFLY, altogether, basically, by and large, generally, largely, mainly, mostly, overall, predominantly, principally, substan-tially

primary 1 · first in some respect (as order, character, or importance) *Syn* primal, prime, primeval, primitive, primordial, pristine *Rel* beginning, commencing, initial, initiating, starting **2** *Syn* HEAD, chief, commanding, first, foremost, high, lead, leading, manag-ing, preeminent, premier, presiding, prime, principal, supreme

prime *n Syn* ELITE, best, choice, cream, elect, fat, flower, pick, upper crust

prime *adj* **1** *Syn* EXCELLENT, A1, bang-up, banner, capital, classic, crackerjack, dandy, divine, fabulous, fine, first-class, first-rate, grand, great, groovy, heavenly, jim-dandy, keen, marvelous (*or* marvellous), mean, neat, nifty, noble, par excellence, sensational, splendid, stellar, sterling, superb, superior, superlative, supernal, swell, terrific, tip-top, top, top-notch, unsurpassed, wonderful *Ant* poor **2** *Syn* HEAD, chief, commanding, first, foremost, high, lead, leading, manag-ing, preeminent, premier, presiding, primary, principal, supreme **3** *Syn* PRIMARY, primal, primeval, primitive, primordial, pristine

prime mover *Syn* ORIGIN, inception, prov-enance, provenience, root, source

primeval *Syn* PRIMARY, primal, prime, primi-tive, primordial, pristine

primitive *Syn* PRIMARY, primal, prime, prime-val, primordial, pristine

primordial 1 *Syn* INITIAL, original *Ant* fi-nal **2** *Syn* PRIMARY, primal, prime, primeval, primitive, pristine

princely *Syn* KINGLY, imperial, queenly, re-gal, royal

principal 1 *Syn* CHIEF, capital, foremost, leading, main *Ant* subordinate **2** *Syn* HEAD, chief, commanding, first, foremost, high, lead, leading, managing, preeminent, pre-mier, presiding, primary, prime, supreme

principally 1 *Syn* CHIEFLY, altogether, ba-sically, by and large, generally, largely, mainly, mostly, overall, predominantly, primarily, substantially **2** *Syn* LARGELY, chiefly, generally, greatly, mainly, mostly

principle · a comprehensive and fundamen-tal rule, doctrine, or assumption *Syn* axiom, fundamental, law, theorem *Rel* basis, founda-tion, ground

principles *Syn* ETHICS, morality, morals, standards

print *Syn* IMPRESSION, impress, imprint, stamp

printing *Syn* EDITION, impression, reissue, re-printing

prior *Syn* PREVIOUS, antecedent, anterior, foregoing, precedent, preceding *Ant* after, ensuing, following, subsequent, succeeding

prior to *Syn* BEFORE, ahead of, ere, of, previ-ous to, to *Ant* after, following

priory *Syn* CLOISTER, abbey, convent, monas-tery, nunnery

prismatic · marked by or displaying a variety of colors *Syn* iridescent, opalescent, opaline

prison *Syn* JAIL, brig, guardroom, hoosegow, jug, lockup, pen, penitentiary, stockade

prissy *Syn* PRIM, priggish, prudish, puritani-cal, straitlaced, stuffy

pristine *Syn* PRIMARY, primal, prime, prime-val, primitive, primordial

privateer *Syn* PIRATE, buccaneer, corsair, freebooter

privation 1 *Syn* LACK, absence, dearth, de-fect, want **2** *Syn* POVERTY, destitution, indi-gence, penury, want *Ant* riches

privilege *Syn* RIGHT, appanage, birthright, perquisite, prerogative

prize *vb Syn* APPRECIATE, cherish, treasure, value *Ant* despise

prize *n* **1** *Syn* AWARD, decoration, distinction, honor, plume, premium **2** *Syn* SPOIL, booty, loot, plunder, swag

probability · a measure of how often an event will occur instead of another *Syn* chance, odds, percentage *Rel* outlook, prospect

probable · almost sure to be or to become true or real *Syn* likely, possible *Rel* believ-able, colorable, credible, plausible *Ant* cer-tain, improbable

probably · without much doubt *Syn* doubtless, likely, presumably *Rel* mayhap, perchance, perhaps, possibly *Ant* improbably

probe *vb* **1** *Syn* ENTER (sense 1), penetrate, pierce *Ant* issue from **2** *Syn* EXPLORE, delve (into), dig (into), inquire (into), investigate, look (into), research

probe *n Syn* INQUIRY, inquest, inquisition, in-vestigation, research

probity *Syn* HONESTY, honor, integrity *Ant* dishonesty

problem *Syn* MYSTERY, conundrum, enigma, puzzle, riddle

problematic *Syn* DOUBTFUL, .dubious, ques-tionable *Ant* cocksure, positive

procedure *Syn* PROCESS, proceeding

proceed *Syn* SPRING, arise, derive, emanate, flow, issue, originate, rise, stem

proceed (along) *Syn* TRAVERSE, cover, criss-cross, cross, cut (across), follow, go, pass (over), travel

proceeding *Syn* PROCESS, procedure

process 1 · the series of actions, operations,

or motions involved in the accomplishment of an end *Syn* procedure, proceeding *Rel* advance, progress **2** *Syn* ADVANCE (sense 2), advancement, furtherance, going, headway, march, onrush, passage, procession, progress, progression *Ant* recession, regression, retrogression

procession **1** · a body (as of persons and vehicles) moving along in a usually ceremonial order *Syn* cavalcade, cortege, motorcade, parade *Rel* sequence, succession, train **2** *Syn* ADVANCE (sense 2), advancement, furtherance, going, headway, march, onrush, passage, process, progress, progression *Ant* recession, regression, retrogression

proclaim *Syn* ANNOUNCE, advertise, blaze, broadcast, declare, enunciate, placard, post, promulgate, publicize, publish, sound

proclamation *Syn* DECLARATION, advertisement, announcement, broadcasting, promulgation, publication

proclivity *Syn* LEANING, flair, penchant, propensity *Ant* distaste

procrastinate *Syn* DELAY (sense 2), dawdle, lag, loiter *Ant* hasten, hurry

procreate *Syn* GENERATE, beget, breed, engender, get, propagate, reproduce, sire

procurator *Syn* AGENT (sense 1), attorney, commissary, delegate, deputy, envoy, factor, proxy, representative

procure **1** *Syn* EARN, acquire, attain, capture, carry, draw, gain, garner, get, land, make, obtain, realize, secure, win *Ant* forfeit, lose **2** *Syn* GET, gain, obtain, secure, win

prod *n Syn* POKE, jog, nudge

prod *vb* **1** *Syn* POKE, jog, nudge **2** *Syn* URGE, egg (on), encourage, exhort, goad, press, prompt

prodigal *adj* **1** · given to spending money freely or foolishly *Syn* extravagant, profligate, spendthrift, squandering, thriftless, unthrifty, wasteful *Rel* improvident, myopic, shortsighted *Ant* conserving, economical, economizing, frugal, scrimping, skimping, thrifty **2** *Syn* PROFUSE, exuberant, lavish, lush, luxuriant *Ant* scant, scanty, spare

prodigal *n* · someone who carelessly spends money *Syn* profligate, spender, spendthrift, squanderer, waster, wastrel *Ant* economizer

prodigious *Syn* MONSTROUS, monumental, stupendous, tremendous

prodigy *Syn* WONDER (sense 1), marvel, miracle, phenomenon

produce *vb* **1** *Syn* BEAR (sense 1), turn out, yield **2** *Syn* EFFECT, bring about, cause, create, effectuate, engender, generate, induce, make, prompt, result (in), spawn, work, yield

produce *n Syn* PRODUCT, production

product **1** · something produced by physical labor or intellectual effort *Syn* produce, production **2** *Syn* WORK (sense 3), artifact, opus, production

production **1** *Syn* PRODUCT, produce **2** *Syn* WORK (sense 3), artifact, opus, product

productive *Syn* FERTILE, fat, fecund, fruitful, luxuriant, prolific, rich *Ant* barren, infertile, sterile, unfruitful, unproductive

profanation · a violation or a misuse of something normally held sacred *Syn* blasphemy, desecration, sacrilege *Rel* contamination, defilement, pollution

profane *adj* **1** · not concerned with religion or religious purposes *Syn* lay, secular, temporal *Rel* earthly, mundane, terrestrial, worldly *Ant* sacred **2** *Syn* IMPIOUS, blasphemous, sacrilegious *Ant* pious, reverent

profane *vb Syn* DESECRATE, defile, violate

profanity *Syn* BLASPHEMY, cursing, swearing *Ant* adoration

profess *Syn* ASSERT, affirm, aver, avouch, avow, declare, predicate, protest, warrant *Ant* controvert, deny

profession **1** *Syn* OCCUPATION, calling, employment, line, trade, vocation, work **2** *Syn* TRADE, art, craft, handicraft

proffer *vb Syn* OFFER, prefer, present, tender

proffer *n Syn* PROPOSAL, offer, proposition, suggestion

proficient · having great knowledge and experience in a trade or profession *Syn* adept, expert, masterly, skilled, skillful *Rel* effective, effectual, efficient *Ant* amateur, amateurish, inexperienced, inexpert, unexperienced, unpracticed, unprofessional, unseasoned, unskilled, unskillful

profile *Syn* OUTLINE, contour, silhouette, skyline

profit *vb Syn* BENEFIT, avail *Ant* harm

profit *n Syn* USE (sense 1), account, advantage, avail, service

profitable **1** *Syn* BENEFICIAL, advantageous, favorable, helpful, salutary *Ant* disadvantageous, unfavorable, unhelpful **2** *Syn* PAYING, gainful, lucrative, remunerative

profligate *adj* **1** *Syn* ABANDONED (sense 1), dissolute, reprobate *Ant* redeemed, regenerate **2** *Syn* PRODIGAL, extravagant, spendthrift, squandering, thriftless, unthrifty, wasteful *Ant* conserving, economical, economizing, frugal, scrimping, skimping, thrifty

profligate *n Syn* PRODIGAL, spender, spendthrift, squanderer, waster, wastrel *Ant* economizer

profound *Syn* DEEP, abysmal

profuse · giving or given out in great abundance *Syn* exuberant, lavish, lush, luxuriant, prodigal *Rel* abundant, copious, plentiful *Ant* scant, scanty, spare

progenitor *Syn* ANCESTOR (sense 1), forebear, forefather *Ant* descendant (*or* descendent)

progeny *Syn* OFFSPRING, descendants, issue, posterity, young

prognosis *Syn* PREDICTION, auguring, cast, forecast, forecasting, foretelling, predicting, presaging, prognosticating, prognostication, prophecy, soothsaying

prognosticate *Syn* FORETELL, augur, forebode, forecast, portend, predict, presage, prophesy

prognosticating *Syn* PREDICTION, auguring, cast, forecast, forecasting, foretelling, predicting, presaging, prognosis, prognostication, prophecy, soothsaying

prognostication *Syn* PREDICTION, auguring, cast, forecast, forecasting, foretelling, predicting, presaging, prognosis, prognosticating, prophecy, soothsaying

prognosticator *Syn* PROPHET, augur, diviner, forecaster, foreseer, foreteller, fortune-teller, futurist, prophesier, seer, soothsayer

program · a formulated plan listing things to be done or to take place especially in chronological order *Syn* agenda, schedule, timetable

progress *Syn* ADVANCE (sense 2), advancement, furtherance, going, headway, march, onrush, passage, process, procession, progression *Ant* recession, regression, retrogression

progression 1 *Syn* ADVANCE (sense 2), advancement, furtherance, going, headway, march, onrush, passage, process, procession, progress *Ant* recession, regression, retrogression 2 *Syn* SUCCESSION, chain, sequence, series, string, train

progressive *Syn* LIBERAL (sense 2), advanced, radical *Ant* authoritarian

prohibit *Syn* FORBID, ban, bar, enjoin, interdict, outlaw, proscribe *Ant* allow, let, permit, suffer

prohibiting *Syn* PROHIBITION (sense 1), banning, barring, enjoining, forbidding, interdicting, interdiction, outlawing, proscribing, proscription *Ant* prescription

prohibition 1 · the act of ordering that something not be done or used *Syn* banning, barring, enjoining, forbidding, interdicting, interdiction, outlawing, prohibiting, proscribing, proscription *Rel* bidding, charging, decreeing, dictation, direction, instruction 2 · an order that something not be done or used *Syn* ban, embargo, interdict, interdiction, proscription, veto *Rel* constraint, denial, deterrent, disallowance, discouragement, inhibition, injunction, limitation, negation, objection, protest, refusal, rejection, repression, restraint, restriction, suppression, taboo *Ant* prescription

project *vb* 1 *Syn* BULGE, beetle, jut, overhang, protrude, stick out 2 *Syn* PLAN, design, plot, scheme

project *n Syn* PLAN, design, plot, scheme

projection · an extension beyond the normal line or surface *Syn* bulge, protrusion, protuberance

proliferate *Syn* INCREASE (sense 2), accumulate, appreciate, balloon, build (up), burgeon,

enlarge, escalate, expand, mount, multiply, mushroom, rise, snowball, swell, wax *Ant* contract, decrease, diminish, lessen, wane

prolific *Syn* FERTILE, fat, fecund, fruitful, luxuriant, productive, rich *Ant* barren, infertile, sterile, unfruitful, unproductive

prolificacy *Syn* FERTILITY, fecundity, fruitfulness *Ant* infertility, sterility

prolix *Syn* WORDY, diffuse, redundant, verbose *Ant* compact, concise, crisp, pithy, succinct, terse

prologue *Syn* INTRODUCTION, exordium, foreword, preamble, preface, prelude

prolong *Syn* EXTEND, elongate, lengthen, protract *Ant* abridge, shorten

prom *Syn* DANCE, ball, cotillion, formal, hop

prominent 1 *Syn* FAMOUS, celebrated, famed, noted, notorious, renowned, star, well-known *Ant* anonymous, obscure, unknown 2 *Syn* NOTICEABLE, arresting, conspicuous, outstanding, remarkable, salient, signal, striking

promiscuous *Syn* MISCELLANEOUS, assorted, heterogeneous, motley

promise *n* · a person's solemn declaration that he or she will do or not do something *Syn* oath, pledge, troth, vow, word *Rel* appointment, arrangement, commitment, engagement

promise *vb* · to give one's word to do, bring about, or provide *Syn* contract, covenant, engage, pledge, plight *Rel* accede, agree, assent, consent

promote *Syn* ADVANCE (sense 1), forward, further *Ant* check, retard

promoter *Syn* EXPONENT, advocate, apostle, backer, booster, champion, friend, proponent, supporter *Ant* adversary, antagonist, opponent

promotion 1 *Syn* ADVANCEMENT, elevation, preferment *Ant* degradation, reduction (*in rank or status*) 2 *Syn* PUBLICITY, ballyhoo, propaganda

prompt *vb* 1 *Syn* EFFECT, bring about, cause, create, effectuate, engender, generate, induce, make, produce, result (in), spawn, work, yield 2 *Syn* URGE, egg (on), encourage, exhort, goad, press, prod

prompt *adj Syn* QUICK, apt, ready *Ant* sluggish

promulgate *Syn* ANNOUNCE, advertise, blaze, broadcast, declare, enunciate, placard, post, proclaim, publicize, publish, sound

promulgation *Syn* DECLARATION, advertisement, announcement, broadcasting, proclamation, publication

prone 1 · having a tendency to be or act in a certain way *Syn* apt, given, inclined, tending *Rel* choosing, preferring 2 · lying down *Syn* couchant, dormant, prostrate, recumbent, supine *Rel* flat, level *Ant* erect 3 *Syn* LIABLE, exposed, open, sensitive, subject, susceptible *Ant* exempt, immune

pronounce *Syn* ARTICULATE, enunciate

pronounced *Syn* EGREGIOUS, blatant, conspicuous, flagrant, glaring, gross, obvious, patent, rank, striking

proof 1 · something that serves as evidence compelling the acceptance of a truth or fact *Syn* demonstration, test, trial 2 *Syn* REASON (sense 1), argument, ground

prop *Syn* SUPPORT (sense 1), bolster, brace, buttress, sustain

propaganda *Syn* PUBLICITY, ballyhoo, promotion

propagate 1 *Syn* GENERATE, beget, breed, engender, get, procreate, reproduce, sire 2 *Syn* SPREAD, circulate, diffuse, disseminate, radiate

propel 1 *Syn* ACTIVATE, actuate, crank (up), drive, move, run, set off, spark, start, touch off, trigger, turn on *Ant* cut, deactivate, kill, shut off, turn off 2 *Syn* PUSH, shove, thrust

propensity *Syn* LEANING, flair, penchant, proclivity *Ant* distaste

proper 1 *Syn* DECOROUS, decent, nice, seemly *Ant* blatant, indecorous 2 *Syn* FIT, appropriate, apt, felicitous, fitting, happy, meet, suitable *Ant* unfit

properly · in a manner suitable for the occasion or purpose *Syn* appropriately, congruously, correctly, fittingly, happily, meetly, rightly, suitably *Rel* well *Ant* improperly, inappropriately, incongruously, incorrectly, unsuitably, wrongly

property *Syn* CHARACTERISTIC, attribute, character, feature, mark, peculiarity, point, quality, trait

prophecy 1 *Syn* PREDICTION, auguring, cast, forecast, forecasting, foretelling, predicting, presaging, prognosis, prognosticating, prognostication, soothsaying 2 *Syn* REVELATION (sense 1), vision

prophesier *Syn* PROPHET, augur, diviner, forecaster, foreseer, foreteller, fortune-teller, futurist, prognosticator, seer, soothsayer

prophesy *Syn* FORETELL, augur, forebode, forecast, portend, predict, presage, prognosticate

prophet · one who predicts future events or developments *Syn* augur, diviner, forecaster, foreseer, foreteller, fortune-teller, futurist, prognosticator, prophesier, seer, soothsayer *Rel* prophetess

propitiate *Syn* PACIFY, appease, conciliate, disarm, mollify, placate *Ant* anger, enrage, incense, infuriate, madden, outrage

propitious *Syn* FAVORABLE, auspicious, benign *Ant* antagonistic, unfavorable

proponent *Syn* EXPONENT, advocate, apostle, backer, booster, champion, friend, promoter, supporter *Ant* adversary, antagonist, opponent

proportion *Syn* SYMMETRY, balance, harmony

proportional · corresponding in size, degree, or intensity *Syn* commensurable, commensurate, proportionate *Rel* correlative, corresponding, reciprocal

proportionate *Syn* PROPORTIONAL, commensurable, commensurate

proposal · something which is presented for consideration *Syn* offer, proffer, proposition, suggestion *Rel* feeler, overture

propose 1 · to set before the mind for consideration *Syn* pose, propound *Rel* state 2 *Syn* INTEND, design, mean, purpose

proposition 1 *Syn* PROPOSAL, offer, proffer, suggestion 2 *Syn* THEORY, hypothesis, supposition

propound *Syn* PROPOSE, pose

proprietor · one who has a legal or rightful claim to ownership *Syn* holder, owner, possessor *Rel* homeowner, landowner

propriety *Syn* DECORUM, decency, dignity, etiquette *Ant* indecorum, license

prorate *Syn* APPORTION, parcel, portion, ration

prosaic · having a plain, practical, everyday character or quality *Syn* matter-of-fact, prosy *Rel* practicable, practical

proscribe 1 *Syn* FORBID, ban, bar, enjoin, interdict, outlaw, prohibit *Ant* allow, let, permit, suffer 2 *Syn* SENTENCE, condemn, damn, doom

proscribing *Syn* PROHIBITION (sense 1), banning, barring, enjoining, forbidding, interdicting, interdiction, outlawing, prohibiting, proscription *Ant* prescription

proscription 1 *Syn* PROHIBITION (sense 1), banning, barring, enjoining, forbidding, interdicting, interdiction, outlawing, prohibiting, proscribing *Ant* prescription 2 *Syn* PROHIBITION (sense 2), ban, embargo, interdict, interdiction, veto *Ant* prescription

prospect 1 · an advance realization of something to come *Syn* anticipation, foretaste, outlook *Rel* expectation, hope 2 *Syn* CANDIDATE, applicant, aspirant, campaigner, contender, hopeful, seeker

prosper *Syn* SUCCEED, flourish, thrive *Ant* attempt, fail

prostration *Syn* FATIGUE, burnout, collapse, exhaustion, lassitude, tiredness, weariness *Ant* refreshment, rejuvenation, revitalization

prosy *Syn* PROSAIC, matter-of-fact

protean *Syn* CHANGEABLE, changeful, mutable, variable *Ant* stable, unchangeable

protect *Syn* DEFEND, guard, safeguard, shield *Ant* attack, combat

protection 1 *Syn* PROTECTOR, custodian, defender, guard 2 *Syn* SAFETY, safeness, security *Ant* danger, distress, endangerment, imperilment, jeopardy, peril, trouble

protector · someone that protects *Syn* custodian, defender, guard, protection *Rel* bodyguard, champion

protest *vb* 1 *Syn* ASSERT, affirm, aver,

avouch, avow, declare, predicate, profess, warrant *Ant* controvert, deny **2** *Syn* OBJECT, expostulate, kick, remonstrate *Ant* acquiesce

protest *n Syn* OBJECTION, challenge, complaint, demur, expostulation, fuss, question, remonstrance

protract *Syn* EXTEND, elongate, lengthen, prolong *Ant* abridge, shorten

protrude *Syn* BULGE, beetle, jut, overhang, project, stick out

protrusion *Syn* PROJECTION, bulge, protuberance

protuberance *Syn* PROJECTION, bulge, protrusion

proud **1** · showing scorn for inferiors *Syn* arrogant, disdainful, haughty, insolent, lordly, overbearing, supercilious *Rel* contemptuous, scornful *Ant* ashamed, humble **2** · having or exhibiting undue or excessive pride especially in one's appearance or achievements *Syn* vain, vainglorious *Rel* aggrandized, exalted, magnified *Ant* ashamed, humble **3** *Syn* CONCEITED, complacent, egoistic, egotistic (*or* egotistical), important, overweening, pompous, prideful, self-conceited, self-important, self-satisfied, smug, stuck-up, vain, vainglorious *Ant* humble, modest

prove **1** · to establish a point by appropriate objective means *Syn* demonstrate, test, try *Rel* confirm, corroborate, substantiate, verify *Ant* disprove **2** *Syn* INDICATE, argue, attest, bespeak, betoken

provenance *Syn* ORIGIN, inception, prime mover, provenience, root, source

provender *Syn* FOOD (sense 1), comestibles, feed, fodder, forage, provisions, viands, victuals

provenience *Syn* ORIGIN, inception, prime mover, provenance, root, source

proverb *Syn* SAYING, adage, aphorism, apothegm, epigram, maxim, motto, saw

provide *Syn* FURNISH (sense 2), deliver, feed, give, hand, hand over, supply *Ant* hold (back), keep (back), reserve, retain, withhold

providence **1** *Syn* ECONOMY, frugality, husbandry, scrimping, skimping, thrift *Ant* wastefulness **2** *Syn* PRUDENCE, discretion, foresight, forethought

provident **1** *Syn* FRUGAL, economical, economizing, scrimping, sparing, thrifty *Ant* prodigal, wasteful **2** *Syn* PRUDENT, discreet, foresighted, forethoughtful

providential *Syn* LUCKY, fortunate, happy *Ant* unlucky

province **1** *Syn* FIELD, bailiwick, domain, sphere, territory **2** *Syn* FUNCTION, duty, office

provincial *n Syn* HICK, bumpkin, clodhopper, countryman, rustic, yokel *Ant* cosmopolitan, sophisticate

provincial *adj Syn* INSULAR, local, parochial, small-town

provision *Syn* CONDITION, proviso, reservation, stipulation, strings, terms

provisional *Syn* TEMPORARY, acting, ad interim *Ant* permanent

provisions *Syn* FOOD (sense 1), comestibles, feed, fodder, forage, provender, viands, victuals

proviso *Syn* CONDITION, provision, reservation, stipulation, strings, terms

provocative · serving or likely to arouse a strong reaction *Syn* exciting, inciting, instigating, piquing, provoking, stimulating *Rel* explosive, fiery, incendiary, inflammatory, triggering

provoke **1** · to arouse as if pricking *Syn* excite, galvanize, pique, quicken, stimulate *Rel* arouse, rouse, stir **2** *Syn* IRRITATE, aggravate, exasperate, nettle, peeve, rile

provoking *Syn* PROVOCATIVE, exciting, inciting, instigating, piquing, stimulating

prowess *Syn* HEROISM, gallantry, valor

prowl *Syn* WANDER, gad, gallivant, meander, ramble, range, roam, rove, stray, traipse

proximity · the state or condition of being near *Syn* closeness, contiguity, immediacy, nearness *Rel* abutment, juxtaposition *Ant* distance, remoteness

proxy *Syn* AGENT (sense 1), attorney, commissary, delegate, deputy, envoy, factor, procurator, representative

prudence **1** good sense or shrewdness in the management of affairs *Syn* discretion, foresight, forethought, providence *Rel* calculation, caution, circumspection **2** *Syn* COMMON SENSE, discreetness, discretion, horse sense, levelheadedness, sense, sensibleness, wisdom, wit *Ant* imprudence, indiscretion

prudent **1** · making provision for the future *Syn* discreet, foresighted, forethoughtful, provident *Rel* calculating, cautious, circumspect, wary **2** *Syn* EXPEDIENT, advisable, desirable, judicious, politic, tactical, wise *Ant* imprudent, inadvisable, inexpedient, injudicious, unwise **3** *Syn* WISE, judicious, sage, sane, sapient, sensible *Ant* simple

prudish *Syn* PRIM, priggish, prissy, puritanical, straitlaced, stuffy

prune *Syn* CLIP, bob, crop, curtail, cut, cut back, dock, lop (off), nip, pare, shave, shear, snip, trim

pry *Syn* INTERFERE, butt in, intrude, meddle, mess, nose, obtrude, poke, snoop

prying **1** *Syn* CURIOUS, inquisitive, nosy, snoopy *Ant* incurious, uninterested **2** *Syn* INTRUSIVE, interfering, intruding, meddlesome, meddling, nosy (*or* nosey), obtrusive, officious, presumptuous, snoopy *Ant* unobtrusive

pseudo *Syn* COUNTERFEIT, bogus, fake, phony, pinchbeck, sham, spurious *Ant* bona fide, genuine

pseudonym · a fictitious or assumed name *Syn* alias, incognito, nom de guerre, nom de plume, pen name

psyche *Syn* MIND, brain, intellect, intelligence, soul, wit

psychic *Syn* MENTAL, cerebral, intellectual, intelligent

psychosis *Syn* INSANITY, lunacy, mania *Ant* sanity

pub *Syn* BARROOM, bar, café, groggery, grogshop, saloon, tavern

puberty *Syn* YOUTH, adolescence, pubescence *Ant* age

pubescence *Syn* YOUTH, adolescence, puberty *Ant* age

publication *Syn* DECLARATION, advertisement, announcement, broadcasting, proclamation, promulgation

publicity · an act or device designed to attract public interest and to mold public opinion *Syn* ballyhoo, promotion, propaganda *Rel* advertisement, announcement, broadcasting, promulgation, publication

publicize *Syn* ANNOUNCE, advertise, blaze, broadcast, declare, enunciate, placard, post, proclaim, promulgate, publish, sound

public servant *Syn* BUREAUCRAT, functionary

publish *Syn* ANNOUNCE, advertise, blaze, broadcast, declare, enunciate, placard, post, proclaim, promulgate, publicize, sound

puerile 1 *Syn* CALLOW, adolescent, green, immature, inexperienced, juvenile, raw, unfledged, unripe, unripened *Ant* adult, experienced, grown-up, mature, ripe 2 *Syn* CHILDISH, adolescent, babyish, immature, infantile, juvenile, kiddish *Ant* adult, grown-up, mature

puff *Syn* CRITICISM, blurb, critique, review

pugnacious *Syn* BELLIGERENT, aggressive, argumentative, bellicose, combative, contentious, discordant, disputatious, gladiatorial, militant, quarrelsome, scrappy, truculent, warlike *Ant* nonbelligerent, pacific, peaceable, peaceful

pugnacity *Syn* BELLIGERENCE, aggression, aggressiveness, bellicosity, combativeness, contentiousness, disputatiousness, fight, militancy, scrappiness, truculence *Ant* pacifism

puissance *Syn* POWER (sense 1), energy, force, might, strength *Ant* impotence

puissant *Syn* POWERFUL, forceful, forcible, potent *Ant* inefficacious, powerless

pull · to cause to move toward or after an applied force *Syn* drag, draw, hale, haul, tow, tug

pulsate · to course or move with or as if with rhythmic strokes *Syn* beat, palpitate, pulse, throb *Rel* fluctuate, oscillate, swing, vibrate, waver

pulsation · a rhythmical movement or one single step in recurring rhythmic steps *Syn* beat, palpitation, pulse, throb

pulse *vb Syn* PULSATE, beat, palpitate, throb

pulse *n Syn* PULSATION, beat, palpitation, throb

pummel *Syn* BEAT, baste, belabor, buffet, pound, thrash

punch *vb* 1 *Syn* PERFORATE, bore, drill, prick, puncture 2 *Syn* STRIKE, box, clout, cuff, hit, slap, slog, slug, smite, swat

punch *n Syn* VIGOR, dash, drive, élan, esprit, spirit, verve, vim

puncheon *Syn* CASK, barrel, firkin, hogshead, keg, pipe

punctilious *Syn* CAREFUL, meticulous, punctual, scrupulous *Ant* careless

punctual *Syn* CAREFUL, meticulous, punctilious, scrupulous *Ant* careless

puncture *Syn* PERFORATE, bore, drill, prick, punch

pungent · sharp and stimulating to the mind or the senses *Syn* piquant, poignant, racy, snappy, spicy *Rel* biting, cutting, incisive, trenchant *Ant* bland

punish · to inflict a penalty on in requital for wrongdoing *Syn* castigate, chasten, chastise, correct, discipline *Rel* amerce, fine, mulct, penalize *Ant* excuse, pardon

punitive · inflicting, involving, or serving as punishment *Syn* castigating, chastening, chastising, correcting, correctional, corrective, disciplinary, disciplining, penal, penalizing *Rel* retaliatory, retributive, retributory, revengeful

puny *Syn* PETTY, measly, paltry, picayune, picayunish, trifling, trivial *Ant* gross, important, momentous

pupil 1 *Syn* STUDENT, scholar 2 *Syn* FOLLOWER, adherent, convert, disciple, partisan, votary *Ant* leader

purchasable *Syn* VENAL, bribable, corruptible *Ant* incorruptible, uncorruptible

purchase *Syn* BUY, pick up, take

pure 1 · containing nothing that does not properly belong *Syn* absolute, sheer, simple *Rel* elemental, elementary *Ant* adulterated, applied (*of science*), contaminated, polluted 2 *Syn* CHASTE, decent, modest *Ant* bizarre (*of style, effect*); immoral, lewd, wanton

purge *Syn* RID, clear, disabuse, unburden

puritanical *Syn* PRIM, priggish, prissy, prudish, straitlaced, stuffy

purity *Syn* CHASTITY, chasteness, modesty *Ant* immodesty, impurity, unchastity

purloin *Syn* STEAL, cop, filch, lift, pilfer, pinch, snitch, swipe

purport *Syn* SUBSTANCE, burden, core, gist, pith

purported *Syn* SUPPOSED, conjectural, hypothetical, putative, reputed, suppositious, suppositious *Ant* certain

purpose *n* 1 *Syn* GOAL, aim, ambition, aspiration, design, dream, end, intent, intention, mark, meaning, object, objective, plan, pretension, target, thing **2** *Syn* ROLE, capacity, function, job, part, place, position, task, work

purpose *vb Syn* INTEND, design, mean, propose

purposefully *Syn* INTENTIONALLY, consciously, deliberately, designedly, knowingly, purposely, willfully, wittingly *Ant* inadvertently, unconsciously, unintentionally, unknowingly, unwittingly

purposely *Syn* INTENTIONALLY, consciously, deliberately, designedly, knowingly, purposefully, willfully, wittingly *Ant* inadvertently, unconsciously, unintentionally, unknowingly, unwittingly

purse • a container for carrying money and small personal items *Syn* bag, handbag, pocketbook *Rel* billfold, wallet

pursuing *Syn* PURSUIT, chase, chasing, dogging, following, hounding, shadowing, tagging, tailing, tracing, tracking, trailing

pursuit 1 • the act of going after or in the tracks of another *Syn* chase, chasing, dogging, following, hounding, pursuing, shadowing, tagging, tailing, tracing, tracking, trailing *Rel* tagging along **2** *Syn* WORK (sense 2), business, calling, employment, occupation

purvey *Syn* CATER, pander

purview *Syn* RANGE, compass, gamut, horizon, ken, orbit, radius, reach, scope, sweep

push • to press against with force so as to cause to move ahead or aside *Syn* propel, shove, thrust *Rel* drive, impel, move

pushing *Syn* AGGRESSIVE (sense 1), assertive, militant, pushy, self-assertive

pushover *Syn* CINCH, breeze, child's play, duck soup, picnic, snap *Ant* chore, headache, labor

pushy *Syn* AGGRESSIVE (sense 1), assertive, militant, pushing, self-assertive

pusillanimous *Syn* COWARDLY, chicken, chickenhearted, craven, dastardly, lily-livered, recreant, spineless, unheroic, yellow *Ant* brave, courageous, daring, dauntless, doughty, fearless, gallant, greathearted, gutsy, hardy, heroic, intrepid, lionhearted, stalwart, stout, stouthearted, valiant, valorous

puss *Syn* FACE, countenance, mug, physiognomy, visage

pustule *Syn* ABSCESS, boil, carbuncle, furuncle, pimple

put 1 *Syn* ESTIMATE (sense 2), calculate, call, conjecture, figure, gauge, guess, judge, make, place, reckon, suppose **2** *Syn* IMPOSE, assess, charge, exact, fine, lay, levy *Ant* remit **3** *Syn* PHRASE, articulate, clothe, couch, express, formulate, say, state, word

putative *Syn* SUPPOSED, conjectural, hypothetical, purported, reputed, supposititious, suppositious *Ant* certain

put by *Syn* HOARD, cache, lay away, lay up, salt away, squirrel (away), stash, stockpile, store, stow

put-down *Syn* INSULT, affront, barb, dart, dig, epithet, indignity, name, offense (*or* offence), outrage, sarcasm, slight, slur

put off *Syn* POSTPONE, defer, delay, hold off (on), hold up, shelve

put on *Syn* OVERSTATE, exaggerate, overdo, overdraw *Ant* understate

put out *Syn* EXERT, apply, exercise, ply, wield

putrefy *Syn* DECAY, crumble, decompose, disintegrate, rot, spoil

putrid *Syn* MALODOROUS, fetid, fusty, musty, noisome, rancid, rank, stinking *Ant* odorous

putsch *Syn* REBELLION, coup, insurrection, mutiny, revolt, revolution, uprising

put up 1 *Syn* BUILD, assemble, construct, erect, fabricate, make, make up, piece, raise, rear, set up *Ant* disassemble, dismantle, take down **2** *Syn* MARKET, deal (in), merchandise, retail, sell, vend *Ant* buy, purchase **3** *Syn* RESIDE, dwell, live, lodge, sojourn, stay, stop

puzzle *vb* **1** • to baffle and disturb mentally *Syn* bewilder, confound, distract, dumbfound, mystify, nonplus, perplex *Rel* amaze, astound, flabbergast, surprise **2** *Syn* SOLVE, answer, break, crack, dope (out), figure out, resolve, riddle, unravel, work, work out

puzzle *n Syn* MYSTERY, conundrum, enigma, problem, riddle

pygmy *Syn* DWARF, midget, runt

Q

quack *Syn* IMPOSTOR, charlatan, faker, mountebank

quail *Syn* RECOIL, blench, flinch, shrink, wince *Ant* confront, defy

quaint *Syn* STRANGE, curious, eccentric, erratic, odd, outlandish, peculiar, queer, singular, unique *Ant* familiar

quake *Syn* SHAKE (sense 1), dither, quaver, quiver, shimmy, shiver, shudder, teeter, totter, tremble, wobble

qualified *Syn* COMPETENT, able, capable, fit, good, qualified, suitable *Ant* incompetent, inept, poor, unfit, unqualified

qualify 1 *Syn* CHARACTERIZE, distinguish, mark **2** *Syn* MODERATE, temper **3** *Syn* PREPARE, condition, fit, ready

quality 1 · a usually high level of merit or superiority *Syn* caliber, stature *Rel* excellence, virtue **2** *Syn* CHARACTERISTIC, attribute, character, feature, mark, peculiarity, point, property, trait

qualm · an uneasy feeling about the rightness of what one is doing or going to do *Syn* compunction, misgiving, scruple *Rel* conscience

quandary *Syn* PREDICAMENT, dilemma, fix, jam, pickle, plight, scrape

quantity 1 *Syn* AMOUNT, measure, volume **2** *Syn* SUM, aggregate, amount, number, total, whole

quarrel · a usually verbal dispute marked by anger or discord *Syn* altercation, bickering, spat, squabble, tiff, wrangle *Rel* brawl, broil, fracas, melee, row, rumpus, scrap

quarrelsome *Syn* BELLIGERENT, aggressive, argumentative, bellicose, combative, contentious, discordant, disputatious, gladiatorial, militant, pugnacious, scrappy, truculent, warlike *Ant* nonbelligerent, pacific, peaceable, peaceful

quarry *Syn* VICTIM, prey

quash 1 *Syn* ABOLISH, abrogate, annul, cancel, dissolve, invalidate, negate, nullify, repeal, rescind, void **2** *Syn* CRUSH (sense 2), extinguish, quell, quench, suppress

quaver *Syn* SHAKE (sense 1), dither, quake, quiver, shimmy, shiver, shudder, teeter, totter, tremble, wobble

quay *Syn* WHARF, berth, dock, jetty, levee, pier, slip

queenly *Syn* KINGLY, imperial, princely, regal, royal

queer *Syn* STRANGE, curious, eccentric, erratic, odd, outlandish, peculiar, quaint, singular, unique *Ant* familiar

quell *Syn* CRUSH (sense 2), extinguish, quash, quench, suppress

quench *Syn* CRUSH (sense 2), extinguish, quash, quell, suppress

querulous *Syn* IRRITABLE, fractious, fretful, huffy, peevish, pettish, petulant, snappish, waspish *Ant* easygoing

query *Syn* ASK (sense 1), catechize, examine, inquire, interrogate, question, quiz

quest *Syn* ADVENTURE, enterprise

question *vb* **1** *Syn* ASK (sense 1), catechize, examine, inquire, interrogate, query, quiz **2** *Syn* DISTRUST, doubt, mistrust, suspect *Ant* trust

question *n* *Syn* OBJECTION, challenge, complaint, demur, expostulation, fuss, protest, remonstrance

questionable 1 *Syn* DOUBTFUL, dubious, problematic *Ant* cocksure, positive **2** *Syn* IMPROBABLE, doubtful, dubious, farfetched, flimsy, unapt, unlikely *Ant* likely, probable

questioner *Syn* SKEPTIC, disbeliever, doubter, unbeliever

quibble · to make often peevish criticisms or objections about matters that are minor, unimportant, or irrelevant *Syn* carp, cavil, fuss, nitpick *Rel* criticize, fault

quick 1 · able to respond without delay or hesitation or indicative of such ability *Syn* apt, prompt, ready *Rel* clever, intelligent, quickwitted, smart *Ant* sluggish **2** *Syn* FAST, expeditious, fleet, hasty, rapid, speedy, swift *Ant* slow

quicken 1 *Syn* ANIMATE, brace, energize, enliven, fire, invigorate, jazz (up), liven (up), pep (up), stimulate, vitalize, vivify *Ant* damp, dampen, deaden, dull **2** *Syn* HURRY (sense 1), accelerate, hasten, rush, speed (up), whisk *Ant* decelerate, retard, slow (down) **3** *Syn* PROVOKE, excite, galvanize, pique, stimulate

quick-witted *Syn* INTELLIGENT, alert, bright, brilliant, clever, knowing, smart *Ant* unintelligent

quiescence *Syn* ABEYANCE, doldrums, dormancy, latency, suspense, suspension *Ant* continuance, continuation

quiescent *Syn* LATENT, abeyant, dormant, potential *Ant* patent

quiet *n* **1** *Syn* CALM, calmness, hush, peace, peacefulness, placidity, quietness, quietude, repose, restfulness, sereneness, serenity, still, stillness, tranquillity (*or* tranquility) *Ant* bustle, commotion, hubbub, hurly-burly, pandemonium, tumult, turmoil, uproar **2** *Syn* SILENCE, hush, quietness, quietude, still, stillness *Ant* noise, sound

quiet *vb Syn* CALM, compose, lull, quieten, settle, soothe, still, tranquilize *Ant* agitate, arouse

quiet *adj* **1** *Syn* SECLUDED, cloistered, covert, isolated, remote, retired, secret, sheltered **2** *Syn* SILENT (sense 2), hushed, muted, noiseless, quieted, soundless, still *Ant* noisy, unquiet **3** *Syn* STILL, noiseless, silent, stilly *Ant* noisy, stirring

quiet (down) *Syn* SHUT UP, clam up, hush *Ant* speak, talk

quieted *Syn* SILENT (sense 2), hushed, muted, noiseless, quiet, soundless, still *Ant* noisy, unquiet

quieten *Syn* CALM, compose, lull, quiet, settle, soothe, still, tranquilize *Ant* agitate, arouse

quietness 1 *Syn* CALM, calmness, hush, peace, peacefulness, placidity, quiet, quietude, repose, restfulness, sereneness, serenity, still, stillness, tranquillity (*or* tranquility) *Ant* bustle, commotion, hubbub, hurly-burly, pandemonium, tumult, turmoil, uproar **2** *Syn* SILENCE, hush, quiet, quietude, still, stillness *Ant* noise, sound

quietude 1 *Syn* CALM, calmness, hush, peace, peacefulness, placidity, quiet, quietness, repose, restfulness, sereneness, serenity, still, stillness, tranquillity (*or* tranquility) **2** *Syn* SILENCE, hush, quiet, quietness, still, stillness *Ant* noise, sound

quip *vb Syn* JOKE, banter, fool, fun, jest, jive, josh, kid, wisecrack

quip *n Syn* JOKE, crack, gag, jape, jest, wisecrack, witticism

quisling *Syn* TRAITOR, betrayer, doublecrosser, recreant, turncoat

quit **1** *Syn* BEHAVE, acquit, comport, conduct, demean, deport *Ant* misbehave **2** *Syn* GO, depart, leave, retire, withdraw *Ant* come **3** *Syn* STOP, cease, desist, discontinue

quiver *Syn* SHAKE (sense 1), dither, quake, quaver, shimmy, shiver, shudder, teeter, totter, tremble, wobble

quixotic *Syn* IMAGINARY, chimerical, fanciful, fantastic, visionary *Ant* actual, real

quiz *Syn* ASK (sense 1), catechize, examine, inquire, interrogate, query, question

quote **1** · to speak or write again something already said or written by another *Syn* cite, repeat *Rel* adduce, advance, allege **2** *Syn* REPEAT (sense 2), echo, parrot

R

rabble-rouser *Syn* AGITATOR, demagogue, exciter, firebrand, fomenter, incendiary, inciter, instigator

rabid **1** *Syn* ANGRY, angered, apoplectic, enraged, foaming, fuming, furious, incensed, indignant, inflamed, infuriated, irate, ireful, mad, outraged, riled, roiled, sore, steaming, wrathful, wroth *Ant* delighted, pleased **2** *Syn* FURIOUS, delirious, frantic, frenetic, frenzied, wild

race *vb Syn* HURRY (sense 2), barrel, bolt, bowl, breeze, career, course, dash, fly, hasten, hotfoot (it), hump, hurtle, hustle, pelt, rip, rocket, run, rush, rustle, scoot, scurry, scuttle, shoot, speed, step (along), tear, trot, whirl, whisk, zip, zoom *Ant* crawl, creep, poke

race *n Syn* VARIETY (sense 2), breed, clone, cultivar, stock, strain, subspecies

rack *Syn* AFFLICT, agonize, bedevil, curse, harrow, martyr, persecute, plague, torment, torture

racket *Syn* DIN, babel, clamor, hubbub, hullabaloo, pandemonium, uproar *Ant* quiet

racking *Syn* EXCRUCIATING, agonizing

racy *Syn* PUNGENT, piquant, poignant, snappy, spicy *Ant* bland

radiant *Syn* BRIGHT, beaming, brilliant, effulgent, incandescent, lambent, lucent, luminous, lustrous, refulgent *Ant* dim, dull

radiate *Syn* SPREAD, circulate, diffuse, disseminate, propagate

radical *n* · a person who favors rapid and sweeping changes especially in laws and methods of government *Syn* extremist, revolutionist *Ant* moderate

radical *adj* **1** *Syn* FUNDAMENTAL, basal, basic, underlying **2** *Syn* LIBERAL (sense 2), advanced, progressive *Ant* authoritarian

radius *Syn* RANGE, compass, gamut, horizon, ken, orbit, purview, reach, scope, sweep

rag *Syn* BANTER, chaff, jolly, josh, kid, rib

rage **1** *Syn* ANGER, angriness, furor, fury, indignation, irateness, ire, outrage, spleen, wrath, wrathfulness *Ant* delight, pleasure **2** *Syn* FASHION, craze, cry, dernier cri, fad, mode, style, vogue **3** *Syn* FRENZY, agitation, delirium, distraction, furor, furore, fury, hysteria, rampage, uproar

raid **1** *Syn* ATTACK (sense 2), aggression, assault, blitzkrieg, charge, descent, offense (*or* offence), offensive, onset, onslaught, rush, strike **2** *Syn* INVASION, incursion, inroad

raider *Syn* AGGRESSOR, invader

rail *n Syn* RAILING, balustrade, banister, guardrail

rail *vb Syn* SCOLD, bawl, berate, chew out, jaw, rate, revile, tongue-lash, upbraid, vituperate, wig

railer *Syn* CRITIC, carper, castigator, caviler (*or* caviller), censurer, faultfinder, nitpicker, scold

railing · a protective barrier consisting of a horizontal bar and its supports *Syn* balustrade, banister, guardrail, rail *Rel* handrail

raillery *Syn* BANTER, chaff, give-and-take, jesting, joshing, persiflage, repartee

raiment *Syn* CLOTHES, apparel, attire, clothing, dress

rain **1** · a steady falling of water from the sky in significant quantity *Syn* cloudburst, deluge, downpour, rainfall, rainstorm, storm, wet *Rel* precipitation, shower **2** · a heavy fall of objects *Syn* hail, shower, storm *Rel* barrage, broadside, cannonade, fusillade, salvo, volley

rainfall *Syn* RAIN (sense 1), cloudburst, deluge, downpour, rainstorm, storm, wet

rainstorm *Syn* RAIN (sense 1), cloudburst, deluge, downpour, rainfall, storm, wet

raise **1** *Syn* BUILD, assemble, construct, erect, fabricate, make, make up, piece, put up, rear, set up *Ant* disassemble, dismantle, take down **2** *Syn* INCREASE (sense 1), add (to), aggrandize, amplify, augment, boost, compound, enlarge, escalate, expand, extend, multiply, swell, up *Ant* abate, contract, decrease, diminish, lessen, lower, reduce, subtract (from) **3** *Syn* LIFT, boost, elevate, heave, hoist, rear *Ant* lower

raised *Syn* ERECT, perpendicular, plumb, standing, upright, upstanding, vertical *Ant* flat, recumbent

rally¹ *vb* **1** *Syn* CONVALESCE, gain, heal, mend, recover, recuperate, snap back **2** *Syn* STIR, arouse, awaken, rouse, waken

rally² *vb* **1** *Syn* RIDICULE, deride, mock, taunt, twit **2** *Syn* TEASE, chaff, jive, josh, kid, razz, rib, ride, roast

ram *Syn* PACK, cram, crowd, stuff, tamp

ramble 1 *Syn* WALK, constitutional, perambulation, range, saunter, stroll, turn **2** *Syn* WANDER, gad, gallivant, meander, prowl, range, roam, rove, stray, traipse

rambler *Syn* NOMAD, drifter, gadabout, roamer, rover, stroller, vagabond, wanderer, wayfarer

rambunctious *Syn* BOISTEROUS, knockabout, raucous, rowdy *Ant* orderly

rampage *Syn* FRENZY, agitation, delirium, distraction, furor, furore, fury, hysteria, rage, uproar

rampart *Syn* BULWARK, bastion, breastwork, parapet

rancid *Syn* MALODOROUS, fetid, fusty, musty, noisome, putrid, rank, stinking *Ant* odorous

rancor *Syn* ENMITY, animosity, animus, antagonism, antipathy, hostility *Ant* amity

random · determined by accident rather than by design *Syn* casual, chance, chancy, desultory, haphazard, happy-go-lucky, hit-or-miss *Rel* accidental, casual, fortuitous *Ant* methodical, nonrandom, orderly, systematic

randomly *Syn* HIT OR MISS, aimlessly, anyhow, anyway, anywise, desultorily, erratically, haphazard, haphazardly, helterskelter, irregularly *Ant* methodically, systematically

range *n* **1** · the extent that lies within the powers of something to cover or control *Syn* compass, gamut, horizon, ken, orbit, purview, radius, reach, scope, sweep *Rel* area, extent **2** *Syn* HABITAT, biotope, station **3** *Syn* WALK, constitutional, perambulation, ramble, saunter, stroll, turn

range *vb* **1** *Syn* LINE, align, array, line up **2** *Syn* WANDER, gad, gallivant, meander, prowl, ramble, roam, rove, stray, traipse

rangy *Syn* LANKY, gangling, gangly, spindling, spindly

rank *vb Syn* CLASS, gradate, grade, graduate, rate

rank *adj* **1** *Syn* EGREGIOUS, blatant, conspicuous, flagrant, glaring, gross, obvious, patent, pronounced, striking **2** *Syn* FLAGRANT, glaring, gross **3** *Syn* MALODOROUS, fetid,

fusty, musty, noisome, putrid, rancid, stinking *Ant* odorous

rank *n Syn* LINE, echelon, file, row, tier

rankle *Syn* ANGER, antagonize, enrage, incense, inflame, infuriate, madden, outrage, rile, roil *Ant* delight, gratify, please

rankling *Syn* ANNOYING, aggravating, bothersome, disturbing, exasperating, frustrating, galling, irksome, irritating, maddening, nettling, peeving, pesty, riling, vexatious, vexing

ransack *Syn* SEEK, comb, ferret out, hunt, rummage, scour, search

ransom *Syn* RESCUE, deliver, reclaim, redeem, save

rant *vb* · to talk loudly and wildly *Syn* bluster, fulminate, rave, spout *Rel* sound off, speak out, speak up

rant *n Syn* BOMBAST, fustian, rhapsody, rodomontade

rap *vb* **1** *Syn* CHAT, babble, blab, cackle, chatter, converse, gab, gabble, gas, jabber, jaw, palaver, patter, prate, prattle, rattle, run on, talk, twitter, visit **2** *Syn* TAP, knock, thud, thump

rap *n* **1** *Syn* CHAT, chatter, chitchat, gabfest, gossip, palaver, small talk, table talk, talk, tête-à-tête **2** *Syn* TAP, knock, thud, thump **3** *Syn* CHARGE, complaint, count, indictment

rapacious *Syn* VORACIOUS, gluttonous, ravening, ravenous

rapaciousness *Syn* GREED, acquisitiveness, avarice, avariciousness, avidity, covetousness, cupidity, greediness, rapacity

rapacity *Syn* GREED, acquisitiveness, avarice, avariciousness, avidity, covetousness, cupidity, greediness, rapaciousness

rapid *Syn* FAST, expeditious, fleet, hasty, quick, speedy, swift *Ant* slow

rapport · a friendly relationship marked by ready communication and mutual understanding *Syn* communion, fellowship, rapprochement *Rel* accord, agreement, concord, harmony

rapprochement *Syn* RAPPORT, communion, fellowship

rapscallion *Syn* VILLAIN, blackguard, knave, miscreant, rascal, rogue, scamp, scoundrel

rapt *Syn* INTENT, absorbed, engrossed *Ant* distracted

rapture *Syn* ECSTASY, elation, euphoria, exhilaration, heaven, intoxication, paradise, rhapsody, transport *Ant* depression

rapturous *Syn* ECSTATIC, elated, enraptured, entranced, euphoric, exhilarated, intoxicated, rhapsodic *Ant* depressed

rare 1 *Syn* CHOICE, dainty, delicate, elegant, exquisite, recherché *Ant* indifferent, medium **2** *Syn* INFREQUENT, occasional, scarce, sporadic, uncommon *Ant* frequent **3** *Syn* THIN, slender, slight, slim, tenuous *Ant* thick

rarefy *Syn* THIN, attenuate, dilute, extenuate *Ant* thicken

rarely *Syn* SELDOM, infrequently, little *Ant* frequently, often

rascal *Syn* VILLAIN, blackguard, knave, miscreant, rapscallion, rogue, scamp, scoundrel

rash *Syn* ADVENTUROUS, daredevil, daring, foolhardy, reckless, venturesome *Ant* cautious, unadventurous

rasp *Syn* SCRAPE, grate, grind, scratch

rate¹ *vb* **1** *Syn* CLASS, gradate, grade, graduate, rank **2** *Syn* DESERVE, earn, merit **3** *Syn* ESTIMATE (sense 1), appraise, assay, assess, evaluate, value

rate² *vb* *Syn* SCOLD, bawl, berate, chew out, jaw, rail, revile, tongue-lash, upbraid, vituperate, wig

ration *n* · an amount allotted or made available especially from a limited supply *Syn* allowance, dole, pittance *Rel* apportionment, portion, portioning

ration *vb* *Syn* APPORTION, parcel, portion, prorate

rationalize *Syn* EXPLAIN (sense 2), account (for), explain away

rattle **1** *Syn* CHAT, babble, blab, cackle, chatter, converse, gab, gabble, gas, jabber, jaw, palaver, patter, prate, prattle, rap, talk, twitter, visit **2** *Syn* EMBARRASS, abash, discomfit, disconcert, faze *Ant* facilitate, relieve

rattling *Syn* VERY, awful, awfully, beastly, deadly, especially, exceedingly, extra, extremely, far, frightfully, full, greatly, heavily, highly, hugely, jolly, mightily, mighty, mortally, most, much, particularly, real, right, so, something, super, terribly, too, whacking *Ant* little, negligibly, nominally, slightly

raucous **1** *Syn* BOISTEROUS, knockabout, rambunctious, rowdy *Ant* orderly **2** *Syn* LOUD, earsplitting, hoarse, stentorian, stertorous, strident *Ant* low, low-pitched

ravage · to lay waste by plundering or destroying *Syn* despoil, devastate, pillage, sack, spoliate, waste *Rel* demolish, destroy, raze

rave **1** *Syn* GUSH (sense 2), enthuse, fuss, rhapsodize, slobber **2** *Syn* RANT, bluster, fulminate, spout

ravening *Syn* VORACIOUS, gluttonous, rapacious, ravenous

ravenous *Syn* VORACIOUS, gluttonous, rapacious, ravening

rave(s) *Syn* APPLAUSE, acclamation, cheering, cheers, ovation, plaudit(s) *Ant* booing, hissing

ravine *Syn* CANYON, defile, flume, gap, gorge, gulch, gulf, notch, pass

ravish *Syn* ENTRANCE, carry away, enrapture, enthrall (*or* enthral), overjoy, transport

ravishing *Syn* BEAUTIFUL, attractive, beauteous, comely, cute, fair, gorgeous, handsome, knockout, lovely, pretty, sightly, stunning, taking *Ant* homely, ill-favored, plain, ugly, unattractive, unbeautiful, unhandsome, unlovely, unpretty, unsightly

raw **1** *Syn* CALLOW, adolescent, green, immature, inexperienced, juvenile, puerile, unfledged, unripe, unripened *Ant* adult, experienced, grown-up, mature, ripe **2** *Syn* RUDE (sense 1), callow, crude, green, rough, uncouth *Ant* civil, urbane

rawboned *Syn* LEAN, angular, gaunt, lank, lanky, scrawny, skinny, spare *Ant* fleshy

raw deal *Syn* DISSERVICE, injury, injustice, wrong *Ant* justice

rawness *Syn* CHILL, bite, bitterness, bleakness, chilliness, nip, sharpness

raze *Syn* DESTROY, demolish

razz *Syn* TEASE, chaff, jive, josh, kid, rally, rib, ride, roast

reach *vb* · to arrive at a point by effort or work *Syn* achieve, attain, compass, gain *Rel* accomplish, effect, execute, fulfill, perform

reach *n* *Syn* RANGE, compass, gamut, horizon, ken, orbit, purview, radius, scope, sweep

react *Syn* ACT (sense 1), behave, function, operate, work

readdress *Syn* RECONSIDER, reanalyze, reconceive, reevaluate, reexamine, rethink, review, reweigh

readily *Syn* EASILY, effortlessly, facilely, fluently, freely, handily, lightly, painlessly, smoothly *Ant* arduously, laboriously

readiness · the power of doing something without evidence of effort *Syn* dexterity, ease, facility *Rel* aptness, promptness, quickness

ready *vb* *Syn* PREPARE, condition, fit, qualify

ready *adj* *Syn* QUICK, apt, prompt *Ant* sluggish

real *adj* *Syn* ACTUAL, concrete, existent, factual, true, very *Ant* conjectural, hypothetical, ideal, nonexistent, possible, potential, theoretical

real *adv* *Syn* VERY, awful, awfully, beastly, deadly, especially, exceedingly, extra, extremely, far, frightfully, full, greatly, heavily, highly, hugely, jolly, mightily, mighty, mortally, most, much, particularly, rattling, right, so, something, super, terribly, too, whacking *Ant* little, negligibly, nominally, slightly

realization *Syn* FRUITION, accomplishment, achievement, actuality, attainment, consummation, fulfillment *Ant* naught, nonfulfillment

realize **1** · to bring into concrete existence something that has existed as an abstraction or a conception or a possibility *Syn* actualize, embody, externalize, hypostatize, incarnate, materialize, objectify, reify *Rel* accomplish, achieve, effect, execute, fulfill, perform **2** *Syn* EARN, acquire, attain, capture, carry, draw, gain, garner, get, land, make, obtain, procure, secure, win *Ant* forfeit, lose **3** *Syn* THINK (sense 1), conceive, envisage, envision, fancy, imagine

reanalyze *Syn* RECONSIDER, readdress, reconceive, reevaluate, reexamine, rethink, review, reweigh

reanimation *Syn* REVIVAL, rebirth, regeneration, rejuvenation, renewal, resurgence, resurrection, resuscitation, revitalization

reap · to do the work of collecting ripened crops *Syn* garner, gather, glean, harvest *Rel* assemble, collect

rear *n* **1** *Syn* BACK, hind, hindmost, posterior, rearward *Ant* anterior, fore, forward, front **2** *Syn* BUTTOCKS, backside, bottom, breech, butt, fanny, hams, haunches, posterior, rump, seat

rear *vb* **1** *Syn* BUILD, assemble, construct, erect, fabricate, make, make up, piece, put up, raise, set up *Ant* disassemble, dismantle, take down **2** *Syn* LIFT, boost, elevate, heave, hoist, raise *Ant* lower

rearward *Syn* BACK, hind, hindmost, posterior, rear *Ant* anterior, fore, forward, front

reason *n* **1** · a point or points that support something open to question *Syn* argument, ground, proof *Rel* explanation, justification, rationalization **2** · the power of the mind by which people attain truth or knowledge *Syn* intuition, understanding *Rel* brain, intellect, intelligence, mind **3** *Syn* CAUSE, antecedent, determinant, occasion **4** *Syn* EXCUSE, alibi, defense, justification, plea

reason *vb* *Syn* THINK (sense 2), cogitate, deliberate, reflect, speculate

reasoned *Syn* DEDUCTIVE, deducible, derivable, inferable

rebate *Syn* DEDUCTION, abatement, discount

rebel · one who rises up against constituted authority or the established order *Syn* iconoclast, insurgent *Rel* adversary, antagonist, opponent

rebellion · an outbreak against authority *Syn* coup, insurrection, mutiny, putsch, revolt, revolution, uprising *Rel* sedition, treason

rebellious **1** *Syn* DISOBEDIENT, balky, contrary, defiant, froward, insubordinate, intractable, recalcitrant, refractory, restive, ungovernable, unruly, untoward, wayward, willful (*or* wilful) *Ant* amenable, compliant, docile, obedient, tractable **2** *Syn* INSUBORDINATE, contumacious, factious, mutinous, seditious

rebelliousness *Syn* DISOBEDIENCE, contrariness, defiance, frowardness, insubordination, intractability, recalcitrance, refractoriness, unruliness, willfulness *Ant* amenability, compliance, docility, obedience

rebirth *Syn* REVIVAL, reanimation, regeneration, rejuvenation, renewal, resurgence, resurrection, resuscitation, revitalization

rebound · to spring back to an original position or shape *Syn* recoil, repercuss, resile, reverberate *Rel* bound, ricochet, skip

rebuild *Syn* MEND, patch, repair

rebuke **1** *Syn* CENSURE, condemnation, denunciation, reprimand, reproach, reproof, stricture *Ant* citation, commendation, endorsement **2** *Syn* REPROVE, admonish, chide, reprimand, reproach

rebut *Syn* DISPROVE, confute, controvert, refute *Ant* demonstrate, prove

recalcitrance *Syn* DISOBEDIENCE, contrariness, defiance, frowardness, insubordination, intractability, rebelliousness, refractoriness, unruliness, willfulness *Ant* amenability, compliance, docility, obedience

recalcitrant **1** *Syn* DISOBEDIENT, balky, contrary, defiant, froward, insubordinate, intractable, rebellious, refractory, restive, ungovernable, unruly, untoward, wayward, willful (*or* wilful) *Ant* amenable, compliant, docile, obedient, tractable **2** *Syn* UNCONTROLLABLE, froward, headstrong, intractable, refractory, ungovernable, unmanageable, unruly, untoward, wayward, willful (*or* wilful) *Ant* controllable, governable, tractable **3** *Syn* UNRULY, headstrong, intractable, refractory, ungovernable, willful *Ant* docile, tractable

recall *n* *Syn* CANCELLATION, abortion, calling, calling off, dropping, repeal, rescission, revocation *Ant* continuation

recall *vb* **1** *Syn* REMEMBER, bethink, mind, recollect, remind, reminisce *Ant* forget **2** *Syn* REVOKE, repeal, rescind, reverse

recant *Syn* ABJURE, forswear, renounce, retract *Ant* pledge (*allegiance, a vow*), elect (*a way of life, a means to an end*)

recap *Syn* SUMMARIZE, abstract, digest, encapsulate, epitomize, outline, recapitulate, sum up, wrap up

recapitulate *Syn* SUMMARIZE, abstract, digest, encapsulate, epitomize, outline, recap, sum up, wrap up

recast *Syn* CHANGE (sense 1), alter, make over, modify, redo, refashion, remake, remodel, revamp, revise, rework, vary *Ant* fix, freeze, set, stabilize

recede · to move backward *Syn* back, retract, retreat, retrograde *Rel* depart, retire, withdraw *Ant* advance, proceed

receipt · a formula or set of directions for the compounding of ingredients especially in cookery and medicine *Syn* prescription, recipe

receive · to bring and accept into one's possession, one's presence, a group, or the mind *Syn* accept, admit, take *Rel* enter, penetrate

receptacle *Syn* CONTAINER, holder, vessel

recess **1** *Syn* ADJOURN, suspend **2** *Syn* PAUSE, break, breath, breather, interruption, lull

recessed *Syn* HOLLOW, concave, dented, depressed, indented, sunken *Ant* bulging, convex, protruding, protuberant

recherché *Syn* CHOICE, dainty, delicate, elegant, exquisite, rare *Ant* indifferent, medium

recipe *Syn* RECEIPT, prescription

reciprocal 1 · shared, felt, or shown by both sides concerned *Syn* common, mutual *Rel* partaken, participated, shared **2** · like, equivalent, or similarly related to each other (as in kind, quality, or value) *Syn* complemental, complementary, convertible, correlative, corresponding *Rel* equivalent, identical, same

reciprocate · to give back usually in kind or in quantity *Syn* requite, retaliate, return *Rel* exchange, interchange

recite *Syn* RELATE, describe, narrate, recount, rehearse, report, state

reckless *Syn* ADVENTUROUS, daredevil, daring, foolhardy, rash, venturesome *Ant* cautious, unadventurous

reckon 1 *Syn* CALCULATE, compute, estimate **2** *Syn* CONSIDER (sense 2), account, deem, regard **3** *Syn* ESTIMATE (sense 2), calculate, call, conjecture, figure, gauge, guess, judge, make, place, put, suppose **4** *Syn* RELY (ON), bank, count, depend, trust

reckoning *Syn* CALCULATION, arithmetic, ciphering, computation, figures, figuring

reclaim *Syn* RESCUE, deliver, ransom, redeem, save

recluse · a person who leads a secluded or solitary life *Syn* anchorite, cenobite, eremite, hermit

recognition · a learning process that relates a perception of something new to knowledge already possessed *Syn* apperception, assimilation, identification

recoil 1 · to draw back in fear or distaste *Syn* blench, flinch, quail, shrink, wince *Rel* falter, hesitate, waver *Ant* confront, defy **2** *Syn* REBOUND, repercuss, resile, reverberate

recollect *Syn* REMEMBER, bethink, mind, recall, remind, reminisce *Ant* forget

recollection *Syn* MEMORY, mind, remembrance, reminiscence, souvenir *Ant* oblivion

recommend *Syn* COMMEND, applaud, compliment *Ant* admonish, censure

recommendation *Syn* CREDENTIAL, character, reference, testimonial

recompense *Syn* PAY, compensate, indemnify, reimburse, remunerate, repay, satisfy

reconceive *Syn* RECONSIDER, readdress, reanalyze, reevaluate, reexamine, rethink, review, reweigh

reconcile *Syn* ADAPT, accommodate, adjust, conform *Ant* unfit

recondite · beyond the reach of the average intelligence *Syn* abstruse, esoteric, occult *Rel* erudite, learned, scholarly

reconsider · to consider again especially with the possibility of change or reversal *Syn* readdress, reanalyze, reconceive, reevaluate, reexamine, rethink, review, reweigh *Rel* reappraise, reassess

record *vb* **1** · to set down in writing usu-ally for the purpose of written evidence or official record of *Syn* catalog, enroll, list, register *Rel* admit, enter, introduce **2** *Syn* RELATE, describe, narrate, recite, rehearse, report, state

record *n Syn* DOCUMENT, archive, monument

recount *Syn* RELATE, describe, narrate, recite, rehearse, report, state

recoup *Syn* RECOVER, recruit, regain, retrieve

recover 1 · to get back again *Syn* recoup, recruit, regain, retrieve *Rel* reclaim, redeem, rescue **2** *Syn* CONVALESCE, gain, heal, mend, rally, recuperate, snap back **3** *Syn* IMPROVE (sense 2), convalesce, gain, recuperate

recreant *adj Syn* COWARDLY, chicken, chickenhearted, craven, dastardly, lily-livered, pusillanimous, spineless, unheroic, yellow *Ant* brave, courageous, daring, dauntless, doughty, fearless, gallant, greathearted, gutsy, hardy, heroic, intrepid, lionhearted, stalwart, stout, stouthearted, valiant, valorous

recreant *n* **1** *Syn* COWARD, chicken, craven, dastard, poltroon *Ant* hero, stalwart, valiant **2** *Syn* RENEGADE, apostate, backslider, turncoat *Ant* adherent, loyalist **3** *Syn* TRAITOR, betrayer, double-crosser, quisling, turncoat

recreate *Syn* AMUSE, divert, entertain *Ant* bore

recreation *Syn* AMUSEMENT, diversion, entertainment *Ant* boredom

recrudesce *Syn* RETURN, recur, revert

recrudescence *Syn* RETURN, recurrence, reversion

recruit *n Syn* BEGINNER, colt, fledgling, freshman, greenhorn, neophyte, newbie, newcomer, novice, rookie, tenderfoot, tyro *Ant* old hand, old-timer, vet, veteran

recruit *vb Syn* RECOVER, recoup, regain, retrieve

rectifiable *Syn* REMEDIABLE, correctable, fixable, repairable, reparable *Ant* incorrigible, irremediable, irreparable

rectify *Syn* CORRECT, amend, emend, redress, reform, remedy, revise

rectitude *Syn* GOODNESS, morality, virtue *Ant* badness, evil

recuperate 1 *Syn* CONVALESCE, gain, heal, mend, rally, recover, snap back **2** *Syn* IMPROVE (sense 2), convalesce, gain, recover

recur *Syn* RETURN, recrudesce, revert

recurrence *Syn* RETURN, recrudescence, reversion

recurrent *Syn* INTERMITTENT, alternate, periodic *Ant* continual, incessant

redact *Syn* EDIT, adapt, compile, revise, rewrite

redden *Syn* BLUSH, bloom, color, crimson, flush, glow

redeem *Syn* RESCUE, deliver, ransom, reclaim, save

redeemer *Syn* SAVIOR, deliverer, rescuer, saver

red-hot 1 *Syn* FERVENT, ardent, blazing,

burning, charged, emotional, fervid, feverish, fiery, flaming, glowing, hot-blooded, impassioned, passionate, vehement, warm, warm-blooded *Ant* cold, cool, dispassionate, impassive, unemotional **2** *Syn* MODERN, contemporary, current, hot, mod, modernistic, new, newfangled, new-fashioned, present-day, space-age, ultramodern, up-to-date *Ant* antiquated, archaic, dated, fusty, musty, noncontemporary, oldfangled, old-fashioned, old-time, out-of-date, passé

redo *Syn* CHANGE (sense 1), alter, make over, modify, recast, refashion, remake, remodel, revamp, revise, rework, vary *Ant* fix, freeze, set, stabilize

redolence *Syn* FRAGRANCE, bouquet, incense, perfume *Ant* stench, stink

redolent **1** *Syn* FRAGRANT, ambrosial, aromatic, perfumed, savory, scented, sweet *Ant* fetid, foul, malodorous, noisome, putrid, rancid, rank, reeking, reeky, smelly, stinking, stinky, strong **2** *Syn* ODOROUS, aromatic, balmy, fragrant *Ant* malodorous, odorless

redress *vb* *Syn* CORRECT, amend, emend, rectify, reform, remedy, revise

redress *n* *Syn* REPARATION, amends, indemnity, restitution

reduce **1** *Syn* CONQUER, beat, defeat, lick, overcome, overthrow, rout, subdue, subjugate, surmount, vanquish **2** *Syn* DECREASE, abate, diminish, dwindle, lessen *Ant* increase **3** *Syn* DEGRADE, declass, demote, disrate *Ant* elevate

redundancy *Syn* VERBIAGE, circumlocution, periphrasis, pleonasm, tautology

redundant *Syn* WORDY, diffuse, prolix, verbose *Ant* compact, concise, crisp, pithy, succinct, terse

reduplication *Syn* COPY, carbon copy, duplicate, duplication, facsimile, imitation, replica, replication, reproduction *Ant* original

reef *Syn* SHOAL, bank, bar

reek *Syn* HAZE (sense 1), fog, mist, murk, smog, soup

reel · to move uncertainly or uncontrollably or unsteadily (as from weakness or intoxication) *Syn* stagger, totter, whirl *Rel* revolve, rotate, spin, turn

reevaluate *Syn* RECONSIDER, readdress, reanalyze, reconceive, reexamine, rethink, review, reweigh

reexamine *Syn* RECONSIDER, readdress, reanalyze, reconceive, reevaluate, rethink, review, reweigh

refashion *Syn* CHANGE (sense 1), alter, make over, modify, recast, redo, remake, remodel, revamp, revise, rework, vary *Ant* fix, freeze, set, stabilize

refer **1** · to call or direct attention to something *Syn* advert, allude *Rel* insert, interpolate, introduce **2** *Syn* ASCRIBE, accredit, assign, attribute, charge, credit, impute **3** *Syn* RESORT, apply, go, turn

referee *Syn* JUDGE, arbiter, arbitrator, umpire

reference *Syn* CREDENTIAL, character, recommendation, testimonial

referendum *Syn* MANDATE, initiative, plebiscite

refined *Syn* CULTIVATED, civilized, cultured, genteel, polished *Ant* philistine, uncivilized, uncultured, unpolished, unrefined

refinement **1** *Syn* ADVANCE (sense 1), advancement, breakthrough, enhancement, improvement *Ant* setback **2** *Syn* CULTURE, breeding, cultivation **3** *Syn* ELEGANCE, class, elegancy, grace, gracefulness, handsomeness, majesty, stateliness

reflect *Syn* THINK (sense 2), cogitate, deliberate, reason, speculate

reflection *Syn* ANIMADVERSION, aspersion, stricture *Ant* commendation

reflective **1** *Syn* CONTEMPLATIVE, meditative, melancholy, pensive, ruminant, thoughtful *Ant* unreflective **2** *Syn* THOUGHTFUL (sense 1), contemplative, meditative, pensive, speculative *Ant* thoughtless

reform *Syn* CORRECT, amend, emend, rectify, redress, remedy, revise

refractoriness *Syn* DISOBEDIENCE, contrariness, defiance, frowardness, insubordination, intractability, rebelliousness, recalcitrance, unruliness, willfulness *Ant* amenability, compliance, docility, obedience

refractory **1** *Syn* DISOBEDIENT, balky, contrary, defiant, froward, insubordinate, intractable, rebellious, recalcitrant, restive, ungovernable, unruly, untoward, wayward, willful (*or* wilful) *Ant* amenable, compliant, docile, obedient, tractable **2** *Syn* UNCONTROLLABLE, froward, headstrong, intractable, recalcitrant, ungovernable, unmanageable, unruly, untoward, wayward, willful (*or* wilful) *Ant* controllable, governable, tractable **3** *Syn* UNRULY, headstrong, intractable, recalcitrant, ungovernable, willful *Ant* docile, tractable

refrain · to hold oneself back from doing or indulging in *Syn* abstain, forbear *Rel* arrest, check, interrupt

refresh *Syn* RENEW, refurbish, rejuvenate, renovate, restore

refreshing *Syn* TONIC, bracing, invigorating, restorative, reviving, stimulating, stimulative, vitalizing

refuge *Syn* SHELTER, asylum, cover, retreat, sanctuary

refulgent *Syn* BRIGHT, beaming, brilliant, effulgent, incandescent, lambent, lucent, luminous, lustrous, radiant *Ant* dim, dull

refund *Syn* REPAY, reimburse

refurbish *Syn* RENEW, refresh, rejuvenate, renovate, restore

refusal *Syn* DENIAL (sense 1), disallowance, nay, no, rejection *Ant* allowance, grant

refuse *n* · matter that is regarded as worthless

and fit only for throwing away *Syn* debris, garbage, offal, rubbish, trash, waste

refuse *vb Syn* DECLINE, reject, repudiate, spurn *Ant* accept

refute *Syn* DISPROVE, confute, controvert, rebut *Ant* demonstrate, prove

regain *Syn* RECOVER, recoup, recruit, retrieve

regal *Syn* KINGLY, imperial, princely, queenly, royal

regale *Syn* PLEASE, delight, gladden, gratify, rejoice, tickle *Ant* anger, displease, vex

regalia *Syn* FINERY, array, best, bravery, caparison, feather, frippery, full dress, gaiety

regard *n* · a feeling of deferential approval and liking *Syn* respect, esteem, admiration *Rel* deference, homage, honor, reverence *Ant* despite

regard *vb* **1** · to recognize the worth of a person or thing *Syn* admire, esteem, respect *Rel* appreciate, cherish, prize, treasure, value *Ant* despise **2** *Syn* CONSIDER (sense 2), account, deem, reckon

regardful *Syn* RESPECTFUL, deferential, dutiful *Ant* disrespectful

regarding *Syn* ABOUT, concerning, respecting

regards *Syn* COMPLIMENTS, congratulations, felicitations, greetings, respects

regeneration *Syn* REVIVAL, reanimation, rebirth, rejuvenation, renewal, resurgence, resurrection, resuscitation, revitalization

regime *Syn* RULE (sense 2), administration, authority, governance, government, jurisdiction, regimen

regimen *Syn* RULE (sense 2), administration, authority, governance, government, jurisdiction, regime

region **1** · a part or portion having no fixed boundaries *Syn* area, demesne, field, zone *Rel* section **2** *Syn* AREA, belt, tract, zone

register *n Syn* LIST, catalog, inventory, roll, roster, schedule, table

register *vb Syn* RECORD, catalog, enroll, list

regress · to go back to a previous and usually lower state or level *Syn* retrogress, revert *Rel* backslide, lapse, relapse *Ant* advance, develop, evolve, progress

regression · the act or an instance of going back to an earlier and lower level especially of intelligence or behavior *Syn* retrogression, reversion *Rel* backslide, lapse, relapse *Ant* advancement, development, evolution, progression

regressive *Syn* BACKWARD, retrograde, retrogressive *Ant* advanced

regret *vb* · to feel sorry or dissatisfied about *Syn* bemoan, deplore, lament, repent, rue *Rel* bewail, grieve (for), mourn, sorrow (for)

regret *n Syn* SORROW, anguish, grief, heartache, heartbreak, woe *Ant* joy

regrettable · of a kind to cause great distress *Syn* deplorable, distressful, distressing, grievous, heartbreaking, heartrending, lam-

entable, unfortunate, woeful *Rel* affecting, moving, poignant, touching

regular **1** · being of the sort or kind that is expected as usual, ordinary, or average *Syn* natural, normal, typical *Rel* customary, habitual, usual *Ant* irregular **2** *Syn* ORDERLY, methodical, systematic *Ant* chaotic, disorderly

regularize *Syn* STANDARDIZE, formalize, homogenize, normalize

regulate *Syn* ADJUST, fix *Ant* derange

regulation **1** *Syn* LAW, canon, ordinance, precept, rule, statute **2** *Syn* RULE (sense 1), bylaw, ground rule

regurgitate *Syn* BELCH, burp, disgorge, spew, throw up, vomit

rehearsal · a private performance or session in preparation for a public appearance *Syn* dry run, practice, trial *Rel* dress rehearsal

rehearse *Syn* RELATE, describe, narrate, recite, recount, report, state

reify *Syn* REALIZE, actualize, embody, externalize, hypostatize, incarnate, materialize, objectify

reimburse **1** *Syn* PAY, compensate, indemnify, recompense, remunerate, repay, satisfy **2** *Syn* REPAY, refund

reinforce *Syn* STRENGTHEN, energize, fortify, invigorate *Ant* weaken

reissue *Syn* EDITION, impression, printing, reprinting

reiterate *Syn* REPEAT (sense 1), ingeminate, iterate

reject *Syn* DECLINE, refuse, repudiate, spurn *Ant* accept

rejected *Syn* ABANDONED (sense 2), derelict, deserted, disused, forgotten, forsaken, vacated

rejection **1** *Syn* DENIAL, disallowance, nay, no, refusal *Ant* allowance, grant **2** *Syn* DENIAL (sense 2), contradiction, disallowance, disavowal, disclaimer, negation, repudiation *Ant* acknowledgment, admission, avowal, confirmation

rejoice *Syn* PLEASE, delight, gladden, gratify, regale, tickle *Ant* anger, displease, vex

rejoicing *Syn* EXULTANT, exulting, glorying, jubilant, triumphant

rejoin *Syn* ANSWER, reply, respond, retort

rejoinder *Syn* ANSWER (sense 1), reply, response, retort

rejuvenate *Syn* RENEW, refresh, refurbish, renovate, restore

rejuvenation *Syn* REVIVAL, reanimation, rebirth, regeneration, renewal, resurgence, resurrection, resuscitation, revitalization

relapse *Syn* LAPSE, backslide

relate **1** · to tell orally or in writing the details or circumstances of a situation *Syn* describe, narrate, recite, recount, rehearse, report, state *Rel* disclose, divulge, reveal, tell **2** *Syn* BEAR (sense 3), appertain, apply, belong, pertain **3** *Syn* JOIN, associate, combine, conjoin, connect, link, unite *Ant* disjoin, part

related · connected by or as if by family ties *Syn* affiliated, allied, cognate, kindred *Rel* associated, connected

relation *Syn* RELATIVE, kin, kinsman

relative *n* · a person connected with another by blood or marriage *Syn* kin, kinsman, relation *Rel* in-law

relative *adj* **1** *Syn* DEPENDENT, conditional, contingent *Ant* absolute, infinite, original **2** *Syn* PERTINENT, applicable, apposite, apropos, germane, material, pointed *Ant* extraneous, immaterial, inapplicable, irrelevant, pointless

relax *Syn* SLACKEN, ease, loosen, slack *Ant* strain, stretch, tense, tighten

relaxation *Syn* REST, comfort, ease, leisure, repose

relaxed *Syn* LOOSE, lax, slack *Ant* strict, tight

release *n* *Syn* ANNOUNCEMENT, ad, advertisement, bulletin, notice, notification, posting

release *vb* *Syn* FREE, discharge, emancipate, liberate, manumit

relegate *Syn* COMMIT (sense 1), confide, consign, entrust

relent *Syn* YIELD, bow, capitulate, cave, defer, submit, succumb

relentless *Syn* GRIM, implacable, merciless, unrelenting *Ant* lenient

relevant *Syn* PERTINENT, applicable, apposite, apropos, germane, material, pointed, relative *Ant* extraneous, immaterial, inapplicable, irrelevant, pointless

reliable *Syn* DEPENDABLE, good, responsible, safe, solid, steady, sure, tried, tried-and-true, true, trustworthy, trusty *Ant* irresponsible, undependable, unreliable, untrustworthy

reliance *Syn* TRUST, confidence, dependence, faith *Ant* mistrust

relic *Syn* VESTIGE, shadow, trace

relief *Syn* SUBSTITUTE, backup, pinch hitter, replacement, reserve, stand-in, sub

relieve · to make something more tolerable or less grievous *Syn* allay, alleviate, assuage, lighten, mitigate *Rel* comfort, console, solace *Ant* alarm, embarrass, intensify

religion · a system of religious belief or the body of persons who accept such a system *Syn* church, communion, creed, denomination, faith, persuasion, sect

religious *n* · a member of a religious order usually bound by monastic vows of poverty, chastity, and obedience *Syn* friar, monk, nun

religious *adj* *Syn* HOLY (sense 1), devout, godly, pious, sainted, saintly *Ant* faithless, godless, impious, irreligious, ungodly, unholy

relinquish · to give up completely *Syn* abandon, cede, leave, resign, surrender, waive, yield *Rel* abdicate, renounce *Ant* keep

relish *vb* *Syn* LIKE, dote, enjoy, fancy, love *Ant* dislike

relish *n* **1** *Syn* LIKING, appetite, fancy, favor, fondness, like, love, partiality, preference, shine, taste, use *Ant* aversion, disfavor, dislike, distaste, hatred, loathing **2** *Syn* TASTE (sense 1), flavor, savor, smack, tang *Ant* antipathy

relishing *Syn* PALATABLE, appetizing, flavorsome, sapid, savory, tasty, toothsome *Ant* distasteful, unpalatable

reluctance · a lack of willingness or desire to do or accept something *Syn* disinclination, hesitance, hesitancy, unwillingness *Rel* faltering, hesitation, indecision, irresolution, shilly-shallying, staggering, vacillation, wavering *Ant* inclination, willingness

reluctant *Syn* DISINCLINED, averse, hesitant, indisposed, loath

rely (on) *or* **rely upon** · to have or place full confidence *Syn* bank, count, depend, reckon, trust *Rel* commit, confide, entrust

remain *Syn* STAY, abide, linger, tarry, wait

remainder · a remaining or left-over group, part, or trace *Syn* balance, leavings, remains, remnant, residue, residuum, rest

remains *Syn* REMAINDER, balance, leavings, remnant, residue, residuum, rest

remake *Syn* CHANGE (sense 1), alter, make over, modify, recast, redo, refashion, remodel, revamp, revise, rework, vary *Ant* fix, freeze, set, stabilize

remark *n* · an expression of opinion or judgment *Syn* comment, commentary, note, obiter dictum, observation

remark *vb* **1** · to make observations and pass judgment thereon *Syn* animadvert, comment, commentate **2** *Syn* SEE (sense 1), behold, contemplate, descry, discern, espy, note, notice, observe, perceive, survey, view

remarkable *Syn* NOTICEABLE, arresting, conspicuous, outstanding, prominent, salient, signal, striking

remediable · capable of being corrected *Syn* correctable, fixable, rectifiable, repairable, reparable *Rel* amendable, improvable, resolvable *Ant* incorrigible, irremediable, irreparable

remedial *Syn* CURATIVE, corrective, restorative, sanative

remedy *n* · something prescribed or used for the treatment of disease *Syn* cure, medicament, medication, medicine, physic, specific

remedy *vb* **1** *Syn* CORRECT, amend, emend, rectify, redress, reform, revise **2** *Syn* CURE, heal

remember · to bring an image or idea from the past into the mind *Syn* bethink, mind, recall, recollect, remind, reminisce *Ant* forget

remembrance 1 *Syn* MEMORIAL, commemorative, keepsake, memento, monument, reminder, souvenir, token **2** *Syn* MEMORY, mind, recollection, reminiscence, souvenir *Ant* oblivion

remind *Syn* REMEMBER, bethink, mind, recall, recollect, reminisce *Ant* forget

reminder *Syn* MEMORIAL, commemorative, keepsake, memento, monument, remembrance, souvenir, token

reminisce *Syn* REMEMBER, bethink, mind, recall, recollect, remind *Ant* forget

reminiscence *Syn* MEMORY, mind, recollection, remembrance, souvenir *Ant* oblivion

remiss *Syn* NEGLIGENT, careless, derelict, lax, neglectful, neglecting, slack *Ant* attentive, careful, conscientious

remission *Syn* PARDON, absolution, amnesty, forgiveness, remittal *Ant* penalty, punishment, retribution

remit 1 *Syn* EXCUSE, condone, forgive, pardon *Ant* punish 2 *Syn* SEND, dispatch, forward, route, ship, transmit *Ant* accept, receive

remittable *Syn* VENIAL, excusable, forgivable, pardonable *Ant* inexcusable, mortal, unforgivable, unpardonable

remittal *Syn* PARDON, absolution, amnesty, forgiveness, remission *Ant* penalty, punishment, retribution

remnant *Syn* REMAINDER, balance, leavings, remains, residue, residuum, rest

remodel *Syn* CHANGE (sense 1), alter, make over, modify, recast, redo, refashion, remake, revamp, revise, rework, vary *Ant* fix, freeze, set, stabilize

remonstrance *Syn* OBJECTION, challenge, complaint, demur, expostulation, fuss, protest, question

remonstrate *Syn* OBJECT, expostulate, kick, protest *Ant* acquiesce

remorse *Syn* PENITENCE, attrition, compunction, contrition, repentance

remorseful *Syn* GUILTY, ashamed, contrite, hangdog, penitent, repentant, shamed, shamefaced *Ant* impenitent, remorseless, shameless, unashamed, unrepentant

remorseless · not sorry for having done wrong *Syn* impenitent, unrepentant *Rel* compassionless, cruel, merciless, pitiless, ruthless, unmerciful *Ant* contrite, guilty, penitent, regretful, remorseful, repentant, sorry

remote 1 *Syn* DISTANT, far, faraway, far-off, removed 2 *Syn* SECLUDED, cloistered, covert, isolated, quiet, retired, secret, sheltered

remove *Syn* MOVE (sense 2), shift, transfer

removed *Syn* DISTANT, far, faraway, far-off, remote

remunerate *Syn* PAY, compensate, indemnify, recompense, reimburse, repay, satisfy

remunerative *Syn* PAYING, gainful, lucrative, profitable

rend *Syn* TEAR, cleave, rip, rive, split

rendezvous 1 *Syn* ENGAGEMENT, appointment, assignation, date, tryst 2 *Syn* HANGOUT, haunt, resort

renegade · a person who forsakes his or her faith, party, cause, or allegiance and aligns with another *Syn* apostate, backslider, recreant, turncoat *Rel* iconoclast, insurgent, rebel *Ant* adherent, loyalist

renege · to break a promise or agreement *Syn* back down, back off, cop out *Rel* chicken (out)

renew 1 · to make like new *Syn* refresh, refurbish, rejuvenate, renovate, restore *Rel* mend, rebuild, repair 2 *Syn* RESUME, continue, reopen, restart

renewal *Syn* REVIVAL, reanimation, rebirth, regeneration, rejuvenation, resurgence, resurrection, resuscitation, revitalization

renounce 1 *Syn* ABDICATE, resign *Ant* assume, usurp 2 *Syn* ABJURE, forswear, recant, retract *Ant* pledge (*allegiance, a vow*), elect (*a way of life, a means to an end*)

renovate *Syn* RENEW, refresh, refurbish, rejuvenate, restore

renown *Syn* FAME, celebrity, éclat, glory, honor, notoriety, reputation, repute *Ant* infamy, obscurity

renowned *Syn* FAMOUS, celebrated, famed, noted, notorious, prominent, star, well-known *Ant* anonymous, obscure, unknown

rent 1 *Syn* HIRE, charter, lease, let 2 *Syn* BREACH, break, rift, rupture, schism, split

renter *Syn* TENANT, boarder, lodger, roomer *Ant* landlord

renunciation · voluntary surrender or putting aside of something desired or desirable *Syn* abnegation, self-abnegation, self-denial *Rel* eschewing, forbearing, forgoing, sacrifice, sacrificing *Ant* indulgence, self-indulgence

reopen *Syn* RESUME, continue, renew, restart

repair *Syn* MEND, patch, rebuild

repairable *Syn* REMEDIABLE, correctable, fixable, rectifiable, reparable *Ant* incorrigible, irremediable, irreparable

reparable *Syn* REMEDIABLE, correctable, fixable, rectifiable, repairable *Ant* incorrigible, irremediable, irreparable

reparation · a return for something lost or suffered, usually through the fault of another *Syn* amends, indemnity, redress, restitution *Rel* atonement, expiation

repartee 1 *Syn* BANTER, chaff, give-and-take, jesting, joshing, persiflage, raillery 2 *Syn* WIT, humor, irony, sarcasm, satire

repast *Syn* MEAL, chow, feed, mess, table

repay 1 · to make a return payment to *Syn* refund, reimburse *Rel* quit, satisfy, settle 2 *Syn* PAY, compensate, indemnify, recompense, reimburse, remunerate, satisfy

repeal *vb* 1 *Syn* ABOLISH, abrogate, annul, cancel, dissolve, invalidate, negate, nullify, quash, rescind, void 2 *Syn* REVOKE, recall, rescind, reverse

repeal *n* *Syn* CANCELLATION, abortion, calling, calling off, dropping, recall, rescission, revocation *Ant* continuation

repeat **1** · to say or do again *Syn* ingeminate, iterate, reiterate *Rel* recrudesce, recur, return, revert **2** · to say after another *Syn* echo, parrot, quote *Rel* mouth **3** *Syn* QUOTE, cite

repel *Syn* DISGUST, nauseate, repulse, revolt, sicken, turn off

repellent *Syn* REPUGNANT, abhorrent, distasteful, invidious, obnoxious *Ant* congenial

repent *Syn* REGRET, bemoan, deplore, lament, rue

repentance *Syn* PENITENCE, attrition, compunction, contrition, remorse

repentant *Syn* GUILTY, ashamed, contrite, hangdog, penitent, remorseful, shamed, shamefaced *Ant* impenitent, remorseless, shameless, unashamed, unrepentant

repercuss *Syn* REBOUND, recoil, resile, reverberate

rephrase *Syn* PARAPHRASE, restate, reword, translate *Ant* quote

repine *Syn* COMPLAIN, beef, bellyache, carp, crab, croak, fuss, gripe, grouse, growl, grumble, kick, moan, murmur, mutter, squawk, wail, whine, yammer *Ant* rejoice

replace · to put out of a usual or proper place or into the place of another *Syn* displace, supersede, supplant *Rel* renew, restore

replacement *Syn* SUBSTITUTE, backup, pinch hitter, relief, reserve, stand-in, sub

replete *Syn* FULL, complete, plenary *Ant* empty

replete *Syn* RIFE, abounding, flush, fraught, swarming, teeming, thick, thronging

replica *Syn* COPY, carbon copy, duplicate, duplication, facsimile, imitation, reduplication, replication, reproduction *Ant* original

replication *Syn* COPY, carbon copy, duplicate, duplication, facsimile, imitation, reduplication, replica, reproduction *Ant* original

reply *vb Syn* ANSWER, rejoin, respond, retort

reply *n Syn* ANSWER (sense 1), rejoinder, response, retort

report *n* **1** · common talk or an instance of it that spreads rapidly *Syn* gossip, hearsay, rumor *Rel* conversation, conversing, speaking, speech, talk, talking **2** *Syn* ACCOUNT, chronicle, story, version **3** *Syn* LETTER, dispatch, epistle, memorandum, message, missive, note

report *vb Syn* RELATE, describe, narrate, recite, recount, rehearse, state

reporter · a person employed by a newspaper, magazine, or radio or television station to gather, write, or report news *Syn* correspondent, journalist *Rel* announcer, broadcaster, newscaster, newsman, newspaperman

repose **1** *Syn* CALM, calmness, hush, peace, peacefulness, placidity, quiet, quietness, quietude, restfulness, sereneness, serenity, still, stillness, tranquillity (*or* tranquility) *Ant* bustle, commotion, hubbub, hurly-burly, pan-

demonium, tumult, turmoil, uproar **2** *Syn* REST, comfort, ease, leisure, relaxation

repository *Syn* STOREHOUSE, depository, depot, magazine, storage, stowage, warehouse

reprehend *Syn* CRITICIZE, blame, censure, condemn, denounce, reprobate

represent · to present an image or lifelike imitation of (as in art) *Syn* delineate, depict, limn, picture, portray *Rel* display, exhibit, show

representative **1** *Syn* AGENT (sense 1), attorney, commissary, delegate, deputy, envoy, factor, procurator, proxy **2** *Syn* AMBASSADOR, delegate, emissary, envoy, legate, minister **3** *Syn* DELEGATE, deputy **4** *Syn* EXAMPLE, case, exemplar, illustration, instance, sample, specimen

reprimand **1** *Syn* CENSURE, condemnation, denunciation, rebuke, reproach, reproof, stricture *Ant* citation, commendation, endorsement **2** *Syn* REPROVE, admonish, chide, rebuke, reproach

reprinting *Syn* EDITION, impression, printing, reissue

reprisal *Syn* RETALIATION, retribution, revenge, vengeance

reproach *n* **1** *Syn* CENSURE, condemnation, denunciation, rebuke, reprimand, reproof, stricture *Ant* citation, commendation, endorsement **2** *Syn* REPROVE, admonish, chide, rebuke, reprimand

reprobate *adj* **1** *Syn* ABANDONED (sense 1), dissolute, profligate *Ant* redeemed, regenerate **2** *Syn* CORRUPT, debased, debauched, decadent, degenerate, degraded, demoralized, depraved, dissipated, dissolute, perverse, perverted, warped *Ant* uncorrupted

reprobate *vb Syn* CRITICIZE, blame, censure, condemn, denounce, reprehend

reprobate *n Syn* OUTCAST, castaway, derelict, pariah, untouchable

reproduce *Syn* GENERATE, beget, breed, engender, get, procreate, propagate, sire

reproduction *Syn* COPY, carbon copy, duplicate, duplication, facsimile, imitation, reduplication, replica, replication *Ant* original

reproof *Syn* CENSURE, condemnation, denunciation, rebuke, reprimand, reproach, stricture *Ant* citation, commendation, endorsement

reprove **1** · to criticize adversely *Syn* admonish, chide, rebuke, reprimand, reproach *Rel* censure, criticize, reprehend, reprobate **2** *Syn* DISAPPROVE (OF), deprecate, discountenance, disfavor, dislike, frown (on) *Ant* approve, favor, like

republican *Syn* DEMOCRATIC, popular, self-governing, self-ruling *Ant* undemocratic

repudiate **1** *Syn* DECLINE, refuse, reject, spurn *Ant* accept **2** *Syn* DISCLAIM, disallow, disavow, disown *Ant* claim

repudiation *Syn* DENIAL (sense 2), contradiction, disallowance, disavowal, disclaimer, negation, rejection *Ant* acknowledgment, admission, avowal, confirmation

repugnance *Syn* DISGUST, aversion, distaste, loathing, nausea, repulsion, revulsion

repugnant 1 · so alien or unlikable as to arouse antagonism and aversion *Syn* abhorrent, distasteful, invidious, obnoxious, repellent *Rel* alien, extraneous, extrinsic, foreign *Ant* congenial 2 *Syn* OFFENSIVE, loathsome, repulsive, revolting

repulse *Syn* DISGUST, turn off

repulsion *Syn* DISGUST, aversion, distaste, loathing, nausea, repugnance, revulsion

repulsive *Syn* OFFENSIVE, loathsome, repugnant, revolting

reputation *Syn* FAME, celebrity, éclat, glory, honor, notoriety, renown, repute *Ant* infamy, obscurity

repute *Syn* FAME, celebrity, éclat, glory, honor, notoriety, renown, reputation *Ant* infamy, obscurity

reputed *Syn* SUPPOSED, conjectural, hypothetical, purported, putative, supposititious, suppositious *Ant* certain

request *Syn* ASK, solicit

require 1 *Syn* DEMAND, claim, exact 2 *Syn* LACK, need, want

required *Syn* MANDATORY, compulsory, forced, imperative, incumbent, involuntary, necessary, nonelective, obligatory, peremptory *Ant* elective, optional, voluntary

requirement · something essential to the existence or occurrence of something else *Syn* prerequisite, requisite

requisite *adj Syn* NEEDFUL, essential, indispensable, necessary

requisite *n Syn* REQUIREMENT, prerequisite

requite *Syn* RECIPROCATE, retaliate, return

rescind 1 *Syn* ABOLISH, abrogate, annul, cancel, dissolve, invalidate, negate, nullify, quash, repeal, void 2 *Syn* REVOKE, recall, repeal, reverse

rescission *Syn* CANCELLATION, abortion, calling, calling off, dropping, recall, repeal, revocation *Ant* continuation

rescue · to set free from confinement or danger *Syn* deliver, ransom, reclaim, redeem, save *Rel* emancipate, free, liberate, manumit, release

rescuer *Syn* SAVIOR, deliverer, redeemer, saver

research *vb Syn* EXPLORE, delve (into), dig (into), inquire (into), investigate, look (into), probe

research *n Syn* INQUIRY, inquest, inquisition, investigation, probe

resemblance *Syn* SIMILARITY, alikeness, community, correspondence, likeness, parallelism, similitude *Ant* dissimilarity, unlikeness

resembling *Syn* ALIKE, akin, analogous, comparable, correspondent, corresponding, like,

matching, parallel, similar, such, suchlike *Ant* different, dissimilar, diverse, unlike

resentful *Syn* ENVIOUS, covetous, invidious, jaundiced, jealous

resentment *Syn* OFFENSE (sense 1), dudgeon, huff, pique, umbrage

reservation *Syn* CONDITION, provision, proviso, stipulation, strings, terms

reserve *vb Syn* KEEP (sense 2), detain, hold back, keep back, keep out, retain, withhold *Ant* relinquish

reserve *n* 1 *Syn* SUBSTITUTE, backup, pinch hitter, relief, replacement, stand-in, sub 1 *Syn* STORE, cache, deposit, hoard

reserved *Syn* SILENT (sense 1), close, close-lipped, closemouthed, reticent, secretive, taciturn, tight-lipped, uncommunicative *Ant* talkative

reside · to have as one's habitation or domicile *Syn* dwell, live, lodge, put up, sojourn, stay, stop *Rel* abide, remain

residence *Syn* HABITATION, abode, domicile, dwelling, home, house

resident *Syn* INHABITANT, denizen, dweller, habitant, occupant, resider *Ant* transient

resider *Syn* INHABITANT, denizen, dweller, habitant, occupant, resident *Ant* transient

residue *Syn* REMAINDER, balance, leavings, remains, remnant, residuum, rest

residuum *Syn* REMAINDER, balance, leavings, remains, remnant, residue, rest

resign 1 *Syn* ABDICATE, renounce *Ant* assume, usurp 2 *Syn* RELINQUISH, abandon, cede, leave, surrender, waive, yield *Ant* keep

resignation 1 *Syn* COMPLIANCE, acquiescence *Ant* forwardness 2 *Syn* PATIENCE, forbearance, longanimity, long-suffering *Ant* impatience

resigned 1 *Syn* COMPLIANT, acquiescent *Ant* forward 2 *Syn* PASSIVE, acquiescent, nonresistant, tolerant, tolerating, unresistant, unresisting, yielding *Ant* protesting, resistant, resisting, unyielding

resile *Syn* REBOUND, recoil, repercuss, reverberate

resilient 1 *Syn* ELASTIC (sense 1), flexible, springy, supple *Ant* rigid 2 *Syn* ELASTIC (sense 2), buoyant, effervescent, expansive, volatile *Ant* depressed

resist · to stand firm against a person or influence *Syn* antagonize, combat, conflict, contest, fight, oppose, withstand *Rel* assail, assault, attack *Ant* submit

resistance · the inclination to resist *Syn* defiance, opposition *Rel* demur, objection, protest, remonstrance *Ant* acquiescence

resolution *Syn* ANALYSIS, breakdown, dissection *Ant* synthesis

resolvable *Syn* SOLVABLE, answerable, explainable, explicable, soluble *Ant* inexplicable, insoluble, unexplainable, unsolvable

resolve 1 *Syn* DECIDE, determine, rule, settle

2 *Syn* SOLVE, answer, break, crack, dope (out), figure out, puzzle (out), riddle, unravel, work, work out

resolved *Syn* DECIDED, decisive, determined

resonant · marked by conspicuously full and rich sounds or tones (as of speech or music) *Syn* orotund, resounding, ringing, sonorous, vibrant *Rel* full, replete

resort *vb* · to betake oneself or to have recourse when in need of help or relief *Syn* apply, go, refer, turn *Rel* address, devote, direct

resort *n* **1** *Syn* HANGOUT, haunt, rendezvous **2** *Syn* RESOURCE, expedient, makeshift, shift, stopgap, substitute, surrogate

resounding *Syn* RESONANT, orotund, ringing, sonorous, vibrant

resource · something one turns to in the absence of the usual means or source of supply *Syn* expedient, makeshift, resort, shift, stopgap, substitute, surrogate *Rel* contraption, contrivance, device

resources *Syn* POSSESSIONS, assets, belongings, effects, means

respect *n* *Syn* REGARD, admiration, esteem *Ant* despite

respect *vb* *Syn* REGARD, admire, esteem *Ant* despise

respectable *Syn* ADEQUATE, acceptable, all right, decent, fine, OK (*or* okay), passable, satisfactory, tolerable *Ant* deficient, inadequate, lacking, unacceptable, unsatisfactory, wanting

respectful · marked by or showing proper regard for another's higher status *Syn* deferential, dutiful, regardful *Rel* reverent, reverential, venerating, worshipful *Ant* disrespectful

respecting *Syn* ABOUT, concerning, regarding

respectively *Syn* EACH, apiece, individually, severally

respects *Syn* COMPLIMENTS, congratulations, felicitations, greetings, regards

resplendence *Syn* MAGNIFICENCE, augustness, brilliance, gloriousness, glory, grandeur, grandness, majesty, nobility, nobleness, splendor, stateliness, stupendousness, sublimeness, superbness

resplendent *Syn* SPLENDID, glorious, gorgeous, sublime, superb

respond *Syn* ANSWER, rejoin, reply, retort

response *Syn* ANSWER (sense 1), rejoinder, reply, retort

responsibility *Syn* OBLIGATION, burden, charge, commitment, duty, need

responsible **1** · subject to being held to account *Syn* accountable, amenable, answerable, liable *Rel* exposed, open, subject **2** *Syn* DEPENDABLE, good, reliable, safe, solid, steady, sure, tried, tried-and-true, true, trustworthy, trusty *Ant* irresponsible, undependable, unreliable, untrustworthy

responsive **1** *Syn* SENTIENT, impressible, impressionable, sensitive, susceptible **2** *Syn* TENDER, compassionate, sympathetic, warm, warmhearted *Ant* callous, severe

rest *n* **1** · freedom from toil or strain *Syn* comfort, ease, leisure, relaxation, repose *Rel* deferring, intermission, intermitting, suspending, suspension **2** *Syn* REMAINDER, balance, leavings, remains, remnant, residue, residuum

rest *vb* *Syn* BASE, found, ground, stay

restart *Syn* RESUME, continue, renew, reopen

restate *Syn* PARAPHRASE, rephrase, reword, translate *Ant* quote

restaurant · a public establishment where meals are served to paying customers for consumption on the premises *Syn* café, diner, grill *Rel* cafeteria, coffeehouse, garden, luncheonette, lunchroom, snack bar, tearoom

restful *Syn* COMFORTABLE, cozy, easy, snug *Ant* miserable, uncomfortable

restfulness *Syn* CALM, calmness, hush, peace, peacefulness, placidity, quiet, quietness, quietude, repose, sereneness, serenity, still, stillness, tranquillity (*or* tranquility) *Ant* bustle, commotion, hubbub, hurly-burly, pandemonium, tumult, turmoil, uproar

restitution *Syn* REPARATION, amends, indemnity, redress

restive **1** *Syn* CONTRARY, balky, froward, perverse, wayward *Ant* complaisant, good-natured **2** *Syn* DISOBEDIENT, balky, contrary, defiant, froward, insubordinate, intractable, rebellious, recalcitrant, refractory, ungovernable, unruly, untoward, wayward, willful (*or* wilful) *Ant* amenable, compliant, docile, obedient, tractable **3** *Syn* IMPATIENT, fidgety, jittery, jumpy, nervous, restless, uneasy, unquiet *Ant* patient

restiveness *Syn* UNREST, disquiet, ferment, restlessness, turmoil, uneasiness *Ant* calm, ease, peace, quiet

restless *Syn* IMPATIENT, fidgety, jittery, jumpy, nervous, restive, uneasy, unquiet *Ant* patient

restlessness *Syn* UNREST, disquiet, ferment, restiveness, turmoil, uneasiness *Ant* calm, ease, peace, quiet

restorative **1** *Syn* CURATIVE, corrective, remedial, sanative **2** *Syn* TONIC, bracing, invigorating, refreshing, reviving, stimulating, stimulative, vitalizing

restore **1** · to help or cause to regain signs of life and vigor *Syn* resuscitate, revive, revivify *Rel* cure, heal, remedy **2** *Syn* RENEW, refresh, refurbish, rejuvenate, renovate

restrain · to hold back from or control in doing something *Syn* bridle, check, curb, inhibit *Rel* arrest, interrupt *Ant* abandon (*oneself*), activate, impel, incite

restraint **1** *Syn* FORCE, coercion, compulsion, constraint, duress, violence **2** *Syn* RESTRICTION, check, condition, constraint, curb, fetter, limitation

restrict *Syn* LIMIT, circumscribe, confine *Ant* widen

restriction · something that limits one's freedom of action or choice *Syn* check, condition, constraint, curb, fetter, limitation, restraint *Rel* stipulation, strings

result 1 *Syn* ANSWER (sense 2), solution **2** *Syn* EFFECT, aftereffect, aftermath, consequence, event, issue, outcome, sequel, upshot *Ant* cause

result (in) *Syn* EFFECT, bring about, cause, create, effectuate, engender, generate, induce, make, produce, prompt, spawn, work, yield

resume · to begin again or return to after an interruption *Syn* continue, renew, reopen, restart *Rel* resuscitate, revive

resurgence *Syn* REVIVAL, reanimation, rebirth, regeneration, rejuvenation, renewal, resurrection, resuscitation, revitalization

resurrection *Syn* REVIVAL, reanimation, rebirth, regeneration, rejuvenation, renewal, resurgence, resuscitation, revitalization

resuscitate *Syn* RESTORE, revive, revivify

resuscitation *Syn* REVIVAL, reanimation, rebirth, regeneration, rejuvenation, renewal, resurgence, resurrection, revitalization

retail *Syn* MARKET, deal (in), merchandise, put up, sell, vend *Ant* buy, purchase

retain *Syn* KEEP (sense 2), detain, hold back, keep back, keep out, reserve, withhold *Ant* relinquish

retainer *Syn* SERVANT, domestic, flunky, lackey, menial, steward *Ant* master

retaliate 1 *Syn* RECIPROCATE, requite, return **2** *Syn* AVENGE, revenge

retaliation · the act of inflicting or the intent to inflict injury in return for injury *Syn* reprisal, retribution, revenge, vengeance *Rel* correcting, correction, discipline, disciplining, punishment

retard 1 *Syn* DELAY (sense 1), detain, slacken, slow *Ant* expedite, hasten **2** *Syn* SLOW, brake, decelerate *Ant* accelerate, hasten, hurry, quicken, rush, speed (up), step up

rethink *Syn* RECONSIDER, readdress, reanalyze, reconceive, reevaluate, reexamine, review, reweigh

reticent 1 *Syn* SECRETIVE, close, closemouthed, dark, uncommunicative *Ant* communicative, open **2** *Syn* SILENT (sense 1), close, close-lipped, closemouthed, reserved, secretive, taciturn, tight-lipped, uncommunicative *Ant* talkative

retire *Syn* GO, depart, leave, quit, withdraw *Ant* come

retired *Syn* SECLUDED, cloistered, covert, isolated, quiet, remote, secret, sheltered

retort *vb Syn* ANSWER, rejoin, reply, respond

retort *n Syn* ANSWER (sense 1), rejoinder, reply, response

retract 1 *Syn* ABJURE, forswear, recant, renounce *Ant* pledge (*allegiance, a vow*), elect

(*a way of life, a means to an end*) **2** *Syn* RECEDE, back, retreat, retreat, retrograde *Ant* advance, proceed

retreat *vb Syn* RECEDE, back, retract, retrograde *Ant* advance, proceed

retreat *n Syn* SHELTER, asylum, cover, refuge, sanctuary

retrench *Syn* SHORTEN, abbreviate, abridge, curtail *Ant* elongate, extend, lengthen, prolong, protract

retribution *Syn* RETALIATION, reprisal, revenge, vengeance

retrieve *Syn* RECOVER, recoup, recruit, regain

retrograde *adj Syn* BACKWARD, regressive, retrogressive *Ant* advanced

retrograde *vb Syn* RECEDE, back, retract, retreat *Ant* advance, proceed

retrogress *Syn* REGRESS, revert *Ant* advance, develop, evolve, progress

retrogression *Syn* REGRESSION, reversion *Ant* advancement, development, evolution, progression

retrogressive *Syn* BACKWARD, regressive, retrograde *Ant* advanced

return *n* · the act of coming back to or from a place or condition *Syn* recrudescence, recurrence, reversion

return *vb* **1** · to go or come back (as to a person, place, or condition) *Syn* recrudesce, recur, revert *Rel* advert **2** *Syn* RECIPROCATE, requite, retaliate

revamp *Syn* CHANGE (sense 1), alter, make over, modify, recast, redo, refashion, remake, remodel, revise, rework, vary *Ant* fix, freeze, set, stabilize

reveal · to make known what has been or should be concealed *Syn* betray, disclose, discover, divulge, tell *Rel* communicate, impart *Ant* conceal

revealing *Syn* EXPRESSIVE, eloquent, meaning, meaningful, pregnant, significant, suggestive

revelation 1 · disclosure or something disclosed by or as if by divine or preternatural means *Syn* prophecy, vision *Ant* adumbration **2** · the act or an instance of making known something previously unknown or concealed *Syn* disclosure, divulgence, exposure *Rel* bombshell, surprise

revenge *vb Syn* AVENGE, retaliate

revenge *n Syn* RETALIATION, reprisal, retribution, vengeance

revengeful *Syn* VINDICTIVE, vengeful

reverberate *Syn* REBOUND, recoil, repercuss, resile

revere · to honor and admire profoundly and respectfully *Syn* adore, reverence, venerate, worship *Rel* admire, esteem, regard, respect *Ant* flout

reverence *n* **1** · a feeling of worshipful respect *Syn* adoration, veneration, worship *Rel* ardor, fervor, passion, zeal **2** · the emotion inspired by what arouses one's deep respect or veneration *Syn* awe, fear **3** *Syn* HONOR, deference, homage, obeisance

reverence *vb Syn* REVERE, adore, venerate, worship *Ant* flout

reverie · the state of being lost in thought *Syn* daydreaming, study, trance, woolgathering *Rel* contemplation, meditation, musing

reverse *vb* **1** · to change to the opposite position *Syn* invert, transpose *Rel* capsize, overturn, upset **2** *Syn* REVOKE, recall, repeal, rescind

reverse *n Syn* OPPOSITE, antipode, antithesis, antonym, contradictory, contrary, converse, counter

reversion **1** *Syn* REGRESSION, retrogression *Ant* advancement, development, evolution, progression **2** *Syn* RETURN, recrudescence, recurrence

revert **1** *Syn* REGRESS, retrogress *Ant* advance, develop, evolve, progress **2** *Syn* RETURN, recrudesce, recur

review *n* **1** *Syn* CRITICISM, blurb, critique, puff **2** *Syn* INSPECTION, audit, check, checkup, examination, scan, scrutiny, survey **3** *Syn* JOURNAL, magazine, newspaper, organ, periodical

review *vb Syn* RECONSIDER, readdress, reanalyze, reconceive, reevaluate, reexamine, rethink, reweigh

revile *Syn* SCOLD, bawl, berate, chew out, jaw, rail, rate, tongue-lash, upbraid, vituperate, wig

revise **1** *Syn* CHANGE (sense 1), alter, make over, modify, recast, redo, refashion, remake, remodel, revamp, rework, vary *Ant* fix, freeze, set, stabilize **2** *Syn* CORRECT, amend, emend, rectify, redress, reform, remedy **3** *Syn* EDIT, adapt, compile, redact, rewrite

revitalization *Syn* REVIVAL, reanimation, rebirth, regeneration, rejuvenation, renewal, resurgence, resurrection, resuscitation

revival · the act or an instance of bringing something back to life, public attention, or vigorous activity *Syn* reanimation, rebirth, regeneration, rejuvenation, renewal, resurgence, resurrection, resuscitation, revitalization *Rel* renaissance, renascence

revive **1** *Syn* COME TO, come around, come round **2** *Syn* RESTORE, resuscitate, revivify

revivify *Syn* RESTORE, resuscitate, revive

reviving *Syn* TONIC, bracing, invigorating, refreshing, restorative, stimulating, stimulative, vitalizing

revocation *Syn* CANCELLATION, abortion, calling, calling off, dropping, recall, repeal, rescission *Ant* continuation

revoke · to annul by recalling or taking back *Syn* recall, repeal, rescind, reverse *Rel* abrogate, annul, void

revolt *vb Syn* DISGUST, nauseate, repel, repulse, sicken, turn off

revolt *n Syn* REBELLION, coup, insurrection, mutiny, putsch, revolution, uprising

revolting *Syn* OFFENSIVE, loathsome, repugnant, repulsive

revolution *Syn* REBELLION, coup, insurrection, mutiny, putsch, revolt, uprising

revolutionary *Syn* RADICAL, extremist, revolutionist *Ant* moderate

revolutionist *Syn* RADICAL, extremist, revolutionary *Ant* moderate

revolve *Syn* TURN (sense 1), circle, eddy, gyrate, pirouette, rotate, spin, swirl, twirl, wheel, whirl

revulsion *Syn* DISGUST, aversion, distaste, loathing, nausea, repugnance, repulsion

rewarding *Syn* HEARTWARMING, cheering, comforting, encouraging, fulfilling, gladdening, gratifying, heartening, satisfying *Ant* depressing, discouraging, disheartening, dispiriting

reweigh *Syn* RECONSIDER, readdress, reanalyze, reconceive, reevaluate, reexamine, rethink, review

reword *Syn* PARAPHRASE, rephrase, restate, translate *Ant* quote

rework *Syn* CHANGE (sense 1), alter, make over, modify, recast, redo, refashion, remake, remodel, revamp, revise, vary *Ant* fix, freeze, set, stabilize

rewrite *Syn* EDIT, adapt, compile, redact, revise

rhapsodic *Syn* ECSTATIC, elated, enraptured, entranced, euphoric, exhilarated, intoxicated, rapturous *Ant* depressed

rhapsodize *Syn* GUSH (sense 2), enthuse, fuss, rave, slobber

rhapsody **1** *Syn* BOMBAST, fustian, rant, rodomontade **2** *Syn* ECSTASY, elation, euphoria, exhilaration, heaven, intoxication, paradise, rapture, transport *Ant* depression

rhetorical · emphasizing style often at the expense of thought *Syn* aureate, bombastic, euphuistic, flowery, grandiloquent, magniloquent *Rel* articulate, eloquent, fluent, glib, vocal, voluble

rhymer *Syn* POET, bard, minstrel, poetaster, rhymester, troubadour, versifier

rhymester *Syn* POET, bard, minstrel, poetaster, rhymer, troubadour, versifier

rhythm · the recurrent pattern formed by a series of sounds having a regular rise and fall in intensity *Syn* beat, cadence, measure, meter *Rel* accent, accentuation, emphasis, stress

rib **1** *Syn* BANTER, chaff, jolly, josh, kid, rag **2** *Syn* TEASE, chaff, jive, josh, kid, rally, razz, ride, roast

ribald *Syn* COARSE, gross, obscene, vulgar *Ant* fine, refined

ribbon *Syn* STRIP, band, fillet, stripe

rich **1** · having goods, property, and money in abundance *Syn* affluent, opulent, wealthy *Ant* poor **2** *Syn* FERTILE, fat, fecund, fruitful, luxuriant, productive, prolific *Ant* barren, infertile, sterile, unfruitful, unproductive

richly *Syn* HIGH, expensively, extravagantly, grandly, lavishly, luxuriously, opulently, sumptuously *Ant* austerely, humbly, modestly, plainly, simply

ricochet *Syn* SKIP, bound, curvet, hop, lollop, lope

rid · to set a person or thing free of something that encumbers *Syn* clear, disabuse, purge, unburden *Rel* free, liberate, release

riddle *n Syn* MYSTERY, conundrum, enigma, problem, puzzle

riddle *vb Syn* SOLVE, answer, break, crack, dope (out), figure out, puzzle (out), resolve, unravel, work, work out

ride 1 *Syn* BAIT, badger, chivy, heckle, hector, hound 2 *Syn* TEASE, chaff, jive, josh, kid, rally, razz, rib, roast

ridicule · to make an object of laughter of *Syn* deride, mock, rally, taunt, twit *Rel* flout, gibe, jeer, scoff

ridiculous *Syn* LAUGHABLE, comic, comical, droll, farcical, funny, ludicrous, risible

rife 1 · possessing or covered with great numbers or amounts of something specified *Syn* abounding, flush, fraught, replete, swarming, teeming, thick, thronging *Rel* alive, animated, astir, brimming, bulging, bursting, bustling, busy, buzzing, chock-full (*or* chockful), clogged, congested, crammed, crowded, fat, filled, full, humming, jam-packed, jammed, lively, loaded, overcrowded, overfilled, overflowing, overfull, overloaded, overstuffed, packed, saturated, stuffed, surfeited 2 *Syn* PREVAILING, current, prevalent

rifle *Syn* ROB, burglarize, loot, plunder

rift *Syn* BREACH, break, rent, rupture, schism, split

rig *Syn* FURNISH (sense 1), accoutre (*or* accouter), equip, fit (out), outfit, supply *Ant* hold (back), keep (back), reserve, retain, withhold

right *n* · something to which one has a just claim *Syn* appanage, birthright, perquisite, prerogative, privilege *Rel* claim, title

right *adj* 1 *Syn* CORRECT, accurate, exact, nice, precise *Ant* incorrect 2 *Syn* SANE, balanced, clearheaded, lucid, normal, stable *Ant* crazed, crazy, demented, deranged, insane, lunatic, mad, maniacal, mental, unbalanced, unsound

right *adv Syn* VERY, awful, awfully, beastly, deadly, especially, exceedingly, extra, extremely, far, frightfully, full, greatly, heavily, highly, hugely, jolly, mightily, mighty, mortally, most, much, particularly, rattling, real, so, something, super, terribly, too, whacking *Ant* little, negligibly, nominally, slightly

righteous *Syn* MORAL, ethical, noble, virtuous

rightful *Syn* DUE, condign

rightly *Syn* PROPERLY, appropriately, congru-

ously, correctly, fittingly, happily, meetly, suitably *Ant* improperly, inappropriately, incongruously, incorrectly, unsuitably, wrongly

rightness *Syn* APPROPRIATENESS, aptness, felicitousness, fitness, fittingness, seemliness, suitability, suitableness *Ant* inappropriateness, inaptness, infelicity, unfitness

rigid 1 · extremely severe or stern *Syn* rigorous, strict, stringent *Rel* adamant, adamantine, inexorable, inflexible, obdurate *Ant* lax 2 *Syn* OBSTINATE, adamant, adamantine, dogged, hard, hardened, hardheaded, hardhearted, headstrong, immovable, implacable, inflexible, mulish, obdurate, opinionated, ossified, pat, peevish, pertinacious, perverse, pigheaded, self-willed, stubborn, unbending, uncompromising, unrelenting, unyielding, willful (*or* wilful) *Ant* acquiescent, agreeable, amenable, compliant, complying, flexible, pliable, pliant, relenting, yielding 3 *Syn* STIFF, inflexible, stark, tense, wooden *Ant* relaxed, supple

rigidity *Syn* SEVERITY, hardness, harshness, inflexibility, rigidness, rigorousness, sternness, strictness *Ant* flexibility, gentleness, laxness, mildness

rigidly *Syn* STRICTLY, exactly, precisely, rigorously *Ant* imprecisely, inexactly, loosely

rigidness *Syn* SEVERITY, hardness, harshness, inflexibility, rigidity, rigorousness, sternness, strictness *Ant* flexibility, gentleness, laxness, mildness

rigor *Syn* DIFFICULTY, hardship, vicissitude

rigorous *Syn* RIGID, strict, stringent *Ant* lax

rigorously *Syn* STRICTLY, exactly, precisely, rigidly *Ant* imprecisely, inexactly, loosely

rigorousness 1 *Syn* PRECISION, accuracy, closeness, delicacy, exactitude, exactness, fineness, preciseness, veracity *Ant* coarseness, impreciseness, imprecision, inaccuracy, inexactness, roughness 2 *Syn* SEVERITY, hardness, harshness, inflexibility, rigidity, rigidness, sternness, strictness *Ant* flexibility, gentleness, laxness, mildness

rile 1 *Syn* ANGER, antagonize, enrage, incense, inflame, infuriate, madden, outrage, rankle, roil *Ant* delight, gratify, please 2 *Syn* IRRITATE, aggravate, exasperate, nettle, peeve, provoke

riled *Syn* ANGRY, angered, apoplectic, enraged, foaming, fuming, furious, incensed, indignant, inflamed, infuriated, irate, ireful, mad, outraged, rabid, roiled, sore, steaming, wrathful, wroth *Ant* delighted, pleased

riling *Syn* ANNOYING, aggravating, bothersome, disturbing, exasperating, frustrating, galling, irksome, irritating, maddening, nettling, peeving, pesty, rankling, vexatious, vexing

rim *vb Syn* BORDER, bound, fringe, margin, skirt

rim *n Syn* BORDER, brim, brink, edge, margin, verge

rind *Syn* SKIN, bark, hide, peel, pelt

ring *n Syn* COMBINATION, bloc, combine, faction, party

ring *vb Syn* SURROUND, circle, compass, encircle, encompass, environ, gird, girdle, hem

ringing *Syn* RESONANT, orotund, resounding, sonorous, vibrant

rip **1** *Syn* HURRY (sense 2), barrel, bolt, bowl, breeze, career, course, dash, fly, hasten, hotfoot (it), hump, hurtle, hustle, pelt, race, rocket, run, rush, rustle, scoot, scurry, scuttle, shoot, speed, step (along), tear, trot, whirl, whisk, zip, zoom *Ant* crawl, creep, poke **2** *Syn* TEAR, cleave, rend, rive, split

ripe *Syn* MATURE, adult, grown-up, matured, mellow *Ant* childish, immature

ripen *Syn* MATURE, age, develop

rise **1** *Syn* ASCEND, arise, climb, lift, mount, soar, up, uprise, upsweep, upturn *Ant* decline, descend, dip, drop, fall (off) **2** *Syn* INCREASE (sense 2), accumulate, appreciate, balloon, build (up), burgeon, enlarge, escalate, expand, mount, multiply, mushroom, proliferate, snowball, swell, wax *Ant* contract, decrease, diminish, lessen, wane **3** *Syn* SPRING, arise, derive, emanate, flow, issue, originate, proceed, stem

risible *Syn* LAUGHABLE, comic, comical, droll, farcical, funny, ludicrous, ridiculous

risk *n* **1** *Syn* DANGER (sense 1), hazard, menace, peril, pitfall, threat, trouble *Ant* safeness, safety, security **2** *Syn* DANGER (sense 2), distress, endangerment, imperilment, jeopardy, peril, trouble *Ant* safeness, safety, security

risk *vb Syn* ENDANGER, adventure, compromise, gamble (with), hazard, imperil, jeopardize, menace, venture

risky *Syn* DANGEROUS, hazardous, perilous, precarious *Ant* safe, secure

rite *Syn* FORM (sense 2), ceremonial, ceremony, formality, liturgy, ritual

ritual *Syn* FORM (sense 2), ceremonial, ceremony, formality, liturgy, rite

rival *vb* **1** · to strive to equal or surpass *Syn* compete, emulate, vie *Rel* attempt, strive, struggle, try **2** *Syn* MATCH, approach, equal, touch

rival *n* **1** *Syn* COMPETITOR, challenger, competition, contender, contestant **2** *Syn* EQUAL, coordinate, counterpart, equivalent, fellow, like, match, parallel, peer

rive *Syn* TEAR, cleave, rend, rip, split

rivet *Syn* SECURE, anchor, moor

riveting *Syn* INTERESTING, absorbing, arresting, engaging, engrossing, enthralling, fascinating, gripping, immersing, intriguing, involving *Ant* boring, drab, dry, dull, heavy, monotonous, tedious, uninteresting

roam *Syn* WANDER, gad, gallivant, meander, prowl, ramble, range, rove, stray, traipse

roamer *Syn* NOMAD, drifter, gadabout, rambler, rover, stroller, vagabond, wanderer, wayfarer

roar *n* · a very loud and often a continuous noise *Syn* bawl, bellow, bluster, ululation, vociferation

roar *vb* · to make a very loud and often a continuous or protracted noise *Syn* bawl, bellow, bluster, clamor, howl, ululate, vociferate *Rel* rebound, repercuss, reverberate

roast *Syn* TEASE, chaff, jive, josh, kid, rally, razz, rib, ride

rob · to take possessions unlawfully *Syn* burglarize, loot, plunder, rifle *Rel* filch, lift, pilfer, purloin, steal

robber *Syn* THIEF, burglar, larcener, larcenist

robbery *Syn* THEFT, burglary, larceny

robe *Syn* CLOTHE, apparel, array, attire, dress *Ant* unclothe

robust *Syn* HEALTHY, hale, sound, well, wholesome *Ant* unhealthy

robustness *Syn* HEALTH, fitness, healthiness, heartiness, soundness, wellness, wholeness, wholesomeness *Ant* illness, sickness, unhealthiness, unsoundness

rock *Syn* SHAKE (sense 2), agitate, convulse

rocket *Syn* HURRY (sense 2), barrel, bolt, bowl, breeze, career, course, dash, fly, hasten, hotfoot (it), hump, hurtle, hustle, pelt, race, rip, run, rush, rustle, scoot, scurry, scuttle, shoot, speed, step (along), tear, trot, whirl, whisk, zip, zoom *Ant* crawl, creep, poke

rococo *Syn* ORNATE, baroque, flamboyant, florid *Ant* austere, chaste

rodomontade *Syn* BOMBAST, fustian, rant, rhapsody

rogue *Syn* VILLAIN, blackguard, knave, miscreant, rapscallion, rascal, scamp, scoundrel

roguish *Syn* PLAYFUL, frolicsome, impish, mischievous, sportive, waggish

roil *Syn* ANGER, antagonize, enrage, incense, inflame, infuriate, madden, outrage, rankle, rile *Ant* delight, gratify, please

roiled *Syn* ANGRY, angered, apoplectic, enraged, foaming, fuming, furious, incensed, indignant, inflamed, infuriated, irate, ireful, mad, outraged, rabid, riled, sore, steaming, wrathful, wroth *Ant* delighted, pleased

roily *Syn* TURBID, muddy *Ant* clear, limpid

role · the action for which a person or thing is specially fitted or used or for which a thing exists *Syn* capacity, function, job, part, place, position, purpose, task, work *Rel* affair, business, concern, involvement, participation

roll *Syn* LIST, catalog, inventory, register, roster, schedule, table

rollick *vb Syn* PLAY, disport, frolic, gambol, romp, sport *Ant* work

rollick *n Syn* PLAY, disport, frolic, gambol, romp, sport

romantic *adj* **1** *Syn* EXOTIC, fantastic, glamorous, marvelous (*or* marvellous), outlandish, strange **2** *Syn* SENTIMENTAL, maudlin, mawkish, mushy, slushy, soppy

romantic *n* *Syn* IDEALIST, dreamer, romanticist, utopian, visionary *Ant* pragmatist, realist

romanticist *Syn* IDEALIST, dreamer, romantic, utopian, visionary *Ant* pragmatist, realist

romanticize *Syn* IDEALIZE, glamorize, glorify

romp *n* *Syn* PLAY, disport, frolic, gambol, rollick, sport *Ant* work

romp *vb* *Syn* PLAY, disport, frolic, gambol, rollick, sport

roof *Syn* CANOPY, awning, ceiling, tent

rook *Syn* FLEECE, bleed, cheat, chisel, cozen, defraud, hustle, mulct, shortchange, skin, squeeze, stick, sting, swindle, victimize

rookie *Syn* BEGINNER, colt, fledgling, freshman, greenhorn, neophyte, newbie, newcomer, novice, recruit, tenderfoot, tyro *Ant* old hand, old-timer, vet, veteran

room **1** · space in a building enclosed or set apart by a partition *Syn* apartment, chamber **2** · enough space or range for free movement *Syn* berth, clearance, elbow room, leeway, margin, play

roomer *Syn* TENANT, boarder, lodger, renter *Ant* landlord

roost *Syn* ALIGHT, land, light, perch, settle, touch down *Ant* take off

root *vb* *Syn* APPLAUD, cheer *Ant* boo, hiss

root *n* *Syn* ORIGIN, inception, prime mover, provenance, provenience, source

rope *Syn* CORD, cable, lace, lacing, line, string, wire

roseate *Syn* HOPEFUL, optimistic, rose-colored *Ant* despairing, hopeless

rose-colored *Syn* HOPEFUL, optimistic, roseate *Ant* despairing, hopeless

roster *Syn* LIST, catalog, inventory, register, roll, schedule, table

rostrum *Syn* PLATFORM, dais, podium, stage, stand

rot *vb* **1** *Syn* DECAY, crumble, decompose, disintegrate, putrefy, spoil **2** *Syn* DETERIORATE, crumble, decay, decline, degenerate, descend, ebb, sink, worsen *Ant* ameliorate, improve, meliorate

rot *n* *Syn* NONSENSE, balderdash, bull, bunk, drivel, gobbledygook, poppycock, trash, twaddle

rotate *Syn* TURN (sense 1), circle, eddy, gyrate, pirouette, revolve, spin, swirl, twirl, wheel, whirl

rotten *Syn* UNPLEASANT, bad, disagreeable, displeasing, distasteful, nasty, sour, uncongenial, unlovely, unpleasing, unsatisfying, unwelcome *Ant* agreeable, congenial, good, grateful, gratifying, nice, palatable, pleasant, pleasing, pleasurable, satisfying, welcome

rotund *Syn* FLESHY, chubby, corpulent, fat, obese, plump, portly, stout *Ant* scrawny, skinny

rough **1** · not smooth or even *Syn* harsh, rugged, scabrous, uneven *Rel* firm, hard, solid *Ant* smooth **2** *Syn* HAIRY (sense 1), bristly, fleecy, furry, hirsute, shaggy, unshorn, woolly *Ant* bald, furless, hairless, shorn, smooth **3** *Syn* HAIRY (sense 2), furry, fuzzy, shaggy, woolly **4** *Syn* RUDE (sense 1), callow, crude, green, raw, uncouth *Ant* civil, urbane

roughhouse *Syn* HORSEPLAY, clowning, foolery, high jinks, horsing (around), monkeying, monkeyshines, roughhousing, shenanigans, skylarking, tomfoolery

roughhousing *Syn* HORSEPLAY, clowning, foolery, high jinks, horsing (around), monkeying, monkeyshines, roughhouse, shenanigans, skylarking, tomfoolery

round *Syn* AROUND (sense 2), about, over, through, throughout

roundabout *Syn* INDIRECT, circuitous *Ant* direct, forthright, straightforward

rouse *Syn* STIR, arouse, awaken, rally, waken

roustabout *Syn* WORKER, artisan, craftsman, hand, handicraftsman, laborer, mechanic, operative, workingman, workman *Ant* idler

rout *vb* *Syn* CONQUER, beat, defeat, lick, overcome, overthrow, reduce, subdue, subjugate, surmount, vanquish

rout *n* *Syn* CROWD, crush, horde, mob, press, throng

route *vb* *Syn* SEND, dispatch, forward, remit, ship, transmit *Ant* accept, receive

route *n* *Syn* WAY, artery, course, pass, passage

rove *Syn* WANDER, gad, gallivant, meander, prowl, ramble, range, roam, stray, traipse

rover *Syn* NOMAD, drifter, gadabout, rambler, roamer, stroller, vagabond, wanderer, wayfarer

row **1** *Syn* BRAWL, broil, fracas, melee, rumpus, scrap **2** *Syn* COMMOTION, bother, bustle, clatter, disturbance, furor, furore, fuss, hubbub, hullabaloo, hurly-burly, pandemonium, pother, ruckus, ruction, rumpus, shindy, squall, stew, stir, storm, to-do, tumult, turmoil, uproar, welter, whirl **3** *Syn* LINE, echelon, file, rank, tier

rowdy *Syn* BOISTEROUS, knockabout, rambunctious, raucous *Ant* orderly

royal *Syn* KINGLY, imperial, princely, queenly, regal

rub *Syn* POLISH, buff, burnish, dress, gloss, grind, shine, smooth

rubbed *Syn* GLOSSY, buffed, burnished, glistening, lustrous, polished, satin, satiny, sleek *Ant* dim, dull, flat, lusterless, matte

rubberneck *Syn* GAPE, gawk, gaze, goggle, peer, stare

rubbish *Syn* REFUSE, debris, garbage, offal, trash, waste

ruckus *Syn* COMMOTION, bother, bustle, clatter, disturbance, furor, furore, fuss, hubbub, hullabaloo, hurly-burly, pandemonium, pother, row, ruction, rumpus, shindy, squall, stew, stir, storm, to-do, tumult, turmoil, uproar, welter, whirl

ruction *Syn* COMMOTION, bother, bustle, clatter, disturbance, furor, furore, fuss, hubbub, hullabaloo, hurly-burly, pandemonium, pother, row, ruckus, rumpus, shindy, squall, stew, stir, storm, to-do, tumult, turmoil, uproar, welter, whirl

rude 1 · lacking in social refinement *Syn* callow, crude, green, raw, rough, uncouth *Rel* boorish, churlish, clownish, loutish **2** *Syn* IMPOLITE, discourteous, ill-bred, ill-mannered, impertinent, inconsiderate, thoughtless, uncalled-for, uncivil, ungracious, unmannerly *Ant* civil, considerate, courteous, genteel, gracious, mannerly, polite, thoughtful, well-bred

rudimentary *Syn* ELEMENTARY, basic, elemental, essential, fundamental, underlying *Ant* advanced

rue *Syn* REGRET, bemoan, deplore, lament, repent

rueful *Syn* MELANCHOLY, doleful, dolorous, lugubrious, plaintive

rugged *Syn* ROUGH, harsh, scabrous, uneven *Ant* smooth

ruin *vb* · to subject to forces that are destructive of soundness, worth, or usefulness *Syn* dilapidate, wreck *Rel* demolish, destroy, raze

ruin *n Syn* DESTRUCTION, annihilation, decimation, demolishment, demolition, desolation, devastation, extermination, extinction, havoc, loss, obliteration, ruination, wastage, wreckage *Ant* building, construction, erection, raising

ruination *Syn* DESTRUCTION, annihilation, decimation, demolishment, demolition, desolation, devastation, extermination, extinction, havoc, loss, obliteration, ruin, wastage, wreckage *Ant* building, construction, erection, raising

rule *n* **1** · a statement spelling out the proper procedure or conduct for an activity *Syn* bylaw, ground rule, regulation *Rel* code, constitution, decalogue **2** · lawful control over the affairs of a political unit (as a nation) *Syn* administration, authority, governance, government, jurisdiction, regime, regimen *Rel* reign **3** *Syn* LAW, canon, ordinance, precept, regulation, statute

rule *vb Syn* DECIDE, determine, resolve, settle

rule out *Syn* EXCLUDE, blackball, debar, disbar, eliminate, shut out, suspend *Ant* admit, include

ruler *Syn* MONARCH, autocrat, sovereign

ruminant *Syn* CONTEMPLATIVE, meditative, melancholy, pensive, reflective, thoughtful *Ant* unreflective

ruminate *Syn* PONDER, meditate, muse

rummage *Syn* SEEK, comb, ferret out, hunt, ransack, scour, search

rumor *vb* · to make (as a piece of information) the subject of common talk without any authority or confirmation of accuracy *Syn* bruit (about), circulate, noise (about), whisper *Rel* bandy (about), blab, gossip

rumor *n Syn* REPORT, gossip, hearsay

rump *Syn* BUTTOCKS, backside, bottom, breech, butt, fanny, hams, haunches, posterior, rear, seat

rumple *Syn* DISORDER, confuse, derange, disarrange, disarray, discompose, dishevel, dislocate, disorganize, disrupt, disturb, hash, jumble, mess (up), mix (up), muddle, muss, scramble, shuffle, tousle, tumble, upset *Ant* arrange, array, draw up, marshal, order, organize, range, regulate, straighten (up), tidy

rumpled *Syn* MESSY, chaotic, cluttered, confused, disarranged, disarrayed, disheveled (*or* dishevelled), disordered, disorderly, higgledy-piggledy, hugger-mugger, jumbled, littered, messed, muddled, mussed, mussy, pell-mell, sloppy, topsy-turvy, tousled, tumbled, unkempt, untidy, upside-down *Ant* neat, ordered, orderly, organized, shipshape, snug, tidied, tidy, trim

rumpus 1 *Syn* BRAWL, broil, fracas, melee, row, scrap **2** *Syn* COMMOTION, bother, bustle, clatter, disturbance, furor, furore, fuss, hubbub, hullabaloo, hurly-burly, pandemonium, pother, row, ruckus, ruction, shindy, squall, stew, stir, storm, to-do, tumult, turmoil, uproar, welter, whirl

run 1 *Syn* ACTIVATE, actuate, crank (up), drive, move, propel, set off, spark, start, touch off, trigger, turn on *Ant* cut, deactivate, kill, shut off, turn off **2** *Syn* BECOME, come, get, go, grow, turn, wax **3** *Syn* HURRY (sense 2), barrel, bolt, bowl, breeze, career, course, dash, fly, hasten, hotfoot (it), hump, hurtle, hustle, pelt, race, rip, rocket, rush, rustle, scoot, scurry, scuttle, shoot, speed, step (along), tear, trot, whirl, whisk, zip, zoom *Ant* crawl, creep, poke

run on *Syn* CHAT, babble, blab, cackle, chatter, converse, gab, gabble, gas, jabber, jaw, palaver, patter, prate, prattle, rap, rattle, talk, twitter, visit

runt *Syn* DWARF, midget, pygmy

rupture *Syn* BREACH, break, rent, rift, schism, split

rural · relating to or characteristic of the country *Syn* bucolic, pastoral, rustic *Ant* urban

ruse *Syn* TRICK, artifice, feint, gambit, maneuver, ploy, stratagem, wile

rush *vb* **1** *Syn* GUSH (sense 1), jet, pour, spew, spout, spurt, squirt *Ant* dribble, drip, drop, trickle **2** *Syn* HURRY (sense 1), accelerate, hasten, quicken, speed (up), whisk

Ant decelerate, retard, slow (down) **3** *Syn* HURRY (sense 2), barrel, bolt, bowl, breeze, career, course, dash, fly, hasten, hotfoot (it), hump, hurtle, hustle, pelt, race, rip, rocket, run, rustle, scoot, scurry, scuttle, shoot, speed, step (along), tear, trot, whirl, whisk, zip, zoom *Ant* crawl, creep, poke

rush *n Syn* ATTACK (sense 2), aggression, assault, blitzkrieg, charge, descent, offense (*or* offence), offensive, onset, onslaught, raid, strike

rustic *n Syn* HICK, bumpkin, clodhopper, coun-

tryman, provincial, yokel *Ant* cosmopolitan, sophisticate

rustic *adj Syn* RURAL, bucolic, pastoral *Ant* urban

rustle *Syn* HURRY (sense 2), barrel, bolt, bowl, breeze, career, course, dash, fly, hasten, hotfoot (it), hump, hurtle, hustle, pelt, race, rip, rocket, run, rush, scoot, scurry, scuttle, shoot, speed, step (along), tear, trot, whirl, whisk, zip, zoom *Ant* crawl, creep, poke

ruth *Syn* SYMPATHY, commiseration, compassion, condolence, empathy, pity

S

saccharine *Syn* CORNY, maudlin, mawkish, mushy, sappy, schmaltzy, sentimental, sloppy, sugarcoated, sugary *Ant* unsentimental

sack *n Syn* BAG, pouch

sack *vb* **1** *Syn* DISMISS, bounce, cashier, discharge, drop, fire **2** *Syn* RAVAGE, despoil, devastate, pillage, spoliate, waste

sacred **1** · protected (as by law, custom, or human respect) against abuse *Syn* inviolable, inviolate, sacrosanct *Rel* defended, guarded, protected, shielded **2** *Syn* HOLY (sense 2), blessed, consecrated, hallowed, sacrosanct, sanctified *Ant* unconsecrated, unhallowed

sacrifice *Syn* FORGO, abnegate, eschew, forbear

sacrilege *Syn* PROFANATION, blasphemy, desecration

sacrilegious *Syn* IMPIOUS, blasphemous, profane *Ant* pious, reverent

sacrosanct **1** *Syn* SACRED, inviolable, inviolate **2** *Syn* HOLY (sense 2), blessed, consecrated, hallowed, sacred, sanctified *Ant* unconsecrated, unhallowed

sad **1** · feeling unhappiness *Syn* bad, blue, brokenhearted, crestfallen, dejected, depressed, despondent, disconsolate, doleful, down, downcast, downhearted, droopy, forlorn, gloomy, glum, heartbroken, heartsick, heartsore, inconsolable, joyless, low, low-spirited, melancholy, miserable, mournful, saddened, sorrowful, sorry, unhappy, woebegone, woeful, wretched *Rel* aggrieved, distressed, troubled *Ant* blissful, buoyant, buoyed, cheerful, cheery, chipper, delighted, glad, gladdened, gladsome, gleeful, happy, joyful, joyous, jubilant, sunny, upbeat **2** · causing unhappiness *Syn* depressing, dismal, drear, dreary, heartbreaking, heartrending, melancholy, pathetic, saddening, sorry, tearful, teary *Rel* discomforting, discomposing,

disquieting, distressing, disturbing, perturbing *Ant* cheering, cheery, glad, happy

saddened *Syn* SAD (sense 1), bad, blue, brokenhearted, crestfallen, dejected, depressed, despondent, disconsolate, doleful, down, downcast, downhearted, droopy, forlorn, gloomy, glum, heartbroken, heartsick, heartsore, inconsolable, joyless, low, low-spirited, melancholy, miserable, mournful, sorrowful, sorry, unhappy, woebegone, woeful, wretched *Ant* blissful, buoyant, buoyed, cheerful, cheery, chipper, delighted, glad, gladdened, gladsome, gleeful, happy, joyful, joyous, jubilant, sunny, upbeat

saddening *Syn* SAD (sense 2), depressing, dismal, drear, dreary, heartbreaking, heartrending, melancholy, pathetic, sorry, tearful, teary *Ant* cheering, cheery, glad, happy

saddle *Syn* BURDEN, charge, cumber, encumber, lade, load, tax, weigh, weight

sadism *Syn* CRUELTY, barbarity, brutality, cruelness, heartlessness, inhumanity, savageness, savagery, viciousness, wantonness *Ant* benignity, compassion, good-heartedness, humanity, kindheartedness, kindness, sympathy

sadness · a state or spell of low spirits *Syn* blues, dejection, depression, desolation, despondency, disconsolateness, dispiritedness, doldrums, downheartedness, dreariness, dumps, forlornness, gloom, gloominess, heartsickness, joylessness, melancholy, mopes, oppression, unhappiness *Rel* melancholia, self-pity *Ant* bliss, blissfulness, ecstasy, elatedness, elation, euphoria, exhilaration, exuberance, exultation, felicity, gladness, gladsomeness, happiness, heaven, intoxication, joy, joyfulness, joyousness, jubilation, rapture, rapturousness

safe *Syn* DEPENDABLE, good, reliable, responsible, solid, steady, sure, tried, tried-and-true,

true, trustworthy, trusty *Ant* irresponsible, undependable, unreliable, untrustworthy

safeguard *Syn* DEFEND, guard, protect, shield *Ant* attack, combat

safekeeping *Syn* CUSTODY, care, guardianship, keeping, trust, ward

safeness *Syn* SAFETY, protection, security *Ant* danger, distress, endangerment, imperilment, jeopardy, peril, trouble

safety · the state of not being exposed to danger *Syn* safeness, security *Rel* aegis, defense, guardianship, ward *Ant* danger, distress, endangerment, imperilment, jeopardy, peril, trouble

sag *Syn* DROOP, flag, wilt

saga *Syn* MYTH, legend

sagacious *Syn* SHREWD, astute, perspicacious

sage *Syn* WISE, judicious, prudent, sane, sapient, sensible *Ant* simple

sail *Syn* FLY, dart, float, scud, shoot, skim

sailor *Syn* MARINER, bluejacket, gob, seaman, tar

sainted *Syn* HOLY (sense 1), devout, godly, pious, religious, saintly *Ant* faithless, godless, impious, irreligious, ungodly, unholy

sainthood *Syn* HOLINESS, blessedness, devoutness, godliness, piety, piousness, saintliness, saintship, sanctity *Ant* godlessness, impiety, ungodliness, unholiness

saintliness *Syn* HOLINESS, blessedness, devoutness, godliness, piety, piousness, sainthood, saintship, sanctity *Ant* godlessness, impiety, ungodliness, unholiness

saintly *Syn* HOLY (sense 1), devout, godly, pious, religious, sainted *Ant* faithless, godless, impious, irreligious, ungodly, unholy

saintship *Syn* HOLINESS, blessedness, devoutness, godliness, piety, piousness, sainthood, saintliness, sanctity *Ant* godlessness, impiety, ungodliness, unholiness

salable *or* **saleable** *Syn* COMMERCIAL, marketable *Ant* noncommercial, nonsalable, uncommercial, unmarketable, unsalable

salary *Syn* WAGE, emolument, fee, hire, pay, stipend

sale · the transfer of ownership of something from one person to another for a price *Syn* deal, trade, transaction *Rel* auction

salient *Syn* NOTICEABLE, arresting, conspicuous, outstanding, prominent, remarkable, signal, striking

saloon *Syn* BARROOM, bar, café, groggery, grogshop, pub, tavern

salt away *Syn* HOARD, cache, lay away, lay up, put by, squirrel (away), stash, stockpile, store, stow

salubrious *Syn* HEALTHFUL, healthy, hygienic, salutary, sanitary, wholesome

salutary **1** *Syn* BENEFICIAL, advantageous, favorable, helpful, profitable *Ant* disadvantageous, unfavorable, unhelpful **2** *Syn* HEALTHFUL, healthy, hygienic, salubrious, sanitary, wholesome

salute **1** *Syn* ACCLAIM, applaud, cheer, hail, laud, praise, tout *Ant* knock, pan, slam **2** *Syn* ADDRESS, accost, greet, hail

salvo *Syn* BARRAGE, bombardment, cannonade, fusillade, hail, shower, storm, volley

same · not different or not differing from one another *Syn* equivalent, identic, identical, selfsame, tantamount, very *Rel* akin, alike, like, parallel, uniform *Ant* different

sample *Syn* EXAMPLE, case, exemplar, illustration, instance, representative, specimen

sanative *Syn* CURATIVE, corrective, remedial, restorative

sanctification *Syn* CONSECRATION, blessing, hallowing

sanctified *Syn* HOLY (sense 1), blessed, consecrated, hallowed, sacred, sacrosanct *Ant* unconsecrated, unhallowed

sanctimoniousness *Syn* HYPOCRISY, cant, dissembling, dissimulation, insincerity, piousness *Ant* genuineness, sincerity

sanction *vb Syn* APPROVE, accredit, certify, endorse *Ant* disapprove

sanction *n Syn* PERMISSION, allowance, authorization, clearance, concurrence, consent, granting, leave, license (*or* licence), sufferance *Ant* interdiction, prohibition, proscription

sanctity *Syn* HOLINESS, blessedness, devoutness, godliness, piety, piousness, sainthood, saintliness, saintship *Ant* godlessness, impiety, ungodliness, unholiness

sanctuary *Syn* SHELTER, asylum, cover, refuge, retreat

sand *Syn* FORTITUDE, backbone, grit, guts, pluck *Ant* pusillanimity

sandy *Syn* BLOND, fair, flaxen, golden, straw, tawny *Ant* dark

sane **1** · having full use of one's mind and control over one's actions *Syn* balanced, clearheaded, lucid, normal, right, stable *Rel* clear, logical, rational, reasonable *Ant* crazed, crazy, demented, deranged, insane, lunatic, mad, maniacal, mental, unbalanced, unsound **2** *Syn* WISE, judicious, prudent, sage, sapient, sensible *Ant* simple

sanguinary **1** *Syn* BLOODTHIRSTY, bloody, homicidal, murdering, murderous, sanguine **2** *Syn* BLOODY, gory, sanguine, sanguineous

sanguine **1** *Syn* BLOODTHIRSTY, bloody, homicidal, murdering, murderous, sanguinary **2** *Syn* BLOODY, gory, sanguinary, sanguineous **3** *Syn* CONFIDENT, assured, presumptuous, sure *Ant* apprehensive, diffident

sanguineous *Syn* BLOODY, gory, sanguinary, sanguine

sanitary **1** · free from filth, infection, or dangers to health *Syn* aseptic, germfree, hygienic, sterile *Rel* antibacterial, antiseptic, germicidal *Ant* insanitary, unhygienic, unsanitary **2** *Syn* HEALTHFUL, healthy, hygienic, salubrious, salutary, wholesome

sanitize *Syn* STERILIZE (sense 2), disinfect, fumigate

sap *n Syn* DUPE, chump, gull, pigeon, sucker, tool

sap *vb Syn* WEAKEN, debilitate, enervate, enfeeble, soften *Ant* strengthen

sapid *Syn* PALATABLE, appetizing, flavorsome, relishing, savory, tasty, toothsome *Ant* distasteful, unpalatable

sapient *Syn* WISE, judicious, prudent, sage, sane, sensible *Ant* simple

sappy *Syn* CORNY, maudlin, mawkish, mushy, saccharine, schmaltzy, sentimental, sloppy, sugarcoated, sugary *Ant* unsentimental

sarcasm 1 *Syn* INSULT, affront, barb, dart, dig, epithet, indignity, name, offense (*or* offence), outrage, put-down, slight, slur 2 *Syn* WIT, humor, irony, repartee, satire

sarcastic · marked by bitterness and a power or will to cut or sting *Syn* ironic, sardonic, satiric *Rel* biting, cutting, trenchant

sardonic *Syn* SARCASTIC, ironic, satiric

sass *Syn* BACK TALK, cheek, impertinence, impudence, insolence, sauce

sate *Syn* SATIATE, cloy, glut, gorge, pall, surfeit

satiate · to fill to repletion *Syn* cloy, glut, gorge, pall, sate, surfeit *Rel* content, satisfy

satin *Syn* GLOSSY, buffed, burnished, glistening, lustrous, polished, rubbed, satiny, sleek *Ant* dim, dull, flat, lusterless, matte

satiny 1 *Syn* GLOSSY, · buffed, burnished, glistening, lustrous, polished, rubbed, satin, sleek *Ant* dim, dull, flat, lusterless, matte 2 *Syn* SLEEK, glossy, silken, silky, slick, velvety

satire *Syn* WIT, humor, irony, repartee, sarcasm

satiric *Syn* SARCASTIC, ironic, sardonic

satisfactoriness *Syn* SUFFICIENCY, acceptability, adequacy *Ant* inadequacy, insufficiency

satisfactory *Syn* ADEQUATE, acceptable, all right, decent, fine, OK (*or* okay), passable, respectable, tolerable *Ant* deficient, inadequate, lacking, unacceptable, unsatisfactory, wanting

satisfied *Syn* CONTENT, contented, gratified, happy, pleased *Ant* discontent, discontented, displeased, dissatisfied, malcontent, unhappy

satisfy 1 · to measure up to a set of criteria or requirements *Syn* answer, fulfill, meet *Rel* demonstrate, prove, test, try 2 *Syn* PAY, compensate, indemnify, recompense, reimburse, remunerate, repay 3 *Syn* PERSUADE, argue, convince, get, induce, move, prevail (on *or* upon), talk (into), win (over)

satisfying 1 *Syn* COGENT, compelling, conclusive, convincing, decisive, effective, forceful, persuasive, strong, telling *Ant* inconclusive, indecisive, ineffective, unconvincing 2 *Syn* HEARTWARMING, cheering, comforting,

encouraging, fulfilling, gladdening, gratifying, heartening, rewarding *Ant* depressing, discouraging, disheartening, dispiriting

saturate 1 *Syn* PERMEATE, impenetrate, impregnate, interpenetrate, penetrate, pervade 2 *Syn* SOAK, drench, impregnate, sop, steep, waterlog

saturnine *Syn* SULLEN, crabbed, dour, gloomy, glum, morose, sulky, surly

sauce 1 *Syn* BACK TALK, cheek, impertinence, impudence, insolence, sass 2 *Syn* EFFRONTERY, audacity, brashness, brass, brassiness, brazenness, cheek, cheekiness, chutzpah, gall, nerve, nerviness, pertness, presumption, presumptuousness, sauciness, temerity

sauciness *Syn* EFFRONTERY, audacity, brashness, brass, brassiness, brazenness, cheek, cheekiness, chutzpah, gall, nerve, nerviness, pertness, presumption, presumptuousness, sauce, temerity

saucy · flippant and bold in manner or attitude *Syn* arch, pert *Rel* flippant, frivolous, light-minded, volatile

saunter *vb* · to walk slowly in an idle or aimless manner *Syn* amble, stroll

saunter *n Syn* WALK, constitutional, perambulation, ramble, range, stroll, turn

savage 1 *Syn* BARBARIAN, barbaric, barbarous *Ant* civilized 2 *Syn* FIERCE, barbarous, cruel, fell, ferocious, inhuman, truculent *Ant* mild, tame

savageness *Syn* CRUELTY, barbarity, brutality, cruelness, heartlessness, inhumanity, sadism, savagery, viciousness, wantonness *Ant* benignity, compassion, good-heartedness, humanity, kindheartedness, kindness, sympathy

savagery *Syn* CRUELTY, barbarity, brutality, cruelness, heartlessness, inhumanity, sadism, savageness, viciousness, wantonness *Ant* benignity, compassion, good-heartedness, humanity, kindheartedness, kindness, sympathy

savanna *Syn* PLAIN, down, grassland, prairie, steppe, tundra, veld (*or* veldt)

save 1 · to keep secure or maintain intact from injury, decay, or loss *Syn* conserve, preserve *Rel* enjoy, have, hold, own, possess *Ant* consume, spend 2 *Syn* ECONOMIZE, scrimp, skimp *Ant* waste 3 *Syn* RESCUE, deliver, ransom, reclaim, redeem

saver *Syn* SAVIOR, deliverer, redeemer, rescuer

savior *or* **saviour** · one that saves from danger or destruction *Syn* deliverer, redeemer, rescuer, saver *Rel* custodian, defender, guard, guardian, keeper, lookout, protector, sentinel, sentry, warden, warder, watch, watchman

savoir faire *Syn* TACT, address, poise *Ant* awkwardness

savor *Syn* TASTE (sense 1), flavor, relish, smack, tang *Ant* antipathy

savory

savory 1 *Syn* FRAGRANT, ambrosial, aromatic, perfumed, redolent, scented, sweet *Ant* fetid, foul, malodorous, noisome, putrid, rancid, rank, reeking, reeky, smelly, stinking, stinky, strong **2** *Syn* PALATABLE, appetizing, flavorsome, relishing, sapid, tasty, toothsome *Ant* distasteful, unpalatable

saw *Syn* SAYING, adage, aphorism, apothegm, epigram, maxim, motto, proverb

say 1 · to express in words *Syn* state, tell, utter *Rel* articulate, enunciate, pronounce **2** *Syn* PHRASE, articulate, clothe, couch, express, formulate, put, state, word

saying · an often repeated statement that usually is brief and expresses a common observation or general truth *Syn* adage, aphorism, apothegm, epigram, maxim, motto, proverb, saw

scabrous *Syn* ROUGH, harsh, rugged, uneven *Ant* smooth

scamp *Syn* VILLAIN, blackguard, knave, miscreant, rapscallion, rascal, rogue, scoundrel

scamper *Syn* SCUTTLE, scurry, skedaddle, sprint

scan *n Syn* INSPECTION, audit, check, checkup, examination, review, scrutiny, survey

scan *vb Syn* SCRUTINIZE, audit, examine, inspect

scandal 1 *Syn* DETRACTION, backbiting, calumny, slander **2** *Syn* OFFENSE (sense 2), crime, sin, vice

scandalous *Syn* LIBELOUS, defamatory, slanderous

scant *Syn* MEAGER, exiguous, scanty, scrimpy, skimpy, spare, sparse *Ant* ample, copious

scantiness *Syn* DEFICIENCY, dearth, deficit, failure, famine, inadequacy, insufficiency, lack, paucity, poverty, scarceness, scarcity, shortage, want *Ant* abundance, adequacy, amplitude, plenitude, plenty, sufficiency

scanty *Syn* MEAGER, exiguous, scant, scrimpy, skimpy, spare, sparse *Ant* ample, copious

scar *Syn* BLEMISH, defect, deformity, disfigurement, fault, flaw, imperfection, mark, pockmark

scarce *Syn* INFREQUENT, occasional, rare, sporadic, uncommon *Ant* frequent

scarceness *Syn* DEFICIENCY, dearth, deficit, failure, famine, inadequacy, insufficiency, lack, paucity, poverty, scantiness, scarcity, shortage, want *Ant* abundance, adequacy, amplitude, plenitude, plenty, sufficiency

scarcity *Syn* DEFICIENCY, dearth, deficit, failure, famine, inadequacy, insufficiency, lack, paucity, poverty, scantiness, scarceness, shortage, want *Ant* abundance, adequacy, amplitude, plenitude, plenty, sufficiency

scare *Syn* FRIGHTEN, affray, affright, alarm, fright, startle, terrify, terrorize *Ant* reassure

scathe *Syn* ATTACK (sense 2), abuse, assail, belabor, blast, castigate, excoriate, jump (on), lambaste (*or* lambast), slam, vituperate

scathing *Syn* CAUSTIC, acrid, mordant *Ant* genial

scatter 1 · to cause to separate or break up *Syn* dispel, disperse, dissipate *Rel* cast, fling, throw, toss **2** · to cover by or as if by scattering something over or on *Syn* bestrew, dot, pepper, sow, spray, sprinkle, strew *Rel* blanket, dust **3** *Syn* STREW, broadcast, sow, straw

scent *Syn* SMELL, aroma, odor

scented *Syn* FRAGRANT, ambrosial, aromatic, perfumed, redolent, savory, sweet *Ant* fetid, foul, malodorous, noisome, putrid, rancid, rank, reeking, reeky, smelly, stinking, stinky, strong

schedule 1 *Syn* LIST, catalog, inventory, register, roll, roster, table **2** *Syn* PROGRAM, agenda, timetable

scheme *n* **1** *Syn* PLAN, design, plot, project **2** *Syn* SYSTEM, complex, network, organism *Ant* chaos

scheme *vb* **1** *Syn* PLAN, design, plot, project **2** *Syn* PLOT, conspire, contrive, intrigue, machinate

schism 1 *Syn* DISCORD, conflict, contention, difference, dissension, strife, variance **2** *Syn* BREACH, break, rent, rift, rupture, split

schismatic *Syn* HERETIC, dissenter, nonconformist, sectarian, sectary *Ant* conformer, conformist

schmaltzy *Syn* CORNY, maudlin, mawkish, mushy, saccharine, sappy, sentimental, sloppy, sugarcoated, sugary *Ant* unsentimental

scholar 1 *Syn* EXPERT, ace, adept, artist, authority, crackerjack, maestro, master, past master, shark, virtuoso, whiz, wizard *Ant* amateur **2** *Syn* STUDENT, pupil

scholarly 1 *Syn* ACADEMIC, educational, scholastic *Ant* nonacademic, unacademic **2** *Syn* EDUCATED, erudite, knowledgeable, learned, literate, well-read *Ant* ignorant, illiterate, uneducated **3** *Syn* LEARNED, erudite

scholarship 1 *Syn* EDUCATION (sense 2), erudition, knowledge, learnedness, learning, science **2** *Syn* KNOWLEDGE, erudition, information, learning, lore, science *Ant* ignorance

scholastic 1 *Syn* ACADEMIC, educational, scholarly *Ant* nonacademic, unacademic **2** *Syn* PEDANTIC, academic, bookish

school *Syn* TEACH, discipline, educate, instruct, train

schooling *Syn* EDUCATION (sense 1), instruction, teaching, training, tutelage, tutoring

schoolteacher *Syn* TEACHER, educator, instructor, pedagogue, preceptor

science 1 *Syn* EDUCATION (sense 2), erudition, knowledge, learnedness, learning, scholarship **2** *Syn* KNOWLEDGE, erudition, information, learning, lore, scholarship *Ant* ignorance

scintillate *Syn* FLASH, coruscate, glance, gleam, glint, glisten, glitter, sparkle, twinkle

scoff · to show one's contempt in derision or mockery *Syn* fleer, flout, gibe, gird, jeer, sneer *Rel* deride, mock, ridicule, taunt

scold *vb* · to reproach angrily and abusively *Syn* bawl, berate, chew out, jaw, rail, rate, revile, tongue-lash, upbraid, vituperate, wig *Rel* blame, censure, criticize, reprehend, reprobate

scold *n Syn* CRITIC, carper, castigator, caviler (*or* caviller), censurer, faultfinder, nitpicker, railer

scoop *Syn* DIP (sense 2), bail, dish, ladle, spoon

scoot *Syn* HURRY (sense 2), barrel, bolt, bowl, breeze, career, course, dash, fly, hasten, hotfoot (it), hump, hurtle, hustle, pelt, race, rip, rocket, run, rush, rustle, scurry, scuttle, shoot, speed, step (along), tear, trot, whirl, whisk, zip, zoom *Ant* crawl, creep, poke

scope *Syn* RANGE, compass, gamut, horizon, ken, orbit, purview, radius, reach, sweep

scorch *Syn* BURN, char, sear, singe

scorn *vb* **1** · to ignore in a disrespectful manner *Syn* despise, disregard, flout *Rel* dismiss, forget, ignore, neglect, overlook, overpass, pass over, slight, slur (over) **2** · to show contempt for *Syn* disdain, high-hat, slight, sniff (at), snub *Rel* scout *Ant* honor, respect **3** *Syn* DESPISE, contemn, disdain, scout *Ant* appreciate

scorn *n Syn* CONTEMPT, despite, despitefulness, disdain *Ant* admiration, esteem, regard, respect

scoundrel *Syn* VILLAIN, blackguard, knave, miscreant, rapscallion, rascal, rogue, scamp

scour *Syn* SEEK, comb, ferret out, hunt, ransack, rummage, search

scout *Syn* DESPISE, contemn, disdain, scorn *Ant* appreciate

scowl *vb Syn* FROWN, glare, gloom, glower, lower *Ant* beam, smile

scowl *n Syn* GRIMACE, face, frown, lower, mouth, pout

scramble *Syn* DISORDER, confuse, derange, disarrange, disarray, discompose, dishevel, dislocate, disorganize, disrupt, disturb, hash, jumble, mess (up), mix (up), muddle, muss, rumple, shuffle, tousle, tumble, upset *Ant* arrange, array, draw up, marshal, order, organize, range, regulate, straighten (up), tidy

scrap *Syn* DISCARD, cast, junk, molt, shed, slough

scrape *vb* · to rub or slide against something that is harsh, rough, or sharp *Syn* grate, grind, rasp, scratch

scrape *n* **1** *Syn* PREDICAMENT, dilemma, fix, jam, pickle, plight, quandary **2** *Syn* BRAWL, broil, fracas, melee, row, rumpus

scrappiness *Syn* BELLIGERENCE, aggression, aggressiveness, bellicosity, combativeness, contentiousness, disputatiousness, fight, militancy, pugnacity, truculence *Ant* pacifism

scrappy *Syn* BELLIGERENT, aggressive, argumentative, bellicose, combative, contentious, discordant, disputatious, gladiatorial, militant, pugnacious, quarrelsome, truculent, warlike *Ant* nonbelligerent, pacific, peaceable, peaceful

scratch *Syn* SCRAPE, grate, grind, rasp

scrawny *Syn* LEAN, angular, gaunt, lank, lanky, rawboned, skinny, spare *Ant* fleshy

scream *vb* **1** · to cry out loudly and emotionally *Syn* howl, screech, shriek, shrill, squall, squeal, yell, yelp *Rel* bawl, bay, call, caterwaul, cry, holler, keen, shout, squawk, vociferate, wail, yawp (*or* yaup), yowl **2** *Syn* SHOUT, holler, screech, shriek, squeal, whoop, yell

scream *n Syn* SHOUT, holler, screech, shriek, squeal, whoop, yell

screech *vb* **1** *Syn* SCREAM, howl, shriek, shrill, squall, squeal, yell, yelp **2** *Syn* SHOUT, holler, scream, shriek, squeal, whoop, yell

screech *n Syn* SHOUT, holler, scream, shriek, squeal, whoop, yell

screeching *Syn* SHRILL, acute, high-pitched, piping, shrieking, squeaking, squeaky, treble, whistling *Ant* bass, deep, low, throaty

screen *vb Syn* HIDE, bury, cache, conceal, ensconce, secrete

screen *n Syn* MOVIE (sense 2), cinema, film, motion pictures, pictures

screwball *Syn* ECCENTRIC, character, codger, crackbrain, crackpot, crank, kook, nut, oddball, weirdo

screwlike *Syn* SPIRAL, coiling, corkscrew, helical, winding

scrimp *Syn* ECONOMIZE, save, skimp *Ant* waste

scrimping *n Syn* ECONOMY, frugality, husbandry, providence, skimping, thrift *Ant* wastefulness

scrimping *adj Syn* FRUGAL, economical, economizing, provident, sparing, thrifty *Ant* prodigal, wasteful

scrimpy *Syn* MEAGER, exiguous, scant, scanty, skimpy, spare, sparse *Ant* ample, copious

scruple *vb Syn* DEMUR, balk, boggle, jib, shy, stick, stickle, strain *Ant* accede

scruple *n Syn* QUALM, compunction, misgiving

scrupulous **1** *Syn* CAREFUL, meticulous, punctilious, punctual *Ant* careless **2** *Syn* UPRIGHT, conscientious, honest, honorable, just

scrutinize · to look at or over *Syn* audit, examine, inspect, scan *Rel* consider, study, weigh

scrutiny *Syn* INSPECTION, audit, check, checkup, examination, review, scan, survey

scud *Syn* FLY, dart, float, sail, shoot, skim

scuffle *Syn* WRESTLE, grapple, tussle

sculpt *Syn* CARVE, chisel, engrave, etch, incise, sculpture

sculpture Syn CARVE, chisel, engrave, etch, incise, sculpt

scum Syn FOAM, froth, lather, spume, suds, yeast

scurrility Syn ABUSE, billingsgate, invective, obloquy, vituperation Ant adulation

scurrilous Syn ABUSIVE, contumelious, opprobrious, vituperative Ant complementary, respectful

scurry 1 Syn HURRY (sense 2), barrel, bolt, bowl, breeze, career, course, dash, fly, hasten, hotfoot (it), hump, hurtle, hustle, pelt, race, rip, rocket, run, rush, rustle, scoot, scuttle, shoot, speed, step (along), tear, trot, whirl, whisk, zip, zoom Ant crawl, creep, poke 2 Syn SCUTTLE, scamper, skedaddle, sprint

scurvy Syn CONTEMPTIBLE, beggarly, cheap, despicable, pitiable, shabby, sorry Ant admirable, estimable, formidable

scuttle 1 · to move with or as if with short brisk steps Syn scamper, scurry, skedaddle, sprint Rel charge, dash, rush, shoot, tear 2 Syn HURRY (sense 2), barrel, bolt, bowl, breeze, career, course, dash, fly, hasten, hotfoot (it), hump, hurtle, hustle, pelt, race, rip, rocket, run, rush, rustle, scoot, scurry, shoot, speed, step (along), tear, trot, whirl, whisk, zip, zoom Ant crawl, creep, poke

seaman Syn MARINER, bluejacket, gob, sailor, tar

sear Syn BURN, char, scorch, singe

search Syn SEEK, comb, ferret out, hunt, ransack, rummage, scour

season Syn HARDEN (sense 2), acclimate, acclimatize Ant soften

seasonable · done or occurring at a good, suitable, or proper time Syn opportune, pat, timely, well-timed Rel apposite, apropos, pertinent, relevant Ant unseasonable

seat 1 Syn BUTTOCKS, backside, bottom, breech, butt, fanny, hams, haunches, posterior, rear, rump 2 Syn CENTER (sense 2), base, capital, core, cynosure, eye, focus, heart, hub, mecca, nucleus

seclude Syn ISOLATE, insulate, segregate, sequester

secluded · hidden from view Syn cloistered, covert, isolated, quiet, remote, retired, secret, sheltered Rel lonely, reclusive, solitary

secludedness Syn ISOLATION, insulation, seclusion, segregation, separateness, sequestration, solitariness, solitude

seclusion Syn ISOLATION, insulation, secludedness, segregation, separateness, sequestration, solitariness, solitude

second Syn INSTANT, flash, jiffy, minute, moment, shake, split second, trice, twinkle, twinkling, wink

secondary Syn SUBORDINATE, collateral, dependent, subject, tributary Ant chief, dominant, leading

second-rate Syn MEDIUM, average, fair, indifferent, mediocre, middling, moderate

secret 1 · done without attracting observation Syn clandestine, covert, furtive, stealthy, surreptitious, underhand, underhanded Rel arcane, inscrutable, mysterious 2 Syn SECLUDED, cloistered, covert, isolated, quiet, remote, retired, sheltered

secrete Syn HIDE, bury, cache, conceal, ensconce, screen

secretive 1 · given to keeping one's activities hidden from public observation or knowledge Syn close, closemouthed, dark, reticent, uncommunicative Rel quiet, reserved, silent, taciturn, tight-lipped Ant communicative, open 2 Syn SILENT (sense 1), close, closelipped, closemouthed, reserved, reticent, taciturn, tight-lipped, uncommunicative Ant talkative

sect 1 Syn FACTION, bloc, body, coalition, party, set, side, wing 2 Syn RELIGION, church, communion, creed, denomination, faith, persuasion

section Syn PART, detail, division, fraction, fragment, member, parcel, piece, portion, sector, segment Ant whole

sector Syn PART, detail, division, fraction, fragment, member, parcel, piece, portion, section, segment Ant whole

secular Syn PROFANE, lay, temporal Ant sacred

secure 1 · to fasten or fix firmly Syn anchor, moor, rivet Rel establish, fix, set, settle 2 Syn EARN, acquire, attain, capture, carry, draw, gain, garner, get, land, make, obtain, procure, realize, win Ant forfeit, lose 3 Syn ENSURE, assure, cinch, guarantee, guaranty, insure 4 Syn GET, gain, obtain, procure, win

security 1 Syn GUARANTEE, bail, bond, guaranty, surety 2 Syn SAFETY, protection, safeness Ant danger, distress, endangerment, imperilment, jeopardy, peril, trouble

sedate Syn SERIOUS, earnest, grave, sober, solemn, somber, staid Ant flippant, light

sediment Syn DEPOSIT, dregs, grounds, lees, precipitate

seditious Syn INSUBORDINATE, contumacious, factious, mutinous, rebellious

seduce Syn LURE, allure, beguile, decoy, entice, lead on, tempt

seductress Syn SIREN, enchantress, temptress

sedulous Syn BUSY, assiduous, diligent, industrious Ant idle, unoccupied

see 1 · to take cognizance of by physical or mental vision Syn behold, contemplate, descry, discern, espy, note, notice, observe, perceive, remark, survey, view Rel examine, inspect, scan, scrutinize 2 · to perceive something by means of the eyes Syn look, watch Rel gape, gaze, glare, stare

seeable Syn VISIBLE, apparent, observable, visual Ant invisible, unseeable

seedy *Syn* SHABBY, dilapidated, dingy, faded, threadbare

seek 1 · to look for *Syn* comb, ferret out, hunt, ransack, rummage, scour, search *Rel* ask, inquire, interrogate, question 2 *Syn* ATTEMPT, assay, endeavor, essay, strive, try

seeker *Syn* CANDIDATE, applicant, aspirant, campaigner, contender, hopeful, prospect

seem · to give the impression of being *Syn* act, appear, look, make, sound *Rel* dissemble, pretend

seeming *Syn* APPARENT, illusory, ostensible *Ant* real

seemingly *Syn* APPARENTLY, evidently, ostensibly, presumably, supposedly

seemliness *Syn* APPROPRIATENESS, aptness, felicitousness, fitness, fittingness, rightness, suitability, suitableness *Ant* inappropriateness, inaptness, infelicity, unfitness

seemly *Syn* DECOROUS, decent, nice, proper *Ant* blatant, indecorous

seep *Syn* EXUDE, bleed, ooze, percolate, strain, sweat, weep

seer *Syn* PROPHET, augur, diviner, forecaster, foreseer, foreteller, fortune-teller, futurist, prognosticator, prophesier, soothsayer

seethe *Syn* BOIL, parboil, simmer, stew

segment *Syn* PART, detail, division, fraction, fragment, member, parcel, piece, portion, section, sector *Ant* whole

segregate *Syn* ISOLATE, insulate, seclude, sequester

segregation *Syn* ISOLATION, insulation, secludedness, seclusion, separateness, sequestration, solitariness, solitude

seize *Syn* TAKE, clutch, grab, grasp, snatch

seizure *Syn* ATTACK (sense 3), bout, case, fit, siege, spell

seldom · not often *Syn* infrequently, little, rarely *Rel* ne'er, never *Ant* frequently, often

select *adj* · chosen from a number or group by fitness, superiority, or preference *Syn* elect, exclusive, picked *Rel* choice, dainty, delicate, exquisite, rare, recherché *Ant* indiscriminate

select *vb Syn* CHOOSE, cull, elect, opt, pick, prefer, single *Ant* eschew, reject

selection *Syn* CHOICE, alternative, election, option, preference

selective · tending to select carefully *Syn* choosy (*or* choosey), particular, picky *Rel* fastidious, finicky, fussy *Ant* nonselective

self-abnegation *Syn* RENUNCIATION, abnegation, self-denial *Ant* indulgence, self-indulgence

self-admiration *Syn* COMPLACENCE, complacency, conceit, conceitedness, ego, egotism, pompousness, pride, pridefulness, self-conceit, self-esteem, self-importance, self-satisfaction, smugness, vaingloriousness, vainglory, vainness, vanity *Ant* humbleness, humility, modesty

self-assertive *Syn* AGGRESSIVE (sense 1), assertive, militant, pushing, pushy

self-assurance *Syn* CONFIDENCE, aplomb, assurance, self-confidence, self-possession *Ant* diffidence

self-centered *Syn* EGOCENTRIC, egoistic, egotistic (*or* egotistical), selfish, self-seeking *Ant* selfless

self-complacent *Syn* COMPLACENT, priggish, self-satisfied, smug

self-conceit *Syn* COMPLACENCE, complacency, conceit, conceitedness, ego, egotism, pompousness, pride, pridefulness, self-admiration, self-esteem, self-importance, self-satisfaction, smugness, vaingloriousness, vainglory, vainness, vanity *Ant* humbleness, humility, modesty

self-conceited *Syn* CONCEITED, complacent, egoistic, egotistic (*or* egotistical), important, overweening, pompous, prideful, proud, self-important, self-satisfied, smug, stuck-up, vain, vainglorious *Ant* humble, modest

self-confidence *Syn* CONFIDENCE, aplomb, assurance, self-assurance, self-possession *Ant* diffidence

self-denial *Syn* RENUNCIATION, abnegation, self-abnegation *Ant* indulgence, self-indulgence

self-esteem 1 *Syn* COMPLACENCE, complacency, conceit, conceitedness, ego, egotism, pompousness, pride, pridefulness, self-admiration, self-conceit, self-importance, self-satisfaction, smugness, vaingloriousness, vainglory, vainness, vanity *Ant* humbleness, humility, modesty 2 *Syn* CONCEIT, amour propre, egoism, egotism, self-love *Ant* humility

self-governing *Syn* DEMOCRATIC, popular, republican, self-ruling *Ant* undemocratic

self-importance *Syn* ARROGANCE, haughtiness, imperiousness, loftiness, lordliness, masterfulness, peremptoriness, pompousness, presumptuousness, pretense (*or* pretence), pretension, pretentiousness, superciliousness, superiority *Ant* humility, modesty

self-importance *Syn* COMPLACENCE, complacency, conceit, conceitedness, ego, egotism, pompousness, pride, pridefulness, self-admiration, self-conceit, self-esteem, self-satisfaction, smugness, vaingloriousness, vainglory, vainness, vanity *Ant* humbleness, humility, modesty

self-important *Syn* CONCEITED, complacent, egoistic, egotistic (*or* egotistical), important, overweening, pompous, prideful, proud, self-conceited, self-satisfied, smug, stuck-up, vain, vainglorious *Ant* humble, modest

selfish *Syn* EGOCENTRIC, egoistic, egotistic (*or* egotistical), self-centered, self-seeking *Ant* selfless

self-love *Syn* CONCEIT, amour propre, egoism, egotism, self-esteem *Ant* humility

self-possession 1 *Syn* CONFIDENCE, aplomb, assurance, self-assurance, self-confidence *Ant* diffidence 2 *Syn* EQUANIMITY, aplomb, calmness, composure, coolheadedness, coolness, imperturbability, placidity, serenity, tranquillity (*or* tranquility) *Ant* agitation, discomposure, perturbation

self-reliant *Syn* SELF-SUFFICIENT, independent, self-supporting *Ant* dependent, reliant

self-ruling *Syn* DEMOCRATIC, popular, republican, self-governing *Ant* undemocratic

selfsame *Syn* SAME, equal, equivalent, identic, identical, tantamount, very *Ant* different

self-satisfaction *Syn* COMPLACENCE, complacency, conceit, conceitedness, ego, egotism, pompousness, pride, pridefulness, self-admiration, self-conceit, self-esteem, self-importance, smugness, vaingloriousness, vainglory, vainness, vanity *Ant* humbleness, humility, modesty

self-satisfied 1 *Syn* COMPLACENT, priggish, self-complacent, smug 2 *Syn* CONCEITED, complacent, egoistic, egotistic (*or* egotistical), important, overweening, pompous, prideful, proud, self-conceited, self-important, smug, stuck-up, vain, vainglorious *Ant* humble, modest

self-seeking *Syn* EGOCENTRIC, egoistic, egotistic (*or* egotistical), self-centered, selfish *Ant* selfless

self-sufficient · able to take care of oneself without outside help *Syn* independent, self-reliant, self-supporting *Rel* potent, powerful, resilient, strong *Ant* dependent, reliant

self-supporting *Syn* SELF-SUFFICIENT, independent, self-reliant *Ant* dependent, reliant

self-willed *Syn* OBSTINATE, adamant, adamantine, dogged, hard, hardened, hardheaded, hardhearted, headstrong, immovable, implacable, inflexible, mulish, obdurate, opinionated, ossified, pat, peevish, pertinacious, perverse, pigheaded, rigid, stubborn, unbending, uncompromising, unrelenting, unyielding, willful (*or* wilful) *Ant* acquiescent, agreeable, amenable, compliant, complying, flexible, pliable, pliant, relenting, yielding

sell *Syn* MARKET, deal (in), merchandise, put up, retail, vend *Ant* buy, purchase

sellout *Syn* BETRAYAL, disloyalty, double cross, faithlessness, falseness, falsity, infidelity, perfidy, treachery, treason, unfaithfulness

semblance *Syn* APPEARANCE, aspect, look

send · to cause to go or be taken from one place, person or condition to another *Syn* dispatch, forward, remit, route, ship, transmit *Rel* quicken, speed *Ant* accept, receive

senescence *Syn* AGE (sense 1), dotage, senility

senility *Syn* AGE (sense 1), dotage, senescence

senior *adj Syn* ELDERLY, aged, aging, ancient, geriatric, long-lived, old, older *Ant* young, youthful

senior *n Syn* SUPERIOR, better, elder *Ant* inferior, subordinate, underling

senior citizen · a person of advanced years *Syn* ancient, elder, golden-ager, oldster, old-timer *Rel* senior *Ant* youngster, youth

sensation 1 · awareness (as of heat or pain) due to stimulation of a sense organ *Syn* image, percept, sense-datum, sensum *Rel* impress, impression, print, stamp 2 · the power to respond or an act of responding to stimuli *Syn* feeling, sense, sensibility *Rel* palpability, palpableness, perceptibility, perceptibleness, ponderability, ponderableness, tangibility, tangibleness

sensational *Syn* EXCELLENT, A1, bang-up, banner, capital, classic, crackerjack, dandy, divine, fabulous, fine, first-class, first-rate, grand, great, groovy, heavenly, jim-dandy, keen, marvelous (*or* marvellous), mean, neat, nifty, noble, par excellence, prime, splendid, stellar, sterling, superb, superior, superlative, supernal, swell, terrific, tip-top, top, top-notch, unsurpassed, wonderful *Ant* poor

sense 1 · the ability to reach intelligent conclusions *Syn* common sense, good sense, gumption, horse sense, judgment, wisdom *Rel* discretion, foresight, prudence 2 *Syn* COMMON SENSE, discreetness, discretion, horse sense, levelheadedness, prudence, sense, sensibleness, wisdom, wit *Ant* imprudence, indiscretion 3 *Syn* MEANING, acceptation, import, significance, signification 4 *Syn* SENSATION (sense 2), feeling, sensibility

sense-datum *Syn* SENSATION (sense 1), image, percept, sensum

senseless *Syn* MEANINGLESS, empty, inane, pointless *Ant* meaningful

sensibility *Syn* SENSATION (sense 2), feeling, sense

sensible 1 *Syn* AWARE, alive, awake, cognizant, conscious *Ant* unaware 2 *Syn* CONSCIOUS, alive, aware, cognizant, mindful, sentient *Ant* insensible, unaware, unconscious, unmindful 3 *Syn* MATERIAL, corporeal, objective, phenomenal, physical *Ant* immaterial 4 *Syn* PERCEPTIBLE, appreciable, detectable, discernible, distinguishable, palpable *Ant* impalpable, imperceptible, inappreciable, indistinguishable, insensible 5 *Syn* WISE, judicious, prudent, sage, sane, sapient *Ant* simple

sensibleness *Syn* COMMON SENSE, discreetness, discretion, horse sense, levelheadedness, prudence, sense, wisdom, wit *Ant* imprudence, indiscretion

sensitive 1 *Syn* LIABLE, exposed, open, prone, subject, susceptible *Ant* exempt, immune 2 *Syn* SENTIENT, impressible, impressionable, responsive, susceptible

sensual *Syn* CARNAL, animal, fleshly *Ant* intellectual, spiritual

sensum *Syn* SENSATION (sense 1), image, percept, sense-datum

sensuous · relating to or providing pleasure through gratification of the senses *Syn* epicurean, luxurious, sybaritic, voluptuous *Rel* imaginal, sensational

sentence · to decree the fate or punishment of one adjudged guilty, unworthy, or unfit *Syn* condemn, damn, doom, proscribe *Rel* adjudge, adjudicate, judge

sentient 1 · readily affected by external stimuli *Syn* impressible, impressionable, responsive, sensitive, susceptible 2 *Syn* CONSCIOUS, alive, aware, cognizant, mindful, sensible *Ant* insensible, unaware, unconscious, unmindful

sentiment 1 *Syn* FEELING, affection, emotion, passion 2 *Syn* OPINION, belief, conviction, persuasion, view

sentimental 1 · unduly or affectedly emotional *Syn* maudlin, mawkish, mushy, romantic, slushy, soppy *Rel* affectionate, emotional, feeling, passionate 2 *Syn* CORNY, maudlin, mawkish, mushy, saccharine, sappy, schmaltzy, sloppy, sugarcoated, sugary *Ant* unsentimental

separate *vb* · to become or cause to become disunited or disjoined *Syn* divide, divorce, part, sever, sunder *Rel* cleave, rend, rive, split, tear *Ant* combine

separate *adj* 1 *Syn* DISTINCT, discrete, several 2 *Syn* SINGLE, lone, particular, sole, solitary, unique *Ant* accompanied, conjugal, supported

separateness *Syn* ISOLATION, insulation, secludedness, seclusion, segregation, sequestration, solitariness, solitude

sequel *Syn* EFFECT, aftereffect, aftermath, consequence, event, issue, outcome, result, upshot *Ant* cause

sequence *Syn* SUCCESSION, chain, progression, series, string, train

sequent *Syn* CONSECUTIVE, sequential, serial, successive *Ant* inconsecutive

sequential *Syn* CONSECUTIVE, sequent, serial, successive *Ant* inconsecutive

sequester *Syn* ISOLATE, insulate, seclude, segregate

sequestration *Syn* ISOLATION, insulation, secludedness, seclusion, segregation, separateness, solitariness, solitude

serene *Syn* CALM, halcyon, peaceful, placid, tranquil *Ant* agitated, stormy

sereneness *Syn* CALM, calmness, hush, peace, peacefulness, placidity, quiet, quietness, quietude, repose, restfulness, serenity, still, stillness, tranquillity (*or* tranquility) *Ant* bustle, commotion, hubbub, hurly-burly, pandemonium, tumult, turmoil, uproar

serenity 1 *Syn* CALM, calmness, hush, peace,

peacefulness, placidity, quiet, quietness, quietude, repose, restfulness, sereneness, still, stillness, tranquillity (*or* tranquility) *Ant* bustle, commotion, hubbub, hurly-burly, pandemonium, tumult, turmoil, uproar 2 *Syn* EQUANIMITY, aplomb, calmness, composure, coolheadedness, coolness, imperturbability, placidity, self-possession, tranquillity (*or* tranquility) *Ant* agitation, discomposure, perturbation

serial *Syn* CONSECUTIVE, sequent, sequential, successive *Ant* inconsecutive

series *Syn* SUCCESSION, chain, progression, sequence, string, train

serious · not light or frivolous (as in disposition, appearance, or manner) *Syn* earnest, grave, sedate, sober, solemn, somber, staid *Rel* ascetic, austere, severe, stern *Ant* flippant, light

seriousness *Syn* EARNESTNESS, gravity, intentness, soberness, sobriety, solemnity *Ant* frivolity, levity, lightheartedness

sermon *Syn* SPEECH, address, harangue, homily, lecture, oration, talk

serpentine *Syn* WINDING, flexuous, sinuous, tortuous *Ant* straight

servant · a person hired to perform household or personal services *Syn* domestic, flunky, lackey, menial, retainer, steward *Rel* butler, footman, handmaiden, houseboy, maid, maidservant, majordomo, man, manservant, servitor, valet, woman *Ant* master

serve *Syn* FUNCTION, act, perform, work

service *Syn* USE (sense 1), account, advantage, avail, profit

servile *Syn* SUBSERVIENT, menial, obsequious, slavish *Ant* domineering, overbearing

set *vb* 1 · to position (something) in a specified place *Syn* establish, fix, settle *Rel* implant 2 *Syn* APPOINT (sense 1), designate, fix, name *Ant* discharge, dismiss, expel, fire 3 *Syn* COAGULATE, clot, congeal, curdle, jell, jelly

set *n* *Syn* FACTION, bloc, body, coalition, party, sect, side, wing

set in *Syn* BEGIN (sense 1), arise, commence, dawn, form, materialize, originate, spring, start *Ant* cease, end, stop

set off *Syn* ACTIVATE, actuate, crank (up), drive, move, propel, run, spark, start, touch off, trigger, turn on *Ant* cut, deactivate, kill, shut off, turn off

settee *Syn* COUCH, chesterfield, davenport, divan, lounge, sofa

setting *Syn* BACKGROUND, backdrop, environment, milieu, mise-en-scène

settle 1 *Syn* ALIGHT, land, light, perch, roost, touch down *Ant* take off 2 *Syn* CALM, compose, lull, quiet, quieten, soothe, still, tranquilize *Ant* agitate, arouse 3 *Syn* DECIDE, determine, resolve, rule 4 *Syn* SET, establish, fix

set up Syn BUILD, assemble, construct, erect, fabricate, make, make up, piece, put up, raise, rear Ant disassemble, dismantle, take down

sever Syn SEPARATE, divide, divorce, part, sunder Ant combine

several 1 Syn DISTINCT, discrete, separate **2** Syn MANY, divers, multifarious, numerous, sundry, various Ant few

severally Syn EACH, apiece, individually, respectively

severe · given to or marked by strict discipline and firm restraint Syn ascetic, austere, stern Rel burdensome, exacting, onerous, oppressive Ant tender, tolerant

severity · the quality or state of being demanding or unyielding (as in discipline or criticism) Syn hardness, harshness, inflexibility, rigidity, rigidness, rigorousness, sternness, strictness Rel hardheartedness, implacability, obduracy Ant flexibility, gentleness, laxness, mildness

shabby 1 being ill-kept and showing signs of wear and tear Syn dilapidated, dingy, faded, seedy, threadbare Rel haggard, worn **2** Syn CONTEMPTIBLE, beggarly, cheap, despicable, pitiable, scurvy, sorry Ant admirable, estimable, formidable

shack · a small, simply constructed, and often temporary dwelling Syn cabin, camp, hovel, hut, hutch, shanty Rel lean-to, shed

shackle Syn HAMPER, clog, fetter, hog-tie, manacle, trammel Ant assist (*persons*), expedite (*work, projects*)

shackles Syn ENCUMBRANCE, bar, block, chain, clog, crimp, deterrent, drag, embarrassment, fetter, handicap, hindrance, hurdle, impediment, inhibition, interference, let, manacle, obstacle, obstruction, stop, stumbling block, trammel Ant aid, assistance, benefit, help

shade 1 · comparative darkness or obscurity due to interception of light rays Syn adumbration, penumbra, shadow, umbra, umbrage Rel darkness, dimness, obscurity **2** Syn COLOR, hue, tinge, tint, tone **3** Syn GHOST, apparition, bogey, phantasm, phantom, poltergeist, shadow, specter (or spectre), spirit, spook, vision, wraith **4** Syn GRADATION, nuance **5** Syn TOUCH, dash, smack, soupçon, spice, strain, streak, suggestion, suspicion, tincture, tinge, vein

shadow n **1** Syn GHOST, apparition, bogey, phantasm, phantom, poltergeist, shade, specter (or spectre), spirit, spook, vision, wraith **2** Syn SHADE, adumbration, penumbra, umbra, umbrage **3** Syn VESTIGE, relic, trace

shadow vb Syn SUGGEST (sense 2), adumbrate Ant manifest

shadowing Syn PURSUIT, chase, chasing, dogging, following, hounding, pursuing, tagging, tailing, tracing, tracking, trailing

shaggy 1 Syn HAIRY (sense 1), bristly, fleecy, furry, hirsute, rough, woolly Ant bald, furless, hairless, shorn, smooth **2** Syn HAIRY (sense 2), furry, fuzzy, rough, woolly

shake vb **1** · to exhibit vibratory, wavering, or oscillating movement often as an evidence of instability Syn dither, quake, quaver, quiver, shimmy, shiver, shudder, teeter, totter, tremble, wobble Rel fluctuate, oscillate, sway, swing, vibrate, waver **2** · to move up and down or to and fro with some violence Syn agitate, convulse, rock Rel drive, impel, move **3** Syn SWING (sense 1), brandish, flourish, thrash, wave

shake n Syn INSTANT, flash, jiffy, minute, moment, second, split second, trice, twinkle, twinkling, wink

shall Syn NEED (sense 1), have (to), must, ought (to), should Ant have, hold

shallow Syn SUPERFICIAL, cursory, uncritical Ant deep, profound

sham vb Syn ASSUME, affect, counterfeit, feign, pretend, simulate

sham adj **1** Syn COUNTERFEIT, bogus, fake, phony, pinchbeck, pseudo, spurious Ant bona fide, genuine **2** Syn IMITATION, artificial, bogus, factitious, fake, false, man-made, mimic, mock, simulated, substitute, synthetic Ant genuine, natural, real

shame Syn DISGRACE, dishonor, disrepute, ignominy, infamy, obloquy, odium, opprobrium Ant esteem, respect

shamed Syn GUILTY, ashamed, contrite, hangdog, penitent, remorseful, repentant, shamefaced Ant impenitent, remorseless, shameless, unashamed, unrepentant

shamefaced Syn GUILTY, ashamed, contrite, hangdog, penitent, remorseful, repentant, shamed Ant impenitent, remorseless, shameless, unashamed, unrepentant

shameless · characterized by or exhibiting boldness and a lack of shame Syn barefaced, brash, brazen, impudent Rel abandoned, dissolute, profligate

shanty Syn SHACK, cabin, camp, hovel, hut, hutch

shape 1 Syn FORM (sense 1), configuration, conformation, figure **2** Syn MAKE, fabricate, fashion, forge, form, manufacture

shapeless Syn FORMLESS, amorphous, unformed, unshaped, unstructured Ant formed, shaped, structured

share · to have, get, or use in common with another or others Syn partake, participate Rel communicate, impart

sharer Syn PARTICIPANT, partaker, participator, party Ant nonparticipant

shark Syn EXPERT, ace, adept, artist, authority, crackerjack, maestro, master, past master, scholar, virtuoso, whiz, wizard Ant amateur

sharp · having or showing alert competence and clear understanding Syn acute, keen Rel biting, cutting, incisive, trenchant *Ant* blunt, dull

sharpen · to make sharp or sharper *Syn* edge, grind, hone, strop, whet *Rel* file *Ant* blunt, dull

sharply *Syn* SMARTLY, dashingly, nattily, sprucely *Ant* sloppily, slovenly

sharpness *Syn* CHILL, bite, bitterness, bleakness, chilliness, nip, rawness

shatter *Syn* BREAK, burst, bust, crack, shiver, snap *Ant* cleave (*together*), keep (*of laws*)

shave **1** *Syn* BRUSH, glance, graze, skim **2** *Syn* CLIP, bob, crop, curtail, cut, cut back, dock, lop (off), nip, pare, prune, shear, snip, trim

shaver *Syn* BOY, lad, laddie, nipper, sonny, stripling, tad, youth

shear *Syn* CLIP, bob, crop, curtail, cut, cut back, dock, lop (off), nip, pare, prune, shave, snip, trim

shed *Syn* DISCARD, cast, junk, molt, scrap, slough

sheen *Syn* LUSTER, glaze, gloss

sheep *Syn* LAMB, angel, dove, innocent *Ant* wolf

sheer *adj* **1** *Syn* PURE, absolute, simple *Ant* adulterated, applied (*of science*), contaminated, polluted **2** *Syn* STEEP, abrupt, precipitous

sheer *vb* *Syn* TURN (sense 2), avert, deflect, divert

shelter *n* · something that covers or affords protection *Syn* asylum, cover, refuge, retreat, sanctuary *Rel* protection, safeguard, safeguarding

shelter *vb* *Syn* HARBOR, board, entertain, house, lodge

sheltered *Syn* SECLUDED, cloistered, covert, isolated, quiet, remote, retired, secret

shelve *Syn* POSTPONE, defer, delay, hold off (on), hold up, put off

shenanigans *Syn* HORSEPLAY, clowning, foolery, high jinks, horsing (around), monkeying, monkeyshines, roughhouse, roughhousing, skylarking, tomfoolery

shibboleth **1** *Syn* CATCHWORD, byword, slogan **2** *Syn* SLOGAN, cry, watchword

shield *Syn* DEFEND, guard, protect, safeguard *Ant* attack, combat

shift *vb* **1** *Syn* CHANGE (sense 2), fluctuate, mutate, vary *Ant* stabilize **2** *Syn* CHANGE (sense 3), commute, exchange, substitute, swap, switch, trade **3** *Syn* MOVE (sense 2), remove, transfer

shift *n* **1** *Syn* RESOURCE, expedient, makeshift, resort, stopgap, substitute, surrogate **2** *Syn* SPELL, bout, go, stint, tour, trick, turn

shilly-shallying *Syn* HESITATION, faltering, hesitance, hesitancy, indecision, irresolution, vacillation, wavering, wobbling

shimmy *Syn* SHAKE (sense 1), dither, quake, quaver, quiver, shiver, shudder, teeter, totter, tremble, wobble

shindy *Syn* COMMOTION, bother, bustle, clatter, disturbance, furor, furore, fuss, hubbub, hullabaloo, hurly-burly, pandemonium, pother, row, ruckus, ruction, rumpus, squall, stew, stir, storm, to-do, tumult, turmoil, uproar, welter, whirl

shine *n* *Syn* LIKING, appetite, fancy, favor, fondness, like, love, partiality, preference, relish, taste, use *Ant* aversion, disfavor, dislike, distaste, hatred, loathing

shine *vb* *Syn* POLISH, buff, burnish, dress, gloss, grind, rub, smooth

ship *n* *Syn* BOAT, craft, vessel

ship *vb* *Syn* SEND, dispatch, forward, remit, route, transmit *Ant* accept, receive

shipshape *Syn* NEAT, snug, spick-and-span, tidy, trig, trim *Ant* filthy

shirk *Syn* DODGE, duck, fence, malinger, parry, sidestep *Ant* face

shiver **1** *Syn* BREAK, burst, bust, crack, shatter, snap *Ant* cleave (*together*), keep (*of laws*) **2** *Syn* SHAKE (sense 1), dither, quake, quaver, quiver, shimmy, shudder, teeter, totter, tremble, wobble

shoal · a shallow place in a body of water *Syn* bank, bar, reef

shock *vb* *Syn* HEAP, bank, cock, mass, pile, stack

shock *n* **1** *Syn* HEAP, bank, cock, mass, pile, stack **2** *Syn* IMPACT, clash, collision, concussion, impingement, jar, jolt, percussion

shocking *Syn* FEARFUL (sense 2), appalling, awful, dreadful, frightful, horrible, horrific, terrible, terrific

shoot *n* · a branch or a part of a plant that is an outgrowth from a main stem *Syn* bough, branch, limb

shoot *vb* **1** *Syn* FLY, dart, float, sail, scud, skim **2** *Syn* HURRY (sense 2), barrel, bolt, bowl, breeze, career, course, dash, fly, hasten, hotfoot (it), hump, hurtle, hustle, pelt, race, rip, rocket, run, rush, rustle, scoot, scurry, scuttle, speed, step (along), tear, trot, whirl, whisk, zip, zoom *Ant* crawl, creep, poke

shop *Syn* STORE, bazaar, emporium

shore · land bordering a usually large body of water *Syn* bank, beach, coast, foreshore, littoral, strand

short *Syn* FRAGILE, brittle, crisp, frangible, friable *Ant* tough

shortage *Syn* DEFICIENCY, dearth, deficit, failure, famine, inadequacy, insufficiency, lack, paucity, poverty, scantiness, scarceness, scarcity, want *Ant* abundance, adequacy, amplitude, plenitude, plenty, sufficiency

shortchange *Syn* FLEECE, bleed, cheat, chisel, cozen, defraud, hustle, mulct, rook, skin, squeeze, stick, sting, swindle, victimize

shortcoming *Syn* IMPERFECTION, deficiency, fault *Ant* perfection

shorten · to reduce in extent *Syn* abbreviate, abridge, curtail, retrench *Rel* decrease, diminish, lessen, reduce *Ant* elongate, extend, lengthen, prolong, protract

short-lived *Syn* MOMENTARY, ephemeral, evanescent, flash, fleeting, fugitive, impermanent, passing, temporary, transient, transitory *Ant* enduring, eternal, everlasting, lasting, long-lived, permanent, perpetual

shortly 1 · at or within a short time *Syn* anon, momentarily, presently, soon *Rel* directly, forthwith, immediately, instantly, now, promptly, pronto, right away, right now, straightaway 2 *Syn* PRESENTLY, directly, soon

shot *Syn* ATTEMPT, crack, endeavor, essay, fling, go, pass, stab, trial, try, whack

should *Syn* NEED (sense 1), have (to), must, ought (to), shall *Ant* have, hold

shout *n* · a sudden loud cry *Syn* holler, scream, screech, shriek, squeal, whoop, yell *Rel* bawl, bellow, clamor, roar, vociferation

shout *vb* · to utter a sudden loud cry (as to attract attention) *Syn* holler, scream, screech, shriek, squeal, whoop, yell *Rel* bawl, bellow, howl, roar

shove *Syn* PUSH, propel, thrust

show *vb* 1 · to reveal outwardly or make apparent *Syn* demonstrate, evidence, evince, manifest *Rel* disclose, discover, reveal 2 · to present so as to invite notice or attention *Syn* display, exhibit, expose, flaunt, parade *Rel* argue, attest, bespeak, betoken, indicate, prove *Ant* disguise

show *n* *Syn* EXHIBITION, exhibit, exposition, fair

shower *n* *Syn* BARRAGE, bombardment, cannonade, fusillade, hail, salvo, storm, volley

shower *vb* *Syn* RAIN (sense 2), hail, storm

showiness *Syn* OSTENTATION, flamboyance, flashiness, garishness, gaudiness, glitz, ostentatiousness, pretentiousness, swank *Ant* austerity, plainness, severity

show off *Syn* CUT UP, act up, clown (around), fool (around), horse (around), monkey (around), skylark

showy · given to excess outward display *Syn* ostentatious, pretentious *Rel* flashy, garish, gaudy, meretricious, tawdry

shrewd · acute in perception and sound in judgment *Syn* astute, perspicacious, sagacious *Rel* clever, intelligent, knowing, quick-witted, smart

shriek *vb* 1 *Syn* SCREAM, howl, screech, shrill, squall, squeal, yell, yelp 2 *Syn* SHOUT, holler, scream, screech, squeal, whoop, yell

shriek *n* *Syn* SHOUT, holler, scream, screech, squeal, whoop, yell

shrieking *Syn* SHRILL, acute, high-pitched, piping, screeching, squeaking, squeaky, treble, whistling *Ant* bass, deep, low, throaty

shrill *adj* · having a high musical pitch or range *Syn* acute, high-pitched, piping, screeching, shrieking, squeaking, squeaky, treble, whistling *Rel* peeping, thin, tinny *Ant* bass, deep, low, throaty

shrill *vb* *Syn* SCREAM, howl, screech, shriek, squeal, yell, yelp

shrink 1 *Syn* CONTRACT, compress, condense, constrict, deflate *Ant* expand 2 *Syn* RECOIL, blench, flinch, quail, wince *Ant* confront, defy

shrivel *Syn* WITHER, wizen

shroud *Syn* COVER, envelop, overspread, veil, wrap *Ant* bare

shudder *Syn* SHAKE (sense 1), dither, quake, quaver, quiver, shimmy, shiver, teeter, totter, tremble, wobble

shuffle *Syn* DISORDER, confuse, derange, disarrange, disarray, discompose, dishevel, dislocate, disorganize, disrupt, disturb, hash, jumble, mess (up), mix (up), muddle, muss, rumple, scramble, tousle, tumble, upset *Ant* arrange, array, draw up, marshal, order, organize, range, regulate, straighten (up), tidy

shun *Syn* ESCAPE (sense 2), avoid, elude, eschew, evade

shut out *Syn* EXCLUDE, blackball, debar, disbar, eliminate, rule out, suspend *Ant* admit, include

shut up · to stop talking *Syn* clam up, hush, quiet (down) *Rel* calm (down), cool (down), settle (down) *Ant* speak, talk

shy *adj* · not inclined to be forward *Syn* bashful, coy, diffident, modest *Rel* timid, timorous *Ant* obtrusive

shy *vb* *Syn* DEMUR, balk, boggle, jib, scruple, stick, stickle, strain *Ant* accede

sicken *Syn* DISGUST, nauseate, repel, repulse, revolt, turn off

sickly *Syn* UNWHOLESOME, diseased, morbid, pathological *Ant* wholesome

side 1 *Syn* FACTION, bloc, body, coalition, party, sect, set, wing 2 *Syn* PHASE, angle, aspect, facet

sideboard *Syn* CABINET, buffet, closet, cupboard, hutch, locker

sidekick *Syn* ASSISTANT, adjutant, aid, aide, apprentice, coadjutor, deputy, helper

sidereal *Syn* STARRY, astral, stellar

sidestep *Syn* DODGE, duck, fence, malinger, parry, shirk *Ant* face

sideways · with one side faced forward *Syn* broadside, edgewise, sidewise *Rel* aslant, indirectly, obliquely

sidewise *Syn* SIDEWAYS, broadside, edgewise

siege *Syn* ATTACK (sense 3), bout, case, fit, seizure, spell

sigh *n* · a usually inarticulate sound indicating mental or physical pain or distress *Syn* groan, moan, sob *Rel* grief, regret, sorrow

sigh *vb* · to let out a deep audible breath (as in weariness or sorrow) *Syn* groan, moan, sob *Rel* bemoan, bewail, deplore, lament

sight *Syn* LOOK, glance, glimpse, peek, peep, view

sightless *Syn* BLIND, eyeless, stone blind *Ant* sighted

sightly *Syn* BEAUTIFUL, attractive, beauteous, comely, cute, fair, gorgeous, handsome, knockout, lovely, pretty, ravishing, stunning, taking *Ant* homely, ill-favored, plain, ugly, unattractive, unbeautiful, unhandsome, unlovely, unpretty, unsightly

sign 1 · a discernible indication of what is not itself directly perceptible *Syn* badge, mark, note, symptom, token *Rel* attestation, attesting, betokening, indication 2 *Syn* CHARACTER, mark, symbol

signal *adj* 1 *Syn* EMINENT, distinguished, illustrious, noble, notable, noteworthy, outstanding, preeminent, prestigious, star, superior 2 *Syn* NOTICEABLE, arresting, conspicuous, outstanding, prominent, remarkable, salient, striking

signal *vb* *Syn* MOTION, beckon, flag, gesture, wave

significance 1 *Syn* IMPORTANCE, consequence, import, moment, weight *Ant* unimportance 2 *Syn* MEANING, acceptation, import, sense, signification

significant *Syn* EXPRESSIVE, eloquent, meaning, meaningful, pregnant, revealing, suggestive

signification *Syn* MEANING, acceptation, import, sense, significance

signify 1 *Syn* MATTER, count, import, mean, weigh 2 *Syn* MEAN, denote, import

silence · the near or complete absence of sound *Syn* hush, quiet, quietness, quietude, still, stillness *Rel* calm, lull, peacefulness, tranquility *Ant* noise, sound

silent 1 · showing restraint in speaking *Syn* close, close-lipped, closemouthed, reserved, reticent, secretive, taciturn, tight-lipped, uncommunicative *Rel* checked, curbed, inhibited, restrained *Ant* talkative 2 · mostly or entirely without sound *Syn* hushed, muted, noiseless, quiet, quieted, soundless, still *Rel* peaceful, tranquil *Ant* noisy, unquiet 3 · deliberately refraining from speech *Syn* dumb, mum, mute, speechless, uncommunicative, wordless *Rel* inarticulate, tongue-tied *Ant* communicative, speaking, talking 4 *Syn* STILL, quiet, stilly *Ant* noisy, stirring

silhouette *Syn* OUTLINE, contour, profile, skyline

silken *Syn* SLEEK, glossy, satiny, silky, slick, velvety

silky *Syn* SLEEK, glossy, satiny, silken, slick, velvety

silly 1 *Syn* FOOLISH, absurd, preposterous *Ant* sensible 2 *Syn* SIMPLE, asinine, fatuous, foolish *Ant* wise

similar *Syn* ALIKE, akin, analogous, comparable, correspondent, corresponding, like, matching, parallel, resembling, such, suchlike *Ant* different, dissimilar, diverse, unlike

similarity · the quality or state of having many qualities in common *Syn* alikeness, community, correspondence, likeness, parallelism, resemblance, similitude *Rel* analogousness *Ant* dissimilarity, unlikeness

simile *Syn* ANALOGY, metaphor

similitude *Syn* SIMILARITY, alikeness, community, correspondence, likeness, parallelism, resemblance *Ant* dissimilarity, unlikeness

simmer *Syn* BOIL, parboil, seethe, stew

simper *n* *Syn* SMILE, grin, smirk *Ant* frown

simper *vb* *Syn* SMILE, grin, smirk *Ant* frown

simple *adj* 1 · actually or apparently deficient in intelligence *Syn* asinine, fatuous, foolish, silly *Rel* childish, childlike *Ant* wise 2 *Syn* EASY, effortless, facile, light, smooth *Ant* hard 3 *Syn* IGNORANT, benighted, dark, illiterate, nonliterate, uneducated, uninstructed, unlearned, unlettered, unread, unschooled, untaught, untutored *Ant* educated, knowledgeable, literate, schooled 4 *Syn* NATURAL, artless, ingenuous, naive, unaffected, unsophisticated 5 *Syn* PLAIN, homely, unpretentious *Ant* lovely 6 *Syn* PURE, absolute, sheer *Ant* adulterated, applied (*of science*), contaminated, polluted

simple *n* *Syn* DRUG, biologic, medicinal, pharmaceutical

simpleton *Syn* FOOL (sense 2), booby, goose, half-wit, jackass, lunatic, nincompoop, ninny, nitwit, nut, turkey, yo-yo

simulate *Syn* ASSUME, affect, counterfeit, feign, pretend, sham

simulated *Syn* IMITATION, artificial, bogus, factitious, fake, false, man-made, mimic, mock, sham, substitute, synthetic *Ant* genuine, natural, real

simultaneous *Syn* CONTEMPORARY, coetaneous, coeval, coincident, concomitant, concurrent, contemporaneous, synchronous

sin 1 *Syn* EVIL, bad, evildoing, ill, immorality, iniquity, villainy, wrong *Ant* good, morality, right, virtue 2 *Syn* OFFENSE (sense 2), crime, scandal, vice

since *Syn* BECAUSE, as, for, inasmuch as

sincere · genuine in feeling *Syn* heartfelt, hearty, unfeigned, wholehearted, wholesouled *Rel* candid, frank, open, plain *Ant* insincere

sincerely *Syn* NATURALLY (sense 3), artlessly, guilelessly, ingenuously, innocently, naively, unaffectedly, unfeignedly, unpretentiously *Ant* affectedly, artificially, hypocritically, insincerely, pretentiously, unnaturally

sinewy *Syn* MUSCULAR, athletic, brawny, burly, husky

sing · to produce musical tones by or as if by means of the voice *Syn* carol, chant, descant, hymn, intone, trill, troll, warble

singe *Syn* BURN, char, scorch, sear

single *adj* **1** · one as distinguished from two or more or all others *Syn* lone, particular, separate, sole, solitary, unique *Rel* especial, individual, special, specific *Ant* accompanied, conjugal, supported **2** *Syn* UNMARRIED, celibate, maiden, virgin

single *vb Syn* CHOOSE, cull, elect, opt, pick, prefer, select *Ant* eschew, reject

singular *adj* **1** *Syn* ONLY, alone, lone, solitary, special, unique **2** *Syn* STRANGE, curious, eccentric, erratic, odd, outlandish, peculiar, quaint, queer, unique *Ant* familiar

sinister **1** · seriously threatening evil or disaster *Syn* baleful, malefic, maleficent, malign *Rel* fateful, inauspicious, ominous, portentous, unpropitious **2** *Syn* OMINOUS, baleful, dire, foreboding, inauspicious, menacing, portentous, threatening

sink **1** *Syn* DETERIORATE, crumble, decay, decline, degenerate, descend, ebb, rot, worsen *Ant* ameliorate, improve, meliorate **2** *Syn* FALL, drop, slump, subside *Ant* rise

sinuous *Syn* WINDING, flexuous, serpentine, tortuous *Ant* straight

siphon *Syn* CHANNEL, channelize, direct, funnel, pipe

sire *Syn* GENERATE, beget, breed, engender, get, procreate, propagate, reproduce

siren · a woman whom men find irresistibly attractive *Syn* enchantress, seductress, temptress *Rel* charmer, seducer

sissy *Syn* COWARD, chicken, craven, dastard, poltroon, recreant *Ant* hero, stalwart, valiant

site *Syn* PLACE, location, position, situation, spot, station

situation **1** *Syn* PLACE, location, position, site, spot, station **2** *Syn* STATE, condition, mode, posture, status

sizable *or* **sizeable** *Syn* LARGE, big, bulky, considerable, goodly, good-sized, grand, great, handsome, hefty, hulking, largish, outsize, oversize (*or* oversized), substantial, tidy, voluminous *Ant* little, puny, small, undersized

size · the amount of measurable space or area occupied by a thing *Syn* area, dimensions, extent, magnitude, volume *Rel* amplitude, expanse, spread, stretch

skedaddle *Syn* SCUTTLE, scamper, scurry, sprint

skeleton *Syn* STRUCTURE, anatomy, framework

skeptic · a person who is always ready to doubt or question the truth or existence of something *Syn* disbeliever, doubter, questioner, unbeliever *Rel* cynic, misanthrope, pessimist

skeptically *Syn* ASKANCE, distrustfully, doubtfully, doubtingly, dubiously, mistrustfully, suspiciously *Ant* trustfully, trustingly

skepticism *Syn* DOUBT, distrust, distrustfulness, incertitude, misgiving, mistrust, mistrustfulness, suspicion, uncertainty *Ant* assurance, belief, certainty, certitude, confidence, conviction, sureness, surety, trust

sketch *n* **1** · a rough drawing representing the chief features of an object or scene *Syn* blueprint, delineation, diagram, draft, outline, plot, tracing *Rel* design, plan, project, scheme **2** *Syn* COMPENDIUM, aperçu, digest, pandect, précis, survey, syllabus

sketch *vb* · to make a sketch, rough draft, or outline of *Syn* blueprint, delineate, diagram, draft, outline, plot, trace *Rel* design, plan, project, scheme

skewbald *Syn* VARIEGATED, checked, checkered, dappled, motley, parti-colored, piebald, pied

skewed *Syn* AWRY, askew, aslant, cockeyed, crooked, listing, lopsided, oblique, slanted, slanting, slantwise, tilted, tipping, uneven *Ant* even, level, straight

skid *Syn* SLIDE, coast, glide, glissade, slip, slither, toboggan

skill *Syn* ART, artifice, craft, cunning

skilled *Syn* PROFICIENT, adept, expert, masterly, skillful *Ant* amateur, amateurish, inexperienced, inexpert, unexperienced, unpracticed, unprofessional, unseasoned, unskilled, unskillful

skillful *Syn* PROFICIENT, adept, expert, masterly, skilled *Ant* amateur, amateurish, inexperienced, inexpert, unexperienced, unpracticed, unprofessional, unseasoned, unskilled, unskillful

skim **1** *Syn* BRUSH, glance, graze, shave **2** *Syn* FLY, dart, float, sail, scud, shoot

skimp *Syn* ECONOMIZE, save, scrimp *Ant* waste

skimping *Syn* ECONOMY, frugality, husbandry, providence, scrimping, thrift *Ant* wastefulness

skimpy *Syn* MEAGER, exiguous, scant, scanty, scrimpy, spare, sparse *Ant* ample, copious

skin *n* · an outer or surface layer especially the outer limiting layer of an animal body *Syn* bark, hide, peel, pelt, rind

skin *vb* **1** · to remove the surface, skin, or thin outer covering of *Syn* decorticate, flay, pare, peel **2** *Syn* FLEECE, bleed, cheat, chisel, cozen, defraud, hustle, mulct, rook, short-change, squeeze, stick, sting, swindle, victimize

skinny *Syn* LEAN, angular, gaunt, lank, lanky, rawboned, scrawny, spare *Ant* fleshy

skip · to move or advance with successive springs or leaps *Syn* bound, curvet, hop, lollop, lope, ricochet

skirmish *Syn* ENCOUNTER, brush

skirt *Syn* BORDER, bound, fringe, margin, rim

skirting *Syn* ADJACENT, abutting, adjoining, bordering, contiguous, flanking, fringing, joining, juxtaposed, touching, verging *Ant* nonadjacent

skittish *Syn* EXCITABLE, flighty, fluttery, high-strung, jittery, jumpy, nervous, spooky *Ant* unflappable

skulk *Syn* LURK, slink, sneak

skylark *Syn* CUT UP, act up, clown (around), fool (around), horse (around), monkey (around), show off

skylarking *Syn* HORSEPLAY, clowning, foolery, high jinks, horsing (around), monkeying, monkeyshines, roughhouse, roughhousing, shenanigans, tomfoolery

skyline *Syn* OUTLINE, contour, profile, silhouette

skyward *Syn* ABOVE, aloft, over, overhead *Ant* below, beneath, under

slack *adj* **1** *Syn* LOOSE, lax, relaxed *Ant* strict, tight **2** *Syn* NEGLIGENT, careless, derelict, lax, neglectful, neglecting, remiss *Ant* attentive, careful, conscientious

slack *vb Syn* SLACKEN, ease, loosen, relax *Ant* strain, stretch, tense, tighten

slacken **1** · to make less taut *Syn* ease, loosen, relax, slack *Rel* detach, free, unbind, undo, unfasten, untie *Ant* strain, stretch, tense, tighten **2** *Syn* DELAY (sense 1), detain, retard, slow *Ant* expedite, hasten

slam *Syn* ATTACK (sense 2), abuse, assail, belabor, blast, castigate, excoriate, jump (on), lambaste (*or* lambast), scathe, vituperate

slander *vb* · to make untrue and harmful statements about *Syn* asperse, blacken, defame, libel, malign, smear, traduce, vilify *Rel* belittle, detract, disparage

slander *n Syn* DETRACTION, backbiting, calumny, scandal

slanderous *Syn* LIBELOUS, defamatory, scandalous

slang *Syn* TERMINOLOGY, argot, cant, dialect, jargon, language, lingo, patois, patter, vocabulary

slant *vb* · to set or be set at an angle *Syn* incline, lean, slope *Rel* deviate, diverge, swerve, veer

slant *n Syn* POINT OF VIEW, angle, standpoint, viewpoint

slanted *Syn* AWRY, askew, aslant, cockeyed, crooked, listing, lopsided, oblique, skewed, slanting, slantwise, tilted, tipping, uneven *Ant* even, level, straight

slanting *Syn* AWRY, askew, aslant, cockeyed, crooked, listing, lopsided, oblique, skewed, slanted, slantwise, tilted, tipping, uneven *Ant* even, level, straight

slantwise *Syn* AWRY, askew, aslant, cockeyed, crooked, listing, lopsided, oblique, skewed, slanted, slanting, tilted, tipping, uneven *Ant* even, level, straight

slap *Syn* STRIKE, box, clout, cuff, hit, punch, slog, slug, smite, swat

slapjack *Syn* PANCAKE, flapjack, griddle cake, hotcake

slapstick *Syn* COMEDY, farce, humor

slash *Syn* CUT, carve, chop, hew, slit

slatternly · being habitually untidy and very dirty especially in dress or appearance *Syn* blowsy, dowdy, frowzy *Rel* disheveled, slipshod, sloppy, slovenly, unkempt

slaughter *vb Syn* MASSACRE, butcher, mow (down)

slaughter *n Syn* MASSACRE, butchery, carnage, pogrom

slave *n* **1** · a person who is considered the property of another person *Syn* bondman, bondsman, chattel, thrall *Rel* domestic, drudge, lackey, menial, servant *Ant* freeman **2** · a person who does very hard or dull work *Syn* drudge, drudger, grubber, laborer, peon, plugger, slogger, toiler, worker *Rel* workhorse

slave *vb Syn* LABOR, drudge, endeavor, grub, hump, hustle, moil, peg (away), plod, plow, plug, slog, strain, strive, struggle, sweat, toil, travail, work *Ant* dabble, fiddle (around), fool (around), mess (around), putter (around)

slavish *Syn* SUBSERVIENT, menial, obsequious, servile *Ant* domineering, overbearing

slay *Syn* KILL, assassinate, dispatch, execute, murder

sleazy *Syn* LIMP, flabby, flaccid, flimsy, floppy

sleek **1** · having a smooth bright surface or appearance *Syn* glossy, satiny, silken, silky, slick, velvety *Rel* bright, brilliant, lustrous **2** *Syn* GLOSSY, buffed, burnished, glistening, lustrous, polished, rubbed, satin, satiny *Ant* dim, dull, flat, lusterless, matte

sleep · to take rest by a suspension of consciousness *Syn* catnap, doze, drowse, nap, slumber, snooze *Rel* relax, repose, rest

sleepiness · the quality or state of desiring or needing sleep *Syn* drowsiness, somnolence *Rel* lassitude, lethargy, sluggishness, torpor *Ant* insomnia, sleeplessness, wakefulness

sleepless *Syn* WAKEFUL, awake, wide-awake *Ant* asleep, dormant, dozing, napping, resting, sleeping, slumbering

sleepy · affected by or inducing of a desire to sleep *Syn* drowsy, slumberous, somnolent *Rel* comatose, lethargic, sluggish

sleight **1** *Syn* DEXTERITY (sense 1), adroitness, cleverness, finesse *Ant* awkwardness, clumsiness, gawkiness **2** *Syn* DEXTERITY (sense 2), agility, deftness, nimbleness, spryness *Ant* awkwardness, clumsiness, gawkiness

slender *Syn* THIN, rare, slight, slim, tenuous *Ant* thick

slick *Syn* SLEEK, glossy, satiny, silken, silky, velvety

slide · to go or progress with a smooth continuous motion *Syn* coast, glide, glissade, skid, slip, slither, toboggan

slight *n Syn* INSULT, affront, barb, dart, dig,

epithet, indignity, name, offense (*or* offence), outrage, put-down, sarcasm, slur

slight *vb Syn* NEGLECT, disregard, forget, ignore, omit, overlook *Ant* cherish

slight *adj* **1** *Syn* THIN, rare, slender, slim, tenuous *Ant* thick **2** *Syn* UNIMPORTANT, frivolous, inconsequential, inconsiderable, insignificant, little, minor, minute, negligible, small, small-fry, trifling, trivial *Ant* big, consequential, eventful, important, major, material, meaningful, momentous, significant, substantial, weighty

slightest *Syn* MINIMAL, least, littlest, lowest, minimum *Ant* full, greatest, largest, maximum, top, topmost, utmost

slighting *Syn* DEROGATORY, depreciative, depreciatory, disparaging, pejorative

slim *Syn* THIN, rare, slender, slight, tenuous *Ant* thick

sling **1** *Syn* HANG, dangle, suspend **2** *Syn* THROW, cast, fling, hurl, pitch, toss

slink *Syn* LURK, skulk, sneak

slip *n* **1** *Syn* ERROR, blunder, bull, faux pas, howler, lapse, mistake **2** *Syn* WHARF, berth, dock, jetty, levee, pier, quay

slip *vb Syn* SLIDE, coast, glide, glissade, skid, slither, toboggan

slipshod · negligent of or marked by lack of neatness and order especially in appearance or dress *Syn* disheveled, sloppy, slovenly, unkempt *Rel* lax, neglectful, negligent, remiss, slack

slit *Syn* CUT, carve, chop, hew, slash

slither *Syn* SLIDE, coast, glide, glissade, skid, slip, toboggan

slobber *Syn* GUSH (sense 2), enthuse, fuss, rave, rhapsodize

slog **1** *Syn* LABOR, drudge, endeavor, grub, hump, hustle, moil, peg (away), plod, plow, plug, slave, strain, strive, struggle, sweat, toil, travail, work *Ant* dabble, fiddle (around), fool (around), mess (around), putter (around) **2** *Syn* STRIKE, box, clout, cuff, hit, punch, slap, slug, smite, swat

slogan **1** an attention-getting word or phrase used to publicize something (as a campaign or product) *Syn* cry, shibboleth, watchword *Rel* tag line **2** *Syn* CATCHWORD, byword, shibboleth

slogger *Syn* SLAVE (sense 2), drudge, drudger, grubber, laborer, peon, plugger, toiler, worker *Ant* freeman

slope *Syn* SLANT, incline, lean

sloppily · in a careless or unfashionable manner *Syn* dowdily, slovenly, unstylishly *Rel* slatternly *Ant* nattily, sharply, smartly, sprucely

sloppy **1** *Syn* CORNY, maudlin, mawkish, mushy, saccharine, sappy, schmaltzy, sentimental, sugarcoated, sugary *Ant* unsentimental **2** *Syn* MESSY, chaotic, cluttered, confused, disarranged, disarrayed, dishev-

eled (*or* dishevelled), disordered, disorderly, higgledy-piggledy, hugger-mugger, jumbled, littered, messed, muddled, mussed, mussy, pell-mell, rumpled, topsy-turvy, tousled, tumbled, unkempt, untidy, upside-down *Ant* neat, ordered, orderly, organized, shipshape, snug, tidied, tidy, trim **3** *Syn* SLIPSHOD, disheveled, slovenly, unkempt

slothful *Syn* LAZY, faineant, indolent *Ant* industrious

slouch *Syn* LAZYBONES, drone, idler, loafer, slug, sluggard *Ant* doer, go-getter, hummer, hustler, rustler, self-starter

slough *vb Syn* DISCARD, cast, junk, molt, scrap, shed

slough *n Syn* SWAMP, bog, fen, marsh, marshland, mire, morass, muskeg, swampland

slovenly *adj Syn* SLIPSHOD, disheveled, sloppy, unkempt

slovenly *adv Syn* SLOPPILY, dowdily, unstylishly *Ant* nattily, sharply, smartly, sprucely

slow *adj* **1** · moving, flowing, or proceeding at less than the usual, desirable, or required speed *Syn* deliberate, dilatory, laggard, leisurely *Ant* fast **2** *Syn* STUPID, crass, dense, dull, dumb *Ant* intelligent

slow *adv* · at a pace that is less than usual, desirable, or expected *Syn* laggardly, leisurely, slowly, sluggishly, tardily *Rel* carefully, cautiously, deliberately, purposefully *Ant* apace, briskly, fast, fleetly, full tilt, hastily, quick, quickly, rapidly, snappily, speedily, swift, swiftly

slow *vb* **1** · to cause to move or proceed at a less rapid pace *Syn* brake, decelerate, retard *Rel* halt, stop *Ant* accelerate, hasten, hurry, quicken, rush, speed (up), step up **2** *Syn* DELAY (sense 1), detain, retard, slacken *Ant* expedite, hasten

slowly *Syn* SLOW, laggardly, leisurely, sluggishly, tardily *Ant* apace, briskly, fast, fleetly, full tilt, hastily, quick, quickly, rapidly, snappily, speedily, swift, swiftly

slug *n Syn* LAZYBONES, drone, idler, loafer, slouch, sluggard *Ant* doer, go-getter, hummer, hustler, rustler, self-starter

slug *vb Syn* STRIKE, box, clout, cuff, hit, punch, slap, slog, smite, swat

sluggard *Syn* LAZYBONES, drone, idler, loafer, slouch, slug *Ant* doer, go-getter, hummer, hustler, rustler, self-starter

sluggish *Syn* LETHARGIC, comatose, torpid *Ant* energetic, vigorous

sluggishly *Syn* SLOW, laggardly, leisurely, slowly, tardily *Ant* apace, briskly, fast, fleetly, full tilt, hastily, quick, quickly, rapidly, snappily, speedily, swift, swiftly

sluice *Syn* POUR, gush, stream

slumber *Syn* SLEEP, catnap, doze, drowse, nap, snooze

slumberous *Syn* SLEEPY, drowsy, somnolent

slump *Syn* FALL, drop, sink, subside *Ant* rise

slur *Syn* INSULT, affront, barb, dart, dig, epithet, indignity, name, offense (*or* offence), outrage, put-down, sarcasm, slight

slushy *Syn* SENTIMENTAL, maudlin, mawkish, mushy, romantic, soppy

sly · attaining or seeking to attain one's ends by devious means *Syn* artful, crafty, cunning, foxy, guileful, insidious, tricky, wily *Rel* clandestine, covert, furtive, secret, stealthy

smack **1** *Syn* TASTE (sense 1), flavor, relish, savor, tang *Ant* antipathy **2** *Syn* TOUCH, dash, shade, soupçon, spice, strain, streak, suggestion, suspicion, tincture, tinge, vein

small *Syn* UNIMPORTANT, frivolous, inconsequential, inconsiderable, insignificant, little, minor, minute, negligible, slight, small-fry, trifling, trivial *Ant* big, consequential, eventful, important, major, material, meaningful, momentous, significant, substantial, weighty

smaller *Syn* LESSER, inferior, junior, less, lower, minor, subordinate, under *Ant* greater, higher, major, more, primary, prime, senior, superior

small-fry *Syn* UNIMPORTANT, frivolous, inconsequential, inconsiderable, insignificant, little, minor, minute, negligible, slight, small, trifling, trivial *Ant* big, consequential, eventful, important, major, material, meaningful, momentous, significant, substantial, weighty

small-minded *Syn* INTOLERANT, bigoted, narrow, narrow-minded, prejudiced *Ant* broadminded, liberal, open-minded, tolerant, unprejudiced

small talk *Syn* CHAT, chatter, chitchat, gabfest, gossip, palaver, rap, table talk, talk, tête-à-tête

small-town *Syn* INSULAR, local, parochial, provincial

smart **1** *Syn* FLIPPANT, facetious, flip, pert, smart-alecky (*or* smart-aleck) *Ant* earnest, sincere **2** *Syn* INTELLIGENT, alert, bright, brilliant, clever, knowing, quick-witted *Ant* unintelligent **3** *Syn* STYLISH, chic, dashing, fashionable, modish **4** *Syn* WORLDLY-WISE, cosmopolitan, sophisticated, worldly *Ant* ingenuous, innocent, naive, unsophisticated, unworldly, wide-eyed

smart aleck · a person who likes to show off in a clever but annoying way *Syn* smarty (*or* smartie), wise guy, wiseacre *Rel* know-it-all

smart-alecky *or* **smart-aleck** *Syn* FLIPPANT, facetious, flip, pert, smart *Ant* earnest, sincere

smartly · in a strikingly neat and trim manner *Syn* dashingly, nattily, sharply, sprucely *Rel* neatly, orderly, tidily, trimly *Ant* sloppily, slovenly

smarty *or* **smartie** *Syn* SMART ALECK, wise guy, wiseacre

smash *Syn* CRUSH (sense 1), bruise, macerate, mash, squash

smear *Syn* SLANDER, asperse, blacken, defame, libel, malign, traduce, vilify

smell · the quality that makes a thing perceptible to the olfactory sense *Syn* aroma, odor, scent *Rel* bouquet, fragrance, incense, perfume, redolence

smidgen *Syn* PARTICLE, atom, bit, iota, jot, mite, tittle, whit

smile *n* · a facial expression in which the lips curve slightly upward especially in expression of pleasure or amusement *Syn* grin, simper, smirk *Ant* frown

smile *vb* · to have, produce, or exhibit a smile *Syn* grin, simper, smirk *Ant* frown

smirch *Syn* DIRTY, befoul, begrime, besmirch, blacken, foul, grime, mire, muddy, smudge, soil, stain, sully *Ant* clean, cleanse

smirk *n Syn* SMILE, grin, simper *Ant* frown

smirk *vb Syn* SMILE, grin, simper

smite *Syn* STRIKE, box, clout, cuff, hit, punch, slap, slog, slug, swat

smog *Syn* HAZE (sense 1), fog, mist, murk, reek, soup

smooth *adj* **1** *Syn* EASY, effortless, facile, light, simple *Ant* hard **2** *Syn* SOFT, balmy, bland, gentle, lenient, mild *Ant* hard, stern **3** *Syn* SUAVE, debonair, sophisticated, urbane *Ant* boorish, churlish, clownish, loutish, uncouth **4** *Syn* LEVEL, even, flat, flush, plain, plane

smooth *vb Syn* POLISH, buff, burnish, dress, gloss, grind, rub, shine

smoothly *Syn* EASILY, effortlessly, facilely, fluently, freely, handily, lightly, painlessly, readily *Ant* arduously, laboriously

smother *Syn* SUFFOCATE, asphyxiate, choke, stifle, strangle, throttle

smudge *Syn* DIRTY, befoul, begrime, besmirch, blacken, foul, grime, mire, muddy, smirch, soil, stain, sully *Ant* clean, cleanse

smug **1** *Syn* COMPLACENT, priggish, self-complacent, self-satisfied **2** *Syn* CONCEITED, complacent, egoistic, egotistic (*or* egotistical), important, overweening, pompous, prideful, proud, self-conceited, self-important, self-satisfied, stuck-up, vain, vainglorious *Ant* humble, modest

smuggled · imported or exported secretly and in violation of the law *Syn* bootleg, contraband

smugness *Syn* COMPLACENCE, complacency, conceit, conceitedness, ego, egotism, pompousness, pride, pridefulness, self-admiration, self-conceit, self-esteem, self-importance, self-satisfaction, vaingloriousness, vainglory, vainness, vanity *Ant* humbleness, humility, modesty

snap *vb* **1** *Syn* BREAK, burst, bust, crack, shatter, shiver *Ant* cleave (*together*), keep (*of laws*) **2** *Syn* JERK, twitch, yank

snap *n Syn* CINCH, breeze, child's play, duck soup, picnic, pushover *Ant* chore, headache, labor

snap back *Syn* CONVALESCE, gain, heal, mend, rally, recover, recuperate

snappish *Syn* IRRITABLE, fractious, fretful, huffy, peevish, pettish, petulant, querulous, waspish *Ant* easygoing

snappy *Syn* PUNGENT, piquant, poignant, racy, spicy *Ant* bland

snare **1** *Syn* CATCH, bag, capture, ensnare, entrap, trap *Ant* miss **2** *Syn* ENTANGLE, enmesh, ensnare, entrap, mesh, tangle, trap *Ant* disentangle

snarl *vb* *Syn* BARK, bay, growl, howl, yap, yelp

snarl *n* *Syn* CONFUSION, chaos, clutter, disarray, disorder, jumble, muddle

snatch *Syn* TAKE, clutch, grab, grasp, seize

sneak *Syn* LURK, skulk, slink

sneer *Syn* SCOFF, fleer, flout, gibe, gird, jeer

snip *Syn* CLIP, bob, crop, curtail, cut, cut back, dock, lop (off), nip, pare, prune, shave, shear, trim

snitch *Syn* STEAL, cop, filch, lift, pilfer, pinch, purloin, swipe

snoop *Syn* INTERFERE, butt in, intrude, meddle, mess, nose, obtrude, poke, pry

snoopy **1** *Syn* CURIOUS, inquisitive, nosy, prying *Ant* incurious, uninterested **2** *Syn* INTRUSIVE, interfering, intruding, meddlesome, meddling, nosy (*or* nosey), obtrusive, officious, presumptuous, prying *Ant* unobtrusive

snooze *Syn* SLEEP, catnap, doze, drowse, nap, slumber

snowball *Syn* INCREASE (sense 2), accumulate, appreciate, balloon, build (up), burgeon, enlarge, escalate, expand, mount, multiply, mushroom, proliferate, rise, swell, wax *Ant* contract, decrease, diminish, lessen, wane

snug **1** *Syn* COMFORTABLE, cozy, easy, restful *Ant* miserable, uncomfortable **2** *Syn* NEAT, shipshape, spick-and-span, tidy, trig, trim *Ant* filthy

so **1** *Syn* THEREFORE, accordingly, consequently, hence, then **2** *Syn* VERY, awful, awfully, beastly, deadly, especially, exceedingly, extra, extremely, far, frightfully, full, greatly, heavily, highly, hugely, jolly, mightily, mighty, mortally, most, much, particularly, rattling, real, right, something, super, terribly, too, whacking *Ant* little, negligibly, nominally, slightly

soak *vb* **1** · to permeate or be permeated with a liquid *Syn* drench, impregnate, saturate, sop, steep, waterlog *Rel* dip, immerse, submerge **2** *Syn* WET, bathe, douse, drench, souse, wash, water *Ant* dry

soak *n* *Syn* DRUNKARD, alcoholic, dipsomaniac, inebriate, sot, tippler, toper, tosspot *Ant* teetotaler

soar *Syn* ASCEND, arise, climb, lift, mount, rise, up, uprise, upsweep, upturn *Ant* decline, descend, dip, drop, fall (off)

sob *vb* *Syn* SIGH, groan, moan

sob *n* *Syn* SIGH, groan, moan

sober **1** · having or exhibiting self-control and avoiding extremes of behavior *Syn* continent, temperate, unimpassioned *Rel* abstaining, forbearing *Ant* drunk, excited **2** *Syn* SERIOUS, earnest, grave, sedate, solemn, somber, staid *Ant* flippant, light

soberness *Syn* EARNESTNESS, gravity, intentness, seriousness, sobriety, solemnity *Ant* frivolity, levity, lightheartedness

sobriety **1** *Syn* EARNESTNESS, gravity, intentness, seriousness, soberness, solemnity *Ant* frivolity, levity, lightheartedness **2** *Syn* TEMPERANCE, abstemiousness, abstinence, continence *Ant* excessiveness, immoderacy, intemperance, intemperateness

sociable **1** *Syn* CONVIVIAL, boon, companionable, extroverted, gregarious, outgoing, social *Ant* antisocial, introverted, reclusive, unsociable **2** *Syn* GRACIOUS, affable, cordial, genial *Ant* ungracious

social *Syn* CONVIVIAL, boon, companionable, extroverted, gregarious, outgoing, sociable *Ant* antisocial, introverted, reclusive, unsociable

socialize · to take part in social activities *Syn* associate, fraternize, hobnob, mingle, mix

society **1** *Syn* ARISTOCRACY, county, elite, gentry, nobility *Ant* people, proletariat **2** *Syn* ASSOCIATION, club, order **3** *Syn* COMPANIONSHIP, camaraderie, company, comradeship, fellowship

sofa *Syn* COUCH, chesterfield, davenport, divan, lounge, settee

soft · free from all harshness, roughness, or intensity *Syn* balmy, bland, gentle, lenient, mild, smooth *Rel* moderated, tempered *Ant* hard, stern

soften **1** *Syn* CUSHION, buffer, gentle **2** *Syn* WEAKEN, debilitate, enervate, enfeeble, sap

soft-soap *Syn* COAX, blandish, blarney, cajole, wheedle

soil *Syn* DIRTY, befoul, begrime, besmirch, blacken, foul, grime, mire, muddy, smirch, smudge, stain, sully *Ant* clean, cleanse

sojourn *Syn* RESIDE, dwell, live, lodge, put up, stay, stop

solace *Syn* COMFORT, console *Ant* afflict, bother

solar plexus *Syn* STOMACH, abdomen, belly, gut, tummy

sole **1** *Syn* ONLY, alone, lone, singular, solitary, special, unique **2** *Syn* SINGLE, lone, particular, separate, solitary, unique *Ant* accompanied, conjugal, supported

solecism **1** *Syn* BARBARISM, corruption, impropriety, vernacularism, vulgarism **2** *Syn* IMPROPRIETY (sense 1), familiarity, gaffe, indiscretion *Ant* amenity, civility, courtesy, formality, gesture

solemn **1** *Syn* CEREMONIAL, ceremonious, conventional, formal **2** *Syn* DIGNIFIED, august, imposing, staid, stately *Ant* flighty, frivolous, giddy, goofy, silly, undignified **3**

Syn SERIOUS, earnest, grave, sedate, sober, somber, staid *Ant* flippant, light

solemnity *Syn* EARNESTNESS, gravity, intentness, seriousness, soberness, sobriety *Ant* frivolity, levity, lightheartedness

solemnize *Syn* KEEP (sense 1), celebrate, commemorate, observe *Ant* break

solicit 1 *Syn* CANVASS, poll, survey **2** *Syn* INVITE, bid, court, woo **3** *Syn* ASK, request

solicitor 1 *Syn* LAWYER, advocate, attorney, barrister, counsel, counselor **2** *Syn* SUPPLICANT, petitioner, pleader, suitor, suppliant

solicitous *Syn* WORRIED, anxious, careful, concerned

solicitude *Syn* CARE, anxiety, concern, worry

solid 1 *Syn* DEPENDABLE, good, reliable, responsible, safe, steady, sure, tried, tried-and-true, true, trustworthy, trusty *Ant* irresponsible, undependable, unreliable, untrustworthy **2** *Syn* FIRM, hard *Ant* flabby, loose

solidarity *Syn* UNITY, integrity, union

solidify *Syn* HARDEN (sense 1), cake, indurate, petrify *Ant* soften

solitariness *Syn* ISOLATION, insulation, secludedness, seclusion, segregation, separateness, sequestration, solitude

solitary 1 *Syn* ALONE, desolate, forlorn, lone, lonely, lonesome, lorn *Ant* accompanied **2** *Syn* ONLY, alone, lone, singular, sole, special, unique **3** *Syn* SINGLE, lone, particular, separate, sole, unique *Ant* accompanied, conjugal, supported

solitude *Syn* ISOLATION, insulation, secludedness, seclusion, segregation, separateness, sequestration, solitariness

soluble *Syn* SOLVABLE, answerable, explainable, explicable, resolvable *Ant* inexplicable, insoluble, unexplainable, unsolvable

solution *Syn* ANSWER (sense 2), result

solvable · capable of having the reason for or cause of determined *Syn* answerable, explainable, explicable, resolvable, soluble *Rel* analyzable, decipherable *Ant* inexplicable, insoluble, unexplainable, unsolvable

solve · to find an answer for through reasoning *Syn* answer, break, crack, dope (out), figure out, puzzle (out), resolve, riddle, unravel, work, work out *Rel* clear (up), iron out, straighten (out), unscramble, untangle, untie

somatic *Syn* BODILY, corporal, corporeal, physical

somber *Syn* SERIOUS, earnest, grave, sedate, sober, solemn, staid *Ant* flippant, light

some *Syn* ALMOST, about, more or less, most, much, near, nearly, next to, nigh, practically, virtually, well-nigh

something *Syn* VERY, awful, awfully, beastly, deadly, especially, exceedingly, extra, extremely, far, frightfully, full, greatly, heavily, highly, hugely, jolly, mightily, mighty, mortally, most, much, particularly,

rattling, real, right, so, super, terribly, too, whacking *Ant* little, negligibly, nominally, slightly

sometime *Syn* FORMER, erstwhile, late, old, onetime, past, whilom

somnolence *Syn* SLEEPINESS, drowsiness *Ant* insomnia, sleeplessness, wakefulness

somnolent *Syn* SLEEPY, drowsy, slumberous

song 1 *Syn* MELODY, air, lay, strain, tune, warble **2** *Syn* POEM, lyric, verse

sonny *Syn* BOY, lad, laddie, nipper, shaver, stripling, tad, youth

sonorous *Syn* RESONANT, orotund, resounding, ringing, vibrant

soon 1 *Syn* EARLY, beforehand, betimes *Ant* late **2** *Syn* PRESENTLY, directly, shortly **3** *Syn* SHORTLY, anon, momentarily, presently

soothe *Syn* CALM, compose, lull, quiet, quieten, settle, still, tranquilize *Ant* agitate, arouse

soothsayer *Syn* PROPHET, augur, diviner, forecaster, foreseer, foreteller, fortune-teller, futurist, prognosticator, prophesier, seer

soothsaying *Syn* PREDICTION, auguring, cast, forecast, forecasting, foretelling, predicting, presaging, prognosis, prognosticating, prognostication, prophecy

sop *Syn* SOAK, drench, impregnate, saturate, steep, waterlog

sophisticate *vb Syn* ADULTERATE, doctor, load, weight *Ant* refine

sophisticate *n Syn* COSMOPOLITAN, metropolitan *Ant* bumpkin, hick, provincial, rustic, yokel

sophisticated 1 *Syn* SUAVE, debonair, smooth, urbane *Ant* boorish, churlish, clownish, loutish, uncouth **2** *Syn* WORLDLY-WISE, cosmopolitan, smart, worldly *Ant* ingenuous, innocent, naive, unsophisticated, unworldly, wide-eyed

soppy *Syn* SENTIMENTAL, maudlin, mawkish, mushy, romantic, slushy

sorcerer *Syn* MAGICIAN (sense 1), charmer, conjurer (*or* conjuror), enchanter, necromancer, voodoo, witch, wizard

sorcery *Syn* MAGIC, alchemy, thaumaturgy, witchcraft, witchery, wizardry

sordid *Syn* MEAN, abject, ignoble

sore *Syn* ANGRY, angered, apoplectic, enraged, foaming, fuming, furious, incensed, indignant, inflamed, infuriated, irate, ireful, mad, outraged, rabid, riled, roiled, steaming, wrathful, wroth *Ant* delighted, pleased

sorrow *n* · distress of mind *Syn* anguish, grief, heartache, heartbreak, regret, woe *Rel* grieving, mourning *Ant* joy

sorrow *vb Syn* GRIEVE, mourn *Ant* rejoice

sorrowful *Syn* SAD (sense 1), bad, blue, brokenhearted, crestfallen, dejected, depressed, despondent, disconsolate, doleful, down, downcast, downhearted, droopy, forlorn, gloomy, glum, heartbroken, heartsick, heartsore, inconsolable, joyless, low, low-spirited, melancholy, miserable, mournful, saddened, sorry, unhappy, woebegone, woeful, wretched *Ant* blissful, buoyant, buoyed, cheerful, cheery, chipper, delighted, glad, gladdened, gladsome, gleeful, happy, joyful, joyous, jubilant, sunny, upbeat

sorry 1 *Syn* CONTEMPTIBLE, beggarly, cheap, despicable, pitiable, scurvy, shabby *Ant* admirable, estimable, formidable 2 *Syn* SAD (sense 1), bad, blue, brokenhearted, crestfallen, dejected, depressed, despondent, disconsolate, doleful, down, downcast, downhearted, droopy, forlorn, gloomy, glum, heartbroken, heartsick, heartsore, inconsolable, joyless, low, low-spirited, melancholy, miserable, mournful, saddened, sorrowful, unhappy, woebegone, woeful, wretched *Ant* blissful, buoyant, buoyed, cheerful, cheery, chipper, delighted, glad, gladdened, gladsome, gleeful, happy, joyful, joyous, jubilant, sunny, upbeat 3 *Syn* SAD (sense 2), depressing, dismal, drear, dreary, heartbreaking, heartrending, melancholy, pathetic, saddening, tearful, teary *Ant* cheering, cheery, glad, happy

sort *vb Syn* ASSORT, classify, pigeonhole

sort *n Syn* TYPE, character, description, ilk, kidney, kind, nature, stripe

sot *Syn* DRUNKARD, alcoholic, dipsomaniac, inebriate, soak, tippler, toper, tosspot *Ant* teetotaler

soul *Syn* MIND, brain, intellect, intelligence, psyche, wit

sound *vb* 1 *Syn* ANNOUNCE, advertise, blaze, broadcast, declare, enunciate, placard, post, proclaim, promulgate, publicize, publish 2 *Syn* FATHOM, plumb 3 *Syn* SEEM, act, appear, look, make

sound *adj Syn* HEALTHY, hale, robust, well, wholesome *Ant* unhealthy

sound *n Syn* STRAIT, channel, narrows, passage

soundless *Syn* SILENT (sense 2), hushed, muted, noiseless, quiet, quieted, still

soundness *Syn* HEALTH, fitness, healthiness, heartiness, robustness, wellness, wholeness, wholesomeness *Ant* illness, sickness, unhealthiness, unsoundness

sound off *Syn* SPEAK UP, speak out, spout (off)

soup *Syn* HAZE (sense 1), fog, mist, murk, reek, smog

soupçon *Syn* TOUCH, dash, shade, smack, spice, strain, streak, suggestion, suspicion, tincture, tinge, vein

sour 1 · having a taste devoid of sweetness *Syn* acid, acidulous, dry, tart *Rel* acrid, bitter 2 *Syn* UNPLEASANT, bad, disagreeable, displeasing, distasteful, nasty, rotten, uncongenial, unlovely, unpleasing, unsatisfying, unwelcome *Ant* agreeable, congenial, good,

grateful, gratifying, nice, palatable, pleasant, pleasing, pleasurable, satisfying, welcome

source *Syn* ORIGIN, inception, prime mover, provenance, provenience, root

souring *Syn* ESTRANGEMENT, disaffection, disgruntlement *Ant* reconciliation

souse 1 *Syn* DIP (sense 1), duck, dunk, immerse, submerge 2 *Syn* WET, bathe, douse, drench, soak, wash, water *Ant* dry

souvenir 1 *Syn* MEMORIAL, commemorative, keepsake, memento, monument, remembrance, reminder, token 2 *Syn* MEMORY, mind, recollection, remembrance, reminiscence *Ant* oblivion

sovereign *adj* 1 *Syn* DOMINANT, paramount, predominant, preponderant, preponderating *Ant* subordinate 2 *Syn* FREE, autarchic, autarkic, autonomous, independent *Ant* bond

sovereign *n Syn* MONARCH, autocrat, ruler

sovereignty 1 *Syn* FREEDOM (sense 1), autarchy, autarky, autonomy, independence *Ant* bondage 2 *Syn* NATION, commonwealth, country, land, state 3 *Syn* SUPREMACY, ascendancy, dominance, dominion, preeminence

sow 1 *Syn* SCATTER (sense 2), bestrew, dot, pepper, spray, sprinkle, strew 2 *Syn* STREW, broadcast, scatter, straw

space-age *Syn* MODERN, contemporary, current, hot, mod, modernistic, new, newfangled, new-fashioned, present-day, red-hot, ultramodern, up-to-date *Ant* antiquated, archaic, dated, fusty, musty, noncontemporary, oldfangled, old-fashioned, old-time, out-of-date, passé

spacious · larger in extent or capacity than the average *Syn* ample, capacious, commodious *Rel* enormous, huge, immense, vast

spade *Syn* DIG, delve, excavate, grub

spangled *Syn* SPOTTED, bespangled, flecked, marbled, mottled, spattered, speckled, sprinkled, stippled

spare 1 *Syn* LEAN, angular, gaunt, lank, lanky, rawboned, scrawny, skinny *Ant* fleshy 2 *Syn* MEAGER, exiguous, scant, scanty, scrimpy, skimpy, sparse *Ant* ample, copious 3 *Syn* SUPERFLUOUS, extra, supernumerary, surplus

sparing *Syn* FRUGAL, economical, economizing, provident, scrimping, thrifty *Ant* prodigal, wasteful

spark *Syn* ACTIVATE, actuate, crank (up), drive, move, propel, run, set off, start, touch off, trigger, turn on *Ant* cut, deactivate, kill, shut off, turn off

sparkle *Syn* FLASH, coruscate, glance, gleam, glint, glisten, glitter, scintillate, twinkle

sparse *Syn* MEAGER, exiguous, scant, scanty, scrimpy, skimpy, spare *Ant* ample, copious

spasm 1 *Syn* CRAMP, charley horse, crick 2 *Syn* FIT, convulsion, paroxysm

spasmodic *Syn* FITFUL, casual, choppy, discontinuous, erratic, intermittent, irregular, occasional, sporadic, spotty, unsteady *Ant* constant, continuous, regular, steady

spat *Syn* QUARREL, altercation, bickering, squabble, tiff, wrangle

spate *Syn* FLOOD, cataract, deluge, inundation, torrent

spattered *Syn* SPOTTED, bespangled, flecked, marbled, mottled, spangled, speckled, sprinkled, stippled

spawn *Syn* EFFECT, bring about, cause, create, effectuate, engender, generate, induce, make, produce, prompt, result (in), work, yield

spay *Syn* STERILIZE (sense 1), alter, castrate, emasculate, geld, mutilate *Ant* fertilize

speak · to articulate words so as to express thoughts *Syn* converse, talk *Rel* articulate, enunciate, pronounce

speak out *Syn* SPEAK UP, sound off, spout (off)

speak up · to voice one's opinions freely with force *Syn* sound off, speak out, spout (off) *Rel* bawl, call, cry, holler, shout, sing (out), vociferate, yell

special 1 of or relating to one thing or class *Syn* especial, individual, particular, specific *Rel* characteristic, distinctive, peculiar 2 *Syn* ONLY, alone, lone, singular, sole, solitary, unique

specie *Syn* MONEY, cash, coin, coinage, currency, legal tender

specific *adj* 1 *Syn* EXPLICIT, categorical, definite, express *Ant* ambiguous 2 *Syn* SPECIAL, especial, individual, particular

specific *n* *Syn* REMEDY, cure, medicament, medication, medicine, physic

specify *Syn* MENTION, instance, name

specimen *Syn* EXAMPLE, case, exemplar, illustration, instance, representative, sample

specious *Syn* PLAUSIBLE, believable, colorable, credible

speck *Syn* SPOT, blotch, dapple, dot, fleck, freckle, marble, mottle, pepper, speckle, splotch, sprinkle, stipple

speckle *Syn* SPOT, blotch, dapple, dot, fleck, freckle, marble, mottle, pepper, speck, splotch, sprinkle, stipple

speckled *Syn* SPOTTED, bespangled, flecked, marbled, mottled, spangled, spattered, sprinkled, stippled

spectator · one who looks on or watches *Syn* beholder, bystander, eyewitness, kibitzer, looker-on, observer, onlooker, witness

specter *or* **spectre** *Syn* GHOST, apparition, bogey, phantasm, phantom, poltergeist, shade, shadow, spirit, spook, vision, wraith

speculate *Syn* THINK (sense 2), cogitate, deliberate, reason, reflect

speculative 1 *Syn* THEORETICAL, academic 2 *Syn* THOUGHTFUL (sense 1), contemplative, meditative, pensive, reflective *Ant* thoughtless

speech 1 · a usually formal discourse delivered to an audience *Syn* address, harangue, homily, lecture, oration, sermon, talk 2 *Syn* LANGUAGE (sense 1), dialect, idiom, tongue

speechless 1 *Syn* MUTE, inarticulate, voiceless 2 *Syn* SILENT (sense 3), dumb, mum, mute, uncommunicative, wordless

speed *n* 1 · rate of motion, performance, or action *Syn* headway, impetus, momentum, pace, velocity 2 *Syn* HASTE, dispatch, expedition, hurry *Ant* deliberation

speed *vb* *Syn* HURRY (sense 2), barrel, bolt, bowl, breeze, career, course, dash, fly, hasten, hotfoot (it), hump, hurtle, hustle, pelt, race, rip, rocket, run, rush, rustle, scoot, scurry, scuttle, shoot, step (along), tear, trot, whirl, whisk, zip, zoom *Ant* crawl, creep, poke

speed (up) *Syn* HURRY (sense 1), accelerate, hasten, quicken, rush, whisk *Ant* decelerate, retard, slow (down)

speedy *Syn* FAST, expeditious, fleet, hasty, quick, rapid, swift *Ant* slow

spell 1 · a limited period or amount of activity *Syn* bout, go, shift, stint, tour, trick, turn *Rel* period 2 *Syn* ATTACK (sense 3), bout, case, fit, seizure, siege

spell out *Syn* EXPLAIN (sense 1), clarify, clear (up), construe, demonstrate, elucidate, explicate, expound, illuminate, illustrate, interpret *Ant* obscure

spend 1 · to use up or pay out *Syn* disburse, expend *Rel* deal, dispense, distribute, divide, dole *Ant* save 2 *Syn* DEPLETE, clean (out), consume, drain, exhaust, expend, use up *Ant* renew, replace

spender *Syn* PRODIGAL, profligate, spendthrift, squanderer, waster, wastrel *Ant* economizer

spendthrift *adj* *Syn* PRODIGAL, extravagant, profligate, squandering, thriftless, unthrifty, wasteful *Ant* conserving, economical, economizing, frugal, scrimping, skimping, thrifty

spendthrift *n* *Syn* PRODIGAL, profligate, spender, squanderer, waster, wastrel *Ant* economizer

spew 1 *Syn* BELCH, burp, disgorge, regurgitate, throw up, vomit 2 *Syn* ERUPT (sense 2), belch, disgorge, eject, expel, jet, spout, spurt 3 *Syn* GUSH (sense 1), jet, pour, rush, spout, spurt, squirt *Ant* dribble, drip, drop, trickle

sphere *Syn* FIELD, bailiwick, domain, province, territory

spice *Syn* TOUCH, dash, shade, smack, soupçon, strain, streak, suggestion, suspicion, tincture, tinge, vein

spick-and-span *Syn* NEAT, shipshape, snug, tidy, trig, trim *Ant* filthy

spicy *Syn* PUNGENT, piquant, poignant, racy, snappy *Ant* bland

spin *n* *Syn* HAZE (sense 2), daze, fog, muddle

spin

spin vb Syn TURN (sense 1), circle, eddy, gyrate, pirouette, revolve, rotate, swirl, twirl, wheel, whirl

spindling Syn LANKY, gangling, gangly, rangy, spindly

spindly Syn LANKY, gangling, gangly, rangy, spindling

spine • the articulated column of bones that is the central and axial feature of a vertebrate skeleton Syn back, backbone, chine, vertebrae

spineless Syn COWARDLY, chicken, chicken-hearted, craven, dastardly, lily-livered, pusillanimous, recreant, unheroic, yellow Ant brave, courageous, daring, dauntless, doughty, fearless, gallant, greathearted, gutsy, hardy, heroic, intrepid, lionhearted, stalwart, stout, stouthearted, valiant, valorous

spin-off Syn DERIVATIVE, by-product, offshoot, outgrowth Ant origin, root, source

spiral • turning around an axis like the thread of a screw Syn coiling, corkscrew, helical, screwlike, winding Rel curling, curving, twisting

spirit 1 Syn GHOST, apparition, bogey, phantasm, phantom, poltergeist, shade, shadow, specter (or spectre), spook, vision, wraith 2 Syn VIGOR, dash, drive, élan, esprit, punch, verve, vim

spirited • full of energy, animation, or courage Syn fiery, gingery, high-spirited, mettlesome, peppery, spunky Rel audacious, bold, brave, courageous, intrepid, valiant Ant spiritless

spiritless Syn LISTLESS, enervated, lackadaisical, languid, languishing, languorous, limp Ant ambitious, animated, energetic, enterprising, motivated

spirits Syn ALCOHOL, booze, drink, grog, intoxicant, liquor, moonshine

spiritual Syn IMMATERIAL, incorporeal Ant material

spite Syn MALICE, despite, grudge, ill will, malevolence, malignancy, malignity, spleen Ant charity

spiteful Syn MALICIOUS, malevolent, malign, malignant

splashy Syn GAUDY, flamboyant, flashy, garish, glitzy, loud, ostentatious, swank (or swanky), tawdry Ant conservative, quiet, understated

spleen 1 Syn ANGER, angriness, furor, fury, indignation, irateness, ire, outrage, rage, wrath, wrathfulness Ant delight, pleasure 2 Syn MALICE, despite, grudge, ill will, malevolence, malignancy, malignity, spite Ant charity

splendid 1 • extraordinarily or transcendently impressive Syn glorious, gorgeous, resplendent, sublime, superb Rel bright, brilliant, effulgent, luminous, radiant 2 Syn EXCELLENT, A1, bang-up, banner, capital, classic, crackerjack, dandy, divine, fabulous, fine, first-class, first-rate, grand, great, groovy, heavenly, jim-dandy, keen, marvelous (or marvellous), mean, neat, nifty, noble, par excellence, prime, sensational, stellar, sterling, superb, superior, superlative, supernal, swell, terrific, tip-top, top, top-notch, unsurpassed, wonderful Ant poor

splendor Syn MAGNIFICENCE, augustness, brilliance, gloriousness, glory, grandeur, grandness, majesty, nobility, nobleness, resplendence, stateliness, stupendousness, sublimeness, superbness

splenetic Syn IRASCIBLE, choleric, cranky, cross, testy, touchy

split vb Syn TEAR, cleave, rend, rip, rive

split n Syn BREACH, break, rent, rift, rupture, schism

split second Syn INSTANT, flash, jiffy, minute, moment, second, shake, trice, twinkle, twinkling, wink

splotch Syn SPOT, blotch, dapple, dot, fleck, freckle, marble, mottle, pepper, speck, speckle, sprinkle, stipple

spoil n • something taken from another by force or craft Syn booty, loot, plunder, prize, swag Rel burglary, larceny, robbery, theft

spoil vb 1 Syn BABY, coddle, dandle, mollycoddle, nurse, pamper Ant abuse, ill-treat, ill-use, maltreat, mishandle, mistreat, misuse 2 Syn DECAY, crumble, decompose, disintegrate, putrefy, rot 3 Syn INJURE, damage, harm, hurt, impair, mar Ant aid

spoken Syn VERBAL, oral, unwritten Ant written

spoliate Syn RAVAGE, despoil, devastate, pillage, sack, waste

sponge Syn PARASITE, bootlicker, favorite, hanger-on, leech, lickspittle, sponger, sycophant, toady

sponger Syn PARASITE, bootlicker, favorite, hanger-on, leech, lickspittle, sponge, sycophant, toady

sponsor • one who assumes responsibility for some other person or thing Syn angel, backer, guarantor, patron, surety Rel advocate, advocator, champion, support, supporter, upholder

spontaneity Syn ABANDON, abandonment, ease, lightheartedness, naturalness, unrestraint Ant constraint, restraint

spontaneous • acting or activated without deliberation Syn automatic, impulsive, instinctive, mechanical Rel extemporaneous, extempore, impromptu, improvised, offhand, unpremeditated

spook Syn GHOST, apparition, bogey, phantasm, phantom, poltergeist, shade, shadow, specter (or spectre), spirit, vision, wraith

spooky 1 Syn EERIE, creepy, haunting, uncanny, unearthly, weird 2 Syn EXCITABLE, flighty, fluttery, high-strung, jittery, jumpy, nervous, skittish Ant unflappable

spoon *Syn* DIP (sense 2), bail, dish, ladle, scoop

sporadic **1** *Syn* FITFUL, casual, choppy, discontinuous, erratic, intermittent, irregular, occasional, spasmodic, spotty, unsteady *Ant* constant, continuous, regular, steady **2** *Syn* INFREQUENT, occasional, rare, scarce, uncommon *Ant* frequent

sport *n* **1** *Syn* FUN, game, jest, play **2** *Syn* PLAY, disport, frolic, gambol, rollick, romp

sport *vb* *Syn* PLAY, disport, frolic, gambol, rollick, romp *Ant* work

sportive *Syn* PLAYFUL, frolicsome, impish, mischievous, roguish, waggish

sports *Syn* ATHLETICS, games

spot *vb* · to mark with small spots especially unevenly *Syn* blotch, dapple, dot, fleck, freckle, marble, mottle, pepper, speck, speckle, splotch, sprinkle, stipple *Rel* blot, dye, stain

spot *n* *Syn* PLACE, location, position, site, situation, station

spotted · marked with spots or streaks *Syn* bespangled, flecked, marbled, mottled, spangled, spattered, speckled, sprinkled, stippled

spotty *Syn* FITFUL, casual, choppy, discontinuous, erratic, intermittent, irregular, occasional, spasmodic, sporadic, unsteady *Ant* constant, continuous, regular, steady

spouse · the person to whom another is married *Syn* consort, mate, partner *Rel* husband, man, old man

spout **1** *Syn* ERUPT (sense 2), belch, disgorge, eject, expel, jet, spew, spurt **2** *Syn* GUSH (sense 1), jet, pour, rush, spew, spurt, squirt *Ant* dribble, drip, drop, trickle **3** *Syn* RANT, bluster, fulminate, rave

spout (off) *Syn* SPEAK UP, sound off, speak out

spray *Syn* SCATTER (sense 2), bestrew, dot, pepper, sow, sprinkle, strew

spread *vb* **1** · to extend or cause to extend over an area or space *Syn* circulate, diffuse, disseminate, propagate, radiate *Rel* deal, dispense, distribute **2** *Syn* COMMUNICATE, convey, impart, transfer, transfuse, transmit

spread *n* *Syn* EXPANSE, amplitude, stretch

sprightly *Syn* LIVELY, animated, gay, vivacious *Ant* dull

spring *vb* **1** · to come up or out of something into existence *Syn* arise, derive, emanate, flow, issue, originate, proceed, rise, stem *Rel* appear, emerge, loom **2** *Syn* BEGIN (sense 1), arise, commence, dawn, form, materialize, originate, set in, start *Ant* cease, end, stop **3** *Syn* JUMP, bound, leap, vault

spring *n* **1** *Syn* JUMP, bound, leap, vault **2** *Syn* MOTIVE, goad, impulse, incentive, inducement, spur

springy *Syn* ELASTIC (sense 1), flexible, resilient, supple *Ant* rigid

sprinkle **1** *Syn* SCATTER (sense 2), bestrew, dot, pepper, sow, spray, strew **2** *Syn* SPOT, blotch, dapple, dot, fleck, freckle, marble, mottle, pepper, speck, speckle, splotch, stipple

sprinkled *Syn* SPOTTED, bespangled, flecked, marbled, mottled, spangled, spattered, speckled, stippled

sprint *Syn* SCUTTLE, scamper, scurry, skedaddle

sprite *Syn* FAIRY, brownie, elf, fay, pixie (*also* pixy)

sprucely *Syn* SMARTLY, dashingly, nattily, sharply *Ant* sloppily, slovenly

spry *Syn* AGILE, brisk, nimble *Ant* torpid

spryness *Syn* DEXTERITY (sense 2), agility, deftness, nimbleness, sleight *Ant* awkwardness, clumsiness, gawkiness

spume *Syn* FOAM, froth, lather, scum, suds, yeast

spunky *Syn* SPIRITED, fiery, gingery, highspirited, mettlesome, peppery *Ant* spiritless

spur *Syn* MOTIVE, goad, impulse, incentive, inducement, spring

spurious *Syn* COUNTERFEIT, bogus, fake, phony, pinchbeck, pseudo, sham *Ant* bona fide, genuine

spurn *Syn* DECLINE, refuse, reject, repudiate *Ant* accept

spurt *vb* **1** *Syn* ERUPT (sense 2), belch, disgorge, eject, expel, jet, spew, spout **2** *Syn* GUSH (sense 1), jet, pour, rush, spew, spout, squirt *Ant* dribble, drip, drop, trickle

spurt *n* *Syn* OUTBREAK, burst, flare, flare-up, flash, flicker, flurry, flutter, outburst

squabble *Syn* QUARREL, altercation, bickering, spat, tiff, wrangle

squalid *Syn* DIRTY, filthy, foul, nasty *Ant* clean

squall *n* *Syn* COMMOTION, bother, bustle, clatter, disturbance, furor, furore, fuss, hubbub, hullabaloo, hurly-burly, pandemonium, pother, row, ruckus, ruction, rumpus, shindy, stew, stir, storm, to-do, tumult, turmoil, uproar, welter, whirl

squall *vb* *Syn* SCREAM, howl, screech, shriek, shrill, squeal, yell, yelp

squander *Syn* WASTE, consume, dissipate, fritter *Ant* conserve, save

squanderer *Syn* PRODIGAL, profligate, spender, spendthrift, waster, wastrel *Ant* economizer

squandering *Syn* PRODIGAL, extravagant, profligate, spendthrift, thriftless, unthrifty, wasteful *Ant* conserving, economical, economizing, frugal, scrimping, skimping, thrifty

square *Syn* AGREE (sense 2), accord, conform, correspond, harmonize, jibe, tally *Ant* differ (from)

squash *Syn* CRUSH (sense 1), bruise, macerate, mash, smash

squat *Syn* STOCKY, chunky, dumpy, stubby, thick, thickset

squawk *Syn* COMPLAIN, beef, bellyache, carp, crab, croak, fuss, gripe, grouse, growl, grumble, kick, moan, murmur, mutter, repine, wail, whine, yammer *Ant* rejoice

squeaking *Syn* SHRILL, acute, high-pitched, piping, screeching, shrieking, squeaky, treble, whistling *Ant* bass, deep, low, throaty

squeaky *Syn* SHRILL, acute, high-pitched, piping, screeching, shrieking, squeaking, treble, whistling *Ant* bass, deep, low, throaty

squeal *vb* 1 *Syn* SCREAM, howl, screech, shriek, shrill, squall, yell, yelp 2 *Syn* SHOUT, holler, scream, screech, shriek, whoop, yell

squeal *n Syn* SHOUT, holler, scream, screech, shriek, whoop, yell

squeamish *Syn* NICE, dainty, fastidious, finical, finicking, finicky, fussy, particular, pernickety, persnickety

squeeze 1 *Syn* FLEECE, bleed, cheat, chisel, cozen, defraud, hustle, mulct, rook, short-change, skin, stick, sting, swindle, victimize 2 *Syn* PRESS, bear, bear down, crowd, jam

squire *Syn* ACCOMPANY, attend, chaperone (*or* chaperon), convoy, escort

squirm *Syn* WRITHE, agonize

squirrel (away) *Syn* HOARD, cache, lay away, lay up, put by, salt away, stash, stockpile, store, stow

squirt *Syn* GUSH (sense 1), jet, pour, rush, spew, spout, spurt *Ant* dribble, drip, drop, trickle

stab *Syn* ATTEMPT, crack, endeavor, essay, fling, go, pass, shot, trial, try, whack

stabilize · to make or become stable, steadfast, or firm *Syn* balance, ballast, poise, steady, trim *Rel* adjust, fix, regulate

stable 1 *Syn* LASTING, durable, perdurable, permanent, perpetual *Ant* fleeting 2 *Syn* SANE, balanced, clearheaded, lucid, normal, right *Ant* crazed, crazy, demented, deranged, insane, lunatic, mad, maniacal, mental, unbalanced, unsound

stack *n Syn* HEAP, bank, cock, mass, pile, shock

stack *vb Syn* HEAP, bank, cock, mass, pile, shock

stage *Syn* PLATFORM, dais, podium, rostrum, stand

stagger *Syn* REEL, totter, whirl

staid 1 *Syn* DIGNIFIED, august, imposing, solemn, stately *Ant* flighty, frivolous, giddy, goofy, silly, undignified 2 *Syn* SERIOUS, earnest, grave, sedate, sober, solemn, somber *Ant* flippant, light

stain *vb Syn* DIRTY, befoul, begrime, besmirch, blacken, foul, grime, mire, muddy, smirch, smudge, soil, sully *Ant* clean, cleanse

stain *n* 1 *Syn* PIGMENT, color, coloring, dye, dyestuff, tincture 2 *Syn* STIGMA, blot, brand

stake *n Syn* BET, ante, pot, wager

stake *vb Syn* BET, gamble, go, lay, wager

stale · used or heard so often as to be dull *Syn* banal, commonplace, hackney, hackneyed, moth-eaten, musty, stereotyped, threadbare, tired, trite *Rel* canned, unimaginative, uninspired, unoriginal *Ant* fresh, new, original

stalemate *Syn* DRAW, deadlock, standoff, tie

stalwart *Syn* STRONG, stout, sturdy, tenacious, tough *Ant* weak

stamp *n* 1 *Syn* IMPRESSION, impress, imprint, print 2 *Syn* MARK, brand, label, tag, ticket

stamp *vb* 1 *Syn* MARK, brand, label, tag, ticket 2 *Syn* TRAMPLE, stomp, tramp, tromp

stand *vb Syn* BEAR (sense 2), abide, brook, endure, suffer, tolerate

stand *n* 1 *Syn* PLATFORM, dais, podium, rostrum, stage 2 *Syn* POSITION, attitude

standard 1 · a means of determining what a thing should be *Syn* criterion, gauge, touchstone, yardstick *Rel* average, mean, median, norm, par 2 *Syn* AVERAGE, norm, normal, par 3 *Syn* FLAG, banner, color, ensign, jack, pendant, pennant, pennon, streamer 4 *Syn* MODEL, beau ideal, example, exemplar, ideal, mirror, pattern

standardize · to make agree with a single established standard or model *Syn* formalize, homogenize, normalize, regularize *Rel* codify, organize, systematize

standards *Syn* ETHICS, morality, morals, principles

stand-in *Syn* SUBSTITUTE, backup, pinch hitter, relief, replacement, reserve, sub

standing *Syn* ERECT, perpendicular, plumb, raised, upright, upstanding, vertical *Ant* flat, recumbent

standoff *Syn* DRAW, deadlock, stalemate, tie

standpoint *Syn* POINT OF VIEW, angle, slant, viewpoint

star 1 *Syn* EMINENT, distinguished, illustrious, noble, notable, noteworthy, outstanding, preeminent, prestigious, signal, superior 2 *Syn* FAMOUS, celebrated, famed, noted, notorious, prominent, renowned, well-known *Ant* anonymous, obscure, unknown

stare 1 *Syn* GAPE, gawk, gaze, goggle, peer, rubberneck 2 *Syn* GAZE, gape, glare, gloat, peer

stark *Syn* STIFF, inflexible, rigid, tense, wooden *Ant* relaxed, supple

starry · of, relating to, or suggestive of a star or group of stars *Syn* astral, sidereal, stellar

start *vb* 1 *Syn* ACTIVATE, actuate, crank (up), drive, move, propel, run, set off, spark, touch off, trigger, turn on *Ant* cut, deactivate, kill, shut off, turn off 2 *Syn* BEGIN (sense 1), arise, commence, dawn, form, materialize, originate, set in, spring *Ant* cease, end, stop 3 *Syn* BEGIN (sense 2), commence, embark (on *or* upon), enter (into *or* upon), get off, kick off, launch, open, strike (into) *Ant* conclude, end, finish, terminate

start *n Syn* BEGINNING, alpha, birth, commencement, dawn, genesis, inception, incipiency, launch, morning, onset, outset, threshold *Ant* close, conclusion, end, ending

startle *Syn* FRIGHTEN, affray, affright, alarm, fright, scare, terrify, terrorize *Ant* reassure

stash *Syn* HOARD, cache, lay away, lay up, put by, salt away, squirrel (away), stockpile, store, stow

state *n* 1 · the way in which one manifests existence or the circumstances under which one exists or by which one is given distinctive character *Syn* condition, mode, posture, situation, status *Rel* aspect, phase 2 *Syn* NATION, commonwealth, country, land, sovereignty

state *vb* 1 *Syn* PHRASE, articulate, clothe, couch, express, formulate, put, say, word 2 *Syn* RELATE, describe, narrate, recite, recount, rehearse, report 3 *Syn* SAY, tell, utter

stateliness 1 *Syn* ELEGANCE, class, elegancy, grace, gracefulness, handsomeness, majesty, refinement 2 *Syn* MAGNIFICENCE, augustness, brilliance, gloriousness, glory, grandeur, grandness, majesty, nobility, nobleness, resplendence, splendor, stupendousness, sublimeness, superbness

stately 1 *Syn* DIGNIFIED, august, imposing, solemn, staid *Ant* flighty, frivolous, giddy, goofy, silly, undignified 2 *Syn* GRAND, august, grandiose, imposing, magnificent, majestic, noble

statesman *Syn* POLITICIAN, politico

station 1 *Syn* HABITAT, biotope, range 2 *Syn* PLACE, location, position, site, situation, spot

statue *Syn* IMAGE, effigy, mask, photograph, portrait

stature *Syn* QUALITY (sense 2), caliber

status *Syn* STATE, condition, mode, posture, situation

statute *Syn* LAW, canon, ordinance, precept, regulation, rule

staunch *or* **stanch** *Syn* FAITHFUL, constant, devoted, devout, fast, good, loyal, pious, steadfast, steady, true, true-blue *Ant* disloyal, faithless, false, fickle, inconstant, perfidious, recreant, traitorous, treacherous, unfaithful, untrue

stay 1 · to continue to be in one place for a noticeable time *Syn* abide, linger, remain, tarry, wait *Rel* delay, lag, loiter, procrastinate 2 *Syn* BASE, found, ground, rest 3 *Syn* RESIDE, dwell, live, lodge, put up, sojourn, stop

steadfast *Syn* FAITHFUL, constant, devoted, devout, fast, good, loyal, pious, staunch (*or* stanch), steady, true, true-blue *Ant* disloyal, faithless, false, fickle, inconstant, perfidious, recreant, traitorous, treacherous, unfaithful, untrue

steady *adj* 1 · not varying throughout a course or extent *Syn* constant, equable, even, uniform *Rel* durable, lasting, perdurable, perpetual, stable *Ant* jumpy, nervous, unsteady 2 *Syn* DEPENDABLE, good, reliable, responsible, safe, solid, sure, tried, tried-and-true, true, trustworthy, trusty *Ant* irresponsible, undependable, unreliable, untrustworthy 3 *Syn* FAITHFUL, constant, devoted, devout, fast, good, loyal, pious, staunch (*or* stanch), steadfast, true, true-blue *Ant* disloyal, faithless, false, fickle, inconstant, perfidious, recreant, traitorous, treacherous, unfaithful, untrue 4 *Syn* UNIFORM, invariant, unchanging, undeviating, unvarying, unwavering *Ant* changing, deviating, varying

steady *vb Syn* STABILIZE, balance, ballast, poise, trim

steal · to take from another without right or without detection *Syn* cop, filch, lift, pilfer, pinch, purloin, snitch, swipe *Rel* burglarize, loot, plunder, rifle, rob

stealthy *Syn* SECRET, clandestine, covert, furtive, surreptitious, underhand, underhanded

steaming *Syn* ANGRY, angered, apoplectic, enraged, foaming, fuming, furious, incensed, indignant, inflamed, infuriated, irate, ireful, mad, outraged, rabid, riled, roiled, sore, wrathful, wroth *Ant* delighted, pleased

steel *Syn* ENCOURAGE, cheer, embolden, hearten, inspirit, nerve *Ant* discourage

steep *adj* · having an incline approaching the perpendicular *Syn* abrupt, precipitous, sheer *Rel* elevated, lifted, raised

steep *vb Syn* SOAK, drench, impregnate, saturate, sop, waterlog

steer *Syn* GUIDE, engineer, lead, pilot *Ant* misguide

stellar 1 *Syn* EXCELLENT, A1, bang-up, banner, capital, classic, crackerjack, dandy, divine, fabulous, fine, first-class, first-rate, grand, great, groovy, heavenly, jim-dandy, keen, marvelous (*or* marvellous), mean, neat, nifty, noble, par excellence, prime, sensational, splendid, sterling, superb, superior, superlative, supernal, swell, terrific, tip-top, top, top-notch, unsurpassed, wonderful *Ant* poor 2 *Syn* STARRY, astral, sidereal

stem *Syn* SPRING, arise, derive, emanate, flow, issue, originate, proceed, rise

stentorian *Syn* LOUD, earsplitting, hoarse, raucous, stertorous, strident *Ant* low, low-pitched

step *Syn* WALK, foot (it), hoof (it), leg (it), pad, traipse, tread

step (along) *Syn* HURRY (sense 2), barrel, bolt, bowl, breeze, career, course, dash, fly, hasten, hotfoot (it), hump, hurtle, hustle, pelt, race, rip, rocket, run, rush, rustle, scoot, scurry, scuttle, shoot, speed, tear, trot, whirl, whisk, zip, zoom *Ant* crawl, creep, poke

step-by-step *Syn* GRADUAL, gradational, incremental, phased, piecemeal *Ant* sudden

steppe *Syn* PLAIN, down, grassland, prairie, savanna, tundra, veld (*or* veldt)

stereotyped Syn STALE, banal, commonplace, hackney, hackneyed, moth-eaten, musty, threadbare, tired, trite Ant fresh, new, original

sterile 1 · not able to bear fruit, crops, or offspring Syn barren, impotent, infertile, unfruitful Rel bald, bare, naked Ant exuberant, fertile **2** Syn SANITARY, aseptic, germfree, hygienic Ant insanitary, unhygienic, unsanitary

sterilize 1 · to make incapable of producing offspring Syn alter, castrate, emasculate, geld, mutilate, spay Ant fertilize **2 ·** to free from living microorganisms Syn disinfect, fumigate, sanitize

sterling Syn EXCELLENT, A1, bang-up, banner, capital, classic, crackerjack, dandy, divine, fabulous, fine, first-class, first-rate, grand, great, groovy, heavenly, jim-dandy, keen, marvelous (or marvellous), mean, neat, nifty, noble, par excellence, prime, sensational, splendid, stellar, superb, superior, superlative, supernal, swell, terrific, tip-top, top, top-notch, unsurpassed, wonderful Ant poor

stern Syn SEVERE, ascetic, austere Ant tender, tolerant

sternness Syn SEVERITY, hardness, harshness, inflexibility, rigidity, rigidness, rigorousness, strictness Ant flexibility, gentleness, laxness, mildness

stertorous Syn LOUD, earsplitting, hoarse, raucous, stentorian, strident Ant low, low-pitched

stew vb Syn BOIL, parboil, seethe, simmer

stew n Syn COMMOTION, bother, bustle, clatter, disturbance, furor, furore, fuss, hubbub, hullabaloo, hurly-burly, pandemonium, pother, row, ruckus, ruction, rumpus, shindy, squall, stir, storm, to-do, tumult, turmoil, uproar, welter, whirl

steward Syn SERVANT, domestic, flunky, lackey, menial, retainer Ant master

stick 1 · to become or cause to become closely and firmly attached Syn adhere, cleave, cling, cohere Rel bind, tie **2** Syn DEMUR, balk, boggle, jib, scruple, shy, stickle, strain Ant accede **3** Syn FLEECE, bleed, cheat, chisel, cozen, defraud, hustle, mulct, rook, shortchange, skin, squeeze, sting, swindle, victimize

stickle Syn DEMUR, balk, boggle, jib, scruple, shy, stick, strain Ant accede

stick out Syn BULGE, beetle, jut, overhang, project, protrude

stiff · difficult to bend Syn inflexible, rigid, stark, tense, wooden Rel stout, strong, tenacious, tough Ant relaxed, supple

stifle Syn SUFFOCATE, asphyxiate, choke, smother, strangle, throttle

stigma · a mark of shame or discredit Syn blot, brand, stain Rel disgrace, dishonor, odium, opprobrium, shame

still adj **1 ·** making no stir or noise Syn noiseless, quiet, silent, stilly Rel calm, peaceful, placid, serene, tranquil Ant noisy, stirring **2** Syn SILENT (sense 2), hushed, muted, noiseless, quiet, quieted, soundless Ant noisy, unquiet

still n **1** Syn CALM, calmness, hush, peace, peace, peacefulness, placidity, quiet, quietness, quietude, repose, restfulness, sereneness, serenity, stillness, tranquillity (or tranquility) Ant bustle, commotion, hubbub, hurly-burly, pandemonium, tumult, turmoil, uproar **2** Syn SILENCE, hush, quiet, quietness, quietude, stillness Ant noise, sound

still vb Syn CALM, compose, lull, quiet, quieten, settle, soothe, tranquilize Ant agitate, arouse

stillness 1 Syn CALM, calmness, hush, peace, peacefulness, placidity, quiet, quietness, quietude, repose, restfulness, sereneness, serenity, still, tranquillity (or tranquility) Ant bustle, commotion, hubbub, hurly-burly, pandemonium, tumult, turmoil, uproar **2** Syn SILENCE, hush, quiet, quietness, quietude, still Ant noise, sound

stilly Syn STILL, noiseless, quiet, silent Ant noisy, stirring

stimulant Syn STIMULUS, excitant, impetus, incitement

stimulate 1 Syn ANIMATE, brace, energize, enliven, fire, invigorate, jazz (up), liven (up), pep (up), quicken, vitalize, vivify Ant damp, dampen, deaden, dull **2** Syn PROVOKE, excite, galvanize, pique, quicken

stimulating 1 Syn PROVOCATIVE, exciting, inciting, instigating, piquing, provoking **2** Syn TONIC, bracing, invigorating, refreshing, restorative, reviving, stimulative, vitalizing

stimulative Syn TONIC, bracing, invigorating, refreshing, restorative, reviving, stimulating, vitalizing

stimulus · something that rouses or incites to activity Syn excitant, impetus, incitement, stimulant Rel goad, incentive, inducement, motive, spur

sting Syn FLEECE, bleed, cheat, chisel, cozen, defraud, hustle, mulct, rook, shortchange, skin, squeeze, stick, swindle, victimize

stingy · being unwilling or showing unwillingness to share with others Syn cheeseparing, close, closefisted, miserly, niggardly, parsimonious, penny-pinching, penurious, tight, tightfisted Rel ignoble, mean, sordid Ant generous

stinking Syn MALODOROUS, fetid, fusty, musty, noisome, putrid, rancid, rank Ant odorous

stint 1 Syn CHORE, assignment, duty, job, task **2** Syn SPELL, bout, go, shift, tour, trick, turn

stipend Syn WAGE, emolument, fee, hire, pay, salary

stipple *Syn* SPOT, blotch, dapple, dot, fleck, freckle, marble, mottle, pepper, speck, speckle, splotch, sprinkle

stippled *Syn* SPOTTED, bespangled, flecked, marbled, mottled, spangled, spattered, speckled, sprinkled

stipulation *Syn* CONDITION, provision, proviso, reservation, strings, terms

stir *n* **1** · signs of excited activity, hurry, or commotion *Syn* ado, bustle, flurry, fuss, pother *Rel* agitation, disquiet, disquieting, disturbance *Ant* tranquillity **2** *Syn* COMMOTION, bother, bustle, clatter, disturbance, furor, furore, fuss, hubbub, hullabaloo, hurlyburly, pandemonium, pother, row, ruckus, ruction, rumpus, shindy, squall, stew, storm, to-do, tumult, turmoil, uproar, welter, whirl **3** *Syn* MOTION, locomotion, move, movement

stir *vb* · to cause to shift from quiescence or torpor into activity *Syn* arouse, awaken, rally, rouse, waken *Rel* excite, galvanize, provoke, quicken, stimulate

stirring *Syn* MOVING, affecting, emotional, impressive, poignant, touching *Ant* unemotional, unimpressive

stitch *Syn* PAIN, ache, pang, throe, twinge

stock **1** *Syn* ANCESTRY, birth, blood, bloodline, breeding, descent, extraction, family tree, genealogy, line, lineage, origin, parentage, pedigree, strain *Ant* issue, posterity, progeny, seed **2** *Syn* VARIETY (sense 2), breed, clone, cultivar, race, strain, subspecies

stockade *Syn* JAIL, brig, guardroom, hoosegow, jug, lockup, pen, penitentiary, prison

stockpile *Syn* HOARD, cache, lay away, lay up, put by, salt away, squirrel (away), stash, store, stow

stocky · compact, sturdy, and relatively thick in build *Syn* chunky, dumpy, squat, stubby, thick, thickset

stodgy *Syn* BORING, drab, dreary, dry, dull, flat, heavy, humdrum, jading, leaden, monotonous, pedestrian, ponderous, stuffy, stupid, tame, tedious, tiresome, tiring, unanimated, uninteresting, wearisome, weary, wearying *Ant* absorbing, engaging, engrossing, gripping, interesting, intriguing, involving

stoic *Syn* IMPASSIVE, apathetic, phlegmatic, stolid *Ant* responsive

stoicism *Syn* IMPASSIVITY, apathy, phlegm, stolidity

stolid *Syn* IMPASSIVE, apathetic, phlegmatic, stoic *Ant* responsive

stolidity *Syn* IMPASSIVITY, apathy, phlegm, stoicism

stomach · the part of the body between the chest and the pelvis *Syn* abdomen, belly, gut, solar plexus, tummy *Rel* middle, midriff, waist

stomp *Syn* TRAMPLE, stamp, tramp, tromp

stone blind *Syn* BLIND, eyeless, sightless *Ant* sighted

stoop · to descend from one's real or pretended level of dignity *Syn* condescend, deign *Rel* abase, demean, humble

stop *vb* **1** · to suspend or cause to suspend activity *Syn* cease, desist, discontinue, quit *Rel* arrest, check, interrupt **2** *Syn* RESIDE, dwell, live, lodge, put up, sojourn, stay

stop *n* *Syn* ENCUMBRANCE, bar, block, chain, clog, crimp, deterrent, drag, embarrassment, fetter, handicap, hindrance, hurdle, impediment, inhibition, interference, let, manacle, obstacle, obstruction, shackles, stumbling block, trammel *Ant* aid, assistance, benefit, help

stopgap *Syn* RESOURCE, expedient, makeshift, resort, shift, substitute, surrogate

storage *Syn* STOREHOUSE, depository, depot, magazine, repository, stowage, warehouse

store *vb* *Syn* HOARD, cache, lay away, lay up, put by, salt away, squirrel (away), stash, stockpile, stow

store *n* **1** · a collection of things kept available for future use or need *Syn* cache, deposit, hoard, reserve *Rel* budget, fund, nest egg, pool, reservoir, stock, stockpile, supply; accumulation, assemblage, collection, gathering **2** · an establishment where goods are sold to consumers *Syn* bazaar, emporium, shop *Rel* boutique, market, marketplace, outlet

storehouse · a building for storing goods *Syn* depository, depot, magazine, repository, storage, stowage, warehouse *Rel* cache, stockroom, storeroom

storm *vb* *Syn* ATTACK (sense 1), assail, assault, bombard

storm *n* **1** *Syn* BARRAGE, bombardment, cannonade, fusillade, hail, salvo, shower, volley **2** *Syn* COMMOTION, bother, bustle, clatter, disturbance, furor, furore, fuss, hubbub, hullabaloo, hurly-burly, pandemonium, pother, row, ruckus, ruction, rumpus, shindy, squall, stew, stir, to-do, tumult, turmoil, uproar, welter, whirl **3** *Syn* CONVULSION, cataclysm, paroxysm, tempest, tumult, upheaval, uproar **4** *Syn* RAIN (sense 1), cloudburst, deluge, downpour, rainfall, rainstorm, wet **5** *Syn* RAIN (sense 2), hail, shower

stormy *Syn* CONVULSIVE, cataclysmal (*or* cataclysmic), tempestuous, tumultuous

story **1** · a recital of happenings less elaborate than a novel *Syn* anecdote, narrative, tale, yarn *Rel* description, narration **2** *Syn* ACCOUNT, chronicle, report, version **3** *Syn* LIE, falsehood, fib, misrepresentation, untruth *Ant* truth **4** *Syn* NEWS, information, intelligence, item, tidings, word

stout **1** *Syn* FLESHY, chubby, corpulent, fat, obese, plump, portly, rotund *Ant* scrawny, skinny **2** *Syn* STRONG, stalwart, sturdy, tenacious, tough *Ant* weak

stoutness *Syn* COURAGE, bravery, courageousness, daring, dauntlessness, doughtiness, fearlessness, gallantry, greatheartedness, guts, hardihood, heart, heroism, intrepidity, intrepidness, nerve, valor *Ant* cowardice, cowardliness, cravenness, dastardliness, spinelessness, yellowness

stow *Syn* HOARD, cache, lay away, lay up, put by, salt away, squirrel (away), stash, stockpile, store

stowage *Syn* STOREHOUSE, depository, depot, magazine, repository, storage, warehouse

straighten · to cause to follow a line that is without bends or curls *Syn* unbend, uncurl *Rel* uncoil, unwind *Ant* bend, crook, curl, curve

straightforward · free from all that is dishonest or secretive *Syn* aboveboard, forthright *Rel* honest, honorable, just, upright *Ant* devious, indirect

straightforwardness *Syn* CANDOR, directness, forthrightness, frankness, openheartedness, openness, plainness *Ant* dissembling, pretense (*or* pretence)

strain *n* **1** *Syn* ANCESTRY, birth, blood, bloodline, breeding, descent, extraction, family tree, genealogy, line, lineage, origin, parentage, pedigree, stock *Ant* issue, posterity, progeny, seed **2** *Syn* MELODY, air, lay, song, tune, warble **3** *Syn* STRESS, pressure, tension **4** *Syn* TOUCH, dash, shade, smack, soupçon, spice, streak, suggestion, suspicion, tincture, tinge, vein **5** *Syn* VARIETY (sense 2), breed, clone, cultivar, race, stock, subspecies

strain *vb* **1** *Syn* DEMUR, balk, boggle, jib, scruple, shy, stick, stickle *Ant* accede **2** *Syn* EXUDE, bleed, ooze, percolate, seep, sweat, weep **3** *Syn* LABOR, drudge, endeavor, grub, hump, hustle, moil, peg (away), plod, plow, plug, slave, slog, strive, struggle, sweat, toil, travail, work *Ant* dabble, fiddle (around), fool (around), mess (around), putter (around)

strained *Syn* FORCED, labored

strait **1** · a comparatively narrow stretch of water connecting two larger bodies of water *Syn* channel, narrows, passage, sound **2** *Syn* JUNCTURE, contingency, crisis, emergency, exigency, pass, pinch

straitlaced *Syn* PRIM, priggish, prissy, prudish, puritanical, stuffy

strand *Syn* SHORE, bank, beach, coast, foreshore, littoral

stranded *Syn* AGROUND, beached, grounded *Ant* afloat

strange **1** · departing from what is ordinary, usual, and to be expected *Syn* curious, eccentric, erratic, odd, outlandish, peculiar, quaint, queer, singular, unique *Rel* aberrant, abnormal, atypical *Ant* familiar **2** *Syn* EXOTIC, fantastic, glamorous, marvelous (*or* marvellous), outlandish, romantic

stranger · a nonresident or an unknown person in a community *Syn* alien, émigré, foreigner, immigrant, outlander, outsider

strangle *Syn* SUFFOCATE, asphyxiate, choke, smother, stifle, throttle

stratagem *Syn* TRICK, artifice, feint, gambit, maneuver, ploy, ruse, wile

strategic · of, relating to, or marked by strategy *Syn* logistic, tactical

strategy · the art of devising or employing plans toward a usually military goal *Syn* logistics, tactics

straw *adj Syn* BLOND, fair, flaxen, golden, sandy, tawny *Ant* dark

straw *vb Syn* STREW, broadcast, scatter, sow

stray *Syn* WANDER, gad, gallivant, meander, prowl, ramble, range, roam, rove, traipse

streak *Syn* TOUCH, dash, shade, smack, soupçon, spice, strain, suggestion, suspicion, tincture, tinge, vein

stream *n Syn* FLOW, current, flood, flux, tide

stream *vb Syn* POUR, gush, sluice

streamer *Syn* FLAG, banner, color, ensign, jack, pendant, pennant, pennon, standard

strength *Syn* POWER (sense 1), energy, force, might, puissance *Ant* impotence

strengthen · to make strong or stronger *Syn* energize, fortify, invigorate, reinforce *Rel* cheer, embolden, encourage, hearten, inspirit, nerve, steel *Ant* weaken

strenuous *Syn* VIGOROUS, energetic, lusty, nervous *Ant* languorous, lethargic

stress *n* **1** · the action or effect of force exerted within or upon a thing *Syn* pressure, strain, tension **2** *Syn* EMPHASIS, accent, accentuation

stress *vb Syn* EMPHASIZE, accentuate, feature, highlight, play (up), point (up), underline, underscore *Ant* play (down)

stretch *Syn* EXPANSE, amplitude, spread

stretching *Syn* EXAGGERATION, caricature, coloring, elaboration, embellishment, embroidering, hyperbole, magnification, overstatement, padding *Ant* understatement

strew **1** · to throw loosely or at intervals *Syn* broadcast, scatter, sow, straw *Rel* disseminate, spread **2** *Syn* SCATTER (sense 2), bestrew, dot, pepper, sow, spray, sprinkle

strict *Syn* RIGID, rigorous, stringent *Ant* lax

strictly · without any relaxation of standards or precision *Syn* exactly, precisely, rigidly, rigorously *Rel* carefully, conscientiously, meticulously, scrupulously *Ant* imprecisely, inexactly, loosely

strictness *Syn* SEVERITY, hardness, harshness, inflexibility, rigidity, rigidness, rigorousness, sternness *Ant* flexibility, gentleness, laxness, mildness

stricture **1** *Syn* ANIMADVERSION, aspersion, reflection *Ant* commendation **2** *Syn* CENSURE, condemnation, denunciation, rebuke, reprimand, reproach, reproof *Ant* citation, commendation, endorsement

strident 1 *Syn* LOUD, earsplitting, hoarse, raucous, stentorian, stertorous *Ant* low, low-pitched 2 *Syn* VOCIFEROUS, blatant, boisterous, clamorous, obstreperous

strife *Syn* DISCORD, conflict, contention, difference, dissension, schism, variance

strike *vb* 1 · to deliver (a blow) in a strong, vigorous manner *Syn* box, clout, cuff, hit, punch, slap, slog, slug, smite, swat *Rel* baste, beat, belabor, buffet, pound, pummel, thrash 2 *Syn* AFFECT, impress, influence, sway, touch 3 *Syn* BEGIN (sense 2), commence, embark (on *or* upon), enter (into *or* upon), get off, kick off, launch, open, start *Ant* conclude, end, finish, terminate

strike *n* 1 *Syn* ATTACK (sense 2), aggression, assault, blitzkrieg, charge, descent, offense (*or* offence), offensive, onset, onslaught, raid, rush 2 *Syn* DISADVANTAGE, drawback, handicap, liability, minus, penalty *Ant* advantage, asset, edge, plus

striking 1 *Syn* EGREGIOUS, blatant, conspicuous, flagrant, glaring, gross, obvious, patent, pronounced, rank 2 *Syn* NOTICEABLE, arresting, conspicuous, outstanding, prominent, remarkable, salient, signal

string 1 *Syn* CORD, cable, lace, lacing, line, rope, wire 2 *Syn* SUCCESSION, chain, progression, sequence, series, train

stringent *Syn* RIGID, rigorous, strict *Ant* lax

strings *Syn* CONDITION, provision, proviso, reservation, stipulation, terms

strip *n* · long narrow piece or area *Syn* band, fillet, ribbon, stripe

strip *vb* · to remove what clothes, furnishes, or invests a person or thing *Syn* bare, denude, dismantle, divest *Rel* despoil, devastate, ravage, spoliate, waste *Ant* furnish, invest

stripe 1 *Syn* STRIP, band, fillet, ribbon 2 *Syn* TYPE, character, description, ilk, kidney, kind, nature, sort

stripling *Syn* BOY, lad, laddie, nipper, shaver, sonny, tad, youth

strive 1 *Syn* ATTEMPT, assay, endeavor, essay, seek, try 2 *Syn* LABOR, drudge, endeavor, grub, hump, hustle, moil, peg (away), plod, plow, plug, slave, slog, strain, struggle, sweat, toil, travail, work *Ant* dabble, fiddle (around), fool (around), mess (around), putter (around)

stroll *vb* *Syn* SAUNTER, amble

stroll *n* *Syn* WALK, constitutional, perambulation, ramble, range, saunter, turn

stroller *Syn* NOMAD, drifter, gadabout, rambler, roamer, rover, vagabond, wanderer, wayfarer

strong 1 · showing power to resist or to endure *Syn* stalwart, stout, sturdy, tenacious, tough *Rel* energetic, lusty, vigorous *Ant* weak 2 *Syn* COGENT, compelling, conclusive, convincing, decisive, effective, forceful, persuasive, satisfying, telling *Ant* inconclusive, indecisive, ineffective, unconvincing

stronghold *Syn* FORT, citadel, fastness, fortress

strop *Syn* SHARPEN, edge, grind, hone, whet *Ant* blunt, dull

structure 1 · something made up of interdependent parts in a definite pattern of organization *Syn* anatomy, framework, skeleton *Rel* articulation, concatenation, integration 2 *Syn* BUILDING, edifice

struggle *Syn* LABOR, drudge, endeavor, grub, hump, hustle, moil, peg (away), plod, plow, plug, slave, slog, strain, strive, sweat, toil, travail, work *Ant* dabble, fiddle (around), fool (around), mess (around), putter (around)

strut · to walk with an air of pomposity or affected dignity *Syn* bridle, bristle, swagger *Rel* exhibit, expose, flaunt, parade, show

stubborn *Syn* OBSTINATE, adamant, adamantine, dogged, hard, hardened, hardheaded, hardhearted, headstrong, immovable, implacable, inflexible, mulish, obdurate, opinionated, ossified, pat, peevish, pertinacious, perverse, pigheaded, rigid, self-willed, unbending, uncompromising, unrelenting, unyielding, willful (*or* wilful) *Ant* acquiescent, agreeable, amenable, compliant, complying, flexible, pliable, pliant, relenting, yielding

stubby *Syn* STOCKY, chunky, dumpy, squat, thick, thickset

stuck-up *Syn* CONCEITED, complacent, egoistic, egotistic (*or* egotistical), important, overweening, pompous, prideful, proud, self-conceited, self-important, self-satisfied, smug, vain, vainglorious *Ant* humble, modest

student *Syn* pupil, scholar *Rel* schoolboy, schoolchild, schoolgirl

studied *Syn* DELIBERATE, advised, considered, designed, premeditated *Ant* casual

study *n* 1 *Syn* ATTENTION (sense 1), application, concentration *Ant* inattention 2 *Syn* REVERIE, daydreaming, trance, woolgathering

study *vb* *Syn* CONSIDER (sense 1), contemplate, excogitate, weigh

stuff *n* *Syn* MATTER, material, substance

stuff *vb* *Syn* PACK, cram, crowd, ram, tamp

stuffer *Syn* GLUTTON, gorger, gormandizer, gourmand, hog, overeater, swiller

stuffy 1 *Syn* BORING, drab, dreary, dry, dull, flat, heavy, humdrum, jading, leaden, monotonous, pedestrian, ponderous, stodgy, stupid, tame, tedious, tiresome, tiring, unanimated, uninteresting, wearisome, weary, wearying *Ant* absorbing, engaging, engrossing, gripping, interesting, intriguing, involving 2 *Syn* PRIM, priggish, prissy, prudish, puritanical, straitlaced

stumble · to move so clumsily or unsteadily as to fall or nearly fall *Syn* blunder, bumble, flounder, galumph, lollop, lumber, lurch, trip *Rel* reel, stagger, totter

stumble (on *or* **onto)** *Syn* HAPPEN (on *or* upon), chance (upon), encounter, find, hit (upon), meet

stumbling block *Syn* ENCUMBRANCE, bar, block, chain, clog, crimp, deterrent, drag, embarrassment, fetter, handicap, hindrance, hurdle, impediment, inhibition, interference, let, manacle, obstacle, obstruction, shackles, stop, trammel *Ant* aid, assistance, benefit, help

stump *Syn* CHALLENGE, dare, defy

stun *Syn* DAZE, bemuse, benumb, paralyze, petrify, stupefy

stunning *Syn* BEAUTIFUL, attractive, beauteous, comely, cute, fair, gorgeous, handsome, knockout, lovely, pretty, ravishing, sightly, taking *Ant* homely, ill-favored, plain, ugly, unattractive, unbeautiful, unhandsome, unlovely, unpretty, unsightly

stupefy *Syn* DAZE, bemuse, benumb, paralyze, petrify, stun

stupendous *Syn* MONSTROUS, monumental, prodigious, tremendous

stupendousness *Syn* MAGNIFICENCE, augustness, brilliance, gloriousness, glory, grandeur, grandness, majesty, nobility, nobleness, resplendence, splendor, stateliness, sublimeness, superbness

stupid **1** · lacking in power to absorb ideas or impressions *Syn* crass, dense, dull, dumb, slow *Rel* asinine, fatuous, foolish, silly, simple *Ant* intelligent **2** *Syn* BORING, drab, dreary, dry, dull, flat, heavy, humdrum, jading, leaden, monotonous, pedestrian, ponderous, stodgy, stuffy, tame, tedious, tiresome, tiring, unanimated, uninteresting, wearisome, weary, wearying *Ant* absorbing, engaging, engrossing, gripping, interesting, intriguing, involving

stupor *Syn* LETHARGY, languor, lassitude, torpidity, torpor *Ant* vigor

sturdy *Syn* STRONG, stalwart, stout, tenacious, tough *Ant* weak

stygian *Syn* INFERNAL, chthonian, chthonic, Hadean, hellish, Tartarean *Ant* supernal

style **1** *Syn* FASHION, craze, cry, dernier cri, fad, mode, rage, vogue **2** *Syn* LANGUAGE (sense 2), diction, phraseology, phrasing, vocabulary **3** *Syn* NAME, appellation, denomination, designation, title

stylish · conforming to current fashion *Syn* chic, dashing, fashionable, modish, smart *Rel* modernistic, new, newfangled, new-fashioned, novel

suave · having or showing very polished and worldly manners *Syn* debonair, smooth, sophisticated, urbane *Rel* glib, slick, unctuous *Ant* boorish, churlish, clownish, loutish, uncouth

sub *Syn* SUBSTITUTE, backup, pinch hitter, relief, replacement, reserve, stand-in

subdue *Syn* CONQUER, beat, defeat, lick, overcome, overthrow, reduce, rout, subjugate, surmount, vanquish

subdued *Syn* TAME, submissive *Ant* fierce

subject *n* **1** · the basic idea or the principal object of attention in a discourse or artistic composition *Syn* argument, leitmotiv, matter, motif, motive, subject matter, text, theme, topic **2** *Syn* CITIZEN, national *Ant* alien

subject *adj* **1** *Syn* LIABLE, exposed, open, prone, sensitive, susceptible *Ant* exempt, immune **2** *Syn* SUBORDINATE, collateral, dependent, secondary, tributary *Ant* chief, dominant, leading

subject matter *Syn* SUBJECT, argument, leitmotiv, matter, motif, motive, text, theme, topic

subjugate *Syn* CONQUER, beat, defeat, lick, overcome, overthrow, reduce, rout, subdue, surmount, vanquish

sublime *Syn* SPLENDID, glorious, gorgeous, resplendent, superb

sublimeness *Syn* MAGNIFICENCE, augustness, brilliance, gloriousness, glory, grandeur, grandness, majesty, nobility, nobleness, resplendence, splendor, stateliness, stupendousness, superbness

sublunary *Syn* EARTHLY, earthy, mundane, terrestrial, worldly

submerge **1** *Syn* DIP (sense 1), duck, dunk, immerse, souse **2** *Syn* FLOOD, deluge, drown, engulf, inundate, overflow, overwhelm, submerse, swamp *Ant* drain

submerse *Syn* FLOOD, deluge, drown, engulf, inundate, overflow, overwhelm, submerge, swamp *Ant* drain

submission *Syn* SURRENDER, capitulation

submissive **1** *Syn* OBEDIENT, amenable, compliant, conformable, docile, law-abiding, tractable *Ant* contrary, disobedient, froward, insubordinate, intractable, rebellious, recalcitrant, refractory, unruly **2** *Syn* TAME, subdued *Ant* fierce

submit *Syn* YIELD, bow, capitulate, cave, defer, relent, succumb

subordinate *adj* **1** · placed in or occupying a lower class, rank, or status *Syn* collateral, dependent, secondary, subject, tributary *Rel* adjuvant, auxiliary, contributory, subservient, subsidiary *Ant* chief, dominant, leading **2** *Syn* LESSER, inferior, junior, less, lower, minor, smaller, under *Ant* greater, higher, major, more, primary, prime, senior, superior

subordinate *n* *Syn* UNDERLING, inferior, junior *Ant* senior, superior

subscribe *Syn* ASSENT, accede, acquiesce, agree, consent *Ant* dissent

subscribe (to) *Syn* APPROVE (OF), accept, care (for), countenance, favor, OK (*or* okay)

Ant disapprove (of), discountenance, disfavor, frown (on *or* upon)

subsequently *Syn* AFTER, afterward (*or* afterwards), later, thereafter *Ant* before, beforehand, earlier, previously

subservient **1** · showing or characterized by extreme compliance or abject obedience *Syn* menial, obsequious, servile, slavish *Rel* cowering, cringing, fawning, truckling *Ant* domineering, overbearing **2** *Syn* AUXILIARY, accessory, adjuvant, ancillary, contributory, subsidiary

subside **1** *Syn* ABATE, ebb, wane *Ant* revive, rise **2** *Syn* FALL, drop, sink, slump *Ant* rise

subsidiary *Syn* AUXILIARY, accessory, adjuvant, ancillary, contributory, subservient

subsidy *Syn* APPROPRIATION, allocation, allotment, annuity, grant

subsist *Syn* BE, exist, live

subsistence **1** *Syn* CONTINUATION, continuance, duration, endurance, persistence *Ant* ending, termination **2** *Syn* LIVING, bread, bread and butter, keep, livelihood, maintenance, support, sustenance

subspecies *Syn* VARIETY (sense 2), breed, clone, cultivar, race, stock, strain

substance **1** · the inner significance or central meaning of something written or said *Syn* burden, core, gist, pith, purport *Rel* center, focus, heart, nucleus **2** *Syn* MATTER, material, stuff

substantial **1** *Syn* LARGE, big, bulky, considerable, goodly, good-sized, grand, great, handsome, hefty, hulking, largish, outsize, oversize (*or* oversized), sizable (*or* sizeable), tidy, voluminous *Ant* little, puny, small, undersized **2** *Syn* MASSIVE, bulky, massy, monumental

substantially *Syn* CHIEFLY, altogether, basically, by and large, generally, largely, mainly, mostly, overall, predominantly, primarily, principally

substantiate **1** *Syn* CONFIRM, authenticate, corroborate, validate, verify *Ant* contradict, deny **2** *Syn* EMBODY (sense 2), epitomize, incarnate, manifest, materialize, personalize, personify

substitute *n* **1** · a person or thing that takes the place of another *Syn* backup, pinch hitter, relief, replacement, reserve, stand-in, sub *Rel* alternate, understudy **2** *Syn* RESOURCE, expedient, makeshift, resort, shift, stopgap, surrogate

substitute *vb Syn* CHANGE (sense 3), commute, exchange, shift, swap, switch, trade

substitute *adj Syn* IMITATION, artificial, bogus, factitious, fake, false, man-made, mimic, mock, sham, simulated, synthetic *Ant* genuine, natural, real

subsume *Syn* INCLUDE, comprehend, embrace, imply, involve *Ant* exclude

subterfuge *Syn* TRICKERY, artifice, chicanery, hanky-panky, jugglery, legerdemain, wile

subtle *Syn* LOGICAL, analytical *Ant* illogical

subvert *Syn* OVERTURN, capsize, overthrow, upset

succeed **1** · to attain or be attaining a desired end *Syn* flourish, prosper, thrive *Rel* achieve, attain, gain, reach *Ant* attempt, fail **2** *Syn* FOLLOW (sense 1), ensue, supervene *Ant* forsake (*a teacher or teachings*), precede

succession · a number of things that follow each other in some order *Syn* chain, progression, sequence, series, string, train *Rel* consecutiveness, successiveness

successive *Syn* CONSECUTIVE, sequent, sequential, serial *Ant* inconsecutive

succinct *Syn* CONCISE, compendious, laconic, pithy, summary, terse *Ant* redundant

succinctly · in a few words *Syn* briefly, compactly, concisely, crisply, laconically, pithily, summarily, tersely *Rel* aphoristically *Ant* diffusely, long-windedly, verbosely, wordily

succumb *Syn* YIELD, bow, capitulate, cave, defer, relent, submit

such *Syn* ALIKE, akin, analogous, comparable, correspondent, corresponding, like, matching, parallel, resembling, similar, suchlike *Ant* different, dissimilar, diverse, unlike

suchlike *Syn* ALIKE, akin, analogous, comparable, correspondent, corresponding, like, matching, parallel, resembling, similar, such *Ant* different, dissimilar, diverse, unlike

sucker *Syn* DUPE, chump, gull, pigeon, sap, tool

sudden *Syn* PRECIPITATE, abrupt, hasty, headlong, impetuous *Ant* deliberate

suddenly *Syn* UNAWARES, aback, unaware, unexpectedly

suds *Syn* FOAM, froth, lather, scum, spume, yeast

sue *Syn* PRAY, appeal, petition, plead

suffer **1** *Syn* BEAR (sense 2), abide, brook, endure, stand, tolerate **2** *Syn* EXPERIENCE, sustain, undergo **3** *Syn* LET, allow, leave, permit

sufferable *Syn* BEARABLE, endurable, supportable, sustainable, tolerable *Ant* insufferable, insupportable, intolerable, unbearable, unendurable, unsupportable

sufferance *Syn* PERMISSION, allowance, authorization, clearance, concurrence, consent, granting, leave, license (*or* licence), sanction *Ant* interdiction, prohibition, proscription

suffering *Syn* DISTRESS, agony, dolor, misery, passion

sufficiency · the quality or state of meeting one's needs adequately *Syn* acceptability, adequacy, satisfactoriness *Rel* appropriateness, correctness, fitness, goodness, properness, rightness, seemliness, suitability, suitableness *Ant* inadequacy, insufficiency

sufficient · being what is necessary or desirable *Syn* adequate, competent, enough

suffocate · to stop the respiration of *Syn* asphyxiate, choke, smother, stifle, strangle, throttle

suffrage · the right, privilege, or power of expressing one's choice or wish (as in an election or in the determination of policy) *Syn* ballot, franchise, vote

suffuse *Syn* INFUSE, imbue, ingrain, inoculate, leaven

sugarcoated *Syn* CORNY, maudlin, mawkish, mushy, saccharine, sappy, schmaltzy, sentimental, sloppy, sugary *Ant* unsentimental

sugary *Syn* CORNY, maudlin, mawkish, mushy, saccharine, sappy, schmaltzy, sentimental, sloppy, sugarcoated *Ant* unsentimental

suggest 1 · to call to mind by thought, through close connection, or by association *Syn* adumbrate, shadow *Ant* manifest **2** *Syn* HINT, allude, imply, indicate, infer, insinuate, intimate

suggestion 1 *Syn* PROPOSAL, offer, proffer, proposition **2** *Syn* TOUCH, dash, shade, smack, soupçon, spice, strain, streak, suspicion, tincture, tinge, vein

suggestive *Syn* EXPRESSIVE, eloquent, meaning, meaningful, pregnant, revealing, significant

suit 1 · a legal proceeding instituted for the sake of demanding justice or enforcing a right *Syn* action, case, cause, lawsuit **2** *Syn* PRAYER, appeal, petition, plea

suitability *Syn* APPROPRIATENESS, aptness, felicitousness, fitness, fittingness, rightness, seemliness, suitableness *Ant* inappropriateness, inaptness, infelicity, unfitness

suitable 1 *Syn* COMPETENT, able, capable, fit, good, qualified *Ant* incompetent, inept, poor, unfit, unqualified **2** *Syn* FIT, appropriate, apt, felicitous, fitting, happy, meet, proper *Ant* unfit

suitableness *Syn* APPROPRIATENESS, aptness, felicitousness, fitness, fittingness, rightness, seemliness, suitability *Ant* inappropriateness, inaptness, infelicity, unfitness

suitably *Syn* PROPERLY, appropriately, congruously, correctly, fittingly, happily, meetly, rightly *Ant* improperly, inappropriately, incongruously, incorrectly, unsuitably, wrongly

suitor *Syn* SUPPLICANT, petitioner, pleader, solicitor, suppliant

sulk · to silently go about in a bad mood *Syn* mope, pout *Rel* brood, dwell (on), mull (over), muse (over), ponder

sulky *Syn* SULLEN, crabbed, dour, gloomy, glum, morose, saturnine, surly

sullen · showing a forbidding or disagreeable mood *Syn* crabbed, dour, gloomy, glum, morose, saturnine, sulky, surly *Rel* frowning, glowering, lowering, scowling

sully *Syn* DIRTY, befoul, begrime, besmirch, blacken, foul, grime, mire, muddy, smirch, smudge, soil, stain *Ant* clean, cleanse

sum *n* · the result of simple addition of all the numbers or particulars in a given group *Syn* aggregate, amount, number, quantity, total, whole

sum *vb Syn* ADD (sense 1), foot (up), total *Ant* deduct, remove, subtract, take

summarily *Syn* SUCCINCTLY, briefly, compactly, concisely, crisply, laconically, pithily, tersely *Ant* diffusely, long-windedly, verbosely, wordily

summarize · to make into a short statement of the main points (as of a report) *Syn* abstract, digest, encapsulate, epitomize, outline, recap, recapitulate, sum up, wrap up *Rel* abridge, condense, curtail, shorten

summary *Syn* CONCISE, compendious, laconic, pithy, succinct, terse *Ant* redundant

summative *Syn* CUMULATIVE, accumulative, additive

summit · the highest point attained or attainable *Syn* acme, apex, apogee, climax, culmination, meridian, peak, pinnacle, zenith

summon, summons · to demand or request the presence or service of *Syn* call, cite, convene, convoke, muster *Rel* bid, command, enjoin, order

sumptuous *Syn* LUXURIOUS, deluxe, lavish, luxuriant, opulent, palatial, plush *Ant* ascetic, austere, humble, Spartan

sumptuously *Syn* HIGH, expensively, extravagantly, grandly, lavishly, luxuriously, opulently, richly *Ant* austerely, humbly, modestly, plainly, simply

sum up *Syn* SUMMARIZE, abstract, digest, encapsulate, epitomize, outline, recap, recapitulate, wrap up

sunder *Syn* SEPARATE, divide, divorce, part, sever *Ant* combine

sundry *Syn* MANY, divers, multifarious, numerous, several, various *Ant* few

sunken *Syn* HOLLOW, concave, dented, depressed, indented, recessed *Ant* bulging, convex, protruding, protuberant

sunny 1 *Syn* CHEERFUL (sense 1), blithe, blithesome, bright, buoyant, cheery, chipper, gay, gladsome, lightsome, upbeat *Ant* dour, gloomy, glum, morose, saturnine, sulky, sullen **2** *Syn* MERRY, blithesome, festive, gay, gleeful, jocose, jocund, jolly, jovial, laughing, mirthful

super *Syn* VERY, awful, awfully, beastly, deadly, especially, exceedingly, extra, extremely, far, frightfully, full, greatly, heavily, highly, hugely, jolly, mightily, mighty, mortally, most, much, particularly, rattling, real, right, so, something, terribly, too, whacking *Ant* little, negligibly, nominally, slightly

superabundance *Syn* EXCESS, fat, overabundance, overage, overflow, overkill, overmuch, oversupply, superfluity, surfeit, surplus *Ant* deficiency, deficit, insufficiency

superb 1 *Syn* EXCELLENT, A1, bang-up,

banner, capital, classic, crackerjack, dandy, divine, fabulous, fine, first-class, first-rate, grand, great, groovy, heavenly, jim-dandy, keen, marvelous (*or* marvellous), mean, neat, nifty, noble, par excellence, prime, sensational, splendid, stellar, sterling, superior, superlative, supernal, swell, terrific, tip-top, top, top-notch, unsurpassed, wonderful *Ant* poor **2** *Syn* SPLENDID, glorious, gorgeous, resplendent, sublime

superbness *Syn* MAGNIFICENCE, augustness, brilliance, gloriousness, glory, grandeur, grandness, majesty, nobility, nobleness, resplendence, splendor, stateliness, stupendousness, sublimeness

supercilious **1** *Syn* ARROGANT, cavalier, haughty, highfalutin, high-handed, high-hat, imperious, important, lofty, lordly, masterful, overweening, peremptory, pompous, presumptuous, pretentious, superior, uppish, uppity *Ant* humble, modest **2** *Syn* PROUD (sense 1), arrogant, disdainful, haughty, insolent, lordly, overbearing *Ant* ashamed, humble

superciliousness *Syn* ARROGANCE, haughtiness, imperiousness, loftiness, lordliness, masterfulness, peremptoriness, pompousness, presumptuousness, pretense (*or* pretence), pretension, pretentiousness, self-importance, superiority *Ant* humility, modesty

supererogatory · given or done without compulsion, need, or warrant *Syn* gratuitous, uncalled-for, wanton *Rel* autonomous, free, independent

superficial · lacking in depth or solidity *Syn* cursory, shallow, uncritical *Ant* deep, profound

superfluity *Syn* EXCESS, fat, overabundance, overage, overflow, overkill, overmuch, oversupply, superabundance, surfeit, surplus *Ant* deficiency, deficit, insufficiency

superfluous · exceeding what is needed or necessary *Syn* extra, spare, supernumerary, surplus *Rel* gratuitous, supererogatory, uncalled-for, wanton

superhuman *Syn* SUPERNATURAL, miraculous, preternatural, supranatural

superimpose *Syn* OVERLAY, appliqué, superpose

superintendent *Syn* EXECUTIVE, administrator, director, manager, supervisor

superior *n* · one who is above another in rank, station, or office *Syn* better, elder, senior *Rel* boss, chief, head, leader, master *Ant* inferior, subordinate, underling

superior *adj* **1** *Syn* ARROGANT, cavalier, haughty, highfalutin, high-handed, high-hat, imperious, important, lofty, lordly, masterful, overweening, peremptory, pompous, presumptuous, pretentious, supercilious, uppish, uppity *Ant* humble, modest **2** *Syn* BETTER, preferable **3** *Syn* EMINENT, distinguished,

illustrious, noble, notable, noteworthy, outstanding, preeminent, prestigious, signal, star **4** *Syn* EXCELLENT, A1, bang-up, banner, capital, classic, crackerjack, dandy, divine, fabulous, fine, first-class, first-rate, grand, great, groovy, heavenly, jim-dandy, keen, marvelous (*or* marvellous), mean, neat, nifty, noble, par excellence, prime, sensational, splendid, stellar, sterling, superb, superlative, supernal, swell, terrific, tip-top, top, top-notch, unsurpassed, wonderful *Ant* poor

superiority *Syn* ARROGANCE, haughtiness, imperiousness, loftiness, lordliness, masterfulness, peremptoriness, pompousness, presumptuousness, pretense (*or* pretence), pretension, pretentiousness, self-importance, superciliousness *Ant* humility, modesty

superlative **1** *Syn* EXCELLENT, A1, bang-up, banner, capital, classic, crackerjack, dandy, divine, fabulous, fine, first-class, first-rate, grand, great, groovy, heavenly, jim-dandy, keen, marvelous (*or* marvellous), mean, neat, nifty, noble, par excellence, prime, sensational, splendid, stellar, sterling, superb, superior, supernal, swell, terrific, tip-top, top, top-notch, unsurpassed, wonderful *Ant* poor **2** *Syn* SUPREME, incomparable, peerless, preeminent, surpassing, transcendent

supernal **1** *Syn* CELESTIAL, Elysian, empyreal, empyrean, heavenly *Ant* hellish, infernal **2** *Syn* EXCELLENT, A1, bang-up, banner, capital, classic, crackerjack, dandy, divine, fabulous, fine, first-class, first-rate, grand, great, groovy, heavenly, jim-dandy, keen, marvelous (*or* marvellous), mean, neat, nifty, noble, par excellence, prime, sensational, splendid, stellar, sterling, superb, superior, superlative, swell, terrific, tip-top, top, top-notch, unsurpassed, wonderful *Ant* poor

supernatural · of or relating to an order of existence beyond the visible observable universe *Syn* miraculous, preternatural, superhuman, supranatural *Rel* blessed, divine, holy, sacred, spiritual

supernumerary *Syn* SUPERFLUOUS, extra, spare, surplus

superpose *Syn* OVERLAY, appliqué, superimpose

supersede *Syn* REPLACE, displace, supplant

supervene *Syn* FOLLOW (sense 1), ensue, succeed *Ant* forsake (*a teacher or teachings*), precede

supervision *Syn* OVERSIGHT, surveillance

supervisor *Syn* EXECUTIVE, administrator, director, manager, superintendent

supine *Syn* INACTIVE, idle, inert, passive *Ant* active, live

supplant *Syn* REPLACE, displace, supersede

supple **1** · able to bend or twist with ease and grace *Syn* limber, lissome, lithe, lithesome *Rel* elegant, graceful **2** *Syn* ELASTIC (sense 1), flexible, resilient, springy *Ant* rigid

3 *Syn* WILLOWY, flexible, limber, lissome, lithe, pliable, pliant *Ant* inflexible, rigid, stiff

supplement *Syn* APPENDIX, addendum

suppliant *Syn* SUPPLICANT, petitioner, pleader, solicitor, suitor

supplicant · one who asks earnestly for a favor or gift *Syn* petitioner, pleader, solicitor, suitor, suppliant *Rel* beggar, mendicant, panhandler

supplicate *Syn* BEG, adjure, beseech, entreat, implore, importune

supply 1 *Syn* FURNISH (sense 1), accoutre (*or* accouter), equip, fit (out), outfit, rig *Ant* hold (back), keep (back), reserve, retain, withhold 2 *Syn* FURNISH (sense 2), deliver, feed, give, hand, hand over, provide *Ant* hold (back), keep (back), reserve, retain, withhold

support *vb* 1 · to hold up in position by serving as a foundation or base for *Syn* bolster, brace, buttress, prop, sustain *Rel* bear, carry, convey 2 · to favor actively one that meets opposition *Syn* advocate, back, champion, uphold *Rel* approve, endorse, sanction

support *n Syn* LIVING, bread, bread and butter, keep, livelihood, maintenance, subsistence, sustenance

supportable 1 *Syn* BEARABLE, endurable, sufferable, sustainable, tolerable *Ant* insufferable, insupportable, intolerable, unbearable, unendurable, unsupportable 2 *Syn* TENABLE, defendable, defensible, justifiable, maintainable, sustainable *Ant* indefensible, insupportable, unjustifiable, untenable

supporter 1 *Syn* ALLY, abettor, backer, confederate, sympathizer 2 *Syn* EXPONENT, advocate, apostle, backer, booster, champion, friend, promoter, proponent *Ant* adversary, antagonist, opponent

suppose 1 *Syn* BELIEVE (sense 1), consider, deem, feel, figure, guess, hold, imagine, think *Ant* disbelieve, discredit, reject 2 *Syn* ESTIMATE (sense 2), calculate, call, conjecture, figure, gauge, guess, judge, make, place, put, reckon

supposed · accepted or advanced as true or real on the basis of less than conclusive evidence *Syn* conjectural, hypothetical, purported, putative, reputed, supposititious, suppositious *Rel* assumed, postulated, presumed, presupposed *Ant* certain

supposedly *Syn* APPARENTLY, evidently, ostensibly, presumably, seemingly

supposition 1 *Syn* CONJECTURE, guess, surmise 2 *Syn* THEORY, hypothesis, proposition

suppositious *Syn* SUPPOSED, conjectural, hypothetical, purported, putative, reputed, supposititious *Ant* certain

supposititious *Syn* SUPPOSED, conjectural, hypothetical, purported, putative, reputed, suppositious *Ant* certain

suppress *Syn* CRUSH (sense 2), extinguish, quash, quell, quench

supranatural *Syn* SUPERNATURAL, miraculous, preternatural, superhuman

supremacy · controlling power or influence over others *Syn* ascendancy, dominance, dominion, predominance, preeminence, sovereignty *Rel* authority, command, control, mastery

supreme 1 · developed to the utmost and not exceeded by any other in degree, quality, or intensity *Syn* incomparable, peerless, preeminent, superlative, surpassing, transcendent 2 *Syn* HEAD, chief, commanding, first, foremost, high, lead, leading, managing, preeminent, premier, presiding, primary, prime, principal

sure 1 · having no doubt or uncertainty *Syn* certain, cocksure, positive *Rel* decided, decisive *Ant* unsure 2 *Syn* CONFIDENT, assured, presumptuous, sanguine *Ant* apprehensive, diffident 3 *Syn* DEPENDABLE, good, reliable, responsible, safe, solid, steady, tried, tried-and-true, true, trustworthy, trusty *Ant* irresponsible, undependable, unreliable, untrustworthy 4 *Syn* INEVITABLE, certain, inescapable, necessary, unavoidable *Ant* avoidable, escapable, uncertain, unsure

surety 1 *Syn* GUARANTEE, bail, bond, guaranty, security 2 *Syn* SPONSOR, angel, backer, guarantor, patron

surfeit *n Syn* EXCESS, fat, overabundance, overage, overflow, overkill, overmuch, oversupply, superabundance, superfluity, surplus *Ant* deficit, insufficiency

surfeit *vb Syn* SATIATE, cloy, glut, gorge, pall, sate

surly *Syn* SULLEN, crabbed, dour, gloomy, glum, morose, saturnine, sulky

surmise *Syn* CONJECTURE, guess, supposition

surmount *Syn* CONQUER, beat, defeat, lick, overcome, overthrow, reduce, rout, subdue, subjugate, vanquish

surpass *Syn* EXCEED, excel, outdo, outstrip, transcend

surpassing *Syn* SUPREME, incomparable, peerless, preeminent, superlative, transcendent

surplus 1 *Syn* EXCESS, fat, overabundance, overage, overflow, overkill, overmuch, oversupply, superabundance, superfluity, surfeit *Ant* deficiency, deficit, insufficiency 2 *Syn* SUPERFLUOUS, extra, spare, supernumerary

surprise 1 · to attack unawares *Syn* ambush, waylay *Rel* capture, catch 2 · to impress forcibly through unexpectedness *Syn* amaze, astonish, astound, flabbergast *Rel* alarm, frighten, scare, startle

surrender *n* · the yielding of one's person, forces, or possessions to another *Syn* capitulation, submission

surrender *vb Syn* RELINQUISH, abandon, cede, leave, resign, waive, yield *Ant* keep

surreptitious *Syn* SECRET, clandestine, covert, furtive, stealthy, underhand, underhanded

surrogate *Syn* RESOURCE, expedient, makeshift, resort, shift, stopgap, substitute

surround • to close in or as if in a ring about something *Syn* circle, compass, encircle, encompass, environ, gird, girdle, hem, ring *Rel* enclose, envelop, fence, wall

surveillance **1** *Syn* OVERSIGHT, supervision **2** *Syn* VIGILANCE, alertness, attentiveness, lookout, watch, watchfulness

survey *vb* **1** *Syn* CANVASS, poll, solicit **2** *Syn* SEE (sense 1), behold, contemplate, descry, discern, espy, note, notice, observe, perceive, remark, view

survey *n* **1** *Syn* COMPENDIUM, aperçu, digest, pandect, précis, sketch, syllabus **2** *Syn* INSPECTION, audit, check, checkup, examination, review, scan, scrutiny

survive *Syn* OUTLIVE, outlast

susceptible **1** *Syn* LIABLE, exposed, open, prone, sensitive, subject *Ant* exempt, immune **2** *Syn* SENTIENT, impressible, impressionable, responsive, sensitive

suspect *Syn* DISTRUST, doubt, mistrust, question *Ant* trust

suspend **1** *Syn* ADJOURN, recess **2** *Syn* EXCLUDE, blackball, debar, disbar, eliminate, rule out, shut out *Ant* admit, include **3** *Syn* HANG, dangle, sling

suspended • hanging from or remaining in place as if hanging from a support *Syn* pendent, pendulous

suspense *Syn* ABEYANCE, doldrums, dormancy, latency, quiescence, suspension *Ant* continuance, continuation

suspension *Syn* ABEYANCE, doldrums, dormancy, latency, quiescence, suspense *Ant* continuance, continuation

suspicion **1** *Syn* DOUBT, distrust, distrustfulness, incertitude, misgiving, mistrust, mistrustfulness, skepticism, uncertainty *Ant* assurance, belief, certainty, certitude, confidence, conviction, sureness, surety, trust **2** *Syn* TOUCH, dash, shade, smack, soupçon, spice, strain, streak, suggestion, tincture, tinge, vein

suspiciously *Syn* ASKANCE, distrustfully, doubtfully, doubtingly, dubiously, mistrustfully, skeptically *Ant* trustfully, trustingly

sustain **1** *Syn* EXPERIENCE, suffer, undergo **2** *Syn* SUPPORT (sense 1), bolster, brace, buttress, prop

sustainable **1** *Syn* BEARABLE, endurable, sufferable, supportable, tolerable *Ant* insufferable, insupportable, intolerable, unbearable, unendurable, unsupportable **2** *Syn* TENABLE, defendable, defensible, justifiable, maintainable, supportable *Ant* indefensible, insupportable, unjustifiable, untenable

sustenance **1** *Syn* FOOD (sense 2), aliment, nourishment, nutriment, pabulum, pap **2**

Syn LIVING, bread, bread and butter, keep, livelihood, maintenance, subsistence, support

suture *Syn* JOINT, articulation

swag *Syn* SPOIL, booty, loot, plunder, prize

swagger *Syn* STRUT, bridle, bristle

swain *Syn* BOYFRIEND, beau, fellow, man

swallow *Syn* EAT, consume, devour, ingest

swamp *n* • spongy land saturated or partially covered with water *Syn* bog, fen, marsh, marshland, mire, morass, muskeg, slough, swampland *Rel* quagmire

swamp *vb* *Syn* FLOOD, deluge, drown, engulf, inundate, overflow, overwhelm, submerge, submerse *Ant* drain

swampland *Syn* SWAMP, bog, fen, marsh, marshland, mire, morass, muskeg, slough

swank *n* *Syn* OSTENTATION, flamboyance, flashiness, garishness, gaudiness, glitz, ostentatiousness, pretentiousness, showiness *Ant* austerity, plainness, severity

swank *or* **swanky** *n* *Syn* GAUDY, flamboyant, flashy, garish, glitzy, loud, ostentatious, splashy, tawdry *Ant* conservative, quiet, understated

swap *Syn* CHANGE (sense 3), commute, exchange, shift, substitute, switch, trade

swarm *Syn* TEEM, abound, overflow

swarming *Syn* RIFE, abounding, flush, fraught, replete, teeming, thick, thronging

swat *Syn* STRIKE, box, clout, cuff, hit, punch, slap, slog, slug, smite

sway **1** *Syn* AFFECT, impress, influence, strike, touch **2** *Syn* SWING (sense 2), fluctuate, oscillate, pendulate, undulate, vibrate, waver

swear *Syn* TESTIFY, attest, depose, witness

swearing *Syn* BLASPHEMY, cursing, profanity *Ant* adoration

sweat **1** *Syn* EXUDE, bleed, ooze, percolate, seep, strain, weep **2** *Syn* LABOR, drudge, endeavor, grub, hump, hustle, moil, peg (away), plod, plow, plug, slave, slog, strain, strive, struggle, toil, travail, work *Ant* dabble, fiddle (around), fool (around), mess (around), putter (around)

sweep *Syn* RANGE, compass, gamut, horizon, ken, orbit, purview, radius, reach, scope

sweeping *Syn* INDISCRIMINATE, wholesale *Ant* discriminating, selective

sweet *adj* **1** • distinctly pleasing or charming *Syn* dulcet, engaging, winning, winsome *Rel* agreeable, grateful, gratifying, pleasant, pleasing, welcome *Ant* bitter, sour **2** *Syn* AMIABLE, affable, agreeable, genial, good-natured, good-tempered, gracious, nice, well-disposed *Ant* disagreeable, ill-natured, ill-tempered, ungracious, unpleasant **3** *Syn* FRAGRANT, ambrosial, aromatic, perfumed, redolent, savory, scented *Ant* fetid, foul, malodorous, noisome, putrid, rancid, rank, reeking, reeky, smelly, stinking, stinky, strong **4** *Syn* LOVABLE, darling, dear, disarming, endearing, precious, winning *Ant* abhorrent, abominable, detestable, hateful, odious, unlovable

sweet *n Syn* SWEETHEART, beloved, darling, dear, flame, honey, love

sweetheart · a person with whom one is in love *Syn* beloved, darling, dear, flame, honey, love, sweet *Rel* beau, boyfriend, fellow, lover, man, swain

swell *adj Syn* EXCELLENT, A1, bang-up, banner, capital, classic, crackerjack, dandy, divine, fabulous, fine, first-class, first-rate, grand, great, groovy, heavenly, jim-dandy, keen, marvelous (*or* marvellous), mean, neat, nifty, noble, par excellence, prime, sensational, splendid, stellar, sterling, superb, superior, superlative, supernal, terrific, tip-top, top, top-notch, unsurpassed, wonderful *Ant* poor

swell *vb* 1 *Syn* EXPAND, amplify, dilate, distend, inflate *Ant* abridge, circumscribe, contract 2 *Syn* INCREASE (sense 1), add (to), aggrandize, amplify, augment, boost, compound, enlarge, escalate, expand, extend, multiply, raise, up *Ant* abate, contract, decrease, diminish, lessen, lower, reduce, subtract (from) 3 *Syn* INCREASE (sense 2), accumulate, appreciate, balloon, build (up), burgeon, enlarge, escalate, expand, mount, multiply, mushroom, proliferate, rise, snowball, wax *Ant* contract, decrease, diminish, lessen, wane

swerve · to turn aside from a straight course *Syn* depart, deviate, digress, diverge, veer *Rel* avert, deflect, divert, sheer, turn

swift *Syn* FAST, expeditious, fleet, hasty, quick, rapid, speedy *Ant* slow

swiller *Syn* GLUTTON, gorger, gormandizer, gourmand, hog, overeater, stuffer

swimming *Syn* GIDDY, dazzled, dizzy, vertiginous

swindle *Syn* FLEECE, bleed, cheat, chisel, cozen, defraud, hustle, mulct, rook, shortchange, skin, squeeze, stick, sting, victimize

swing 1 · to wield or cause to move to and fro or up and down *Syn* brandish, flourish, shake, thrash, wave *Rel* display, exhibit, flaunt, parade, show 2 · to move from one direction to its opposite *Syn* fluctuate, oscillate, pendulate, sway, undulate, vibrate, waver *Rel* gyrate, revolve, rotate, spin, turn, wheel, whirl 3 *Syn* HANDLE, manipulate, ply, wield

swipe *Syn* STEAL, cop, filch, lift, pilfer, pinch, purloin, snitch

swirl *Syn* TURN (sense 1), circle, eddy, gyrate, pirouette, revolve, rotate, spin, twirl, wheel, whirl

switch *Syn* CHANGE (sense 3), commute, exchange, shift, substitute, swap, trade

swoon *n Syn* FAINT, blackout, coma, insensibility, knockout

swoon *vb Syn* FAINT, black out, pass out *Ant* come around, come round, come to, revive

sybaritic *Syn* SENSUOUS, epicurean, luxurious, voluptuous

sycophant 1 · a person who flatters another in order to get ahead *Syn* fawner, flunky, toady *Rel* yes-man 2 *Syn* PARASITE, bootlicker, favorite, hanger-on, leech, lickspittle, sponge, sponger, toady

syllabus *Syn* COMPENDIUM, aperçu, digest, pandect, précis, sketch, survey

symbol 1 · something concrete that represents or suggests another thing that cannot in itself be pictured *Syn* attribute, emblem, type *Rel* badge, mark, sign, token 2 *Syn* CHARACTER, mark, sign

symmetry · beauty of form or arrangement arising from balanced proportions *Syn* balance, harmony, proportion

sympathetic 1 *Syn* CONSONANT, compatible, congenial, congruous, consistent *Ant* dissonant (*in music*), inconstant 2 *Syn* TENDER, compassionate, responsive, warm, warmhearted *Ant* callous, severe

sympathizer *Syn* ALLY, abettor, backer, confederate, supporter

sympathy 1 · the act or capacity for sharing in the interests and especially in the painful experiences of another *Syn* commiseration, compassion, condolence, empathy, pity, ruth *Rel* responsiveness, tenderness, warmheartedness, warmth 2 *Syn* ATTRACTION, affinity

symptom *Syn* SIGN (sense 1), badge, mark, note, token

synchronous *Syn* CONTEMPORARY, coetaneous, coeval, coincident, concomitant, concurrent, contemporaneous, simultaneous

syndicate 1 *Syn* CARTEL, combination, combine, trust 2 *Syn* MONOPOLY, cartel, corner, pool, trust

syndrome *Syn* DISEASE, ailment, complaint, condition, disorder, distemper, malady

synopsis *Syn* ABRIDGMENT, abstract, brief, conspectus, epitome *Ant* expansion

synthetic 1 *Syn* ARTIFICIAL, ersatz, factitious *Ant* natural 2 *Syn* IMITATION, artificial, bogus, factitious, fake, false, man-made, mimic, mock, sham, simulated, substitute *Ant* genuine, natural, real

system 1 · an organized integrated whole made up of diverse but interrelated and interdependent parts *Syn* complex, network, organism, scheme *Ant* chaos 2 *Syn* METHOD, fashion, manner, mode, way

systematic *Syn* ORDERLY, methodical, regular *Ant* chaotic, disorderly

systematize *Syn* ORDER, arrange, marshal, methodize, organize

T

table 1 *Syn* LIST, catalog, inventory, register, roll, roster, schedule 2 *Syn* MEAL, chow, feed, mess, repast

tablet *Syn* PILL, capsule, lozenge

table talk *Syn* CHAT, chatter, chitchat, gabfest, gossip, palaver, rap, small talk, talk, tête-à-tête

tacit *Syn* IMPLICIT, implied, unexpressed, unspoken, unvoiced, wordless *Ant* explicit, express, expressed, spoken, stated

taciturn *Syn* SILENT (sense 1), close, close-lipped, closemouthed, reserved, reticent, secretive, tight-lipped, uncommunicative *Ant* talkative

tackle *Syn* EQUIPMENT, apparatus, gear, machinery, matériel, outfit, paraphernalia

tack (on) *Syn* ADD (sense 2), adjoin, annex, append *Ant* deduct, remove, subtract, take

tact · skill and grace in dealing with others *Syn* address, poise, savoir faire *Rel* diplomacy, policy, suavity, urbanity *Ant* awkwardness

tactical 1 *Syn* EXPEDIENT, advisable, desirable, judicious, politic, prudent, wise *Ant* imprudent, inadvisable, inexpedient, injudicious, unwise 2 *Syn* STRATEGIC, logistic

tactics *Syn* STRATEGY, logistics

tactless *Syn* INDISCREET, ill-advised, imprudent, inadvisable, injudicious, unadvisable, unwise *Ant* advisable, discreet, judicious, prudent, tactful, wise

tad *Syn* BOY, lad, laddie, nipper, shaver, sonny, stripling, youth

tag *n Syn* MARK, brand, label, stamp, ticket

tag *vb Syn* MARK, brand, label, stamp, ticket

tagging *Syn* PURSUIT, chase, chasing, dogging, following, hounding, pursuing, shadowing, tailing, tracing, tracking, trailing

tailing *Syn* PURSUIT, chase, chasing, dogging, following, hounding, pursuing, shadowing, tagging, tracing, tracking, trailing

taint *Syn* CONTAMINATE, befoul, defile, foul, poison, pollute *Ant* decontaminate, purify

tainted *Syn* IMPURE, adulterated, alloyed, contaminated, dilute, diluted, polluted, thinned, weakened *Ant* pure, unadulterated, unalloyed, uncontaminated, undiluted, unpolluted, untainted

take 1 · to get hold of by or as if by catching up with the hand *Syn* clutch, grab, grasp, seize, snatch *Rel* have, hold, own, possess 2 *Syn* BRING, fetch *Ant* remove, withdraw 3 *Syn* BUY, pick up, purchase 4 *Syn* RECEIVE, accept, admit

taking *Syn* BEAUTIFUL, attractive, beauteous, comely, cute, fair, gorgeous, handsome, knockout, lovely, pretty, ravishing, sightly, stunning *Ant* homely, ill-favored, plain, ugly, unattractive, unbeautiful, unhandsome, unlovely, unpretty, unsightly

tale *Syn* STORY, anecdote, narrative, yarn

talent *Syn* GIFT (sense 2), aptitude, bent, faculty, genius, knack, turn

talisman *Syn* FETISH, amulet, charm

talk *vb* 1 *Syn* CHAT, babble, blab, cackle, chatter, converse, gab, gabble, gas, jabber, jaw, palaver, patter, prate, prattle, rap, rattle, run on, twitter, visit 2 *Syn* SPEAK, converse

talk *n* 1 *Syn* CHAT, chatter, chitchat, gabfest, gossip, palaver, rap, small, table talk, talk, tête-à-tête 2 *Syn* SPEECH, address, harangue, homily, lecture, oration, sermon

talkative · given to talk or talking *Syn* garrulous, glib, loquacious, voluble *Rel* articulate, eloquent, fluent, vocal *Ant* closemouthed, laconic, reserved, reticent, taciturn, tight-lipped

talkativeness · the inclination to talk or to talking *Syn* garrulity, garrulousness, glibness, loquaciousness, loquacity, volubility *Rel* articulateness, eloquence, fluency *Ant* silence

talk (into) *Syn* PERSUADE, argue, convince, get, induce, move, prevail (on *or* upon), satisfy, win (over)

tall *Syn* HIGH, lofty *Ant* low

tally *Syn* AGREE (sense 2), accord, conform, correspond, harmonize, jibe, square *Ant* differ (from)

tame 1 · made docile and tractable *Syn* subdued, submissive *Rel* amenable, biddable, docile, obedient, tractable *Ant* fierce 2 *Syn* BORING, drab, dreary, dry, dull, flat, heavy, humdrum, jading, leaden, monotonous, pedestrian, ponderous, stodgy, stuffy, stupid, tedious, tiresome, tiring, unanimated, uninteresting, wearisome, weary, wearying *Ant* absorbing, engaging, engrossing, gripping, interesting, intriguing, involving

tamp *Syn* PACK, cram, crowd, ram, stuff

tang *Syn* TASTE (sense 1), flavor, relish, savor, smack *Ant* antipathy

tangible · capable of being perceived by the sense of touch *Syn* palpable, touchable *Rel* tactile *Ant* impalpable, intangible

tangle *Syn* ENTANGLE, enmesh, ensnare, entrap, mesh, snare, trap *Ant* disentangle

tantalize *Syn* WORRY, annoy, harass, harry, pester, plague, tease

tantamount *Syn* SAME, equal, equivalent, identic, identical, selfsame, very *Ant* different

tap *n* · a light usually audible blow or the sound made by such a blow *Syn* knock, rap, thud, thump

tap *vb* · to strike or hit audibly *Syn* knock, rap, thud, thump *Rel* smite, strike

tar *Syn* MARINER, bluejacket, gob, sailor, seaman

tardily *Syn* SLOW, laggardly, leisurely, slowly, sluggishly *Ant* apace, briskly, fast, fleetly, full tilt, hastily, quick, quickly, rapidly, snappily, speedily, swift, swiftly

tardy · not arriving, occurring, or done at the set, due, or expected time *Syn* behindhand, late, overdue *Rel* dilatory, laggard, slow *Ant* prompt

target **1** *Syn* GOAL, aim, ambition, aspiration, design, dream, end, intent, intention, mark, meaning, object, objective, plan, pretension, purpose, thing **2** *Syn* LAUGHINGSTOCK, butt, mark, mock, mockery

tarry *Syn* STAY, abide, linger, remain, wait

tart *Syn* SOUR, acid, acidulous, dry

Tartarean *Syn* INFERNAL, chthonian, chthonic, Hadean, hellish, stygian *Ant* supernal

task **1** *Syn* CHORE, assignment, duty, job, stint **2** *Syn* ROLE, capacity, function, job, part, place, position, purpose, work

taskmaster *Syn* BOSS, captain, chief, foreman, head, headman, helmsman, kingpin, leader, master

taste **1** · the property of a substance which makes it perceptible to the gustatory sense *Syn* flavor, relish, savor, smack, tang **2** · a liking for or enjoyment of something because of the pleasure it gives *Syn* gusto, palate, relish, zest *Rel* partiality, predilection, prepossession *Ant* antipathy **3** *Syn* LIKING, appetite, fancy, favor, fondness, like, love, partiality, preference, relish, shine, use *Ant* aversion, disfavor, dislike, distaste, hatred, loathing

tasty *Syn* PALATABLE, appetizing, flavorsome, relishing, sapid, savory, toothsome *Ant* distasteful, unpalatable

tat *Syn* WEAVE, braid, crochet, knit, plait

tattle *Syn* GOSSIP, blab

taunt *Syn* RIDICULE, deride, mock, rally, twit

taut *Syn* TIGHT, tense *Ant* loose

tautology *Syn* VERBIAGE, circumlocution, periphrasis, pleonasm, redundancy

tavern *Syn* BARROOM, bar, café, groggery, grogshop, pub, saloon

tawdry *Syn* GAUDY, flamboyant, flashy, garish, glitzy, loud, ostentatious, splashy, swank (*or* swanky) *Ant* conservative, quiet, understated

tawny *Syn* BLOND, fair, flaxen, golden, sandy, straw *Ant* dark

tax *n* · a charge usually of money collected by the government from people or businesses for public use *Syn* assessment, duty, imposition, impost, levy *Rel* custom(s), excise, income tax, poll tax, sales tax, tariff, toll, tribute, withholding tax

tax *vb* *Syn* BURDEN, charge, cumber, encumber, lade, load, saddle, weigh, weight

teach · to cause to acquire knowledge or skill *Syn* discipline, educate, instruct, school, train *Rel* communicate, impart

teacher · a person whose occupation is to give formal instruction in a school *Syn* educator, instructor, pedagogue, preceptor, schoolteacher *Rel* headmaster, master, schoolmaster

teaching *Syn* EDUCATION (sense 1), instruction, schooling, training, tutelage, tutoring

tear **1** · to separate forcibly *Syn* cleave, rend, rip, rive, split *Rel* cut, slash, slit **2** *Syn* HURRY (sense 2), barrel, bolt, bowl, breeze, career, course, dash, fly, hasten, hotfoot (it), hump, hurtle, hustle, pelt, race, rip, rocket, run, rush, rustle, scoot, scurry, scuttle, shoot, speed, step (along), trot, whirl, whisk, zip, zoom *Ant* crawl, creep, poke

tearful *Syn* SAD (sense 2), depressing, dismal, drear, dreary, heartbreaking, heartrending, melancholy, pathetic, saddening, sorry, teary *Ant* cheering, cheery, glad, happy

teary *Syn* SAD (sense 2), depressing, dismal, drear, dreary, heartbreaking, heartrending, melancholy, pathetic, saddening, sorry, tearful *Ant* cheering, cheery, glad, happy

tease **1** · to make fun of in a good-natured way *Syn* chaff, jive, josh, kid, rally, razz, rib, ride, roast *Rel* banter, joke **2** *Syn* WORRY, annoy, harass, harry, pester, plague, tantalize

tedious *Syn* BORING, drab, dreary, dry, dull, flat, heavy, humdrum, jading, leaden, monotonous, pedestrian, ponderous, stodgy, stuffy, stupid, tame, tiresome, tiring, unanimated, uninteresting, wearisome, weary, wearying *Ant* absorbing, engaging, engrossing, gripping, interesting, intriguing, involving

tedium · a state of dissatisfaction and weariness *Syn* boredom, doldrums, ennui *Rel* irksomeness, tediousness, tiresomeness, wearisomeness

teem · to be present in large quantity *Syn* abound, overflow, swarm *Rel* bear, produce, turn out, yield

teeming *Syn* RIFE, abounding, flush, fraught, replete, swarming, thick, thronging

teeny *Syn* TINY, atomic, bitty, infinitesimal, microminiature, microscopic, miniature, minute, teeny-weeny, wee *Ant* astronomical, colossal, cosmic, elephantine, enormous, giant, gigantic, herculean, heroic, huge, immense, mammoth, massive, monster, monstrous, monumental, mountainous, prodigious, titanic, tremendous

teeny-weeny *Syn* TINY, atomic, bitty, infinitesimal, microminiature, microscopic, miniature, minute, teeny, wee *Ant* astronomical, colossal, cosmic, elephantine, enormous, giant, gigantic, herculean, heroic, huge, immense, mammoth, massive, monster, monstrous, monumental, mountainous, prodigious, titanic, tremendous

teeter *Syn* SHAKE (sense 1), dither, quake, quaver, quiver, shimmy, shiver, shudder, totter, tremble, wobble

tell 1 *Syn* COUNT, enumerate, number 2 *Syn* ENLIGHTEN (sense 1), acquaint, advise, apprise, brief, clue, familiarize, fill in, inform, instruct, wise (up) 3 *Syn* REVEAL, betray, disclose, discover, divulge *Ant* conceal 4 *Syn* SAY, state, utter

telling *Syn* COGENT, compelling, conclusive, convincing, decisive, effective, forceful, persuasive, satisfying, strong *Ant* inconclusive, indecisive, ineffective, unconvincing

temerity *Syn* EFFRONTERY, audacity, brashness, brass, brassiness, brazenness, cheek, cheekiness, chutzpah, gall, nerve, nerviness, pertness, presumption, presumptuousness, sauce, sauciness

temper *n* 1 *Syn* AURA, air, atmosphere, climate, flavor, mood, note 2 *Syn* DISPOSITION, character, complexion, individuality, personality, temperament 3 *Syn* MOOD, humor, vein

temper *vb Syn* MODERATE, qualify

temperament *Syn* DISPOSITION, character, complexion, individuality, personality, temper

temperance · self-restraint in the gratification of appetites or passions *Syn* abstinence, abstemiousness, continence, sobriety *Rel* eschewal, forbearance, forbearing, forgoing, sacrifice, sacrificing *Ant* excessiveness, immoderacy, intemperance, intemperateness

temperate 1 *Syn* CLEMENT, balmy, equable, gentle, mild, moderate *Ant* harsh, inclement, intemperate, severe 2 *Syn* SOBER, continent, unimpassioned *Ant* drunk, excited

tempest *Syn* CONVULSION, cataclysm, paroxysm, storm, tumult, upheaval, uproar

tempestuous *Syn* CONVULSIVE, cataclysmal (*or* cataclysmic), stormy, tumultuous

temporal *Syn* PROFANE, lay, secular *Ant* sacred

temporary 1 · lasting, continuing, or serving for a limited time *Syn* acting, ad interim, provisional *Ant* permanent 2 *Syn* MOMENTARY, ephemeral, evanescent, flash, fleeting, fugitive, impermanent, passing, short-lived, transient, transitory *Ant* enduring, eternal, everlasting, lasting, long-lived, permanent, perpetual

tempt *Syn* LURE, allure, beguile, decoy, entice, lead on, seduce

temptress *Syn* SIREN, enchantress, seductress

tenable · capable of being defended with good reasoning against verbal attack *Syn* defendable, defensible, justifiable, maintainable, supportable, sustainable *Rel* rational, reasonable, sensible *Ant* indefensible, insupportable, unjustifiable, untenable

tenacious 1 *Syn* PERSISTENT, dogged, insistent, patient, persevering, pertinacious 2 *Syn* STRONG, stalwart, stout, sturdy, tough *Ant* weak

tenant · one who rents a room or apartment in another's house *Syn* boarder, lodger, renter, roomer *Rel* roommate *Ant* landlord

tend · to supervise or take charge of *Syn* attend, mind, watch *Rel* defend, guard, protect, safeguard, shield

tendency · movement in a particular direction *Syn* drift, tenor, trend *Rel* leaning, penchant, proclivity, propensity

tender *adj* · showing or expressing interest in another *Syn* compassionate, responsive, sympathetic, warm, warmhearted *Rel* gentle, lenient, mild, soft *Ant* callous, severe

tender *vb Syn* OFFER, prefer, present, proffer

tender *n Syn* OVERTURE, advance, approach, bid

tenderfoot *Syn* BEGINNER, colt, fledgling, freshman, greenhorn, neophyte, newbie, newcomer, novice, recruit, rookie, tyro *Ant* old hand, old-timer, vet, veteran

tending *Syn* PRONE (sense 1), apt, given, inclined

tenet *Syn* DOCTRINE, dogma

tenor *Syn* TENDENCY, drift, trend

tense 1 *Syn* STIFF, inflexible, rigid, stark, wooden *Ant* relaxed, supple 2 *Syn* TIGHT, taut *Ant* loose

tension 1 *Syn* BALANCE, equilibrium, equipoise, poise 2 *Syn* STRESS, pressure, strain

tent *Syn* CANOPY, awning, ceiling, roof

tenuous *Syn* THIN, rare, slender, slight, slim *Ant* thick

term 1 *Syn* LIMIT, bound, confine, end 2 *Syn* WORD, vocable

terminal *Syn* LAST, concluding, eventual, final, latest, ultimate *Ant* first

terminate *Syn* CONCLUDE (sense 1), complete, end, finish

termination *Syn* END, ending, terminus *Ant* beginning

terminology · the special terms or expressions of a particular group or field *Syn* argot, cant, dialect, jargon, language, lingo, patois, patter, slang, vocabulary *Rel* colloquialism, idiom, localism, parlance, pidgin, provincialism, regionalism, speech, vernacular

terminus *Syn* END, ending, termination *Ant* beginning

terms *Syn* CONDITION, provision, proviso, reservation, stipulation, strings

terrestrial *Syn* EARTHLY, earthy, mundane, sublunary, worldly

terrible *Syn* FEARFUL (sense 2), appalling, awful, dreadful, frightful, horrible, horrific, shocking, terrific

terribly *Syn* VERY, awful, awfully, beastly, deadly, especially, exceedingly, extra, extremely, far, frightfully, full, greatly, heavily,

terrific

highly, hugely, jolly, mightily, mighty, mortally, most, much, particularly, rattling, real, right, so, something, super, too, whacking *Ant* little, negligibly, nominally, slightly

terrific **1** *Syn* EXCELLENT, A1, bang-up, banner, capital, classic, crackerjack, dandy, divine, fabulous, fine, first-class, first-rate, grand, great, groovy, heavenly, jim-dandy, keen, marvelous (*or* marvellous), mean, neat, nifty, noble, par excellence, prime, sensational, splendid, stellar, sterling, superb, superior, superlative, supernal, swell, tip-top, top, top-notch, unsurpassed, wonderful *Ant* poor **2** *Syn* FEARFUL (sense 2), appalling, awful, dreadful, frightful, horrible, horrific, shocking, terrible

terrify *Syn* FRIGHTEN, affray, affright, alarm, fright, scare, startle, terrorize *Ant* reassure

territory *Syn* FIELD, bailiwick, domain, province, sphere

terror *Syn* FEAR, alarm, consternation, dismay, dread, fright, horror, panic, trepidation *Ant* fearlessness

terrorize *Syn* FRIGHTEN, affray, affright, alarm, fright, scare, startle, terrify *Ant* reassure

terse *Syn* CONCISE, compendious, laconic, pithy, succinct, summary *Ant* redundant

tersely *Syn* SUCCINCTLY, briefly, compactly, concisely, crisply, laconically, pithily, summarily *Ant* diffusely, long-windedly, verbosely, wordily

test *n* *Syn* PROOF, demonstration, trial

test *vb* *Syn* PROVE, demonstrate, try *Ant* disprove

testify · to make a solemn declaration under oath for the purpose of establishing a fact *Syn* attest, depose, swear, witness *Rel* vouch

testimonial *Syn* CREDENTIAL, character, recommendation, reference

testy *Syn* IRASCIBLE, choleric, cranky, cross, splenetic, touchy

tête-à-tête *Syn* CHAT, chatter, chitchat, gabfest, gossip, palaver, rap, small talk, table talk, talk

text *Syn* SUBJECT, argument, leitmotiv, matter, motif, motive, subject matter, theme, topic

thankfulness *Syn* THANKS, appreciation, appreciativeness, gratefulness, gratitude *Ant* ingratitude, thanklessness, ungratefulness

thankless · not showing gratitude *Syn* unappreciative, ungrateful *Rel* rude, thoughtless, ungracious *Ant* appreciative, grateful, obliged, thankful

thanks · acknowledgment of having received something good from another *Syn* appreciation, appreciativeness, gratefulness, gratitude, thankfulness *Rel* thanksgiving *Ant* ingratitude, thanklessness, ungratefulness

thaumaturgy *Syn* MAGIC, alchemy, sorcery, witchcraft, witchery, wizardry

thaw *Syn* LIQUEFY, deliquesce, fuse, melt

theatrical *Syn* DRAMATIC, dramaturgic, histrionic, melodramatic

theft · an unlawful taking of property especially personal property stolen from its rightful owner *Syn* burglary, larceny, robbery

theme **1** *Syn* ESSAY, article, composition, paper **2** *Syn* SUBJECT, argument, leitmotiv, matter, motif, motive, subject matter, text, topic

then *Syn* THEREFORE, accordingly, consequently, hence, so

theorem *Syn* PRINCIPLE, axiom, fundamental, law

theoretical **1** · concerned principally with abstractions and theories *Syn* academic, speculative *Rel* conjectural, hypothetical, supposed **2** *Syn* ABSTRACT (sense 2), conceptual *Ant* concrete

theory · an idea that is the starting point for making a case or conducting an investigation *Syn* hypothesis, proposition, supposition *Rel* assumption, concession, premise, presumption, presupposition

thereafter *Syn* AFTER, afterward (*or* afterwards), later, subsequently *Ant* before, beforehand, earlier, previously

therefore · for this or that reason *Syn* accordingly, consequently, hence, so, then

thesis *Syn* DISCOURSE, disquisition, dissertation, monograph, treatise

thespian *Syn* ACTOR, impersonator, mime, mimic, mummer, performer, player, trouper

thick *n* · the most intense or characteristic phase of something *Syn* deep, depth, height, middle, midst *Rel* center, heart

thick *adj* **1** *Syn* CLOSE (sense 2), compact, dense *Ant* open **2** *Syn* FAMILIAR, chummy, close, confidential, intimate *Ant* aloof **3** *Syn* RIFE, abounding, flush, fraught, replete, swarming, teeming, thronging **4** *Syn* STOCKY, chunky, dumpy, squat, stubby, thickset

thicket · a thick patch of shrubbery, small trees, or underbrush *Syn* brake, brushwood, chaparral, coppice, copse, covert *Rel* canebrake

thickset *Syn* STOCKY, chunky, dumpy, squat, stubby, thick

thief · one that steals especially stealthily or secretly *Syn* burglar, larcener, larcenist, robber

thin *adj* · not thick, broad, abundant, or dense *Syn* rare, slender, slight, slim, tenuous *Rel* gaunt, lank, lanky, lean, spare *Ant* thick

thin *vb* · to make thin or thinner or less dense *Syn* attenuate, dilute, extenuate, rarefy *Rel* decrease, diminish, lessen, reduce *Ant* thicken

thing **1** · whatever is apprehended as having actual, distinct, and demonstrable existence *Syn* article, object *Rel* detail, item, particular

2 *Syn* AFFAIR, business, concern, matter **3** *Syn* GOAL, aim, ambition, aspiration, design, dream, end, intent, intention, mark, meaning, object, objective, plan, pretension, purpose, target

think 1 · to form an idea of *Syn* conceive, envisage, envision, fancy, imagine, realize *Rel* consider, contemplate, study, weigh **2 ·** to use one's powers of conception, judgment, or inference *Syn* cogitate, deliberate, reason, reflect, speculate *Rel* meditate, muse, ponder, ruminate **3** *Syn* BELIEVE (sense 1), consider, deem, feel, figure, guess, hold, imagine, suppose *Ant* disbelieve, discredit, reject

think (up) *Syn* INVENT, concoct, contrive, cook (up), devise, fabricate, make up, manufacture

thinned *Syn* IMPURE, adulterated, alloyed, contaminated, dilute, diluted, polluted, tainted, weakened *Ant* pure, unadulterated, unalloyed, uncontaminated, undiluted, unpolluted, untainted

thirst *Syn* LONG, hanker, hunger, pine, yearn

thorough *Syn* EXHAUSTIVE, comprehensive, full-scale, out-and-out, thoroughgoing, total

thoroughgoing *Syn* EXHAUSTIVE, all-out, clean, complete, comprehensive, full-scale, out-and-out, thorough, total

though *Syn* ALTHOUGH, albeit, howbeit, when, while

thought *Syn* IDEA, concept, conception, impression, notion

thoughtful 1 · characterized by or exhibiting the power to think *Syn* contemplative, meditative, pensive, reflective, speculative *Rel* earnest, grave, serious, sober **2 ·** mindful of others *Syn* attentive, considerate *Rel* anxious, careful, concerned, solicitous *Ant* thoughtless **3** *Syn* CONTEMPLATIVE, meditative, melancholy, pensive, reflective, ruminant *Ant* unreflective

thoughtless 1 *Syn* CARELESS, heedless, inadvertent *Ant* careful **2** *Syn* IMPOLITE, discourteous, ill-bred, ill-mannered, impertinent, inconsiderate, rude, uncalled-for, uncivil, ungracious, unmannerly *Ant* civil, considerate, courteous, genteel, gracious, mannerly, polite, thoughtful, well-bred

thrall *Syn* SLAVE (sense 1), bondman, bondsman, chattel *Ant* freeman

thrash 1 *Syn* BEAT, baste, belabor, buffet, pound, pummel **2** *Syn* SWING (sense 1), brandish, flourish, shake, wave

threadbare 1 *Syn* SHABBY, dilapidated, dingy, faded, seedy **2** *Syn* STALE, banal, commonplace, hackney, hackneyed, motheaten, musty, stereotyped, tired, trite *Ant* fresh, new, original

threat *Syn* DANGER (sense 1), hazard, menace, peril, pitfall, risk, trouble *Ant* safeness, safety, security

threatening *Syn* OMINOUS, baleful, dire, foreboding, inauspicious, menacing, portentous, sinister

threshold *Syn* BEGINNING, alpha, birth, commencement, dawn, genesis, inception, incipiency, launch, morning, onset, outset, start *Ant* close, conclusion, end, ending

thrift *Syn* ECONOMY, frugality, husbandry, providence, scrimping, skimping *Ant* wastefulness

thriftless *Syn* PRODIGAL, extravagant, profligate, spendthrift, squandering, unthrifty, wasteful *Ant* conserving, economical, economizing, frugal, scrimping, skimping, thrifty

thrifty *Syn* FRUGAL, economical, economizing, provident, scrimping, sparing *Ant* prodigal, wasteful

thrill *n ·* a pleasurably intense stimulation of the feelings *Syn* bang, exhilaration, kick, titillation *Rel* arousal, electrification, intoxication, stimulation

thrill *vb ·* to excite with emotions that provoke pleasurable sensations or to be so excited *Syn* electrify, enthuse *Rel* excite, galvanize, provoke, quicken, stimulate

thrive *Syn* SUCCEED, flourish, prosper *Ant* attempt, fail

throb *vb Syn* PULSATE, beat, palpitate, pulse

throb *n Syn* PULSATION, beat, palpitation, pulse

throe *Syn* PAIN, ache, pang, stitch, twinge

throng *Syn* CROWD, crush, horde, mob, press, rout

thronging *Syn* RIFE, abounding, flush, fraught, replete, swarming, teeming, thick

throttle *Syn* SUFFOCATE, asphyxiate, choke, smother, stifle, strangle

through 1 *Syn* AMONG, amid (*or* amidst), mid, midst **2** *Syn* BECAUSE OF, due to, owing to, with **3** *Syn* AROUND (sense 2), about, over, round, throughout **4** *Syn* BY, with

throughout *Syn* AROUND (sense 2), about, over, round, through

throw · to cause to move swiftly through space by a propulsive movement or a propelling force *Syn* cast, fling, hurl, pitch, sling, toss *Rel* drive, impel

throw up *Syn* BELCH, burp, disgorge, regurgitate, spew, vomit

thrust *Syn* PUSH, propel, shove

thud *n Syn* TAP, knock, rap, thump

thud *vb Syn* TAP, knock, rap, thump

thump *n Syn* TAP, knock, rap, thud

thump *vb Syn* TAP, knock, rap, thud

thwart *Syn* FRUSTRATE, baffle, balk, circumvent, foil, outwit *Ant* fulfill

ticket *n Syn* MARK, brand, label, stamp, tag

ticket *vb Syn* MARK, brand, label, stamp, tag

tickle *Syn* PLEASE, delight, gladden, gratify, regale, rejoice *Ant* anger, displease, vex

tide *Syn* FLOW, current, flood, flux, stream

tidings

tidings *Syn* NEWS, information, intelligence, item, story, word

tidy **1** *Syn* LARGE, big, bulky, considerable, goodly, good-sized, grand, great, handsome, hefty, hulking, largish, outsize, oversize (*or* oversized), sizable (*or* sizeable), substantial, voluminous *Ant* little, puny, small, undersized **2** *Syn* NEAT, shipshape, snug, spick-and-span, trig, trim *Ant* filthy

tie **1** *Syn* BOND, band **2** *Syn* DRAW, deadlock, stalemate, standoff

tier *Syn* LINE, echelon, file, rank, row

tiff *Syn* QUARREL, altercation, bickering, spat, squabble, wrangle

tight **1** · fitting, drawn, or stretched so that there is no slackness or looseness *Syn* taut, tense *Rel* rigid, strict, stringent *Ant* loose **2** *Syn* DRUNK, drunken, inebriated, intoxicated, tipsy *Ant* sober **3** *Syn* STINGY, cheeseparing, close, closefisted, miserly, niggardly, parsimonious, penny-pinching, penurious, tightfisted

tightfisted *Syn* STINGY, cheeseparing, close, closefisted, miserly, niggardly, parsimonious, penny-pinching, penurious, tight *Ant* generous

tight-lipped *Syn* SILENT (sense 1), close, close-lipped, closemouthed, reserved, reticent, secretive, taciturn, uncommunicative *Ant* talkative

tilted *Syn* AWRY, askew, aslant, cockeyed, crooked, listing, lopsided, oblique, skewed, slanted, slanting, slantwise, tipping, uneven *Ant* even, level, straight

time **1** *Syn* AGE (sense 3), day, epoch, era, period **2** *Syn* OPPORTUNITY, break, chance, occasion

timely *Syn* SEASONABLE, opportune, pat, well-timed *Ant* unseasonable

timetable *Syn* PROGRAM, agenda, schedule

timidity · lack of willingness to assert oneself and take risks *Syn* faintheartedness, timidness, timorousness *Rel* bashfulness, constraint, embarrassment, inhibition, restraint, shyness, skittishness *Ant* audaciousness, audacity, boldness, guts, nerve

timidness *Syn* TIMIDITY, faintheartedness, timorousness *Ant* audaciousness, audacity, boldness, guts, nerve

timorousness *Syn* TIMIDITY, faintheartedness, timidness *Ant* audaciousness, audacity, boldness, guts, nerve

tincture **1** *Syn* PIGMENT, color, coloring, dye, dyestuff, stain **2** *Syn* TOUCH, dash, shade, smack, soupçon, spice, strain, streak, suggestion, suspicion, tinge, vein

tinge **1** *Syn* COLOR, hue, shade, tint, tone **2** *Syn* TOUCH, dash, shade, smack, soupçon, spice, strain, streak, suggestion, suspicion, tincture, vein

tint *Syn* COLOR, hue, shade, tinge, tone

tiny · very small in size *Syn* atomic, bitty, in-finitesimal, microminiature, microscopic, miniature, minute, teeny, teeny-weeny, wee *Rel* diminutive, dinky, dwarf, dwarfish, insignificant, little, midget, model, petite, pint-size (*or* pint-sized), pocket, pocket-size, puny, pygmy, scrubby, small, smallish, undersized *Ant* astronomical, colossal, cosmic, elephantine, enormous, giant, gigantic, herculean, heroic, huge, immense, mammoth, massive, monster, monstrous, monumental, mountainous, prodigious, titanic, tremendous

tip *Syn* BONUS, dividend, extra, gratuity, gravy, lagniappe, perquisite

tipping *Syn* AWRY, askew, aslant, cockeyed, crooked, listing, lopsided, oblique, skewed, slanted, slanting, slantwise, tilted, uneven *Ant* even, level, straight

tippler *Syn* DRUNKARD, alcoholic, dipsomaniac, inebriate, soak, sot, toper, tosspot *Ant* teetotaler

tipsy *Syn* DRUNK, drunken, inebriated, intoxicated, tight *Ant* sober

tip-top *Syn* EXCELLENT, A1, bang-up, banner, capital, classic, crackerjack, dandy, divine, fabulous, fine, first-class, first-rate, grand, great, groovy, heavenly, jim-dandy, keen, marvelous (*or* marvellous), mean, neat, nifty, noble, par excellence, prime, sensational, splendid, stellar, sterling, superb, superior, superlative, supernal, swell, terrific, top, top-notch, unsurpassed, wonderful *Ant* poor

tirade · a violent, often long-winded, and usually denunciatory speech or writing *Syn* diatribe, jeremiad, philippic *Rel* harangue, oration, speech *Ant* eulogy

tire · to make or become unable or unwilling to continue (as from a loss of physical strength or endurance) *Syn* exhaust, fatigue, jade, tucker, weary *Rel* annoy, bother, irk, vex

tired *Syn* STALE, banal, commonplace, hackney, hackneyed, moth-eaten, musty, stereotyped, threadbare, trite *Ant* fresh, new, original

tiredness *Syn* FATIGUE, burnout, collapse, exhaustion, lassitude, prostration, weariness *Ant* refreshment, rejuvenation, revitalization

tireless *Syn* INDEFATIGABLE, unflagging, untiring, unwearied, unwearying, weariless

tiresome *Syn* BORING, drab, dreary, dry, dull, flat, heavy, humdrum, jading, leaden, monotonous, pedestrian, ponderous, stodgy, stuffy, stupid, tame, tedious, tiring, unanimated, uninteresting, wearisome, weary, wearying *Ant* absorbing, engaging, engrossing, gripping, interesting, intriguing, involving

tiring *Syn* BORING, drab, dreary, dry, dull, flat, heavy, humdrum, jading, leaden, monotonous, pedestrian, ponderous, stodgy, stuffy, stupid, tame, tedious, tiresome, unanimated, uninteresting, wearisome, weary, wearying

Ant absorbing, engaging, engrossing, gripping, interesting, intriguing, involving

titan *Syn* GIANT, behemoth, blockbuster, colossus, jumbo, leviathan, mammoth, monster, whale, whopper *Ant* dwarf, midget, mini, miniature, peewee, pygmy, runt, shrimp

titanic *Syn* HUGE, Brobdingnagian, colossal, cyclopean, elephantine, enormous, gargantuan, giant, gigantean, gigantic, Herculean, immense, mammoth, vast *Ant* bitty, diminutive, microscopic (*or* microscopical), midget, miniature, minute, pocket, pygmy, teeny, teeny-weeny, tiny, wee

titillation *Syn* THRILL, bang, exhilaration, kick

title **1** *Syn* CLAIM, pretense, pretension **2** *Syn* NAME, appellation, denomination, designation, style

tittle *Syn* PARTICLE, atom, bit, iota, jot, mite, smidgen, whit

to *Syn* BEFORE, ahead of, ere, of, previous, prior to, to *Ant* after, following

toady *vb Syn* FAWN, cower, cringe, truckle *Ant* domineer

toady *n* **1** *Syn* PARASITE, bootlicker, favorite, hanger-on, leech, lickspittle, sponge, sponger, sycophant **2** *Syn* SYCOPHANT, fawner, flunky

toboggan *Syn* SLIDE, coast, glide, glissade, skid, slip, slither

to-do *Syn* COMMOTION, bother, bustle, clatter, disturbance, furor, furore, fuss, hubbub, hullabaloo, hurly-burly, pandemonium, pother, row, ruckus, ruction, rumpus, shindy, squall, stew, stir, storm, tumult, turmoil, uproar, welter, whirl

toil *vb Syn* LABOR, drudge, endeavor, grub, hump, hustle, moil, peg (away), plod, plow, plug, slave, slog, strain, strive, struggle, sweat, travail, work *Ant* dabble, fiddle (around), fool (around), mess (around), putter (around)

toil *n Syn* WORK (sense 1), drudgery, grind, labor, travail *Ant* play

toiler *Syn* SLAVE (sense 2), drudge, drudger, grubber, laborer, peon, plugger, slogger, worker *Ant* freeman

token **1** *Syn* MEMORIAL, commemorative, keepsake, memento, monument, remembrance, reminder, souvenir **2** *Syn* PLEDGE, earnest, hostage, pawn **3** *Syn* SIGN (sense 1), badge, mark, note, symptom

tolerable **1** *Syn* ADEQUATE, acceptable, all right, decent, fine, OK (*or* okay), passable, respectable, satisfactory *Ant* deficient, inadequate, lacking, unacceptable, unsatisfactory, wanting **2** *Syn* BEARABLE, endurable, sufferable, supportable, sustainable *Ant* insufferable, insupportable, intolerable, unbearable, unendurable, unsupportable

tolerance *Syn* FORBEARANCE, clemency, indulgence, leniency, mercifulness *Ant* anger, vindictiveness

tolerant **1** *Syn* FORBEARING, clement, indulgent, lenient, merciful *Ant* unrelenting **2** *Syn* PASSIVE, acquiescent, nonresistant, resigned, tolerating, unresistant, unresisting, yielding *Ant* protesting, resistant, resisting, unyielding

tolerantly *Syn* FORBEARINGLY, clemently, indulgently, leniently, mercifully

tolerate *Syn* BEAR (sense 2), abide, brook, endure, stand, suffer

tolerating *Syn* PASSIVE, acquiescent, nonresistant, resigned, tolerant, unresistant, unresisting, yielding *Ant* protesting, resistant, resisting, unyielding

tomfoolery *Syn* HORSEPLAY, clowning, foolery, high jinks, horsing (around), monkeying, monkeyshines, roughhouse, roughhousing, shenanigans, skylarking

tone *Syn* COLOR, hue, shade, tinge, tint

tongue *Syn* LANGUAGE (sense 1), dialect, idiom, speech

tongue-lash *Syn* SCOLD, bawl, berate, chew out, jaw, rail, rate, revile, upbraid, vituperate, wig

tonic · having a renewing effect on the state of the body or mind *Syn* bracing, invigorating, refreshing, restorative, reviving, stimulating, stimulative, vitalizing *Rel* conditioning, strengthening

too *Syn* VERY, awful, awfully, beastly, deadly, especially, exceedingly, extra, extremely, far, frightfully, full, greatly, heavily, highly, hugely, jolly, mightily, mighty, mortally, most, much, particularly, rattling, real, right, so, something, super, terribly, whacking *Ant* little, negligibly, nominally, slightly

tool **1** *Syn* DUPE, chump, gull, pigeon, sap, sucker **2** *Syn* IMPLEMENT, appliance, instrument, utensil

toothsome *Syn* PALATABLE, appetizing, flavorsome, relishing, sapid, savory, tasty *Ant* distasteful, unpalatable

top *Syn* EXCELLENT, A1, bang-up, banner, capital, classic, crackerjack, dandy, divine, fabulous, fine, first-class, first-rate, grand, great, groovy, heavenly, jim-dandy, keen, marvelous (*or* marvellous), mean, neat, nifty, noble, par excellence, prime, sensational, splendid, stellar, sterling, superb, superior, superlative, supernal, swell, terrific, tip-top, top-notch, unsurpassed, wonderful *Ant* poor

toper *Syn* DRUNKARD, alcoholic, dipsomaniac, inebriate, soak, sot, tippler, tosspot *Ant* teetotaler

topic *Syn* SUBJECT, argument, leitmotiv, matter, motif, motive, subject matter, text, theme

top-notch *Syn* EXCELLENT, A1, bang-up, banner, capital, classic, crackerjack, dandy, divine, fabulous, fine, first-class, first-rate, grand, great, groovy, heavenly, jim-dandy, keen, marvelous (*or* marvellous), mean, neat, nifty, noble, par excellence, prime, sensational, splendid, stellar, sterling, superb, superior, superlative, supernal, swell, terrific, tip-top, top, unsurpassed, wonderful *Ant* poor

topsy-turvy *Syn* MESSY, chaotic, cluttered, confused, disarranged, disarrayed, disheveled (*or* dishevelled), disordered, disorderly, higgledy-piggledy, hugger-mugger, jumbled, littered, messed, muddled, mussed, mussy, pell-mell, rumpled, sloppy, tousled, tumbled, unkempt, untidy, upside-down *Ant* neat, ordered, orderly, organized, shipshape, snug, tidied, tidy, trim

torment *Syn* AFFLICT, agonize, bedevil, curse, harrow, martyr, persecute, plague, rack, torture

tornado · a violent whirling wind accompanied by a funnel-shaped cloud *Syn* cyclone, twister *Rel* whirlwind, whirly

torpid *Syn* LETHARGIC, comatose, sluggish *Ant* energetic, vigorous

torpidity *Syn* LETHARGY, languor, lassitude, stupor, torpor *Ant* vigor

torpor *Syn* LETHARGY, languor, lassitude, stupor, torpidity *Ant* vigor

torrent *Syn* FLOOD, cataract, deluge, inundation, spate

tortuous *Syn* WINDING, flexuous, serpentine, sinuous *Ant* straight

torture *Syn* AFFLICT, agonize, bedevil, devil, harrow, martyr, persecute, plague, rack, torment

toss *Syn* THROW, cast, fling, hurl, pitch, sling

tosspot *Syn* DRUNKARD, alcoholic, dipsomaniac, inebriate, soak, sot, tippler, toper *Ant* teetotaler

total *vb Syn* ADD (sense 1), foot (up), sum *Ant* deduct, remove, subtract, take

total *adj* **1** *Syn* EXHAUSTIVE, all-out, clean, complete, comprehensive, full-scale, out-and-out, thorough, thoroughgoing **2** *Syn* WHOLE, all, entire, gross *Ant* partial

total *n Syn* SUM, aggregate, amount, number, quantity, whole

totter **1** *Syn* REEL, stagger, whirl **2** *Syn* SHAKE (sense 1), dither, quake, quaver, quiver, shimmy, shiver, shudder, teeter, tremble, wobble

touch *n* · a very small amount or perceptible trace of something added *Syn* dash, shade, smack, soupçon, spice, strain, streak, suggestion, suspicion, tincture, tinge, vein *Rel* trace, vestige

touch *vb* **1** · to probe with a sensitive part of the body (as a finger) so as to get or produce a sensation often in the course of examining or exploring *Syn* feel, handle, palpate, paw *Rel* examine, inspect, scrutinize **2** *Syn* AFFECT, impress, influence, strike, sway **3** *Syn* MATCH, approach, equal, rival

touchable *Syn* TANGIBLE, palpable *Ant* impalpable, intangible

touch down *Syn* ALIGHT, land, light, perch, roost, settle *Ant* take off

touching **1** *Syn* ADJACENT, abutting, adjoining, bordering, contiguous, flanking, fringing, joining, juxtaposed, skirting, verging *Ant* nonadjacent **2** *Syn* MOVING, affecting, emotional, impressive, poignant, stirring *Ant* unemotional, unimpressive

touch off *Syn* ACTIVATE, actuate, crank (up), drive, move, propel, run, set off, spark, start, trigger, turn on *Ant* cut, deactivate, kill, shut off, turn off

touchstone *Syn* STANDARD, criterion, gauge, yardstick

touchy *Syn* IRASCIBLE, choleric, cranky, cross, splenetic, testy

tough *Syn* STRONG, stalwart, stout, sturdy, tenacious *Ant* weak

tour **1** *Syn* JOURNEY, cruise, excursion, expedition, jaunt, pilgrimage, trip, voyage **2** *Syn* SPELL, bout, go, shift, stint, trick, turn

tousle *Syn* DISORDER, confuse, derange, disarrange, disarray, discompose, dishevel, dislocate, disorganize, disrupt, disturb, hash, jumble, mess (up), mix (up), muddle, muss, rumple, scramble, shuffle, tumble, upset *Ant* arrange, array, draw up, marshal, order, organize, range, regulate, straighten (up), tidy

tousled *Syn* MESSY, chaotic, cluttered, confused, disarranged, disarrayed, disheveled (*or* dishevelled), disordered, disorderly, higgledy-piggledy, hugger-mugger, jumbled, littered, messed, muddled, mussed, mussy, pell-mell, rumpled, sloppy, topsy-turvy, tumbled, unkempt, untidy, upside-down *Ant* neat, ordered, orderly, organized, shipshape, snug, tidied, tidy, trim

tout *Syn* ACCLAIM, applaud, cheer, hail, laud, praise, salute *Ant* knock, pan, slam

tow *Syn* PULL, drag, draw, hale, haul, tug

town *Syn* CITY, burg, megalopolis, metropolis, municipality

toxic *Syn* POISONOUS, mephitic, miasmal, miasmatic, miasmic, pestilent, pestilential, venomous, virulent *Ant* nonpoisonous, nontoxic, nonvenomous

toxin *Syn* POISON, bane, venom, virus

trace *vb Syn* SKETCH, blueprint, delineate, diagram, draft, outline, plot

trace *n Syn* VESTIGE, relic, shadow

tracing **1** *Syn* PURSUIT, chase, chasing, dogging, following, hounding, pursuing, shadowing, tagging, tailing, tracking, trailing **2** *Syn* SKETCH, blueprint, delineation, diagram, draft, outline, plot

tracking *Syn* PURSUIT, chase, chasing, dogging, following, hounding, pursuing, shadowing, tagging, tailing, tracing, trailing

tract *Syn* AREA, belt, region, zone

tractable *Syn* OBEDIENT, amenable, compliant, conformable, docile, law-abiding, submissive *Ant* contrary, disobedient, froward, insubordinate, intractable, rebellious, recalcitrant, refractory, unruly

trade *n* **1 ·** a pursuit followed as an occupation or means of livelihood and requiring technical knowledge and skill *Syn* art, craft, handicraft, profession *Rel* employment, occupation, pursuit, work **2** *Syn* BUSINESS, commerce, industry, traffic **3** *Syn* OCCUPATION, calling, employment, line, profession, vocation, work **4** *Syn* SALE, deal, transaction

trade *vb Syn* CHANGE (sense 3), commute, exchange, shift, substitute, swap, switch

trader *Syn* MERCHANT, dealer, merchandiser, tradesman, trafficker

tradesman 1 *Syn* ARTISAN, artificer, craftsman, handicrafter **2** *Syn* MERCHANT, dealer, merchandiser, trader, trafficker

tradition *Syn* FOLKLORE, legend, lore, myth, mythology

traditional *Syn* CONSERVATIVE, orthodox *Ant* liberal, nontraditional, progressive

traduce *Syn* SLANDER, asperse, blacken, defame, libel, malign, smear, vilify

traffic *Syn* BUSINESS, commerce, industry, trade

trafficker *Syn* MERCHANT, dealer, merchandiser, trader, tradesman

trailer *Syn* CAMPER, caravan, mobile home, motor home

trailing *Syn* PURSUIT, chase, chasing, dogging, following, hounding, pursuing, shadowing, tagging, tailing, tracing, tracking

train *n Syn* SUCCESSION, chain, progression, sequence, series, string

train *vb Syn* TEACH, discipline, educate, instruct, school

training *Syn* EDUCATION (sense 1), instruction, schooling, teaching, tutelage, tutoring

traipse 1 *Syn* WALK, foot (it), hoof (it), leg (it), pad, step, tread **2** *Syn* WANDER, gad, gallivant, meander, prowl, ramble, range, roam, rove, stray

trait *Syn* CHARACTERISTIC, attribute, character, feature, mark, peculiarity, point, property, quality

traitor · one who betrays a trust or an allegiance *Syn* betrayer, double-crosser, quisling, recreant, turncoat *Rel* collaborationist, collaborator, subversive

traitorous *Syn* FAITHLESS, disloyal, false, perfidious, treacherous *Ant* faithful

trammel *n Syn* ENCUMBRANCE, bar, block, chain, clog, crimp, deterrent, drag, embarrassment, fetter, handicap, hindrance, hurdle, impediment, inhibition, interference, let, manacle, obstacle, obstruction, shackles, stop, stumbling block *Ant* aid, assistance, benefit, help

trammel *vb Syn* HAMPER, clog, fetter, hog-tie, manacle, shackle *Ant* assist (*persons*), expedite (*work, projects*)

tramp *vb Syn* TRAMPLE, stamp, stomp, tromp

tramp *n Syn* VAGABOND, bum, hobo, truant, vagrant

trample · to tread on heavily so as to crush or injure *Syn* stamp, stomp, tramp, tromp *Rel* override, run down, run over, step (on)

trance *Syn* REVERIE, daydreaming, study, woolgathering

tranquil *Syn* CALM, halcyon, peaceful, placid, serene *Ant* agitated, stormy

tranquilize *Syn* CALM, compose, lull, quiet, quieten, settle, soothe, still *Ant* agitate, arouse

tranquillity *or* **tranquility 1** *Syn* CALM, calmness, hush, peace, peacefulness, placidity, quiet, quietness, quietude, repose, restfulness, sereneness, serenity, still, stillness *Ant* bustle, commotion, hubbub, hurly-burly, pandemonium, tumult, turmoil, uproar **2** *Syn* EQUANIMITY, aplomb, calmness, composure, coolheadedness, coolness, imperturbability, placidity, self-possession, serenity *Ant* agitation, discomposure, perturbation

transaction *Syn* SALE, deal, trade

transcend *Syn* EXCEED, excel, outdo, outstrip, surpass

transcendent 1 *Syn* ABSTRACT (sense 1), ideal, transcendental *Ant* concrete **2** *Syn* SUPREME, incomparable, peerless, preeminent, superlative, surpassing

transcendental *Syn* ABSTRACT (sense 1), ideal, transcendent *Ant* concrete

transfer 1 · to shift title or possession from one owner to another *Syn* alienate, convey, deed **2** *Syn* COMMUNICATE, convey, impart, spread, transfuse, transmit **3** *Syn* MOVE (sense 2), remove, shift

transfiguration *Syn* TRANSFORMATION, conversion, metamorphosis, transmogrification, transmutation

transfigure 1 *Syn* CONVERT, make over, metamorphose, transform **2** *Syn* TRANSFORM, convert, metamorphose, transmogrify, transmute

transform 1 · to change a thing into a different thing *Syn* convert, metamorphose, transfigure, transmogrify, transmute *Rel* alter, change, modify, vary **2** *Syn* CONVERT, make over, metamorphose, transfigure

transformation · a change of one thing into another different thing *Syn* conversion, metamorphosis, transfiguration, transmutation *Rel* alteration, change, modification, variation

transfuse *Syn* COMMUNICATE, convey, impart, spread, transfer, transmit

transgression *Syn* BREACH (sense 1), contravention, infraction, infringement, trespass, violation

transient *Syn* MOMENTARY, ephemeral, evanescent, flash, fleeting, fugitive, impermanent, passing, short-lived, temporary, transitory *Ant* enduring, eternal, everlasting, lasting, long-lived, permanent, perpetual

transitory *Syn* MOMENTARY, ephemeral, evanescent, flash, fleeting, fugitive, impermanent, passing, short-lived, temporary, transient *Ant* eternal, everlasting, lasting, long-lived, permanent, perpetual

translate *Syn* PARAPHRASE, rephrase, restate, reword *Ant* quote

translation · a restating often in a simpler language of something previously stated or written *Syn* metaphrase, paraphrase, version

translucent *Syn* CLEAR (sense 1), diaphanous, limpid, lucid, pellucid, transparent *Ant* confused, turbid

transmit 1 *Syn* CARRY, bear, convey, transport 2 *Syn* COMMUNICATE, convey, impart, spread, transfer, transfuse 3 *Syn* SEND, dispatch, forward, remit, route, ship *Ant* accept, receive

transmogrification *Syn* TRANSFORMATION, conversion, metamorphosis, transfiguration, transmutation

transmogrify *Syn* TRANSFORM, convert, metamorphose, transfigure, transmute

transmutation *Syn* TRANSFORMATION, conversion, metamorphosis, transfiguration

transmute *Syn* TRANSFORM, convert, metamorphose, transfigure, transmogrify

transparent *Syn* CLEAR (sense 1), diaphanous, limpid, lucid, pellucid, translucent *Ant* confused, turbid

transpire *Syn* HAPPEN, befall, betide, chance, occur

transport *vb* 1 · to carry away by strong and usually pleasurable emotion *Syn* enrapture, entrance, ravish *Rel* excite, provoke, quicken, stimulate 2 *Syn* BANISH, deport, exile, expatriate, extradite, ostracize 3 *Syn* CARRY, bear, convey, transmit 4 *Syn* ELATE, elevate, enrapture, exhilarate, overjoy *Ant* depress 5 *Syn* ENTRANCE, carry away, enrapture, enthrall (*or* enthral), overjoy, ravish

transport *n Syn* ECSTASY, elation, euphoria, exhilaration, heaven, intoxication, paradise, rapture, rhapsody *Ant* depression

transpose *Syn* REVERSE, invert

trap 1 *Syn* CATCH, bag, capture, ensnare, entrap, snare *Ant* miss 2 *Syn* ENTANGLE, enmesh, ensnare, entrap, mesh, snare, tangle *Ant* disentangle

trash 1 *Syn* NONSENSE, balderdash, bull, bunk, drivel, gobbledygook, poppycock, rot, twaddle 2 *Syn* REFUSE, debris, garbage, offal, rubbish, waste

trauma *Syn* WOUND, bruise, contusion, lesion, traumatism

traumatism *Syn* WOUND, bruise, contusion, lesion, trauma

travail *vb Syn* LABOR, drudge, endeavor, grub, hump, hustle, moil, peg (away), plod, plow,

plug, slave, slog, strain, strive, struggle, sweat, toil, work *Ant* dabble, fiddle (around), fool (around), mess (around), putter (around)

travail *n Syn* WORK (sense 1), drudgery, grind, labor, toil *Ant* play

travel *Syn* TRAVERSE, cover, crisscross, cross, cut (across), follow, go, pass (over), proceed (along)

traverse 1 · to make one's way through, across, or over *Syn* cover, crisscross, cross, cut (across), follow, go, pass (over), proceed (along), travel *Rel* hike, tread, walk 2 *Syn* DENY, contradict, contravene, gainsay, impugn, negative *Ant* concede, confirm

travesty *n Syn* CARICATURE, burlesque, parody

travesty *vb Syn* CARICATURE, burlesque, parody

treacherous *Syn* FAITHLESS, disloyal, false, perfidious, traitorous *Ant* faithful

treachery *Syn* BETRAYAL, disloyalty, double cross, faithlessness, falseness, falsity, infidelity, perfidy, sellout, treason, unfaithfulness

tread *Syn* WALK, foot (it), hoof (it), leg (it), pad, step, traipse

treason *Syn* BETRAYAL, disloyalty, double cross, faithlessness, falseness, falsity, infidelity, perfidy, sellout, treachery, unfaithfulness

treasure *Syn* APPRECIATE, cherish, prize, value *Ant* despise

treat · to have to do with or behave toward (a person or thing) in a specified manner *Syn* deal, handle *Rel* conduct, manage

treatise *Syn* DISCOURSE, disquisition, dissertation, monograph, thesis

treaty *Syn* CONTRACT, bargain, cartel, compact, concordat, convention, entente, pact

treble *Syn* SHRILL, acute, high-pitched, piping, screeching, shrieking, squeaking, squeaky, whistling *Ant* bass, deep, low, throaty

tremble *Syn* SHAKE (sense 1), dither, quake, quaver, quiver, shimmy, shiver, shudder, teeter, totter, wobble

tremendous *Syn* MONSTROUS, monumental, prodigious, stupendous

trenchant *Syn* INCISIVE, biting, clear-cut, crisp, cutting

trend *Syn* TENDENCY, drift, tenor

trepidation *Syn* FEAR, alarm, consternation, dismay, dread, fright, horror, panic, terror *Ant* fearlessness

trespass *vb* · to make inroads upon the property, territory, or rights of another *Syn* encroach, entrench, infringe, invade *Rel* butt in, interlope, intrude, obtrude

trespass *n Syn* BREACH (sense 1), contravention, infraction, infringement, transgression, violation

trial 1 · the state or fact of being tested (as by suffering) *Syn* affliction, cross, tribulation, visitation *Rel* agony, distress, misery,

suffering 2 *Syn* ATTEMPT, crack, endeavor, essay, fling, go, pass, shot, stab, try, whack 3 *Syn* PROOF, demonstration, test 4 *Syn* REHEARSAL, dry run, practice

tribulation *Syn* TRIAL, affliction, cross, visitation

tributary *Syn* SUBORDINATE, collateral, dependent, secondary, subject *Ant* chief, dominant, leading

tribute *Syn* ENCOMIUM, citation, eulogy, panegyric

trice *Syn* INSTANT, flash, jiffy, minute, moment, second, shake, split second, twinkle, twinkling, wink

trick *n* 1 · an indirect means to gain an end *Syn* artifice, feint, gambit, maneuver, ploy, ruse, stratagem, wile *Rel* cheat, counterfeit, deceit, deception, fake, fraud, humbug, imposture 2 *Syn* HABIT, custom, fashion, pattern, practice, way, wont 3 *Syn* SPELL, bout, go, shift, stint, tour, turn

trick *vb Syn* DUPE, bamboozle, befool, gull, hoax, hoodwink

trickery 1 · the use of clever underhanded actions to achieve an end *Syn* artifice, chicanery, hanky-panky, jugglery, legerdemain, subterfuge, wile *Rel* artfulness, caginess, craftiness, cunning, deviousness, foxiness, shadiness, sharpness, shiftiness, slickness, slipperiness, slyness, sneakiness, treachery, underhandedness, wiliness 2 *Syn* DECEPTION, chicane, chicanery, double-dealing, fraud

trickster *Syn* MAGICIAN (sense 2), conjurer (*or* conjuror), prestidigitator

tricky *Syn* SLY, artful, crafty, cunning, foxy, guileful, insidious, wily

tried *Syn* DEPENDABLE, good, reliable, responsible, safe, solid, steady, sure, tried-and-true, true, trustworthy, trusty *Ant* irresponsible, undependable, unreliable, untrustworthy

tried-and-true *Syn* DEPENDABLE, good, reliable, responsible, safe, solid, steady, sure, tried, true, trustworthy, trusty *Ant* irresponsible, undependable, unreliable, untrustworthy

trifle *n* · something of little importance *Syn* child's play, frippery, nothing, triviality *Rel* naught, nothingness, smoke, zero

trifle *vb Syn* FLIRT, dally, frivol

trifling 1 *Syn* PETTY, measly, paltry, picayune, picayunish, puny, trivial *Ant* gross, important, momentous 2 *Syn* UNIMPORTANT, frivolous, inconsequential, inconsiderable, insignificant, little, minor, minute, negligible, slight, small, small-fry, trivial *Ant* big, consequential, eventful, important, major, material, meaningful, momentous, significant, substantial, weighty

trig *Syn* NEAT, shipshape, snug, spick-and-span, tidy, trim *Ant* filthy

trigger *Syn* ACTIVATE, actuate, crank (up),

drive, move, propel, run, set off, spark, start, touch off, turn on *Ant* cut, deactivate, kill, shut off, turn off

trill *Syn* SING, carol, chant, descant, hymn, intone, troll, warble

trim *vb* 1 *Syn* CLIP, bob, crop, curtail, cut, cut back, dock, lop (off), nip, pare, prune, shave, shear, snip 2 *Syn* STABILIZE, balance, ballast, poise, steady

trim *adj Syn* NEAT, shipshape, snug, spick-and-span, tidy, trig *Ant* filthy

trinket *Syn* KNICKKNACK, bauble, curio, curiosity, gaud, gewgaw, novelty, ornamental

trip *n Syn* JOURNEY, cruise, excursion, expedition, jaunt, pilgrimage, tour, voyage

trip *vb Syn* STUMBLE, blunder, bumble, flounder, galumph, lollop, lumber, lurch

trite *Syn* STALE, banal, commonplace, hackney, hackneyed, moth-eaten, musty, stereotyped, threadbare, tired *Ant* fresh, new, original

triumph *Syn* VICTORY, conquest *Ant* defeat

triumphant *Syn* EXULTANT, exulting, glorying, jubilant, rejoicing

trivial 1 *Syn* PETTY, measly, paltry, picayune, picayunish, puny, trifling *Ant* gross, important, momentous 2 *Syn* UNIMPORTANT, frivolous, inconsequential, inconsiderable, insignificant, little, minor, minute, negligible, slight, small, small-fry, trifling *Ant* big, consequential, eventful, important, major, material, meaningful, momentous, significant, substantial, weighty

triviality *Syn* TRIFLE, child's play, frippery, nothing

troll *Syn* SING, carol, chant, descant, hymn, intone, trill, warble

tromp *Syn* TRAMPLE, stamp, stomp, tramp

troop *Syn* COMPANY, band, party, troupe

tropical storm *Syn* HURRICANE, typhoon

trot *Syn* HURRY (sense 2), barrel, bolt, bowl, breeze, career, course, dash, fly, hasten, hotfoot (it), hump, hurtle, hustle, pelt, race, rip, rocket, run, rush, rustle, scoot, scurry, scuttle, shoot, speed, step (along), tear, whirl, whisk, zip, zoom *Ant* crawl, creep, poke

troth *Syn* PROMISE, oath, pledge, vow, word

troubadour *Syn* POET, bard, minstrel, poetaster, rhymer, rhymester, versifier

trouble *vb* 1 · to cause to be uneasy or upset *Syn* ail, distress *Rel* agitate, discompose, disquiet, disturb, perturb, upset 2 *Syn* INCONVENIENCE, discommode, disoblige, disturb, incommode *Ant* accommodate, oblige

trouble *n* 1 *Syn* DANGER (sense 1), hazard, menace, peril, pitfall, risk, threat *Ant* safeness, safety, security 2 *Syn* EFFORT, exertion, pains *Ant* ease 3 *Syn* DANGER (sense 2), distress, endangerment, imperilment, jeopardy, peril, risk *Ant* safeness, safety, security

troublesome · causing worry or anxiety *Syn*

discomforting, discomposing, disquieting, distressing, disturbing, perturbing, troubling, troublous, unsettling, upsetting, worrisome *Rel* daunting, demoralizing, discomfiting, disconcerting, discouraging, disheartening, dismaying, dispiriting *Ant* reassuring, untroublesome

troubling *Syn* TROUBLESOME, discomforting, discomposing, disquieting, distressing, disturbing, perturbing, troublous, unsettling, upsetting, worrisome *Ant* reassuring, untroublesome

troublous *Syn* TROUBLESOME, discomforting, discomposing, disquieting, distressing, disturbing, perturbing, troubling, unsettling, upsetting, worrisome *Ant* reassuring, untroublesome

troupe *Syn* COMPANY, band, party, troop

trouper *Syn* ACTOR, impersonator, mime, mimic, mummer, performer, player, thespian

truant *Syn* VAGABOND, bum, hobo, tramp, vagrant

truce · a suspension of or an agreement for suspending hostilities *Syn* armistice, ceasefire, peace

truckle *Syn* FAWN, cower, cringe, toady *Ant* domineer

truculence *Syn* BELLIGERENCE, aggression, aggressiveness, bellicosity, combativeness, contentiousness, disputatiousness, fight, militancy, pugnacity, scrappiness *Ant* pacifism

truculent 1 *Syn* BELLIGERENT, aggressive, argumentative, bellicose, combative, contentious, discordant, disputatious, gladiatorial, militant, pugnacious, quarrelsome, scrappy, warlike *Ant* nonbelligerent, pacific, peaceable, peaceful 2 *Syn* FIERCE, barbarous, cruel, fell, ferocious, inhuman, savage *Ant* mild, tame

true 1 *Syn* ACTUAL, concrete, existent, factual, real, very *Ant* conjectural, hypothetical, ideal, nonexistent, possible, potential, theoretical 2 *Syn* DEPENDABLE, good, reliable, responsible, safe, solid, steady, sure, tried, trustworthy *Ant* irresponsible, undependable, unreliable, untrustworthy 3 *Syn* FAITHFUL, constant, devoted, devout, fast, good, loyal, pious, staunch (*or* stanch), steadfast, steady, true-blue *Ant* disloyal, faithless, false, fickle, inconstant, perfidious, recreant, traitorous, treacherous, unfaithful, untrue

true-blue *Syn* FAITHFUL, constant, devoted, devout, fast, good, loyal, pious, staunch (*or* stanch), steadfast, steady, true *Ant* disloyal, faithless, false, fickle, inconstant, perfidious, recreant, traitorous, treacherous, unfaithful, untrue

truism *Syn* COMMONPLACE, bromide, cliché, platitude

trunk *Syn* CHEST, box, caddy, case, casket, locker

trust *vb* 1 · assured reliance on the character, ability, strength, or truth of someone or something *Syn* confidence, dependence, faith, reliance *Rel* assurance, certainty, certitude, conviction *Ant* mistrust 2 *Syn* CARTEL, combination, combine, syndicate 3 *Syn* CUSTODY, care, guardianship, keeping, safekeeping, ward 4 *Syn* MONOPOLY, cartel, corner, pool, syndicate

trust *n Syn* RELY (ON), bank, count, depend, reckon

trustworthy *Syn* DEPENDABLE, good, reliable, responsible, safe, solid, steady, sure, tried, tried-and-true, true, trusty *Ant* irresponsible, undependable, unreliable, untrustworthy

trusty *Syn* DEPENDABLE, good, reliable, responsible, safe, solid, steady, sure, tried, tried-and-true, true, trustworthy *Ant* irresponsible, undependable, unreliable, untrustworthy

truth · the quality or state of keeping close to fact and avoiding distortion or misrepresentation *Syn* veracity, verisimilitude, verity *Rel* correctness, exactness, precision, rightness *Ant* falsehood, lie, untruth

truthful · being in the habit of telling the truth *Syn* honest, veracious *Rel* candid, frank, open, plainspoken *Ant* dishonest, fibbing, lying, mendacious, prevaricating, untruthful

try *vb* 1 *Syn* ATTEMPT, assay, endeavor, essay, seek, strive 2 *Syn* PROVE, demonstrate, test *Ant* disprove

try *n Syn* ATTEMPT, crack, endeavor, essay, fling, go, pass, shot, stab, trial, whack

tryst *Syn* ENGAGEMENT, appointment, assignation, date, rendezvous

tucker *Syn* TIRE, exhaust, fatigue, jade, weary

tug *Syn* PULL, drag, draw, hale, haul, tow

tumble *Syn* DISORDER, confuse, derange, disarrange, disarray, discompose, dishevel, dislocate, disorganize, disrupt, disturb, hash, jumble, mess (up), mix (up), muddle, muss, rumple, scramble, shuffle, tousle, upset *Ant* arrange, array, draw up, marshal, order, organize, range, regulate, straighten (up), tidy

tumbled *Syn* MESSY, chaotic, cluttered, confused, disarranged, disarrayed, disheveled (*or* dishevelled), disordered, disorderly, higgledy-piggledy, hugger-mugger, jumbled, littered, messed, muddled, mussed, mussy, pell-mell, rumpled, sloppy, topsy-turvy, tousled, unkempt, untidy, upside-down *Ant* neat, ordered, orderly, organized, shipshape, snug, tidied, tidy, trim

tumid *Syn* INFLATED, flatulent, turgid *Ant* pithy

tummy *Syn* STOMACH, abdomen, belly, gut, solar plexus

tumult 1 *Syn* COMMOTION, bother, bustle, clatter, disturbance, furor, furore, fuss, hubbub, hullabaloo, hurly-burly, pandemonium, pother, row, ruckus, ruction, rumpus, shindy, squall, stew, stir, storm, to-do, turmoil, uproar, welter, whirl **2** *Syn* CONVULSION, cataclysm, paroxysm, storm, tempest, upheaval, uproar

tumultuous *Syn* CONVULSIVE, cataclysmal (*or* cataclysmic), stormy, tempestuous

tundra *Syn* PLAIN, down, grassland, prairie, savanna, steppe, veld (*or* veldt)

tune *vb Syn* HARMONIZE, attune

tune *n Syn* MELODY, air, lay, song, strain, warble

turbid · not clear or translucent but clouded with or as if with sediment *Syn* muddy, roily *Rel* dark, murky, obscure *Ant* clear, limpid

turgid *Syn* INFLATED, flatulent, tumid *Ant* pithy

turkey *Syn* FOOL (sense 2), booby, goose, half-wit, jackass, lunatic, nincompoop, ninny, nitwit, nut, simpleton, yo-yo

turmoil **1** *Syn* COMMOTION, bother, bustle, clatter, disturbance, furor, furore, fuss, hubbub, hullabaloo, hurly-burly, pandemonium, pother, row, ruckus, ruction, rumpus, shindy, squall, stew, stir, storm, to-do, tumult, uproar, welter, whirl **2** *Syn* UNREST, disquiet, ferment, restiveness, restlessness, uneasiness *Ant* calm, ease, peace, quiet

turn *vb* **1** · to move or cause to move in a curved or circular path on or as if on an axis *Syn* circle, eddy, gyrate, pirouette, revolve, rotate, spin, swirl, twirl, wheel, whirl *Rel* fluctuate, oscillate, pendulate, swing, undulate, vibrate **2** · to change or cause to change course or direction *Syn* avert, deflect, divert, sheer *Rel* depart, deviate, digress, diverge, swerve, veer **3** *Syn* BECOME, come, get, go, grow, run, wax **4** *Syn* DEPEND (sense 1), hang, hinge **5** *Syn* RESORT, apply, go, refer

turn *n* **1** *Syn* GIFT (sense 2), aptitude, bent, faculty, genius, knack, talent **2** *Syn* SPELL, bout, go, shift, stint, tour, trick **3** *Syn* WALK, constitutional, perambulation, ramble, range, saunter, stroll

turncoat **1** *Syn* RENEGADE, apostate, backslider, recreant *Ant* adherent, loyalist **2** *Syn* TRAITOR, betrayer, double-crosser, quisling, recreant

turning point · a point in a chain of events at which an important change (as in one's fortunes) occurs *Syn* climax, landmark, milestone *Rel* break, clincher, highlight

turn off *Syn* DISGUST, nauseate, repel, repulse, revolt, sicken

turn on *Syn* ACTIVATE, actuate, crank (up), drive, move, propel, run, set off, spark, start, touch off, trigger *Ant* cut, deactivate, kill, shut off, turn off

turn out *Syn* BEAR (sense 1), produce, yield

tussle *Syn* WRESTLE, grapple, scuffle

tutelage *Syn* EDUCATION (sense 1), instruction, schooling, teaching, training, tutoring

tutoring *Syn* EDUCATION (sense 1), instruction, schooling, teaching, training, tutelage

twaddle *Syn* NONSENSE, balderdash, bull, bunk, drivel, gobbledygook, poppycock, rot, trash

twain *Syn* PAIR, brace, couple, duo, twosome

tweet *vb Syn* CHIRP, cheep, chirrup, chitter, peep, twitter

tweet *n Syn* CHIRP, cheep, chirrup, chitter, peep, twitter

twin *Syn* DOUBLE, binary, bipartite, dual, duplex *Ant* single

twine *Syn* WIND, coil, curl, entwine, twist, wreathe

twinge *Syn* PAIN, ache, pang, stitch, throe

twinkle *vb Syn* FLASH, coruscate, glance, gleam, glint, glisten, glitter, scintillate, sparkle

twinkle *n Syn* INSTANT, flash, jiffy, minute, moment, second, shake, split second, trice, twinkling, wink

twinkling *Syn* INSTANT, flash, jiffy, minute, moment, second, shake, split second, trice, twinkle, wink

twirl *Syn* TURN (sense 1), circle, eddy, gyrate, pirouette, revolve, rotate, spin, swirl, wheel, whirl

twist **1** *Syn* CURVE, bend **2** *Syn* WIND, coil, curl, entwine, twine, wreathe

twister *Syn* TORNADO, cyclone

twit *Syn* RIDICULE, deride, mock, rally, taunt

twitch *Syn* JERK, snap, yank

twitter *vb* **1** *Syn* CHAT, babble, blab, cackle, chatter, converse, gab, gabble, gas, jabber, jaw, palaver, patter, prate, prattle, rap, rattle, run on, talk, visit **2** *Syn* CHIRP, cheep, chirrup, chitter, peep, tweet

twitter *n Syn* CHIRP, cheep, chirrup, chitter, peep, tweet

two-faced *Syn* INSINCERE, artificial, backhanded, double-dealing, feigned, hypocritical, left-handed, mealy, mealymouthed, unctuous *Ant* genuine, heartfelt, honest, sincere, unfeigned

twosome *Syn* PAIR, brace, couple, duo, twain

type **1** · a number of individuals thought of as a group because of a common quality or qualities *Syn* character, description, ilk, kidney, kind, nature, sort, stripe *Rel* example, exemplar, model, pattern **2** *Syn* SYMBOL, attribute, emblem

typhoon *Syn* HURRICANE, tropical storm

typical *Syn* REGULAR, natural, normal *Ant* irregular

typically *Syn* NATURALLY (sense 1), commonly, generally, normally, ordinarily, usually *Ant* abnormally, atypically, extraordinarily, uncommonly, unusually

tyrannical **1** *Syn* ABSOLUTE, arbitrary, autocratic, despotic, tyrannous *Ant* limited, restrained 2 *Syn* BOSSY, authoritarian, autocratic, despotic, dictatorial, domineering, imperious, masterful, overbearing, peremptory, tyrannous

tyrannous 1 *Syn* ABSOLUTE, arbitrary, autocratic, despotic, tyrannical *Ant* limited, restrained 2 *Syn* BOSSY, authoritarian, autocratic, despotic, dictatorial, domineering, imperious, masterful, overbearing, peremptory, tyrannical

tyro 1 *Syn* AMATEUR, dabbler, dilettante *Ant* expert, professional 2 *Syn* BEGINNER, colt, fledgling, freshman, greenhorn, neophyte, newbie, newcomer, novice, recruit, rookie, tenderfoot *Ant* old hand, old-timer, vet, veteran

U

ugly · unpleasing to the sight *Syn* hideous, ill-favored, unsightly *Rel* homely, plain *Ant* beautiful

ultimate 1 · being so fundamental as to represent the extreme limit of actual or possible knowledge *Syn* absolute, categorical 2 *Syn* LAST, concluding, eventual, final, latest, terminal *Ant* first

ultramodern *Syn* MODERN, contemporary, current, hot, mod, modernistic, new, newfangled, new-fashioned, present-day, red-hot, space-age, up-to-date *Ant* antiquated, archaic, dated, fusty, musty, noncontemporary, oldfangled, old-fashioned, old-time, out-of-date, passé

ululate *Syn* ROAR, bawl, bellow, bluster, clamor, howl, vociferate

ululation *Syn* ROAR, bawl, bellow, bluster, vociferation

umbra *Syn* SHADE, adumbration, penumbra, shadow, umbrage

umbrage 1 *Syn* OFFENSE (sense 1), dudgeon, huff, pique, resentment 2 *Syn* SHADE, adumbration, penumbra, shadow, umbra

umpire *Syn* JUDGE, arbiter, arbitrator, referee

unabashed · not embarrassed or ashamed *Syn* unashamed, unblushing, unembarrassed *Rel* prideful, proud *Ant* abashed, ashamed, embarrassed, shamefaced, sheepish

unacceptable *Syn* OBJECTIONABLE, exceptionable, undesirable, unwanted, unwelcome

unacceptably *Syn* BADLY, inadequately, poorly, unsatisfactorily *Ant* acceptably, adequately, all right, fine, good, palatably, passably, so-so, tolerably

unachievable *Syn* IMPOSSIBLE, hopeless, unattainable, unsolvable *Ant* achievable, attainable, doable, feasible, possible, realizable, workable

unadvisable *Syn* INDISCREET, ill-advised, imprudent, inadvisable, injudicious, tactless, unwise *Ant* advisable, discreet, judicious, prudent, tactful, wise

unaffected *Syn* NATURAL, artless, ingenuous, naive, simple, unsophisticated

unaffectedly *Syn* NATURALLY (sense 3), artlessly, guilelessly, ingenuously, innocently, naively, sincerely, unpretentiously *Ant* affectedly, artificially, hypocritically, insincerely, pretentiously, unnaturally

unafraid *Syn* BRAVE, audacious, bold, courageous, dauntless, doughty, fearless, intrepid, undaunted, valiant, valorous *Ant* craven

unanimated *Syn* BORING, drab, dreary, dry, dull, flat, heavy, humdrum, jading, leaden, monotonous, pedestrian, ponderous, stodgy, stuffy, stupid, tame, tedious, tiresome, tiring, uninteresting, wearisome, weary, wearying *Ant* absorbing, engaging, engrossing, gripping, interesting, intriguing, involving

unanswerable *Syn* IRREFUTABLE, incontestable, incontrovertible, indisputable, indubitable, undeniable, unquestionable *Ant* answerable, debatable, disputable, questionable

unanticipated *Syn* UNEXPECTED, unforeseen, unlooked-for *Ant* anticipated, expected, foreseen

unappreciative *Syn* THANKLESS, ungrateful *Ant* appreciative, grateful, obliged, thankful

unapt 1 *Syn* IMPROBABLE, doubtful, dubious, far-fetched, flimsy, questionable, unlikely *Ant* likely, probable 2 *Syn* INAPPROPRIATE, graceless, improper, inapt, incongruous, incorrect, indecorous, inept, infelicitous, unbecoming, unfit, unhappy, unseemly, unsuitable, wrong *Ant* appropriate, becoming, befitting, correct, decorous, felicitous, fit, fitting, genteel, happy, meet, proper, right, seemly, suitable

unashamed *Syn* UNABASHED, unblushing, unembarrassed *Ant* abashed, ashamed, embarrassed, shamefaced, sheepish

unassailable *Syn* INVINCIBLE, impregnable, indomitable, inexpugnable, invulnerable, unconquerable

unattached *Syn* UNMARRIED, single, unwed *Ant* espoused, married

unattainable *Syn* IMPOSSIBLE, hopeless, unachievable, unsolvable *Ant* achievable, attainable, doable, feasible, possible, realizable, workable

unavoidable *Syn* INEVITABLE, certain, inescapable, necessary, sure *Ant* avoidable, escapable, uncertain, unsure

unaware *Syn* UNAWARES, aback, suddenly, unexpectedly

unawares · without warning *Syn* aback, suddenly, unaware, unexpectedly *Rel* abruptly, short

unbearable · more than can be put up with *Syn* insufferable, insupportable, intolerable, unendurable, unsupportable *Rel* unacceptable *Ant* endurable, sufferable, supportable, tolerable

unbecoming *Syn* INAPPROPRIATE, graceless, improper, inapt, incongruous, incorrect, indecorous, inept, infelicitous, unapt, unfit, unhappy, unseemly, unsuitable, wrong *Ant* appropriate, becoming, befitting, correct, decorous, felicitous, fit, fitting, genteel, happy, meet, proper, right, seemly, suitable

unbelief · the attitude or state of mind of one who does not believe *Syn* disbelief, incredulity *Rel* doubt, dubiety, dubiosity, skepticism, uncertainty *Ant* belief

unbeliever *Syn* SKEPTIC, disbeliever, doubter, questioner

unbend *Syn* STRAIGHTEN, uncurl *Ant* bend, crook, curl, curve

unbending *Syn* OBSTINATE, adamant, adamantine, dogged, hard, hardened, hardheaded, hardhearted, headstrong, immovable, implacable, inflexible, mulish, obdurate, opinionated, ossified, pat, peevish, pertinacious, perverse, pigheaded, rigid, self-willed, stubborn, uncompromising, unrelenting, unyielding, willful (*or* wilful) *Ant* acquiescent, agreeable, amenable, compliant, complying, flexible, pliable, pliant, relenting, yielding

unbiased *Syn* FAIR, dispassionate, equitable, impartial, just, objective, uncolored *Ant* unfair

unblushing *Syn* UNABASHED, unashamed, unembarrassed *Ant* abashed, ashamed, embarrassed, shamefaced, sheepish

unbounded *Syn* INFINITE, boundless, endless, illimitable, immeasurable, indefinite, limitless, measureless, unfathomable, unlimited *Ant* bounded, circumscribed, confined, definite, finite, limited, restricted

unburden *Syn* RID, clear, disabuse, purge

uncalled-for 1 *Syn* IMPOLITE, discourteous, ill-bred, ill-mannered, impertinent, inconsiderate, rude, thoughtless, uncivil, ungracious, unmannerly *Ant* civil, considerate, courteous, genteel, gracious, mannerly, polite, thoughtful, well-bred 2 *Syn* UNNECESSARY, dispensable, gratuitous, needless, nonessential, unessential, unwarranted *Ant* essential,

indispensable, necessary, needed, needful, required

uncanny *Syn* EERIE, creepy, haunting, spooky, unearthly, weird

unceasing *Syn* EVERLASTING, endless, interminable *Ant* transitory

uncertainty *Syn* DOUBT, distrust, distrustfulness, incertitude, misgiving, mistrust, mistrustfulness, skepticism, suspicion *Ant* assurance, belief, certainty, certitude, confidence, conviction, sureness, surety, trust

unchanging *Syn* UNIFORM, invariant, steady, undeviating, unvarying, unwavering *Ant* changing, deviating, varying

uncivil *Syn* IMPOLITE, discourteous, ill-bred, ill-mannered, impertinent, inconsiderate, rude, thoughtless, uncalled-for, ungracious, unmannerly *Ant* civil, considerate, courteous, genteel, gracious, mannerly, polite, thoughtful, well-bred

uncolored 1 *Syn* COLORLESS, undyed, unpainted, unstained, white *Ant* colored, dyed, painted, stained, tinged, tinted 2 *Syn* FAIR, dispassionate, equitable, impartial, just, objective, unbiased *Ant* unfair

uncommon *Syn* INFREQUENT, occasional, rare, scarce, sporadic *Ant* frequent

uncommunicative 1 *Syn* SECRETIVE, close, closemouthed, dark, reticent *Ant* communicative, open 2 *Syn* SILENT (sense 1), close, close-lipped, closemouthed, reserved, reticent, secretive, taciturn, tight-lipped *Ant* talkative 3 *Syn* SILENT (sense 3), dumb, mum, mute, speechless, wordless *Ant* communicative, speaking, talking

uncompromising *Syn* OBSTINATE, adamant, adamantine, dogged, hard, hardened, hardheaded, hardhearted, headstrong, immovable, implacable, inflexible, mulish, obdurate, opinionated, ossified, pat, peevish, pertinacious, perverse, pigheaded, rigid, self-willed, stubborn, unbending, unrelenting, unyielding, willful (*or* wilful) *Ant* acquiescent, agreeable, amenable, compliant, complying, flexible, pliable, pliant, relenting, yielding

unconcern *Syn* INDIFFERENCE, apathy, casualness, disinterestedness, disregard, insouciance, nonchalance *Ant* concern, interest, regard

unconcerned 1 *Syn* CAREFREE, careless, cavalier, devil-may-care, easygoing, gay, happy-go-lucky, insouciant, lighthearted *Ant* careworn 2 *Syn* INDIFFERENT, aloof, detached, disinterested, incurious, uninterested *Ant* avid

uncongenial 1 *Syn* INCONSONANT, discordant, discrepant, incompatible, incongruous, inconsistent, unsympathetic *Ant* consonant 2 *Syn* UNPLEASANT, bad, disagreeable, displeasing, distasteful, nasty, rotten, sour, unlovely, unpleasing, unsatisfying, unwelcome *Ant* agreeable, congenial, good, grateful, gratifying, nice, palatable, pleasant, pleasing, pleasurable, satisfying, welcome

unconquerable *Syn* INVINCIBLE, impregnable, indomitable, inexpugnable, invulnerable, unassailable

unconscionable *Syn* UNPRINCIPLED, cutthroat, immoral, Machiavellian, unethical, unmoral, unscrupulous *Ant* ethical, moral, principled, scrupulous

uncontrollable · given to resisting control or discipline by others *Syn* froward, headstrong, intractable, recalcitrant, refractory, ungovernable, unmanageable, unruly, untoward, wayward, willful (*or* wilful) *Rel* contrary, incorrigible, obstinate, perverse, self-willed, stubborn *Ant* controllable, governable, tractable

uncountable *Syn* COUNTLESS, innumerable, numberless, uncounted, unnumbered, untold *Ant* countable

uncounted *Syn* COUNTLESS, innumerable, numberless, uncountable, unnumbered, untold *Ant* countable

uncouth 1 *Syn* CLOWNISH, boorish, churlish, cloddish, loutish *Ant* civil, courteous, courtly, cultivated, genteel, gentlemanly, ladylike, polished, polite, refined, well-bred 2 *Syn* RUDE (sense 1), callow, crude, green, raw, rough *Ant* civil, urbane

uncritical *Syn* SUPERFICIAL, cursory, shallow *Ant* deep, profound

unctuous *Syn* INSINCERE, artificial, backhanded, double-dealing, feigned, hypocritical, left-handed, mealy, mealymouthed, two-faced *Ant* genuine, heartfelt, honest, sincere, unfeigned

uncurl *Syn* STRAIGHTEN, unbend *Ant* bend, crook, curl, curve

undaunted *Syn* BRAVE, audacious, bold, courageous, dauntless, doughty, fearless, intrepid, unafraid, valiant, valorous *Ant* craven

undeniable *Syn* IRREFUTABLE, incontestable, incontrovertible, indisputable, indubitable, unanswerable, unquestionable *Ant* answerable, debatable, disputable, questionable

under 1 *Syn* BELOW, beneath, underneath *Ant* above 2 *Syn* LESSER, inferior, junior, less, lower, minor, smaller, subordinate *Ant* greater, higher, major, more, primary, prime, senior, superior

undergo *Syn* EXPERIENCE, suffer, sustain

underhand *Syn* SECRET, clandestine, covert, furtive, stealthy, surreptitious, underhanded

underhanded *Syn* SECRET, clandestine, covert, furtive, stealthy, surreptitious, underhand

underline *Syn* EMPHASIZE, accent, accentuate, feature, highlight, play (up), point (up), stress, underscore *Ant* play (down)

underling · one who is of lower rank and typically under the authority of another *Syn* inferior, junior, subordinate *Rel* attendant, follower, retainer *Ant* senior, superior

underlying 1 *Syn* ELEMENTARY, basic, elemental, essential, fundamental, rudimentary *Ant* advanced 2 *Syn* FUNDAMENTAL, basal, basic, radical

underneath *Syn* BELOW, beneath, under *Ant* above

underprivileged *Syn* DEPRIVED, disadvantaged *Ant* privileged

underscore *Syn* EMPHASIZE, accent, accentuate, feature, highlight, play (up), point (up), stress, underline *Ant* play (down)

understand · to have a clear or complete idea of *Syn* appreciate, comprehend *Rel* conceive, envisage, envision, realize, think

understanding 1 *Syn* AGREEMENT, accord 2 *Syn* COMPREHENSION, appreciation, apprehension, grasp, grip, perception 3 *Syn* REASON (sense 2), intuition

undesirable *Syn* OBJECTIONABLE, exceptionable, unacceptable, unwanted, unwelcome

undeviating *Syn* UNIFORM, invariant, steady, unchanging, unvarying, unwavering *Ant* changing, deviating, varying

undulate *Syn* SWING (sense 2), fluctuate, oscillate, pendulate, sway, vibrate, waver

undyed *Syn* COLORLESS, uncolored, unpainted, unstained, white *Ant* colored, dyed, painted, stained, tinged, tinted

undying *Syn* IMMORTAL, deathless, unfading *Ant* mortal

unearth *Syn* DISCOVER, ascertain, determine, learn

unearthly *Syn* EERIE, creepy, haunting, spooky, uncanny, weird

uneasiness *Syn* UNREST, disquiet, ferment, restiveness, restlessness, turmoil *Ant* calm, ease, peace, quiet

uneasy *Syn* IMPATIENT, fidgety, jittery, jumpy, nervous, restive, restless, unquiet *Ant* patient

uneducated *Syn* IGNORANT, benighted, dark, illiterate, nonliterate, simple, uninstructed, unlearned, unlettered, unread, unschooled, untaught, untutored *Ant* educated, knowledged

unembarrassed *Syn* UNABASHED, unashamed, unblushing *Ant* abashed, ashamed, embarrassed, shamefaced, sheepish

unendurable *Syn* UNBEARABLE, insufferable, insupportable, intolerable, unsupportable *Ant* endurable, sufferable, supportable, tolerable

unerring *Syn* INFALLIBLE, inerrable, inerrant *Ant* fallible

unessential *Syn* UNNECESSARY, dispensable, gratuitous, needless, nonessential, uncalled-for, unwarranted *Ant* essential, indispensable, necessary, needed, needful, required

unethical *Syn* UNPRINCIPLED, cutthroat, immoral, Machiavellian, unconscionable, unmoral, unscrupulous *Ant* ethical, moral, principled, scrupulous

uneven 1 *Syn* AWRY, askew, aslant, cockeyed, crooked, listing, lopsided, oblique, skewed, slanted, slanting, slantwise, tilted, tipping *Ant* even, level, straight **2** *Syn* ROUGH, harsh, rugged, scabrous *Ant* smooth

unexpected · not expected *Syn* unanticipated, unforeseen, unlooked-for *Rel* unintended, unplanned *Ant* anticipated, expected, foreseen

unexpectedly *Syn* UNAWARES, aback, suddenly, unaware

unexpressed *Syn* IMPLICIT, implied, tacit, unspoken, unvoiced, wordless *Ant* explicit, express, expressed, spoken, stated

unfading *Syn* IMMORTAL, deathless, undying *Ant* mortal

unfaithfulness *Syn* BETRAYAL, disloyalty, double cross, faithlessness, falseness, falsity, infidelity, perfidy, sellout, treachery, treason

unfathomable **1** *Syn* INCOMPREHENSIBLE, impenetrable, unintelligible *Ant* fathomable, intelligible, understandable **2** *Syn* INFINITE, boundless, endless, illimitable, immeasurable, indefinite, limitless, measureless, unbounded, unlimited *Ant* bounded, circumscribed, confined, definite, finite, limited, restricted

unfeeling *Syn* NUMB, asleep, benumbed, dead, insensitive, numbed *Ant* feeling, sensitive

unfeigned *Syn* SINCERE, heartfelt, hearty, wholehearted, whole-souled *Ant* insincere

unfeignedly *Syn* NATURALLY (sense 3), artlessly, guilelessly, ingenuously, innocently, naively, sincerely, unaffectedly, unpretentiously *Ant* affectedly, artificially, hypocritically, insincerely, pretentiously, unnaturally

unfit **1** · not adapted or appropriate to a particular end or purpose *Syn* improper, inappropriate, inapt, infelicitous, unfitting, unhappy, unsuitable *Ant* fit **2** *Syn* INAPPROPRIATE, graceless, improper, inapt, incongruous, incorrect, indecorous, inept, infelicitous, unapt, unbecoming, unhappy, unseemly, unsuitable, wrong *Ant* appropriate, becoming, befitting, correct, decorous, felicitous, fit, fitting, genteel, happy, meet, proper, right, seemly, suitable **3** *Syn* INCOMPETENT, incapable, inept, inexpert, unqualified, unskilled, unskillful *Ant* able, capable, competent, expert, fit, qualified, skilled, skillful

unfitness *Syn* IMPROPRIETY (sense 2), inappropriateness, incorrectness, indecency *Ant* appropriateness, correctness, decency, decorousness, fitness, propriety, rightness, seemliness, suitability

unfitting *Syn* UNFIT, improper, inappropriate, inapt, infelicitous, unhappy, unsuitable *Ant* fit

unflagging *Syn* INDEFATIGABLE, tireless, untiring, unwearied, unwearying, weariless

unflappable **1** · not easily panicked or upset *Syn* imperturbable, nerveless, unshakable *Rel* calm, collected, composed, cool, coolheaded, nonchalant, placid, self-possessed, serene, tranquil, undisturbed, unperturbed, unruffled, unshaken, untroubled, unworried *Ant* perturbable, shakable **2** *Syn* COOL, collected, composed, imperturbable, nonchalant, unruffled *Ant* agitated, ardent

unfledged *Syn* CALLOW, adolescent, green, immature, inexperienced, juvenile, puerile, raw, unripe, unripened *Ant* adult, experienced, grown-up, mature, ripe

unfold · to disclose by degrees to the sight or understanding *Syn* develop, elaborate, evolve, perfect *Rel* demonstrate, evidence, evince, manifest, show

unforeseen *Syn* UNEXPECTED, unanticipated, unlooked-for *Ant* anticipated, expected, foreseen

unforgivable *Syn* INEXCUSABLE, indefensible, unjustifiable, unpardonable, unwarrantable *Ant* defensible, excusable, forgivable, justifiable, pardonable

unformed *Syn* FORMLESS, amorphous, shapeless, unshaped, unstructured *Ant* formed, shaped, structured

unfortunate **1** *Syn* REGRETTABLE, deplorable, distressful, distressing, grievous, heartbreaking, heartrending, lamentable, woeful **2** *Syn* UNLUCKY, calamitous, disastrous, hapless, ill-fated, ill-starred, luckless *Ant* fortunate, happy, lucky

unfounded **1** *Syn* BASELESS, groundless, unwarranted **2** *Syn* GROUNDLESS, invalid, nonvalid, ungrounded, unreasonable, unsubstantiated, unsupported, unwarranted *Ant* good, hard, just, justified, reasonable, reasoned, substantiated, valid, well-founded

unfruitful *Syn* STERILE, barren, impotent, infertile *Ant* exuberant, fertile

ungainly *Syn* CUMBERSOME, awkward, clumsy, cranky, cumbrous, unhandy, unwieldy *Ant* handy

ungodly *Syn* IRRELIGIOUS, godless, nonreligious, unreligious *Ant* religious

ungovernable **1** *Syn* DISOBEDIENT, balky, contrary, defiant, froward, insubordinate, intractable, rebellious, recalcitrant, refractory, restive, unruly, untoward, wayward, willful (*or* wilful) *Ant* amenable, compliant, docile, obedient, tractable **2** *Syn* UNCONTROLLABLE, froward, headstrong, intractable, recalcitrant, refractory, unmanageable, unruly, untoward, wayward, willful (*or* wilful) *Ant* controllable, governable, tractable **3** *Syn* UNRULY, headstrong, intractable, recalcitrant, refractory, willful *Ant* docile, tractable

ungracious *Syn* IMPOLITE, discourteous, ill-bred, ill-mannered, impertinent, inconsiderate, rude, thoughtless, uncalled-for, uncivil, ungracious, unmannerly *Ant* civil, considerate, courteous, genteel, gracious, mannerly, polite, thoughtful, well-bred

ungrateful *Syn* THANKLESS, unappreciative *Ant* appreciative, grateful, obliged, thankful

ungrounded *Syn* GROUNDLESS, invalid, nonvalid, unfounded, unreasonable, unsubstantiated, unsupported, unwarranted *Ant* good, hard, just, justified, reasonable, reasoned, substantiated, valid, well-founded

unhandy *Syn* CUMBERSOME, awkward, clumsy, cranky, cumbrous, ungainly, unwieldy *Ant* handy

unhappiness *Syn* SADNESS, blues, dejection, depression, desolation, despondency, disconsolateness, dispiritedness, doldrums, downheartedness, dreariness, dumps, forlornness, gloom, gloominess, heartsickness, joylessness, melancholy, mopes, oppression *Ant* bliss, blissfulness, ecstasy, elatedness, elation, euphoria, exhilaration, exuberance, exultation, felicity, gladness, gladsomeness, happiness, heaven, intoxication, joy, joyfulness, joyousness, jubilation, rapture, rapturousness

unhappy 1 *Syn* INAPPROPRIATE, graceless, improper, inapt, incongruous, incorrect, indecorous, inept, infelicitous, unapt, unbecoming, unfit, unseemly, unsuitable, wrong *Ant* appropriate, becoming, befitting, correct, decorous, felicitous, fit, fitting, genteel, happy, meet, proper, right, seemly, suitable **2** *Syn* SAD (sense 1), bad, blue, brokenhearted, crestfallen, dejected, depressed, despondent, disconsolate, doleful, down, downcast, downhearted, droopy, forlorn, gloomy, glum, heartbroken, heartsick, heartsore, inconsolable, joyless, low, lowspirited, melancholy, miserable, mournful, saddened, sorrowful, sorry, woebegone, woeful, wretched *Ant* blissful, buoyant, buoyed, cheerful, cheery, chipper, delighted, glad, gladdened, gladsome, gleeful, happy, joyful, joyous, jubilant, sunny, upbeat **3** *Syn* UNFIT, improper, inappropriate, inapt, infelicitous, unfitting, unsuitable *Ant* fit

unheroic *Syn* COWARDLY, chicken, chickenhearted, craven, dastardly, lily-livered, pusillanimous, recreant, spineless, yellow *Ant* brave, courageous, daring, dauntless, doughty, fearless, gallant, greathearted, gutsy, hardy, heroic, intrepid, lionhearted, stalwart, stout, stouthearted, valiant, valorous

uniform 1 · not varying *Syn* invariant, steady, unchanging, undeviating, unvarying, unwavering *Rel* immutable, invariable, unalterable, unchangeable *Ant* changing, deviating, varying **2** *Syn* STEADY, constant, equable, even *Ant* jumpy, nervous, unsteady

unify *Syn* COMPACT, concentrate, consolidate

unimpassioned *Syn* SOBER, continent, temperate *Ant* drunk, excited

unimportant · lacking importance *Syn* frivolous, inconsequential, inconsiderable, insignificant, little, minor, minute, negligible, slight, small, small-fry, trifling, trivial *Rel* jerkwater, one-horse *Ant* big, consequential, eventful, important, major, material, meaningful, momentous, significant, substantial, weighty

uninhibited *Syn* DEMONSTRATIVE, effusive, emotional, unreserved, unrestrained *Ant* inhibited, reserved, restrained, undemonstrative, unemotional

uninstructed *Syn* IGNORANT, benighted, dark, illiterate, nonliterate, simple, uneducated, unlearned, unlettered, unread, unschooled, untaught, untutored *Ant* educated, knowledgeable, literate, schooled

unintelligible *Syn* INCOMPREHENSIBLE, impenetrable, unfathomable *Ant* fathomable, intelligible, understandable

unintended *Syn* ACCIDENTAL, casual, chance, fluky, fortuitous, inadvertent, incidental, unintentional, unplanned, unpremeditated, unwitting *Ant* deliberate, intended, intentional, planned, premeditated

unintentional *Syn* ACCIDENTAL, casual, chance, fluky, fortuitous, inadvertent, incidental, unintended, unplanned, unpremeditated, unwitting *Ant* deliberate, intended, intentional, planned, premeditated

uninterested *Syn* INDIFFERENT, aloof, detached, disinterested, incurious, unconcerned *Ant* avid

uninteresting *Syn* BORING, drab, dreary, dry, dull, flat, heavy, humdrum, jading, leaden, monotonous, pedestrian, ponderous, stodgy, stuffy, stupid, tame, tedious, tiresome, tiring, unanimated, wearisome, weary, wearying *Ant* absorbing, engaging, engrossing, gripping, interesting, intriguing, involving

union *Syn* UNITY, integrity, solidarity

unique 1 *Syn* ONLY, alone, lone, singular, sole, solitary, special **2** *Syn* SINGLE, lone, particular, separate, sole, solitary *Ant* accompanied, conjugal, supported **3** *Syn* STRANGE, curious, eccentric, erratic, odd, outlandish, peculiar, quaint, queer, singular *Ant* familiar

unite 1 · to join forces or act in concert *Syn* combine, concur, conjoin, cooperate *Rel* coalesce, commingle, fuse, mingle *Ant* part **2** *Syn* ALLY, associate, band, club, confederate, conjoin, cooperate, federate, league *Ant* break up, disband **3** *Syn* JOIN, associate, combine, conjoin, connect, link, relate *Ant* disjoin, part

unity · the character of a thing that is a whole composed of many parts *Syn* integrity, solidarity, union *Rel* assimilation, embodiment, identification, incorporation

universal 1 · present or significant throughout the world *Syn* catholic, cosmic, cosmopolitan, ecumenical *Rel* earthly, mundane, terrestrial, worldly **2** · of, belonging, or relating to all or the whole *Syn* common, general, generic *Ant* particular **3** *Syn* EN-

305 unpleasant

CYCLOPEDIC, compendious, complete, comprehensive, full, global, inclusive, in-depth, omnibus, panoramic **4** *Syn* GENERAL (sense 1), blanket, common, generic, global, overall *Ant* individual, particular

unjustifiable *Syn* INEXCUSABLE, indefensible, unforgivable, unpardonable, unwarrantable *Ant* defensible, excusable, forgivable, justifiable, pardonable

unkempt 1 *Syn* MESSY, chaotic, cluttered, confused, disarranged, disarrayed, disheveled (*or* dishevelled), disordered, disorderly, higgledy-piggledy, hugger-mugger, jumbled, littered, messed, muddled, mussed, mussy, pell-mell, rumpled, sloppy, topsy-turvy, tousled, tumbled, untidy, upside-down *Ant* neat, ordered, orderly, organized, shipshape, snug, tidied, tidy, trim **2** *Syn* SLIPSHOD, disheveled, sloppy, slovenly

unlawful · contrary to or prohibited by the law *Syn* illegal, illegitimate, illicit *Rel* flagitious, iniquitous, nefarious *Ant* lawful

unlearned *Syn* IGNORANT, benighted, dark, illiterate, nonliterate, simple, uneducated, uninstructed, unlettered, unread, unschooled, untaught, untutored *Ant* educated, knowledgeable, literate, schooled

unlettered *Syn* IGNORANT, benighted, dark, illiterate, nonliterate, simple, uneducated, uninstructed, unlearned, unread, unschooled, untaught, untutored *Ant* educated, knowledgeable, literate, schooled

unlikely *Syn* IMPROBABLE, doubtful, dubious, far-fetched, flimsy, questionable, unapt *Ant* likely, probable

unlikeness *Syn* DISSIMILARITY, difference, distinction, divergence, divergency *Ant* similarity

unlimited *Syn* INFINITE, boundless, endless, illimitable, immeasurable, indefinite, limitless, measureless, unbounded, unfathomable *Ant* bounded, circumscribed, confined, definite, finite, limited, restricted

unlooked-for *Syn* UNEXPECTED, unanticipated, unforeseen *Ant* anticipated, expected, foreseen

unlovely *Syn* UNPLEASANT, bad, disagreeable, displeasing, distasteful, nasty, rotten, sour, uncongenial, unpleasing, unsatisfying, unwelcome *Ant* agreeable, congenial, good, grateful, gratifying, nice, palatable, pleasant, pleasing, pleasurable, satisfying, welcome

unlucky · involving or suffering misfortune that results from chance *Syn* calamitous, disastrous, hapless, ill-fated, ill-starred, luckless, unfortunate *Rel* awkward, inept *Ant* fortunate, happy, lucky

unmanageable *Syn* UNCONTROLLABLE, froward, headstrong, intractable, recalcitrant, refractory, ungovernable, unruly, untoward, wayward, willful (*or* wilful) *Ant* controllable, governable, tractable

unmannerly *Syn* IMPOLITE, discourteous, ill-bred, ill-mannered, impertinent, inconsiderate, rude, thoughtless, uncalled-for, uncivil, ungracious *Ant* civil, considerate, courteous, genteel, gracious, mannerly, polite, thoughtful, well-bred

unmarried · being without a spouse *Syn* single, unattached, unwed *Ant* espoused, married

unmatured *Syn* IMMATURE, unmellow, unripe *Ant* mature

unmellow *Syn* IMMATURE, unmatured, unripe *Ant* mature

unmindful *Syn* FORGETFUL, oblivious

unmitigated *Syn* OUTRIGHT, arrant, out-and-out

unmoral *Syn* UNPRINCIPLED, cutthroat, immoral, Machiavellian, unconscionable, unethical, unscrupulous *Ant* ethical, moral, principled, scrupulous

unnatural 1 *Syn* DEVIANT, aberrant, abnormal, anomalous, atypical, irregular *Ant* natural, normal, regular, standard, typical **2** *Syn* IRREGULAR, anomalous *Ant* regular

unnecessary · not needed by the circumstances or to accomplish an end *Syn* dispensable, gratuitous, needless, nonessential, uncalled-for, unessential, unwarranted *Rel* discretionary, elective, optional *Ant* essential, indispensable, necessary, needed, needful, required

unnerve *Syn* DISCOURAGE (sense 1), daunt, demoralize, dishearten, dismay, dispirit *Ant* embolden, encourage, hearten, nerve, steel

unnoticeable *Syn* UNOBTRUSIVE, inconspicuous *Ant* conspicuous, noticeable

unnumbered *Syn* COUNTLESS, innumerable, numberless, uncountable, uncounted, untold *Ant* countable

unobtrusive · not readily seen or noticed *Syn* inconspicuous, unnoticeable *Rel* unnoticed *Ant* conspicuous, noticeable

unoffending *Syn* HARMLESS, innocent, innocuous, inoffensive *Ant* harmful

unpainted *Syn* COLORLESS, uncolored, undyed, unstained, white *Ant* colored, dyed, painted, stained, tinged, tinted

unpardonable *Syn* INEXCUSABLE, indefensible, unforgivable, unjustifiable, unwarrantable *Ant* defensible, excusable, forgivable, justifiable, pardonable

unplanned *Syn* ACCIDENTAL, casual, chance, fluky, fortuitous, inadvertent, incidental, unintended, unintentional, unpremeditated, unwitting *Ant* deliberate, intended, intentional, planned, premeditated

unpleasant · not giving pleasure to the mind or senses *Syn* bad, disagreeable, displeasing, distasteful, nasty, rotten, sour, uncongenial, unlovely, unpleasing, unsatisfying, unwelcome *Rel* abhorrent, abominable, annoying, appalling, awful, beastly, disgusting, dreadful, foul, galling, hideous, horrendous, horrible, horrid, invidious, irritating, loathsome, noisome, obnoxious, obscene, odious, repellent, repugnant, repulsive, revolting, scandalous, shocking, sickening, ugly, vexing, villainous *Ant* agreeable, congenial, good, grateful, gratifying, nice, palatable, pleasant, pleasing, pleasurable, satisfying, welcome

unpleasing *Syn* UNPLEASANT, bad, disagreeable, displeasing, distasteful, nasty, rotten, sour, uncongenial, unlovely, unsatisfying, unwelcome *Ant* agreeable, congenial, good, grateful, gratifying, nice, palatable, pleasant, pleasing, pleasurable, satisfying, welcome

unpremeditated 1 *Syn* ACCIDENTAL, casual, chance, fluky, fortuitous, inadvertent, incidental, unintended, unintentional, unplanned, unwitting *Ant* deliberate, intended, intentional, planned, premeditated 2 *Syn* EXTEMPORANEOUS, extemporary, extempore, impromptu, improvised, offhand *Ant* premeditated

unpretentious *Syn* PLAIN, homely, simple *Ant* lovely

unpretentiously *Syn* NATURALLY (sense 3), artlessly, guilelessly, ingenuously, innocently, naively, sincerely, unaffectedly, unfeignedly *Ant* affectedly, artificially, hypocritically, insincerely, pretentiously, unnaturally

unprincipled · not guided by or showing a concern for what is right *Syn* cutthroat, immoral, Machiavellian, unconscionable, unethical, unmoral, unscrupulous *Rel* calculating, intriguing, opportunistic, scheming *Ant* ethical, moral, principled, scrupulous

unprofessional *Syn* AMATEURISH, amateur, dilettante, inexperienced, inexpert, nonprofessional, unskilled, unskillful *Ant* ace, adept, consummate, crackerjack, expert, master, masterful, masterly, professional, virtuoso

unqualified *Syn* INCOMPETENT, incapable, inept, inexpert, unfit, unskilled, unskillful *Ant* able, capable, competent, expert, fit, qualified, skilled, skillful

unquestionable *Syn* IRREFUTABLE, incontestable, incontrovertible, indisputable, indubitable, unanswerable, undeniable *Ant* answerable, debatable, disputable, questionable

unquiet *Syn* IMPATIENT, fidgety, jittery, jumpy, nervous, restive, restless, uneasy *Ant* patient

unravel *Syn* SOLVE, answer, break, crack, dope (out), figure out, puzzle (out), resolve, riddle, work, work out

unread *Syn* IGNORANT, benighted, dark, illiterate, nonliterate, simple, uneducated, uninstructed, unlearned, unlettered, unschooled, untaught, untutored *Ant* educated, knowledgeable, literate, schooled

unreasonable 1 *Syn* GROUNDLESS, invalid,

nonvalid, unfounded, ungrounded, unsubstantiated, unsupported, unwarranted *Ant* good, hard, just, justified, reasonable, reasoned, substantiated, valid, well-founded 2 *Syn* ILLOGICAL, fallacious, invalid, irrational, nonrational, unreasoning, unsound, weak *Ant* logical, rational, reasonable, sound, valid

unreasoning *Syn* ILLOGICAL, fallacious, invalid, irrational, nonrational, unreasonable, unsound, weak *Ant* logical, rational, reasonable, sound, valid

unrelenting 1 *Syn* GRIM, implacable, merciless, relentless *Ant* lenient 2 *Syn* OBSTINATE, adamant, adamantine, dogged, hard, hardened, hardheaded, hardhearted, headstrong, immovable, implacable, inflexible, mulish, obdurate, opinionated, ossified, pat, peevish, pertinacious, perverse, pigheaded, rigid, self-willed, stubborn, unbending, uncompromising, unyielding, willful (*or* wilful) *Ant* acquiescent, agreeable, amenable, compliant, complying, flexible, pliable, pliant, relenting, yielding

unreligious *Syn* IRRELIGIOUS, godless, nonreligious, ungodly *Ant* religious

unremitting *Syn* CONTINUAL, constant, continuous, incessant, perennial, perpetual *Ant* intermittent

unrepentant *Syn* REMORSELESS, impenitent *Ant* contrite, guilty, penitent, regretful, remorseful, repentant, sorry

unreserved *Syn* DEMONSTRATIVE, effusive, emotional, uninhibited, unrestrained *Ant* inhibited, reserved, restrained, undemonstrative, unemotional

unresistant *Syn* PASSIVE, acquiescent, nonresistant, resigned, tolerant, tolerating, unresisting, yielding *Ant* protesting, resistant, resisting, unyielding

unresisting *Syn* PASSIVE, acquiescent, nonresistant, resigned, tolerant, tolerating, unresistant, yielding *Ant* protesting, resistant, resisting, unyielding

unrest · a disturbed or uneasy state *Syn* disquiet, ferment, restiveness, restlessness, turmoil, uneasiness *Rel* fidgets *Ant* calm, ease, peace, quiet

unrestrained *Syn* DEMONSTRATIVE, effusive, emotional, uninhibited, unreserved *Ant* inhibited, reserved, restrained, undemonstrative, unemotional

unrestraint *Syn* ABANDON, abandonment, ease, lightheartedness, naturalness, spontaneity *Ant* constraint, restraint

unripe 1 *Syn* CALLOW, adolescent, green, immature, inexperienced, juvenile, puerile, raw, unfledged, unripened *Ant* adult, experienced, grown-up, mature, ripe 2 *Syn* IMMATURE, unmatured, unmellow *Ant* mature

unripened *Syn* CALLOW, adolescent, green, immature, inexperienced, juvenile, puerile, raw, unfledged, unripe *Ant* adult, experienced, grown-up, mature, ripe

unruffled *Syn* COOL, collected, composed, imperturbable, nonchalant, unflappable *Ant* agitated, ardent

unruliness *Syn* DISOBEDIENCE, contrariness, defiance, frowardness, insubordination, intractability, rebelliousness, recalcitrance, refractoriness, willfulness *Ant* amenability, compliance, docility, obedience

unruly 1 · not submissive to government or control *Syn* headstrong, intractable, recalcitrant, refractory, ungovernable, willful *Rel* contumacious, insubordinate, rebellious *Ant* docile, tractable **2** *Syn* DISOBEDIENT, balky, contrary, defiant, froward, insubordinate, intractable, rebellious, recalcitrant, refractory, restive, ungovernable, untoward, wayward, willful (*or* wilful) *Ant* amenable, compliant, docile, obedient, tractable **3** *Syn* LAWLESS, anarchic, disorderly, lawbreaking *Ant* lawabiding, orderly **4** *Syn* UNCONTROLLABLE, froward, headstrong, intractable, recalcitrant, refractory, ungovernable, unmanageable, unruly, untoward, wayward, willful (*or* wilful) *Ant* controllable, governable, tractable

unsatisfactorily *Syn* BADLY, inadequately, poorly, unacceptably *Ant* acceptably, adequately, all right, fine, good, palatably, passably, so-so, tolerably

unsatisfying *Syn* UNPLEASANT, bad, disagreeable, displeasing, distasteful, nasty, rotten, sour, uncongenial, unlovely, unpleasing, unwelcome *Ant* agreeable, congenial, good, grateful, gratifying, nice, palatable, pleasant, pleasing, pleasurable, satisfying, welcome

unschooled *Syn* IGNORANT, benighted, dark, illiterate, nonliterate, simple, uneducated, uninstructed, unlearned, unlettered, unread, untaught, untutored *Ant* educated, knowledgeable, literate, schooled

unscrupulous *Syn* UNPRINCIPLED, cutthroat, immoral, Machiavellian, unconscionable, unethical, unmoral *Ant* ethical, moral, principled, scrupulous

unseemly *Syn* INAPPROPRIATE, graceless, improper, inapt, incongruous, incorrect, indecorous, inept, infelicitous, unapt, unbecoming, unfit, unhappy, unsuitable, wrong *Ant* appropriate, becoming, befitting, correct, decorous, felicitous, fit, fitting, genteel, happy, meet, proper, right, seemly, suitable

unsettling *Syn* TROUBLESOME, discomforting, discomposing, disquieting, distressing, disturbing, perturbing, troubling, troublous, upsetting, worrisome *Ant* reassuring, untroublesome

unshakable *Syn* UNFLAPPABLE, imperturbable, nerveless *Ant* perturbable, shakable

unshaped *Syn* FORMLESS, amorphous, shapeless, unformed, unstructured *Ant* formed, shaped, structured

unshorn *Syn* HAIRY (sense 1), bristly, fleecy, furry, hirsute, rough, shaggy, woolly *Ant* bald, furless, hairless, shorn, smooth

unsightly *Syn* UGLY, hideous, ill-favored *Ant* beautiful

unskilled 1 *Syn* AMATEURISH, amateur, dilettante, inexperienced, inexpert, nonprofessional, unprofessional, unskillful *Ant* ace, adept, consummate, crackerjack, expert, master, masterful, masterly, professional, virtuoso **2** *Syn* INCOMPETENT, incapable, inept, inexpert, unfit, unqualified, unskillful *Ant* able, capable, competent, expert, fit, qualified, skilled, skillful

unskillful 1 *Syn* AMATEURISH, amateur, dilettante, inexperienced, inexpert, nonprofessional, unprofessional, unskilled *Ant* ace, adept, consummate, crackerjack, expert, master, masterful, masterly, professional, virtuoso **2** *Syn* INCOMPETENT, incapable, inept, inexpert, unfit, unqualified, unskilled *Ant* able, capable, competent, expert, fit, qualified, skilled, skillful

unsocial · disliking or avoiding the company of others *Syn* antisocial, asocial, nonsocial *Ant* social

unsolvable *Syn* IMPOSSIBLE, hopeless, unachievable, unattainable *Ant* achievable, attainable, doable, feasible, possible, realizable, workable

unsophisticated *Syn* NATURAL, artless, ingenuous, naive, simple, unaffected

unsound *Syn* ILLOGICAL, fallacious, invalid, irrational, nonrational, unreasonable, unreasoning, weak *Ant* logical, rational, reasonable, sound, valid

unspeakable *Syn* UNUTTERABLE, indefinable, indescribable, ineffable, inexpressible

unspoken *Syn* IMPLICIT, implied, tacit, unexpressed, unvoiced, wordless *Ant* explicit, express, expressed, spoken, stated

unstable *Syn* INCONSTANT, capricious, fickle, mercurial *Ant* constant

unstained *Syn* COLORLESS, uncolored, undyed, unpainted, white *Ant* colored, dyed, painted, stained, tinged, tinted

unsteady *Syn* FITFUL, casual, choppy, discontinuous, erratic, intermittent, irregular, occasional, spasmodic, sporadic, spotty *Ant* constant, continuous, regular, steady

unstructured *Syn* FORMLESS, amorphous, shapeless, unformed, unshaped *Ant* formed, shaped, structured

unstylishly *Syn* SLOPPILY, dowdily, slovenly *Ant* nattily, sharply, smartly, sprucely

unsubstantiated *Syn* GROUNDLESS, invalid, nonvalid, unfounded, ungrounded, unreasonable, unsupported, unwarranted *Ant* good, hard, just, justified, reasonable, reasoned, substantiated, valid, well-founded

unsuitable 1 *Syn* INAPPROPRIATE, graceless, improper, inapt, incongruous, incorrect, indecorous, inept, infelicitous, unapt, unbecoming, unfit, unhappy, unseemly, wrong *Ant* appropriate, becoming, befitting, correct, decorous, felicitous, fit, fitting, genteel, happy, meet, proper, right, seemly, suitable **2** *Syn* UNFIT, improper, inappropriate, inapt, infelicitous, unfitting, unhappy *Ant* fit

unsupportable *Syn* UNBEARABLE, insufferable, insupportable, intolerable, unendurable *Ant* endurable, sufferable, supportable, tolerable

unsupported *Syn* GROUNDLESS, invalid, nonvalid, ungrounded, unreasonable, unsubstantiated, unwarranted *Ant* good, hard, just, justified, reasonable, reasoned, substantiated, valid, well-founded

unsurpassed *Syn* EXCELLENT, A1, bang-up, banner, capital, classic, crackerjack, dandy, divine, fabulous, fine, first-class, first-rate, grand, great, groovy, heavenly, jim-dandy, keen, marvelous (*or* marvellous), mean, neat, nifty, noble, par excellence, prime, sensational, splendid, stellar, sterling, superb, superior, superlative, supernal, swell, terrific, tip-top, top, top-notch, wonderful *Ant* poor

unsympathetic *Syn* INCONSONANT, discordant, discrepant, incompatible, incongruous, inconsistent, uncongenial *Ant* consonant

untangle *Syn* EXTRICATE, disembarrass, disencumber, disentangle

untaught *Syn* IGNORANT, benighted, dark, illiterate, nonliterate, simple, uneducated, uninstructed, unlearned, unlettered, unread, unschooled, untutored *Ant* educated, knowledgeable, literate, schooled

unthrifty *Syn* PRODIGAL, extravagant, profligate, spendthrift, squandering, thriftless, wasteful *Ant* conserving, economical, economizing, frugal, scrimping, skimping, thrifty

untidy *Syn* MESSY, chaotic, cluttered, confused, disarranged, disarrayed, disheveled (*or* dishevelled), disordered, disorderly, higgledy-piggledy, hugger-mugger, jumbled, littered, messed, muddled, mussed, mussy, pell-mell, rumpled, sloppy, topsy-turvy, tousled, tumbled, unkempt, upside-down *Ant* neat, ordered, orderly, organized, shipshape, snug, tidied, tidy, trim

untimely *Syn* PREMATURE, advanced, forward, precocious *Ant* matured

untiring *Syn* INDEFATIGABLE, tireless, unflagging, unwearied, unwearying, weariless

untold *Syn* COUNTLESS, innumerable, numberless, uncountable, uncounted, unnumbered *Ant* countable

untouchable *Syn* OUTCAST, derelict, pariah, reprobate

untoward **1** *Syn* DISOBEDIENT, balky, contrary, defiant, froward, insubordinate, intractable, rebellious, recalcitrant, refractory, restive, ungovernable, unruly, wayward, willful (*or* wilful) *Ant* amenable, compliant,

docile, obedient, tractable **2** *Syn* UNCONTROLLABLE, froward, headstrong, intractable, recalcitrant, refractory, ungovernable, unmanageable, unruly, wayward, willful (*or* wilful) *Ant* controllable, governable, tractable

untruth **1** *Syn* FALLACY (sense 1), error, falsehood, falsity, illusion, misconception, myth, old wives' tale *Ant* truth, verity **2** *Syn* FALLACY (sense 2), erroneousness, fallaciousness, falseness, falsity *Ant* truth **3** *Syn* LIE, falsehood, fib, misrepresentation, story *Ant* truth

untutored *Syn* IGNORANT, benighted, dark, illiterate, nonliterate, simple, uneducated, uninstructed, unlearned, unlettered, unread, unschooled, untaught *Ant* educated, knowledgeable, literate, schooled

unusable *Syn* IMPRACTICAL, impracticable, inoperable, nonpractical, unworkable, useless *Ant* applicable, feasible, functional, operable, operational, practicable, practical, usable, useful, workable

unusual *Syn* EXCEPTIONAL, extraordinary, phenomenal, unwonted *Ant* average, common

unutterable · not capable of being put into words *Syn* indefinable, indescribable, ineffable, inexpressible, unspeakable

unvarying *Syn* UNIFORM, invariant, steady, unchanging, undeviating, unwavering *Ant* changing, deviating, varying

unvoiced *Syn* IMPLICIT, implied, tacit, unexpressed, unspoken, wordless *Ant* explicit, express, expressed, spoken, stated

unwanted *Syn* OBJECTIONABLE, exceptionable, unacceptable, undesirable, unwelcome

unwarrantable *Syn* INEXCUSABLE, indefensible, unforgivable, unjustifiable, unpardonable *Ant* defensible, excusable, forgivable, justifiable, pardonable

unwarranted **1** *Syn* BASELESS, groundless, unfounded **2** *Syn* GROUNDLESS, invalid, nonvalid, unfounded, ungrounded, unreasonable, unsubstantiated, unsupported *Ant* good, hard, just, justified, reasonable, reasoned, substantiated, valid, well-founded **3** *Syn* UNNECESSARY, dispensable, gratuitous, needless, nonessential, uncalled-for, unessential *Ant* essential, indispensable, necessary, needed, needful, required

unwavering *Syn* UNIFORM, invariant, steady, unchanging, undeviating, unvarying *Ant* changing, deviating, varying

unwearied *Syn* INDEFATIGABLE, tireless, unflagging, untiring, unwearying, weariless

unwearying *Syn* INDEFATIGABLE, tireless, unflagging, untiring, unwearied, weariless

unwed *Syn* UNMARRIED, single, unattached *Ant* espoused, married

unwelcome **1** *Syn* OBJECTIONABLE, exceptionable, unacceptable, undesirable,

unwanted **2** *Syn* UNPLEASANT, bad, disagreeable, displeasing, distasteful, nasty, rotten, sour, uncongenial, unlovely, unpleasing, unsatisfying *Ant* agreeable, congenial, good, grateful, gratifying, nice, palatable, pleasant, pleasing, pleasurable, satisfying, welcome

unwholesome · detrimental to physical, mental, or moral well-being *Syn* diseased, morbid, pathological, sickly *Rel* baneful, deleterious, detrimental, noxious, pernicious *Ant* wholesome

unwieldy *Syn* CUMBERSOME, awkward, clumsy, cranky, cumbrous, ungainly, unhandy *Ant* handy

unwillingness *Syn* RELUCTANCE, disinclination, hesitance, hesitancy *Ant* inclination, willingness

unwise *Syn* INDISCREET, ill-advised, imprudent, inadvisable, injudicious, tactless, unadvisable *Ant* advisable, discreet, judicious, prudent, tactful, wise

unwitting *Syn* ACCIDENTAL, casual, chance, fluky, fortuitous, inadvertent, incidental, unintended, unintentional, unplanned, unpremeditated *Ant* deliberate, intended, intentional, planned, premeditated

unwonted *Syn* EXCEPTIONAL, extraordinary, phenomenal, unusual *Ant* average, common

unworkable *Syn* IMPRACTICAL, impracticable, inoperable, nonpractical, unusable, useless *Ant* applicable, feasible, functional, operable, operational, practicable, practical, usable, useful, workable

unwritten *Syn* VERBAL, oral, spoken *Ant* written

unyielding *Syn* OBSTINATE, adamant, adamantine, dogged, hard, hardened, hardheaded, hardhearted, headstrong, immovable, implacable, inflexible, mulish, obdurate, opinionated, ossified, pat, peevish, pertinacious, perverse, pigheaded, rigid, self-willed, stubborn, unbending, uncompromising, unrelenting, willful (*or* wilful) *Ant* acquiescent, agreeable, amenable, compliant, complying, flexible, pliable, pliant, relenting, yielding

up **1** *Syn* ASCEND, arise, climb, lift, mount, rise, soar, uprise, upsweep, upturn *Ant* decline, descend, dip, drop, fall (off) **2** *Syn* INCREASE (sense 1), add (to), aggrandize, amplify, augment, boost, compound, enlarge, escalate, expand, extend, multiply, raise, swell *Ant* abate, contract, decrease, diminish, lessen, lower, reduce, subtract (from)

upbeat *Syn* CHEERFUL (sense 1), blithe, blithesome, bright, buoyant, cheery, chipper, gay, gladsome, lightsome, sunny *Ant* dour, gloomy, glum, morose, saturnine, sulky, sullen

upbraid *Syn* SCOLD, bawl, berate, chew out, jaw, rail, rate, revile, tongue-lash, vituperate, wig

upcoming *Syn* FORTHCOMING, approaching, coming, imminent, impending, nearing, oncoming, pending *Ant* late, recent

up-country *Syn* FRONTIER, backwater, backwoods, bush, hinterland

upheaval *Syn* CONVULSION, cataclysm, paroxysm, storm, tempest, tumult, uproar

uphold *Syn* SUPPORT (sense 2), advocate, back, champion

upon *Syn* AGAINST, on

upper crust *Syn* ELITE, best, choice, cream, elect, fat, flower, pick, prime

uppish *Syn* ARROGANT, cavalier, haughty, highfalutin, high-handed, high-hat, imperious, important, lofty, lordly, masterful, overweening, peremptory, pompous, presumptuous, pretentious, supercilious, superior, uppity *Ant* humble, modest

uppity *Syn* ARROGANT, cavalier, haughty, highfalutin, high-handed, high-hat, imperious, important, lofty, lordly, masterful, overweening, peremptory, pompous, presumptuous, pretentious, supercilious, superior, uppish *Ant* humble, modest

upright **1** · having or showing a strict regard for what is morally right *Syn* conscientious, honest, honorable, just, scrupulous *Rel* ethical, righteous, virtuous **2** *Syn* ERECT, perpendicular, plumb, raised, standing, upstanding, vertical *Ant* flat, recumbent

uprise *Syn* ASCEND, arise, climb, lift, mount, rise, soar, up, upsweep, upturn *Ant* decline, descend, dip, drop, fall (off)

uprising *Syn* REBELLION, coup, insurrection, mutiny, putsch, revolt, revolution

uproar **1** *Syn* COMMOTION, bother, bustle, clatter, disturbance, furor, furore, fuss, hubbub, hullabaloo, hurly-burly, pandemonium, pother, row, ruckus, ruction, rumpus, shindy, squall, stew, stir, storm, to-do, tumult, turmoil, welter, whirl **2** *Syn* CONVULSION, cataclysm, paroxysm, storm, tempest, tumult, upheaval **3** *Syn* DIN, babel, clamor, hubbub, hullabaloo, pandemonium, racket *Ant* quiet **4** *Syn* FRENZY, agitation, delirium, distraction, furor, furore, fury, hysteria, rage, rampage

uproot *Syn* EXTERMINATE, deracinate, eradicate, extirpate, wipe

upset *vb Syn* DISCOMPOSE, agitate, disquiet, disturb, flurry, fluster, perturb

upset *n Syn* DISORDER, confuse, derange, disarrange, disarray, discompose, dishevel, dislocate, disorganize, disrupt, disturb, hash, jumble, mess (up), mix (up), muddle, muss, rumple, scramble, shuffle, tousle, tumble *Ant* arrange, array, draw up, marshal, order, organize, range, regulate, straighten (up), tidy

upset *Syn* OVERTURN, capsize, overthrow, subvert

upsetting *Syn* TROUBLESOME, discomforting, discomposing, disquieting, distressing, disturbing, perturbing, troubling, troublous, unsettling, worrisome *Ant* reassuring, untroublesome

upshot *Syn* EFFECT, aftereffect, aftermath, consequence, event, issue, outcome, result, sequel *Ant* cause

upside-down *Syn* MESSY, chaotic, cluttered, confused, disarranged, disarrayed, disheveled (*or* dishevelled), disordered, disorderly, higgledy-piggledy, hugger-mugger, jumbled, littered, messed, muddled, mussed, mussy, pell-mell, rumpled, sloppy, topsy-turvy, tousled, tumbled, unkempt, untidy *Ant* neat, ordered, orderly, organized, shipshape, snug, tidied, tidy, trim

upstanding *Syn* ERECT, perpendicular, plumb, raised, standing, upright, vertical *Ant* flat, recumbent

upsweep *Syn* ASCEND, arise, climb, lift, mount, rise, soar, up, uprise, upturn *Ant* decline, descend, dip, drop, fall (off)

up-to-date *Syn* MODERN, contemporary, current, hot, mod, modernistic, new, newfangled, new-fashioned, present-day, red-hot, space-age, ultramodern *Ant* antiquated, archaic, dated, fusty, musty, noncontemporary, oldfangled, old-fashioned, old-time, out-of-date, passé

upturn *Syn* ASCEND, arise, climb, lift, mount, rise, soar, up, uprise, upsweep *Ant* decline, descend, dip, drop, fall (off)

urbane *Syn* SUAVE, debonair, smooth, sophisticated *Ant* boorish, churlish, clownish, loutish, uncouth

urge *vb* · to try to persuade (someone) through earnest appeals to follow a course of action *Syn* egg (on), encourage, exhort, goad, press, prod, prompt *Rel* drive, propel, spur, stimulate

urge *n Syn* DESIRE, appetite, lust, passion *Ant* distaste

urgent *Syn* PRESSING, crying, exigent, imperative, importunate, insistent, instant

usage *Syn* FORM (sense 3), convenance, convention

use *n* **1** · a useful or valuable end, result, or purpose *Syn* account, advantage, avail, profit, service *Rel* benefit **2** · a capacity for serving an end or purpose *Syn* usefulness, utility *Rel* applicability, pertinence, relevance **3** *Syn* LIKING, appetite, fancy, favor, fondness, like, love, partiality, preference, relish, shine, taste *Ant* aversion, disfavor, dislike, distaste, hatred, loathing

use *vb* · to put into service especially to attain an end *Syn* apply, avail, employ, utilize *Rel* handle, manipulate, ply, wield

used *Syn* ACCUSTOMED, given, habituated, wont *Ant* unaccustomed, unused

usefulness *Syn* USE (sense 2), utility

useless *Syn* IMPRACTICAL, impracticable, inoperable, nonpractical, unusable, unworkable *Ant* applicable, feasible, functional, operable, operational, practicable, practical, usable, useful, workable

use up *Syn* DEPLETE, clean (out), consume, drain, exhaust, expend, spend *Ant* renew, replace

usual · familiar through frequent or regular repetition *Syn* accustomed, customary, habitual, wont, wonted *Rel* natural, normal, regular, typical

usually *Syn* NATURALLY (sense 1), commonly, generally, normally, ordinarily, typically *Ant* abnormally, atypically, extraordinarily, uncommonly, unusually

usurp *Syn* ARROGATE, appropriate, confiscate, preempt *Ant* renounce, yield

utensil *Syn* IMPLEMENT, appliance, instrument, tool

utility *Syn* USE (sense 2), usefulness

utilize *Syn* USE, apply, avail, employ

utopian *adj Syn* AMBITIOUS (sense 2), pretentious *Ant* modest

utopian *n Syn* IDEALIST, dreamer, romantic, romanticist, visionary

utter **1** *Syn* EXPRESS, air, broach, vent, ventilate, voice *Ant* imply **2** *Syn* SAY, state, tell

uttered *Syn* VOCAL (sense 1), oral, voiced *Ant* nonvocal

V

vacancy **1** · empty space *Syn* blank, blankness, emptiness, vacuity, void *Rel* nothingness **2** · the quality or state of being empty *Syn* bareness, emptiness, vacuity *Rel* hollowness *Ant* fullness

vacant *Syn* EMPTY, blank, vacuous, void *Ant* full

vacate *Syn* EMPTY, clear, evacuate, void *Ant* fill, load

vacated *Syn* ABANDONED (sense 2), derelict, deserted, disused, forgotten, forsaken, rejected

vacillate *Syn* HESITATE, falter, waver *Ant* dive (in), plunge (in)

vacillation *Syn* HESITATION, faltering, hesitance, hesitancy, indecision, irresolution, shilly-shallying, wavering, wobbling

vacuity **1** *Syn* VACANCY (sense 1), blank,

blankness, emptiness, void *Ant* fullness **2** *Syn* VACANCY (sense 2), bareness, emptiness *Ant* fullness

vacuous *Syn* EMPTY, blank, vacant, void *Ant* full

vacuum *Syn* HOLE, cavity, hollow, pocket, void

vagabond **1** · a person who wanders at will or as a habit *Syn* bum, hobo, tramp, truant, vagrant *Rel* roamer, rover, wanderer **2** *Syn* NOMAD, drifter, gadabout, rambler, roamer, rover, stroller, wanderer, wayfarer

vagary *Syn* WHIM, caprice, fancy, freak, notion, whimsy

vagrant *adj Syn* ITINERANT, ambulant, ambulatory, nomadic, peripatetic

vagrant *n Syn* VAGABOND, bum, hobo, tramp, truant

vague *Syn* OBSCURE, ambiguous, cryptic, dark, enigmatic, equivocal *Ant* distinct, obvious

vain **1** · being without worth or significance *Syn* empty, hollow, idle, nugatory, otiose **2** *Syn* CONCEITED, complacent, egoistic, egotistic (*or* egotistical), important, overweening, pompous, prideful, proud, self-conceited, self-important, self-satisfied, smug, stuck-up, vainglorious *Ant* humble, modest **3** *Syn* FUTILE, abortive, bootless, fruitless *Ant* effective, effectual, efficacious, efficient, fruitful, productive, profitable, successful **4** *Syn* PROUD (sense 2), vainglorious *Ant* ashamed, humble

vainglorious **1** *Syn* CONCEITED, complacent, egoistic, egotistic (*or* egotistical), important, overweening, pompous, prideful, proud, self-conceited, self-important, self-satisfied, smug, stuck-up, vain *Ant* humble, modest **2** *Syn* PROUD (sense 2), vain *Ant* ashamed, humble

vaingloriousness *Syn* COMPLACENCE, complacency, conceit, conceitedness, ego, egotism, pompousness, pride, pridefulness, self-admiration, self-conceit, self-esteem, self-importance, self-satisfaction, smugness, vainglory, vainness, vanity *Ant* humbleness, humility, modesty

vainglory **1** *Syn* COMPLACENCE, complacency, conceit, conceitedness, ego, egotism, pompousness, pride, pridefulness, self-admiration, self-conceit, self-esteem, self-importance, self-satisfaction, smugness, vaingloriousness, vainness, vanity *Ant* humbleness, humility, modesty **2** *Syn* PRIDE, vanity *Ant* humility, shame

vainness *Syn* COMPLACENCE, complacency, conceit, conceitedness, ego, egotism, pompousness, pride, pridefulness, self-admiration, self-conceit, self-esteem, self-importance, self-satisfaction, smugness, vaingloriousness, vainglory, vanity *Ant* humbleness, humility, modesty

valiant *Syn* BRAVE, audacious, bold, courageous, dauntless, doughty, fearless, intrepid, unafraid, undaunted, valorous *Ant* craven

validate *Syn* CONFIRM, authenticate, corroborate, substantiate, verify *Ant* contradict, deny

valor **1** *Syn* COURAGE, bravery, courageousness, daring, dauntlessness, doughtiness, fearlessness, gallantry, greatheartedness, guts, hardihood, heart, heroism, intrepidity, intrepidness, nerve, stoutness *Ant* cowardice, cowardliness, cravenness, dastardliness, spinelessness, yellowness **2** *Syn* HEROISM, gallantry, prowess

valorous *Syn* BRAVE, audacious, bold, courageous, dauntless, doughty, fearless, intrepid, unafraid, undaunted, valiant *Ant* craven

valuable *Syn* COSTLY, dear, expensive, invaluable, precious, priceless *Ant* cheap

value *vb* **1** *Syn* APPRECIATE, cherish, prize, treasure *Ant* despise **2** *Syn* ESTIMATE (sense 1), appraise, assay, assess, evaluate, rate

value *adj Syn* EXCELLENCE, distinction, excellency, merit, virtue *Ant* deficiency

vanish · to pass from view or out of existence *Syn* disappear, evanesce, evaporate, fade *Rel* escape, flee, fly *Ant* appear, loom

vanished *Syn* EXTINCT, bygone, dead, defunct, departed, expired, gone *Ant* alive, existent, existing, extant, living

vanity **1** *Syn* COMPLACENCE, complacency, conceit, conceitedness, ego, egotism, pompousness, pride, pridefulness, self-admiration, self-conceit, self-esteem, self-importance, self-satisfaction, smugness, vaingloriousness, vainglory, vainness *Ant* humbleness, humility, modesty **2** *Syn* PRIDE, vainglory *Ant* humility, shame

vanquish *Syn* CONQUER, beat, defeat, lick, overcome, overthrow, reduce, rout, subdue, subjugate, surmount

vanquisher *Syn* VICTOR, champion, conqueror, winner

vapid *Syn* INSIPID, banal, flat, inane, jejune, wishy-washy *Ant* sapid, zestful

variable *Syn* CHANGEABLE, changeful, mutable, protean *Ant* stable, unchangeable

variance *Syn* DISCORD, conflict, contention, difference, dissension, schism, strife

variation *Syn* CHANGE (sense 1), alteration, modification *Ant* monotony, uniformity

varicolored *Syn* COLORFUL, motley, multicolored, polychromatic, polychrome, variegated *Ant* colorless, monochromatic, solid

variegated **1** · having a pattern involving different colors or shades of color *Syn* checked, checkered, dappled, motley, particolored, piebald, pied, skewbald *Rel* flecked, marbled, mottled, spattered, spotted, stippled **2** *Syn* COLORFUL, motley, multicolored, polychromatic, polychrome, varicolored *Ant* colorless, monochromatic, solid

variety · a group of related plants or animals

narrower in scope than a species *Syn* breed, clone, cultivar, race, stock, strain, subspecies

various 1 *Syn* DIFFERENT, disparate, divergent, diverse *Ant* alike, identical, same **2** *Syn* MANY, divers, multifarious, numerous, several, sundry *Ant* few

vary 1 *Syn* CHANGE (sense 1), alter, make over, modify, recast, redo, refashion, remake, remodel, revamp, revise, rework *Ant* fix, freeze, set, stabilize **2** *Syn* CHANGE (sense 2), fluctuate, mutate, shift *Ant* stabilize **3** *Syn* DIFFER, disagree, dissent *Ant* agree

vast *Syn* HUGE, Brobdingnagian, colossal, cyclopean, elephantine, enormous, gargantuan, giant, gigantean, gigantic, Herculean, immense, mammoth, titanic *Ant* bitty, diminutive, microscopic (*or* microscopical), midget, miniature, minute, pocket, pygmy, teeny, teeny-weeny, tiny, wee

vault *vb Syn* JUMP, bound, leap, spring

vault *n Syn* JUMP, bound, leap, spring

vaunt *Syn* BOAST, brag, crow, gasconade *Ant* depreciate (*oneself, one's accomplishments*)

veer *Syn* SWERVE, depart, deviate, digress, diverge

vehement 1 *Syn* FERVENT, ardent, blazing, burning, charged, emotional, fervid, feverish, fiery, flaming, glowing, hot-blooded, impassioned, passionate, red-hot, warm, warm-blooded *Ant* cold, cool, dispassionate, impassive, unemotional **2** *Syn* INTENSE, exquisite, fierce, violent *Ant* subdued

vehicle *Syn* AGENT (sense 2), agency, instrument, instrumentality, machinery, means, medium, organ

veil *Syn* COVER, envelop, overspread, shroud, wrap *Ant* bare

vein 1 *Syn* MOOD, humor, temper **2** *Syn* TOUCH, dash, shade, smack, soupçon, spice, strain, streak, suggestion, suspicion, tincture, tinge

veld *or* **veldt** *Syn* PLAIN, down, grassland, prairie, savanna, steppe, tundra

velocity *Syn* SPEED, headway, impetus, momentum, pace

velvety *Syn* SLEEK, glossy, satiny, silken, silky, slick

venal · open to improper influence and especially bribery *Syn* bribable, corruptible, purchasable *Rel* hack, mercenary *Ant* incorruptible, uncorruptible

vend *Syn* MARKET, deal (in), merchandise, put up, retail, sell *Ant* buy, purchase

venerate *Syn* REVERE, adore, reverence, worship *Ant* flout

veneration *Syn* REVERENCE (sense 1), adoration, worship

vengeance *Syn* RETALIATION, reprisal, retribution, revenge

vengeful *Syn* VINDICTIVE, revengeful

venial · worthy of forgiveness *Syn* excusable, forgivable, pardonable, remittable *Rel* justifiable, redeemable *Ant* inexcusable, mortal, unforgivable, unpardonable

venom *Syn* POISON, bane, toxin, virus

venomous *Syn* POISONOUS, mephitic, miasmal, miasmatic, miasmic, pestilent, pestilential, toxic, virulent *Ant* nonpoisonous, nontoxic, nonvenomous

vent *Syn* EXPRESS, air, broach, utter, ventilate, voice *Ant* imply

ventilate *Syn* EXPRESS, air, broach, utter, vent, voice *Ant* imply

venture *Syn* ENDANGER, adventure, compromise, gamble (with), hazard, imperil, jeopardize, menace, risk

venturesome *Syn* ADVENTUROUS, daredevil, daring, foolhardy, rash, reckless *Ant* cautious, unadventurous

veracious *Syn* TRUTHFUL, honest *Ant* dishonest, fibbing, lying, mendacious, prevaricating, untruthful

veracity 1 *Syn* PRECISION, accuracy, closeness, delicacy, exactitude, exactness, fineness, preciseness, rigorousness *Ant* coarseness, impreciseness, imprecision, inaccuracy, inexactness, roughness **2** *Syn* TRUTH, verisimilitude, verity *Ant* falsehood, lie, untruth

verbal · made or carried on through speaking rather than in writing *Syn* oral, spoken, unwritten *Rel* implicit, informal *Ant* written

verbiage · an excess of words usually of little or obscure content *Syn* circumlocution, periphrasis, pleonasm, redundancy, tautology *Rel* diffuseness, prolixity, verboseness, wordiness

verbose *Syn* WORDY, diffuse, prolix, redundant *Ant* compact, concise, crisp, pithy, succinct, terse

verge *Syn* BORDER, brim, brink, edge, margin, rim

verging *Syn* ADJACENT, abutting, adjoining, bordering, contiguous, flanking, fringing, joining, juxtaposed, skirting, touching *Ant* nonadjacent

verify *Syn* CONFIRM, authenticate, corroborate, substantiate, validate *Ant* contradict, deny

verisimilitude *Syn* TRUTH, veracity, verity *Ant* falsehood, lie, untruth

veritable *Syn* AUTHENTIC, bona fide, genuine *Ant* spurious

verity *Syn* TRUTH, veracity, verisimilitude *Ant* falsehood, lie, untruth

vernacularism *Syn* BARBARISM, corruption, impropriety, solecism, vulgarism

versatile · having a wide range of skills or abilities or many different uses *Syn* all-around, many-sided *Rel* gifted, talented

verse 1 *Syn* PARAGRAPH, article, clause, count, plank **2** *Syn* POEM, lyric, song

versifier *Syn* POET, bard, minstrel, poetaster, rhymer, rhymester, troubadour

version **1** *Syn* ACCOUNT, chronicle, report, story **2** *Syn* TRANSLATION, metaphrase, paraphrase

vertebrae *Syn* SPINE, back, backbone, chine

vertical **1** · being at right angles to a base line *Syn* perpendicular, plumb *Ant* horizontal **2** *Syn* ERECT, perpendicular, plumb, raised, standing, upright, upstanding *Ant* flat, recumbent

vertiginous *Syn* GIDDY, dazzled, dizzy, swimming

verve *Syn* VIGOR, dash, drive, élan, esprit, punch, spirit, vim

very *adv* · to a great degree *Syn* awful, awfully, beastly, deadly, especially, exceedingly, extra, extremely, far, frightfully, full, greatly, heavily, highly, hugely, jolly, mightily, mighty, mortally, most, much, particularly, rattling, real, right, so, something, super, terribly, too, whacking *Rel* completely, entirely, purely, thoroughly, totally, utterly *Ant* little, negligibly, nominally, slightly

very *adj* **1** *Syn* ACTUAL, concrete, existent, factual, real, true *Ant* conjectural, hypothetical, ideal, nonexistent, possible, potential, theoretical **2** *Syn* MERE, bare **3** *Syn* SAME, equal, equivalent, identic, identical, selfsame, tantamount *Ant* different

vessel **1** *Syn* BOAT, craft, ship **2** *Syn* CONTAINER, holder, receptacle

vestige · a tiny often physical indication of something lost or vanished *Syn* relic, shadow, trace *Rel* memento, remembrance, reminder

veto *Syn* PROHIBITION (sense 2), ban, embargo, interdict, interdiction, proscription *Ant* prescription

vex *Syn* ANNOY, bother, irk *Ant* soothe

vexatious *Syn* ANNOYING, aggravating, bothersome, disturbing, exasperating, frustrating, galling, irksome, irritating, maddening, nettling, peeving, pesty, rankling, riling, vexing

vexing *Syn* ANNOYING, aggravating, bothersome, disturbing, exasperating, frustrating, galling, irksome, irritating, maddening, nettling, peeving, pesty, rankling, riling, vexatious

viands *Syn* FOOD (sense 1), comestibles, feed, fodder, forage, provender, provisions, victuals

vibrant *Syn* RESONANT, orotund, resounding, ringing, sonorous

vibrate *Syn* SWING (sense 2), fluctuate, oscillate, pendulate, sway, undulate, waver

vice **1** *Syn* FAULT, failing, foible, frailty *Ant* merit **2** *Syn* OFFENSE (sense 2), crime, scandal, sin

vicinity *Syn* LOCALITY, district, neighborhood

vicious · highly reprehensible or offensive in character, nature, or conduct *Syn* corrupt, degenerate, flagitious, infamous, iniquitous, nefarious, villainous *Rel* debased, debauched, depraved, perverted *Ant* virtuous

viciousness *Syn* CRUELTY, barbarity, brutality, cruelness, heartlessness, inhumanity, sadism, savageness, savagery, wantonness *Ant* benignity, compassion, good-heartedness, humanity, kindheartedness, kindness, sympathy

vicissitude **1** *Syn* CHANGE (sense 2), alternation, mutation, permutation **2** *Syn* DIFFICULTY, hardship, rigor

victim · one killed or injured for the ends of the one who kills or injures *Syn* prey, quarry

victimize *Syn* FLEECE, bleed, cheat, chisel, cozen, defraud, hustle, mulct, rook, shortchange, skin, squeeze, stick, sting, swindle

victor · one that defeats an enemy or opponent *Syn* champion, conqueror, vanquisher, winner

victory · a successful outcome in a contest or struggle *Syn* conquest, triumph *Rel* gaining, winning *Ant* defeat

victuals *Syn* FOOD (sense 1), comestibles, feed, fodder, forage, provender, provisions, viands

vie *Syn* RIVAL, compete, emulate

view *vb* **1** *Syn* LOOK, glance, glimpse, peek, peep, sight **2** *Syn* SEE (sense 1), behold, contemplate, descry, discern, espy, note, notice, observe, perceive, remark, survey

view *n* *Syn* OPINION, belief, conviction, persuasion, sentiment

viewpoint *Syn* POINT OF VIEW, angle, slant, standpoint

vigilance · the act or state of being constantly attentive and responsive to signs of opportunity, activity, or danger *Syn* alertness, attentiveness, lookout, surveillance, watch, watchfulness *Rel* aliveness, awareness, consciousness, sensitivity

vigilant *Syn* WATCHFUL, alert, wide-awake

vigor · a quality of force, forcefulness, or energy *Syn* dash, drive, élan, esprit, punch, spirit, verve, vim *Rel* energy, force, might, power, strength

vigorous · having or showing great vitality and force *Syn* energetic, lusty, nervous, strenuous *Rel* manful, manly, virile *Ant* languorous, lethargic

vile *Syn* BASE, low *Ant* noble

vilify *Syn* SLANDER, asperse, blacken, defame, libel, malign, smear, traduce

villa *Syn* MANSION, castle, château, country-seat, estate, hacienda, hall, manor, manor house, palace

villain · a low, mean, reprehensible person utterly lacking in principles *Syn* blackguard, knave, miscreant, rapscallion, rascal, rogue, scamp, scoundrel *Rel* offender, sinner

villainous *Syn* VICIOUS, corrupt, degenerate,

flagitious, infamous, iniquitous, nefarious *Ant* virtuous

villainy *Syn* EVIL, bad, evildoing, ill, immorality, iniquity, sin, wrong *Ant* good, morality, right, virtue

vim *Syn* VIGOR, dash, drive, élan, esprit, punch, spirit, verve

vindicate 1 *Syn* EXCULPATE, absolve, acquit, exonerate *Ant* accuse, inculpate 2 *Syn* MAINTAIN, assert, defend, justify

vindictive · showing or motivated by a desire for vengeance *Syn* revengeful, vengeful *Rel* grim, implacable, merciless, relentless, unrelenting

violate *Syn* DESECRATE, defile, profane

violation *Syn* BREACH (sense 1), contravention, infraction, infringement, transgression, trespass

violence *Syn* FORCE, coercion, compulsion, constraint, duress, restraint

violent *Syn* INTENSE, exquisite, fierce, vehement *Ant* subdued

virile *Syn* MALE, manful, manlike, manly, mannish, masculine *Ant* female

virility · the set of qualities considered appropriate for or characteristic of men *Syn* manhood, manliness, masculinity *Rel* maleness *Ant* femininity

virtually 1 · not absolutely or actually, yet so nearly so that the difference is negligible *Syn* morally, practically 2 *Syn* ALMOST, about, more or less, most, much, near, nearly, next to, nigh, practically, some, well-nigh

virtue 1 *Syn* EXCELLENCE, distinction, excellency, merit, value *Ant* deficiency 2 *Syn* GOODNESS, morality, rectitude *Ant* badness, evil

virtuoso *Syn* EXPERT, ace, adept, artist, authority, crackerjack, maestro, master, past master, scholar, shark, whiz, wizard *Ant* amateur

virtuous *Syn* MORAL, ethical, noble, righteous

virulent *Syn* POISONOUS, mephitic, miasmal, miasmatic, miasmic, pestilent, pestilential, toxic, venomous *Ant* nonpoisonous, nontoxic, nonvenomous

virus *Syn* POISON, bane, toxin, venom

visage *Syn* FACE, countenance, mug, physiognomy, puss

visible · capable of being seen *Syn* apparent, observable, seeable, visual *Rel* external, outer, outward *Ant* invisible, unseeable

vision 1 *Syn* FANCY, daydream, dream, fantasy, nightmare, phantasm, phantasy *Ant* reality 2 *Syn* GHOST, apparition, bogey, phantasm, phantom, poltergeist, shade, shadow, specter (*or* spectre), spirit, spook, wraith 3 *Syn* REVELATION (sense 1), prophecy

visionary *adj Syn* IDEALIST, dreamer, romantic, romanticist, utopian *Ant* pragmatist, realist

visionary *n Syn* IMAGINARY, chimerical, fanciful, fantastic, quixotic *Ant* actual, real

visit *n* · a usually brief stay with another as an act of friendship or courtesy *Syn* call, visitation

visit *vb Syn* CHAT, babble, blab, cackle, chatter, converse, gab, gabble, gas, jabber, jaw, palaver, patter, prate, prattle, rap, rattle, run on, talk, twitter

visitant *Syn* VISITOR, caller, guest

visitation 1 *Syn* TRIAL, affliction, cross, tribulation 2 *Syn* VISIT, call

visitor · one who visits another *Syn* caller, guest, visitant

visual *Syn* VISIBLE, apparent, observable, seeable *Ant* invisible, unseeable

vital 1 *Syn* CRUCIAL, critical, key, pivotal 2 *Syn* DEADLY, baleful, deathly, fatal, fell, killer, lethal, mortal, murderous, pestilent *Ant* healthful, healthy, nonfatal, nonlethal, wholesome 3 *Syn* ESSENTIAL, cardinal, fundamental 4 *Syn* LIVING, alive, animate, animated *Ant* lifeless

vitalize 1 · to arouse to activity, animation, or life *Syn* activate, energize *Rel* animate, enliven, quicken, vivify *Ant* atrophy 2 *Syn* ANIMATE, brace, energize, enliven, fire, invigorate, jazz (up), liven (up), pep (up), quicken, stimulate, vivify *Ant* damp, dampen, deaden, dull

vitalizing *Syn* TONIC, bracing, invigorating, refreshing, restorative, reviving, stimulating, stimulative

vitiate *Syn* DEBASE, corrupt, debauch, deprave, pervert *Ant* amend (*morals, character*), elevate (*taste, way of life*)

vitiated *Syn* DEBASED, corrupted, debauched, depraved, perverted

vituperate 1 *Syn* ATTACK (sense 2), abuse, assail, belabor, blast, castigate, excoriate, jump (on), lambaste (*or* lambast), scathe, slam 2 *Syn* SCOLD, bawl, berate, chew out, jaw, rail, rate, revile, tongue-lash, upbraid, wig

vituperation *Syn* ABUSE, billingsgate, invective, obloquy, scurrility *Ant* adulation

vituperative *Syn* ABUSIVE, contumelious, opprobrious, scurrilous *Ant* complementary, respectful

vivacious *Syn* LIVELY, animated, gay, sprightly *Ant* dull

vivid *Syn* GRAPHIC, pictorial, picturesque

vivify *Syn* ANIMATE, brace, energize, enliven, fire, invigorate, jazz (up), liven (up), pep (up), quicken, stimulate, vitalize *Ant* damp, dampen, deaden, dull

vocable *Syn* WORD, term

vocabulary 1 *Syn* LANGUAGE (sense 2), diction, phraseology, phrasing, style 2 *Syn* TERMINOLOGY, argot, cant, dialect, jargon, language, lingo, patois, patter, slang

vocal · uttered by the voice or having to do with such utterance *Syn* oral, uttered, voiced *Rel* articulate, articulated, spoken *Ant* nonvocal

vocation *Syn* OCCUPATION, calling, employment, line, profession, trade, work

vociferate *Syn* ROAR, bawl, bellow, bluster, clamor, howl, ululate

vociferation *Syn* ROAR, bawl, bellow, bluster, ululation

vociferous · so loud or insistent as to compel attention *Syn* blatant, boisterous, clamorous, obstreperous, strident *Rel* noisy, sounding

vogue **1** *Syn* FASHION, craze, cry, dernier cri, fad, mode, rage, style **2** *Syn* POPULARITY, fashionableness, favor, hotness, modishness *Ant* disfavor, unpopularity

voice *Syn* EXPRESS, air, broach, utter, vent, ventilate *Ant* imply

voiced *Syn* VOCAL (sense 1), oral, uttered *Ant* nonvocal

voiceless *Syn* MUTE, inarticulate, speechless

void *vb* **1** *Syn* ABOLISH, abrogate, annul, cancel, dissolve, invalidate, negate, nullify, quash, repeal, rescind **2** *Syn* EMPTY, clear, evacuate, vacate *Ant* fill, load

void *adj* **1** *Syn* DEVOID, destitute **2** *Syn* EMPTY, blank, vacant, vacuous *Ant* full

void *n* **1** *Syn* HOLE, cavity, hollow, pocket, vacuum **2** *Syn* VACANCY (sense 1), blank, blankness, emptiness, vacuity *Ant* fullness

volatile *Syn* ELASTIC (sense 2), buoyant, effervescent, expansive, resilient *Ant* depressed

volatility *Syn* LIGHTNESS, flightiness, flippancy, frivolity, levity, light-mindedness *Ant* seriousness

volcano *Syn* MOUNTAIN, alp, mesa, mount, peak

volition *Syn* WILL, conation

volley *Syn* BARRAGE, bombardment, cannonade, fusillade, hail, salvo, shower, storm

volubility *Syn* TALKATIVENESS, garrulity, garrulousness, glibness, loquaciousness, loquacity *Ant* silence

voluble *Syn* TALKATIVE, garrulous, glib, loquacious *Ant* closemouthed, laconic, reserved, reticent, taciturn, tight-lipped

volume **1** *Syn* AMOUNT, measure, quantity **2** *Syn* BULK, mass **3** *Syn* SIZE, area, dimensions, extent, magnitude

voluminous *Syn* LARGE, big, bulky, considerable, goodly, good-sized, grand, great, handsome, hefty, hulking, largish, outsize, oversize (*or* oversized), sizable (*or* sizeable), substantial, tidy *Ant* little, puny, small, undersized

voluntary **1** · done or brought about of one's own will *Syn* deliberate, intentional, willful, willing *Rel* chosen, elected, opted *Ant* instinctive, involuntary **2** *Syn* OPTIONAL, discretionary, elective *Ant* compulsory, mandatory, nonelective, obligatory, required

voluptuous *Syn* SENSUOUS, epicurean, luxurious, sybaritic

vomit *Syn* BELCH, burp, disgorge, regurgitate, spew, throw up

voodoo *Syn* MAGICIAN (sense 1), charmer, conjurer (*or* conjuror), enchanter, necromancer, sorcerer, witch, wizard

voracious · excessively greedy *Syn* gluttonous, rapacious, ravening, ravenous *Rel* acquisitive, covetous, grasping, greedy

vortex *Syn* EDDY, maelstrom, whirlpool

votary **1** *Syn* ADDICT, devotee, habitué **2** *Syn* FOLLOWER, adherent, convert, disciple, partisan, pupil *Ant* leader

vote *Syn* SUFFRAGE, ballot, franchise

vouch *Syn* CERTIFY, attest, witness

vouchsafe *Syn* GRANT (sense 1), accord, award, concede

vow *Syn* PROMISE, oath, pledge, troth, word

voyage *Syn* JOURNEY, cruise, excursion, expedition, jaunt, pilgrimage, tour, trip

vulgar **1** *Syn* COARSE, gross, obscene, ribald *Ant* fine, refined **2** *Syn* COMMON, familiar, ordinary, popular *Ant* exceptional, uncommon

vulgarism *Syn* BARBARISM, corruption, impropriety, solecism, vernacularism

W

wage, wages · the price paid a person for his or her labor or services *Syn* emolument, fee, hire, pay, salary, stipend *Rel* recompense, recompensing, remuneration

wager *n Syn* BET, ante, pot, stake

wager *vb Syn* BET, gamble, go, lay, stake

wagerer *Syn* BETTOR, gambler

waggish *Syn* PLAYFUL, frolicsome, impish, mischievous, roguish, sportive

wail *vb* **1** *Syn* COMPLAIN, beef, bellyache, carp, crab, croak, fuss, gripe, grouse, growl, grumble, kick, moan, murmur, mutter, repine, squawk, whine, yammer **2** *Syn* CRY, blubber, keen, weep, whimper

wail *n Syn* LAMENT, groan, howl, keen, lamentation, moan, plaint *Ant* exultation, rejoicing

wait *n Syn* DELAY, detainment, holdup

wait vb Syn STAY, abide, linger, remain, tarry

waive Syn RELINQUISH, abandon, cede, leave, resign, surrender, yield Ant keep

wakeful · not sleeping or able to sleep Syn awake, sleepless, wide-awake Rel aroused, awakened, roused, wakened Ant asleep, dormant, dozing, napping, resting, sleeping, slumbering

waken Syn STIR, arouse, awaken, rally, rouse

walk n · a relaxed journey on foot for exercise or pleasure Syn constitutional, perambulation, ramble, range, saunter, stroll, turn Rel parade, promenade

walk vb · to go on foot Syn foot (it), hoof (it), leg (it), pad, step, traipse, tread Rel parade, promenade

wall n Syn BARRIER, barricade, fence, hedge

wall vb Syn ENCLOSE, cage, coop, corral, envelop, fence, pen

wallow · to move clumsily and in a debased or pitable condition Syn grovel, welter Rel crawl, creep

wan Syn PALE (sense 1), ashen, ashy, livid, pallid Ant florid, flush, rubicund, ruddy, sanguine

wander · to move about from place to place more or less aimlessly and without a plan Syn gad, gallivant, meander, prowl, ramble, range, roam, rove, stray, traipse

wanderer Syn NOMAD, drifter, gadabout, rambler, roamer, rover, stroller, vagabond, wayfarer

wane Syn ABATE, ebb, subside Ant revive, rise

wangle Syn ENGINEER, contrive, finagle, finesse, frame, machinate, maneuver, manipulate, mastermind, negotiate

want n **1** Syn DEFICIENCY, dearth, deficit, failure, famine, inadequacy, insufficiency, lack, paucity, poverty, scantiness, scarceness, scarcity, shortage Ant abundance, adequacy, amplitude, plenitude, plenty, sufficiency **2** Syn LACK, absence, dearth, defect, privation **3** Syn POVERTY, destitution, indigence, penury, privation Ant riches

want vb **1** Syn DESIRE, covet, crave, wish **2** Syn LACK, need, require

wanton 1 Syn LICENTIOUS, lascivious, lecherous, lewd, libertine, libidinous, lustful Ant continent **2** Syn SUPEREROGATORY, gratuitous, uncalled-for

wantonness Syn CRUELTY, barbarity, brutality, cruelness, heartlessness, inhumanity, sadism, savageness, savagery, viciousness Ant benignity, compassion, good-heartedness, humanity, kindheartedness, kindness, sympathy

war Syn CONTEND, battle, fight

warble n Syn MELODY, air, lay, song, strain, tune

warble vb Syn SING, carol, chant, descant, hymn, intone, trill, troll

ward Syn CUSTODY, care, guardianship, keeping, safekeeping, trust

warehouse Syn STOREHOUSE, depository, depot, magazine, repository, storage, stowage

wariness Syn CAUTION, calculation, chariness, circumspection Ant adventurousness, temerity

warlike 1 Syn BELLIGERENT, aggressive, argumentative, bellicose, combative, contentious, discordant, disputatious, gladiatorial, militant, pugnacious, quarrelsome, scrappy, truculent Ant nonbelligerent, pacific, peaceable, peaceful **2** Syn MARTIAL, military

warm 1 Syn FERVENT, ardent, blazing, burning, charged, emotional, fervid, feverish, fiery, flaming, glowing, hot-blooded, impassioned, passionate, red-hot, vehement, warm-blooded Ant cold, cool, dispassionate, impassive, unemotional **2** Syn TENDER, compassionate, responsive, sympathetic, warmhearted Ant callous, severe

warm-blooded Syn FERVENT, ardent, blazing, burning, charged, emotional, fervid, feverish, fiery, flaming, glowing, hot-blooded, impassioned, passionate, red-hot, vehement, warm Ant cold, cool, dispassionate, impassive, unemotional

warmhearted Syn TENDER, compassionate, responsive, sympathetic, warm Ant callous, severe

warn · to let one know of approaching danger or risk Syn alert, caution, forewarn Rel advise, apprise, inform, notify

warning n · the act or an instance of telling beforehand of danger or risk Syn admonition, alarm, alert, caution, forewarning, notice Rel auguring, augury, forecasting, foretelling, predicting, prediction, presaging, prognosticating, prophecy, prophesying

warning adj Syn CAUTIONARY, admonishing, admonitory, cautioning

warp Syn DEFORM, contort, distort

warped Syn CORRUPT, debased, debauched, decadent, degenerate, degraded, demoralized, depraved, dissipated, dissolute, perverse, perverted, reprobate Ant uncorrupted

warrant Syn ASSERT, affirm, aver, avouch, avow, declare, predicate, profess, protest Ant controvert, deny

wary Syn CAUTIOUS, calculating, chary, circumspect Ant adventurous, temerarious

wash Syn WET, bathe, douse, drench, soak, souse, water Ant dry

wash out Syn WHITEN, blanch, bleach, blench, decolorize, dull, fade, pale Ant blacken, darken, deepen

waspish Syn IRRITABLE, fractious, fretful, huffy, peevish, pettish, petulant, querulous, snappish Ant easygoing

wastage Syn DESTRUCTION, annihilation, decimation, demolishment, demolition, desolation, devastation, extermination, extinction, havoc, loss, obliteration, ruin, ruination, wreckage *Ant* building, construction, erection, raising

waste *n* **1** · an area of the earth unsuitable for cultivation or general habitation *Syn* badlands, desert, wilderness **2** *Syn* REFUSE, debris, garbage, offal, rubbish, trash

waste *vb* **1** · to spend or expend freely and usually foolishly or futilely *Syn* consume, dissipate, fritter, squander *Rel* disburse, expend, spend *Ant* conserve, save **2** *Syn* RAVAGE, despoil, devastate, pillage, sack, spoliate

wasted *Syn* HAGGARD, cadaverous, careworn, pinched, worn

wasteful *Syn* PRODIGAL, extravagant, profligate, spendthrift, squandering, thriftless, unthrifty *Ant* conserving, economical, economizing, frugal, scrimping, skimping, thrifty

waster *Syn* PRODIGAL, profligate, spender, spendthrift, squanderer, wastrel *Ant* economizer

wastrel *Syn* PRODIGAL, profligate, spender, spendthrift, squanderer, waster *Ant* economizer

watch *vb* **1** *Syn* SEE (sense 2), look **2** *Syn* TEND, attend, mind

watch *n* *Syn* VIGILANCE, alertness, attentiveness, lookout, surveillance, watchfulness

watchful · on the lookout especially for danger or for opportunities *Syn* alert, vigilant, wide-awake *Rel* cautious, chary, circumspect, wary

watchfulness *Syn* VIGILANCE, alertness, attentiveness, lookout, surveillance, watch

watchword *Syn* SLOGAN, cry, shibboleth

water *Syn* WET, bathe, douse, drench, soak, souse, wash *Ant* dry

waterfall · a fall of water usually from a great height *Syn* cascade, cataract, fall(s) *Rel* rapid(s), white water

waterlog *Syn* SOAK, drench, impregnate, saturate, sop, steep

wave **1** *Syn* MOTION, beckon, flag, gesture, signal **2** *Syn* SWING (sense 1), brandish, flourish, shake, thrash

waver **1** *Syn* HESITATE, falter, vacillate *Ant* dive (in), plunge (in) **2** *Syn* SWING (sense 2), fluctuate, oscillate, pendulate, sway, undulate, vibrate

wavering *Syn* HESITATION, faltering, hesitance, hesitancy, indecision, irresolution, shilly-shallying, vacillation, wobbling

wax **1** *Syn* BECOME, come, get, go, grow, run, turn **2** *Syn* INCREASE (sense 2), accumulate, appreciate, balloon, build (up), burgeon, enlarge, escalate, expand, mount, multiply, mushroom, proliferate, rise, snowball, swell *Ant* contract, decrease, diminish, lessen, wane

way **1** · a track or path traversed in going from one place to another *Syn* artery, course,

pass, passage, route **2** *Syn* HABIT, custom, fashion, pattern, practice, trick, wont **3** *Syn* METHOD, fashion, manner, mode, system

wayfarer *Syn* NOMAD, drifter, gadabout, rambler, roamer, rover, stroller, vagabond, wanderer

waylay *Syn* SURPRISE (sense 1), ambush

wayward **1** *Syn* CONTRARY, balky, froward, perverse, restive *Ant* complaisant, good-natured **2** *Syn* DISOBEDIENT, balky, contrary, defiant, froward, insubordinate, intractable, rebellious, recalcitrant, refractory, restive, ungovernable, unruly, untoward, willful (*or* wilful) *Ant* amenable, compliant, docile, obedient, tractable **3** *Syn* UNCONTROLLABLE, froward, headstrong, intractable, recalcitrant, refractory, ungovernable, unmanageable, unruly, untoward, willful (*or* wilful) *Ant* controllable, governable, tractable

weak **1** · lacking physical, mental, or moral strength *Syn* decrepit, feeble, fragile, frail, infirm *Rel* debilitated, enfeebled, weakened *Ant* strong **2** *Syn* ILLOGICAL, fallacious, invalid, irrational, nonrational, unreasonable, unreasoning, unsound *Ant* logical, rational, reasonable, sound, valid **3** *Syn* POWERLESS, helpless, impotent *Ant* mighty, potent, powerful, puissant, strong

weaken · to diminish the strength or vigor of *Syn* debilitate, enervate, enfeeble, sap, soften *Rel* cripple, disable, emasculate, unman, unnerve *Ant* strengthen

weakened *Syn* IMPURE, adulterated, alloyed, contaminated, dilute, diluted, polluted, tainted, thinned *Ant* pure, unadulterated, unalloyed, uncontaminated, undiluted, unpolluted, untainted

wealthy *Syn* RICH, affluent, opulent *Ant* poor

wean *Syn* ESTRANGE, alienate, disaffect *Ant* reconcile

weariless *Syn* INDEFATIGABLE, tireless, unflagging, untiring, unwearied, unwearying

weariness *Syn* FATIGUE, burnout, collapse, exhaustion, lassitude, prostration, tiredness *Ant* refreshment, rejuvenation, revitalization

wearisome *Syn* BORING, drab, dreary, dry, dull, flat, heavy, humdrum, jading, leaden, monotonous, pedestrian, ponderous, stodgy, stuffy, stupid, tame, tedious, tiresome, tiring, unanimated, uninteresting, weary, wearying *Ant* absorbing, engaging, engrossing, gripping, interesting, intriguing, involving

weary *adj* *Syn* BORING, drab, dreary, dry, dull, flat, heavy, humdrum, jading, leaden, monotonous, pedestrian, ponderous, stodgy, stuffy, stupid, tame, tedious, tiresome, tiring, unanimated, uninteresting, wearisome, wearying *Ant* absorbing, engaging, engrossing, gripping, interesting, intriguing, involving

weary *vb* *Syn* TIRE, exhaust, fatigue, jade, tucker

wearying *Syn* BORING, drab, dreary, dry, dull,

flat, heavy, humdrum, jading, leaden, monotonous, pedestrian, ponderous, stodgy, stuffy, stupid, tame, tedious, tiresome, tiring, unanimated, uninteresting, wearisome, weary

weave · to make a textile or to form an article by interlacing threads or strands of material *Syn* braid, crochet, knit, plait, tat

wedded *Syn* MARITAL, conjugal, connubial, married, matrimonial, nuptial

wedding *Syn* MARRIAGE, espousal, matrimony, nuptial, wedlock

wedlock *Syn* MARRIAGE, espousal, matrimony, nuptial, wedding

wee *Syn* TINY, atomic, bitty, infinitesimal, microminiature, microscopic, miniature, minute, teeny, teeny-weeny *Ant* astronomical, colossal, cosmic, elephantine, enormous, giant, gigantic, herculean, heroic, huge, immense, mammoth, massive, monster, monstrous, monumental, mountainous, prodigious, titanic, tremendous

weep 1 *Syn* CRY, blubber, keen, wail, whimper **2** *Syn* EXUDE, bleed, ooze, percolate, seep, strain, sweat

weigh 1 *Syn* BURDEN, charge, cumber, encumber, lade, load, saddle, tax, weight **2** *Syn* CONSIDER (sense 1), contemplate, excogitate, study **3** *Syn* DEPRESS, oppress *Ant* cheer, elate **4** *Syn* MATTER, count, import, mean, signify

weight *vb* **1** *Syn* ADULTERATE, doctor, load, sophisticate *Ant* refine **2** *Syn* BURDEN, charge, cumber, encumber, lade, load, saddle, tax, weigh

weight *n* **1** *Syn* IMPORTANCE, consequence, import, moment, significance *Ant* unimportance **2** *Syn* INFLUENCE, authority, credit, prestige

weighty *Syn* HEAVY, cumbersome, cumbrous, hefty, ponderous *Ant* light

weird *Syn* EERIE, creepy, haunting, spooky, uncanny, unearthly

weirdo *Syn* ECCENTRIC, character, codger, crackbrain, crackpot, crank, kook, nut, oddball, screwball

welcome *Syn* PLEASANT, agreeable, grateful, gratifying, pleasing *Ant* distasteful, harsh, unpleasant

well *Syn* HEALTHY, hale, robust, sound, wholesome *Ant* unhealthy

well-disposed *Syn* AMIABLE, affable, agreeable, genial, good-natured, good-tempered, gracious, nice, sweet *Ant* disagreeable, ill-natured, ill-tempered, ungracious, unpleasant

well-known *Syn* FAMOUS, celebrated, famed, noted, notorious, prominent, renowned, star *Ant* anonymous, obscure, unknown

wellness *Syn* HEALTH, fitness, healthiness, heartiness, robustness, soundness, wholeness, wholesomeness *Ant* illness, sickness, unhealthiness, unsoundness

well-nigh *Syn* ALMOST, about, more or less, most, much, near, nearly, next to, nigh, practically, some, virtually

well-read *Syn* EDUCATED, erudite, knowledgeable, learned, literate, scholarly *Ant* ignorant, illiterate, uneducated

well-spoken *Syn* ARTICULATE, eloquent, fluent *Ant* inarticulate

well-timed *Syn* SEASONABLE, opportune, pat, timely *Ant* unseasonable

welter *n Syn* COMMOTION, bother, bustle, clatter, disturbance, furor, furore, fuss, hubbub, hullabaloo, hurly-burly, pandemonium, pother, row, ruckus, ruction, rumpus, shindy, squall, stew, stir, storm, to-do, tumult, turmoil, uproar, whirl

welter *vb Syn* WALLOW, grovel

wet *adj* · covered or more or less soaked with liquid *Syn* damp, dank, humid, moist *Rel* drenched, saturated, soaked, waterlogged *Ant* dry

wet *vb* · to make wet *Syn* bathe, douse, drench, soak, souse, wash, water *Rel* damp, dampen, humidify, hydrate, moisten *Ant* dry

wet *n Syn* RAIN (sense 1), cloudburst, deluge, downpour, rainstorm, storm

whack *Syn* ATTEMPT, crack, endeavor, essay, fling, go, pass, shot, stab, trial, try

whacking *Syn* VERY, awful, awfully, beastly, deadly, especially, exceedingly, extra, extremely, far, frightfully, full, greatly, heavily, highly, hugely, jolly, mightily, mighty, mortally, most, much, particularly, rattling, real, right, so, something, super, terribly, too *Ant* little, negligibly, nominally, slightly

whale *Syn* GIANT, behemoth, blockbuster, colossus, jumbo, leviathan, mammoth, monster, titan, whopper *Ant* dwarf, midget, mini, miniature, peewee, pygmy, runt, shrimp

wharf · a structure used by boats and ships for taking on or landing cargo or passengers *Syn* berth, dock, jetty, levee, pier, quay, slip

wheedle *Syn* COAX, blandish, blarney, cajole, soft-soap

wheel *Syn* TURN (sense 1), circle, eddy, gyrate, pirouette, revolve, rotate, spin, swirl, twirl, whirl

when *Syn* ALTHOUGH, albeit, howbeit, though, while

whet *Syn* SHARPEN, edge, grind, hone, strop *Ant* blunt, dull

while *vb* · to pass time, and especially leisure time, without boredom or in pleasant ways *Syn* beguile, fleet, wile *Rel* amuse, divert, entertain

while *conj Syn* ALTHOUGH, albeit, howbeit, though, when

whilom *Syn* FORMER, erstwhile, late, old, onetime, past, sometime

whim · a sudden impulsive and apparently unmotivated idea or action *Syn* caprice, fancy, freak, notion, vagary, whimsy *Rel* capriciousness, freakishness, whimsicality

whimper *Syn* CRY, blubber, keen, wail, weep

whimsical · prone to sudden illogical changes of mind, ideas, or actions *Syn* capricious, freakish, impulsive *Rel* mercurial, moody, temperamental, volatile

whimsy *Syn* WHIM, caprice, fancy, freak, notion, vagary

whine *Syn* COMPLAIN, beef, bellyache, carp, crab, croak, fuss, gripe, grouse, growl, grumble, kick, moan, murmur, mutter, repine, squawk, wail, yammer *Ant* rejoice

whiner *Syn* GROUCH, bear, complainer, crab, crank, croaker, curmudgeon, fusser, griper, grouser, growler, grumbler, grump, murmurer, mutterer

whirl *n Syn* COMMOTION, bother, bustle, clatter, disturbance, furor, furore, fuss, hubbub, hullabaloo, hurly-burly, pandemonium, pother, row, ruckus, ruction, rumpus, shindy, squall, stew, stir, storm, to-do, tumult, turmoil, uproar, welter

whirl *vb* **1** *Syn* HURRY (sense 2), barrel, bolt, bowl, breeze, career, course, dash, fly, hasten, hotfoot (it), hump, hurtle, hustle, pelt, race, rip, rocket, run, rush, rustle, scoot, scurry, scuttle, shoot, speed, step (along), tear, trot, whisk, zip, zoom *Ant* crawl, creep, poke **2** *Syn* REEL, stagger, totter **3** *Syn* TURN (sense 1), circle, eddy, gyrate, pirouette, revolve, rotate, spin, swirl, twirl, wheel

whirlpool *Syn* EDDY, maelstrom, vortex

whisk **1** *Syn* HURRY (sense 1), accelerate, hasten, quicken, rush, speed (up) *Ant* decelerate, retard, slow (down) **2** *Syn* HURRY (sense 2), barrel, bolt, bowl, breeze, career, course, dash, fly, hasten, hotfoot (it), hump, hurtle, hustle, pelt, race, rip, rocket, run, rush, rustle, scoot, scurry, scuttle, shoot, speed, step (along), tear, trot, whirl, zip, zoom *Ant* crawl, creep, poke

whisper *Syn* RUMOR, bruit (about), circulate, noise (about)

whistling *Syn* SHRILL, acute, high-pitched, piping, screeching, shrieking, squeaking, squeaky, treble *Ant* bass, deep, low, throaty

whit *Syn* PARTICLE, atom, bit, iota, jot, mite, smidgen, tittle

white *Syn* COLORLESS, uncolored, undyed, unpainted, unstained *Ant* colored, dyed, painted, stained, tinged, tinted

whiten **1** · to make white or whiter by removing color *Syn* blanch, bleach, blench, decolorize, dull, fade, pale, wash out *Rel* brighten, lighten *Ant* blacken, darken, deepen **2** *Syn* PALLIATE, extenuate, gloss, gloze, whitewash

whitewash *Syn* PALLIATE, extenuate, gloss, gloze, whiten

whiz *Syn* EXPERT, ace, adept, artist, authority, crackerjack, maestro, master, past master, scholar, shark, virtuoso, wizard *Ant* amateur

whole *adj* **1** · having every constituent element or individual *Syn* all, entire, gross, total *Ant* partial **2** *Syn* PERFECT, entire, intact *Ant* imperfect

whole *n Syn* SUM, aggregate, amount, number, quantity, total

wholehearted *Syn* SINCERE, heartfelt, hearty, unfeigned, whole-souled *Ant* insincere

wholeness *Syn* HEALTH, fitness, healthiness, heartiness, robustness, soundness, wellness, wholesomeness *Ant* illness, sickness, unhealthiness, unsoundness

wholesale *Syn* INDISCRIMINATE, sweeping *Ant* discriminating, selective

wholesome **1** *Syn* HEALTHFUL, healthy, hygienic, salubrious, salutary, sanitary **2** *Syn* HEALTHY, hale, robust, sound, well *Ant* unhealthy

wholesomeness *Syn* HEALTH, fitness, healthiness, heartiness, robustness, soundness, wellness, wholeness *Ant* illness, sickness, unhealthiness, unsoundness

whole-souled *Syn* SINCERE, heartfelt, hearty, unfeigned, wholehearted *Ant* insincere

whoop *vb Syn* SHOUT, holler, scream, screech, shriek, squeal, yell

whoop *n Syn* SHOUT, holler, scream, screech, shriek, squeal, yell

whopper *Syn* GIANT, behemoth, blockbuster, colossus, jumbo, leviathan, mammoth, monster, titan, whale *Ant* dwarf, midget, mini, miniature, peewee, pygmy, runt, shrimp

wicked *Syn* BAD (sense 1), evil, ill, naughty *Ant* good

wide **1** *Syn* BROAD, deep *Ant* narrow **2** *Syn* EXTENSIVE, broad, expansive, extended, far-flung, far-reaching, widespread *Ant* narrow

wide-awake **1** *Syn* WAKEFUL, awake, sleepless *Ant* asleep, dormant, dozing, napping, resting, sleeping, slumbering **2** *Syn* WATCHFUL, alert, vigilant

widespread *Syn* EXTENSIVE, broad, expansive, extended, far-flung, far-reaching, wide *Ant* narrow

wield **1** *Syn* EXERT, apply, exercise, ply, put out **2** *Syn* HANDLE, manipulate, ply, swing

wig *Syn* SCOLD, bawl, berate, chew out, jaw, rail, rate, revile, tongue-lash, upbraid, vituperate

wild *Syn* FURIOUS, delirious, frantic, frenetic, frenzied, rabid

wilderness *Syn* WASTE, badlands, desert

wile **1** *Syn* TRICKERY, artifice, chicanery, hanky-panky, jugglery, legerdemain, subterfuge **2** *Syn* TRICK, artifice, feint, gambit, maneuver, ploy, ruse, stratagem

will *n* · the power or act of making or effecting a choice or decision *Syn* conation, volition *Rel* design, intent, intention, purpose

will *vb* · to give to another by will *Syn* bequeath, devise, leave, legate

willful **1** *Syn* VOLUNTARY, deliberate, intentional, willing *Ant* instinctive, involuntary **2** *Syn* DISOBEDIENT, balky, contrary, defiant, froward, insubordinate, intractable, rebellious, recalcitrant, refractory, restive, ungovernable, unruly, untoward, wayward *Ant* amenable, compliant, docile, obedient, tractable **3** *Syn* OBSTINATE, adamant, adamantine, dogged, hard, hardened, hardheaded, hardhearted, headstrong, immovable, implacable, inflexible, mulish, obdurate, opinionated, ossified, pat, peevish, pertinacious, perverse, pigheaded, rigid, self-willed, stubborn, unbending, uncompromising, unrelenting, unyielding *Ant* acquiescent, agreeable, amenable, compliant, complying, flexible, pliable, pliant, relenting, yielding **4** *Syn* UNCONTROLLABLE, froward, headstrong, intractable, recalcitrant, refractory, ungovernable, unmanageable, unruly, untoward, wayward *Ant* controllable, governable, tractable **5** *Syn* UNRULY, headstrong, intractable, recalcitrant, refractory, ungovernable *Ant* docile, tractable

willfully *Syn* INTENTIONALLY, consciously, deliberately, designedly, knowingly, purposefully, purposely, wittingly *Ant* inadvertently, unconsciously, unintentionally, unknowingly, unwittingly

willfulness *Syn* DISOBEDIENCE, contrariness, defiance, frowardness, insubordination, intractability, rebelliousness, recalcitrance, refractoriness, unruliness *Ant* amenability, compliance, docility, obedience

willing *Syn* VOLUNTARY, deliberate, intentional, willful *Ant* instinctive, involuntary

willingness *Syn* ALACRITY, amenability, gameness, goodwill

willowy · able to bend easily without breaking *Syn* flexible, limber, lissome, lithe, pliable, pliant, supple *Rel* adaptable, ductile, elastic, fluid, malleable, modifiable, plastic, variable, yielding *Ant* inflexible, rigid, stiff

wilt *Syn* DROOP, flag, sag

wily *Syn* SLY, artful, crafty, cunning, foxy, guileful, insidious, tricky

win 1 *Syn* EARN, acquire, attain, capture, carry, draw, gain, garner, get, land, make, obtain, procure, realize, secure *Ant* forfeit, lose **2** *Syn* GET, gain, obtain, procure, secure

wince *Syn* RECOIL, blench, flinch, quail, shrink *Ant* confront, defy

wind · to follow a circular, spiral, or writhing course *Syn* coil, curl, entwine, twine, twist, wreathe *Rel* bend, curve

winding 1 · curving repeatedly first one way and then another *Syn* flexuous, serpentine, sinuous, tortuous *Rel* bending, curving, twisting *Ant* straight **2** *Syn* SPIRAL, coiling, corkscrew, helical, screwlike

window · an opening in the wall of a building that is usually covered with glass and serves to admit light and air *Syn* casement, oriel

windup *Syn* FINALE, close, closing, conclusion, consummation, end, ending, finis, finish *Ant* beginning, dawn, opening, start

wing 1 *Syn* ANNEX, ell, extension **2** *Syn* FACTION, bloc, body, coalition, party, sect, set, side

wink *Syn* INSTANT, flash, jiffy, minute, moment, second, shake, split second, trice, twinkle, twinkling

winner *Syn* VICTOR, champion, conqueror, vanquisher

winning 1 *Syn* LOVABLE, adorable, darling, dear, disarming, endearing, precious, sweet *Ant* abhorrent, abominable, detestable, hateful, odious, unlovable **2** *Syn* SWEET, dulcet, engaging, winsome *Ant* bitter, sour

win (over) *Syn* PERSUADE, argue, convince, get, induce, move, prevail (on *or* upon), satisfy, talk (into)

winsome *Syn* SWEET, dulcet, engaging, winning *Ant* bitter, sour

wipe *Syn* EXTERMINATE, deracinate, eradicate, extirpate, uproot

wire *Syn* CORD, cable, lace, lacing, line, rope, string

wisdom 1 *Syn* COMMON SENSE, discreetness, discretion, horse sense, levelheadedness, prudence, sense, sensibleness, wit *Ant* imprudence, indiscretion **2** *Syn* SENSE, common sense, good sense, gumption, horse sense, judgment

wise 1 · exercising or involving sound judgment *Syn* judicious, prudent, sage, sane, sapient, sensible *Rel* discreet, foresighted, prudent *Ant* simple **2** *Syn* EXPEDIENT, advisable, desirable, judicious, politic, prudent, tactical *Ant* imprudent, inadvisable, inexpedient, injudicious, unwise

wiseacre *Syn* SMART ALECK, smarty (*or* smartie), wise guy

wisecrack *vb Syn* JOKE, banter, fool, fun, jest, jive, josh, kid, quip

wisecrack *n Syn* JOKE, crack, gag, jape, jest, quip, witticism

wise guy *Syn* SMART ALECK, smarty (*or* smartie), wiseacre

wise (up) *Syn* ENLIGHTEN (sense 1), acquaint, advise, apprise, brief, clue, familiarize, fill in, inform, instruct, tell

wish *Syn* DESIRE, covet, crave, want

wishy-washy *Syn* INSIPID, banal, flat, inane, jejune, vapid *Ant* sapid, zestful

wit 1 · a mode of expression intended to arouse amusement *Syn* humor, irony, repartee, sarcasm, satire *Rel* alertness, brightness, brilliancy, cleverness, intelligence, quick-wittedness, smartness **2** *Syn* COMMON SENSE, discreetness, discretion, horse sense, levelheadedness, prudence, sense, sensibleness, wisdom *Ant* imprudence, indiscretion **3** *Syn* MIND, brain, intellect, intelligence, psyche, soul

witch *Syn* MAGICIAN (sense 1), charmer, conjurer (*or* conjuror), enchanter, necromancer, sorcerer, voodoo, wizard

witchcraft *Syn* MAGIC, alchemy, sorcery, thaumaturgy, witchery, wizardry

witchery *Syn* MAGIC, alchemy, sorcery, thaumaturgy, witchcraft, wizardry

with 1 *Syn* BECAUSE OF, due to, owing to, through 2 *Syn* BY, through

withdraw *Syn* GO, depart, leave, quit, retire *Ant* come

wither · to lose freshness and substance by or as if by loss of natural moisture *Syn* shrivel, wizen *Rel* desiccate, dry, parch

withhold *Syn* KEEP (sense 2), detain, hold back, keep back, keep out, reserve, retain *Ant* relinquish

without *Syn* BEYOND (sense 2), outside, outside of *Ant* within

withstand *Syn* RESIST, antagonize, combat, conflict, contest, fight, oppose *Ant* abide, submit

witness *vb* 1 *Syn* CERTIFY, attest, vouch 2 *Syn* TESTIFY, attest, depose, swear

witness *n* *Syn* SPECTATOR, beholder, bystander, eyewitness, kibitzer, looker-on, observer, onlooker

witticism *Syn* JOKE, crack, gag, jape, jest, quip, wisecrack

wittingly *Syn* INTENTIONALLY, consciously, deliberately, designedly, knowingly, purposefully, purposely, willfully *Ant* inadvertently, unconsciously, unintentionally, unknowingly, unwittingly

witty · provoking or intended to provoke laughter *Syn* facetious, humorous, jocose, jocular *Rel* amusing, diverting, entertaining

wizard 1 *Syn* EXPERT, ace, adept, artist, authority, crackerjack, maestro, master, past master, scholar, shark, virtuoso, whiz *Ant* amateur 2 *Syn* MAGICIAN (sense 1), charmer, conjurer (*or* conjuror), enchanter, necromancer, sorcerer, voodoo, witch

wizardry *Syn* MAGIC, alchemy, sorcery, thaumaturgy, witchcraft, witchery

wizen *Syn* WITHER, shrivel

wobble *Syn* SHAKE (sense 1), dither, quake, quaver, quiver, shimmy, shiver, shudder, teeter, totter, tremble

wobbling *Syn* HESITATION, faltering, hesitance, hesitancy, indecision, irresolution, shilly-shallying, vacillation, wavering

woe *Syn* SORROW, anguish, grief, heartache, heartbreak, regret *Ant* joy

woebegone *Syn* SAD (sense 1), bad, blue, brokenhearted, crestfallen, dejected, depressed, despondent, disconsolate, doleful, down, downcast, downhearted, droopy, forlorn, gloomy, glum, heartbroken, heartsick, heartsore, inconsolable, joyless, low, low-spirited, melancholy, miserable, mournful, saddened, sorrowful, sorry, unhappy, woeful, wretched *Ant* blissful, buoyant, buoyed, cheerful, cheery, chipper, delighted, glad, gladdened, gladsome, gleeful, happy, joyful, joyous, jubilant, sunny, upbeat

woeful 1 *Syn* REGRETTABLE, deplorable, distressful, distressing, grievous, heartbreaking, heartrending, lamentable, unfortunate 2 *Syn* SAD (sense 1), bad, blue, brokenhearted, crestfallen, dejected, depressed, despondent, disconsolate, doleful, down, downcast, downhearted, droopy, forlorn, gloomy, glum, heartbroken, heartsick, heartsore, inconsolable, joyless, low, low-spirited, melancholy, miserable, mournful, saddened, sorrowful, sorry, unhappy, woebegone, wretched *Ant* blissful, buoyant, buoyed, cheerful, cheery, chipper, delighted, glad, gladdened, gladsome, gleeful, happy, joyful, joyous, jubilant, sunny, upbeat

woman 1 · an adult female human being *Syn* FEMALE, lady 2 *Syn* GIRLFRIEND, gal, lady

womanish *Syn* FEMALE, feminine, ladylike, womanlike, womanly *Ant* male

womanlike *Syn* FEMALE, feminine, ladylike, womanish, womanly *Ant* male

womanly *Syn* FEMALE, feminine, ladylike, womanish, womanlike *Ant* male

wonder 1 · something that causes astonishment or admiration *Syn* marvel, miracle, phenomenon, prodigy 2 · the complex emotion aroused by the incomprehensible and especially the awe-inspiring *Syn* admiration, amazement, awe, wonderment *Rel* awe, fear, reverence

wonderful *Syn* EXCELLENT, A1, bang-up, banner, capital, classic, crackerjack, dandy, divine, fabulous, fine, first-class, first-rate, grand, great, groovy, heavenly, jim-dandy, keen, marvelous (*or* marvellous), mean, neat, nifty, noble, par excellence, prime, sensational, splendid, stellar, sterling, superb, superior, superlative, supernal, swell, terrific, tip-top, top, top-notch, unsurpassed *Ant* poor

wonderment *Syn* WONDER (sense 2), admiration, amazement, awe

wont *adj* *Syn* ACCUSTOMED, given, habituated, used *Ant* unaccustomed, unused

wont *n* *Syn* HABIT, custom, fashion, pattern, practice, trick, way

wonted *Syn* USUAL, accustomed, customary, habitual

woo *Syn* INVITE, bid, court, solicit

wooden *Syn* STIFF, inflexible, rigid, stark, tense *Ant* relaxed, supple

woolgathering *Syn* REVERIE, daydreaming, study, trance

woolly 1 *Syn* HAIRY (sense 1), bristly, fleecy, furry, hirsute, rough, shaggy, unshorn *Ant* bald, furless, hairless, shorn, smooth 2 *Syn* HAIRY (sense 2), furry, fuzzy, rough, shaggy

word *n* 1 · a pronounceable sound or combination of sounds that expresses and symbolizes an idea *Syn* term, vocable *Rel* expression, idiom, locution, phrase **2** *Syn* NEWS, information, intelligence, item, story, tidings **3** *Syn* PROMISE, oath, pledge, troth, vow

word *vb* *Syn* PHRASE, articulate, clothe, couch, express, formulate, put, say, state

wordless 1 *Syn* IMPLICIT, implied, tacit, unexpressed, unspoken, unvoiced *Ant* explicit, express, expressed, spoken, stated **2** *Syn* SILENT (sense 3), dumb, mum, mute, speechless, uncommunicative *Ant* communicative, speaking, talking

wordy · using or marked by the use of more words than are necessary to express the thought *Syn* diffuse, prolix, redundant, verbose *Rel* flatulent, inflated, tumid, turgid *Ant* compact, concise, crisp, pithy, succinct, terse

work *n* **1** · strenuous activity that involves difficulty and effort and usually affords no pleasure *Syn* drudgery, grind, labor, toil, travail *Rel* effort, exertion, pains, trouble *Ant* fun, play **2** · a sustained activity that affords one a livelihood *Syn* business, calling, employment, occupation, pursuit *Rel* art, craft, handicraft, profession, trade **3** · something brought into being by the exertion of effort and the exercise of skill *Syn* artifact, opus, product, production *Rel* article, object, thing **4** *Syn* OCCUPATION, calling, employment, line, profession, trade, vocation **5** *Syn* ROLE, capacity, function, job, part, place, position, purpose, task

work *vb* **1** *Syn* ACT (sense 1), behave, function, operate, react **2** *Syn* EFFECT, bring about, cause, create, effectuate, engender, generate, induce, make, produce, prompt, result (in), spawn, yield **3** *Syn* FUNCTION, act, perform, serve **4** *Syn* LABOR, drudge, endeavor, grub, hump, hustle, moil, peg (away), plod, plow, plug, slave, slog, strain, strive, struggle, sweat, toil, travail *Ant* dabble, fiddle (around), fool (around), mess (around), putter (around) **5** *Syn* SOLVE, answer, break, crack, dope (out), figure out, puzzle (out), resolve, riddle, unravel, work out

worker 1 · one who earns his living by labor and especially by manual labor *Syn* artisan, craftsman, hand, handicraftsman, laborer, mechanic, operative, roustabout, workingman, workman *Ant* idler **2** *Syn* SLAVE (sense 2), drudge, drudger, grubber, laborer, peon, plugger, slogger, toiler *Ant* freeman

workingman *Syn* WORKER, artisan, craftsman, hand, handicraftsman, laborer, mechanic, operative, roustabout, workman *Ant* idler

workman *Syn* WORKER, artisan, craftsman, hand, handicraftsman, laborer, mechanic, operative, roustabout, workingman *Ant* idler

work out *Syn* SOLVE, answer, break, crack, dope (out), figure out, puzzle (out), resolve, riddle, unravel, work

world *Syn* EARTH, globe, planet

worldly 1 *Syn* EARTHLY, earthy, mundane, sublunary, terrestrial **2** *Syn* WORLDLY-WISE, cosmopolitan, smart, sophisticated *Ant* ingenuous, innocent, naive, unsophisticated, unworldly, wide-eyed

worldly-wise · having a wide and refined knowledge of the world especially from personal experience *Syn* cosmopolitan, smart, sophisticated, worldly *Rel* suave, urbane *Ant* ingenuous, innocent, naive, unsophisticated, unworldly, wide-eyed

worn *Syn* HAGGARD, cadaverous, careworn, pinched, wasted

worried · distressed or troubled usually about something anticipated *Syn* anxious, careful, concerned, solicitous *Rel* afraid, apprehensive, fearful

worrisome *Syn* TROUBLESOME, discomforting, discomposing, disquieting, distressing, disturbing, perturbing, troubling, troublous, unsettling, upsetting *Ant* reassuring, untroublesome

worry *vb* · to disturb one or destroy one's peace of mind by repeated or persistent tormenting attacks *Syn* annoy, harass, harry, pester, plague, tantalize, tease *Rel* agitate, discompose, disquiet, disturb, perturb, upset

worry *n* *Syn* CARE, anxiety, concern, solicitude

worsen *Syn* DETERIORATE, crumble, decay, decline, degenerate, descend, ebb, rot, sink *Ant* ameliorate, improve, meliorate

worship *n* **1** · excessive admiration of or devotion to a person *Syn* adulation, deification, idolatry, idolization, worshipping *Rel* adoration, deference, glorification, reverence, veneration **2** *Syn* REVERENCE (sense 1), adoration, veneration

worship *vb* **1** *Syn* IDOLIZE, adore, adulate, canonize, deify, dote (on) **2** *Syn* REVERE, adore, reverence, venerate *Ant* flout

worshipping *Syn* WORSHIP, adulation, deification, idolatry, idolization

worthy · having sufficient worth or merit to receive one's honor, esteem, or reward *Syn* deserving, good, meritorious *Rel* admirable, commendable, creditable, laudable, praiseworthy *Ant* no-good, undeserving, valueless, worthless

wound · an injury to the body *Syn* bruise, contusion, lesion, trauma, traumatism *Rel* hurt, injury

wraith *Syn* GHOST, apparition, bogey, phantasm, phantom, poltergeist, shade, shadow, specter (*or* spectre), spirit, spook, vision

wrangle *Syn* QUARREL, altercation, bickering, spat, squabble, tiff